# OXFORD

The world's most trusted dictionaries

# School
# German
# Dictionary

**Editors**
Valerie Grundy

Nicholas Rollin
with the assistance of Marie-Louise Wasmeier

*G rares*

# OXFORD
UNIVERSITY PRESS

*70 16*

# OXFORD
## UNIVERSITY PRESS

Great Clarendon Street, Oxford OX2 6DP

Oxford University Press is a department of the University of Oxford.
It furthers the University's objective of excellence in research,
scholarship, and education by publishing worldwide in

Oxford   New York

Auckland  Cape Town   Dar es Salaam  Hong Kong  Karachi
Kuala Lumpur  Madrid  Melbourne  Mexico City  Nairobi
New Delhi  Shanghai  Taipei  Toronto

With offices in

Argentina  Austria  Brazil  Chile  Czech Republic  France  Greece
Guatemala  Hungary  Italy  Japan  Poland  Portugal  Singapore
South Korea  Switzerland  Thailand  Turkey  Ukraine  Vietnam

Oxford is a registered trade mark of Oxford University Press
in the UK and in certain other countries

British Library Cataloguing in Publication Data
Data available

ISBN: 978-0-19-840800-0

10 9 8 7 6 5

Printed in Great Britain by Bell and Bain Ltd, Glasgow

MIX
Paper from
responsible sources
FSC® C007785

# Introduction

This dictionary has been specially written for students who are in their first years of learning German all the way through to preparing for exams. We have paid particular attention to making the dictionary user-friendly. With the help of colour headwords, alphabet tabs, easy-to-follow signposts and examples, the right translation can quickly be found. The things students need to know about words in German are clearly shown. These include main parts of irregular verbs, noun plurals, and the case taken by prepositions.

Throughout the writing of this dictionary we have worked in close consultation with students, teachers, and examining boards. We gratefully acknowledge the examining boards AQA, OCR, and EDEXCEL, who have read and commented on the dictionary text.

Since the first edition of this dictionary there have been many changes in German life. This new edition of the dictionary takes full account of these changes and many new words and examples have been included in order to provide the best possible learner's dictionary of German at this level.

# How a bilingual dictionary works

A bilingual dictionary contains two languages. When you look up a word in one of the languages, it gives the translation for that word in the other language. This dictionary is divided into two halves which are separated by a section of verb tables. In the first half you look up German words, which are in alphabetical order, to find out what they mean in English and in the second half you look up English words, also in alphabetical order, to find out how to say them in German.

At the entry, you will find not only translations but also other information that will help you get the right word and use it correctly. Here is a guide to the different things you will find in an entry:

| | |
|---|---|
| **headword** | a word you look up in the dictionary |
| **translation** | In this dictionary all the German words are in blue and all the English words are in black |
| *NOUN* | word class (part of speech): tells you whether the word you are looking up is a noun, a verb, an adjective, or another part of speech. A headword can be more than one part of speech. For instance, **book** can be a noun **she was reading a book** or a verb **I've booked the seats** |
| *(informal)* | helpful information: to guide you to the right translation, to show you how to use the translation, or to give you extra information about either the headword or the translation |
| example | a phrase or sentence using the word you have looked up. You should read through them carefully to see if they are close to what you want to understand or say |
| der/die/das | gender: after a German noun to tell you whether it is masculine (der), feminine (die), or neuter (das) |
| *(PLURAL* die ...) | shows the plural form of a German noun |
| • | indicates a phrasal verb such as • **to carry on** or an idiomatic expression such as • **to be over the moon** |
| [27] | verb number – tells you which verb pattern to look at in the central pages of the dictionary |
| ◇ | indicates an irregular German verb |
| *(SEP)* | indicates that a German verb is separable such as **ablenken** *(PERF* **lenkt ab***)* |
| *(+DAT) (+ACC)* *(+GEN)* | indicates whether dative, accusative or genitive forms are needed |

# Using the dictionary

## To find out what a German word means

Suppose you want to find out what the German word **Tor** means. You need to use the first half of the dictionary to find the German word that you are looking for. To help you do this, the guide words at the top of each page show the alphabetical range of words on the pages you have open. You will know that all German nouns start with a capital letter. Notice that this makes no difference to the alphabetical order, nor do accented letters like ü.

When you find the entry for **Tor** you will find the translation, but you will also see what the gender of **Tor** is. Nouns in German are either masculine, feminine, or neuter. These are shown in the dictionary as der, die, or das. You can see that **Tor** says das so it is neuter.

However, it often happens that a German word has more than one translation in English so you will see that the translation for **Tor** is divided into sections numbered ❶ and ❷.

**Tor** das *(PLURAL* die **Tore)** ❶ gate
❷ **goal**; mit 3 zu 2 Toren gewinnen
to win by 3 goals to 2

The first translation is **gate** and the second is **goal**. You will need to look at both translations and see which fits best in the German sentence you are trying to understand, so:

Uli hat das Tor geöffnet *means* Uli opened the gate

*but*

Uli steht im Tor *means* Uli's in goal

In English, the plural of most nouns is formed by adding **-s**. In German there are quite a lot of ways of forming the plural and these are not always easy to recognize. To help you with this, we show the plural form after every noun headword. For instance, if you are trying to find out what the German word **Häuser** means, you can see immediately that it is the plural of **Haus** and so it means **houses**.

**Haus** das *(PLURAL* die **Häuser)**
❶ **house** ❷ nach Hause home, zu
Hause at home

German like English has certain words that you would use when chatting with friends but not in more formal situations. German words like this are marked *(informal)* like **flitzen** here:

**flitzen** *VERB (informal) (PERF* **ist**
**geflitzt)** ❶ to dash ❷ to whizz

You can think of a dictionary entry as being made out of different sorts of building bricks. In the entries below you can see how they fit together to help you find what you need. The more you use your dictionary the more confident you will feel about finding your way around it.

# German—English

*German entries have blue tabs*

## Aa

**Aal** der *(PLURAL die* **Aale)** eel

**ab** *PREPOSITION (+DAT)* **from;** ab Montag from Monday, Kinder ab sechs Jahren children from the age of six

[word class (part of speech)]

**ab** *ADVERB* **❶ off;** der Henkel ist ab the handle has come off, ab ins Bett! *(informal)* off (you go) to bed! **❷** ab und zu now and again

[German headwords in blue for easy look-up]

**abbiegen** *◇VERB (IMP* **bog ab,** *PERF* **ist abgebogen) ❶** to turn off; nach rechts abbiegen to turn off to the right **❷** biegen Sie an der Ampel (nach) links ab turn left at the lights

[main forms of irregular verbs]

**Abbildung** die *(PLURAL die* **Abbildungen)** illustration

**abbrechen** *◇VERB (PRES* **bricht ab,** *IMP* **brach ab,** *PERF* **hat abgebrochen) ❶** to break off *(a branch, negotiations);* Ruth brach ein paar Zweige ab Ruth broke off a few branches **❷** to pull down *(a building)* **❸** to cut short; leider mussten wir unsere Ferien vorzeitig abbrechen unfortunately we had to cut short our holidays, er hat sein Studium aus finanziellen Gründen abgebrochen he left university for financial reasons **❹** *(PERF* **ist abgebrochen)** der Ast ist abgebrochen the branch has broken off

[typical examples to show German in context]

**Abend** der *(PLURAL die* **Abende)** evening; am Abend in the evening, heute Abend this evening, tonight,

[noun plurals in full for easy look-up]

gestern Abend yesterday evening, last night, wann esst ihr zu Abend? when do you have dinner?

**Abendbrot** das evening meal

**Abendessen** das *(PLURAL die* **Abendessen)** supper, dinner *(in the evening);* was gibt es zum Abendessen? what are we having for supper?

**Abendkurs** der *(PLURAL die* **Abendkurse)** evening course

**abends** *ADVERB* in the evening

**Abenteuer** das *(PLURAL die* **Abenteuer)** adventure

**Abenteuerfilm** der *(PLURAL die* **Abenteuerfilme)** adventure film

**aber** *CONJUNCTION* **but;** es ist zwar nützlich, aber zu teuer it's useful, but too expensive

**aber** *ADVERB* **really;** das ist aber sehr nett von dir that's really nice of you, du bist aber groß! aren't you tall!, aber ja! but of course!, jetzt ist aber Schluss! that's it now!

**abergläubisch** *ADJECTIVE* **superstitious**

**abfahren** *◇VERB (PRES* **fährt ab,** *IMP* **fuhr ab,** *PERF* **ist abgefahren)** to leave; Peter fährt morgen ganz früh ab Peter is leaving very early tomorrow morning, wann fährt der Zug nach Berlin ab? when does the Berlin train leave?

**Abfahrt** die *(PLURAL die* **Abfahrten) ❶ departure ❷ run** *(on a ski slope)* **❸ exit** *(on a motorway)*

**Abfall** der *(PLURAL die* **Abfälle)** rubbish

**Abfalleimer** der *(PLURAL die* **Abfalleimer)** rubbish bin

[gender]

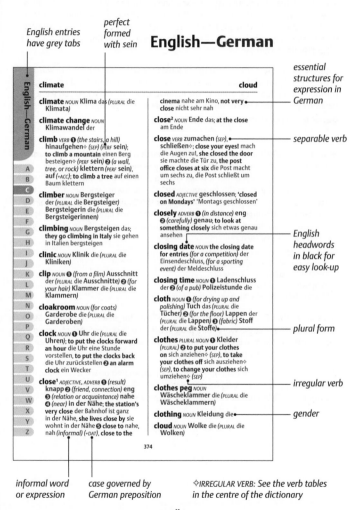

*English entries have grey tabs*

*perfect formed with sein*

# English—German

*essential structures for expression in German*

**climate** NOUN Klima das (PLURAL die Klimata)

**climate change** NOUN Klimawandel der

**climb** VERB ❶ (the stairs, a hill) hinaufgehen◇ (SEP) (PERF sein); **to climb a mountain** einen Berg besteigen◇ (PERF sein) ❷ (a wall, tree, or rock) klettern (PERF sein), auf (+ACC); **to climb a tree** auf einen Baum klettern

**climber** NOUN Bergsteiger der (PLURAL die Bergsteiger) Bergsteigerin die (PLURAL die Bergsteigerinnen)

**climbing** NOUN Bergsteigen das; **they go climbing in Italy** sie gehen in Italien bergsteigen

**clinic** NOUN Klinik die (PLURAL die Kliniken)

**clip** NOUN ❶ (from a film) Ausschnitt der (PLURAL die Ausschnitte) ❷ (for your hair) Klammer die (PLURAL die Klammern)

**cloakroom** NOUN (for coats) Garderobe die (PLURAL die Garderoben)

**clock** NOUN ❶ Uhr die (PLURAL die Uhren); **to put the clocks forward an hour** die Uhr eine Stunde vorstellen, **to put the clocks back** die Uhr zurückstellen ❷ **an alarm clock** ein Wecker

**close¹** ADJECTIVE, ADVERB ❶ (result) knapp ❷ (friend, connection) eng ❸ (relation or acquaintance) nahe ❹ (near) in der Nähe; **the station's very close** der Bahnhof ist ganz in der Nähe, **she lives close by** sie wohnt in der Nähe ❺ **close to** nahe, nah (informal) (+DAT), **close to the**

**cinema** nahe am Kino, **not very close** nicht sehr nah

**close²** NOUN Ende das; **at the close** am Ende

**close** VERB ❶ **to close** zumachen (SEP), schließen◇; **close your eyes!** mach die Augen zu!, **she closed the door** sie machte die Tür zu, **the post office closes at six** die Post macht um sechs zu, die Post schließt um sechs

**closed** ADJECTIVE geschlossen; **'closed on Mondays'** 'Montags geschlossen'

**closely** ADVERB ❶ (in distance) eng ❷ (carefully) genau; **to look at something closely** sich etwas genau ansehen

**closing date** NOUN **the closing date for entries** (for a competition) der Einsendeschluss, (for a sporting event) der Meldeschluss

**closing time** NOUN ❶ Ladenschluss der ❷ (of a pub) Polizeistunde die

**cloth** NOUN ❶ (for drying up and polishing) Tuch das (PLURAL die Tücher) ❷ (for the floor) Lappen der (PLURAL die Lappen) ❸ (fabric) Stoff der (PLURAL die Stoffe)

**clothes** PLURAL NOUN ❶ Kleider (PLURAL) ❷ **to put your clothes on** sich anziehen◇ (SEP), **to take your clothes off** sich ausziehen◇ (SEP), **to change your clothes** sich umziehen◇ (SEP)

**clothes peg** NOUN Wäscheklammer die (PLURAL die Wäscheklammern)

**clothing** NOUN Kleidung die

**cloud** NOUN Wolke die (PLURAL die Wolken)

*separable verb*

*English headwords in black for easy look-up*

*plural form*

*irregular verb*

*gender*

374

*informal word or expression*

*case governed by German preposition*

◇IRREGULAR VERB: See the verb tables in the centre of the dictionary

**vii**

## Finding an English word and how to say it in German

You can see that it is quite easy once you know how the dictionary works, to look up a German word and find out what it means. Students usually find it harder to use the dictionary to find out how to say something in German. This dictionary is written specially to help you do this and to make it easy to find the right way of saying things in German.

Suppose you want to know how to say **garden** in German. Look up the word in the second part of the dictionary. If you follow the same method of going through the alphabetical order of the headwords as you did when you were looking up a German word, you will find **garden** on page 433.

**garden** *NOUN* **Garten** der *(PLURAL* die Gärten*)*

Now you can see that the German word for **garden** is Garten. But if you want to make a sentence using a noun like Garten you need to know its gender. The dictionary shows you that it is der Garten so **in the garden** will be im Garten. It is not always as easy as this to know which German word you need. Sometimes there will be more than one German word for the English word you are looking up. When the dictionary entry gives you more than just one translation, it is very important to take the time to read through the whole entry. If you look up **plug** the entry looks like this:

**plug** *NOUN* ❶ *(electrical)* **Stecker** der *(PLURAL* die Stecker*)* ❷ *(in a bath or sink)* **Stöpsel** der *(PLURAL* die Stöpsel)*; **to pull out the plug** den Stöpsel herausziehen

You can see that ❶ tells you that the German word for an electrial **plug** is Stecker and ❷ tells you that the word for a **plug** in a bath or a sink is Stöpsel. Remember that information which is either in brackets or italics or both is there to help you, but it *will never* be the translation itself.

Wherever there is more than one translation, depending on what meaning of the English word you are looking for, the dictionary will always help you to choose the right one. Often it is not enough to find the translation of one word.

In the case of more common words the dictionary also gives you a selection of phrases you will often want to use. In the entry for **hair** below you can find out how to use the translation Haare in different expressions:

**hair** *NOUN* ❶ Haare *(plural)*; **to comb your hair** sich *(DAT)* die Haare kämmen, **to wash your hair** sich *(DAT)* die Haare waschen, **to have your hair cut** sich *(DAT)* die Haare schneiden lassen, **she's had her hair cut** sie hat sich die Haare schneiden lassen ❷ **a hair** ein Haar

## Note on the German Spelling Reform

The German spelling reform was adopted by German-speaking countries in July 1996. You will find all the new spellings in this dictionary. However, since you may come across old spellings if you are reading pre-reform German material, we have also given all the most frequent old spellings as headwords to help you locate the entry. These are cross-referred to the new spellings. Thus **As** is cross-referred to **Ass** but the old spelling of **Ausschuss (Ausschuß)** is not shown.

**Aal** der *(PLURAL* die **Aale)** eel

**ab** *PREPOSITION (+DAT)* from; ab Montag from Monday, Kinder ab sechs Jahren children from the age of six

**ab** *ADVERB* ❶ off; der Henkel ist ab the handle has come off, ab ins Bett! *(informal)* off (you go) to bed! ❷ ab und zu now and again

**abbiegen** ◇*VERB (IMP* **bog ab,** *PERF* **ist abgebogen)** ❶ to turn off; nach rechts abbiegen to turn off to the right ❷ biegen Sie an der Ampel (nach) links ab turn left at the lights

**Abbildung** die *(PLURAL* die **Abbildungen)** illustration

**abbrechen** ◇*VERB (PRES* **bricht ab,** *IMP* **brach ab,** *PERF* **hat abgebrochen)** ❶ to break off *(a branch, negotiations)*; Ruth brach ein paar Zweige ab Ruth broke off a few branches ❷ to pull down *(a building)* ❸ to cut short; leider mussten wir unsere Ferien vorzeitig abbrechen unfortunately we had to cut short our holidays, er hat sein Studium aus finanziellen Gründen abgebrochen he left university for financial reasons ❹ *(PERF* **ist abgebrochen)** der Ast ist abgebrochen the branch has broken off

**Abend** der *(PLURAL* die **Abende)** evening; am Abend in the evening, heute Abend this evening, tonight,

gestern Abend yesterday evening, last night, wann esst ihr zu Abend? when do you have dinner?

**Abendbrot** das evening meal

**Abendessen** das *(PLURAL* die **Abendessen)** supper, dinner *(in the evening)*; was gibt es zum Abendessen? what are we having for supper?

**Abendkurs** der *(PLURAL* die **Abendkurse)** evening course

**abends** *ADVERB* in the evening

**Abenteuer** das *(PLURAL* die **Abenteuer)** adventure

**Abenteurfilm** der *(PLURAL* die **Abenteuerfilme)** adventure film

**aber** *CONJUNCTION* but; es ist zwar nützlich, aber zu teuer it's useful, but too expensive

**aber** *ADVERB* really; das ist aber sehr nett von dir that's really nice of you, du bist aber groß! aren't you tall!, aber ja! but of course!, jetzt ist aber Schluss! that's it now!

**abergläubisch** *ADJECTIVE* superstitious

**abfahren** ◇*VERB (PRES* **fährt ab,** *IMP* **fuhr ab,** *PERF* **ist abgefahren)** to leave; Peter fährt morgen ganz früh ab Peter is leaving very early tomorrow morning, wann fährt der Zug nach Berlin ab? when does the Berlin train leave?

**Abfahrt** die *(PLURAL* die **Abfahrten)** ❶ departure ❷ run *(on a ski slope)* ❸ exit *(on a motorway)*

**Abfall** der *(PLURAL* die **Abfälle)** rubbish

**Abfalleimer** der *(PLURAL* die **Abfalleimer)** rubbish bin

**abfliegen** ◇*VERB (IMP* **flog ab***, PERF* **ist abgeflogen) ❶ to take off**; die Maschine ist mit zehn Minuten Verspätung abgeflogen the plane took off ten minutes late ❷ **to leave** *(by plane)*; ich fliege um elf Uhr ab my plane leaves at 11 o'clock

**Abflug** der *(PLURAL die* **Abflüge)** **departure**

**Abflussrohr** das *(PLURAL die* **Abflussrohre)** **outlet**, **drain**

**abfragen** *VERB (PERF* **hat abgefragt)** ❶ **to test**; sie fragt ihn Vokabeln ab she's testing him on his vocabulary ❷ **to call up** *(on a computer)*; Adressen am Computer abfragen to call up addresses on the computer

**Abgase** *PLURAL NOUN* **exhaust fumes**

**abgeben** ◇*VERB (PRES* **gibt ab***, IMP* **gab ab***, PERF* **hat abgegeben) ❶ to hand in** *(homework, an application, lost property)* ❷ **to pass** *(in football)*; den Ball abgeben to pass the ball ❸ sich mit etwas abgeben to spend time on something, mit solchen Typen würde ich mich nicht abgeben I wouldn't want to associate with blokes like that ❹ jemandem etwas abgeben to give someone something, gib mir ein Stück von deiner Schokolade ab give me a piece of your chocolate ❺ er wird einen guten Lehrer abgeben he'll make a good teacher

**abgelegen** *ADJECTIVE* **remote**

**abgemacht** *ADJECTIVE* **agreed**

**Abgeordnete** der/die *(PLURAL die* **Abgeordneten)** **member of parliament**

**abgießen** *VERB (IMP* **goss ab***, PERF* **hat abgegossen) ❶ to pour away** ❷ **to drain** *(vegetables)*

**Abhang** der *(PLURAL die* **Abhänge)** **slope**

**abhängen¹** ◇*VERB (IMP* **hing ab***, PERF* **hat abgehangen)** von jemandem abhängen to depend on somebody, von etwas abhängen to depend on something, es hängt vom Wetter ab, ob wir am Wochenende nach Wales fahren whether or not we are going to Wales at the weekend depends on the weather

**abhängen²** *VERB (PERF* **hat abgehängt) ❶ to unhitch** *(a trailer)* ❷ **to uncouple** *(a train carriage)* ❸ *(informal)* **to shake off**; die Einbrecher hängten die Polizei schnell ab the burglars soon shook off the police

**abhängig** *ADJECTIVE* **dependent**

**abheben** ◇*VERB (IMP* **hob ab***, PERF* **hat abgehoben) ❶ to lift off** ❷ **to withdraw** *(money)* ❸ **to answer the phone**; ich habe schon zweimal angerufen, aber niemand hat abgehoben I've rung twice before, but nobody answered

**abholen** *VERB (PERF* **hat abgeholt)** ❶ **to collect** ❷ **to pick up**; ich hole dich am Bahnhof ab I'll pick you up at the station

**Abitur** das *(PLURAL die* **Abiture)** **A levels** *(German students usually take Abitur at 19, sitting exams in four subjects, which they have to pass to go on to university)*; sein Abitur machen to do your A levels

**Abiturient** der *(PLURAL die* **Abiturienten)** **A-level student**

**Abiturientin** die *(PLURAL* die **Abiturientinnen)** A-level student

**Abkommen** das *(PLURAL* die **Abkommen)** agreement

**abkürzen** *VERB (PERF* hat abgekürzt) **❶** to abbreviate; wie kürzt man das Wort ab? how do you abbreviate that word? **❷** den Weg abkürzen to take a short cut

**Abkürzung** die *(PLURAL* die **Abkürzungen)** **❶** abbreviation; die Abkürzung für Europäische Union is EU the abbreviation for European Union is EU **❷** short cut

**abladen** ◇*VERB (PRES* lädt ab, *IMP* lud ab, *PERF* hat abgeladen) to unload

**Ablaufdatum** der *(PLURAL* die **Ablaufdaten)** expiry date

**ablaufen** ◇*VERB (PRES* läuft ab, *IMP* lief ab, *PERF* ist abgelaufen) **❶** to expire *(passport, contract)* **❷** to drain off; das Badewasser ablaufen lassen to let the bathwater out **❸** to go off; wie ist die Besprechung abgelaufen? how did the meeting go?

**ablegen** *VERB (PERF* hat abgelegt) **❶** to take off **❷** abgelegte Kleidung cast-offs

**ablehnen** *VERB (PERF* hat abgelehnt) **❶** to turn down *(a position, money, an invitation)* **❷** to reject *(an applicant, a suggestion)*

**ablenken** *VERB (PERF* hat abgelenkt) **❶** to distract; jemanden von seiner Arbeit ablenken to distract somebody from their work **❷** jemanden von seinen Sorgen ablenken to take somebody's mind off their worries **❸** to divert *(attention, suspicion)*; vom Thema ablenken to change the subject

**abliefern** *VERB (PERF* hat abgeliefert) **❶** to deliver **❷** to hand in *(an essay, a form, lost property)* **❸** to drop off; die Kinder abliefern to drop the children off

**abmachen** *VERB (PERF* hat abgemacht) **❶** to take off; kannst du den Deckel abmachen? can you take off the lid? **❷** to agree; wir müssen noch einen Termin für unser nächstes Treffen abmachen we still have to agree on a date for our next meeting, abgemacht! agreed! **❸** to sort out; das müsst ihr untereinander abmachen you'll have to sort that out amongst yourselves

**Abmachung** die *(PLURAL* die **Abmachungen)** agreement

**abnehmen** ◇*VERB (PRES* nimmt ab, *IMP* nahm ab, *PERF* hat abgenommen) **❶** to take off *(remove)* **❷** kann ich dir etwas abnehmen? *(carry)* can I take something (for you)?, *(help)* can I do anything for you? **❸** jemandem etwas abnehmen to take something off somebody, sie nehmen einem schnell zwanzig Euro ab they'll soon take 20 euros off you **❹** to buy **❺** to decrease *(in number)* **❻** to diminish **❼** to lose weight; er hat schon vier Kilo abgenommen he's already lost four kilos **❽** to answer the phone **❾** das nehme ich dir nicht ab *(informal)* I don't buy that

**Abonnement** das *(PLURAL* die **Abonnements)** subscription

**abonnieren** *VERB (PERF* hat abonniert) to subscribe to

**abraten** ◇VERB (PRES **rät ab**, IMP **riet ab**, PERF **hat abgeraten**) jemandem von etwas abraten to advise somebody against something

**abräumen** VERB (PERF **hat abgeräumt**) to clear away; den Tisch abräumen to clear the table

**abreagieren** VERB (PERF **hat abreagiert**) ❶ seine Wut an jemandem abreagieren to take your anger out on somebody ❷ sich abreagieren to calm down

**Abreise** die departure

**abreisen** VERB (PERF **ist abgereist**) to leave

**abreißen** ◇VERB (IMP **riss ab**, PERF **hat abgerissen**) ❶ to tear down (a poster, notice) ❷ to demolish (a building) ❸ (PERF **ist abgerissen**) to come off (a button, for example)

**Absage** die (PLURAL die **Absagen**) refusal

**absagen** VERB (PERF **hat abgesagt**) ❶ to cancel ❷ eine Einladung absagen to turn down an invitation

**Absatz** der (PLURAL die **Absätze**) ❶ heel (of a shoe) ❷ paragraph

**abschaffen** VERB (PERF **hat abgeschafft**) ❶ to abolish (a regulation, capital punishment) ❷ to get rid of; wir haben unseren Hund abgeschafft we got rid of our dog

**abscheulich** ADJECTIVE horrible

**abschicken** VERB (PERF **hat abgeschickt**) to send off

**Abschied** der (PLURAL die **Abschiede**) ❶ parting ❷ farewell ❸ Abschied nehmen to say goodbye

**Abschleppdienst** der breakdown service

**abschleppen** VERB (PERF **hat abgeschleppt**) ❶ to tow away ❷ sich mit den Koffern abschleppen (informal) to struggle along with the suitcases ❸ jemanden abschleppen (informal) to pick somebody up

**Abschleppwagen** der (PLURAL die **Abschleppwagen**) breakdown truck

**abschließen** ◇VERB (IMP **schloss ab**, PERF **hat abgeschlossen**) to lock

**Abschlussprüfung** die (PLURAL die **Abschlussprüfungen**) final exam

**abschneiden** ◇VERB (IMP **schnitt ab**, PERF **hat abgeschnitten**) ❶ to cut off; ich schneide dir eine Scheibe Brot ab I'll cut you a slice of bread ❷ gut/schlecht abschneiden to do well/badly

**abschrecken** VERB (PERF **hat abgeschreckt**) to deter

**abschreiben** ◇VERB (IMP **schrieb ab**, PERF **hat abgeschrieben**) to copy

**Abseilen** das abseiling

**abseits** ADVERB ❶ far away; etwas abseits a little way away ❷ offside (in soccer)

**Absender** der (PLURAL die **Absender**) sender

**absetzen** VERB (PERF **hat abgesetzt**) ❶ to take off (your hat, glasses) ❷ to put down (a bag, suitcase) ❸ to drop off; ich setze euch am Bahnhof ab I'll drop you off at the station ❹ die Pille absetzen to stop taking the pill

**Absicht** die (PLURAL die **Absichten**) intention

**absichtlich** ADVERB intentionally

**absolut** *ADJECTIVE* **absolute**

**absolut** *ADVERB* **absolutely**; das ist absolut unmöglich that's absolutely impossible

**abspülen** *VERB (PERF* hat abgespült) **❶** to rinse, to rinse off **❷** to do the washing up

**Abstand** der *(PLURAL* die **Abstände)** **❶** distance; in zwanzig Meter Abstand at a distance of 20 metres, Abstand halten to keep your distance **❷** interval

**abstauben** *VERB (PERF* hat abgestaubt) to dust

**abstellen** *VERB (PERF* hat abgestellt) **❶** to turn off *(the radio, a tap)* **❷** to put down *(a suitcase, the shopping)* **❸** to park *(the car)*

**Abstimmung** die *(PLURAL* die **Abstimmungen)** vote

**abstreiten** ◇*VERB (IMP* stritt ab, *PERF* hat abgestritten) to deny

**abstürzen** *VERB (PERF* ist abgestürzt) **❶** to fall **❷** to crash *(a plane)*

**Abszess** der *(PLURAL* die **Abszesse)** abscess

**abtauen** *VERB (PERF* hat abgetaut) to defrost *(the fridge)*

**Abteil** das *(PLURAL* die **Abteile)** compartment

**abteilen** *VERB (PERF* hat abgeteilt) **❶** to divide up **❷** to divide off

**Abteilung** die *(PLURAL* die **Abteilungen)** department

**Abtreibung** die *(PLURAL* die **Abtreibungen)** abortion

**abtrocknen** *VERB (PERF* hat abgetrocknet) **❶** to dry up **❷** sich abtrocknen to dry yourself

**abwägen** *VERB (IMP* wog ab, *PERF* hat abgewogen) to weigh up

**abwärts** *ADVERB* **down**

**Abwasch** der **washing-up**

**abwaschen** ◇*VERB (PRES* wäscht ab, *IMP* wusch ab, *PERF* hat abgewaschen) **❶** to wash up *(the dishes)* **❷** to wash off *(dirt, marks)*

**Abwasser** das *(PLURAL* die **Abwässer)** sewage

**Abwechslung** die *(PLURAL* die **Abwechslungen)** change; zur Abwechslung for a change

**abwerten** *VERB (PERF* hat abgewertet) to devalue

**abwertend** *ADJECTIVE* **pejorative**

**abwesend** *ADJECTIVE* **absent**

**Abwesenheit** die **absence**

**abwischen** *VERB (PERF* hat abgewischt) to wipe

**abzählen** *VERB (PERF* hat abgezählt) to count

**Abzeichen** das *(PLURAL* die **Abzeichen)** badge

**abziehen** ◇*VERB (IMP* zog ab, *PERF* hat abgezogen) **❶** to take off *(a sheet, backing)*; die Betten abziehen to strip the beds **❷** to take out *(a key)* **❸** to deduct, to take away **❹** to withdraw *(troops)* **❺** *(PERF* ist abgezogen) to escape *(steam or smoke, for example)* **❻** *(PERF* ist abgezogen) sie sind gleich nach dem Essen abgezogen *(informal)* they pushed off straight after the meal

**abzielen** *VERB (PERF* hat abgezielt) etwas zielt auf etwas ab something is aimed at something

**Abzweigung** die *(PLURAL* die **Abzweigungen)** turning

**ach** *EXCLAMATION* **oh!**

**Achsel** die *(PLURAL* die **Achseln)** shoulder

**acht** *NUMBER* **eight**; um acht (Uhr) at eight (o'clock), um halb acht at half past seven

**Acht**[1] die *(PLURAL* die **Achten)** eight; eine Acht schreiben to write an eight

**Acht**[2] die ❶ Acht geben to pay attention, er sollte in der Schule besser Acht geben he should pay more attention at school ❷ auf etwas/jemanden Acht geben to look after something/somebody ❸ gib Acht! watch out! ❹ sich in Acht nehmen to be careful ❺ etwas außer Acht lassen to disregard something

**Achtel** das *(PLURAL* die **Achtel)** eighth

**achten** *VERB (PERF* hat **geachtet)** ❶ to respect *(a person, an opinion)* ❷ auf etwas achten to pay attention to something ❸ auf jemanden achten to look after somebody ❹ achte nicht darauf! don't take any notice of it!

**achter, achte, achtes** *ADJECTIVE* **eighth**; jede achte Kiste every eighth crate, mein achter Geburtstag my eighth birthday, sie ging als Achte durchs Ziel she finished eighth

**Achterbahn** die *(PLURAL* die **Achterbahnen)** roller coaster

**achtgeben** ▸ SEE **Acht**[2]

**achthundert** *NUMBER* **eight hundred**

**achtmal** *ADVERB* **eight times**

**Achtung** die ❶ respect; Achtung vor jemandem haben to have respect for somebody ❷ Achtung! look out!, Achtung, fertig, los! on your marks, get set, go!, 'Achtung Stufe' 'mind the step'

**achtzehn** *NUMBER* **eighteen**

**achtzig** *NUMBER* **eighty**

**Acker** der *(PLURAL* die **Äcker)** field

**addieren** *VERB (PERF* hat **addiert)** to add

**Ader** die *(PLURAL* die **Adern)** vein

**Adjektiv** das *(PLURAL* die **Adjektive)** adjective

**Adler** der *(PLURAL* die **Adler)** eagle

**adoptieren** *VERB (PERF* hat **adoptiert)** to adopt

**Adoption** die *(PLURAL* die **Adoptionen)** adoption

**Adoptiveltern** *PLURAL NOUN* adoptive parents

**Adoptivkind** das *(PLURAL* die **Adoptivkinder)** adopted child

**Adresse** die *(PLURAL* die **Adressen)** address

**adressieren** *VERB (PERF* hat **adressiert)** to address; an wen soll ich den Brief adressieren? who shall I address the letter to?

**Advent** der Advent

**Adventskalender** der *(PLURAL* die **Adventskalender)** Advent calendar

**Adventskranz** der *(PLURAL* die **Adventskränze)** Advent wreath

**Adverb** das *(PLURAL* die **Adverbien)** adverb

**Aerobic** das aerobics

**Affe** der *(PLURAL* die **Affen)** ❶ monkey ❷ ape

**Afrika** das Africa; aus Afrika from Africa, nach Afrika to Africa

**Afrikaner** der (PLURAL die **Afrikaner**) African

**Afrikanerin** die (PLURAL die **Afrikanerinnen**) African

**afrikanisch** ADJECTIVE African

**AG¹** die (PLURAL die **AGs**) (short for Aktiengesellschaft) Plc (short for Public limited company)

**AG²** die (PLURAL die **AGs**) ❶ work group ❷ school club

**Agentur** die (PLURAL die **Agenturen**) agency

**aggressiv** ADJECTIVE aggressive

**ähneln** VERB (PERF **hat geähnelt**) ❶ to resemble; er ähnelt seinem Vater sehr he's very like his father ❷ sich ähneln to be alike

**ahnen** VERB (PERF **hat geahnt**) ❶ to know; das konnte ich wirklich nicht ahnen I had no way of knowing that, wer soll denn ahnen, dass ...? who would know that ...? ❷ to suspect; so etwas habe ich doch schon geahnt I did suspect something like that

**ähnlich** ADJECTIVE ❶ similar ❷ jemandem ähnlich sein to be like somebody, jemandem ähnlich sehen to look like somebody ❸ ähnlich wie like ❹ das sieht dir ähnlich! (informal) that's just like you!

**Ähnlichkeit** die (PLURAL die **Ähnlichkeiten**) similarity

**Ahnung** die ❶ idea; hast du eine Ahnung, wie er heißt? have you got any idea what he's called? ❷ keine Ahnung! no idea!, er hat von Mode absolut keine Ahnung he doesn't know a thing about fashion ❸ premonition

**ahnungslos** ADJECTIVE unsuspecting

**Ahorn** der (PLURAL die **Ahorne**) maple

**Aids** das Aids

**Akademiker** der (PLURAL die **Akademiker**) university graduate

**Akademikerin** die (PLURAL die **Akademikerinnen**) university graduate

**akademisch** ADJECTIVE academic

**Akkusativ** der (PLURAL die **Akkusative**) accusative

**Akne** die acne

**Akte** die (PLURAL die **Akten**) file

**Aktentasche** die (PLURAL die **Aktentaschen**) briefcase

**Aktion** die (PLURAL die **Aktionen**) ❶ action; in Aktion treten to go into action ❷ campaign

**aktiv** ADJECTIVE active

**Aktiv** das active

**Aktualisierung** die (PLURAL die **Aktualisierungen**) ❶ up-date ❷ updating

**aktuell** ADJECTIVE ❶ topical; ein aktuelles Thema a topical issue ❷ nicht mehr aktuell no longer relevant ❸ current; eine aktuelle Sendung a current-affairs programme

**Akzent** der (PLURAL die **Akzente**) ❶ accent; mit starkem Akzent sprechen to speak with a strong accent ❷ accent (on a letter) ❸ stress; den Akzent auf etwas legen to stress something

**albern** ADJECTIVE silly

**albern** ADVERB in a silly way

**Albtraum** der (PLURAL die **Albträume**) nightmare

**Album** | **alltäglich**

**Album** das *(PLURAL die* **Alben***)* album

**Algebra** die algebra

**Alkohol** der alcohol

**alkoholfrei** *ADJECTIVE* non-alcoholic

**Alkoholiker** der *(PLURAL die* **Alkoholiker***)* alcoholic

**Alkoholikerin** die *(PLURAL die* **Alkoholikerinnen***)* alcoholic

**alkoholisch** *ADJECTIVE* alcoholic

**All** das space; einen Satelliten ins All schicken to send a satellite into space

**alle** ▸ SEE **aller**

**Allee** die *(PLURAL die* **Alleen***)* avenue

**allein** *ADJECTIVE, ADVERB* ❶ alone; sie waren allein im Zimmer they were alone in the room, jemanden allein lassen to leave somebody alone ❷ on your own; sie hat das ganz allein gezeichnet she drew it all on her own ❸ von allein by yourself, by itself *(automatically)* ❹ allein stehend single ❺ eine allein erziehende Mutter a single mother, der/die allein Erziehende single parent ❻ nicht allein not only ❼ allein der Gedanke the mere thought

**alleinerziehend, alleinstehend** ▸ SEE **allein**

**aller, alle, alles** *PRONOUN* ❶ all; alle meine Freunde all my friends, alles Geld all the money, alle miteinander all together ❷ alle Jungen in der Schule all the boys in the school, alle Bewohner der Stadt sind dagegen all the people of the town are against it, alles Gute! all the best!, Getränke aller Art all kinds of drinks ❸ alle *PLURAL* all,

alle waren da they were all there, wir alle all of us, wir haben alle gesehen we saw all of them ❹ ohne allen Grund without any reason ❺ alle beide both of them ❻ every; alle Tage every day, alle fünf Minuten every five minutes ❼ alles everything, everybody *(people)*

**alle** *ADJECTIVE* alle sein *(informal)* to be all gone

**allerbester, allerbeste, allerbestes** *ADJECTIVE* ❶ very best ❷ am allerbesten best of all

**allerdings** *ADVERB* ❶ though; das Essen ist gut, allerdings ziemlich teuer the food's good, though rather expensive ❷ certainly *(yes)*; 'tut das weh?' – 'allerdings!' 'does it hurt?' – 'it certainly does!'

**Allergie** die *(PLURAL die* **Allergien***)* allergy

**allergisch** *ADJECTIVE* allergic

**Allerheiligen** das All Saints' Day

**allerlei** *ADJECTIVE* all sorts of; allerlei Ausreden all sorts of excuses

**allerletzter, allerletzte, allerletztes** *ADJECTIVE* very last

**alles** ▸ SEE **aller**

**allgemein** *ADJECTIVE* ❶ general ❷ im Allgemeinen in general

**allgemein** *ADVERB* ❶ generally ❷ es ist allgemein bekannt, dass ... it is common knowledge that ...

**allmählich** *ADJECTIVE* gradual

**allmählich** *ADVERB* gradually; wir sollten allmählich gehen it's time we got going

**Alltag** der ❶ daily routine ❷ weekday

**alltäglich** *ADJECTIVE* everyday *(event, sight)*

8

**alltags** *ADVERB* on weekdays

**Alpen** *PLURAL NOUN* die Alpen the Alps

**Alphabet** das *(PLURAL* die **Alphabete)** alphabet

**alphabetisch** *ADJECTIVE* alphabetical

**als** *CONJUNCTION* **❶** when; als meine Freundin hier war when my friend was here, erst als only when **❷** than *(as a comparison);* er ist jünger als sie he's younger than her **❸** lieber ... als ... than ..., ich würde lieber ins Kino gehen, als zum Essen I'd rather go to the cinema than for a meal **❹** as; als Frau kann ich das verstehen as a woman, I can sympathize, gerade als ich gehen wollte just as I was about to leave **❺** als ob as if, als ob ich das nicht wüsste! as if I didn't know that!

**also** *ADVERB, CONJUNCTION* **❶** so; ich konnte ihn telefonisch nicht erreichen, also habe ich ihm ein E-mail geschickt I couldn't get through to him on the phone, so I sent him an email **❷** then; also kommst du mit? you're coming too, then?, also gut all right then **❸** well; also, wie gesagt well, as I said before **❹** na also! there you are!

**alt** *ADJECTIVE* **❶** old; wie alt bist du? how old are you?, alt werden to grow old **❷** alles beim Alten lassen to leave everything as it was

**Altar** der *(PLURAL* die **Altäre)** altar

**Altenheim** das *(PLURAL* die **Altenheime)** old people's home

**Alter** das *(PLURAL* die **Alter) ❶** age; in deinem Alter at your age, im Alter von zwanzig at the age of twenty **❷** old age; im Alter in old age

**älter** *ADJECTIVE* **❶** older; mein Rad ist älter als deins my bike is older than yours **❷** elder; mein älterer Bruder my elder brother **❸** elderly

**altern** *VERB (PERF* ist gealtert*)* to age

**Alternative** die *(PLURAL* die **Alternativen)** alternative

**Altersgenosse** der *(PLURAL* die **Altersgenossen)** person of one's own age

**Altersgenossin** der *(PLURAL* die **Altersgenossinnen)** person of one's own age

**Altersgrenze** die *(PLURAL* die **Altersgrenzen)** age limit

**Altersheim** das *(PLURAL* die **Altersheime)** old people's home

**ältester, älteste, ältestes** *ADJECTIVE* **❶** oldest **❷** eldest; der älteste Sohn the eldest son

**Altglas** das used glass

**Altglascontainer** der *(PLURAL* die **Altglascontainer)** bottle bank

**altmodisch** *ADJECTIVE* old-fashioned

**Altpapier** das waste paper

**Altstadt** die *(PLURAL* die **Altstädte)** old town

**Alufolie** die tin foil

**Aluminium** das aluminium

**am** an dem; **❶** am Freitag on Friday **❷** am besten the best **❸** am teuersten (the) most expensive **❹** am höchsten the highest **❺** am Abend in the evening

**Ameise** die *(PLURAL* die **Ameisen)** ant

**Amerika** das America

**Amerikaner** der *(PLURAL* die **Amerikaner)** American

**Amerikanerin** die *(PLURAL* die **Amerikanerinnen)** American

a
b
c
d
e
f
g
h
i
j
k
l
m
n
o
p
q
r
s
t
u
v
w
x
y
z

**amerikanisch** *ADJECTIVE* **American**

**Ampel** die *(PLURAL* die **Ampeln)** traffic lights

**Amsel** die *(PLURAL* die **Amseln)** blackbird

**Amt** das *(PLURAL* die **Ämter) ❶** office **❷** exchange *(telephone)*

**amtlich** *ADJECTIVE* **official**

**amüsant** *ADJECTIVE* **amusing**

**amüsieren** *VERB (PERF* **hat amüsiert) ❶** to amuse **❷** sich amüsieren to enjoy oneself, amüsier dich gut! enjoy yourself! **❸** sich über etwas amüsieren to find something funny

**an** *PREPOSITION (+DAT or +ACC)* **❶** *(the dative is used when talking about position; the accusative shows movement or a change of place)* at; an der Spitze at the top, sich an den Tisch setzen to sit down at the table, er arbeitet an der Schule he works at the school **❷** on *(attached to, when talking about time)*; das Bild hängt an der Wand the picture is on the wall, an dem Tag on that day, ich habe am fünften März Geburtstag my birthday is on the fifth of March **❸** to; einen Brief an jemanden schicken to send a letter to somebody **❹** an einer Krankheit sterben to die of a disease **❺** an jemanden denken to think of somebody **❻** sich an etwas erinnern to remember something **❼** an (und für) sich actually, an sich ist das kein Problem actually, it's no problem **❽** es liegt an dir, jetzt etwas zu unternehmen it's up to you to do something now

**an** *ADVERB* **❶** on; das Licht ist an the light's on **❷** ohne etwas an with nothing on **❸** an die dreißig Euro about thirty euros **❹** von heute an from today

**analysieren** *VERB (PERF* **hat analysiert)** to analyse

**Ananas** die *(PLURAL* die **Ananas)** pineapple

**Anästhetikum** das *(PLURAL* die **Anästhetika)** anaesthetic

**anbieten** ⬦*VERB (IMP* **bot an,** *PERF* **hat angeboten)** to offer; Anna bot mir an, mich nach Hause zu bringen Anna offered to take me home

**Anblick** der *(PLURAL* die **Anblicke)** sight

**anbrennen** ⬦*VERB (IMP* **brannte an,** *PERF* **ist angebrannt)** to burn; das Essen ist angebrannt the food's burnt

**Andenken** das *(PLURAL* die **Andenken) ❶** souvenir **❷** zum Andenken an unsere Ferien to remind us of our holiday

**anderer, andere, anderes** *ADJECTIVE* **❶** other; ich nehme das andere T-Shirt I'll have the other T-shirt **❷** different **❸** ein anderer/ eine andere/ein anderes another, ein anderes Mal another time

**andere** *PRONOUN* **❶** der/die/das andere the other one, nicht dieses Buch, sondern das andere not that book, but the other one, die anderen the others, die anderen kommen später the others are coming later **❷** andere other ones *(things, toys, etc.)* **❸** ein anderer/ eine andere/ein anderes a different one *(thing)*, someone else *(person)* **❹** kein anderer no one else **❺** unter anderem among other things **❻** etwas anderes something else **❼** alles andere everything else

**andererseits** ADVERB on the other hand

**andermal** ADVERB ein andermal another time

**ändern** VERB (PERF hat geändert) ❶ to change ❷ to alter (a garment) ❸ sich ändern to change, sie hat sich sehr geändert she's changed a lot

**anders** ADVERB ❶ differently ❷ anders aussehen to look different ❸ niemand anders nobody else, jemand anders somebody else ❹ anders als different from, du bist ganz anders als ich you're quite different from me ❺ irgendwo anders somewhere else

**anderthalb** NUMBER one and a half

**Anerkennung** die ❶ appreciation ❷ recognition (of a king, state)

**Anfall** der (PLURAL die **Anfälle**) fit

**Anfang** der (PLURAL die **Anfänge**) ❶ beginning, start; am Anfang at the beginning, von Anfang an from the start ❷ zu Anfang at first

**anfangen** ◇VERB (PRES **fängt an**, IMP **fing an**, PERF **hat angefangen**) ❶ to begin, to start; die Schule fängt um acht an school starts at eight, mit etwas anfangen to start (on) something ❷ bei einer Firma anfangen to start working for a firm ❸ was soll ich damit anfangen? what am I supposed to do with that? ❹ damit kann ich nichts anfangen that's no good to me (it's no use), it doesn't mean anything to me (I don't understand it)

**Anfänger** der (PLURAL die **Anfänger**) beginner

**Anfängerin** die (PLURAL die **Anfängerinnen**) beginner

**anfassen** VERB (PERF **hat angefasst**) ❶ to touch ❷ to tackle (a problem, a task) ❸ to treat (a person) ❹ mit anfassen to lend a hand ❺ sich anfassen to feel, es fasst sich weich an it feels soft ❻ jemanden anfassen to take somebody's hand, sie hat ihre Mutter angefasst she took her mother's hand, fasst euch an! hold hands!

**anfragen** VERB (PERF **hat angefragt**) to enquire, to ask

**anfreunden** VERB (PERF **hat sich angefreundet**) ❶ sich anfreunden to make friends, sie freundet sich mit allen möglichen Leuten an she makes friends with all sorts of people ❷ sich anfreunden to become friends, wir haben uns angefreundet we've become friends

**Anführungszeichen** PLURAL NOUN inverted commas

**Angabe** die (PLURAL die **Angaben**) ❶ piece of information ❷ serve (in tennis) ❸ showing off; das ist nur Angabe he is/she is/they are only showing off

**angeben** ◇VERB (PRES **gibt an**, IMP **gab an**, PERF **hat angegeben**) ❶ to give (your name, a reason) ❷ to show off ❸ to indicate (on a map) ❹ to serve (in tennis)

**Angeber** der (PLURAL die **Angeber**) show-off

**Angeberin** die (PLURAL die **Angeberinnen**) show-off

**Angebot** das (PLURAL die **Angebote**) offer

**angehen** ◇VERB (IMP **ging an**, PERF **ist angegangen**) ❶ to come on (a radio, heating, a light) ❷ to concern; das geht auch dich etwas an it concerns you too, das geht dich nichts an it's none of your business ❸ (PERF **hat angegangen**) to tackle (problems, difficulty, work)

**Angehörige** der/die (PLURAL die **Angehörigen**) relative

**Angel** die (PLURAL die **Angeln**) fishing rod

**Angelegenheit** die (PLURAL die **Angelegenheiten**) ❶ matter ❷ business; das ist meine Angelegenheit that's my business

**angeln** VERB (PERF **hat geangelt**) ❶ to fish; angeln gehen to go fishing ❷ to catch (a fish)

**Angelrute** die (PLURAL die **Angelruten**) fishing rod

**angemessen** ADJECTIVE adequate

**angenehm** ADJECTIVE pleasant

**angenehm** EXCLAMATION pleased to meet you! (when introduced to somebody)

**Angestellte** der/die (PLURAL die **Angestellten**) employee

**angewiesen** ADJECTIVE dependent; auf etwas angewiesen sein to be dependent on something, auf jemanden angewiesen sein to be dependent on somebody

**angewöhnen** VERB (PERF **hat angewöhnt**) ❶ jemandem etwas angewöhnen to get somebody used to something ❷ sich etwas angewöhnen to get into the habit of doing something, ich habe es mir angewöhnt, früh aufzustehen I've got into the habit of getting up early

**Angewohnheit** die (PLURAL die **Angewohnheiten**) habit

**angreifen** ◇VERB (IMP **griff an**, PERF **hat angegriffen**) ❶ to attack ❷ to affect (your health, voice)

**Angriff** der (PLURAL die **Angriffe**) attack

**Angst** die (PLURAL die **Ängste**) ❶ fear ❷ Angst haben to be afraid, vor jemandem Angst haben to be afraid of somebody, mir ist Angst I'm afraid ❸ jemandem Angst machen to frighten somebody ❹ Angst vor einer Prüfung haben to be worried about an exam, Angst um jemanden haben to be worried about somebody

**ängstlich** ADJECTIVE ❶ nervous ❷ frightened ❸ anxious

**anhaben** ◇VERB (informal) (PRES **hat an**, IMP **hatte an**, PERF **hat angehabt**) to have on; sie hat heute das neue Kleid an she's got her new dress on today

**anhalten** ◇VERB (PRES **hält an**, IMP **hielt an**, PERF **hat angehalten**) ❶ to stop ❷ den Atem anhalten to hold your breath ❸ to last; das schöne Wetter wird nicht lange anhalten the nice weather won't last long ❹ jemanden zur Arbeit anhalten to urge somebody to work

**Anhalter** der (PLURAL die **Anhalter**) hitchhiker; per Anhalter fahren to hitchhike

**Anhalterin** die (PLURAL die **Anhalterinnen**) hitchhiker

**Anhang** der (PLURAL die **Anhänge**) appendix

**Anhänger** der (PLURAL die **Anhänger**) ❶ supporter ❷ trailer ❸ label (on a suitcase) ❹ pendant ❺ loop (for hanging up)

**Anhängerin** die *(PLURAL* die **Anhängerinnen)** supporter

**anhören** *VERB (PERF* hat angehört) ❶ to listen to *(music)*; sich etwas anhören to listen to something, ich kann ihn mir nicht länger anhören I can't listen to him any longer ❷ sich anhören to sound, sich gut anhören to sound good ❸ jemandem etwas anhören to hear something in somebody's voice, man hörte ihr die Verzweiflung an you could hear the despair in her voice

**anklagen** *VERB (PERF* hat angeklagt) to accuse

**Ankleidekabine** die *(PLURAL* die **Ankleidekabinen)** changing cubicle

**anklicken** *VERB (PERF* hat angeklickt) etwas anklicken to click on something, das Icon anklicken to click on the icon

**ankommen** ◇*VERB (IMP* kam an, *PERF* ist angekommen) ❶ to arrive; gut ankommen to arrive safely ❷ (bei jemandem) gut ankommen *(informal)* to go down well (with somebody) ❸ ankommen auf to depend on, es kommt ganz darauf an it all depends ❹ es drauf ankommen lassen *(informal)* to take a chance ❺ auf ein paar Minuten kommt es nicht an a few minutes don't matter

**ankündigen** *VERB (PERF* hat angekündigt) to announce

**Ankunft** die *(PLURAL* die **Ankünfte)** arrival

**Ankunftstafel** die *(PLURAL* die **Ankunftstafeln)** arrivals board

**Ankunftszeit** die *(PLURAL* die **Ankunftszeiten)** time of arrival

**Anlage** die *(PLURAL* die **Anlagen)** ❶ gardens ❷ investment; das Haus ist eine gute Anlage the house is a good investment ❸ plant *(industrial, for recycling, for example)* ❹ enclosure; als Anlage enclosed ❺ system *(music, loudspeakers, etc.)* ❻ installation *(military)*

**Anlass** der *(PLURAL* die **Anlässe)** ❶ cause; der Anlass ihres Streits the cause of their row, Anlass zu etwas geben to give cause for something ❷ occasion; ein festlicher Anlass a festive occasion, aus Anlass ihres Geburtstags on the occasion of her birthday

**Anleitung** die *(PLURAL* die **Anleitungen)** instructions

**anmachen** *VERB (PERF* hat angemacht) ❶ to turn on *(the light, radio, TV)* ❷ to light *(a fire)* ❸ to dress *(salad)* ❹ *(informal)* to chat up *(a person)*

**Anmeldeformular** das *(PLURAL* die **Anmeldeformulare)** registration form

**anmelden** *VERB (PERF* hat angemeldet) ❶ to register *(a car, change of address)* ❷ jemanden anmelden to enrol somebody ❸ jemanden anmelden to make an appointment for somebody, sind Sie angemeldet? do you have an appointment? ❹ ein Gespräch anmelden to book a call *(on the phone)* ❺ sich anmelden to say that you're coming ❻ sich anmelden to register your new address *(in Germany a change of address has to be registered at the 'Einwohnermeldeamt')*, sich polizeilich anmelden to register with the police ❼ sich anmelden to make an appointment, sich

a
b
c
d
e
f
g
h
i
j
k
l
m
n
o
p
q
r
s
t
u
v
w
x
y
z

beim Arzt anmelden to make an appointment with the doctor ❽ sich anmelden to check in *(at a hotel)* ❾ sich anmelden to enrol, sich zu einem Abendkurs anmelden to enrol for an evening course

**Anmeldung** die *(PLURAL die Anmeldungen)* ❶ registration ❷ appointment

**annehmbar** *ADJECTIVE* acceptable

**annehmen** ⬦*VERB (PRES nimmt an, IMP nahm an, PERF hat angenommen)* ❶ to accept *(an invitation, help, a verdict)* ❷ to take *(a call, name)* ❸ to adopt *(a child, habit)* ❹ to assume; angenommen, dass ... assuming that ... ❺ to suppose

**Annonce** die *(PLURAL die Annoncen)* (small) ad

**Anorak** der *(PLURAL die Anoraks)* ❶ anorak ❷ cagoule

**anordnen** *VERB (PERF hat angeordnet)* ❶ to arrange ❷ to order

**anpassen** *VERB (PERF hat sich angepasst)* sich anpassen to adapt

**anpassungsfähig** *ADJECTIVE* adaptable

**anprobieren** *VERB (PERF hat anprobiert)* to try on

**Anruf** der *(PLURAL die Anrufe)* (phone) call

**Anrufbeantworter** der *(PLURAL die Anrufbeantworter)* answering machine

**anrufen** ⬦*VERB (IMP rief an, PERF hat angerufen)* ❶ to ring, to phone; ich rufe schnell mal meine Mutter an I'll just quickly ring my mother ❷ to call to *(a passer-by)*

**ans** an das; ans Telefon gehen to answer the phone

**Ansage** die *(PLURAL die Ansagen)* announcement

**Ansager** der *(PLURAL die Ansager)* announcer

**Ansagerin** die *(PLURAL die Ansagerinnen)* announcer

**anschalten** *VERB (PERF hat angeschaltet)* to switch on

**anschauen** *VERB (PERF hat angeschaut)* ❶ to look at ❷ sich etwas anschauen to look at something, to watch something *(on TV)*, sie schauten sich den neuen Film an they saw the new film

**anscheinend** *ADVERB* apparently

**Anschlag** der *(PLURAL die Anschläge)* ❶ notice ❷ attack; ein Anschlag auf den Präsidenten an attack on the president

**Anschlagbrett** das *(PLURAL die Anschlagbretter)* notice board

**anschlagen** ⬦*VERB (PRES schlägt an, IMP schlug an, PERF hat angeschlagen)* ❶ to put up *(a notice, an announcement)* ❷ to chip

**anschließen** ⬦*VERB (IMP schloss an, PERF hat angeschlossen)* ❶ to connect ❷ sich an etwas anschließen to follow something, an den Vortrag schließt sich eine Diskussion an the talk will be followed by a discussion ❸ sich jemandem anschließen to join somebody, sich einer Gruppe anschließen to join a group

**anschließend** *ADVERB* ❶ afterwards ❷ anschließend an das Essen after the meal

**Anschluss** der *(PLURAL die Anschlüsse)* ❶ connection

❷ **Anschluss finden** to make friends ❸ **den Anschluss verlieren** to lose contact ❹ **im Anschluss an** after

**anschnallen** VERB *(PERF* **hat sich angeschnallt)** **sich anschnallen** to fasten your seat belt

**Anschrift** die *(PLURAL die* **Anschriften)** address

**Anschuldigung** die *(PLURAL die* **Anschuldigungen)** accusation

**ansehen** ◇VERB *(PRES* **sieht an**, *IMP* **sah an**, *PERF* **hat angesehen)** ❶ to look at; **sie sah mich nicht an** she didn't look at me ❷ **sich etwas ansehen** to look at something *(on TV)* to **watch something; sich einen Film ansehen** to see a film ❸ **sich eine Stadt ansehen** to look round a town ❹ to regard; **ich sehe ihn als meinen Freund an** I regard him as a friend

**Ansehen** das ❶ respect ❷ reputation

**Ansicht** die *(PLURAL die* **Ansichten)** view; **meiner Ansicht nach** in my view

**Ansichtskarte** die *(PLURAL die* **Ansichtskarten)** picture postcard

**ansprechen** ◇VERB *(PRES* **spricht an**, *IMP* **sprach an**, *PERF* **hat angesprochen)** ❶ to speak to ❷ to appeal to; **die Musik spricht mich an** the music appeals to me ❸ to mention; **er hat den Skandal, in den sie verwickelt war, angesprochen** he mentioned the scandal she was involved in ❹ **auf etwas ansprechen** to respond to something *(a treatment, for example)*

**Anspruch** der *(PLURAL die* **Ansprüche)** ❶ demand;

**keine Ansprüche stellen** to make no demands ❷ **claim** *(for compensation)* ❸ **Anspruch auf etwas haben** to be entitled to something ❹ **viel Zeit in Anspruch nehmen** to take up a lot of time ❺ **etwas in Anspruch nehmen** to take advantage of something *(an offer, for example)*

**anständig** ADJECTIVE ❶ decent ❷ respectable

**anstarren** VERB *(PERF* **hat angestarrt)** to stare at

**anstatt** PREPOSITION *(+GEN)* instead of

**anstatt** CONJUNCTION **anstatt zu arbeiten** instead of working

**ansteckend** ADJECTIVE infectious

**anstelle** PREPOSITION *(+GEN)* instead of

**anstellen** VERB *(PERF* **hat angestellt)** ❶ to employ ❷ to turn on *(the TV, radio)* ❸ *(informal)* to do; **was stellt ihr heute Abend noch an?** what are you doing tonight?, **wie kann ich es nur anstellen, dass ...?** what can I do to ...? ❹ **sich anstellen** to queue ❺ **sich anstellen** to make a fuss, **stell dich nicht so an!** don't make such a fuss!

**Anstieg** der *(PLURAL die* **Anstiege)** ❶ increase ❷ way up, ascent

**anstreichen** ◇VERB *(IMP* **strich an**, *PERF* **hat angestrichen)** to paint

**anstrengen** VERB *(PERF* **hat angestrengt)** ❶ to tire; **ihr Besuch hat mich sehr angestrengt** their visit tired me out ❷ **sich anstrengen** to make an effort

**anstrengend** ADJECTIVE tiring

**Anstrengung** die *(PLURAL die* **Anstrengungen)** effort

**Antarktis** die (PLURAL die Antarktis) the Antarctic

**Anteil** der (PLURAL die **Anteile**) ❶ share; mein Anteil an dem Gewinn my share of the profit ❷ Anteil nehmen to sympathize ❸ Anteil nehmen an to take an interest in

**Antenne** die (PLURAL die **Antennen**) aerial

**Antibiotikum** das (PLURAL die **Antibiotika**) antibiotic

**antik** ADJECTIVE antique

**Antiquitäten** PLURAL NOUN antiques

**Antiseptikum** das (PLURAL die **Antiseptika**) antiseptic

**Antivirenprogramm** das (PLURAL die **Antivirenprogramme**) anti-virus software

**Antrag** der (PLURAL die **Anträge**) application; einen Antrag stellen to make an application

**Antragsformular** das (PLURAL die **Antragsformulare**) application form

**Antwort** die (PLURAL die **Antworten**) answer, reply; jemandem eine Antwort geben to give somebody an answer

**antworten** VERB (PERF hat geantwortet) to answer, to reply; auf etwas antworten to answer something, jemandem antworten to reply to somebody

**Anwalt** der (PLURAL die **Anwälte**) lawyer

**Anwältin** die (PLURAL die **Anwältinnen**) lawyer

**Anweisung** die (PLURAL die **Anweisungen**) instruction

**anwenden** VERB (PERF hat angewendet) ❶ to use (a method, process, medicine) ❷ to apply (a rule, law)

**Anwendung** die (PLURAL die **Anwendungen**) ❶ use ❷ (on mobile phone) application

**anwesend** ADJECTIVE present

**Anwesenheit** die presence; er gab es in meiner Anwesenheit zu he admitted it in my presence

**Anzahl** die number

**anzahlen** VERB (PERF hat angezahlt) to pay a deposit; hundert Euro anzahlen to pay a deposit of a hundred euros, ein Auto anzahlen to pay a deposit on a car

**Anzahlung** die (PLURAL die **Anzahlungen**) deposit

**Anzeichen** das (PLURAL die **Anzeichen**) sign

**Anzeige** die (PLURAL die **Anzeigen**) ❶ advertisement ❷ report (to the police); (eine) Anzeige gegen jemanden erstatten to report somebody to the police

**anzeigen** VERB (PERF hat angezeigt) ❶ to report; jemanden anzeigen to report somebody to the police ❷ to show (the time, a date)

**anziehen** ◇VERB (IMP zog an, PERF hat angezogen) ❶ to attract ❷ to put on (clothes, the brakes) ❸ to dress (a child or doll); gut angezogen well dressed ❹ to tighten (a knot, a screw) ❺ sich anziehen to get dressed ❻ was soll ich anziehen? what shall I wear?

**Anzug** der (PLURAL die **Anzüge**) suit

**anzünden** VERB (PERF hat angezündet) to light

**Apfel** der *(PLURAL* die **Äpfel)** apple

**Apfelsaft** der *(PLURAL* die **Apfelsäfte)** apple juice

**Apfelsine** die *(PLURAL* die **Apfelsinen)** orange

**Apotheke** die *(PLURAL* die **Apotheken)** chemist's, pharmacy

**Apotheker** der *(PLURAL* die **Apotheker)** chemist, pharmacist

**Apothekerin** die *(PLURAL* die **Apothekerinnen)** chemist, pharmacist

**App** die *(PLURAL* die **Apps)** app

**Apparat** der *(PLURAL* die **Apparate)** ❶ set *(TV, radio)* ❷ camera ❸ phone; am Apparat! speaking! ❹ gadget

**Appartement** das *(PLURAL* die **Appartements)** flat

**Appetit** der appetite; guten Appetit! enjoy your meal!

**Aprikose** die *(PLURAL* die **Aprikosen)** apricot

**April** der April; am ersten April on the first of April, April, April! April fool! jemanden in den April schicken to play an April fool trick on somebody

**Aquarium** das *(PLURAL* die **Aquarien)** ❶ aquarium ❷ tank *(for fish)*

**Äquator** der equator

**Araber** der *(PLURAL* die **Araber)** Arab

**Araberin** die *(PLURAL* die **Araberinnen)** Arab

**arabisch** *ADJECTIVE* ❶ Arab; die arabischen Länder the Arab countries ❷ Arabian ❸ Arabic *(number)*; die arabische Sprache Arabic

**Arbeit** die *(PLURAL* die **Arbeiten)** ❶ work; viel Arbeit haben to have a lot of work, von der Arbeit kommen to come from work ❷ job ❸ test *(at school)* ❹ sich viel Arbeit machen to go to a lot of trouble

**arbeiten** *VERB (PERF* hat gearbeitet) to work

**Arbeiter** der *(PLURAL* die **Arbeiter)** worker

**Arbeiterin** die *(PLURAL* die **Arbeiterinnen)** worker

**Arbeitgeber** der *(PLURAL* die **Arbeitgeber)** employer

**Arbeitnehmer** der *(PLURAL* die **Arbeitnehmer)** employee

**Arbeitsamt** das *(PLURAL* die **Arbeitsämter)** job centre

**arbeitslos** *ADJECTIVE* unemployed

**Arbeitslose** der/die *(PLURAL* die **Arbeitslosen)** unemployed person; die Arbeitslosen the unemployed

**Arbeitslosigkeit** die unemployment

**Arbeitsplatz** der *(PLURAL* die **Arbeitsplätze)** ❶ job ❷ desk

**Arbeitspraktikum** das *(PLURAL* die **Arbeitspraktika)** work experience

**Arbeitsstunde** die *(PLURAL* die **Arbeitsstunden)** working hour

**Arbeitszeit** die *(PLURAL* die **Arbeitszeiten)** working hours

**Arbeitszimmer** das *(PLURAL* die **Arbeitszimmer)** study

**Architekt** der *(PLURAL* die **Architekten)** architect

**Architektin** die *(PLURAL* die **Architektinnen)** architect

**Architektur** die architecture

a
b
c
d
e
f
g
h
i
j
k
l
m
n
o
p
q
r
s
t
u
v
w
x
y
z

**Ärger** der ❶ annoyance ❷ trouble; Ärger mit dem Auto haben to have trouble with the car

**ärgerlich** ADJECTIVE ❶ annoying ❷ annoyed; er war darüber sehr ärgerlich he was very annoyed about it

**ärgern** VERB (PERF hat geärgert) ❶ to annoy ❷ sich ärgern to be annoyed, to get annoyed, ich habe mich darüber geärgert I was annoyed about it, sich über jemanden ärgern to get annoyed with somebody

**Arktis** die die Arktis the Arctic, in der Arktis in the Arctic

**arm** ADJECTIVE poor

**Arm** der (PLURAL die Arme) arm; jemanden auf den Arm nehmen (informal) to pull somebody's leg

**Armband** das (PLURAL die Armbänder) bracelet

**Armbanduhr** die (PLURAL die Armbanduhren) wrist-watch

**Armee** die (PLURAL die Armeen) army

**Ärmel** der (PLURAL die Ärmel) sleeve

**Ärmelkanal** der (English) Channel

**Armut** die poverty

**arrangieren** VERB (PERF hat arrangiert) ❶ to arrange ❷ sich arrangieren to come to an arrangement

**Art** die (PLURAL die Arten) ❶ way; auf diese Art in this way, auf seine Art in his own way ❷ kind; diese Art (von) Buch this kind of book, Bücher aller Art books of all kinds ❸ species; eine gefährdete Art an endangered species ❹ nature; es ist nicht seine Art, das zu tun it's not (in) his nature to do that

**Arterie** die (PLURAL die Arterien) artery

**artig** ADJECTIVE well-behaved

**Artikel** der (PLURAL die Artikel) article; der bestimmte/ unbestimmte Artikel the definite/ indefinite article

**Arznei** die (PLURAL die Arzneien) medicine

**Arzneimittel** das (PLURAL die Arzneimittel) drug

**Arzt** der (PLURAL die Ärzte) doctor

**Ärztin** die (PLURAL die Ärztinnen) doctor

**ärztlich** ADJECTIVE medical

**ärztlich** ADVERB sich ärztlich behandeln lassen to have medical treatment

**As** ▸ SEE **Ass**

**Asche** die (PLURAL die Aschen) ash

**Aschenbecher** der (PLURAL die Aschenbecher) ashtray

**Aschermittwoch** der Ash Wednesday

**Asiat** der (PLURAL die Asiaten) Asian

**Asiatin** die (PLURAL die Asiatinnen) Asian

**asiatisch** ADJECTIVE Asian

**Asien** das Asia; nach Asien to Asia

**Ass** das (PLURAL die Asse) ace

**aß** ▸ SEE **essen**

**Assistent** der (PLURAL die Assistenten) assistant

**Assistentin** die (PLURAL die Assistentinnen) assistant

**Ast** der (PLURAL die Äste) branch

**Asthma** das asthma

**Astrologie** die astrology

**Astronaut** der (PLURAL die Astronauten) astronaut

**Astronomie** die astronomy

**Asyl** das ❶ asylum; um politisches Asyl bitten to apply for political asylum ❷ hostel *(for the homeless)*

**Asylant** der *(PLURAL die Asylanten)* asylum-seeker

**Atelier** das *(PLURAL die Ateliers)* *(artist's)* studio

**Atem** der breath; außer Atem sein to be out of breath

**atemlos** ADJECTIVE breathless

**Atemlosigkeit** die breathlessness

**Athlet** der *(PLURAL die Athleten)* athlete

**Athletin** die *(PLURAL die Athletinnen)* athlete

**Atlantik** der der Atlantik the Atlantic (Ocean), im Atlantik in the Atlantic

**Atlas** der *(PLURAL die Atlanten)* atlas

**atmen** VERB *(PERF hat geatmet)* to breathe

**Atmosphäre** die *(PLURAL die Atmosphären)* atmosphere

**Atom** das *(PLURAL die Atome)* atom

**atomar** ADJECTIVE atomic

**Atombombe** die *(PLURAL die Atombomben)* atomic bomb

**Atomwaffen** PLURAL NOUN nuclear weapons

**atomwaffenfrei** ADJECTIVE nuclear-free

**attraktiv** ADJECTIVE attractive

**ätzend** ADJECTIVE ❶ corrosive ❷ caustic *(wit, remark)*

**au** EXCLAMATION ❶ ouch! ❷ oh! *(when surprised or enthusiastic)*; au ja! oh yes!

**auch** ADVERB ❶ also, too; Sophie war auch dabei Sophie was also there, Sophie was there too, ich auch me too, nicht nur ... sondern auch ... not only ... but also ... ❷ 'ich gehe jetzt' - 'ich auch' 'I'm going now' - 'so am I', 'er schläft' - 'sie auch' 'he's asleep' - 'so is she' ❸ 'ich bin nicht müde' - 'ich auch nicht' 'I'm not tired' - 'neither am I', das weiß ich auch nicht I don't know either ❹ auch wenn even if ❺ wann auch whenever, was auch whatever, wo auch wherever, wer auch whoever ❻ wie dem auch sei however that may be ❼ lügst du auch nicht? you're not lying, are you?

**auf** PREPOSITION *(+DAT or +ACC)* ❶ *(the dative is used when talking about position; the accusative shows movement or a change of place)* on; das Buch liegt auf dem Tisch the book's on the table, er hat das Buch auf den Tisch gelegt he put the book on the table ❷ ich war auf der Party I was at the party, ich gehe auf eine Party I'm going to a party, ich war auf der Post I was at the post office, er ist auf die Post gegangen he went to the post office ❸ auf der Straße in the street ❹ auf diese Art in this way, auf Deutsch in German ❺ for *(indicating time or distance)*; er ist auf ein paar Tage verreist he's gone away for a few days ❻ auf seinen Rat hin on his advice ❼ auf Wiedersehen! goodbye!

**auf** ADVERB ❶ open; die Tür ist auf the door is open, Mund auf! open your mouth! ❷ up *(out of bed)*; auf sein to be up, er ist schon auf he's already up ❸ auf einmal suddenly ❹ auf einmal at once *(at the same time)* ❺ auf und ab up and down ❻ sich auf und davon machen to make off

19

**aufbekommen** ◇*VERB (IMP* **bekam auf,** *PERF* **hat aufbekommen)** ❶ to get open ❷ Hausaufgaben aufbekommen to be given homework

**aufbewahren** *VERB (PERF* **hat aufbewahrt)** to keep

**aufblasen** ◇*VERB (PRES* **bläst auf,** *IMP* **blies auf,** *PERF* **hat aufgeblasen)** to blow up

**aufbleiben** ◇*VERB (IMP* **blieb auf,** *PERF* **ist aufgeblieben)** ❶ to stay open; wie lange bleiben die Geschäfte auf? how long do the shops stay open? ❷ to stay up *(not go to bed)*

**aufbringen** ◇*VERB (IMP* **brachte auf,** *PERF* **hat aufgebracht)** ❶ to raise *(money)* ❷ to find *(patience, strength)* ❸ to open; ich bringe die Tür nicht auf I can't open the door ❹ jemanden aufbringen to make somebody angry ❺ Verständnis für etwas aufbringen to be able to understand something

**aufeinander** *ADVERB* ❶ one on top of the other; die Bretter aufeinander legen to put the planks one on top of the other ❷ aufeinander liegen to lie on top of each other ❸ aufeinander folgen to follow one another ❹ aufeinander warten to wait for each other ❺ aufeinander schießen to shoot at each other ❻ aufeinander fahren to collide with each other

**Aufenthalt** der *(PLURAL* die **Aufenthalte)** ❶ stay ❷ stop *(pause in a journey)*; zehn Minuten Aufenthalt haben to stop for ten minutes

**Aufenthaltsraum** der *(PLURAL* die **Aufenthaltsräume)** ❶ lounge ❷ recreation room

**Auffahrt** die *(PLURAL* die **Auffahrten)** ❶ drive ❷ slip road

**auffallend** *ADJECTIVE* striking

**auffangen** ◇*VERB (PRES* **fängt auf,** *IMP* **fing auf,** *PERF* **hat aufgefangen)** to catch

**aufführen** *VERB (PERF* **hat aufgeführt)** ❶ to perform *(a play)* ❷ to list *(words, items)* ❸ sich aufführen to behave

**Aufführung** die *(PLURAL* die **Aufführungen)** performance

**auffüllen** *VERB (PERF* **hat aufgefüllt)** ❶ to fill up ❷ to stock up

**Aufgabe** die *(PLURAL* die **Aufgaben)** ❶ task ❷ exercise *(at school)* ❸ question *(in a test or an exam)* ❹ Aufgaben homework

**aufgeben** ◇*VERB (PRES* **gibt auf,** *IMP* **gab auf,** *PERF* **hat aufgegeben)** ❶ to give up; ich gebe auf! I give up! ❷ to post ❸ to check in *(luggage)* ❹ to place *(an advertisement, order)* ❺ Hausaufgaben aufgeben to set homework

**aufgehen** ◇*VERB (IMP* **ging auf,** *PERF* **ist aufgegangen)** ❶ to open *(of a door or flower, for example)* ❷ to come undone *(of a knot or zip, for example)* ❸ to rise *(of the sun, moon)* ❹ to realize; es ist mir aufgegangen, dass ... I've realized that ... ❺ to work out *(in maths)*; zehn durch drei geht nicht auf three into ten won't go

**aufgeregt** *ADJECTIVE* excited

**aufgeschlossen** *ADJECTIVE* open-minded

**aufgrund** *PREPOSITION (+GEN)* ❶ because of ❷ on the strength of

20

**aufhaben** ◇*VERB (PRES* **hat auf***, IMP* **hatte auf***, PERF* **hat aufgehabt)* **❶ to have on** *(a hat)* **❷ den Mund aufhaben** to have your mouth open **❸ etwas aufhaben** to have homework to do, **viel aufhaben** to have a lot of homework **❹ to be open**; **der Laden hat abends auf** the shop is open in the evening

**aufhalten** ◇*VERB (PRES* **hält auf***, IMP* **hielt auf***, PERF* **hat aufgehalten)* **❶ to hold open** *(a door)* **❷ to hold up, to keep** *(somebody from doing something)* **❸ die Hand aufhalten** to hold out your hand **❹ die Augen aufhalten** to keep your eyes open **❺ to check** *(inflation, an advance, unemployment)* **❻ sich aufhalten** to stay **❼ sich mit etwas aufhalten** to spend your time on something

**aufhängen** *VERB (PERF* **hat aufgehängt)* **❶ to hang up** *(washing)* **❷ sich aufhängen** to hang yourself

**aufheben** ◇*VERB (IMP* **hob auf***, PERF* **hat aufgehoben)* **❶ to pick up** *(from the ground)* **❷ to keep ❸ to abolish** *(a law)* **❹ gut aufgehoben sein** to be well looked after

**aufheitern** *VERB (PERF* **hat aufgeheitert)* **❶ to cheer up ❷ sich aufheitern** to brighten up *(of the weather)*

**aufhören** *VERB (PERF* **hat aufgehört)* **to stop**; **aufhören zu arbeiten** to stop working

**aufklären** *VERB (PERF* **hat aufgeklärt)* **❶ to solve** *(a crime)* **❷ to explain** *(an event, incident)* **❸ ein Kind aufklären** to tell a child the facts of life **❹ sich aufklären** to be solved *(a misunderstanding or mystery)* **❺ sich aufklären** to clear up, das

Wetter klärt sich auf the weather is clearing up

**Aufkleber** der *(PLURAL* die **Aufkleber)** **sticker**

**auflegen** *VERB (PERF* **hat aufgelegt)* **❶ to put on ❷ to hang up** *(when phoning)* **❸ to lay**; **noch ein Gedeck auflegen** to lay another place *(at table)* **❹ to publish**; **ein Buch neu auflegen** to reprint a book

**auflösen** *VERB (PERF* **hat aufgelöst)* **❶ to dissolve ❷ to close** *(an account)* **❸ sich auflösen** to dissolve **❹ sich auflösen** to break up *(of a crowd, demonstration)* **❺ der Nebel hat sich aufgelöst** the fog has lifted **❻ in Tränen aufgelöst sein** to be in floods of tears

**aufmachen** *VERB (PERF* **hat aufgemacht)* **❶ to open ❷ jemandem aufmachen** to open the door to somebody **❸ to undo** *(a zip, knot)* **❹ sich aufmachen** to set out

**aufmerksam** *ADJECTIVE* **❶ attentive ❷ auf etwas aufmerksam werden** to notice something **❸ jemanden auf etwas aufmerksam machen** to draw somebody's attention to something

**aufmuntern** *VERB (PERF* **hat aufgemuntert)* **to cheer up**

**Aufnahme** die *(PLURAL* die **Aufnahmen)** **❶ photograph ❷ recording ❸ admission** *(to hospital, to a club)* **❹ welcome**

**Aufnahmeprüfung** die *(PLURAL* die **Aufnahmeprüfungen)** **entrance exam**

**Aufnahmetaste** die *(PLURAL* die **Aufnahmetasten)** **record button**

**aufnehmen** ◇*VERB (PRES* **nimmt auf,** *IMP* **nahm auf,** *PERF* **hat aufgenommen)** ❶ to receive *(guests)* ❷ to take up *(an idea, activity, a theme)* ❸ to admit *(to hospital, to a club)* ❹ to photograph ❺ to film ❻ to record *(a song, a programme, a film)* ❼ es mit jemandem aufnehmen können to be a match for somebody ❽ to take *(food, news)*; etwas gelassen aufnehmen to take something calmly

**aufpassen** *VERB (PERF* **hat aufgepasst)** ❶ to pay attention ❷ to watch out ❸ auf jemanden aufpassen to look after somebody ❹ auf etwas aufpassen to keep an eye on something, pass auf meine Tasche auf keep an eye on my bag

**aufräumen** *VERB (PERF* **hat aufgeräumt)** to tidy up

**aufrecht** *ADJECTIVE* **upright**

**aufregen** *VERB (PERF* **hat aufgeregt)** ❶ to excite ❷ to annoy ❸ sich aufregen to get worked up

**aufregend** *ADJECTIVE* **exciting**

**aufs** on the ▸ SEE **auf**

**Aufsatz** der *(PLURAL* die **Aufsätze)** essay

**aufschieben** ◇*VERB (IMP* **schob auf,** *PERF* **hat aufgeschoben)** ❶ to put off *(an arrangement)* ❷ to slide open

**aufschlagen** *VERB (PRES* **schlägt auf,** *IMP* **schlug auf,** *PERF* **hat aufgeschlagen)** to open

**aufschließen** ◇*VERB (IMP* **schloss auf,** *PERF* **hat aufgeschlossen)** to unlock

**Aufschnitt** der sliced cold meat and cheese

**aufschreiben** ◇*VERB (IMP* **schrieb auf,** *PERF* **hat aufgeschrieben)** to write down

**aufsehen** ◇*VERB (PRES* **sieht auf,** *IMP* **sah auf,** *PERF* **hat aufgesehen)** to look up

**Aufsehen** das sensation, stir; Aufsehen erregen to cause a stir

**Aufseher** der *(PLURAL* die **Aufseher)** ❶ supervisor ❷ warder *(in a prison)* ❸ attendant *(in a museum)*

**Aufseherin** die *(PLURAL* die **Aufseherinnen)** ❶ supervisor ❷ warder *(in a prison)* ❸ attendant *(in a museum)*

**aufsetzen** *VERB (PERF* **hat aufgesetzt)** ❶ to put on ❷ to draft ❸ sich aufsetzen to sit up

**Aufsicht** die ❶ supervision ❷ supervisor

**Aufstand** der *(PLURAL* die **Aufstände)** rebellion

**aufstehen** ◇*VERB (IMP* **stand auf,** *PERF* **ist aufgestanden)** ❶ to get up ❷ *(PERF* hat aufgestanden) to be open

**aufstellen** *VERB (PERF* **hat aufgestellt)** ❶ to put up ❷ to set up *(skittles, chess pieces)* ❸ eine Mannschaft aufstellen to pick a team ❹ eine Liste aufstellen to draw up a list ❺ sich aufstellen to line up

**auftauen** *VERB (PERF* **ist aufgetaut)** ❶ to thaw ❷ to defrost; die Erdbeeren sind aufgetaut the strawberries have defrosted ❸ *(PERF* hat aufgetaut) to defrost; ich habe die Erbeeren aufgetaut I've defrosted the strawberries

**aufteilen** *VERB (PERF* **hat aufgeteilt)** to divide up

**Auftrag** der (PLURAL die **Aufträge**)
**❶ job ❷ order** (in business);
etwas in Auftrag geben to order
something **❸ instructions**; einen
Auftrag ausführen to carry out an
instruction **❹ im Auftrag von** on
behalf of

**auftreten** ◇VERB (PRES **tritt auf**, IMP
**trat auf**, PERF **ist aufgetreten**)
**❶ to appear** (on stage) **❷ to arise**
(a problem, difficulty) **❸ to behave**
**❹ to tread**

**aufwachen** VERB (PERF **ist**
**aufgewacht**) to wake up

**aufwachsen** ◇VERB (PRES **wächst**
**auf**, IMP **wuchs auf**, PERF **ist**
**aufgewachsen**) to grow up

**aufwecken** VERB (PERF **hat**
**aufgeweckt**) to wake up

**aufziehen** ◇VERB (IMP **zog auf**, PERF
**hat aufgezogen**) **❶ to wind up** (a
clock or toy) **❷ to draw** (curtains)
**❸ jemanden aufziehen** (informal)
to tease somebody **❹ to bring up**
(a child)

**Aufzug** der (PLURAL die **Aufzüge**) **lift**;
ich fahre mit dem Aufzug runter
I'm going down in the lift

**Auge** das (PLURAL die **Augen**) **❶ eye**
**❷ unter vier Augen** in private

**Augenarzt** der (PLURAL die
**Augenärzte**) ophthalmologist

**Augenärztin** die (PLURAL
die **Augenärztinnen**)
ophthalmologist

**Augenblick** der (PLURAL die
**Augenblicke**) moment; im
Augenblick at the moment

**Augenbraue** die (PLURAL die
**Augenbrauen**) eyebrow

**August** der August

**aus** PREPOSITION (+DAT) **❶ out of**; er
hat es aus dem Fenster geworfen
he threw it out of the window
**❷ from**; aus Spanien from Spain,
aus Erfahrung from experience
**❸ made of**; aus Holz made of wood
**❹ aus Spaß** for fun **❺ aus der Mode**
out of fashion **❻ aus Versehen** by
mistake **❼ aus welchem Grund?**
for what reason? **❽ aus ihr ist eine**
gute Rechtsanwältin geworden
she made a good lawyer, aus ihm
ist nichts geworden he never made
anything of his life

**aus** ADVERB **❶ off** (of a TV, radio); das
Licht ist aus the light is off, Licht
aus! lights out! **❷ finished**; wenn
das Spiel aus ist when the game has
finished **❸ von mir aus** as far as I'm
concerned **❹ von sich aus** of your
own accord

**ausbauen** VERB (PERF **hat ausgebaut**)
**❶ to extend** (a building) **❷ to**
**build up**

**ausbeuten** VERB (PERF **hat**
**ausgebeutet**) to exploit

**ausbilden** VERB (PERF **hat**
**ausgebildet**) to train

**Ausbildung** die **❶ training**
**❷ education**

**ausbreiten** VERB (PERF **hat**
**ausgebreitet**) **❶ to unfold ❷ to**
**spread ❸ to stretch** (one's arms
etc)

**ausbuhen** VERB (PERF **hat ausgebuht**)
to boo; die Menge buhte den
Schiedsrichter aus the crowd booed
the referee

**ausdehnen** VERB (PERF **hat**
**ausgedehnt**) **❶ to extend, to**
**prolong ❷ to expand**

a
b
c
d
e
f
g
h
i
j
k
l
m
n
o
p
q
r
s
t
u
v
w
x
y
z

**Ausdruck¹** der *(PLURAL* die **Ausdrücke)** expression; etwas zum Ausdruck bringen to express something

**Ausdruck²** der *(PLURAL* die **Ausdrucke)** print-out

**ausdrucken** VERB *(PERF* **hat ausgedruckt)** to print out

**ausdrücken** VERB *(PERF* **hat ausgedrückt)** ❶ to squeeze *(oranges, lemons)* ❷ to express ❸ sich ausdrücken to express oneself

**auseinander** ADVERB ❶ apart; etwas auseinander nehmen to take something apart, auseinander halten to tell apart ❷ auseinander gehen to part ❸ auseinander schreiben to write as separate words ❹ sich mit einem Problem auseinander setzen to come to grips with a problem ❺ sich mit jemandem auseinander setzen to have it out with somebody

**Ausfahrt** die *(PLURAL* die **Ausfahrten)** ❶ exit ❷ 'Ausfahrt freihalten' 'keep clear'

**Ausfall** der *(PLURAL* die **Ausfälle)** ❶ result ❷ failure, breakdown ❸ loss *(of hair, teeth)* ❹ cancellation

**ausfallen** ◇VERB *(PRES* **fällt aus,** *IMP* **fiel aus,** *PERF* **ist ausgefallen)** ❶ to be cancelled; etwas ausfallen lassen to cancel something ❷ to fall out *(hair)* ❸ to fail *(an engine, brakes, a signal)* ❹ to break down *(a machine, a car, heating)* ❺ to turn out; gut ausfallen to turn out well

**Ausflug** der *(PLURAL* die **Ausflüge)** outing, trip; einen Ausflug machen to go on an outing

**Ausfuhr** die export

**ausführen** VERB *(PERF* **hat ausgeführt)** ❶ to carry out *(a plan)* ❷ to export *(goods)* ❸ to take out; er hat seine Freundin zum Essen ausgeführt he took his girlfriend out for a meal ❹ den Hund ausführen to take the dog for a walk

**ausführlich** ADJECTIVE detailed

**ausführlich** ADVERB in detail

**ausfüllen** VERB *(PERF* **hat ausgefüllt)** ❶ to fill in; ein Formular ausfüllen to fill in a form ❷ ihr Beruf als Lehrerin füllt sie ganz aus teaching gives her great satisfaction

**Ausgabe** die *(PLURAL* die **Ausgaben)** ❶ edition ❷ issue ❸ Ausgaben expenditure

**Ausgang** der *(PLURAL* die **Ausgänge)** ❶ exit; 'kein Ausgang' 'no exit' ❷ end, ending ❸ result *(of a game, discussion)*

**ausgeben** ◇VERB *(PRES* **gibt aus,** *IMP* **gab aus,** *PERF* **hat ausgegeben)** ❶ to spend ❷ to hand out ❸ Fahrkarten ausgeben to issue tickets ❹ to serve *(food)* ❺ sich ausgeben als to pretend to be ❻ einen ausgeben *(informal)* to treat everybody *(to a round of drinks for example)*

**ausgebucht** ADJECTIVE fully booked

**ausgehen** ◇VERB *(PRES* **geht aus,** *IMP* **ging aus,** *PERF* **ist ausgegangen)** ❶ to go out; mit Freunden ausgehen to go out with friends ❷ to run out *(of supplies)* ❸ to end; schlecht ausgehen to end badly ❹ davon ausgehen, dass ... to assume that ...

**ausgerechnet** *ADVERB*
❶ ausgerechnet heute today of all days ❷ ausgerechnet sie she of all people

**ausgeschlossen** *ADJECTIVE* out of the question

**ausgestorben** *ADJECTIVE* ❶ dead ❷ extinct

**ausgewogen** *ADJECTIVE* balanced

**ausgezeichnet** *ADJECTIVE* excellent

**ausgleichen** *VERB (IMP* glich aus, *PERF* hat ausgeglichen*)* to equalize; sie haben in der letzten Minute ausgeglichen they equalized in the last minute

**aushalten** ◇*VERB (PRES* hält aus, *IMP* hielt aus, *PERF* hat ausgehalten*)* ❶ to stand ❷ es ist nicht zum Aushalten it's unbearable

**Aushilfe** die *(PLURAL* die **Aushilfen***)* temporary assistant, temp

**aushöhlen** *VERB (PERF* hat ausgehöhlt*)* to hollow out

**auskennen** ◇*VERB (IMP* kannte sich aus, *PERF* hat sich ausgekannt*)* ❶ sich auskennen to know your way around ❷ sich gut mit etwas auskennen to know a lot about something

**auskommen** ◇*VERB (IMP* kam aus, *PERF* ist ausgekommen*)* ❶ to manage; mit fünfzig Euro auskommen to manage on fifty euros ❷ mit jemandem gut auskommen to get on well with somebody

**Auskunft** die *(PLURAL* die **Auskünfte***)* ❶ information ❷ information desk ❸ enquiries *(when phoning)*

**auslachen** *VERB (PERF* hat ausgelacht*)* to laugh at

**ausladen** ◇*VERB (PRES* lädt aus, *IMP* lud aus, *PERF* hat ausgeladen*)* ❶ to unload ❷ jemanden ausladen *(informal)* to put somebody off

**Ausland** das im Ausland abroad, ins Ausland reisen to travel abroad

**Ausländer** der *(PLURAL* die **Ausländer***)* foreigner

**Ausländerin** die *(PLURAL* die **Ausländerinnen***)* foreigner

**ausländisch** *ADJECTIVE* foreign

**Auslandsgespräch** das *(PLURAL* die **Auslandsgespräche***)* international call

**ausleeren** *VERB (PERF* hat ausgeleert*)* to empty

**ausleihen** ◇*VERB (IMP* lieh aus, *PERF* hat ausgeliehen*)* ❶ to lend ❷ sich etwas ausleihen to borrow something

**ausmachen** *VERB (PERF* hat ausgemacht*)* ❶ to turn off ❷ to put out ❸ to arrange; wir haben ausgemacht, dass wir uns heute Abend treffen we've arranged to meet up this evening ❹ das macht mir nichts aus I don't mind, macht es Ihnen etwas aus, wenn …? would you mind if …? ❺ viel ausmachen to make a great difference

**Ausnahme** die *(PLURAL* die **Ausnahmen***)* exception

**ausnutzen** *VERB (PERF* hat ausgenutzt*)* ❶ to use ❷ to take advantage of ❸ to exploit

**auspacken** *VERB (PERF* hat ausgepackt*)* to unpack

**Auspuff** der *(PLURAL die **Auspuffe**)* exhaust

**ausrechnen** *VERB (PERF* **hat ausgerechnet)** to work out

**Ausrede** die *(PLURAL die **Ausreden**)* excuse

**ausreichend** *ADJECTIVE* **❶ sufficient ❷ fair, pass** *(as a mark at school)*

**Ausreise** die *(PLURAL die **Ausreisen**)* departure *(from a country)*

**ausrichten** *VERB (PERF* **hat ausgerichtet)** jemandem etwas ausrichten to tell somebody something

**ausrufen** *VERB (IMP* **rief aus**, *PERF* **hat ausgerufen) ❶** to call out **❷** to call, to declare; allgemeine Wahlen ausrufen to call a general election

**Ausrufezeichen** das *(PLURAL die **Ausrufezeichen**)* exclamation mark

**ausruhen** *VERB (PERF* **hat sich ausgeruht)** sich ausruhen to have a rest

**ausrüsten** *VERB (PERF* **hat ausgerüstet)** to equip

**Ausrüstung** die equipment

**ausschalten** *VERB (PERF* **hat ausgeschaltet) ❶** to switch off **❷** to eliminate

**ausschneiden** ◇*VERB (IMP* **schnitt aus**, *PERF* **hat ausgeschnitten)** to cut out

**Ausschuss** der *(PLURAL die **Ausschüsse**)* committee

**aussehen** ◇*VERB (PRES* **sieht aus**, *IMP* **sah aus**, *PERF* **hat ausgesehen)** to look

**Aussehen** das appearance

**außen** *ADVERB* **❶ (on the) outside**; von außen from the outside **❷** nach außen outwards

**Außenminister** der *(PLURAL die **Außenminister**)* Foreign Secretary, Foreign Minister

**außer** *PREPOSITION (+DAT)* **❶ apart from, except (for)**; alle außer ihm everyone except (for) him **❷ out of**; außer Sicht out of sight, außer Betrieb out of order **❸** außer Haus out **❹** außer sich sein to be beside yourself

**außer** *CONJUNCTION* **❶ except**; außer sonntags except Sundays **❷** außer wenn unless

**außerdem** *ADVERB* **❶ as well ❷ besides**

**äußerer, äußere, äußeres** *ADJECTIVE* **❶ external** *(injury, circumstances)* **❷ outer** *(layer, circle)* **❸ outward** *(appearance, effect)*

**außergewöhnlich** *ADJECTIVE* unusual

**außerhalb** *PREPOSITION (+GEN)* outside

**außerhalb** *ADVERB* außerhalb wohnen to live out of town

**Außerirdische** der/die *(PLURAL die **Außerirdischen**)* alien *(from outer space)*

**äußerlich** *ADJECTIVE* **❶ external ❷ outward** *(appearance)*

**außerordentlich** *ADJECTIVE* extraordinary

**äußerst** *ADVERB* extremely

**Äußerung** die *(PLURAL die **Äußerungen**)* remark

**Aussicht** die *(PLURAL die **Aussichten**)* **❶ prospect**; etwas in Aussicht haben to have the prospect of something, keine Aussichten auf Erfolg haben to have no chance of success **②** view; ein Zimmer mit Aussicht aufs Meer a room with a view of the sea

**Aussprache** die (PLURAL die **Aussprachen**) **①** pronunciation **②** talk

**aussprechen** ◇VERB (PRES **spricht aus**, IMP **sprach aus**, PERF **hat ausgesprochen**) **①** to pronounce **②** to express **③** lassen Sie ihn aussprechen let him finish (speaking) **④** sich aussprechen to talk, sich mit jemandem aussprechen to have a talk with somebody **⑤** sich gegen etwas aussprechen to come out against something, sich für etwas aussprechen to come out in favour of something **⑥** sich lobend über jemanden aussprechen to speak highly of somebody

**aussteigen** ◇VERB (IMP **stieg aus**, PERF **ist ausgestiegen**) **①** to get out **②** to get off

**ausstellen** VERB (PERF **hat ausgestellt**) **①** to display (in a shop) **②** to exhibit **③** to make out (a certificate, bill) **④** to issue (a passport) **⑤** to switch off

**Ausstellung** die (PLURAL die **Ausstellungen**) exhibition

**ausstreichen** ◇VERB (IMP **strich aus**, PERF **hat ausgestrichen**) to cross out

**aussuchen** VERB (PERF **hat ausgesucht**) **①** to choose **②** sich etwas aussuchen to choose something

**Austausch** der (PERF **hat**

**austauschen** VERB (PERF **hat ausgetauscht**) **①** to exchange **②** to replace **③** to substitute (a player)

**Auster** die (PLURAL die **Austern**) oyster

**austragen** ◇VERB (PRES **trägt aus**, IMP **trug aus**, PERF **hat ausgetragen**) **①** to deliver (post, newspapers) **②** to hold (a race)

**Australien** das **Australia**; aus Australien from Australia

**Australier** der (PLURAL die **Australier**) Australian

**Australierin** die (PLURAL die **Australierinnen**) Australian

**australisch** ADJECTIVE Australian

**austreten** ◇VERB (PRES **tritt aus**, IMP **trat aus**, PERF **hat ausgetreten**) **①** to stamp out (a cigarette or fire) **②** to wear out (shoes) **③** (PERF **ist ausgetreten**) aus einem Klub austreten to leave a club, ich trete aus I'm leaving **④** (informal) (PERF **ist ausgetreten**) to go to the loo

**austrinken** ◇VERB (IMP **trank aus**, PERF **hat ausgetrunken**) to drink up

**Ausverkauf** der (PLURAL die **Ausverkäufe**) sale

**ausverkauft** ADJECTIVE **①** sold out **②** ein ausverkauftes Haus a full house (at the cinema or theatre)

**Auswahl** die (PLURAL die **Auswahlen**) choice, selection; wenig Auswahl haben to have a limited selection

**Auswanderer** der (PLURAL die **Auswanderer**) emigrant

**Auswanderin** die (PLURAL die **Auswanderinnen**) emigrant

**Axt**

**auswandern** VERB (PERF **ist ausgewandert**) to emigrate; **nach Amerika auswandern** to emigrate to America

**Auswanderung** die emigration

**auswärts** ADVERB ❶ away (in sport); **auswärts spielen** to play away ❷ **auswärts essen** to eat out ❸ **sie arbeitet auswärts** she doesn't work locally

**Auswärtsspiel** das (PLURAL die **Auswärtsspiele**) away game

**Ausweg** der (PLURAL die **Auswege**) way out

**Ausweis** der (PLURAL die **Ausweise**) ❶ identity card ❷ card (for students or members) ❸ pass

**auswendig** ADVERB by heart

**auswirken** VERB (PERF **hat sich ausgewirkt**) **sich auf etwas auswirken** to have an effect on something

**ausziehen** ◇VERB (IMP **zog aus**, PERF **hat ausgezogen**) ❶ to take off (clothes) ❷ to undress ❸ **sich ausziehen** to get undressed ❹ (PERF **ist ausgezogen**) to move out (move house); **wir ziehen nächste Woche aus** we're moving out next week

**Auszubildende** der/die (PLURAL die **Auszubildenden**) trainee

**Auto** das (PLURAL die **Autos**) car; **Auto fahren** to drive, **das Auto waschen** to wash the car

**Autobahn** die (PLURAL die **Autobahnen**) motorway

**Autobahnraststätte** die (PLURAL die **Autobahnraststätten**) motorway service area

**Autofahrer** der (PLURAL die **Autofahrer**) motorist

**Autogramm** das (PLURAL die **Autogramme**) autograph

**Automat** der (PLURAL die **Automaten**) machine

**automatisch** ADJECTIVE automatic

**Autor** der (PLURAL die **Autoren**) author

**Autorin** die (PLURAL die **Autorinnen**) authoress

**Autorität** die authority

**Autoskooter** der (PLURAL die **Autoskooter**) bumper car, dodgem car

**Autostopp** der **per Autostopp fahren** to hitchhike

**Autounfall** der (PLURAL die **Autounfälle**) car accident

**Autoverleih** der (PLURAL die **Autoverleihe**) car hire (firm)

**Axt** die (PLURAL die **Äxte**) axe

# Bb

**Baby** das (PLURAL die **Babys**) baby

**Babysitting** das babysitting; Babysitting machen to babysit

**Bach** der (PLURAL die **Bäche**) stream

**Backe** die (PLURAL die **Backen**) cheek

**backen** ◇VERB (PRES **bäckt**, IMP **backte**, PERF **hat gebacken**) to bake

**Bäcker** der (PLURAL die **Bäcker**) ❶ baker ❷ beim Bäcker at the baker's

**Bäckerei** die (PLURAL die **Bäckereien**) baker's

**Backofen** der (PLURAL die **Backöfen**) oven

**Backpflaume** die (PLURAL die **Backpflaumen**) prune

**Bad** das (PLURAL die **Bäder**) ❶ bath ❷ bathroom ❸ pool (for swimming)

**Badeanzug** der (PLURAL die **Badeanzüge**) swimsuit

**Badehose** die (PLURAL die **Badehosen**) swimming trunks

**Bademeister** der (PLURAL die **Bademeister**) swimming-pool attendant

**Bademeisterin** die (PLURAL die **Bademeisterinnen**) swimming-pool attendant

**Bademütze** die (PLURAL die **Bademützen**) bathing cap

**baden** VERB (PERF **hat gebadet**) ❶ to have a bath ❷ to bathe (in the sea) ❸ to bath (wash somebody)

**Badetuch** das (PLURAL die **Badetücher**) bath towel

**Badewanne** die (PLURAL die **Badewannen**) bath (tub)

**Badezimmer** das (PLURAL die **Badezimmer**) bathroom

**Bahn** die (PLURAL die **Bahnen**) ❶ railway ❷ train; mit der Bahn fahren to go by train ❸ tram ❹ track (in sport) ❺ lane (on a track) ❻ path; auf die schiefe Bahn geraten to go off the rails

**Bahnhof** der (PLURAL die **Bahnhöfe**) (railway) station

**Bahnsteig** der (PLURAL die **Bahnsteige**) platform

**Bahnübergang** der (PLURAL die **Bahnübergänge**) level crossing

**bald** ADVERB ❶ soon; bis bald! see you soon! ❷ wird's bald! (informal) get a move on! ❸ almost; ich hätte bald vergessen, ihn anzurufen I almost forgot to ring him

**baldig** ADJECTIVE speedy

**Balken** der (PLURAL die **Balken**) beam

**Balkon** der (PLURAL die **Balkons**) balcony

**Ball** der (PLURAL die **Bälle**) ❶ ball; Ball spielen to play ball ❷ ball; auf dem Ball at the ball

**Ballett** das (PLURAL die **Ballette**) ballet

**Balletttänzer** der (PLURAL die **Balletttänzer**) ballet dancer

a
**b**
c
d
e
f
g
h
i
j
k
l
m
n
o
p
q
r
s
t
u
v
w
x
y
z

**Balletttänzerin** die *(PLURAL die Balletttänzerinnen)* ballet dancer

**Ballon** der *(PLURAL die Ballons)* balloon

**Banane** die *(PLURAL die Bananen)* banana

**band** ▸ SEE **binden**

**Band¹** das *(PLURAL die Bänder)* ❶ ribbon ❷ tape *(for recording)*; etwas auf Band aufnehmen to tape something ❸ production line; am Band arbeiten to work on the production line ❹ am laufenden Band *(informal)* nonstop

**Band²** der *(PLURAL die Bände)* volume

**Band³** die *(PLURAL die Bands)* band

**Bank¹** die *(PLURAL die Bänke)* bench

**Bank²** die *(PLURAL die Banken)* bank; ich muss erst zur Bank gehen I have to go to the bank first

**Bankkauffrau** die *(PLURAL die Bankkauffrauen)* bank clerk

**Bankkaufmann** der *(PLURAL die Bankkaufleute)* bank clerk

**Bankkonto** das *(PLURAL die Bankkonten)* bank account

**Banknote** die *(PLURAL die Banknoten)* banknote

**bankrott** *ADJECTIVE* bankrupt; bankrott gehen/machen to go bankrupt

**bar** *ADJECTIVE* (in) cash

**Bar** die *(PLURAL die Bars)* bar

**Bär** der *(PLURAL die Bären)* bear

**Bardame** die *(PLURAL die Bardamen)* barmaid

**barfuß** *ADJECTIVE* barefoot

**Bargeld** das cash

**Barkeeper** der *(PLURAL die Barkeeper)* barman

**Barren** der *(PLURAL die Barren)* ❶ bar ❷ parallel bars

**Bart** der *(PLURAL die Bärte)* beard

**bärtig** *ADJECTIVE* bearded

**Basel** das Basle

**Basis** die *(PLURAL die Basen)* basis

**Bass** der *(PLURAL die Bässe)* bass

**basta** *EXCLAMATION* and that's that!

**basteln** *VERB (PERF hat gebastelt)* ❶ to make *(things)* ❷ sie bastelt gern she likes making things

**bat** ▸ SEE **bitten**

**Batterie** die *(PLURAL die Batterien)* battery

**Bau** der *(PLURAL die Bauten)* ❶ construction; im Bau sein to be under construction ❷ building ❸ building site; auf dem Bau arbeiten to work on a building site

**Bauarbeiten** *PLURAL NOUN* building work

**Bauarbeiter** der *(PLURAL die Bauarbeiter)* builder

**Bauarbeiterin** die *(PLURAL die Bauarbeiterinnen)* builder

**Bauch** der *(PLURAL die Bäuche)* stomach, belly

**Bauchschmerzen** *PLURAL NOUN* stomachache

**bauen** *VERB (PERF hat gebaut)* ❶ to build ❷ einen Unfall bauen *(informal)* to have an accident

**Bauer** der (PLURAL die **Bauern**)
❶ farmer ❷ pawn (in chess)

**Bäuerin** die (PLURAL die **Bäuerinnen**)
❶ farmer ❷ farmer's wife

**Bauernhof** der (PLURAL die
**Bauernhöfe**) farm

**Baum** der (PLURAL die **Bäume**) tree

**Baumwolle** die cotton

**Bausparkasse** die (PLURAL die
**Bausparkassen**) building society

**Baustelle** die (PLURAL die **Baustellen**)
building site

**bay(e)risch** ADJECTIVE Bavarian

**Bayer** der (PLURAL die **Bayern**)
Bavarian

**Bayerin** die (PLURAL die **Bayerinnen**)
Bavarian

**Bayern** das Bavaria; aus Bayern
from Bavaria

**beabsichtigen** VERB (PERF hat
**beabsichtigt**) to intend

**beachten** VERB (PERF hat beachtet)
❶ to take notice of; beachte ihn
einfach nicht just don't take any
notice of him ❷ to observe ❸ to
follow (a rule, advice) ❹ to obey;
die Verkehrsregeln beachten to
obey traffic regulations

**Beamte** der (PLURAL die **Beamten**)
❶ civil servant (in Germany all
public employees, such as teachers
and policemen, are 'Beamte')
❷ official

**Beamtin** die (PLURAL die
**Beamtinnen**) ❶ civil servant
❷ official

**beanspruchen** VERB (PERF hat
**beansprucht**) ❶ to claim
(benefit) ❷ to take up (time,
space); jemanden beanspruchen
to take up somebody's time ❸ to
demand (energy, attention); die
Arbeit beansprucht sie sehr her
work is very demanding ❹ to take
advantage of (hospitality, services,
help); ich möchte Ihre Geduld nicht
zu sehr beanspruchen I don't want
to try your patience

**Beanstandung** die (PLURAL die
**Beanstandungen**) complaint

**beantragen** VERB (PERF hat
**beantragt**) to apply for

**beantworten** VERB (PERF hat
**beantwortet**) to answer

**bearbeiten** VERB (PERF hat
**bearbeitet**) ❶ to deal with; einen
Antrag bearbeiten to deal with
an application ❷ to adapt (a play)
❸ to treat (wood, for example);
er hat die Oberfläche mit Wachs
bearbeitet he's treated the surface
with wax ❹ jemanden bearbeiten,
dass er etwas macht (informal) to
work on somebody so that he does
something (persuade)

**beaufsichtigen** VERB (PERF hat
**beaufsichtigt**) to supervise

**Becher** der (PLURAL die **Becher**)
❶ beaker, mug ❷ pot, carton
(of yoghurt, cream)

**Becherglas** das (PLURAL die
**Bechergläser**) tumbler

**Becken** das (PLURAL die **Becken**)
❶ basin ❷ pool (for swimming)
❸ pelvis

**bedanken** VERB (PERF hat sich
**bedankt**) sich bedanken to say
thank you, vergiss nicht, dich zu
bedanken don't forget to say thank
you, ich habe mich bei ihm bedankt
I thanked him

**Bedarf** der ❶ **need** ❷ bei Bedarf if required ❸ **demand**; je nach Bedarf according to demand

**bedauerlicherweise** ADVERB **unfortunately**

**bedauern** VERB (PERF hat bedauert) ❶ **to regret**; ich bedaure kein Wort I don't regret a single word ❷ ich bedaure sehr, dass du nicht kommen kannst I'm very sorry that you can't come, bedaure! sorry! ❸ jemanden bedauern to feel sorry for somebody

**bedecken** VERB (PERF hat bedeckt) **to cover**

**bedeckt** ADJECTIVE ❶ **covered** ❷ **overcast** (weather); gestern war es den ganzen Tag bedeckt it was overcast all day yesterday

**bedenken** ◇VERB (IMP **bedachte**, PERF hat **bedacht**) **to consider**

**Bedenken** PLUAL NOUN ❶ **doubts**; Bedenken haben to have doubts ❷ ohne Bedenken without hesitation

**bedenklich** ADJECTIVE ❶ **worrying**; die Situation ist sehr bedenklich the situation is very worrying ❷ **dubious**; er hat bedenkliche Mittel angewendet, um sein Ziel zu erreichen he's used dubious methods to achieve his aims ❸ **serious**

**bedeuten** VERB (PERF hat bedeutet) **to mean**

**bedeutend** ADJECTIVE ❶ **important** ❷ **considerable**

**Bedeutung** die (PLURAL die Bedeutungen) ❶ **meaning** ❷ **importance**

**bedienen** VERB (PERF hat bedient) ❶ **to serve**; hier wird man sehr schnell bedient you get served very quickly here ❷ **to operate** ❸ sich bedienen to help oneself

**Bedienstete** der/die (PLURAL die Bediensteten) **servant**

**Bedienung** die (PLURAL die Bedienungen) ❶ **service**; Bedienung inbegriffen service included ❷ **waiter, waitress** ❸ **shop assistant** ❹ **operation** (of a machine)

**Bedingung** die (PLURAL die Bedingungen) **condition**; nur unter der Bedingung, dass du mitkommst only on condition that you're coming with us

**bedrohen** VERB (PERF hat bedroht) **to threaten**

**bedroht** ADJECTIVE **endangered**

**Bedrohung** die (PLURAL die Bedrohungen) **threat**

**Bedürfnis** das (PLURAL die Bedürfnisse) **need**

**beeilen** VERB (PERF hat sich beeilt) sich beeilen to hurry (up) beeilt euch! hurry up!

**beeindrucken** VERB (PERF hat beeindruckt) **to impress**

**beeinflussen** VERB (PERF hat beeinflusst) **to influence**

**beenden** VERB (PERF hat beendet) **to end**

**Beerdigung** die (PLURAL die Beerdigungen) **funeral**

**Beere** die (PLURAL die Beeren) **berry**

**Beet** das (PLURAL die Beete) ❶ **bed** (of flowers) ❷ **patch** (of vegetables)

**befahl** ▸ SEE **befehlen**

**Befehl** der (PLURAL die **Befehle**)
❶ order ❷ command; den
Befehl über etwas haben to be in
command of something

**befehlen** ◇VERB (PRES **befiehlt**,
IMP **befahl**, PERF **hat befohlen**)
❶ jemandem befehlen, etwas
zu tun to order somebody to do
something ❷ to give orders

**befestigen** VERB (PERF **hat befestigt**)
❶ to fix; etwas an der Wand
befestigen to fix something to the
wall ❷ to fasten

**befinden** ◇VERB (IMP **befand sich**, PERF
**hat sich befunden**) sich befinden
to be, sie befindet sich zur Zeit in
Deutschland she's in Germany at
the moment

**befolgen** VERB (PERF **hat befolgt**) to
follow

**befördern** VERB (PERF **hat befördert**)
❶ to carry (people by bus or train)
❷ to transport (goods by train or
lorry) ❸ to promote; er ist zum
Kommissar befördert worden he's
been promoted to superintendent

**befragen** VERB (PERF **hat befragt**) to
question

**befreien** VERB (PERF **hat befreit**) ❶ to
free ❷ to exempt; jemanden vom
Wehrdienst befreien to exempt
somebody from military service
❸ sich befreien to free oneself

**Befreiung** die liberation

**befreunden** VERB (PERF **hat sich
befreundet**) sich befreunden to
make friends

**befreundet** ADJECTIVE mit jemandem
befreundet sein to be friends with
somebody, wir sind schon lange

gut befreundet we've been close
friends for a long time

**befriedigen** VERB (PERF **hat
befriedigt**) to satisfy

**befriedigend** ADJECTIVE satisfactory

**Befugnis** die (PLURAL die **Befugnisse**)
authority

**begabt** ADJECTIVE gifted, talented

**Begabung** die gift, talent

**begann** ▸ SEE **beginnen**

**begegnen** VERB (PERF **ist begegnet**)
❶ jemandem begegnen to meet
somebody, etwas begegnen to
meet something ❷ sich begegnen
to meet (each other)

**Begegnung** die (PLURAL die
**Begegnungen**) meeting

**begehen** ◇VERB (IMP **beging**, PERF **hat
begangen**) to commit

**begeistern** VERB (PERF **hat
begeistert**) ❶ jemanden für etwas
begeistern to fill somebody with
enthusiasm for something ❷ sich
begeistern to get enthusiastic

**begeistert** ADJECTIVE enthusiastic

**Begeisterung** die enthusiasm

**Beginn** der beginning; zu Beginn at
the beginning

**beginnen** ◇VERB (IMP **begann**, PERF
**hat begonnen**) to begin, to start

**begleiten** VERB (PERF **hat begleitet**)
to accompany; jemanden
begleiten to accompany somebody,
er hat mich nach Hause begleitet
he took me home

**beglückwünschen** VERB (PERF
**hat beglückwünscht**) to
congratulate

**begonnen** ▸SEE **beginnen**

**begraben** ◇*VERB* (*PRES* **begräbt**, *IMP* **begrub**, *PERF* **hat begraben**) to bury

**begreifen** ◇*VERB* (*IMP* **begriff**, *PERF* **hat begriffen**) to understand

**begrenzen** *VERB* (*PERF* **hat begrenzt**) to limit

**Begriff** der (*PLURAL* die **Begriffe**) ❶ concept; davon kann ich mir keinen Begriff machen I can't imagine that ❷ term; ein Begriff aus der Malerei a painting term ❸ im Begriff sein, etwas zu tun to be about to do something ❹ für meine Begriffe to my mind ❺ schwer von Begriff (*informal*) slow on the uptake

**Begründung** die (*PLURAL* die **Begründungen**) reason

**begrüßen** *VERB* (*PERF* **hat begrüßt**) ❶ to greet ❷ to welcome

**Begrüßung** die welcome

**begünstigen** *VERB* (*PERF* **hat begünstigt**) to favour

**behaart** *ADJECTIVE* hairy

**behaglich** *ADJECTIVE* cosy

**behalten** ◇*VERB* (*PRES* **behält**, *IMP* **behielt**, *PERF* **hat behalten**) ❶ to keep; du kannst die CD behalten you can keep the CD ❷ to remember (*a name*)

**Behälter** der (*PLURAL* die **Behälter**) container

**behandeln** *VERB* (*PERF* **hat behandelt**) ❶ to treat; er ist sehr schlecht behandelt worden he's been treated very badly, einen Patienten behandeln to treat a patient ❷ to deal with (*a subject, question*)

**Behandlung** die (*PLURAL* die **Behandlungen**) treatment

**behaupten** *VERB* (*PERF* **hat behauptet**) ❶ to claim ❷ sich behaupten to assert oneself

**Behauptung** die (*PLURAL* die **Behauptungen**) claim

**beherrschen** *VERB* (*PERF* **hat beherrscht**) ❶ to rule over (*a country, people*) ❷ to control ❸ to know ❹ sich beherrschen to control oneself

**behilflich** *ADJECTIVE* jemandem behilflich sein to help somebody

**behindert** *ADJECTIVE* disabled; ist er behindert? does he have a disability?

**Behinderte** der/die (*PLURAL* die **Behinderten**) disabled person

**Behindertenheim** das (*PLURAL* die **Behindertenheime**) home for disabled people

**Behinderung** die ❶ obstruction ❷ disability

**Behörde** die (*PLURAL* die **Behörden**) authority, authorities

**behüten** *VERB* (*PERF* **hat behütet**) to protect

**bei** *PREPOSITION* (+*DAT*) ❶ near; die Diskothek beim Bahnhof the disco near the station ❷ at (*indicating a place or time*); bei mir at my place, beim Arzt at the doctor's, bei Beginn at the beginning ❸ bei seinen Eltern wohnen to live with your parents ❹ bei uns in der Firma in our firm, bei guter Gesundheit in good health ❺ bei einem Verlag arbeiten to work for a publisher ❻ bei Regen if it rains, bei Nebel in fog, bei Tag by day ❼ etwas bei sich haben to have something on you ❽ bei Morris c/o Morris ❾ sich bei jemandem entschuldigen to apologize to somebody ❿ bei der hohen Miete with the high rent ⓫ beim Fahren while driving, beim Lesen sein to be reading, beim Frühstück at breakfast ⓬ bei der Ankunft on arrival

**beibringen** ◇*VERB (PRES* **bringt bei**, *IMP* **brachte bei**, *PERF* **hat beigebracht)** jemandem etwas beibringen to teach somebody something

**Beichte** die *(PLURAL die* **Beichten)** confession

**beichten** *VERB (PERF* **hat gebeichtet)** to confess

**beide** *ADJECTIVE, PRONOUN* ❶ both; ihr beide both of you, er hat seine beiden Eltern verloren he has lost both his parents ❷ die ersten beiden the first two ❸ eins von beiden one of the two ❸ keiner von beiden neither (of them) ❹ beides both, er kann beides – Klavier und Gitarre spielen he can do both – play the piano and the guitar ❺ dreißig beide thirty all *(in tennis)*

**beieinander** *ADVERB* **together**

**Beifahrer** der *(PLURAL die* **Beifahrer)** passenger

**Beifahrerin** die *(PLURAL die* **Beifahrerinnen)** passenger

**Beifall** der **applause**

**Beil** das *(PLURAL die* **Beile)** axe

**Beilage** die *(PLURAL die* **Beilagen)** ❶ **supplement** *(to a paper)* ❷ side-dish; als Beilage Reis und Spinat served with rice and spinach

**beiläufig** *ADJECTIVE* **casual**

**beilegen** *VERB (PERF* **hat beigelegt)** to enclose

**Beileid** das **condolences**; jemandem sein Beileid aussprechen to offer your condolences to somebody

**beiliegen** ◇*VERB (PRES* **liegt bei**, *IMP* **lag bei**, *PERF* **hat beigelegen)** to be enclosed; ein Scheck liegt bei please find enclosed a cheque

**beiliegend** *ADJECTIVE* **enclosed**

**beim** bei dem **at the** ▸ SEE **bei**

**Bein** das *(PLURAL die* **Beine)** leg

**beinahe** *ADVERB* **almost**

**Beinbruch** der *(PLURAL die* **Beinbrüche)** broken leg; das ist doch kein Beinbruch *(informal)* it's not the end of the world

**beisammen** *ADVERB* **together**

**beiseite** *ADVERB* ❶ aside; etwas beiseite schieben to push something aside ❷ etwas beiseite legen to put something by ❸ das Geld beiseite schaffen to hide the money away

**Beispiel** das *(PLURAL die* **Beispiele)** example; zum Beispiel for example, mit gutem Beispiel vorangehen to set a good example

**beispielsweise** *ADVERB* **for example**

**beißen** ◇*VERB (IMP* **biss**, *PERF* **hat gebissen)** ❶ to bite ❷ to sting *(of smoke, for example)* ❸ sich beißen to clash, die Farben beißen sich the colours clash

**Beitrag** der *(PLURAL die* **Beiträge)** ❶ **contribution** ❷ **subscription** ❸ **premium** *(insurance fee)* ❹ **article** *(in a newspaper)*

A
**B**
C
D
E
F
G
H
I
J
K
L
M
N
O
P
Q
R
S
T
U
V
W
X
Y
Z

**beitragen** ◇*VERB* (*PRES* **trägt bei**, *IMP* **trug bei**, *PERF* **hat beigetragen**) zu etwas beitragen to contribute to something

**beitreten** ◇*VERB* (*PRES* **tritt bei**, *IMP* **trat bei**, *PERF* **ist beigetreten**) to join; ich trete dem Fußballverein bei I'm joining the football club

**bekam** ▸ SEE **bekommen**

**bekämpfen** *VERB* (*PERF* **hat bekämpft**) ❶ to fight ❷ sich bekämpfen to fight

**bekannt** *ADJECTIVE* ❶ well known ❷ familiar; das kommt mir bekannt vor that seems familiar ❸ mit jemandem bekannt sein to know somebody ❹ für etwas bekannt sein to be (well) known for something ❺ jemanden bekannt machen to introduce somebody ❻ das ist mir bekannt I know that ❼ etwas bekannt geben/machen to announce something, sie gab ihre Verlobung bekannt she announced her engagement ❽ bekannt werden to become known

**Bekannte** der/die (*PLURAL* die **Bekannten**) ❶ acquaintance ❷ friend

**bekannt geben** *VERB* (*PRES* **gibt bekannt**, *IMP* **gab bekannt**, *PERF* **hat bekannt gegeben**) to announce ▸ SEE **bekannt**

**bekanntlich** *ADVERB* Rauchen ist bekanntlich schädlich as you know, smoking is bad for you

**beklagen** *VERB* (*PERF* **hat sich beklagt**) sich beklagen to complain

**Bekleidung** die clothes, clothing

**bekommen** ◇*VERB* (*IMP* **bekam**, *PERF* **hat bekommen**) ❶ to get; Angst bekommen to get frightened ❷ to catch (*a cold, the train*) ❸ ein Kind bekommen to have a baby ❹ was bekommen Sie? (*in a shop*) can I help you? (*in a restaurant*) what would you like? ❺ was bekommen Sie dafür? how much is it? ❻ (*PERF* **ist bekommen**) fettes Essen bekommt mir nicht fatty food doesn't agree with me ❼ (*PERF* **ist bekommen**) die Ferien sind mir gut bekommen the holiday did me good

**Belag** der (*PLURAL* die **Beläge**) ❶ covering ❷ coating ❸ topping (*on bread*) ❹ lining (*of brakes*)

**belasten** *VERB* (*PERF* **hat belastet**) ❶ to burden ❷ to put weight on (*foot*) ❸ to pollute (*the atmosphere*) ❹ to debit (*an account*) ❺ to incriminate

**belästigen** *VERB* (*PERF* **hat belästigt**) ❶ to bother ❷ to harass

**Belastung** die ❶ strain ❷ load ❸ burden ❹ pollution

**belaufen** ◇*VERB* (*PRES* **beläuft**, *IMP* **belief**, *PERF* **belaufen**) sich auf etwas belaufen to amount to something, die Rechnung beläuft sich auf fünfhundert Euro the bill amounts to five hundred euros

**belegen** *VERB* (*PERF* **hat belegt**) ❶ to cover ❷ eine Scheibe Brot mit Käse belegen to put some cheese on a slice of bread ❸ to enrol for (*a course*) ❹ to reserve (*a seat*) ❺ den ersten Platz belegen to come first ❻ to prove (*facts*)

**belegt** *ADJECTIVE* ❶ occupied ❷ der Platz ist belegt this seat is taken ❸ ein belegtes Brot an open sandwich ❹ die Nummer ist belegt (*when phoning*) the number's engaged

**beleidigen** *VERB (PERF* **hat beleidigt)**
to insult

**Beleidigung** die *(PLURAL* die
**Beleidigungen)** insult

**Beleuchtung** die lighting

**Belgien** das Belgium

**Belgier** der *(PLURAL* die **Belgier)**
Belgian

**Belgierin** die *(PLURAL* die
**Belgierinnen)** Belgian

**belgisch** *ADJECTIVE* Belgian

**Belichtung** die exposure

**beliebig** *ADJECTIVE* any; eine beliebige
Zahl any number you like

**beliebig** *ADVERB* beliebig lange
as long as you like, beliebig viele
as many as you like

**beliebt** *ADJECTIVE* popular

**Beliebtheit** die popularity

**bellen** *VERB (PERF* **hat gebellt)** to bark

**belohnen** *VERB (PERF* **hat belohnt)**
to reward

**Belohnung** die *(PLURAL* die
**Belohnungen)** reward

**belügen** *VERB (IMP* **belog,** *PERF* **hat
belogen)** to lie to

**bemerkbar** *ADJECTIVE* sich
bemerkbar machen to attract
attention, to become noticeable

**bemerken** *VERB (PERF* **hat bemerkt)**
❶ to notice ❷ to remark
❸ nebenbei bemerkt by the way

**Bemerkung** die *(PLURAL* die
**Bemerkungen)** remark

**bemitleiden** *VERB (PERF* **hat
bemitleidet)** to pity

**bemühen** *VERB (PERF* **hat sich
bemüht)** ❶ sich bemühen to try,
sich sehr bemühen to try hard,
er bemüht sich um eine Stelle
he's trying to get a job ❷ sich um
jemanden bemühen to try to help
somebody ❸ bitte, bemühen Sie
sich nicht please don't trouble
yourself

**Bemühung** die *(PLURAL* die
**Bemühungen)** effort

**benachrichtigen** *VERB (PERF* **hat
benachrichtigt)** ❶ to inform ❷ to
notify *(officially)*

**benachteiligt** *ADJECTIVE*
disadvantaged

**benehmen** ◇*VERB (PRES* **benimmt
sich,** *IMP* **benahm sich,** *PERF* **hat
sich benommen)** sich benehmen
to behave, benimm dich! behave
yourself!

**Benehmen** das behaviour

**beneiden** *VERB (PERF* **hat beneidet)**
to envy; jemanden um etwas
beneiden to envy somebody
something

**benoten** *VERB (PERF* **hat benotet)**
to mark

**benutzen** *VERB (PERF* **hat benutzt)**
to use

**Benutzer** der *(PLURAL* die **Benutzer)**
user

**benutzerfreundlich** *ADJECTIVE*
user-friendly

**Benutzerin** die *(PLURAL* die
**Benutzerinnen)** user

**Benutzung** die use

**Benzin** das petrol

**beobachten** *VERB (PERF* **hat
beobachtet)** to observe, to
watch; Vögel beobachten to watch
birds

**bequem** *ADJECTIVE* ❶ comfortable
❷ machen Sie es sich bequem
make yourself at home ❸ lazy
❹ easy; eine bequeme Lösung
finden to find an easy way out

**beraten** ◇*VERB (PRES* **berät,** *IMP*
**beriet,** *PERF* **hat beraten)** ❶ to
advise ❷ jemanden gut/schlecht
beraten to give somebody good/
bad advice ❸ sich beraten lassen to
get advice ❹ gut beraten sein to be
well advised ❺ to discuss *(a plan,
matter)* ❻ sich über etwas beraten
to discuss something

**Berater** der *(PLURAL die* **Berater)**
adviser

**Beratung** die *(PLURAL die*
**Beratungen)** ❶ advice
❷ discussion ❸ consultation
*(with a doctor)*

**berauben** *VERB (PERF* **hat beraubt)**
to rob

**berechnen** *VERB (PERF* **hat**
**berechnet)** ❶ to charge;
jemandem zehn Euro für etwas
berechnen to charge somebody ten
euros for something ❷ jemandem
zu viel berechnen to overcharge
somebody ❸ to calculate

**berechtigen** *VERB (PERF* **hat**
**berechtigt)** jemanden
berechtigen, etwas zu tun to give
someone the right to do something

**berechtigt** *ADJECTIVE* justified

**Bereich** der *(PLURAL die* **Bereiche)**
❶ area ❷ field *(in a profession)*; im
Bereich Tourismus in the field of
tourism

**bereit** *ADJECTIVE* ready

**bereiten** *VERB (PERF* **hat bereitet)**
❶ to make *(coffee, tea)* ❷ to cause

*(trouble, difficulty)*; leider hat es
uns Schwierigkeiten bereitet
unfortunately it caused us some
trouble ❸ to give *(a surprise,
pleasure)*

**bereits** *ADVERB* already

**bereuen** *VERB (PERF* **hat bereut)** to
regret

**Berg** der *(PLURAL die* **Berge)**
❶ mountain ❷ hill

**bergab** *ADVERB* downhill

**Bergarbeiter** der *(PLURAL die*
**Bergarbeiter)** miner

**bergauf** *ADVERB* uphill

**bergen** ◇*VERB (PRES* **birgt,** *IMP* **barg,**
*PERF* **hat geborgen)** to rescue

**Bergsteigen** das mountaineering

**Bergsteiger** der *(PLURAL die*
**Bergsteiger)** mountaineer,
climber

**Bergsteigerin** die *(PLURAL die*
**Bergsteigerinnen)** mountaineer,
climber

**Bergwacht** die mountain rescue

**Bergwerk** das *(PLURAL die*
**Bergwerke)** mine

**Bericht** der *(PLURAL die* **Berichte)**
report

**berichten** *VERB (PERF* **hat berichtet)**
❶ to report; die Zeitungen
haben nichts davon berichtet the
newspapers didn't report anything
about it ❷ jemandem über etwas
berichten to tell somebody about
something, er hat mir über seine
Ferien in Amerika berichtet he told
me about his holiday in America

**berücksichtigen** *VERB (PERF* **hat**
**berücksichtigt)** to take into
account

**Beruf** der (PLURAL die **Berufe**)
❶ occupation ❷ profession; ich
bin Lehrerin von Beruf I'm a teacher
by profession ❸ trade ❹ was sind
Sie von Beruf? what do you do for
a living?

**beruflich** ADJECTIVE ❶ professional
❷ vocational (training)

**beruflich** ADVERB ❶ beruflich
erfolgreich sein to be successful
in your career ❷ viel beruflich
unterwegs sein to be away a lot on
business

**Berufsberatung** die careers
advice

**Berufsschule** die (PLURAL die
**Berufsschulen**) technical college

**berufstätig** ADJECTIVE working

**Berufsverkehr** der rush-hour
traffic

**beruhigen** VERB (PERF hat beruhigt)
❶ to calm down ❷ to reassure
❸ sich beruhigen to calm down

**Beruhigungsmittel** das (PLURAL
die **Beruhigungsmittel**) sedative,
tranquillizer

**berühmt** ADJECTIVE famous

**berühren** VERB (PERF hat berührt)
❶ to touch ❷ to touch on (a
topic, an issue) ❸ to affect; ihre
Geschichte berührte ihn seltsam he
was strangely affected by her story
❹ sich berühren to touch

**besaß** ▸ SEE besitzen

**beschädigen** VERB (PERF hat
beschädigt) to damage

**Beschädigung** die (PLURAL die
**Beschädigungen**) damage; der
Sturm verursachte zahlreiche
Beschädigungen the storm caused
considerable damage

**beschaffen¹** VERB (PERF hat
beschafft) to get; kannst du mir
nicht einen Job beschaffen? can't
you get me a job?

**beschaffen²** ADJECTIVE so beschaffen
sein, dass ... to be such that ...

**beschäftigen** VERB (PERF hat
beschäftigt) ❶ to occupy (keep
busy) ❷ to employ (people) ❸ sich
beschäftigen to occupy yourself
❹ ich beschäftige mich mit den
Kindern I'm busy with the children
❺ sich mit einem Fall beschäftigen
to deal with a case, sein Aufsatz
beschäftigt sich mit der
Umweltverschmutzung his essay
deals with environmental pollution

**beschäftigt** ADJECTIVE ❶ busy
❷ employed

**Beschäftigung** die (PLURAL die
**Beschäftigungen**) ❶ occupation
❷ activity

**Bescheid** der (PLURAL die **Bescheide**)
❶ information ❷ jemandem
Bescheid sagen to let somebody
know ❸ über etwas Bescheid
wissen to know about something

**bescheiden** ADJECTIVE modest

**Bescheinigung** die (PLURAL die
**Bescheinigungen**) ❶ certificate;
eine Bescheinigung des Arztes a
doctor's certificate ❷ (written)
confirmation

**beschimpfen** VERB (PERF hat
beschimpft) to abuse

**beschlagnahmen** VERB (PERF hat
beschlagnahmt) to confiscate

**beschleunigen** VERB (PERF hat
beschleunigt) ❶ to speed up ❷ to
accelerate; der Lastwagen hinter
uns hat plötzlich beschleunigt

a b c d e f g h i j k l m n o p q r s t u v w x y z

the lorry behind us suddenly
accelerated

**beschließen** ⬦*VERB* *(IMP* **beschloss**,
*PERF* **hat beschlossen**) to decide

**Beschluss** der *(PLURAL* die
**Beschlüsse)** decision

**beschränken** *VERB* *(PERF* **hat
beschränkt)** to limit

**beschränkt** *ADJECTIVE* ❶ narrow-
minded ❷ dim; sie ist ein bisschen
beschränkt she's a bit dim

**beschreiben** ⬦*VERB* *(IMP* **beschrieb**,
*PERF* **hat beschrieben**) to describe

**Beschreibung** die *(PLURAL* die
**Beschreibungen)** description

**beschuldigen** *VERB* *(PERF* **hat
beschuldigt)** to accuse

**Beschuldigung** die *(PLURAL* die
**Beschuldigungen)** accusation

**beschützen** *VERB* *(PERF* **hat
beschützt)** to protect

**Beschwerde** die *(PLURAL* die
**Beschwerden)** complaint

**beschweren** *VERB* *(PERF* **hat sich
beschwert)** sich beschweren to
complain, ich habe mich bei den
Nachbarn über ihn beschwert
I've complained to the neighbours
about him

**beschwipst** *ADJECTIVE* tipsy

**beseitigen** *VERB* *(PERF* **hat beseitigt)**
to remove

**Besen** der *(PLURAL* die **Besen)** broom

**besetzen** *VERB* *(PERF* **hat besetzt)**
❶ to occupy ❷ to fill *(a post, role)*
❸ to trim, to edge *(with lace or fur)*

**besetzt** *ADJECTIVE* ❶ occupied
❷ besetzt sein to be engaged

*(a phone, toilet)* ❸ taken *(a table,
seat)*; der Platz ist besetzt this seat
is taken ❹ full *(of a train, bus)*; der
Zug ist voll besetzt the train is full up

**Besetztzeichen** das *(PLURAL* die
**Besetztzeichen)** engaged tone

**Besetzung** die *(PLURAL* die
**Besetzungen)** ❶ cast ❷ team
❸ occupation

**besichtigen** *VERB* *(PERF* **hat
besichtigt)** ❶ to look round *(a
town, museum)* ❷ to see *(sights, a
house)*

**Besichtigung** die *(PLURAL* die
**Besichtigungen)** visit

**besinnungslos** *ADJECTIVE*
unconscious

**Besitz** der ❶ property ❷ im Besitz
einer Sache sein to be in possession
of something

**besitzen** ⬦*VERB* *(IMP* **besaß**, *PERF* **hat
besessen)** ❶ to own; sie besitzen
ein Haus in Italien they own a
house in Italy ❷ to have *(talent,
a quality)*

**Besitzer** der *(PLURAL* die **Besitzer)**
owner

**Besitzerin** die *(PLURAL* die
**Besitzerinnen)** owner

**besonderer, besondere,
besonderes** *ADJECTIVE* ❶ special;
unter besonderen Umständen in
special circumstances ❷ particular;
ohne besondere Begeisterung
without any particular enthusiasm
❸ keine besonderen Kennzeichen
no distinguishing features

**Besonderheit** die *(PLURAL* die
**Besonderheiten)** ❶ special
feature ❷ peculiarity

**besonders** *ADVERB* **particularly**

**besorgen** *VERB (PERF* **hat besorgt)**
to get; ich kann dir Karten besorgen
I can get you tickets

**besorgt** *ADJECTIVE* **worried**

**besprechen** ◇*VERB (PRES* **bespricht,**
*IMP* **besprach,** *PERF* **hat besprochen)**
❶ to discuss; ich muss es erst mit
meinen Eltern besprechen I'll have
to discuss it with my parents first
❷ to review *(a book, film)*

**Besprechung** die *(PLURAL* die
**Besprechungen)** ❶ meeting *(at
work)* ❷ discussion ❸ review *(of a
film, play)*

**besser** *ADJECTIVE, ADVERB* **better**; alles
besser wissen to know better

**Besserung** die ❶ improvement
❷ gute Besserung! get well soon!

**beständig** *ADJECTIVE* ❶ constant
❷ settled *(weather)*

**Bestandteil** der *(PLURAL* die
**Bestandteile)** component

**bestätigen** *VERB (PERF* **hat bestätigt)**
❶ to confirm ❷ to acknowledge
*(receipt)* ❸ sich bestätigen to be
confirmed, to prove to be true

**beste** ▸ SEE **bester**

**bestechen** ◇*VERB (PRES* **besticht,** *IMP*
**bestach,** *PERF* **hat bestochen)** ❶ to
bribe ❷ to win over

**Bestechung** die *(PLURAL* die
**Bestechungen)** bribery

**Besteck** das *(PLURAL* die **Bestecke)**
cutlery

**bestehen** ◇*VERB (IMP* **bestand,** *PERF*
**hat bestanden)** ❶ to exist ❷ es
besteht die Gefahr, dass ... there
is a danger that ..., noch besteht

die Hoffnung, dass ... there is
still hope that ... ❸ to pass; eine
Prüfung bestehen to pass an exam
❹ auf etwas bestehen to insist on
something ❺ aus etwas bestehen
to consist of something ❻ aus
etwas bestehen to be made of
something

**bestellen** *VERB (PERF* **hat bestellt)**
❶ to order *(goods)* ❷ to reserve
*(tickets)* ❸ to tell; jemandem
etwas bestellen to tell somebody
something ❹ bestell ihm schöne
Grüße give him my regards ❺ kann
ich etwas bestellen? can I take a
message? ❻ to send for; jemanden
zu sich bestellen to send for
somebody

**Bestellung** die *(PLURAL* die
**Bestellungen)** ❶ order *(for goods)*
❷ reservation *(for tickets)*

**bestens** *ADVERB* **very well**; das hat ja
bestens geklappt that worked out
very well

**bester, beste, bestes** *ADJECTIVE*
❶ best; sein bestes Buch his best
book ❷ ich halte es für das Beste,
wenn ... I think it would be best
if ..., sein Bestes tun to do your best
❸ einen Witz zum Besten geben to
tell a joke ❹ jemanden zum Besten
halten to pull somebody's leg

**am besten** *ADVERB* **best**; du bleibst
am besten zu Hause you'd best stay
at home, es ist am besten, wenn
wir gleich anfangen it's best if we
get started straight away

**bestimmen** *VERB (PERF* **hat
bestimmt)** ❶ to fix *(a time,
price)* ❷ to decide (on); etwas
allein bestimmen to decide
(on) something on your own, er
bestimmt immer, was wir machen
he always decides what we're going

41

to do **❸ to be in charge ❹** für
jemanden bestimmt sein to be
meant for somebody **❺** für etwas
bestimmt sein to be intended for
something *(a donation for a good
cause, for example)*

**bestimmt** *ADJECTIVE* **❶ certain**;
zu einer bestimmten Zeit at a
certain time **❷ particular**; suchen
Sie etwas Bestimmtes? are you
looking for anything in particular?
**❸ definite**

**bestimmt** *ADVERB* **❶ certainly,
definitely**; ich komme ganz
bestimmt I'm definitely coming
**❷** er hat es bestimmt vergessen
he's bound to have forgotten **❸** du
weißt es doch bestimmt noch
surely you must remember it

**Bestimmung** die *(PLURAL* die
**Bestimmungen) regulation**

**bestrafen** *VERB (PERF* **hat bestraft)
to punish**

**bestreiten** ◇*VERB (IMP* **bestritt,** *PERF*
**hat bestritten) ❶ to deny ❷ to
dispute**; das möchte ich nicht
bestreiten I'm not disputing it **❸ to
pay for**

**bestürzt** *ADJECTIVE* **upset**

**Besuch** der *(PLURAL* die **Besuche)
❶ visit ❷ attendance** *(at school)*
**❸** Besuch haben to have visitors/a
visitor **❹** bei Freunden zu Besuch
sein to be staying with friends, zu
Besuch kommen to be visiting

**besuchen** *VERB (PERF* **hat besucht)
❶ to visit ❷ to go to** *(an exhibition,
the theatre)*; die Schule besuchen to
go to school **❸ to attend** *(a lecture)*

**Besucher** der *(PLURAL* die **Besucher)
visitor**

**Besucherin** die *(PLURAL* die
**Besucherinnen) visitor**

**betätigen** *VERB (PERF* **hat betätigt)
❶ to operate ❷** die Bremse
betätigen to apply the brakes
**❸** sich politisch betätigen to
be involved in politics **❹** sich
künstlerisch betätigen to do art
**❺** sich als Reporter betätigen to
work as a reporter

**Betäubungsmittel** das *(PLURAL* die
**Betäubungsmittel) anaesthetic**

**Bete** die Rote Bete beetroot

**beteiligen** *VERB (PERF* **hat beteiligt)
❶ to give a share to**; jemanden
mit zehn Prozent an einem
Geschäft beteiligen to give
somebody a ten percent share of a
business **❷** sich an etwas beteiligen
to take part in something **❸** kann
ich mich an eurem Spiel beteiligen?
can I join in your game?

**beten** *VERB (PERF* **hat gebetet)
to pray**

**Beton** der **concrete**

**betonen** *VERB (PERF* **hat betont)
to stress**

**Betonung** die *(PLURAL* die
**Betonungen) stress**

**Betrag** der *(PLURAL* die **Beträge)
amount**

**betragen** ◇*VERB (PRES* **beträgt,** *IMP*
**betrug,** *PERF* **hat betragen) ❶ to
amount to, to come to ❷** sich
betragen to behave, haben sich
die Kinder gut betragen? did the
children behave well?

**Betragen** das **behaviour**

**betreffen** ◇*VERB (PRES* **betrifft,**
*IMP* **betraf,** *PERF* **hat betroffen) to**

**concern**; was mich betrifft as far as I'm concerned

**betreten** ◇ *VERB (PRES* **betritt**, *IMP* **betrat**, *PERF* **hat betreten)** ❶ to enter ❷ 'Betreten verboten' 'keep out', 'keep off' *(the grass, for example)*

**Betrieb** der *(PLURAL* die **Betriebe)** ❶ **business**, **firm** ❷ **activity**; es war viel Betrieb it was very busy ❸ in Betrieb sein to be working *(of a machine)* ❹ außer Betrieb sein to be out of order ❺ eine Maschine in Betrieb setzen to start up a machine

**Betriebsferien** *PLURAL NOUN* firm's holiday; 'Betriebsferien' 'closed for the holidays'

**Betriebspraktikum** das *(PLURAL* die **Betriebspraktika)** **training course**

**betrinken** ◇ *VERB (IMP* **betrank sich**, *PERF* **hat sich betrunken)** sich betrinken to get drunk

**betrog** ▸ SEE **betrügen**

**Betrug** der ❶ **deception** ❷ **fraud**; was für ein Betrug what a swindle!

**betrügen** ◇ *VERB (IMP* **betrog**, *PERF* **hat betrogen)** ❶ to cheat; jemanden um tausend Euro betrügen to cheat somebody out of a thousand euros ❷ to be unfaithful to, to cheat on; sie hat ihren Mann betrogen she's been unfaithful to her husband

**betrunken** *ADJECTIVE* **drunk**

**Bett** das *(PLURAL* die **Betten)** bed; ins Bett gehen to go to bed, das Bett machen to make the bed

**Bettbezug** der *(PLURAL* die **Bettbezüge)** **duvet cover**

**Bettdecke** die *(PLURAL* die **Bettdecken)** **duvet**

**betteln** *VERB (PERF* **hat gebettelt)** to beg

**Bettlaken** das *(PLURAL* die **Bettlaken)** **sheet**

**Bettler** der *(PLURAL* die **Bettler)** **beggar**

**Bettlerin** die *(PLURAL* die **Bettlerinnen)** **beggar**

**Bettwäsche** die **bed linen**

**Bettzeug** das **bedding**

**beugen** *VERB (PERF* **hat gebeugt)** ❶ to bend ❷ to decline, to conjugate *(in grammar)* ❸ sich nach vorn beugen to bend forwards, sich über etwas beugen to bend over something ❹ sich aus dem Fenster beugen to lean out of the window ❺ sich beugen to submit

**Beule** die *(PLURAL* die **Beulen)** ❶ **bump** ❷ **lump** ❸ **dent**

**beurteilen** *VERB (PERF* **hat beurteilt)** to judge

**Beutel** der *(PLURAL* die **Beutel)** **bag**

**Bevölkerung** die *(PLURAL* die **Bevölkerungen)** **population**

**bevor** *CONJUNCTION* ❶ **before** ❷ bevor nicht until, bevor er nicht unterschrieben hat until he has signed

**bevorzugen** *VERB (PERF* **hat bevorzugt)** to prefer

**bewachen** *VERB (PERF* **hat bewacht)** to guard

**bewaffnen** *VERB (PERF* **hat bewaffnet)** to arm

**bewaffnet** *ADJECTIVE* **armed**

**bewahren** VERB (PERF **hat bewahrt**) jemanden vor etwas bewahren to protect someone from something

**bewährt** ADJECTIVE ❶ reliable ❷ proven (method, design) ❸ ein bewährtes Rezept a well-tried recipe

**bewegen**[1] VERB (PERF **hat bewegt**) ❶ to move ❷ sich bewegen to take exercise ❸ sich bewegen to move

**bewegen**[2] ◇VERB (IMP **bewog**, PERF **hat bewogen**) jemanden dazu bewegen, etwas zu tun to persuade somebody to do something

**bewegt** ADJECTIVE eventful

**Bewegung** die (PLURAL die **Bewegungen**) ❶ movement ❷ exercise ❸ eine Maschine in Bewegung setzen to start (up) a machine ❹ sich in Bewegung setzen to start to move

**Beweis** der (PLURAL die **Beweise**) ❶ proof ❷ belastende Beweise incriminating evidence ❸ token, sign

**beweisen** ◇VERB (IMP **bewies**, PERF **hat bewiesen**) ❶ to prove ❷ to show

**bewerben** ◇VERB (PRES **bewirbt sich**, IMP **bewarb sich**, PERF **hat sich beworben**) sich bewerben to apply, sich um eine Stelle bewerben to apply for a job

**Bewerber** der (PLURAL die **Bewerber**) applicant

**Bewerberin** die (PLURAL die **Bewerberinnen**) applicant

**Bewerbung** die (PLURAL die **Bewerbungen**) application

**Bewerbungsformular** das (PLURAL

die **Bewerbungsformulare**) application form

**bewohnen** VERB (PERF **hat bewohnt**) to live in

**Bewohner** der (PLURAL die **Bewohner**) ❶ resident ❷ inhabitant (of a region)

**Bewohnerin** die (PLURAL die **Bewohnerinnen**) ❶ resident ❷ inhabitant (of a region)

**bewölkt** ADJECTIVE cloudy

**Bewölkung** die clouds

**bewundern** VERB (PERF **hat bewundert**) to admire

**Bewunderung** die admiration

**bewusst** ADJECTIVE ❶ conscious ❷ deliberate ❸ sich etwas bewusst sein to be aware of something, ich war mir der Folgen bewusst I was aware of the consequences

**bewusstlos** ADJECTIVE unconscious

**Bewusstsein** das ❶ consciousness ❷ bei vollem Bewusstsein sein to be fully conscious ❸ mir kam zu(m) Bewusstsein, dass ... I realized that ...

**bezahlbar** ADJECTIVE affordable

**bezahlen** VERB (PERF **hat bezahlt**) ❶ to pay; für etwas 10 Euro bezahlen to pay 10 euros for something ❷ to pay for (goods, food); er hat das Essen bezahlt he paid for the meal

**Bezahlung** die payment

**bezeichnend** ADJECTIVE typical

**beziehen** ◇VERB (IMP **bezog**, PERF **hat bezogen**) ❶ to cover ❷ das Bett frisch beziehen to put clean sheets on the bed ❸ to move into; wann kannst du die neue Wohnung beziehen? when will you be able to move into the new flat? ❹ to get (goods, a pension) ❺ to take (a newspaper) ❻ sich auf etwas/jemanden beziehen to refer to something/somebody ❼ es bezieht sich it's clouding over

**Beziehung** die (PLURAL die Beziehungen) ❶ connection ❷ relationship ❸ Beziehungen contacts, Anna hat gute Beziehungen Anna has good contacts ❹ diplomatische Beziehungen diplomatic relations ❺ in dieser Beziehung in this respect ❻ eine Beziehung zu etwas haben to be able to relate to something (to art, pop music, for example)

**beziehungsweise** CONJUNCTION ❶ or rather ❷ respectively

**Bezirk** der (PLURAL die Bezirke) district

**Bezug** der (PLURAL die Bezüge) ❶ cover (of a cushion, duvet, etc.) ❷ connection; keinen Bezug zu etwas haben to be unable to relate to something ❸ auf etwas Bezug nehmen to refer to something ❹ in Bezug auf regarding ❺ mit Bezug auf Ihr Angebot with reference to your offer

**bezweifeln** VERB (PERF hat bezweifelt) to doubt

**BH** der (PLURAL die BHs) bra

**Bibel** die (PLURAL die Bibeln) bible; die Bibel the Bible

**Bibliothek** die (PLURAL die Bibliotheken) library

**Bibliothekar** der (PLURAL die Bibliothekare) librarian

**Bibliothekarin** die (PLURAL die Bibliothekarinnen) librarian

**biegen** ◇VERB (IMP bog, PERF hat gebogen) ❶ to bend ❷ sich biegen to bend ❸ (PERF ist gebogen) to turn; um die Ecke biegen to turn the corner

**Biene** die (PLURAL die Bienen) bee

**Bier** das (PLURAL die Biere) beer

**Bierdeckel** der (PLURAL die Bierdeckel) beer mat

**bieten** ◇VERB (IMP bot, PERF hat geboten) ❶ to offer ❷ to bid (at an auction) ❸ es bietet sich die Möglichkeit there is a possibility ❹ to present (a sight) ❺ das lasse ich mir nicht bieten! I won't put up with it!

**Bikini** der (PLURAL die Bikinis) bikini

**Bild** das (PLURAL die Bilder) ❶ picture; jemanden ins Bild setzen to put somebody in the picture ❷ scene

**bilden** VERB (PERF hat gebildet) ❶ to form ❷ sich bilden to form ❸ sich bilden to educate yourself

**Bildschirm** der (PLURAL die Bildschirme) screen

**bildschön** ADJECTIVE (very) beautiful

**Bildung** die ❶ formation ❷ education

**billig** ADJECTIVE cheap

**Billion** die (PLURAL die Billionen) billion (a million million); drei Billionen Euro three Billion euros

**bin** ▸ SEE sein

**Binde** die (PLURAL die Binden) ❶ bandage ❷ sanitary towel

**binden** ◇VERB (IMP band, PERF hat gebunden) ❶ to tie ❷ to bind

A
**B**
C
D
E
F
G
H
I
J
K
L
M
N
O
P
Q
R
S
T
U
V
W
X
Y
Z

*(a book)* ❸ **to make up** *(a bouquet)* ❹ **to thicken** *(a sauce)* ❺ **sich binden** to commit oneself

**Bindestrich** der *(PLURAL die Bindestriche)* **hyphen**

**Bindfaden** der *(PLURAL die Bindfäden)* **(piece of) string**

**Bindung** die *(PLURAL die Bindungen)* ❶ **tie** ❷ **relationship** ❸ **binding** *(on a ski)*

**Biokost** die **health food**

**Biologie** die **biology**

**biologisch** ADJECTIVE **biological**

**Biomüll** der **organic waste**

**Birke** die *(PLURAL die Birken)* **birch tree**

**Birne** die *(PLURAL die Birnen)* ❶ **pear** ❷ **bulb**

**bis** PREPOSITION *(+ACC)* ❶ **as far as**; dieser Zug fährt nur bis Passau this train only goes as far as Passau ❷ **up to**; Kinder bis zehn zahlen die Hälfte children up to ten pay half, bis jetzt up to now, bis zu up to ❸ **until, till** *(with time)* ❹ **by**; bis dahin by then ❺ **bis auf except for**, alle sind durchgefallen bis auf die zwei Mädchen everyone failed except for the two girls ❻ **bis bald!** see you soon! ❼ von München bis Salzburg from Munich to Salzburg, von Montag bis Freitag from Monday to Friday, zwei bis drei Euro two to three euros

**bis** CONJUNCTION **until, till**; sie bleibt, bis es dunkel wird she's staying until it gets dark

**Bischof** der *(PLURAL die Bischöfe)* **bishop**

**bisher** ADVERB **so far**

**bisherig** ADJECTIVE **previous**

**biss** ▸ SEE **beißen**

**Biss** der *(PLURAL die Bisse)* **bite**

**bisschen** PRONOUN ❶ **ein bisschen** a bit, ein bisschen Brot a bit of bread ❷ **kein bisschen** not a bit

**bissig** ADJECTIVE ❶ **vicious**; 'Vorsicht bissiger Hund!' 'beware of the dog!' ❷ **cutting** *(remark, tone)*

**bist** ▸ SEE **sein**

**bitte** ADVERB ❶ **please**; 'möchten Sie Kuchen?' – 'ja bitte' 'would you like some cake?' – 'yes please' ❷ **you're welcome** *(in reply to thanks)* ❸ **come in** *(after a knock on the door)* ❹ *(in a shop)* bitte? yes, please? ❺ wie bitte? sorry?

**Bitte** die *(PLURAL die Bitten)* **request**

**bitten** ◇VERB *(IMP bat, PERF hat gebeten)* **to ask**; jemanden um etwas bitten to ask somebody for something

**bitter** ADJECTIVE **bitter**

**blamieren** VERB *(PERF hat blamiert)* ❶ **to disgrace** ❷ **jemanden blamieren to embarrass somebody** ❸ **sich blamieren to make a fool of yourself**

**Blase** die *(PLURAL die Blasen)* ❶ **bubble** ❷ **blister** ❸ **bladder**

**blasen** ◇VERB *(PRES bläst, IMP bliest, PERF hat geblasen)* **to blow**

**Blasinstrument** das *(PLURAL die Blasinstrumente)* **wind instrument**

**Blaskapelle** die *(PLURAL die Blaskapellen)* **brass band**

**blass** ADJECTIVE **pale**

46

**Blatt** das *(PLURAL* die **Blätter)** ❶ leaf ❷ sheet; ein Blatt Papier a sheet of paper ❸ page ❹ newspaper

**blau** *ADJECTIVE* ❶ blue; ein blau gestreiftes Kleid a dress with blue stripes ❷ ein blaues Auge haben to have a black eye ❸ ein blauer Fleck a bruise ❹ blau sein *(informal)* to be tight ❺ eine Fahrt ins Blaue a mystery tour

**Blech** das *(PLURAL* die **Bleche)** ❶ sheet metal ❷ tin ❸ baking tray ❹ brass *(in music)*

**Blei** das lead

**bleiben** ◇*VERB (IMP* **blieb,** *PERF* **ist geblieben)** ❶ to stay, to remain ❷ to be left ❸ bleiben Sie am Apparat hold the line ❹ bei etwas bleiben to stick to something ❺ ruhig bleiben to keep calm ❻ wo bleibt er so lange? where has he got to? ❼ etwas bleiben lassen to not do something, wenn du nicht mitkommen willst, dann lass es eben bleiben if you don't want to come, then don't

**bleich** *ADJECTIVE* pale

**Bleichmittel** das *(PLURAL* die **Bleichmittel)** bleach

**bleifrei** *ADJECTIVE* unleaded

**Bleistift** der *(PLURAL* die **Bleistifte)** pencil

**Bleistiftspitzer** der *(PLURAL* die **Bleistiftspitzer)** pencil sharpener

**blenden** *VERB (PERF* **hat geblendet)** ❶ to dazzle ❷ to blind

**blendend** *ADJECTIVE* ❶ marvellous ❷ es geht mir blendend I feel great, wir haben uns blendend amüsiert we had a great time

**Blick** der *(PLURAL* die **Blicke)** ❶ look ❷ glance ❸ auf den ersten Blick at first sight ❹ view; ein Zimmer mit Blick aufs Meer a room with a sea view

**blicken** *VERB (PERF* **hat geblickt)** ❶ to look ❷ sich blicken lassen to show your face

**blieb** ▸ SEE **bleiben**

**blies** ▸ SEE **blasen**

**blind** *ADJECTIVE* blind

**Blinddarm** der *(PLURAL* die **Blinddärme)** appendix

**Blinddarmentzündung** die *(PLURAL* die **Blinddarmentzündungen)** appendicitis

**Blinde** der/die *(PLURAL* die **Blinden)** blind person, blind man/woman

**blinken** *VERB (PERF* **hat geblinkt)** ❶ to flash ❷ to indicate *(of a car)*

**Blinker** der *(PLURAL* die **Blinker)** indicator

**blinzeln** *VERB (PERF* **hat geblinzelt)** to blink

**Blitz** der *(PLURAL* die **Blitze)** ❶ (flash of) lightning ❷ flash

**blitzen** *VERB (PERF* **hat geblitzt)** ❶ to flash ❷ to sparkle ❸ es hat geblitzt there was a flash of lightning

**Block** der *(PLURAL* die **Blöcke)** ❶ pad *(for writing on)* ❷ *(PLURAL* die **Blocks)** block *(of flats)*

**Blockflöte** die *(PLURAL* die **Blockflöten)** recorder

**blöd** *ADJECTIVE* stupid

**Blödsinn** der nonsense

**Blog** das or der *(PLURAL* die **Blogs)** blog

a
**b**
c
d
e
f
g
h
i
j
k
l
m
n
o
p
q
r
s
t
u
v
w
x
y
z

**blond** | **böse**

**blond** ADJECTIVE blonde, fair-haired

**bloß** ADVERB ❶ only; es kostet bloß fünf Euro it's only five euros ❷ warum hat er das bloß gemacht? why on earth did he do it? ❸ was mache ich bloß? whatever shall I do? ❹ fass das bloß nicht an! don't touch it!

**bloß** ADJECTIVE ❶ bare (feet); mit bloßem Auge with the naked eye ❷ mere (words, suspicion); der bloße Gedanke daran the mere thought of it

**Blume** die (PLURAL die Blumen) flower

**Blumenkohl** der cauliflower

**Bluse** die (PLURAL die Blusen) blouse

**Blut** das blood

**Blutdruck** der blood pressure

**Blüte** die (PLURAL die Blüten) blossom

**bluten** VERB (PERF hat geblutet) to bleed

**Blutgefäß** das (PLURAL die Blutgefäße) bloodvessel

**Blutprobe** die (PLURAL die Blutproben) blood test

**Blutwurst** die (PLURAL die Blutwürste) black pudding

**Bock** der (PLURAL die Böcke) ❶ buck ❷ billy-goat ❸ ram ❹ Bock auf etwas haben (informal) to fancy something ❺ einen Bock schießen (informal) to make a blunder

**Bockwurst** die (PLURAL die Bockwürste) frankfurter

**Boden** der (PLURAL die Böden) ❶ ground ❷ floor ❸ bottom (of a container) ❹ loft, attic

**Bodensee** der Lake Constance

**bog** ▸ SEE **biegen**

**Bogen** der (PLURAL die Bögen) ❶ curve ❷ arch ❸ turn (in skiing)

**Bohne** die (PLURAL die Bohnen) bean

**bohren** VERB (PERF hat gebohrt) to drill

**Bohrer** der (PLURAL die Bohrer) drill

**Bohrinsel** die (PLURAL die Bohrinseln) oil rig

**Bohrmaschine** die (PLURAL die Bohrmaschinen) electric drill

**Bombe** die (PLURAL die Bomben) bomb

**Bonbon** der (PLURAL die Bonbons) sweet

**Boot** das (PLURAL die Boote) boat

**Bord**¹ das (PLURAL die Borde) shelf

**Bord**² der an Bord on board, über Bord overboard

**Bordkarte** die (PLURAL die Bordkarten) boarding card

**borgen** (PERF hat geborgt) ❶ to borrow ❷ sich etwas borgen to borrow something, ich habe es mir von ihr geborgt I borrowed it from her ❸ jemandem etwas borgen to lend somebody something, Evi hat mir ihr Buch geborgt Evi lent me her book

**Börse** die (PLURAL die Börsen) stock exchange

**Börsenmakler** der (PLURAL die Börsenmakler) stock broker

**Borste** die (PLURAL die Borsten) bristle

**böse** ADJECTIVE ❶ bad ❷ wicked ❸ naughty (child) ❹ angry; böse werden to get angry, ich bin ihm böse I'm angry with him ❺ auf

48

jemanden böse sein to be cross with somebody

**boshaft** *ADJECTIVE* malicious

**bot** ▸ SEE **bieten**

**Bote** der *(PLURAL* die **Boten)** messenger

**Botin** die *(PLURAL* die **Botinnen)** messenger

**Botschaft** die *(PLURAL* die **Botschaften)** ❶ message ❷ embassy; die britische Botschaft the British Embassy

**Botschafter** der *(PLURAL* die **Botschafter)** ambassador

**Botschafterin** die *(PLURAL* die **Botschafterinnen)** ambassador

**Bowle** die *(PLURAL* die **Bowlen)** punch *(for drinking)*

**boxen** *VERB (PERF* hat geboxt*)* ❶ to box ❷ to punch

**Boxer** der *(PLURAL* die **Boxer)** boxer

**brach** ▸ SEE **brechen**

**brachte** ▸ SEE **bringen**

**Branche** die *(PLURAL* die **Branchen)** (line of) business

**Branchenverzeichnis** das *(PLURAL* die **Branchenverzeichnisse)** classified directory

**Brand** der *(PLURAL* die **Brände)** fire

**Brandung** die surf

**brannte** ▸ SEE **brennen**

**Brasilianer** der *(PLURAL* die **Brasilianer)** Brazilian

**Brasilianerin** die *(PLURAL* die **Brasilianerinnen)** Brazilian

**Brasilien** Brazil

**braten** ◇*VERB (PRES* **brät**, *IMP* **briet**, *PERF* **hat gebraten)** ❶ to fry ❷ to roast

**Braten** der *(PLURAL* die **Braten)** ❶ roast ❷ joint

**Brathähnchen** das *(PLURAL* die **Brathähnchen)** roast chicken

**Bratkartoffeln** *PLURAL NOUN* fried potatoes

**Bratpfanne** die *(PLURAL* die **Bratpfannen)** frying pan

**Bratwurst** die *(PLURAL* die **Bratwürste)** fried sausage

**Brauch** der *(PLURAL* die **Bräuche)** custom

**brauchbar** *ADJECTIVE* ❶ usable ❷ useful

**brauchen** *VERB (PERF* hat gebraucht*)* ❶ need; ich brauche eine neue Birne für meine Lampe I need a new bulb for my light, du brauchst nur auf den Knopf zu drücken all you need to do is press the button, du brauchst nicht zu gehen you needn't go ❷ sie braucht es nur zu sagen she only has to say ❸ to take *(time)*; wie lange braucht du mit dem Auto? how long does it take you by car? ❹ ich könnte es gut brauchen I could do with it

**brauen** *VERB (PERF* hat gebraut*)* to brew

**Brauerei** die *(PLURAL* die **Brauereien)** brewery

**braun** *ADJECTIVE* ❶ brown ❷ braun werden to get a tan, braun (gebrannt) sein to be tanned

**Bräune** die tan

**Brause** die *(PLURAL* die **Brausen)** fizzy drink

**Braut** die *(PLURAL die* **Bräute**) bride

**Bräutigam** der *(PLURAL die* **Bräutigame**) bridegroom

**Brautjungfer** die *(PLURAL die* **Brautjungfern**) bridesmaid

**Brautpaar** das *(PLURAL die* **Brautpaare**) bride and groom

**brav** ADJECTIVE **good**

**BRD** die *(short for Bundesrepublik Deutschland)* **FRG** *(short for Federal Republic of Germany)*

**brechen** ◇VERB *(PRES* **bricht**, *IMP* **brach**, *PERF* **hat gebrochen**) ❶ to break *(an agreement, a record)* ❷ sich den Arm brechen to break your arm ❸ to vomit ❹ *(PERF* **ist gebrochen**) to break; der Ast ist gebrochen the branch broke

**breit** ADJECTIVE ❶ wide ❷ broad ❸ die breite Masse the general public

**Breite** die *(PLURAL die* **Breiten**) width

**Bremse** die *(PLURAL die* **Bremsen**) ❶ brake ❷ horsefly

**bremsen** VERB *(PERF* **hat gebremst**) ❶ to brake ❷ to slow down *(development, production)* ❸ jemanden bremsen *(informal)* to stop somebody, er ist nicht mehr zu bremsen there's no stopping him

**Bremslicht** das *(PLURAL die* **Bremslichter**) brake light

**Bremspedal** das *(PLURAL die* **Bremspedale**) brake pedal

**brennen** ◇VERB *(IMP* **brannte**, *PERF* **hat gebrannt**) ❶ to burn ❷ to be on *(of a light)*; das Licht brennen lassen to leave the light on ❸ to sting *(of a wound or sore)* ❹ das Haus brennt the house is on fire, es brennt! fire!

❺ darauf brennen, etwas zu tun to be dying to do something

**Brennnessel** die *(PLURAL die* **Brennnesseln**) stinging nettle

**Brennpunkt** der *(PLURAL die* **Brennpunkte**) focus

**Brett** das *(PLURAL die* **Bretter**) ❶ board ❷ plank ❸ shelf

**Brettspiel** das *(PLURAL die* **Brettspiele**) board game

**Brezel** die *(PLURAL die* **Brezeln**) pretzel

**bricht** ▸ SEE **brechen**

**Brief** der *(PLURAL die* **Briefe**) letter

**Brieffreund** der *(PLURAL die* **Brieffreunde**) pen friend

**Brieffreundin** die *(PLURAL die* **Brieffreundinnen**) pen friend

**Briefkasten** der *(PLURAL die* **Briefkästen**) ❶ letterbox ❷ postbox

**Briefmarke** die *(PLURAL die* **Briefmarken**) stamp

**Brieftasche** die *(PLURAL die* **Brieftaschen**) wallet

**Briefträger** der *(PLURAL die* **Briefträger**) postman

**Briefträgerin** die *(PLURAL die* **Briefträgerinnen**) postwoman

**Briefumschlag** der *(PLURAL die* **Briefumschläge**) envelope

**Briefwechsel** der correspondence

**briet** ▸ SEE **braten**

**Brillant** der *(PLURAL die* **Brillanten**) diamond

**Brille** die *(PLURAL die* **Brillen**) glasses, spectacles

**bringen** ◇*VERB (IMP* **brachte**, *PERF* **hat gebracht)** ❶ to bring ❷ to take; Peter bringt dich nach Hause Peter will take you home ❸ die Kinder ins Bett bringen to put the children to bed ❹ einen Film im Fernsehen bringen to show a film on television ❺ to publish *(an article)* ❻ to yield *(interest, a profit)* ❼ jemanden dazu bringen, etwas zu tun to get somebody to do something ❽ mit sich bringen to entail ❾ etwas hinter sich bringen to get something over and done with ❿ es weit bringen to go far ⓫ jemanden auf eine Idee bringen to give somebody an idea ⓬ es zu nichts bringen to get nowhere ⓭ das bringt's nicht! *(informal)* that's no use!

**Brise** die *(PLURAL* die **Brisen)** breeze

**Brite** der *(PLURAL* die **Briten)** Briton; die Briten the British

**Britin** die *(PLURAL* die **Britinnen)** Briton

**britisch** *ADJECTIVE* British

**Brokkoli** der broccoli

**Brombeere** die *(PLURAL* die **Brombeeren)** blackberry

**Brosche** die *(PLURAL* die **Broschen)** brooch

**Broschüre** die *(PLURAL* die **Broschüren)** brochure

**Brot** das *(PLURAL* die **Brote)** ❶ bread; ein Brot a loaf of bread ❷ ein Brot a slice of bread

**Brötchen** das *(PLURAL* die **Brötchen)** roll

**Bruch** der *(PLURAL* die **Brüche)** ❶ break ❷ fracture ❸ hernia ❹ fraction

**Bruchteil** der *(PLURAL* die **Bruchteile)** fraction

**Brücke** die *(PLURAL* die **Brücken)** bridge

**Bruder** der *(PLURAL* die **Brüder)** brother

**Brühe** die *(PLURAL* die **Brühen)** ❶ broth ❷ stock *(for cooking)*

**Brühwürfel** der *(PLURAL* die **Brühwürfel)** stock cube

**brüllen** *VERB (PERF* **hat gebrüllt)** to roar

**brummen** *VERB (PERF* **hat gebrummt)** ❶ to buzz ❷ to growl *(of a bear)* ❸ to hum *(of an engine)*

**Brunnen** der *(PLURAL* die **Brunnen)** ❶ well ❷ fountain

**Brüssel** das Brussels

**Brust** die *(PLURAL* die **Brüste)** ❶ chest ❷ breast

**Brustschwimmen** das breaststroke

**brutto** *ADVERB* gross

**BSE** das *(short for bovine spongiforme Enzephalopathie)* BSE

**Bub** der *(PLURAL* die **Buben)** boy

**Buch** das *(PLURAL* die **Bücher)** book

**Buche** die *(PLURAL* die **Buchen)** beech

**buchen** *VERB (PERF* **hat gebucht)** to book

**Bücherei** die *(PLURAL* die **Büchereien)** library

**Bücherregal** das *(PLURAL* die **Bücherregale)** bookcase

**Buchhalter** der *(PLURAL* die **Buchhalter)** accountant, bookkeeper

**Buchhalterin** die *(PLURAL* die **Buchhalterinnen)** accountant, bookkeeper

**Buchhandlung** die *(PLURAL* die **Buchhandlungen)** bookshop

**Büchse** die *(PLURAL* die **Büchsen)** tin, can

**Büchsenöffner** der *(PLURAL* die **Büchsenöffner)** tin opener

**Buchstabe** der *(PLURAL* die **Buchstaben)** letter *(of the alphabet)*; ein großer Buchstabe a capital letter, ein kleiner Buchstabe a small letter

**buchstabieren** *VERB (PERF* **hat buchstabiert)** to spell

**Bucht** die *(PLURAL* die **Buchten)** bay

**Buchung** die *(PLURAL* die **Buchungen)** booking, reservation

**bücken** *(PERF* **hat sich gebückt)** sich bücken to bend down

**Buddhismus** der Buddhism

**Bude** die *(PLURAL* die **Buden)** ❶ hut ❷ stall ❸ meine Bude *(informal)* my room, my pad

**Büfett** das *(PLURAL* die **Büfetts)** buffet

**Bügel** der *(PLURAL* die **Bügel)** hanger

**Bügeleisen** das *(PLURAL* die **Bügeleisen)** iron

**bügeln** *VERB (PERF* **hat gebügelt)** to iron

**Bühne** die *(PLURAL* die **Bühnen)** stage

**Bulgarien** das Bulgaria

**Bulle** der *(PLURAL* die **Bullen)** ❶ bull ❷ *(informal)* cop

**Bummel** der *(PLURAL* die **Bummel)** stroll *(around town)*

**bummeln** *VERB (PERF* **ist gebummelt)** ❶ to stroll; wir sind durch die Stadt gebummelt we strolled around town ❷ *(PERF* **hat gebummelt)** to dawdle

**Bund**[1] der *(PLURAL* die **Bünde)** ❶ association ❷ waistband

**Bund**[2] das *(PLURAL* die **Bunde)** bunch

**Bundesbürger** der *(PLURAL* die **Bundesbürger)** German citizen

**Bundeskanzler** der *(PLURAL* die **Bundeskanzler)** Federal Chancellor

**Bundeskanzlerin** die *(PLURAL* die **Bundeskanzlerinnen)** Federal Chancellor

**Bundesland** das *(PLURAL* die **Bundesländer)** (federal) state

**Bundesliga** die (German) national football league

**Bundespräsident** der *(PLURAL* die **Bundespräsidenten)** German president

**Bundesrat** der Upper House *(of the German Parliament)*

**Bundesregierung** die German government

**Bundesrepublik** die Federal Republic

**Bundesstraße** die *(PLURAL* die **Bundesstraßen)** A road, major road

**Bundestag** der Lower House *(of the German Parliament)*

**Bundeswehr** die (German) Army

**Bungalow** der *(PLURAL* die **Bungalows)** bungalow

**bunt** *ADJECTIVE* colourful

**Buntstift** der *(PLURAL* die **Buntstifte)** coloured pencil

**Burg** die *(PLURAL* die **Burgen)** castle

**Bürger** der *(PLURAL* die **Bürger)** citizen

**Bürgerin** die *(PLURAL* die **Bürgerinnen)** citizen

**Bürgermeister** der *(PLURAL* die **Bürgermeister)** mayor

**Bürgersteig** der *(PLURAL* die **Bürgersteige)** pavement

**Büro** das *(PLURAL* die **Büros)** office

**Büroklammer** die *(PLURAL* die **Büroklammern)** paper clip

**Bürste** die *(PLURAL* die **Bürsten)** brush

**bürsten** *VERB (PERF* **hat gebürstet)** to brush

**Bus** der *(PLURAL* die **Busse)** bus; ich fahre mit dem Bus I'm going by bus

**Busbahnhof** der *(PLURAL* die **Busbahnhöfe)** bus station

**Busch** der *(PLURAL* die **Büsche)** bush

**Busen** der *(PLURAL* die **Busen)** bosom

**Busfahrer** der *(PLURAL* die **Busfahrer)** bus driver

**Busfahrerin** die *(PLURAL* die **Busfahrerinnen)** bus driver

**Busfahrkarte** die *(PLURAL* die **Busfahrkarten)** bus ticket

**Bushaltestelle** die *(PLURAL* die **Bushaltestellen)** bus stop

**Buslinie** die *(PLURAL* die **Buslinien)** bus route

**Bussard** der *(PLURAL* die **Bussarde)** buzzard

**Bußgeld** das *(PLURAL* die **Bußgelder)** fine

**Büstenhalter** der *(PLURAL* die **Büstenhalter)** bra

**Busverbindung** die *(PLURAL* die **Busverbindungen)* ❶ bus connection ❷ bus line

**Butter** die butter

**Butterbrot** das *(PLURAL* die **Butterbrote)** sandwich, bread and butter

**bzw.** ▸ SEE beziehungsweise

# Cc

**Café** das *(PLURAL* die **Cafés)** cafe

**Cafeteria** die *(PLURAL* die **Cafeterias)** cafeteria

**campen** *VERB (PERF* **hat gecampt)** to camp

**Camper** der *(PLURAL* die **Camper)** camper

**Camperin** die *(PLURAL* die **Camperinnen)** camper

**Camping** das camping

**Campingbus** der *(PLURAL* die **Campingbusse)** camper *(vehicle)*

**Campingkocher** der *(PLURAL* die **Campingkocher)** camping stove

**Campingplatz** der *(PLURAL* die **Campingplätze)** campsite

**CD** die *(PLURAL* die **CDs)** CD

**CD-ROM** die *(PLURAL* die **CD-ROMs)** CD-ROM

**CD-Spieler** der *(PLURAL* die **CD-Spieler)** CD player

**Cello** das *(PLURAL* die **Cellos)** cello

**Cent** der *(PLURAL* die **Cents)** cent *(in euro and dollar systems)*; 25 Cent 25 cents

**Champignon** der *(PLURAL* die **Champignons)** mushroom

**Chance** die *(PLURAL* die **Chancen)** chance

**Chaos** das chaos

**chaotisch** *ADJECTIVE* chaotic

**Charakter** der *(PLURAL* die **Charaktere)** character

**charmant** *ADJECTIVE* charming

**Charterflug** der *(PLURAL* die **Charterflüge)** charter flight

**Chatroom** der *(PLURAL* die **Chatrooms)** chatroom

**chatten** *VERB (PERF* **hat gechattet)** to chat

**Chauvinist** der *(PLURAL* die **Chauvinisten)** chauvinist

**Chef** der *(PLURAL* die **Chefs)** ❶ head *(of a firm)* ❷ boss

**Chefin** die *(PLURAL* die **Chefinnen)** ❶ head *(of a firm)* ❷ boss

**Chemie** die chemistry

**Chemikalie** die *(PLURAL* die **Chemikalien)** chemical

**Chemiker** der *(PLURAL* die **Chemiker)** chemist

**Chemikerin** die *(PLURAL* die **Chemikerinnen)** chemist

**chemisch** *ADJECTIVE* ❶ chemical ❷ chemische Reinigung dry-cleaning, dry-cleaner's

**Chicorée** der chicory

**China** das China

**Chinese** der *(PLURAL* die **Chinesen)** Chinese; die Chinesen the Chinese

**Chinesin** die *(PLURAL* die **Chinesinnen)** Chinese

**chinesisch** *ADJECTIVE* Chinese

**Chipkarte** die *(PLURAL* die **Chipkarten)** smart card

**Chips** *PLURAL NOUN* crisps

**Chirurg** der *(PLURAL* die **Chirurgen)** surgeon

**Chirurgin** die *(PLURAL* die **Chirurginnen)** surgeon

**Chlor** das chlorine

**Chor** der *(PLURAL* die **Chöre)** choir

**Christ** der *(PLURAL* die **Christen)** Christian

**Christentum** das Christianity

**Christin** die *(PLURAL* die **Christinnen)** Christian

**christlich** *ADJECTIVE* Christian

**Christus** der Christ

**circa** *ADVERB* approximately

**Clique** die *(PLURAL* die **Cliquen)** ❶ gang ❷ clique

**Clown** der *(PLURAL* die **Clowns)** clown

**Cola** die *(PLURAL* die **Colas)** Coke

**Comic** der *(PLURAL* die **Comics)** cartoon

**Comicheft** das *(PLURAL* die **Comichefte)** comic

**Computer** der *(PLURAL* die **Computer)** computer; ich spiele am Computer I'm playing on the computer

**Computerprogramm** das *(PLURAL* die **Computerprogramme)** computer program

**Computerspiel** das *(PLURAL* die **Computerspiele)** computer game

**Container** der *(PLURAL* die **Container)** ❶ container ❷ skip

**Cordsamt** der corduroy

**Couch** die *(PLURAL* die **Couchs)** sofa

**Couchtisch** der *(PLURAL* die **Couchtische)** coffee table

**Cousin** der *(PLURAL* die **Cousins)** cousin

**Cousine** die *(PLURAL* die **Cousinen)** cousin
▸ SEE **Kusine**

**Creme** die *(PLURAL* die **Cremes)** ❶ cream ❷ cream dessert

**Curry** das ❶ curry ❷ curry powder

**Currywurst** die *(PLURAL* die **Currywürste)** curried sausage

**Cursor** der *(PLURAL* die **Cursors)** cursor

**Cybermobbing** das cyberbullying

a
b
c
d
e
f
g
h
i
j
k
l
m
n
o
p
q
r
s
t
u
v
w
x
y
z

# Dd

**da** ADVERB ❶ there; **da draußen** out there, **da drüben** over there, **da sein** to be there, **man muss pünktlich da sein** you have to be there on time ❷ **ist noch Brot da?** is there any bread left? ❸ here; **sind alle da?** is everyone here?, **da sind deine Handschuhe** here are your gloves ❹ **ist Sabine da?** is Sabine about? ❺ **von da an** from then on ❻ **ich bin wieder da** I'm back ❼ so (therefore); **der Bus war weg, da bin ich gelaufen** the bus had gone, so I walked ❽ **da kann man nichts machen** there's nothing you can do about it ❾ **da, wo die Straße nach Stuttgart abzweigt** at the turning for Stuttgart

**da** CONJUNCTION as, since; **da es gerade regnet** as it's raining

**dabei** ADVERB ❶ (included or next to) with it/him/her/them; **sie hatten die Kinder dabei** they had the children with them ❷ **dicht dabei** close by ❸ (referring to something already mentioned) about it; **das Wichtigste dabei** the most important thing about it ❹ at the same time; **er malte ein Bild und sang dabei** he painted a picture and sang at the same time ❺ during this ❻ **jemandem dabei helfen, etwas zu tun** to help somebody do something ❼ **was hast du dir denn dabei gedacht?** what were you thinking of? ❽ **dabei sein** to be there, **er ist dabei gewesen** he

was there ❾ **was ist denn dabei?** so what? ❿ **dabei sein, etwas zu tun** to be just doing something, **ich war gerade dabei zu gehen** I was just about to leave ⓫ **dabei bleiben** to stick with it (an opinion, for example) ⓬ and yet, even though

**dabeibleiben** ⬦VERB (IMP **blieb dabei**, PERF **ist dabeigeblieben**) ❶ to stay on (at an organisation) ❷ **er hat mit dem Training begonnen, ist aber nicht dabeigeblieben** he started training, but didn't keep it up

**dabeisein** ▸ SEE **dabei**

**Dach** das (PLURAL die **Dächer**) roof

**Dachboden** der (PLURAL die **Dachböden**) loft, attic

**Dachgeschoss** das (PLURAL die **Dachgeschosse**) attic

**Dachrinne** die (PLURAL die **Dachrinnen**) gutter (on roof edge)

**dachte** ▸ SEE **denken**

**Dackel** der (PLURAL die **Dackel**) dachshund

**dadurch** ADVERB ❶ through it/them; **das Wasser muss dadurch gelaufen sein** the water must have run through it ❷ as a result ❸ in this way; **ich nehme die U-Bahn, dadurch bin ich eine halbe Stunde eher da** I'll take the tube, that way I'll be there half an hour earlier

**dadurch** CONJUNCTION **dadurch, dass** because

**dafür** ADVERB ❶ for it/them; **dafür kriegt man nicht viel** you won't get much for it/them ❷ instead; **wenn er schon nicht auf die Party gehen will, kann er dich dafür zum Essen einladen** if he doesn't want to go to the party he can take you for a meal instead ❸ **but then** (on the other hand) ❹ **dafür, dass** considering (that) **ich kann nichts dafür** it's not my fault

**dagegen** ADVERB ❶ **against it/them**; **ich bin dagegen** I'm against it ❷ **for it/them** (when swapping) ❸ **into it**; **das Auto ist dagegen gefahren** the car drove into it ❹ **by comparison** ❺ **hast du was dagegen?** do you mind? ❻ **however**

**daheim** ADVERB **at home**

**daher** ADVERB ❶ **from there** ❷ **that's why**

**dahin** ADVERB ❶ **there** ❷ **bis dahin** (in the past) **until then**, (in the future) **by then** ❸ **jemanden dahin bringen, dass er etwas tut** to get somebody to do something

**dahinten** ADVERB **over there**

**dahinter** ADVERB ❶ **behind it/them** ❷ **dahinter kommen** to get to the bottom of it, **ich bin endlich dahinter gekommen** I finally got to the bottom of it

**dalassen** ◇VERB (PRES **lässt da**, IMP **ließ da**, PERF **hat dagelassen**) to **leave there**

**damals** ADVERB **at that time, then**; **wir wohnten damals in Berlin** we were then living in Berlin

**Dame** die (PLURAL die **Damen**) ❶ **lady** ❷ **queen** (in chess or cards) ❸ **draughts**

**Damenbinde** die (PLURAL die **Damenbinden**) **sanitary towel**

**damit** ADVERB ❶ **with it/them**; **ich will damit spielen** I want to play with it, **hör auf damit!** stop it! ❷ **by it**; **was meinst du damit?** what do

you mean by that? ❸ **damit hat es noch Zeit** there's no hurry (about that) ❹ **therefore, because of that**; **sie hat den zweiten Satz verloren und damit das Spiel** she lost the second set and because of it the match

**damit** CONJUNCTION **so that**; **ich habe es aufgeschrieben, damit du es nicht vergisst** I wrote it down so that you won't forget

**Damm** der (PLURAL die **Dämme**) ❶ **dam** ❷ **embankment**

**dämmern** VERB (PERF **hat gedämmert**) **es dämmert** it is getting light, it is getting dark

**Dämmerung** die ❶ **dawn** ❷ **dusk**

**Dampf** der (PLURAL die **Dämpfe**) **steam**

**dampfen** VERB (PERF **hat gedampft**) to **steam**

**dämpfen** VERB (PERF **hat gedämpft**) ❶ to **steam** (in cooking) ❷ to **muffle** (a sound) ❸ to **dampen** (somebody's enthusiasm)

**Dampfer** der (PLURAL die **Dampfer**) **steamer**

**danach** ADVERB ❶ **after it/them** ❷ **afterwards**; **kurz danach** shortly afterwards ❸ **danach suchen** to look for it/them ❹ **danach riechen** to smell of it ❺ **accordingly** ❻ **es sieht danach aus** it looks like it

**Däne** der (PLURAL die **Dänen**) **Dane**

**daneben** ADVERB ❶ **next to it/them** ❷ **by comparison**

**Dänemark** das **Denmark**

**Dänin** die (PLURAL die **Däninnen**) **Dane**

**dänisch** *ADJECTIVE* **Danish**

**dank** *PREPOSITION* (+GEN or +DAT) **thanks to**

**Dank** der ❶ **thanks**; mit Dank zurück thanks for the loan ❷ vielen Dank thank you very much

**dankbar** *ADJECTIVE* ❶ **grateful** ❷ **rewarding**

**danke** *EXCLAMATION* **thank you, thanks**; danke schön thank you very much, (nein) danke no thank you, no thanks

**danken** *VERB* (PERF hat gedankt) ❶ **to thank** ❷ nichts zu danken don't mention it

**dann** *ADVERB* **then**

**daran** *ADVERB* ❶ **on it/them** ❷ daran denken to think of it/them ❸ dicht daran close to it/them ❹ nahe daran sein, etwas zu tun to be on the point of doing something ❺ **about it/them** ❻ es liegt daran, dass ... it is because ... ❼ er ist daran gestorben he died of it

**darauf** *ADVERB* ❶ **on it/them** ❷ darauf warten to wait for it ❸ darauf antworten to reply to it ❹ **after that**; kurz darauf shortly after that ❺ am Tag darauf the day after ❻ am darauf folgenden Tag the following day ❼ es kommt darauf an, ob ... it depends whether ...

**daraufhin** *ADVERB* **as a result**

**daraus** *ADVERB* ❶ **out of it/them, from it/them** ❷ was ist daraus geworden? what has become of it/them? ❸ mach dir nichts daraus don't worry about it

**darf, darfst** ▸ SEE **dürfen**

**darin** *ADVERB* ❶ **in it/them** ❷ **in that respect**; der Unterschied liegt darin, dass ... the difference is that ...

**Darm** der (PLURAL die **Därme**) **intestine(s)**

**darstellen** *VERB* (PERF hat dargestellt) ❶ **to represent** ❷ **to portray**; dieses Gemälde stellt Szenen aus dem Bürgerkrieg dar this painting portrays scenes from the civil war ❸ **to describe**; er stellt es so dar, als sei es meine Schuld the way he describes it, it's all my fault ❹ **to play** (in the theatre)

**Darsteller** der (PLURAL die **Darsteller**) **actor**

**Darstellerin** die (PLURAL die **Darstellerinnen**) **actress**

**darüber** *ADVERB* ❶ **over it/them** ❷ **about it**; darüber sprechen to talk about it ❸ **more**; dreißig Euro oder darüber thirty euros or more

**darum** *ADVERB* ❶ **round it/them** ❷ darum bitten to ask for it ❸ **that's why**; darum komme ich nicht that's why I'm not coming ❹ ich sorge mich darum I worry about it ❺ es geht darum, zu gewinnen the main thing is to win ❻ darum geht es nicht that's not the point ❼ **because of that**; darum, weil because

**darunter** *ADVERB* ❶ **under it/them** ❷ im Stock darunter on the floor below ❸ **among them**; mehrere Schüler, darunter zwei Zehnjährige a number of pupils, among them two ten year olds ❹ **less**; dreißig Euro oder darunter thirty euros or less **❺** was verstehen Sie darunter? what do you understand by that?

**das** *ARTICLE* **❶** *(neuter)* **the**; das Haus the house **❷** that; das Mädchen war es it was that girl, das da that one

**das** *PRONOUN* **❶** which, that; das Kleid, das ich im Schaufenster gesehen habe the dress which I saw in the window **❷** das mit der Spitze the one with the lace **❸** who; das Mädchen, das gegenüber wohnt the girl who lives opposite **❹** that; das wusste ich nicht I didn't know that, das geht that's all right

**dasein** ▸ SEE **da**

**Dasein** das **existence**

**dass** *CONJUNCTION* **❶** that; ich freue mich, dass … I'm very pleased that … **❷** ich verstehe nicht, dass Karin ihn mag I don't understand why Karin likes him

**dasselbe** *PRONOUN* the same, the same one

**Date** die *(PLURAL* die **Dateien)** file

**Daten** *PLURAL NOUN* data

**Datenbank** die *(PLURAL* die **Datenbanken)** database

**Datenverarbeitung** die data processing

**datieren** *VERB (PERF* hat datiert) to date

**Dativ** der *(PLURAL* die **Dative)** dative

**Datum** das *(PLURAL* die **Daten)** date

**Dauer** die **❶** duration **❷** length **❸** für die Dauer von fünf Jahren for (a period of) five years **❹** von Dauer sein to last **❺** auf die Dauer in the long run, auf Dauer permanently

**Dauerkarte** die *(PLURAL* die **Dauerkarten)** season ticket

**dauern** *VERB (PERF* hat gedauert) **❶** to last **❷** lange dauern to take a long time, es hat vier Wochen gedauert, bis der Brief hier ankam it took four weeks for the letter to arrive

**dauernd** *ADJECTIVE* constant

**dauernd** *ADVERB* constantly

**Dauerwelle** die *(PLURAL* die **Dauerwellen)** perm

**Daumen** der *(PLURAL* die **Daumen)** thumb

**Daunendecke** die *(PLURAL* die **Daunendecken)** duvet

**davon** *ADVERB* **❶** from it/them **❷** about it; ich weiß nichts davon I don't know anything about it **❸** of it/them; die Hälfte davon half of it/them **❹** das kommt davon *(informal)* it serves you right **❺** was habe ich davon? what's the point? **❻** abgesehen davon apart from that

**davor** *ADVERB* **❶** in front of it/them **❷** beforehand **❸** Angst davor haben to be frightened of it/them **❹** kurz davor sein, etwas zu tun to be on the point of doing something

**dazu** *ADVERB* **❶** to it/them **❷** in addition; noch dazu in addition (to it) **❸** with it; was isst du dazu? what are you having with it? **❹** ich habe keine Lust dazu I don't feel like it **❺** jemanden dazu bringen, etwas zu tun to get somebody to do something **❻** ich bin nicht dazu gekommen I didn't get round to it **❼** er ist nicht dazu bereit he's not prepared to do it

**dazugeben** ◇*VERB* (*PRES* **gibt dazu**, *IMP* **gab dazu**, *PERF* **hat dazugegeben**) to add

**dazugehören** *VERB* (*PERF* **hat dazugehört**) ❶ to belong to it/them ❷ to go with it/them (*of accessories*); **alles, was dazugehört** everything that goes with it

**dazukommen** ◇*VERB* (*IMP* **kam dazu**, *PERF* **ist dazugekommen**) ❶ to arrive ❷ to be added ❸ **kommt noch etwas dazu?** would you like anything else?

**dazwischen** *ADVERB* ❶ in between ❷ between them; **der Unterschied dazwischen** the difference between them

**dazwischenkommen** ◇*VERB* (*PRES* **kommt dazwischen**, *IMP* **kam dazwischen**, *PERF* **ist dazwischengekommen**) to crop up

**DB** die (*Deutsche Bundesbahn*) German railways

**DDR** die (*Deutsche Demokratische Republik*) GDR, East Germany; **in der ehemaligen DDR** in the former East Germany

**Debatte** die (*PLURAL* die **Debatten**) debate

**Decke** die (*PLURAL* die **Decken**) ❶ blanket, cover ❷ (table)cloth; **ich habe eine neue Decke aufgelegt** I've put on a new tablecloth ❸ ceiling

**Deckel** der (*PLURAL* die **Deckel**) ❶ lid ❷ top

**decken** *VERB* (*PERF* **hat gedeckt**) ❶ to cover ❷ **ein Tuch über etwas decken** to spread a cloth over something ❸ **den Tisch decken** to lay the table ❹ **jemanden decken** to cover up for somebody ❺ **einen Spieler decken** to mark a player (*in sport*)

**definieren** *VERB* (*PERF* **hat definiert**) to define

**Definition** die (*PLURAL* die **Definitionen**) definition

**dehnbar** *ADJECTIVE* elastic

**dehnen** *VERB* (*PERF* **hat gedehnt**) to stretch

**dein** *ADJECTIVE* your

**deiner, deine, deins** *PRONOUN* yours; **meine Uhr ist kaputt, kann ich deine haben?** my watch is broken, can I take yours?

**deinetwegen** *ADVERB* ❶ because of you ❷ for your sake

**deins** ► SEE **deiner**

**deklinieren** *VERB* (*PERF* **hat dekliniert**) to decline

**Delfin** der (*PLURAL* die **Delfine**) dolphin

**Delle** die (*PLURAL* die **Dellen**) dent

**Delphin** der (*PLURAL* die **Delphine**) dolphin

**dem** *ARTICLE* ❶ (*dative*) (to) the ❷ **es liegt auf dem Tisch** it's on the table

**dem** *PRONOUN* ❶ to him; **gib es dem** give it to him ❷ to it, to that one ❸ to whom; **der Mann, dem ich das Geld gegeben habe** the man I gave the money to ❹ which; **das Messer, mit dem ich Zwiebeln schneide** the knife that I cut onions with

**demnächst** *ADVERB* shortly

**Demokratie** die (*PLURAL* die **Demokratien**) democracy

**demokratisch** *ADJECTIVE* **democratic**

**Demonstrant** der *(PLURAL* die **Demonstranten)* demonstrator**

**Demonstrantin** die *(PLURAL* die **Demonstrantinnen)* demonstrator**

**Demonstration** die *(PLURAL* die **Demonstrationen)* demonstration**

**demonstrieren** *VERB (PERF* **hat demonstriert)* to demonstrate**

**den** *ARTICLE* ❶ *(ACCUSATIVE)* **the** ❷ **ich habe mir den Arm gebrochen** I've broken my arm

**den** *PRONOUN* ❶ **him; kennst du den?** do you know him? ❷ **it, that one; den kannst du gerne haben** you're welcome to it, **ich nehme den** I'll take that one ❸ **who(m)** ❹ **which; der Mantel, den ich mir gekauft habe** the coat I bought

**denen** *PRONOUN* ❶ *(dative plural)* **(to) them** ❷ **that, (to) whom; die Menschen, denen sie geholfen hat** the people she helped

**denkbar** *ADJECTIVE* **conceivable**

**denken** ⬦*VERB (IMP* **dachte,** *PERF* **hat gedacht)* ❶ to think; ich denke oft an dich** I often think of you ❷ **das kann ich mir denken** I can imagine

**Denkmal** das *(PLURAL* die **Denkmäler)* monument**

**denn** *CONJUNCTION* ❶ **because, for** ❷ **mehr denn je** more than ever

**denn** *ADVERB* ❶ **wo denn?** where? ❷ **was ist denn los?** so what's the matter? ❸ **warum denn nicht?** why ever not? ❹ **es sei denn** unless

**dennoch** *CONJUNCTION* **nevertheless**

**deprimierend** *ADJECTIVE* **depressing**

**deprimiert** *ADJECTIVE* **depressed**

**der** *ARTICLE* ❶ *(masculine)* **the; der Mann** the man ❷ *(feminine and plural genitive)* **of the; die Katze der Frau** the woman's cat, **der Ball der Kinder** the children's ball ❸ *(dative)* **(to) the; ich gab es der Frau** I gave it to the woman

**der** *PRONOUN* ❶ **who; der Mann, der hier wohnt** the man who lives here ❷ **which; der Regenschirm, der mir gehört** the umbrella which is mine ❸ **der da** that one ❹ **him, he**

**deren** *PRONOUN* ❶ **their; die Kinder und deren Hund** the children and their dog ❷ **whose** ❸ **of which**

**derselbe** *PRONOUN* **the same, the same one**

**des** *ARTICLE* ❶ *(masculine and neuter genitive singular)* **of the; das Klingeln des Telefons** the ringing of the phone ❷ **der Ball des Jungen** the boy's ball

**deshalb** *ADVERB* ❶ **therefore** ❷ **that's why**

**Desinfektionsmittel** das *(PLURAL* die **Desinfektionsmittel)* disinfectant**

**desinfizieren** *VERB (PERF* **hat desinfiziert)* to disinfect**

**dessen** *PRONOUN* ❶ **his** ❷ **its** ❸ **whose; der Junge, dessen Mutter weint** the boy whose mother is crying ❹ **of which**

**desto** *ADVERB* **the; je mehr, desto besser** the more the better

**deswegen** *CONJUNCTION* ❶ **therefore** ❷ **that's why**

a
b
c
d
e
f
g
h
i
j
k
l
m
n
o
p
q
r
s
t
u
v
w
x
y
z

**Detektiv** der (PLURAL die **Detektive**) detective

**deutlich** ADJECTIVE **clear**

**deutlich** ADVERB ich konnte ihn deutlich sehen I could clearly see him

**deutsch** ADJECTIVE **German**

**Deutsch** das German; auf Deutsch in German, fließend Deutsch sprechen to speak fluent German

**Deutsche** der/die (PLURAL die **Deutschen**) German; er ist Deutscher he's German

**Deutschland** das Germany; nach Deutschland to Germany

**Devisen** PLURAL NOUN **foreign currency**

**Dezember** der December; am ersten Dezember on the first of December, im Dezember in December

**Dezimalzahl** die (PLURAL die **Dezimalzahlen**) decimal (number)

**d. h.** (short for das heißt) **i.e.**

**Dia** das (PLURAL die **Dias**) slide

**Diagnose** die (PLURAL die **Diagnosen**) diagnosis

**diagonal** ADJECTIVE **diagonal**

**Diagramm** das (PLURAL die **Diagramme**) diagram

**Dialekt** der (PLURAL die **Dialekte**) dialect

**Dialog** der (PLURAL die **Dialoge**) dialogue

**Diamant** der (PLURAL die **Diamanten**) diamond

**Diät** die (PLURAL die **Diäten**) diet; jemanden auf Diät setzen to put somebody on a diet

**dich** PRONOUN ❶ you ❷ yourself

**dicht** ADJECTIVE ❶ thick (fog) ❷ dense ❸ watertight ❹ airtight ❺ er ist nicht ganz dicht (informal) he's off his head

**dicht** ADVERB ❶ densely ❷ tightly ❸ close; geh nicht so dicht an den Käfig don't go so close to the cage, dicht bei close to

**Dichter** der (PLURAL die **Dichter**) poet

**Dichterin** die (PLURAL die **Dichterinnen**) poet

**Dichtung** die (PLURAL die **Dichtungen**) ❶ poetry ❷ seal, washer

**dick** ADJECTIVE ❶ thick ❷ swollen (ankle, tonsils) ❸ fat (person)

**Dickkopf** der (PLURAL die **Dickköpfe**) ❶ stubborn person ❷ einen Dickkopf haben to be stubborn

**die** ARTICLE (FEM & PLURAL) the; die Frau the woman, die Bücher the books

**die** PRONOUN ❶ (FEM & PLURAL) who; die Frau, die hier wohnt the woman who lives here, die Frau, die ich kenne the woman I know, die Kinder, die ich gefragt habe the children I asked ❷ which; die Tasche, die ich gekauft habe the bag I bought ❸ she, her ❹ them; ich meine die I mean them ❺ die da that one, (plural) those

**Dieb** der (PLURAL die **Diebe**) thief

**Diebin** die (PLURAL die **Diebinnen**) thief

**Diebstahl** der (PLURAL die **Diebstähle**) theft

**Diele** die *(PLURAL* die **Dielen)** ❶ hall ❷ floorboard

**dienen** *VERB (PERF* **hat gedient)** to serve

**Dienst** der *(PLURAL* die **Dienste)** service; Dienst haben to work, to be on duty *(of a soldier or doctor)*

**Dienstag** der *(PLURAL* die **Dienstage)** Tuesday; am Dienstag on Tuesday

**dienstags** *ADVERB* on Tuesdays

**dienstfrei** *ADJECTIVE*
❶ ein dienstfreier Tag a day off
❷ dienstfrei haben to have time off, to be off duty

**dienstlich** *ADVERB* on business

**Dienstreise** die *(PLURAL* die **Dienstreisen)** business trip

**diese** ► SEE **dieser**

**Diesel** der **diesel**

**dieselbe** *PRONOUN* the same, the same one

**dieser, diese, dieses** *ADJECTIVE*
❶ this ❷ these; diese Äpfel these apples

**dieses** *PRONOUN* ❶ this one; mir gefällt dieses am besten I like this one best ❷ these ones

**diesmal** *ADVERB* this time

**digital** *ADJECTIVE* digital

**Digitaluhr** die *(PLURAL* die **Digitaluhren)** ❶ digital watch ❷ digital clock

**Diktat** das *(PLURAL* die **Diktate)** dictation

**Ding** das *(PLURAL* die **Dinge)** thing; vor allen Dingen above all, das war ein Ding *(informal)* that was quite something

**Dings** der/die/das **thingummy**

**Dinosaurier** der *(PLURAL* die **Dinosaurier)** dinosaur

**Diplom** das *(PLURAL* die **Diplome)** diploma

**dir** *PRONOUN* ❶ you, to you; sie hat es dir gegeben she gave it to you, ich verspreche dir, dass ... I promise you that ... ❷ Freunde von dir friends of yours ❸ yourself

**direkt** *ADJECTIVE* direct

**direkt** *ADVERB* direct; der Bus fährt direkt zum Flughafen the bus goes direct to the airport

**Direktor** der *(PLURAL* die **Direktoren)** ❶ director ❷ headmaster, principal ❸ manager *(of a bank, theatre)*

**Direktorin** die *(PLURAL* die **Direktorinnen)** ❶ director ❷ headmistress, principal ❸ manager *(of a bank, theatre)*

**Direktübertragung** die *(PLURAL* die **Direktübertragungen)** live transmission

**Dirigent** der *(PLURAL* die **Dirigenten)** conductor

**dirigieren** *VERB (PERF* **hat dirigiert)** to conduct

**Diskette** die *(PLURAL* die **Disketten)** floppy disk

**Diskettenlaufwerk** das *(PLURAL* die **Diskettenlaufwerke)** disk drive

**Disko** die *(PLURAL* die **Diskos)** disco

**Diskothek** die *(PLURAL* die **Diskotheken)** disco, discotheque

**Diskriminierung** die discrimination; die Diskriminierung von Frauen discrimination against women

**Diskussion** die (PLURAL die **Diskussionen**) discussion; zur Diskussion stehen to be under discussion

**diskutieren** VERB (PERF **hat diskutiert**) to discuss

**Disziplin** die (PLURAL die **Disziplinen**) discipline

**DJH** die (short for Deutsche Jugendherberge) German youth hostel (association)

**DM** die (short for Deutschemark) DM, **Deutschmark**
▸ SEE **Mark**

**D-Mark** die (PLURAL die **D-Mark**) **Deutschmark**, German mark
▸ SEE **Mark**

**doch** ADVERB ❶ yes (when you are contradicting somebody); 'hast du keinen Hunger?' – 'doch!' 'aren't you hungry?' – 'yes, I am!' ❷ after all; sie hat ihn doch eingeladen she invited him after all, sie ist doch nicht gekommen she hasn't come after all ❸ er hat doch meinen Brief bekommen? he did get my letter, didn't he?, sie kommt doch? she's coming, isn't she? ❹ anyway; du hörst ja doch nicht auf mich you won't listen to me anyway ❺ pass doch auf! do be careful!

**doch** CONJUNCTION but

**Doktor** der (PLURAL die **Doktoren**) doctor; den Doktor machen to do a doctorate

**Dokument** das (PLURAL die **Dokumente**) document

**Dokumentarfilm** der (PLURAL die **Dokumentarfilme**) documentary

**Dokumentarsendung** die (PLURAL die **Dokumentarsendungen**) documentary (programme)

**dolmetschen** VERB (PERF **hat gedolmetscht**) to interpret

**Dolmetscher** der (PLURAL die **Dolmetscher**) interpreter

**Dolmetscherin** die (PLURAL die **Dolmetscherinnen**) interpreter

**Dom** der (PLURAL die **Dome**) cathedral

**Donau** die Danube

**Donner** der thunder

**donnern** VERB (PERF **hat gedonnert**) to thunder

**Donnerstag** der (PLURAL die **Donnerstage**) Thursday; am Donnerstag on Thursday

**donnerstags** ADVERB on Thursdays

**doof** ADJECTIVE (informal) stupid

**Doppel** das (PLURAL die **Doppel**) ❶ duplicate ❷ doubles (in sport)

**Doppelbett** das (PLURAL die **Doppelbetten**) double bed

**Doppelfenster** das (PLURAL die **Doppelfenster**) double-glazed window; wir haben Doppelfenster we've got double glazing

**Doppelhaus** das (PLURAL die **Doppelhäuser**) semi-detached house

**Doppelklick** der (PLURAL die **Doppelklicks**) double-click (with mouse)

**Doppelpunkt** der (PLURAL die **Doppelpunkte**) colon

**doppelt** ADJECTIVE ❶ double ❷ in doppelter Ausführung in duplicate ❸ die doppelte Menge twice the amount

**doppelt** *ADVERB* ❶ doubly ❷ twice; doppelt so viel twice as much, sich doppelt anstrengen to try twice as hard

**Doppelzimmer** das *(PLURAL die Doppelzimmer)* double room

**Dorf** das *(PLURAL die Dörfer)* village

**Dorn** der *(PLURAL die Dornen)* thorn

**dort** *ADVERB* there; dort drüben over there

**dorther** *ADVERB* from there

**dorthin** *ADVERB* there; geht ihr jetzt dorthin? are you going there now?

**Dose** die *(PLURAL die Dosen)* tin, can

**dösen** *VERB (PERF hat gedöst)* to doze

**Dosenöffner** der *(PLURAL die Dosenöffner)* tin opener

**Dosierung** die *(PLURAL die Dosierungen)* dose

**Dosis** die *(PLURAL die Dosen)* dose

**Dotter** der *(PLURAL die Dotter)* yolk

**downloaden** *VERB (PERF hat downgeloadet)* to download

**Dozent** der *(PLURAL die Dozenten)* lecturer

**Dozentin** die *(PLURAL die Dozentinnen)* lecturer

**Drache** der *(PLURAL die Drachen)* dragon

**Drachen** der *(PLURAL die Drachen)* kite

**Drachenfliegen** das hang-gliding; Drachenfliegen gehen to go hang-gliding

**Draht** der *(PLURAL die Drähte)* ❶ wire ❷ er ist auf Draht *(informal)* he's on the ball

**Drama** das *(PLURAL die Dramen)* drama

**Dramatik** die drama

**dran** *ADVERB ▸ SEE* daran ❶ ich bin dran it's my turn, wer ist dran? whose turn is it? ❷ gut dran sein to be well off ❸ arm dran sein to be in a bad way ❹ spät dran sein to be late

**drängen** *VERB (PERF hat gedrängt)* ❶ to push ❷ to press, to urge *(somebody)* ❸ sich drängen to crowd, die Leute drängten sich vor der Kasse people crowded around the box-office

**drankommen** *⬦VERB (IMP kam dran, PERF ist drangekommen)* to have your turn; wer kommt dran? whose turn is it?

**drauf** *ADVERB ▸ SEE* darauf ❶ drauf und dran sein, etwas zu tun to be on the point of doing something ❷ gut drauf sein *(informal)* to be in a good mood

**draußen** *ADVERB* outside

**Dreck** der dirt

**dreckig** *ADJECTIVE* dirty, filthy

**Drehbuch** das *(PLURAL die Drehbücher)* ❶ screenplay ❷ script

**drehen** *VERB (PERF hat gedreht)* ❶ to turn; an etwas drehen to turn something ❷ to shoot *(a film)* ❸ sich drehen to turn ❹ sich im Kreis drehen to rotate ❺ es dreht sich um ihr Taschengeld it's about her pocket money

**drei** *NUMBER* three

**Drei** die *(PLURAL die Dreien)* three

**Dreieck** das *(PLURAL* die **Dreiecke)** triangle

**dreieckig** *ADJECTIVE* triangular

**dreifach** *ADJECTIVE* triple

**dreihundert** *NUMBER* three hundred

**dreimal** *ADVERB* three times

**Dreirad** das *(PLURAL* die **Dreiräder)** tricycle

**dreißig** *NUMBER* thirty

**drei viertel** *NUMBER* three-quarters

**Dreiviertelstunde** die *(PLURAL* die **Dreiviertelstunden)** three-quarters of an hour

**dreizehn** *NUMBER* thirteen

**drin** *ADVERB* ▸ SEE **darin** drin sein to be inside

**dringend** *ADJECTIVE* urgent

**drinnen** *ADVERB* ❶ inside ❷ indoors

**dritt** *ADVERB* sie sind zu dritt there are three of them

**dritte** ▸ SEE **dritter**

**Drittel** das *(PLURAL* die **Drittel)** third

**drittens** *ADVERB* thirdly

**dritter, dritte, drittes** *ADJECTIVE* third; zum dritten Mal for the third time, ein Dritter a third person, jeder Dritte, der mitwollte every third person who wanted to come, die Dritte Welt the Third World

**Droge** die *(PLURAL* die **Drogen)** drug

**drogenabhängig** *ADJECTIVE* addicted to drugs

**Drogenabhängige** der/die *(PLURAL* die **Drogenabhängigen)** drug addict

**Drogenabhängigkeit** die drug addiction

**drogensüchtig** *ADJECTIVE* addicted to drugs

**Drogensüchtige** der/die *(PLURAL* die **Drogensüchtigen)** drug addict

**Drogerie** die *(PLURAL* die **Drogerien)** chemist's

**Drogist** der *(PLURAL* die **Drogisten)** chemist

**Drogistin** die *(PLURAL* die **Drogistinnen)** chemist

**drohen** *VERB (PERF* hat gedroht) to threaten; jemandem drohen to threaten somebody

**Drohung** die *(PLURAL* die **Drohungen)** threat

**Drossel** die *(PLURAL* die **Drosseln)** ❶ thrush *(bird)* ❷ throttle

**drüben** *ADVERB* over there

**Druck** der ❶ pressure; jemanden unter Druck setzen to put pressure on somebody ❷ printing ❸ *(PLURAL* die **Drucke)** print

**drucken** *VERB (PERF* hat gedruckt) to print

**drücken** *VERB (PERF* hat gedrückt) ❶ to press ❷ an der Tür drücken to push the door, 'bitte drücken' 'push' ❸ to hug ❹ to pinch *(of shoes)* ❺ die Preise drücken to force down prices ❻ sich vor etwas drücken *(informal)* to get out of something, du hast dich mal wieder vor dem Aufräumen gedrückt you've got out of tidying up again

**Drucker** der *(PLURAL* die **Drucker)** printer

**Druckknopf** der *(PLURAL die Druckknöpfe)* press stud

**Druckluftmesser** der *(PLURAL die Druckluftmesser)* pressure gauge

**Drucksache** die *(PLURAL die Drucksachen)* printed matter

**Druckschrift** die *(PLURAL die Druckschriften)* ❶ block letters ❷ type ❸ pamphlet

**Drüse** die *(PLURAL die Drüsen)* gland

**Dschungel** der *(PLURAL die Dschungel)* jungle

**du** PRONOUN ❶ you ❷ du sagen to say 'du' (to each other), per du sein to be on familiar terms *('du' is used when talking to family members, close friends, or people of your own age; otherwise 'Sie' is used)*

**Dudelsack** der *(PLURAL die Dudelsäcke)* bagpipes

**Duft** der *(PLURAL die Düfte)* fragrance, scent

**duften** VERB *(PERF hat geduftet)* to smell; nach Lavendel duften to smell of lavender

**dumm** ADJECTIVE ❶ stupid ❷ das wird mir jetzt zu dumm *(informal)* I've had enough of it ❸ so etwas Dummes! how annoying! ❹ der Dumme sein to draw the short straw

**dummerweise** ADVERB stupidly

**Dummheit** die *(PLURAL die Dummheiten)* ❶ stupidity ❷ stupid thing; mach keine Dummheiten don't do anything stupid

**Dummkopf** der *(PLURAL die Dummköpfe)* fool

**Dünger** der *(PLURAL die Dünger)* fertilizer

**dunkel** ADJECTIVE ❶ dark; ein dunkler Anzug a dark suit ❷ im Dunkeln in the dark ❸ vague *(idea)* ❹ shady *(business)* ❺ deep *(voice)*

**Dunkelheit** die darkness, dark; bei Einbruch der Dunkelheit at dusk

**dünn** ADJECTIVE ❶ thin ❷ weak *(coffee, tea)*

**Dunst** der *(PLURAL die Dünste)* haze

**Duo** das *(PLURAL die Duos)* duet

**durch** PREPOSITION *(+ACC)* ❶ through; er ist durch das Fernsehen bekannt geworden he's become famous through television ❷ by; durch Boten by courier ❸ acht durch zwei ist vier eight divided by two is four ❹ due to

**durch** ADVERB ❶ through; die ganze Nacht durch all through the night ❷ den Winter durch throughout the winter ❸ durch und durch completely ❹ es war acht Uhr durch *(informal)* it was gone eight o'clock

**durcharbeiten** VERB *(PERF hat durchgearbeitet)* ❶ to work through; die Nacht durcharbeiten to work through the night ❷ sich durch etwas durcharbeiten to work your way through something

**durchaus** ADVERB absolutely

**durchblicken** VERB *(PERF hat durchgeblickt)* ❶ *(informal)* to understand ❷ durchblicken lassen, dass ... to hint that ...

**durchbrechen** ◇VERB *(PRES bricht durch, IMP brach durch, PERF hat durchgebrochen)* ❶ to snap, to break in two ❷ *(PERF ist*

**durchgebrochen)** das Brett ist durchgebrochen the board has snapped

**durcheinander** *ADVERB* ❶ in a mess; mein Zimmer ist durcheinander my room is (in) a mess ❷ die Akten durcheinander bringen to muddle up the files, Karl hat ihre Namen durcheinander gebracht Karl got their names mixed up ❸ confused; bring mich nicht durcheinander don't confuse me ❹ sie haben alle durcheinander geredet they all talked at once

**Durcheinander** das ❶ muddle ❷ mess; in der Wohnung herrschte ein fürchterliches Durcheinander the flat was a terrible mess ❸ confusion; im allgemeinen Durcheinander in the general confusion

**durcheinanderbringen**
▸ SEE **durcheinander**

**durchfahren** ◇*VERB* (*PRES* **fährt durch**, *IMP* **fuhr durch**, *PERF* **ist durchgefahren)** ❶ to drive through ❷ to go through ❸ der Zug fährt (in Stuttgart) durch the train doesn't stop (in Stuttgart)

**Durchfall** der diarrhoea

**durchfallen** ◇*VERB* (*PRES* **fällt durch**, *IMP* **fiel durch**, *PERF* **ist durchgefallen)** ❶ to fall through ❷ to fail (an exam)

**durchführen** *VERB* (*PERF* **hat durchgeführt)** to carry out

**Durchgang** der (*PLURAL* die **Durchgänge)** ❶ passage ❷ 'Durchgang verboten' 'no entry' ❸ round (in sport)

**Durchgangsverkehr** der through traffic

**durchgehen** ◇*VERB* (*IMP* **ging durch**, *PERF* **ist durchgegangen)** ❶ to go through ❷ (informal) to escape ❸ jemandem etwas durchgehen lassen to let somebody get away with something

**durchkommen** ◇*VERB* (*IMP* **kam durch**, *PERF* **ist durchgekommen)** ❶ to come through ❷ to get through (on the phone, in an exam) ❸ to pull through (after an illness)

**durchlassen** ◇*VERB* (*PRES* **lässt durch**, *IMP* **ließ durch**, *PERF* **hat durchgelassen)** ❶ to let through ❷ to let in

**durchmachen** *VERB* (*PERF* **hat durchgemacht)** ❶ to go through ❷ to work through (your lunch break, for example) ❸ wir haben die Nacht durchgemacht we made a night of it

**Durchmesser** der (*PLURAL* die **Durchmesser)** diameter

**durchnehmen** ◇*VERB* (*PRES* **nimmt durch**, *IMP* **nahm durch**, *PERF* **hat durchgenommen)** to do (a topic at school)

**durchs** durch das through the
▸ SEE **durch**

**Durchsage** die (*PLURAL* die **Durchsagen)** announcement

**Durchschnitt** der (*PLURAL* die **Durchschnitte)** average; im Durchschnitt on average

**durchschnittlich** *ADJECTIVE* average

**durchschnittlich** *ADVERB* on average

**durchsetzen** *VERB* (*PERF* **hat durchgesetzt)** ❶ to carry through ❷ sich durchsetzen to assert yourself ❸ sich durchsetzen to catch on (of a fashion, an idea)

**durchsichtig** *ADJECTIVE* **transparent**

**durchstreichen** ◇*VERB (IMP* **strich durch**, *PERF* **hat durchgestrichen)** **to cross out**

**Durchzug** der **draught**

**dürfen** ◇*VERB (PRES* **darf**, *IMP* **durfte**, *PERF* **hat gedurft**, *PERF* **hat dürfen)** ❶ **to be allowed**; sie darf das nicht she's not allowed to do that, er hat nicht gedurft he wasn't allowed to ❷ Klaus hat sie im Krankenhaus besuchen dürfen Klaus was allowed to visit her in hospital ❸ darf ich? may I? ❹ das dürfen Sie nicht vergessen you mustn't forget that, du darfst es nicht alles so ernst nehmen you mustn't take it all so seriously ❺ du darfst froh sein, dass sonst nichts passiert ist you should be glad that nothing else happened, das darf einfach nicht passieren that just shouldn't happen, das dürfte nicht schwierig sein that shouldn't be difficult ❻ das darf nicht wahr sein! I don't believe it! ❼ was darf es sein? can I help you? ❽ das dürfte der Grund sein that's probably the reason

**durfte, durften, durftest, durftet** ▸ SEE **dürfen**

**dürftig** *ADJECTIVE* **poor, meagre**

**Dürre** die *(PLURAL* die **Dürren)** **drought**

**Durst** der **thirst**; Durst haben to be thirsty

**durstig** *ADJECTIVE* **thirsty**

**Dusche** die *(PLURAL* die **Duschen)** **shower**

**duschen** *VERB (PERF* **hat geduscht)** ❶ **to have a shower** ❷ sich duschen to have a shower

**Düsenflugzeug** das *(PLURAL* die **Düsenflugzeuge)** **jet (plane)**

**düster** *ADJECTIVE* ❶ **gloomy** *(future, thoughts)* ❷ **dark**

**Dutzend** das *(PLURAL* die **Dutzende)** **dozen**

**duzen** *VERB (PERF* **hat geduzt)** **to call somebody 'du'**; wollen wir uns duzen? shall we say 'du' to each other? *('du' is used when talking to family members, close friends, or people of your own age)*

**dynamisch** *ADJECTIVE* **dynamic**

**D-Zug** der *(PLURAL* die **D-Züge)** **fast train, express**

# Ee

A
B
C
D
E
F
G
H
I
J
K
L
M
N
O
P
Q
R
S
T
U
V
W
X
Y
Z

**Ebbe** die (PLURAL die **Ebben**) low tide; es ist Ebbe the tide is out

**eben** ADJECTIVE ❶ flat ❷ level

**eben** ADVERB ❶ just; Gabi war eben hier Gabi was just here, eben noch just now ❷ eben! exactly!

**Ebene** die (PLURAL die **Ebenen**) ❶ plain ❷ level ❸ plane (in geometry)

**ebenso** ADVERB just as; Ulla hat den Film ebenso oft gesehen wie du Ulla's seen the film just as often as you, ich habe ebenso viel Arbeit wie du I've got just as much work as you

**Echo** das (PLURAL die **Echos**) echo

**echt** ADJECTIVE real, genuine; die Kette ist aus echtem Gold the necklace is real gold

**echt** ADVERB (informal) really; das ist echt gut that's really good

**Eckball** der (PLURAL die **Eckbälle**) corner (kick)

**Ecke** die (PLURAL die **Ecken**) corner; um die Ecke round the corner

**eckig** ADJECTIVE square

**Edelstein** der (PLURAL die **Edelsteine**) precious stone

**EDV** die (short for elektronische Datenverarbeitung) electronic data processing, EDP

**Efeu** der (PLURAL die **Efeus**) ivy

**Effekt** der (PLURAL die **Effekte**) effect

**effektiv** ADJECTIVE effective

**effektiv** ADVERB really, actually

**EG** die (short for Europäische Gemeinschaft) EC

**egal** ADJECTIVE ❶ das ist mir egal it's all the same to me ❷ egal, wie groß no matter how big, egal, ob er es will oder nicht (it doesn't matter) whether he wants to or not

**egoistisch** ADJECTIVE selfish

**ehe** CONJUNCTION before; ehe ich nicht weiß, was er will, mache ich nichts I won't do anything before I know what he wants

**Ehe** die (PLURAL die **Ehen**) marriage

**Ehefrau** die (PLURAL die **Ehefrauen**) wife

**ehemalig** ADJECTIVE former

**Ehemann** der (PLURAL die **Ehemänner**) husband

**Ehepaar** das (PLURAL die **Ehepaare**) married couple

**eher** ADVERB ❶ earlier, sooner; je eher, desto besser the sooner the better ❷ rather; eher gehe ich zu Fuß, als Geld für ein Taxi auszugeben I'd rather walk than pay for a taxi ❸ more; das ist schon eher möglich that's more likely

**Ehre** die (PLURAL die **Ehren**) honour

**ehrenamtlich** ADJECTIVE honorary

**Ehrgeiz** der ambition

**ehrgeizig** ADJECTIVE ambitious

**ehrlich** ADJECTIVE honest

**Ehrlichkeit** die honesty

**Ei** das *(PLURAL die Eier)* egg

**Eiche** die *(PLURAL die Eichen)* oak

**Eichhörnchen** das *(PLURAL die Eichhörnchen)* squirrel

**Eid** der *(PLURAL die Eide)* oath

**Eidechse** die *(PLURAL die Eidechsen)* lizard

**Eidotter** das *(PLURAL die Eidotter)* egg yolk

**Eierbecher** der *(PLURAL die Eierbecher)* egg-cup

**Eierschale** die *(PLURAL die Eierschalen)* eggshell

**Eifer** der eagerness

**Eifersucht** die jealousy

**eifersüchtig** *ADJECTIVE* jealous; auf jemanden eifersüchtig sein to be jealous of somebody

**eifrig** *ADJECTIVE* eager

**Eigelb** das *(PLURAL die Eigelb(e))* egg yolk

**eigen** *ADJECTIVE* own; sie ist erst siebzehn und hat schon ihr eigenes Auto she's only seventeen and she's already got her own car

**Eigenart** die *(PLURAL die Eigenarten)* peculiarity

**eigenartig** *ADJECTIVE* peculiar

**Eigenschaft** die *(PLURAL die Eigenschaften)* ❶ quality ❷ characteristic

**eigensinnig** *ADJECTIVE* obstinate

**eigentlich** *ADJECTIVE* actual

**eigentlich** *ADVERB* actually; eigentlich habe ich keine Lust, heute ins Kino zu gehen actually I don't fancy going to the cinema today

**Eigentum** das property

**Eigentümer** der *(PLURAL die Eigentümer)* owner

**eignen** *VERB (PERF hat sich geeignet)* sich eignen to be suitable

**Eile** die hurry

**eilen** *VERB* ❶ *(PERF ist geeilt)* to hurry ❷ *(PERF hat geeilt)* to be urgent; das eilt nicht it's not urgent

**eilig** *ADJECTIVE* ❶ urgent ❷ hurried ❸ es eilig haben to be in a hurry

**Eilzug** der *(PLURAL die Eilzüge)* fast stopping train

**Eimer** der *(PLURAL die Eimer)* bucket

**ein, eine, ein** *ARTICLE* a, an; ein Haus a house, eine Allergie an allergy, ein bisschen mehr a bit more, was für ein Kleid hast du gekauft? what sort of dress did you buy?

**ein** *ADJECTIVE* ❶ one; sie haben nur ein Kind they've got just one child, eines Abends one evening ❷ einer Meinung sein to be of the same opinion ❸ ein für alle Mal once and for all

**einander** *PRONOUN* each other, one another

**einatmen** *VERB (PERF hat eingeatmet)* to breathe in

**Einbahnstraße** die *(PLURAL die Einbahnstraßen)* one-way street

**Einband** der *(PLURAL die Einbände)* cover

**einbauen** *VERB (PERF hat eingebaut)* ❶ to fit ❷ to install

**Einbauküche** die *(PLURAL die Einbauküchen)* fitted kitchen

**einbiegen** ◇*VERB (IMP* **bog ein**, *PERF* **ist eingebogen) to turn**; der Radfahrer bog langsam in die Seitenstraße ein the cyclist turned slowly down the side street

**einbilden** *VERB (PERF* **hat sich eingebildet) ❶** sich einbilden to imagine, das bildest du dir nur ein you're only imagining it **❷** Till bildet sich viel ein Till is very conceited

**Einbildung** die **imagination**; das ist alles nur Einbildung it's all in the mind

**einbrechen** ◇*VERB (PRES* **bricht ein**, *IMP* **brach ein**, *PERF* **ist eingebrochen) to break in**; in unserem Haus sind Diebe eingebrochen thieves broke into our house, bei unseren Nachbarn ist eingebrochen worden our neighbours have been burgled

**Einbrecher** der *(PLURAL* die **Einbrecher) burglar**

**einbringen** *VERB (IMP* **brachte ein**, *PERF* **hat eingebracht) to bring in**; die Ernte einbringen to gather in the harvest

**Einbruch** der *(PLURAL* die **Einbrüche) ❶ burglary ❷** vor Einbruch der Dunkelheit before it gets dark **❸** bei Einbruch der Nacht at nightfall

**einchecken** *VERB (PERF* **hat eingecheckt)** am Flughafen einchecken to check in at the airport

**eindeutig** *ADJECTIVE* **❶ clear ❷ definite** *(proof)*

**Eindruck** der *(PLURAL* die **Eindrücke) impression**; einen guten Eindruck auf jemanden machen to make a good impression on somebody

**eindrucksvoll** *ADJECTIVE* **impressive**

**eine** ▸ SEE **ein, einer**

**eineinhalb** *NUMBER* **one and a half**

**einer, eine, ein(e)s** *PRONOUN* **❶ one**; einer von uns one of us, wie soll das einer wissen? how is one supposed to know? **❷ somebody ❸** kaum einer hardly anyone **❹ you**; das macht einen müde it makes you tired

**einerseits** *ADVERB* **on the one hand**; einerseits sagt sie, dass sie kein Geld hat, andererseits kauft sie sich dauernd neue Sachen on the one hand she claims to have no money, on the other hand she's constantly buying new things

**eines** ▸ SEE **einer**

**einfach** *ADJECTIVE* **❶ simple ❷ easy ❸ single** *(ticket, knot)*

**einfach** *ADVERB* **simply**

**Einfachheit** die **simplicity**

**Einfahrt** die *(PLURAL* die **Einfahrten) ❶ entrance ❷ arrival** *(of a train)* **❸ slip road** *(on a motorway)*

**Einfall** der *(PLURAL* die **Einfälle) idea**

**einfallen** ◇*VERB (PRES* **fällt ein**, *IMP* **fiel ein**, *PERF* **ist eingefallen) ❶** jemandem einfallen to occur to somebody **❷** ihr Name fällt mir nicht ein I can't think of her name **❸** was fällt dir eigentlich ein? what do you think you're doing? **❹** sich etwas einfallen lassen to think of something

**Einfamilienhaus** das *(PLURAL* die **Einfamilienhäuser) detached family house**

**Einfluss** der (PLURAL die **Einflüsse**) influence

**einfrieren** ◇VERB (IMP **fror ein**, PERF **ist eingefroren**) **❶** to freeze **❷** (PERF **hat eingefroren**) to freeze (food in the freezer)

**Einfuhr** die (PLURAL die **Einfuhren**) import

**einführen** VERB (PERF **hat eingeführt**) **❶** to import **❷** to introduce

**Einführung** die (PLURAL die **Einführungen**) introduction

**Eingabe** die **input** (of data)

**Eingang** der (PLURAL die **Eingänge**) entrance

**Eingangshalle** die (PLURAL die **Eingangshallen**) hallway

**eingeben** ◇VERB (PRES **gibt ein**, IMP **gab ein**, PERF **hat eingegeben**) **❶** to hand in **❷** to input, to key in

**eingebildet** ADJECTIVE **❶** conceited **❷** imaginary (illness)

**Eingeborene** der/die (PLURAL die **Eingeborenen**) native

**eingehen** ◇VERB (IMP **ging ein**, PERF **ist eingegangen**) **❶** to shrink (of clothes) **❷** to die (of plants) **❸** to arrive (of goods) **❹** auf etwas eingehen to go into something, sie ging näher darauf ein she went into it in more detail **❺** auf etwas nicht eingehen to ignore something **❻** auf etwas eingehen to agree to something, Oliver ist auf unseren Plan eingegangen Oliver agreed to our plan **❼** ein Risiko eingehen to take a risk

**eingeschrieben** ADJECTIVE **registered**; ein eingeschriebener Brief a registered letter

**eingestellt** ADJECTIVE **❶** auf etwas eingestellt sein to be prepared for something **❷** fortschrittlich eingestellt sein to be progressively minded

**eingewöhnen** VERB (PERF **hat sich eingewöhnt**) sich eingewöhnen to settle in

**eingießen** ◇VERB (IMP **goss ein**, PERF **hat eingegossen**) to pour

**Eingriff** der (PLURAL die **Eingriffe**) **❶** intervention **❷** operation (surgical)

**einheimisch** ADJECTIVE **❶** native **❷** local

**Einheit** die (PLURAL die **Einheiten**) **❶** unity **❷** unit (of drink, soldiers)

**Einheitspreis** der (PLURAL die **Einheitspreise**) **❶** standard price **❷** flat fare

**einholen** VERB (PERF **hat eingeholt**) **❶** to catch up with **❷** to make up (time, a delay) **❸** to buy; einholen gehen to go shopping

**einhundert** NUMBER one hundred

**einige** ▸SEE **einiger**

**einigen** VERB (PERF **hat sich geeinigt**) sich einigen to come to an agreement, sich auf etwas einigen to agree on something

**einiger**, **einige**, **einiges** ADJECTIVE, PRONOUN **❶** some; vor einiger Zeit some time ago **❷** several **❸** nur einige waren noch da there were only a few left **❹** einiges quite a lot, wir haben einiges gesehen we saw quite a lot (of things) **❺** einiges some things, einiges hat uns nicht gefallen there were some things we didn't like

73

a b c d e f g h i j k l m n o p q r s t u v w x y z

**einigermaßen** *ADVERB* ❶ **fairly**
❷ **fairly well** ❸ 'wie geht es dir?'
– 'einigermaßen' 'how are you?'
– 'so-so'

**einiges** ▸ SEE **einiger**

**Einigung** die **agreement**

**Einkauf** der *(PLURAL* die **Einkäufe)*
❶ **purchase** ❷ **shopping**; Einkäufe
machen to do some shopping

**einkaufen** *VERB (PERF* hat
**eingekauft)* ❶ **to buy**; ich habe
vergessen Milch einzukaufen I
forgot to buy milk ❷ **to shop**; wir
kaufen meist im Supermarkt ein
we usually shop at the supermarket,
einkaufen gehen to go shopping

**Einkaufsbummel** der *(PLURAL* die
**Einkaufsbummel)* **shopping
spree**

**Einkaufswagen** der *(PLURAL* die
**Einkaufswagen)* **shopping trolley**

**Einkaufszentrum** das *(PLURAL*
die **Einkaufszentren)* **shopping
centre**

**Einkommen** das *(PLURAL* die
**Einkommen)* **income**

**einladen** ◇*VERB (PRES* **lädt ein**, *IMP*
**lud ein**, *PERF* hat **eingeladen)* ❶ **to
invite**; jemanden zum Abendessen
einladen to invite somebody
for dinner ❷ jemanden ins Kino
einladen to take sombody to the
cinema ❸ **to treat**; ich lade euch
ein I'll treat you ❹ **to load** *(goods)*

**Einladung** die *(PLURAL* die
**Einladungen)* **invitation**

**einleben** *VERB (PERF* hat sich
**eingelebt)* sich einleben to settle
down

**Einleitung** die *(PLURAL* die
**Einleitungen)* **introduction**

**einlösen** *VERB (PERF* hat **eingelöst)*
**to cash**

**einmal** *ADVERB* ❶ **once** *(in the past)*; es
war einmal ... once upon a time ...
❷ **one day** *(in the future)* ❸ auf
einmal **suddenly** ❹ auf einmal **at
the same time**, sie kamen alle auf
einmal they all came at the same
time ❺ nicht einmal **not even**
❻ noch einmal **again** ❼ es geht nun
einmal nicht it's just not possible

**einmalig** *ADJECTIVE* ❶ **unique**
❷ **fantastic** ❸ **single, one-off**
*(payment)*

**einmischen** *VERB (PERF* hat sich
**eingemischt)* sich einmischen to
interfere

**Einmündung** die *(PLURAL* die
**Einmündungen)* ❶ **junction** *(of
roads)* ❷ **confluence** *(of rivers)*

**einordnen** *VERB (PERF* hat
**eingeordnet)* ❶ **to put in order**
❷ sich einordnen **to fit in** *(with
other people)* ❸ sich einordnen **to
get in lane** *(when driving)*

**einpacken** *VERB (PERF* hat
**eingepackt)* ❶ **to pack** ❷ **to wrap**

**einreichen** *VERB (PERF* hat
**eingereicht)* **to hand in**

**Einreise** die *(PLURAL* die **Einreisen)*
**entry**

**einreisen** *VERB (PERF* ist **eingereist)*
**to enter a country**; er reiste nach
Italien ein he entered Italy

**einrichten** *VERB (PERF* hat
**eingerichtet)* ❶ **to furnish**
❷ **to set up** *(an organisation)*
❸ **to arrange**; kannst du es so
einrichten, dass du vormittags da
bist? can you arrange to be here
in the morning? ❹ sich einrichten

to furnish your home ❺ sich einrichten to economize ❻ sich auf etwas einrichten to prepare for something

**Einrichtung** die (PLURAL die Einrichtungen) ❶ furnishing ❷ furnishings ❸ setting up ❹ institution; staatliche Einrichtungen state institutions

**eins** NUMBER one; eins zu eins one all, es ist eins it's one o'clock

**eins** PRONOUN ▸ SEE **einer**

**eins** ADJECTIVE mir ist alles eins it's all the same to me

**Eins** die (PLURAL die Einsen) one

**einsam** ADJECTIVE lonely

**einsammeln** VERB (PERF hat eingesammelt) to collect

**Einsatz** der ❶ use ❷ stake (when betting)

**einschalten** VERB (PERF hat eingeschaltet) ❶ to switch on (a radio, TV) ❷ sich einschalten to intervene

**einschlafen** ◇VERB (PRES schläft ein, IMP schlief ein, PERF ist eingeschlafen) to go to sleep

**einschließen** ◇VERB (IMP schloss ein, PERF hat eingeschlossen) ❶ to lock in ❷ to include ❸ sich einschließen to lock yourself in

**einschließlich** PREPOSITION (+GEN) including; einschließlich der Unkosten including expenses

**einschließlich** ADVERB inclusive

**einschränken** VERB (PERF hat eingeschränkt) ❶ to restrict ❷ to cut back ❸ sich einschränken to economize

**einschreiben** ◇VERB (IMP schrieb sich ein, PERF hat sich eingeschrieben) ❶ sich einschreiben to enrol (at university) ❷ sich einschreiben to put your name down

**Einschreiben** das (PLURAL die Einschreiben) registered letter, registered parcel; per Einschreiben registered

**einsehen** ◇VERB (PRES sieht ein, IMP sah ein, PERF hat eingesehen) ❶ to realize ❷ to see; das sehe ich nicht ein I don't see why

**einseitig** ADJECTIVE one-sided

**einsenden** ◇VERB (IMP sendete ein/ sandte ein, PERF hat eingesendet/ hat eingesandt) to send in

**einsetzen** VERB (PERF hat eingesetzt) ❶ to put in (a missing part) to insert ❷ to use, während der Weltmeisterschaft wurden Sonderzüge eingesetzt special trains were put on during the World Cup ❸ to stake (money) ❹ to start (of rain, snow) ❺ sich für jemanden einsetzen to support somebody

**Einsicht** die ❶ insight ❷ sense ❸ zu der Einsicht kommen, dass ... to come to realize that ...

**einsperren** VERB (PERF hat eingesperrt) to lock up

**Einspruch** der (PLURAL die Einsprüche) objection

**einst** ADVERB ❶ once ❷ one day (in the future)

**einstecken** VERB (PERF hat eingesteckt) ❶ to put in (a coin) ❷ einen Brief einstecken to post a letter ❸ to plug in ❹ etwas einstecken to put something in your pocket or bag, to take something **❺** (informal) to take (insults)

**einsteigen** ◇VERB (IMP **stieg ein**, PERF **ist eingestiegen**) **❶** to get in **❷** to get on (a bus or train)

**einstellen** VERB (PERF **hat eingestellt**) **❶** to employ (in a job) **❷** to adjust (a machine) **❸** to focus (a camera) **❹** to tune into (a radio station) **❺** to stop **❻** sich auf etwas einstellen to prepare yourself for something **❼** sich schnell auf eine neue Situation einstellen to adjust quickly to a new situation

**Einstellung** die (PLURAL die **Einstellungen**) **❶** employment **❷** adjustment **❸** stopping **❹** take (of a film) **❺** attitude; seine politische Einstellung his political views

**Einstieg** der (PLURAL die **Einstiege**) entrance

**einstürzen** VERB (PERF **ist eingestürzt**) to collapse

**einstweilen** ADVERB **❶** for the time being **❷** meanwhile

**eintausend** NUMBER one thousand

**einteilen** VERB (PERF **hat eingeteilt**) **❶** to divide up **❷** sich seine Zeit gut einteilen to organize your time well

**Eintopf** der (PLURAL die **Eintöpfe**) stew

**Eintrag** der (PLURAL die **Einträge**) entry

**eintragen** ◇VERB (PRES **trägt ein**, IMP **trug ein**, PERF **hat eingetragen**) **❶** to enter, to write **❷** sich eintragen to put your name down

**einträglich** ADJECTIVE **profitable**

**eintreffen** ◇VERB (PRES **trifft ein**, IMP **traf ein**, PERF **ist eingetroffen**) **❶** to arrive **❷** to come true

**eintreten** ◇VERB (PRES **tritt ein**, IMP **trat ein**, PERF **ist eingetreten**) **❶** to enter **❷** in einen Klub eintreten to join a club **❸** für jemanden eintreten to stand up for somebody

**Eintritt** der **❶** entrance **❷** admission; 'Eintritt frei' 'admission free'

**Eintrittskarte** die (PLURAL die **Eintrittskarten**) (admission) ticket

**Eintrittspreis** der (PLURAL die **Eintrittspreise**) admission charge

**einverstanden** ADJECTIVE **❶** einverstanden sein to agree, einverstanden! okay! **❷** mit jemandem einverstanden sein to approve of somebody

**Einwand** der (PLURAL die **Einwände**) objection

**Einwanderer** der (PLURAL die **Einwanderer**) immigrant

**Einwanderin** die (PLURAL die **Einwanderinnen**) immigrant

**einwandern** VERB (PERF **ist eingewandert**) to immigrate; nach Europa einwandern to immigrate into Europe

**Einwanderung** die immigration

**einwärts** ADVERB inwards

**einweichen** VERB (PERF **hat eingeweicht**) to soak (washing)

**einwerfen** ◇VERB (PRES **wirft ein**, IMP **warf ein**, PERF **hat eingeworfen**)

**❶** to post **❷** to put in *(a coin, money)* **❸** to throw in **❹** to smash

**Einwohner** der *(PLURAL die Einwohner)* inhabitant

**Einzahl** die singular

**einzahlen** *VERB (PERF* **hat eingezahlt)** to pay in

**Einzel** das *(PLURAL die Einzel)* singles *(in sport)*

**Einzelheit** die *(PLURAL die Einzelheiten)* detail

**Einzelkarte** die *(PLURAL die Einzelkarten)* single ticket

**Einzelkind** das *(PLURAL die Einzelkinder)* only child

**einzeln** *ADJECTIVE* **❶** single **❷** individual **❸** odd *(sock, for example)*

**einzeln** *ADVERB* **❶** individually **❷** separately, one at a time; bitte einzeln eintreten please enter one at a time

**Einzelne** der/die/das *(PLURAL die Einzelnen)* **❶** der/die Einzelne the individual **❷** Einzelne some **❸** ein Einzelner/eine Einzelne/ ein Einzelnes a single one, jeder/ jede/jedes Einzelne every single one **❹** im Einzelnen in detail, ins Einzelne gehen to go into detail

**Einzelzimmer** das *(PLURAL die Einzelzimmer)* single room

**einziehen** ◇*VERB (IMP* **zog ein,** *PERF* **hat eingezogen) ❶** to collect *(payment)* **❷** to draw in *(its feelers, claws)* **❸** den Kopf einziehen to duck **❹** *(PERF* **ist eingezogen)** to move in; wann zieht ihr in die neue Wohnung ein? when are you moving into your new flat? **❺** *(PERF* **ist eingezogen)** to soak in

**einzig** *ADJECTIVE* only; ein einziges Mal only once

**Einzige** der/die/das *(PLURAL die Einzigen)* **❶** der/die/das Einzige the only one **❷** ein Einziger/eine Einzige/ein Einziges a single one, kein Einziger/keine Einzige/kein Einziges not a single one **❸** das Einzige, was mich stört the only thing that bothers me

**Eis** das **❶** ice **❷** ice cream

**Eisbahn** die *(PLURAL die Eisbahnen)* skating rink

**Eisbär** der *(PLURAL die Eisbären)* polar bear

**Eisbecher** der *(PLURAL die Eisbecher)* ice-cream sundae

**Eisdiele** die *(PLURAL die Eisdielen)* ice-cream parlour

**Eisen** das iron

**Eisenbahn** die *(PLURAL die Eisenbahnen)* railway

**eisern** *ADJECTIVE* iron

**Eishockey** das ice hockey

**eisig** *ADJECTIVE* icy

**eiskalt** *ADJECTIVE* **❶** ice-cold *(drink)* **❷** freezing cold

**Eislaufen** das ice-skating

**Eisläufer** der *(PLURAL die Eisläufer)* skater *(on ice)*

**Eisläuferin** die *(PLURAL die Eisläuferinnen)* skater *(on ice)*

**Eisportionierer** der *(PLURAL die Eisportionierer)* scoop

**Eiswürfel** der *(PLURAL die Eiswürfel)* ice cube

**Eiszapfen** der (PLURAL die **Eiszapfen**) icicle

**eitel** ADJECTIVE vain

**Eitelkeit** die vanity

**Eiter** der pus

**Eiweiß** das ❶ egg-white ❷ protein

**Ekel** der disgust

**ekelhaft** ADJECTIVE disgusting

**ekeln** VERB (PERF hat sich geekelt) sich vor etwas ekeln to find something disgusting

**eklig** ADJECTIVE disgusting

**Ekzem** das (PLURAL die **Ekzeme**) eczema

**Elefant** der (PLURAL die **Elefanten**) elephant

**elegant** ADJECTIVE elegant, stylish

**Elektriker** der (PLURAL die **Elektriker**) electrician

**elektrisch** ADJECTIVE electrical

**Elektrizität** die electricity

**Elektroherd** der (PLURAL die **Elektroherde**) electric cooker

**Elektronik** die electronics

**elektronisch** ADJECTIVE electronic

**Elektrorasierer** der (PLURAL die **Elektrorasierer**) electric razor

**elend** ADJECTIVE ❶ miserable ❷ terrible

**Elend** das misery

**elf** NUMBER eleven

**Elfe** die (PLURAL die **Elfen**) fairy

**Elfmeter** der (PLURAL die **Elfmeter**) penalty (in soccer)

**Ellbogen** der (PLURAL die **Ellbogen**) elbow

**Eltern** PLURAL NOUN parents

**Email** das (PLURAL die **Emails**) enamel

**E-Mail** die (PLURAL die **E-Mails**) email

**empfahl** ▸ SEE empfehlen

**Empfang** der (PLURAL die **Empfänge**) ❶ reception ❷ receipt (of goods or a letter)

**empfangen** ◇VERB (PRES **empfängt**, IMP **empfing**, PERF **hat empfangen**) to receive

**Empfängnisverhütung** die contraception

**Empfangsdame** die (PLURAL die **Empfangsdamen**) receptionist

**empfehlen** ◇VERB (PRES **empfiehlt**, IMP **empfahl**, PERF **hat empfohlen**) to recommend

**empfindlich** ADJECTIVE ❶ sensitive ❷ delicate ❸ touchy

**empfing** ▸ SEE empfangen

**empfohlen** ▸ SEE empfehlen

**empört** ADJECTIVE indignant

**Ende** das (PLURAL die **Enden**) ❶ end; Ende April at the end of April, am Ende der Straße at the end of the road ❷ am Ende in the end ❸ ending (of a film, novel) ❹ zu Ende sein to be finished, to be over ❺ Ende gut, alles gut all's well that ends well

**enden** VERB (PERF **hat geendet**) to end

**endgültig** ADJECTIVE ❶ final (consent, decision) ❷ definite

**Endivie** die (PLURAL die **Endivien**) endive

**endlich** *ADVERB* finally, at last, na endlich! at last!

**endlos** *ADJECTIVE* **endless**

**Endspiel** das (*PLURAL* die **Endspiele**) final

**Endstation** die (*PLURAL* die **Endstationen**) terminus

**Endung** die (*PLURAL* die **Endungen**) ending

**Energie** die energy

**energisch** *ADJECTIVE* **energetic**

**eng** *ADJECTIVE* ❶ narrow ❷ tight ❸ close; eng befreundet sein to be close friends

**Engel** der (*PLURAL* die **Engel**) angel

**England** das England; aus England from England

**Engländer** der (*PLURAL* die **Engländer**) Englishman

**Engländerin** die (*PLURAL* die **Engländerinnen**) Englishwoman

**englisch** *ADJECTIVE* **English**

**Englisch** das English; auf Englisch in English

**Enkel** der (*PLURAL* die **Enkel**) grandson

**Enkelin** die (*PLURAL* die **Enkelinnen**) granddaughter

**Enkelkind** das (*PLURAL* die **Enkelkinder**) grandchild

**entdecken** *VERB* (*PERF* hat entdeckt) to discover

**Entdeckung** die (*PLURAL* die **Entdeckungen**) discovery

**Ente** die (*PLURAL* die **Enten**) duck

**entfernen** *VERB* (*PERF* hat entfernt) to remove

**entfernt** *ADJECTIVE* ❶ distant ❷ zehn Kilometer entfernt ten kilometres away

**entfernt** *ADVERB* entfernt verwandt sein to be distantly related

**Entfernung** die (*PLURAL* die **Entfernungen**) distance

**entführen** *VERB* (*PERF* hat entführt) ❶ to kidnap ❷ to hijack

**Entführer** der (*PLURAL* die **Entführer**) ❶ hijacker ❷ kidnapper

**Entführerin** die (*PLURAL* die **Entführerinnen**) ❶ hijacker ❷ kidnapper

**Entführung** die (*PLURAL* die **Entführungen**) ❶ hijacking ❷ kidnapping

**entgegen** *PREPOSITION* (+*DAT*) contrary to

**entgegengesetzt** *ADJECTIVE* ❶ opposite ❷ opposing (views)

**entgegenkommen** ⬦*VERB* (*IMP* kam entgegen, *PERF* ist entgegengekommen) ❶ to come towards ❷ jemandem entgegenkommen to come to meet somebody ❸ jemandem auf halbem Wege entgegenkommen to meet somebody halfway ❹ jemandem freundlich entgegenkommen to be accommodating towards somebody

**entgegenkommend** *ADJECTIVE* ❶ obliging ❷ der entgegenkommende Verkehr the oncoming traffic

**Entgelt** das payment

**Enthaarungsmittel** das (*PLURAL* die **Enthaarungsmittel**) hair remover, depilatory

**enthalten** ◇*VERB* (*PRES* **enthält**, *IMP* **enthielt**, *PERF* **hat enthalten**) **❶** to contain **❷** sich einer Sache enthalten to abstain from something, sich der Stimme enthalten to abstain **❸** (*PERF* **ist enthalten**) in etwas enthalten sein to be included in something, im Preis enthalten included in the price

**entkommen** ◇*VERB* (*IMP* **entkam**, *PERF* **ist entkommen**) to escape

**entlang** *PREPOSITION* (*+ACC* or *+DAT*) along; die Straße entlang along the road, am Fluss entlang along the river

**entlanggehen** ◇*VERB* (*IMP* **ging entlang**, *PERF* **ist entlanggegangen**) to walk along

**entlanglaufen** ◇*VERB* (*PRES* **läuft entlang**, *IMP* **lief entlang**, *PERF* **ist entlanggelaufen**) to run along

**entlassen** ◇*VERB* (*PRES* **entlässt**, *IMP* **entließ**, *PERF* **hat entlassen**) **❶** to dismiss (*from a job*) **❷** to discharge (*from hospital*) **❸** to release (*from prison*)

**Entlassung** die (*PLURAL* die **Entlassungen**) **❶** dismissal **❷** discharge **❸** release

**entmutigen** *VERB* (*PERF* **hat entmutigt**) to discourage

**entschädigen** *VERB* (*PERF* **hat entschädigt**) to compensate

**Entschädigung** die compensation

**entscheiden** ◇*VERB* (*IMP* **entschied**, *PERF* **hat entschieden**) **❶** to decide (on) **❷** sich entscheiden to decide

**entscheidend** *ADJECTIVE* decisive, crucial

**Entscheidung** die (*PLURAL* die **Entscheidungen**) decision

**Entschiedenheit** die decisiveness

**entschließen** ◇*VERB* (*IMP* **entschloss sich**, *PERF* **hat sich entschlossen**) **❶** sich entschließen to decide **❷** sich anders entschließen to change your mind, Karl hat sich anders entschlossen Karl has changed his mind

**entschlossen** *ADJECTIVE* determined

**Entschluss** der (*PLURAL* die **Entschlüsse**) decision

**entschuldigen** *VERB* (*PERF* **hat entschuldigt**) **❶** to excuse; entschuldigen Sie bitte excuse me **❷** sich entschuldigen to apologize, ich habe mich bei Michi entschuldigt I apologized to Michi

**Entschuldigung** die (*PLURAL* die **Entschuldigungen**) **❶** apology **❷** jemanden um Entschuldigung bitten to apologize to somebody **❸** Entschuldigung! sorry! **❹** Entschuldigung (*with a question or request*) excuse me, Entschuldigung, können Sie mir sagen, wie ich zum Bahnhof komme? excuse me, could you tell me the way to the station? **❺** excuse

**Entsetzen** das horror

**entsetzlich** *ADJECTIVE* **❶** horrible **❷** terrible

**entsetzt** *ADJECTIVE* horrified

**entspannen** *VERB* (*PERF* **hat sich entspannt**) **❶** sich entspannen to relax **❷** sich entspannen to ease (*of a situation*)

**entspannend** *ADJECTIVE* relaxing

**entsprechen** ◇*VERB* *(PRES* **entspricht**, *IMP* **entsprach**, *PERF* **hat entsprochen)* ❶ den Anforderungen entsprechen to meet the requirements ❷ einer Sache entsprechen to correspond to something ❸ to agree with *(the truth, a description)* ❹ to comply with *(certain standards)*

**entsprechend** *ADJECTIVE* ❶ corresponding ❷ appropriate

**entsprechend** *PREPOSITION* *(+DAT)* in accordance with

**entstehen** ◇*VERB* *(IMP* **entstand**, *PERF* **ist entstanden)** ❶ to develop ❷ to result *(of damage)*

**enttäuschen** *VERB* *(PERF* **hat enttäuscht)** to disappoint

**Enttäuschung** die *(PLURAL* die **Enttäuschungen)** disappointment

**entweder** *CONJUNCTION* either; entweder heute oder morgen either today or tomorrow

**entwerten** *VERB* *(PERF* **hat entwertet)** ❶ to devalue ❷ to punch *(a ticket in a machine found on trains, trams, buses, and on the platform; you have to punch your ticket before each journey)*

**Entwerter** der *(PLURAL* die **Entwerter)** ticket-punching machine *(these machines are found on trains, trams, buses, and on the platform; you have to punch your ticket before each journey)*

**entwickeln** *VERB* *(PERF* **hat entwickelt)** ❶ to develop ❷ to display *(ability, a characteristic)* ❸ sich entwickeln to develop

**Entwicklung** die *(PLURAL* die **Entwicklungen)** ❶ development ❷ developing

**Entwicklungsland** das *(PLURAL* die **Entwicklungsländer)** developing country

**Entwurf** der *(PLURAL* die **Entwürfe)** ❶ design ❷ draft

**entzückend** *ADJECTIVE* delightful

**entzünden** *VERB* *(PERF* **hat entzündet)** ❶ to light *(a fire, match)* ❷ sich entzünden to become inflamed ❸ sich entzünden to ignite

**Entzündung** die *(PLURAL* die **Entzündungen)** inflammation

**Enzian** der *(PLURAL* die **Enziane)** gentian

**Epidemie** die *(PLURAL* die **Epidemien)** epidemic

**er** *PRONOUN* ❶ he ❷ it; 'wo ist mein Mantel?' – 'er liegt auf dem Stuhl' 'where's my coat?' – 'it's on the chair' ❸ him *(stressed)*; er war es it was him

**erben** *VERB* *(PERF* **hat geerbt)** to inherit

**erblich** *ADJECTIVE* hereditary

**erbrechen** *VERB* *(PRES* **erbricht**, *IMP* **erbrach**, *PERF* **hat erbrochen)** ❶ to brng up *(food)* ❷ sich erbrechen to be sick

**Erbschaft** die *(PLURAL* die **Erbschaften)** inheritance

**Erbse** die *(PLURAL* die **Erbsen)** pea

**Erdbeben** das *(PLURAL* die **Erdbeben)** earthquake

**Erdbeere** die *(PLURAL* die **Erdbeeren)** strawberry

a
b
c
d
e
f
g
h
i
j
k
l
m
n
o
p
q
r
s
t
u
v
w
x
y
z

**Erde** die ❶ earth, soil ❷ ground; auf der Erde on the ground ❸ Earth ❹ earth (for electricity)

**Erdgeschoss** das (PLURAL die Erdgeschosse) ground floor; im Erdgeschoss on the ground floor

**Erdkunde** die geography

**Erdnuss** die (PLURAL die Erdnüsse) peanut

**ereignen** VERB (PERF hat sich ereignet) sich ereignen to happen

**Ereignis** das (PLURAL die Ereignisse) event

**erfahren** ◇VERB (PRES erfährt, IMP erfuhr, PERF hat erfahren) ❶ to hear, to learn ❷ to experience

**erfahren** ADJECTIVE experienced

**Erfahrung** die (PLURAL die Erfahrungen) experience

**erfinden** ◇VERB (IMP erfand, PERF hat erfunden) to invent

**Erfindung** die (PLURAL die Erfindungen) invention

**Erfolg** der (PLURAL die Erfolge) ❶ success; Erfolg haben to be successful ❷ Erfolg versprechend promising ❸ viel Erfolg! good luck!

**erfolglos** ADJECTIVE unsuccessful

**erfolgreich** ADJECTIVE successful

**erfolgversprechend** ▸ SEE Erfolg

**erforderlich** ADJECTIVE necessary

**erforschen** VERB (PERF hat erforscht) ❶ to explore ❷ to investigate

**erfreulicherweise** ADVERB happily

**erfreut** ADJECTIVE pleased

**Erfrischung** die (PLURAL die Erfrischungen) refreshment

**Erfrischungsgetränk** das (PLURAL die Erfrischungsgetränke) soft drink

**erfüllen** VERB (PERF hat erfüllt) to fulfil; sich erfüllen to come true

**Ergebnis** das (PLURAL die Ergebnisse) result

**ergreifen** ◇VERB (IMP ergriff, PERF hat ergriffen) ❶ to seize, to grab ❷ to take (measures, an opportunity) ❸ to take up (a job, career) ❹ to move; die Nachricht von ihrem Tod hat uns tief ergriffen the news of her death moved us deeply ❺ die Flucht ergreifen to flee

**ergreifend** ADJECTIVE moving

**erhalten** ◇VERB (PRES erhält, IMP erhielt, PERF hat erhalten) ❶ to receive ❷ to preserve

**erhältlich** ADJECTIVE obtainable

**Erhaltung** die ❶ preservation ❷ conservation ❸ maintenance

**erheben** ◇VERB (IMP erhob, PERF hat erhoben) ❶ to raise ❷ to charge (a fee) ❸ Protest erheben to protest ❹ sich erheben to rise up (in a rebellion)

**erheblich** ADJECTIVE considerable

**erheitern** VERB (PERF hat erheitert) to amuse

**erhitzen** VERB (PERF hat erhitzt) to heat

**erhöhen** VERB (PERF hat erhöht) ❶ to increase ❷ sich erhöhen to rise

**Erhöhung** die (PLURAL die Erhöhungen) increase

**erholen** VERB (PERF hat sich erholt) ❶ sich erholen to have a rest, ich habe mich in den Ferien gut erholt

I had a good rest on holiday ❷ sich von einer Krankheit erholen to recover from an illness

**erholsam** *ADJECTIVE* **restful**

**Erholung** die **rest**; Iris ist zur Erholung in die Berge gefahren Iris went to the mountains for a rest

**erinnern** *VERB (PERF* **hat erinnert)** ❶ to remind ❷ sich erinnern to remember

**Erinnerung** die *(PLURAL die* **Erinnerungen)** ❶ memory ❷ souvenir

**erkälten** *VERB (PERF* **hat sich erkältet)** ❶ sich erkälten to catch a cold ❷ erkältet sein to have a cold, Ben ist erkältet Ben has a cold

**Erkältung** die *(PLURAL die* **Erkältungen)** **cold**

**erkennbar** *ADJECTIVE* **recognizable**

**erkennen** ⬦*VERB (IMP* **erkannte,** *PERF* **hat erkannt)** ❶ to recognize ❷ to realize

**erklären** *VERB (PERF* **hat erklärt)** ❶ to explain ❷ to declare ❸ sich zu etwas bereit erklären to agree to something

**Erklärung** die *(PLURAL die* **Erklärungen)** ❶ explanation ❷ declaration ❸ eine öffentliche Erklärung a public statement

**erkundigen** *VERB (PERF* **hat sich erkundigt)** ❶ sich erkundigen to enquire, ich werde mich nach den Zügen erkundigen I'm going to enquire about the trains ❷ to ask about; Susi hat sich nach dir erkundigt Susi was asking about you

**Erkundigung** die *(PLURAL die* **Erkundigungen)** **enquiry**

**erlauben** *VERB (PERF* **hat erlaubt)** ❶ to allow; jemandem etwas erlauben to allow somebody to do something ❷ sich etwas erlauben to allow yourself something ❸ sich alles erlauben to do as you please ❹ erlauben Sie mal! *(informal)* do you mind!

**Erlaubnis** die **permission**

**erleben** *VERB (PERF* **hat erlebt)** ❶ to experience ❷ to have *(a disappointment, an experience)*; eine Überraschung erleben to have a surprise ❸ er hat die Geburt seines Enkels nicht mehr erlebt he didn't live to see the birth of his grandson

**Erlebnis** das *(PLURAL die* **Erlebnisse)** **experience**

**erledigen** *VERB (PERF* **hat erledigt)** to deal with, to do

**erledigt** *ADJECTIVE* ❶ settled ❷ *(informal)* worn out

**erleichtert** *ADJECTIVE* **relieved**

**Erleichterung** die **relief**

**erleiden** ⬦*VERB (IMP* **erlitt,** *PERF* **hat erlitten)** to suffer

**Erlös** der *(PLURAL die* **Erlöse)** proceeds

**erloschen** *ADJECTIVE* ❶ out, extinguished ❷ extinct

**ermäßigen** *VERB (PERF* **hat ermäßigt)** to reduce

**Ermäßigung** die *(PLURAL die* **Ermäßigungen)** reduction

**ermorden** *VERB (PERF* **hat ermordet)** to murder

**ermutigen** *VERB (PERF* **hat ermutigt)** to encourage

# ernähren | erst

**ernähren** VERB (PERF **hat ernährt**) ❶ to feed ❷ sich von Nudeln ernähren to live on pasta ❸ to support *(a family)*

**Ernährung** die ❶ diet; eine gesunde Ernährung a healthy diet ❷ nutrition

**erneuern** VERB (PERF **hat erneuert**) to renew

**erneut** ADJECTIVE renewed

**erneut** ADVERB once again

**ernst** ADJECTIVE serious

**Ernst** der ❶ seriousness ❷ im Ernst seriously ❸ ist das dein Ernst? are you serious?

**ernsthaft** ADJECTIVE serious

**ernstlich** ADJECTIVE serious

**Ernte** die (PLURAL die **Ernten**) harvest; die Ernte einbringen to gather in the harvest

**ernten** VERB (PERF **hat geerntet**) to harvest

**erobern** VERB (PERF **hat erobert**) to conquer

**Eroberung** die (PLURAL die **Eroberungen**) conquest

**eröffnen** (PERF **hat eröffnet**) to open

**Eröffnung** die (PLURAL die **Eröffnungen**) opening

**erraten** ◇VERB (PRES **errät**, IMP **erriet**, PERF **hat erraten**) to guess

**erregen** VERB (PERF **hat erregt**) ❶ to arouse ❷ to cause; sie erregte viel Aufsehen she caused a sensation

**Erreger** der (PLURAL die **Erreger**) germ

**Erregung** die excitement

**erreichen** VERB (PERF **hat erreicht**) ❶ to reach ❷ den Zug erreichen to catch the train ❸ to achieve *(a goal, aim)* ❹ Irene ist telefonisch zu erreichen Irene can be contacted by phone

**erröten** VERB (PERF **ist errötet**) to blush

**Ersatz** der replacement, substitute

**Ersatzmann** der (PLURAL die **Ersatzmänner**) substitute *(in sport)*

**Ersatzmittel** das (PLURAL die **Ersatzmittel**) substitute *(material, ingredient)*

**Ersatzreifen** der (PLURAL die **Ersatzreifen**) spare tyre

**Ersatzteil** das (PLURAL die **Ersatzteile**) spare part

**erschaffen** VERB (IMP **erschuf**, PERF **erschaffen**) to create

**erscheinen** ◇VERB (IMP **erschien**, PERF **ist erschienen**) to appear

**erschöpft** ADJECTIVE exhausted

**erschrecken** VERB ❶ (PERF **hat erschreckt**) to scare ❷ (PRES **erschrickt**, IMP **erschrak**, PERF **ist erschrocken**) to get a fright

**erschreckend** ADJECTIVE alarming

**erschrocken** ADJECTIVE ❶ frightened ❷ startled

**ersetzen** VERB (PERF **hat ersetzt**) to replace; jemandem einen Schaden ersetzen to compensate somebody for damages

**Ersparnisse** PLURAL NOUN savings

**erst** ADVERB ❶ first; erst einmal first

of all ❷ only; eben erst only just
❸ not until; erst nächste Woche
not until next week, Oma war erst
zufrieden, als die ganze Familie da
war granny was not happy until all
the family were there

**erstatten** VERB (PERF **hat erstattet**)
to reimburse

**Erstattung** die (PLURAL die
**Erstattungen**) reimbursement

**erstaunen** VERB (PERF **hat erstaunt**)
to astonish

**erstaunlich** ADJECTIVE **astonishing**

**erstaunt** ADJECTIVE **amazed**; über
etwas erstaunt sein to be amazed
about something

**Erste** der/die/das (PLURAL die **Ersten**)
❶ der/die Erste the first (one),
das Erste the first (thing) ❷ Dirk
kam als Erster Dirk arrived first,
Marianne ging als Erste Marianne
left first ❸ als Erster/Erste etwas
tun to be the first to do something
❹ als Erstes first of all ❺ fürs Erste
for the time being

**erstens** ADVERB **firstly**

**erster, erste, erstes** ADJECTIVE **first**;
mein erstes Rad war rot my first
bike was red, der erste April the
first of April, erste Hilfe first aid

**erstklassig** ADJECTIVE **first-class**

**erstmals** ADVERB **for the first time**

**erteilen** VERB (PERF **hat erteilt**) to
give (advice, information)

**ertragen** ◇VERB (PRES **erträgt**, IMP
**ertrug**, PERF **hat ertragen**) to bear

**ertrinken** ◇VERB (IMP **ertrank**, PERF **ist
ertrunken**) to drown; sie ertrank
im See she drowned in the lake

**erwachsen** ADJECTIVE **grown-up**

**Erwachsene** der/die (PLURAL die
**Erwachsenen**) adult, grown-up

**Erwachsenenbildung** die adult
education

**erwähnen** VERB (PERF **hat erwähnt**)
to mention

**erwarten** VERB (PERF **hat erwartet**)
to expect

**Erwartung** die (PLURAL die
**Erwartungen**) expectation

**erwürgen** VERB (PERF **hat erwürgt**)
to strangle

**erzählen** VERB (PERF **hat erzählt**)
to tell

**Erzählung** die (PLURAL die
**Erzählungen**) story

**Erzeugnis** das (PLURAL die
**Erzeugnisse**) product

**erziehen** ◇VERB (IMP **erzog**, PERF **hat
erzogen**) ❶ to bring up ❷ to
educate

**Erzieher** der (PLURAL die **Erzieher**)
teacher

**Erzieherin** die (PLURAL die
**Erzieherinnen**) teacher

**Erziehung** die ❶ upbringing
❷ education

**es** PRONOUN ❶ it; es regnet it is raining
❷ es gibt there is, there are ❸ 'wo
ist das Baby?' – 'es schläft' 'where's
the baby?' – 'he's/she's asleep'

**Esel** der (PLURAL die **Esel**) donkey

**essbar** ADJECTIVE **edible**

**essen** ◇VERB (PRES **isst**, IMP **aß**, PERF
**hat gegessen**) to eat; iss keine
Bonbons don't eat sweets

**Essen** das ❶ meal ❷ food

**Essig** der vinegar

**Essiggurke** die *(PLURAL die Essiggurken)* gherkin

**Esskastanie** die *(PLURAL die Esskastanien)* sweet chestnut

**Esszimmer** das *(PLURAL die Esszimmer)* dining room

**Etage** die *(PLURAL die Etagen)* floor; in der zweiten Etage on the second floor

**Etagenbett** das *(PLURAL die Etagenbetten)* bunk beds

**ethnisch** *ADJECTIVE* ethnic

**Etikett** das *(PLURAL die Etikette(n))* label

**Etui** das *(PLURAL die Etuis)* case

**etwa** *ADVERB* ❶ about; er ist etwa so groß wie du he's about as tall as you ❷ for example ❸ nicht etwa, dass ... not that ... ❹ hat Klaus etwa Angst gehabt? Klaus wasn't scared, was he?

**etwas** *PRONOUN, ADVERB* ❶ something ❷ anything; sonst noch etwas? anything else? ❸ some; etwas von dem Geld some of the money, noch etwas Kaffee? (some) more coffee? ❹ a little; nur etwas Zucker only a little sugar, etwas lauter singen to sing a little louder

**EU** die *(short for Europäische Union)* EU

**euch** *PRONOUN* ❶ you; ich habe euch eingeladen I've invited you ❷ to you; Eva hat es euch geschenkt Eva gave it to you ❸ *(reflexive)* yourselves

**euer** *ADJECTIVE* your

**Eule** die *(PLURAL die Eulen)* owl

**eurer, eure, eures** *PRONOUN* yours

**Euro** der *(PLURAL die Euros)* euro; ein Euro hat hundert Cent the euro is divided into a hundred cents, es kostet 3 Euro it costs 3 euros

**Eurocent** der *(PLURAL die Eurocents)* cent; 50 Eurocent 50 cents

**Euroland** das eurozone

**Europa** das Europe

**Europäer** der *(PLURAL die Europäer)* European

**Europäerin** die *(PLURAL die Europäerinnen)* European

**europäisch** *ADJECTIVE* European

**Eurostar** der Eurostar; mit dem Eurostar fahren to go by Eurostar

**Eurostück** das *(PLURAL die Eurostücke)* one-euro coin

**Eurotunnel** der Channel Tunnel

**evangelisch** *ADJECTIVE* Protestant

**eventuell** *ADJECTIVE* possible

**eventuell** *ADVERB* possibly

**ewig** *ADJECTIVE* eternal

**ewig** *ADVERB* forever

**Ewigkeit** die eternity

**Examen** das *(PLURAL die Examen)* examination, exam

**Exemplar** das *(PLURAL die Exemplare)* ❶ copy ❷ specimen

**existieren** *VERB (PERF* hat existiert*)* to exist

**Expedition** die *(PLURAL die Expeditionen)* expedition

**explodieren** *VERB (PERF* ist explodiert*)* to explode

**Explosion** die *(PLURAL die Explosionen)* explosion

**Export** der *(PLURAL die Exporte)* export

**exportieren** VERB *(PERF hat exportiert)* to export; Russland exportiert viel Öl und Holz Russia exports a lot of oil and timber

**extra** ADVERB ❶ separately ❷ extra ❸ specially ❹ *(informal)* on purpose

**extrem** ADJECTIVE extreme

**fabelhaft** ADJECTIVE fabulous, fantastic

**Fabrik** die *(PLURAL die Fabriken)* factory

**Fach** das *(PLURAL die Fächer)* ❶ compartment ❷ drawer ❸ subject *(at school)*

**Facharzt** der *(PLURAL die Fachärzte)* specialist

**Fachärztin** die *(PLURAL die Fachärztinnen)* specialist

**Fachfrau** die *(PLURAL die Fachfrauen)* expert

**Fachmann** der *(PLURAL die Fachleute)* expert

**fade** ADJECTIVE tasteless

**Faden** der *(PLURAL die Fäden)* thread

**fähig** ADJECTIVE ❶ capable ❷ able

**Fähigkeit** die *(PLURAL die Fähigkeiten)* ability

**Fahne** die *(PLURAL die Fahnen)* flag

**Fahrausweis** der *(PLURAL die Fahrausweise)* ticket

**Fahrbahn** die *(PLURAL die Fahrbahnen)* ❶ carriageway ❷ road

**Fähre** die *(PLURAL die Fähren)* ferry

**fahren** ◇ VERB *(PRES fährt, IMP fuhr, PERF ist gefahren)* ❶ to go; mit

a
b
c
d
e
f
g
h
i
j
k
l
m
n
o
p
q
r
s
t
u
v
w
x
y
z

**Fahrer** | **fallen**

dem Zug nach Wien fahren to go to Vienna by train, ich bin mit dem Auto gefahren I went by car ❷ **to drive**; Hanna ist sehr schnell gefahren Hanna drove very fast ❸ **to ride** *(of a cyclist)* ❹ **to run** *(of a train, bus)*; der Zug fährt nicht an Sonn- und Feiertagen the train doesn't run on Sundays and public holidays ❺ **to leave**; wann fahrt ihr? when are you leaving? ❻ was ist in sie gefahren? *(informal)* what's got into her? ❼ *(PERF* **hat gefahren) to drive**; er hat Doris nach Hause gefahren he drove Doris home, ich habe das Auto in die Garage gefahren I drove the car into the garage

**Fahrer** der *(PLURAL* die **Fahrer)** **driver**

**Fahrerflucht** die **hit-and-run driving**; Fahrerflucht begehen to be involved in a hit-and-run

**Fahrerin** die *(PLURAL* die **Fahrerinnen)** **driver**

**Fahrgast** der *(PLURAL* die **Fahrgäste)** **passenger**

**Fahrkarte** die *(PLURAL* die **Fahrkarten)** **ticket**

**Fahrkartenausgabe** die **ticket office**

**Fahrkartenautomat** der *(PLURAL* die **Fahrkartenautomaten)** **ticket machine**

**Fahrkartenschalter** der *(PLURAL* die **Fahrkartenschalter)** **ticket office**

**fahrlässig** *ADJECTIVE* **negligent**

**Fahrlehrer** der *(PLURAL* die **Fahrlehrer)** **driving instructor**

**Fahrplan** der *(PLURAL* die **Fahrpläne)** **timetable**

**Fahrpreis** der *(PLURAL* die **Fahrpreise)** **fare**

**Fahrprüfung** die *(PLURAL* die **Fahrprüfungen)** **driving test**; die Fahrprüfung machen to take your driving test

**Fahrrad** das *(PLURAL* die **Fahrräder)** **bicycle**

**Fahrradfahrer** der *(PLURAL* die **Fahrradfahrer)** **cyclist**

**Fahrradfahrerin** die *(PLURAL* die **Fahrradfahrerinnen)** **cyclist**

**Fahrradweg** der *(PLURAL* die **Fahrradwege)** **cycle lane**

**Fahrschein** der *(PLURAL* die **Fahrscheine)** **ticket**

**Fahrschule** die *(PLURAL* die **Fahrschulen)** **driving school**

**Fahrstuhl** der *(PLURAL* die **Fahrstühle)** **lift**

**Fahrt** die *(PLURAL* die **Fahrten)** ❶ **journey**; gute Fahrt! have a good journey! ❷ **trip** ❸ **drive** ❹ in voller Fahrt at full speed

**Fahrzeug** das *(PLURAL* die **Fahrzeuge)** **vehicle**

**fair** *ADJECTIVE* **fair**

**Faktor** der *(PLURAL* die **Faktoren)** **factor**

**Falke** der *(PLURAL* die **Falken)** **falcon**

**Fall** der *(PLURAL* die **Fälle)** ❶ **case**; in diesem Fall in this case, auf alle Fälle, auf jeden Fall in any case, für alle Fälle just in case ❷ auf jeden Fall definitely ❸ auf keinen Fall on no account ❹ **fall**

**Falle** die *(PLURAL* die **Fallen)** **trap**

**fallen** ◇*VERB (PRES* **fällt,** *IMP* **fiel,** *PERF* **ist gefallen) ❶ to fall ❷** etwas fallen lassen to drop something, wir haben den Plan fallen lassen we've dropped the idea ❸ eine Bemerkung fallen lassen to make a comment

**fällen** *VERB* (*PERF* **hat gefällt**) to fell, to cut down (*trees*)

**fallenlassen** ▸ *SEE* **fallen**

**fällig** *ADJECTIVE* **due**

**falls** *CONJUNCTION* ❶ if ❷ in case

**Fallschirm** der (*PLURAL* die Fallschirme) parachute

**falsch** *ADJECTIVE* ❶ wrong; du hast ihn falsch verstanden you got him wrong ❷ false (*teeth, etc.*) ❸ forged

**fälschen** *VERB* (*PERF* **hat gefälscht**) to forge

**Fälschung** die (*PLURAL* die Fälschungen) ❶ fake ❷ forgery

**Falte** die (*PLURAL* die Falten) ❶ fold ❷ crease ❸ pleat ❹ wrinkle

**falten** *VERB* (*PERF* **hat gefaltet**) to fold

**faltig** *ADJECTIVE* ❶ wrinkled ❷ creased

**familiär** *ADJECTIVE* **familiar**

**Familie** die (*PLURAL* die Familien) family

**Familienname** der (*PLURAL* die Familiennamen) surname

**Fan** der (*PLURAL* die Fans) fan

**fand** ▸ *SEE* **finden**

**fangen** ◇*VERB* (*PRES* **fängt**, *IMP* **fing**, *PERF* **hat gefangen**) to catch

**Fantasie** die ❶ imagination ❷ Fantasien *PLURAL* fantasies

**fantasievoll** *ADJECTIVE* **imaginative**

**fantastisch** *ADJECTIVE* **fantastic**

**Farbe** die (*PLURAL* die Farben) ❶ colour ❷ paint ❸ dye ❹ suit (*in playing cards*)

**farbecht** *ADJECTIVE* **colour fast**

**färben** *VERB* (*PERF* **hat gefärbt**) ❶ to dye ❷ sich die Haare färben to dye your hair ❸ das Sweatshirt färbt this sweatshirt runs

**farbenblind** *ADJECTIVE* **colour blind**

**Farbfernsehen** das television

**Farbfilm** der (*PLURAL* die Farbfilme) colour film

**farbig** *ADJECTIVE* **coloured**

**farblos** *ADJECTIVE* **colourless**

**Farbstift** der (*PLURAL* die Farbstifte) coloured pencil

**Farbstoff** der (*PLURAL* die Farbstoffe) ❶ dye ❷ colouring (*for food*)

**Farbton** der (*PLURAL* die Farbtöne) shade

**Fasan** der (*PLURAL* die Fasane) pheasant

**Fasching** der (*PLURAL* die Faschinge) carnival

**Faser** die (*PLURAL* die Fasern) fibre

**Fass** das (*PLURAL* die Fässer) barrel; Bier vom Fass draught beer

**fassen** *VERB* (*PERF* **hat gefasst**) ❶ to grasp ❷ einen Dieb fassen to catch a thief ❸ to hold (*of a container*) ❹ to understand ❺ nicht zu fassen unbelievable ❻ sich fassen to compose yourself ❼ einen Entschluss fassen to make a decision ❽ sich kurz fassen to be brief

**Fassung** | **feindlich**

**Fassung** die (PLURAL die **Fassungen**) ❶ version ❷ composure ❸ jemanden aus der Fassung bringen to throw somebody, to upset somebody ❹ setting (for gems)

**fassungslos** ADJECTIVE speechless

**fast** ADVERB ❶ almost ❷ fast nie hardly ever

**Fastenzeit** die (PLURAL die **Fastenzeiten**) Lent

**Fastfood** das fast food

**Fastnacht** die carnival

**faul** ADJECTIVE ❶ lazy ❷ rotten ❸ eine faule Ausrede a lame excuse ❹ an der Sache ist etwas faul (informal) there's something fishy about it

**faulen** VERB (PERF ist gefault) to rot

**faulenzen** VERB (PERF hat gefaulenzt) to laze about

**Faust** die (PLURAL die **Fäuste**) ❶ fist ❷ auf eigene Faust off your own bat

**Februar** der February

**fechten** ◇VERB (PRES **ficht**, IMP **focht**, PERF **hat gefochten**) to fence

**Feder** die (PLURAL die **Federn**) ❶ feather ❷ spring ❸ nib (of a pen)

**Federball** der (PLURAL die **Federbälle**) ❶ badminton ❷ shuttlecock

**Federhalter** der (PLURAL die **Federhalter**) fountain pen

**Federmäppchen** das (PLURAL die **Federmäppchen**) pencil case

**Fee** die (PLURAL die **Feen**) fairy

**fegen** VERB (PERF hat gefegt) to sweep

**fehl** ADJECTIVE fehl am Platz out of place

**fehlen** VERB (PERF hat gefehlt) ❶ to be missing ❷ to be lacking ❸ to be absent (from school) ❹ mir fehlt die Zeit I haven't got the time, es fehlt ihnen einfach das Geld für ein neues Auto they simply haven't got the money for a new car ❺ was fehlt dir? what's the matter? ❻ Rudi fehlt mir I miss Rudi

**Fehler** der (PLURAL die **Fehler**) ❶ mistake ❷ fault

**Feier** die (PLURAL die **Feiern**) ❶ party ❷ celebration

**Feierabend** der (PLURAL die **Feierabende**) ❶ finishing time ❷ nach Feierabend after work

**Feierlichkeiten** PLURAL NOUN festivities

**feiern** VERB (PERF hat gefeiert) to celebrate

**Feiertag** der (PLURAL die **Feiertage**) ❶ holiday; ein gesetzlicher Feiertag a public holiday ❷ am ersten Feiertag on Christmas Day, der zweite Feiertag Boxing Day

**feige** ADJECTIVE cowardly; du bist feige you're a coward

**Feige** die (PLURAL die **Feigen**) fig

**Feigenbaum** der (PLURAL die **Feigenbäume**) fig tree

**Feigling** der (PLURAL die **Feiglinge**) coward

**Feile** die (PLURAL die **Feilen**) file

**fein** ADJECTIVE ❶ fine ❷ delicate ❸ refined ❹ sich fein machen to dress up

**Feind** der (PLURAL die **Feinde**) enemy

**feindlich** ADJECTIVE hostile

**Feld** das *(PLURAL* die **Felder)** ❶ field ❷ pitch ❸ box *(on a form)* ❹ square *(on a board game)*

**Fell** das *(PLURAL* die **Felle)** fur, skin

**Fels** der rock

**Felsen** der *(PLURAL* die **Felsen)** cliff

**feminin** *ADJECTIVE* feminine

**Feminist** der *(PLURAL* die **Feministen)** feminist

**Feministin** die *(PLURAL* die **Feministinnen)** feminist

**Fenster** das *(PLURAL* die **Fenster)** window

**Fensterladen** der *(PLURAL* die **Fensterläden)** shutter

**Ferien** *PLURAL NOUN* holidays; Ferien haben to be on holiday

**Ferienhaus** das *(PLURAL* die **Ferienhäuser)** holiday home

**fern** *ADJECTIVE* ❶ distant ❷ sich fern halten to keep away, jemanden von etwas fern halten to keep somebody away from something

**fern** *ADVERB* far away

**Fernbedienung** die remote control

**Ferngespräch** das *(PLURAL* die **Ferngespräche)** long-distance call

**ferngesteuert** *ADJECTIVE* remote-controlled

**Fernglas** das *(PLURAL* die **Ferngläser)** binoculars

**fernhalten** ▸ SEE **fern**

**Fernost** das Far East

**Fernrohr** das *(PLURAL* die **Fernrohre)** telescope

**Fernsehapparat** der *(PLURAL* die **Fernsehapparate)** television set

**fernsehen** ◇*VERB (PRES* **sieht fern**, *IMP* **sah fern**, *PERF* **hat ferngesehen)** to watch television

**Fernsehen** das television; im Fernsehen on television

**Fernseher** der *(PLURAL* die **Fernseher)** television (set)

**Fernsehsendung** die *(PLURAL* die **Fernsehsendungen)** television programme

**Fernsehturm** der *(PLURAL* die **Fernsehtürme)** television tower

**Fernsprecher** der *(PLURAL* die **Fernsprecher)** telephone

**Ferse** die *(PLURAL* die **Fersen)** heel

**fertig** *ADJECTIVE* ❶ finished; mit den Hausaufgaben fertig werden to finish your homework, fertig sein to be finished ❷ mit jemandem fertig sein *(informal)* to be through with somebody ❸ völlig fertig sein to be completely worn out ❹ mit etwas fertig werden to cope with something *(problems, for example)* ❺ ready; das Essen ist fertig food's ready ❻ etwas fertig machen *(prepare)* to get something ready, *(complete)* to finish something, sich fertig machen to get ready ❼ jemanden fertig machen to wear somebody out, to wear somebody down, der ständige Stress macht mich fertig this constant stress is wearing me down ❽ es fertig bringen, etwas zu tun to bring yourself to do something, ich bringe es einfach nicht fertig I just can't bring myself to do it

**fertig** *ADVERB* fertig essen to finish eating

**fertigbringen** ▸ SEE **fertig**

**Fertiggericht** das *(PLURAL* die **Fertiggerichte)** ready-to-serve meal

**fertigmachen** ▸ SEE **fertig**

**fest** *ADJECTIVE* ❶ firm ❷ fixed *(salary, address)* ❸ solid; feste Nahrung solids ❹ fest werden to harden

**fest** *ADVERB* ❶ fest schlafen to be fast asleep ❷ fest befreundet sein to be close friends ❸ fest angestellt sein to be in permanent employment

**Fest** das *(PLURAL* die **Feste)** ❶ party ❷ celebration ❸ festival

**festbinden** ◇*VERB (IMP* **band fest,** *PERF* **hat festgebunden)** to tie (up)

**festhalten** ◇*VERB (PRES* **hält fest,** *IMP* **hielt fest,** *PERF* **hat festgehalten)** ❶ to hold on to ❷ sich festhalten to hold on
halt dich an mir fest hold on to me

**Festigkeit** die strength

**festlegen** *VERB (PERF* **hat festgelegt)** ❶ to fix ❷ sich auf etwas festlegen to commit yourself to something

**Festlegung** die *(PLURAL* die **Festlegungen)** establishment

**festlich** *ADJECTIVE* festive

**festmachen** *VERB (PERF* **hat festgemacht)** ❶ to fix; ich mache gleich einen Termin fest I'll fix a date straight away ❷ to fasten

**Festnahme** die *(PLURAL* die **Festnahmen)** arrest

**festnehmen** ◇*VERB (PRES* **nimmt fest,** *IMP* **nahm fest,** *PERF* **hat festgenommen)** to arrest

**Festplatte** die *(PLURAL* die **Festplatten)** hard disk

**feststehen** ◇*VERB (IMP* **stand fest,** *PERF* **hat festgestanden)** to be certain; eins steht fest, Daniel lade ich nicht mehr ein one thing's certain, I'm not going to invite Daniel again

**feststellen** *VERB (PERF* **hat festgestellt)** ❶ to establish ❷ to notice

**Fete** die *(PLURAL* die **Feten)** party

**fett** *ADJECTIVE* ❶ fat *(person)* ❷ greasy, fatty *(food)* ❸ bold *(type)*

**Fett** das *(PLURAL* die **Fette)** ❶ fat ❷ grease

**fettarm** *ADJECTIVE* low-fat; fettarme Milch skimmed milk

**fettig** *ADJECTIVE* greasy

**Fetzen** der *(PLURAL* die **Fetzen)** ❶ scrap ❷ rag

**feucht** *ADJECTIVE* ❶ damp ❷ humid

**Feuchtigkeit** die ❶ moisture ❷ humidity

**Feuer** das ❶ fire ❷ hast du Feuer? have you got a light?

**Feuerlöscher** der *(PLURAL* die **Feuerlöscher)** fire extinguisher

**Feuermelder** der *(PLURAL* die **Feuermelder)** fire alarm

**Feuertreppe** die *(PLURAL* die **Feuertreppen)** fire escape

**Feuerwehr** die *(PLURAL* die **Feuerwehren)** fire brigade

**Feuerwehrauto** das *(PLURAL* die **Feuerwehrautos)** fire engine

**Feuerwehrmann** der *(PLURAL* die **Feuerwehrleute)** fireman

**Feuerwerk** das fireworks

**Feuerzeug** das *(PLURAL* die **Feuerzeuge)** lighter

**ficht** ▸ SEE **fechten**

**Fieber** das **(high) temperature, fever**; (hohes) Fieber haben to have a (high) temperature

**fiel** ▸ SEE **fallen**

**fies** *ADJECTIVE (informal)* **nasty**

**Figur** die *(PLURAL* die **Figuren)** ❶ figure ❷ character

**Filiale** die *(PLURAL* die **Filialen)** branch

**Film** der *(PLURAL* die **Filme)** film

**filmen** *VERB (PERF* hat gefilmt*)* to film

**Filter** der *(PLURAL* die **Filter)** filter

**Filzstift** der *(PLURAL* die **Filzstifte)** felt pen

**Finale** das *(PLURAL* die **Finale)** final

**finanziell** *ADJECTIVE* financial

**finanzieren** *VERB (PERF* hat finanziert*)* to finance

**finden** ◇*VERB (IMP* fand, *PERF* hat gefunden*)* ❶ to find ❷ to think; wie findest du das? what do you think of it?, findest du? do you think so? ❸ ich finde nichts dabei I don't mind

**fing** ▸ SEE **fangen**

**Finger** der *(PLURAL* die **Finger)** finger

**Fingernagel** der *(PLURAL* die **Fingernägel)** fingernail

**Finne** der *(PLURAL* die **Finnen)** Finn

**Finnin** die *(PLURAL* die **Finninnen)** Finn

**Finnland** das **Finland**

**finster** *ADJECTIVE* ❶ dark; im Finstern in the dark ❷ sinister

**Finsternis** die **darkness**

**Firma** die *(PLURAL* die **Firmen)** firm, company

**Fisch** der *(PLURAL* die **Fische)** ❶ fish ❷ Fische Pisces, Helmut ist Fisch Helmut is Pisces

**Fischer** der *(PLURAL* die **Fischer)** fisherman

**fit** *ADJECTIVE* fit; er hält sich durch Jogging fit he keeps fit by jogging

**Fitnesscenter** das *(PLURAL* die **Fitnesscenter)** gym

**Fitnesstraining** das **keep fit**

**fix** *ADJECTIVE* ❶ quick ❷ fix und fertig all finished, all ready ❸ ich bin fix und fertig *(informal)* I'm shattered

**flach** *ADJECTIVE* ❶ flat ❷ low ❸ shallow; die Erdbeeren kommen in die flache Schüssel the strawberries go into the shallow bowl

**Fläche** die *(PLURAL* die **Flächen)** ❶ surface ❷ area

**flackern** *VERB (PERF* hat geflackert*)* to flicker

**Flagge** die *(PLURAL* die **Flaggen)** flag

**Flamme** die *(PLURAL* die **Flammen)** flame

**Flasche** die *(PLURAL* die **Flaschen)** bottle

**Flaschenöffner** der *(PLURAL* die **Flaschenöffner)** bottle opener

**flauschig** *ADJECTIVE* ❶ fluffy ❷ fleecy

**Fleck** der *(PLURAL* die **Flecken)** ❶ stain ❷ spot ❸ ein blauer Fleck a bruise

a b c d e f g h i j k l m n o p q r s t u v w x y z

**fleckig** ADJECTIVE ❶ stained ❷ blotchy *(skin)*

**Fledermaus** die *(PLURAL* die **Fledermäuse)** bat

**Fleisch** das ❶ meat ❷ flesh

**Fleischer** der *(PLURAL* die **Fleischer)** butcher

**Fleischerei** die *(PLURAL* die **Fleischereien)** butcher's

**Fleiß** der hard work

**fleißig** ADJECTIVE hard-working

**flicken** VERB *(PERF* hat geflickt) to mend

**Flicken** der *(PLURAL* die **Flicken)** patch *(for mending)*

**Fliege** die *(PLURAL* die **Fliegen)** ❶ fly ❷ bow tie

**fliegen** ◇VERB *(IMP* flog, *PERF* ist geflogen) ❶ to fly ❷ ich bin geflogen *(informal)* I fell ❸ Manfred ist geflogen *(informal)* Manfred has been fired ❹ *(PERF* hat geflogen) to fly *(a plane)*

**fliehen** ◇VERB *(IMP* floh, *PERF* ist geflohen) to flee

**Fliese** die *(PLURAL* die **Fliesen)** tile

**Fließband** das *(PLURAL* die **Fließbänder)** ❶ conveyor belt ❷ assembly line

**fließen** ◇VERB *(IMP* floss, *PERF* ist geflossen) to flow

**fließend** ADJECTIVE ❶ running ❷ fluent; fließendes Deutsch fluent German ❸ moving *(traffic)*

**Flitterwochen** PLURAL NOUN honeymoon; sie fahren nach Ägyten für ihre Flitterwochen they're going to Egypt for their honeymoon

**flitzen** VERB *(informal)* *(PERF* ist geflitzt) ❶ to dash ❷ to whizz

**Flocke** die *(PLURAL* die **Flocken)** flake

**flog** ▸ SEE **fliegen**

**floh** ▸ SEE **fliehen**

**Floh** der *(PLURAL* die **Flöhe)** flee

**Flohmarkt** der *(PLURAL* die **Flohmärkte)** flea market

**floss** ▸ SEE **fließen**

**Flosse** die *(PLURAL* die **Flossen)** ❶ fin ❷ flipper

**Flöte** die *(PLURAL* die **Flöten)** flute

**fluchen** VERB *(PERF* hat geflucht) to curse

**Flüchtling** der *(PLURAL* die **Flüchtlinge)** refugee

**Flug** der *(PLURAL* die **Flüge)** flight

**Flugbegleiter** der *(PLURAL* die **Flugbegleiter)** flight attendant

**Flugbegleiterin** die *(PLURAL* die **Flugbegleiterinnen)** flight attendant

**Flugblatt** das *(PLURAL* die **Flugblätter)** pamphlet

**Flugdienstleiter** der *(PLURAL* die **Flugdienstleiter)** air-traffic controller

**Flugdienstleiterin** die *(PLURAL* die **Flugdienstleiterinnen)** air-traffic controller

**Flügel** der *(PLURAL* die **Flügel)** ❶ wing ❷ grand piano

**Fluggast** der *(PLURAL* die **Fluggäste)** (air) passenger

**Fluggesellschaft** die *(PLURAL* die **Fluggesellschaften)** airline

**Flughafen** der *(PLURAL die Flughäfen)* airport

**Fluglotse** der *(PLURAL die Fluglotsen)* air-traffic controller

**Fluglotsin** der *(PLURAL die Fluglotsinnen)* air-traffic controller

**Flugplatz** der *(PLURAL die Flugplätze)* ❶ airport ❷ airfield

**Flugzeug** das *(PLURAL die Flugzeuge)* aeroplane; mit dem Flugzeug fliegen to go by air

**Fluor** das fluoride

**Flur** der *(PLURAL die Flure)* ❶ hall ❷ corridor

**Fluss** der *(PLURAL die Flüsse)* river

**flüssig** *ADJECTIVE* liquid

**Flüssigkeit** die *(PLURAL die Flüssigkeiten)* liquid

**flüstern** *VERB (PERF hat geflüstert)* to whisper

**Flut** die *(PLURAL die Fluten)* ❶ high tide; bei Flut at high tide ❷ flood *(of letters, complaints)*

**Flutlicht** das floodlight

**focht** ▸ SEE fechten

**Föhn** der *(PLURAL die Föhne)* hair drier

**föhnen** *VERB (PERF hat geföhnt)* to blow-dry

**Folge** die *(PLURAL die Folgen)* ❶ consequence ❷ episode ❸ etwas zur Folge haben to result in something ❹ an den Folgen eines Unfalls sterben to die as the result of an accident

**folgen** *VERB (PERF ist gefolgt)* ❶ to follow; daraus folgt, dass ... it

follows that ..., ich kann dir nicht folgen I can't follow what you're saying ❷ *(PERF hat gefolgt)* to obey

**folgend** *ADJECTIVE* ❶ following ❷ Folgendes the following

**Folgerung** die *(PLURAL die Folgerungen)* conclusion

**folgsam** *ADJECTIVE* obedient

**Folie** die *(PLURAL die Folien)* foil

**Folienkartoffel** die *(PLURAL die Folienkartoffeln)* jacket potato

**Folterkammer** die *(PLURAL die Folterkammern)* torture chamber

**Fön** ▸ SEE Föhn

**fönen** ▸ SEE föhnen

**fordern** *VERB (PERF hat gefordert)* to demand

**fördern** *VERB (PERF hat gefördert)* ❶ to promote ❷ to sponsor

**Forderung** die *(PLURAL die Forderungen)* ❶ demand ❷ claim

**Forelle** die *(PLURAL die Forellen)* trout

**Form** die *(PLURAL die Formen)* ❶ shape ❷ form; in Form sein to be on form ❸ tin *(for baking)*

**Format** das *(PLURAL die Formate)* format

**formatieren** *VERB (PERF hat formatiert)* to format

**formen** *VERB (PERF hat geformt)* ❶ to form ❷ sich formen to take shape

**förmlich** *ADJECTIVE* formal

**förmlich** *ADVERB* ❶ formally ❷ jemanden förmlich zwingen, etwas zu tun to positively force

somebody to do something, ich
hätte förmlich schreien können
I really could have screamed

**Formular** das *(PLURAL die Formulare)*
form

**Forscher** der *(PLURAL die Forscher)*
❶ researcher, research scientist
❷ explorer

**Forschung** die *(PLURAL die Forschungen)* research

**Forst** der *(PLURAL die Forste(n))*
forest

**Förster** der *(PLURAL die Förster)*
forester

**fort** *ADVERB* ❶ away ❷ fort sein to
have gone ❸ und so fort and so on
❹ in einem fort on and on

**fortbewegen** *VERB (PERF hat
fortbewegt)* ❶ to move ❷ sich
fortbewegen to move

**fortfahren** *◇VERB (PRES fährt fort,
IMP fuhr fort, PERF ist fortgefahren)*
❶ to leave; wann fahrt ihr fort?
when are you leaving? ❷ to
continue

**fortgeschritten** *ADJECTIVE*
advanced

**Fortpflanzung** die *(PLURAL
die Fortpflanzungen)*
❶ reproduction ❷ propagation

**Fortschritt** der *(PLURAL die
Fortschritte)* progress;
Fortschritte machen to make
progress

**fortsetzen** *VERB (PERF hat
fortgesetzt)* to continue

**Fortsetzung** die *(PLURAL die
Fortsetzungen)* ❶ continuation
❷ instalment

**Foto** das *(PLURAL die Fotos)* photo

**Fotoapparat** der *(PLURAL die
Fotoapparate)* camera

**Fotograf** der *(PLURAL die Fotografen)*
photographer

**Fotografie** die *(PLURAL die
Fotografien)* ❶ photography
❷ photograph

**fotografieren** *VERB (PERF hat
fotografiert)* ❶ to photograph,
to take a photograph of ❷ to
take photographs

**Fotografin** die *(PLURAL die
Fotografinnen)* photographer

**Fotokopie** die *(PLURAL die
Fotokopien)* photocopy

**fotokopieren** *VERB (PERF hat
fotokopiert)* to photocopy

**Fracht** die *(PLURAL die Frachten)*
freight, cargo

**Frage** die *(PLURAL die Fragen)*
question; eine Frage stellen to ask
a question, etwas in Frage stellen
to question something, das kommt
nicht in Frage that's out of the
question

**Fragebogen** der *(PLURAL die
Fragebogen)* questionnaire

**fragen** *VERB (PERF hat gefragt)* ❶ to
ask ❷ sich fragen to wonder

**Fragezeichen** das *(PLURAL die
Fragezeichen)* question mark

**fraglich** *ADJECTIVE* doubtful

**Franken¹** der *(PLURAL die Franken)*
(Swiss) franc

**Franken²** das Franconia

**Frankreich** das France

**Franzose** der *(PLURAL die Franzosen)*
Frenchman

**Französin** die *(PLURAL* die **Französinnen)** Frenchwoman

**französisch** *ADJECTIVE* **French**

**Französisch** das **French**

**fraß** ▸ SEE **fressen**

**Frau** die *(PLURAL* die **Frauen)**
❶ woman ❷ wife ❸ Mrs, Ms
*('Frau' is usually used to address both married and unmarried women)*

**Fräulein** das *(PLURAL* die **Fräulein)**
❶ young lady ❷ Miss; Fräulein Schmidt Miss Schmidt

**frech** *ADJECTIVE* **cheeky**

**Frechheit** die *(PLURAL* die **Frechheiten)** ❶ cheek ❷ cheeky remark

**Frechheit** *(PLURAL* die **Frechheiten)** ❶ cheeky remark ❷ cheekiness

**frei** *ADJECTIVE* ❶ free ❷ freelance ❸ ist dieser Platz frei? is this seat taken? ❹ ein freier Tag a day off, sich frei nehmen to take a day off ❺ 'Zimmer frei' 'vacancies'

**Freibad** das *(PLURAL* die **Freibäder)** open-air swimming pool

**Freie** das im Freien in the open air

**freigebig** *ADJECTIVE* **generous**

**Freiheit** die *(PLURAL* die **Freiheiten)** ❶ freedom ❷ liberty; sich Freiheiten erlauben to take liberties

**freimachen** *VERB (PERF* hat freigemacht) ❶ to take time off ❷ sich freimachen to take time off

**Freistoß** der *(PLURAL* die **Freistöße)** free kick

**Freistunde** die *(PLURAL* die **Freistunden)** free period

**Freitag** der *(PLURAL* die **Freitage)** Friday

**freitags** *ADVERB* on Fridays

**freiwillig** *ADJECTIVE* **voluntary**

**Freiwillige** der/die *(PLURAL* die **Freiwilligen)** volunteer

**Freizeit** die ❶ spare time ❷ leisure

**Freizeitkleidung** die leisure wear, casual clothes

**fremd** *ADJECTIVE* ❶ foreign ❷ strange; fremde Leute strangers, ich bin hier fremd I'm a stranger here

**Fremde** der/die *(PLURAL* die **Fremden)** ❶ foreigner ❷ stranger

**Fremdenverkehr** der tourism

**Fremdenverkehrsbüro** das *(PLURAL* die **Fremdenverkehrsbüros)** tourist office

**Fremdenzimmer** das *(PLURAL* die **Fremdenzimmer)** room (to let)

**Fremdsprache** die *(PLURAL* die **Fremdsprachen)** foreign language

**fressen** ◇*VERB (PRES* frisst, *IMP* fraß, *PERF* hat gefressen) to eat

**Freude** die *(PLURAL* die **Freuden)** ❶ joy ❷ pleasure; mit Freuden with pleasure ❸ an etwas Freude haben to be delighted with something ❹ jemandem eine Freude machen to please somebody

**freuen** *VERB (PERF* hat sich gefreut) ❶ sich freuen to be pleased, sich über etwas freuen to be pleased about something ❷ sich auf etwas freuen to look forward to something

**Freund** der *(PLURAL* die **Freunde)** ❶ friend ❷ boyfriend

**Freundin** die (PLURAL die Freundinnen) ❶ friend ❷ girlfriend

**freundlich** ADJECTIVE ❶ friendly ❷ kind

**freundlicherweise** ADVERB kindly

**Freundlichkeit** die friendliness

**Freundschaft** die (PLURAL die Freundschaften) friendship; mit jemandem Freundschaft schließen to make friends with somebody

**Frieden** der peace

**Friedhof** der (PLURAL die Friedhöfe) cemetery

**friedlich** ADJECTIVE peaceful

**frieren** ⬦VERB (IMP fror, PERF hat gefroren) ❶ to be cold; frierst du? are you cold? ❷ es friert it's freezing, it's frosty ❸ (PERF ist gefroren) to freeze

**Frikadelle** die (PLURAL die Frikadellen) rissole

**frisch** ADJECTIVE fresh; sich frisch machen to freshen up

**frisch** ADVERB freshly; 'frisch gestrichen' 'wet paint'

**Friseur** der (PLURAL die Friseure) hairdresser

**Friseuse** die (PLURAL die Friseusen) hairdresser

**frisieren** VERB (PERF hat frisiert) ❶ jemanden frisieren to do somebody's hair ❷ sich frisieren to do your hair

**frisst** ▸ SEE fressen

**Frisur** die (PLURAL die Frisuren) hairstyle, hairdo

**froh** ADJECTIVE ❶ happy; frohe Weihnachten! happy Christmas! ❷ über etwas froh sein to be glad about something

**fröhlich** ADJECTIVE cheerful

**Fröhlichkeit** die cheerfulness

**fromm** ADJECTIVE devout

**fror** ▸ SEE frieren

**Frosch** der (PLURAL die Frösche) frog

**Frost** der (PLURAL die Fröste) frost

**frostig** ADJECTIVE frosty

**Frottee** das (PLURAL die Frottees) towelling

**Frottiertuch** das (PLURAL die Frottiertücher) towel

**Frucht** die (PLURAL die Früchte) fruit

**fruchtbar** ADJECTIVE fertile

**Fruchtsaft** der (PLURAL die Fruchtsäfte) fruit juice

**früh** ADJECTIVE, ADVERB ❶ early; von früh auf from an early age ❷ heute früh this morning

**Frühe** die in aller Frühe at the crack of dawn

**früher** ADJECTIVE ❶ earlier ❷ former

**früher** ADVERB ❶ earlier ❷ formerly ❸ früher war sie ganz anders she used to be quite different, das war früher ein Blumengeschäft it used to be a florist's

**frühestens** ADVERB at the earliest

**Frühjahr** das (PLURAL die Frühjahre) spring; im Frühjahr in spring

**Frühling** der (PLURAL die Frühlinge) spring; im Frühling in spring

**Frühstück** das *(PLURAL* die **Frühstücke)** breakfast

**frühstücken** *VERB (PERF* **hat gefrühstückt)** to have breakfast

**frühzeitig** *ADJECTIVE* **early**

**Fuchs** der *(PLURAL* die **Füchse)** fox

**fühlen** *VERB (PERF* **hat gefühlt)** ❶ to feel ❷ sich krank fühlen to feel ill

**fuhr** ▸ SEE **fahren**

**führen** *VERB (PERF* **hat geführt)** ❶ to lead; sie führt mit fünf Punkten she is five points in the lead, unsere Mannschaft führt our team's winning ❷ to run *(a shop or business)* ❸ to show round ❹ to keep *(a diary, list)* ❺ ein Telefongespräch führen to make a phone call

**Führer** der *(PLURAL* die **Führer)** ❶ leader ❷ guide

**Führerschein** der *(PLURAL* die **Führerscheine)** driving licence; den Führerschein machen to take your driving test

**Führung** die *(PLURAL* die **Führungen)** ❶ leadership ❷ guided tour ❸ management *(of a shop)* ❹ in Führung in the lead

**Führungsposition** die *(PLURAL* die **Führungspositionen)** ❶ top position ❷ pole position

**füllen** *VERB (PERF* **hat gefüllt)** ❶ to fill ❷ to stuff *(a turkey, peppers)* ❸ sich füllen to fill (up)

**Füller** der *(PLURAL* die **Füller)** fountain pen

**Füllfederhalter** der *(PLURAL* die **Füllfederhalter)** fountain pen

**Füllung** die *(PLURAL* die **Füllungen)** filling

**Fundament** das *(PLURAL* die **Fundamente)** foundations

**Fundbüro** das *(PLURAL* die **Fundbüros)** lost property office

**fünf** *NUMBER* **five**

**fünfhundert** *NUMBER* **five hundred**

**Fünftel** das *(PLURAL* die **Fünftel)** fifth

**fünfter, fünfte, fünftes** *ADJECTIVE* **fifth**

**fünfzehn** *NUMBER* **fifteen**

**fünfzig** *NUMBER* **fifty**

**Funke** der *(PLURAL* die **Funken)** spark

**funkeln** *VERB (PERF* **hat gefunkelt)** ❶ to sparkle ❷ to twinkle *(of a star)*

**funktionieren** *VERB (PERF* **hat funktioniert)** to work

**für** *PREPOSITION (+ACC)* ❶ for ❷ was für ein ...? what sort of ... ? ❸ für sich by yourself, jetzt habe ich das Haus ganz für mich now I've got the house to myself ❹ das Für und Wider the pros and cons

**Furcht** die **fear**

**furchtbar** *ADJECTIVE* **terrible**

**fürchten** *VERB (PERF* **hat gefürchtet)** ❶ to fear ❷ sich fürchten to be afraid, ich fürchte mich vor ihm I'm afraid of him, ich fürchte, das geht nicht I'm afraid that's not possible

**fürchterlich** *ADJECTIVE* **dreadful**

**füreinander** *ADVERB* **for each other**

**fürs** für das ▸ SEE **für**

**Fürsorge** die ❶ care ❷ welfare ❸ *(informal)* social security

**Fuß** der *(PLURAL die Füße)* ❶ foot; zu Fuß on foot, zu Fuß gehen to walk ❷ base

**Fußabdruck** der *(PLURAL die Fußabdrücke)* footprint

**Fußball** der *(PLURAL die Fußbälle)* football

**Fußballplatz** der *(PLURAL die Fußballplätze)* football pitch

**Fußballspiel** das *(PLURAL die Fußballspiele)* football match

**Fußballspieler** der *(PLURAL die Fußballspieler)* footballer

**Fußboden** der *(PLURAL die Fußböden)* floor

**Fußgänger** der *(PLURAL die Fußgänger)* pedestrian

**Fußgängerzone** die *(PLURAL die Fußgängerzonen)* pedestrian precinct

**Fußweg** der *(PLURAL die Fußwege)* footpath

**Futter** das ❶ feed; ich habe dem Hund schon Futter gegeben I've already given the dog his food ❷ lining *(of clothes)*

**füttern** VERB *(PERF hat gefüttert)* ❶ to feed; den Hund und die Katze füttern to feed the dog and the cat ❷ to line

**Futur** das *(PLURAL die Future)* future *(tense)*

# Gg

**gab** ▸ SEE **geben**

**Gabel** die *(PLURAL die Gabeln)* fork

**gähnen** VERB *(PERF hat gegähnt)* to yawn

**Galerie** die *(PLURAL die Galerien)* gallery

**galoppieren** VERB *(PERF ist galoppiert)* to gallop

**Gammler** der *(PLURAL die Gammler)* drop-out

**Gammlerin** die *(PLURAL die Gammlerinnen)* drop-out

**Gang** der *(PLURAL die Gänge)* ❶ walk ❷ errand ❸ corridor ❹ ein Platz am Gang an aisle seat ❺ course *(of a meal)* ❻ gear *(of a car)* ❼ in Gang setzen to get going ❽ im Gange in progress

**gängig** ADJECTIVE ❶ common ❷ popular *(goods)*

**Gans** die *(PLURAL die Gänse)* goose

**Gänseblümchen** das *(PLURAL die Gänseblümchen)* daisy

**Gänsehaut** die goose pimples

**ganz** ADJECTIVE ❶ whole; ganz Deutschland the whole of Germany ❷ im Großen und Ganzen on the whole ❸ eine ganze Menge quite a lot ❹ all; mein ganzes Geld all my money, die ganzen Leute all the people ❺ etwas wieder ganz machen to mend something

**ganz** *ADVERB* ❶ quite; es war ganz gut it was quite good ❷ ganz und gar completely ❸ ganz und gar nicht not at all

**ganztägig** *ADJECTIVE, ADVERB* ❶ full-time ❷ all-day; ganztägig geöffnet open all day

**ganztags** *ADVERB* ❶ full time ❷ all day

**Ganztagsschule** die *(PLURAL die Ganztagsschulen)* ❶ all-day school ❷ all-day schooling

**gar** *ADJECTIVE* done, cooked

**gar** *ADVERB* ❶ gar nicht not at all, gar nichts nothing ❷ oder gar or even

**Garage** die *(PLURAL die Garagen)* garage

**Garantie** die *(PLURAL die Garantien)* guarantee

**garantieren** *VERB (PERF hat garantiert)* to guarantee

**Garderobe** die *(PLURAL die Garderoben)* cloakroom; wir können die Mäntel an der Garderobe abgeben we can leave the coats in the cloakroom

**Gardine** die *(PLURAL die Gardinen)* curtain

**Garn** das *(PLURAL die Garne)* thread

**Garnele** die *(PLURAL die Garnelen)* ❶ shrimp ❷ prawn

**Garten** der *(PLURAL die Gärten)* garden

**Gärtner** der *(PLURAL die Gärtner)* gardener

**Gärtnerin** die *(PLURAL die Gärtnerinnen)* gardener

**Gas** das *(PLURAL die Gase)* ❶ gas ❷ Gas geben to accelerate

**Gasherd** der *(PLURAL die Gasherde)* gas cooker

**Gaspedal** das *(PLURAL die Gaspedale)* accelerator

**Gasse** die *(PLURAL die Gassen)* lane

**Gast** der *(PLURAL die Gäste)* ❶ guest; wir haben heute Abend Gäste we've got guests tonight ❷ bei jemandem zu Gast sein to be staying with somebody

**Gastarbeiter** der *(PLURAL die Gastarbeiter)* foreign worker, guest worker

**Gästezimmer** das *(PLURAL die Gästezimmer)* ❶ (hotel) room ❷ spare room

**Gastfamilie** die *(PLURAL die Gastfamilien)* host family

**gastfreundlich** *ADJECTIVE* hospitable

**Gastfreundschaft** die hospitality

**Gastgeber** der *(PLURAL die Gastgeber)* host

**Gastgeberin** die *(PLURAL die Gastgeberinnen)* host

**Gasthaus** das *(PLURAL die Gasthäuser)* inn

**Gasthof** der *(PLURAL die Gasthöfe)* inn

**Gaststätte** die *(PLURAL die Gaststätten)* restaurant

**Gauner** der *(PLURAL die Gauner)* crook

**Gebäck** das ❶ pastries ❷ biscuits

**gebären** ◇*VERB (IMP gebar, PERF hat geboren)* ❶ to give birth to ❷ geboren werden to be born

# Gebäude

## gedacht

**Gebäude** das *(PLURAL* die **Gebäude)** building

**geben** ◇*VERB (PRES* **gibt**, *IMP* **gab**, *PERF* **hat gegeben)** ❶ to give ❷ to deal *(cards)* ❸ to teach *(at school)* ❹ geben Sie mir bitte Frau Scheck please put me through to Mrs Scheck ❺ es gibt there is, there are, es gibt viele gute Restaurants in München there are lots of good restaurants in Munich, was gibts or gibt's im Kino? what's on at the cinema?, was gibt es zum Mittagessen? what are we having for lunch? ❻ was gibts or gibt's Neues? what's the news?, what's new? ❼ sich geschlagen geben to admit defeat ❽ das gibt sich wieder it'll get better ❾ das gibts or gibt's doch nicht! I don't believe it!

**Gebet** das *(PLURAL* die **Gebete)** prayer

**gebeten** ▸ see **bitten**

**Gebiet** das *(PLURAL* die **Gebiete)** ❶ area ❷ field

**gebildet** *ADJECTIVE* educated

**Gebirge** das *(PLURAL* die **Gebirge)** mountain range; im Gebirge in the mountains

**Gebiss** das *(PLURAL* die **Gebisse)** ❶ teeth ❷ false teeth, dentures

**gebissen** ▸ see **beißen**

**geblieben** ▸ see **bleiben**

**geboren** *VERB* ▸ see **gebären**

**geboren** *ADJECTIVE* ❶ born ❷ née; Frau Hahn, geborene Müller Mrs Hahn, née Müller

**geborgen** *ADJECTIVE* safe

**geboten** ▸ see **bieten**

**gebracht** ▸ see **bringen**

**gebraten** *ADJECTIVE* fried

**Gebrauch** der *(PLURAL* die **Gebräuche)** ❶ use; vor Gebrauch schütteln shake before use ❷ custom

**gebrauchen** *VERB (PERF* **hat gebraucht)** to use

**Gebrauchsanweisung** die *(PLURAL* die **Gebrauchsanweisungen)** instructions (for use)

**gebraucht** *ADJECTIVE* used, second-hand

**Gebrauchtwagen** der *(PLURAL* die **Gebrauchtwagen)** second-hand car

**gebrochen** ▸ see **brechen**

**Gebühr** die *(PLURAL* die **Gebühren)** fee, charge

**gebührenfrei** *ADJECTIVE* free (of charge)

**gebührenpflichtig** *ADJECTIVE* ❶ subject to a charge ❷ eine gebührenpflichtige Straße a toll road

**gebunden** ▸ see **binden**

**Geburt** die *(PLURAL* die **Geburten)** birth

**Geburtenregelung** die birth control

**Geburtsdatum** das *(PLURAL* die **Geburtsdaten)** date of birth

**Geburtsort** der *(PLURAL* die **Geburtsorte)** place of birth

**Geburtstag** der *(PLURAL* die **Geburtstage)** birthday

**Geburtsurkunde** die *(PLURAL* die **Geburtsurkunden)** birth certificate

**gedacht** ▸ see **denken**

**Gedächtnis** das *(PLURAL* die **Gedächtnisse)** memory

**Gedanke** der *(PLURAL* die **Gedanken)**
❶ thought; in Gedanken versunken sein to be lost in thought ❷ sich Gedanken machen to worry ❸ jemanden auf andere Gedanken bringen to take somebody's mind off things

**gedankenlos** *ADJECTIVE* thoughtless

**gedankenlos** *ADVERB* without thinking

**Gedeck** das *(PLURAL* die **Gedecke)**
❶ place setting ❷ set meal

**Gedicht** das *(PLURAL* die **Gedichte)** poem

**Geduld** die patience

**geduldig** *ADJECTIVE* patient

**gedurft** ▸ SEE **dürfen**

**geehrt** *ADJECTIVE* ❶ honoured ❷ Sehr geehrte Frau Ross Dear Mrs Ross

**geeignet** *ADJECTIVE* ❶ suitable ❷ right

**Gefahr** die *(PLURAL* die **Gefahren)**
❶ danger; außer Gefahr out of danger ❷ auf eigene Gefahr at your own risk, Gefahr laufen, etwas zu tun to run the risk of doing something

**gefährdet** *ADJECTIVE* at risk, endangered; eine gefährdete Art an endangered species

**gefährlich** *ADJECTIVE* dangerous

**gefallen¹** ▸ SEE **fallen**

**gefallen²** ◇ *VERB (PRES* **gefällt**, *IMP* **gefiel**, *PERF* **hat gefallen)** ❶ es gefällt mir I like it, es hat mir sehr gut gefallen I liked it a lot ❷ sich etwas gefallen lassen to put up with something

**Gefallen¹** der *(PLURAL* die **Gefallen)** favour

**Gefallen²** das pleasure; dir zu Gefallen to please you

**Gefangene** der/die *(PLURAL* die **Gefangenen)** prisoner

**Gefängnis** das *(PLURAL* die **Gefängnisse)** prison

**Gefäß** das *(PLURAL* die **Gefäße)** container

**gefasst** *ADJECTIVE* ❶ calm, composed ❷ auf etwas gefasst sein to be prepared for something

**gefiel** ▸ SEE **gefallen**

**geflogen** ▸ SEE **fliegen**

**geflossen** ▸ SEE **fließen**

**Geflügel** das poultry

**gefochten** ▸ SEE **fechten**

**gefräßig** *ADJECTIVE* (informal) greedy

**gefrieren** ◇ *VERB (IMP* **gefror**, *PERF* **ist gefroren)** to freeze

**Gefrierfach** das *(PLURAL* die **Gefrierfächer)** freezer (compartment)

**gefroren** *ADJECTIVE* **frozen**

**Gefühl** das *(PLURAL* die **Gefühle)**
❶ feeling ❷ etwas im Gefühl haben to have a feel for something

**gefüllt** *ADJECTIVE* stuffed *(peppers, for example)*

**gefunden** ▸ SEE **finden**

**gegangen** ▸ SEE **gehen**

**gegeben** ▸ SEE **geben**

**gegebenenfalls** *ADVERB* if need be

**gegen** *PREPOSITION (+ACC)* ❶ against ❷ gegen die Mauer fahren to drive into the wall ❸ ein Mittel gegen Grippe a cure for flu ❹ towards; gegen Abend towards evening ❺ gegen vier Uhr around four o'clock ❻ compared with ❼ versus *(in sport)*

**Gegend** die *(PLURAL die Gegenden)* ❶ area ❷ neighbourhood

**gegeneinander** *ADVERB* against each other, against one another

**Gegenmittel** das *(PLURAL die Gegenmittel)* ❶ remedy ❷ antidote

**Gegensatz** der *(PLURAL die Gegensätze)* ❶ contrast ❷ opposite ❸ im Gegensatz zu mir unlike me

**gegenseitig** *ADJECTIVE* mutual

**gegenseitig** *ADVERB* sich gegenseitig helfen to help each other

**Gegenstand** der *(PLURAL die Gegenstände)* ❶ object ❷ subject *(in grammar or of a discussion)*

**Gegenteil** das *(PLURAL die Gegenteile)* ❶ opposite ❷ im Gegenteil on the contrary

**gegenüber** *PREPOSITION (+DAT)* ❶ opposite; Susi saß mir gegenüber Susi sat opposite me ❷ compared with ❸ towards; jemandem gegenüber freundlich sein to be friendly towards somebody

**gegenüber** *ADVERB* opposite; meine Freundin wohnt gegenüber my friend lives opposite

**Gegenwart** die ❶ present ❷ presence

**gegessen** ▸ SEE **essen**

**Gegner** der *(PLURAL die Gegner)* opponent

**Gegnerin** die *(PLURAL die Gegnerinnen)* opponent

**gegrillt** *ADJECTIVE* grilled

**Gehackte** das mince

**Gehalt** das *(PLURAL die Gehälter)* salary

**gehässig** *ADJECTIVE* spiteful

**geheim** *ADJECTIVE* secret

**Geheimnis** das *(PLURAL die Geheimnisse)* secret

**geheimnisvoll** *ADJECTIVE* mysterious

**gehen** ◇*VERB (IMP* **ging***, PERF* **ist gegangen)** ❶ to go; schlafen gehen to go to bed ❷ to walk ❸ über die Straße gehen to cross the road ❹ es geht ihr gut she's well, wie geht es Ihnen? how are you?, es geht it's not too bad ❺ das geht nicht that's impossible ❻ um etwas gehen to be about something, worum gehts or geht's hier? what's it all about? ❼ die Uhr geht falsch the clock's wrong

**Gehirn** das *(PLURAL die Gehirne)* brain

**Gehirnerschütterung** die *(PLURAL die Gehirnerschütterungen)* concussion

**gehoben** ▸ SEE **heben**

**geholfen** ▸ SEE **helfen**

**Gehör** das hearing

**gehorchen** *VERB (PERF* **hat gehorcht)** to obey

**gehören** *VERB (PERF* **hat gehört)** ❶ to belong; es gehört mir it belongs to me ❷ dazu gehört Mut that takes courage ❸ es gehört sich nicht it isn't done

**gehorsam** *ADJECTIVE* obedient

**Gehsteig** der *(PLURAL* die **Gehsteige)** pavement

**Geier** der *(PLURAL* die **Geier)** vulture

**Geige** die *(PLURAL* die **Geigen)** violin

**geil** *ADJECTIVE (informal)* **wicked**, **amazing**

**Geisel** die *(PLURAL* die **Geiseln)** hostage

**Geist** der *(PLURAL* die **Geister)** ❶ mind ❷ ghost ❸ wit

**geistesabwesend** *ADJECTIVE* absent-minded

**Geisteskrankheit** die *(PLURAL* die **Geisteskrankheiten)** mental illness

**Geisteswissenschaften** *PLURAL NOUN* arts, humanities

**geistig** *ADJECTIVE* mental

**geistreich** *ADJECTIVE* witty, clever

**geizig** *ADJECTIVE* mean

**gekannt** ▸ SEE **kennen**

**gekonnt** ▸ SEE **können**

**Gel** das *(PLURAL* die **Gele)** gel

**Gelächter** das *(PLURAL* die **Gelächter)** laughter

**geladen** ▸ SEE **laden**

**gelähmt** *ADJECTIVE* paralysed

**Gelände** das *(PLURAL* die **Gelände)** ❶ ground ❷ area

**Geländer** das *(PLURAL* die **Geländer)** ❶ banister(s) ❷ railing(s)

**gelangweilt** *ADJECTIVE* bored

**gelassen** *VERB* ▸ SEE **lassen**

**gelassen** *ADJECTIVE* calm

**geläufig** *ADJECTIVE* ❶ common ❷ das ist mir nicht geläufig I'm not familiar with it

**gelaunt** *ADJECTIVE* gut gelaunt sein to be in a good mood

**gelb** *ADJECTIVE* yellow

**Geld** das *(PLURAL* die **Gelder)** money

**Geldautomat** der *(PLURAL* die **Geldautomaten)** cash dispenser

**Geldbörse** die *(PLURAL* die **Geldbörsen)** purse

**Geldschein** der *(PLURAL* die **Geldscheine)** banknote

**Geldstrafe** die *(PLURAL* die **Geldstrafen)** fine

**Geldwechsel** der ❶ bureau de change ❷ currency exchange

**gelegen** ▸ SEE **liegen**

**Gelegenheit** die *(PLURAL* die **Gelegenheiten)** ❶ opportunity ❷ occasion

**gelegentlich** *ADVERB* occasionally

**Gelenk** das *(PLURAL* die **Gelenke)** joint

**Geliebte** der/die *(PLURAL* die **Geliebten)** lover

**geliehen** ▸ SEE **leihen**

**gelingen** ◇ *VERB (IMP* **gelang**, *PERF* **ist gelungen)** to succeed; es ist mir gelungen, sie zu überreden I succeeded in persuading her

**gelten** ◇ *VERB (PRES* **gilt**, *IMP* **galt**, *PERF* **hat gegolten)** ❶ to be valid ❷ to apply *(of a rule)* ❸ jemandem gelten to be directed at somebody ❹ sein Wort gilt viel his word is worth a lot ❺ das gilt nicht that doesn't count ❻ als etwas gelten to be regarded as something gelungen *VERB* ▸ SEE **gelingen**

gelungen *ADJECTIVE* successful

**Gemälde** das *(PLURAL* die **Gemälde)** painting

**gemein** *ADJECTIVE* mean

**Gemeinde** die *(PLURAL* die **Gemeinden)** ❶ community ❷ congregation

**gemeinsam** *ADJECTIVE* ❶ common ❷ joint

**gemeinsam** *ADVERB* together; gemeinsam essen to eat together

**Gemeinschaft** die *(PLURAL* die **Gemeinschaften)** community

**gemischt** *ADJECTIVE* mixed

**gemocht** ▸ SEE **mögen**

**Gemüse** das *(PLURAL* die **Gemüse)** vegetables

**Gemüsehändler** der *(PLURAL* die **Gemüsehändler)** greengrocer

**Gemüseladen** der *(PLURAL* die **Gemüseläden)** greengrocer's shop

**gemusst** ▸ SEE **müssen**

**gemustert** *ADJECTIVE* patterned

**gemütlich** *ADJECTIVE* ❶ cosy ❷ mach es dir gemütlich make yourself comfortable

**genannt** ▸ SEE **nennen**

**genau** *ADJECTIVE* ❶ exact ❷ accurate *(scales, description)* ❸ meticulous ❹ ich weiß nichts Genaues I don't know any details

**genau** *ADVERB* ❶ exactly; sich etwas genau ansehen to look at something carefully ❷ genau genommen strictly speaking

**Genauigkeit** die accuracy

**genauso** *ADVERB* ❶ just the same ❷ genauso gut just as good, genauso viel just as much, just as many, genauso lange just as long

**Genehmigung** die *(PLURAL* die **Genehmigungen)** ❶ permission ❷ permit ❸ licence

**Generation** die *(PLURAL* die **Generationen)** generation

**Generator** der *(PLURAL* die **Generatoren)** generator

**generell** *ADJECTIVE* general

**Genetik** die genetics

**Genf** das Geneva

**Genfer See** der Lake Geneva

**genial** *ADJECTIVE* brilliant

**Genick** das *(PLURAL* die **Genicke)** (back of the) neck

**Genie** das *(PLURAL* die **Genies)** genius

**genießbar** *ADJECTIVE* edible

**genießen** ◇*VERB* *(IMP* genoss, *PERF* hat genossen) to enjoy

**genommen** ▸ SEE **nehmen**

**genug** *ADVERB* enough

**genügen** *VERB* *(PERF* hat genügt) to be enough

**genügend** *ADJECTIVE* ❶ enough ❷ sufficient

**Genuss** der *(PLURAL* die **Genüsse)** ❶ enjoyment ❷ consumption *(of alcohol)*

**geöffnet** *ADJECTIVE* open

**Geometrie** die geometry

**Gepäck** das luggage

**Gepäckaufbewahrung** die *(PLURAL* die **Gepäckaufbewahrungen)** left-luggage office

**Gepäckausgabe** die left-luggage office

**Gepäckträger** der *(PLURAL die Gepäckträger)* ❶ porter ❷ roof rack ❸ carrier *(on a bike)*

**gerade** *ADJECTIVE* ❶ straight ❷ etwas gerade biegen to straighten something ❸ upright ❹ eine gerade Zahl an even number

**gerade** *ADVERB* ❶ just; gerade erst only just ❷ es war nicht gerade billig it wasn't exactly cheap

**geradeaus** *ADVERB* straight ahead

**geradebiegen** ▸ SEE gerade

**gerannt** ▸ SEE rennen

**Gerät** das *(PLURAL die Geräte)* ❶ appliance ❷ set *(TV or radio)* ❸ tool ❹ gadget ❺ die Geräte apparatus *(in gymnastics)*

**geraten** ◇*VERB (PRES* gerät, *IMP* geriet, *PERF* ist geraten)* ❶ to get *(somewhere, the wrong side of the road etc.)*; in etwas geraten to get into something, in Wut geraten to get angry ❷ an den Richtigen geraten to come to the right person ❸ gut/schlecht geraten to turn out well/badly ❹ nach jemandem geraten to take after somebody

**Gerätetauchen** das scuba diving

**geräuchert** *ADJECTIVE* smoked

**geräumig** *ADJECTIVE* spacious

**Geräusch** das *(PLURAL die Geräusche)* noise

**gerecht** *ADJECTIVE* ❶ just ❷ fair

**Gerechtigkeit** die justice

**Gerede** das gossip

**Gericht** das *(PLURAL die Gerichte)* ❶ court ❷ dish

**gerieben** ▸ SEE reiben

**gering** *ADJECTIVE* ❶ small *(amount)* ❷ low *(value)* ❸ short *(time, distance)*

**Gerippe** das *(PLURAL die Gerippe)* skeleton

**gerissen** *ADJECTIVE* crafty

**geritten** ▸ SEE reiten

**gern(e)** *ADVERB* ❶ gladly ❷ jemanden gern haben to like somebody, etwas gern tun to like doing something ich tanze gern I like dancing, ich hätte gerne einen Kaffee I'd like a coffee, welchen Belag hättest du gerne? which topping would you like? ❸ ja, gern! yes, I'd love to! ❹ das glaube ich gern I can well believe that

**Gerste** die barley

**Geruch** der *(PLURAL die Gerüche)* smell

**Gerücht** das *(PLURAL die Gerüchte)* rumour

**Gerümpel** das junk

**gesalzen** *VERB* ▸ SEE salzen

**gesalzen** *ADJECTIVE* ❶ salted ❷ gesalzene Preise *(informal)* steep prices

**gesamt** *ADJECTIVE* ❶ whole ❷ die gesamten Kosten the total cost ❸ die gesamten Werke the complete works

**Gesamtschule** die *(PLURAL die Gesamtschulen)* comprehensive school

**gesandt** ▸ SEE senden

**Geschäft** das *(PLURAL die Geschäfte)* ❶ shop ❷ business ❸ deal

**Geschäftsfrau** die *(PLURAL die Geschäftsfrauen)* businesswoman

**Geschäftsführer** der (PLURAL die Geschäftsführer) **manager**

**Geschäftsführerin** die (PLURAL die Geschäftsführerinnen) **manageress**

**Geschäftsmann** der (PLURAL die Geschäftsleute) **businessman**

**Geschäftszeiten** PLURAL NOUN **business hours**

**geschehen** ◇VERB (PRES **geschieht**, IMP **geschah**, PERF **ist geschehen**) **to happen**

**gescheit** ADJECTIVE **clever**

**Geschenk** das (PLURAL die Geschenke) **present, gift**

**Geschichte** die (PLURAL die Geschichten) ❶ **story** ❷ **history** ❸ mach bloß keine große Geschichte daraus **don't make such a thing of it**

**Geschick** das ❶ **skill** ❷ **fate**

**geschickt** ADJECTIVE ❶ **skilful** ❷ **clever**

**geschieden** VERB ▸ SEE **scheiden**

**geschieden** ADJECTIVE **divorced**; meine Eltern sind geschieden **my parents are divorced**

**geschienen** ▸ SEE **scheinen**

**Geschirr** das ❶ **crockery** ❷ **dishes**

**Geschirrspülmaschine** die (PLURAL die Geschirrspülmaschinen) **dishwasher**

**Geschirrtuch** das (PLURAL die Geschirrtücher) **tea towel**

**Geschlecht** das (PLURAL die Geschlechter) ❶ **sex** ❷ **gender**

**geschlossen** VERB ▸ SEE **schließen**

**geschlossen** ADJECTIVE **closed**

**Geschmack** der (PLURAL die Geschmäcke) **taste**

**geschmacklos** ADJECTIVE ❶ **tasteless** ❷ geschmacklos sein **to be in bad taste**

**geschnitten** ▸ SEE **schneiden**

**geschossen** ▸ SEE **schießen**

**geschrieben** ▸ SEE **schreiben**

**geschrien** ▸ SEE **schreien**

**Geschwätz** das **talk**

**geschwätzig** ADJECTIVE **talkative**

**Geschwindigkeit** die (PLURAL die Geschwindigkeiten) **speed**

**Geschwindigkeitsbeschränkung** die (PLURAL die Geschwindigkeitsbeschränkungen) **speed limit**

**Geschwister** PLURAL NOUN **brothers and sisters, siblings**

**geschwommen** ▸ SEE **schwimmen**

**Geschwür** das (PLURAL die Geschwüre) **ulcer**

**gesellig** ADJECTIVE **sociable**

**Gesellschaft** die (PLURAL die Gesellschaften) ❶ **society** ❷ **company**; ich leiste dir Gesellschaft **I'll keep you company** ❸ **party**

**gesessen** ▸ SEE **sitzen**

**Gesetz** das (PLURAL die Gesetze) **law**

**gesetzlich** ADJECTIVE **legal**; ein gesetzlicher Feiertag **a public holiday**

**gesetzlich** ADVERB **legally, by law**

**Gesicht** das (PLURAL die Gesichter) **face**

**Gesichtsausdruck** der (facial) **expression**

**gesollt** ▸ SEE **sollen**

**gespannt** ADJECTIVE ❶ **eager** ❷ auf etwas gespannt sein **to look**

forward eagerly to something, auf jemanden gespannt sein to look forward to seeing somebody **❸** ich bin gespannt, ob ... I wonder whether ... **❹** tense; in Südafrika ist die Lage immer noch gespannt the situation in South Africa is still tense

**Gespenst** das *(PLURAL* die **Gespenster)** ghost

**Gespräch** das *(PLURAL* die **Gespräche)** **❶** conversation **❷** call *(on the phone)*

**gesprächig** *ADJECTIVE* talkative

**gesprochen** ▸ SEE **sprechen**

**gesprungen** ▸ SEE **springen**

**Gestalt** die *(PLURAL* die **Gestalten)** **❶** figure **❷** form

**gestanden** ▸ SEE **stehen, gestehen**

**Geständnis** das *(PLURAL* die **Geständnisse)** confession

**gestatten** *VERB (PERF* hat gestattet) **❶** to permit **❷** nicht gestattet prohibited **❸** gestatten Sie? may I?

**Geste** die *(PLURAL* die **Gesten)** gesture

**gestehen** ◇*VERB (IMP* gestand, *PERF* hat gestanden) to confess

**Gestell** das *(PLURAL* die **Gestelle)** **❶** rack **❷** stand **❸** frame

**gestern** *ADVERB* **❶** yesterday **❷** gestern Nacht last night

**gestohlen** ▸ SEE **stehlen**

**gestorben** ▸ SEE **sterben**

**gestreift** *ADJECTIVE* striped

**gesund** *ADJECTIVE* **❶** healthy **❷** wieder gesund werden to get well again **❸** Schwimmen ist gesund swimming is good for you

**Gesundheit** die **❶** health **❷** Gesundheit! bless you! *(said after someone sneezes)*

**gesungen** ▸ SEE **singen**

**getan** ▸ SEE **tun**

**Getränk** das *(PLURAL* die **Getränke)** drink

**Getränkekarte** die *(PLURAL* die **Getränkekarten)** wine list

**getrauen** *VERB (PERF* hat sich getraut) sich getrauen to dare

**Getreide** das grain

**getrennt** *ADJECTIVE* separated

**Getriebe** das *(PLURAL* die **Getriebe)** gearbox

**getrieben** ▸ SEE **treiben**

**getroffen** ▸ SEE **treffen**

**getrunken** ▸ SEE **trinken**

**Getue** das fuss

**geübt** *ADJECTIVE* **❶** accomplished **❷** mit geübtem Auge with a practised eye

**Gewächshaus** das *(PLURAL* die **Gewächshäuser)** greenhouse

**Gewalt** die **❶** power **❷** force; mit Gewalt by force **❸** violence

**gewaltig** *ADJECTIVE* enormous

**gewalttätig** *ADJECTIVE* violent

**gewann** ▸ SEE **gewinnen**

**Gewebe** das *(PLURAL* die **Gewebe)** **❶** fabric **❷** tissue

**Gewehr** das *(PLURAL* die **Gewehre)** rifle, gun

**Gewerkschaft** die *(PLURAL* die **Gewerkschaften)** trade union

**gewesen** ▸ SEE **sein**

**Gewicht** das *(PLURAL* die **Gewichte)** weight

**Gewinn** der *(PLURAL* die **Gewinne)** ❶ profit ❷ winnings ❸ prize

**gewinnen** ◇*VERB (IMP* **gewann,** *PERF* **hat gewonnen)** ❶ to win; mit 3 zu 2 Toren gewinnen to win by 3 goals to 2 ❷ to gain *(time or influence)*; an Bedeutung gewinnen to gain in importance

**Gewinner** der *(PLURAL* die **Gewinner)** winner

**Gewinnerin** die *(PLURAL* die **Gewinnerinnen)** winner

**gewiss** *ADJECTIVE* certain; ein gewisser Herr Schmidt möchte Sie sprechen a Mr Schmidt would like to speak to you

**gewiss** *ADVERB* certainly; 'darf ich?' 'aber gewiss doch' 'may I?' 'but of course'

**Gewissen** das *(PLURAL* die **Gewissen)** conscience

**gewissenhaft** *ADJECTIVE* conscientious

**gewissermaßen** *ADVERB* ❶ more or less ❷ as it were

**Gewitter** das *(PLURAL* die **Gewitter)** thunderstorm

**gewittrig** *ADJECTIVE* thundery

**gewöhnen** *VERB (PERF* **hat gewöhnt)** ❶ jemanden an etwas gewöhnen to get somebody used to something ❷ an etwas gewöhnt sein to be used to something ❸ sich an etwas gewöhnen to get used to something

**Gewohnheit** die *(PLURAL* die **Gewohnheiten)** habit

**gewöhnlich** *ADJECTIVE* ❶ usual ❷ ordinary

**gewöhnlich** *ADVERB* usually; wie gewöhnlich as usual

**gewohnt** *ADJECTIVE* ❶ usual ❷ etwas gewohnt sein to be used to something, Renate ist es nicht gewohnt, früh aufzustehen Renate isn't used to getting up early

**gewollt** ▸ SEE **wollen**

**gewonnen** ▸ SEE **gewinnen**

**geworden** ▸ SEE **werden**

**geworfen** ▸ SEE **werfen**

**Gewürz** das *(PLURAL* die **Gewürze)** spice

**gewusst** ▸ SEE **wissen**

**Gezeiten** *PLURAL NOUN* tides

**gezogen** ▸ SEE **ziehen**

**gezwungen** ▸ SEE **zwingen**

**gibt** ▸ SEE **geben**

**gierig** *ADJECTIVE* greedy

**gießen** ◇*VERB (IMP* **goss,** *PERF* **hat gegossen)** ❶ to pour; es gießt it's pouring ❷ to water; vergiss nicht, die Blumen zu gießen don't forget to water the flowers

**Gießkanne** die *(PLURAL* die **Gießkannen)** watering can

**Gift** das *(PLURAL* die **Gifte)** poison

**giftig** *ADJECTIVE* ❶ poisonous ❷ toxic

**Gigabyte** das *(PLURAL* die **Gigabytes)** gigabyte; eine Festplatte mit 20 Gigabyte Speicherkapazität a twenty gigabyte hard disk

**ging** ▸ SEE **gehen**

**Gipfel** der *(PLURAL* die **Gipfel)** ❶ peak, summit ❷ der Gipfel der Geschmacklosigkeit the height of bad taste

**Gips** der plaster

**Giraffe** die *(PLURAL* die **Giraffen)** giraffe

**Girokonto** das *(PLURAL* die **Girokonten)** current account

**Gitarre** die *(PLURAL* die **Gitarren)** guitar

**Gitarrist** der *(PLURAL* die **Gitarristen)** guitarist, guitar player

**Gitter** das *(PLURAL* die **Gitter)** ❶ grid ❷ bars

**glänzen** *VERB (PERF* **hat geglänzt)** to shine

**glänzend** *ADJECTIVE* ❶ shining ❷ brilliant; ein glänzender Erfolg a brilliant success

**Glas** das *(PLURAL* die **Gläser)** ❶ glass *(the material)* ❷ glass *(for a drink)* ❸ jar

**Glasscheibe** die *(PLURAL* die **Glasscheiben)** pane (of glass)

**Glasur** die ❶ icing ❷ glaze

**glatt** *ADJECTIVE* ❶ smooth ❷ slippery ❸ eine glatte Absage a flat refusal

**glatt** *ADVERB* ❶ smoothly ❷ flatly; etwas glatt ablehnen to flatly reject something ❸ das ist glatt gelogen that's a downright lie ❹ ich habe ihren Geburtstag glatt vergessen I totally forgot about her birthday

**Glatteis** das **(black) ice**

**Glatze** die *(PLURAL* die **Glatzen)** eine Glatze haben to be bald, eine Glatze bekommen to go bald

**glauben** *VERB (PERF* **hat geglaubt)** ❶ to believe; an Gott glauben to believe in God ❷ to think ❸ nicht zu glauben! incredible!

**gleich** *ADJECTIVE* ❶ same ❷ identical ❸ gleich bleibend constant ❹ das ist mir gleich it's all the same to me,

ganz gleich, wer anruft no matter who calls

**gleich** *ADVERB* ❶ the same ❷ equally ❸ immediately; gleich danach immediately afterwards, gleich neben right next to, ich komme gleich I'm coming (right away), er ist gleich fertig he'll be ready in a minute

**gleichartig** *ADJECTIVE* similar

**gleichberechtigt** *ADJECTIVE* equal

**Gleichberechtigung** die equality

**gleichbleibend** ▸ SEE gleich

**gleichen** ◇*VERB (IMP* **glich**, *PERF* **hat geglichen)** ❶ to be like ❷ sich gleichen to be alike

**gleichfalls** *ADVERB* ❶ also ❷ danke gleichfalls! the same to you!

**Gleichgewicht** das balance

**gleichgültig** *ADJECTIVE* indifferent; das ist doch gleichgültig it's not important

**gleichwertig** *ADJECTIVE* ❶ equivalent ❷ of the same value ❸ of the same standard

**gleichzeitig** *ADVERB* at the same time

**Gleis** das *(PLURAL* die **Gleise)** ❶ track, line ❷ platform; Gleis vier platform four

**glich** ▸ SEE gleichen

**Glied** das *(PLURAL* die **Glieder)** ❶ limb ❷ link

**glitschig** *ADJECTIVE* slippery

**glitzern** *VERB (PERF* **hat geglitzert)** to glitter

**global** *ADJECTIVE* global, general; der globale Temperaturanstieg global warming

**Glocke** die *(PLURAL* die **Glocken)** bell

**Glück** das ❶ luck; viel Glück! good
luck!, Glück haben to be lucky, zum
Glück luckily ❷ happiness

**glücklich** *ADJECTIVE* ❶ lucky; es war
ein glücklicher Zufall, dass ich ihn
heute in der Stadt getroffen habe it
was a lucky coincidence that I met
him in town today ❷ happy

**glücklicherweise** *ADVERB* luckily,
fortunately

**Glückwunsch** der *(PLURAL* die
**Glückwünsche)** congratulations;
herzlichen Glückwunsch zum
Geburtstag! happy birthday!

**Glückwunschkarte** die *(PLURAL* die
**Glückwunschkarten)** greetings
card

**Glühbirne** die *(PLURAL* die
**Glühbirnen)** light bulb

**glühen** *VERB (PERF* **hat geglüht)** to
glow

**Gokart** der *(PLURAL* die **Gokarts)** gokart; Gokart gehen to go karting

**Gold** das gold

**golden** *ADJECTIVE* ❶ gold ❷ golden

**Goldfisch** der *(PLURAL* die **Goldfische)**
goldfish

**Golf**[1] der *(PLURAL* die **Golfe)** gulf

**Golf**[2] das golf

**Golfplatz** der *(PLURAL* die **Golfplätze)**
golf course

**Golfschläger** der *(PLURAL* die
**Golfschläger)** golf club

**Golfspieler** der *(PLURAL* die
**Golfspieler)** golfer

**Golfspielerin** die *(PLURAL* die
**Golfspielerinnen)** golfer

**Gorilla** der *(PLURAL* die **Gorillas)**
gorilla

**goss** ▸ SEE **gießen**

**Gosse** die *(PLURAL* die **Gossen)** gutter
*(in street)*

**Gott** der *(PLURAL* die **Götter)** god

**Gottesdienst** der *(PLURAL* die
**Gottesdienste)** service

**Göttin** die *(PLURAL* die **Göttinnen)**
goddess

**Grab** das *(PLURAL* die **Gräber)** grave

**graben** *VERB (PRES* **gräbt,** *IMP* **grub,**
*PERF* **hat gegraben)** to dig

**Grad** der *(PLURAL* die **Grade)** degree

**Grafik** die *(PLURAL* die **Grafiken)**
graphics

**Gramm** das *(PLURAL* die **Gramme)**
gram

**Grammatik** die *(PLURAL* die
**Grammatiken)** grammar

**grammatikalisch**
*ADJECTIVE* grammatical; ein
grammatikalischer Fehler
a grammatical error

**grantig** *ADJECTIVE* grumpy

**Gras** das *(PLURAL* die **Gräser)** grass

**grässlich** *ADJECTIVE* horrible

**Gräte** die *(PLURAL* die **Gräten)** (fish)
bone

**gratis** *ADVERB* free of charge

**gratulieren** *VERB (PERF* **hat
gratuliert)** ❶ to congratulate
❷ ich habe Gabi zum Geburtstag
gratuliert I wished Gabi happy
birthday ❸ wir gratulieren!
congratulations!

**grau** *ADJECTIVE* grey

**Gräuel** der horror

**grauen** VERB (PERF **hat gegraut**) mir graut es davor I dread it

**grauenvoll** ADJECTIVE ❶ grim ❷ horrific

**grauhaarig** ADJECTIVE grey-haired

**grausam** ADJECTIVE cruel

**Grausamkeit** die cruelty

**graziös** ADJECTIVE graceful

**greifen** ◇VERB (IMP **griff**, PERF **hat gegriffen**) ❶ to take hold of ❷ to catch ❸ nach etwas greifen to reach for something ❹ um sich greifen to spread (of fire)

**grell** ADJECTIVE ❶ glaring ❷ garish ❸ shrill

**Grenze** die (PLURAL die **Grenzen**) ❶ border ❷ boundary ❸ limit

**grenzen** VERB (PERF **hat gegrenzt**) an etwas grenzen to border on something

**Greuel** ▸ SEE **Gräuel**

**Grieche** der (PLURAL die **Griechen**) Greek

**Griechenland** das Greece

**Griechin** die (PLURAL die **Griechinnen**) Greek

**griechisch** ADJECTIVE Greek

**griff** ▸ SEE **greifen**

**Griff** der (PLURAL die **Griffe**) ❶ grasp ❷ handle

**griffbereit** ADJECTIVE handy; sie hat den Korkenzieher immer griffbereit she always keeps the corkscrew handy

**Grill** der (PLURAL die **Grills**) ❶ grill ❷ barbecue

**Grille** die (PLURAL die **Grillen**) cricket (the insect)

**grillen** VERB (PERF **hat gegrillt**) ❶ to grill ❷ to have a barbecue

**Grillfest** das (PLURAL die **Grillfeste**) barbecue

**grinsen** VERB (PERF **hat gegrinst**) to grin

**Grippe** die (PLURAL die **Grippen**) flu

**grob** ADJECTIVE ❶ coarse ❷ rough ❸ rude ❹ ein grober Fehler a bad mistake

**Groschen** der (PLURAL die **Groschen**) ❶ groschen (one hundredth of a Schilling in the former Austrian currency) ▸ SEE **Schilling** ❷ (informal) der Groschen ist gefallen the penny's dropped

**groß** ADJECTIVE ❶ big ❷ great; Gisela hatte große Angst Gisela was very frightened ❸ tall ❹ ein großer Buchstabe a capital letter ❺ groß werden to grow up ❻ die großen Ferien the summer holidays ❼ im Großen und Ganzen on the whole ❽ Groß und Klein young and old

**groß** ADVERB was soll man da schon groß machen? what are you supposed to do?

**großartig** ADJECTIVE great

**Großbritannien** das Great Britain

**Großbuchstabe** der (PLURAL die **Großbuchstaben**) capital (letter)

**Größe** die (PLURAL die **Größen**) ❶ size ❷ height ❸ greatness

**Großeltern** PLURAL NOUN grandparents

**großenteils** ADVERB largely

**Großmarkt** der (PLURAL die **Großmärkte**) hypermarket

**Großmutter** die *(PLURAL* die **Großmütter)** grandmother

**großschreiben** ◇*VERB (IMP* **großschrieb,** *PERF* **hat großgeschrieben)** ein Wort großschreiben to write a word with a capital

**Großstadt** die *(PLURAL* die **Großstädte)** city

**Großvater** der *(PLURAL* die **Großväter)** grandfather

**großzügig** *ADJECTIVE* **generous**

**grub** ▸ SEE **graben**

**grün** *ADJECTIVE* ❶ green ❷ im Grünen in the country ❸ die Grünen the Greens

**Grund** der *(PLURAL* die **Gründe)** ❶ ground ❷ bottom ❸ reason; aus diesem Grund for this reason ❹ im Grunde genommen basically

**gründen** *VERB (PERF* **hat gegründet)** ❶ to set up, to found ❷ sich auf etwas gründen to be based on something

**Grundlage** die *(PLURAL* die **Grundlagen)** basis

**gründlich** *ADJECTIVE* **thorough**

**grundsätzlich** *ADJECTIVE* ❶ fundamental ❷ basic

**grundsätzlich** *ADVERB* ❶ basically ❷ on principle

**Grundschule** die *(PLURAL* die **Grundschulen)** primary school

**Grundstück** das *(PLURAL* die **Grundstücke)** plot (of land)

**Gruppe** die *(PLURAL* die **Gruppen)** group

**Gruß** der *(PLURAL* die **Grüße)** greeting; einen schönen Gruß an Lars give my regards to Lars, mit herzlichen Grüßen with best wishes

**grüßen** *VERB (PERF* **hat gegrüßt)** ❶ to greet ❷ to say hello ❸ grüß Gott! hello ❹ grüße Thomas von mir give Thomas my regards, Gisela lässt grüßen Gisela sends her regards

**gucken** *VERB (PERF* **hat geguckt)** to look

**gültig** *ADJECTIVE* **valid**

**Gültigkeit** die validity

**Gummi** der *(PLURAL* die **Gummis)** rubber

**Gummiband** das *(PLURAL* die **Gummibänder)** rubber band

**Gummistiefel** der *(PLURAL* die **Gummistiefel)** wellington (boot)

**günstig** *ADJECTIVE* ❶ favourable ❷ convenient

**Gurgel** die *(PLURAL* die **Gurgeln)** throat

**gurgeln** *VERB (PERF* **hat gegurgelt)** to gargle

**Gurke** die *(PLURAL* die **Gurken)** ❶ cucumber ❷ gherkin

**Gürtel** der *(PLURAL* die **Gürtel)** belt

**Gürteltasche** die *(PLURAL* die **Gürteltaschen)** bum bag

**gut** *ADJECTIVE* ❶ good ❷ guten Appetit! enjoy your meal! ❸ schon gut that's all right, also gut all right ❹ im Guten amicably ❺ alles Gute! all the best!

**gut** *ADVERB* ❶ well ❷ gut schmecken to taste good ❸ gut zwei Stunden a good two hours ❹ uns geht's gut we're fine, ihm geht es nicht gut he's not well

**Gut** das (PLURAL die **Güter**)
**❶** property **❷** estate **❸** (plural),
goods, freight

**Güte** die **❶** goodness; du meine
Güte! my goodness! **❷** quality

**Güterzug** der (PLURAL die **Güterzüge**)
goods train

**gutgehen** ▸ SEE gut

**gutmütig** ADJECTIVE good-natured

**Gutschein** der (PLURAL die
**Gutscheine**) **❶** voucher **❷** coupon

**Gymnasium** das (PLURAL die
**Gymnasien**) grammar school

**Gymnastik** die **❶** gymnastics
**❷** keep-fit (exercises)

**Haar** das (PLURAL die **Haare**) **❶** hair;
sich die Haare waschen to wash
your hair **❷** um ein Haar (informal)
very nearly

**Haarbürste** die (PLURAL die
**Haarbürsten**) hairbrush

**haarig** ADJECTIVE hairy

**Haarschnitt** der (PLURAL die
**Haarschnitte**) haircut

**Haarwaschmittel** das (PLURAL die
**Haarwaschmittel**) shampoo

**haben** ◇ VERB (PRES **hat**, IMP **hatte**,
PERF **hat gehabt**) **❶** to have (got);
ich habe ein neues Auto I have (
I've got) a new car, etwas gegen
jemanden haben to have something
against somebody **❷** (used with
another verb, like 'have' in English, to
form past tenses) ich habe Werners
Adresse verloren I've lost Werner's
address, ich habe deine Mutter
gestern angerufen I rang your
mother yesterday **❸** Angst haben
to be frightened, Hunger haben
to be hungry, Husten haben to
have a cough **❹** heute haben wir
Mittwoch it's Wednesday today
**❺** die Kinder haben Ferien the
children are on holiday **❻** was hat
sie? what's the matter with her?
**❼** ich hätte gern ... I'd like ..., ich
hätte ihr geholfen I would have
helped her **❽** sich haben (informal)
to make a fuss

**Habicht** der *(PLURAL die Habichte)* hawk

**hacken** VERB *(PERF hat gehackt)* **❶** to chop (up) **❷** to peck *(of a bird)*

**Hackfleisch** das minced meat

**Hacksteak** das *(PLURAL die Hacksteaks)* beefburger *(without bread)*

**Hafen** der *(PLURAL die Häfen)* harbour

**Haferflocken** PLURAL NOUN porridge oats

**haftbar** ADJECTIVE für etwas haftbar sein to be liable for something

**haften** VERB *(PERF hat gehaftet)* **❶** to stick **❷** für etwas haften to be responsible for something

**Hagel** der hail

**hageln** VERB *(PERF hat gehagelt)* to hail

**Hagelschauer** der *(PLURAL die Hagelschauer)* hailstorm

**Hahn** der *(PLURAL die Hähne)* **❶** cock **❷** tap

**Hähnchen** das *(PLURAL die Hähnchen)* chicken

**Hai** der *(PLURAL die Haie)* shark

**Haken** der *(PLURAL die Haken)* **❶** hook **❷** tick **❸** catch; da muss ein Haken dran sein there must be a catch

**halb** ADJECTIVE half; zum halben Preis at half price, halb eins half past twelve

**Halbbruder** der *(PLURAL die Halbbrüder)* half-brother

**Halbfinale** das *(PLURAL die Halbfinale)* semi-final

**halbieren** VERB *(PERF hat halbiert)* to halve

**Halbkreis** der *(PLURAL die Halbkreise)* semicircle

**Halbpension** die half board

**Halbschwester** die *(PLURAL die Halbschwestern)* half-sister

**halbtags** ADVERB part-time

**halbwegs** ADVERB **❶** half-way **❷** more or less

**Halbzeit** die *(PLURAL die Halbzeiten)* **❶** half **❷** half-time; während der Halbzeit during half-time

**half** ▸ SEE **helfen**

**Hälfte** die *(PLURAL die Hälften)* half; zur Hälfte half

**Halle** die *(PLURAL die Hallen)* **❶** hall **❷** foyer

**Hallenbad** das *(PLURAL die Hallenbäder)* indoor swimming pool

**hallo** EXCLAMATION hello!

**Hals** der *(PLURAL die Hälse)* **❶** neck **❷** throat; mir tut der Hals weh I've got a sore throat **❸** aus vollem Hals schreien to shout at the top of your voice **❹** Hals über Kopf in a rush

**Halsband** das *(PLURAL die Halsbänder)* collar

**Halsschmerzen** PLURAL NOUN sore throat; Paul hat Halsschmerzen Paul's got a sore throat

**Halstuch** das *(PLURAL die Halstücher)* scarf

**halt** EXCLAMATION stop!

**Halt** der **❶** hold; jetzt hat es einen besseren Halt it holds better now **❷** Halt machen to stop

**haltbar** *ADJECTIVE* **❶** hard-wearing **❷** durable **❸** mindestens haltbar bis … best before …

**halten** ◇*VERB (PRES* **hält**, *IMP* **hielt**, *PERF* **hat gehalten) ❶** to hold **❷** to keep; sein Versprechen halten to keep your promise, warm halten to keep warm **❸** to stop; der Bus hält direkt vor seiner Haustür the bus stops right outside his door **❹** to save *(in sport)* **❺** to take *(a paper, magazine)* **❻** ich habe ihn für deinen Bruder gehalten I took him for your brother **❼** viel von jemandem halten to think a lot of somebody, jemanden für ehrlich halten to think somebody is honest **❽** zu jemandem halten to stand by somebody **❾** eine Rede halten to make a speech **❿** sich halten to keep *(of milk, fruit, etc.)* **⓫** sich links/rechts halten to keep left/right **⓬** sich gut halten to do well **⓭** sich an etwas halten to keep to something

**Haltestelle** die *(PLURAL* die **Haltestellen)** stop

**haltmachen** ▸ SEE **Halt**

**Haltung** die *(PLURAL* die **Haltungen) ❶** posture **❷** attitude **❸** composure

**Hammelfleisch** das mutton

**Hammer** der *(PLURAL* die **Hämmer)** hammer

**hämmern** *VERB (PERF* **hat gehämmert)** to hammer

**Hamster** der *(PLURAL* die **Hamster)** hamster

**Hand** die *(PLURAL* die **Hände)** hand; jemandem die Hand geben to shake hands with somebody

**Handarbeit** die *(PLURAL* die **Handarbeiten) ❶** handicraft **❷** hand-made article

**Handball** der handball

**Handbremse** die *(PLURAL* die **Handbremsen)** handbrake; die Handbremse ziehen to pull the handbrake

**Handbuch** das *(PLURAL* die **Handbücher)** manual

**Handel** der **❶** trade **❷** deal **❸** in den Handel kommen to come on the market

**handeln** *VERB (PERF* **hat gehandelt) ❶** to trade, to deal **❷** mit jemandem handeln to bargain with somebody **❸** to act **❹** von etwas handeln to be about something **❺** es handelt sich um … it's about …, worum handelt es sich? what's it about?

**Handelsschule** die *(PLURAL* die **Handelsschulen)** business school, vocational college

**Handfläche** die *(PLURAL* die **Handflächen)** palm

**Handgelenk** das *(PLURAL* die **Handgelenke)** wrist

**Handgepäck** das hand luggage

**handhaben** *VERB (PERF* **hat gehandhabt)** to handle

**Händler** der *(PLURAL* die **Händler)** dealer

**handlich** *ADJECTIVE* handy

**Handlung** die *(PLURAL* die **Handlungen) ❶** act **❷** action **❸** plot

**Handschellen** *PLURAL NOUN* handcuffs

**Handschrift** die *(PLURAL die Handschriften)* handwriting

**Handschuh** der *(PLURAL die Handschuhe)* glove

**Handtasche** die *(PLURAL die Handtaschen)* bag

**Handtrommel** die *(PLURAL die Handtrommeln)* tambourine

**Handtuch** das *(PLURAL die Handtücher)* towel

**Handwerker** der *(PLURAL die Handwerker)* ❶ craftsman ❷ workman

**Handwerkszeug** das tools

**Handy** das *(PLURAL die Handys)* mobile (phone)

**Hang** der *(PLURAL die Hänge)* slope

**Hängematte** die *(PLURAL die Hängematten)* hammock

**hängen**[1] *VERB (PERF hat gehängt)* ❶ to hang; Florian hat das Bild an die Wand gehängt Florian hung the picture on the wall, sie hängte ihren Mantel in den Schrank she hung her coat up in the cupboard ❷ sie haben den Wohnwagen an das Auto gehängt they attached the caravan to the car ❸ sich an jemanden hängen to latch on to somebody

**hängen**[2] ◇*VERB (IMP hing, PERF hat gehangen)* ❶ to hang; mein Bild hat immer hier gehangen my picture used to hang here ❷ an seinen Eltern hängen to be attached to your parents, sie hängt sehr an ihrer Mutter she's very attached to her mother ❸ an etwas hängen bleiben to catch on something, to stick to something, ich bin mit dem Ärmel am Zaun

hängen geblieben I got my sleeve caught on the fence

**hängenbleiben** ▸ SEE **hängen**[2]

**Hansaplast** das plaster

**Happen** der *(PLURAL die Happen)* mouthful; ich habe heute keinen Happen gegessen I haven't had a bite to eat all day

**Harfe** die *(PLURAL die Harfen)* harp

**Harke** die *(PLURAL die Harken)* rake

**harmlos** *ADJECTIVE* harmless

**hart** *ADJECTIVE* ❶ hard ❷ harsh

**hart gekocht** *ADJECTIVE* hard-boiled

**Häschen** das *(PLURAL die Häschen)* bunny rabbit

**Hase** der *(PLURAL die Hasen)* hare

**Haselnuss** die *(PLURAL die Hasselnüsse)* hazelnut

**Hass** der hatred

**hassen** *VERB (PERF hat gehasst)* to hate

**hässlich** *ADJECTIVE* ❶ ugly; sie hat ein hässliches Gesicht she's got an ugly face ❷ nasty; das war sehr hässlich von dir that was very nasty of you

**hast** ▸ SEE **haben**

**hastig** *ADJECTIVE* hasty

**hat, hatte, hatten, hattest, hattet** ▸ SEE **haben**

**Haube** die *(PLURAL die Hauben)* ❶ bonnet ❷ cap

**hauen** ◇*VERB (PRES haut, IMP haute, PERF hat gehauen)* ❶ to beat ❷ to thump, to bang ❸ sich hauen to fight ❹ jemanden übers Ohr hauen *(informal)* to cheat somebody

**Haufen** der *(PLURAL* die **Haufen)** **❶** heap **❷** crowd *(of people)* **❸** ein Haufen *(informal)* heaps of, ein Haufen Geld heaps of money

**haufenweise** *ADVERB* heaps of; Gabi hat haufenweise CDs Gabi has heaps of CDs

**häufig** *ADJECTIVE* frequent

**Häufigkeit** die frequency

**Hauptbahnhof** der *(PLURAL* die **Hauptbahnhöfe)** main station

**Hauptgericht** das *(PLURAL* die **Hauptgerichte)** main course

**Hauptrolle** die *(PLURAL* die **Hauptrollen)** lead

**Hauptsache** die *(PLURAL* die **Hauptsachen)** main thing

**hauptsächlich** *ADJECTIVE* main

**hauptsächlich** *ADVERB* mainly

**Hauptschule** die secondary school

**Hauptstadt** die *(PLURAL* die **Hauptstädte)** capital

**Hauptstraße** die *(PLURAL* die **Hauptstraßen)** main road

**Hauptverkehrszeit** die *(PLURAL* die **Hauptverkehrszeiten)** rush hour

**Hauptwort** das *(PLURAL* die **Hauptwörter)** noun

**Haus** das *(PLURAL* die **Häuser)** **❶** house **❷** nach Hause home, zu Hause at home

**Hausarbeit** die *(PLURAL* die **Hausarbeiten)** **❶** housework; die Kinder müssen bei der Hausarbeit helfen the children have to help with the housework **❷** homework

**Hausaufgaben** *PLURAL NOUN* homework; hast du deine Hausaufgaben gemacht? have you done your homework?

**Hausfrau** die *(PLURAL* die **Hausfrauen)** housewife

**Haushalt** der *(PLURAL* die **Haushalte)** **❶** household **❷** den Haushalt machen to do the housework, im Haushalt helfen to help with the housework **❸** budget

**Haushaltswarengeschäft** das *(PLURAL* die **Haushaltswaren-geschäfte)** hardware shop

**Hausmeister** der *(PLURAL* die **Hausmeister)** caretaker

**Hausnummer** die house number

**Hausschlüssel** der *(PLURAL* die **Hausschlüssel)** front-door key

**Hausschuh** der *(PLURAL* die **Hausschuhe)** slipper

**Haustier** das *(PLURAL* die **Haustiere)** pet

**Haustür** die *(PLURAL* die **Haustüren)** front door

**Haut** die *(PLURAL* die **Häute)** skin; aus der Haut fahren *(informal)* to go up the wall

**Hebamme** die *(PLURAL* die **Hebammen)** midwife

**Hebel** der *(PLURAL* die **Hebel)** lever

**heben** ⋄*VERB (IMP* hob, *PERF* hat gehoben) **❶** to lift **❷** sich heben to rise

**Hecke** die *(PLURAL* die **Hecken)** hedge

**Heer** das *(PLURAL* die **Heere)** army

**Hefe** die *(PLURAL* die **Hefen)** yeast

**Heft** das *(PLURAL* die **Hefte)** **❶** exercise book **❷** issue *(of a magazine)*

**heften** VERB (PERF **hat geheftet**) ❶ to pin ❷ to tack (by sewing) ❸ to clip ❹ to staple

**heftig** ADJECTIVE ❶ violent ❷ heavy (snow, rain)

**Heftklammer** die (PLURAL die **Heftklammern**) staple

**Heftpflaster** das (PLURAL die **Heftpflaster**) sticking plaster

**Heftzwecke** die (PLURAL die **Heftzwecken**) drawing pin

**Heide** die heath

**Heidekraut** das heather

**Heidelbeere** die (PLURAL die **Heidelbeeren**) bilberry

**heilen** VERB (PERF **hat geheilt**) ❶ to cure ❷ to heal

**heilig** ADJECTIVE ❶ holy ❷ heilig halten to hold sacred ❸ der heilige Franz von Assisi Saint Francis of Assisi

**Heiligabend** der (PLURAL die **Heiligabende**) Christmas Eve

**Heilige** der/die (PLURAL die **Heiligen**) saint

**Heilmittel** das (PLURAL die **Heilmittel**) remedy

**heim** ADVERB home

**Heim** das (PLURAL die **Heime**) ❶ home ❷ hostel

**Heimat** die (PLURAL die **Heimaten**) ❶ home ❷ native land

**Heimatstadt** die home town

**Heimfahrt** die (PLURAL die **Heimfahrten**) ❶ journey home ❷ way home

**heimgehen** ◇VERB (IMP **ging heim**, PERF **ist heimgegangen**) to go home

**heimlich** ADJECTIVE secret

**heimlich** ADVERB secretly

**Heimspiel** das (PLURAL die **Heimspiele**) home game

**Heimweg** der (PLURAL die **Heimwege**) way home

**Heimweh** das homesickness; Heimweh haben to be homesick

**Heirat** die (PLURAL die **Heiraten**) marriage

**heiraten** VERB (PERF **hat geheiratet**) to marry

**heiser** ADJECTIVE hoarse

**heiß** ADJECTIVE hot

**heißen** ◇VERB (IMP **hieß**, PERF **hat geheißen**) ❶ to be called; wie heißt du? what's your name? ❷ to mean ❸ das heißt that is ❹ es heißt it is said ❺ wie heißt 'dog' auf Deutsch? what's the German for 'dog'?

**heiter** ADJECTIVE ❶ bright ❷ cheerful

**heizen** VERB (PERF **hat geheizt**) ❶ to heat (a room) ❷ to put the heating on ❸ to have the heating on

**Heizkörper** der (PLURAL die **Heizkörper**) radiator

**Heizung** die heating

**hektisch** ADJECTIVE hectic

**Held** der (PLURAL die **Helden**) hero

**Heldin** die (PLURAL die **Heldinnen**) heroine

**helfen** ◇VERB (PRES **hilft**, IMP **half**, PERF **hat geholfen**) ❶ to help; Lisa hilft mir Lisa is helping me ❷ es hilft nichts it's no good ❸ sich zu helfen wissen to know what to do, ich weiß mir nicht zu helfen I don't know what to do

**Helfer** der (PLURAL die **Helfer**)
❶ helper ❷ assistant

**Helferin** die (PLURAL die **Helferinnen**)
❶ helper ❷ assistant

**hell** ADJECTIVE ❶ light (colour)
❷ bright ❸ eine helle Stimme a clear voice ❹ helles Bier lager ❺ da ist heller Wahnsinn (informal) that's sheer madness

**hellwach** ADJECTIVE wide awake

**Helm** der (PLURAL die **Helme**) helmet

**Hemd** das (PLURAL die **Hemden**)
❶ shirt ❷ vest

**Henkel** der (PLURAL die **Henkel**) handle

**Henne** die (PLURAL die **Hennen**) hen

**her** ADVERB ❶ here; komm her come here ❷ vor jemandem her in front of somebody ❸ hinter etwas her sein to be after something ❹ von der Farbe her as far as the colour is concerned ❺ wo bist du her? where do you come from? ❻ wo hat Klaus das her? where did Klaus get it from? ❼ her damit! (informal) give it to me! ❽ ago; das ist schon lange her it was a long time ago, das ist drei Tage her it was three days ago

**herab** ADVERB down

**herablassend** ADJECTIVE condescending

**herabsetzen** VERB (PERF hat herabgesetzt) ❶ to reduce ❷ to belittle

**heran** ADVERB ❶ an etwas heran close to something, right up to something, bis an die Wand heran up to the wall ❷ immer heran! come closer!

**herankommen** ◇VERB (IMP kam heran, PERF ist herangekommen)
❶ to come near ❷ herankommen an to come up to ❸ ich komme nicht heran I can't get at it

**herauf** ADVERB up

**heraufkommen** ◇VERB (IMP kam herauf, PERF ist heraufgekommen) to come up

**heraus** ADVERB out

**herausbekommen** ◇VERB (IMP bekam heraus, PERF hat herausbekommen) ❶ to get out ❷ to find out ❸ to solve ❹ Geld herausbekommen to get change

**herausbringen** VERB (IMP brachte heraus, PERF hat herausgebracht) ❶ to publish (a book) ❷ to release (an album) ❸ to launch

**herausfinden** ◇VERB (IMP fand heraus, PERF hat herausgefunden) ❶ to find out ❷ to find your way out

**herausgeben** ◇VERB (PRES gibt heraus, IMP gab heraus, PERF hat herausgegeben) ❶ to hand over ❷ to bring out

**herauskommen** ◇VERB (IMP kam heraus, PERF ist herausgekommen) to come out

**herausnehmen** ◇VERB (PRES nimmt heraus, IMP nahm heraus, PERF hat herausgenommen) ❶ to take out; sie hat ihren Lippenstift aus der Tasche herausgenommen she took her lipstick out of the bag ❷ sich die Mandeln herausnehmen lassen to have your tonsils out ❸ es sich herausnehmen, etwas zu tun to have the nerve to do something, du nimmst dir zu viel heraus you're going too far

**herausstellen** VERB (PERF **hat herausgestellt**) ❶ to put out ❷ **sich herausstellen** to turn out, **es stellte sich heraus, dass ...** it turned out that ...

**herausziehen** ◇VERB (IMP **zog heraus**, PERF **hat herausgezogen**) to pull out

**herb** ADJECTIVE ❶ sharp ❷ dry (wine)

**herbei** ADVERB over (here); **kommt herbei!** come over here!

**Herberge** die (PLURAL die **Herbergen**) hostel

**Herbergsmutter** die (PLURAL die **Herbergsmütter**) warden (in a youth hostel)

**Herbergsvater** der (PLURAL die **Herbergsväter**) warden (in a youth hostel)

**herbringen** ◇VERB (IMP **brachte her**, PERF **hat hergebracht**) to bring (here)

**Herbst** der (PLURAL die **Herbste**) autumn; **im Herbst** in autumn

**Herd** der (PLURAL die **Herde**) cooker

**Herde** die (PLURAL die **Herden**) ❶ herd ❷ flock

**herein** ADVERB in; **herein!** come in!

**hereinfallen** ◇VERB (PRES **fällt herein**, IMP **fiel herein**, PERF **ist hereingefallen**) to be taken in; **auf einen Betrüger hereinfallen** to be taken in by a swindler

**hereinkommen** ◇VERB (IMP **kam herein**, PERF **ist hereingekommen**) to come in

**hereinlassen** ◇VERB (PRES **lässt herein**, IMP **ließ herein**, PERF **hat hereingelassen**) to let in; **Max**

lässt mich nicht ins Zimmer herein Max won't let me into the room

**Herfahrt** die (PLURAL die **Herfahrten**) ❶ journey here ❷ way here

**hergeben** ◇VERB (PRES **gibt her**, IMP **gab her**, PERF **hat hergegeben**) ❶ to hand over; **gib die Tasche her!** hand over the bag! ❷ to give away ❸ **sich für etwas hergeben** to get involved in something, **dazu gebe ich mich nicht her** I won't have anything to do with it

**Hering** der (PLURAL die **Heringe**) herring

**herkommen** ◇VERB (IMP **kam her**, PERF **ist hergekommen**) to come (here); **wo kommt das her?** where does it come from?

**Herkunft** die (PLURAL die **Herkünfte**) ❶ origin ❷ background

**Heroin** das heroin

**Herr** der (PLURAL die **Herren**) ❶ gentleman ❷ **Herr Huber** Mr Huber ❸ **Sehr geehrte Herren** Dear Sirs (in a letter) ❹ **meine Herren!** gentlemen! ❺ master ❻ **der Herr** the Lord

**herrichten** VERB (PERF **hat hergerichtet**) to get ready, to prepare; **sie richtet die Betten für die Gäste her** she's getting the beds for the guests ready

**herrlich** ADJECTIVE marvellous

**herrschen** VERB (PERF **hat geherrscht**) ❶ to rule ❷ to be; **es herrschte große Aufregung** there was great excitement

**herstellen** VERB (PERF **hat hergestellt**) to manufacture, to make; **in Deutschland hergestellt** made in Germany

**Herstellung** die *(PLURAL* die **Herstellungen)** manufacture, production

**herüber** *ADVERB* over (here)

**herum** *ADVERB* um ... herum round, falsch herum the wrong way round, im Kreis herum in a circle

**herumdrehen** *VERB (PERF* **hat herumgedreht)** ❶ to turn (over or round) ❷ sich herumdrehen to turn round

**herumführen** *VERB (PERF* **hat herumgeführt)** to show around

**herumgehen** ◇*VERB (IMP* **ging herum**, *PERF* **ist herumgegangen)** ❶ to go round ❷ to walk around; im Park herumgehen to walk around the park ❸ to pass *(of time)*

**herunter** *ADVERB* down; die Treppe herunter down the stairs

**herunterfallen** ◇*VERB (PRES* **fällt herunter**, *IMP* **fiel herunter**, *PERF* **ist heruntergefallen)** ❶ to fall down ❷ to fall off

**herunterkommen** ◇*VERB (IMP* **kam herunter**, *PERF* **ist heruntergekommen)** ❶ to come down ❷ *(informal)* to go to rack and ruin

**herunterladen** *VERB (PRES* **lädt herunter**, *IMPERF* **lud herunter**, *PERF* **hat heruntergeladen)** to download

**herunterlassen** ◇*VERB (PRES* **lässt herunter**, *IMP* **ließ herunter**, *PERF* **hat heruntergelassen)** to let down, to lower

**hervor** *ADVERB* out

**hervorragend** *ADJECTIVE* outstanding

**hervorragend** *ADVERB* outstandingly well

**hervorrufen** ◇*VERB (IMP* **rief hervor**, *PERF* **hat hervorgerufen)** to cause

**Herz** das *(PLURAL* die **Herzen)** ❶ heart ❷ hearts *(in cards)*

**Herzanfall** der *(PLURAL* die **Herzanfälle)** heart attack

**Herzinfarkt** der *(PLURAL* die **Herzinfarkte)** heart attack

**herzlich** *ADJECTIVE* ❶ warm ❷ sincere ❸ herzlichen Dank many thanks ❹ herzliche Grüße best wishes ❺ herzlichen Glückwunsch! congratulations! ❻ herzlich willkommen in Passau! welcome to Passau!

**herzlos** *ADJECTIVE* heartless

**Herzschlag** der *(PLURAL* die **Herzschläge)** ❶ heartbeat ❷ heart failure; er hat einen Herzschlag bekommen he had a heart attack

**heterosexuell** *ADJECTIVE* heterosexual

**Heterosexuelle** der/die *(PLURAL* die **Heterosexuellen)** heterosexual

**Heu** das hay

**heulen** *VERB (PERF* **hat geheult)** ❶ to howl ❷ *(informal)* to cry

**Heuschnupfen** der hayfever; ich habe Heuschnupfen I suffer from hayfever

**heute** *ADVERB* today; heute Abend this evening, heute Morgen this morning

**heutig** *ADJECTIVE* ❶ today's ❷ in der heutigen Zeit nowadays

**heutzutage** nowadays; heutzutage sind sie häufig they're common nowadays

**Hexe** die *(PLURAL* die **Hexen)** witch

**Hexenschuss** der **lumbago**

**hielt** ▸ SEE **halten**

**hier** *ADVERB* here

**hierher** *ADVERB* here; komm sofort hierher! come here immediately!

**hierhin** *ADVERB* here

**hieß** ▸ SEE **heißen**

**Hilfe** die *(PLURAL* die **Hilfen)** ❶ help ❷ aid

**hilflos** *ADJECTIVE* helpless

**hilfsbereit** *ADJECTIVE* helpful

**hilft** ▸ SEE **helfen**

**Himbeere** die *(PLURAL* die **Himbeeren)** raspberry

**Himmel** der *(PLURAL* die **Himmel)** ❶ sky ❷ heaven

**himmlisch** *ADJECTIVE* heavenly

**hin** *ADVERB* ❶ there; hin und zurück there and back ❷ hin und wieder now and again ❸ hin und her back and forth, to and fro ❹ auf meinen Rat hin on my advice, auf Ihren Brief hin in reply to your letter ❺ wo ist Dominik hin? where's Dominik gone? ❻ es ist nicht mehr lange hin it's not long to go ❼ ich bin hin *(informal)* I'm worn out

**hinauf** *ADVERB* up; die Straße hinauf up the road

**hinaufgehen** ◇*VERB (IMP* ging hinauf, *PERF* ist hinaufgegangen) to go up

**hinaus** *ADVERB* ❶ out ❷ auf Jahre hinaus for years to come

**hinausbringen** ◇*VERB (IMP* brachte hinaus, *PERF* hat hinausgebracht) ❶ to see out *(a person)* ❷ to take out; den Abfall hinausbringen to take the rubbish out

**hinausgehen** ◇*VERB (IMP* ging hinaus, *PERF* ist hinausgegangen) ❶ to go out ❷ über etwas hinausgehen to exceed something ❸ das Zimmer geht nach Norden hinaus the room faces north

**hindern** *VERB (PERF* hat gehindert) to stop; jemanden daran hindern, etwas zu tun to stop somebody from doing something

**Hindernis** das *(PLURAL* die **Hindernisse)** obstacle

**hinduistisch** *ADJECTIVE* Hindu

**hindurch** *ADVERB* ❶ through it/ them ❷ das ganze Jahr hindurch throughout the year

**hinein** *ADVERB* ❶ in ❷ in etwas hinein into something

**hineingehen** ◇*VERB (IMP* ging hinein, *PERF* ist hineingegangen) ❶ to go in ❷ in etwas hineingehen to go into something

**hinfahren** ◇*VERB (PRES* fährt hin, *IMP* fuhr hin, *PERF* ist hingefahren) ❶ to go/drive there ❷ *(PERF* hat hingefahren) to take/drive there

**Hinfahrt** die *(PLURAL* die **Hinfahrten)** ❶ journey there, way there ❷ outward journey

**hinfallen** ◇*VERB (PRES* fällt hin, *IMP* fiel hin, *PERF* ist hingefallen) to fall over

**hing** ▸ SEE **hängen**

**hingehen** ◇*VERB (IMP* ging hin, *PERF* ist hingegangen) ❶ to go there;

wo geht ihr hin? where are you going? **❷ to go by** (of time)

**hinken** VERB (PERF **hat/ist gehinkt**) to limp

**hinkommen** ◇VERB (IMP **kam hin**, PERF **ist hingekommen**) **❶ to get there ❷ to go**; wo kommt das Buch hin? where does the book go? **❸ mit etwas hinkommen** (informal) to manage (with something)

**hinlegen** VERB (PERF **hat hingelegt**) **❶ to put down**; leg die Zeitung unten hin put the paper down there **❷ sich hinlegen** to lie down

**hinsetzen** VERB (PERF **hat sich hingesetzt**) sich hinsetzen to sit down, Petra setzte sich neben ihm hin Petra sat down next to him

**hinten** ADVERB **at the back**; von hinten from behind

**hinter** PREPOSITION **❶** (+DAT or +ACC) **behind ❷** etwas hinter sich bringen to get something over with

**hintere** ▸ SEE **hinterer**

**hintereinander** ADVERB **❶ one behind the other ❷ one after the other**; dreimal hintereinander three times in a row

**hinterer, hintere, hinteres** ADJECTIVE **❶ back ❷** am hinteren Ende at the far end

**Hintergrund** der (PLURAL die **Hintergründe**) **background**

**hinterher** ADVERB **afterwards**

**Hintern** der (PLURAL die **Hintern**) **bottom**

**Hinterrad** das (PLURAL die **Hinterräder**) **back wheel**

**hinters** hinter das ▸ SEE **hinter**

**hinüber** ADVERB **❶ over (there), across (there) ❷** das Radio ist hinüber (informal) the radio has had it

**hinübergehen** ◇VERB (IMP **ging hinüber**, PERF **ist hinübergegangen**) **to go over, to go across**

**hinunter** ADVERB **down**

**Hinweg** der (PLURAL die **Hinwege**) **way there**; auf dem Hinweg on the way there

**Hinweis** der (PLURAL die **Hinweise**) **❶ hint**; das war ein deutlicher Hinweis, dass er lieber allein fährt it was an obvious hint that he prefers to go on his own **❷ reference ❸** Hinweise zur Bedienung operating instructions

**hinweisen** ◇VERB (IMP **wies hin**, PERF **hat hingewiesen**) **to point**; jemanden auf etwas hinweisen to point something out to somebody

**Hirn** das (PLURAL die **Hirne**) **brain**

**Hirnhautentzündung** die **meningitis**

**Hirsch** der (PLURAL die **Hirsche**) **❶ deer ❷ stag ❸ venison**

**Hirt** der (PLURAL die **Hirten**) **shepherd**

**Hirtin** die (PLURAL die **Hirtinnen**) **shepherd**

**Historiker** der (PLURAL die **Historiker**) **historian**

**historisch** ADJECTIVE **historical**

**Hitze** die **heat**

**hitzefrei** ADJECTIVE hitzefrei haben to be sent home early from school because of hot weather

**Hitzewelle** die (PLURAL die **Hitzewellen**) **heatwave**

a
b
c
d
e
f
g
h
i
j
k
l
m
n
o
p
q
r
s
t
u
v
w
x
y
z

**Hitzschlag** der *(PLURAL die Hitzschläge)* heatstroke

**hob** ▸SEE **heben**

**Hobby** das *(PLURAL die Hobbys)* hobby

**hoch** *ADJECTIVE (with endings) ('hoch' becomes 'hoher/hohe/hohes')* ❶ high; der Zaun ist zu hoch the fence is too high, ein hoher Zaun a high fence ❷ deep *(snow)* ❸ great *(age, weight)*

**hoch** *ADVERB* ❶ highly; hoch begabt highly gifted ❷ die Treppe hoch up the stairs

**Hoch** das *(PLURAL die Hochs)* ❶ cheer; ein dreifaches Hoch für das Geburtstagskind three cheers for the birthday girl/boy ❷ high *(pressure)*

**hochachtungsvoll** *ADVERB* Hochachtungsvoll Yours faithfully

**hochhackig** *ADJECTIVE* high-heeled; hochhackige Schuhe high-heeled shoes

**Hochhaus** das *(PLURAL die Hochhäuser)* high-rise building

**hochheben** ◇*VERB (IMP hob hoch, PERF hat hochgehoben)* to lift up; sie hob das Kind hoch she lifted up the child

**hochladen** *VERB (PRES lädt hoch, IMPERF lud hoch, PERF hat hochgeladen)* to upload

**hochnäsig** *ADJECTIVE* stuck-up

**Hochschule** die *(PLURAL die Hochschulen)* university, college

**Hochsprung** der high jump

**höchst** *ADVERB* extremely

**höchstens** *ADVERB* ❶ at most ❷ except perhaps

**höchster, höchste, höchstes** *ADJECTIVE* highest; der Mount Everest ist der der höchste Berg der Welt Mount Everest is the highest mountain in the world, es ist höchste Zeit it is high time

**Höchstgeschwindigkeit** die maximum speed

**höchstmöglich** *ADJECTIVE* highest possible; die höchstmögliche Geschwindigkeit the highest possible speed

**Höchsttemperatur** die *(PLURAL die Höchsttemperaturen)* maximum temperature

**Hochzeit** die *(PLURAL die Hochzeiten)* wedding

**Hochzeitstag** der *(PLURAL die Hochzeitstage)* ❶ wedding day ❷ wedding anniversary

**Hocker** der *(PLURAL die Hocker)* stool

**Hockey** das hockey

**Hockeyschläger** der *(PLURAL die Hockeyschläger)* hockey stick

**Hof** der *(PLURAL die Höfe)* ❶ yard ❷ farm

**hoffen** *VERB (PERF hat gehofft)* to hope; auf etwas hoffen to hope for something

**hoffentlich** *ADVERB* hopefully; hoffentlich nicht I hope not

**Hoffnung** die *(PLURAL die Hoffnungen)* hope

**hoffnungslos** *ADJECTIVE* hopeless

**höflich** *ADJECTIVE* polite

**Höflichkeit** die *(PLURAL die Höflichkeiten)* politeness, courtesy

**Höhe** die *(PLURAL* die **Höhen)**
❶ height ❷ das ist die Höhe!
*(informal)* that's the limit!

**hoher, hohe, hohes** ▸ SEE **hoch**

**höher** *ADJECTIVE* ❶ higher ❷ deeper

**hohl** *ADJECTIVE* hollow

**Höhle** die *(PLURAL* die **Höhlen)** ❶ cave
❷ den

**holen** *VERB (PERF* hat geholt) ❶ to
get, to fetch ❷ jemanden holen
lassen to send for somebody ❸ sich
etwas holen to get something

**Holland** das Holland

**Holländer** der *(PLURAL* die **Holländer)**
Dutchman

**Holländerin** die *(PLURAL* die
**Holländerinnen)** Dutchwoman

**holländisch** *ADJECTIVE* Dutch

**Hölle** die *(PLURAL* die **Höllen)** hell

**Holz** das *(PLURAL* die **Hölzer)** wood

**Holzkohle** die charcoal

**homöopathisch** *ADJECTIVE*
homeopathic

**homosexuell** *ADJECTIVE* homosexual

**Homosexuelle** der/die *(PLURAL* die
**Homosexuellen)** homosexual

**Honig** der *(PLURAL* die **Honige)** honey

**horchen** *VERB (PERF* hat gehorcht)
❶ to listen ❷ to eavesdrop

**hören** *VERB (PERF* hat gehört) ❶ to
hear ❷ to listen (to); Musik hören
to listen to music

**Hörer** der *(PLURAL* die **Hörer)**
❶ listener ❷ receiver *(of a phone)*

**Hörerin** die *(PLURAL* die **Hörerinnen)**
listener

**Hörgerät** das *(PLURAL* die **Hörgeräte)**
hearing aid

**Horizont** der *(PLURAL* die **Horizonte)**
horizon

**horizontal** *ADJECTIVE* horizontal

**Horn** das *(PLURAL* die **Hörner)** horn

**Horoskop** das *(PLURAL* die
**Horoskope)** horoscope

**Horrorfilm** der *(PLURAL* die
**Horrorfilme)** horror film

**Hose** die *(PLURAL* die **Hosen)** trousers

**Hosenträger** *PLURAL NOUN* braces

**Hotdog** das or der *(PLURAL* die
**Hotdogs)** hot dog

**Hotel** das *(PLURAL* die **Hotels)** hotel

**Hotelverzeichnis** das *(PLURAL* die
**Hotelverzeichnisse)** list of hotels

**hübsch** *ADJECTIVE* ❶ pretty ❷ nice

**Hubschrauber** der *(PLURAL* die
**Hubschrauber)** helicopter

**Huf** der *(PLURAL* die **Hufe)** hoof

**Hufeisen** das *(PLURAL* die **Hufeisen)**
horseshoe

**Hüfte** die *(PLURAL* die **Hüften)** hip

**Hügel** der *(PLURAL* die **Hügel)** hill

**Huhn** das *(PLURAL* die **Hühner)**
❶ chicken ❷ hen

**Hummel** die *(PLURAL* die **Hummeln)**
bumble-bee

**Hummer** der *(PLURAL* die **Hummer)**
lobster

**Humor** der humour; Humor haben
to have a sense of humour

**Hund** der *(PLURAL* die **Hunde)** dog;
den Hund ausführen to take the
dog for a walk

**Hundehütte** die *(PLURAL* die
**Hundehütten)** kennel

a
b
c
d
e
f
g
h
i
j
k
l
m
n
o
p
q
r
s
t
u
v
w
x
y
z

**hundemüde** *ADJECTIVE (informal)*
dog-tired

**Hundepension** die *(PLURAL die*
**Hundepensionen)** kennels *(for*
*boarding)*

**hundert** *NUMBER* a hundred, one
hundred

**Hunger** der hunger; Hunger haben
to be hungry

**hungrig** *ADJECTIVE* hungry

**Hupe** die *(PLURAL die Hupen)* horn

**hurra** *EXCLAMATION* hooray!

**husten** *VERB (PERF hat gehustet)*
to cough

**Husten** der cough

**Hut** der *(PLURAL die Hüte)* hat

**hüten** *VERB (PERF hat gehütet)* ❶ to
look after *(a child, children)* ❷ sich
hüten to be on your guard ❸ sich
hüten, etwas zu tun to take care
not to do something

**Hütte** die *(PLURAL die Hütten)* hut

**Hygiene** die ❶ hygiene ❷ health
care

**hygienisch** *ADJECTIVE* hygienic

**hypnotisieren** *VERB (PERF hat*
*hypnotisiert)* to hypnotize

**Hypothek** die *(PLURAL die*
**Hypotheken)** mortgage

**hysterisch** *ADJECTIVE* hysterical

**ich** *PRONOUN* I

**Icon** das *(PLURAL die Icons)* icon; das
Icon anklicken to click the icon

**IC-Zug** der *(PLURAL die IC-Züge) (short*
*for Intercityzug)* intercity train

**ideal** *ADJECTIVE* ideal

**Idee** die *(PLURAL die Ideen)* idea

**identifizieren** *VERB (PERF hat*
*identifiziert)* to identify

**identisch** *ADJECTIVE* identical

**Idiot** der *(PLURAL die Idioten)* idiot

**idiotisch** *ADJECTIVE* idiotic

**idyllisch** *ADJECTIVE* idyllic

**Igel** der *(PLURAL die Igel)* hedgehog

**ihm** *PRONOUN* ❶ him, to him ❷ it,
to it

**ihn** *PRONOUN* ❶ him ❷ it

**ihnen** *PRONOUN* them, to them

**ihr** *PRONOUN* ❶ you *(plural)* ❷ her,
to her ❸ *(standing for an object)*
it, to it

**ihr** *ADJECTIVE* ❶ her ❷ its ❸ their; sie
haben ihr Auto verkauft they sold
their car

**Ihr** *ADJECTIVE* your; Ihr Sohn hat mir
geschrieben your son wrote to me

**ihrer, ihre, ihr(e)s** *PRONOUN* ❶ hers;
mein Rad ist rot, ihrs ist blau my

bike is red, hers is blue **❷ theirs**; das ist nicht ihre Katze, ihre ist schwarz that's not their cat, theirs is black

**Ihrer, Ihre, Ihr(e)s** *PRONOUN* **yours**; mein Job ist nicht so interessant wie Ihrer my job's not as interesting as yours

**ihretwegen** *ADVERB* **❶ for her sake ❷ for their sake ❸ because of her ❹ because of them**

**Ihretwegen** *ADVERB* **❶ for your sake ❷ because of you**

**Illusion** die *(PLURAL* die **Illusionen)** **illusion**

**Illustration** die *(PLURAL* die **Illustrationen)** **illustration**

**Illustrierte** die *(PLURAL* die **Illustrierten)** **magazine**

**im** in dem; was läuft im Kino? what's on at the cinema?, im August in August

**Imbiss** der *(PLURAL* die **Imbisse)** **❶ snack ❷ snack bar**

**Imbissstube** die *(PLURAL* die **Imbissstuben)** **snack bar**

**Imitator** der *(PLURAL* die **Imitatoren)** **mimic, impressionist**

**imitieren** *VERB (PERF* hat **imitiert)** **to imitate**

**immer** *ADVERB* **❶ always ❷ immer wieder again and again ❸ immer mehr more and more**, immer dunkler darker and darker **❹ immer noch still ❺ immer, wenn er anruft every time he rings ❻ wo/wer/ wann immer wherever/whoever/ whenever ❼ für immer for ever**

**immerhin** *ADVERB* **at least**

**immerzu** *ADVERB* **all the time**

**Imperfekt** das **imperfect**; 'ich schlug' steht im Imperfekt 'ich schlug' is in the imperfect

**Impfausweis** der *(PLURAL* die **Impfausweise)** **vaccination certificate**

**impfen** *VERB (PERF* hat **geimpft)** **to vaccinate**

**Impfung** die *(PLURAL* die **Impfungen)** **vaccination**

**imponieren** *VERB (PERF* hat **imponiert)** **to impress**; jemandem imponieren to impress somebody

**Import** der *(PLURAL* die **Importe)** **import**

**Importeur** der *(PLURAL* die **Importeure)** **importer**

**importieren** *VERB (PERF* hat **importiert)** **to import**

**imprägniert** *ADJECTIVE* **waterproof**

**imstande** *ADVERB* imstande sein, etwas zu tun to be able to do something, er ist nicht imstande, seine Hausaufgaben allein zu machen he's not able to do his homework on his own

**in** *PREPOSITION (+DAT or +ACC)* **❶** *(the dative is used when talking about position; the accusative shows movement towards something)* **in**; es ist in der Küche it's in the kitchen **❷ into**; ich habe es in meine Tasche gesteckt I've put it in my bag **❸** in die Schule gehen to go to school **❹** Susi ist in der Schule Susi is at school **❺** in diesem Jahr this year **❻** in sein to be in, Rap ist in rap is in

A
B
C
D
E
F
G
H
I
J
K
L
M
N
O
P
Q
R
S
T
U
V
W
X
Y
Z

**inbegriffen** *ADJECTIVE* **included**;
Essen ist inbegriffen food is
included

**indem** *CONJUNCTION* ❶ **while** ❷ **by**

**Inder** der *(PLURAL die Inder)* **Indian**

**Inderin** die *(PLURAL die Inderinnen)*
**Indian**

**Indianer** der *(PLURAL die Indianer)*
**(American) Indian, native
American**

**Indianerin** die *(PLURAL die
Indianerinnen)* **(American)
Indian, native American**

**indianisch** *ADJECTIVE* **(American)
Indian, native American**

**Indien** das **India**

**indisch** *ADJECTIVE* **Indian**

**indiskutabel** *ADJECTIVE* **out of the
question**

**individuell** *ADJECTIVE* **individual**

**Individuum** das *(PLURAL die
Individuen)* **individual**

**Industrie** die *(PLURAL die Industrien)*
**industry**

**industriell** *ADJECTIVE* **industrial**

**Infektion** die *(PLURAL die
Infektionen)* **infection**

**Infinitiv** der *(PLURAL die Infinitive)*
**infinitive**

**infizieren** *VERB (PERF hat infiziert)*
❶ **to infect** ❷ sich bei jemandem
infizieren **to be infected by
somebody**

**Inflation** die *(PLURAL die Inflationen)*
**inflation**

**infolge** *PREPOSITION (+GEN)* **as a result
of**

**infolgedessen** *ADVERB*
**consequently**

**Informatik** die **computer science**

**Informatiker** der *(PLURAL die
Informatiker)* **computer scientist**

**Informatikerin** die *(PLURAL die
Informatikerinnen)* **computer
scientist**

**Information** die *(PLURAL die
Informationen)* **(piece of)
information**

**Informationsbüro** das *(PLURAL die
Informationsbüros)* **(tourist)
information office**

**informieren** *VERB (PERF hat
informiert)* ❶ **to inform**
❷ informiert sein **to be aware**, da
bist du falsch informiert **you've
been wrongly informed** ❸ sich
über etwas informieren **to find out
about something**, ich habe mich
darüber genau informieren lassen
**I found out all about it**

**Ingenieur** der *(PLURAL die
Ingenieure)* **engineer**

**Ingenieurin** die *(PLURAL die
Ingenieurinnen)* **engineer**

**Ingwer** der **ginger**

**Inhaber** der *(PLURAL die Inhaber)*
❶ **owner** *(of a shop)* ❷ **holder**
*(of an office)*

**Inhaberin** die *(PLURAL die
Inhaberinnen)* ❶ **owner** *(of a shop)*
❷ **holder** *(of a position)*

**Inhalt** der *(PLURAL die Inhalte)*
❶ **contents**; den Inhalt der Dose
mit etwas Wasser verdünnen **dilute
the contents of the tin with a little
water** ❷ **content** *(of a story, film)*; er
hat den Inhalt der Geschichte kurz

für uns zusammengefasst he gave us a quick summary of the content of the story ❸ **volume** ❹ **area** *(of a rectangle, circle, etc.)*

**Initiative** die *(PLURAL die* **Initiativen)** **initiative**; die Initiative ergreifen to take the initiative

**inklusive** *PREPOSITION (+GEN)* **including**

**inklusive** *ADVERB* **inclusive**

**innen** *ADVERB* **inside**; nach innen inwards

**Innenstadt** die *(PLURAL die* **Innenstädte)** **town centre, city centre**

**Innere** das ❶ **interior** ❷ **inside**

**innerer, innere, inneres** *ADJECTIVE* ❶ **inner** ❷ **inside** ❸ **internal** *(injuries)*

**innerhalb** *PREPOSITION (+GEN)* ❶ **within** ❷ **during**

**innerhalb** *ADVERB* innerhalb von **within**

**innerlich** *ADJECTIVE* ❶ **internal** ❷ **inner**

**innerlich** *ADVERB* ❶ **internally** ❷ **inwardly**

**ins** in das; ins Theater gehen to go to the theatre

**Insekt** das *(PLURAL die* **Insekten)** **insect**

**Insel** die *(PLURAL die* **Inseln)** **island**

**Inserat** das *(PLURAL die* **Inserate)** **advertisement**

**inserieren** *VERB (PERF* hat inseriert) **to advertise**

**insgesamt** *ADVERB* **in all**

**Instinkt** der *(PLURAL die* **Instinkte)** **instinct**

**instinktiv** *ADJECTIVE* **instinctive**

**Instrument** das *(PLURAL die* **Instrumente)** **instrument**; ein Instrument spielen to play an instrument

**intelligent** *ADJECTIVE* **intelligent**

**Intelligenz** die **intelligence**

**Intensivpflege** die **intensive care**

**Intensivstation** die *(PLURAL die* **Intensivstationen)** **intensive care unit**

**Intercityzug** der *(PLURAL die* **Intercityzüge)** **intercity train**

**interessant** *ADJECTIVE* **interesting**

**Interesse** das *(PLURAL die* **Interessen)** **interest**; Interesse für jemanden/ etwas haben to be interested in somebody/something

**interessieren** *VERB (PERF* **hat interessiert)** ❶ **to interest** ❷ sich für etwas interessieren to be interested in something

**Internat** das *(PLURAL die* **Internate)** **boarding school**

**international** *ADJECTIVE* **international**

**Internet** das **Internet**

**Interview** das *(PLURAL die* **Interviews)** **interview**

**inzwischen** *ADVERB* **in the meantime, meanwhile**

**Irak** der **Iraq**

**Iran** der **Iran**

**Ire** der *(PLURAL die* **Iren)** **Irishman**; die Iren the Irish

a
b
c
d
e
f
g
h
i
j
k
l
m
n
o
p
q
r
s
t
u
v
w
x
y
z

**irgend** *ADVERB* ❶ **at all**; wenn irgend möglich if at all possible, wenn du irgend kannst if you could possibly manage it ❷ irgend so ein Idiot some such idiot

**irgendein** *ADJECTIVE* ❶ **some** ❷ **any** ❸ irgendein anderer someone else, anyone else

**irgendeiner, irgendeine, irgendein(e)s** *PRONOUN* ❶ **any one**; 'welche möchten Sie?' – 'irgendeine' 'which one would you like?' – 'any one' ❷ **somebody, someone** ❸ **anybody, anyone**; hat irgendeiner angerufen? has anybody phoned?

**irgendetwas** *PRONOUN* ❶ **something** ❷ **anything**

**irgendjemand** *PRONOUN* ❶ **somebody** ❷ **anybody, anyone**

**irgendwann** *ADVERB* ❶ **some time, at some time** ❷ **any time, at any time**

**irgendwas** *(informal)* ▸ SEE **irgendetwas**

**irgendwie** *ADVERB* **somehow**

**irgendwo** *ADVERB* ❶ **somewhere** ❷ **anywhere**

**Irin** die *(PLURAL* die **Irinnen)** **Irishwoman**

**irisch** *ADJECTIVE* **Irish**

**Irisch** das **Irish** *(language)*

**Irland** das **Ireland**

**ironisch** *ADJECTIVE* **ironic**

**irre** *ADJECTIVE* ❶ **mad** ❷ *(informal)* **incredible, fantastic** *(party, song)*

**irre** *ADVERB* irre gut incredibly good

**irren** *VERB (PERF* **ist geirrt)** ❶ **to wander (about)** *(when lost)* ❷ *(PERF* **hat sich geirrt)** sich irren to be mistaken, to be wrong

**irrsinnig** *ADJECTIVE* ❶ **mad** ❷ *(informal)* **incredible**

**Irrtum** der *(PLURAL* die **Irrtümer)** **mistake**

**Islam** der **Islam**

**Israel** das **Israel**

**isst** ▸ SEE **essen**

**ist** ▸ SEE **sein**

**Italien** das **Italy**

**Italiener** der *(PLURAL* die **Italiener)** **Italian**

**Italienerin** die *(PLURAL* die **Italienerinnen)** **Italian**

**italienisch** *ADJECTIVE* **Italian**

**ja** *ADVERB* **❶** yes **❷** ich glaube ja I think so **❸** du kommst doch, ja? you'll come, won't you?, es passt doch, ja? it fits, doesn't it? **❹** sag's ihm ja nicht! don't (you dare) tell him, whatever you do!, seid ja vorsichtig! do be careful! **❺** es ist ja noch früh it's still early, ich kann ihn ja mal fragen, ob er mitkommen will I could always ask him if he wants to come

**Jacht** die *(PLURAL* die **Jachten)** yacht

**Jacke** die *(PLURAL* die **Jacken)** **❶** jacket **❷** cardigan

**Jackett** das *(PLURAL* die **Jacketts)** jacket

**Jagd** die *(PLURAL* die **Jagden)** **❶** hunt **❷** hunting

**jagen** *VERB (PERF* hat gejagt) **❶** to hunt **❷** to chase; drei Polizisten jagten den Einbrecher, aber er hängte sie schnell ab three policemen chased the burglar, but he soon shook them off, meine Mutter hat mich aus dem Bett gejagt *(informal)* my mother chased me out of bed **❸** jemanden aus dem Haus jagen to throw somebody out of the house **❹** damit kannst du mich jagen *(informal)* I can't stand that

**Jäger** der *(PLURAL* die **Jäger)** **❶** hunter **❷** fighter *(aircraft)*

**jäh** *ADJECTIVE* **sudden**

**Jahr** das *(PLURAL* die **Jahre)** **❶** year; in den sechzigen Jahren in the sixties, Kinder bis zu zwölf Jahren children up to the age of twelve **❷** ein freiwilliges soziales Jahr (FSJ) gap year *(during which socially useful work is done for subsistence payment)*

**jahrelang** *ADVERB* for years

**Jahrestag** der *(PLURAL* die **Jahrestage)** anniversary

**Jahrestag** *(PLURAL* die **Jahrestage)** anniversary

**Jahreszeit** die *(PLURAL* die **Jahreszeiten)** season

**Jahrgang** der *(PLURAL* die **Jahrgänge)** **❶** year **❷** vintage

**Jahrhundert** das *(PLURAL* die **Jahrhunderte)** century

**-jährig** *ADJECTIVE* eine dreißigjährige Frau a woman aged thirty, eine zweijährige Verspätung a two-year delay

**jährlich** *ADJECTIVE, ADVERB* yearly; zweimal jährlich twice a year

**Jahrmarkt** der *(PLURAL* die **Jahrmärkte)** fair

**Jahrtausend** das *(PLURAL* die **Jahrtausende)** millennium

**Jahrzehnt** das *(PLURAL* die **Jahrzehnte)** decade

**jähzornig** *ADJECTIVE* hot-tempered

**jammern** *VERB (PERF* hat gejammert) to moan

**Januar** der January

**Japan** das Japan

a b c d e f g h i j k l m n o p q r s t u v w x y z

**Japaner** der *(PLURAL* die **Japaner)** Japanese

**Japanerin** die *(PLURAL* die **Japanerinnen)** Japanese

**japanisch** *ADJECTIVE* Japanese

**jawohl** *ADVERB* **❶** yes **❷** certainly

**je** *ADVERB* **❶** ever; besser denn je better than ever **❷** each; sie kosten je zwanzig Euro they are twenty euros each **❸** seit eh und je always **❹** je nach depending on

**je** *PREPOSITION (+ACC)* **per**

**je** *CONJUNCTION* **❶** je mehr, desto besser the more the better **❷** je nachdem it depends

**Jeans** *PLURAL NOUN* **jeans**

**jede ▸** SEE **jeder**

**jedenfalls** *ADVERB* in any case

**jeder, jede, jedes** *ADJECTIVE* **❶** every; jedes Mal every time **❷** each **❸** any; ohne jeden Grund without any reason

**jedes** *PRONOUN* **❶** everybody, everyone **❷** each one **❸** anybody, anyone; das kann jeder anybody can do that

**jedermann** *PRONOUN* everybody, everyone

**jederzeit** *ADVERB* at any time

**jedes ▸** SEE **jeder**

**jedesmal ▸** SEE **jeder**

**jedoch** *ADVERB* however

**jemals** *ADVERB* ever

**jemand** *PRONOUN* **❶** somebody, someone; jemand hat das für dich abgegeben sombody left this for you **❷** anybody, anyone; hat jemand angerufen? did anybody call?

**jener, jene, jenes** *ADJECTIVE* **❶** (used in elevated language and in literature) **that ❷** those (plural)

**jenes** *PRONOUN* **❶** that one **❷** those (plural)

**jenseits** *PREPOSITION (+GEN)* **(on) the other side of**

**Jetlag** der jet lag

**jetzt** *ADVERB* now

**Job** der *(PLURAL* die **Jobs)** job

**jobben** *VERB* (informal) (PERF **hat gejobbt)** to work

**joggen** *VERB* (PERF **ist gejoggt)** to jog

**Jogginganzug** der *(PLURAL* die **Jogginganzüge)** tracksuit

**Joghurt** der *(PLURAL* die **Joghurt(s))** yoghurt

**Johannisbeere** die *(PLURAL* die **Johannisbeeren)** **❶** rote Johannisbeeren redcurrants **❷** schwarze Johannisbeeren blackcurrants

**Journalist** der *(PLURAL* die **Journalisten)** journalist

**Journalistin** die *(PLURAL* die **Journalistinnen)** journalist

**Joystick** der *(PLURAL* die **Joysticks)** joystick (for computer games)

**jubeln** *VERB* (PERF **hat gejubelt)** **❶** to cheer **❷** Beifall jubeln to applaud

**Jubiläum** das *(PLURAL* die **Jubiläen)** **❶** anniversary **❷** jubilee

**Jude** der *(PLURAL* die **Juden)** Jew

**Judentum** das Judaism

**Jüdin** die *(PLURAL* die **Jüdinnen)** Jew

**jüdisch** *ADJECTIVE* **Jewish**

**Jugend** die **youth**

**Jugendherberge** die *(PLURAL* die **Jugendherbergen)** **youth hostel**

**Jugendklub** der *(PLURAL* die **Jugendklubs)** **youth club**

**Jugendliche** der/die *(PLURAL* die **Jugendlichen)** ❶ **young man/ woman** ❷ die **Jugendlichen youth, young people**

**Jugendzentrum** das *(PLURAL* die **Jugendzentren)** **youth centre**

**Jugoslawien** das **Yugoslavia**

**jugoslawisch** *ADJECTIVE* **Yugoslavian**

**Juli** der **July**

**jung** *ADJECTIVE* ❶ **young** ❷ **Jung und Alt young and old**

**Junge**¹ der *(PLURAL* die **Jungen)** **boy**

**Junge**² das *(PLURAL* die **Jungen)** **young (animal)**

**Jungfrau** die *(PLURAL* die **Jungfrauen)** ❶ **virgin** ❷ **Virgo**

**jüngster, jüngste, jüngstes** *ADJECTIVE* ❶ **youngest** ❷ **latest** *(news, developments)* ❸ **in jüngster Zeit recently**

**Juni** der **June**

**Jury** die *(PLURAL* die **Jurys)** ❶ **jury** ❷ **judges** *(in sport)*

**Juwelier** der *(PLURAL* die **Juweliere)** **jeweller**

**Jux** der *(informal)* **laugh; aus Jux for a laugh**

# Kk

**Kabel** das *(PLURAL* die **Kabel)** ❶ **cable** ❷ **wire**

**Kabelfernsehen** das **cable television**

**Kabeljau** der *(PLURAL* die **Kabeljaus)** **cod**

**Kabine** die *(PLURAL* die **Kabinen)** ❶ **cabin** ❷ **cubicle** *(for changing)* ❸ **car** *(of a cable car)*

**Kachel** die *(PLURAL* die **Kacheln)** **tile**

**Käfer** der *(PLURAL* die **Käfer)** **beetle**

**Kaffee** der *(PLURAL* die **Kaffee(s))** **coffee; zwei Kaffee mit Milch bitte two white coffees please**

**Kaffeekanne** die *(PLURAL* die **Kaffeekannen)** **coffee-pot**

**Käfig** der *(PLURAL* die **Käfige)** **cage**

**kahl** *ADJECTIVE* ❶ **bald** *(head)* ❷ **bare** *(tree, walls)*

**Kahn** der *(PLURAL* die **Kähne)** ❶ **barge** ❷ **rowing boat**

**Kaiser** der *(PLURAL* die **Kaiser)** **emperor**

**Kaiserin** die *(PLURAL* die **Kaiserinnen)** **empress**

**Kakao** der *(PLURAL* die **Kakao(s))** **cocoa; zwei Kakao bitte two cups of cocoa please**

**Kakerlak** der *(PLURAL* die **Kakerlaken)** **cockroach**

a
b
c
d
e
f
g
h
i
j
k
l
m
n
o
p
q
r
s
t
u
v
w
x
y
z

**Kaktus** der *(PLURAL* die **Kakteen)**
cactus

**Kalb** das *(PLURAL* die **Kälber) ❶** calf
**❷** veal

**Kalbfleisch** das veal

**Kalender** der *(PLURAL* die **Kalender)**
**❶** calendar **❷** diary

**Kalk** der **❶** lime **❷** limescale
**❸** calcium

**Kalorie** die *(PLURAL* die **Kalorien)**
calorie

**kalorienarm** *ADJECTIVE* **low-calorie,**
low in calories

**kalorienreich** *ADJECTIVE* **high-**
calorie, rich in calories

**kalt** *ADJECTIVE* **cold;** ist dir kalt? are
you cold?, stell die Heizung an, den
Kindern ist kalt put on the heating,
the children are cold, abends essen
wir kalt we have a cold meal in the
evening, den Wein kalt stellen to
chill the wine

**Kälte** die **❶** cold **❷** coldness **❸** fünf
Grad Kälte five degrees below zero

**kam** ▸ SEE **kommen**

**Kamel** das *(PLURAL* die **Kamele)** camel

**Kamera** die *(PLURAL* die **Kameras)**
camera

**Kamerad** der *(PLURAL* die
**Kameraden)** friend

**Kameradin** die *(PLURAL* die
**Kameradinnen)** friend

**Kameramann** der *(PLURAL* die
**Kameramänner)** cameraman

**Kamin** der *(PLURAL* die **Kamine)**
fireplace; wir saßen am Kamin we
sat by the fire

**Kamm** der *(PLURAL* die **Kämme)**
**❶** comb **❷** ridge *(of a mountain)*

**kämmen** *VERB (PERF* **hat gekämmt)**
**❶** to comb **❷** sich kämmen to
comb your hair

**Kammer** die *(PLURAL* die **Kammern)**
**❶** store room **❷** chamber

**Kampagne** die *(PLURAL* die
**Kampagnen)** campaign

**Kampf** der *(PLURAL* die **Kämpfe)**
**❶** fight **❷** contest **❸** struggle

**kämpfen** *VERB (PERF* **hat gekämpft)**
to fight

**Kanada** das Canada

**Kanadier** der *(PLURAL* die **Kanadier)**
Canadian

**Kanadierin** die *(PLURAL* die
**Kanadierinnen)** Canadian

**kanadisch** *ADJECTIVE* **Canadian**

**Kanal** der *(PLURAL* die **Kanäle)**
**❶** canal **❷** channel *(radio, TV)*
**❸** der Kanal the (English) Channel
**❹** sewer, drain

**Kanalinseln** *PLURAL NOUN* Channel
Islands

**Kanalisation** die sewers, drains

**Kanaltunnel** der Channel Tunnel

**Kanarienvogel** der *(PLURAL* die
**Kanarienvögel)** canary

**Kandidat** der *(PLURAL* die
**Kandidaten)** candidate

**Kandidatin** die *(PLURAL* die
**Kandidatinnen)** candidate

**Känguru** das *(PLURAL* die **Kängurus)**
kangaroo

**Kaninchen** das *(PLURAL* die
**Kaninchen)** rabbit

**kann** ▸ SEE **können**

**Kännchen** das *(PLURAL* die

**Kännchen)** ❶ pot; ein Kännchen Kaffee bitte a pot of coffee please ❷ jug (of milk)

**Kanne** die (PLURAL die **Kannen**) ❶ pot (for coffee, tea) ❷ jug (for water) ❸ can (for oil) ❹ churn (for milk) ❺ watering can

**kannst** ▸ SEE **können**

**kannte** ▸ SEE **kennen**

**Kante** die (PLURAL die **Kanten**) edge

**Kantine** die (PLURAL die **Kantinen**) canteen; wir essen immer in der Kantine zu Mittag we always have lunch in the canteen

**Kanu** das (PLURAL die **Kanus**) canoe; Kanu fahren to go canoeing

**Kapelle** die (PLURAL die **Kapellen**) ❶ chapel ❷ (brass) band

**kapieren** VERB (informal) (PERF hat kapiert) to understand; er hat es mir schon dreimal erklärt, aber ich kapier es einfach nicht he's already explained it to me three times, but I still don't get it

**Kapital** das capital

**Kapitalismus** der capitalism

**Kapitän** der (PLURAL die **Kapitäne**) captain

**Kapitel** das (PLURAL die **Kapitel**) chapter

**Kappe** die (PLURAL die **Kappen**) cap

**kaputt** ADJECTIVE ❶ broken ❷ an meinem Computer ist etwas kaputt there's something wrong with my computer ❸ ich bin kaputt (informal) I'm shattered

**kaputtgehen** ◇VERB (informal) (IMP ging kaputt, PERF ist kaputtgegangen) ❶ to break

❷ to pack up; mein Fernseher ist mitten im Fußballspiel kaputtgegangen the television packed up in the middle of the football match ❸ to wear out (of clothing) ❹ to break up (of a marriage or friendship)

**kaputtmachen** VERB (informal) (PERF hat kaputtgemacht) ❶ to break; er macht alle seine Spielsachen kaputt he breaks all his toys ❷ to ruin (clothes, furniture) ❸ to finish off (a person); die viele Arbeit macht mich ganz kaputt all this work is wearing me out ❹ sich kaputtmachen to wear yourself out

**Kapuze** die (PLURAL die **Kapuzen**) hood

**Karamell** der (PLURAL die **Karamells**) caramel

**Karfreitag** der Good Friday

**Karibik** die die Karibik the Caribbean

**karibisch** ADJECTIVE Caribbean

**kariert** ADJECTIVE ❶ check; ein karierter Rock a check skirt ❷ squared (paper)

**Karneval** der (PLURAL die **Karnevale**) carnival

**Karo** das (PLURAL die **Karos**) ❶ square ❷ diamonds (in cards)

**Karotte** die (PLURAL die **Karotten**) carrot

**Karpfen** der (PLURAL die **Karpfen**) carp

**Karriere** die (PLURAL die **Karrieren**) career; Karriere machen to get to the top

**Karte** die (PLURAL die **Karten**) ❶ card; ich schicke euch eine Karte aus Italien I'll send you a card from Italy

**❷ card** (for playing); **wir haben den ganzen Abend Karten gespielt** we played cards all evening; **gute/schlechte Karten haben** to have a good/bad hand **❸ ticket**; **gibt es noch Karten für das Popfestival?** can you still get tickets for the pop festival? **❹ menu ❺ map**; **ich kann Oberammergau nicht auf der Karte finden** I can't find Oberammergau on the map **❻ alles auf eine Karte setzen** to put all your eggs in one basket

**Kartenspiel** das (PLURAL die **Kartenspiele**) **❶ card game ❷ pack of cards**

**Kartoffel** die (PLURAL die **Kartoffeln**) potato

**Kartoffelbrei** der **mashed potatoes**

**Kartoffelchips** PLURAL NOUN **potato crisps**

**Karton** der (PLURAL die **Kartons**) **❶ cardboard ❷ cardboard box**

**Karussell** das (PLURAL die **Karussells**) **merry-go-round**; **Karussell fahren** to go on the merry-go-round

**Käse** der **cheese**

**Käsekuchen** der (PLURAL die **Käsekuchen**) **cheesecake**

**Kaserne** die (PLURAL die **Kasernen**) **barracks**

**Kasse** die (PLURAL die **Kassen**) **❶ till ❷ checkout**; **an der Kasse zahlen** pay at the checkout **❸ cash desk** (in a bank) **❹ box-office**; **Sie können die Karten an der Kasse abholen** you can collect the tickets from the box office **❺ ticket office** (at a sports stadium); **Sie müssen sich an der Kasse anstellen** you

have to queue at the ticket office **❻ health insurance ❼ knapp bei Kasse sein** (informal) to be short of money, **gut bei Kasse sein** (informal) to be in the money

**Kassenzettel** der (PLURAL die **Kassenzettel**) **receipt**

**Kassette** die (PLURAL die **Kassetten**) **box** (for money, jewellery)

**kassieren** VERB (PERF **hat kassiert**) **❶ to collect the money ❷ to collect the fares ❸ wie viel hat er kassiert?** how much did he charge you? **❹ darf ich bei Ihnen kassieren?** would you like to pay now? (your bill in a restaurant) **❺** (informal) **to take away** (a driving licence, for example)

**Kassierer** der (PLURAL die **Kassierer**) **cashier**

**Kassiererin** die (PLURAL die **Kassiererinnen**) **cashier**

**Kastanie** die (PLURAL die **Kastanien**) **chestnut**

**Kasten** der (PLURAL die **Kästen**) **❶ box ❷ crate**; **ein Kasten Bier** a crate of beer **❸ bin ❹ letter-box ❺ was auf dem Kasten haben** (informal) to be brainy

**Katalog** der (PLURAL die **Kataloge**) **catalogue**

**Katalysator** der (PLURAL die **Katalysatoren**) **catalytic converter**

**katastrophal** ADJECTIVE, ADVERB **❶ catastrophic ❷ sie hat katastrophal schlecht abgeschnitten** she came out terribly badly

**Katastrophe** die (PLURAL die **Katastrophen**) **catastrophe**

German—English

**Kategorie** die *(PLURAL* die **Kategorien)** category

**Kater** der *(PLURAL* die **Kater)** ❶ tom-cat ❷ einen Kater haben *(informal)* to have a hangover

**Kathedrale** die *(PLURAL* die **Kathedralen)** cathedral

**Katholik** der *(PLURAL* die **Katholiken)** Catholic

**Katholikin** die *(PLURAL* die **Katholikinnen)** Catholic

**katholisch** *ADJECTIVE* Catholic

**Kätzchen** das *(PLURAL* die **Kätzchen)** kitten

**Katze** die *(PLURAL* die **Katzen)** cat

**kauen** *VERB (PERF* **hat gekaut)** to chew

**kauern** *VERB (PERF* **hat gekauert)** to crouch

**Kauf** der *(PLURAL* die **Käufe)** ❶ purchase ❷ ein guter Kauf a bargain ❸ etwas in Kauf nehmen to put up with something

**kaufen** *VERB (PERF* **hat gekauft)** to buy

**Käufer** der *(PLURAL* die **Käufer)** buyer

**Käuferin** die *(PLURAL* die **Käuferinnen)** buyer

**Kauffrau** die *(PLURAL* die **Kauffrauen)** businesswoman

**Kaufhaus** das *(PLURAL* die **Kaufhäuser)** department store

**Kaufmann** der *(PLURAL* die **Kaufleute)** businessman

**Kaugummi** der *(PLURAL* die **Kaugummis)** chewing gum

**Kaulquappe** die *(PLURAL* die **Kaulquappen)** tadpole

**kaum** *ADVERB* hardly, scarcely

**Kaution** die *(PLURAL* die **Kautionen)** ❶ deposit ❷ bail

**Kegel** der *(PLURAL* die **Kegel)** ❶ cone ❷ skittle

**Kegelbahn** die skittle alley

**kegeln** *VERB (PERF* **hat gekegelt)** to play skittles

**Kehle** die *(PLURAL* die **Kehlen)** throat

**Keim** der *(PLURAL* die **Keime)** ❶ shoot ❷ germ

**kein** *ADJECTIVE* ❶ no; auf keinen Fall on no account ❷ ich habe keine Zeit I haven't got any time, er hat kein Geld he hasn't got any money ❸ keine zehn Minuten less than ten minutes

**keiner, keine, kein(e)s** *PRONOUN* ❶ nobody, no one ❷ none, not one ❸ von diesen Kleidern gefällt mir keins I don't like any of these dresses ❹ keiner von beiden neither (of them)

**keinesfalls** *ADVERB* on no account

**keineswegs** *ADVERB* by no means

**keinmal** *ADVERB* not once

**keins** ▸ SEE **keiner**

**Keks** der *(PLURAL* die **Kekse)** biscuit

**Keller** der *(PLURAL* die **Keller)** cellar

**Kellergeschoss** das *(PLURAL* die **Kellergeschosse)** basement

**Kellner** der *(PLURAL* die **Kellner)** waiter

**Kellnerin** die *(PLURAL* die **Kellnerinnen)** waitress

a
b
c
d
e
f
g
h
i
j
k
l
m
n
o
p
q
r
s
t
u
v
w
x
y
z

**kennen** ◇VERB (IMP **kannte**, PERF **hat gekannt**) ❶ to know ❷ kennen lernen to get to know, sich kennen lernen to get to know each other ❸ kennen lernen to meet, ich habe Ulrike in London kennen gelernt I met Ulrike in London, wo habt ihr euch kennen gelernt? where did you meet?

**kennenlernen** ▸SEE **kennen**

**Kenntnis** die (PLURAL die **Kenntnisse**) ❶ knowledge ❷ etwas zur Kenntnis nehmen to take note of something

**Kennzeichen** das (PLURAL die **Kennzeichen**) ❶ mark ❷ characteristic ❸ registration (number) (of a vehicle)

**Kerl** der (PLURAL die **Kerle**) ❶ bloke ❷ Eva ist ein netter Kerl Eva's a nice girl

**Kern** der (PLURAL die **Kerne**) ❶ pip ❷ stone (of an apricot, peach) ❸ kernel (of a nut)

**Kernenergie** die nuclear power

**Kernkraftwerk** das (PLURAL die **Kernkraftwerke**) nuclear power station

**Kernwaffen** PLURAL NOUN nuclear weapons

**Kerze** die (PLURAL die **Kerzen**) candle

**Kerzenhalter** der (PLURAL die **Kerzenhalter**) candlestick

**Kessel** der (PLURAL die **Kessel**) ❶ kettle ❷ boiler

**Kette** die (PLURAL die **Ketten**) chain

**Keule** die (PLURAL die **Keulen**) ❶ club ❷ leg (of lamb) ❸ drumstick (of chicken)

**kichern** VERB (PERF **hat gekichert**) to giggle

**Kiefer**[1] der (PLURAL die **Kiefer**) jaw

**Kiefer**[2] die (PLURAL die **Kiefern**) pine tree

**Kiefernzapfen** der (PLURAL die **Kiefernzapfen**) cone

**Kieselstein** der (PLURAL die **Kieselsteine**) pebble

**Kilo** das (PLURAL die **Kilo(s)**) kilo

**Kilogramm** das (PLURAL die **Kilogramme**) kilogram

**Kilometer** der (PLURAL die **Kilometer**) kilometre

**Kind** das (PLURAL die **Kinder**) child

**Kindergarten** der (PLURAL die **Kindergärten**) nursery school

**Kindergeld** das child benefit

**Kinderkrippe** die (PLURAL die **Kinderkrippen**) crèche

**kinderleicht** ADJECTIVE very easy; das ist kinderleicht it's child's play

**Kindertagesstätte** die (PLURAL die **Kindertagesstätten**) day nursery

**Kinderwagen** der (PLURAL die **Kinderwagen**) pram

**Kindheit** die childhood

**kindisch** ADJECTIVE childish

**Kinn** das (PLURAL die **Kinne**) chin

**Kino** das (PLURAL die **Kinos**) cinema

**Kiosk** das (PLURAL die **Kioske**) kiosk (for newspapers or snacks)

**kippen** VERB (PERF **hat gekippt**) ❶ to tip ❷ (PERF **ist gekippt**) to topple

**Kirche** die *(PLURAL die **Kirchen**)* church

**Kirsche** die *(PLURAL die **Kirschen**)* cherry

**Kissen** das *(PLURAL die **Kissen**)* ❶ cushion ❷ pillow

**Kiste** die *(PLURAL die **Kisten**)* ❶ crate ❷ box

**kitzeln** VERB *(PERF hat gekitzelt)* to tickle

**kitzlig** ADJECTIVE ticklish

**Kiwi** die *(PLURAL die **Kiwis**)* kiwi fruit

**klagen** VERB *(PERF hat geklagt)* to complain

**Klammer** die *(PLURAL die **Klammern**)* ❶ peg *(for washing)* ❷ grip *(for hair)* ❸ bracket

**Klammeraffe** die *(PLURAL die **Klammeraffen**)* at, @ *(in email addresses)*; dieter-punkt-schmidt-Klammeraffe-einfachkom-punkt-com dieter-dot-schmidt-at-einfachkom-dot-com

**Klamotten** PLURAL NOUN gear *(clothes)*

**klang** ▸ SEE **klingen**

**Klang** der *(PLURAL die **Klänge**)* sound

**Klappe** die *(PLURAL die **Klappen**)* ❶ flap ❷ clapperboard ❸ *(informal)* trap *(mouth)*; halt die Klappe! shut up!

**klappen** VERB *(PERF hat geklappt)* ❶ nach vorne klappen to tilt forward ❷ nach hinten klappen to tip back ❸ nach oben klappen to lift up ❹ nach unten klappen to put down ❺ to work out; hoffentlich klappt es I hope it'll work out

**Klappstuhl** der *(PLURAL die **Klappstühle**)* folding chair

**klar** ADJECTIVE ❶ clear *(water, answer)*; klar werden to become clear ❷ jetzt ist mir alles klar now I understand ❸ sich klar werden to make up your mind ❹ sich über etwas im Klaren sein to realize something

**klar** ADVERB clearly; na klar! *(informal)* of course!

**klären** VERB *(PERF hat geklärt)* ❶ to clarify ❷ to sort out ❸ to purify *(sewage)* ❹ sich klären to clear *(of the weather or the sky)* ❺ sich klären to resolve itself, to be settled

**Klarinette** die *(PLURAL die **Klarinetten**)* clarinet

**klarwerden** ▸ SEE **klar**

**klasse** ADJECTIVE *(informal)* great, smashing

**Klasse** die *(PLURAL die **Klassen**)* ❶ class; erster Klasse reisen to travel first class ❷ year; in die sechste Klasse gehen to be in year six

**Klassenarbeit** die *(PLURAL die **Klassenarbeiten**)* (written) test

**Klassenbuch** das *(PLURAL die **Klassenbücher**)* register *(kept by the teacher, it also contains notes about students' achievements)*

**Klassenfahrt** die *(PLURAL die **Klassenfahrten**)* school trip

**Klassenkamerad** der *(PLURAL die **Klassenkameraden**)* class-mate

**Klassenkameradin** die *(PLURAL die **Klassenkameradinnen**)* class-mate

**Klassensprecher** der *(PLURAL die **Klassensprecher**)* class representative

**Klassensprecherin** die (PLURAL die **Klassensprecherinnen**) class representative

**Klassenzimmer** das (PLURAL die **Klassenzimmer**) classroom

**klassisch** ADJECTIVE classical

**Klatsch** der gossip

**klatschen** VERB (PERF hat geklatscht) ❶ to clap; jemandem Beifall klatschen to clap somebody, to applaud somebody ❷ to slap ❸ to gossip

**klauen** VERB (informal) (PERF hat geklaut) to pinch

**Klavier** das (PLURAL die **Klaviere**) piano

**kleben** VERB (PERF hat geklebt) ❶ to stick ❷ to glue ❸ jemandem eine kleben (informal) to belt somebody one

**klebrig** ADJECTIVE sticky

**Klebstoff** der (PLURAL die **Klebstoffe**) glue

**Klebstreifen** der (PLURAL die **Klebstreifen**) sticky tape

**Klecks** der (PLURAL die **Kleckse**) stain

**Kleid** das (PLURAL die **Kleider**) ❶ dress; Uschi hat sich zwei neue Kleider gekauft Uschi bought two new dresses ❷ Kleider clothes

**Kleiderbügel** der (PLURAL die **Kleiderbügel**) coat hanger

**Kleiderschrank** der (PLURAL die **Kleiderschränke**) wardrobe

**Kleidung** die clothes, clothing

**klein** ADJECTIVE ❶ small, little; etwas klein schneiden to cut something up small ❷ short; Peter ist kleiner als Klaus Peter is shorter than Klaus

**Kleingarten** der (PLURAL die **Kleingärten**) allotment (used mainly as garden)

**Kleingeld** das change

**Klempner** der (PLURAL die **Klempner**) plumber

**klettern** VERB (PERF ist geklettert) to climb

**Klick** der (PLURAL die **Klicks**) click (with mouse)

**Klicken** das click (noise)

**Klient** der (PLURAL die **Klienten**) client

**Klientin** die (PLURAL die **Klientinnen**) client

**Klima** das (PLURAL die **Klimas**) climate

**Klimaanlage** die (PLURAL die **Klimaanlagen**) air conditioning

**Klimawandel** der climate change

**Klinge** die (PLURAL die **Klingen**) blade

**Klingel** die (PLURAL die **Klingeln**) bell

**klingeln** VERB (PERF hat geklingelt) to ring; es klingelt there's a ring at the door

**Klingelton** der (PLURAL die **Klingeltone**) ringtone

**klingen** ◇VERB (IMP klang, PERF hat geklungen) to sound

**Klinik** die (PLURAL die **Kliniken**) clinic

**Klinke** die (PLURAL die **Klinken**) handle

**Klippe** die (PLURAL die **Klippen**) rock

**Klo** das (informal) (PLURAL die **Klos**) loo

**klopfen** VERB (PERF hat geklopft) ❶ to knock ❷ to beat

**Klosett** das *(PLURAL die* **Klosetts)** lavatory

**Kloß** der *(PLURAL die* **Klöße)** dumpling

**Kloster** das *(PLURAL die* **Kloster)** ❶ monastery ❷ convent

**Klotz** der *(PLURAL die* **Klötze)** block

**Klub** der *(PLURAL die* **Klubs)** club

**klug** *ADJECTIVE* ❶ clever ❷ ich werde daraus nicht klug I don't understand it

**Klugheit** die cleverness

**Klumpen** der *(PLURAL die* **Klumpen)** lump

**knabbern** *VERB (PERF* **hat geknabbert)** to nibble

**Knäckebrot** das *(PLURAL die* **Knäckebrote)** crispbread

**knacken** *VERB (PERF* **hat geknackt)** to crack

**Knall** der *(PLURAL die* **Knalle)** bang

**knallen** *VERB (PERF* **hat geknallt)** ❶ to go bang ❷ to pop *(of a cork)* ❸ to slam *(of a door)* ❹ to crack *(of a whip)*

**knapp** *ADJECTIVE* ❶ scarce ❷ tight *(skirt, top)* ❸ knapp bei Kasse sein to be short of money ❹ mit knapper Mehrheit by a narrow majority ❺ just; eine knappe Stunde just under an hour, sie haben knapp verloren they only just lost ❻ das war knapp *(informal)* that was a close shave

**knarren** *VERB (PERF* **hat geknarrt)** to creak

**Knauf** der *(PLURAL die* **Knäufe)** knob

**knautschen** *VERB (PERF* **hat geknautscht)** ❶ to crumple ❷ to crease

**kneifen** ◇*VERB (IMP* **kniff,** *PERF* **hat gekniffen)** ❶ to pinch ❷ *(informal)* to chicken out; sie hat mal wieder gekniffen und nichts gesagt she's chickened out yet again and didn't say anything

**Kneipe** die *(PLURAL die* **Kneipen)** pub

**kneten** *VERB (PERF* **hat geknetet)** to knead

**knicken** *VERB (PERF* **hat geknickt)** ❶ to bend ❷ to fold

**Knie** das *(PLURAL die* **Knie)** knee

**knien** *VERB (PERF* **hat gekniet)** ❶ to kneel ❷ sich knien to kneel down

**kniff** ▸ SEE **kneifen**

**knipsen** *VERB (PERF* **hat geknipst)** *(to photograph)* to take a snap, to take snaps

**Knoblauch** der garlic

**Knoblauchzehe** die *(PLURAL die* **Knoblauchzehen)** clove of garlic

**Knöchel** der *(PLURAL die* **Knöchel)** ❶ ankle ❷ knuckle; Mario hat sich beim Jogging den Knöchel verstaucht Mario sprained his ankle when jogging

**Knochen** der *(PLURAL die* **Knochen)** bone

**Knopf** der *(PLURAL die* **Knöpfe)** button

**Knoten** der *(PLURAL die* **Knoten)** ❶ knot ❷ bun *(as a hairstyle)* ❸ lump

**Knüller** der *(PLURAL die* **Knüller)** scoop *(in journalism)*

**knurren** *VERB (PERF* **hat geknurrt)**
❶ to growl ❷ to rumble ❸ to
grumble

**knusprig** *ADJECTIVE* **crisp, crusty**
*(bread)*

**Koalabär** der *(PLURAL* die
**Koalabären)** koala bear

**Koch** der *(PLURAL* die **Köche)** ❶ cook
❷ chef

**Kochbuch** das *(PLURAL* die
**Kochbücher)** cookery book

**kochen** *VERB (PERF* **hat gekocht)** ❶ to
cook ❷ to boil; das Wasser kocht
the water's boiling

**Köchin** die *(PLURAL* die **Köchinnen)**
cook

**Kochtopf** der *(PLURAL* die **Kochtöpfe)**
saucepan

**Koffer** der *(PLURAL* die **Koffer)**
suitcase

**Kofferkuli** der *(PLURAL* die
**Kofferkulis)** baggage trolley

**Kofferraum** der *(PLURAL* die
**Kofferräume)** boot

**Kohl** der ❶ cabbage ❷ *(informal)*
rubbish; rede keinen Kohl don't
talk rubbish

**Kohle** die *(PLURAL* die **Kohlen)** coal

**Kohlrübe** die *(PLURAL* die **Kohlrüben)**
swede

**Kokain** das cocaine

**Kokosnuss** die *(PLURAL* die
**Kokosnüsse)** coconut

**Kollege** der *(PLURAL* die **Kollegen)**
colleague

**Kollegin** die *(PLURAL* die **Kolleginnen)**
colleague

**Köln** das Cologne

**Kölnischwasser** das eau de
cologne

**Kombination** die *(PLURAL* die
**Kombinationen)** combination

**Komfort** der comfort

**Komiker** der *(PLURAL* die **Komiker)**
comedian

**komisch** *ADJECTIVE* funny

**Komma** das *(PLURAL* die **Kommas)**
❶ comma ❷ decimal point; zwei
Komma fünf two point five

**kommen** ◇*VERB (IMP* **kam,** *PERF* **ist
gekommen)** ❶ to come ❷ to
get; wie komme ich zur U-Bahn?
how do I get to the tube station?,
kommt gut nach Hause! have a safe
journey home! ❸ etwas kommen
lassen to send for something ❹ wie
kommst du darauf? what gave you
that idea? ❺ hinter etwas kommen
to find out about something ❻ zur
Schule kommen to start school
❼ to go; die Gabeln kommen
in die Schublade the forks go
in the drawer, ins Krankenhaus
kommen to go to hospital ❽ wer
kommt zuerst? who's first?, du
kommst an die Reihe it's your
turn ❾ wie kommt das? why is
that? ❿ zu etwas kommen to
acquire something ⓫ wieder zu
sich kommen to come round *(after
fainting or anaesthetic)* ⓬ dazu
kommen, etwas zu tun to get
round to doing something,
ich komme einfach nicht zum
Einkaufen I just can't get round to
doing the shopping ⓭ das kommt
davon! see what happens!

**Kommissar** der *(PLURAL* die
**Kommissare)** superintendent

**Kommode** die *(PLURAL die Kommoden)* chest of drawers

**Kommunismus** der communism

**Kommunist** der *(PLURAL die Kommunisten)* communist

**Kommunistin** die *(PLURAL die Kommunistinnen)* communist

**kommunizieren** *VERB (PERF hat kommuniziert)* to communicate

**Komödie** die *(PLURAL die Komödien)* comedy

**Kompass** der *(PLURAL die Kompasse)* compass

**komplett** *ADJECTIVE* complete

**Kompliment** das *(PLURAL die Komplimente)* compliment

**kompliziert** *ADJECTIVE* complicated

**Komponist** der *(PLURAL die Komponisten)* composer

**Komponistin** die *(PLURAL die Komponistinnen)* composer

**Kompott** das *(PLURAL die Kompotte)* stewed fruit

**Kompromiss** der *(PLURAL die Kompromisse)* compromise; einen Kompromiss schließen to compromise

**Konditional** das *(verb tense)* conditional

**Konditorei** die *(PLURAL die Konditoreien)* patisserie, cake shop

**Kondom** das *(PLURAL die Kondome)* condom

**Konfektion** die ready-made clothes

**Konferenz** die *(PLURAL die Konferenzen)* conference

**Konflikt** der *(PLURAL die Konflikte)* conflict

**König** der *(PLURAL die Könige)* king

**Königin** die *(PLURAL die Königinnen)* queen

**königlich** *ADJECTIVE* royal

**Königreich** das *(PLURAL die Königreiche)* kingdom

**Konjunktion** die *(PLURAL die Konjunktionen)* conjunction

**Konkurrent** der *(PLURAL die Konkurrenten)* competitor

**Konkurrentin** die *(PLURAL die Konkurrentinnen)* competitor

**Konkurrenz** die competition

**können** ⬦*VERB (PRES kann, IMP konnte, PERF hat gekonnt)* ❶ can; kann ich Ihnen helfen? can I help you?, kannst du Auto fahren? can you drive?, kannst du Deutsch? can you speak German?, ich konnte nicht früher kommen I couldn't come any earlier, das kann ich nicht I can't do that ❷ etwas können to be able to do something, er wird es vor Dienstag nicht machen können he won't be able to do it before Tuesday ❸ das kann gut sein that may well be so, es kann sein, dass ... it may be that ... ❹ ich kann nichts dafür it's not my fault

**Können** das ability

**Könner** der *(PLURAL die Könner)* expert

**könnt** ▸ SEE **können**

**konnte**, **konnten**, **konntest**, **konntet** ▸ SEE **können**

**Konrektor** der *(PLURAL die Konrektoren)* deputy

headteacher, deputy headmaster

**Konrektorin** die *(PLURAL die Konrektorinnen)* deputy headteacher

**Konserven** *PLURAL NOUN* tinned food

**Konsonant** der *(PLURAL die Konsonanten)* consonant

**Konstruktion** die *(PLURAL die Konstruktionen)* construction *(in grammar)*

**Konsul** der *(PLURAL die Konsuln)* consul

**Konsulat** das *(PLURAL die Konsulate)* consulate

**konsultieren** *VERB (PERF hat konsultiert)* to consult

**Kontakt** der *(PLURAL die Kontakte)* contact

**Kontaktlinse** die *(PLURAL die Kontaktlinsen)* contact lens

**Kontinent** der *(PLURAL die Kontinente)* continent

**Konto** das *(PLURAL die Konten)* account

**Kontrolle** die *(PLURAL die Kontrollen)* ❶ check ❷ control

**Kontrolleur** der *(PLURAL die Kontrolleure)* inspector

**kontrollieren** *VERB (PERF hat kontrolliert)* ❶ to check ❷ to control

**konzentrieren** *VERB (PERF hat konzentriert)* ❶ to concentrate ❷ sich konzentrieren to concentrate

**Konzert** das *(PLURAL die Konzerte)* ❶ concert ❷ concerto

**Kopf** der *(PLURAL die Köpfe)* ❶ head ❷ sich den Kopf zerbrechen to rack your brains ❸ seinen Kopf durchsetzen to get your own way ❹ sich den Kopf waschen to wash your hair ❺ auf dem Kopf upside down ❻ ein Kopf Salat a lettuce

**köpfen** *VERB (PERF hat geköpft)* ❶ to head *(in football)* ❷ to behead

**Kopfhörer** der *(PLURAL die Kopfhörer)* headphones

**Kopfkissen** das *(PLURAL die Kopfkissen)* pillow

**Kopfsalat** der *(PLURAL die Kopfsalate)* lettuce

**Kopfschmerzen** *PLURAL NOUN* headache

**Kopie** die *(PLURAL die Kopien)* copy

**kopieren** *VERB (PERF hat kopiert)* ❶ to copy ❷ to photocopy

**Kopiergerät** das *(PLURAL die Kopiergeräte)* photocopier

**Korb** der *(PLURAL die Körbe)* ❶ basket ❷ jemandem einen Korb geben to turn somebody down

**Kork** der *(PLURAL die Korke)* cork

**Korken** der *(PLURAL die Korken)* cork

**Korkenzieher** der *(PLURAL die Korkenzieher)* corkscrew

**Korn** das *(PLURAL die Körner)* ❶ corn *(in general)* ❷ grain *(a seed)*

**Körper** der *(PLURAL die Körper)* body

**körperbehindert** *ADJECTIVE* disabled

**Körpergeruch** der *(PLURAL die Körpergerüche)* body odour

**körperlich** *ADJECTIVE* physical

**Korrektur** die *(PLURAL* die **Korrekturen)** correction

**korrigieren** *VERB (PERF* **hat korrigiert)** to correct

**Korsika** das **Corsica**

**koscher** *ADJECTIVE* **kosher**

**Kosmetik** die *(PLURAL* die **Kosmetika)** ❶ cosmetics ❷ beauty care

**Kost** die **food**

**kostbar** *ADJECTIVE* **precious**

**kosten** *VERB (PERF* **hat gekostet)** ❶ to cost ❷ wie viel kostet es? how much is it? ❸ to taste

**Kosten** *PLURAL NOUN* ❶ cost ❷ expenses

**kostenlos** *ADJECTIVE* **free (of charge)**

**köstlich** *ADJECTIVE* ❶ delicious ❷ funny

**Kostüm** das *(PLURAL* die **Kostüme)** ❶ suit ❷ costume

**Kotelett** das *(PLURAL* die **Koteletts)** chop

**Krabbe** die *(PLURAL* die **Krabben)** ❶ crab ❷ shrimp

**krabbeln** *VERB (PERF* **ist gekrabbelt)** to crawl

**Krach** der ❶ row ❷ noise ❸ crash

**krachen** *VERB (PERF* **hat gekracht)** ❶ to crash ❷ *(PERF* **ist gekracht)** to crack; er ist gegen die Mauer gekracht he crashed into the wall

**krächzen** *VERB (PERF* **hat gekrächzt)** to croak

**Kraft** die *(PLURAL* die **Kräfte)** ❶ strength; er hat nicht viel Kraft he's not very strong ❷ force; in Kraft treten to come into force ❸ geistige Kräfte mental powers ❹ worker

**kräftig** *ADJECTIVE* ❶ strong ❷ nourishing

**kräftig** *ADVERB* ❶ strongly ❷ hard; kräftig schütteln shake hard

**Kraftwerk** das *(PLURAL* die **Kraftwerke)** power station

**Kragen** der *(PLURAL* die **Kragen)** collar

**Krähe** die *(PLURAL* die **Krähen)** crow

**Kralle** die *(PLURAL* die **Krallen)** claw

**Kram** der **stuff**; mach deinen Kram allein! *(informal)* do it yourself!

**kramen** *VERB (PERF* **hat gekramt)** to rummage about

**Krampf** der *(PLURAL* die **Krämpfe)** cramp

**Kran** der *(PLURAL* die **Kräne)** crane *(machine)*

**Kranich** der *(PLURAL* die **Kraniche)** crane *(bird)*

**krank** *ADJECTIVE* **ill, sick**; krank werden to fall ill

**Kranke** der/die *(PLURAL* die **Kranken)** patient

**kränken** *VERB (PERF* **hat gekränkt)** to hurt

**Krankenhaus** das *(PLURAL* die **Krankenhäuser)** hospital; sie haben ihn gestern ins Krankenhaus eingeliefert he was taken to hospital yesterday

**Krankenkasse** die **health insurance**; bei welcher Krankenkasse sind Sie versichert? what health insurance have you got?

**Krankenpfleger** der (PLURAL die Krankenpfleger) (male) nurse

**Krankenpflegerin** die (PLURAL die Krankenpflegerinnen) nurse

**Krankenschwester** die (PLURAL die Krankenschwestern) nurse; Ulrike ist Krankenschwester Ulrike is a nurse

**Krankenversicherung** die (PLURAL die Krankenversicherungen) medical insurance

**Krankenwagen** der (PLURAL die Krankenwagen) ambulance

**Krankheit** die (PLURAL die Krankheiten) illness, disease

**krass** ADJECTIVE (informal) wicked, amazing

**kratzen** VERB (PERF hat gekratzt) to scratch

**Kratzer** der (PLURAL die Kratzer) scratch

**kraus** ADJECTIVE frizzy

**Kraut** das (PLURAL die Kräuter) ❶ herb ❷ sauerkraut ❸ cabbage

**Kräutertee** der (PLURAL die Kräutertees) herbal tea

**Krawall** der (PLURAL die Krawalle) ❶ riot ❷ row

**Krawatte** die (PLURAL die Krawatten) tie

**kreativ** ADJECTIVE creative

**Krebs** der (PLURAL die Krebse) ❶ crab ❷ cancer ❸ Cancer

**Kredit** der (PLURAL die Kredite) ❶ loan (by a bank); auf Kredit on credit ❷ credit (reputation)

**Kreditkarte** die (PLURAL die Kreditkarten) credit card

**Kreide** die (PLURAL die Kreiden) chalk

**kreieren** VERB (PERF hat kreiert) to create

**Kreis** der (PLURAL die Kreise) ❶ circle ❷ district

**Kreislauf** der ❶ cycle ❷ circulation

**Kreuz** das (PLURAL die Kreuze) ❶ cross ❷ (small of the) back ❸ intersection (of a motorway) ❹ clubs (in cards)

**kreuzen** VERB (PERF hat gekreuzt) ❶ to cross ❷ sich kreuzen to cross

**Kreuzfahrt** die (PLURAL die Kreuzfahrten) ❶ cruise; eine Kreuzfahrt machen to go on a cruise ❷ crusade

**Kreuzung** die (PLURAL die Kreuzungen) ❶ crossroads ❷ cross (of plants, animals)

**Kreuzworträtsel** das (PLURAL die Kreuzworträtsel) crossword (puzzle)

**kriechen** ◇VERB (IMP kroch, PERF ist gekrochen) to crawl

**Krieg** der (PLURAL die Kriege) war

**kriegen** VERB (informal) (PERF hat gekriegt) ❶ to get ❷ ein Kind kriegen to have a baby

**Krimi** der (PLURAL die Krimis) thriller

**Kriminalroman** der (PLURAL die Kriminalromane) crime novel

**kriminell** ADJECTIVE criminal

**Kriminelle** der/die (PLURAL die Kriminellen) criminal

**Krippe** die (PLURAL die Krippen) ❶ manger ❷ crib ❸ crèche

**Krise** die (PLURAL die Krisen) crisis

**Kristall**[1] der *(PLURAL die Kristalle)* crystal

**Kristall**[2] das *(glass)* crystal

**kritisch** *ADJECTIVE* critical

**kritisieren** *VERB (PERF hat kritisiert)* ❶ to criticize ❷ to review

**kroch** ▸ SEE **kriechen**

**Krokodil** das *(PLURAL die Krokodile)* crocodile

**Krone** die *(PLURAL die Kronen)* crown

**Kröte** die *(PLURAL die Kröten)* toad

**Krücke** die *(PLURAL die Krücken)* crutch

**Krug** der *(PLURAL die Krüge)* ❶ jug ❷ mug

**Krümel** der *(PLURAL die Krümel)* crumb

**krümelig** *ADJECTIVE* crumbly

**krumm** *ADJECTIVE* ❶ bent ❷ crooked

**Kruste** die *(PLURAL die Krusten)* crust

**Küche** die *(PLURAL die Küchen)* ❶ kitchen ❷ cooking; die italienische Küche Italian cooking ❸ warme Küche hot food

**Kuchen** der *(PLURAL die Kuchen)* cake

**Kuckuck** der *(PLURAL die Kuckucke)* cuckoo

**Kugel** die *(PLURAL die Kugeln)* ❶ ball ❷ bullet ❸ sphere; wieviele Kugeln Eis möchtest du? how many scoops of ice-cream would you like?

**Kugelschreiber** der *(PLURAL die Kugelschreiber)* ballpoint pen, biro

**Kuh** die *(PLURAL die Kühe)* cow

**kühl** *ADJECTIVE* cool

**kühlen** *VERB (PERF hat gekühlt)* ❶ to cool, to chill ❷ to refrigerate

**Kühler** der *(PLURAL die Kühler)* radiator

**Kühlerhaube** die *(PLURAL die Kühlerhauben)* bonnet

**Kühlschrank** der *(PLURAL die Kühlschränke)* fridge

**Kühltruhe** die *(PLURAL die Kühltruhen)* freezer

**Küken** das *(PLURAL die Küken)* chick

**Kuli** der *(PLURAL die Kulis)* biro

**Kultur** die *(PLURAL die Kulturen)* ❶ culture ❷ civilization

**Kulturbeutel** der *(PLURAL die Kulturbeutel)* toilet bag

**kulturell** *ADJECTIVE* cultural

**Kummer** der ❶ sorrow ❷ worry ❸ trouble

**kümmern** *VERB (PERF hat gekümmert)* ❶ to concern ❷ sich um jemanden kümmern to look after somebody, sich um den Garten kümmern to look after the garden ❸ sich darum kümmern, dass ... to see to it that ... ❹ kümmere dich um deine eigenen Angelegenheiten mind your own business

**Kunde** der *(PLURAL die Kunden)* ❶ customer ❷ client

**Kundendienst** der ❶ customer services (department) ❷ after-sales service

**kündigen** *VERB (PERF hat gekündigt)* ❶ to cancel ❷ to give notice; die Firma hat ihm gekündigt the company gave him his notice ❸ seine Stellung kündigen to hand in your notice

**Kundin** die *(PLURAL* die **Kundinnen)**
❶ customer ❷ client

**Kundschaft** die customers

**Kunst** die *(PLURAL* die **Künste)** ❶ art
❷ skill

**Kunstausstellung** die *(PLURAL*
die **Kunstausstellungen)** art
exhibition

**Künstler** der *(PLURAL* die **Künstler)**
artist

**Künstlerin** die *(PLURAL* die
**Künstlerinnen)** artist

**künstlerisch** *ADJECTIVE* artistic

**künstlich** *ADJECTIVE* artificial

**Kunststoff** der *(PLURAL* die
**Kunststoffe)** plastic

**Kunststück** das *(PLURAL* die
**Kunststücke)** ❶ trick ❷ feat

**Kunstwerk** das *(PLURAL* die
**Kunstwerke)** work of art

**Kupfer** das copper

**Kupplung** die *(PLURAL* die
**Kupplungen)** ❶ clutch *(of a car)*
❷ coupling

**Kürbis** der *(PLURAL* die **Kürbisse)**
pumpkin

**Kurier** der *(PLURAL* die **Kuriere)**
courier *(delivery person)*

**Kurierdienst** der *(PLURAL* die
**Kurierdienste)** courier service

**Kurort** der *(PLURAL* die **Kurorte)**
health resort

**Kurs** der *(PLURAL* die **Kurse)** ❶ course
❷ exchange rate ❸ price
*(of shares)*

**Kurve** die *(PLURAL* die **Kurven)**
❶ curve ❷ bend

**kurz** *ADJECTIVE* ❶ short; vor kurzem a
short time ago ❷ zu kurz kommen
to get less than your fair share, to
come off badly

**kurz** *ADVERB* ❶ shortly ❷ briefly
❸ kurz gesagt in a word

**Kurzarbeit** die short-time
working

**kurzärmelig** *ADJECTIVE* short-
sleeved

**kürzen** *VERB* *(PERF* hat gekürzt)
❶ to shorten ❷ to cut

**kurzfristig** *ADJECTIVE* short-term

**kurzfristig** *ADVERB* at short notice

**kürzlich** *ADVERB* recently

**kurzsichtig** *ADJECTIVE* short-sighted

**Kurzwaren** *PLURAL NOUN*
haberdashery

**Kusine** die *(PLURAL* die **Kusinen)**
cousin

**Kuss** der *(PLURAL* die **Küsse)** kiss

**küssen** *VERB* *(PERF* hat geküsst)
❶ to kiss ❷ sich küssen to kiss

**Küste** die *(PLURAL* die **Küsten)** coast

**Kuvert** das *(PLURAL* die **Kuverts)**
envelope

**Labor** das (PLURAL die **Labors**) laboratory

**Lache** die (PLURAL die **Lachen**) pool

**lächeln** VERB (PERF **hat gelächelt**) to smile

**lachen** VERB (PERF **hat gelacht**) to laugh

**lächerlich** ADJECTIVE ridiculous

**Lachs** der (PLURAL die **Lachse**) salmon

**Lack** der (PLURAL die **Lacke**) ❶ varnish ❷ paint

**lackieren** VERB (PERF **hat lackiert**) ❶ to varnish ❷ to spray (with paint)

**laden** ◇VERB (PRES **lädt**, IMP **lud**, PERF **hat geladen**) ❶ to load; wir haben die Möbel in den Möbelwagen geladen we loaded the furniture into the removal van ❷ eine Batterie laden to charge a battery ❸ to summon; mein Bruder wurde als Zeuge geladen my brother was summoned as a witness

**Laden** der (PLURAL die **Läden**) ❶ shop; wann macht der Laden zu? when does the shop close? ❷ shutter; wenn es heiß ist, lassen wir die Läden den ganzen Tag zu when it's hot we keep the shutters closed all day

**Ladendieb** der (PLURAL die **Ladendiebe**) shoplifter

**Ladung** die (PLURAL die **Ladungen**) ❶ cargo ❷ charge (of dynamite or shot) ❸ summons ❹ load

**lag** ▸ SEE **liegen**

**Lage** die (PLURAL die **Lagen**) ❶ situation; nicht in der Lage sein, etwas zu tun not be in a position to do something ❷ layer

**Lager** das (PLURAL die **Lager**) ❶ camp ❷ warehouse ❸ stock; etwas auf Lager haben to have something in stock ❹ stock-room ❺ bearing (in a machine)

**lagern** VERB (PERF **hat gelagert**) ❶ to store ❷ to camp

**lahm** ADJECTIVE lame

**lähmen** VERB (PERF **hat gelähmt**) to paralyse

**Lähmung** die paralysis

**Laib** der (PLURAL die **Laibe**) loaf

**Laken** das (PLURAL die **Laken**) sheet

**Lakritze** die liquorice

**Lamm** das (PLURAL die **Lämmer**) lamb

**Lampe** die (PLURAL die **Lampen**) lamp

**Lampenschirm** der (PLURAL die **Lampenschirme**) lampshade

**Lancieren** das launch (of product)

**Land** das (PLURAL die **Länder**) ❶ country; auf dem Land in the country ❷ land ❸ state (there are 16 Länder in Germany)

**Landebahn** die (PLURAL die **Landebahnen**) runway

**landen** VERB (PERF **ist gelandet**) ❶ to land ❷ im Krankenhaus landen (informal) to end up in hospital

**Landkarte** die (PLURAL die **Landkarten**) map

a b c d e f g h i j k l m n o p q r s t u v w x y z

**Landkreis** der *(PLURAL* die **Landkreise)** district

**ländlich** *ADJECTIVE* **rural**

**Landschaft** die *(PLURAL* die **Landschaften)** ❶ countryside ❷ landscape

**Landschaftsschutzgebiet** das *(PLURAL* die **Landschaftsschutzgebiete)** conservation area

**Landstraße** die *(PLURAL* die **Landstraßen)** country road

**landswirtschaftlich** *ADJECTIVE* agricultural

**Landtag** der state parliament

**Landwirtschaft** die agriculture, farming

**lang** *ADJECTIVE* ❶ long; seit langem for a long time ❷ tall

**lang** *ADVERB* eine Woche lang for a week

**langärmelig** *ADJECTIVE* long-sleeved

**lange** *ADVERB* ❶ a long time; lange nicht not for a long time ❷ so lange wie möglich as long as possible ❸ er ist lange nicht so reich he's nowhere near as rich

**Länge** die *(PLURAL* die **Längen)** ❶ length ❷ longitude

**langen** *VERB (PERF* hat gelangt) ❶ to be enough; das Geld langt nicht *(informal)* it's not enough money, mir langt's *(informal)* I've had enough ❷ to reach; nach etwas langen to reach for something ❸ jemandem eine langen *(informal)* to slap somebody's face

**Langlauf** der cross-country *(in skiing)*

**langsam** *ADJECTIVE, ADVERB* **slow**; die Musik geht mir langsam auf die Nerven the music is slowly getting on my nerves

**längst** *ADVERB* ❶ a long time ago; das habe ich schon längst gemacht I did it a long time ago ❷ for a long time; er weiß es schon längst he's known it for a long time ❸ längst nicht nowhere near, not nearly

**längster, längste, längstes** *ADJECTIVE* **longest**; Marion hat den längsten Aufsatz geschrieben Marion wrote the longest essay

**langweilen** *VERB (PERF* hat gelangweilt) ❶ to bore ❷ sich langweilen to be bored

**langweilig** *ADJECTIVE* **boring**

**Lappen** der *(PLURAL* die **Lappen)** cloth, rag

**Laptop** der *(PLURAL* die **Laptops)** laptop

**Lärm** der noise; sich über den Lärm beschweren to complain about the noise

**las** ▸ SEE **lesen**

**Laser** der *(PLURAL* die **Laser)** laser

**Laserdrucker** der *(PLURAL* die **Laserdrucker)** laser printer

**Laseroperation** die laser surgery

**Laserstrahl** der *(PLURAL* die **Laserstrahlen)** laser beam

**lassen** ◇*VERB (PRES* lässt, *IMP* ließ, *PERF* hat gelassen) ❶ to let; jemanden schlafen lassen to let somebody sleep, lass uns jetzt gehen let's go now ❷ jemandem etwas lassen to let somebody have something ❸ to leave; die Kinder zu Hause lassen to leave the children at home, lass mich! leave me! **❹** jemanden warten lassen to keep somebody waiting **❺** etwas reparieren lassen to have something repaired **❻** lass das! stop it! **❼** die Tür lässt sich leicht öffnen the door opens easily, das lässt sich alles machen that can all be arranged

**lässig** *ADJECTIVE* casual

**Last** die *(PLURAL die* **Lasten)** **❶** load **❷** jemandem zur Last fallen to be a burden on somebody

**lästig** *ADJECTIVE* troublesome

**Lastwagen** der *(PLURAL die* **Lastwagen)** lorry, truck

**Latein** das Latin

**Laterne** die *(PLURAL die* **Laternen)** **❶** lantern **❷** street lamp

**Laub** das leaves

**Lauch** der leek(s)

**Lauf** der *(PLURAL die* **Läufe)** **❶** run **❷** course; im Laufe der Zeit in the course of time, im Laufe der Jahre over the years **❸** race **❹** barrel *(of a gun)*

**Laufbahn** die *(PLURAL die* **Laufbahnen)** career

**laufen** ◇*VERB (PRES* **läuft**, *IMP* **lief**, *PERF* **ist gelaufen)** **❶** to run; sie kann viel schneller laufen als ihr Bruder she can run much faster than her brother **❷** to walk; du kannst nach Hause laufen oder mit dem Bus fahren you can walk home or go on the bus **❸** to be valid **❹** Ski laufen to ski **❺** to be on *(of a film, programme, or machine)*

**laufend** *ADJECTIVE* **❶** running **❷** current *(issue, month)* **❸** auf dem Laufenden sein to be up to date,

Anita hält mich auf dem Laufenden Anita keeps me up to date

**laufend** *ADVERB* continually, constantly

**Läufer** der *(PLURAL die* **Läufer)** **❶** runner **❷** rug **❸** bishop *(in chess)*

**Läuferin** die *(PLURAL die* **Läuferinnen)** runner

**Laufmasche** die *(PLURAL die* **Laufmaschen)** ladder *(in your tights)*

**Laufwerk** das *(PLURAL die* **Laufwerke)** drive *(on a computer)*

**Laune** die *(PLURAL die* **Launen)** mood

**launisch** *ADJECTIVE* moody

**Laus** die *(PLURAL die* **Läuse)** louse

**laut** *ADJECTIVE* **❶** loud **❷** noisy

**laut** *ADVERB* **❶** loudly **❷** laut lesen to read aloud **❸** lauter stellen to turn up

**laut** *PREPOSITION (+GEN or +DAT)* according to

**Laut** der *(PLURAL die* **Laute)** sound

**lauten** *VERB (PERF* **hat gelautet)** **❶** to be **❷** to go

**läuten** *VERB (PERF* **hat geläutet)** to ring

**lauter** *ADJECTIVE* nothing but

**Lautsprecher** der *(PLURAL die* **Lautsprecher)** (loud)speaker

**Lautstärke** die volume

**lauwarm** *ADJECTIVE* lukewarm

**Lavendel** der lavender

**Lawine** die *(PLURAL die* **Lawinen)** avalanche

**leben** VERB (PERF **hat gelebt**) ❶ to live ❷ to be alive ❸ leb wohl! farewell!

**Leben** das (PLURAL die **Leben**) life; am Leben sein to be alive, ums Leben kommen to lose your life

**lebend** ADJECTIVE **living**

**lebendig** ADJECTIVE ❶ living ❷ lebendig sein to be alive ❸ lively

**Lebensgefahr** die **mortal danger**; sein Vater ist in Lebensgefahr his father is critically ill

**lebensgefährlich** ADJECTIVE ❶ extremely dangerous ❷ critical; lebensgefährlich verletzt critically injured

**Lebenshaltungskosten** PLURAL NOUN cost of living

**lebenslänglich** ADJECTIVE **life**

**lebenslänglich** ADVERB **for life**

**Lebenslauf** der (PLURAL die **Lebensläufe**) CV

**Lebensmittel** PLURAL NOUN **food, groceries**

**Lebensmittelgeschäft** das (PLURAL die **Lebensmittelgeschäfte**) grocer's (shop)

**Lebensmittelvergiftung** die (PLURAL die **Lebensmittelvergiftungen**) food poisoning

**Lebensunterhalt** der **livelihood**; seinen Lebensunterhalt verdienen to earn one's living

**Leber** die (PLURAL die **Lebern**) liver

**Leberfleck** der (PLURAL die **Leberflecke**) mole

**Leberwurst** die **liver sausage**

**Lebewesen** das (PLURAL die **Lebewesen**) living being, living thing

**lebhaft** ADJECTIVE ❶ lively ❷ vivid (idea, colour)

**Lebkuchen** der (PLURAL die **Lebkuchen**) gingerbread

**leblos** ADJECTIVE **lifeless**

**Leck** das (PLURAL die **Lecks**) leak

**lecken** VERB (PERF **hat geleckt**) ❶ to lick; die Katze leckte ihre Jungen the cat licked the kittens, an etwas lecken to lick something ❷ to leak

**lecker** ADJECTIVE **delicious**

**Leder** das (PLURAL die **Leder**) leather

**ledig** ADJECTIVE **single**

**lediglich** ADVERB **merely**

**leer** ADJECTIVE **empty**; leer machen to empty

**leeren** VERB (PERF **hat geleert**) ❶ to empty ❷ ein leeres Blatt Papier a blank sheet of paper ❸ sich leeren to empty

**Leerlauf** der **neutral** (gear)

**Leerung** die (PLURAL die **Leerungen**) collection

**legal** ADJECTIVE **legal**

**legen** VERB (PERF **hat gelegt**) ❶ to put ❷ to lay ❸ sich legen to lie down ❹ sich legen to die down (of a storm, noise), unsere Begeisterung hat sich gelegt our enthusiasm has worn off

**leger** ADJECTIVE, ADVERB **casual**; leger gekleidet sein to be casually dressed

**Lehm** der **clay**

**Lehne** die (PLURAL die **Lehnen**) ❶ back (of a chair) ❷ arm (of a sofa or chair)

**lehnen** *VERB (PERF* **hat gelehnt)** ❶ to lean ❷ sich an etwas lehnen to lean against something

**Lehrbuch** das *(PLURAL die* **Lehrbücher)** textbook

**lehren** *VERB (PERF* **hat gelehrt)** to teach

**Lehrer** der *(PLURAL die* **Lehrer)** ❶ teacher ❷ instructor

**Lehrerin** die *(PLURAL die* **Lehrerinnen)** ❶ teacher ❷ instructor

**Lehrerzimmer** das *(PLURAL die* **Lehrerzimmer)** staffroom

**Lehrling** der *(PLURAL die* **Lehrlinge)** ❶ apprentice ❷ trainee

**Lehrplan** der *(PLURAL die* **Lehrpläne)** syllabus

**Lehrstelle** die *(PLURAL die* **Lehrstellen)** apprenticeship, trainee post

**Leibwächter** der *(PLURAL die* **Leibwächter)** bodyguard

**Leiche** die *(PLURAL die* **Leichen)** (dead) body, corpse

**leicht** *ADJECTIVE* ❶ light ❷ easy; jemandem leicht fallen to be easy for somebody, es ist ihm nicht leicht gefallen it wasn't easy for him, Markus macht es sich immer leicht Markus always takes the easy way out ❸ ein leichter Akzent a slight accent

**Leichtathletik** die athletics

**leichtfallen** ▸ SEE **leicht**

**Leichtsinn** der ❶ carelessness ❷ recklessness

**leichtsinnig** *ADJECTIVE* ❶ careless ❷ reckless

**leid** *ADJECTIVE* jemanden leid sein to be fed up with somebody, etwas leid sein to be fed up with something

**Leid** das ❶ sorrow ❷ harm ❸ es tut mir Leid I'm sorry, Andreas tut mir Leid I feel sorry for Andreas

**leiden** ◇ *VERB (IMP* **litt,** *PERF* **hat gelitten)** ❶ to suffer ❷ jemanden gut leiden können to like somebody ❸ ich kann Erika nicht leiden I can't stand Erika

**leidenschaftlich** *ADJECTIVE* passionate

**leider** *ADVERB* ❶ unfortunately ❷ leider ja I'm afraid so, leider nicht I'm afraid not

**leihen** ◇ *VERB (IMP* **lieh,** *PERF* **hat geliehen)** ❶ to lend ❷ sich etwas leihen to borrow something, ich habe mir das Buch von Alex geliehen I borrowed the book from Alex

**Leihgabe** die *(PLURAL die* **Leihgaben)** loan *(by a bank)*

**Leihwagen** der *(PLURAL die* **Leihwagen)** hire car

**Leim** der *(PLURAL die* **Leime)** glue

**Leine** die *(PLURAL die* **Leinen)** ❶ rope ❷ line *(for washing)* ❸ lead *(for a dog)*

**Leinen** das *(PLURAL die* **Leinen)** linen

**Leinwand** die *(PLURAL die* **Leinwände)** screen *(in a cinema)*

**leise** *ADJECTIVE* quiet

**leise** *ADVERB* ❶ quietly ❷ die Musik leiser stellen to turn the music down

**leisten** *VERB (PERF* **hat geleistet)** ❶ to achieve ❷ jemandem

Hilfe leisten to help somebody
**❸** jemandem Gesellschaft leisten
to keep somebody company **❹** sich
etwas leisten to treat yourself to
something **❺** sich etwas leisten
können to be able to afford
something, ich kann mir kein neues
Auto leisten I can't afford a new car

**Leistung** die *(PLURAL die Leistungen)*
**❶** achievement **❷** performance
**❸** Leistungen payment

**Leistungskurs** der *(PLURAL die Leistungskurse)* main subject

**leiten** *VERB (PERF hat geleitet)* **❶** to lead **❷** to direct **❸** to manage, run *(a business)* **❹** to conduct

**Leiter**[1] die *(PLURAL die Leitern)* ladder

**Leiter**[2] der *(PLURAL die Leiter)*
**❶** leader **❷** head **❸** manager
**❹** director **❺** conductor *(of an orchestra or electricity)*

**Leiterin** die *(PLURAL die Leiterinnen)*
**❶** leader **❷** head **❸** manageress
**❹** director

**Leitung** die *(PLURAL die Leitungen)*
**❶** direction **❷** management
**❸** *(phone)* line **❹** *(electric)* lead
**❺** cable **❻** pipe **❼** unter der
Leitung von conducted by

**Leitungswasser** das tap water

**Lektion** die *(PLURAL die Lektionen)*
lesson

**lenken** *VERB (PERF hat gelenkt)* **❶** to steer **❷** to guide **❸** den Verdacht auf jemanden lenken to throw suspicion on somebody

**Lenkrad** das *(PLURAL die Lenkräder)*
steering wheel

**Lenkstange** die *(PLURAL die Lenkstangen)* handlebars

**lernen** *VERB (PERF hat gelernt)* **❶** to learn; schwimmen lernen to learn to swim **❷** to study

**lesbisch** *ADJECTIVE* lesbian

**lesen** ◇*VERB (PRES liest, IMP las, PERF hat gelesen)* to read

**Leser** der *(PLURAL die Leser)* reader

**Leseratte** die *(PLURAL die Leseratten)*
bookworm

**Leserin** die *(PLURAL die Leserinnen)*
reader

**letzte** ▸ SEE **letzter**

**Letzte** der/die/das *(PLURAL die Letzten)* **❶** der/die Letzte the last (one), das Letzte the last (thing)
**❷** Boris kam als Letzter Boris arrived last

**letztens** *ADVERB* **❶** recently **❷** lastly

**letzter, letzte, letztes** *ADJECTIVE*
**❶** last; zum letzten Mal for the last time, das letzte Mal the last time
**❷** latest *(news, information)* **❸** in letzter Zeit recently

**leuchten** *VERB (PERF hat geleuchtet)*
to shine

**Leuchter** der *(PLURAL die Leuchter)*
candlestick

**Leuchtreklame** die neon sign

**Leuchtturm** der *(PLURAL die Leuchttürme)* lighthouse

**leugnen** *VERB (PERF hat geleugnet)*
to deny

**Leukämie** die leukaemia

**Leute** *PLURAL NOUN* people

**Lexikon** das *(PLURAL die Lexika)*
**❶** encyclopaedia **❷** dictionary

**Licht** das *(PLURAL die Lichter)* light

**Lichtbild** das (PLURAL die **Lichtbilder**) photograph

**Lichtschalter** der (PLURAL die **Lichtschalter**) light switch

**Lid** das (PLURAL die **Lider**) (eye)lid

**Lidschatten** der (PLURAL die **Lidschatten**) eye shadow

**lieb** ADJECTIVE ❶ dear; liebe Gabi dear Gabi ❷ nice; das ist lieb von euch that's nice of you ❸ jemanden lieb haben to be fond of somebody ❹ es wäre mir lieber, wenn … I'd prefer it if … ❺ ihr liebstes Spielzeug her favourite toy

**Liebe** die (PLURAL die **Lieben**) love

**lieben** VERB (PERF **hat geliebt**) to love

**liebenswürdig** ADJECTIVE kind

**lieber** ADVERB ❶ rather ❷ lieber mögen to like better ❸ lass das lieber you'd better not do that ❹ ich trinke lieber Kaffee I prefer coffee

**Liebesbrief** der (PLURAL die **Liebesbriefe**) love letter

**Liebesfilm** der (PLURAL die **Liebesfilme**) romantic film

**Liebeskummer** der Liebeskummer haben to be lovesick

**liebevoll** ADJECTIVE loving

**liebhaben** ▸ SEE **lieb**

**Liebling** der (PLURAL die **Lieblinge**) ❶ darling ❷ favourite

**Lieblings-** PREFIX favourite

**liebster, liebste, liebstes** ADJECTIVE ❶ dearest ❷ favourite

**liebstes** ADVERB am liebsten best (of all), ich mag Max am liebsten I like Max best

**Lied** das (PLURAL die **Lieder**) song

**lief** ▸ SEE **laufen**

**liefern** VERB (PERF **hat geliefert**) ❶ to deliver ❷ to supply

**Lieferung** die (PLURAL die **Lieferungen**) delivery

**Lieferwagen** der (PLURAL die **Lieferwagen**) (delivery) van

**liegen** ◇VERB (IMP **lag**, PERF **hat gelegen**) ❶ to lie; der Brief liegt auf dem Tisch the letter is on the table, es liegt viel Schnee there's lots of snow ❷ to be, to be situated ❸ liegen bleiben to stay (in bed), er ist liegen geblieben he didn't get up ❹ etwas bleibt liegen something is left behind, die Arbeit ist liegen geblieben the job was left undone ❺ der Schnee bleibt liegen the snow is settling ❻ liegen lassen to leave ❼ es liegt mir nicht it doesn't suit me ❽ an etwas liegen to be due to something ❾ das liegt an ihm it's up to him

**liegenbleiben, liegenlassen** ▸ SEE **liegen**

**Liegestuhl** der (PLURAL die **Liegestühle**) deckchair

**Liegewagen** der (PLURAL die **Liegewagen**) couchette (car)

**ließ** ▸ SEE **lassen**

**liest** ▸ SEE **lesen**

**Lift** der (PLURAL die **Lifte**) lift

**Liga** die (PLURAL die **Ligen**) league

**lila** ADJECTIVE ❶ purple ❷ mauve

**Limo** die (PLURAL die **Limo(s)**) ▸ SEE **Limonade**

**Limonade** die (PLURAL die **Limonaden**) ❶ fizzy drink ❷ lemonade

**Limone** die (PLURAL die **Limonen**) lime

**Lineal** das (PLURAL die **Lineale**) ruler

**Linie** die (PLURAL die **Linien**) ❶ line ❷ route (of a bus); Linie 6 number 6

**Linienflug** der (PLURAL die **Linienflüge**) scheduled flight

**Linke** die ❶ left; zu meiner Linken on my left ❷ left hand ❸ left side ❹ die Linke the left (in politics)

**linker, linke, linkes** ADJECTIVE ❶ left ❷ left-wing

**links** ADVERB ❶ on the left; links fahren to drive on the left, links abbiegen to turn left, nach links left, von links from the left ❷ links sein to be left-wing ❸ zwei links, zwei rechts stricken to purl two, knit two ❹ (clothing) inside out

**Linkshänder** der (PLURAL die **Linkshänder**) left-hander

**Linkshänderin** die (PLURAL die **Linkshänderinnen**) left-hander

**Linse** die (PLURAL die **Linsen**) ❶ lens ❷ lentil

**Lippe** die (PLURAL die **Lippen**) lip

**Lippenstift** der (PLURAL die **Lippenstifte**) lipstick

**Liste** die (PLURAL die **Listen**) list

**listig** ADJECTIVE cunning

**Liter** der (PLURAL die **Liter**) litre

**Literatur** die literature

**litt** ▸ SEE **leiden**

**Livesendung** die (PLURAL die **Livesendungen**) live programme

**Lizenz** die (PLURAL die **Lizenzen**) licence

**Lkw** der (PLURAL die **Lkws**) (short for Lastkraftwagen) lorry, truck

**Lob** das praise

**loben** VERB (PERF hat gelobt) to praise

**Loch** das (PLURAL die **Löcher**) hole

**Locke** die (PLURAL die **Locken**) curl

**locken** VERB (PERF hat gelockt) ❶ to tempt ❷ to curl

**locker** ADJECTIVE ❶ loose ❷ slack (rope) ❸ relaxed (atmosphere, person)

**lockerlassen** ◇VERB (PRES **lässt locker**, IMP **ließ locker**, PERF **hat lockergelassen**) nicht lockerlassen (informal) not to let up

**lockig** ADJECTIVE curly

**Löffel** der (PLURAL die **Löffel**) ❶ spoon ❷ ein Löffel Mehl a spoonful of flour

**log** ▸ SEE **lügen**

**Logik** die logic

**logisch** ADJECTIVE ❶ logical ❷ ja, logisch! yes, of course!

**Lohn** der (PLURAL die **Löhne**) ❶ wages ❷ reward

**lohnen** VERB (PERF hat sich gelohnt) sich lohnen to be worth it

**Lokal** das (PLURAL die **Lokale**) ❶ bar ❷ restaurant

**Lokomotive** die (PLURAL die **Lokomotiven**) locomotive, engine

**Lorbeerblatt** das (PLURAL die **Lorbeerblätter**) bay leaf

**los** ADJECTIVE ❶ der Hund ist los the dog is off the lead ❷ die Schraube ist los the screw's loose ❸ es ist viel los there's a lot going on ❹ etwas los sein to be rid of something ❺ was ist los? what's the matter?

**los** *ADVERB* ❶ los! go on! ❷ Achtung, fertig, los! ready, steady, go!

**Los** das (*PLURAL* die **Lose**) ❶ (lottery) ticket ❷ das große Los ziehen to hit the jackpot ❸ lot

**losbinden** ◇*VERB* (*IMP* **band los**, *PERF* **hat losgebunden**) to untie

**löschen** *VERB* (*PERF* **hat gelöscht**) ❶ to put out ❷ seinen Durst löschen to quench your thirst ❸ to delete, to cancel ❹ to erase

**lose** *ADJECTIVE* **loose**

**lösen** *VERB* (*PERF* **hat gelöst**) ❶ to solve ❷ to undo ❸ to buy; eine Fahrkarte lösen to buy a ticket ❹ to release ❺ to remove ❻ sich lösen to come undone ❼ sich lösen to be solved (*of a puzzle or mystery*), sich von selbst lösen to be resolved (*of a problem*) ❽ sich in Wasser lösen to dissolve in water

**losfahren** ◇*VERB* (*PRES* **fährt los**, *IMP* **fuhr los**, *PERF* **ist losgefahren**) ❶ to set off ❷ to drive off

**losgehen** ◇*VERB* (*IMP* **ging los**, *PERF* **ist losgegangen**) ❶ to set off ❷ to start ❸ to come off (*of a button*) ❹ to go off (*of a bomb*) ❺ auf jemanden losgehen to go for somebody

**loslassen** ◇*VERB* (*PRES* **lässt los**, *IMP* **ließ los**, *PERF* **hat losgelassen**) ❶ to let go of ❷ to let go

**Losung** die (*PLURAL* die **Losungen**) ❶ slogan ❷ password; die Losung nennen to give the password

**Lösung** die (*PLURAL* die **Lösungen**) solution

**loswerden** ◇*VERB* (*PRES* **wird los**, *IMP* **wurde los**, *PERF* **ist losgeworden**) to get rid of

**Lotterie** die (*PLURAL* die **Lotterien**) lottery

**Lotto** das (*PLURAL* die **Lottos**) (national) lottery

**Löwe** der (*PLURAL* die **Löwen**) ❶ lion ❷ Leo; Wilhelm ist Löwe Wilhelm's a Leo

**Loyalität** die **loyalty**

**Lücke** die (*PLURAL* die **Lücken**) gap

**Luft** die (*PLURAL* die **Lüfte**) ❶ air ❷ die Luft anhalten to hold your breath ❸ in die Luft gehen (*informal*) to blow your top ❹ jemanden wie Luft behandeln to ignore somebody

**Luftballon** der (*PLURAL* die **Luftballons**) balloon

**Luftdruck** der air pressure

**Luftmatratze** die (*PLURAL* die **Luftmatratzen**) air-bed

**Luftpost** die airmail; per Luftpost by airmail

**Luftverschmutzung** die air pollution

**Luftwaffe** die air force

**Lüge** die (*PLURAL* die **Lügen**) lie

**lügen** ◇*VERB* (*IMP* **log**, *PERF* **hat gelogen**) to lie

**Lügner** der (*PLURAL* die **Lügner**) liar

**Lügnerin** die (*PLURAL* die **Lügnerinnen**) liar

**Lunge** die (*PLURAL* die **Lungen**) lungs

**Lungenentzündung** die pneumonia

a b c d e f g h i j k l m n o p q r s t u v w x y z

**Lupe** die *(PLURAL die **Lupen**)*
magnifying glass

**Lust** die ❶ pleasure ❷ Lust haben,
etwas zu tun to feel like doing
something, ich habe keine Lust
I don't feel like it, Lust auf etwas
haben to feel like something

**lustig** *ADJECTIVE* ❶ jolly ❷ funny
❸ Dieter hat sich über mich lustig
gemacht Dieter made fun of me

**lutschen** *VERB (PERF **hat gelutscht**)*
to suck

**Lutscher** der *(PLURAL die **Lutscher**)*
lollipop

**Luxemburg** das Luxembourg

**Luxus** der luxury

# Mm

**machen** *VERB (PERF **hat gemacht**)*
❶ to make ❷ to do; was machst
du da? what are you doing? ❸ was
macht die Arbeit? how's work?,
was macht Karin? how's Karin?
❹ sich an die Arbeit machen to get
down to work ❺ schnell machen
to hurry ❻ das macht nichts it
doesn't matter ❼ to come to; das
macht fünf Euro that comes to
five euros ❽ sich nichts aus etwas
machen to not be very keen on
something, Gisela macht sich nichts
aus Schokolade Gisela isn't keen on
chocolate

**Macht** die *(PLURAL die **Mächte**)*
power; an die Macht kommen
to come to power

**Mädchen** das *(PLURAL die **Mädchen**)*
girl

**Mädchenname** der *(PLURAL die
**Mädchennamen**)* maiden name

**Made** die *(PLURAL die **Maden**)*
maggot

**mag** ▸ SEE **mögen**

**Magazin** das *(PLURAL die **Magazine**)*
magazine

**Magen** der *(PLURAL die **Mägen**)*
stomach

**Magenschmerzen** *PLURAL NOUN*
stomach-ache

**mager** *ADJECTIVE* ❶ thin ❷ lean ❸ low-fat

**magersüchtig** *ADJECTIVE* anorexic

**Magie** die magic

**Magnet** der *(PLURAL die Magnete(n))* magnet

**magnetisch** *ADJECTIVE* magnetic

**magst** ▸ SEE **mögen**

**Mahagoni** das mahogany

**mähen** *VERB (PERF hat gemäht)* to mow; den Rasen mähen to mow the lawn

**mahlen** ◇*VERB (PERF hat gemahlen)* to grind

**Mahlzeit** die *(PLURAL die Mahlzeiten)* meal; Mahlzeit! enjoy your meal!

**Mai** der May; der Erste Mai May Day

**Maiglöckchen** das *(PLURAL die Maiglöckchen)* lily of the valley

**mailen** *VERB (PERF hat gemailt)* to email

**Mais** der maize

**Majonäse** die mayonnaise

**Majoran** der marjoram

**Makkaroni** *PLURAL NOUN* macaroni

**Makler** der *(PLURAL die Makler)* estate agent

**Makrele** die *(PLURAL die Makrelen)* mackerel

**mal** *ADVERB* ❶ times; zwei mal drei two times three ❷ by *(with measurements)* ❸ sometime *(in the future)*; ich möchte mal nach Brasilien fahren I'd like to go to Brazil sometime ❹ schon mal ever ❺ ich war schon mal da I've been once before ❻ nicht mal not even ❼ komm mal her! come here!

**Mal** das *(PLURAL die Male)* ❶ time; nächstes Mal next time, zum ersten Mal for the first time ❷ mark ❸ mole

**malen** *VERB (PERF hat gemalt)* to paint

**Maler** der *(PLURAL die Maler)* painter

**Malerei** die painting

**Malerin** die *(PLURAL die Malerinnen)* painter

**Mallorca** das Majorca

**Mama** die *(PLURAL die Mamas)* mum

**Mami** die *(PLURAL die Mamis)* mummy

**man** *PRONOUN* ❶ you, one, wie macht man das? how do you do it?, man kann ja nie wissen one can never tell ❷ they, people; man sagt they say ❸ man hat mir gesagt I was told

**Manager** der *(PLURAL die Manager)* manager

**Managerin** die *(PLURAL die Managerinnen)* manageress

**mancher, manche, manches** *ADJECTIVE* ❶ many a; so manchen Tag many a day ❷ manche *(plural)* some, an manchen Tagen some days

**manches** *PRONOUN* ❶ many a person ❷ manche *(plural)* some people ❸ manches some things

**manchmal** *ADVERB* sometimes

**Mandarine** die *(PLURAL die Mandarinen)* mandarin

**Mandel** die *(PLURAL die Mandeln)* ❶ almond ❷ tonsil

**Mandelentzündung** die tonsillitis

a b c d e f g h i j k l m n o p q r s t u v w x y z

**Mangel** der (PLURAL die **Mängel**)
**❶** lack **❷** shortage **❸** defect, fault

**mangelhaft** ADJECTIVE **❶** faulty
**❷** unsatisfactory (school mark)

**Manie** die (PLURAL die **Manien**) mania

**Manieren** PLURAL NOUN manners;
er hat keine Manieren he's got no
manners

**Mann** der (PLURAL die **Männer**)
**❶** man **❷** husband

**Männchen** das (PLURAL die
**Männchen**) male (animal)

**Mannequin** das (PLURAL die
**Mannequins**) model

**männlich** ADJECTIVE **❶** male **❷** manly
**❸** masculine

**Mannschaft** die (PLURAL die
**Mannschaften**) **❶** team **❷** crew

**Manschette** die (PLURAL die
**Manschetten**) cuff

**Mantel** der (PLURAL die **Mäntel**) coat

**Mappe** die (PLURAL die **Mappen**)
**❶** folder **❷** briefcase **❸** bag

**Märchen** das (PLURAL die **Märchen**)
fairy tale

**Margarine** die margarine

**Marienkäfer** der (PLURAL die
**Marienkäfer**) ladybird

**Marine** die (PLURAL die **Marinen**)
navy

**Mark** die (PLURAL die **Mark**) mark
(German currency until replaced
by the euro; one hundred marks
= €51.13 euros)

**Marke** die (PLURAL die **Marken**)
**❶** make, brand; meine Mutter
fährt seit Jahren die gleiche Marke
my mother has been driving the

same make of car for years, Adidas
ist eine führende Marke Adidas is a
leading brand **❷** tag **❸** stamp (for
letters) **❹** coupon

**markieren** VERB (PERF **hat markiert**)
**❶** to mark **❷** to fake

**Markt** der (PLURAL die **Märkte**)
market; auf den Markt bringen
to launch (a product)

**Marktplatz** der (PLURAL die
**Marktplätze**) market-place

**Marmelade** die (PLURAL die
**Marmeladen**) jam

**Marmor** der marble

**Marokko** das Morocco

**Marsch** der (PLURAL die **Märsche**)
march

**März** der March

**Masche** die (PLURAL die **Maschen**)
**❶** stitch **❷** mesh **❸** (informal)
trick; die Masche raushaben
to know how to do it, das ist die
neueste Masche that's the latest
thing

**Maschine** die (PLURAL die
**Maschinen**) **❶** machine **❷** plane
**❸** typewriter; Maschine schreiben
to type

**Masern** PLURAL NOUN measles

**Maske** die (PLURAL die **Masken**) mask

**maskieren** VERB (PERF **hat sich
maskiert**) **❶** sich maskieren
to dress up **❷** sich maskieren
to disguise yourself

**maß** ▸ SEE messen

**Maß¹** das (PLURAL die **Maße**)
**❶** measure **❷** measurement
**❸** extent; in hohem Maße to a
high degree **❹** Maß halten to show
moderation

**Maß²** die *(PLURAL* die **Maß)** litre (of beer)

**Masse** die *(PLURAL* die **Massen)**
❶ mass; eine Masse Arbeit masses of work ❷ crowd ❸ mixture *(in cooking)*

**massenhaft** *ADJECTIVE* masses of

**Massenvernichtungswaffen**
*PLURAL NOUN* weapons of mass destruction

**massieren** *VERB (PERF* hat massiert) to massage

**mäßig** *ADJECTIVE* moderate

**Maßnahme** die *(PLURAL* die **Maßnahmen)** measure

**Maßstab** der *(PLURAL* die **Maßstäbe)**
❶ standard ❷ scale

**Mast** der *(PLURAL* die **Masten)** ❶ mast
❷ pole ❸ pylon

**Material** das *(PLURAL* die **Materialien)** ❶ material
❷ materials

**Mathe** die *(informal)* maths

**Mathematik** die mathematics

**Matratze** die *(PLURAL* die **Matratzen)** mattress

**Matrose** der *(PLURAL* die **Matrosen)** sailor

**Matsch** der ❶ mud ❷ slush

**matschig** *ADJECTIVE* ❶ muddy
❷ slushy

**matt** *ADJECTIVE* ❶ weak ❷ matt
❸ dull ❹ matt! checkmate!

**Matte** die *(PLURAL* die **Matten)** mat

**Mauer** die *(PLURAL* die **Mauern)** wall

**Maul** das *(PLURAL* die **Mäuler)** mouth;
halt's Maul! *(informal)* shut up!

**Maulkorb** der *(PLURAL* die **Maulkörbe)** muzzle

**Maulwurf** der *(PLURAL* die **Maulwürfe)** mole

**Maulwurfshügel** der *(PLURAL* die **Maulwurfshügel)** molehill

**Maurer** der *(PLURAL* die **Maurer)** bricklayer

**Maus** die *(PLURAL* die **Mäuse)** mouse

**Mausklick** der *(PLURAL* die **Mausklicks)** mouse click

**Maximum** das *(PLURAL* die **Maxima)** maximum

**Mayonnaise** die mayonnaise

**Mechaniker** der *(PLURAL* die **Mechaniker)** mechanic

**Mechanikerin** die *(PLURAL* die **Mechanikerinnen)** mechanic

**mechanisch** *ADJECTIVE* mechanical

**meckern** *VERB (PERF* hat gemeckert)
❶ to bleat ❷ to grumble

**Medaille** die *(PLURAL* die **Medaillen)** medal

**Medien** *PLURAL NOUN* media

**Medikament** das *(PLURAL* die **Medikamente)** medicine, drug

**Medizin** die *(PLURAL* die **Medizinen)** medicine

**Meer** das *(PLURAL* die **Meere)** sea

**Meeresfrüchte** *PLURAL NOUN* seafood

**Meerschweinchen** das *(PLURAL* die **Meerschweinchen)** guinea pig

**Megabyte** das *(PLURAL* die **Megabytes)** megabyte

**Mehl** das flour

**mehr** *ADVERB, PRONOUN* **more**; nichts mehr no more, nie mehr never again

**mehrere** *PRONOUN* **several**

**mehreres** *PRONOUN* **several things**

**mehrfach** *ADJECTIVE* ❶ **multiple**, **many** ❷ **repeated**

**mehrfach** *ADVERB* **several times**

**Mehrheit** die *(PLURAL die Mehrheiten)* **majority**

**mehrmalig** *ADJECTIVE* **repeated**

**mehrmals** *ADVERB* **several times**

**Mehrwertsteuer** die **value added tax**

**Mehrzahl** die ❶ **majority** ❷ **plural**

**meiden** ◇*VERB (IMP* **mied**, *PERF* **hat gemieden)** **to avoid**

**Meile** die *(PLURAL die Meilen)* **mile**

**mein** *ADJECTIVE* **my**

**meine** ▸ SEE **meiner**

**meinen** *VERB (PERF* **hat gemeint)** ❶ **to think** ❷ **to mean**; es gut meinen to mean well ❸ **to say**

**meiner, meine, mein(e)s** *PRONOUN* **mine**

**meinetwegen** *ADVERB* ❶ **for my sake** ❷ **because of me** ❸ **as far as I'm concerned**; 'kann ich das Auto haben?' – 'meinetwegen' 'can I take the car?' – 'I don't mind'

**meins** ▸ SEE **meiner**

**Meinung** die *(PLURAL die Meinungen)* **opinion**

**meist** *ADVERB* ❶ **mostly** ❷ **usually**

**meiste** *ADJECTIVE, PRONOUN* **der/die/das meiste most**, die meisten most, am meisten most, the most

**meistens** *ADVERB* ❶ **mostly** ❷ **usually**

**Meister** der *(PLURAL die Meister)* ❶ **master** ❷ **champion**

**Meisterin** die *(PLURAL die Meisterinnen)* **champion**

**Meisterschaft** die *(PLURAL die Meisterschaften)* **championship**

**Meisterstück** das *(PLURAL die Meisterstücke)* ❶ **masterpiece** ❷ **masterstroke**

**Meisterwerk** das *(PLURAL die Meisterwerke)* **masterpiece**

**melden** *VERB (PERF* **hat gemeldet)** ❶ **to report** ❷ **to register** ❸ sich melden to report, *(on the phone)* to answer, Luise hat sich gemeldet *(in school)* Luise put up her hand ❹ sich bei jemandem melden to get in touch with somebody

**Melodie** die *(PLURAL die Melodien)* **melody, tune**

**Melone** die *(PLURAL die Melonen)* ❶ **melon** ❷ **bowler (hat)**

**Menge** die *(PLURAL die Mengen)* ❶ **quantity**; eine Menge Geld a lot of money ❷ **crowd** ❸ **set** *(in maths)*

**Mensch** der *(PLURAL die Menschen)* ❶ **human being** ❷ **person**; kein Mensch nobody, jeder Mensch everybody ❸ die Menschen people, wie viele Menschen? how many people? ❹ *(as an exclamation)* Mensch! *(informal)* wow!, hey!, Mensch, hab ich mich geärgert! *(informal)* I was damn annoyed

**menschenleer** *ADJECTIVE* **deserted**

**Menschenverstand** der gesunder Menschenverstand **common sense**

**Menschheit** die **mankind**

**menschlich** *ADJECTIVE* ❶ human ❷ humane

**Mentalität** die *(PLURAL die Mentalitäten)* mentality

**Menü** das *(PLURAL die Menüs)* ❶ set menu *(in restaurant)* ❷ menu *(of computer program)*

**merken** *VERB (PERF hat gemerkt)* ❶ to notice ❷ sich etwas merken to remember something

**Merkmal** das *(PLURAL die Merkmale)* feature

**merkwürdig** *ADJECTIVE* strange, odd

**Messe** die *(PLURAL die Messen)* ❶ mass ❷ trade fair

**messen** ◇*VERB (PRES misst, IMP maß, PERF hat gemessen)* ❶ to measure; (bei jemandem) Fieber messen to take somebody's temperature ❷ sich mit jemandem messen können to be as good as somebody

**Messer** das *(PLURAL die Messer)* knife

**Messing** das brass

**Metall** das *(PLURAL die Metalle)* metal

**Meter** der *(PLURAL die Meter)* metre

**Metermaß** das *(PLURAL die Metermaße)* tape measure

**Methode** die *(PLURAL die Methoden)* method

**metrisch** *ADJECTIVE* metric

**Metzger** der *(PLURAL die Metzger)* butcher

**Metzgerei** die *(PLURAL die Metzgereien)* butcher's (shop)

**Mexiko** das Mexico

**miauen** *VERB (PERF hat miaut)* to miaow

**mich** *PRONOUN* ❶ me ❷ myself

**mied** ▸ SEE meiden

**Miete** die *(PLURAL die Mieten)* ❶ rent; zur Miete wohnen to live in rented accommodation ❷ hire charge

**mieten** *VERB (PERF hat gemietet)* ❶ to rent ❷ to hire

**Mieter** der *(PLURAL die Mieter)* tenant

**Mieterin** die *(PLURAL die Mieterinnen)* tenant

**Mietshaus** das *(PLURAL die Mietshäuser)* block of rented flats

**Mietvertrag** der *(PLURAL die Mietverträge)* lease

**Mietwagen** der *(PLURAL die Mietwagen)* hire car

**Migräne** die *(PLURAL die Migränen)* migraine

**Mikrochip** der *(PLURAL die Mikrochips)* microchip

**Mikrofon** das *(PLURAL die Mikrofone)* microphone

**Mikroskop** das *(PLURAL die Mikroskope)* microscope

**Mikrowellenherd** der *(PLURAL die Mikrowellenherde)* microwave oven

**Milch** die milk

**Milchshake** der *(PLURAL die Milchshakes)* milk shake

**mild** *ADJECTIVE* mild

**Militär** das army

**militärisch** *ADJECTIVE* military

a
b
c
d
e
f
g
h
i
j
k
l
m
n
o
p
q
r
s
t
u
v
w
x
y
z

**Milliarde** die *(PLURAL* die **Milliarden)** thousand million, billion; zwei Milliarden Euro two billion euros

**Millimeter** der *(PLURAL* die **Millimeter)** millimetre

**Million** die *(PLURAL* die **Millionen)** million

**Millionär** der *(PLURAL* die **Millionäre)** millionaire

**Millionärin** die *(PLURAL* die **Millionärinnen)** millionairess

**Minderheit** die *(PLURAL* die **Minderheiten)** minority

**minderjährig** *ADJECTIVE* under age

**mindestens** *ADVERB* at least

**mindester, mindeste, mindestes** *ADJECTIVE* least

**mindestes** *PRONOUN* ❶ der/die/das Mindeste the least, zum Mindesten at least ❷ nicht im Mindesten not in the least

**Mine** die *(PLURAL* die **Minen)** ❶ mine ❷ lead *(in a pencil)* ❸ refill *(for a ball-point)*

**Mineralwasser** das *(PLURAL* die **Mineralwässer)** mineral water

**Minirock** der *(PLURAL* die **Miniröcke)** miniskirt

**Minister** der *(PLURAL* die **Minister)** minister

**Ministerin** die *(PLURAL* die **Ministerinnen)** minister

**Ministerium** das *(PLURAL* die **Ministerien)** ministry, department

**minus** *ADVERB* minus

**Minute** die *(PLURAL* die **Minuten)** minute

**mir** *PRONOUN* ❶ me, to me ❷ myself

**mischen** *VERB (PERF* hat gemischt*)* ❶ to mix ❷ die Karten mischen to shuffle the cards ❸ sich mischen to mix

**Mischung** die *(PLURAL* die **Mischungen)** ❶ mixture ❷ blend

**miserabel** *ADJECTIVE (informal)* ❶ hopeless ❷ dreadful

**missbilligen** *VERB (PERF* hat missbilligt*)* to disapprove

**Missbrauch** der abuse

**missbrauchen** *VERB (PERF* hat missbraucht*)* to abuse

**Misserfolg** der *(PLURAL* die **Misserfolge)** failure

**Missgeschick** das *(PLURAL* die **Missgeschicke)** ❶ misfortune ❷ mishap

**misshandeln** *VERB (PRES* hat misshandelt*)* to ill-treat

**misslingen** ◇*VERB (IMP* misslang, *PERF* ist misslungen*)* to fail; es misslang ihr she failed

**misst** ▸ *SEE* messen

**misstrauen** *VERB (PERF* hat misstraut*)* jemandem misstrauen to mistrust somebody

**Misstrauen** das ❶ mistrust ❷ distrust

**misstrauisch** *ADJECTIVE* suspicious

**Missverständnis** das *(PLURAL* die **Missverständnisse)** misunderstanding

**missverstehen** ◇*VERB (IMP* missverstand, *PERF* hat missverstanden*)* to misunderstand

**Mist** der ❶ **manure** ❷ *(informal)* **rubbish**

**Mistel** die *(PLURAL* die **Misteln)* **mistletoe**

**mit** *PREPOSITION (+DAT)* ❶ **with** ❷ **mit der Bahn fahren** to go by train, **mit dem Boot fahran** to go by boat ❸ **mit sechs Jahren** at the age of six ❹ **mit jemandem sprechen** to speak to somebody ❺ **mit Bleistift** in pencil ❻ **mit lauter Stimme** in a loud voice

**mit** *ADVERB* **as well**, **too**; **warst du mit dabei?** were you there too?

**Mitarbeiter** der *(PLURAL* die **Mitarbeiter)* ❶ **colleague** ❷ **employee**

**Mitarbeiterin** die *(PLURAL* die **Mitarbeiterinnen)* ❶ **colleague** ❷ **employee**

**mitbringen** ◇*VERB (IMP* **brachte mit**, *PERF* **hat mitgebracht)* to **bring**, to **bring along**; **ich bringe den Kindern Schokolade mit** I'm taking the children some chocolate

**miteinander** *ADVERB* **with each other**, **with one another**

**Mitesser** der *(PLURAL* die **Mitesser)* **blackhead**

**mitfahren** ◇*VERB (PRES* **fährt mit**, *IMP* **fuhr mit**, *PERF* **ist mitgefahren)* ❶ **mit jemandem mitfahren** to go with somebody, **die Kinder fahren mit uns mit** the children are coming with us ❷ **bei jemandem mitfahren** to get a lift with somebody, **jemanden mitfahren lassen** to give somebody a lift

**mitgeben** ◇*VERB (PRES* **gibt mit**, *IMP* **gab mit**, *PERF* **hat mitgegeben)* to **give**

**Mitglied** das *(PLURAL* die **Mitglieder)* **member**

**mithalten** ◇*VERB (PRES* **hält mit**, *IMP* **hielt mit**, *PERF* **hat mitgehalten)* to **keep up**

**mitkommen** ◇*VERB (IMP* **kam mit**, *PERF* **ist mitgekommen)* ❶ to **come too** ❷ to **keep up**

**Mitleid** das **pity**; **kein Mitleid mit jemandem haben** not to feel any sympathy for somebody

**mitmachen** *VERB (PERF* **hat mitgemacht)* ❶ to **join in**; **hast du Lust, bei dem Spiel mitzumachen?** do you want to join in the game? ❷ to **take part in** ❸ to **go through** *(experiences, troubles)*; **sie hat viel mitgemacht** she's gone through a lot

**mitnehmen** ◇*VERB (PRES* **nimmt mit**, *IMP* **nahm mit**, *PERF* **hat mitgenommen)* ❶ to **take**, to **take along**; **Anni hat die Kinder auf den Spielplatz mitgenommen** Anni has taken the children to the playground ❷ to **give a lift to** ❸ to **affect (badly)** ❹ **zum Mitnehmen** to take away

**Mitschüler** der *(PLURAL* die **Mitschüler)* **schoolfriend**

**Mitschülerin** die *(PLURAL* die **Mitschülerinnen)* **schoolfriend**

**mitsingen** *VERB (IMP* **sang mit**, *PERF* **hat mitgesungen)* to **sing along**

**mitspielen** *VERB (PERF* **hat mitgespielt)* ❶ to **play**; **wer spielt bei dem Fußballspiel mit?** who's playing in the football match?, **willst du mitspielen?** do you want to join in? ❷ **in einem Film mitspielen** to be in a film

**Mittag** der *(PLURAL* die **Mittage)**
❶ midday ❷ lunch; zu Mittag
essen to have lunch ❸ lunch-break

**Mittagessen** das *(PLURAL* die
**Mittagessen)** lunch; beim
Mittagessen at lunch

**mittags** *ADVERB* ❶ at lunchtime, at
midday ❷ um zwölf Uhr mittags
at noon

**Mittagspause** die *(PLURAL* die
**Mittagspausen)** lunch-break

**Mitte** die *(PLURAL* die **Mitten)**
❶ middle ❷ centre

**mitteilen** *VERB (PERF* **hat mitgeteilt)**
to tell; jemandem etwas mitteilen
mitteilen to tell somebody
something

**Mitteilung** die *(PLURAL* die
**Mitteilungen)** ❶ announcement
❷ communication

**Mittel** das *(PLURAL* die **Mittel)**
❶ means ❷ ein Mittel gegen
Husten a cough remedy
❸ öffentliche Mittel public funds

**Mittelalter** das Middle Ages

**Mitteleuropa** das Central Europe

**mittelgroß** *ADJECTIVE* medium-sized

**mittelmäßig** *ADJECTIVE* mediocre

**Mittelmeer** das Mediterranean

**Mittelpunkt** der *(PLURAL* die
**Mittelpunkte)** centre; im
Mittelpunkt stehen to be the
centre of attention

**Mittelstand** der middle class

**Mittelstürmer** der *(PLURAL* die
**Mittelstürmer)** centre-forward

**mitten** *ADVERB* mitten in/auf in the
middle of, mitten in der Nacht
in the middle of the night

**Mitternacht** die midnight

**mittlerer, mittlere, mittleres**
*ADJECTIVE* ❶ middle ❷ medium
*(quality, size)* ❸ average

**mittlerweile** *ADVERB* ❶ meanwhile
❷ by now

**Mittwoch** der *(PLURAL* die
**Mittwoche)** Wednesday

**mittwochs** *ADVERB* on Wednesdays

**Mixer** der *(PLURAL* die **Mixer)**
liquidizer

**Möbel** *PLURAL NOUN* furniture

**Möbelwagen** der *(PLURAL* die
**Möbelwagen)** removal van

**Mobiltelefon** das *(PLURAL* die
**Mobiltelefone)** mobile phone

**möbliert** *ADJECTIVE* furnished

**mochte, möchte** ▸ SEE **mögen**

**Mode** die *(PLURAL* die **Moden)** fashion

**Modell** das *(PLURAL* die **Modelle)**
model

**Moderator** der *(PLURAL* die
**Moderatoren)** presenter *(on TV)*

**Moderatorin** die *(PLURAL* die
**Moderatorinnen)** presenter
*(on TV)*

**modern** *ADJECTIVE* modern

**modernisieren** *VERB (PERF* **hat
modernisiert)** to modernize

**modisch** *ADJECTIVE* fashionable

**Mofa** die *(PLURAL* die **Mofas)** moped

**mogeln** *VERB (PERF* **hat gemogelt)**
to cheat

**mögen** ◇*VERB* (*PRES* **mag**, *IMP* **mochte**, *PERF* **hat gemocht**) ❶ to like; ich mag ihn nicht I don't like him, ich möchte I'd like, ich möchte gern wissen I'd like to know, möchtest du nach Hause? would you like to go home? ❷ lieber mögen to prefer, ich möchte lieber Tee I would prefer tea ❸ etwas nicht tun mögen not to want to do something, ich mag nicht fragen I don't want to ask, ich mag nicht mehr I've had enough ❹ das mag sein maybe ❺ was mag das sein? whatever can it be?

**möglich** *ADJECTIVE* **possible**; alles Mögliche all sorts of things

**möglicherweise** *ADVERB* **possibly**

**Möglichkeit** die (*PLURAL* die **Möglichkeiten**) possibility

**möglichst** *ADVERB* **if possible**; möglichst früh as early as possible

**Möhre** die (*PLURAL* die **Möhren**) carrot

**Mokka** der (*PLURAL* die **Mokkas**) mocca

**Molekül** das (*PLURAL* die **Moleküle**) molecule

**Moment** der (*PLURAL* die **Momente**) moment; im Moment at the moment
Moment (mal)! just a moment!

**momentan** *ADJECTIVE* ❶ temporary ❷ current

**momentan** *ADVERB* ❶ temporarily ❷ at the moment

**Monat** der (*PLURAL* die **Monate**) month

**monatelang** *ADVERB* **for months**

**monatlich** *ADJECTIVE, ADVERB* **monthly**

**Mönch** der (*PLURAL* die **Mönche**) monk

**Mond** der (*PLURAL* die **Monde**) moon

**Mondschein** der **moonlight**; im Mondschein by moonlight

**Montag** der (*PLURAL* die **Montage**) Monday

**montags** *ADVERB* **on Mondays**

**Moped** das (*PLURAL* die **Mopeds**) moped

**Moral** die ❶ moral ❷ morale ❸ morals

**moralisch** *ADJECTIVE* **moral**

**Mord** der (*PLURAL* die **Morde**) murder

**Mörder** der (*PLURAL* die **Mörder**) murderer

**Mörderin** die (*PLURAL* die **Mörderinnen**) murderer

**morgen** *ADVERB* **tomorrow**; morgen Abend tomorrow evening

**Morgen** der (*PLURAL* die **Morgen**) morning; am Morgen in the morning, heute Morgen this morning, guten Morgen! good morning!

**morgens** *ADVERB* **in the morning**

**Moschee** die (*PLURAL* die **Moscheen**) mosque

**Mosel** die (River) Moselle

**Moskau** das Moscow

**Moslem** der (*PLURAL* die **Moslems**) Muslim

**moslemisch** *ADJECTIVE* **Muslim**

**Moslenin** die (*PLURAL* die **Mosleninnen**) Muslim

**Motiv** das (*PLURAL* die **Motive**) ❶ motive ❷ motif

**Motivation** die motivation

**Motor** der *(PLURAL* die **Motoren)** engine, motor

**Motorrad** das *(PLURAL* die **Motorräder)** motorcycle, motorbike

**Mousse** die *(PLURAL* die **Mouses)** mousse

**Möwe** die *(PLURAL* die **Möwen)** seagull

**Mücke** die *(PLURAL* die **Mücken)** ❶ midge ❷ mosquito

**müde** *ADJECTIVE* tired

**Müdigkeit** die tiredness

**Mühe** die *(PLURAL* die **Mühen)** ❶ effort; sich Mühe geben to make an effort ❷ trouble; machen Sie sich keine Mühe don't go to any trouble ❸ mit Müh und Not only just

**Mühle** die *(PLURAL* die **Mühlen)** ❶ mill ❷ grinder *(for coffee)*

**mühsam** *ADJECTIVE* laborious

**Müll** der rubbish

**Müllabfuhr** die refuse collection

**Mülleimer** der *(PLURAL* die **Mülleimer)** rubbish bin

**Mülltonne** die *(PLURAL* die **Mülltonnen)** dustbin

**multikulturell** *ADJECTIVE* multicultural

**Mumps** der mumps

**München** das Munich

**Mund** der *(PLURAL* die **Münder)** mouth; halt den Mund! *(informal)* shut up!

**Mundharmonika** die *(PLURAL* die **Mundharmonikas)** mouth organ

**mündlich** *ADJECTIVE* oral

**Münster** das *(PLURAL* die **Münster)** cathedral

**Münze** die *(PLURAL* die **Münzen)** coin

**Münzfernsprecher** der *(PLURAL* die **Münzfernsprecher)** payphone

**murmeln** *VERB (PERF* hat gemurmelt*)* to mumble

**mürrisch** *ADJECTIVE* surly

**Muschel** die *(PLURAL* die **Muscheln)** ❶ mussel ❷ (sea) shell ❸ mouthpiece *(of a phone)*

**Museum** das *(PLURAL* die **Museen)** museum

**Musik** die music

**Musikal** das *(PLURAL* die **Musikals)** musical

**musikalisch** *ADJECTIVE* musical

**Musiker** der *(PLURAL* die **Musiker)** musician

**Musikerin** die *(PLURAL* die **Musikerinnen)** musician

**Muskat** der nutmeg

**Muskel** der *(PLURAL* die **Muskeln)** muscle

**Müsli** das muesli

**Muslim** der *(PLURAL* die **Muslims)** Muslim

**Muslimin** die *(PLURAL* die **Musliminnen)** Muslim

**muss** ▸ SEE **müssen**

**müssen** ◇*VERB (PRES* **muss**, *IMP* **musste**, *PERF* **hat gemusst)** ❶ etwas tun müssen to have to do something, sie muss es tun she's got to do it, she must do it, muss ich? do I have to?, muss das sein? is that necessary? ❷ Sie müssten es mal versuchen you should try it ❸ sie müssen gleich hier sein they'll be here at any moment ❹ ich muss mal *(informal)* I need (to go to) the loo

**Muster** das *(PLURAL* die **Muster)* ❶ pattern ❷ sample

**Mut** der courage; jemandem Mut machen to encourage somebody

**mutig** *ADJECTIVE* courageous

**Mutter**[1] die *(PLURAL* die **Mütter)* mother

**Mutter**[2] die *(PLURAL* die **Muttern)* nut

**Muttersprache** die *(PLURAL* die **Muttersprachen)* mother tongue, native language

**Muttertag** der *(PLURAL* die **Muttertage)* Mother's Day

**Mutti** die *(PLURAL* die **Muttis)* mum

**Mütze** die *(PLURAL* die **Mützen)* cap

**MwSt.** *(Mehrwertsteuer)* VAT

**Mythos** der *(PLURAL* die **Mythen)* myth

**na** *EXCLAMATION* well; na und? so what?, na gut all right then

**Nabel** der *(PLURAL* die **Nabel)* navel

**nach** *PREPOSITION (+DAT)* ❶ to; nach Hause gehen to go home, nach oben up, nach hinten back, nach rechts abbiegen to turn right ❷ after; nach Ihnen after you, zehn nach eins ten past one, nach etwas greifen to reach for something ❸ according to; meiner Meinung nach in my opinion

**nach** *ADVERB* nach und nach bit by bit, gradually, nach wie vor still

**nachahmen** *VERB (PERF* hat **nachgeahmt)* to imitate

**Nachbar** der *(PLURAL* die **Nachbarn)* neighbour

**Nachbarin** die *(PLURAL* die **Nachbarinnen)* neighbour

**Nachbarschaft** die neighbourhood

**nachdem** *CONJUNCTION* ❶ after ❷ je nachdem it depends, je nachdem, wie schnell du damit fertig wirst it depends on how quicky you can finish it

**nachdenken** ◇*VERB (IMP* dachte nach, *PERF* hat nachgedacht) to think; über etwas nachdenken to think about something, ich habe lange über ihr Angebot nachgedacht und mich schließlich

a
b
c
d
e
f
g
h
i
j
k
l
m
n
o
p
q
r
s
t
u
v
w
x
y
z

dagegen entschieden I've thought a long time about her offer and finally decided against it

**nachdenklich** ADJECTIVE thoughtful

**nacheinander** ADVERB one after the other; die Bewerber kamen nacheinander herein the applicants came in one after the other

**Nachfrage** die (PLURAL die Nachfragen) demand; es besteht keine Nachfrage there's no demand for it

**nachgehen** ◇VERB (IMP ging nach, PERF ist nachgegangen) ❶ to be slow; meine Uhr geht nach my watch is slow ❷ jemandem nachgehen to follow somebody, einer Sache nachgehen to look into something

**nachher** ADVERB afterwards; erst gehen wir ins Kino und nachher könnten wir essen gehen we go to the cinema first and afterwards we could go for a meal; bis nachher! see you later!

**Nachhilfe** die private tuition

**nachholen** VERB (PERF hat nachgeholt) ❶ to catch up on; ich hatte Grippe und muss jetzt viel Mathe nachholen I've had flu and now I've got a lot of maths to catch up on ❷ to make up for (something missed) ❸ eine Prüfung nachholen to do an exam at a later date

**nachkommen** ◇VERB (IMP kam nach, PERF ist nachgekommen) ❶ to come later, to follow ❷ ich komme nicht nach I can't keep up ❸ einem Versprechen nachkommen to carry out a promise, seinen Verpflichtungen nachkommen to meet your commitments

**nachlassen** ◇VERB (PRES lässt nach, IMP ließ nach, PERF hat nachgelassen) ❶ to ease; meine Zahnschmerzen lassen langsam nach my toothache is getting better ❷ to let up; sobald die Kälte nachlässt as soon as it gets warmer ❸ to deteriorate ❹ etwas vom Preis nachlassen to take something off the price, jemandem zwanzig Euro nachlassen to give somebody twenty euros off

**nachlässig** ADJECTIVE careless

**nachlaufen** ◇VERB (PRES läuft nach, IMP lief nach, PERF ist nachgelaufen) jemandem nachlaufen to run after somebody, Philipp läuft allen Mädchen nach (informal) Philipp chases all the girls

**nachmachen** VERB (PERF hat nachgemacht) to copy

**Nachmittag** der (PLURAL die Nachmittage) afternoon

**nachmittags** ADVERB in the afternoon

**Nachnahme** die per Nachnahme cash on delivery

**Nachname** der (PLURAL die Nachnamen) surname

**nachprüfen** VERB (PERF hat nachgeprüft) to check; er prüft nach, ob es stimmt he's going to check if it is correct

**Nachricht** die (PLURAL die Nachrichten) ❶ news; ich warte noch immer auf eine Nachricht von ihm I'm still waiting for news of him, eine Nachricht hinterlassen to leave a message ❷ die Nachrichten the news, das kam in den Nachrichten it was on the news

**Nachrichtensprecher** der *(PLURAL die* **Nachrichtensprecher)** newsreader

**Nachrichtensprecherin** die *(PLURAL die* **Nachrichtensprecherinnen)** newsreader

**nachschlagen** ◇*VERB (PRES* **schlägt nach,** *IMP* **schlug nach,** *PERF* **hat nachgeschlagen)** to look up

**nachsehen** ◇*VERB (PRES* **sieht nach,** *IMP* **sah nach,** *PERF* **hat nachgesehen)** ❶ to check; sieh nach, wer da ist go and see who's there ❷ to look up ❸ jemandem etwas nachsehen to let somebody get away with something

**nachsitzen** ◇*VERB (IMP* **saß nach,** *PERF* **hat nachgesessen)** to be in detention; Jan muss nachsitzen Jan has detention

**Nachspeise** die *(PLURAL die* **Nachspeisen)** dessert, pudding

**nächste** ▸ SEE **nächster**

**nächstens** *ADVERB* shortly

**nächster, nächste, nächstes** *ADJECTIVE* ❶ next ❷ nearest; am nächsten sein to be nearest ❸ in nächster Nähe close by

**nächstes** *PRONOUN* der/die/das Nächste (the) next, als Nächstes next

**Nacht** die *(PLURAL die* **Nächte)** night

**Nachteil** der *(PLURAL die* **Nachteile)** disadvantage

**Nachtfalter** der *(PLURAL die* **Nachtfalter)** moth

**Nachthemd** das *(PLURAL die* **Nachthemden)** nightdress, nightshirt

**Nachtigall** die *(PLURAL die* **Nachtigallen)** nightingale

**Nachtisch** der *(PLURAL die* **Nachtische)** dessert, pudding

**Nachtklub** der *(PLURAL die* **Nachtklubs)** night club

**Nachtleben** das nightlife

**nachträglich** *ADJECTIVE* ❶ subsequent ❷ belated

**nachträglich** *ADVERB* ❶ later ❷ belatedly

**nachts** *ADVERB* at night; um zwei Uhr nachts at two o'clock in the morning

**Nacken** der *(PLURAL die* **Nacken)** neck

**nackt** *ADJECTIVE* ❶ naked ❷ bare

**Nacktschnecke** die *(PLURAL die* **Nacktschnecken)** slug

**Nadel** die *(PLURAL die* **Nadeln)** ❶ needle ❷ pin

**Nagel** der *(PLURAL die* **Nägel)** nail

**Nagelbürste** die *(PLURAL die* **Nagelbürsten)** nailbrush

**Nagelfeile** die *(PLURAL die* **Nagelfeilen)** nailfile

**Nagellack** der *(PLURAL die* **Nagellacke)** nail varnish

**nagelneu** *ADJECTIVE* brand-new

**Nagelschere** die *(PLURAL die* **Nagelscheren)** nail scissors

**nahe, nah** *ADJECTIVE, ADVERB* ❶ near, nearby; der Nahe Osten the Middle East, nahe daran sein, etwas zu tun to nearly do something ❷ close; nahe bei close to, nahe verwandt sein to be closely related ❸ jemandem nahe legen, etwas zu tun to urge somebody to do

a
b
c
d
e
f
g
h
i
j
k
l
m
**n**
o
p
q
r
s
t
u
v
w
x
y
z

something **❹** nahe liegend obvious

**nah** PREPOSITION (+DAT) **near, close to**

**Nähe** die **❶ proximity ❷** in der Nähe der Kirche near the church, ganz in der Nähe nearby **❸** aus der Nähe close up

**nahelegen, naheliegend**
▸SEE **nahe**

**nähen** VERB (PERF **hat genäht**) **❶ to sew ❷ to stitch** (a wound)

**näher** ADJECTIVE **❶ closer ❷** nähere Einzelheiten further details **❸ shorter** (way, road)

**näher** ADVERB **❶ closer;** näher kommen to come closer **❷ more closely ❸** Näheres further details

**nähern** VERB (PERF **hat sich genähert**) sich nähern to approach, wir näherten uns dem Dorf we were approaching the village

**Nähgarn** das **cotton**

**nahm** ▸SEE **nehmen**

**Nähmaschine** die (PLURAL die **Nähmaschinen**) **sewing machine**

**Nahrung** die **food**

**Naht** die (PLURAL die **Nähte**) **seam**

**Nahverkehrszug** der (PLURAL die **Nahverkehrszüge**) **local train**

**Name** der (PLURAL die **Namen**) **name;** im Namen von on behalf of, ich rufe im Namen von Herrn und Frau Schmidt an I'm calling on behalf of Mr and Mrs Schmidt

**nämlich** ADVERB **❶ because ❷ namely ❸** das war nämlich ganz anders it was quite different actually

**nannte** ▸SEE **nennen**

**nanu** EXCLAMATION **well, well!**

**Narbe** die (PLURAL die **Narben**) **scar**

**Narr** der (PLURAL die **Narren**) **fool**

**Närrin** die (PLURAL die **Närrinnen**) **fool**

**Nase** die (PLURAL die **Nasen**) **nose;** die Nase voll haben (informal) to have had enough

**Nasenbluten** das **nosebleed**

**Nashorn** das (PLURAL die **Nashörner**) **rhinoceros**

**nass** ADJECTIVE **wet**

**Nation** die (PLURAL die **Nationen**) **nation**

**Nationalhymne** die (PLURAL die **Nationalhymnen**) **national anthem**

**Nationalität** die (PLURAL die **Nationalitäten**) **nationality**

**Natur** die **❶ nature;** von Natur aus by nature **❷** die freie Natur the open countryside

**Naturlehrpfad** der (PLURAL die **Naturlehrpfade**) **nature trail**

**natürlich** ADJECTIVE **natural**

**natürlich** ADVERB **of course, naturally**

**Natürlichkeit** die **naturalness**

**Naturschützer** der (PLURAL die **Naturschützer**) **conservationist**

**Naturschützerin** der (PLURAL die **Naturschützerinnen**) **conservationist**

**Naturschutzgebiet** das (PLURAL die **Naturschutzgebiete**) **nature reserve**

**Naturwissenschaft** die **natural science**

**Nebel** der (PLURAL die **Nebel**) ❶ fog ❷ mist

**nebelig** ADJECTIVE ▸ SEE **neblig**

**neben** PREPOSITION ❶ (+DAT or +ACC with movement towards a place) next to; er hat neben mir gesessen he sat next to me, er hat sich neben mich gesetzt he sat down next to me ❷ apart from

**nebenan** ADVERB next door

**nebenbei** ADVERB ❶ as well, at the same time; er liest die Zeitung und hört nebenbei Musik he reads the newspaper and listens to music at the same time ❷ on the side; nebenbei arbeite ich noch in einem Blumengeschäft I work in a florist's on the side, das mache ich so nebenbei (informal) that's just a sideline ❸ in passing; nebenbei bemerkt by the way

**nebeneinander** ADVERB next to each other

**nebenhergehen** ◇VERB (IMP ging nebenher, PERF ist nebenhergegangen) to walk alongside

**neblig** ADJECTIVE ❶ foggy ❷ misty

**necken** VERB (PERF hat geneckt) to tease

**Neffe** der (PLURAL die **Neffen**) nephew

**negativ** ADJECTIVE negative

**Negativ** das (PLURAL die **Negative**) negative

**nehmen** ◇VERB (PRES nimmt, IMP nahm, PERF hat genommen) ❶ to take ❷ ich nehme eine Suppe I'll have soup ❸ was nehmen Sie dafür? how much do you want for it? ❹ jemanden zu sich nehmen to have somebody live with you ❺ sich etwas nehmen to take something, nimm dir ein Stück Kuchen help yourself to a piece of cake

**Neid** der envy, jealousy

**neidisch** ADJECTIVE envious, jealous

**nein** ADVERB no

**Nelke** die (PLURAL die **Nelken**) carnation

**nennen** ◇VERB (IMP nannte, PERF hat genannt) ❶ to call ❷ to name ❸ ihr Name wurde nicht genannt her name wasn't mentioned ❹ sich nennen to call yourself

**Nerv** der (PLURAL die **Nerven**) nerve; Gabi geht mir auf die Nerven Gabi gets on my nerves

**nervig** ADJECTIVE nerve-wracking

**nervös** ADJECTIVE nervous

**Nervosität** die nervousness

**Nessel** die (PLURAL die **Nesseln**) nettle

**Nest** das (PLURAL die **Nester**) ❶ nest ❷ little place (a village)

**nett** ADJECTIVE nice

**netto** ADVERB net

**Netz** das (PLURAL die **Netze**) ❶ net ❷ network ❸ string bag ❹ (spider's) web

**Netzkamera** die (PLURAL die **Netzkameras**) webcam

**Netzkarte** die (PLURAL die **Netzkarten**) unlimited travel ticket (over a transport network)

**Netzwerk** das (PLURAL die **Netzwerke**) network

**neu** ADJECTIVE ❶ new; wie neu as good as new, neue Sprachen modern languages ❷ seit neuestem recently ❸ die neueste Mode the latest fashion, das Neueste the latest news, das Neueste an Audioausrüstung the latest in audio equipment ❹ das ist mir neu that's news to me

**neu** ADVERB ❶ newly ❷ only just; es ist neu eingetroffen it has only just come in ❸ etwas neu schreiben to rewrite something

**neuartig** ADJECTIVE new; ein neuartiger Flaschenöffner a new kind of bottle opener

**neuerdings** ADVERB recently

**Neugier** die curiosity

**neugierig** ADJECTIVE curious, inquisitive

**Neuigkeit** die (PLURAL die Neuigkeiten) piece of news; gibt es irgendwelche Neuigkeiten? is there any news?

**Neujahr** das New Year, New Year's Day

**neulich** ADVERB the other day

**neun** NUMBER nine

**neunter, neunte, neuntes** ADJECTIVE ninth

**neunzehn** NUMBER nineteen

**neunzig** NUMBER ninety

**Neuseeland** das New Zealand

**nicht** ADVERB ❶ not; ich kann nicht I can't Iris hat nicht angerufen Iris didn't ring, bitte nicht please don't, nicht! don't!, nicht berühren! don't touch! ❷ 'ich mag das nicht' – 'ich auch nicht' 'I don't like it' – 'neither do I' ❸ nicht (wahr)? isn't he/she/it?, du kennst ihn doch, nicht? you know him, don't you? ❹ gar nicht not at all ❺ nicht mehr no more

**Nichte** die (PLURAL die Nichten) niece

**Nichtraucher** der (PLURAL die Nichtraucher) non-smoker

**Nichtraucherabteil** das (PLURAL die Nichtraucherabteile) no-smoking compartment

**Nichtraucherin** die (PLURAL die Nichtraucherinnen) non-smoker

**nichts** PRONOUN ❶ nothing ❷ ich habe nichts gewusst I didn't know anything ❸ nichts mehr no more ❹ das macht nichts it doesn't matter ❺ nichts ahnend unsuspecting

**nichtsahnend** ▸ SEE **nichts**

**Nichtschwimmerbecken** das (PLURAL die Nichtschwimmerbecken) shallow swimming pool (for non-swimmers and learners)

**nicken** VERB (PERF hat genickt) to nod

**Nickerchen** das (PLURAL die Nickerchen) nap; ein Nickerchen machen to have a nap

**nie** ADVERB never

**nieder** ADJECTIVE low

**nieder** ADVERB down

**Niederlage** die (PLURAL die Niederlagen) defeat

**Niederlande** PLURAL NOUN die Niederlande the Netherlands

**Niederländer** der (PLURAL die Niederländer) Dutchman; die Niederländer the Dutch

**Niederländerin** die (PLURAL die **Niederländerinnen**) Dutchwoman

**niederländisch** ADJECTIVE Dutch

**niedlich** ADJECTIVE sweet

**niedrig** ADJECTIVE ❶ low ❷ base

**niemals** ADVERB never

**niemand** PRONOUN nobody; wir haben niemand or niemanden gesehen we didn't see anybody

**Niere** die (PLURAL die **Nieren**) kidney

**nieseln** VERB (PERF **hat genieselt**) to drizzle; es nieselt it's drizzling

**niesen** VERB (PERF **hat geniest**) to sneeze

**Nil** der der Nil the River Nile

**Nilpferd** das (PLURAL die **Nilpferde**) hippopotamus

**nimmt** ▸ SEE nehmen

**nirgends**, **nirgendwo** ADVERB nowhere

**Niveau** das (PLURAL die **Niveaus**) ❶ level ❷ standard

**noch** ADVERB ❶ still; immer noch still ❷ even; noch besser even better ❸ noch nicht not yet, noch nie never ❹ gerade noch only just ❺ wer war noch da? who else was there?, was noch? what else? ❻ noch einmal again ❼ noch ein Bier another beer, noch etwas Kaffee? (would you like some) more coffee? ❽ noch gestern only yesterday ❾ noch und noch Geld loads of money

**noch** CONJUNCTION nor; weder ... noch neither ... nor

**nochmals** ADVERB again

**Nominativ** der (PLURAL die **Nominative**) nominative

**Nonne** die (PLURAL die **Nonnen**) nun

**Nordamerika** das North America

**Nordamerikaner** der (PLURAL die **Nordamerikaner**) North American

**Nordamerikanerin** die (PLURAL die **Nordamerikanerinnen**) North American

**nordamerikanisch** ADJECTIVE North American

**Norden** der north

**Nordirland** das Northern Ireland

**nördlich** ADJECTIVE ❶ northern ❷ northerly (direction)

**nördlich** ADVERB, PREPOSITION (+GEN) nördlich von Wien to the north of Vienna, nördlich der Stadt north of the town

**Nordosten** der north-east

**Nordpol** der North Pole

**Nordsee** die North Sea

**Nordwesten** der north-west

**nörgeln** VERB (PERF **hat genörgelt**) to grumble

**Norm** die (PLURAL die **Normen**) ❶ norm ❷ standard

**normal** ADJECTIVE normal

**normalerweise** ADVERB normally

**Norwegen** das Norway

**Norweger** der (PLURAL die **Norweger**) Norwegian

**Norwegerin** die (PLURAL die **Norwegerinnen**) Norwegian

a
b
c
d
e
f
g
h
i
j
k
l
m
n
o
p
q
r
s
t
u
v
w
x
y
z

**norwegisch** ADJECTIVE **Norwegian**

**Not** die (PLURAL die **Nöte**) ❶ **need**; zur Not if necessary, at a pinch, mit knapper Not only just ❷ **hardship**

**Notaufnahme** die (PLURAL die **Notaufnahmen**) **accident & emergency** (hospital department)

**Notausgang** der (PLURAL die **Notausgänge**) **emergency exit**

**Notdienst** der Notdienst haben to be on call

**Note** die (PLURAL die **Noten**) ❶ **note**; Noten lesen to read music ❷ **mark**

**Notfall** der (PLURAL die **Notfälle**) **emergency**

**notfalls** ADVERB **if need be**

**notieren** VERB (PERF hat notiert) ❶ to **note down** ❷ sich etwas notieren to make a note of something

**nötig** ADJECTIVE **necessary**

**nötig** ADVERB **urgently**

**Notiz** die (PLURAL die **Notizen**) ❶ **note** ❷ keine Notiz von etwas nehmen to take no notice of something ❸ **item** (in a newspaper)

**Notizblock** der (PLURAL die **Notizblöcke**) **notepad**

**Notizbuch** das (PLURAL die **Notizbücher**) **notebook**

**Notlage** die (PLURAL die **Notlagen**) **crisis**

**Notruf** der (PLURAL die **Notrufe**) ❶ **emergency call** ❷ **emergency number**

**notwendig** ADJECTIVE **necessary**

**November** der **November**

**nüchtern** ADJECTIVE ❶ **sober**; wieder nüchtern werden to sober up ❷ auf nüchternen Magen on an empty stomach ❸ **down-to-earth**

**Nudeln** PLURAL NOUN ❶ **noodles** ❷ **pasta**

**null** NUMBER ❶ **nought**; unter null below zero ❷ **nil**; zwei zu null two nil ❸ **love** (in tennis) ❹ null Fehler haben to have no mistakes, ich habe null Ahnung (informal) I haven't got a clue ❺ in null Komma nichts (informal) in less than no time

**Null** die (PLURAL die **Nullen**) ❶ **zero**, **nought** ❷ **failure**

**numerieren** ▸ SEE **nummerieren**

**Nummer** die (PLURAL die **Nummern**) ❶ **number** ❷ **issue** (of a magazine) ❸ **size** (of clothing) ❹ **act** ❺ auf Nummer sicher gehen to play safe

**nummerieren** VERB (PERF hat nummeriert) to **number**

**Nummernschild** das (PLURAL die **Nummernschilder**) **number plate**

**nun** ADVERB **now**

**nun** EXCLAMATION **well**; nun ja ... well, yes ...

**nur** ADVERB ❶ **only** ❷ was sollen wir nur tun? what on earth are we going to do?, sie soll es nur versuchen! just let her try! ❸ nur zu! go ahead!

**Nürnberg** das **Nuremberg**

**Nuss** die (PLURAL die **Nüsse**) **nut**

**nutzen**, **nützen** VERB (PERF hat genutzt/genützt) ❶ to **use**; etwas nutzen to take advantage of something **②** to be useful **③** nichts nutzen to be no use, das nutzt mir nichts that won't help me **④** das nutzt ja doch nichts it's pointless

**Nutzen** der benefit; von Nutzen sein to be useful

**nützlich** *ADJECTIVE* useful

**nutzlos** *ADJECTIVE* useless

**ob** *CONJUNCTION* **①** whether; wissen Sie, ob heute noch ein Zug nach Freising fährt? do you know if there is another train to Freising today? **②** ob Alex noch anruft? I wonder if Alex will ring **③** und ob! you bet!

**obdachlos** *ADJECTIVE* homeless

**Obdachlose** der/die *(PLURAL* die **Obdachlosen)* homeless person; die Obdachlosen the homeless

**oben** *ADVERB* **①** on top; oben auf on top of, die Vase steht oben auf dem Schrank the vase is on top of the cupboard **②** at the top; von oben bis unten from top to bottom, er hat uns von oben bis unten gemustert he looked us up and down **③** upstairs **④** nach oben up, upstairs, er ist nach oben in sein Zimmer gegangen he went up into his room, geht der Fahrstuhl nach oben? is the lift going up?, hier oben up here, da oben up there **⑤** siehe oben see above *(on a page)*, oben erwähnt above mentioned **⑥** oben ohne *(informal)* topless

**obenerwähnt** ▸ SEE oben

**Ober** der *(PLURAL* die **Ober)** waiter; Herr Ober! waiter!

**oberer, obere, oberes** *ADJECTIVE* upper, top

**Oberfläche** die *(PLURAL* die **Oberflächen)** surface

**oberflächlich** ADJECTIVE **superficial**

**Oberhaupt** das (PLURAL die Oberhäupter) **head**

**Oberhemd** das (PLURAL die Oberhemden) **shirt**

**Oberschenkel** der (PLURAL die Oberschenkel) **thigh**

**Oberschule** die (PLURAL die Oberschulen) **secondary school**

**oberster, oberste, oberstes** ADJECTIVE **top**

**Oberstufe** die (PLURAL die Oberstufen) **upper school**

**Oberweite** die (PLURAL die Oberweiten) **chest size, bust measurement**

**Objekt** das (PLURAL die Objekte) **object**

**objektiv** ADJECTIVE **objective**

**Objektiv** das (PLURAL die Objektive) **lens**

**Oboe** die (PLURAL die Oboen) **oboe**; Oboe spielen **to play the oboe**

**Obst** das **fruit**

**Obstbaum** der (PLURAL die Obstbäume) **fruit tree**

**Obstsalat** der (PLURAL die Obstsalate) **fruit salad**

**obszön** ADJECTIVE **obscene**

**obwohl** CONJUNCTION **although**

**öde** ADJECTIVE ❶ **desolate** ❷ **dreary**; das ist so ein furchtbar öder Job **it's such terribly dull job**

**oder** CONJUNCTION ❶ **or** ❷ du kennst sie doch, oder? **you know her, don't you?**

**Ofen** der (PLURAL die Öfen) ❶ **oven** ❷ **stove** ❸ **heater**

**offen** ADJECTIVE ❶ **open**; offen haben **to be open**, Tag der offenen Tür **open day** ❷ **frank** ❸ **vacant**; eine offene Stelle **a vacancy** ❹ offen bleiben **to stay open** ❺ offen bleiben **to remain open** (of a question, possibility)

**offen** ADVERB ❶ **openly** ❷ **frankly**; offen gesagt **frankly**

**offenbar** ADJECTIVE **obvious**

**offenbar** ADVERB ❶ **apparently** ❷ da hast du dich offenbar geirrt **you seem to have made a mistake**, sie hat offenbar den Zug verpasst **she must have missed the train**

**offenbleiben** ▸ SEE **offen**

**offensichtlich** ADJECTIVE **obvious**

**öffentlich** ADJECTIVE **public**

**Öffentlichkeit** die **public**; in aller Öffentlichkeit **in public**

**offiziell** ADJECTIVE **official**

**Offizier** der (PLURAL die Offiziere) **officer**

**öffnen** VERB (PERF hat geöffnet) **to open**; jemandem die Tür öffnen **to open the door for somebody**

**Öffner** der (PLURAL die Öffner) **opener**

**Öffnung** die (PLURAL die Öffnungen) **opening**

**Öffnungszeiten** PLURAL NOUN **opening times**

**oft** ADVERB **often**

**öfter, öfters** ADVERB **quite often**; ich habe ihn öfters mal getroffen **I used to meet him quite often**

**ohne** *PREPOSITION (+ACC)* ❶ without; ohne mich count me out ❷ ohne weiteres easily ❸ oben ohne *(informal)* topless ❹ das ist nicht ohne *(informal)* it's not bad

**ohne** *CONJUNCTION* without; ohne zu überlegen without thinking

**Ohnmacht** die in Ohnmacht fallen to faint

**ohnmächtig** *ADJECTIVE* ❶ unconscious ❷ ohnmächtig werden to faint, Gisela ist ohnmächtig Gisela's fainted

**Ohr** das *(PLURAL die Ohren)* ear

**Ohrenschmerzen** *PLURAL NOUN* earache

**Ohrhörer** der *(PLURAL die Ohrhörer)* earphone

**Ohrring** der *(PLURAL die Ohrringe)* earring

**oje** *EXCLAMATION* oh dear!

**Ökoladen** der *(PLURAL die Ökoläden)* health-food shop

**Ökologie** die ecology

**ökologisch** *ADJECTIVE* ecological

**Oktober** der October

**Öl** das *(PLURAL die Öle)* oil

**Ölfarbe** die *(PLURAL die Ölfarben)* oil-paint

**Ölgemälde** das *(PLURAL die Ölgemälde)* oil painting

**ölig** *ADJECTIVE* oily

**Olive** die *(PLURAL die Oliven)* olive

**Olivenöl** das *(PLURAL die Olivenöle)* olive oil

**Ölteppich** der *(PLURAL die Ölteppiche)* oil slick

**Olympiade** die *(PLURAL die Olympiaden)* Olympic Games; die Olympiade findet alle vier Jahre statt the Olympic Games take place every four years

**olympisch** *ADJECTIVE* Olympic

**Oma** die *(PLURAL die Omas)* granny

**Omelett** das *(PLURAL die Omeletts)* omelette

**Omi** die *(PLURAL die Omis)* granny

**Onkel** der *(PLURAL die Onkel)* uncle

**online** *ADVERB* online

**Opa** der *(PLURAL die Opas)* grandpa

**Oper** die *(PLURAL die Opern)* opera

**Operation** die *(PLURAL die Operationen)* operation

**Operationssaal** der *(PLURAL die Operationssäle)* operating theatre

**operieren** *VERB (PERF hat operiert)* ❶ to operate on; sich operieren lassen to have an operation, sie wurde am Magen operiert she had a stomach operation ❷ to operate

**Opfer** das *(PLURAL die Opfer)* ❶ sacrifice ❷ victim; das Erdbeben forderte viele Opfer the earthquake claimed many victims

**Optiker** der *(PLURAL die Optiker)* optician

**Optikerin** die *(PLURAL die Optikerinnen)* optician

**Optimist** der *(PLURAL die Optimisten)* optimist

**optimistisch** *ADJECTIVE* optimistic

**orange** *ADJECTIVE* orange

**Orange** die *(PLURAL die Orangen)* orange

a
b
c
d
e
f
g
h
i
j
k
l
m
n
o
p
q
r
s
t
u
v
w
x
y
z

**Orangensaft** der *(PLURAL die Orangensäfte)* orange juice

**Orchester** das *(PLURAL die Orchester)* orchestra

**ordentlich** ADJECTIVE ❶ tidy ❷ respectable ❸ proper *(meal, job, salary)* ❹ eine ordentliche Tracht Prügel *(informal)* a good hiding

**ordentlich** ADVERB ❶ tidily; ordentlich schreiben to write neatly ❷ respectably ❸ properly ❹ ordentlich feiern *(informal)* to have a really good celebration, wir sind ordentlich nass geworden *(informal)* we got soaked

**ordinär** ADJECTIVE vulgar

**ordnen** VERB *(PERF hat geordnet)* ❶ to arrange ❷ to put in order

**Ordner** der *(PLURAL die Ordner)* file

**Ordnung** die ❶ order; Ordnung halten to keep order ❷ Ordnung machen to tidy up, die Wohnung in Ordnung bringen to tidy up the flat ❸ mit der Waschmaschine ist etwas nicht in Ordnung there's something wrong with the washing machine ❹ etwas in Ordnung bringen to put something right, die Waschmaschine in Ordnung bringen to repair the washing machine ❺ in Ordnung! okay! ❻ er ist in Ordnung he's all right

**Organ** das *(PLURAL die Organe)* ❶ organ ❷ *(informal)* voice

**Organisation** die *(PLURAL die Organisationen)* organization

**organisch** ADJECTIVE organic

**organisieren** VERB *(PERF hat organisiert)* ❶ to organize ❷ *(informal)* to get (hold of)

**Orgel** die *(PLURAL die Orgeln)* organ

**orientieren** VERB *(PERF hat sich orientiert)* ❶ sich orientieren to get your bearings ❷ sich über etwas orientieren to inform yourself about something

**Orientierung** die ❶ orientation; die Orientierung verlieren to lose your bearings ❷ zu Ihrer Orientierung for your information

**Orientierungsjahr** das *(PLURAL die Orientierungsjahre)* gap year

**Orientierungspunkt** der *(PLURAL die Orientierungspunkte)* landmark, reference point

**Orientierungsrennen** das orienteering

**Orientierungssinn** der sense of direction

**originell** ADJECTIVE original

**Orkan** der *(PLURAL die Orkane)* hurricane

**Ort** der *(PLURAL die Orte)* ❶ place; an Ort und Stelle on the spot ❷ (small) town

**Orthografie**, **Orthographie** die spelling

**örtlich** ADJECTIVE local

**Ortschaft** die *(PLURAL die Ortschaften)* village

**Ortsgespräch** das *(PLURAL die Ortsgespräche)* local call

**Ossi** der *(informal)* *(PLURAL die Ossis)* East German

**Osten** der east

**Osterei** das *(PLURAL die Ostereier)* Easter egg

**Osterhase** die Easter bunny

**Ostern** das Easter

**Österreich** das Austria

**Österreicher** der *(PLURAL* die **Österreicher)** Austrian

**Österreicherin** die *(PLURAL* die **Österreicherinnen)** Austrian

**österreichisch** *ADJECTIVE* Austrian

**östlich** *ADJECTIVE* ❶ eastern ❷ easterly

**östlich** *ADVERB, PREPOSITION (+GEN)* östlich von Wien to the east of Vienna, östlich der Stadt east of the town

**Ostsee** die Baltic (Sea)

**oval** *ADJECTIVE* oval

**Ozean** der *(PLURAL* die **Ozeane)** ocean

**Ozon** das ozone

**Ozonschicht** die ozone layer

**paar** *PRONOUN* ein paar a few, ein paar Mal a few times, alle paar Tage every few days

**Paar** das *(PLURAL* die **Paare)** ❶ pair; ein Paar Schuhe a pair of shoes ❷ couple

**paarmal** ▸ SEE paar

**paarweise** *ADJECTIVE* in pairs; die Kinder stellten sich paarweise auf the children lined up in pairs

**Päckchen** das *(PLURAL* die **Päckchen)** ❶ package, packet ❷ small parcel

**packen** *VERB (PERF* hat gepackt*)* ❶ to pack; ich muss jetzt meinen Koffer packen I must pack my case now ❷ to grab (hold of); von Furcht gepackt seized with fear

**Packung** die *(PLURAL* die **Packungen)** packet, pack

**Pädagoge** der *(PLURAL* die **Pädagogen)** ❶ educationalist ❷ teacher

**pädagogisch** *ADJECTIVE* educational

**Paddel** das *(PLURAL* die **Paddel)** paddle

**paddeln** *VERB* ❶ *(PERF* hat gepaddelt*)* to paddle *(a canoe)* ❷ *(PERF* ist gepaddelt*)* to paddle *(along a lake, river)*

**Paket** das *(PLURAL* die **Pakete)**

a
b
c
d
e
f
g
h
i
j
k
l
m
n
o
p
q
r
s
t
u
v
w
x
y
z

**Paket** das (*PLURAL* die **Pakete**) ❶ parcel; Gabi hat mir ein Paket geschickt Gabi sent me a parcel ❷ packet; kaufe bitte ein Paket Waschpulver für mich can you please buy a packet of washing powder for me

**Pakistan** das Pakistan

**Pakistaner** der (*PLURAL* die **Pakistaner**) Pakistani

**Pakistanerin** die (*PLURAL* die **Pakistanerinnen**) Pakistani

**pakistanisch** *ADJECTIVE* Pakistani

**Palast** der (*PLURAL* die **Paläste**) palace

**Palme** die (*PLURAL* die **Palmen**) palm (tree)

**Pampelmuse** die (*PLURAL* die **Pampelmusen**) grapefruit

**Panik** die panic; in Panik geraten to panic

**Panne** die (*PLURAL* die **Pannen**) ❶ breakdown; wir haben auf dem Rückweg eine Panne gehabt we had a breakdown on the way back ❷ mishap; uns ist eine Panne passiert we had a mishap

**Panzer** der (*PLURAL* die **Panzer**) tank (*military*)

**Papa** der (*PLURAL* die **Papas**) daddy

**Papagei** der (*PLURAL* die **Papageien**) parrot

**Papier** das (*PLURAL* die **Papiere**) paper

**Papierkorb** der (*PLURAL* die **Papierkörbe**) waste-paper basket

**Papiertüte** die (*PLURAL* die **Papiertüten**) paper bag

**Pappe** die (*PLURAL* die **Pappen**) cardboard

**Paprika** der (*PLURAL* die **Paprikas**) ❶ pepper ❷ paprika

**Papst** der (*PLURAL* die **Päpste**) pope

**Parabolantenne** die (*PLURAL* die **Parabolantennen**) satellite dish

**Paradies** das paradise

**Paragraph** der (*PLURAL* die **Paragraphen**) ❶ section ❷ clause

**parallel** *ADJECTIVE* parallel

**Pärchen** das (*PLURAL* die **Pärchen**) couple

**Parfüm** das (*PLURAL* die **Parfüms**) perfume

**Park** der (*PLURAL* die **Parks**) park

**Parkanlage** die (*PLURAL* die **Parkanlagen**) park

**parken** *VERB* (*PERF* hat geparkt) to park

**Parkett** das (*PLURAL* die **Parkette**) ❶ (*in a theatre*) stalls ❷ parquet floor

**Parkhaus** das (*PLURAL* die **Parkhäuser**) multi-storey car park

**Parklücke** die (*PLURAL* die **Parklücken**) parking space

**Parkplatz** der (*PLURAL* die **Parkplätze**) ❶ car park ❷ parking space

**Parkschein** der (*PLURAL* die **Parkscheine**) car-park ticket

**Parkuhr** die (*PLURAL* die **Parkuhren**) parking meter

**Parkverbot** das 'Parkverbot' 'no parking', in der Innenstadt ist

Parkverbot you can't park in the town centre

**Parlament** das (PLURAL die **Parlamente**) parliament

**Parole** die (PLURAL die **Parolen**) slogan

**Partei** die (PLURAL die **Parteien**) ❶ party ❷ für jemanden Partei ergreifen to side with somebody

**Parterre** das (PLURAL die **Parterres**) ground floor

**Partie** die (PLURAL die **Partien**) ❶ part ❷ game (of tennis, chess)

**Partner** der (PLURAL die **Partner**) partner

**Partnerin** die (PLURAL die **Partnerinnen**) partner

**Partnerstadt** die (PLURAL die **Partnerstädte**) twin town

**Party** die (PLURAL die **Partys**) party

**Pass** der (PLURAL die **Pässe**) ❶ passport ❷ pass

**Passage** die (PLURAL die **Passagen**) ❶ shopping arcade ❷ passage (of text) ❸ sequence (of music, film)

**Passagier** der (PLURAL die **Passagiere**) passenger

**Passant** der (PLURAL die **Passanten**) passer-by

**Passantin** die (PLURAL die **Passantinnen**) passer-by

**passen** (PERF hat gepasst) ❶ to fit; jemandem passen to fit somebody ❷ to suit; jemandem passen to suit somebody, Freitag passt mir nicht Friday doesn't suit me, seine Art passt mir nicht I don't like his manner ❸ zu etwas passen to go with something, zu jemandem passen to be right for somebody

**passend** ADJECTIVE ❶ suitable ❷ matching

**passieren** VERB (PERF ist passiert) to happen

**passiv** ADJECTIVE passive

**Passiv** das passive

**Passkontrolle** die passport control

**Passwort** das (PLURAL die **Passwörter**) password (in computing); das Passwort eingeben to give the password

**Paste** die (PLURAL die **Pasten**) paste

**Pastete** die (PLURAL die **Pasteten**) pie

**Pate** der (PLURAL die **Paten**) godfather

**Patenkind** das (PLURAL die **Patenkinder**) godchild

**patent** ADJECTIVE capable, clever

**Patentante** die (PLURAL die **Patentanten**) godmother

**Patient** der (PLURAL die **Patienten**) patient

**Patientin** die (PLURAL die **Patientinnen**) patient

**Patin** die (PLURAL die **Patinnen**) godmother

**patschnass** ADJECTIVE soaking wet

**pauken** VERB (informal) (PERF hat gepaukt) to swot

**pauschal** ADJECTIVE all-inclusive

**Pauschalreise** die (PLURAL die **Pauschalreisen**) package tour

**Pause** die (PLURAL die **Pausen**) ❶ break ❷ pause ❸ interval

a
b
c
d
e
f
g
h
i
j
k
l
m
n
o
p
q
r
s
t
u
v
w
x
y
z

A
B
C
D
E
F
G
H
I
J
K
L
M
N
O
P
Q
R
S
T
U
V
W
X
Y
Z

**Pazifik** der der Pazifik the Pacific (Ocean)

**PC** der *(PLURAL die PCs)* PC

**Pech** das ❶ bad luck; Pech haben to be unlucky ❷ pitch

**Pedal** das *(PLURAL die Pedale)* pedal

**peinlich** *ADJECTIVE* ❶ embarrassing; es war mir sehr peinlich I felt very embarrassed about it ❷ awkward ❸ meticulous

**Peitsche** die *(PLURAL die Peitschen)* whip

**Pelle** die skin

**Pelz** der *(PLURAL die Pelze)* fur

**pendeln** *VERB* ❶ *(PERF ist gependelt)* to commute ❷ *(PERF hat gependelt)* to swing

**Pendelverkehr** der ❶ commuter traffic ❷ shuttle service

**Pendler** der *(PLURAL die Pendler)* commuter

**penetrant** *ADJECTIVE* ❶ overpowering *(odour, perfume)* ❷ pushy *(person)*

**Penis** der *(PLURAL die Penisse)* penis

**pennen** *VERB (informal) (PERF hat gepennt)* to sleep, to kip

**Pension** die *(PLURAL die Pensionen)* ❶ guesthouse ❷ volle Pension full board ❸ pension; eine schöne Pension haben to get a good pension, in Pension gehen to retire

**pensioniert** *ADJECTIVE* retired

**per** *PREPOSITION (+ACC)* ❶ by; per Luftpost by airmail ❷ per

**perfekt** *ADJECTIVE* perfect

**Perfekt** das *(PLURAL die Perfekte)* perfect

**Periode** die *(PLURAL die Perioden)* period

**Perle** die *(PLURAL die Perlen)* ❶ pearl ❷ bead

**Person** die *(PLURAL die Personen)* person; für vier Personen for four people, ich für meine Person personally

**Personal** das staff, personnel

**Personalausweis** der *(PLURAL die Personalausweise)* identity card

**Personenzug** der *(PLURAL die Personenzüge)* stopping train

**persönlich** *ADJECTIVE* personal

**persönlich** *ADVERB* ❶ personally ❷ in person

**Persönlichkeit** die *(PLURAL die Persönlichkeiten)* personality

**Perücke** die *(PLURAL die Perücken)* wig

**Pessimist** der *(PLURAL die Pessimisten)* pessimist

**pessimistisch** *ADJECTIVE* pessimistic

**Petersilie** die parsley

**Petroleum** das paraffin

**Pfad** der *(PLURAL die Pfade)* path

**Pfadfinder** der *(PLURAL die Pfadfinder)* (Boy) Scout

**Pfadfinderin** die *(PLURAL die Pfadfinderinnen)* (Girl) Guide

**Pfand** das *(PLURAL die Pfänder)* ❶ forfeit ❷ deposit *(on a bottle)* ❸ pledge

**Pfandflasche** die *(PLURAL die Pfandflaschen)* returnable bottle

**Pfanne** die *(PLURAL die Pfannen)* (frying) pan

**Pfannkuchen** der *(PLURAL die Pfannkuchen)* pancake

**Pfarrer** der *(PLURAL die* **Pfarrer)**
❶ vicar ❷ priest

**Pfau** der *(PLURAL die* **Pfauen)** peacock

**Pfauhenne** die *(PLURAL die* **Pfauhennen)** peahen

**Pfeffer** der pepper

**Pfefferkorn** das *(PLURAL die* **Pfefferkörner)** peppercorn

**Pfefferkuchen** der gingerbread

**Pfefferminzbonbon** der *(PLURAL die* **Pfefferminzbonbons)** mint

**Pfefferminze** die peppermint

**Pfeffermühle** die *(PLURAL die* **Pfeffermühlen)** peppermill

**Pfeife** die *(PLURAL die* **Pfeifen)**
❶ whistle ❷ pipe

**pfeifen** ◇*VERB (IMP* **pfiff,** *PERF* **hat gepfiffen)** to whistle

**Pfeil** der *(PLURAL die* **Pfeile)** arrow

**Pfeiler** der *(PLURAL die* **Pfeiler)**
❶ pillar ❷ pier

**Pfennig** der *(PLURAL die* **Pfennige)** pfennig *(one hundredth of a mark in the former German currency)*; ich habe keinen Pfennig mehr I haven't got a penny left
▸ SEE **Mark**

**Pferd** das *(PLURAL die* **Pferde)** horse

**Pferderennen** das *(PLURAL die* **Pferderennen)** horse race

**Pferdeschwanz** der *(PLURAL die* **Pferdeschwänze)** ponytail

**pfiff** ▸ SEE **pfeifen**

**Pfingsten** das *(PLURAL die* **Pfingsten)** Whitsun

**Pfirsich** der *(PLURAL die* **Pfirsiche)** peach

**Pflanze** die *(PLURAL die* **Pflanzen)** plant

**pflanzen** *VERB (PERF* **hat gepflanzt)** to plant; pflanze mehr Bäume plant more trees

**Pflaster** das *(PLURAL die* **Pflaster)**
❶ pavement ❷ plaster

**Pflaume** die *(PLURAL die* **Pflaumen)** plum

**Pflege** die ❶ care ❷ nursing ❸ ein Kind in Pflege nehmen to foster a child

**Pflegeeltern** *PLURAL NOUN* foster parents

**Pflegeheim** das *(PLURAL die* **Pflegeheime)** nursing home

**Pflegekind** das *(PLURAL die* **Pflegekinder)** foster child

**pflegeleicht** *ADJECTIVE* easy-care *(fabric)*

**pflegen** *VERB (PERF* **hat gepflegt)**
❶ to look after, to care for; eine Freundschaft pflegen to foster a friendship ❷ to nurse

**Pfleger** der *(PLURAL die* **Pfleger)** (male) nurse

**Pflicht** die *(PLURAL die* **Pflichten)** duty; Pflicht sein to be compulsory

**pflichtbewusst** *ADJECTIVE* conscientious

**Pflichtfach** das *(PLURAL die* **Pflichtfächer)** compulsory subject

**pflücken** *VERB (PERF* **hat gepflückt)** to pick

**Pflug** der *(PLURAL die* **Pflüge)** plough

**pflügen** *VERB (PERF* **hat gepflügt)** to plough

a
b
c
d
e
f
g
h
i
j
k
l
m
n
o
**p**
q
r
s
t
u
v
w
x
y
z

**Pforte** die *(PLURAL die Pforten)* gate

**Pförtner** der *(PLURAL die Pförtner)* porter

**Pfosten** der *(PLURAL die Pfosten)* post

**Pfote** die *(PLURAL die Pfoten)* paw

**pfui** *EXCLAMATION* ugh!

**Pfund** das *(PLURAL die Pfund(e))* pound

**Pfütze** die *(PLURAL die Pfützen)* puddle

**Phantasie** die ▸ SEE **Fantasie**

**phantasievoll** *ADJECTIVE* ▸ SEE **Fantasievoll**

**phantastisch** *ADJECTIVE* fantastic

**Philosoph** der *(PLURAL die Philosophen)* philosopher

**Philosophie** die *(PLURAL die Philosophien)* philosophy

**Photo** das *(PLURAL die Photos)* ▸ SEE **Foto**

**Phrase** die *(PLURAL die Phrasen)* ❶ phrase ❷ cliché

**Physik** die physics

**Physiker** der *(PLURAL die Physiker)* physicist

**Physikerin** die *(PLURAL die Physikerinnen)* physicist

**Pickel** der *(PLURAL die Pickel)* spot, pimple

**Picknick** das *(PLURAL die Picknicks)* picnic

**Pik** das spades *(in cards)*

**pikant** *ADJECTIVE* spicy

**Pille** die *(PLURAL die Pillen)* pill

**Pilot** der *(PLURAL die Piloten)* pilot

**Pilotin** die *(PLURAL die Pilotinnen)* pilot

**Pilz** der *(PLURAL die Pilze)* ❶ mushroom ❷ fungus

**Pinguin** der *(PLURAL die Pinguine)* penguin

**pinkeln** *VERB (informal) (PERF hat gepinkelt)* to pee

**Pinnwand** die *(PLURAL die Pinnwände)* noticeboard

**Pinsel** der *(PLURAL die Pinsel)* brush

**Pinzette** die *(PLURAL die Pinzetten)* tweezers

**Pirat** der *(PLURAL die Piraten)* pirate

**Piste** die *(PLURAL die Pisten)* ❶ run, piste ❷ track ❸ runway

**Pizza** die *(PLURAL die Pizzas)* pizza

**Pkw** der *(PLURAL die Pkws) (short for Personenkraftwagen)* car

**plagen** *VERB (PERF hat geplagt)* ❶ to bother, to torment ❷ to pester ❸ sich plagen to struggle sich in der Schule plagen to struggle at school, er muss sich plagen he has to work hard

**Plakat** das *(PLURAL die Plakate)* poster

**Plan** der *(PLURAL die Pläne)* ❶ plan ❷ map

**planen** *VERB (PERF hat geplant)* to plan

**Planierraupe** die *(PLURAL die Planierraupen)* bulldozer

**planmäßig** *ADJECTIVE* scheduled

**planmäßig** *ADVERB* ❶ according to plan; alles läuft planmäßig everything is going according to plan ❷ on schedule; der Zug ist planmäßig abgefahren the train left on schedule

**Plastik**[1] das **plastic**

**Plastik**[2] die *(PLURAL die **Plastiken**)* **sculpture**

**Plastiktüte** die *(PLURAL die **Plastiktüten**)* **plastic bag**

**Platin** das **platinum**

**platt** *ADJECTIVE* **flat**; platt sein *(informal)* to be flabbergasted

**plattdeutsch** *ADJECTIVE* **low German**

**Platte** die *(PLURAL die **Platten**)* ❶ **plate** ❷ **dish**; kalte Platte cold meats and cheeses ❸ **hotplate** ❹ **record** ❺ **board** *(made of wood)* ❻ **slab** *(made of stone)* ❼ **sheet** *(made of metal or glass)* ❽ **top** *(of a table)*

**Plattenspieler** der *(PLURAL die **Plattenspieler**)* **record player**

**Platz** der *(PLURAL die **Plätze**)* ❶ **place**; viel Platz haben to have a lot of room, Platz lassen to leave room, auf die Plätze, fertig, los! on your marks, get set, go! ❷ **seat**; Platz nehmen to take a seat ❸ **square** *(in a town)* ❹ **ground, pitch**; einen Spieler vom Platz stellen to send a player off ❺ **court** *(for tennis)* ❻ **course** *(for golf)*

**Plätzchen** das *(PLURAL die **Plätzchen**)* ❶ **biscuit** ❷ **spot**

**platzen** *VERB (PERF **ist geplatzt**)* ❶ to **burst** ❷ der Plan ist geplatzt *(informal)* the plan fell through ❸ vor Neugier platzen to be bursting with curiosity

**plaudern** *VERB (PERF **hat geplaudert**)* to **chat**

**pleite** *ADJECTIVE (informal)* **broke**

**Plombe** die *(PLURAL die **Plomben**)* **filling**

**plombieren** *VERB (PERF **hat plombiert**)* to **fill**

**plötzlich** *ADJECTIVE* **sudden**

**plötzlich** *ADVERB* **suddenly**

**plump** *ADJECTIVE* ❶ **plump** ❷ **clumsy**

**Plural** der *(PLURAL die **Plurale**)* **plural**

**plus** *ADVERB* **plus**

**Plus** das ❶ **plus** ❷ **profit** ❸ **advantage**

**PLZ** ▸ SEE **Postleitzahl**

**Po** der *(informal) (PLURAL die **Pos**)* **bottom**

**Poesie** die **poetry**

**Pokal** der *(PLURAL die **Pokale**)* ❶ **cup** ❷ **goblet**

**Pokalspiel** das *(PLURAL die **Pokalspiele**)* **cup-tie**

**Pole** der *(PLURAL die **Polen**)* **Pole**

**Polen** das **Poland**

**polieren** *VERB (PERF **hat poliert**)* to **polish**

**Polin** die *(PLURAL die **Polinnen**)* **Pole**

**Politik** die ❶ **politics** ❷ **policy**

**Politiker** der *(PLURAL die **Politiker**)* **politician**

**Politikerin** die *(PLURAL die **Politikerinnen**)* **politician**

**politisch** *ADJECTIVE* **political**

**Politur** die *(PLURAL die **Polituren**)* **polish**

**Polizei** die **police**

**polizeilich** *ADJECTIVE* **police**

189

**polizeilich** *ADVERB* by the police; sich polizeilich anmelden to register with the police

**Polizeiwache** die *(PLURAL* die **Polizeiwachen)** police station

**Polizist** der *(PLURAL* die **Polizisten)** policeman

**Polizistin** die *(PLURAL* die **Polizistinnen)** policewoman

**polnisch** *ADJECTIVE* Polish

**Pommes frites** *PLURAL NOUN* chips, French fries

**Pony¹** das *(PLURAL* die **Ponys)** pony

**Pony²** der *(PLURAL* die **Ponys)** fringe

**Popgruppe** die *(PLURAL* die **Popgruppen)** pop group

**Popkonzert** das *(PLURAL* die **Popkonzerte)** pop concert

**Popmusik** die pop music

**poppig** *ADJECTIVE* bright; Natalie hat immer poppige Socken an Natalie always wears bright socks

**Popstar** der *(PLURAL* die **Popstars)** pop star

**Porree** der *(PLURAL* die **Porrees)** leek; eine Stange Porree a leek

**Portemonnaie** das ►SEE **Portmonee**

**Portier** der *(PLURAL* die **Portiers)** porter

**Portion** die *(PLURAL* die **Portionen)** portion; möchtest du eine zweite Portion? would you like a second helping?

**Portmonee** das *(PLURAL* die **Portmonees)** purse

**Porto** das postage

**Porträt** das *(PLURAL* die **Porträts)** portrait

**Portugal** das Portugal

**Portugiese** der *(PLURAL* die **Portugiesen)** Portuguese

**Portugiesin** die *(PLURAL* die **Portugiesinnen)** Portuguese

**portugiesisch** *ADJECTIVE* Portuguese

**Posaune** die *(PLURAL* die **Posaunen)** trombone

**Post** die **❶** post; mit der Post by post **❷** post office

**Postamt** das *(PLURAL* die **Postämter)** post office

**Postbote** der *(PLURAL* die **Postboten)** postman

**Poster** das *(PLURAL* die **Poster)** poster

**Postkarte** die *(PLURAL* die **Postkarten)** postcard

**Postleitzahl** die *(PLURAL* die **Postleitzahlen)** postcode

**Pracht** die splendour

**prächtig** *ADJECTIVE* splendid

**prahlen** *VERB* *(PERF* hat geprahlt) to boast

**praktisch** *ADJECTIVE* **❶** practical; praktische Erfahrung practical experience **❷** handy **❸** ein praktischer Arzt a general practitioner

**praktisch** *ADVERB* **❶** practically **❷** in practice

**Praline** die *(PLURAL* die **Pralinen)** chocolate

**Präposition** die *(PLURAL* die **Präpositionen)** preposition

**Präsens** das present (tense)

**Präservativ** das (PLURAL die Präservative) condom

**Präsident** der (PLURAL die Präsidenten) president

**Präsidentin** die (PLURAL die Präsidentinnen) president

**Pratikum** das (PLURAL die Praktika) practical training

**Praxis** die (PLURAL die Praxen) ❶ practice ❷ practical experience ❸ surgery

**Preis** der (PLURAL die Preise) ❶ price; um keinen Preis not at any price ❷ prize

**Preisausschreiben** das (PLURAL die Preisausschreiben) competition

**Preiselbeere** die (PLURAL die Preiselbeeren) cranberry

**preiswert** ADJECTIVE reasonable, cheap

**Prellung** die (PLURAL die Prellungen) bruise

**Premierminister** der (PLURAL die Premierminister) prime minister

**Presse** die press

**Priester** der (PLURAL die Priester) priest

**prima** ADJECTIVE (informal) brilliant

**Prinz** der (PLURAL die Prinzen) prince

**Prinzessin** die (PLURAL die Prinzessinnen) princess

**Prise** die (PLURAL die Prisen) pinch; eine Prise Salz a pinch of salt

**privat** ADJECTIVE private

**Privileg** das (PLURAL die Privilegien) privilege

**pro** PREPOSITION (+ACC) per

**Probe** die (PLURAL die Proben) ❶ test; jemanden auf die Probe stellen to test somebody, ein Auto Probe fahren to test-drive a car ❷ sample ❸ rehearsal

**probefahren** ▸ SEE Probe

**probieren** VERB (PERF hat probiert) ❶ to try ❷ to taste

**Problem** das (PLURAL die Probleme) problem

**Produkt** das (PLURAL die Produkte) product

**Produzent** der (PLURAL die Produzenten) producer

**produzieren** VERB (PERF hat produziert) to produce

**Profi** der (PLURAL die Profis) pro

**Profil** das (PLURAL die Profile) ❶ profile ❷ tread (of a tyre)

**Programm** das (PLURAL die Programme) ❶ programme ❷ program (in computing) ❸ channel (on TV)

**programmieren** VERB (PERF hat programmiert) to program

**Programmierer** der (PLURAL die Programmierer) programmer

**Programmiererin** die (PLURAL die Programmiererinnen) programmer

**Projekt** das (PLURAL die Projekte) project

**Promille** das (PLURAL die Promille) alcohol level; zuviel Promille haben to be over the limit

**Prominente** der (PLURAL die Prominenten) ❶ VIP ❷ celebrity

**Pronomen** das *(PLURAL* die **Pronomen)** pronoun

**Prospekt** der *(PLURAL* die **Prospekte)** brochure

**prost** *EXCLAMATION* cheers!

**Protein** das *(PLURAL* die **Proteine)** protein

**Protest** der *(PLURAL* die **Proteste)** protest

**protestantisch** *ADJECTIVE* Protestant

**protestieren** *VERB (PERF* hat **protestiert)** to protest

**Protokoll** das *(PLURAL* die **Protokolle)** ❶ minutes, transcript ❷ record *(in court)* ❸ protocol

**protzen** *VERB (PERF* hat **geprotzt)** to show off; Klaus protzt mit seinem neuen Auto Klaus is showing off with his new car

**Proviant** der provisions

**Prozent** das *(PLURAL* die **Prozente)** ❶ per cent; zehn Prozent ten per cent ❷ Prozente bekommen *(informal)* to get a discount

**Prozentsatz** der *(PLURAL* die **Prozentsätze)** percentage

**Prozess** der *(PLURAL* die **Prozesse)** ❶ court case; einen Prozess gewinnen to win a case ❷ trial ❸ process

**Prozession** die *(PLURAL* die **Prozessionen)** procession

**prüfen** *VERB (PERF* hat **geprüft)** ❶ to test, to examine *(at school)* ❷ to check; hast du die Reifen geprüft? have you checked the tyres?

**Prüfung** die *(PLURAL* die **Prüfungen)** ❶ examination, exam; eine Prüfung bestehen to pass an examination, sie ist durch die Prüfung gefallen she failed the exam ❷ check

**Prügel** der *(PLURAL* die **Prügel)** ❶ stick ❷ Prügel bekommen to get a beating

**Prügelei** die *(PLURAL* die **Prügeleien)** fight

**prügeln** *VERB (PERF* hat **geprügelt)** ❶ to beat ❷ sich prügeln to fight, sich um etwas prügeln to fight for something

**Psychiater** der *(PLURAL* die **Psychiater)** psychiatrist

**Psychiaterin** die *(PLURAL* die **Psychiaterinnen)** psychiatrist

**psychisch** *ADJECTIVE* psychological

**Psychologe** der *(PLURAL* die **Psychologen)** psychologist

**Psychologie** die psychology

**Psychologin** die *(PLURAL* die **Psychologinnen)** psychologist

**Publikum** das ❶ audience, crowd ❷ public

**Pudding** der *(PLURAL* die **Puddinge)** ❶ blancmange ❷ pudding *(steamed)*

**Pudel** der *(PLURAL* die **Pudel)** poodle

**Puder** der *(PLURAL* die **Puder)** powder

**Puffmais** der popcorn

**Pulli** der *(PLURAL* die **Pullis)** pullover

**Pullover** der *(PLURAL* die **Pullover)** pullover

**Puls** der *(PLURAL* die **Pulse)** pulse; der Arzt maß meinen Puls the doctor took my pulse

**Pult** das *(PLURAL* die **Pulte)** desk

**Pulver** das *(PLURAL* die **Pulver)** powder

**Pulverkaffee** der instant coffee

**Pumpe** die *(PLURAL* die **Pumpen)** pump

**pumpen** *VERB (PERF* **hat gepumpt)** ❶ to pump ❷ *(informal)* to lend; jemandem Geld pumpen to lend somebody money ❸ *(informal)* to borrow; sich etwas pumpen to borrow something

**Punker** der *(PLURAL* die **Punker)** punk

**Punkerin** die *(PLURAL* die **Punkerinnen)** punk

**Punkt** der *(PLURAL* die **Punkte)** ❶ dot, spot; Punkt sechs Uhr at six o'clock on the dot ❷ full stop ❸ point; nach Punkten siegen to win on points

**pünktlich** *ADJECTIVE* punctual

**Puppe** die *(PLURAL* die **Puppen)** ❶ doll ❷ puppet

**pur** *ADJECTIVE* ❶ pure ❷ Whisky pur neat whisky

**Purzelbaum** der *(PLURAL* die **Purzelbäume)** somersault

**pusten** *VERB (PERF* **hat gepustet)** to blow

**Pute** die *(PLURAL* die **Puten)** turkey

**putzen** *VERB (PERF* **hat geputzt)** ❶ to clean; putz dir die Zähne clean your teeth, putzen gehen to work as a cleaner ❷ sich die Nase putzen to blow your nose

**Putzfrau** die *(PLURAL* die **Putzfrauen)** cleaning lady, cleaner

**putzig** *ADJECTIVE* cute

**Puzzle** das *(PLURAL* die **Puzzles)** jigsaw (puzzle)

**Pyjama** der *(PLURAL* die **Pyjamas)** pyjamas

**Pyramide** die *(PLURAL* die **Pyramiden)** pyramid

**Pyrenäen** *PLURAL NOUN* die Pyrenäen the Pyrenees

# Qq

**Quadrat** das *(PLURAL die* **Quadrate)** square

**quadratisch** *ADJECTIVE* **square**

**Quadratmeter** der *(PLURAL die* **Quadratmeter)** square metre

**quaken** *VERB (PERF* **hat gequakt) ❶** to quack **❷** to croak *(of a frog)*

**Qual** die *(PLURAL die* **Qualen) ❶** torment **❷** agony; es war eine Qual, das ansehen zu müssen it was agony to watch

**quälen** *VERB (PERF* **hat gequält) ❶** to torment **❷** to torture **❸** to pester **❹** sich quälen to suffer **❺** sich mit etwas quälen to struggle with something, sich durch ein Buch quälen to struggle (your way) through a book

**Quälgeist** der *(informal) (PLURAL die* **Quälgeister)** pest

**Qualifikation** die *(PLURAL die* **Qualifikationen)** qualification

**qualifizieren** *VERB (PERF* **hat qualifiziert)** sich qualifizieren to qualify, sie haben sich für die dritte Runde qualifiziert they qualified for the third round

**Qualität** die *(PLURAL die* **Qualitäten)** quality

**Qualle** die *(PLURAL die* **Quallen)** jellyfish

**Qualm** der thick smoke

**qualmen** *VERB (PERF* **hat gequalmt)** to give off clouds of smoke; sie qualmt wie ein Schlot *(informal)* she smokes like a chimney

**Quarantäne** die **quarantine**

**Quark** der *(curd cheese)* **quark**

**Quartett** das *(PLURAL die* **Quartette)** quartet

**Quartier** das *(PLURAL die* **Quartiere) ❶** accommodation **❷** quarters

**quasseln** *VERB (informal) (PERF* **hat gequasselt)** to natter

**Quatsch** der *(informal)* **rubbish**

**quatschen** *VERB (informal) (PERF* **hat gequatscht)** to chat

**Quelle** die *(PLURAL die* **Quellen) ❶** source **❷** spring

**quer** *ADVERB* **❶** across **❷** crosswise **❸** diagonally; quer gestreift with diagonal stripes **❹** quer durch straight through

**quergestreift** ▸ SEE **quer**

**Querstraße** die *(PLURAL die* **Querstraßen)** side street; die erste Querstraße rechts the first turning on the right

**quetschen** *VERB (PERF* **hat gequetscht) ❶** to crush **❷** to squash **❸** ich habe mich in meine Jeans gequetscht I squeezed into my jeans

**Quetschung** die *(PLURAL die* **Quetschungen)** bruise

**quietschen** *VERB (PERF* **hat gequietscht)** to squeak

**quitt** *ADJECTIVE* **quits**

**Quittung** die *(PLURAL die* **Quittungen)** receipt

**Quiz** das *(PLURAL die* **Quiz)** quiz

# Rr

**Rabatt** der (PLURAL die **Rabatte**) discount

**Rache** die revenge

**rächen** VERB (PERF **hat gerächt**) ❶ to avenge ❷ sich an jemandem rächen to take revenge on somebody ❸ das wird sich rächen you'll have to pay for it

**Rad** das (PLURAL die **Räder**) ❶ wheel ❷ bike; Julia ist mit dem Rad gekommen Julia came by bike ❸ Rad fahren to cycle

**Radar** der radar

**Radarschirm** der (PLURAL die **Radarschirme**) radar screen

**radeln** VERB (PERF **ist geradelt**) to cycle; Max ist ins Dorf geradelt Max cycled into the village

**radfahren** ▶ SEE **Rad**

**Radfahrer** der (PLURAL die **Radfahrer**) cyclist

**Radfahrerin** die (PLURAL die **Radfahrerinnen**) cyclist

**Radfahrweg** der (PLURAL die **Radfahrwege**) cycle lane

**Radiergummi** der (PLURAL die **Radiergummis**) rubber

**Radieschen** das (PLURAL die **Radieschen**) radish

**Radio** das (PLURAL die **Radios**) radio

**radioaktiv** ADJECTIVE radioactive

**Radiosendung** die (PLURAL die **Radiosendungen**) radio broadcast

**Radler** der (PLURAL die **Radler**) cyclist

**Radlerin** die (PLURAL die **Radlerinnen**) cyclist

**Radrennen** das ❶ cycle race; Maria hat das Radrennen gewonnen Maria won the cycle race ❷ cycle racing

**Radweg** der (PLURAL die **Radwege**) cycle path

**raffiniert** ADJECTIVE crafty

**Rahm** der cream

**rahmen** VERB (PERF **hat gerahmt**) to frame (a picture)

**Rahmen** der (PLURAL die **Rahmen**) ❶ frame ❷ framework ❸ limits; im Rahmen des Möglichen within the bounds of possibility

**Rakete** die (PLURAL die **Raketen**) rocket

**ran** (informal) ▶ SEE **heran**

**Rand** der (PLURAL die **Ränder**) ❶ edge ❷ rim; der Rand der Tasse war angeschlagen the rim of the cup was chipped ❸ ring, mark ❹ margin (of a page); du musst einen Rand für die Korrekturen lassen you must leave a margin for the corrections ❺ outskirts (of a town) ❻ etwas am Rande erwähnen to mention something in passing ❼ am Rande der Pleite sein to be on the verge of bankruptcy ❽ außer Rand und Band geraten (informal) to go wild

**Randstreifen** der (PLURAL die **Randstreifen**) hard shoulder

**Rang** der (PLURAL die **Ränge**) ❶ rank ❷ (in a theatre) circle

a
b
c
d
e
f
g
h
i
j
k
l
m
n
o
p
q
r
s
t
u
v
w
x
y
z

**rannte** ▸ SEE **rennen**

**rasch** ADJECTIVE **quick**

**rasen** VERB (PERF **ist gerast**) **to tear along, to rush**; gegen eine Mauer rasen to career into a wall

**Rasen** der (PLURAL die **Rasen**) **lawn, grass**

**Rasenmäher** der (PLURAL die **Rasenmäher**) **lawnmower**

**Rasierapparat** der (PLURAL die **Rasierapparate**) ❶ **shaver** ❷ **razor**

**Rasiercreme** die (PLURAL die **Rasiercremes**) **shaving cream**

**rasieren** VERB (PERF **hat rasiert**) ❶ **to shave** ❷ sich rasieren to shave

**Rasierklinge** die (PLURAL die **Rasierklingen**) **razor blade**

**Rasierwasser** das **aftershave**

**Rasse** die (PLURAL die **Rassen**) ❶ **race** ❷ **breed**; ich weiß nicht, was für eine Rasse unser Hund ist I don't know what breed our dog is

**Rassenhass** der **racial hatred**

**rassisch** ADJECTIVE **racial**

**Rassismus** der **racism**

**Rassist** der (PLURAL die **Rassisten**) **racist**

**Rassistin** die (PLURAL die **Rassistinnen**) **racist**

**rassistisch** ADJECTIVE **racist**

**rasten** VERB (PERF **hat gerastet**) **to rest**

**Rastplatz** der (PLURAL die **Rastplätze**) **picnic area** (on a motorway)

**Raststätte** die (PLURAL die **Raststätten**) **services** (on a motorway)

**Rat** der ❶ **advice**; ein Rat a piece of advice, jemanden zu Rate ziehen to ask somebody's advice ❷ sich keinen Rat wissen not to know what to do ❸ **council**

**Rate** die (PLURAL die **Raten**) **instalment**; in monatlichen Raten abzahlen to pay in monthly instalments

**raten** ◇ VERB (PRES **rät**, IMP **riet**, PERF **hat geraten**) ❶ jemandem raten to advise somebody, was rätst du mir? what do you advise me to do? ❷ **to guess**; richtig raten to guess right

**Ratespiel** das (PLURAL die **Ratespiele**) **guessing game**

**Rathaus** das (PLURAL die **Rathäuser**) **town hall**

**rationell** ADJECTIVE **efficient**

**ratlos** ADJECTIVE **helpless**; Emma hat mich ratlos angesehen Emma gave me a helpless look, ratlos sein not to know what to do

**ratsam** ADJECTIVE **advisable**; es wäre ratsam, früher zu fahren it would be advisable to leave earlier

**Ratschlag** der (PLURAL die **Ratschläge**) **piece of advice, advice**; deine klugen Ratschläge kannst du dir sparen you can keep your advice to yourself

**Rätsel** das (PLURAL die **Rätsel**) ❶ **puzzle** ❷ **mystery**

**rätselhaft** ADJECTIVE **mysterious**

**Ratte** die (PLURAL die **Ratten**) **rat**

**rau** ADJECTIVE ❶ **rough** ❷ **harsh** ❸ eine raue Stimme a husky voice ❹ einen rauen Hals haben to have a sore throat

**Raub** der **robbery**

**Raubdruck** der *(PLURAL die Raubdrucke)* pirated edition

**Räuber** der *(PLURAL die Räuber)* robber

**Rauch** der smoke

**rauchen** *VERB (PERF hat geraucht)* to smoke; 'Rauchen verboten' 'no smoking'

**Rauchen** das smoking; passives Rauchen passive smoking

**Raucher** der *(PLURAL die Raucher)* smoker

**Raucherin** die *(PLURAL die Raucherinnen)* smoker

**Räucherlachs** der smoked salmon

**räuchern** *VERB (PERF hat geräuchert)* to smoke *(fish, meat)*

**rauf** *(informal)* ▸ SEE **herauf, hinauf**

**rauh** *ADJECTIVE* ▸ SEE **rau**

**Raum** der *(PLURAL die Räume)* ❶ room; das Haus hat sehr große Räume the house has very big rooms ❷ space; wir brauchen mehr Raum we need more space ❸ die Rakete ist im Raum explodiert the rocket exploded in space ❹ area; im Raum Berlin in the area of Berlin

**räumen** *VERB (PERF hat geräumt)* ❶ to clear; das Geschirr vom Tisch räumen to clear away the dishes ❷ die Hemden in den Schrank räumen to put the shirts in the cupboard, seine Sachen beiseite räumen to put your things to one side, die Akten aus dem Schrank räumen to take the files out of the cabinet ❸ to vacate

**Raumfahrt** die space travel

**Raumschiff** das *(PLURAL die Raumschiffe)* space ship

**Räumungsverkauf** der closing-down sale

**Raupe** die *(PLURAL die Raupen)* caterpillar

**raus** *(informal)* ▸ SEE **heraus, hinaus**

**Rauschgift** das *(PLURAL die Rauschgifte)* drug; Rauschgift nehmen to take drugs

**Rauschgiftsüchtige** der/die *(PLURAL die Rauschgiftsüchtigen)* drug addict

**rauskriegen** *VERB (informal) (PERF hat rausgekriegt)* ❶ to get out ❷ ein Geheimnis rauskriegen to find out a secret ❸ ich kann die Aufgabe nicht rauskriegen I can't do the exercise

**räuspern** *VERB (PERF hat sich geräuspert)* sich räuspern to clear your throat

**reagieren** *VERB (PERF hat reagiert)* to react

**Reaktion** die *(PLURAL die Reaktionen)* reaction

**realisieren** *VERB (PERF hat realisiert)* ❶ to realize ❷ to implement

**Reality-Show** die *(PLURAL die Reality-Shows)* reality show

**Realschule** die *(PLURAL die Realschulen)* secondary school

**rebellieren** *VERB (PERF hat rebelliert)* to rebel

**Rechen** der *(PLURAL die Rechen)* rake

**Recherche** die *(PLURAL die Recherchen)* investigation

**rechnen** *VERB (PERF hat gerechnet)* ❶ to do arithmetic; Peter kann gut rechnen Peter's good at arithmetic, Peter's good at figures ❷ to reckon; mit etwas rechnen to reckon with something ❸ er wird zu den besten Schauspielern gerechnet he's reckoned to be one of the best actors ❹ **to count**; jemanden zu seinen Freunden rechnen to count somebody as a friend ❺ mit etwas rechnen to expect something ❻ auf jemanden rechnen to count on somebody

**Rechner** der (PLURAL die **Rechner**) ❶ **calculator** ❷ **computer**

**Rechnung** die (PLURAL die **Rechnungen**) ❶ **bill** ❷ **invoice**; die Rechnung liegt bei the invoice is enclosed ❸ **calculation**

**recht** ADJECTIVE ❶ **right**; jemandem recht sein to be all right with somebody, wenn es dir recht ist if it's all right with you ❷ der/die Rechte the right man/woman ❸ das Rechte the right thing, etwas Rechtes something proper, ich habe nichts Rechtes gegessen I haven't had a proper meal, etwas Rechtes lernen to learn something useful ❹ **real**; ich habe keine rechte Lust I don't really feel like it

**recht** ADVERB ❶ **correctly** ❷ **quite**; recht einfach quite simple ❸ **really** ❹ recht vielen Dank many thanks ❺ das geschieht dir recht! (it) serves you right! ❻ man kann es nicht allen recht machen you can't please everyone

**Recht** das (PLURAL die **Rechte**) ❶ **law**; nach deutschem Recht under German law ❷ **right**; Recht haben to be right, im Recht sein to be in the right, Recht bekommen to be proved right ❸ jemandem Recht geben to agree with somebody ❹ mit Recht rightly, du hast dich mit Recht beschwert you were right to complain

**rechte** ▸ SEE **rechter**

**Rechte** die ❶ **right (side)**; zu meiner Rechten on my right ❷ **right hand** ❸ die Rechte the right (in politics)

**Rechteck** das (PLURAL die **Rechtecke**) **rectangle**

**rechteckig** ADJECTIVE **rectangular**

**rechter, rechte, rechtes** ADJECTIVE ❶ **right**; auf der rechten Seite on the right ❷ **right-wing**

**rechtfertigen** VERB ❶ (PERF hat gerechtfertigt) **to justify** ❷ sich rechtfertigen to justify yourself

**rechtlich** ADJECTIVE **legal**

**rechts** ADVERB **on the right**; nimm die dritte Abzweigung rechts take the third turning on the right, von rechts from the right, rechts abbiegen to turn right

**Rechtsanwalt** der (PLURAL die **Rechtsanwälte**) **lawyer**

**Rechtsanwältin** die (PLURAL die **Rechtsanwältinnen**) **lawyer**

**Rechtschreibprogramm** das (PLURAL die **Rechtschreibprogramme**) **spell checker**

**Rechtschreibung** die **spelling**

**Rechtshänder** der (PLURAL die **Rechtshänder**) Klaus ist Rechtshänder Klaus is right-handed

**Rechtshänderin** die (PLURAL die **Rechtshänderinnen**) Beate ist Rechtshänderin Beate is right-handed

**rechtzeitig** ADJECTIVE **timely**

**rechtzeitig** ADVERB **in time**; wir sind gerade noch rechtzeitig angekommen we got there just in time

**recyceln** VERB (PERF hat recycelt) **to recycle**

**Redakteur** der *(PLURAL die Redakteure)* editor

**Redakteurin** die *(PLURAL die Redakteurinnen)* editor

**Rede** die *(PLURAL die Reden)* ❶ speech; eine Rede halten to make a speech ❷ nicht der Rede wert not worth mentioning, davon kann keine Rede sein it's out of the question, jemanden zur Rede stellen to take somebody to task

**reden** *VERB (PERF hat geredet)* ❶ to talk ❷ to speak; mit jemandem reden to speak to somebody ❸ sie hat kein Wort geredet she didn't say a word ❹ mir ist egal, was über mich geredet wird I don't care what people say about me

**Redewendung** die *(PLURAL die Redewendungen)* idiom, expression

**redigieren** *VERB (PERF hat redigiert)* to edit

**redlich** *ADJECTIVE* honest

**Redlichkeit** die honesty

**Redner** der *(PLURAL die Redner)* speaker

**Rednerin** die *(PLURAL die Rednerinnen)* speaker

**reduzieren** *VERB (PERF hat reduziert)* to reduce

**reflexiv** *ADJECTIVE* reflexive

**Reformhaus** das *(PLURAL die Reformhäuser)* health-food shop

**Regal** das *(PLURAL die Regale)* ❶ shelf ❷ shelves, bookcase

**Regel** die *(PLURAL die Regeln)* ❶ rule; in der Regel as a rule ❷ period *(menstruation)*

**regelmäßig** *ADJECTIVE* regular

**regeln** *VERB (PERF hat geregelt)* ❶ to regulate ❷ to direct *(the traffic)* ❸ to settle *(a matter)*; wir haben die Sache so geregelt, dass ... we've arranged things so that ... ❹ sich von selbst regeln to sort itself out

**Regelung** die *(PLURAL die Regelungen)* ❶ regulation ❷ settlement

**Regen** der rain

**Regenbogen** der *(PLURAL die Regenbogen)* rainbow

**Regenmantel** der *(PLURAL die Regenmäntel)* raincoat

**Regenschirm** der *(PLURAL die Regenschirme)* umbrella

**Regenwurm** der *(PLURAL die Regenwürmer)* earthworm

**regieren** *VERB (PERF hat regiert)* ❶ to govern ❷ to rule, to reign

**Regierung** die *(PLURAL die Regierungen)* ❶ government ❷ reign

**Regisseur** der *(PLURAL die Regisseure)* director

**Regisseurin** die *(PLURAL die Regisseurinnen)* director

**Register** das *(PLURAL die Register)* ❶ index ❷ register

**regnen** *VERB (PERF hat geregnet)* to rain

**regnerisch** *ADJECTIVE* rainy

**Reh** das *(PLURAL die Rehe)* deer

**reiben** ◇*VERB (IMP rieb, PERF hat gerieben)* ❶ to rub ❷ to grate

**reibungslos** *ADJECTIVE* smooth

**reich** *ADJECTIVE* rich

**Reich** das *(PLURAL die* **Reiche)**
❶ **empire**; das Römische Reich the
Roman Empire ❷ **kingdom, realm**

**reichen** *VERB (PERF* **hat gereicht)** ❶ **to
hand, to pass** ❷ **to be enough**;
mit dem Geld reichen to have
enough money ❸ bis zu etwas
reichen to reach up to something,
er reicht seinem Vater bis zur
Schulter he comes up to his father's
shoulder, die Felder reichen bis
zum Wald the fields extend as far
as go right up to the forest ❹ mir
reichts! *(informal)* I've had enough!

**reichlich** *ADJECTIVE* ❶ **large** ❷ **ample**
*(space)*

**reichlich** *ADVERB* **plenty of**

**Reichstag** der **German parliament**

**Reichtum** der *(PLURAL die*
**Reichtümer)* wealth**

**Reichweite** die ❶ **reach**; außer
Reichweite out of reach ❷ **range**

**reif** *ADJECTIVE* ❶ **ripe** ❷ **mature**

**Reife** die **maturity**; mittlere Reife
exams taken after five years of
secondary schooling

**Reifen** der *(PLURAL die* **Reifen)** ❶ **tyre**
❷ **hoop**

**Reifendruck** der **tyre pressure**

**Reifenpanne** die *(PLURAL die*
**Reifenpannen)* puncture**

**Reihe** die *(PLURAL die* **Reihen)**
❶ **row** ❷ **series**; eine Reihe von
Ereignissen a series of events ❸ der
Reihe nach in turn, außer der Reihe
out of turn, du bist an der Reihe it's
your turn

**Reihenfolge** die *(PLURAL die*
**Reihenfolgen)* order**; in der
richtigen Reihenfolge in the right
order

**Reihenhaus** das *(PLURAL die*
**Reihenhäuser)* terraced house**

**Reim** der *(PLURAL die* **Reime)* rhyme**

**reimen** *VERB (PERF* **hat gereimt)** ❶ **to
rhyme** ❷ sich reimen **to rhyme**

**rein**¹ *ADJECTIVE* ❶ **pure** ❷ **clean**
❸ **sheer** *(madness)* ❹ etwas ins
Reine schreiben to make a fair
copy of something, etwas ins Reine
bringen to sort something out

**rein** *ADVERB* ❶ **purely** ❷ **absolutely**;
rein gar nichts absolutely nothing

**rein**² *(informal)* ▸ SEE **herein, hinein**

**reinigen** *VERB (PERF* **hat gereinigt)**
**to clean**

**Reinigung** die *(PLURAL die*
**Reinigungen)** ❶ **cleaning**
❷ **cleaner's**

**Reis** der **rice**

**Reise** die *(PLURAL die* **Reisen)**
❶ **journey, trip**; gute Reise! have a
good journey!, auf meinen Reisen
on my travels ❷ **voyage**

**Reiseandenken** das *(PLURAL die*
**Reiseandenken)* souvenir**

**Reisebüro** das *(PLURAL die*
**Reisebüros)* travel agency**

**Reisebus** der *(PLURAL die* **Reisebusse)**
**coach**

**Reiseführer** der *(PLURAL die*
**Reiseführer)** ❶ **guidebook**
❷ **(travel) guide**

**reisekrank** *ADJECTIVE* **travel-sick**;
reisekrank werden to get
travel-sick

**Reiseleiter** der *(PLURAL die*
**Reiseleiter)* (travel) guide**

**Reiseleiterin** die *(PLURAL die*
**Reiseleiterinnen)* tourist guide**

**reisen** *VERB* *(PERF* **ist gereist)**
to travel

**Reisende** der/die *(PLURAL* die
**Reisenden)** traveller

**Reisepass** der *(PLURAL* die
**Reisepässe)** passport

**Reisescheck** der *(PLURAL* die
**Reiseschecks)** traveller's cheque

**Reiseziel** das *(PLURAL* die **Reiseziele)**
destination

**reißen** ⋄*VERB* *(IMP* **riss***, PERF* **hat
gerissen)** ❶ to tear ❷ to snatch
❸ to pull; an etwas reißen to pull
at something ❹ mit sich reißen to
sweep away ❺ etwas an sich reißen
to snatch something, die Macht an
sich reißen to seize power ❻ Witze
reißen to crack jokes ❼ sich um
etwas reißen to fight for something
❽ *(PERF* **ist gerissen)** hin und her
gerissen sein to be torn ❾ *(PERF* **ist
gerissen)** to tear, to break

**Reißverschluss** der *(PLURAL* die
**Reißverschlüsse)** zip

**Reißzwecke** die *(PLURAL* die
**Reißzwecken)** drawing pin

**reiten** ⋄*VERB* *(IMP* **ritt***, PERF* **hat/ist
geritten)** to ride

**Reiter** der *(PLURAL* die **Reiter)** rider

**Reiterin** die *(PLURAL* die **Reiterinnen)**
rider

**Reitschule** die *(PLURAL* die
**Reitschulen)** riding school

**Reiz** der *(PLURAL* die **Reize)**
❶ attraction, appeal ❷ charm

**reizen** *VERB* *(PERF* **hat gereizt)** ❶ to
appeal to, to tempt; das reizt
mich sehr it's very tempting ❷ to
annoy; jemanden zum Zorn reizen
to provoke somebody to anger ❸ to

irritate *(the skin, eyes)* ❹ to bid
*(when playing cards)*

**reizend** *ADJECTIVE* **charming**

**reizvoll** *ADJECTIVE* **attractive**

**Reklame** die *(PLURAL* die
**Reklamen)** ❶ advertisement,
advert; für etwas Reklame
machen to advertise something
❷ commercial *(on TV)*

**Rekord** der *(PLURAL* die **Rekorde)**
record

**Rektor** der *(PLURAL* die **Rektoren)**
❶ head *(of a school)* ❷ vice-
chancellor *(of a university)*

**Religion** die *(PLURAL* die **Religionen)**
religion

**religiös** *ADJECTIVE* **religious**

**Rendezvous** das *(PLURAL* die
**Rendezvous)** date

**Rennbahn** die *(PLURAL* die
**Rennbahnen)** racetrack

**rennen** ⋄*VERB* *(IMP* **rannte***, PERF* **ist
gerannt)** to run

**Rennen** das *(PLURAL* die **Rennen)** race

**Rennfahrer** der *(PLURAL* die
**Rennfahrer)** racing driver

**Rennwagen** der *(PLURAL* die
**Rennwagen)** racing car

**renovieren** *VERB* *(PERF* **hat
renoviert)** to renovate, to
redecorate

**rentabel** *ADJECTIVE* **profitable**

**Rente** die *(PLURAL* die **Renten)**
pension; in Rente gehen to retire

**Rentner** der *(PLURAL* die **Rentner)**
pensioner

**Rentnerin** die *(PLURAL* die
**Rentnerinnen)** pensioner

**Reparatur** die *(PLURAL* die
**Reparaturen)** repair

**reparieren** VERB (PERF **hat repariert**)
to repair

**Reportage** die (PLURAL die
**Reportagen**) ❶ report ❷ live
commentary

**Reporter** der (PLURAL die **Reporter**)
reporter

**Reporterin** die (PLURAL die
**Reporterinnen**) reporter

**Reptil** das (PLURAL die **Reptile**) reptile

**Republik** die (PLURAL die **Republiken**)
republic

**Reservat** das (PLURAL die **Reservate**)
reservation

**Reserverad** das (PLURAL die
**Reserveräder**) spare wheel

**reservieren** VERB (PERF **hat
reserviert**) to reserve

**Reservierung** die (PLURAL die
**Reservierungen**) reservation

**Reservoir** das (PLURAL die
**Reservoirs**) reservoir

**Respekt** der respect

**respektieren** VERB (PERF **hat
respektiert**) to respect

**Rest** der (PLURAL die **Reste**) ❶ rest,
remainder ❷ left-over; zum
Mittagessen gibts die Reste we're
having the leftovers for lunch ❸ die
Reste the remains

**Restaurant** das (PLURAL die
**Restaurants**) restaurant

**restlich** ADJECTIVE remaining

**restlos** ADJECTIVE complete

**Resultat** das (PLURAL die **Resultate**)
result

**retten** VERB (PERF **hat gerettet**) ❶ to
save, to rescue; jemandem das
Leben retten to save somebody's
life ❷ sich retten to escape

**Rettich** der (PLURAL die **Rettiche**)
radish

**Rettung** die rescue

**Rettungsboot** das (PLURAL die
**Rettungsboote**) life boat

**Rettungsring** der (PLURAL die
**Rettungsringe**) lifebelt

**Rettungsschwimmer** der (PLURAL
die **Rettungsschwimmer**)
lifeguard; gibt es einen
Rettungsschwimmer im
Schwimmbad? is there a lifeguard
at the pool?

**Rettungsschwimmerin**
die (PLURAL die
**Rettungsschwimmerinnen**)
lifeguard

**Rettungswagen** der (PLURAL die
**Rettungswagen**) ambulance

**Rezept** das (PLURAL die **Rezepte**)
❶ prescription ❷ recipe

**Rezeption** die (PLURAL die
**Rezeptionen**) reception; bitte
geben Sie Ihren Schlüssel an der
Rezeption ab please leave your key
at reception

**R-Gespräch** das (PLURAL die
**R-Gespräche**) reverse-charge call

**Rhabarber** der rhubarb

**Rhein** der Rhine

**Rheuma** das rheumatism

**Rhythmus** der (PLURAL die
**Rhythmen**) rhythm

**richten** VERB (PERF **hat gerichtet**)
❶ to direct, to point (a torch,
telescope, gun) ❷ eine Frage an
jemanden richten to put a question
to somebody ❸ to address (a letter,
remarks) ❹ to prepare (a meal,
room) ❺ sich auf etwas richten
to be directed towards something
❻ sich nach jemandem richten

to fit in with somebody's wishes, sich nach den Vorschriften richten to follow the rules **❼** sich nach etwas richten to depend on something

**Richter** der *(PLURAL die* **Richter***)* judge

**richtig** *ADJECTIVE* **❶** right **❷** das Richtige the right thing, der/die Richtige the right man/woman **❸** real, proper

**richtig** *ADVERB* **❶** correctly; hast du das Formular richtig ausgefüllt? have you filled in the form correctly? **❷** really **❸** richtig stellen to put right, die Uhr geht richtig the clock is telling the right time

**Richtlinie** die *(PLURAL die* **Richtlinien***)* guideline

**Richtung** die *(PLURAL die* **Richtungen***)* **❶** direction **❷** trend

**rieb** ▸ SEE **reiben**

**riechen** ◇*VERB (IMP* **roch***, PERF* hat **gerochen***)* **❶** to smell **❷** ich kann ihn nicht riechen *(informal)* I can't stand him

**rief** ▸ SEE **rufen**

**Riegel** der *(PLURAL die* **Riegel***)* **❶** bolt **❷** ein Riegel Schokolade a bar of chocolate

**Riemen** der *(PLURAL die* **Riemen***)* strap

**Riese** der *(PLURAL die* **Riesen***)* giant

**riesengroß** *ADJECTIVE* gigantic

**riesig** *ADJECTIVE* gigantic, huge; ein riesiger Lastwagen a gigantic lorry

**riet** ▸ SEE **raten**

**Rind** das *(PLURAL die* **Rinder***)* **❶** ox **❷** cow; Rinder cattle **❸** beef

**Rinde** die *(PLURAL die* **Rinden***)* **❶** bark **❷** rind **❸** crust

**Rinderbraten** der *(PLURAL die* **Rinderbraten***)* roast beef

**Rindfleisch** das beef

**Ring** der *(PLURAL die* **Ringe***)* ring

**Ringbuch** das *(PLURAL die* **Ringbücher***)* ring binder

**Ringen** das wrestling

**Rinne** die *(PLURAL die* **Rinnen***)* **❶** gutter **❷** drainpipe, channel

**Rippe** die *(PLURAL die* **Rippen***)* rib

**Risiko** das *(PLURAL die* **Risiken***)* risk

**riskant** *ADJECTIVE* risky

**riskieren** *VERB (PERF* hat **riskiert***)* to risk, to put at risk

**riss** ▸ SEE **reißen**

**Riss** der *(PLURAL die* **Risse***)* **❶** tear **❷** crack

**ritt** ▸ SEE **reiten**

**Rivale** der *(PLURAL die* **Rivalen***)* rival

**Rivalin** die *(PLURAL die* **Rivalinnen***)* rival

**Robbe** die *(PLURAL die* **Robben***)* seal

**Roboter** der *(PLURAL die* **Roboter***)* robot

**roch** ▸ SEE **riechen**

**Rock** der *(PLURAL die* **Röcke***)* skirt

**Roggen** der rye

**roh** *ADJECTIVE* **❶** raw **❷** rough **❸** brutal

**Rohr** das *(PLURAL die* **Rohre***)* **❶** pipe **❷** reed **❸** cane

**Rohstoff** der *(PLURAL die* **Rohstoffe***)* raw material

**Rolladen** ▸ SEE **Rollladen**

**Rolle** die *(PLURAL die* **Rollen***)* **❶** roll **❷** reel **❸** role, part **❹** es spielt keine Rolle it doesn't matter

a
b
c
d
e
f
g
h
i
j
k
l
m
n
o
p
q
r
s
t
u
v
w
x
y
z

**rollen** VERB (PERF **hat gerollt**) ❶ to roll ❷ (PERF **ist gerollt**) to roll

**Roller** der (PLURAL die **Roller**) scooter

**Rollkragen** der (PLURAL die **Rollkrägen**) polo neck

**Rollladen** der (PLURAL die **Rollläden**) shutter

**Rollschuh** der (PLURAL die **Rollschuhe**) roller-skate

**Rollschuhfahrer** der (PLURAL die **Rollschuhfahrer**) skater (on rollerskates)

**Rollschuhfahrerin** die (PLURAL die **Rollschuhfahrerinnen**) skater (on rollerskates)

**Rollschuhlaufen** das roller-skating

**Rollstuhl** der (PLURAL die **Rollstühle**) wheelchair

**Rolltreppe** die (PLURAL die **Rolltreppen**) escalator

**Rom** das Rome

**Roman** der (PLURAL die **Romane**) novel

**romantisch** ADJECTIVE romantic

**Römer** der (PLURAL die **Römer**) Roman

**Römerin** die (PLURAL die **Römerinnen**) Roman

**röntgen** VERB (PERF **hat geröntgt**) to X-ray

**rosa** ADJECTIVE pink

**Rose** die (PLURAL die **Rosen**) rose

**Rosenkohl** der (Brussels) sprouts

**Rosine** die (PLURAL die **Rosinen**) raisin

**Rosmarin** der rosemary

**Rosskastanie** die (PLURAL die **Rosskastanien**) horse-chestnut, conker

**Rost** der (PLURAL die **Roste**) ❶ rust ❷ grate, grill

**rosten** VERB (PERF **ist gerostet**) to rust

**rösten** (PERF **hat geröstet**) ❶ to roast ❷ to toast

**rostig** ADJECTIVE rusty

**Röstkartoffeln** PLURAL NOUN roast potatoes

**rot** ADJECTIVE red

**Röteln** PLURAL NOUN German measles

**rothaarig** ADJECTIVE red-haired

**Rotkehlchen** das (PLURAL die **Rotkehlchen**) robin

**Rotkohl** der red cabbage

**Rotwein** der (PLURAL die **Rotweine**) red wine

**Routine** die routine

**rüber** ADVERB (informal) over; komm zu uns rüber come over to us

**Rückblende** die (PLURAL die **Rückblenden**) flashback

**rücken** VERB (PERF **hat gerückt**) to move; kannst du ein wenig rücken? can you move over a bit?

**Rücken** der (PLURAL die **Rücken**) ❶ back ❷ spine (of a book)

**Rückfahrkarte** die (PLURAL die **Rückfahrkarten**) return ticket; eine Rückfahrkarte nach München a return ticket to Munich

**Rückfahrt** die return journey; auf der Rückfahrt on the way back

**Rückgabe** die (PLURAL die **Rückgaben**) return

**Rückgang** der (PLURAL die **Rückgänge**) decrease; ein Rückgang in der Anzahl der Unfälle a decrease in the number of accidents

**rückgängig** *ADJECTIVE* etwas rückgängig machen to cancel something

**Rückhand** die **backhand** *(in tennis)*

**Rückkehr** die **return**

**Rückreise** die **return journey**

**Rucksack** der *(PLURAL die* **Rucksäcke)** **rucksack**

**Rückseite** die *(PLURAL die* **Rückseiten)** **back**

**Rücksicht** die **consideration**

**rücksichtslos** *ADJECTIVE* **❶ inconsiderate**; ein rücksichtsloser Fahrer a reckless driver **❷ ruthless**

**rücksichtsvoll** *ADJECTIVE* **considerate**

**Rücksitz** der *(PLURAL die* **Rücksitze)** **back seat**

**rückwärts** *ADVERB* **backwards**

**Rückwärtsgang** der *(PLURAL die* **Rückwärtsgänge)** **reverse (gear)**

**Rückweg** der *(PLURAL die* **Rückwege)** **❶ way back ❷ return journey**

**Rückzahlung** die *(PLURAL die* **Rückzahlungen)** **refund, repayment**

**Ruder** das *(PLURAL die* **Ruder)** **❶ oar ❷ rudder**

**Ruderboot** das *(PLURAL die* **Ruderboote)** **rowing boat**

**rudern** *VERB (PERF* **ist gerudert)** **❶ to row**; ich bin über den See gerudert I rowed across the lake **❷** *(PERF* **hat gerudert)** **to row**; ich habe Monika über den See gerudert I rowed Monika across the lake

**Rudern** das **rowing**; du bist mit dem Rudern dran it's your turn to row

**Ruf** der *(PLURAL die* **Rufe)** **❶ call**, **shout ❷ reputation ❸ phone number**

**rufen** ◇*VERB (IMP* **rief**, *PERF* **hat gerufen)** **to call**; den Arzt rufen to send for the doctor

**Rufnummer** die *(PLURAL die* **Rufnummern)** **phone number**

**Ruhe** die **❶ silence**; Ruhe bitte! quiet please! **❷ rest ❸ peace**; jemanden in Ruhe lassen to leave somebody in peace, in aller Ruhe calmly **❹** sich nicht aus der Ruhe bringen lassen to not get worked up **❺** sich zur Ruhe setzen to retire

**ruhen** *VERB (PERF* **hat geruht)** **to rest**; hier ruht ... here lies ...

**Ruhestand** der im Ruhestand **retired**

**Ruhetag** der *(PLURAL die* **Ruhetage)** **closing day**; 'Dienstag Ruhetag' 'closed on Tuesdays'

**ruhig** *ADJECTIVE* **❶ quiet ❷ peaceful ❸ calm**

**ruhig** *ADVERB* **❶ quietly**; sich ruhig verhalten to keep quiet **❷ calmly**; ruhig bleiben to remain calm **❸** sehen Sie sich ruhig um you're welcome to look around, du kannst es ihm ruhig sagen it's OK, you can tell him

**Ruhm** der **fame**

**Rührei** das **scrambled eggs**

**rühren** *VERB (PERF* **hat gerührt)** **❶ to move ❷ to stir ❸** sich rühren to move **❹** an etwas rühren to touch, to touch on

**Ruine** die *(PLURAL die* **Ruinen)** **ruin**

**ruinieren** *VERB (PERF* **hat ruiniert)** **to ruin**

a
b
c
d
e
f
g
h
i
j
k
l
m
n
o
p
q
r
s
t
u
v
w
x
y
z

**rülpsen** VERB (PERF **hat gerülpst**) to belch

**Rum** der rum

**Rumänien** das Romania

**rumänisch** ADJECTIVE Romanian

**Rummel** der ❶ hustle and bustle ❷ fuss ❸ fair

**Rummelplatz** der (PLURAL die **Rummelplätze**) fairground

**rund** ADJECTIVE round

**rund** ADVERB about; rund um around

**Runde** die (PLURAL die **Runden**) ❶ round ❷ lap ❸ circle, group ❹ über die Runden kommen (informal) to get by

**Rundfahrt** die (PLURAL die **Rundfahrten**) tour

**Rundfrage** die (PLURAL die **Rundfragen**) poll

**Rundfunk** der radio; im Rundfunk on the radio

**rundherum** ADVERB all around

**Rundkurs** der (PLURAL die **Rundkurse**) (motor racing) circuit

**runter** ADVERB (informal) ▸SEE **herunter, hinunter** runter da! get off!

**runzlig** ADJECTIVE wrinkled

**Rüsche** die (PLURAL die **Rüschen**) frill

**Russe** der (PLURAL die **Russen**) Russian

**Rüssel** der (PLURAL die **Rüssel**) trunk

**Russin** die (PLURAL die **Russinnen**) Russian

**russisch** ADJECTIVE Russian

**Russland** das Russia

**Rüstung** die (PLURAL die **Rüstungen**)

❶ armament ❷ arms ❸ (suit of) armour

**Rutschbahn** die (PLURAL die **Rutschbahnen**) slide

**rutschen** VERB (PERF **ist gerutscht**) ❶ to slide ❷ to slip ❸ rutsch mal! move over!

**rutschig** ADJECTIVE slippery

**rütteln** VERB (PERF **hat gerüttelt**) to shake; an der Tür rütteln to rattle at the door

# Ss

**Saal** der *(PLURAL die Säle)* hall

**Saatkrähe** die *(PLURAL die Saatkrähen)* rook

**Sabbat** der *(PLURAL die Sabbate)* Sabbath

**Sache** die *(PLURAL die Sachen)* ❶ matter; das ist eine andere Sache that's a different matter ❷ business; das ist seine Sache that's his business ❸ thing; meine Sachen my things *(clothing)*, sie räumt nie ihre Sachen weg she never puts away her things ❹ zur Sache kommen to get to the point ❺ das ist so 'ne Sache *(informal)* it's a bit tricky

**Sachgebiet** das *(PLURAL die Sachgebiete)* field, area

**sachlich** *ADJECTIVE* ❶ objective ❷ factual

**sächlich** *ADJECTIVE* neuter

**Sachsen** das Saxony

**Sack** der *(PLURAL die Säcke)* ❶ sack ❷ bag

**Sackgasse** die *(PLURAL die Sackgassen)* dead end, cul-de-sac

**Saft** der *(PLURAL die Säfte)* ❶ juice ❷ sap

**saftig** *ADJECTIVE* juicy

**Säge** die *(PLURAL die Sägen)* saw

**Sägemehl** das sawdust

**sagen** *VERB (PERF hat gesagt)* ❶ to say; man sagt, dass ... it's said that ... ❷ was ich noch sagen wollte by the way, unter uns gesagt between you and me ❸ to tell; jemandem etwas sagen to tell somebody something, sag mal tell me, was sagen Sie dazu? what do you think about it? ❹ to mean; das hat nichts zu sagen it doesn't mean anything ❺ zu jemandem Tante sagen to call somebody aunt ❻ ihr Gesicht sagte alles it was written all over her face

**sägen** *VERB (PERF hat gesägt)* to saw

**sagenhaft** *ADJECTIVE* ❶ legendary ❷ *(informal)* brilliant

**sah** ▸ SEE **sehen**

**Sahne** die cream

**Saison** die *(PLURAL die Saisons)* season

**Saite** die *(PLURAL die Saiten)* string

**Sakko** das *(PLURAL die Sakkos)* jacket

**Salami** die *(PLURAL die Salamis)* salami

**Salat** der *(PLURAL die Salate)* ❶ lettuce; ein grüner Salat a lettuce ❷ salad

**Salatsoße** die *(PLURAL die Salatsoßen)* salad dressing

**Salbe** die *(PLURAL die Salben)* ointment

**Salbei** der sage

**salopp** *ADJECTIVE* casual, informal

**Salz** das salt

**salzen** *VERB (PERF hat gesalzen)* to salt

**salzig** *ADJECTIVE* salty

**Salzkartoffeln** *PLURAL NOUN* **boiled potatoes**

**Salzwasser** das ❶ **salt water** ❷ **salted water** *(for cooking)*

**Samen** der *(PLURAL die* **Samen)** ❶ **seed** ❷ **sperm, semen**

**Sammelalbum** das *(PLURAL die* **Sammelalben)** **scrapbook**

**sammeln** *VERB (PERF* **hat gesammelt)** ❶ **to collect;** Martin sammelt Briefmarken Martin collects stamps ❷ **to gather** ❸ sich sammeln **to gather,** seine Gedanken sammeln to gather your thoughts

**Sammler** der *(PLURAL die* **Sammler)** **collector**

**Sammlerin** die *(PLURAL die* **Sammlerinnen)** **collector**

**Sammlung** die *(PLURAL die* **Sammlungen)** **collection;** eine Sammlung für einen guten Zweck a collection for a good cause

**Samstag** der *(PLURAL die* **Samstage)** **Saturday**

**samstags** *ADVERB* **on Saturdays**

**samt** *PREPOSITION (+DAT)* **(together) with;** Mimi kam samt Puppen und Katze Mimi arrived with her dolls and cat

**Samt** der *(PLURAL die* **Samte)** **velvet**

**sämtlicher, sämtliche, sämtliches** *ADJECTIVE* **all the;** meine sämtlichen Bücher all my books

**Sand** der **sand**

**Sandale** die *(PLURAL die* **Sandalen)** **sandal**

**sandig** *ADJECTIVE* **sandy**

**Sandpapier** das *(PLURAL die* **Sandpapiere)** **sandpaper**

**sandte** ▸ see **senden**

**sanft** *ADJECTIVE* **gentle;** eine sanfte Stimme a soft voice

**sang** ▸ see **singen**

**Sänger** der *(PLURAL die* **Sänger)** **singer**

**Sängerin** die *(PLURAL die* **Sängerinnen)** **singer**

**sank** ▸ see **sinken**

**Sardelle** die *(PLURAL die* **Sardellen)** **anchovy**

**Sardine** die *(PLURAL die* **Sardinen)** **sardine**

**Sarg** der *(PLURAL die* **Särge)** **coffin**

**Sarkasmus** der **sarcasm**

**sarkastisch** *ADJECTIVE* **sarcastic**

**SARS** das **SARS** *(the disease)*

**saß** ▸ see **sitzen**

**Satellit** der *(PLURAL die* **Satelliten)** **satellite**

**Satellitenfernsehen** das **satellite television**

**satt** *ADJECTIVE* ❶ **full (up);** bist du satt geworden? have you had enough to eat?, sich satt essen to eat as much as one wants, satt machen to be filling ❷ etwas satt haben *(informal)* to be fed up with something

**Sattel** der *(PLURAL die* **Sättel)** **saddle**

**Satteltasche** die *(PLURAL die* **Satteltaschen)** **saddlebag**

**Satz** der *(PLURAL die* **Sätze)** ❶ **sentence** ❷ **set** *(of things or in tennis);* ein Satz Reifen a set of tyres

❸ movement *(in music)* ❹ rate *(of tax, interest)* ❺ leap

**sauber** *ADJECTIVE* ❶ clean ❷ neat ❸ *(informal)* fine *(expressing irony)* ❹ sauber machen to clean

**Sauberkeit** die cleanliness, cleanness

**saubermachen** ▸ SEE **sauber**

**Sauce** die *(PLURAL die* **Saucen)** ▸ SEE **Soße**

**sauer** *ADJECTIVE* ❶ sour ❷ pickled ❸ acid; saurer Regen acid rain ❹ sauer sein *(informal)* to be annoyed
ich bin sauer auf Eva I'm annoyed with Eva

**Sauerei** die *(informal)* *(PLURAL die* **Sauereien)** ❶ mess ❷ disgrace, scandal ❸ obscenity

**Sauerstoff** der oxygen

**saufen** ◇*VERB (informal)* *(PRES* **säuft**, *IMP* **soff**, *PERF* **hat gesoffen)** to drink, to booze

**saugen** *VERB (PERF* **hat gesaugt)** ❶ to suck ❷ to vacuum, to hoover

**Säugetier** das *(PLURAL die* **Säugetiere)** mammal

**Säugling** der *(PLURAL die* **Säuglinge)** baby, infant

**Säule** die *(PLURAL die* **Säulen)** column, pillar

**Saum** der *(PLURAL die* **Säume)** hem

**Säure** die *(PLURAL die* **Säuren)** acid

**Saxofon** das *(PLURAL die* **Saxofone)** saxophone

**S-Bahn** die *(PLURAL die* **S-Bahnen)** city and suburban railway

**Scanner** der *(PLURAL die* **Scanner)** scanner

**schäbig** *ADJECTIVE* shabby

**Schach** das chess; Schach! check!

**Schachbrett** das *(PLURAL die* **Schachbretter)** chessboard

**Schachfigur** die *(PLURAL die* **Schachfiguren)** chess piece

**Schachtel** die *(PLURAL die* **Schachteln)** box

**schade** *ADJECTIVE* ❶ schade sein to be a pity, schade! (what a) pity! ❷ zu schade für jemanden sein to be too good for somebody

**Schädel** der *(PLURAL die* **Schädel)** skull

**schaden** *VERB (PERF* **hat geschadet)** ❶ to damage; das hat seinem Ruf geschadet it damaged his reputation ❷ jemandem schaden to harm somebody ❸ das schadet nichts it doesn't matter

**Schaden** der *(PLURAL die* **Schäden)** ❶ damage ❷ disadvantage

**schädlich** *ADJECTIVE* harmful

**Schaf** das *(PLURAL die* **Schafe)** sheep

**Schäfer** der *(PLURAL die* **Schäfer)** shepherd

**Schäferhund** der *(PLURAL die* **Schäferhunde)** sheepdog

**schaffen¹** ◇*VERB (IMP* **schuf**, *PERF* **hat geschaffen)** to create; wie geschaffen für made for

**schaffen²** *VERB (PERF* **hat geschafft)** ❶ to manage; es schaffen, etwas zu tun to manage to do something ❷ eine Prüfung schaffen to pass an exam ❸ jemandem zu schaffen machen to cause somebody trouble ❹ geschafft sein *(informal)* to be worn out

**Schaffner** der *(PLURAL* die **Schaffner)** ❶ conductor ❷ (ticket) inspector

**Schaffnerin** die *(PLURAL* die **Schaffnerinnen)** ❶ conductress ❷ (ticket) inspector

**Schakal** der *(PLURAL* die **Schakale)** jackal

**Schal** der *(PLURAL* die **Schals)** scarf

**Schale** die *(PLURAL* die **Schalen)** ❶ skin ❷ peel ❸ shell ❹ dish, bowl; eine Schale Obst a bowl of fruit

**schälen** *VERB (PERF* **hat geschält)** ❶ to peel; er hat ihr eine Orange geschält he peeled an orange for her ❷ sich schälen to peel, mein Rücken schält sich my back's peeling

**Schall** der sound

**Schallplatte** die *(PLURAL* die **Schallplatten)** record

**schalten** *VERB (PERF* **hat geschaltet)** ❶ to switch; auf etwas schalten to turn to something ❷ to change gear ❸ schnell schalten *(informal)* to catch on quickly

**Schalter** der *(PLURAL* die **Schalter)** ❶ switch ❷ counter

**Schaltjahr** das *(PLURAL* die **Schaltjahre)** leap year

**schämen** *VERB (PERF* **hat sich geschämt)** sich schämen to be ashamed

**Schampon** das *(PLURAL* die **Schampons)** ▸ SEE **Shampoo**

**Schande** die ❶ disgrace ❷ shame

**scharf** *ADJECTIVE* ❶ sharp ❷ hot *(food)*; ein scharfer Wind a biting wind ❸ fierce *(dog, frost)* ❹ scharf nachdenken to think hard ❺ *(in photography)* scharf sein to be in focus, scharf einstellen to focus ❻ scharf schießen to fire live ammunition ❼ scharf auf etwas sein *(informal)* to be really keen on something, sie ist scharf auf Bernd *(informal)* she fancies Bernd

**Schaschlik** der *(PLURAL* die **Schaschliks)** kebab

**Schatten** der *(PLURAL* die **Schatten)** ❶ shadow ❷ shade

**schattig** *ADJECTIVE* shady

**Schatz** der *(PLURAL* die **Schätze)** ❶ treasure ❷ darling

**Schätzchen** das *(PLURAL* die **Schätzchen)** darling

**schätzen** *VERB (PERF* **hat geschätzt)** ❶ to estimate ❷ to value ❸ to reckon, to guess; schätz mal! guess! ❹ etwas zu schätzen wissen to appreciate something

**Schau** die *(PLURAL* die **Schauen)** show

**schauen** *VERB (PERF* **hat geschaut)** ❶ to look ❷ to watch; Fernsehen schauen to watch television

**Schauer** der *(PLURAL* die **Schauer)** shower

**Schauergeschichte** die *(PLURAL* die **Schauergeschichten)** horror story

**Schaufel** die *(PLURAL* die **Schaufeln)** ❶ shovel ❷ dustpan

**Schaufenster** das *(PLURAL* die **Schaufenster)** shop window

**Schaukel** die *(PLURAL* die **Schaukeln)** swing

**schaukeln** *VERB (PERF* **hat geschaukelt)** to swing

**Schaukelstuhl** der (PLURAL die Schaukelstühle) rocking chair

**Schaum** der ❶ foam ❷ froth ❸ lather

**schäumen** VERB (PERF hat geschäumt) ❶ to foam ❷ to froth (up)

**Schauplatz** der (PLURAL die Schauplätze) scene

**Schauspiel** das (PLURAL die Schauspiele) ❶ play ❷ spectacle

**Schauspieler** der (PLURAL die Schauspieler) actor

**Schauspielerin** die (PLURAL die Schauspielerinnen) actress

**Schauspielkunst** die dramatic art, acting

**Scheck** der (PLURAL die Schecks) cheque

**Scheckbuch** das (PLURAL die Scheckbücher) chequebook

**Scheckkarte** die (PLURAL die Scheckkarten) cheque card

**Scheibe** die (PLURAL die Scheiben) ❶ pane (of a window, car) ❷ slice; eine Scheibe Schinken a slice of ham, die Salami in Scheiben schneiden to slice the salami, du könntest dir eine Scheibe von ihr abschneiden (informal) you could take a leaf out of her book ❸ disc

**Scheibenwischer** der (PLURAL die Scheibenwischer) windscreen wiper

**scheiden** ◇VERB (IMP schied, PERF hat geschieden) ❶ to separate; sich scheiden lassen to get divorced, sie haben sich im Juli scheiden lassen they got divorced in July ❷ geschieden sein to be divorced

**Scheidung** die (PLURAL die Scheidungen) divorce

**Schein** der (PLURAL die Scheine) ❶ light ❷ appearance; etwas nur zum Schein machen to only pretend to do something ❸ certificate ❹ note (money)

**scheinbar** ADVERB apparently

**scheinen** ◇VERB (IMP schien, PERF hat geschienen) ❶ to shine ❷ to seem; mir scheint it seems to me

**Scheinwerfer** der (PLURAL die Scheinwerfer) ❶ headlamp, headlight ❷ floodlight, spotlight

**Scheitel** der (PLURAL die Scheitel) parting (in your hair)

**scheitern** VERB (PERF ist gescheitert) to fail

**Schenkel** der (PLURAL die Schenkel) thigh

**schenken** VERB (PERF hat geschenkt) ❶ to give; etwas geschenkt bekommen to be given something ❷ sich etwas schenken to give something a miss ❸ das ist ja geschenkt! (informal) it's a gift!

**Schere** die (PLURAL die Scheren) ❶ (pair of) scissors ❷ shears ❸ claw (of a crab)

**scheren** VERB (informal) (PERF hat geschert) to bother; sich nicht um etwas scheren not to care about something, scher dich um deine eigenen Angelegenheiten! mind your own business!, scher dich zum Teufel! go to hell!

**Scherz** der (PLURAL die Scherze) joke

**scheu** ADJECTIVE shy

**scheuern** VERB (PERF hat gescheuert) ❶ to scrub ❷ to rub

**Scheune** die *(PLURAL die **Scheunen**)* barn

**scheußlich** ADJECTIVE horrible

**Schi** der *(PLURAL die **Schi(er)**)* ▸ SEE **Ski**

**Schicht** die *(PLURAL die **Schichten**)* ❶ layer ❷ class ❸ shift

**Schicht** *(PLURAL die **Schichten**)* ❶ stratum ❷ section ❸ shift *(in factory etc)*

**schick** ADJECTIVE ❶ stylish, smart ❷ *(informal)* great

**schicken** VERB *(PERF hat **geschickt**)* to send

**Schicksal** das *(PLURAL die **Schicksale**)* fate

**Schiebedach** das *(PLURAL die **Schiebedächer**)* sunroof

**schieben** ◇VERB *(IMP **schob**, PERF hat **geschoben**)* ❶ to push ❷ etwas auf etwas schieben to blame something for something, die Schuld auf jemanden schieben to put the blame on somebody

**schied** ▸ SEE **scheiden**

**Schiedsrichter** der *(PLURAL die **Schiedsrichter**)* referee, umpire

**schief** ADJECTIVE crooked; ein schiefer Blick a funny look

**schief** ADVERB ❶ das Bild hängt schief the picture is not straight ❷ schief gehen to go wrong

**Schiefer** der slate

**schiefgehen** ▸ SEE **schief**

**schielen** VERB *(PERF hat **geschielt**)* to squint

**schien** ▸ SEE **scheinen**

**Schienbein** das *(PLURAL die **Schienbeine**)* shin

**Schiene** die *(PLURAL die **Schienen**)* ❶ rail ❷ splint

**schießen** ◇VERB *(IMP **schoss**, PERF hat **geschossen**)* ❶ to shoot; auf jemanden schießen to shoot at somebody, ein Tor schießen to score a goal ❷ *(PERF ist **geschossen**)* to shoot (along); Andrea ist in die Höhe geschossen Andrea's shot up *(has got a lot taller)*

**Schiff** das *(PLURAL die **Schiffe**)* ship; ein Schiff zu Wasser lassen to launch a ship

**Schifffahrt** die *(PLURAL die **Schifffahrten**)* boat trip

**schikanieren** VERB *(PERF hat **schikaniert**)* to bully

**Schikoree** der ▸ SEE **Chicorée**

**Schild**¹ das *(PLURAL die **Schilder**)* ❶ sign ❷ badge ❸ label

**Schild**² der *(PLURAL die **Schilde**)* shield

**Schildkröte** die *(PLURAL die **Schildkröten**)* ❶ tortoise ❷ turtle

**Schilling** der *(PLURAL die **Schilling(e)**)* Schilling *(the currency of Austria until replaced by the euro; 100 Schillings = €7.26 euros)*

**Schimmel** der *(PLURAL die **Schimmel**)* ❶ mould ❷ white horse

**Schimpanse** der *(PLURAL die **Schimpansen**)* chimpanzee

**schimpfen** VERB *(PERF hat **geschimpft**)* ❶ to tell off ❷ to grumble

**Schinken** der *(PLURAL die **Schinken**)* ham; ein Schinkenbrötchen a ham roll

**Schirm** der (PLURAL die **Schirme**)
❶ umbrella ❷ sunshade ❸ shade
(of a lamp) ❹ peak (of a cap)

**Schlaf** der sleep

**Schlafanzug** der (PLURAL die
**Schlafanzüge**) pyjamas

**Schlafcouch** die (PLURAL die
**Schlafcouchs**) sofa bed

**schlafen** ◇VERB (PRES **schläft**, IMP
**schlief**, PERF **hat geschlafen**) ❶ to
sleep ❷ to be asleep; das Baby
schläft the baby's asleep ❸ schlafen
gehen to go to bed

**schlaff** ADJECTIVE ❶ slack (rope)
❷ limp (handshake, body)
❸ lethargic

**schläfrig** ADJECTIVE sleepy; ich bin
schläfrig I'm sleepy

**Schlafsaal** der (PLURAL die
**Schlafsäle**) dormitory

**Schlafsack** der (PLURAL die
**Schlafsäcke**) sleeping bag

**Schlafwagen** der (PLURAL die
**Schlafwagen**) sleeper

**Schlafzimmer** das (PLURAL die
**Schlafzimmer**) bedroom

**Schlag** der (PLURAL die **Schläge**)
❶ blow, punch; Schläge kriegen to
get a beating ❷ stroke ❸ (electric)
shock ❹ Schlag auf Schlag in quick
succession, auf einen Schlag all at
once

**schlagen** ◇VERB (PRES **schlägt**, IMP
**schlug**, PERF **hat geschlagen**)
❶ to hit; einen Nagel in die Wand
schlagen to knock a nail into the
wall ❷ to beat ❸ to bang; mit
dem Kopf gegen etwas schlagen to
bang your head against something
❹ to strike (of a clock) ❺ to whip

(cream) ❻ sich schlagen to fight
❼ sich geschlagen geben to admit
defeat

**Schlager** der (PLURAL die **Schlager**)
hit

**Schläger** der (PLURAL die **Schläger**)
❶ racket (in tennis) ❷ bat (in
baseball) ❸ club (in golf) ❹ stick
(in hockey) ❺ thug

**Schlägerei** die (PLURAL die
**Schlägereien**) fight

**Schlagsahne** die ❶ whipping
cream ❷ whipped cream

**Schlagzeile** die (PLURAL die
**Schlagzeilen**) headline

**Schlagzeug** das (PLURAL die
**Schlagzeuge**) drums

**Schlagzeuger** der (PLURAL die
**Schlagzeuger**) drummer

**Schlamm** der mud

**schlampen** VERB (PERF **hat
geschlampt**) to be sloppy

**Schlamperei** die (PLURAL die
**Schlampereien**) ❶ sloppiness
❷ mess

**schlampig** ADJECTIVE sloppy

**Schlange** die (PLURAL die **Schlangen**)
❶ snake ❷ queue; Schlange
stehen to queue

**schlank** ADJECTIVE slim

**Schlankheitskur** die (PLURAL die
**Schlankheitskuren**) diet; eine
Schlankeitskur machen to be on
a diet

**schlapp** ADJECTIVE worn out, tired
out

**schlau** ADJECTIVE ❶ crafty ❷ clever;
ich werde nicht schlau daraus
I can't make head nor tail of it

**Schlauch** der (PLURAL die **Schläuche**) hose

**schlauchlos** ADJECTIVE tubeless

**schlecht** ADJECTIVE ❶ bad; schlecht werden to go bad ❷ mir ist schlecht I feel sick ❸ jemanden schlecht machen to run somebody down

**schlecht** ADVERB ❶ badly; schlecht gelaunt in a bad mood ❷ es geht ihm schlecht he's not well

**schleichen** ◇VERB (IMP schlich, PERF ist geschlichen) ❶ to creep ❷ to crawl (in traffic) ❸ sich schleichen to creep

**Schleife** die (PLURAL die **Schleifen**) ❶ bow ❷ loop

**Schlepper** der (PLURAL die **Schlepper**) ❶ tug ❷ tractor

**Schleuder** die (PLURAL die Schleudern) ❶ catapult ❷ spin-dryer

**schleudern** VERB (PERF hat geschleudert) ❶ to hurl ❷ to spin (washing) ❸ (PERF ist geschleudert) to skid

**schlich** ▸ SEE schleichen

**schlicht** ADJECTIVE plain, simple

**schlief** ▸ SEE schlafen

**schließen** ◇VERB (IMP schloss, PERF hat geschlossen) ❶ to close, to shut ❷ to close down ❸ to lock ❹ to conclude; aus etwas schließen, dass ... to conclude from something that ... ❺ einen Vertrag schließen to enter into a contract ❻ Freundschaft mit jemandem schließen to make friends with somebody ❼ sich schließen to close

**Schließfach** das (PLURAL die **Schließfächer**) locker

**schließlich** ADVERB ❶ finally ❷ after all; er hat sie schließlich doch eingeladen he's invited her after all

**schlimm** ADJECTIVE bad

**schlimmstenfalls** ADVERB if the worst comes to the worst

**Schlips** der (PLURAL die **Schlipse**) tie

**Schlitten** der (PLURAL die **Schlitten**) sledge; Schlitten fahren gehen to go sledging

**Schlittschuh** der (PLURAL die **Schlittschuhe**) skate; Schlittschuh laufen to skate

**Schlittschuhlaufen** das ice-skating

**Schlitz** der (PLURAL die **Schlitze**) ❶ slit ❷ flies (in trousers) ❸ slot

**schloss** ▸ SEE schließen

**Schloss** das (PLURAL die **Schlösser**) ❶ lock ❷ castle

**Schluck** der (PLURAL die **Schlucke**) ❶ mouthful ❷ gulp

**Schluckauf** der hiccups

**schlucken** VERB (PERF hat geschluckt) to swallow

**schlug** ▸ SEE schlagen

**Schlüpfer** der (PLURAL die **Schlüpfer**) knickers

**Schluss** der (PLURAL die **Schlüsse**) ❶ end, ending; zum Schluss in the end
Schluss machen to stop, mit jemandem Schluss machen to finish with somebody ❷ conclusion

**Schlüssel** der (PLURAL die **Schlüssel**) ❶ key ❷ spanner

**Schlüsselwort** das *(PLURAL die Schlüsselwörter)* keyword

**Schlussverkauf** der sales

**schmal** *ADJECTIVE* ❶ narrow ❷ thin *(face, nose)* ❸ sie ist schmäler geworden she's lost weight

**schmecken** *VERB (PERF hat geschmeckt)* to taste; die Suppe schmeckt gut the soup tastes good, das schmeckt mir nicht I don't like it, das Eis schmeckt nach Zitrone the ice cream tastes of lemon

**schmeicheln** *VERB (PERF hat geschmeichelt)* to flatter; jemandem schmeicheln to flatter somebody

**schmeißen** ◇*VERB (informal) (IMP schmiss, PERF hat geschmissen)* to chuck; mit etwas schmeißen to chuck something

**schmelzen** ◇*VERB (PRES schmilzt, IMP schmolz, PERF ist geschmolzen)* ❶ to melt; der Schnee ist geschmolzen the snow has melted ❷ *(PERF hat geschmolzen)* to melt *(snow, ice)* ❸ *(PERF hat geschmolzen)* to smelt *(ore)*

**Schmerz** der *(PLURAL die Schmerzen)* ❶ pain ❷ grief

**schmerzen** *VERB (PERF hat geschmerzt)* to hurt; mein Kopf schmerzt my head is aching

**schmerzhaft** *ADJECTIVE* painful

**schmerzlos** *ADJECTIVE* painless

**Schmerzmittel** das *(PLURAL die Schmerzmittel)* painkiller

**Schmerzschwelle** das *(PLURAL die Schmerzschwellen)* painthreshold

**Schmetterling** der *(PLURAL die Schmetterlinge)* butterfly

**schmettern** *VERB (PERF hat geschmettert)* ❶ to hurl ❷ to smash *(in tennis)* ❸ to blare out *(music, orders)*

**schmieren** *VERB (PERF hat geschmiert)* ❶ to lubricate ❷ to spread *(butter, jam)*; Brote schmieren to spread slices of bread, jemandem eine schmieren *(informal)* to clout somebody ❸ to scrawl ❹ to smudge

**schmilzt** ▸ SEE **schmelzen**

**Schminke** die make-up

**schminken** *VERB (PERF hat geschminkt)* ❶ to make up ❷ sich schminken to put on make-up

**schmiss** ▸ SEE **schmeißen**

**schmolz** ▸ SEE **schmelzen**

**Schmuck** der ❶ jewellery ❷ decoration

**schmücken** *VERB (PERF hat geschmückt)* to decorate

**schmuggeln** *VERB (PERF hat geschmuggelt)* to smuggle

**schmusen** *VERB (PERF hat geschmust)* to cuddle; Gabi hat mit Max geschmust Gabi cuddled Max

**Schmutz** der dirt

**schmutzig** *ADJECTIVE* dirty

**Schmutzigkeit** die dirtiness

**Schnabel** der *(PLURAL die Schnäbel)* beak

**Schnalle** die *(PLURAL die Schnallen)* buckle

**schnallen** *VERB (PERF hat geschnallt)* ❶ to fasten ❷ to buckle

**schnarchen** *VERB (PERF hat geschnarcht)* to snore

**Schnauze** die *(PLURAL die Schnauzen)* ❶ muzzle; eine kalte Schnauze a cold nose ❷ die Schnauze halten *(informal)* to keep your mouth shut

**schnäuzen** *(PERF hat sich geschnäuzt)* sich schnäuzen to blow your nose

**Schnecke** die *(PLURAL die Schnecken)* snail

**Schnee** der snow

**Schneeregen** der sleet

**Schneesturm** der *(PLURAL die Schneestürme)* blizzard

**Schneewehe** die *(PLURAL die Schneewehen)* snow drift

**schneiden** ◇*VERB (IMP schnitt, PERF hat geschnitten)* ❶ to cut; ich kann dir die Haare schneiden I can cut your hair, Evi hat sich die Haare kurz schneiden lassen Evi had her hair cut short, in Scheiben schneiden to slice ❷ sich schneiden to cut yourself, ich habe mich in den Finger geschnitten I've cut my finger ❸ sich schneiden to intersect ❹ Gesichter schneiden to pull faces

**Schneider** der *(PLURAL die Schneider)* tailor

**Schneiderin** die *(PLURAL die Schneiderinnen)* dressmaker

**schneien** *VERB (PERF hat geschneit)* to snow; es schneit it's snowing

**schnell** *ADJECTIVE* quick, fast

**schnell** *ADVERB* quickly; mach schnell! hurry up!

**Schnelligkeit** die speed

**Schnellimbiss** der *(PLURAL die Schnellimbisse)* snack bar

**schnellstens** *ADVERB* as quickly as possible

**Schnellzug** der *(PLURAL die Schnellzüge)* express (train)

**schneuzen** ▸ SEE **schnäuzen**

**schnitt** ▸ SEE **schneiden**

**Schnitt** der *(PLURAL die Schnitte)* ❶ cut; er hat einen tiefen Schnitt im Finger he's got a deep cut in his finger, das Kostüm hat einen sehr guten Schnitt the suit is well cut ❷ cutting *(of a film)* ❸ im Schnitt on average ❹ pattern

**Schnittlauch** der chives

**Schnitzel** das *(PLURAL die Schnitzel)* ❶ escalope ❷ scrap

**schnitzen** *VERB (PERF hat geschnitzt)* to carve

**Schnorchel** der *(PLURAL die Schnorchel)* snorkel

**schnüffeln** *VERB (PERF hat geschnüffelt)* ❶ to sniff ❷ to snoop around

**Schnuller** der *(PLURAL die Schnuller)* dummy

**Schnupfen** der *(PLURAL die Schnupfen)* cold

**Schnur** die *(PLURAL die Schnüre)* ❶ (piece of) string ❷ flex ❸ cord

**Schnurrbart** der *(PLURAL die Schnurrbärte)* moustache

**schnurren** *VERB (PERF hat geschnurrt)* to purr

**Schnurrhaar** das *(PLURAL die Schnurrhaare)* whisker

**Schnürsenkel** der *(PLURAL die Schnürsenkel)* shoelace

**schob** ▸ SEE **schieben**

**Schock** der (PLURAL die **Schocks**) shock

**schockieren** VERB (PERF hat **schockiert**) to shock

**Schokolade** die (PLURAL die **Schokoladen**) chocolate

**schon** ADVERB ❶ already ('schon' is often not translated); schon wieder again, schon oft often, du wirst schon sehen you'll see, ja schon, aber ... well yes, but ..., nun geh schon! go on then! ❷ yet; hast du sie schon gesehen? have you seen her yet?, du weißt schon you know ❸ even ❹ komm schon! come on! ❺ schon deshalb for that reason alone ❻ das ist schon möglich that's quite possible ❼ er war schon mal da he's been there before

**schön** ADJECTIVE ❶ beautiful ❷ nice; schönes Wochenende! have a nice weekend! ❸ good; na schön all right then ❹ schönen Dank thank you very much, schöne Grüße best wishes

**schonen** VERB (PERF hat **geschont**) ❶ to look after ❷ sich schonen to take things easy

**Schönheit** die (PLURAL die **Schönheiten**) beauty

**Schornstein** der (PLURAL die **Schornsteine**) chimney, funnel

**schoss** ▸ SEE **schießen**

**Schoß** der (PLURAL die **Schöße**) lap

**Schotte** der (PLURAL die **Schotten**) Scot, Scotsman

**Schottin** die (PLURAL die **Schottinnen**) Scot, Scotswoman

**schottisch** ADJECTIVE Scottish

**Schottland** das Scotland

**schräg** ADJECTIVE ❶ diagonal ❷ sloping

**schräg** ADVERB etwas schräg halten to tilt something, etwas schräg stellen to put something at an angle

**Schrägstrich** der (PLURAL die **Schrägstriche**) forward slash

**Schrank** der (PLURAL die **Schränke**) ❶ cupboard ❷ wardrobe

**Schranke** die (PLURAL die **Schranken**) barrier

**Schraube** die (PLURAL die **Schrauben**) screw

**schrauben** VERB (PERF hat **geschraubt**) to screw

**Schraubenschlüssel** der (PLURAL die **Schraubenschlüssel**) spanner

**Schraubenzieher** der (PLURAL die **Schraubenzieher**) screwdriver

**Schreck** der (PLURAL die **Schrecke**) fright; jemandem einen Schreck einjagen to give somebody a fright, ich habe einen Schreck bekommen I got a fright

**schrecklich** ADJECTIVE terrible

**Schrei** der (PLURAL die **Schreie**) ❶ cry, shout ❷ scream ❸ der letzte Schrei (informal) the latest thing

**Schreibblock** der (PLURAL die **Schreibblöcke**) writing pad

**schreiben** ◇VERB (IMP **schrieb**, PERF hat **geschrieben**) ❶ to write; David hat mir einen Brief geschrieben David wrote a letter to me, einen Test schreiben to do a test ❷ to spell; wie schreibt man das? how is it spelt? ❸ to type

**Schreibmaschine** die (PLURAL die **Schreibmaschinen**) typewriter

**Schreibpapier** das **writing paper**

**Schreibtisch** der (PLURAL die **Schreibtische**) **desk**

**Schreibwaren** PLURAL NOUN **stationery**

**schreien** ◇VERB (IMP **schrie**, PERF **hat geschrien**) ❶ to cry, to shout; das Baby schreit the baby's crying ❷ to scream; vor Lachen schreien to scream with laughter, zum Schreien sein (informal) to be a scream

**Schreiner** der (PLURAL die **Schreiner**) **joiner**

**schrie** ▸ SEE **schreien**

**schrieb** ▸ SEE **schreiben**

**Schrift** die (PLURAL die **Schriften**) ❶ writing ❷ type ❸ script

**schriftlich** ADJECTIVE **written**

**schriftlich** ADVERB in writing; das lasse ich mir schriftlich geben I'll get that in writing, jemanden schriftlich einladen to send somebody a written invitation

**Schriftsteller** der (PLURAL die **Schriftsteller**) **writer**

**Schriftstellerin** die (PLURAL die **Schriftstellerinnen**) **writer**

**Schritt** der (PLURAL die **Schritte**) ❶ step ❷ footstep

**schrumpfen** VERB (PERF ist **geschrumpft**) ❶ to shrink ❷ to shrivel

**Schublade** die (PLURAL die **Schubladen**) **drawer**

**schubsen** VERB (PERF hat **geschubst**) **to shove**

**schüchtern** ADJECTIVE **shy**

**schuf** ▸ SEE **schaffen**

**Schuh** der (PLURAL die **Schuhe**) **shoe**

**Schuhgröße** die (PLURAL die **Schuhgrößen**) **shoe size**

**Schulabschluss** der (PLURAL die **Schulabschlusse**) **school-leaving qualification**

**Schularbeiten** PLURAL NOUN **homework**

**Schulaufgaben** PLURAL NOUN **homework**

**Schulbuch** das (PLURAL die **Schulbücher**) **schoolbook**

**schuld** ADJECTIVE schuld sein to be to blame, du bist schuld daran it's your fault

**Schuld** die (PLURAL die **Schulden**) ❶ blame; Schuld haben to be to blame, jemandem Schuld geben to blame somebody ❷ fault; es war seine Schuld it was his fault ❸ guilt ❹ debt; Schulden haben to be in debt, Schulden machen to get into debt

**schulden** VERB (PERF hat **geschuldet**) **to owe**

**schuldig** ADJECTIVE ❶ guilty ❷ jemandem etwas schuldig sein to owe somebody something

**Schule** die (PLURAL die **Schulen**) **school**; in die Schule gehen to go to school

**schulen** VERB (PERF hat **geschult**) **to train**

**Schüler** der (PLURAL die **Schüler**) **pupil, student**

**Schülerin** die (PLURAL die **Schülerinnen**) **pupil, student**

**Schulferien** PLURAL NOUN **school holidays**

**schulfrei** *ADJECTIVE* ein schulfreier Tag a day off school, wir haben heute schulfrei there's no school today

**Schulfreund** der *(PLURAL die Schulfreunde)* schoolfriend

**Schulfreundin** die *(PLURAL die Schulfreundinnen)* schoolfriend

**Schulheft** das *(PLURAL die Schulhefte)* exercise book

**Schulhof** der *(PLURAL die Schulhöfe)* playground

**Schuljahr** das *(PLURAL die Schuljahre)* school year

**Schulleiter** der *(PLURAL die Schulleiter)* headmaster

**Schulleiterin** die *(PLURAL die Schulleiterinnen)* headmistress

**Schulschwänzer** der *(PLURAL die Schulschwänzer)* truant

**Schulschwänzerin** die *(PLURAL die Schulschwänzerinnen)* truant

**Schulstunde** die *(PLURAL die Schulstunden)* period

**Schultag** der *(PLURAL die Schultage)* school day

**Schultasche** die *(PLURAL die Schultaschen)* schoolbag

**Schulter** die *(PLURAL die Schultern)* shoulder

**schummeln** *VERB (PERF hat geschummelt)* to cheat

**Schuppe** die *(PLURAL die Schuppen)* ❶ scale ❷ Schuppen dandruff

**Schuppen** der *(PLURAL die Schuppen)* shed

**Schürze** die *(PLURAL die Schürzen)* apron

**Schuss** der *(PLURAL die Schüsse)* ❶ shot ❷ dash *(of brandy, vinegar)* ❸ schuss *(in skiing)*

**Schüssel** die *(PLURAL die Schüsseln)* bowl, dish

**Schuster** der *(PLURAL die Schuster)* shoemaker

**schütteln** *VERB (PERF hat geschüttelt)* ❶ to shake ❷ sich schütteln to shake yourself, sich vor Ekel schütteln to shudder

**schütten** *VERB (PERF hat geschüttet)* ❶ to pour; es schüttet *(informal)* it's pouring (down) ❷ to tip ❸ to spill

**Schutz** der ❶ protection ❷ shelter ❸ conservation

**Schutzbrille** die *(PLURAL die Schutzbrillen)* goggles

**Schütze** der *(PLURAL die Schützen)* ❶ marksman ❷ Sagittarius; Daniel ist Schütze Daniel's Sagittarius

**schützen** *VERB (PERF hat geschützt)* ❶ to protect; die meisten Cremes schützen die Haut gegen Sonnenbrand most creams protect the skin from sunburn ❷ gesetzlich geschützt registered *(as a trademark)*

**Schutzhütte** die *(PLURAL die Schutzhütten)* ❶ mountain refuge ❷ shelter

**schwach** *ADJECTIVE* ❶ weak ❷ dim *(light)* ❸ poor *(performance, memory)*

**Schwäche** die *(PLURAL die Schwächen)* weakness

**schwachsinnig** *ADJECTIVE* idiotic

**Schwager** der *(PLURAL die Schwäger)* brother-in-law

**Schwägerin** die *(PLURAL* die **Schwägerinnen)** sister-in-law

**Schwalbe** die *(PLURAL* die **Schwalben)** swallow

**schwamm** ▸ SEE **schwimmen**

**Schwamm** der *(PLURAL* die **Schwämme)** sponge

**Schwan** der *(PLURAL* die **Schwäne)** swan

**schwanger** *ADJECTIVE* **pregnant**

**Schwangerschaft** die *(PLURAL* die **Schwangerschaften)** pregnancy

**schwanken** *VERB (PERF* **hat geschwankt) ❶** to sway **❷** to fluctuate **❸** to waver **❹** *(PERF* **ist geschwankt)** to stagger

**Schwanz** der *(PLURAL* die **Schwänze)** tail

**schwänzen** *VERB (PERF* **hat geschwänzt)** to skip, to skive off; die Schule schwänzen to play truant

**Schwarm** der *(PLURAL* die **Schwärme)** swarm

**schwarz** *ADJECTIVE, ADVERB* **❶** black; schwarz gekleidet dressed in black, ein schwarz gestreiftes Kleid a dress with black stripes, das habe ich schwarz auf weiß I have it in black and white **❷** ins Schwarze treffen to hit the nail on the head, to score a bull's eye **❸** schwarz sehen to be pessimistic **❹** etwas schwarz machen to do something illegally

**Schwarze** der/die *(PLURAL* die **Schwarzen)** black

**schwarzsehen** ▸ SEE **schwarz**

**Schwarzwald** der Black Forest

**schwätzen** *VERB (PERF* **hat geschwätzt)** to chatter

**Schwede** der *(PLURAL* die **Schweden)** Swede

**Schweden** das Sweden

**Schwedin** die *(PLURAL* die **Schwedinnen)** Swede

**schwedisch** *ADJECTIVE* **Swedish**

**schweigen** ◇*VERB (IMP* **schwieg,** *PERF* **hat geschwiegen)** to be silent; ganz zu schweigen von ... not to mention ...

**Schwein** das *(PLURAL* die **Schweine)** **❶** pig **❷** pork **❸** du Schwein! *(informal)* you swine!, Schwein haben *(informal)* to be lucky

**Schweinefleisch** das pork

**Schweinekotelett** das *(PLURAL* die **Schweinekoteletts)** pork chop

**Schweiß** der sweat

**Schweiz** die die Schweiz Switzerland

**Schweizer** der *(PLURAL* die **Schweizer)** Swiss

**Schweizerin** die *(PLURAL* die **Schweizerinnen)** Swiss

**schweizerisch** *ADJECTIVE* **Swiss**

**Schwelle** der *(PLURAL* die **Schwellen)** threshold

**Schwellung** die *(PLURAL* die **Schwellungen)** swelling

**schwer** *ADJECTIVE* **❶** heavy; zwei Pfund schwer sein to weigh two pounds **❷** difficult **❸** serious

**schwer** *ADVERB* **❶** heavily **❷** seriously; schwer krank seriously ill **❸** schwer arbeiten to work hard, jemandem schwer fallen to be hard for somebody

**❹** sich mit etwas schwer tun to have difficulty with something

**schwerfallen** ▸ SEE **schwer**

**schwerhörig** ADJECTIVE hard of hearing

**Schwert** das (PLURAL die **Schwerter**) sword

**schwertun** ▸ SEE **schwer**

**Schwester** die (PLURAL die **Schwestern**) sister

**schwieg** ▸ SEE **schweigen**

**Schwiegereltern** PLURAL NOUN parents-in-law

**Schwiegermutter** die (PLURAL die **Schwiegermütter**) mother-in-law

**Schwiegersohn** der (PLURAL die **Schwiegersöhne**) son-in-law

**Schwiegertochter** die (PLURAL die **Schwiegertöchter**) daughter-in-law

**Schwiegervater** der (PLURAL die **Schwiegerväter**) father-in-law

**schwierig** ADJECTIVE difficult

**Schwierigkeit** die (PLURAL die **Schwierigkeiten**) difficulty

**Schwimmbad** das (PLURAL die **Schwimmbäder**) swimming baths

**schwimmen** ◇VERB (IMP **schwamm**, PERF **ist/hat geschwommen**) ❶ to swim ❷ to float

**Schwimmer** der (PLURAL die **Schwimmer**) swimmer

**Schwimmerbecken** das (PLURAL die **Schwimmbecken**) swimming pool (for experienced swimmers)

**Schwimmerin** die (PLURAL die **Schwimmerinnen**) swimmer

**Schwimmweste** die (PLURAL die **Schwimmwesten**) life-jacket

**schwindlig** ADJECTIVE dizzy; mir ist schwindlig I feel dizzy

**Schwips** der (PLURAL die **Schwipse**) einen Schwips haben to be tipsy

**schwitzen** VERB (PERF **hat geschwitzt**) to sweat

**schwören** ◇VERB (IMP **schwor**, PERF **hat geschworen**) to swear

**schwul** ADJECTIVE gay

**schwül** ADJECTIVE close

**Schwule** der (PLURAL die **Schwulen**) gay

**Schwung** der (PLURAL die **Schwünge**) ❶ swing ❷ drive; die Party in Schwung bringen to get the party going

**sechs** NUMBER six

**sechster, sechste, sechstes** ADJECTIVE sixth

**sechzehn** NUMBER sixteen

**sechzig** NUMBER sixty

**See**[1] der (PLURAL die **Seen**) lake

**See**[2] die sea

**Seehund** der (PLURAL die **Seehunde**) seal

**seekrank** ADJECTIVE seasick

**Seele** die (PLURAL die **Seelen**) soul

**Seemann** der (PLURAL die **Seeleute**) seaman, sailor

**Seetang** der seaweed

**Segel** das (PLURAL die **Segel**) sail

**Segelboot** das *(PLURAL die Segelboote)* sailing boat

**Segelfliegen** das gliding

**Segelflugzeug** das *(PLURAL die Segelflugzeuge)* glider

**Segellehrer** der *(PLURAL die Segellehrer)* sailing instructor

**Segellehrerin** die *(PLURAL die Segellehrerinnen)* sailing instructor

**segeln** *VERB (PERF ist gesegelt)* to sail

**sehen** *◇VERB (PRES sieht, IMP sah, PERF hat gesehen)* **❶** to see; jemanden wieder sehen to see somebody again, mal sehen, ob ... let's see if ... **❷** to look **❸** eine Fernsehsendung sehen to watch a television programme **❹** gut/schlecht sehen to have good/bad eyesight **❺** nach jemandem sehen to look after somebody

**sehenswert** *ADJECTIVE* worth seeing

**Sehenswürdigkeiten** *PLURAL NOUN* sights

**Sehnsucht** die longing; Sehnsucht nach jemandem haben to long to see somebody

**sehr** *ADVERB* **❶** very; sehr gut very good **❷** danke sehr thank you very much **❸** ich habe Karin sehr gern I like Karin a lot **❹** Sehr geehrte Frau Huber Dear Mrs Huber

**seid** ▸ SEE sein

**Seide** die *(PLURAL die Seiden)* silk

**Seife** die *(PLURAL die Seifen)* soap

**Seifenoper** die *(PLURAL die Seifenopern)* soap opera

**Seil** das *(PLURAL die Seile)* **❶** rope **❷** cable

**Seilbahn** die *(PLURAL die Seilbahnen)* cable railway

**sein¹** *◇VERB (PRES ist, IMP war, PERF ist gewesen)* **❶** to be; wir sind in der Küche we're in the kitchen, Rosi ist krank Rosi is ill, mir ist schlecht I feel sick, mir ist kalt/heiß I'm cold/hot **❷** sie ist Lehrerin she's a teacher **❸** es ist drei Uhr it's three o'clock, Karl ist aus München Karl's from Munich, es war viel zu tun there was a lot to be done **❹** aus Seide sein to be made of silk **❺** etwas sein lassen to stop something, lass das sein! stop it! **❻** es sei denn, dass ... unless ... **❼** *(used with certain verbs to form past tenses)* ich bin nach Berlin gefahren I went to Berlin, wir sind kurz vor acht nach Hause gekommen we got home shortly before eight o'clock, er ist abgeholt worden he's been collected

**sein²** *ADJECTIVE* **❶** his **❷** *(of a thing or animal)* its; der Hund ist in seiner Hütte the dog is in its kennel **❸** *(after the pronoun 'man')* your, one's wenn man sich seine Eltern aussuchen könnte if you could choose your parents

**seiner, seine, sein(e)s** *PRONOUN* **❶** his; das ist nicht meine CD, das ist seine it's not my CD, it's his, du kannst seins nehmen you can take his **❷** *(after the pronoun 'man')* your own, one's own; das Seine tun to do one's share

**seinetwegen** *ADVERB* **❶** for his sake **❷** because of him **❸** on his account

**seinlassen** ▸ SEE sein

**seins** ▸ SEE seiner

**seit** *PREPOSITION (+DAT) CONJUNCTION* **❶** since; seit etwa einer Woche since about a week, seit du hier wohnst since you've been living here, seit wann? since when? **❷** ich bin seit zwei Wochen hier I've been here for two weeks, seit einiger Zeit for some time

**seitdem** *ADVERB* since then; ich habe sie seitdem nicht mehr gesehen I haven't seen her since

**seitdem** *CONJUNCTION* since

**Seite** die *(PLURAL* die **Seiten)* **❶** side; auf der einen Seite on the one hand **❷** page; das steht auf Seite zwanzig it's on page twenty

**Seitenstechen** das stich; ich habe Seitenstechen I've got a stitch

**Seitenstraße** die *(PLURAL* die **Seitenstraßen)* side street

**seither** *ADVERB* since then

**Sekretär** der *(PLURAL* die **Sekretäre)* secretary

**Sekretärin** die *(PLURAL* die **Sekretärinnen)* secretary

**Sekt** der *(PLURAL* die **Sekte)* sparkling wine

**Sekte** die *(PLURAL* die **Sekten)* sect

**Sekunde** die *(PLURAL* die **Sekunden)* second

**selbst** *PRONOUN* **❶** ich selbst I myself, er selbst he himself, wir selbst we ourselves, Sie selbst you yourself, you yourselves **❷** von selbst by itself **❸** sie schneidet sich die Haare selbst she cuts her own hair **❹** on one's own; ich kann es selbst machen I can do it on my own **❺** selbst gemacht home-made

**selbst** *ADVERB* **even**; selbst wenn even if

**selbständig** ▸ SEE **selbstständig**

**Selbstbedienung** die **self-service**

**selbstbewusst** *ADJECTIVE* **self-confident**

**Selbstbewusstsein** das **❶** self-confidence **❷** self-awareness

**selbstgemacht** ▸ SEE **selbst**

**Selbstmord** der *(PLURAL* die **Selbstmorde)* suicide; Selbstmord begehen to commit suicide

**selbstsicher** *ADJECTIVE* **self-confident**

**selbstständig** *ADJECTIVE* **❶** independent **❷** self-employed; sich selbstständig machen to set up on your own

**selbstverständlich** *ADJECTIVE* **natural**; etwas für selbstverständlich halten to take something for granted, das ist selbstverständlich it goes without saying

**selbstverständlich** *ADVERB* **naturally, of course**; wir haben ihn selbstverständlich auf die Party eingeladen of course we invited him to the party

**selten** *ADJECTIVE* **rare**

**selten** *ADVERB* **rarely**

**seltsam** *ADJECTIVE* **strange, odd**

**Semester** das *(PLURAL* die **Semester)* **semester, term**

**Semikolon** das *(PLURAL* die **Semikolons)* **semicolon**

**Semmel** die *(PLURAL* die **Semmeln)* **roll**

**senden** VERB (PERF **hat gesendet**)
❶ to send; etwas an jemanden
senden to send something to
somebody ❷ to broadcast; seine
Rede wird im ersten Programm
gesendet his speech will be
broadcast on channel one ❸ to
transmit

**Sendung** die (PLURAL die **Sendungen**)
❶ programme ❷ consignment

**Senf** der (PLURAL die **Senfe**) mustard

**Senior** der (PLURAL die **Senioren**)
❶ senior ❷ Senioren senior citizens

**Seniorenheim** das (PLURAL die
**Seniorenheime**) old peoeple's
home

**senkrecht** ADJECTIVE vertical

**Sensation** die (PLURAL die
**Sensationen**) sensation, stir

**sensationell** ADJECTIVE sensational

**sensibel** ADJECTIVE sensitive

**sentimental** ADJECTIVE sentimental

**September** der September

**Sequenz** die (PLURAL die **Sequenzen**)
sequence (in a film)

**Serie** die (PLURAL die **Serien**) ❶ series
❷ serial

**Service**¹ das (PLURAL die **Service**) set
(of china, for example)

**Service**² der service; das Essen im
Hotel ist gut, aber der Service ist
furchtbar the food in the hotel is
good but the service is appalling

**servieren** VERB (PERF **hat serviert**)
to serve

**Serviette** die (PLURAL die **Servietten**)
napkin

**Sessel** der (PLURAL die **Sessel**)
armchair

**Sessellift** der (PLURAL die **Sessellifte**)
chair-lift

**setzen** VERB (PERF **hat gesetzt**) ❶ to
put; ein Komma setzen to put
a comma, vergiss nicht, deinen
Namen auf die Liste zu setzen
don't forget to put your name on
the list ❷ to move (a counter in
games) ❸ auf etwas setzen to bet
on something, auf ein Pferd setzen
to back a horse ❹ sich setzen to sit
down, sich auf einen Stuhl setzen
to sit down on a chair

**seufzen** VERB (PERF **hat geseufzt**)
to sigh

**Seufzer** der (PLURAL die **Seufzer**) sigh

**Sex** der sex; Sex mit jemandem
haben to have sex with somebody

**Sexismus** der sexism

**sexistisch** ADJECTIVE sexist

**sexuell** ADJECTIVE sexual

**Shampoo** das (PLURAL die **Shampoos**)
shampoo

**Shuttledienst** der (PLURAL die
**Shuttledienste**) shuttle service

**sich** PRONOUN ❶ (with 'er/sie/es')
himself/herself/itself; sie hat sich
eingeschlossen she locked herself
in ❷ (with plural 'sie') themselves
❸ (with 'Sie') yourself, yourselves
(plural) ❹ each other, one
another; sich kennen to know each
other, Petra und Werner lieben sich
Petra and Werner love each other
❺ (not translated with certain verbs)
sich freuen to be pleased, sich
wundern to be surprised ❻ Anita
wäscht sich die Haare Anita is
washing her hair, sich den Arm
brechen to break your arm ❼ sich
gut verkaufen to sell well ❽ von
sich aus of your own accord

**sicher** *ADJECTIVE* ❶ safe ❷ certain; bist du sicher? are you sure?

**sicher** *ADVERB* ❶ safely ❷ certainly, surely; sicher! certainly!

**Sicherheit** die ❶ safety; zur Sicherheit for safety's sake, schnallen Sie sich zur Ihrer eigenen Sicherheit an fasten your seat belt for your own safety, etwas in Sicherheit bringen to rescue something, in Sicherheit sein to be safe ❷ security; die Sicherheit der Arbeitsplätze job security ❸ certainty; mit Sicherheit! certainly! *(as a reply)*

**Sicherheitsgurt** der *(PLURAL die Sicherheitsgurte)* seatbelt

**Sicherheitsnadel** die *(PLURAL die Sicherheitsnadeln)* safety pin

**sicherlich** *ADVERB* certainly

**sichern** *VERB (PERF hat gesichert)* to secure; jemandem etwas sichern to secure something for somebody

**Sicherung** die *(PLURAL die Sicherungen)* ❶ fuse; die Sicherung is durchgebrannt the fuse has blown ❷ safeguard; die Sicherung der Arbeitsplätze safeguarding jobs ❸ safety catch

**Sicht** die ❶ view; ich hatte eine gute Sicht auf den See I had a good view of the lake, auf lange Sicht in the long term ❷ aus meiner Sicht as I see it ❸ visibility; gute/schlechte Sicht good/poor visibility

**sichtbar** *ADJECTIVE* visible

**sie** *PRONOUN* ❶ she ❷ her; ich kenne sie I know her ❸ it; so eine hübsche Bluse, war sie teuer? what a pretty blouse, was it expensive? ❹ they; sie sind in der Küche they're in

the kitchen ❺ them; ich habe sie gestern abgeschickt I posted them yesterday

**Sie** *PRONOUN* you; kommen Sie herein! come in!

**Sieb** das *(PLURAL die Siebe)* ❶ sieve ❷ strainer

**sieben** *NUMBER* seven

**siebter, siebte, siebtes** *ADJECTIVE* seventh

**siebzehn** *NUMBER* seventeen

**siebzig** *NUMBER* seventy

**Siedlung** die *(PLURAL die Siedlungen)* ❶ (housing) estate ❷ settlement

**Sieg** der *(PLURAL die Siege)* victory, win

**Siegel** das *(PLURAL die Siegel)* seal

**siegen** *VERB (PERF hat gesiegt)* to win

**Sieger** der *(PLURAL die Sieger)* winner

**Siegerin** die *(PLURAL die Siegerinnen)* winner

**sieht** ▸ SEE sehen

**siezen** *VERB (PERF hat gesiezt)* to address as 'Sie'

**Silbe** die *(PLURAL die Silben)* syllable

**Silber** das silver

**silbern** *ADJECTIVE* silver

**Silvester** das New Year's Eve

**simsen** *VERB (PERF hat gesimst)* to text

**sind** ▸ SEE sein

**Sinfonie** die *(PLURAL die Sinfonien)* symphony

**singen** ◇*VERB (IMP sang, PERF hat gesungen)* to sing

**sinken** ◇*VERB* (*IMP* **sank**, *PERF* **ist gesunken**) ❶ to sink ❷ to go down

**Sinn** der (*PLURAL* die **Sinne**) ❶ sense ❷ meaning ❸ point; das hat keinen Sinn there's no point

**sinnlos** *ADJECTIVE* pointless

**sinnvoll** *ADJECTIVE* ❶ sensible ❷ meaningful

**Situation** die (*PLURAL* die **Situationen**) situation

**Sitz** der (*PLURAL* die **Sitze**) ❶ seat ❷ fit (*of clothes*)

**sitzen** ◇*VERB* (*IMP* **saß**, *PERF* **hat gesessen**) ❶ to sit; sitzen bleiben to remain seated ❷ sitzen bleiben to have to repeat a year, to stay down (*at school*) ❸ er sitzt (*informal*) he's in jail ❹ jemanden sitzen lassen (*informal*) to leave somebody in the lurch ❺ to fit (*of clothes*); der Mantel sitzt gut the coat fits well

**Sitzplatz** der (*PLURAL* die **Sitzplätze**) seat

**Sitzung** die (*PLURAL* die **Sitzungen**) ❶ meeting ❷ session

**Sizilien** das Sicily

**Skandal** der (*PLURAL* die **Skandale**) scandal

**Skandinavien** das Scandinavia

**skandinavisch** *ADJECTIVE* Scandinavian

**Skateboard** der (*PLURAL* die **Skateboards**) skateboard; Skateboard fahren to skateboard

**Skater** der (*PLURAL* die **Skater**) skater (*on a skateboard*)

**Skelett** das (*PLURAL* die **Skelette**) skeleton

**skeptisch** *ADJECTIVE* sceptical

**Ski** der (*PLURAL* die **Ski(er)**) ski; Ski fahren/laufen to ski

**Skianzug** der (*PLURAL* die **Skianzüge**) ski suit

**Skibrille** die (*PLURAL* die **Skibrillen**) skiing goggles

**Skifahren** das skiing

**Skifahrer** der (*PLURAL* die **Skifahrer**) skier

**Skifahrerin** die (*PLURAL* die **Skifahrerinnen**) skier

**Skilaufen** das skiing

**Skiläufer** der (*PLURAL* die **Skiläufer**) skier

**Skiläuferin** die (*PLURAL* die **Skiläuferinnen**) skier

**Skilehrer** der (*PLURAL* die **Skilehrer**) ski instructor

**Skizze** die (*PLURAL* die **Skizzen**) sketch

**Skooter** der (*PLURAL* die **Skooter**) bumper car, dodgem car

**Skorpion** der (*PLURAL* die **Skorpione**) ❶ scorpion ❷ Scorpio

**Skulptur** die (*PLURAL* die **Skulpturen**) sculpture

**Slip** der (*PLURAL* die **Slips**) briefs, pants

**Slowake** der (*PLURAL* die **Slowaken**) Slovak

**Slowakei** die Slovakia

**Slowakin** die (*PLURAL* die **Slowakinnen**) Slovak

**slowakisch** *ADJECTIVE* **Slovak**

**Slowenien** das **Slovenia**

**Smoking** der *(PLURAL* die **Smokings)** **dinner jacket**

**SMS** die *(PLURAL* die **SMS)** **text message**

**so** *ADVERB* ❶ **so**; nicht so viel not so much, und so weiter and so on ❷ **like this, like that**; so nicht not like that ❸ **as**; so bald wie as soon as ❹ **such**; so ein Zufall! what a coincidence! ❺ das kriegst du so *(informal)* you get it for nothing ❻ so um zwanzig Euro *(informal)* about twenty euros

**so** *CONJUNCTION* so dass so that

**so** *EXCLAMATION* **right!, well!**; so? really?

**sobald** *CONJUNCTION* **as soon as**

**Socke** die *(PLURAL* die **Socken)** **sock**

**Sofa** das *(PLURAL* die **Sofas)** **sofa**

**sofort** *ADVERB* **immediately**

**Software** die **software**

**sogar** *ADVERB* **even**

**sogleich** *ADVERB* **at once**

**Sohle** die *(PLURAL* die **Sohlen)** **sole**

**Sohn** der *(PLURAL* die **Söhne)** **son**

**Soja** die **soy**

**solange** *CONJUNCTION* **as long as**

**solch** *PRONOUN* **such**; solch einer/eine/eins one like that, somebody like that

**solcher, solche, solches** *ADJECTIVE, PRONOUN* ❶ **such**; ich habe solche Angst I'm so frightened ❷ ein solcher Mann a man like that, eine solche Frage a question like that,

ein solches Haus a house like that ❸ solche *PLURAL* **those,** solche wie die people like that

**Soldat** der *(PLURAL* die **Soldaten)** **soldier**

**solide** *ADJECTIVE* ❶ **solid** ❷ **respectable**

**Solist** der *(PLURAL* die **Solisten)** **soloist**

**Solistin** die *(PLURAL* die **Solistinnen)** **soloist**

**sollen** ◇*VERB (PRES* **soll,** *IMP* **sollte,** *PERF* **hat gesollt)** ❶ **should**; sollte es regnen if it should rain ❷ **to be supposed to**; was soll das heißen? what's that supposed to mean? ❸ sagen Sie ihr, sie soll anrufen tell her to ring ❹ was soll ich machen? what shall I do?, soll ich? shall I? ❺ was soll's! so what!

**sollte, sollten, solltest, solltet** ▸SEE **sollen**

**Sommer** der *(PLURAL* die **Sommer)** **summer**

**Sommerferien** *PLURAL NOUN* **summer holidays**

**sommerlich** *ADJECTIVE* **summery, summer**

**Sommersprossen** *PLURAL NOUN* **freckles**

**Sonderangebot** das *(PLURAL* die **Sonderangebote)** **special offer**; im Sonderangebot on special offer

**sonderbar** *ADJECTIVE* **strange, odd**

**sondern** *CONJUNCTION* **but**; nicht nur ..., sondern auch ... not only ..., but also ...

**Song** der *(PLURAL* die **Songs)** **song**

**Sonnabend** der *(PLURAL* die **Sonnabende)** **Saturday**

German—English

**sonnabends** *ADVERB* on Saturdays

**Sonne** die *(PLURAL* die **Sonnen)** sun

**sonnen** *VERB (PERF* hat sich gesonnt) sich sonnen to sun yourself

**Sonnenaufgang** der sunrise

**Sonnenbrand** der sunburn

**Sonnenbrille** die *(PLURAL* die **Sonnenbrillen)** sunglasses

**Sonnencreme** die *(PLURAL* die **Sonnencremes)** suntan lotion

**Sonnenenergie** die solar energy

**Sonnenmilch** die suntan lotion

**Sonnenöl** das suntan oil

**Sonnenschein** der sunshine

**Sonnenstich** der sunstroke

**sonnig** *ADJECTIVE* sunny

**Sonntag** der *(PLURAL* die **Sonntage)** Sunday

**sonntags** *ADVERB* on Sundays

**sonst** *ADVERB* ❶ usually ❷ else; wer sonst? who else?, was sonst? what else? ❸ sonst noch etwas? anything else?, sonst noch jemand? anybody else? ❹ sonst wo somewhere, es kann sonst wo sein it could be anywhere ❺ otherwise; geh jetzt, sonst verpasst du den Bus go now, otherwise you'll miss the bus

**sonstwo** ▸ SEE **sonst**

**sooft** *CONJUNCTION* whenever

**Sorge** die *(PLURAL* die **Sorgen)** worry; sich Sorgen machen to worry

**sorgen** *VERB (PERF* hat gesorgt) ❶ für etwas sorgen to take care of something, für die Musik sorgen to see to the music, für jemanden sorgen to look after somebody

❷ dafür sorgen, dass ... to make sure that ... ❸ sich sorgen to worry, ich sorge mich um meine Eltern I worry about my parents

**sorgfältig** *ADJECTIVE* careful

**Sorte** die *(PLURAL* die **Sorten)** ❶ kind ❷ brand

**Soße** die *(PLURAL* die **Soßen)** ❶ sauce ❷ gravy ❸ dressing

**Souvenir** das *(PLURAL* die **Souvenirs)** souvenir

**soviel** *CONJUNCTION* as far as; soviel ich weiß as far as I know

**soviel** *ADVERB* ▸ SEE **viel**

**soweit** *CONJUNCTION* as far as; soweit ich weiß, ist er in Ferien as far as I know, he's on holiday

**soweit** *ADVERB* ▸ SEE **weit**

**sowenig** ▸ SEE **wenig**

**sowie** *CONJUNCTION* ❶ as well as ❷ as soon as

**sowieso** *ADVERB* anyway

**sowohl** *ADVERB* sowohl ... als auch ... both ... and ..., sowohl er wie auch sein Freund both he and his friend

**sozial** *ADJECTIVE* social

**Sozialarbeiter** der *(PLURAL* die **Sozialarbeiter)** social worker

**Sozialarbeiterin** die *(PLURAL* die **Sozialarbeiterinnen)** social worker

**Sozialhilfe** die social security

**Sozialismus** der socialism

**sozialistisch** *ADJECTIVE* socialist

**Sozialkunde** die social studies

**Sozialwohnung** die *(PLURAL die Sozialwohnungen)* council flat

**Soziologie** die sociology

**sozusagen** *ADVERB* so to speak

**Spalte** die *(PLURAL die Spalten)* ❶ crack ❷ column *(in text)*

**spalten** *VERB (PERF hat gespalten)* to split

**Spaniel** der *(PLURAL die Spaniels)* Spaniel

**Spanien** das Spain

**Spanier** der *(PLURAL die Spanier)* Spaniard

**Spanierin** die *(PLURAL die Spanierinnen)* Spaniard

**spanisch** *ADJECTIVE* Spanish

**Spanisch** das Spanish *(language)*

**spann** ▸ SEE **spinnen**

**spannend** *ADJECTIVE* exciting

**Spannung** die *(PLURAL die Spannungen)* ❶ tension ❷ suspense *(in a film or novel, for example)*; ich erwarte seine Antwort mit Spannung I can't wait for his answer ❸ voltage

**Sparbüchse** die *(PLURAL die Sparbüchsen)* money box

**sparen** *VERB (PERF hat gespart)* ❶ to save; auf etwas sparen to save up for something ❷ sich etwas sparen not to bother with something, sich die Mühe sparen to save yourself the trouble ❸ an etwas sparen to economize on something

**Spargel** der asparagus

**Sparkasse** die savings bank

**sparsam** *ADJECTIVE* ❶ economical ❷ thrifty

**Sparschwein** das *(PLURAL die Sparschweine)* piggy bank

**Spaß** der *(PLURAL die Späße)* ❶ fun; zum/aus Spaß for fun, das macht Spaß it's fun, Segeln macht mir keinen Spaß I don't like sailing ❷ viel Spaß! have a good time! ❸ joke; er macht nur Spaß he's only joking

**spät** *ADJECTIVE, ADVERB* late; zu spät kommen to be late, wie spät ist es? what time is it?

**Spaten** der *(PLURAL die Spaten)* spade

**später** *ADJECTIVE* later

**spätestens** *ADVERB* at the latest

**Spatz** der *(PLURAL die Spatzen)* sparrow

**Spätzle** *PLURAL NOUN* noodles *(South German dish)*

**spazieren** *VERB (PERF ist spaziert)* ❶ to stroll ❷ spazieren gehen to go for a walk, hast du Lust, spazieren zu gehen? would you like to go for a walk?

**spazierengehen** ▸ SEE **spazieren**

**Spaziergang** der *(PLURAL die Spaziergänge)* walk; einen Spaziergang machen to go for a walk

**Speck** der bacon

**Speiche** die *(PLURAL die Speichen)* spoke

**Speicher** der *(PLURAL die Speicher)* ❶ loft, attic ❷ memory *(in computing)*

**Speicherkapazität** die storage capacity *(on hard disk)*

**Speicherkarte** die *(PLURAL die Speicherkarten)* memory card

**speichern** VERB (PERF hat gespeichert) ❶ to store ❷ to save (in computing)

**Speise** die (PLURAL die Speisen) ❶ food ❷ dish

**Speisekarte** die (PLURAL die Speisekarten) menu

**Speisesaal** der (PLURAL die Speisesäle) ❶ dining hall ❷ dining room

**Speisewagen** der (PLURAL die Speisewagen) dining car

**Spende** die (PLURAL die Spenden) donation

**spenden** VERB (PERF hat gespendet) ❶ to donate ❷ to give

**spendieren** VERB (PERF hat spendiert) jemandem etwas spendieren to treat somebody to something

**Sperling** der (PLURAL die Sperlinge) sparrow

**Sperre** die (PLURAL die Sperren) ❶ barrier ❷ ban

**sperren** VERB (PERF hat gesperrt) ❶ to close ❷ to block (an entrance, access) ❸ den Strom sperren to cut off the electricity ❹ einen Scheck sperren to stop a cheque ❺ ein Tier in einen Käfig sperren to shut an animal (up) in a cage

**spezialisieren** VERB (PERF hat spezialisiert) sich spezialisieren to specialize

**Spezialität** die (PLURAL die Spezialitäten) speciality

**speziell** ADJECTIVE special

**Spezies** die (PLURAL die Spezies) species

**Spiegel** der (PLURAL die Spiegel) mirror

**Spiegelbild** das (PLURAL die Spiegelbilder) reflection

**Spiegelei** das (PLURAL die Spiegeleier) fried egg

**spiegeln** VERB (PERF hat gespiegelt) ❶ to reflect ❷ sich spiegeln to be reflected

**Spiel** das (PLURAL die Spiele) ❶ game ❷ ein Spiel Karten a pack of cards ❸ es steht viel auf dem Spiel there's a lot at stake

**Spielautomat** der (PLURAL die Spielautomaten) gaming machine

**spielen** VERB (PERF hat gespielt) ❶ to play; wir spielen morgen Fußball we're playing football tomorrow ❷ to gamble ❸ to act; das Stück war gut gespielt the play was well acted ❹ der Film spielt in Rom the film is set in Rome

**spielend** ADVERB easily

**Spieler** der (PLURAL die Spieler) ❶ player ❷ gambler

**Spielerin** die (PLURAL die Spielerinnen) ❶ player ❷ gambler

**Spielfeld** das (PLURAL die Spielfelder) pitch, field

**Spielhalle** die (PLURAL die Spielhallen) amusement arcade

**Spielkonsole** die (PLURAL die Spielkonsolen) games console

**Spielplatz** der (PLURAL die Spielplätze) playground

**Spielverderber** der (PLURAL die Spielverderber) spoilsport

**Spielverderberin** die *(PLURAL* die **Spielverderberinnen)** spoilsport

**Spielwaren** *PLURAL NOUN* **toys**

**Spielzeug** das ❶ toy ❷ toys

**Spinat** der spinach

**Spinne** die *(PLURAL* die **Spinnen)** spider

**spinnen** ◇*VERB (IMP* **spann**, *PERF* **hat gesponnen)** ❶ to spin ❷ du spinnst! *(informal)* you're mad!

**Spinnennetz** das *(PLURAL* die **Spinnennetze)** ❶ spider's web ❷ cobweb

**Spion** der *(PLURAL* die **Spione)** spy

**Spionage** die spying, espionage

**spionieren** *VERB (PERF* **hat spioniert)** to spy

**Spirituosen** *PLURAL NOUN* **spirits** *(alcohol)*

**spitz** *ADJECTIVE* **pointed**

**Spitze** die *(PLURAL* die **Spitzen)** ❶ point ❷ top; Schalke liegt jetzt an der Spitze Schalke is top of the league at the moment ❸ peak; von hier kann man die schneebedeckten Spitzen sehen you can see the snow-covered peaks from here ❹ front; an der Spitze liegen to be in the lead ❺ lace ❻ Spitze sein *(informal)* to be great

**spitzen** *VERB (PERF* **hat gespitzt)** ❶ to sharpen ❷ sich auf etwas spitzen *(informal)* to look forward to something

**Spitzname** der *(PLURAL* die **Spitznamen)** nickname

**Splitter** der *(PLURAL* die **Splitter)** splinter

**splittern** *VERB (PERF* **hat/ist gesplittert)** ❶ to splinter ❷ to shatter

**sponsern** *VERB (PERF* **hat gesponsert)** to sponsor

**Sport** der sport

**Sportgeschäft** das *(PLURAL* die **Sportgeschäfte)** sports shop

**Sporthalle** die *(PLURAL* die **Sporthallen)** sports hall

**Sportler** der *(PLURAL* die **Sportler)** sportsman

**Sportlerin** die *(PLURAL* die **Sportlerinnen)** sportswoman

**sportlich** *ADJECTIVE* ❶ sporting ❷ sporty

**Sportplatz** der *(PLURAL* die **Sportplätze)** sports field, sports ground

**Sportschuh** der *(PLURAL* die **Sportschuhe)** trainer

**Sportverein** der *(PLURAL* die **Sportvereine)** sports club

**Sportwagen** der *(PLURAL* die **Sportwagen)** ❶ sports car ❷ pushchair

**Sportzentrum** das *(PLURAL* die **Sportzentren)** sports centre

**spotten** *VERB (PERF* **hat gespottet)** to mock

**sprach** ▸ SEE **sprechen**

**Sprache** die *(PLURAL* die **Sprachen)** ❶ language ❷ speech; etwas zur Sprache bringen to bring something up

**Sprachführer** der *(PLURAL* die **Sprachführer)** phrase-book

**sprachlos** *ADJECTIVE* speechless

**sprang** ▸ SEE **springen**

**Sprechblase** die *(PLURAL die Sprechblasen)* speech bubble

**sprechen** ◇VERB *(PRES* **spricht***, IMP* **sprach***, PERF* **hat gesprochen)* **❶ to speak**; Deutsch sprechen to speak German, mit wem spreche ich? who's speaking? *(on the phone)*, jemanden sprechen to speak to somebody **❷** Frau Hahn ist nicht zu sprechen Mrs Hahn is not available **❸ to talk**; mit jemandem über etwas sprechen to talk to somebody about something **❹ to say** *(a word, sentence)*

**Sprecher** der *(PLURAL die Sprecher)* **❶ spokesman ❷** *(on TV)* **announcer ❸** *(in a film)* **narrator ❹ speaker**

**Sprecherin** die *(PLURAL die Sprecherinnen)* **❶ spokeswoman ❷** *(on TV)* **announcer ❸** *(in a film)* **narrator ❹ speaker**

**Sprechstunde** die *(PLURAL die Sprechstunden)* surgery

**spricht** ▸ SEE **sprechen**

**Sprichwort** das *(PLURAL die Sprichwörter)* proverb

**springen** ◇VERB *(IMP* **sprang***, PERF* **ist gesprungen)* **❶ to jump ❷ to bounce** *(of a ball)* **❸ to dive ❹ to crack**

**Spritze** die *(PLURAL die Spritzen)* **❶ syringe ❷ injection ❸ hose**

**spritzen** VERB *(PERF* **hat gespritzt)* **❶ to inject ❷ to splash**; du hast mich nass gespritzt you've splashed me **❸ to spray ❹ to spit** *(of fat)* **❺** *(PERF* **ist gespritzt)* **to splash up**

**Sprudel** der *(PLURAL die Sprudel)* sparkling mineral water

**sprühen** VERB *(PERF* **hat gesprüht)* **❶ to spray ❷ to sparkle** *(of eyes)* **❸** *(PERF* **ist gesprüht)* **to fly** *(of sparks)*; die Funken sind in alle Richtungen gesprüht sparks flew in all directions

**Sprung** der *(PLURAL die Sprünge)* **❶ jump ❷ dive ❸ crack** *(in china, glass)*

**Sprungbrett** das *(PLURAL die Sprungbretter)* diving board

**spucken** VERB *(PERF* **hat gespuckt)* to spit

**Spülbecken** das *(PLURAL die Spülbecken)* sink

**spülen** VERB *(PERF* **hat gespült)* **❶ to rinse ❷ to wash up ❸ to flush**

**Spülmaschine** die *(PLURAL die Spülmaschinen)* dishwasher

**Spülmittel** das *(PLURAL die Spülmittel)* washing-up liquid

**Spültuch** das *(PLURAL die Spültücher)* dishcloth

**Spur** die *(PLURAL die Spuren)* **❶ track**; auf der falschen Spur sein to be on the wrong track, jemandem auf die Spur kommen to get on to somebody **❷ lane**; in der Spur bleiben to keep in lane **❸ trail ❹ trace**

**spüren** VERB *(PERF* **hat gespürt)* **❶ to feel ❷ to sense**

**Staat** der *(PLURAL die Staaten)* state

**staatlich** ADJECTIVE **state**; eine staatliche Schule a state school

**staatlich** ADVERB by the state

**Staatsangehörigkeit** die *(PLURAL die Staatsangehörigkeiten)* nationality

German—English

**stabil** ADJECTIVE ❶ stable ❷ sturdy

**stach** ▸ SEE **stechen**

**Stachel** der (PLURAL die **Stacheln**)
❶ spine ❷ spike ❸ sting

**Stachelbeere** die (PLURAL die
**Stachelbeeren**) gooseberry

**Stacheldraht** der barbed wire

**Stadion** das (PLURAL die **Stadien**)
stadium

**Stadium** das (PLURAL die **Stadien**)
stage

**Stadt** die (PLURAL die **Städte**) town,
city

**Stadtbummel** der (PLURAL die
**Stadtbummel**) wander around
town; einen Stadtbummel machen
Stadtbummel to have a wander
around town

**städtisch** ADJECTIVE ❶ urban
❷ municipal

**Stadtmitte** die town centre

**Stadtplan** der (PLURAL die
**Stadtpläne**) street map

**Stadtrand** der outskirts (of town);
am Stadtrand von Lübeck on the
outskirts of Lübeck

**Stadtrat** der (PLURAL die **Stadträte**)
town or city council

**Stadtrundfahrt** die (PLURAL die
**Stadtrundfahrten**) sightseeing
tour (of a town)

**Stadtteil** der (PLURAL die **Stadtteile**)
district

**Stadtzentrum** das (PLURAL die
**Stadtzentren**) town centre

**stahl** ▸ SEE **stehlen**

**Stahl** der steel

**Stall** der (PLURAL die **Ställe**) ❶ stable
❷ cowshed ❸ pigsty

**Stamm** der (PLURAL die **Stämme**)
❶ trunk ❷ tribe ❸ stem (of a
word)

**Stammbaum** der (PLURAL die
**Stammbäume**) family tree

**stammen** VERB (PERF **hat gestammt**)
aus Deutschland stammen to come
from Germany

**Stammgast** der (PLURAL die
**Stammgäste**) regular customer
(in a pub or restaurant)

**stand** ▸ SEE **stehen**

**Stand** der (PLURAL die **Stände**)
❶ state; etwas auf den neuesten
Stand bringen to bring something
up to date ❷ stall (for a horse) ❸ stall (in a
fair) ❹ stand (in a
fair) ❺ level (of water, of a river)

**ständig** ADJECTIVE constant

**Standort** der (PLURAL die **Standorte**)
position, location; von ihrem
Standort aus konnte sie nichts
sehen she couldn't see anything
from where she was standing

**Stange** die (PLURAL die **Stangen**)
❶ bar ❷ pole

**stank** ▸ SEE **stinken**

**starb** ▸ SEE **sterben**

**stark** ADJECTIVE ❶ strong ❷ heavy
(rain, traffic) ❸ severe (frost, pain)
❹ (informal) great; das ist stark!
that's great!

**Stärke** die (PLURAL die **Stärken**)
❶ strength ❷ starch

**starrsinnig** ADJECTIVE obstinate

**Start** der (PLURAL die **Starts**) ❶ start
❷ take-off

a
b
c
d
e
f
g
h
i
j
k
l
m
n
o
p
q
r
s
t
u
v
w
x
y
z

**Startbahn** die (PLURAL die **Startbahnen**) runway

**starten** VERB (PERF **ist gestartet**) ❶ (of a plane) to take off ❷ (PERF **hat gestartet**) to start, to launch (a campaign)

**Station** die (PLURAL die **Stationen**) ❶ station ❷ stop; Station machen to stop over ❸ ward (in hospital)

**statt** CONJUNCTION, PREPOSITION (+GEN) instead of; statt zu arbeiten instead of working, sie ging statt ihrer Schwester she went instead of her sister

**stattdessen** CONJUNCTION instead

**stattfinden** ◇VERB (IMP **fand statt**, PERF **hat stattgefunden**) to take place

**Stau** der (PLURAL die **Staus**) ❶ congestion ❷ traffic jam

**Staub** der dust

**staubig** ADJECTIVE dusty

**staubsaugen** VERB (PERF **hat staubgesaugt**) to vacuum

**Staubsauger** der (PLURAL die **Staubsauger**) vacuum cleaner

**staunen** VERB (PERF **hat gestaunt**) to be amazed

**Steak** das (PLURAL die **Steaks**) steak

**stechen** ◇VERB (PRES **sticht**, IMP **stach**, PERF **hat gestochen**) ❶ to prick; sich in den Finger stechen to prick your finger ❷ to sting, to bite (of an insect) ❸ mit etwas in etwas stechen to jab something into something

**Steckbrief** der (PLURAL die **Steckbriefe**) description (of a wanted person)

**Steckdose** die (PLURAL die **Steckdosen**) socket

**stecken** VERB (PERF **hat gesteckt**) ❶ to put; du musst die Münze in den Schlitz stecken put the coin into the slot ❷ to pin ❸ wo steckt er? where is he? ❹ stecken bleiben to get stuck, den Schlüssel stecken lassen to leave the key in the lock

**Stecker** der (PLURAL die **Stecker**) plug

**Stecknadel** die (PLURAL die **Stecknadeln**) pin

**Steckrübe** die (PLURAL die **Steckrüben**) turnip

**stehen** ◇VERB (IMP **stand**, PERF **hat gestanden**) ❶ to stand ❷ to be; es steht zwei zu zwei the score is two all, wie steht's? what's the score? ❸ to have stopped (of a clock or a machine) ❹ es steht schlecht um ihn he's in a bad way, na, wie steht's? how are you? ❺ stehen bleiben to stop, die Uhr ist stehen geblieben the clock has stopped ❻ in der Zeitung steht, dass ... it says in the paper that ... ❼ jemandem (gut) stehen to suit somebody ❽ zu jemandem stehen to stand by somebody ❾ sich gut stehen to be on good terms ❿ zum Stehen kommen to come to a standstill

**stehenbleiben** ▸ SEE stehen

**stehlen** ◇VERB (PRES **stiehlt**, IMP **stahl**, PERF **hat gestohlen**) to steal

**steif** ADJECTIVE stiff

**steigen** VERB (IMP **stieg**, PERF **ist gestiegen**) ❶ to climb; auf eine Leiter steigen to climb up a ladder, auf ein Fahrrad steigen to get on a bike, in den Bus steigen to get on the bus ❷ to rise

**steil** *ADJECTIVE* **steep**

**Stein** der *(PLURAL* die **Steine)** stone

**Steinbock** der *(PLURAL* die **Steinböcke)** ❶ ibex ❷ Capricorn; Petra ist Steinbock Petra's Capricorn

**Steinbruch** der *(PLURAL* die **Steinbrüche)** quarry

**Stelle** die *(PLURAL* die **Stellen)** ❶ place, spot; an deiner Stelle in your place, an dritter Stelle liegen to be in third place ❷ job; eine freie Stelle a vacancy ❸ authority ❹ auf der Stelle immediately

**stellen** *VERB (PERF* **hat gestellt)** ❶ to put ❷ to set *(a watch, task)* ❸ zur Verfügung stellen to provide ❹ lauter stellen to turn up, leiser stellen to turn down, die Heizung höher stellen to turn the heating up ❺ sich krank stellen to pretend to be ill ❻ sich stellen to give yourself up ❼ die Kinder stellten sich an die Wand the children stood against the wall

**Stellenanzeige** die *(PLURAL* die **Stellenanzeigen)** job advertisement

**Stellplatz** der *(PLURAL* die **Stellplätze)** pitch *(for a tent)*

**Stellung** die *(PLURAL* die **Stellungen)** position

**stellvertretend** *ADJECTIVE* ❶ acting ❷ deputy; der stellvertretende Feuerwehrhauptmann the deputy chief fire officer

**Stellvertreter** der *(PLURAL* die **Stellvertreter)** ❶ deputy ❷ representative

**Stellvertreterin** die *(PLURAL* die **Stellvertreterinnen)** ❶ deputy

❷ representative

**Stempel** der *(PLURAL* die **Stempel)** ❶ stamp ❷ postmark

**stempeln** *VERB (PERF* **hat gestempelt)** to stamp

**Steppdecke** die *(PLURAL* die **Steppdecken)** quilt

**sterben** ◇*VERB (PRES* **stirbt**, *IMP* **starb**, *PERF* **ist gestorben)** to die

**Stereoanlage** die *(PLURAL* die **Stereoanlagen)** stereo (system)

**Stern** der *(PLURAL* die **Sterne)** star

**Sternzeichen** das *(PLURAL* die **Sternzeichen)** star sign; was ist dein Sternzeichen? what star sign are you?

**Steuer**[1] das *(PLURAL* die **Steuer)** ❶ (steering) wheel ❷ helm

**Steuer**[2] die *(PLURAL* die **Steuern)** tax

**steuern** *VERB (PERF* **hat gesteuert)** ❶ to steer ❷ to control ❸ *(PERF* ist gesteuert) to head

**Stewardess** die *(PLURAL* die **Stewardessen)** stewardess, air hostess

**Stich** der *(PLURAL* die **Stiche)** ❶ prick ❷ stab ❸ sting, bite *(of an insect)* ❹ stitch ❺ trick *(when playing cards)* ❻ engraving ❼ jemanden im Stich lassen to leave somebody in the lurch

**sticht** ▸ SEE **stechen**

**sticken** *VERB (PERF* **hat gestickt)** to embroider

**Stickstoff** der nitrogen

**Stiefbruder** der *(PLURAL* die **Stiefbrüder)** stepbrother

**Stiefel** der *(PLURAL* die **Stiefel)** boot

**Stiefkind** das *(PLURAL die Stiefkinder)* stepchild

**Stiefmutter** die *(PLURAL die Stiefmütter)* stepmother

**Stiefschwester** die *(PLURAL die Stiefschwestern)* stepsister

**Stiefvater** der *(PLURAL die Stiefväter)* stepfather

**stieg** ▸ SEE **steigen**

**stiehlt** ▸ SEE **stehlen**

**Stiel** der *(PLURAL die Stiele)* ❶ handle ❷ stem

**Stier** der *(PLURAL die Stiere)* ❶ bull ❷ Taurus; Andrea ist Stier Andrea's Taurus

**stieß** ▸ SEE **stoßen**

**Stift** der *(PLURAL die Stifte)* ❶ pencil ❷ crayon ❸ tack *(nail)*

**Stil** der *(PLURAL die Stile)* style

**still** ADJECTIVE ❶ quiet ❷ still

**stillen** VERB *(PERF hat gestillt)* ❶ to quench ❷ to breast-feed

**stillhalten** ◇VERB *(PRES hält still, IMP hielt still, PERF hat stillgehalten)* to keep still

**Stimme** die *(PLURAL die Stimmen)* ❶ voice ❷ vote

**stimmen** VERB *(PERF hat gestimmt)* ❶ to be right; stimmt das? is that right? ❷ to vote ❸ to tune

**Stimmung** die *(PLURAL die Stimmungen)* ❶ mood ❷ atmosphere

**stinken** ◇VERB *(IMP stank, PERF hat gestunken)* to smell, to stink

**Stipendium** das *(PLURAL die Stipendien)* ❶ scholarship ❷ grant

**stirbt** ▸ SEE **sterben**

**Stirn** die *(PLURAL die Stirnen)* forehead

**Stock**[1] der *(PLURAL die Stöcke)* stick

**Stock**[2] der *(PLURAL die Stock)* floor; im ersten Stock on the first floor

**Stockwerk** das *(PLURAL die Stockwerke)* floor

**Stoff** der *(PLURAL die Stoffe)* ❶ material, fabric ❷ substance

**stöhnen** VERB *(PERF hat gestöhnt)* to groan

**stolpern** VERB *(PERF ist gestolpert)* ❶ to stumble ❷ to trip; ich bin über einen Stein gestolpert I tripped on a stone

**stolz** ADJECTIVE **proud**

**stoppen** VERB *(PERF hat gestoppt)* to stop

**Stöpsel** der *(PLURAL die Stöpsel)* ❶ plug ❷ stopper

**stören** VERB *(PERF hat gestört)* ❶ to disturb; Bitte nicht stören please do not disturb ❷ to bother; das stört mich nicht that doesn't bother me ❸ stört es Sie, wenn ich das Fenster aufmache? do you mind if I open the window?, der Empfang ist gestört *(on a TV)* there's interference

**Störung** die *(PLURAL die Störungen)* ❶ disturbance, interruption; entschuldigen Sie die Störung I'm sorry to bother you ❷ interference; eine technische Störung a technical fault

**Stoß** der *(PLURAL die Stöße)* ❶ push ❷ pile; ein Stoß Handtücher a pile of towels

**stoßen** ◇VERB *(PRES stößt, IMP stieß, PERF hat gestoßen)* ❶ to push

**❷ to kick ❸** sich den Kopf stoßen to hit your head, ich habe mir den Kopf an dem Balken gestoßen I hit my head on the beam, sich stoßen to bump yourself **❹** sich an etwas stoßen to object to something **❺** (PERF **ist gestoßen**) gegen etwas stoßen to bump into something **❻** (PERF **ist gestoßen**) auf etwas stoßen to come across something

**Stoßstange** die (PLURAL die **Stoßstangen**) bumper

**Stoßzeit** die (PLURAL die **Stoßzeiten**) rush hour

**stottern** VERB (PERF **hat gestottert**) to stutter

**Strafe** die (PLURAL die **Strafen**) **❶ punishment ❷ fine ❸ penalty**

**Straftat** die (PLURAL die **Straftaten**) crime

**Strahl** der (PLURAL die **Strahlen**) **❶ ray, beam ❷ jet**

**strahlen** VERB (PERF **hat gestrahlt**) **❶ to shine ❷ to beam**

**Strahlung** die (PLURAL die **Strahlungen**) radiation

**Strand** der (PLURAL die **Strände**) beach

**Straße** die (PLURAL die **Straßen**) street, road; in welcher Straße ist der Supermarkt? which street is the supermarket in?, über die Straße gehen to cross the road, jemanden auf die Straße setzen (informal) to give somebody the sack, mein Wirt hat mich einfach auf die Straße gesetzt (informal) my landlord just turned me out (of a flat or room)

**Straßenbahn** die (PLURAL die **Straßenbahnen**) tram; mit der Straßenbahn fahren to go by tram

**Straßenraub** der **❶ mugging ❷ street robbery**

**Straßenräuber** der (PLURAL die **Straßenräuber**) mugger

**Straßenüberführung** die (PLURAL die **Straßenüberführungen**) **❶ footbrige ❷ roadbridge**

**Straßenunterführung** die (PLURAL die **Straßenunterführungen**) **❶ subway ❷ underpass**

**Strauch** der (PLURAL die **Sträucher**) bush

**Strauß**¹ der (PLURAL die **Sträuße**) bunch of flowers, bouquet

**Strauß**² der (PLURAL die **Strauße**) ostrich

**Streber** der (PLURAL die **Streber**) swot

**Strecke** die (PLURAL die **Strecken**) **❶ distance ❷ route ❸ line** (rail)

**strecken** VERB (PERF **hat gestreckt**) **❶ to stretch** (your arms, legs) **❷ sich strecken to stretch**

**Streich** der (PLURAL die **Streiche**) trick

**streicheln** VERB (PERF **hat gestreichelt**) to stroke

**streichen** ◇VERB (IMP **strich**, PERF **hat gestrichen**) **❶ to paint**; 'frisch gestrichen' 'wet paint' **❷ to spread** (with butter) **❸ to delete ❹ to cancel** (a flight) **❺** jemandem über den Kopf streichen to stroke somebody's head

**Streichholz** das (PLURAL die **Streichhölzer**) match

**Streifen** der (PLURAL die **Streifen**) **❶ stripe ❷ strip**

**Streik** der (PLURAL die **Streiks**) strike

**streiken** *VERB (PERF* **hat gestreikt)**
to strike

**Streit** der *(PLURAL* die **Streite)**
quarrel, argument

**streiten** ◇*VERB (IMP* **stritt,** *PERF* **hat
gestritten)** ❶ to quarrel, to argue
❷ **sich streiten** to quarrel, to argue

**streng** *ADJECTIVE* **strict**

**Stress** der **stress**

**stressig** *ADJECTIVE* **stressful**

**streuen** *VERB (PERF* **hat gestreut)**
❶ to spread; **die Straßen streuen**
to grit the roads ❷ to sprinkle

**strich** ▸ SEE **streichen**

**Strich** der *(PLURAL* die **Striche)** ❶ line
❷ stroke

**Strichpunkt** der *(PLURAL* die
**Strichpunkte)** semicolon

**stricken** *VERB (PERF* **hat gestrickt)**
to knit

**Strickjacke** die *(PLURAL* die
**Strickjacken)** cardigan

**stritt** ▸ SEE **streiten**

**Stroh** das **straw**

**Strohhalm** der *(PLURAL* die
**Strohhalme)** straw *(for drinking)*

**Strom** der *(PLURAL* die **Ströme)**
❶ river ❷ stream *(of people or
blood)*; **es regnet in Strömen** it's
pouring with rain ❸ current

**Stromausfall** der *(PLURAL* die
**Stromausfälle)** power failure

**strömen** *VERB (PERF* **ist geströmt)**
to stream

**Strömung** die *(PLURAL* die
**Strömungen)** current

**Strudel** der *(PLURAL* die **Strudel)**
strudel *(kind of Austrian cake)*

**Strumpf** der *(PLURAL* die **Strümpfe)**
❶ stocking ❷ sock

**Strumpfhose** die *(PLURAL* die
**Strumpfhosen)** tights

**Stube** die *(PLURAL* die **Stuben)** room

**Stück** das *(PLURAL* die **Stücke)** ❶ piece
❷ item; **ein Euro das Stück** one
euro each ❸ play

**Stückchen** das *(PLURAL* die
**Stückchen)** little piece

**Student** der *(PLURAL* die **Studenten)**
student

**Studentin** die *(PLURAL* die
**Studentinnen)** student

**studieren** *VERB (PERF* **hat studiert)** to
study; **Horst studiert Mathematik**
Horst is studying mathematics

**Studium** das *(PLURAL* die **Studien)**
studies

**Stufe** die *(PLURAL* die **Stufen)** ❶ step;
'**Vorsicht Stufe**' 'mind the step'
❷ stage *(of development)*

**Stuhl** der *(PLURAL* die **Stühle)** chair

**stumm** *ADJECTIVE* ❶ dumb ❷ silent

**stumpf** *ADJECTIVE* ❶ blunt ❷ dull
❸ **ein stumpfer Winkel** an obtuse
angle

**Stunde** die *(PLURAL* die **Stunden)**
❶ hour ❷ lesson

**stundenlang** *ADVERB* **for hours**

**Stundenplan** der *(PLURAL* die
**Stundenpläne)** timetable

**stündlich** *ADJECTIVE* **hourly**

**stur** *ADJECTIVE* **stubborn**

**Sturm** der *(PLURAL* die **Stürme)** storm

**stürmisch** *ADJECTIVE* **stormy**

**Sturz** der *(PLURAL* die **Stürze)** ❶ fall
❷ overthrow

**stürzen** *VERB (PERF* **ist gestürzt)** ❶ to fall ❷ to rush *(into a room)* ❸ *(PERF* **hat gestürzt)** to overthrow ❹ *(PERF* **hat sich gestürzt)** er hat sich aus dem Fenster gestürzt he threw himself out of the window, sich auf jemanden stürzen to pounce on somebody

**Sturzhelm** der *(PLURAL die* **Sturzhelme)** crash helmet

**stützen** *VERB (PERF* **hat gestützt)** to support; sich auf jemanden stützen to lean on somebody

**Subjekt** das *(PLURAL die* **Subjekte)** subject

**Substantiv** das *(PLURAL die* **Substantive)** noun

**subtil** *ADJECTIVE* subtle

**Subvention** die *(PLURAL die* **Subventionen)** subsidy

**subventionieren** *VERB (PERF* **hat subventioniert)** to subsidize

**Suche** die *(PLURAL die* **Suchen)** search

**suchen** *VERB (PERF* **hat gesucht)** ❶ to look for; 'Zimmer gesucht' 'room wanted' ❷ to search

**süchtig** *ADJECTIVE* addicted

**Süchtige** der/die *(PLURAL die* **Süchtigen)** addict

**Südafrika** das South Africa

**Südamerika** das South America

**Süden** der south

**südlich** *ADJECTIVE* ❶ southern ❷ southerly

**südlich** *ADVERB, PREPOSITION (+GEN)* südlich von Wien south of Vienna, südlich der Stadt to the south of the town

**Südosten** der south-east

**Südpol** der South Pole

**Südwesten** der south-west

**Summe** die *(PLURAL die* **Summen)** sum

**summen** *VERB (PERF* **hat gesummt)** ❶ to hum ❷ to buzz

**Sünde** die *(PLURAL die* **Sünden)** sin

**super** *ADJECTIVE (informal)* great

**Supermarkt** der *(PLURAL die* **Supermärkte)** supermarket

**Suppe** die *(PLURAL die* **Suppen)** soup

**surfen** *VERB (PERF* **hat gesurft)** to surf *(in the sea, on the Internet)*; im Internet surfen to surf the Internet

**Surfen** das surf

**Surfer** der *(PLURAL die* **Surfer)** surfer *(on the sea and Internet)*

**Surferin** die *(PLURAL die* **Surferinnen)** surfer *(on the sea and Internet)*

**süß** *ADJECTIVE* sweet

**Süßigkeit** die *(PLURAL die* **Süßigkeiten)** sweet

**Sweatshirt** die *(PLURAL die* **Sweatshirts)** sweatshirt

**symbolisch** *ADJECTIVE* symbolic

**sympathisch** *ADJECTIVE* likeable

**Symphonie** die *(PLURAL die* **Symphonien)** ▸ SEE Sinfonie

**Synagoge** die *(PLURAL die* **Synagogen)** synagogue

**synthetisch** *ADJECTIVE* synthetic

**System** das *(PLURAL die* **Systeme)** system

**Szene** die *(PLURAL die* **Szenen)** scene

# Tt

**Tabak** der (PLURAL die **Tabake**) tobacco

**Tabelle** die (PLURAL die **Tabellen**) table

**Tablett** das (PLURAL die **Tabletts**) tray

**Tablette** die (PLURAL die **Tabletten**) tablet

**Tafel** die (PLURAL die **Tafeln**) ❶ board, blackboard; ein Wort an die Tafel schreiben to write a word on the blackboard ❷ eine Tafel Schokolade a bar of chocolate

**Tag** der (PLURAL die **Tage**) day; guten Tag hello, am Tag in the daytime

**Tagebuch** das (PLURAL die **Tagebücher**) diary

**tagelang** ADVERB for days

**Tagesanbruch** der dawn

**Tagesausflug** der (PLURAL die **Tagesausflüge**) day trip

**Tageskarte** die (PLURAL die **Tageskarten**) ❶ today's menu ❷ day ticket

**Tageslicht** das daylight

**Tageslichtprojektor** der (PLURAL die **Tageslichtprojektoren**) overhead projector

**Tagesmutter** die (PLURAL die **Tagesmütter**) childminder

**Tagesschau** die (PLURAL die **Tagesschauen**) news (on television)

**Tageszeitung** die (PLURAL die **Tageszeitungen**) daily paper

**täglich** ADJECTIVE daily; sein täglicher Besuch his daily visit

**täglich** ADVERB daily; zweimal täglich twice daily, twice a day

**tagsüber** ADVERB during the day

**Taille** die (PLURAL die **Taillen**) waist

**Takt** der (PLURAL die **Takte**) ❶ tact ❷ time; im Takt in time to the music ❸ rhythm

**taktlos** ADJECTIVE tactless

**taktvoll** ADJECTIVE tactful

**Tal** das (PLURAL die **Täler**) valley

**Talent** das (PLURAL die **Talente**) talent

**Tampon** der (PLURAL die **Tampons**) tampon

**Tang** der seaweed

**Tank** der (PLURAL die **Tanks**) tank

**tanken** VERB (PERF **hat getankt**) to fill up (with petrol) to get petrol

**Tanker** der (PLURAL die **Tanker**) tanker (on sea)

**Tankstelle** die (PLURAL die **Tankstellen**) petrol station

**Tankwagen** der (PLURAL die **Tankwagen**) tanker (on road)

**Tankwart** der (PLURAL die **Tankwarte**) petrol-pump attendant

**Tanne** die (PLURAL die **Tannen**) fir

**Tannenbaum** der (PLURAL die **Tannenbäume**) ❶ fir tree ❷ Christmas tree

A B C D E F G H I J K L M N O P Q R S T U V W X Y Z

**Tante** die *(PLURAL* die **Tanten)** aunt

**Tanz** der *(PLURAL* die **Tänze)** dance

**tanzen** *VERB (PERF* **hat getanzt)**
to dance

**Tänzer** der *(PLURAL* die **Tänzer)**
dancer

**Tänzerin** die *(PLURAL* die
**Tänzerinnen)** dancer

**Tapete** die *(PLURAL* die **Tapeten)**
wallpaper

**tapezieren** *VERB (PERF* **hat tapeziert)**
to (wall)paper

**tapfer** *ADJECTIVE* brave

**Tapferkeit** die bravery

**Tarif** der *(PLURAL* die **Tarife)** ❶ tariff
❷ rate

**Tasche** die *(PLURAL* die **Taschen)**
❶ bag ❷ pocket; er hat es aus
eigener Tasche bezahlt he paid
for it out of his own pocket, Max
hat mir fünf Euro aus der Tasche
gezogen *(informal)* Max wangled
five euros out of me

**Taschenbuch** das *(PLURAL* die
**Taschenbücher)** paperback

**Taschendieb** der *(PLURAL* die
**Taschendiebe)** pickpocket

**Taschengeld** das pocket money

**Taschenlampe** die *(PLURAL* die
**Taschenlampen)** torch

**Taschenmesser** das *(PLURAL* die
**Taschenmesser)** penknife

**Taschenrechner** der *(PLURAL*
die **Taschenrechner)** pocket
calculator

**Taschentuch** das *(PLURAL* die
**Taschentücher)** handkerchief

**Tasse** die *(PLURAL* die **Tassen)** cup

**Tastatur** die *(PLURAL* die **Tastaturen)**
keyboard

**Taste** die *(PLURAL* die **Tasten)** ❶ key
❷ button *(on a phone or a machine)*

**tasten** *VERB (PERF* **hat getastet)** ❶ to
feel ❷ sich tasten to feel your way

**tat** ▸ SEE **tun**

**Tat** die *(PLURAL* die **Taten)** ❶ action
❷ eine gute Tat a good deed
❸ crime ❹ in der Tat indeed

**Täter** der *(PLURAL* die **Täter)** ❶ culprit
❷ offender

**Täterin** die *(PLURAL* die **Täterinnen)**
❶ culprit ❷ offender

**tätig** *ADJECTIVE* active

**Tätigkeit** die *(PLURAL* die
**Tätigkeiten)** ❶ activity ❷ job

**Tätigkeit** *(PLURAL* die **Tätigkeiten)**
activity

**Tätowierung** die *(PLURAL* die
**Tätowierungen)** tattoo

**Tatsache** die *(PLURAL* die **Tatsachen)**
fact

**tatsächlich** *ADJECTIVE* actual

**tatsächlich** *ADVERB* ❶ actually
❷ really

**Tau¹** der dew

**Tau²** das *(PLURAL* die **Taue)** rope

**taub** *ADJECTIVE* deaf

**Taube** die *(PLURAL* die **Tauben)**
❶ pigeon ❷ dove

**tauchen** *VERB (PERF* **hat getaucht)**
❶ to dip ❷ *(PERF* **hat/ist getaucht)**
*('ist getaucht' is used when
movement is described)* to dive

**Taucher** der *(PLURAL* die **Taucher)** diver

**Taucherbrille** die *(PLURAL* die **Taucherbrillen)** diving goggles

**Taucherin** die *(PLURAL* die **Taucherinnen)** diver

**tauen** *VERB (PERF* **ist getaut) ❶** to melt **❷** es taut it's thawing

**Taufe** die *(PLURAL* die **Taufen)** christening

**taufen** *VERB (PERF* **hat getauft) ❶** to christen **❷** to baptize

**taugen** *VERB (PERF* **hat getaugt)** nichts taugen to be no good

**tauschen** *VERB (PERF* **hat getauscht)** to exchange, to swap

**tausend** *NUMBER* a thousand

**Taxi** das *(PLURAL* die **Taxis)** taxi

**Taxifahrer** der *(PLURAL* die **Taxifahrer)** taxi driver

**Taxifahrerin** die *(PLURAL* die **Taxifahrerinnen)** taxi driver

**Taxistand** der *(PLURAL* die **Taxistände)** taxi rank

**Technik** die *(PLURAL* die **Techniken)** **❶** technology **❷** technique

**Techniker** der *(PLURAL* die **Techniker)** technician

**Technikerin** die *(PLURAL* die **Technikerinnen)** technician

**technisch** *ADJECTIVE* **❶** technical **❷** technological

**Technologie** die technology

**technologisch** *ADJECTIVE* technological

**Teddybär** der *(PLURAL* die **Teddybären)** teddy bear

**Tee** der *(PLURAL* die **Tee(s))** tea; ein Tee mit Zitrone one lemon tea, ein Tee mit Milch one tea with milk

**Teebeutel** der *(PLURAL* die **Teebeutel)** tea bag

**Teekanne** die *(PLURAL* die **Teekannen)** teapot

**Teelöffel** der *(PLURAL* die **Teelöffel)** teaspoon

**Teenager** der *(PLURAL* die **Teenager)** teenager

**Teich** der *(PLURAL* die **Teiche)** pond

**Teig** der *(PLURAL* die **Teige) ❶** dough **❷** pastry **❸** mixture

**Teigwaren** *PLURAL NOUN* pasta

**Teil**[1] der *(PLURAL* die **Teile) ❶** part; der zweite Teil the second part, zum größten Teil for the most part **❷** zum Teil partly **❸** share; mein Teil am Gewinn my share of the profit

**Teil**[2] das *(PLURAL* die **Teile) ❶** spare part **❷** part *(of a car, machine)* **❸** unit *(of furniture)*

**teilen** *VERB (PERF* **hat geteilt) ❶** to divide **❷** sich etwas mit jemandem teilen to share something with somebody

**teilnehmen** ◇*VERB (PRES* **nimmt teil,** *IMP* **nahm teil,** *PERF* **hat teilgenommen)** an etwas teilnehmen to take part in something

**Teilnehmer** der *(PLURAL* die **Teilnehmer) ❶** participant **❷** competitor

**Teilnehmerin** die *(PLURAL* die **Teilnehmerinnen) ❶** participant **❷** competitor

**teils** *ADVERB* partly

**Teilung** die *(PLURAL* die **Teilungen)** division

**Teilzeitarbeit** die part-time work

**Telefon** das *(PLURAL* die **Telefone)** telephone

**Telefonanruf** der *(PLURAL* die **Telefonanrufe)** phone call

**Telefonbuch** das *(PLURAL* die **Telefonbücher)** telephone directory, phone book

**Telefongespräch** das *(PLURAL* die **Telefongespräche)** telephone call

**Telefonhörer** der *(PLURAL* die **Telefonhörer)** receiver

**telefonieren** *VERB (PERF* hat telefoniert) to telephone, to make a phone call

**telefonisch** *ADJECTIVE* telephone

**telefonisch** *ADVERB* by telephone; er ist telefonisch nicht erreichbar he can't be contacted by phone

**Telefonnummer** die *(PLURAL* die **Telefonnummern)** telephone number

**Telefonzelle** die *(PLURAL* die **Telefonzellen)** phone box, call box

**Teleskop** das *(PLURAL* die **Teleskope)** telescope

**Teller** der *(PLURAL* die **Teller)** plate

**Temperatur** die *(PLURAL* die **Temperaturen)** temperature

**Tempo** das *(PLURAL* die **Tempos)** speed; Tempo Tempo! *(informal)* hurry up!

**Tendenz** die *(PLURAL* die **Tendenzen)** ❶ trend ❷ tendency

**tendieren** *VERB (PERF* hat tendiert) zu etwas tendieren to tend towards something

**Tennis** das tennis

**Tennisplatz** der *(PLURAL* die **Tennisplätze)** tennis court

**Tennisschläger** der *(PLURAL* die **Tennisschläger)** tennis racket

**Tennisspieler** der *(PLURAL* die **Tennisspieler)** tennis player

**Tennisspielerin** die *(PLURAL* die **Tennisspielerinnen)** tennis player

**Teppich** der *(PLURAL* die **Teppiche)** ❶ carpet ❷ rug

**Termin** der *(PLURAL* die **Termine)** ❶ date; einen Termin vereinbaren to fix a date ❷ appointment ❸ der letzte Termin the deadline

**Terminal**[1] der *(PLURAL* die **Terminals)** terminal

**Terminal**[2] das *(PLURAL* die **Terminals)** (computer) terminal

**Terrasse** die *(PLURAL* die **Terrassen)** terrace

**Terror** der terror

**Terrorismus** der terrorism

**Terrorist** der *(PLURAL* die **Terroristen)** terrorist

**Terroristin** die *(PLURAL* die **Terroristinnen)** terrorist

**Tesafilm** der Sellotape

**Test** der *(PLURAL* die **Tests)** test; ein Test zum Hörverständnis a listening comprehension test

**testen** *VERB (PERF* hat getestet) to test

**teuer** *ADJECTIVE* **expensive**; wie teuer? how much?

**Teufel** der *(PLURAL die Teufel)* devil

**Text** der *(PLURAL die Texte)* ❶ text
❷ lyrics ❸ caption

**Textverarbeitung** die word processing

**Theater** das *(PLURAL die Theater)*
❶ theatre ❷ *(informal)* fuss

**Theaterstück** das *(PLURAL die Theaterstücke)* play

**Theke** die *(PLURAL die Theken)* ❶ bar
❷ counter

**Thema** das *(PLURAL die Themen)* subject, topic

**Themenpark** der *(PLURAL die Themenparks)* theme park

**Themse** die Thames

**theoretisch** *ADJECTIVE* theoretical

**theoretisch** *ADVERB* in theory

**Theorie** die *(PLURAL die Theorien)* theory

**Therapie** die *(PLURAL die Therapien)* therapy

**Thermometer** das *(PLURAL die Thermometer)* thermometer

**Thron** der *(PLURAL die Throne)* throne

**Thunfisch** der *(PLURAL die Thunfische)* tuna

**Thymian** der thyme

**tief** *ADJECTIVE* ❶ deep ❷ low

**Tiefe** die *(PLURAL die Tiefen)* depth

**Tiefgarage** die *(PLURAL die Tiefgaragen)* underground car park

**Tiefkühlfach** das *(PLURAL die Tiefkühlfächer)* freezer compartment

**Tiefkühlkost** die frozen food

**Tiefkühltruhe** die *(PLURAL die Tiefkühltruhen)* freezer

**Tiefsttemperatur** die *(PLURAL die Tiefsttemperaturen)* minimum temperature

**Tier** das *(PLURAL die Tiere)* animal

**Tierarzt** der *(PLURAL die Tierärzte)* vet

**Tierärztin** die *(PLURAL die Tierärztinnen)* vet

**Tiergarten** der *(PLURAL die Tiergärten)* zoo

**Tierkreis** der zodiac

**Tierpark** der *(PLURAL die Tierparks)* zoo

**Tiger** der *(PLURAL die Tiger)* tiger

**Tinte** die *(PLURAL die Tinten)* ink

**Tintenfisch** der *(PLURAL die Tintenfische)* ❶ octopus ❷ squid

**Tipp** der *(PLURAL die Tipps)* tip

**tippen** *VERB (PERF hat getippt)* ❶ to type ❷ to tap ❸ auf etwas tippen to bet on something, ich tippe auf ihn I'm tipping him to win, im Lotto tippen to do the lottery

**Tisch** der *(PLURAL die Tische)* ❶ table
❷ nach Tisch after the meal

**Tischdecke** die *(PLURAL die Tischdecken)* tablecloth

**Tischler** der *(PLURAL die Tischler)* joiner, carpenter

**Tischtennis** das table tennis

**Tischtuch** das *(PLURAL die Tischtücher)* tablecloth

**Titel** der *(PLURAL die Titel)* title

**Toast** der *(PLURAL die* **Toasts***)* toast

**toben** *VERB (PERF* hat getobt*)* ❶ to rage ❷ to go mad ❸ to charge about

**Tochter** die *(PLURAL die* **Töchter***)* daughter

**Tod** der *(PLURAL die* **Tode***)* death

**Todesstrafe** die death penalty

**tödlich** *ADJECTIVE* ❶ fatal ❷ deadly

**todmüde** *ADJECTIVE (informal)* dead tired

**todschick** *ADJECTIVE (informal)* trendy

**Toilette** die *(PLURAL die* **Toiletten***)* toilet; auf die Toilette gehen to go to the toilet

**Toilettenpapier** das toilet paper

**toll** *ADJECTIVE (informal)* brilliant

**Tollwut** die rabies

**Tomate** die *(PLURAL die* **Tomaten***)* tomato

**Tomatenmark** das tomato purée

**Ton**[1] der *(PLURAL die* **Töne***)* ❶ sound; er hat keinen Ton gesagt he didn't make a sound ❷ große Töne spucken *(informal)* to talk big ❸ tone; einen frechen Ton anschlagen to adopt a cheeky tone ❹ note ❺ shade *(of colour)* ❻ stress *(in pronunciation)*

**Ton**[2] der clay

**Tonband** das *(PLURAL die* **Tonbänder***)* tape

**Tonne** die *(PLURAL die* **Tonnen***)* ❶ barrel ❷ bin *(for rubbish)* ❸ tonne, ton

**Topf** der *(PLURAL die* **Töpfe***)* ❶ pot ❷ pan

**Töpferei** die *(PLURAL die* **Töpfereien***)* pottery

**Tor** das *(PLURAL die* **Tore***)* ❶ gate ❷ goal; mit 3 zu 2 Toren gewinnen to win by 3 goals to 2

**Torte** die *(PLURAL die* **Torten***)* ❶ gateau ❷ cake

**Torwart** der *(PLURAL die* **Torwarte***)* goalkeeper

**tot** *ADJECTIVE* dead

**total** *ADJECTIVE* complete

**total** *ADVERB* completely; du bist total verrückt you're totally mad

**Tote** der/die *(PLURAL die* **Toten***)* ❶ dead man/woman; die Toten the dead ❷ fatality

**töten** *VERB (PERF* hat getötet*)* to kill

**totlachen** *VERB (informal) (PERF* hat sich totgelacht*)* sich totlachen to laugh your head off

**Touchscreen** der *(PLURAL die* **Touchscreens***)* touchscreen

**Tour** die *(PLURAL die* **Touren***)* ❶ tour ❷ trip ❸ auf diese Tour *(informal)* in this way

**Tourismus** der tourism

**Tourist** der *(PLURAL die* **Touristen***)* tourist

**Touristeninformation** die *(PLURAL die* **Touristeninformationen***)* ❶ tourist information office ❷ tourist information

**Touristin** die *(PLURAL die* **Touristinnen***)* tourist

**Tournee** die *(PLURAL die* **Tournees***)* tour

**traben** *VERB (PERF* ist getrabt*)* to trot

**Tradition** die *(PLURAL die Traditionen)* tradition

**traditionell** *ADJECTIVE* traditional

**traf** ▸ SEE **treffen**

**tragbar** *ADJECTIVE* ❶ portable ❷ wearable

**tragen** ◇*VERB (PRES* **trägt**, *IMP* **trug**, *PERF* **hat getragen)** ❶ to carry ❷ to wear; sie trug ein weißes Kleid she wore a white dress, man trägt wieder kurz short skirts are in fashion again ❸ to bear; die Verantwortung für etwas tragen to be responsible for something ❹ to support; die Organisation trägt sich selbst the organization is self-supporting

**Träger** der *(PLURAL die Träger)* ❶ porter ❷ bearer *(of a name, title)* ❸ strap *(of a dress)* ❹ girder

**Tragetasche** die *(PLURAL die Tragetaschen)* carrier bag

**tragisch** *ADJECTIVE* tragic

**Tragödie** die *(PLURAL die Tragödien)* tragedy

**Trainer** der *(PLURAL die Trainer)* coach, trainer

**trainieren** *VERB (PERF* **hat trainiert)** ❶ to coach ❷ to train

**Training** das training

**Trainingsanzug** der *(PLURAL die Trainingsanzüge)* tracksuit

**Trainingsschuh** der *(PLURAL die Trainingsschuhe)* trainer *(shoe)*

**Traktor** der *(PLURAL die Traktoren)* tractor

**trampen** *VERB (PERF* **ist getrampt)** to hitchhike

**Trampen** das hitchhiking

**Tramper** der *(PLURAL die Tramper)* hitchhiker

**Tramperin** die *(PLURAL die Tramperinnen)* hitchhiker

**Träne** die *(PLURAL die Tränen)* tear

**trank** ▸ SEE **trinken**

**Transplantation** die *(PLURAL die Transplantationen)* transplant

**Transport** der *(PLURAL die Transporte)* ❶ transport ❷ consignment

**transportieren** *VERB (PERF* **hat transportiert)** to transport

**trat** ▸ SEE **treten**

**Traube** die *(PLURAL die Trauben)* grape

**trauen** *VERB (PERF* **hat getraut)** ❶ to trust; jemandem trauen to trust somebody ❷ sich trauen to dare, Ich trau mich nicht I don't dare ❸ to marry

**Trauer** die ❶ grief ❷ mourning

**Traum** der *(PLURAL die Träume)* dream

**träumen** *VERB (PERF* **hat geträumt)** to dream

**traumhaft** *ADJECTIVE* fabulous

**traurig** *ADJECTIVE* sad

**Traurigkeit** die sadness

**Trauung** die *(PLURAL die Trauungen)* wedding

**Trauzeuge** der *(PLURAL die Trauzeugen)* witness *(at a wedding ceremony)*

**treffen** ◇*VERB (PRES* **trifft**, *IMP* **traf**, *PERF* **hat getroffen)** ❶ to hit ❷ to meet ❸ to make *(arrangements, a decision)* ❹ sich mit jemandem treffen to meet somebody ❺ sich gut treffen to be convenient ❻ *(PERF* ist getroffen) auf etwas treffen to meet with *(resistance, difficulties)*

**Treffen** das *(PLURAL die* **Treffen)** meeting

**Treffer** der *(PLURAL die* **Treffer)** ❶ hit ❷ winner ❸ goal

**Treffpunkt** der *(PLURAL die* **Treffpunkte)** meeting place

**treiben** ◇*VERB (IMP* **trieb,** *PERF* **hat getrieben)** ❶ to drive ❷ to do; viel Sport treiben to do a lot of sport, Handel treiben to trade ❸ jemanden zur Eile treiben to hurry somebody up ❹ Unsinn treiben to mess about ❺ *(PERF* ist getrieben) to drift

**Treibhaus** das *(PLURAL die* **Treibhäuser)** hothouse

**Treibhauseffekt** der greenhouse effect

**Treibstoff** der fuel

**trennen** *VERB (PERF* hat getrennt) ❶ to separate ❷ to divide *(words, parts of a room)* ❸ sich trennen to separate, wir haben uns getrennt we've separated, Jutta hat sich von ihm getrennt Jutta has left him ❹ sich von etwas trennen to part with something

**Trennung** die *(PLURAL die* **Trennungen)** ❶ separation ❷ division

**Treppe** die *(PLURAL die* **Treppen)** stairs; eine Treppe a flight of stairs

**Treppenhaus** das stairwell; im Treppenhaus on the stairs

**treten** ◇*VERB (PRES* **tritt,** *IMP* **trat,** *PERF* **ist getreten)** ❶ to step ❷ to tread ❸ to kick ❹ mit jemandem in Verbindung treten to get in touch with somebody

**treu** *ADJECTIVE* faithful

**Treuekarte** die *(PLURAL die* **Treuekarten)** loyalty card

**Tribüne** die *(PLURAL die* **Tribünen)** ❶ stand *(in a stadium)* ❷ platform

**Trick** der *(PLURAL die* **Tricks)** trick

**Trickfilm** der *(PLURAL die* **Trickfilme)** cartoon

**trieb** ▸ SEE **treiben**

**trifft** ▸ SEE **treffen**

**Trimm-dich-Pfad** der *(PLURAL die* **Trimm-dich-Pfade)** keep-fit trail

**trimmen** *VERB (PERF* hat getrimmt) ❶ to trim ❷ sich trimmen to keep fit

**trinken** ◇*VERB (IMP* **trank,** *PERF* **hat getrunken)** to drink

**Trinkgeld** das *(PLURAL die* **Trinkgelder)** tip

**Trinkschokolade** die drinking chocolate

**Trinkwasser** das drinking water

**tritt** ▸ SEE **treten**

**Tritt** der *(PLURAL die* **Tritte)** ❶ step ❷ kick

**Triumph** der *(PLURAL die* **Triumphe)** triumph

**trocken** *ADJECTIVE* dry

**trockenlegen** *VERB (PERF* hat trockengelegt) to drain *(a marsh, a pond)*

**trocknen** *VERB (PERF* hat getrocknet) to dry

a b c d e f g h i j k l m n o p q r s **t** u v w x y z

**Trockner** der *(PLURAL* die **Trockner)** drier

**Trödel** der *(informal)* junk

**Trödelmarkt** der *(PLURAL* die **Trödelmärkte)** flea market

**Trommel** die *(PLURAL* die **Trommeln)** drum

**trommeln** VERB *(PERF* hat getrommelt) to drum

**Trompete** die *(PLURAL* die **Trompeten)** trumpet

**Tropen** PLURAL NOUN die Tropen the tropics

**tropfen** VERB *(PERF* hat getropft) to drip

**Tropfen** der *(PLURAL* die **Tropfen)** drop

**Trophäe** die *(PLURAL* die **Trophäen)** trophy

**tropisch** ADJECTIVE tropical

**trösten** VERB *(PERF* hat getröstet) to console, to comfort

**trotz** PREPOSITION *(+GEN)* despite, in spite of

**trotzdem** ADVERB nevertheless

**trüb** ADJECTIVE ❶ dull, dismal ❷ cloudy *(liquid)*

**trübsinnig** ADJECTIVE gloomy

**trug** ▸ SEE tragen

**Truhe** die *(PLURAL* die **Truhen)** chest

**Trümmer** PLURAL NOUN ruins

**Trumpf** der *(PLURAL* die **Trümpfe)** ❶ trump (card) ❷ trumps

**Trunkenheit** die drunkenness; Trunkenheit am Steuer drink-driving

**Truppen** PLURAL NOUN troops

**Truthahn** der *(PLURAL* die **Truthähne)** turkey

**Tscheche** der *(PLURAL* die **Tschechen)** Czech

**Tschechin** die *(PLURAL* die **Tschechinnen)** Czech

**tschechisch** ADJECTIVE Czech

**Tschechische Republik** die Czech Republic

**tschüss** EXCLAMATION bye!

**T-Shirt** das *(PLURAL* die **T-Shirts)** T-shirt

**Tube** die *(PLURAL* die **Tuben)** tube

**Tuberkulose** die tuberculosis

**Tuch** das *(PLURAL* die **Tücher)** ❶ cloth ❷ scarf

**tüchtig** ADJECTIVE ❶ efficient ❷ competent

**Tüchtigkeit** die ❶ efficiency ❷ competence

**Tulpe** die *(PLURAL* die **Tulpen)** tulip

**Tumor** der *(PLURAL* die **Tumoren)** tumour

**tun** ◇VERB *(PRES* tut, IMP tat, PERF getan) ❶ to do; das tut man nicht it isn't done, das tut's *(informal)* that'll do ❷ to put; die Butter in den Kühlschrank tun to put the butter in the fridge ❸ to pretend; er tut nur so he's only pretending ❹ to act; freundlich tun to act friendly ❺ jemandem etwas tun to hurt somebody ❻ mit jemandem etwas zu tun haben to have dealings with somebody, das hat nichts damit zu tun it's got nothing to do with it ❼ das tut nichts it doesn't matter, es hat sich viel getan lots has happened

**Tunesien** das Tunisia

**Tunesier** der *(PLURAL* die **Tunesier)** Tunisian

**Tunesierin** die *(PLURAL* die **Tunesierinnen)** Tunisian

**tunesisch** *ADJECTIVE* Tunisian

**Tunfisch** der *(PLURAL* die **Tunfische)** tuna

**Tunnel** der *(PLURAL* die **Tunnel)** tunnel

**tupfen** *VERB (PERF* hat **getupft)** to dab

**Tupfen** der *(PLURAL* die **Tupfen)** dot

**Tür** die *(PLURAL* die **Türen)** door

**Türke** der *(PLURAL* die **Türken)** Turk

**Türkei** die Turkey

**Türkin** die *(PLURAL* die **Türkinnen)** Turk

**türkis** *ADJECTIVE* turquoise

**türkisch** *ADJECTIVE* Turkish

**Turm** der *(PLURAL* die **Türme)** ❶ tower ❷ steeple ❸ rook, castle *(in chess)*

**Turnanzug** der *(PLURAL* die **Turnanzüge)** leotard

**turnen** *VERB (PERF* hat **geturnt)** to do gymnastics

**Turnen** das ❶ gymnastics ❷ physical education, PE

**Turnhalle** die *(PLURAL* die **Turnhallen)** gymnasium, gym

**Turnier** das *(PLURAL* die **Turniere)** tournament

**Turnschuh** der *(PLURAL* die **Turnschuhe)** ❶ trainer ❷ gym shoe

**Turnverein** der *(PLURAL* die **Turnvereine)** gymnastics club

**tuscheln** *VERB (PERF* hat **getuschelt)** to whisper

**tut** ▸ SEE **tun**

**Tüte** die *(PLURAL* die **Tüten)** bag

**Typ** der *(PLURAL* die **Typen)** ❶ type ❷ *(informal)* bloke

**typisch** *ADJECTIVE* typical

a
b
c
d
e
f
g
h
i
j
k
l
m
n
o
p
q
r
s
t
u
v
w
x
y
z

# Uu

**U-Bahn** die *(PLURAL* die **U-Bahnen)** underground

**übel** *ADJECTIVE* ❶ **bad** ❷ **mir ist übel** I feel sick ❸ **etwas übel nehmen** to take offence at something, **jemandem etwas übel nehmen** to hold something against somebody

**Übelkeit** die **nausea**

**übelnehmen** ▸ SEE **übel**

**üben** *VERB (PERF* **hat geübt)** to practise

**über** *PREPOSITION* ❶ *(+DAT, or +ACC with movement towards a place)* **over**; **über Weihnachten** over Christmas ❷ **above**; **er wohnt über uns** he lives above us, **fünf Grad über Null** five degrees above zero ❸ **about**; **über etwas schreiben** to write about something ❹ **for**; **ein Scheck über hundert Euro** a cheque for one hundred euros ❺ **across** *(a field, the street)* ❻ **über Frankfurt fahren** to go via Frankfurt ❼ **über die Straße gehen** to cross the road

**über** *ADVERB* ❶ **über und über** over and over ❷ **jemandem über sein** to be better than somebody ❸ **über sein** *(informal)* to be left over ❹ **jemandem ist etwas über** *(informal)* somebody is fed up with something ❺ **etwas über haben** *(informal)* to be fed up with something, **Nudeln habe ich über** I'm getting fed up with pasta

**überall** *ADVERB* **everywhere**

**überarbeiten** *VERB (PERF* **hat überarbeitet))** to revise *(a text)*

**Überblick** der *(PLURAL* die **Überblicke)** ❶ **einen guten Überblick über etwas haben** to have a good view of something ❷ **overall view**; **den Überblick verlieren** to lose track of things ❸ **summary**

**überblicken** *VERB (PERF* **hat überblickt)** ❶ to overlook ❷ to assess

**Überdosis** die *(PLURAL* die **Überdosen)** **overdose**

**Überdruss** der **bis zum Überdruss** ad nauseam

**übereinander** *ADVERB* ❶ **one on top of the other** ❷ **übereinander sprechen** to talk about each other

**übereinstimmen** *VERB (PERF* **hat übereingestimmt)** to agree

**überempfindlich** *ADJECTIVE* **hypersensitive**

**überfahren** ◇*VERB (PRES* **überfährt**, *IMP* **überfuhr**, *PERF* **hat überfahren)** to run over; **das Kind ist von einem Auto überfahren worden** the child was run over by a car

**Überfahrt** die *(PLURAL* die **Überfahrten)** **crossing**

**Überfall** der *(PLURAL* die **Überfälle)** ❶ **attack** ❷ **raid**

**überfallen** ◇*VERB (PRES* **überfällt**, *IMP* **überfiel**, *PERF* **hat überfallen)** ❶ to attack, to mug ❷ to raid ❸ **jemanden mit Fragen überfallen** to bombard somebody with questions

**überfällig** ADJECTIVE **overdue**

**überflüssig** ADJECTIVE **superfluous**

**Überführung** die (PLURAL die Überführungen) ❶ transfer ❷ flyover ❸ footbridge

**überfüllt** ADJECTIVE ❶ crowded ❷ oversubscribed

**Übergang** der (PLURAL die Übergänge) ❶ crossing ❷ transition

**übergeben** ◇VERB (PRES **übergibt**, IMP **übergab**, PERF **hat übergeben**) ❶ to hand over ❷ sich übergeben to be sick

**übergewichtig** ADJECTIVE overweight

**überhaben** ▸SEE **über**

**überhaupt** ADVERB ❶ in general ❷ anyway; was will er überhaupt? what does he want anyway? ❸ überhaupt nicht not at all, überhaupt nichts nothing at all, überhaupt keine Zeit haben to have no time at all

**überholen** VERB (PERF **hat überholt**) ❶ to overtake ❷ to overhaul

**überholt** ADJECTIVE out-of-date

**überlassen** ◇VERB (PRES **überlässt**, IMP **überließ**, PERF **hat überlassen**) ❶ jemandem etwas überlassen to let somebody have something ❷ etwas jemandem überlassen to leave something up to somebody (a decision, for example), das bleibt dir überlassen it's up to you

**überlaufen** ◇VERB (PRES **läuft über**, IMP **lief über**, PERF **ist übergelaufen**) to overflow

**überleben** VERB (PERF **hat überlebt**) to survive

**überlegen**[1] VERB (PERF **hat überlegt**) ❶ to think; sich etwas überlegen to think something over, ohne zu überlegen without thinking ❷ ich habe es mir anders überlegt I've changed my mind

**überlegen**[2] ADJECTIVE ❶ superior; jemandem überlegen sein to be superior to somebody ❷ convincing (victory)

**überm** über dem ▸SEE **über**

**übermäßig** ADJECTIVE excessive

**übermorgen** ADVERB the day after tomorrow

**übernächster, übernächste, übernächstes** ADJECTIVE next but one; übernächstes Jahr the year after next

**übernachten** VERB (PERF **hat übernachtet**) to stay the night; bei jemandem übernachten to stay the night at somebody's house

**übernehmen** ◇VERB (PRES **übernimmt**, IMP **übernahm**, PERF **hat übernommen**) ❶ to take over ❷ to take on ❸ sich übernehmen to take on too much

**überqueren** VERB (PERF **hat überquert**) to cross

**überraschen** VERB (PERF **hat überrascht**) to surprise

**Überraschung** die (PLURAL die Überraschungen) surprise

**überreden** VERB (PERF **hat überredet**) to persuade

**übers** über das.

**Überschrift** die *(PLURAL* die Überschriften) heading

**überschüssig** *ADJECTIVE* surplus

**überschütten** *VERB (PERF* hat überschüttet) jemanden mit etwas überschütten to shower somebody with something

**Überschwemmung** die *(PLURAL* die Überschwemmungen) flood

**übersehen**[1] *◇VERB (PRES* **übersieht**, *IMP* **übersah**, *PERF* hat übersehen) ❶ to overlook; *(informal)* einen Fehler übersehen to overlook a mistake ❷ to assess *(consequences, damages)*

**übersehen**[2] *◇VERB (PRES* **sieht sich über**, *IMP* **sah sich über**, *PERF* hat sich übergesehen)* sich etwas übersehen *(informal)* to get fed up of seeing something

**übersetzen** *VERB (PERF* hat übersetzt) to translate

**Übersetzer** der *(PLURAL* die Übersetzer) translator

**Übersetzerin** die *(PLURAL* die Übersetzerinnen) translator

**Übersetzung** die *(PLURAL* die Übersetzungen) translation

**Übersicht** die ❶ overall view ❷ summary

**überspringen** *◇VERB (IMP* **übersprang**, *PERF* hat übersprungen) ❶ to jump (over) ❷ to skip *(a chapter)*

**überstehen** *◇VERB (IMP* **überstand**, *PERF* hat überstanden) ❶ to get over ❷ to survive

**Überstunden** *PLURAL NOUN* overtime; Überstunden machen to work overtime

**übertragen** *◇VERB (PRES* **überträgt**, *IMP* **übertrug**, *PERF* hat übertragen) ❶ to transfer ❷ to transmit ❸ to broadcast ❹ etwas ins Reine übertragen to make a fair copy of something ❺ sich auf jemanden übertragen to communicate itself to somebody *(of enthusiasm or nervousness)*

**Übertragung** die *(PLURAL* die Übertragungen) ❶ broadcast ❷ transmission

**übertreiben** *◇VERB (IMP* **übertrieb**, *PERF* hat übertrieben) ❶ to exaggerate ❷ to overdo

**Übertreibung** die *(PLURAL* die Übertreibungen) exaggeration

**überwältigend** *ADJECTIVE* overwhelming

**überweisen** *◇VERB (IMP* **überwies**, *PERF* hat überwiesen) ❶ to transfer ❷ to refer *(a patient)*

**überzeugen** *VERB (PERF* hat überzeugt) ❶ to convince ❷ sich selbst überzeugen to satisfy yourself

**überzeugend** *ADJECTIVE* convincing

**Überzeugung** die *(PLURAL* die Überzeugungen) conviction

**überziehen**[1] *◇VERB (IMP* **zog über**, *PERF* hat übergezogen) to put on *(a cardigan, jacket)*

**überziehen**[2] *◇VERB (IMP* **überzog**, *PERF* hat überzogen) ❶ to overdraw ❷ to cover *(with icing, for example)*

**üblich** *ADJECTIVE* usual

**U-Boot** das *(PLURAL* die U-Boote) submarine

**übrig** *ADJECTIVE* ❶ remaining ❷ übrig sein to be left over ❸ etwas übrig lassen to leave something (over) ❹ uns blieb nichts anderes übrig we had no other choice ❺ alles Übrige the rest, die Übrigen the others ❻ im Übrigen besides

**übrigens** *ADVERB* by the way

**übriglassen** ▸ SEE **übrig**

**Übung** die *(PLURAL die* **Übungen***)* ❶ exercise ❷ practice; aus der Übung sein to be out of practice

**Ufer** das *(PLURAL die* **Ufer***)* ❶ bank *(of a river)* ❷ shore

**Uhr** die *(PLURAL die* **Uhren***)* ❶ clock ❷ watch ❸ *(in time phrases)* es ist ein Uhr it's one o'clock wie viel Uhr ist es? what's the time?, um sechzehn Uhr at four o'clock (in the afternoon)

**Uhrzeiger** der *(PLURAL die* **Uhrzeiger***)* hand *(of a clock or watch)*

**Uhrzeigersinn** der im Uhrzeigersinn clockwise, entgegen dem Uhrzeigersinn anti-clockwise

**Uhrzeit** die time; jemanden nach der Uhrzeit fragen to ask somebody the time

**ulkig** *ADJECTIVE* funny

**um** *PREPOSITION (+ACC)* ❶ round, around; um das Haus herum around the house ❷ at; um fünf Uhr at five o'clock ❸ around (about) ❹ for; um etwas bitten to ask for something, um seinetwillen for his sake ❺ sich um jemanden sorgen to worry about somebody ❻ by *(indicating difference)*; um vieles besser better by far, um so besser so much the better

**um** *ADVERB* ❶ about, around; um

die dreihundert Euro herum about three hundred euros, um Weihnachten around Christmas ❷ um sein *(informal)* to be over

**um** *CONJUNCTION* um zu (in order) to, er ist noch zu klein, um in die Schule zu gehen he's too young to go to school

**umarmen** *VERB (PERF* **hat umarmt***)* to hug

**Umbau** der *(PLURAL die* **Umbauten***)* ❶ renovation ❷ conversion

**umbinden** ⬦*VERB (IMP* **band um***, PERF* **hat umgebunden***)* to put on

**umblättern** *VERB (PERF* **hat umgeblättert***)* to turn over

**umbringen** ⬦*VERB (IMP* **brachte um***, PERF* **hat umgebracht***)* to kill

**umdrehen** *VERB (PERF* **hat umgedreht***)* ❶ to turn (round) ❷ sich umdrehen to turn round, to turn over

**umfallen** ⬦*VERB (PRES* **fällt um***, IMP* **fiel um***, PERF* **ist umgefallen***)* to fall down

**Umfrage** die *(PLURAL die* **Umfragen***)* survey

**umgänglich** *ADJECTIVE* sociable

**Umgangsformen** *PLURAL NOUN* manners

**Umgangssprache** die slang, colloquial language

**umgeben** ⬦*VERB (PRES* **umgibt***, IMP* **umgab***, PERF* **hat umgeben***)* to surround

**Umgebung** die *(PLURAL die* **Umgebungen***)* ❶ surroundings ❷ neighbourhood

a
b
c
d
e
f
g
h
i
j
k
l
m
n
o
p
q
r
s
t
**u**
v
w
x
y
z

**umgehen**[1] ◇*VERB* (*IMP* **ging um**, *PERF* **ist umgegangen**) ❶ to go round (*of a rumour, an illness*) ❷ mit jemandem streng umgehen to treat somebody strictly ❸ er kann mit Geld nicht umgehen he can't handle money, mit seinen Sachen sorgfältig umgehen to handle one's things carefully

**umgehen**[2] ◇*VERB* (*IMP* **umging**, *PERF* **hat umgangen**) to avoid

**Umgehungsstraße** die (*PLURAL* die **Umgehungsstraßen**) bypass

**umgekehrt** *ADJECTIVE* ❶ opposite ❷ reverse (*order*) ❸ es war umgekehrt it was the other way round

**umgekehrt** *ADVERB* ❶ und umgekehrt and vice versa ❷ the other way round; warum machst du es nicht umgekehrt? why don't you do it the other way round?

**umkehren** *VERB* (*PERF* **ist umgekehrt**) ❶ to turn back; nach zehn Minuten sind wir wieder umgekehrt ten minutes later we turned back again ❷ to turn round (*a picture, book*) ❸ to turn inside out (*a bag, for example*) ❹ sie hat das ganze Zimmer umgekehrt (*informal*) she turned the whole room upside down

**Umkleidekabine** die (*PLURAL* die **Umkleidekabinen**) changing cubicle

**Umkleideraum** der (*PLURAL* die **Umkleideräume**) changing room

**umkommen** ◇*VERB* (*IMP* **kam um**, *PERF* **ist umgekommen**) to be killed

**Umlaut** der (*PLURAL* die **Umlaute**) umlaut

**umlegen** *VERB* (*PERF* **hat umgelegt**) ❶ to put on (*a scarf*) ❷ to transfer (*a patient, call*) ❸ jemanden umlegen (*informal*) to bump somebody off

**Umleitung** die (*PLURAL* die **Umleitungen**) diversion

**umrechnen** *VERB* (*PERF* **hat umgerechnet**) to convert

**Umrechnung** die conversion

**Umrechnungskurs** der exchange rate

**Umriss** der (*PLURAL* die **Umrisse**) outline

**umrühren** *VERB* (*PERF* **hat umgerührt**) to stir

**ums** um das.

**umschalten** *VERB* (*PERF* **hat umgeschaltet**) ❶ to turn over; vom ersten aufs zweite Programm umschalten to turn from channel one to channel two ❷ auf Rot umschalten to change to red

**Umschlag** der (*PLURAL* die **Umschläge**) ❶ envelope ❷ cover

**umsehen** ◇*VERB* (*PRES* **sieht sich um**, *IMP* **sah sich um**, *PERF* **hat sich umgesehen**) sich umsehen to look round

**umso** *ADVERB* umso besser all the better, je mehr, umso besser the more the better

**umsonst** *ADVERB* ❶ in vain ❷ free, for nothing

**Umstand** der (*PLURAL* die **Umstände**) ❶ circumstance; unter diesen Umständen under these circumstances ❷ unter Umständen possibly ❸ jemandem Umstände machen to put somebody to trouble, das macht gar keine Umstände it's no trouble at all **❹** in anderen Umständen sein to be pregnant

**umständlich** ADJECTIVE **❶** laborious **❷** complicated

**umsteigen** ◇VERB (IMP **stieg um**, PERF ist **umgestiegen**) to change

**umstellen¹** VERB (PERF **hat umgestellt**) **❶** to rearrange **❷** to reset **❸** to change over **❹** sich umstellen to adjust

**umstellen²** VERB (PERF **hat umstellt**) to surround

**Umtausch** der exchange

**umtauschen** VERB (PERF **hat umgetauscht**) to change, to exchange

**Umweg** der (PLURAL die **Umwege**) detour

**Umwelt** die environment

**umweltfeindlich** ADJECTIVE environmentally unfriendly

**umweltfreundlich** ADJECTIVE environmentally friendly

**Umweltschützer** der (PLURAL die **Umweltschützer**) environmentalist

**Umweltschützerin** die (PLURAL die **Umweltschützerinnen**) environmentalist

**Umweltverschmutzung** die pollution

**umwerfen** ◇VERB (PRES **wirft um**, IMP **warf um**, PERF **hat umgeworfen**) **❶** to knock over **❷** to upset (a plan); das hat mich umgeworfen it's thrown me

**umwerfend** ADJECTIVE fantastic

**umziehen** ◇VERB (IMP **zog um**, PERF ist **umgezogen**) **❶** to move; sie ziehen nächste Woche um they're moving next week **❷** (PERF **hat umgezogen**) to change **❸** (PERF **hat sich umgezogen**) sich umziehen to get changed

**Umzug** der (PLURAL die **Umzüge**) **❶** move **❷** procession

**unabhängig** ADJECTIVE independent

**Unabhängigkeit** die independence

**unangenehm** ADJECTIVE **❶** unpleasant **❷** embarrassing (question, situation)

**unartig** ADJECTIVE naughty

**unbedeutend** ADJECTIVE insignificant

**unbedeutend** ADVERB slightly

**unbedingt** ADJECTIVE absolute

**unbedingt** ADVERB really; ich muss ihn unbedingt sprechen I really must talk to him, nicht unbedingt not necessarily

**unbefriedigend** ADJECTIVE unsatisfactory

**unbefriedigt** ADJECTIVE unsatisfied

**unbegrenzt** ADJECTIVE unlimited

**unbehaglich** ADJECTIVE **❶** uncomfortable **❷** uneasy

**unbekannt** ADJECTIVE unknown

**unbeliebt** ADJECTIVE unpopular

**unbequem** ADJECTIVE uncomfortable

**unbestimmt** ADJECTIVE **❶** indefinite; auf unbestimmte Zeit for an indefinite period **❷** uncertain

**unbestimmt** *ADVERB* **vaguely**; etwas unbestimmt lassen to leave something open

**unbewusst** *ADJECTIVE* **unconscious**

**und** *CONJUNCTION* **and**; und so weiter and so on, na und? so what?

**undankbar** *ADJECTIVE* **ungrateful**

**undeutlich** *ADJECTIVE* **unclear**

**undicht** *ADJECTIVE* **leaking, leaky**; eine undichte Stelle a leak

**uneben** *ADJECTIVE* **uneven**

**unehrlich** *ADJECTIVE* **dishonest**

**unempfindlich** *ADJECTIVE* ❶ **hard-wearing, easy-care** ❷ **immune**; gegen Kälte unempfindlich sein not to feel the cold

**unentbehrlich** *ADJECTIVE* **indispensable**

**unentschieden** *ADJECTIVE* **undecided**; unentschieden spielen to draw

**unerträglich** *ADJECTIVE* **unbearable**

**unerwartet** *ADJECTIVE* **unexpected**

**unfähig** *ADJECTIVE* ❶ **incompetent** ❷ unfähig sein, etwas zu tun to be incapable of doing something

**unfair** *ADJECTIVE* **unfair**

**Unfall** der *(PLURAL die* **Unfälle***)* **accident**

**unfreundlich** *ADJECTIVE* **unfriendly**

**Unfug** der ❶ **nonsense** ❷ **mischief**; Unfug machen to get up to mischief

**Ungar** der *(PLURAL die* **Ungarn***)* **Hungarian**

**Ungarin** die *(PLURAL die* **Ungarinnen***)* **Hungarian**

**ungarisch** *ADJECTIVE* **Hungarian**

**Ungarn** das **Hungary**

**Ungeduld** die **impatience**

**ungeduldig** *ADJECTIVE* **impatient**

**ungeeignet** *ADJECTIVE* **unsuitable**

**ungefähr** *ADJECTIVE* **approximate**

**ungefähr** *ADVERB* **approximately, about**

**ungefährlich** *ADJECTIVE* **safe, harmless**

**ungeheuer** *ADJECTIVE* **enormous**

**Ungeheuer** das *(PLURAL die* **Ungeheuer***)* **monster**

**ungehorsam** *ADJECTIVE* **disobedient**

**ungelegen** *ADJECTIVE* **inconvenient**

**ungemütlich** *ADJECTIVE* **uncomfortable**

**ungenau** *ADJECTIVE* ❶ **inaccurate** ❷ **vague**

**ungenießbar** *ADJECTIVE* ❶ **inedible** ❷ **undrinkable** ❸ Bernd ist heute aber ungenießbar *(informal)* Bernd is quite unbearable today

**ungenügend** *ADJECTIVE* ❶ **insufficient** ❷ **unsatisfactory** *(mark at school)*

**ungerade** *ADJECTIVE* eine ungerade Zahl an odd number

**ungerecht** *ADJECTIVE* **unjust**

**ungern** *ADVERB* **reluctantly**

**ungeschickt** *ADJECTIVE* **clumsy**

**ungesund** *ADJECTIVE* **unhealthy**

**ungewöhnlich** *ADJECTIVE* **unusual**

**Ungeziefer** das **vermin**

**ungezwungen** *ADJECTIVE*
❶ informal ❷ natural

**unglaublich** *ADJECTIVE* incredible

**Unglück** das *(PLURAL* die **Unglücke)**
❶ accident ❷ misfortune ❸ bad
luck; das bringt Unglück that's
unlucky

**unglücklich** *ADJECTIVE* ❶ unhappy
❷ unfortunate

**unglücklicherweise** *ADVERB*
unfortunately

**unheilbar** *ADJECTIVE* incurable

**unheimlich** *ADJECTIVE* eerie

**unheimlich** *ADVERB* ❶ eerily
❷ *(informal)* incredibly; unheimlich
viel an incredible amount

**unhöflich** *ADJECTIVE* impolite

**Uniform** die *(PLURAL* die **Uniformen)**
uniform

**uninteressant** *ADJECTIVE*
uninteresting

**Universität** die *(PLURAL* die
**Universitäten)** university

**Unkenntnis** die ignorance

**unklar** *ADJECTIVE* unclear

**Unkosten** *PLURAL NOUN* expenses

**Unkraut** das weed

**unleserlich** *ADJECTIVE* illegible

**unlogisch** *ADJECTIVE* illogical

**unmittelbar** *ADJECTIVE* immediate,
direct

**unmodern** *ADJECTIVE* old-fashioned

**unmöglich** *ADJECTIVE* impossible

**Unmöglichkeit** die impossibility

**unnötig** *ADJECTIVE* unnecessary

**unordentlich** *ADJECTIVE* untidy

**Unordnung** die ❶ disorder ❷ mess

**unpraktisch** *ADJECTIVE* impractical

**unpünktlich** *ADJECTIVE* unpunctual;
unpünktlich sein to be late

**unrecht** *ADJECTIVE* wrong; jemandem
unrecht tun to do somebody an
injustice

**Unrecht** das ❶ wrong; zu Unrecht
wrongly, Unrecht haben to be
wrong ❷ jemandem Unrecht geben
to disagree with somebody

**unregelmäßig** *ADJECTIVE* irregular

**unreif** *ADJECTIVE* ❶ unripe
❷ immature

**Unruhe** die *(PLURAL* die **Unruhen)**
❶ restlessness ❷ agitation
❸ Unruhen unrest

**Unruhestifter** der *(PLURAL* die
**Unruhestifter)** troublemaker

**unruhig** *ADJECTIVE* restless

**uns** *PRONOUN* ❶ us; gib es uns give it
to us, sie kommen mit uns they're
coming with us ❷ ourselves; wir
waschen uns die Hände we are
washing our hands ❸ each other;
wir kennen uns we know each
other

**unscharf** *ADJECTIVE* blurred,
indistinct

**unschuldig** *ADJECTIVE* innocent

**unser** *PRONOUN* our

**unserer, unsere, unser(e)s**
*PRONOUN* ours

**unsertwegen** *ADVERB* ❶ for our
sake ❷ because of us ❸ as far as
we're concerned

**unsicher** ADJECTIVE ❶ uncertain ❷ insecure

**unsicher** ADVERB unsteadily

**unsichtbar** ADJECTIVE invisible

**Unsinn** der nonsense

**unsrer** ▸ SEE unserer

**unsympathisch** ADJECTIVE unpleasant; Tobias ist mir unsympathisch I don't like Tobias

**unten** ADVERB ❶ at the bottom ❷ underneath ❸ downstairs; hier unten down here, nach unten down

**unter** PREPOSITION ❶ (+DAT or +ACC with movement towards a place) under, below ❷ among; unter anderem among other things ❸ unter sich by themselves, unter uns gesagt between ourselves ❹ unter der Woche during the week

**Unterbewusstsein** das subconscious

**unterbrechen** ◇VERB (PRES unterbricht, IMP unterbrach, PERF hat unterbrochen) to interrupt

**Unterbrechung** die (PLURAL die Unterbrechungen) interruption

**unterbringen** ◇VERB (IMP brachte unter, PERF hat untergebracht) ❶ to put ❷ to put up (a guest)

**untere** ▸ SEE unterer

**untereinander** ADVERB ❶ among ourselves/yourselves/ themselves ❷ one below the other

**unterer, untere, unteres** ADJECTIVE lower

**Unterführung** die (PLURAL die Unterführungen) subway

**untergehen** ◇VERB (IMP ging unter, PERF ist untergegangen) ❶ to set (of the sun) ❷ to sink, to drown ❸ to come to an end

**Untergrundbahn** die (PLURAL die Untergrundbahnen) underground

**unterhalb** PREPOSITION (+GEN) below

**unterhalten** ◇VERB (PRES unterhält, IMP unterhielt, PERF hat unterhalten) ❶ to support ❷ to run (a hotel, leisure centre) ❸ to entertain ❹ sich über etwas unterhalten to talk about something ❺ sich unterhalten to enjoy yourself

**unterhaltsam** ADJECTIVE entertaining

**Unterhaltung** die (PLURAL die Unterhaltungen) ❶ conversation ❷ entertainment

**Unterhemd** das (PLURAL die Unterhemden) vest

**Unterhose** die (PLURAL die Unterhosen) underpants

**Unterkunft** die (PLURAL die Unterkünfte) accommodation

**Unterlagen** PLURAL NOUN documents, papers

**Untermieter** der (PLURAL die Untermieter) lodger

**Untermieterin** die (PLURAL die Untermieterinnen) lodger

**unternehmen** ◇VERB (PRES unternimmt, IMP unternahm, PERF hat unternommen) ❶ to undertake ❷ nichts unternehmen to do nothing, was unternehmt ihr heute? what are you doing today?

**Unternehmen** das (PLURAL die Unternehmen) ❶ enterprise ❷ concern

**Unterricht** der ➊ lessons; heute haben wir keinen Unterricht we've got no lessons today ➋ teaching

**unterrichten** VERB (PERF hat unterrichtet) ➊ to teach ➋ to inform ➌ sich unterrichten to inform yourself

**Unterrichtsfach** das (PLURAL die Unterrichtsfächer) subject

**Unterrock** der (PLURAL die Unterröcke) slip

**unterscheiden** ◇VERB (IMP unterschied, PERF hat unterschieden) ➊ to distinguish, to tell apart ➋ sich unterscheiden to differ

**Unterschied** der (PLURAL die Unterschiede) difference

**unterschiedlich** ADJECTIVE different; das ist unterschiedlich it varies

**unterschreiben** ◇VERB (IMP unterschrieb, PERF hat unterschrieben) to sign

**Unterschrift** die (PLURAL die Unterschriften) signature

**Unterseeboot** (PLURAL die Unterseeboote) submarine

**unterster, unterste, unterstes** ADJECTIVE bottom, lowest

**unterstreichen** ◇VERB (IMP unterstrich, PERF hat unterstrichen) to underline

**unterstützen** VERB (PERF hat unterstüzt) to support

**Unterstützung** die support

**untersuchen** VERB (PERF hat untersucht) ➊ to examine ➋ to investigate

**Untersuchung** die (PLURAL die Untersuchungen) ➊ examination, check-up ➋ investigation

**Untertasse** die (PLURAL die Untertassen) saucer

**Untertitel** der (PLURAL die Untertitel) subtitle

**Unterwäsche** die underwear

**unterwegs** ADVERB on the way; den ganzen Tag unterwegs sein to be out all day

**untreu** ADJECTIVE ➊ unfaithful ➋ disloyal

**untüchtig** ADJECTIVE ➊ inefficient ➋ incompetent

**ununterbrochen** ADJECTIVE uninterrupted

**unverbleit** ADJECTIVE unleaded

**unvergleichlich** ADJECTIVE incomparable

**unverheiratet** ADJECTIVE unmarried

**unverkäuflich** ADJECTIVE not for sale; ein unverkäufliches Muster a free sample

**unverschämt** ADJECTIVE impertinent

**unverständlich** ADJECTIVE incomprehensible

**unverzüglich** ADJECTIVE promptly; bitte antworten Sie unverzüglich please reply promptly

**unvorsichtig** ADJECTIVE careless

**unwahr** ADJECTIVE untrue

**unwahrscheinlich** ADJECTIVE ➊ unlikely ➋ incredible

**unwahrscheinlich** ADVERB (informal) incredibly; unwahrscheinlich schön incredibly beautiful

259

**Unwetter** das (PLURAL die **Unwetter**)
storm

**unwichtig** ADJECTIVE unimportant

**unzählig** ADJECTIVE countless

**unzerbrechlich** ADJECTIVE
unbreakable

**unzertrennlich** ADJECTIVE
inseparable

**unzufrieden** ADJECTIVE dissatisfied

**uploaden** VERB (PERF hat
**upgeloadet**) to upload

**üppig** ADJECTIVE lavish

**uralt** ADJECTIVE ancient

**Urenkel** der (PLURAL die **Urenkel**)
great-grandson; die Urenkel the
great-grandchildren

**Urenkelin** die (PLURAL die
**Urenkelinnen**) great-
granddaughter

**Urkunde** die (PLURAL die **Urkunden**)
certificate

**Urlaub** der (PLURAL die **Urlaube**)
holiday; Urlaub haben to be on
holiday, auf/im Urlaub on holiday

**Urlauber** der (PLURAL die **Urlauber**)
holidaymaker

**Ursache** die (PLURAL die **Ursachen**)
cause; keine Ursache! don't
mention it!

**Ursprung** der (PLURAL die
**Ursprünge**) origin

**ursprünglich** ADJECTIVE original

**ursprünglich** ADVERB originally

**Urteil** das (PLURAL die **Urteile**)
❶ judgement ❷ opinion
❸ verdict

**urteilen** VERB (PERF hat **geurteilt**)
to judge

**Urwald** der (PLURAL die **Urwälder**)
jungle

**USA** PLURAL NOUN USA

**usw.** (short for und so weiter) etc.

# Vv

**vage** *ADJECTIVE* **vague**

**Vagina** die *(PLURAL die **Vaginen**)* vagina

**Valentinskarte** die *(PLURAL die **Valentinskarten**)* valentine card

**Valentinstag** der **Valentine's Day**

**Vandalismus** der **vandalism**

**Vanille** die **vanilla**

**Variante** DIE *(PLURAL die **Varianten**)* variety

**Vase** die *(PLURAL die **Vasen**)* vase

**Vater** der *(PLURAL die **Väter**)* father

**Vaterunser** das **Lord's Prayer**

**Vati** der *(PLURAL die **Vatis**)* dad

**Veganer** der *(PLURAL die **Veganer**)* vegan

**Vegetarier** der *(PLURAL die **Vegetarier**)* vegetarian

**Vegetarierin** die *(PLURAL die **Vegetarierinnen**)* vegetarian

**vegetarisch** *ADJECTIVE* **vegetarian**

**Veilchen** das *(PLURAL die **Veilchen**)* violet

**Vene** die *(PLURAL die **Venen**)* vein

**Ventil** das *(PLURAL die **Ventile**)* valve

**Ventilator** der *(PLURAL die **Ventilatoren**)* fan

**verabreden** VERB *(PERF **hat verabredet**)* ❶ to arrange; was habt ihr verabredet? what did you arrange?, mit jemandem verabredet sein to have arranged to meet somebody, Laura ist mit Frank verabredet Laura has a date with Frank ❷ sich mit jemandem verabreden to arrange to meet somebody, ich habe mich mit Oliver zum Tennis verabredet I've arranged to play tennis with Oliver

**Verabredung** die *(PLURAL die **Verabredungen**)* ❶ appointment ❷ date ❸ arrangement

**verabschieden** VERB *(PERF **hat verabschiedet**)* ❶ to say goodbye to ❷ sich verabschieden to say goodbye

**Verachtung** die **contempt**

**verallgemeinern** VERB *(PERF **hat verallgemeinert**)* to generalize

**veralten** VERB *(PERF **ist veraltet**)* to become obsolete

**veränderlich** *ADJECTIVE* **changeable**

**verändern** VERB *(PERF **hat verändert**)* ❶ to change ❷ sich verändern to change

**Veränderung** die *(PLURAL die **Veränderungen**)* change

**veranstalten** VERB *(PERF **hat veranstaltet**)* to organize

**Veranstalter** der *(PLURAL die **Veranstalter**)* organizer

**Veranstaltung** die *(PLURAL die **Veranstaltungen**)* event

**verantwortlich** *ADJECTIVE* **responsible**

**Verantwortung** die **responsibility**

**verantwortungsbewusst**
*ADJECTIVE* **responsible**

**verantwortungslos** *ADJECTIVE*
**irresponsible**

**verarbeiten** *VERB (PERF* **hat
verarbeitet) ❶ to process**; etwas
zu etwas verarbeiten to make
something into something **❷ to
digest** *(food, information)*

**Verarbeitung** die **❶ use
❷ digestion ❸ processing of data**

**verärgern** *VERB (PERF* **hat verärgert)**
**to annoy**

**Verb** das *(PLURAL* die **Verben) verb**

**verband ▸** SEE **verbinden**

**Verband** der *(PLURAL* die **Verbände)**
**❶ association**; sich zu einem
Verband zusammenschließen to
form an associaton **❷ bandage,
dressing**; einen Verband anlegen
to apply a dressing

**verbergen** ◇*VERB (PRES* **verbirgt,** *IMP*
**verbarg,** *PERF* **hat verborgen) ❶ to
hide ❷ sich verbergen to hide**

**verbessern** *VERB (PERF* **hat
verbessert) ❶ to improve ❷ to
correct ❸ sich verbessern to
improve**

**Verbesserung** die *(PLURAL*
die **Verbesserungen)**
**❶ improvement ❷ correction**

**verbiegen** ◇*VERB (IMP* **verbog,** *PERF*
**hat verbogen) ❶ to bend ❷ sich
verbiegen to bend**

**verbieten** ◇*VERB (IMP* **verbot,** *PERF*
**hat verboten) ❶ to forbid**; sie
hat ihm verboten, das Haus zu
betreten she forbade him to enter
the house, meine Eltern verbieten
mir, am Abend wegzugehen my

parents don't allow me to go out in
the evening **❷ to ban**

**verbilligt** *ADJECTIVE* **reduced**

**verbinden** ◇*VERB (IMP* **verband,** *PERF*
**hat verbunden) ❶ to connect, to
join ❷ to combine ❸ to bandage,
to dress** *(a wound)*; jemandem
die Augen verbinden to blindfold
somebody **❹ jemanden verbinden
to put somebody through** *(on the
phone)*, ich verbinde I'm putting
you through

**verbindlich** *ADJECTIVE* **❶ friendly
❷ binding** *(agreement, decision)*

**Verbindung** die *(PLURAL* die
**Verbindungen) ❶ connection
❷** gute Verbindungen haben
to have good contacts, sich mit
jemandem in Verbindung setzen
to get in touch with somebody
**❸ combination ❹** eine chemische
Verbindung a chemical compound

**verbirgt ▸** SEE **verbergen**

**verbleit** *ADJECTIVE* **leaded**

**verblüffen** *VERB (PERF* **hat verblüfft)**
**to amaze**

**verbog ▸** SEE **verbiegen**

**verbogen** *ADJECTIVE* **hidden**

**verbot ▸** SEE **verbieten**

**Verbot** das *(PLURAL* die **Verbote) ban**

**verboten** *ADJECTIVE* **forbidden**;
'Rauchen verboten' 'no smoking'

**verbracht, verbrachte
▸** SEE **verbringen**

**verbrannt, verbrannte
▸** SEE **verbrennen**

**Verbrauch** der **consumption**

**verbrauchen** *VERB (PERF* **hat verbraucht)** to use, to use up; die Waschmaschine verbraucht nicht viel Strom the washing machine doesn't use up much electricity

**Verbraucher** der *(PLURAL* die **Verbraucher)** consumer

**Verbrechen** das *(PLURAL* die **Verbrechen)** crime

**Verbrecher** der *(PLURAL* die **Verbrecher)** criminal

**verbreiten** *VERB (PERF* **hat verbreitet)** ❶ to spread; eine Krankheit verbreiten to spread an illness ❷ eine Meldung über den Rundfunk verbreiten to broadcast a message ❸ sich verbreiten to spread, die Neuigkeit hat sich schnell verbreitet the news spread quickly

**verbreitet** *ADJECTIVE* widespread

**verbrennen** ◇*VERB (IMP* **verbrannte,** *PERF* **ist verbrannt)** ❶ to burn ❷ *(PERF* **hat verbrannt)** to burn *(rubbish, leaves)* ❸ *(PERF* **hat verbrannt)** to cremate ❹ *(PERF* **hat verbrannt)** sich die Hand verbrennen to burn your hand

**verbringen** ◇*VERB (IMP* **verbrachte,** *PERF* **hat verbracht)** to spend; wir haben schöne Ferien in Bayern verbracht we spent a nice holiday in Bavaria

**verbunden** ▸ SEE **verbinden**

**Verdacht** der suspicion

**verdächtig** *ADJECTIVE* suspicious

**verdächtigen** *VERB (PERF* **hat verdächtigt)** to suspect

**verdammt** *ADJECTIVE, ADVERB (informal)* damned; verdammt! damn!

**verdarb** ▸ SEE **verderben**

**Verdauung** die digestion

**verderben** ◇*VERB (PRES* **verdirbt,** *IMP* **verdarb,** *PERF* **hat verdorben)** ❶ to spoil, to ruin; das hat mir den Abend verdorben it ruined the evening for me, ich habe mir den Magen verdorben I have an upset stomach ❷ es sich mit jemandem verderben to get into somebody's bad books ❸ *(PERF* **ist verdorben)** to go off; die Milch verdirbt, wenn du sie nicht in den Kühlschrank stellst the milk will go off if you don't put it in the fridge

**verdienen** *VERB (PERF* **hat verdient)** ❶ to earn ❷ to deserve

**Verdienst** der *(PLURAL* die **Verdienste)** ❶ salary ❷ achievement

**verdirbt** ▸ SEE **verderben**

**verdoppeln** *VERB (PERF* **hat verdoppelt)** ❶ to double ❷ sich verdoppeln to double

**verdorben** ▸ SEE **verderben**

**verdünnen** *VERB (PERF* **hat verdünnt)** to dilute

**verehren** *VERB (PERF* **hat verehrt)** to worship

**Verehrer** der *(PLURAL* die **Verehrer)** admirer

**Verehrerin** die *(PLURAL* die **Verehrerinnen)** admirer

**Verein** der *(PLURAL* die **Vereine)** ❶ society ❷ organization ❸ club

**vereinbaren** *VERB (PERF* **hat vereinbart)** to arrange

**Vereinbarung** die *(PLURAL* die **Vereinbarungen)** ❶ agreement ❷ arrangement

a
b
c
d
e
f
g
h
i
j
k
l
m
n
o
p
q
r
s
t
u
v
w
x
y
z

**vereinfachen** *VERB (PERF* **hat vereinfacht)** to simplify

**vereinigen** *VERB (PERF* **hat vereinigt)** to unite; ein Land wieder vereinigen to reunify a country

**Vereinigte Staaten** *PLURAL NOUN* United States

**Vereinigung** die *(PLURAL* die Vereinigungen) organization

**verfahren** ◇*VERB (PRES* **verfährt,** *IMP* **verfuhr,** *PERF* **ist verfahren)** ❶ to proceed ❷ ich habe mich verfahren I've lost my way

**verfallen** ◇*VERB (PRES* **verfällt,** *IMP* **verfiel,** *PERF* **ist verfallen)** ❶ to decay ❷ to expire *(of a passport or ticket)*

**Verfallsdatum** das *(PLURAL* die Verfallsdaten) use-by date

**Verfassung** die *(PLURAL* die Verfassungen) ❶ constitution ❷ state *(of a person)*

**verfaulen** *VERB (PERF* **ist verfault)** to rot

**verfiel** ▸ see **verfallen**

**verfolgen** *VERB (PERF* **hat verfolgt)** ❶ to follow ❷ to persecute

**Verfolgung** die *(PLURAL* die Verfolgungen) ❶ pursuit, hunt ❷ persecution

**verfügbar** *ADJECTIVE* available

**Verfügung** die jemandem etwas zur Verfügung stellen to put something at somebody's disposal, jemandem zur Verfügung stehen to be at somebody's disposal

**verfuhr** ▸ see **verfahren**

**verführen** *VERB (PERF* **hat verführt)** ❶ to tempt ❷ to seduce

**Verführung** die *(PLURAL* die Verführungen) ❶ temptation ❷ seduction

**vergab** ▸ see **vergeben**

**vergangen** *VERB* ▸ see **vergehen**

**vergangen** *ADJECTIVE* last

**Vergangenheit** die ❶ past ❷ past tense

**vergaß** ▸ see **vergessen**

**vergeben** ◇*VERB (PRES* **vergibt,** *IMP* **vergab,** *PERF* **hat vergeben)** ❶ to forgive; jemandem etwas vergeben to forgive somebody for something ❷ to give away, to award ❸ vergeben sein to be taken, das Zimmer ist schon vergeben the room's already taken

**vergeblich** *ADVERB* in vain

**vergehen** ◇*VERB (IMP* **verging,** *PERF* **ist vergangen)** to pass

**vergessen** ◇*VERB (PRES* **vergisst,** *IMP* **vergaß,** *PERF* **hat vergessen)** to forget

**vergesslich** *ADJECTIVE* forgetful

**vergewaltigen** *VERB (PERF* **hat vergewaltigt)** to rape

**Vergewaltigung** die *(PLURAL* die Vergewaltigungen) rape

**vergibt** ▸ see **vergeben**

**vergiften** *VERB (PERF* **hat vergiftet)** to poison

**verging** ▸ see **vergehen**

**vergisst** ▸ see **vergessen**

**Vergleich** der *(PLURAL* die Vergleiche) comparison

**vergleichen** ◇*VERB (IMP* **verglich,** *PERF* **hat verglichen)** to compare

**vergnügen** *VERB (PERF* **hat sich vergnügt)** sich vergnügen to have fun

**Vergnügen** das *(PLURAL die* **Vergnügen)** pleasure; viel Vergnügen! have fun!

**vergnügt** *ADJECTIVE* **cheerful**

**vergrößern** *VERB (PERF* **hat vergrößert)** ❶ to enlarge ❷ to increase ❸ to magnify ❹ to extend *(a room, building)* ❺ sich vergrößern to expand, to grow bigger

**Vergrößerung** die *(PLURAL die* **Vergrößerungen)** ❶ expansion ❷ enlargement *(of a photograph)*

**verhaften** *VERB (PERF* **hat verhaftet)** to arrest; er ist verhaftet worden he was arrested

**verhalten** ◇*VERB (PRES* **verhält sich,** *IMP* **verhielt sich,** *PERF* **hat sich verhalten)** sich verhalten to behave

**Verhalten** das behaviour

**Verhältnis** das *(PLURAL die* **Verhältnisse)** ❶ relationship; sie hat ein gutes Verhältnis zu ihren Eltern she has a good relationship with her parents ❷ affair; Gabi hat ein Verhältnis mit einem verheirateten Mann Gabi is having an affair with a married man ❸ ratio *(in maths)* ❹ in keinem Verhältnis zu etwas stehen to be out of all proportion to something ❺ Verhältnisse conditions, über seine Verhältnisse leben to live beyond your means

**verhältnismäßig** *ADVERB* relatively

**verhandeln** *VERB (PERF* **hat verhandelt)** to negotiate; über

etwas verhandeln to negotiate something

**Verhandlung** die *(PLURAL die* **Verhandlungen)** ❶ negotiation ❷ hearing ❸ trial

**verhauen** *VERB (PERF* **hat verhauen)** ❶ to beat up ❷ die Prüfung verhauen *(informal)* to make a mess of the exam

**verheimlichen** *VERB (PERF* **hat verheimlicht)** to keep secret

**verheiratet** *ADJECTIVE* married

**verhext** *ADJECTIVE* bewitched

**verhielt** ▸ SEE **verhalten**

**verhindern** *VERB (PERF* **hat verhindert)** ❶ to prevent ❷ verhindert sein to be unable to make it, Petra ist verhindert Petra won't be able to make it

**verhungern** *VERB (PERF* **ist verhungert)** to starve

**Verhütungsmittel** das *(PLURAL die* **Verhütungsmittel)** contraceptive

**verirren** *VERB (PERF* **hat sich verirrt)** sich verirren to get lost

**verkam** ▸ SEE **verkommen**

**Verkauf** der *(PLURAL die* **Verkäufe)** sale; zum Verkauf for sale

**verkaufen** *VERB (PERF* **hat verkauft)** to sell; zu verkaufen for sale

**Verkäufer** der *(PLURAL die* **Verkäufer)** ❶ seller ❷ sales assistant

**Verkäuferin** die *(PLURAL die* **Verkäuferinnen)** ❶ seller ❷ sales assistant

**Verkaufsautomat** der (PLURAL die Verkuaufsautomaten) vending machine

**Verkehr** der traffic

**Verkehrsampel** die (PLURAL die Verkehrsampeln) traffic lights

**Verkehrsamt** das (PLURAL die Verkehrsämter) tourist office

**Verkehrsinsel** die (PLURAL die Verkehrsinseln) traffic island

**Verkehrsmittel** das (PLURAL die Verkehrsmittel) means of transport

**Verkehrsunfall** der (PLURAL die Verkehrsunfälle) road accident

**Verkehrszeichen** das (PLURAL die Verkehrszeichen) traffic sign, road sign

**verkehrt** ADJECTIVE ❶ wrong ❷ verkehrt herum inside out, the wrong way round

**verklagen** VERB (PERF hat verklagt) to sue

**verkleiden** VERB (PERF hat sich verkleidet) sich verkleiden to dress up

**Verkleidung** die (PLURAL die Verkleidungen) disguise, fancy dress

**verkommen** ◇VERB (IMP verkam, PERF ist verkommen) ❶ to go off (of food) ❷ to become dilapidated (of a house) ❸ to go to the bad

**verkratzt** ADJECTIVE scratched

**Verlag** der (PLURAL die Verlage) publisher's

**verlangen** VERB (PERF hat verlangt) ❶ to ask for, to require; am Telefon verlangt werden to

be wanted on the phone ❷ to demand ❸ to charge

**verlängern** VERB (PERF hat verlängert) ❶ to extend ❷ to lengthen ❸ to renew (a passport, driving licence)

**Verlängerung** die (PLURAL die Verlängerungen) ❶ extension ❷ renewal ❸ extra time (in sport)

**verlassen**¹ ◇VERB (PRES verlässt, IMP verließ, PERF hat verlassen) ❶ to leave; jemanden verlassen to leave somebody ❷ sich auf etwas verlassen to rely on something, du kannst dich auf ihn verlassen you can rely on him

**verlassen**² ADJECTIVE deserted

**verlaufen** ◇VERB (PRES verläuft, IMP verlief, PERF ist verlaufen) ❶ to go; es ist gut verlaufen it went well ❷ sich verlaufen to lose your way ❸ die Menge verlief sich schnell the crowd quickly dispersed

**verlegen**¹ ADJECTIVE embarrassed

**verlegen**² VERB (PERF hat verlegt) ❶ to mislay ❷ to postpone ❸ to publish ❹ to lay (a carpet, cable)

**Verlegenheit** die embarrassment

**Verleih** der (PLURAL die Verleihe) ❶ renting out, hiring out ❷ rental firm, hire shop

**verleihen** ◇VERB (IMP verlieh, PERF hat verliehen) ❶ to hire out ❷ to lend ❸ to award

**verlernen** VERB (PERF hat verlernt) to forget

**verletzen** VERB (PERF hat verletzt) ❶ to injure ❷ to hurt ❸ to violate (a law) ❹ sich verletzen to hurt yourself

**Verletzte** der/die *(PLURAL die Verletzten)* ❶ injured person ❷ casualty

**Verletzung** die *(PLURAL die Verletzungen)* injury

**verlieben** *VERB (PERF* hat sich verliebt*)* sich verlieben to fall in love

**verlief** ▸ SEE **verlaufen**

**verlieh** ▸ SEE **verleihen**

**verlieren** ◇*VERB (IMP* verlor, *PERF* hat verloren*)* to lose

**verließ** ▸ SEE **verlassen**

**verloben** *VERB (PERF* hat sich verlobt*)* sich verloben to get engaged

**Verlobte** der/die *(PLURAL die Verlobten)* fiancé, fiancée

**Verlobung** die *(PLURAL die Verlobungen)* engagement

**verlocken** *VERB (PERF* hat verlockt*)* to tempt, to entice

**verlor, verloren** ▸ SEE **verlieren**

**Verlosung** die *(PLURAL die Verlosungen)* prize draw

**Verlust** der *(PLURAL die Verluste)* loss

**vermeiden** ◇*VERB (IMP* vermied, *PERF* hat vermieden*)* to avoid

**vermieten** *VERB (PERF* hat vermietet*)* ❶ to rent out, to hire out ❷ to let; Zimmer zu vermieten rooms to let

**Vermieter** der *(PLURAL die Vermieter)* landlord

**Vermieterin** die *(PLURAL die Vermieterinnen)* landlady

**vermissen** *VERB (PERF* hat vermisst*)* to miss

**Vermittlung** die *(PLURAL die Vermittlungen)* ❶ arrangement ❷ agency ❸ switchboard ❹ telephone exchange ❺ mediation

**Vermögen** das *(PLURAL die Vermögen)* fortune; ein Vermögen machen to make a fortune

**vermuten** *VERB (PERF* hat vermutet*)* to suspect

**vermutlich** *ADJECTIVE* probable

**vermutlich** *ADVERB* probably

**vernachlässigen** *VERB (PERF* hat vernachlässigt*)* to neglect

**vernichten** *VERB (PERF* hat vernichtet*)* ❶ to destroy ❷ to exterminate

**Vernunft** die reason

**vernünftig** *ADJECTIVE* sensible

**verpacken** *VERB (PERF* hat verpackt*)* ❶ to pack ❷ to wrap up

**Verpackung** die *(PLURAL die Verpackungen)* packaging

**verpassen** *VERB (PERF* hat verpasst*)* to miss

**verpesten** *VERB (PERF* hat verpestet*)* to pollute

**Verpflegung** die food; Unterkunft und Verpflegung board and lodging

**verpflichten** *VERB (PERF* hat verpflichtet*)* ❶ sich verpflichten to promise ❷ sich vertraglich verpflichten to sign a contract ❸ verpflichtet sein, etwas zu tun to be obliged to do something, jemandem zu Dank verpflichtet sein to be obliged to somebody ❹ verpflichtend binding

a
b
c
d
e
f
g
h
i
j
k
l
m
n
o
p
q
r
s
t
u
**v**
w
x
y
z

**Verpflichtung** die *(PLURAL* die Verpflichtungen*)* ❶ obligation ❷ commitment

**verprügeln** VERB *(PERF* hat verprügelt*)* to beat up

**verraten** ◇VERB *(PRES* verrät, *IMP* verriet, *PERF* hat verraten*)* ❶ to betray ❷ to give away ❸ to tell ❹ sich verraten to give yourself away

**verrechnen** VERB *(PERF* hat sich verrechnet*)* sich verrechnen to make a mistake

**verregnet** ADJECTIVE rainy

**verreisen** VERB *(PERF* ist verreist*)* to go away; verreist sein to be away

**verriet** ▸ SEE verraten

**verrosten** VERB *(PERF* ist verrostet*)* to rust

**verrostet** ADJECTIVE rusty

**verrückt** ADJECTIVE mad, crazy

**Verrückte** der/die *(PLURAL* die Verrückten*)* maniac

**versagen** VERB *(PERF* hat versagt*)* to fail

**versammeln** VERB *(PERF* hat versammelt*)* ❶ to assemble ❷ sich versammeln to assemble

**Versammlung** die *(PLURAL* die Versammlungen*)* meeting

**versäumen** VERB *(PERF* hat versäumt*)* to miss; es versäumen, etwas zu tun to fail to do something

**verschenken** VERB *(PERF* hat verschenkt*)* to give away

**verschieben** ◇VERB *(IMP* verschob, *PERF* hat verschoben*)* to postpone

**verschieden** ADJECTIVE ❶ different ❷ various

**verschlafen** ◇VERB *(PRES* verschläft, *IMP* verschlief, *PERF* hat verschlafen*)* ❶ to oversleep ❷ to sleep through *(the day)* ❸ to miss *(a date, the train)*

**verschlechtern** VERB *(PERF* hat verschlechtert*)* ❶ to make worse ❷ sich verschlechtern to get worse

**verschlief** ▸ SEE verschlafen

**verschließen** ◇VERB *(IMP* verschloss, *PERF* hat verschlossen*)* ❶ to close *(a tin, package)* ❷ to lock *(a door, drawer)*

**verschlimmern** VERB *(PERF* hat verschlimmert*)* ❶ to make worse ❷ sich verschlimmern to get worse

**verschloss** ▸ SEE verschließen

**verschlucken** VERB *(PERF* hat verschluckt*)* ❶ to swallow ❷ sich verschlucken to choke

**Verschluss** der *(PLURAL* die Verschlüsse*)* ❶ fastener, clasp ❷ top *(of a bottle)*

**verschmutzen** VERB *(PERF* hat verschmutzt*)* to soil; die Umwelt verschmutzen to pollute the environment

**Verschmutzung** die pollution

**verschob** ▸ SEE verschieben

**verschreiben** ◇VERB *(IMP* verschrieb, *PERF* hat verschrieben*)* ❶ to prescribe ❷ sich verschreiben to make a mistake

**verschütten** VERB *(PERF* hat verschüttet*)* to spill

**verschwand** ▸ SEE verschwinden

**verschwenden** VERB (PERF **hat verschwendet**) to waste

**Verschwendung** die waste

**verschwinden** ◇VERB (IMP **verschwand**, PERF **ist verschwunden**) to disappear

**verschwommen** ADJECTIVE blurred

**Versehen** das (PLURAL die **Versehen**) oversight; aus Versehen by mistake

**versehentlich** ADVERB by mistake

**versetzen** VERB (PERF **hat versetzt**) ❶ to move, to transfer (a person) ❷ to move up (into the next class at school) ❸ jemanden versetzen to stand somebody up ❹ jemandem einen Schreck versetzen to give somebody a fright, jemandem einen Tritt versetzen to kick somebody ❺ sich in jemandes Lage versetzen to put yourself in somebody's position

**verseuchen** VERB (PERF **hat verseucht**) to contaminate

**Verseuchung** die (PLURAL die **Verseuchungen**) contamination

**versichern** VERB (PERF **hat versichert**) ❶ to insure ❷ to assert; jemandem versichern, dass ... to assure somebody that ...

**Versicherung** die (PLURAL die **Versicherungen**) ❶ insurance ❷ assurance

**Versicherungsgesellschaft** die (PLURAL die **Versicherungsgesell-schaften**) insurance company

**Versicherungsschein** der (PLURAL die **Versicherungsscheine**) insurance policy document

**versöhnen** VERB (PERF **hat sich versöhnt**) sich versöhnen to make up, sich mit jemandem versöhnen to make it up with somebody

**versorgen** VERB (PERF **hat versorgt**) ❶ to supply ❷ to provide for ❸ to look after

**verspäten** VERB (PERF **hat sich verspätet**) sich verspäten to be late

**Verspätung** die lateness, delay; Verspätung haben to be late

**versprechen** ◇VERB (PRES **verspricht**, IMP **versprach**, PERF **hat versprochen**) ❶ to promise ❷ sich viel von etwas versprechen to have high hopes of something ❸ sich versprechen to make a slip of the tongue

**Versprechen** das (PLURAL die **Versprechen**) promise

**verstand** ▸ SEE **verstehen**

**Verstand** der ❶ mind; den Verstand verlieren to go out of your mind ❷ reason

**verstanden** ▸ SEE **verstehen**

**verständigen** VERB (PERF **hat verständigt**) ❶ to notify ❷ sich verständigen to communicate, to make yourself understood ❸ sich über etwas verständigen to agree on something

**Verständigung** die ❶ communication ❷ notification

**verständlich** ADJECTIVE ❶ understandable; jemandem etwas verständlich machen to make something clear to somebody ❷ comprehensible

a
b
c
d
e
f
g
h
i
j
k
l
m
n
o
p
q
r
s
t
u
v
w
x
y
z

**Verständnis** das (PLURAL die Verständnisse) ❶ comprehension ❷ understanding

**Verstärker** der (PLURAL die Verstärker) amplifier

**verstauchen** VERB (PERF hat verstaucht) to sprain; sich den Fuß verstauchen to sprain your ankle

**Versteck** das (PLURAL die Verstecke) hiding place

**verstecken** VERB (PERF hat versteckt) ❶ to hide ❷ sich verstecken to hide

**verstehen** ◇VERB (IMP verstand, PERF hat verstanden) ❶ to understand; etwas falsch verstehen to misunderstand something ❷ sich gut verstehen to get on well ❸ das versteht sich von selbst that goes without saying

**verstellbar** ADJECTIVE adjustable

**verstellen** VERB (PERF hat verstellt) ❶ to adjust ❷ to block ❸ to disguise ❹ sich verstellen to pretend

**verstimmt** ADJECTIVE ❶ out of tune ❷ peeved ❸ ein verstimmter Magen an upset stomach

**verstopft** ADJECTIVE constipated

**Versuch** der (PLURAL die Versuche) ❶ attempt ❷ experiment

**versuchen** VERB (PERF hat versucht) to try

**verteidigen** VERB (PERF hat verteidigt) to defend

**Verteidiger** der (PLURAL die Verteidiger) ❶ defender ❷ defence counsel

**Verteidigung** die defence

**verteilen** VERB (PERF hat verteilt) to distribute

**Vertrag** der (PLURAL die Verträge) ❶ contract ❷ treaty

**vertragen** ◇VERB (PRES verträgt, IMP vertrug, PERF hat vertragen) ❶ to stand, to take ❷ ich vertrage keinen Kaffee coffee disagrees with me ❸ sich vertragen to get on, sich wieder vertragen to make it up

**vertrat** ▸ SEE vertreten

**vertrauen** VERB (PERF hat vertraut) to trust

**Vertrauen** das trust; im Vertrauen in confidence

**vertraulich** ADJECTIVE ❶ confidential ❷ familiar

**vertreten** ◇VERB (PRES vertritt, IMP vertrat, PERF hat vertreten) ❶ to stand in for ❷ to represent ❸ eine Meinung vertreten to hold an opinion ❹ sich die Beine vertreten to stretch your legs

**Vertreter** der (PLURAL die Vertreter) ❶ representative ❷ deputy

**Vertreterin** die (PLURAL die Vertreterinnen) ❶ representative ❷ deputy

**vertritt** ▸ SEE vertreten

**vertrug** ▸ SEE vertragen

**verunglücken** VERB (PERF ist verunglückt) to have an accident

**verursachen** VERB (PERF hat verursacht) to cause

**verurteilen** VERB (PERF hat verurteilt) ❶ to sentence ❷ to condemn

**Verwaltung** die (*PLURAL* die Verwaltungen) administration

**verwandt** *ADJECTIVE* related

**Verwandte** der/die (*PLURAL* die Verwandten) relative

**Verwandtschaft** die relatives

**verwechseln** *VERB* (*PERF* hat verwechselt) to mix up, to confuse; jemanden mit jemandem verwechseln to mistake somebody for somebody, ich verwechsele ihn mit seinem Bruder I mistake him for his brother

**verwenden** *VERB* (*PERF* hat verwendet) to use

**Verwendung** die use

**verwickelt** *ADJECTIVE* complicated

**verwirren** *VERB* (*PERF* hat verwirrt) ❶ to confuse ❷ to tangle up

**verwirrt** *ADJECTIVE* confused

**verwöhnen** *VERB* (*PERF* hat verwöhnt) to spoil

**verwunden** *VERB* (*PERF* hat verwundet) to wound

**Verwundete** der/die (*PLURAL* die Verwundeten) casualty, injured person

**Verwundung** die (*PLURAL* die Verwundungen) injury, wound

**verzählen** *VERB* (*PERF* hat sich verzählt) sich verzählen to miscount

**Verzeichnis** das (*PLURAL* die Verzeichnisse) ❶ list ❷ index

**verzeihen** *VERB* (*IMP* verzieh, *PERF* hat verziehen) to forgive; verzeihen Sie, können Sie mir sagen ...? excuse me, could you tell me ...?

**Verzeihung** die forgiveness; jemanden um Verzeihung bitten to apologize to somebody Verzeihung! sorry!

**verzichten** *VERB* (*PERF* hat verzichtet) ❶ to do without; ich verzichte auf deine Hilfe I can do without your help ❷ auf etwas verzichten to give up something (*smoking or your share of something*), to relinquish something (*a right or privilege*)

**verzieh, verziehen** ► SEE verzeihen

**verzögern** *VERB* (*PERF* hat verzögert) ❶ to delay ❷ sich verzögern to be delayed

**Verzögerung** die (*PLURAL* die Verzögerungen) delay

**verzollen** *VERB* (*PERF* hat verzollt) to pay duty on; haben Sie etwas zu verzollen? have you anything to declare?

**verzweifeln** *VERB* (*PERF* ist verzweifelt) to despair

**verzweifelt** *ADJECTIVE* desperate

**Verzweiflung** die despair

**Vetter** der (*PLURAL* die Vettern) cousin

**Video** das (*PLURAL* die Videos) video

**Videokamera** die (*PLURAL* die Videokameras) video camera

**Videorekorder** der (*PLURAL* die Videorekorder) video recorder

**Videospiel** das (*PLURAL* die Videospiele) video game

**Videothek** die (*PLURAL* die Videotheken) video shop

**Vieh** das cattle

a b c d e f g h i j k l m n o p q r s t u **v** w x y z

**viel** *ADJECTIVE, PRONOUN* **❶** a lot of; Erika hat viel Arbeit Erika's got a lot of work **❷** viele *(plural)* many, a lot of, viele Leute many people **❸** much, a lot; wie viel? how much?, how many?, zu viel too much, vielen Dank thank you very much, viel Spaß! have fun!, viel Glück! good luck! **❹** das viele Geld all that money

**viel** *ADVERB* **❶** much, a lot; viel weniger much less, so viel wie möglich as much as possible, sie redet viel she talks a lot **❷** viel zu groß far too big, much too big, das dauert viel zu lange it'll take far too long

**vielleicht** *ADVERB* perhaps

**vielmals** *ADVERB* danke vielmals thanks a lot

**vier** *NUMBER* four

**Viereck** das *(PLURAL die Vierecke)* **❶** rectangle **❷** square

**viereckig** *ADJECTIVE* **❶** rectangular **❷** square

**vierte** ▸ SEE **vierter**

**viertel** *ADJECTIVE* quarter; wir treffen uns um viertel acht we'll meet at quarter past seven, um drei viertel acht at quarter to eight

**Viertel** das *(PLURAL die Viertel)* quarter; es ist Viertel vor acht it's quarter to eight

**Viertelfinale** das *(PLURAL die Viertelfinale)* quarter finals

**Viertelstunde** die *(PLURAL die Viertelstunden)* quarter of an hour

**vierter, vierte, viertes** *ADJECTIVE* fourth

**vierzehn** *NUMBER* fourteen

**vierzig** *NUMBER* forty

**Villa** die *(PLURAL die Villen)* villa

**virtuell** *ADJECTIVE* virtual; virtuelle Realität virtual reality

**Virus** das *(PLURAL die Viren)* virus

**visuell** *ADJECTIVE* visual

**Visum** das *(PLURAL die Visa)* visa

**Vitamin** das *(PLURAL die Vitamine)* vitamin

**vitaminarm** *ADJECTIVE* low in vitamins

**vitaminreich** *ADJECTIVE* rich in vitamins

**Vogel** der *(PLURAL die Vögel)* bird

**Vogelbeobachter** der *(PLURAL die Vogelbeobachter)* birdwatcher

**Vogelbeobachterin** die *(PLURAL die Vogelbeobachterinnen)* birdwatcher

**Vogelscheuche** die *(PLURAL die Vogelscheuchen)* scarecrow

**Vokabel** die *(PLURAL die Vokabeln)* word; Vokabeln vocabulary

**Vokal** der *(PLURAL die Vokale)* vowel

**Volk** das *(PLURAL die Völker)* people

**Volkshochschule** die adult education centre; ein Kurs an der Volkshochschule an adult education class

**Volkslied** das *(PLURAL die Volkslieder)* folk song

**Volksmusik** die folk music

**Volkswirtschaft** die economics

**voll** *ADJECTIVE* **❶ full**; ein Korb voll Äpfel a basket full of apples, die volle Wahrheit the whole truth **❷** etwas voll machen to fill something up, voll tanken to fill up with petrol

**voll** *ADVERB* **❶ fully, completely**; voll und ganz completely **❷** jemanden nicht für voll nehmen *(informal)* not to take somebody seriously

**Volleyball** der **volleyball**; Volleyball spielen to play volleyball

**völlig** *ADJECTIVE* **complete**

**völlig** *ADVERB* **completely**

**vollkommen** *ADJECTIVE* **❶ perfect ❷ complete**

**vollkommen** *ADVERB* **completely**

**Vollkornbrot** das **wholemeal bread**

**vollmachen** ▸ SEE **voll**

**Vollpension** die **full board**

**vollständig** *ADJECTIVE* **complete**

**volltanken** ▸ SEE **voll**

**Vollzeitarbeit** die **full-time work**

**vom** von dem.

**von** *PREPOSITION* (+DAT) **❶ from**; von heute an from today, von hier bis ... from here to ... **❷ of**; eine Freundin von mir a friend of mine **❸ about**; Peter hat mir von dem neuen Haus erzählt Peter told me about the new house **❹ by**; ein Theaterstück von Brecht a play by Brecht **❺** von mir aus I don't mind

**voneinander** *ADVERB* **from each other**; sie sind voneinander abhängig they depend on each other

**vor** *PREPOSITION* **❶** (+DAT or +ACC with movement towards a place) **in front of ❷ before**; Manfred war vor euch da Manfred arrived before you, kurz vor der Ampel shortly before the lights **❸ with**; vor Angst zittern to tremble with fear **❹** (with clock time) zehn vor fünf ten to five **❺ ago**; vor zwei Jahren two years ago **❻** sich vor jemandem fürchten to be frightened of somebody **❼** vor allen Dingen above all **❽** vor sich hin summen to hum to yourself

**vor** *ADVERB* **forward**; vor und zurück backwards and forwards

**voraus** *ADVERB* **❶ ahead ❷** im Voraus in advance

**vorausgehen** ◇*VERB* (IMP **ging voraus**, PERF **ist vorausgegangen**) **❶** to go on ahead **❷** to precede

**voraussetzen** *VERB* (PERF **hat vorausgesetzt**) **❶** to take for granted **❷** to require **❸** vorausgesetzt, dass ... provided that ...

**Voraussetzung** die (PLURAL die **Voraussetzungen**) **❶ condition ❷ assumption**

**vorbei** *ADVERB* **❶ past ❷ over**; vorbei sein to be over

**vorbeifahren** ◇*VERB* (PRES **fährt vorbei**, IMP **fuhr vorbei**, PERF **ist vorbeigefahren**) to drive past, to pass

**vorbeigehen** ◇*VERB* (IMP **ging vorbei**, PERF **ist vorbeigegangen**) **❶** to go past **❷** to drop in; ich gehe bei Anne vorbei I'll drop in on Anne

**vorbeikommen** ◇*VERB* (IMP **kam vorbei**, PERF **ist vorbeigekommen**) **❶** to pass **❷** to get past **❸** to drop in

**vorbereiten** *VERB (PERF* **hat vorbereitet)** ❶ to prepare ❷ **sich vorbereiten** to prepare

**Vorbereitung** die *(PLURAL* die **Vorbereitungen)** preparation

**vorbeugen** *VERB (PERF* **hat vorgebeugt)** ❶ to prevent ❷ **sich vorbeugen** to lean forward

**Vorbild** das *(PLURAL* die **Vorbilder)** example

**vorderer, vordere, vorderes** *ADJECTIVE* front

**Vordergrund** der foreground; **im Vordergrund** in the foreground

**Vorderseite** die front

**vorderster, vorderste, vorderstes** *ADJECTIVE* front

**Vorfahr** der *(PLURAL* die **Vorfahren)** ancestor

**Vorfahrt** die right of way; 'Vorfahrt beachten/gewähren' 'give way'

**Vorfall** der *(PLURAL* die **Vorfälle)** incident

**Vorführung** die *(PLURAL* die **Vorführungen)** ❶ performance ❷ demonstration

**Vorgänger** der *(PLURAL* die **Vorgänger)** predecessor

**Vorgängerin** die *(PLURAL* die **Vorgängerinnen)** predecessor

**vorgehen** *◇VERB (IMP* **ging vor,** *PERF* **ist vorgegangen)** ❶ to go on ahead ❷ to go forward ❸ to proceed ❹ **die Uhr geht vor** the clock is fast ❺ **was geht hier vor?** what's going on here?

**Vorgehensweise** die *(PLURAL* die **Vorgehensweisen)** policy

**vorgestern** *ADVERB* the day before yesterday

**vorhaben** *◇VERB (PRES* **hat vor,** *IMP* **hatte vor,** *PERF* **hat vorgehabt)** ❶ to intend ❷ **etwas vorhaben** to have something planned

**Vorhang** der *(PLURAL* die **Vorhänge)** curtain

**Vorhängeschloss** das *(PLURAL* die **Vorhängeschlösser)** padlock

**vorher** *ADVERB* beforehand, before

**Vorhersage** die *(PLURAL* die **Vorhersagen)** ❶ forecast ❷ prediction

**vorhin** *ADVERB* just now

**voriger, vorige, voriges** *ADJECTIVE* last

**vorkommen** *◇VERB (IMP* **kam vor,** *PERF* **ist vorgekommen)** ❶ to happen ❷ to occur ❸ to come forward ❹ to come out *(from behind somewhere)* ❺ to seem; **jemandem bekannt vorkommen** to seem familiar to somebody ❻ **sich alt vorkommen** to feel old

**Vorlauf** der fast forward *(on video)*

**vorläufig** *ADJECTIVE* temporary

**vorlesen** *◇VERB (PRES* **liest vor,** *IMP* **las vor,** *PERF* **hat vorgelesen)** ❶ to read (out) ❷ **jemandem vorlesen** to read to somebody

**vorletzter, vorletzte, vorletztes** *ADJECTIVE* last but one; **vorletztes Jahr** the year before last

**Vormittag** der *(PLURAL* die **Vormittage)** morning

**vormittags** *ADVERB* in the morning

**vorn** *ADVERB* ❶ at the front; **nach vorn** to the front ❷ **von vorn** from the beginning, **wieder von vorn anfangen** to start again at the beginning, **da vorn** over there

**Vorname** der *(PLURAL die* **Vornamen)** first name

**vorne** ▸ SEE **vorn**

**vornehm** *ADJECTIVE* ❶ elegant ❷ distinguished

**vornehmen** ◇*VERB (PRES* **nimmt vor**, *IMP* **nahm vor**, *PERF* **hat vorgenommen)** ❶ to carry out ❷ **sich vornehmen, etwas zu tun** to plan to do something

**Vorort** der *(PLURAL die* **Vororte)** suburb

**Vorrat** der *(PLURAL die* **Vorräte)** supply, stock

**Vorsatz** der *(PLURAL die* **Vorsätze)** intention

**Vorschau** die ❶ preview ❷ trailer *(of a film)*

**Vorschlag** der *(PLURAL die* **Vorschläge)** suggestion

**vorschlagen** ◇*VERB (PRES* **schlägt vor**, *IMP* **schlug vor**, *PERF* **hat vorgeschlagen)** to suggest

**Vorschrift** die *(PLURAL die* **Vorschriften)** ❶ regulation ❷ instruction

**Vorschule** die *(PLURAL die* **Vorschulen)** infant school

**vorsehen** ◇*VERB (PRES* **sieht sich vor**, *IMP* **sah sich vor**, *PERF* **hat sich vorgesehen)** **sich vorsehen** to be careful

**Vorsicht** die care; **Vorsicht!** careful!, *(on a sign)* caution!

**vorsichtig** *ADJECTIVE* careful

**vorsichtshalber** *ADVERB* to be on the safe side

**Vorsichtsmaßnahme** die *(PLURAL die* **Vorsichtsmaßnahmen)** precaution; **Vorsichtsmaßnahmen gegen etwas ergreifen** to take precautions against something

**Vorspeise** die *(PLURAL die* **Vorspeisen)** starter

**Vorsprung** der *(PLURAL die* **Vorsprünge)** ❶ ledge *(of a rock)* ❷ lead *(over somebody)*

**vorstellen** *VERB (PERF* **hat vorgestellt)** ❶ to introduce; **darf ich Ihnen Herrn Schulz vorstellen?** may I introduce Mr Schulz? ❷ **die Uhr vorstellen** to put the clock forward ❸ **sich vorstellen** to introduce yourself ❹ **sich beim Personalchef vorstellen** to go for an interview with the personnel manager ❺ **sich etwas vorstellen** to imagine something, **stell dir vor!** can you imagine?

**Vorstellung** die *(PLURAL die* **Vorstellungen)** ❶ performance ❷ introduction ❸ interview *(for a job)* ❹ idea ❺ imagination

**Vorstellungsgespräch** DAS *(PLURAL die* **Vorstellungsgespräche)** interview

**Vorteil** der *(PLURAL die* **Vorteile)** advantage

**Vortrag** der *(PLURAL die* **Vorträge)** talk

**vorüber** *ADVERB* **vorüber sein** to be over

**vorübergehend** *ADJECTIVE* temporary

**vorübergehend** *ADVERB* temporarily

a
b
c
d
e
f
g
h
i
j
k
l
m
n
o
p
q
r
s
t
u
v
w
x
y
z

**Vorurteil** das *(PLURAL die* **Vorurteile)** prejudice

**Vorwahl** die *(PLURAL die* **Vorwahlen)** dialling code; wählen Sie die Vorwahl 00 44 für Großbritannien dial 00 44 for Britain

**vorwärts** *ADVERB* forward(s)

**vorwiegend** *ADVERB* predominantly

**Vorwurf** der *(PLURAL die* **Vorwürfe)** reproach; jemandem Vorwürfe machen to reproach somebody

**vorzeigen** *VERB* *(PERF* **hat vorgezeigt)** to show

**vorziehen** ⬦*VERB* *(PRES* **zieht vor,** *IMP* **zog vor,** *PERF* **hat vorgezogen)** ❶ to prefer ❷ to pull up *(a chair)* ❸ den Vorhang vorziehen to draw the curtain

**vorzüglich** *ADJECTIVE* excellent

**vulgär** *ADJECTIVE* vulgar

**Vulkan** der *(PLURAL die* **Vulkane)** volcano

**Waage** die *(PLURAL die* **Waagen)** ❶ scales ❷ Libra; Gabi ist Waage Gabi's Libra

**waagerecht** *ADJECTIVE* horizontal

**wach** *ADJECTIVE* awake; wach sein to be awake, wach werden to wake up

**Wache** die *(PLURAL die* **Wachen)** ❶ guard ❷ (police) station

**Wachhund** der *(PLURAL die* **Wachhunde)** guard dog

**Wachs** das wax

**wachsen** ⬦*VERB* *(PRES* **wächst,** *IMP* **wuchs,** *PERF* **ist gewachsen)** to grow

**Wachstum** das growth

**wackelig** *ADJECTIVE* wobbly

**wackeln** *VERB* *(PERF* **hat gewackelt)** to wobble

**Wade** die *(PLURAL die* **Waden)** calf

**Waffe** die *(PLURAL die* **Waffen)** weapon

**Waffel** die *(PLURAL die* **Waffeln)** waffle

**Waffenhandel** der arms trade

**wagen** *VERB* *(PERF* **hat gewagt)** ❶ to risk ❷ es wagen, etwas zu tun to dare to do something, sich nicht irgendwohin wagen not dare to go somewhere

**Wagen** der (PLURAL die **Wagen**)
❶ car; nimmst du den Wagen? are
you going by car? ❷ carriage (of a
train) ❸ cart

**Wagenheber** der (PLURAL die
**Wagenheber**) jack

**Wahl** die (PLURAL die **Wahlen**)
❶ choice; er hat die Wahl it's his
choice ❷ election; die nächsten
Wahlen sind im Herbst the next
election is in autumn

**wählen** VERB (PERF **hat gewählt**)
❶ to choose; zwischen zwei
Möglichkeiten wählen to choose
between two possibilities ❷ haben
Sie schon gewählt? are you ready to
order? (in a restaurant) ❸ to elect
❹ to vote, to vote for; sie wählt
immer grün she always votes green,
wählt Schröder! vote for Schröder
❺ to dial; ich muss die falsche
Nummer gewählt haben I must
have dialled the wrong number

**Wahlfach** das (PLURAL die
**Wahlfächer**) optional subject,
option

**Wahnsinn** der madness

**wahnsinnig** ADJECTIVE ❶ mad;
wahnsinnig werden to go mad
❷ wahnsinnigen Durst haben
to be terribly thirsty, der Film
war wahnsinnig gut the film was
incredibly good

**wahr** ADJECTIVE ❶ true ❷ du kommst
doch, nicht wahr? you're coming,
aren't you?

**während** PREPOSITION (+GEN) during

**während** CONJUNCTION ❶ while
❷ whereas

**Wahrheit** die (PLURAL die
**Wahrheiten**) truth

**Wahrsager** der (PLURAL die
**Wahrsager**) fortune-teller

**Wahrsagerin** die (PLURAL die
**Wahrsagerinnen**) fortune-teller

**wahrscheinlich** ADJECTIVE probable,
likely

**wahrscheinlich** ADVERB probably

**Währung** die (PLURAL die
**Währungen**) currency

**Waise** die (PLURAL die **Waisen**)
orphan; er ist Waise he's an orphan

**Wal** der (PLURAL die **Wale**) whale

**Wald** der (PLURAL die **Wälder**) wood,
forest

**Waliser** der (PLURAL die **Waliser**)
Welshman

**Waliserin** die (PLURAL die
**Waliserinnen**) Welshwoman

**walisisch** ADJECTIVE Welsh

**Walkman** der (PLURAL die
**Walkmans**) walkman

**Walnuss** die (PLURAL die **Walnüsse**)
walnut

**Wand** die (PLURAL die **Wände**) wall

**Wanderer** der (PLURAL die
**Wanderer**) ❶ hiker ❷ rambler

**Wanderin** die (PLURAL die
**Wanderinnen**) ❶ hiker
❷ rambler

**wandern** VERB (PERF **ist gewandert**)
❶ to hike ❷ to go walking

**Wandern** das hiking

**Wanderung** die (PLURAL die
**Wanderungen**) ❶ hike ❷ walking
tour

**Wandteppich** der (PLURAL die
**Wandteppiche**) tapestry

a
b
c
d
e
f
g
h
i
j
k
l
m
n
o
p
q
r
s
t
u
v
w
x
y
z

**wann** *ADVERB* **when**

**Wanne** die *(PLURAL* die **Wannen)**
❶ tub ❷ bath

**war** ▸ SEE **sein**

**warb** ▸ SEE **werben**

**Ware** die *(PLURAL* die **Waren)**
❶ article ❷ Waren goods

**waren** ▸ SEE **sein**

**Warenhaus** das *(PLURAL* die
**Warenhäuser)** department store

**warf** ▸ SEE **werfen**

**warm** *ADJECTIVE* **warm**; eine warme
Mahlzeit a hot meal, das Essen
warm machen to heat up the food

**Wärme** die warmth

**wärmen** *VERB (PERF* hat gewärmt) to
warm, to heat

**Warndreieck** das *(PLURAL* die
**Warndreiecke)** warning triangle

**warnen** *VERB (PERF* hat gewarnt) to
warn; jemanden vor etwas warnen
to warn somebody of something

**Warnung** die *(PLURAL* die
**Warnungen)** warning

**warst, wart** ▸ SEE **sein**

**Warteliste** die *(PLURAL* die
**Wartelisten)** waiting list

**warten** *VERB (PERF* hat gewartet)
❶ to wait; auf jemanden warten
to wait for somebody ❷ auf sich
warten lassen to take your time

**Wärter** der *(PLURAL* die **Wärter)**
❶ keeper ❷ attendant ❸ warder

**Warteraum** der *(PLURAL* die
**Warteräume)** waiting room

**Wärterin** die *(PLURAL* die
**Wärterinnen)** ❶ keeper
❷ attendant ❸ warder

**Wartezeit** die **wait**; eine Stunde
Wartezeit an hour's wait

**Wartezimmer** das *(PLURAL* die
**Wartezimmer)** waiting room

**warum** *ADVERB* **why**

**Warze** die *(PLURAL* die **Warzen)** wart

**was** *PRONOUN* ❶ **what**; was für ein/
eine ...? what kind of ...?, was für
ein Fahrrad hast du? what kind
of bike do you have?, was für ein
Glück! what luck!, was kostet
das? how much is it? ❷ that;
alles, was wir brauchen all (that)
we need, alles, was du willst
all (that) you want ❸ *(short for
'etwas')* **something**; heute gibts
was Gutes im Fernsehen there's
something good on television today
❹ *(short for 'etwas' in questions and
negatives)* **anything**; hast du was
für mich? have you got anything
for me?

**Waschbecken** das *(PLURAL* die
**Waschbecken)** washbasin

**Wäsche** die ❶ washing
❷ underwear

**waschen** ◇*VERB (PRES* wäscht, *IMP*
wusch, *PERF* hat gewaschen) ❶ to
wash ❷ sich waschen to have a
wash, sich die Hände waschen to
wash your hands

**Wäscheraum** DER *(PLURAL* die
**Wäscheräume)** laundry room

**Wäscherei** die *(PLURAL* die
**Wäschereien)** laundry

**Waschlappen** der *(PLURAL* die
**Waschlappen)** flannel

**Waschmaschine** die *(PLURAL* die
**Waschmaschinen)** washing
machine

**Waschpulver** das *(PLURAL* die **Waschpulver)** washing powder

**Waschsalon** der *(PLURAL* die **Waschsalons)** launderette

**Wasser** das water

**wasserdicht** *ADJECTIVE* waterproof

**Wasserfall** der *(PLURAL* die **Wasserfälle)** waterfall

**Wasserfarbe** die *(PLURAL* die **Wasserfarben)** watercolour

**Wasserhahn** der *(PLURAL* die **Wasserhähne)** tap

**Wassermann** der **Aquarius**; Lisa ist Wassermann Lisa's Aquarius

**Wassermelone** die *(PLURAL* die **Wassermelonen)** water melon

**Wasserskifahren** das water-skiing

**Wassersport** der water sport

**Wassertiefe** die depth (of water); Wassertiefe: 2 Meter depth: 2 metres

**Watte** die cotton wool

**wattiert** *ADJECTIVE* padded

**WC** das *(PLURAL* die **WCs)** WC, toilet

**Webcam** die *(PLURAL* die **Webcams)** webcam

**weben** *VERB (PERF* **hat gewebt)** to weave

**Webseite** die *(PLURAL* die **Webseiten)** web page

**Website** die *(PLURAL* die **Websites)** web site

**Wechselkurs** der *(PLURAL* die **Wechselkurse)** exchange rate

**wechseln** *VERB (PERF* **hat gewechselt) ❶** to change; kannst du mir zehn Euro wechseln? have you got change for ten euros? **❷ to exchange** *(glances, letters)*

**Wechselstube** die *(PLURAL* die **Wechselstuben)** bureau de change

**wecken** *VERB (PERF* **hat geweckt)** to wake (up)

**Wecker** der *(PLURAL* die **Wecker)** alarm clock; Max geht mir auf den Wecker *(informal)* Max gets on my nerves

**weder** *CONJUNCTION* weder … noch neither … nor

**weg** *ADVERB* **❶** away; geh weg! go away!, Hände weg! hands off! **❷** gone; der Ring ist weg the ring's gone, Heidi ist schon weg Heidi's already gone

**Weg** der *(PLURAL* die **Wege) ❶** way; auf dem Weg nach Hause on the way home **❷** path **❸** sich auf den Weg machen to set off **❹** im Weg sein to be in the way

**wegen** *PREPOSITION (+GEN)* because of

**wegfahren** ⋄*VERB (PRES* **fährt weg,** *IMP* **fuhr weg,** *PERF* **ist weggefahren) ❶** to leave; sie fahren gerade weg they are leaving just now **❷** *(PERF* **hat weggefahren)** to drive away *(a car or things)*

**weggehen** ⋄*VERB (IMP* **ging weg,** *PERF* **ist weggegangen) ❶** to go away **❷** to leave **❸** to go out; wir gehen heute Abend weg we're going out tonight **❹** to come out *(of a stain)*

**weglassen** ⋄*VERB (PRES* **lässt weg,** *IMP* **ließ weg,** *PERF* **hat weggelassen) ❶** to let go **❷** to leave out

**weglaufen** ◇*VERB (PRES* **läuft weg,** *IMP* **lief weg,** *PERF* **ist weggelaufen)** to run away

**weglegen** *VERB (PERF* **hat weggelegt) ❶** to put down **❷** to put away

**wegmachen** *VERB (PERF* **hat weggemacht)** to get rid of *(a stain or wart, for example)*

**wegmüssen** ◇*VERB (informal) (PRES* **muss weg,** *IMP* **musste weg,** *PERF* **hat weggemusst)** to have to go

**wegnehmen** ◇*VERB (PRES* **nimmt weg,** *IMP* **nahm weg,** *PERF* **hat weggenommen)** to take away

**wegräumen** *VERB (PERF* **hat weggeräumt)** to clear away

**wegschicken** *VERB (PERF* **hat weggeschickt) ❶** to send away **❷** to send off

**wegtun** ◇*VERB (IMP* **tat weg,** *PERF* **hat weggetan)** to put away

**Wegweiser** der *(PLURAL* die **Wegweiser)** signpost

**wegwerfen** ◇*VERB (PRES* **wirft weg,** *IMP* **warf weg,** *PERF* **hat weggeworfen)** to throw away

**weh** *ADJECTIVE* **❶** sore **❷** oh weh! oh dear! **❸** es tut weh it hurts

**wehen** *VERB (PERF* **hat geweht)** to blow

**Wehrdienst** der **military service**

**wehren** *VERB (PERF* **hat sich gewehrt)** sich wehren to defend yourself

**wehrlos** *ADJECTIVE* **defenceless**

**wehtun** ◇*VERB (PRES* **tut weh,** *IMP* **tat weh,** *PERF* **hat wehgetan) ❶** to hurt; mein Arm tut weh my arm hurts, jemandem wehtun to hurt

somebody **❷** sich wehtun to hurt yourself

**Weibchen** das *(PLURAL* die **Weibchen)** female

**weiblich** *ADJECTIVE* **❶** female **❷** feminine *(NOUN)*

**weich** *ADJECTIVE* **soft**

**Weide** die *(PLURAL* die **Weiden) ❶** willow **❷** pasture

**weigern** *VERB (PERF* **hat sich geweigert)** sich weigern to refuse

**Weihnachten** das *(PLURAL* die **Weihnachten)** Christmas; Frohe Weihnachten! Merry Christmas!

**Weihnachtskrippe** die *(PLURAL* die **Weihnachtskrippen)** Christmas crib scene

**Weihnachtslied** das *(PLURAL* die **Weihnachtslieder)** Christmas carol

**Weihnachtsmann** der *(PLURAL* die **Weihnachtsmänner)** Father Christmas

**Weihnachtstag** der *(PLURAL* die **Weihnachtstage)** Christmas Day; zweiter Weihnachtstag Boxing Day

**weil** *CONJUNCTION* **because**

**Weile** die **while**

**Wein** der *(PLURAL* die **Weine)** wine

**Weinberg** der *(PLURAL* die **Weinberge)** vineyard

**Weinbergschnecke** die *(PLURAL* die **Weinbergschnecken)** snail

**Weinbrand** der *(PLURAL* die **Weinbrände)** brandy

**weinen** *VERB (PERF* **hat geweint)** to cry

**Weinkarte** die (PLURAL die **Weinkarten**) wine list

**Weinkeller** der (PLURAL die **Weinkeller**) wine cellar

**Weinstube** die (PLURAL die **Weinstuben**) wine bar

**Weintraube** die (PLURAL die **Weintrauben**) grape

**weise** ADJECTIVE **wise**

**Weise** die (PLURAL die **Weisen**) way; auf diese Weise in this way

**Weisheit** die (PLURAL die **Weisheiten**) wisdom

**weiß**[1] ▸ SEE wissen

**weiß**[2] ADJECTIVE white

**Weißwein** der (PLURAL die **Weißweine**) white wine

**weit** ADJECTIVE, ADVERB ❶ **wide**, **loose** (clothes) ❷ long; eine weite Reise a long journey ❸ far; wie weit ist es? how far is it?, ist es noch weit? is it much further?, so weit wie möglich as far as possible, bei weitem by far ❹ von weitem from a distance ❺ ich bin so weit I'm ready ❻ weit verbreitet widespread ❼ zu weit gehen to go too far

**weiten** VERB (PERF **hat sich geweitet**) sich weiten to stretch

**weiter** ADJECTIVE, ADVERB ❶ **further** ❷ in addition ❸ etwas weiter tun to go on doing something, weiter nichts nothing else weiter niemand nobody else ❹ und so weiter and so on

**weiterer, weitere, weiteres** ADJECTIVE ❶ **further** ❷ ohne weiteres just like that, easily ❸ bis auf weiteres for the time being

**weiterfahren** ◇VERB (PRES **fährt weiter**, IMP **fuhr weiter**, PERF **ist weitergefahren**) to go on

**weitergehen** ◇VERB (IMP **ging weiter**, PERF **ist weitergegangen**) to go on

**weiterhin** ADVERB ❶ **still** ❷ in future ❸ etwas weiterhin tun to go on doing something

**weitermachen** VERB (PERF **hat weitergemacht**) to carry on

**Weitsprung** der long jump

**Weizen** der wheat

**welcher, welche, welches** ADJECTIVE **which**; welches Kleid? which dress?, um welche Zeit? at what time?

**welches** PRONOUN ❶ **which (one)** ❷ some; brauchst du Briefmarken? ich habe welche do you need stamps? I've got some ❸ any; hast du welche? have you got any?

**Welle** die (PLURAL die **Wellen**) wave

**Wellensittich** der (PLURAL die **Wellensittiche**) budgerigar

**wellig** ADJECTIVE wavy

**Welt** die (PLURAL die **Welten**) world; auf der ganzen Welt in the whole world

**Weltall** das universe

**Weltkrieg** der (PLURAL die **Weltkriege**) world war

**Weltmeister** der (PLURAL die **Weltmeister**) world champion

**Weltmeisterin** die (PLURAL die **Weltmeisterinnen**) world champion

**Weltmeisterschaft** die (PLURAL

die **Weltmeisterschaften)**
**❶** world championship **❷** die
Weltmeisterschaft *(football)* the
World Cup

**Weltraum** der space

**Weltreise** DIE *(PLURAL* die
**Weltreisen)** world tour

**wem** *PRONOUN* to whom; wem hat er
das Geld gegeben? who did he give
the money to?

**wen** *PRONOUN* whom, who; wen hast
du eingeladen? who did you invite?

**Wende** die **❶** change
**❷** reunification *(of Germany)*

**wenig** *PRONOUN, ADJECTIVE* **❶** little;
zu wenig too little, not enough
**❷** wenige few, in wenigen Wochen
in a few weeks

**wenig** *ADVERB* little; so wenig wie
möglich as little as possible

**weniger** *PRONOUN, ADJECTIVE* less,
fewer; sie hat weniger Geschenke
bekommen she got fewer presents,
immer weniger Geld less and less
money, immer weniger Häuser
fewer and fewer houses

**weniger** *ADVERB, CONJUNCTION* less;
zehn weniger fünf ten minus five

**wenigste** ▸ SEE **wenigster**

**wenigstens** *ADVERB* at least

**wenigster, wenigste,**
**wenigstes** *ADJECTIVE, PRONOUN*
least; am wenigsten least, sein
Geschenk hat mir am wenigsten
gefallen I liked his present least

**wenn** *CONJUNCTION* **❶** when; wenn ich
in München bin, schreibe ich dir I'll
write to you when I'm in Munich,
immer, wenn whenever **❷** if; wenn
es regnet if it rains **❸** außer wenn
unless

**wer** *PRONOUN* who

**werben** ◇*VERB (PRES* **wirbt,** *IMP*
**warb,** *PERF* **hat geworben)** **❶** to
advertise **❷** to recruit *(members)*

**Werbespot** der *(PLURAL* die
**Werbespots)** commercial, advert

**Werbung** die **❶** advertising; in
der Werbung arbeiten to work in
advertising **❷** advertisement;
im Fernsehen kommt viel Werbung
there are many advertisements
on television, Werbung für etwas
machen to advertise something

**werden** ◇*VERB (PRES* **wird,** *IMP* **wurde,**
*PERF* **ist geworden)** **❶** to become;
Arzt werden to become a doctor
**❷** müde werden to get tired, alt
werden to get old, mir wird kalt I'm
getting cold **❸** mir wurde schlecht
I felt sick, blass werden to turn pale
**❹** wach werden to wake up **❺** *(used
to form the future tense)* will, shall;
sie wird anrufen she'll ring, sie wird
gleich da sein she'll be here in a
minute **❻** *(used to form the passive)*
to be; gerufen werden to be called,
er wurde gefragt he was asked
**❼** *(used to form the conditional)* sie
würde kommen she would come,
ich würde gern kommen, aber ...
I'd like to come but ...

**werfen** ◇*VERB (PRES* **wirft,** *IMP* **warf,**
*PERF* **hat geworfen)** to throw

**Werk** das *(PLURAL* die **Werke)** **❶** work
**❷** works *(a factory)*

**Werken** das handicraft

**Werkstatt** die *(PLURAL* die
**Werkstätten)** workshop

**Werktag** der *(PLURAL* die **Werktage)**
weekday

**werktags** *ADVERB* on weekdays

**Werkzeug** das *(PLURAL die Werkzeuge)* tool

**Werkzeugkasten** der *(PLURAL die Werkzeugkästen)* tool box

**wert** *ADJECTIVE* viel wert sein to be worth a lot, nichts wert sein to be worthless

**Wert** der *(PLURAL die Werte)* ❶ value; im Wert von hundert Euros worth one hundred euros ❷ auf etwas Wert legen to attach importance to something ❸ es hat doch keinen Wert there's no point

**wertlos** *ADJECTIVE* worthless

**wertvoll** *ADJECTIVE* valuable

**Wesen** das *(PLURAL die Wesen)* ❶ nature, manner ❷ creature

**wesentlich** *ADJECTIVE* essential; im Wesentlichen essentially

**wesentlich** *ADVERB* considerably

**weshalb** *ADVERB* why

**Wespe** die *(PLURAL die Wespen)* wasp

**wessen** *PRONOUN* whose

**Wessi** der *(informal) (PLURAL die Wessis)* West German

**Weste** die *(PLURAL die Westen)* waistcoat

**Westen** der west

**Western** der *(PLURAL die Western)* western *(film)*

**Westinder** der *(PLURAL die Westinder)* West Indian

**Westinderin** die *(PLURAL die Westinderinnen)* West Indian

**westlich** *ADJECTIVE* ❶ western ❷ westerly

**westlich** *ADVERB, PREPOSITION (+GEN)* westlich von Wien west of Vienna, westlich der Stadt to the west of the town

**weswegen** *ADVERB* why

**Wettbewerb** der *(PLURAL die Wettbewerbe)* competition, contest

**Wette** die *(PLURAL die Wetten)* bet; mit jemandem um die Wette laufen to race somebody

**wetten** *VERB (PERF hat gewettet)* to bet; mit jemandem um etwas wetten to bet somebody something

**Wetter** das weather

**Wetterbericht** der *(PLURAL die Wetterberichte)* weather report

**Wettervorhersage** die weather forecast

**Wettkampf** der *(PLURAL die Wettkämpfe)* contest

**Wettlauf** der race

**wichtig** *ADJECTIVE* important; das wichtigste Exportgut ist Wolle the most important export is wool

**wickeln** *VERB (PERF hat gewickelt)* ❶ to wind ❷ ein Kind wickeln to change a baby

**Widder** der *(PLURAL die Widder)* ❶ ram ❷ Aries; Jan ist Widder Jan's Aries

**widerlich** *ADJECTIVE* disgusting

**widersprechen** ◇*VERB (PRES widerspricht, IMP widersprach, PERF hat widersprochen)* to contradict

**Widerspruch** der *(PLURAL die Widersprüche)* contradiction

A B C D E F G H I J K L M N O P Q R S T U V **W** X Y Z

**Widerstand** der resistance

**widerstehen** ◇*VERB* (*IMP* **widerstand**, *PERF* hat **widerstanden**) to resist

**widmen** *VERB* (*PERF* hat **gewidmet**) ❶ to dedicate ❷ to devote ❸ sich einer Sache widmen to devote yourself to something

**wie** *ADVERB* ❶ how; wie geht's? how are you?, wie viel? how much?, wie viele Leute waren da? how many people were there?, um wie viel Uhr kommst du? (at) what time are you coming? ❷ wie ist Ihr Name? what is your name?, wie ist das Wetter? what's the weather like? ❸ wie bitte? sorry?

**wie** *CONJUNCTION* ❶ as; so schnell wie möglich as quickly as possible ❷ like; wie du like you ❸ wie zum Beispiel such as

**wieder** *ADVERB* ❶ again; sie ist wieder da she's back again ❷ jemanden wieder erkennen to recognize somebody, etwas wieder finden to find something (again), etwas wieder verwerten to recycle something, jemanden wieder beleben to revive somebody

**wiederbekommen** ◇*VERB* (*IMP* **bekam wieder**, *PERF* hat **wiederbekommen**) to get back

**wiederbeleben** *VERB* (*PERF* hat **wiederbelebt**) ▸ SEE **wieder**

**wiedererkennen** ▸ SEE **wieder**

**wiederfinden** ▸ SEE **wieder**

**wiederholen** *VERB* (*PERF* hat **wiederholt**) ❶ to repeat ❷ to bring back ❸ to revise (*schoolwork*) ❹ sich wiederholen to recur, er hat sich wiederholt he's repeated himself

**Wiederholung** die (*PLURAL* die

**Wiederholungen**) ❶ repetition ❷ repeat performance ❸ replay ❹ revision (*at school*)

**Wiederhören** das auf Wiederhören! (*said on the phone*) goodbye!

**wiederkommen** ◇*VERB* (*IMP* **kam wieder**, *PERF* **ist wiedergekommen**) ❶ to come back ❷ to come again

**wiedersehen** ▸ SEE **sehen**

**Wiedersehen** das (*PLURAL* die **Wiedersehen**) ❶ reunion ❷ auf Wiedersehen! goodbye!

**wiedervereinigen** ▸ SEE **vereinigen**

**Wiedervereinigung** die reunification

**wiederverwerten** ▸ SEE **wieder**

**Wiege** die (*PLURAL* die **Wiegen**) cradle

**wiegen** ◇*VERB* (*IMP* **wog**, *PERF* hat **gewogen**) to weigh

**Wiegenlied** das (*PLURAL* die **Wiegenlieder**) lullaby

**Wien** das Vienna

**Wiese** die (*PLURAL* die **Wiesen**) meadow

**wieso** *ADVERB* why

**wieviel** ▸ SEE **wie**

**wievielmal** *ADVERB* how often

**wievielter**, **wievielte**, **wievieltes** *ADJECTIVE* ❶ which ❷ die wievielte Querstraße ist das von hier aus? how many roads is that from here?, der Wievielte ist heute? what's the date today?

**wild** *ADJECTIVE* wild

**Wildleder** das **suede**

**Wildpark** der (PLURAL die **Wildparks**) **wildlife park**

**Wildschwein** DAS (PLURAL die **Wildschweine**) **wild boar**

**will** ▸ SEE **wollen**

**Wille** der **will**; seinen Willen durchsetzen **to get your own way**

**willkommen** ADJECTIVE **welcome**

**willst** ▸ SEE **wollen**

**Wimper** die (PLURAL die **Wimpern**) **eyelash**

**Wimperntusche** die (PLURAL die **Wimperntuschen**) **mascara**

**Wind** der (PLURAL die **Winde**) **wind**

**Windel** die (PLURAL die **Windeln**) **nappy**

**Windhund** der (PLURAL die **Windhunde**) **greyhound**

**windig** ADJECTIVE **windy**

**Windmühle** die (PLURAL die **Windmühlen**) **windmill**

**Windpark** der (PLURAL die **Windparks**) **wind farm**

**Windpocken** PLURAL NOUN **chickenpox**

**Windschutzscheibe** die (PLURAL die **Windschutzscheiben**) **windscreen**

**Windsurfen** das **windsurfing**; Windsurfen gehen **to go windsurfing**

**Winkel** der (PLURAL die **Winkel**) ❶ **angle** ❷ **corner**

**winken** VERB (PERF **hat gewinkt**) **to wave**

**Winter** der (PLURAL die **Winter**) **winter**

**winzig** ADJECTIVE **tiny**

**Wippe** die (PLURAL die **Wippen**) **seesaw**

**wir** PRONOUN **we**; wir sind es **it's us**, wir alle **all of us**

**Wirbel** der (PLURAL die **Wirbel**) ❶ **whirl** ❷ **whirlwind** ❸ **whirlpool** ❹ **commotion**

**Wirbelsäule** die (PLURAL die **Wirbelsäulen**) **spine**

**wirbt** ▸ SEE **werben**

**wird** ▸ SEE **werden**

**wirft** ▸ SEE **werfen**

**wirken** VERB (PERF **hat gewirkt**) ❶ **to have an effect** ❷ gegen etwas wirken **to be effective against something** ❸ **to seem** (sad, happy)

**wirklich** ADJECTIVE **real**

**wirklich** ADVERB **really**

**Wirklichkeit** die **reality**

**wirksam** ADJECTIVE **effective**

**Wirkung** die (PLURAL die **Wirkungen**) **effect**

**wirst** ▸ SEE **werden**

**Wirt** der (PLURAL die **Wirte**) **landlord**

**Wirtin** die (PLURAL die **Wirtinnen**) **landlady**

**Wirtschaft** die (PLURAL die **Wirtschaften**) ❶ **economy** ❷ **pub**

**wirtschaftlich** ADJECTIVE **economic**

**Wirtschaftswissenschaften** PLURAL NOUN **business studies**

**Wirtshaus** das (PLURAL die **Wirtshäuser**) **pub**

**wischen** VERB (PERF **hat gewischt**) **to wipe**

a
b
c
d
e
f
g
h
i
j
k
l
m
n
o
p
q
r
s
t
u
v
**w**
x
y
z

**wissen** ◇VERB (PRES **weiß**, IMP **wusste**, PERF **hat gewusst**) to know; ich weiß, dass er in London wohnt I know he lives in London, ich wüsste gern ... I'd like to know ..., von etwas wissen to know about something, weißt du was? you know what?

**Wissen** das **knowledge**

**Wissenschaft** die (PLURAL die **Wissenschaften**) **science**

**Wissenschaftler** der (PLURAL die **Wissenschaftler**) **scientist**

**Wissenschaftlerin** die (PLURAL die **Wissenschaftlerinnen**) **scientist**

**wissenschaftlich** ADJECTIVE **scientific**

**Witwe** die (PLURAL die **Witwen**) **widow**

**Witwer** der (PLURAL die **Witwer**) **widower**

**Witz** der (PLURAL die **Witze**) **joke**

**witzig** ADJECTIVE **funny**

**WLAN** das **wifi**

**wo** ADVERB **where**; wo seid ihr gewesen? where have you been?, in München, wo Markus seit einem Jahr lebt in Munich, where Markus has been living for a year, wo immer **wherever**

**wo** CONJUNCTION ❶ **seeing that** ❷ **although**; jetzt ist sie mir böse, wo ich doch so nett zu ihr war now she's angry with me, although I've been so nice to her

**woanders** ADVERB **elsewhere**

**Woche** die (PLURAL die **Wochen**) **week**

**Wochenende** das (PLURAL die **Wochenenden**) **weekend**

**wochenlang** ADVERB **for weeks**

**Wochentag** der (PLURAL die **Wochentage**) **weekday**

**wochentags** ADVERB **on weekdays**

**wöchentlich** ADJECTIVE **weekly**

**wofür** ADVERB **what ... for**; wofür brauchst du das Geld? what do you need the money for?

**wog** ▸SEE **wiegen**

**woher** ADVERB **where ... from**; woher ist er? where does he come from?, woher weißt du das? how do you know?

**wohin** ADVERB **where ... (to)**; wohin geht ihr? where are you going?

**wohl** ADVERB ❶ **well**; sich wohl fühlen to feel well, ich fühle mich heute nicht wohl I don't feel well today ❷ sich wohl fühlen to be happy, Anni fühlt sich in London wohl Anni is happy in London ❸ jemandem wohl tun to do somebody good ❹ **probably**; er hat den Zug wohl verpasst he probably missed the train, du bist wohl verrückt! you must be mad! ❺ wohl kaum **hardly**

**Wohl** das ❶ **welfare, well-being** ❷ zu seinem Wohl for his benefit ❸ zum Wohl! cheers!

**wohlhabend** ADJECTIVE **well-off**

**Wohltätigkeitsverein** der (PLURAL die **Wohltätigkeitsvereine**) **charity**

**wohltun** ▸SEE **wohl**

**wohnen** VERB (PERF **hat gewohnt**) ❶ **to live** ❷ **to stay** (for a short time)

**Wohngemeinschaft** die (PLURAL die **Wohngemeinschaften**) **people**

sharing a flat/house; wir wohnen in einer Wohngemeinschaft we share a flat

**wohnhaft** *ADJECTIVE* resident

**Wohnheim** das *(PLURAL die Wohnheime)* ❶ hostel ❷ home *(for old people)*

**Wohnmobil** das *(PLURAL die Wohnmobile)* motor home

**Wohnort** der *(PLURAL die Wohnorte)* place of residence

**Wohnsiedlung** die *(PLURAL die Wohnsiedlung)* housing estate

**Wohnsitz** der *(PLURAL die Wohnsitze)* place of residence

**Wohnung** die *(PLURAL die Wohnungen)* flat, apartment

**Wohnwagen** der *(PLURAL die Wohnwagen)* caravan

**Wohnzimmer** das *(PLURAL die Wohnzimmer)* living room

**Wolf** der *(PLURAL die Wölfe)* wolf

**Wolke** die *(PLURAL die Wolken)* cloud

**Wolkenkratzer** der *(PLURAL die Wolkenkratzer)* skyscraper

**wolkig** *ADJECTIVE* cloudy

**Wolldecke** die *(PLURAL die Wolldecken)* blanket

**Wolle** die wool

**wollen** ⬦*VERB (PRES will, IMP wollte, PERF hat gewollt)* ❶ to want; Anne will einen Hund Anne wants a dog, ich will nach Hause I want to go home ❷ sie wollte gerade gehen she was just about to go ❸ ganz wie du willst as you like

**womit** *ADVERB* ❶ what ... with; womit hast du das gewaschen?

what did you wash it with? ❷ with which

**womöglich** *ADVERB* possibly

**wonach** *ADVERB* ❶ what ... for; wonach suchst du? what are you looking for?, wonach riecht es? what does it smell of? ❷ after which, according to which; eine Regelung, wonach wir eine Stunde mehr arbeiten müssen a rule according to which we have to work an extra hour

**woran** *ADVERB* ❶ what ... of; woran denkst du? what are you thinking of?, woran hast du ihn erkannt? how did you recognize him? ❷ on which, of which; nichts, woran man sich verletzen könnte nothing you could hurt yourself on

**worauf** *ADVERB* ❶ what ... on, what ... for; worauf hast du die Vase gestellt? what did you put the vase on?, worauf wartet ihr? what are you waiting for? ❷ on which, for which; das Regal, worauf das Radio steht the shelf the radio is on, das Einzige, worauf ich mich freue the only thing I'm looking forward to

**woraus** *ADVERB* ❶ what ... from, what ... of; woraus ist das? what's it made of? ❷ from which; es gibt nichts, woraus wir trinken können there isn't anything we can drink out of

**worin** *ADVERB* ❶ what ... in, in what ❷ in which; die Punkte, worin ich mit dir übereinstimme the points I agree with you on

**Wort** das *(PLURAL die Worte/Wörter)* word; mir fehlen die Worte I'm lost for words, ich habe heute zwanzig neue Wörter gelernt I've learnt twenty new words today

**Wörterbuch** das (PLURAL die Wörterbücher) dictionary

**wörtlich** ADJECTIVE word for word

**Wortschatz** der vocabulary

**Wortspiel** das (PLURAL die Wortspiele) pun

**Wortstellung** die word order

**worüber** ADVERB ❶ what ... over, what ... about; worüber lacht ihr? what are you laughing about? ❷ over which, about which

**worum** ADVERB ❶ about what; worum geht es? what's it about?, worum hat sie dich gebeten? what did she ask you for? ❷ for which ❸ round which

**wovon** ADVERB ❶ what ... from, what ... about; wovon redet ihr? what are you talking about? ❷ from which, about which; der Geruch, wovon mir schlecht geworden ist the smell which made me feel sick

**wovor** ADVERB ❶ what ... of; wovor hast du Angst? what are you frightened of? ❷ in front of what ❸ of which ❹ in front of which; der Turm, wovor wir stehen the tower we are standing in front of

**wozu** ADVERB ❶ what ... for, why; wozu brauchst du das? what do you need it for?, wozu? what for? ❷ to which, for which; wozu ich dir raten würde which I would advise

**Wrack** das (PLURAL die Wracks) wreck

**wuchs** ▸ SEE wachsen

**Wuchs** der growth

**wund** ADJECTIVE sore

**Wunde** die (PLURAL die Wunden) wound

**Wunder** das (PLURAL die Wunder) miracle; kein Wunder! no wonder!

**wunderbar** ADJECTIVE wonderful

**wundern** VERB (PERF hat sich gewundert) sich wundern to be surprised

**wunderschön** ADJECTIVE beautiful

**wundervoll** ADJECTIVE wonderful

**Wundschorf** der (PLURAL die Wundschorfe) scab

**Wunsch** der (PLURAL die Wünsche) wish; auf Wunsch on request, haben Sie sonst noch einen Wunsch? will there be anything else?

**wünschen** VERB (PERF hat gewünscht) ❶ to wish; ich wünsche dir alles Gute zum Geburtstag I wish you a happy birthday, ich wünschte, ich könnte ... I wish I could ..., was wünschen Sie? can I help you? ❷ sich etwas wünschen to want something

**wünschenswert** ADJECTIVE desirable

**wurde**, **würde**, **wurden**, **würden**, **wurdest**, **würdest**, **wurdet**, **würdet** ▸ SEE werden

**Wurf** der (PLURAL die Würfe) throw

**Würfel** der (PLURAL die Würfel) ❶ dice (in games) ❷ cube

**würfeln** VERB (PERF hat gewürfelt) to throw the dice

**Würfelspiel** das (PLURAL die Würfelspiele) game of dice

**Wurm** der (PLURAL die Würmer) worm

**Wurst** die *(PLURAL* die **Würste)**
❶ sausage ❷ das ist mir Wurst
*(informal)* I couldn't care less

**Würstchen** das *(PLURAL* die
**Würstchen)** **(little) sausage**

**Wurzel** die *(PLURAL* die **Wurzeln)**
**root**

**würzen** *VERB (PERF* **hat gewürzt)**
**to season**

**würzig** *ADJECTIVE* **spicy**

**wusch** ▸ SEE **waschen**

**wusste** ▸ SEE **wissen**

**Wüste** die *(PLURAL* die **Wüsten)**
**desert**

**Wut** die **rage;** eine Wut auf
jemanden haben to be furious with
somebody

**wütend** *ADJECTIVE* **furious**

**x-beliebig** *ADJECTIVE (informal)* **any;**
eine x-beliebige Zahl any number
(you like)

**x-mal** *ADVERB (informal)* **umpteen
times;** zum x-ten Mal for the
umpteenth time

**Xylophon** das *(PLURAL* die
**Xylophone)** **xylophone**

# Yy

# Zz

**Yoga** das yoga

**Ypsilon** das *(PLURAL* die **Ypsilons)** Y

**zaghaft** *ADJECTIVE* ❶ timid ❷ tentative

**zäh** *ADJECTIVE* tough

**Zahl** die *(PLURAL* die **Zahlen)** ❶ number ❷ figure

**zahlen** *VERB (PERF* hat gezahlt) ❶ to pay; hast du schon gezahlt? have you paid? ❷ to pay for; bitte zahlen! the bill please!

**zählen** *VERB (PERF* hat gezählt) ❶ to count; auf jemanden zählen to count on somebody, jemanden zu seinen Freunden zählen to count somebody among your friends ❷ zählen zu to be one of

**Zähler** der *(PLURAL* die **Zähler)** meter

**zahlreich** *ADJECTIVE* numerous

**Zahlung** die *(PLURAL* die **Zahlungen)** payment

**Zählung** die *(PLURAL* die **Zählungen)** ❶ count ❷ census

**zahm** *ADJECTIVE* tame

**Zahn** der *(PLURAL* die **Zähne)** tooth

**Zahnarzt** der *(PLURAL* die **Zahnärzte)** dentist

**Zahnärztin** die *(PLURAL* die **Zahnärztinnen)** dentist

**Zahnbürste** die *(PLURAL* die **Zahnbürsten)** toothbrush

**Zahnfleisch** das gums

**Zahnpasta** die *(PLURAL* die **Zahnpasten)** toothpaste

**Zahnschmerzen** *PLURAL NOUN* toothache

**Zahnspange** die *(PLURAL* die **Zahnspangen)** brace *(for teeth)*

**Zange** die *(PLURAL* die **Zangen)** pliers

**zanken** *VERB (PERF* hat sich gezankt) sich zanken to squabble

**Zapfen** der *(PLURAL* die **Zapfen)** ❶ cone ❷ icicle

**zappeln** *VERB (PERF* hat gezappelt) ❶ to wriggle ❷ to fidget

**zart** *ADJECTIVE* ❶ delicate, soft ❷ gentle ❸ tender

**zärtlich** *ADJECTIVE* affectionate

**Zauber** der ❶ magic ❷ spell

**Zauberer** der *(PLURAL* die **Zauberer)** magician, conjurer

**Zaubererin** die *(PLURAL* die **Zaubererinnen)** magician, conjurer

**zauberhaft** *ADJECTIVE* enchanting

**zaubern** *VERB (PERF* hat gezaubert) to do magic

**Zaumzeug** das *(PLURAL* die **Zaumzeuge)** bridle

**Zaun** der *(PLURAL* die **Zäune)** fence

**z. B.** *(short for zum Beispiel)* e.g.

**Zebra** das *(PLURAL* die **Zebras)** zebra

**Zebrastreifen** der *(PLURAL* die **Zebrastreifen)** zebra crossing

**Zeh** der *(PLURAL* die **Zehen)** toe

**Zehe** die *(PLURAL* die **Zehen)** ❶ toe ❷ clove *(of garlic)*

**Zehenspitze** die *PLURAL* die **Zehenspitzen**; auf Zehenspitzen on tiptoes

**zehn** *NUMBER* ten

**Zehntel** das *(PLURAL* die **Zehntel)** tenth

**zehnter**, **zehnte**, **zehntes** *ADJECTIVE* tenth

**Zeichen** das *(PLURAL* die **Zeichen)** ❶ sign ❷ signal

**Zeichentrickfilm** *DER (PLURAL* die **Zeichentrickfilme)** cartoon film

**zeichnen** *VERB (PERF* hat gezeichnet) to draw

**Zeichnung** die *(PLURAL* die **Zeichnungen)** drawing

**Zeigefinger** der *(PLURAL* die **Zeigefinger)** index finger

**zeigen** *VERB (PERF* hat gezeigt) ❶ to show; Peter hat uns sein neues Auto gezeigt Peter showed us his new car ❷ to point; auf jemanden zeigen to point at somebody ❸ sich zeigen to appear ❹ es hat sich gezeigt, dass … it has become clear that …, es wird sich zeigen time will tell

**Zeiger** der *(PLURAL* die **Zeiger)** hand

**Zeile** die *(PLURAL* die **Zeilen)** line

**Zeit** die *(PLURAL* die **Zeiten)** ❶ time; sich Zeit lassen to take your time, ich habe keine Zeit mehr I haven't got any more time, eine Zeit lang for a time ❷ es hat Zeit there's no hurry, die erste Zeit at first, in nächster Zeit in the near future

**Zeitalter** das *(PLURAL* die **Zeitalter)** age

**Zeitlang** die ▸ SEE **Zeit**

**Zeitlupe** die **slow motion**; in Zeitlupe **in slow motion**

**Zeitraum** der *(PLURAL* die **Zeiträume)** **period**

**Zeitschrift** die *(PLURAL* die **Zeitschriften)** **magazine**

**Zeitung** die *(PLURAL* die **Zeitungen)** **newspaper**

**Zeitungshändler** der *(PLURAL* die **Zeitungshändler)** **newsagent**

**Zeitverschwendung** die **waste of time**

**zeitweise** *ADVERB* **at times**

**Zelle** die *(PLURAL* die **Zellen)** **❶ cell** **❷ booth**

**Zelt** das *(PLURAL* die **Zelte)** **tent**

**zelten** *VERB (PERF* **hat gezeltet)** **to camp**

**Zeltplatz** der *(PLURAL* die **Zeltplätze)** **campsite**

**Zement** der **cement**

**Zentimeter** der *(PLURAL* die **Zentimeter)** **centimetre**

**Zentimetermaß** das *(PLURAL* die **Zentimetermaße)** **tape measure**

**zentral** *ADJECTIVE* **central**

**Zentrale** die *(PLURAL* die **Zentralen)** **❶ central office, head office** **❷ headquarters ❸ (telephone) exchange, switchboard**

**Zentralheizung** die **central heating**

**Zentrum** das *(PLURAL* die **Zentren)** **centre**

**zerbrechen** ◇*VERB (PRES* **zerbricht,** *IMP* **zerbrach,** *PERF* **hat zerbrochen)** **❶ to break**; Irene hat meine Vase

zerbrochen Irene broke my vase **❷** *(PERF* **ist zerbrochen)** **to break**; die Untertasse ist zerbrochen the saucer broke

**zerbrechlich** *ADJECTIVE* **fragile**

**Zerbrechlichkeit** die **fragility**

**Zeremonie** die *(PLURAL* die **Zeremonien)** **ceremony**

**zerfallen** *VERB (PRES* **zerfällt,** *IMP* **zerfiel,** *PERF* **ist zerfallen)** **to disintegrate, to decay**

**zerreißen** ◇*VERB (IMP* **zerriss,** *PERF* **hat zerrissen)** **❶ to tear**; sie hat sich das Kleid zerrissen she tore her dress **❷ to tear up**; Anna hat seinen Brief zerrissen Anna tore up his letter **❸** *(PERF* **ist zerrissen)** **to tear**; das Hemd ist in der Wäsche zerrissen the shirt got torn in the washing

**zerschlagen** ◇*VERB (PRES* **zerschlägt,** *IMP* **zerschlug,** *PERF* **hat zerschlagen)** **❶ to smash, to smash up ❷ sich zerschlagen to fall through** *(of plans)*, meine Hoffnungen haben sich zerschlagen my hopes were dashed

**zerschneiden** *VERB (IMP* **zerschnitt,** *PERF* **zerschnitten)** **to cut up, to cut to pieces**

**zerstören** *VERB (PERF* **hat zerstört)** **to destroy**

**Zerstörung** die **destruction**

**zerstreuen** *VERB (PERF* **hat zerstreut)** **❶ to scatter ❷ jemanden zerstreuen to entertain somebody ❸ sich zerstreuen to take your mind off things ❹ die Menge hat sich zerstreut the crowd's dispersed**

**zerstreut** *ADJECTIVE* **absent-minded**

**Zettel** der (PLURAL die **Zettel**) ❶ piece of paper ❷ note ❸ leaflet

**Zeug** das (informal) ❶ stuff ❷ things, gear ❸ dummes Zeug nonsense

**Zeuge** der (PLURAL die **Zeugen**) witness

**Zeugin** die (PLURAL die **Zeuginnen**) witness

**Zeugnis** das (PLURAL die **Zeugnisse**) ❶ certificate ❷ report (at school)

**Zickzack** der (PLURAL die **Zickzacke**) zigzag; im Zickzack laufen to zigzag

**Ziege** die (PLURAL die **Ziegen**) goat

**Ziegel** der (PLURAL die **Ziegel**) ❶ brick ❷ tile

**ziehen** ◇VERB (IMP **zog**, PERF **hat gezogen**) ❶ to pull; an etwas ziehen to pull on something, einen Zahn ziehen to pull out a tooth ❷ to draw; einen Strich ziehen to draw a line, eine Niete ziehen to draw a blank ❸ die Bremse ziehen to put on the brakes ❹ to grow (vegetables, flowers) ❺ sich ziehen to run (of a path, road) ❻ (PERF **ist gezogen**) to move; sie sind nach Berlin gezogen they've moved to Berlin

**Ziel** das (PLURAL die **Ziele**) ❶ destination ❷ goal, aim ❸ finish (in sport)

**zielen** VERB (PERF **hat gezielt**) to aim; auf etwas zielen to aim at something

**Zielscheibe** die (PLURAL die **Zielscheiben**) target

**zielstrebig** ADJECTIVE determined

**ziemlich** ADJECTIVE fair

**ziemlich** ADVERB ❶ quite; ziemlich viel quite a lot ❷ fairly; ihre Eltern haben ein ziemlich großes Haus her parents have a fairly large house

**zierlich** ADJECTIVE dainty

**Ziffer** die (PLURAL die **Ziffern**) figure

**Zifferblatt** das (PLURAL die **Zifferblätter**) face, dial

**zig** ADJECTIVE (informal) umpteen

**Zigarette** die (PLURAL die **Zigaretten**) cigarette

**Zigarre** die (PLURAL die **Zigarren**) cigar

**Zigeuner** der (PLURAL die **Zigeuner**) gypsy

**Zigeunerin** die (PLURAL die **Zigeunerinnen**) gypsy

**Zimmer** das (PLURAL die **Zimmer**) room; Zimmer mit Frühstück bed and breakfast, 'Zimmer frei' 'vacancies'

**Zimmermädchen** das (PLURAL die **Zimmermädchen**) chambermaid

**Zimt** der cinnamon

**Zink** das zinc

**zirka** ADVERB about

**Zirkel** der (PLURAL die **Zirkel**) pair of compasses

**Zirkus** der (PLURAL die **Zirkusse**) circus

**zischen** VERB (PERF **hat gezischt**) to hiss

**Zitat** das (PLURAL die **Zitate**) quotation

**zitieren** VERB (PERF **hat zitiert**) to quote

**Zitrone** die (PLURAL die **Zitronen**) lemon

**Zitronensaft** der *(PLURAL* die **Zitronensäfte)** lemon juice

**zittern** *VERB (PERF* **hat gezittert)** to tremble; vor Kälte zittern to shiver

**Zivildienst** der **community service**

**Zivilisation** die *(PLURAL* die **Zivilisationen)** civilization

**zog** ▸ SEE **ziehen**

**zögern** *VERB (PERF* **hat gezögert)** to hesitate

**Zoll** der *(PLURAL* die **Zölle)** ❶ customs; am Zoll at customs ❷ duty; Zoll auf etwas bezahlen to pay duty on something

**Zollbeamte** der *(PLURAL* die **Zollbeamten)** customs officer

**Zollbeamtin** die *(PLURAL* die **Zollbeamtinnen)** customs officer

**zollfrei** *ADJECTIVE* **duty-free**

**Zollkontrolle** die *(PLURAL* die **Zollkontrollen)** customs check

**Zone** die *(PLURAL* die **Zonen)** zone

**Zoo** der *(PLURAL* die **Zoos)** Zoo

**Zoomobjektiv** das *(PLURAL* die **Zoomobjektive)** zoom lens

**Zopf** der *(PLURAL* die **Zöpfe)** plait

**Zorn** der **anger**

**zornig** *ADJECTIVE* **angry**

**zu** *PREPOSITION (+DAT)* ❶ to; ich gehe zum Arzt I'm going to the doctor's, zu einer Party eingeladen sein to be invited to a party ❷ zu ... hin towards, zum Fenster hin towards the window, er kam zu dieser Tür herein he came in through this door ❸ with; das passt nicht zu meinem Mantel it doesn't go with my coat, es gab Wein zum Käse there was

wine with the cheese ❹ at; zu Weihnachten at Christmas, zu Hause at home ❺ zu etwas werden to turn into something ❻ zu diesem Zweck for this purpose, was schenkst du Karin zum Geburtstag? what are you giving Karin for her birthday?, zum Spaß for fun, zum ersten Mal for the first time ❼ sich zu etwas äußern to comment on something, Papier zum Schreiben paper to write on ❽ nett zu jemandem sein to be nice to somebody ❾ sie waren zu zweit there were two of them, eine Marke zu achtzig Cent an 80-Cent stamp, es steht drei zu zwei the score is 3-2 ❿ zu Fuß on foot

**zu** *ADVERB* ❶ too; zu groß too big ❷ closed; zu haben to be closed, Tür zu! *(informal)* shut the door! ❸ zu sein to be closed, alle Läden sind zu gewesen the shops were all closed ❹ towards *(indicating direction)* ❺ mach zu! *(informal)* hurry up!

**zu** *CONJUNCTION* **to**; nichts zu essen nothing to eat, zu verkaufen for sale

**zuallererst** *ADVERB* **first of all**

**zuallerletzt** *ADVERB* **last of all**

**Zubehör** das **accessories**

**zubereiten** *VERB (PERF* **hat zubereitet)** to prepare; sie bereitet das Essen zu she's preparing the meal

**zubinden** ◇*VERB (IMP* **band zu**, *PERF* **hat zugebunden)** to tie, to tie up

**zubringen** ◇*VERB (IMP* **brachte zu**, *PERF* **hat zugebracht)** to spend; sie bringt viel Zeit bei ihrem Freund zu she spends a lot of time with her boyfriend

**Zucchini** *PLURAL NOUN* **courgettes**

**Zucht** die *(PLURAL* die **Zuchten)** **❶ breed**, **species ❷ breeding** *(of animals)* **❸ breeding establishment**

**züchten** *VERB (PERF* **hat gezüchtet)** **to breed**

**zucken** *VERB (PERF* **hat gezuckt)** **to twitch**

**Zucker** der **sugar**

**Zuckerguss** der **icing**

**zuckerkrank** *ADJECTIVE* **diabetic**

**zudecken** *VERB (PERF* **hat zugedeckt)** **❶ to cover up**, **to cover ❷ to tuck up** *(in bed)*

**zueinander** *ADVERB* **❶ to one another**; **lieb zueinander sein** to be nice to one another **❷ together** **zueinander passen** to go together, **zueinander halten** to stick together

**zuerst** *ADVERB* **❶ first ❷ at first**

**Zufahrt** die *(PLURAL* die **Zufahrten)** **❶ access ❷ drive(way)**

**Zufall** der *(PLURAL* die **Zufälle)** **❶ chance**; **durch Zufall** by chance **❷ coincidence**; **so ein komischer Zufall** such a strange coincidence, **per Zufall traf ich ihn in der U-Bahn** by coincidence I met him in the tube

**zufällig** *ADJECTIVE* **chance**; **das war rein zufällig** it was purely by chance

**zufällig** *ADVERB* **by chance**; **kannst du mir zufällig zehn Euro leihen?** could you lend me ten euros by any chance?

**Zuflucht** die **refuge**

**zufrieden** *ADJECTIVE* **❶ content ❷ satisfied**; **mit etwas zufrieden sein** to be satisfied with something

**zufrieden** *ADVERB* **jemanden zufrieden lassen** to leave somebody in peace, **jemanden zufrieden stellen** to satisfy somebody

**zufriedenlassen, zufriedenstellen** ▸ SEE **zufrieden**

**Zug** der *(PLURAL* die **Züge)** **❶ train ❷ procession ❸ characteristic**, **trait ❹ move** *(in games)* **❺ swig** *(when drinking)* **❻ drag** *(when smoking)* **❼ in einem Zug** in one go

**Zugabe** die *(PLURAL* die **Zugaben)** **❶ free gift ❷ encore**

**Zugang** der *(PLURAL* die **Zugänge)** **access**

**zugeben** ◇*VERB (PRES* **gibt zu**, *IMP* **gab zu**, *PERF* **hat zugegeben)** **❶ to add ❷ to admit**

**zugehen** ◇*VERB (IMP* **ging zu**, *PERF* **ist zugegangen)** **❶ to close**, **to shut**; **die Tür geht nicht zu** the door won't shut **❷ auf etwas zugehen** to go towards something, **auf jemanden zugehen** to walk up to somebody **❸ jemandem zugehen** to be sent to somebody **❹ auf der Party ging es lustig zu** the party was good fun **❺ dem Ende zugehen** to be nearing the end

**zügig** *ADJECTIVE* **quick**

**zugreifen** ◇*VERB (IMP* **griff zu**, *PERF* **hat zugegriffen)** **❶ to grab it/ them ❷ to help yourself ❸ to lend a hand**

**zugunsten** *PREPOSITION (+GEN)* **in favour of**

**zuhaben** ▸ SEE **zu**

**Zuhause** das **home**

**zuhören** *VERB (PERF* **hat zugehört)** **to listen**

**Zuhörer** der *(PLURAL die Zuhörer)* listener

**Zuhörerin** die *(PLURAL die Zuhörerinnen)* listener

**zukleben** VERB *(PERF hat zugeklebt)* to seal *(an envelope)*

**zukommen** ◇VERB *(IMP kam zu, PERF ist zugekommen)* ❶ auf jemanden zukommen to come up to somebody, nächstes Jahr kommt eine Menge Arbeit auf mich zu I'm in for a lot of work next year ❷ jemandem etwas zukommen lassen to give somebody something ❸ etwas auf sich zukommen lassen to take things as they come

**Zukunft** die future

**zukünftig** ADJECTIVE future

**zulassen** ◇VERB *(PRES lässt zu, IMP ließ zu, PERF hat zugelassen)* ❶ to allow ❷ to register *(a car)* ❸ to leave closed

**Zulassung** die *(PLURAL die Zulassungen)* ❶ registration ❷ admission

**zuletzt** ADVERB ❶ last ❷ in the end

**zum** zu dem; ❶ etwas zum Lesen something to read ❷ spätestens zum fünften März by 5 March at the latest ❸ er hat es zum Fenster hinausgeworfen he threw it out of the window

**zumachen** VERB *(PERF hat zugemacht)* ❶ to close, to shut ❷ to fasten

**zumindest** ADVERB at least

**zunächst** ADVERB ❶ first (of all) ❷ at first

**Zunahme** die *(PLURAL die Zunahmen)* increase

**Zuname** der *(PLURAL die Zunamen)* surname

**zunehmen** ◇VERB *(PRES nimmt zu, IMP nahm zu, PERF hat zugenommen)* ❶ to increase ❷ to put on weight

**Zunge** die *(PLURAL die Zungen)* tongue

**zur** zu der ▸ SEE zu

**zurechtkommen** ◇VERB *(IMP kam zurecht, PERF ist zurechtgekommen)* to cope, to manage

**zurechtlegen** VERB *(PERF hat zurechtgelegt)* ❶ to put out ready ❷ sich eine Ausrede zurechtlegen to think up an excuse

**zurück** ADVERB ❶ back ❷ Hamburg, hin und zurück a return to Hamburg

**zurückbekommen** ◇VERB *(IMP bekam zurück, PERF hat zurückbekommen)* to get back; zehn Pfennig zurückbekommen to get 10 pfennigs change

**zurückbringen** ◇VERB *(IMP brachte zurück, PERF hat zurückgebracht)* ❶ to bring back ❷ to take back

**zurückfahren** ◇VERB *(PRES fährt zurück, IMP fuhr zurück, PERF ist zurückgefahren)* ❶ to go back ❷ to drive back ❸ *(PERF hat zurückgefahren)* to drive back; jemanden zurückfahren to drive somebody back

**zurückgeben** ◇VERB *(PRES gibt zurück, IMP gab zurück, PERF hat zurückgegeben)* to give back

**zurückgehen** ◇VERB *(IMP ging zurück, PERF ist zurückgegangen)* ❶ to go back; zurückgehen auf to go back to ❷ to go down ❸ to decrease

**zurückhalten** ◇*VERB (PRES* **hält zurück**, *IMP* **hielt zurück**, *PERF* **hat zurückgehalten**) ❶ to hold back ❷ **sich zurückhalten** to restrain yourself

**zurückkommen** ◇*VERB (IMP* **kam zurück**, *PERF* **ist zurückgekommen**) ❶ to come back; **nach Hause zurückkommen** to return home ❷ to get back

**zurücklassen** ◇*VERB (PRES* **lässt zurück**, *IMP* **ließ zurück**, *PERF* **hat zurückgelassen**) to leave behind

**zurücklegen** *VERB (PERF* **hat zurückgelegt**) ❶ to put back ❷ to keep, to put aside ❸ **Geld für etwas zurücklegen** to put money by for something ❹ to cover *(a distance)* ❺ **sich zurücklegen** to lie back

**zurücknehmen** ◇*VERB (PRES* **nimmt zurück**, *IMP* **nahm zurück**, *PERF* **hat zurückgenommen**) to take back

**zurückrufen** ◇*VERB (IMP* **rief zurück**, *PERF* **hat zurückgerufen**) to call back

**zurücktreten** ◇*VERB (PRES* **tritt zurück**, *IMP* **trat zurück**, *PERF* **ist zurückgetreten**) ❶ to step back ❷ to resign

**zurückzahlen** *VERB (PERF* **hat zurückgezahlt**) to pay back

**zurückziehen** ◇*VERB (IMP* **zog zurück**, *PERF* **hat zurückgezogen**) ❶ to draw back ❷ to withdraw *(an offer)* ❸ **sich zurückziehen** to withdraw, to retire

**zurzeit** *ADVERB* at the moment

**Zusage** die *(PLURAL die* **Zusagen**) acceptance

**zusammen** *ADVERB* ❶ together; **zusammen sein** to be together ❷ altogether

**Zusammenarbeit** die co-operation

**zusammenarbeiten** *VERB (PERF* **hat zusammengearbeitet**) to co-operate

**zusammenbleiben** ◇*VERB (IMP* **blieb zusammen**, *PERF* **ist zusammengeblieben**) to stay together

**zusammenbrechen** ◇*VERB (PRES* **bricht zusammen**, *IMP* **brach zusammen**, *PERF* **ist zusammengebrochen**) to collapse

**zusammenfassen** *VERB (PERF* **hat zusammengefasst**) to summarize

**Zusammenfassung** die *(PLURAL die* **Zusammenfassungen**) summary

**zusammenhalten** ◇*VERB (PRES* **hält zusammen**, *IMP* **hielt zusammen**, *PERF* **hat zusammengehalten**) ❶ to hold together ❷ to keep together ❸ **die Kinder haben zusammengehalten** the children stuck together

**Zusammenhang** der *(PLURAL die* **Zusammenhänge**) ❶ context ❷ connection

**zusammenkommen** ◇*VERB (IMP* **kam zusammen**, *PERF* **ist zusammengekommen**) ❶ to meet ❷ to accumulate

**Zusammenkunft** die *(PLURAL die* **Zusammenkünfte**) meeting

**zusammenlegen** *VERB (PERF* **hat**

a
b
c
d
e
f
g
h
i
j
k
l
m
n
o
p
q
r
s
t
u
v
w
x
y
z

zusammengelegt) ❶ to put together ❷ to fold up ❸ to club together

**zusammennehmen** ◇VERB (PRES **nimmt zusammen,** IMP **nahm zusammen,** PERF **hat zusammengenommen**) ❶ to gather up ❷ to summon up, to collect ❸ sich zusammennehmen to pull yourself together

**zusammenpassen** VERB (PERF **hat zusammengepasst**) ❶ to match ❷ to be well matched (of people) ❸ to fit together

**Zusammensein** das get-together

**Zusammenstoß** der (PLURAL die **Zusammenstöße**) collision, crash

**zusammenstoßen** ◇VERB (PRES **stößt zusammen,** IMP **stieß zusammen,** PERF **ist zusammengestoßen**) to collide, to crash

**zusammenzählen** VERB (PERF **hat zusammengezählt**) to add up

**zusätzlich** ADJECTIVE additional, extra

**zusätzlich** ADVERB in addition, extra

**zuschauen** VERB (PERF **hat zugeschaut**) to watch

**Zuschauer** der (PLURAL die **Zuschauer**) ❶ spectator ❷ viewer ❸ die Zuschauer the audience

**Zuschauerin** die (PLURAL die **Zuschauerinnen**) ❶ spectator ❷ viewer

**Zuschlag** der (PLURAL die **Zuschläge**) ❶ surcharge ❷ supplement

**Zuschuss** der (PLURAL die **Zuschüsse**) ❶ contribution ❷ grant

**zusehen** ◇VERB (PRES **sieht zu,** IMP **sah zu,** PERF **hat zugesehen**) ❶ to watch ❷ zusehen, dass ... to see (to it) that ...

**zusein** ▸ SEE zu

**zusenden** VERB (PERF **hat zugesendet**) to send; jemandem etwas zusenden to send something to somebody

**Zustand** der (PLURAL die **Zustände**) ❶ condition ❷ state

**zustande** ADVERB zustande bringen to bring about, zustande kommen to come about

**zuständig** ADJECTIVE responsible

**Zustellung** die (PLURAL die **Zustellungen**) delivery

**zustimmen** VERB (PERF **hat zugestimmt**) to agree

**Zustimmung** die (PLURAL die **Zustimmungen**) ❶ agreement ❷ approval

**zustoßen** ◇VERB (PRES **stößt zu,** IMP **stieß zu,** PERF **ist zugestoßen**) to happen

**Zutat** die (PLURAL die **Zutaten**) ingredient

**zutreffen** ◇VERB (PRES **trifft zu,** IMP **traf zu,** PERF **hat zugetroffen**) auf etwas zutreffen to apply to something

**Zutritt** der entry; Zutritt haben to have access

**zuverlässig** ADJECTIVE reliable

**zuversichtlich** ADJECTIVE confident, optimistic

**Zuversichtlichkeit** die confidence

**zuviel** ▸ SEE viel

**zuvor** *ADVERB* ❶ **before**; der Tag zuvor the day before ❷ **first**

**zuwenig** ▸ SEE **wenig**

**zuzahlen** *VERB* (*PERF* **hat zugezahlt**) to pay extra

**zuziehen** ◇*VERB* (*IMP* **zog zu**, *PERF* **hat zugezogen**) ❶ to pull tight ❷ to draw *(curtains)* ❸ to call in *(an expert etc.)* ❹ (*PERF* **ist zugezogen**) to move into an area ❺ sich eine Verletzung zuziehen to sustain an injury
sich eine Erkältung zuziehen to catch a cold

**zuzüglich** *PREPOSITION* (*+GEN*) **plus**

**zwang** ▸ SEE **zwingen**

**Zwang** der (*PLURAL* die **Zwänge**) ❶ **compulsion** ❷ **urge** ❸ **obligation**

**zwängen** *VERB* (*PERF* **hat gezwängt**) to squeeze

**zwanglos** *ADJECTIVE* **casual, informal**

**zwar** *ADVERB* ❶ **admittedly** ❷ ich war zwar dabei, habe aber nichts gesehen I was there, but I didn't see anything ❸ und zwar to be exact

**Zweck** der (*PLURAL* die **Zwecke**) ❶ **purpose** ❷ **point**; es hat keinen Zweck there's no point

**zwecklos** *ADJECTIVE* **pointless**

**zwei** *NUMBER* **two**

**zweideutig** *ADJECTIVE* **ambiguous**

**zweifach** *ADJECTIVE* **twice**

**Zweifel** der (*PLURAL* die **Zweifel**) **doubt**

**zweifelhaft** *ADJECTIVE* ❶ **doubtful** ❷ **dubious**

**zweifellos** *ADVERB* **undoubtedly**

**zweifeln** *VERB* (*PERF* **hat gezweifelt**) to doubt; an etwas zweifeln to doubt something

**Zweig** der (*PLURAL* die **Zweige**) ❶ **branch** ❷ **twig**

**zweihundert** *NUMBER* **two hundred**

**zweimal** *ADVERB* **twice**

**zweisprachig** *ADJECTIVE* **bilingual**

**zweispurig** *ADJECTIVE* **two-track** *(railway, recording, road)*; eine zweispurigen Straße a dual carriageway

**zweit** *ADVERB* zu zweit in twos, wir sind zu zweit there are two of us

**zweite** ▸ SEE **zweiter**

**zweitens** *ADVERB* **secondly**

**zweiter, zweite, zweites** *ADJECTIVE* **second**; Mario kam als Zweiter Mario was the second to arrive

**Zwerg** der (*PLURAL* die **Zwerge**) **dwarf**

**Zwiebel** die (*PLURAL* die **Zwiebeln**) ❶ **onion** ❷ **bulb**

**Zwilling** der (*PLURAL* die **Zwillinge**) ❶ **twin** ❷ Zwillinge Gemini, Markus ist Zwilling Markus is Gemini

**zwingen** ◇*VERB* (*IMP* **zwang**, *PERF* **hat gezwungen**) ❶ to force ❷ sich zwingen to force yourself

**zwinkern** *VERB* (*PERF* **hat gezwinkert**) to wink

**zwischen** *PREPOSITION* ❶ (*+DAT, or +ACC with movement towards a place*) **between** ❷ **among** *(a crowd)*

**zwischendurch** *ADVERB* ❶ **in between** ❷ **now and again**

a
b
c
d
e
f
g
h
i
j
k
l
m
n
o
p
q
r
s
t
u
v
w
x
y
z

**Zwischenfall** der *(PLURAL* die Zwischenfälle*)* **incident**

**Zwischenlandung** die *(PLURAL* die Zwischenlandungen*)* **stop-over**

**Zwischenraum** der *(PLURAL* die Zwischenräume*)* **gap**, **space**

**Zwischenzeit** die in der Zwischenzeit **in the meantime**

**zwo** *NUMBER* **two**

**zwölf** *NUMBER* **twelve**

**zwoter**, **zwote**, **zwotes** *ADJECTIVE* **second**

# VERB TABLES

On the following pages you will find forms for a **regular German verb machen** followed by the forms for a **reflexive verb sich waschen** and then the forms for twelve important **irregular verbs** in alphabetical order: **dürfen, essen, fahren, gehen, haben, kommen, können, müssen, sein, sollen, werden** and **wissen**.

After these, the main forms for other **irregular verbs** are given. Note that the forms for **separable verbs** such as **aufstehen** are not given as they can be looked up under the base form, for example **stehen**.

## Guide to the verb tables

### Personal pronouns

| | | | |
|---|---|---|---|
| ich | = I | ihr | = you *(plural)* |
| du | = you *(singular)* | Sie | = you *(polite form / singular and plural)* |
| er / sie / es | = he / she / it | | |
| wir | = we | sie | = they |

### Perfect and Imperfect tense

In German, both these tenses are **past tenses**. The **Perfect tense** is usually used in spoken German or informal letters. The **Imperfect tense** is usually used when writing formal letters or stories. When you are translating sentences with 'already' or 'yet' in them (German **schon**), the **English Perfect tense** should be translated with the **German Perfect tense**, not the **Imperfect**. For example:

I saw the film yesterday.
**Ich habe den Film gestern gesehen** or **Ich sah den Film gestern.**

I have seen the film already.
**Ich habe den Film schon gesehen.**

### Translation of Perfect and Imperfect tense

Both German past tenses can sometimes be translated into English with the 'I was doing' form of the verb. For example:

**Wir spielten Tischtennis, als er ankam. / Wir haben Tischtennis gespielt, als er ankam.** We were playing table tennis when he arrived.

### Imperative

The imperative form does not make sense with all verbs. Therefore it has only been given where it makes sense. For example:

| | | |
|---|---|---|
| **Frag!** | Ask! | *(speaking to one friend)* |
| **Fragt!** | Ask! | *(speaking to two or more friends)* |
| **Fragen Sie!** | Ask! | *(polite form)* |
| **Fragen wir!** | Let's ask! | *(speaking to yourself and others)* |

## [1]

## machen
to make *or* to do

**Imperative**
Mach!
Make! *or* Do!
Macht!
Make! *or* Do!
Machen Sie!
Make! *or* Do!
Machen wir!
Let's make! *or* Let's do!

**Past participle**
gemacht
made *or* done

### Present

| ich | mache | I make *or* |
|-----|-------|-------------|
|     |       | I do        |
| du  | machst |            |
| er* | macht |             |
| wir | machen |            |
| ihr | macht |             |
| sie* | machen |           |

### Perfect

| ich | habe gemacht | I made *or* |
|-----|--------------|-------------|
|     |              | I did       |
| du  | hast gemacht |             |
| er  | hat gemacht  |             |
| wir | haben gemacht |            |
| ihr | habt gemacht |             |
| sie | haben gemacht |            |

### Future

| ich | werde machen | I will make *or* |
|-----|--------------|------------------|
|     |              | I will do        |
| du  | wirst machen |                  |
| er  | wird machen  |                  |
| wir | werden machen |                 |
| ihr | werdet machen |                 |
| sie | werden machen |                 |

### Present subjunctive

| ich | mache | I make *or* |
|-----|-------|-------------|
|     |       | I do        |
| du  | machest |           |
| er  | mache |             |
| wir | machen |            |
| ihr | machet |            |
| sie | machen |            |

### Imperfect

| ich | machte | I made *or* I did |
|-----|--------|-------------------|
| du  | machtest |                 |
| er  | machte |                 |
| wir | machten |                |
| ihr | machtet |                |
| sie | machten |                |

### Conditional

| ich | würde machen | I would make *or* |
|-----|--------------|-------------------|
|     |              | I would do        |
| du  | würdest machen |                 |
| er  | würde machen |                  |
| wir | würden machen |                 |
| ihr | würdet machen |                 |
| sie | würden machen |                 |

* In these tables er should be read as er / sie / es and sie should be read as sie / Sie.

**Imperative**
Wasch dich!
Wash!
Wascht euch!
Wash!
Waschen Sie sich!
Wash!
Waschen wir uns!
Let's wash!

**Past participle**
gewaschen
washed

## sich waschen

to wash (yourself)

| **Present** | | **Present subjunctive** | |
|---|---|---|---|
| ich wasche mich | I wash | ich wasche mich | I wash |
| du wäschst dich | | du waschest dich | |
| er* wäscht sich | | er wasche sich | |
| wir waschen uns | | wir waschen uns | |
| ihr wascht euch | | ihr waschet euch | |
| sie* waschen sich | | sie waschen sich | |

| **Perfect** | | **Imperfect** | |
|---|---|---|---|
| ich habe mich gewaschen | I washed | ich wusch mich | I washed |
| du hast dich gewaschen | | du wuschst dich | |
| er hat sich gewaschen | | er wusch sich | |
| wir haben uns gewaschen | | wir wuschen uns | |
| ihr habt euch gewaschen | | ihr wuscht euch | |
| sie haben sich gewaschen | | sie wuschen sich | |

| **Future** | | **Conditional** | |
|---|---|---|---|
| ich werde mich waschen | I will wash | ich würde mich waschen | I would wash |
| du wirst dich waschen | | du würdest dich waschen | |
| er wird sich waschen | | er würde sich waschen | |
| wir werden uns waschen | | wir würden uns waschen | |
| ihr werdet euch waschen | | ihr würdet euch waschen | |
| sie werden sich waschen | | sie würden sich waschen | |

* In these tables **er** should be read as **er / sie / es** and **sie** should be read as **sie / Sie**.

## [3]
### dürfen
to be allowed

**Imperative**
The imperative of
dürfen is not used.

**Past participle**
gedurft
allowed
dürfen
allowed

**Present**

| ich | darf | I am allowed |
|-----|------|--------------|
| du | darfst | |
| er* | darf | |
| wir | dürfen | |
| ihr | dürft | |
| sie* | dürfen | |

**Present subjunctive**

| ich | dürfe | I am allowed |
|-----|-------|--------------|
| du | dürfest | |
| er | dürfe | |
| wir | dürfen | |
| ihr | dürfet | |
| sie | dürfen | |

**Perfect**

| ich | habe gedurft | I was allowed |
|-----|--------------|---------------|
| du | hast gedurft | |
| er | hat gedurft | |
| wir | haben gedurft | |
| ihr | habt gedurft | |
| sie | haben gedurft | |

**Imperfect**

| ich | durfte | I was allowed |
|-----|--------|---------------|
| du | durftest | |
| er | durfte | |
| wir | durften | |
| ihr | durftet | |
| sie | durften | |

**Future**

| ich | werde dürfen | I will be allowed |
|-----|--------------|-------------------|
| du | wirst dürfen | |
| er | wird dürfen | |
| wir | werden dürfen | |
| ihr | werdet dürfen | |
| sie | werden dürfen | |

**Conditional**

| ich | würde dürfen | I would be allowed |
|-----|--------------|--------------------|
| du | würdest dürfen | |
| er | würde dürfen | |
| wir | würden dürfen | |
| ihr | würdet dürfen | |
| sie | würden dürfen | |

* In these tables **er** should be read as **er / sie / es** and **sie** should be read as **sie / Sie**.

| **Imperative** | **Past participle** |
|---|---|
| Iss! | gegessen |
| Eat! | eaten |
| Esst! | |
| Eat! | |
| Essen Sie! | |
| Eat! | |
| Essen wir! | |
| Let's eat! | |

## Present

| ich | esse | I eat |
|---|---|---|
| du | isst | |
| er* | isst | |
| wir | essen | |
| ihr | esst | |
| sie* | essen | |

## Present subjunctive

| ich | esse | I eat |
|---|---|---|
| du | essest | |
| er | esse | |
| wir | essen | |
| ihr | esset | |
| sie | essen | |

## Perfect

| ich | habe gegessen | I ate |
|---|---|---|
| du | hast gegessen | |
| er | hat gegessen | |
| wir | haben gegessen | |
| ihr | habt gegessen | |
| sie | haben gegessen | |

## Imperfect

| ich | aß | I ate |
|---|---|---|
| du | aßest | |
| er | aß | |
| wir | aßen | |
| ihr | aßt | |
| sie | aßen | |

## Future

| ich | werde essen | I will eat |
|---|---|---|
| du | wirst essen | |
| er | wird essen | |
| wir | werden essen | |
| ihr | werdet essen | |
| sie | werden essen | |

## Conditional

| ich | würde essen | I would eat |
|---|---|---|
| du | würdest essen | |
| er | würde essen | |
| wir | würden essen | |
| ihr | würdet essen | |
| sie | würden essen | |

* In these tables **er** should be read as **er / sie / es** and **sie** should be read as **sie / Sie**.

# [5]

## fahren
to drive *or* to go

**Imperative**
Fahr!
Drive! *or* Go!
Fahrt!
Drive! *or* Go!
Fahren Sie!
Drive! *or* Go!
Fahren wir!
Let's drive! *or* Let's go!

**Past participle**
gefahren
driven *or* gone

### Present

| ich fahre | I drive *or* I go |
| du fährst | |
| er* fährt | |
| wir fahren | |
| ihr fahrt | |
| sie* fahren | |

### Present subjunctive

| ich fahre | I drive *or* I go |
| du fahrest | |
| er fahre | |
| wir fahren | |
| ihr fahret | |
| sie fahren | |

### Perfect

| ich bin gefahren | I drove *or* I went |
| du bist gefahren | |
| er ist gefahren | |
| wir sind gefahren | |
| ihr seid gefahren | |
| sie sind gefahren | |

### Imperfect

| ich fuhr | I drove *or* I went |
| du fuhrst | |
| er fuhr | |
| wir fuhren | |
| ihr fuhrt | |
| sie fuhren | |

### Future

| ich werde fahren | I will drive *or* I will go |
| du wirst fahren | |
| er wird fahren | |
| wir werden fahren | |
| ihr werdet fahren | |
| sie werden fahren | |

### Conditional

| ich würde fahren | I would drive *or* I would go |
| du würdest fahren | |
| er würde fahren | |
| wir würden fahren | |
| ihr würdet fahren | |
| sie würden fahren | |

* In these tables **er** should be read as **er / sie / es** and **sie** should be read as **sie / Sie**.

| **Imperative** | **Past participle** |
| --- | --- |
| Geh! | gegangen |
| Go! | gone |
| Geht! | |
| Go! | |
| Gehen Sie! | |
| Go! | |
| Gehen wir! | |
| Let's go! | |

## [6]

### gehen
to go *or* to leave

### Present

| ich | gehe | I go |
| --- | --- | --- |
| du | gehst | |
| er* | geht | |
| wir | gehen | |
| ihr | geht | |
| sie* | gehen | |

### Present subjunctive

| ich | gehe | I go |
| --- | --- | --- |
| du | gehest | |
| er | gehe | |
| wir | gehen | |
| ihr | gehet | |
| sie | gehen | |

### Perfect

| ich | bin gegangen | I went |
| --- | --- | --- |
| du | bist gegangen | |
| er | ist gegangen | |
| wir | sind gegangen | |
| ihr | seid gegangen | |
| sie | sind gegangen | |

### Imperfect

| ich | ging | I went |
| --- | --- | --- |
| du | gingst | |
| er | ging | |
| wir | gingen | |
| ihr | gingt | |
| sie | gingen | |

### Future

| ich | werde gehen | I will go |
| --- | --- | --- |
| du | wirst gehen | |
| er | wird gehen | |
| wir | werden gehen | |
| ihr | werdet gehen | |
| sie | werden gehen | |

### Conditional

| ich | würde gehen | I would go |
| --- | --- | --- |
| du | würdest gehen | |
| er | würde gehen | |
| wir | würden gehen | |
| ihr | würdet gehen | |
| sie | würden gehen | |

* In these tables **er** should be read as **er** / **sie** / **es** and **sie** should be read as **sie** / **Sie**.

**[7]**

**haben**
to have

| **Imperative** | **Past participle** |
|---|---|
| Hab! | gehabt |
| Have! | had |
| Habt! | |
| Have! | |
| Haben Sie! | |
| Have! | |
| Haben wir! | |
| Let's have! | |

## Present

| ich | habe | I have |
|---|---|---|
| du | hast | |
| er* | hat | |
| wir | haben | |
| ihr | habt | |
| sie* | haben | |

## Present subjunctive

| ich | habe | I have |
|---|---|---|
| du | habest | |
| er | habe | |
| wir | haben | |
| ihr | habet | |
| sie | haben | |

## Perfect

| ich | habe gehabt | I had |
|---|---|---|
| du | hast gehabt | |
| er | hat gehabt | |
| wir | haben gehabt | |
| ihr | habt gehabt | |
| sie | haben gehabt | |

## Imperfect

| ich | hatte | I had |
|---|---|---|
| du | hattest | |
| er | hatte | |
| wir | hatten | |
| ihr | hattet | |
| sie | hatten | |

## Future

| ich | werde haben | I will have |
|---|---|---|
| du | wirst haben | |
| er | wird haben | |
| wir | werden haben | |
| ihr | werdet haben | |
| sie | werden haben | |

## Imperfect subjunctive

| ich | hätte | I would have+ |
|---|---|---|
| du | hättest | |
| er | hätte | |
| wir | hätten | |
| ihr | hättet | |
| sie | hätten | |

## Conditional

| ich | würde haben | I would have |
|---|---|---|
| du | würdest haben | |
| er | würde haben | |
| wir | würden haben | |
| ihr | würdet haben | |
| sie | würden haben | |

---

* In these tables er should be read as er / sie / es and sie should be read as sie / Sie.
+ 'Ich hätte' can also be translated as 'I had', e.g. Wenn ich viel Geld hätte … If I had lots of money …

| **Imperative** | **Past participle** |
|---|---|
| Komm! | gekommen |
| Come! | come |
| Kommt! | |
| Come! | |
| Kommen Sie! | |
| Come! | |
| Kommen wir! | |
| Let's come! | |

**Present**

| ich komme | I come |
|---|---|
| du kommst | |
| er* kommt | |
| wir kommen | |
| ihr kommt | |
| sie* kommen | |

**Present subjunctive**

| ich komme | I come |
|---|---|
| du kommest | |
| er komme | |
| wir kommen | |
| ihr kommet | |
| sie kommen | |

**Perfect**

| ich bin gekommen | I came |
|---|---|
| du bist gekommen | |
| er ist gekommen | |
| wir sind gekommen | |
| ihr seid gekommen | |
| sie sind gekommen | |

**Imperfect**

| ich kam | I came |
|---|---|
| du kamst | |
| er kam | |
| wir kamen | |
| ihr kamt | |
| sie kamen | |

**Future**

| ich werde kommen | I will come |
|---|---|
| du wirst kommen | |
| er wird kommen | |
| wir werden kommen | |
| ihr werdet kommen | |
| sie werden kommen | |

**Conditional**

| ich würde kommen | I will come |
|---|---|
| du würdest kommen | |
| er würde kommen | |
| wir würden kommen | |
| ihr würdet kommen | |
| sie würden kommen | |

* In these tables **er** should be read as **er / sie / es** and **sie** should be read as **sie / Sie**.

# [9]

## können

can *or*
to be able to

**Imperative**
The imperative of
können is not used.

**Past participle**
gekonnt
been able to
hätte können
been able to

## Present

| ich | kann | I can *or* I am able to |
| du | kannst | |
| er* | kann | |
| wir | können | |
| ihr | könnt | |
| sie* | können | |

## Perfect

| ich | habe gekonnt | I could *or* I was able to |
| du | hast gekonnt | |
| er | hat gekonnt | |
| wir | haben gekonnt | |
| ihr | habt gekonnt | |
| sie | haben gekonnt | |

## Future

| ich | werde können | I will be able to |
| du | wirst können | |
| er | wird können | |
| wir | werden können | |
| ihr | werdet können | |
| sie | werden können | |

## Present subjunctive

| ich | könne | I can *or* I am able to |
| du | könnest | |
| er | könne | |
| wir | können | |
| ihr | könnet | |
| sie | können | |

## Imperfect

| ich | konnte | I could *or* I was able to |
| du | konntest | |
| er | konnte | |
| wir | konnten | |
| ihr | konntet | |
| sie | konnten | |

## Imperfect subjunctive

| ich | könnte | I could *or* I would be able to |
| du | könntest | |
| er | könnte | |
| wir | könnten | |
| ihr | könntet | |
| sie | könnten | |

## Conditional

| ich | würde können | I could *or* I would be able to |
| du | würdest können | |
| er | würde können | |
| wir | würden können | |
| ihr | würdet können | |
| sie | würden können | |

* In these tables **er** should be read as **er / sie / es** and **sie** should be read as **sie / Sie**.

**Imperative**
The imperative of
müssen is not used.

**Past participle**
gemusst
had to
müssen
had to

## Present

| ich | muss | I must *or* I have to |
| du | musst | |
| er* | muss | |
| wir | müssen | |
| ihr | müsst | |
| sie* | müssen | |

## Perfect

| ich | habe gemusst | I had to |
| du | hast gemusst | |
| er | hat gemusst | |
| wir | haben gemusst | |
| ihr | habt gemusst | |
| sie | haben gemusst | |

## Future

| ich | werde müssen | I will have to |
| du | wirst müssen | |
| er | wird müssen | |
| wir | werden müssen | |
| ihr | werdet müssen | |
| sie | werden müssen | |

## Present subjunctive

| ich | müsse | I must *or* I have to |
| du | müssest | |
| er | müsse | |
| wir | müssen | |
| ihr | müsset | |
| sie | müssen | |

## Imperfect

| ich | musste | I had to |
| du | musstest | |
| er | musste | |
| wir | mussten | |
| ihr | musstet | |
| sie | mussten | |

## Imperfect subjunctive

| ich | müsste | I would have to |
| du | müsstest | |
| er | müsste | |
| wir | müssten | |
| ihr | müsstet | |
| sie | müssten | |

## Conditional

| ich | würde müssen | I would have to |
| du | würdest müssen | |
| er | würde müssen | |
| wir | würden müssen | |
| ihr | würdet müssen | |
| sie | würden müssen | |

* In these tables **er** should be read as **er / sie / es** and **sie** should be read as **sie / Sie**.

**[11]**

**sein**
to be

| **Imperative** | **Past participle** |
|---|---|
| Sei! | gewesen    been |
| Be! | |
| Seid! | |
| Be! | |
| Seien Sie! | |
| Be! | |
| Seien wir! | |
| Let's be! | |

**Present**

| ich | bin | I am |
|---|---|---|
| du | bist | |
| er* | ist | |
| wir | sind | |
| ihr | seid | |
| sie* | sind | |

**Present subjunctive**

| ich | sei | I am |
|---|---|---|
| du | seist / seiest | |
| er | sei | |
| wir | seien | |
| ihr | seiet | |
| sie | seien | |

**Perfect**

| ich | bin gewesen | I was |
|---|---|---|
| du | bist gewesen | |
| er | ist gewesen | |
| wir | sind gewesen | |
| ihr | seid gewesen | |
| sie | sind gewesen | |

**Imperfect**

| ich | war | I was |
|---|---|---|
| du | warst | |
| er | war | |
| wir | waren | |
| ihr | wart | |
| sie | waren | |

**Future**

| ich | werde sein | I will be |
|---|---|---|
| du | wirst sein | |
| er | wird sein | |
| wir | werden sein | |
| ihr | werdet sein | |
| sie | werden sein | |

**Imperfect subjunctive**

| ich | wäre | I would be⁺ |
|---|---|---|
| du | wärst / wärest | |
| er | wäre | |
| wir | wären | |
| ihr | wärt / wäret | |
| sie | wären | |

**Conditional**

| ich | würde sein | I would be |
|---|---|---|
| du | würdest sein | |
| er | würde sein | |
| wir | würden sein | |
| ihr | würdet sein | |
| sie | würden sein | |

* In these tables **er** should be read as **er / sie / es** and **sie** should be read as **sie / Sie**.
⁺ 'Ich wäre' can also be translated as 'I were', e.g. Wenn ich du wäre ...
 If I were you ...

312

**Imperative**
The imperative of
sollen is not used.

**Past participle**
gesollt
had to
sollen
had to

## [12]

**sollen**

should *or*
to have to

| **Present** | | **Present subjunctive** | |
|---|---|---|---|
| ich soll | I should | ich solle | I should |
| du sollst | | du sollest | |
| er* soll | | er solle | |
| wir sollen | | wir sollen | |
| ihr sollt | | ihr sollet | |
| sie* sollen | | sie sollen | |

| **Perfect** | | **Imperfect** | |
|---|---|---|---|
| ich habe gesollt | I had to | ich sollte | I had to |
| du hast gesollt | | du solltest | |
| er hat gesollt | | er sollte | |
| wir haben gesollt | | wir sollten | |
| ihr habt gesollt | | ihr solltet | |
| sie haben gesollt | | sie sollten | |

| **Future** | | **Imperfect subjunctive** | |
|---|---|---|---|
| ich werde sollen | I will have to | ich sollte | I should |
| du wirst sollen | | du solltest | |
| er wird sollen | | er sollte | |
| wir werden sollen | | wir sollten | |
| ihr werdet sollen | | ihr solltet | |
| sie werden sollen | | sie sollten | |

| **Conditional** | |
|---|---|
| ich würde sollen | I would have to |
| du würdest sollen | |
| er würde sollen | |
| wir würden sollen | |
| ihr würdet sollen | |
| sie würden sollen | |

* In these tables **er** should be read as **er / sie / es** and **sie** should be read as **sie / Sie**.

## [13]

### werden
to become *or*
to get

**Imperative**
Werde!
Become! *or* Get!
Werdet!
Become! *or* Get!
Werden Sie!
Become! *or* Get!
Werden wir!
Let's become! *or* Let's get!

**Past participle**
geworden
become *or* got

### Present

| ich werde | I become *or* I get |
| du wirst | |
| er* wird | |
| wir werden | |
| ihr werdet | |
| sie* werden | |

### Present subjunctive

| ich werde | I become *or* I get |
| du werdest | |
| er werde | |
| wir werden | |
| ihr werdet | |
| sie werden | |

### Perfect

| ich bin geworden | I became *or* I got |
| du bist geworden | |
| er ist geworden | |
| wir sind geworden | |
| ihr seid geworden | |
| sie sind geworden | |

### Imperfect

| ich wurde | I became *or* I got |
| du wurdest | |
| er wurde | |
| wir wurden | |
| ihr wurdet | |
| sie wurden | |

### Future

| ich werde werden | I will become *or* I will get |
| du wirst werden | |
| er wird werden | |
| wir werden werden | |
| ihr werdet werden | |
| sie werden werden | |

### Conditional

| ich würde werden | I would become *or* I would get |
| du würdest werden | |
| er würde werden | |
| wir würden werden | |
| ihr würdet werden | |
| sie würden werden | |

* In these tables **er** should be read as **er / sie / es** and **sie** should be read as **sie / Sie**.

**Imperative**
The imperative of
wissen is not used.

**Past participle**
gewusst
known

### Present

| | | |
|---|---|---|
| ich | weiß | I know |
| du | weißt | |
| er* | weiß | |
| wir | wissen | |
| ihr | wisst | |
| sie* | wissen | |

### Present subjunctive

| | | |
|---|---|---|
| ich | wisse | I know |
| du | wissest | |
| er | wisse | |
| wir | wissen | |
| ihr | wisset | |
| sie | wissen | |

### Perfect

| | | |
|---|---|---|
| ich | habe gewusst | I knew |
| du | hast gewusst | |
| er | hat gewusst | |
| wir | haben gewusst | |
| ihr | habt gewusst | |
| sie | haben gewusst | |

### Imperfect

| | | |
|---|---|---|
| ich | wusste | I knew |
| du | wusstest | |
| er | wusste | |
| wir | wussten | |
| ihr | wusstet | |
| sie | wussten | |

### Future

| | | |
|---|---|---|
| ich | werde wissen | I will know |
| du | wirst wissen | |
| er | wird wissen | |
| wir | werden wissen | |
| ihr | werdet wissen | |
| sie | werden wissen | |

### Conditional

| | | |
|---|---|---|
| ich | würde wissen | I would know |
| du | würdest wissen | |
| er | würde wissen | |
| wir | würden wissen | |
| ihr | würdet wissen | |
| sie | würden wissen | |

* In these tables **er** should be read as **er / sie / es** and **sie** should be read as **sie / Sie**.

## German irregular verb forms

The list shows the main forms of irregular verbs.

| Infinitive | Present<br>ich, du, er / sie / es | Imperfect<br>er / sie / es | Perfect<br>er / sie / es |
|---|---|---|---|
| bekommen | bekomme, bekommst, bekommt | bekam | hat bekommen |
| bergen | berge, birgst, birgt | barg | hat geborgen |
| besitzen | besitze, besitzst, besitzt | besaß | hat besessen |
| betrügen | betrüge, betrügst, betrügt | betrog | hat betrogen |
| biegen | biege, biegst, biegt | bog | hat or ist gebogen |
| bieten | biete, bietest, bietet | bot | hat geboten |
| binden | binde, bindest, bindet | band | hat gebunden |
| bitten | bitte, bittest, bittet | bat | hat gebeten |
| blasen | blase, bläst, bläst | blies | hat geblasen |
| bleiben | bleibe, bleibst, bleibt | blieb | ist geblieben |
| braten | brate, brätst, brät | briet | hat gebraten |
| brechen | breche, brichst, bricht | brach | hat or ist gebrochen |
| brennen | brenne, brennst, brennt | brannte | hat gebrannt |
| bringen | bringe, bringst, bringt | brachte | hat gebracht |
| denken | denke, denkst, denkt | dachte | hat gedacht |
| dürfen | darf, darfst, darf | durfte | hat gedurft |
| einladen | lade ein, lädst ein, lädt ein | lud ein | hat eingeladen |
| empfangen | empfange, empfängst, empfängt | empfing | hat empfangen |
| empfehlen | empfehle, empfiehlst, empfiehlt | empfahl | hat empfohlen |
| entscheiden | entscheide, entscheidest, entscheidet | entschied | hat entschieden |

| Infinitive | Present<br>ich, du, er / sie / es | Imperfect<br>er / sie / es | Perfect<br>er / sie / es |
|---|---|---|---|
| erfahren | erfahre, erfährst, erfährt | erfuhr | hat erfahren |
| erfinden | erfinde, erfindest, erfindet | erfand | hat erfunden |
| erschrecken | erschrecke, erschrickst, erschrickt | erschrak | ist erschrocken |
| ertrinken | ertrinke, ertrinkst, ertrinkt | ertrank | ist ertrunken |
| essen | esse, isst, isst | aß | hat gegessen |
| | | | |
| fahren | fahre, fährst, fährt | fuhr | ist *or* hat<br>gefahren |
| fallen | falle, fällst, fällt | fiel | ist gefallen |
| fangen | fange, fängst, fängt | fing | hat gefangen |
| fechten | fechte, fichtst, ficht | focht | hat gefochten |
| finden | finde, findest, findet | fand | hat gefunden |
| fliegen | fliege, fliegst, fliegt | flog | ist *or* hat geflogen |
| fliehen | fliehe, fliehst, flieht | floh | ist geflohen |
| fließen | fließe, fließt, fließt | floss | ist geflossen |
| fressen | fresse, frisst, frisst | fraß | hat gefressen |
| frieren | friere, frierst, friert | fror | hat *or* ist gefroren |
| | | | |
| geben | gebe, gibst, gibt | gab | hat gegeben |
| gefallen | gefalle, gefällst, gefällt | gefiel | hat gefallen |
| gehen | gehe, gehst, geht | ging | ist gegangen |
| gelingen | es gelingt mir/dir/ihm, ihr, ihm | gelang | ist gelungen |
| gelten | gelte, giltst, gilt | galt | hat gegolten |
| genießen | genieße, genießt, genießt | genoss | hat genossen |
| geraten | gerate, gerätst, gerät | geriet | ist geraten |
| geschehen | es geschieht | geschah | ist geschehen |
| gewinnen | gewinne, gewinnst, gewinnt | gewann | hat gewonnen |
| gießen | gieße, gießt, gießt | goss | hat gegossen |
| gleichen | gleiche, gleichst, gleicht | glich | hat geglichen |
| graben | grabe, gräbst, gräbt | grub | hat gegraben |
| greifen | greife, greifst, greift | griff | hat gegriffen |

317

| Infinitive | Present<br>ich, du, er / sie / es | Imperfect<br>er / sie / es | Perfect<br>er / sie / es |
|---|---|---|---|
| helfen | helfe, hilfst, hilft | half | hat geholfen |
| hinweisen | weise hin, weist hin, weist hin | wies hin | hat hingewiesen |
| kennen | kenne, kennst, kennt | kannte | hat gekannt |
| klingen | klinge, klingst, klingt | klang | hat geklungen |
| kneifen | kneife, kneifst, kneift | kniff | hat gekniffen |
| kommen | komme, kommst, kommt | kam | ist gekommen |
| können | kann, kannst, kann | konnte | hat gekonnt |
| kriechen | krieche, kriechst, kriecht | kroch | ist gekrochen |
| lassen | lasse, lässt, lässt | ließ | hat gelassen |
| laufen | laufe, läufst, läuft | lief | ist gelaufen |
| leiden | leide, leidest, leidet | litt | hat gelitten |
| leihen | leihe, leihst, leiht | lieh | hat geliehen |
| lesen | lese, liest, liest | las | hat gelesen |
| liegen | liege, liegst, liegt | lag | hat gelegen |
| lügen | lüge, lügst, lügt | log | hat gelogen |
| mahlen | mahle, mahlst, mahlt | mahlte | hat gemahlen |
| meiden | meide, meidest, meidet | mied | hat gemieden |
| messen | messe, misst, misst | maß | hat gemessen |
| misslingen | es misslingt mir/dir/ihm, ihr, ihm | misslang | ist misslungen |
| mögen | mag, magst, mag | mochte | hat gemocht |
| müssen | muss, musst, muss | musste | hat gemusst |
| nehmen | nehme, nimmst, nimmt | nahm | hat genommen |
| nennen | nenne, nennst, nennt | nannte | hat genannt |
| pfeifen | pfeife, pfeifst, pfeift | pfiff | hat gepfiffen |
| raten | rate, rätst, rät | riet | hat geraten |
| reiben | reibe, reibst, reibt | rieb | hat gerieben |
| reißen | reiße, reißt, reißt | riss | hat or ist gerissen |

318

| Infinitive | Present<br>ich, du, er / sie / es | Imperfect<br>er / sie / es | Perfect<br>er / sie / es |
|---|---|---|---|
| reiten | reite, reitest, reitet | ritt | hat or ist geritten |
| rennen | renne, rennst, rennt | rannte | ist gerannt |
| riechen | rieche, riechst, riecht | roch | hat gerochen |
| rufen | rufe, rufst, ruft | rief | hat gerufen |
| saufen | saufe, säufst, säuft | soff | hat gesoffen |
| schaffen | schaffe, schaffst, schafft | schuf | hat geschaffen |
| scheiden | scheide, scheidest, scheidet | schied | hat or ist geschieden |
| scheinen | scheine, scheinst, scheint | schien | hat geschienen |
| schieben | schiebe, schiebst, schiebt | schob | hat geschoben |
| schießen | schieße, schießt, schießt | schoss | hat or ist geschossen |
| schlafen | schlafe, schläfst, schläft | schlief | hat geschlafen |
| schlagen | schlage, schlägst, schlägt | schlug | hat geschlagen |
| schleichen | schleiche, schleichst, schleicht | schlich | ist geschlichen |
| schließen | schließe, schließt, schließt | schloss | hat geschlossen |
| schmeißen | schmeiße, schmeißt, schmeißt | schmiss | hat geschmissen |
| schmelzen | schmelze, schmilzt, schmilzt | schmolz | ist geschmolzen |
| schneiden | schneide, schneidest, schneidet | schnitt | hat geschnitten |
| schreiben | schreibe, schreibst, schreibt | schrieb | hat geschrieben |
| schreien | schreie, schreist, schreit | schrie | hat geschrien |
| schweigen | schweige, schweigst, schweigt | schwieg | hat geschwiegen |
| schwimmen | schwimme, schwimmst, schwimmt | schwamm | ist or hat geschwommen |
| schwören | schwöre, schwörst, schwört | schwor | hat geschworen |
| sehen | sehe, siehst, sieht | sah | hat gesehen |
| sein | bin, bist, ist | war | ist gewesen |
| singen | singe, singst, singt | sang | hat gesungen |
| sinken | sinke, sinkst, sinkt | sank | ist gesunken |
| sitzen | sitze, sitzt, sitzt | saß | hat gesessen |
| sollen | soll, sollst, soll | sollte | hat gesollt |

| Infinitive | Present<br>ich, du, er / sie / es | Imperfect<br>er / sie / es | Perfect<br>er / sie / es |
|---|---|---|---|
| spinnen | spinne, spinnst, spinnt | spann | hat gesponnen |
| springen | springe, springst, springt | sprang | ist gesprungen |
| stechen | steche, stichst, sticht | stach | hat gestochen |
| stehen | stehe, stehst, steht | stand | hat gestanden |
| sprechen | spreche, sprichst, spricht | sprach | hat gesprochen |
| stehlen | stehle, stiehlst, stiehlt | stahl | hat gestohlen |
| steigen | steige, steigst, steigt | stieg | ist gestiegen |
| sterben | sterbe, stirbst, stirbt | starb | ist gestorben |
| stinken | stinke, stinkst, stinkt | stank | hat gestunken |
| stoßen | stoße, stößt, stößt | stieß | hat or ist gestoßen |
| streichen | streiche, streichst, streicht | strich | hat gestrichen |
| streiten | streite, streitest, streitet | stritt | hat gestritten |
| tragen | trage, trägst, trägt | trug | hat getragen |
| treffen | treffe, triffst, trifft | traf | hat getroffen |
| treiben | treibe, treibst, treibt | trieb | hat getrieben |
| treten | trete, trittst, tritt | trat | hat or ist getreten |
| trinken | trinke, trinkst, trinkt | trank | hat getrunken |
| tun | tue, tust, tut | tat | hat getan |
| überweisen | überweise, überweist, überweist | überwies | hat überwiesen |
| umziehen | ziehe um, ziehst um, zieht um | zog um | ist or hat umgezogen |
| verbieten | verbiete, verbietest, verbietet | verbot | hat verboten |
| verderben | verderbe, verdirbst, verdirbt | verdarb | hat or ist verdorben |
| vergessen | vergesse, vergisst, vergisst | vergaß | hat vergessen |
| verlieren | verliere, verlierst, verliert | verlor | hat verloren |
| verschwinden | verschwinde, verschwindest, verschwindet | verschwand | ist verschwunden |
| verzeihen | verzeihe, verzeihst, verzeiht | verzieh | hat verziehen |

| Infinitive | Present ich, du, er / sie / es | Imperfect er / sie / es | Perfect er / sie / es |
|---|---|---|---|
| verstehen | verstehe, verstehst, versteht | verstand | hat verstanden |
| wachsen | wachse, wächst, wächst | wuchs | ist gewachsen |
| waschen | wasche, wäschst, wäscht | wusch | hat gewaschen |
| werben | werbe, wirbst, wirbt | warb | hat geworben |
| werden | werde, wirst, wird | wurde | ist geworden |
| werfen | werfe, wirfst, wirft | warf | hat geworfen |
| wiegen | wiege, wiegst, wiegt | wog | hat gewogen |
| wissen | weiß, weißt, weiß | wusste | hat gewusst |
| wollen | will, willst, will | wollte | hat gewollt |
| ziehen | ziehe, ziehst, zieht | zog | hat or ist gezogen |
| zwingen | zwinge, zwingst, zwingt | zwang | hat gezwungen |

# Aa

**a** _DETERMINER_ ❶ (before a noun which is masculine in German) ein; **a tree** ein Baum ❷ (before a noun which is feminine in German) eine; **a story** eine Geschichte ❸ (before a noun which is neuter in German) ein; **a dress** ein Kleid ❹ not a kein, **the party was not a success** die Party war kein Erfolg, **he didn't say a word** er hat kein Wort gesagt ❺ **ten euros a metre** zehn Euro den Meter ❻ **fifty kilometres an hour** fünfzig Stundenkilometer ❼ **three times a day** dreimal täglich

**abandon** _VERB_ ❶ aufgeben⬦ (SEP); **they abandoned the plan** sie gaben den Plan auf ❷ verlassen⬦, **they abandoned the city** sie verließen die Stadt

**abbey** _NOUN_ Abtei die (PLURAL die Abteien)

**abbreviation** _NOUN_ Abkürzung die (PLURAL die Abkürzungen)

**ability** _NOUN_ Fähigkeit die (PLURAL die Fähigkeiten); **to have the ability to do something** etwas tun können

**able** _ADJECTIVE_ fähig; **to be able to do something** etwas tun können, **she wasn't able to come** sie konnte nicht kommen

**abortion** _NOUN_ Abtreibung die (PLURAL die Abtreibungen)

**about** _PREPOSITION_ ❶ über (+ACC); **a film about space** ein Film über den Weltraum, **to talk about something/somebody** über etwas/jemanden reden
**what is she talking about?** worüber redet sie? ❷ um (+ACC); **to be about something** um etwas gehen
**what's it about?** worum geht es? ❸ **to know about something** von etwas (DAT) wissen
**she didn't know about the party** sie wusste nichts von der Party
**he knows nothing about it** er weiß nichts davon ❹ **to think about something/somebody** an etwas/jemanden (+ACC) denken, **I'm thinking about you** ich denke an dich

**about** _ADVERB_ ❶ (approximately) ungefähr; **about sixty people** ungefähr sechzig Leute
**in about a week** in ungefähr einer Woche ❷ (when talking about time) gegen; **about three o'clock** gegen drei Uhr ❸ **to be about to do something** gerade etwas tun wollen, **I was (just) about to leave** ich wollte gerade gehen

**above** _PREPOSITION_ ❶ über (+DAT); **the lamp above the table** die Lampe über dem Tisch ❷ **above all** vor allem

**abroad** _ADVERB_ im Ausland; **to live abroad** im Ausland leben, **to go abroad** ins Ausland fahren

**abscess** _NOUN_ Abszess der (PLURAL die Abszesse)

**abseiling** _NOUN_ Abseilen das

**absent** _ADJECTIVE_ abwesend; **to be absent from school** in der Schule fehlen

**absent-minded** ADJECTIVE zerstreut

**absolute** ADJECTIVE absolut; **an absolute disaster** eine absolute Katastrophe

**absolutely** ADVERB ❶ wirklich; **it's absolutely dreadful** das ist wirklich furchtbar ❷ völlig; **you're absolutely right** du hast völlig Recht

**abuse** NOUN ❶ Missbrauch der; **drug abuse** Der Drogenmissbrauch ❷ (insults) Beschimpfungen (plural)

**abuse** VERB ❶ **to abuse somebody** jemanden missbrauchen ❷ (to insult) beschimpfen

**accelerate** VERB beschleunigen

**accelerator** NOUN Gaspedal das (PLURAL die Gaspedale)

**accent** NOUN Akzent der (PLURAL die Akzente); **to speak with a German accent** mit deutschem Akzent sprechen

**accept** VERB annehmen◇ (SEP); **he accepted the invitation** er nahm die Einladung an

**acceptable** ADJECTIVE annehmbar

**access** NOUN Zugang der

**access** VERB **to access data** auf Daten zugreifen

**accessory** NOUN ❶ Zubehörteil das; **accessories** Zubehör das ❷ accessories (fashion items) Accessoires (plural)

**accident** NOUN ❶ Unfall der (PLURAL die Unfälle); **to have an accident** einen Unfall haben, **road accident** der Verkehrsunfall, **car accident** der Autounfall ❷ Zufall der (PLURAL die Zufälle); **by accident** zufällig, **I found it by accident** ich habe es zufällig gefunden

**accident & emergency** NOUN Notaufnahme die

**accidental** ADJECTIVE zufällig; **an accidental discovery** eine zufällige Entdeckung

**accidentally** ADVERB ❶ (without meaning to) versehentlich; **I accidentally threw it away** ich habe es versehentlich weggeworfen ❷ (by chance) zufällig; **I accidentally discovered that ...** ich habe zufällig herausgefunden, dass ...

**accommodation** NOUN Unterkunft die; **accommodation is free** Unterkunft ist kostenlos, **I'm looking for accommodation** (when looking for a room) ich suche ein Zimmer

**accompany** VERB begleiten; **to accompany somebody** jemanden begleiten

**according** IN PHRASE **according to** laut (+DAT), **according to Sophie** laut Sophie

**accordion** NOUN Akkordeon das (PLURAL die Akkordeons)

**account** NOUN ❶ (in a bank, shop, or post office) Konto das (PLURAL die Konten); **bank account** das Bankkonto, **to open an account** ein Konto eröffnen, **I have fifty pounds in my account** ich habe fünfzig Pfund auf meinem Konto ❷ (an explanation) Darstellung die (PLURAL die Darstellungen); **I want to hear his account of what happened** ich möchte seine Darstellung der

Ereignisse hören ❸ **on account of** wegen *(+GEN)* ❹ **to take something into account** etwas berücksichtigen

**accountant** *NOUN* Buchhalter der *(PLURAL* die **Buchhalter)** Buchhalterin die *(PLURAL* die **Buchhalterinnen)**; **she's an accountant** sie ist Buchhalterin

**accurate** *ADJECTIVE* genau

**accurately** *ADVERB* genau

**accuse** *VERB* beschuldigen; **she accused me of stealing her pen** sie beschuldigte mich, ihren Kugelschreiber gestohlen zu haben

**ace** *NOUN* Ass das *(PLURAL* die **Asse)**; **the ace of hearts** das Herzass

**ace** *ADJECTIVE* klasse *(informal)*; **he's an ace drummer** er spielt klasse Schlagzeug

**ache** *VERB* schmerzen; **my head aches** mein Kopf schmerzt

**achieve** *VERB* ❶ leisten; **she's achieved a great deal** sie hat eine Menge geleistet ❷ erreichen *(an aim)*; **he achieved what he wanted** er hat erreicht, was er wollte

**achievement** *NOUN* Leistung die *(PLURAL* die **Leistungen)**; **it's a great achievement** das ist eine große Leistung

**acid** *NOUN* Säure die *(PLURAL* die **Säuren)**

**acne** *NOUN* Akne die

**across** *PREPOSITION* ❶ *(over to the other side of)* über *(+ACC)*; **to run across the road** über die Straße laufen, **we walked across the park** wir sind durch den Park gegangen ❷ *(on the other side of)* auf der anderen

Seite *(+GEN)*; **he lives across the river** er wohnt auf der anderen Seite des Flusses ❸ **they live across the street** sie wohnen gegenüber

**act** *NOUN (deed)* Tat die *(PLURAL* die **Taten)**

**act** *VERB (in a play or film)* spielen; **to act the part of the hero** die Rolle des Helden spielen

**action** *NOUN* ❶ Handlung die *(PLURAL* die **Handlungen)** ❷ **to take action** etwas unternehmen

**action replay** *NOUN* Wiederholung die *(PLURAL* die **Wiederholungen)**

**active** *ADJECTIVE* aktiv

**activity** *NOUN* Aktivität die *(PLURAL* die **Aktivitäten)**

**actor** *NOUN* Schauspieler der *(PLURAL* die **Schauspieler)**

**actress** *NOUN* Schauspielerin die *(PLURAL* die **Schauspielerinnen)**

**actual** *ADJECTIVE* **what were his actual words?** was genau hat er gesagt?, **in actual fact** eigentlich

**actually** *ADVERB* ❶ *(in fact, as it happens)* eigentlich; **actually, I've changed my mind** ich habe mich eigentlich anders entschlossen ❷ *(really and truly)* wirklich; **did she actually say that?** hat sie das wirklich gesagt?

**ad** *NOUN* ❶ *(on TV)* Werbespot der *(PLURAL* die **Werbespots)** ❷ *(in a newspaper)* Anzeige die *(PLURAL* die **Anzeigen)**; **to put an ad in the paper** eine Anzeige in die Zeitung setzen, **the small ads** die Kleinanzeigen

**AD** (short for **Anno Domini**) n. Chr., (short for nach Christus); **in 400 AD** 400 n. Chr

**adapt** VERB ❶ to adapt something (a book or film) etwas bearbeiten ❷ to adapt to sich anpassen (SEP) (+DAT), **she's adapted to her new surroundings** sie hat sich der neuen Umgebung angepasst

**adaptor** NOUN ❶ Adapter der (PLURAL die Adapter) ❷ (for two plugs) Doppelstecker der (PLURAL die Doppelstecker)

**add** VERB ❶ hinzufügen (SEP); **to add an introduction to something** etwas (DAT) eine Einleitung hinzufügen ❷ dazugeben◇ (SEP); **add three eggs** geben Sie drei Eier dazu
• **to add up** zusammenzählen (SEP)

**addict** NOUN ❶ (drug addict) Süchtige der/die (PLURAL die Süchtigen) ❷ **she's a telly addict** sie ist fernsehsüchtig, **he's a football addict** er ist ein Fußballnarr

**addicted** ADJECTIVE ❶ **to become addicted to drugs** drogensüchtig werden ❷ **he's addicted to football** Fußball ist bei ihm zur Sucht geworden ❸ **I'm addicted to sweets** ich bin nach Süßigkeiten süchtig

**addition** NOUN ❶ (adding up) Addition die ❷ **in addition** außerdem ❸ **in addition to** zusätzlich zu (+DAT)

**additional** ADJECTIVE zusätzlich

**additive** NOUN Zusatz der (PLURAL die Zusätze)

**address** NOUN Adresse die (PLURAL die Adressen); **do you know his**

**address?** weißt du seine Adresse?, **to change address** die Adresse wechseln

**address book** NOUN Adressbuch das (PLURAL die Adressbücher)

**adequate** ADJECTIVE angemessen

**adhesive** NOUN Klebstoff der

**adhesive** ADJECTIVE **adhesive tape** der Klebstreifen

**adjective** NOUN Adjektiv das (PLURAL die Adjektive)

**adjust** VERB ❶ to adjust something etwas einstellen (SEP) **he adjusted the set** er stellte das Gerät ein, **to adjust the distance** auf die (richtige) Entfernung einstellen ❷ to adjust to something sich an etwas (DAT) gewöhnen

**adjustable** ADJECTIVE verstellbar

**administration** NOUN Verwaltung die

**admiration** NOUN Bewunderung die

**admire** VERB bewundern

**admission** NOUN Eintritt der; **'admission free'** 'Eintritt frei'

**admit** VERB ❶ (confess, concede) zugeben◇ (SEP); **she admits she lied** sie gibt zu, dass sie gelogen hat ❷ (allow to enter) hereinlassen◇ (SEP); **to admit somebody to a restaurant** jemanden in ein Restaurant lassen ❸ **to be admitted to hospital** ins Krankenhaus eingeliefert werden

**adolescence** NOUN Jugend die

**adolescent** NOUN Jugendliche der/die (PLURAL die Jugendlichen)

**adopt** *VERB* adoptieren

**adopted** *ADJECTIVE* adoptiert

**adoption** *NOUN* Adoption die (*PLURAL* die Adoptionen)

**adore** *VERB* lieben

**adult** *NOUN* Erwachsene der/die (*PLURAL* die Erwachsenen)

**adult** *ADJECTIVE* the adult population Erwachsene (*plural*)

**Adult Education** *NOUN* Erwachsenenbildung die

**advance** *NOUN* Fortschritt der (*PLURAL* die Fortschritte); **advances in technology** technologische Fortschritte

**advance** *VERB* ❶ (*make progress*) Fortschritte machen ❷ (*move forward*) (*of a group or an army*) vorrücken (*SEP*) (*PERF* sein)

**advanced** *ADJECTIVE* fortgeschritten (*student, age*)

**advantage** *NOUN* ❶ Vorteil der (*PLURAL* die Vorteile); **there are several advantages** es gibt verschiedene Vorteile ❷ **to take advantage of something** etwas ausnutzen (*SEP*) **I always take advantage of the sales to buy myself some shoes** ich warte immer bis zum Schlussverkauf, um mir Schuhe zu kaufen ❸ **to take advantage of somebody** (*unfairly*) jemanden ausnutzen (*SEP*)

**Advent** *NOUN* Advent der

**adventure** *NOUN* Abenteuer das (*PLURAL* die Abenteuer)

**adverb** *NOUN* Adverb das (*PLURAL* die Adverbien)

**advert**, **advertisement** *NOUN* ❶ (*at the cinema or on television*) Werbespot der (*PLURAL* die Werbespots) ❷ (*in a newspaper for a job, article for sale, etc.*) Anzeige die (*PLURAL* die Anzeigen); **she answered a job advertisement** sie meldete sich auf eine Stellenanzeige

**advertise** *VERB* **to advertise something in the newspaper** (*in the small ads*) etwas in der Zeitung inserieren, **I saw a bike advertised in the paper** ich habe ein Rad in der Zeitung inseriert gesehen

**advertising** *NOUN* Werbung die

**advice** *NOUN* Rat der; **to ask somebody's advice** jemanden um Rat fragen, **a piece of advice** ein Ratschlag

**advise** *VERB* raten◇ (*+DAT*); **to advise somebody to do something** jemandem raten, etwas zu tun, **I advised him to stop** ich riet ihm anzuhalten, **I advised her not to buy the car** ich habe ihr geraten, das Auto nicht zu kaufen

**aerial** *NOUN* Antenne die (*PLURAL* die Antennen)

**aerobics** *NOUN* Aerobic das; **to do aerobics** Aerobic machen

**aeroplane** *NOUN* Flugzeug das (*PLURAL* die Flugzeuge)

**aerosol** *NOUN* **an aerosol can** eine Spraydose

**affair** *NOUN* ❶ Angelegenheit die (*PLURAL* die Angelegenheiten); **international affairs** internationale Angelegenheiten

**current affairs** die Tagespolitik
**❷ love affair** das Liebesverhältnis

**affect** *VERB* beeinflussen

**affectionate** *ADJECTIVE* liebevoll

**afford** *VERB* **to be able to afford
something** sich *(DAT)* etwas leisten
können, **we can't afford to go
out much** wir können es uns nicht
leisten, oft auszugehen, **I can't
afford a new bike** ich kann mir kein
neues Rad leisten

**afraid** *ADJECTIVE* **❶ to be afraid of
something** Angst vor etwas *(DAT)*
haben, **she's afraid of dogs** sie hat
Angst vor Hunden **❷ I'm afraid I
can't help you** ich kann dir leider
nicht helfen, **I'm afraid so** leider ja,
**I'm afraid not** leider nicht

**Africa** *NOUN* Afrika das; **to Africa**
nach Afrika

**African** *NOUN* Afrikaner der *(PLURAL*
die **Afrikaner)** Afrikanerin die
*(PLURAL* die **Afrikanerinnen)**

**African** *ADJECTIVE* afrikanisch; **she is
African** sie ist Afrikanerin

**after** *PREPOSITION, ADVERB* **❶** nach *(+DAT)*;
**after 10 o'clock** nach zehn Uhr,
**after lunch** nach dem Mittagessen,
**after school** nach der Schule **❷ the
day after tomorrow** übermorgen,
**soon after** kurz danach **❸ to
run after somebody** jemandem
hinterherlaufen◇ *(SEP)*

**after** *CONJUNCTION* nachdem; **after I'd
finished my homework** nachdem
ich meine Hausaufgaben gemacht
hatte

**after all** *ADVERB* schließlich; **after
all, she's only six** sie ist schließlich
erst sechs

**afternoon** *NOUN* **❶** Nachmittag
der *(PLURAL* die **Nachmittage)**; **in
the afternoon** am Nachmittag,
**every afternoon** jeden Nachmittag
**❷ this afternoon** heute Nachmittag,
**on Sunday afternoon** am
Sonntagnachmittag **❸ on Saturday
afternoons** samstagsnachmittags,
**at four o' clock in the afternoon** um
vier Uhr nachmittags

**after-shave** *NOUN* Rasierwasser das
*(PLURAL* die **Rasierwasser)**

**afterwards** *ADVERB* danach; **shortly
afterwards** kurz danach

**again** *ADVERB* **❶** wieder; **she's ill
again** sie ist wieder krank **❷ I saw
her again yesterday** ich habe sie
gestern wieder gesehen **❸ never
again!** nie wieder!, **again and again**
immer wieder **❹** *(one more time)*
**noch einmal**; **try again** versuche
es noch einmal, **you should ask her
again** du solltest sie noch einmal
fragen

**against** *PREPOSITION* gegen *(+ACC)*;
**against the wall** gegen die Wand,
**to lean against the wall** sich gegen
die Wand lehnen, **I'm against the
idea** ich bin gegen die Idee

**age** *NOUN* **❶** Alter das; **at the age of
fifty** im Alter von fünfzig, **she's the
same age as me** sie ist genauso
alt wie ich, **to be under age**
minderjährig sein **❷ I haven't seen
Johnny for ages** ich habe Johnny
schon ewig nicht mehr gesehen, **I
haven't been to London for ages**
ich bin schon ewig nicht mehr in
London gewesen

**aged** *ADJECTIVE* alt; **a woman aged
thirty** eine dreißigjährige Frau

**agent** NOUN Vertreter der (PLURAL die Vertreter) Vertreterin die (PLURAL die Vertreterinnen); **an estate agent** ein Immobilienmakler, **a travel agent's** ein Reisebüro

**aggressive** ADJECTIVE aggressiv

**ago** ADVERB vor (+DAT); **an hour ago** vor einer Stunde, **three days ago** vor drei Tagen, **a long time ago** vor langer Zeit, **not long ago** vor kurzem, **how long ago was it?** wie lange ist das her?

**agree** VERB ❶ **to agree with somebody** mit jemandem gleicher Meinung sein, **I agree with Laura** ich stimme Laura zu ❷ **I agree** ich bin der gleichen Meinung, **I don't agree** ich bin anderer Meinung ❸ **to agree that …** zugeben◇ (SEP), dass …, **I agree that it's too late now** ich gebe zu, dass es jetzt zu spät ist ❹ **to agree to something** mit etwas einverstanden sein, **Steve's agreed to help me** Steve hat sich einverstanden erklärt, mir zu helfen ❺ **coffee doesn't agree with me** Kaffee bekommt mir nicht

**agreement** NOUN ❶ (when sharing an opinion) Übereinstimmung die ❷ (contract) Abkommen das (PLURAL die Abkommen)

**agriculture** NOUN Landwirtschaft die

**ahead** ADVERB ❶ **go ahead!** bitte! ❷ **straight ahead** geradeaus, **keep going straight ahead until you get to the crossroads** gehen Sie immer geradeaus bis zur Kreuzung ❸ **our team was ten points ahead** unsere Mannschaft hatte zehn Punkte Vorsprung ❹ **ahead of time** früher als geplant ❺ **the people ahead of me** die Leute vor mir

**aid** NOUN ❶ Hilfe die; **aid to developing countries** die Entwicklungshilfe ❷ **in aid of** zugunsten (+GEN), **in aid of the homeless** zugunsten der Obdachlosen

**Aids** NOUN Aids das; **to have Aids** Aids haben

**aim** NOUN ❶ Ziel das (PLURAL die Ziele); **their aim is to control pollution** ihr Ziel ist es, die Umweltverschmutzung unter Kontrolle zu bringen

**aim** VERB ❶ **to aim to do something** beabsichtigen, etwas zu tun, **we're aiming to finish it today** wir beabsichtigen, es heute fertig zu machen ❷ **the campaign is aimed at young people** die Kampagne zielt auf junge Leute ab

**air** NOUN ❶ Luft die; **in the open air** im Freien, **to go out for a breath of air** frische Luft schöpfen gehen ❷ **to travel by air** fliegen◇ (PERF sein)

**air-conditioned** ADJECTIVE klimatisiert

**air conditioning** NOUN Klimaanlage die

**Air Force** NOUN Luftwaffe die

**air hostess** NOUN Stewardess die (PLURAL die Stewardessen); **she's an air hostess** sie ist Stewardess

**airline** NOUN Fluggesellschaft die (PLURAL die Fluggesellschaften)

**airmail** NOUN **by airmail** per Luftpost

**air pollution** NOUN Luftverschmutzung die

**airport** NOUN Flughafen der (PLURAL die Flughäfen)

a
b
c
d
e
f
g
h
i
j
k
l
m
n
o
p
q
r
s
t
u
v
w
x
y
z

**alarm**                                        **all right**

**alarm** NOUN Alarm der (PLURAL die Alarme); **fire alarm** der Feuermelder, **burglar alarm** die Alarmanlage

**alarm clock** NOUN Wecker der (PLURAL die Wecker)

**album** NOUN Album das (PLURAL die Alben)

**alcohol** NOUN Alkohol der

**alcoholic** NOUN Alkoholiker der (PLURAL die Alkoholiker), Alkoholikerin die (PLURAL die Alkoholikerinnen)

**alcoholic** ADJECTIVE alkoholisch

**A levels** NOUN Abitur das (Students take 'Abitur' at about 19 years of age. You can explain A levels briefly as follows: Diese Prüfungen werden in zwei Schritten abgelegt: AS und A2. AS Prüfungen finden nach einjähriger Vorbereitungszeit statt, und umfassen normalerweise vier bis fünf Fächer. A2 Prüfungen macht man in weniger Fächern als man für die AS Prüfungen belegt hatte. AS und A2 Prüfungen werden benotet von A (beste Note) bis N (nicht bestanden). A levels stellen eine Zugangsberechtigung für die Universität dar)
▸ SEE **Abitur**

**alien** NOUN ❶ (foreigner) Ausländer der (PLURAL die Ausländer), Ausländerin die (PLURAL die Ausländerinnen) ❷ (from outer space) Außerirdische der/die (PLURAL die Außerirdischen)

**alike** ADJECTIVE ❶ gleich ❷ they're all **alike** sie sind alle gleich ❸ to look **alike** sich (DAT) ähnlich sehen, **the two brothers look alike** die beiden Brüder sehen sich ähnlich

**alive** ADJECTIVE ❶ to be alive leben, to stay alive am Leben bleiben ❷ (lively) lebendig

**all** ADJECTIVE ❶ (with a singular noun) ganz; **all the time** die ganze Zeit **all day** den ganzen Tag ❷ (with a plural noun) alle; **all the knives** alle Messer, **all our friends** alle unsere Freunde

**all** PRONOUN ❶ (everything) alles; **they've eaten it all** sie haben alles aufgegessen ❷ (everybody) alle **all of us** wir alle **they're all there** sie sind alle da ❸ **not at all** gar nicht

**all** ADVERB ❶ ganz; **all alone** ganz allein ❷ **three all** drei beide

**all along** ADVERB die ganze Zeit; **I knew it all along** ich habe es die ganze Zeit gewusst

**allergic** ADJECTIVE allergisch; **to be allergic to something** gegen etwas (ACC) allergisch sein

**allow** VERB ❶ to allow somebody to do something jemandem erlauben, etwas zu tun, **the teacher allowed them to go home** der Lehrer erlaubte ihnen, nach Hause zu gehen ❷ to be allowed to dürfen◇, **I'm not allowed to go to the cinema during the week** ich darf während der Woche nicht ins Kino gehen

**all right** ADVERB ❶ (yes) ist gut, okay (informal); **'come round to my house around six' – 'all right'** 'komm um sechs bei mir vorbei' – 'okay' ❷ (fine) in Ordnung, okay (informal); **is everything all right?** ist alles okay?, **she's all right again** es geht ihr wieder gut, **it's all right by me** das geht in Ordnung, **is it**

all right if I come later? ist es in Ordnung, wenn ich später komme? ❸ *(not bad)* gut, okay *(informal)*; **the meal was all right** das Essen war okay ❹ **'how are you?' – 'I'm all right'** 'wie geht's dir?' – 'mir geht's gut'

**almost** *ADVERB* fast; **almost every day** fast jeden Tag, **almost everybody** fast alle

**alone** *ADJECTIVE* ❶ allein; **he lives alone** er lebt allein ❷ **leave me alone!** lass mich in Ruhe!

**along** *PREPOSITION* ❶ entlang *(+ACC or +DAT)*; **there are trees all along the river** am Fluss entlang stehen Bäume, **to go for a walk along the beach** am Strand entlang spazieren gehen ❷ *(there is often no direct translation for 'along', so the sentence has to be expressed differently)* **she lives along the road from me** sie wohnt in der gleichen Straße wie ich **I'll bring it along** ich bringe es mit

**aloud** *ADVERB* laut; **to read something aloud** etwas vorlesen◇ *(SEP)*

**alphabet** *NOUN* Alphabet das *(PLURAL die Alphabete)*

**Alps** *PLURAL NOUN* **the Alps** die Alpen

**already** *ADVERB* schon; **they've already left** sie sind schon weggegangen, **it's six o'clock already** es ist schon sechs Uhr

**Alsatian** *NOUN* Schäferhund der *(PLURAL die Schäferhunde)*

**also** *ADVERB* auch; **I've also invited Karen** ich habe Karen auch eingeladen

**alter** *VERB* ❶ ändern *(a report, a dress)* ❷ *(to change)* sich verändern

**alternative** *NOUN* ❶ Alternative die *(PLURAL die Alternativen)*; **there are several alternatives** es gibt mehrere Alternativen ❷ **we have no alternative** wir haben keine andere Wahl

**alternative** *ADJECTIVE* anderer/andere/anderes *(masculine/feminine/neuter)*; **to find an alternative solution** eine andere Lösung finden

**alternative medicine** *NOUN* Alternativmedizin die

**although** *CONJUNCTION* obwohl; **although she's ill, she wants to help us** obwohl sie krank ist, will sie uns helfen

**altogether** *ADVERB* ❶ insgesamt; **I've spent thirty pounds altogether** insgesamt habe ich dreißig Pfund ausgegeben ❷ *(completely)* ganz; **I'm not altogether convinced** ich bin nicht ganz überzeugt

**always** *ADVERB* immer; **I always leave at five** ich gehe immer um fünf (weg)

**am** *VERB* ▸ SEE **be**

**a.m.** *ABBREVIATION* vormittags; **at 8 a.m.** um acht Uhr morgens

**amateur** *NOUN* ❶ Amateur der *(PLURAL die Amateure)*, Amateurin die *(PLURAL die Amateurinnen)* ❷ **amateur dramatics** das Laientheater

**amaze** *VERB* erstaunen; **what amazes me is ...** was mich erstaunt, ist ...

**amazed** *ADJECTIVE* erstaunt; **I was amazed to see her** ich war erstaunt, sie zu sehen

**amazing** ADJECTIVE ❶ (terrific) fantastisch; they've got an amazing house sie haben ein fantastisches Haus ❷ (extraordinary) erstaunlich; she has an amazing number of friends sie hat erstaunlich viele Freunde

**ambition** NOUN Ehrgeiz der

**ambitious** ADJECTIVE ehrgeizig

**ambulance** NOUN Krankenwagen der (PLURAL die Krankenwagen)

**America** NOUN Amerika das; in America in Amerika, to America nach Amerika

**American** NOUN Amerikaner der (PLURAL die Amerikaner), Amerikanerin die (PLURAL die Amerikanerinnen)

**American** ADJECTIVE amerikanisch; she's American sie ist Amerikanerin

**among, amongst** PREPOSITION ❶ unter (+DAT); I found it amongst my books ich habe das unter meinen Büchern gefunden, amongst other things unter anderem ❷ (between) among yourselves untereinander

**amount** NOUN ❶ Menge die (PLURAL die Mengen); a huge amount of work eine Menge Arbeit ❷ (of money) Betrag der (PLURAL die Beträge); a large amount of money ein sehr hoher Betrag

**amount** VERB to amount to sich belaufen◇, the bill amounts to five hundred euros die Rechnung beläuft sich auf fünfhundert Euro

**amp** NOUN (amplifier) Verstärker der (PLURAL die Verstärker)

**amplifier** NOUN Verstärker der (PLURAL die Verstärker)

**amuse** VERB amüsieren

**amusement arcade** NOUN Spielhalle die (PLURAL die Spielhallen)

**amusing** ADJECTIVE amüsant

**an** ARTICLE ▸ SEE a

**anaesthetic** NOUN Narkose die (PLURAL die Narkosen)

**analyse** VERB analysieren

**ancestor** NOUN Vorfahr der (PLURAL die Vorfahren)

**anchovy** NOUN Sardelle die (PLURAL die Sardellen)

**ancient** ADJECTIVE ❶ alt; ancient Greece das alte Griechenland ❷ (very old) uralt; an ancient pair of jeans uralte Jeans

**and** CONJUNCTION ❶ und; Rosie and I Rosie und ich, girls and boys Mädchen und Jungen ❷ louder and louder immer lauter ❸ try and come versuche zu kommen

**angel** NOUN Engel der (PLURAL die Engel)

**anger** NOUN Zorn der

**angle** NOUN Winkel der (PLURAL die Winkel)

**angrily** ADVERB wütend

**angry** ADJECTIVE to be angry böse sein, she was angry with me sie war böse auf mich, to get angry böse werden

**animal** NOUN Tier das (PLURAL die Tiere)

**ankle** NOUN Knöchel der (PLURAL die Knöchel)

**anniversary** NOUN ❶ Jahrestag der (PLURAL die Jahrestage) ❷ our wedding anniversary unser Hochzeitstag

**announce** VERB bekanntgeben◇ (SEP); she announced her engagement sie gab ihre Verlobung bekannt

**annoy** VERB to be annoyed verärgert sein, to get annoyed with somebody sich über jemanden ärgern, she got annoyed about it sie hat sich darüber geärgert

**annoying** ADJECTIVE ärgerlich

**annual** ADJECTIVE jährlich

**anorak** NOUN Anorak der (PLURAL die Anoraks)

**anorexia** NOUN Magersucht die

**another** ADJECTIVE ❶ (additional) noch ein/noch eine/noch ein; would you like another cup of tea? möchtest du noch eine Tasse Tee?, we need another three chairs wir brauchen noch drei Stühle ❷ (different) ein anderer/ eine andere/ein anderes; we saw another film wir haben einen anderen Film gesehen ❸ in another two years in zwei weiteren Jahren

**answer** NOUN ❶ Antwort die (PLURAL die Antworten); the right answer die richtige Antwort, the wrong answer die falsche Antwort ❷ the answer to a problem die Lösung eines Problems

**answer** VERB ❶ antworten (+DAT); why don't you answer him? warum antwortest du ihm nicht?

❷ beantworten (a letter, a question); he hasn't answered our letter er hat unseren Brief nicht beantwortet

**answering machine** NOUN Anrufbeantworter der (PLURAL die Anrufbeantworter)

**ant** NOUN Ameise die (PLURAL die Ameisen)

**anthem** NOUN the national anthem die Nationalhymne

**antibiotic** NOUN Antibiotikum das (PLURAL die Antibiotika)

**antique** NOUN antiques Antiquitäten (plural)

**antique** ADJECTIVE antik; an antique table ein antiker Tisch

**antique shop** NOUN Antiquitätengeschäft das (PLURAL die Antiquitätengeschäfte)

**antiseptic** NOUN Antiseptikum das (PLURAL die Antiseptika)

**anxious** ADJECTIVE ❶ (worried) besorgt ❷ (keen) she was anxious to see him sie wollte ihn unbedingt sehen

**anxiously** ADVERB ängstlich

**any** ADJECTIVE ❶ irgendein; if they had any plan wenn sie irgendeinen Plan hätten ❷ (with plural nouns) irgendwelche; if they had any plans wenn sie irgendwelche Pläne hätten ❸ (in questions 'any' is often not translated) have you got any stamps? haben Sie Briefmarken?, have we got any milk? haben wir Milch? ❹ not any kein, they haven't made any plans sie haben nichts geplant, we haven't got any milk wir haben keine Milch ❺ (no matter

333

*which)* jeder beliebige/jede beliebige/jedes beliebige; **you can have any colour** du kannst jede beliebige Farbe haben

**any** PRONOUN ❶ *(in questions, replacing the noun)* welcher/welche/welches, *(replacing a plural noun)* welche; **I need some flour, have you got any?** ich brauche Mehl, hast du welches? ❷ **not any** keiner/keine/keins, *(replacing a plural noun)* keine, **I don't want any** ich will keins haben, **there aren't any** es gibt keine ❸ *(no matter which one)* irgendein; **'which chair can I take?' – 'take any of them'** 'welchen Stuhl kann ich nehmen?' – 'nimm irgendeinen'

**any** ADVERB ❶ *(in questions)* noch; **would you like any more?** möchtest du noch etwas? ❷ *(with negatives)* **I can't see him any more** ich kann ihn nicht mehr sehen

**anybody**, **anyone** PRONOUN ❶ *(in questions)* jemand; **does anybody want some tea?** möchte jemand Tee?, **is anybody in?** ist irgendjemand da? ❷ **not anybody** niemand, **there isn't anybody in the office** niemand ist im Büro ❸ *(absolutely anybody)* jeder; **anybody can do it** das kann jeder

**anyhow** ADVERB ▸ SEE **anyway**

**anyone** PRONOUN ▸ SEE **anybody**

**anything** PRONOUN ❶ *(in questions)* irgendetwas; **is there anything I can do to help?** kann ich irgendwie helfen? ❷ **not anything** nichts, **there isn't anything on the table** auf dem Tisch liegt nichts ❸ *(anything at all)* alles; **I'll do anything to help him** ich werde alles tun, um ihm zu helfen

**anyway**, **anyhow** ADVERB ❶ jedenfalls; **anyway, I'll ring you before I leave** jedenfalls ruf ich dich an, bevor ich fahre ❷ sowieso

**anywhere** ADVERB ❶ *(in questions)* irgendwo; **have you seen my keys anywhere?** hast du meine Schlüssel irgendwo gesehen? ❷ **not anywhere** nirgends, **I can't find my keys anywhere** ich kann meine Schlüssel nirgends finden ❸ *(to any place)* irgendwohin; **are you going anywhere tomorrow?** fahrt ihr morgen irgendwohin?, **put your cases down anywhere** stell deine Koffer irgendwohin ❹ *(in any place)* überall; **you can get that anywhere** das kann man überall kriegen

**apart** ADJECTIVE, ADVERB ❶ *(separate)* auseinander; **they've been apart for some time** sie sind schon lange auseinander ❷ **to be two metres apart** zwei Meter auseinander liegen ❸ **apart from** außer (+DAT), **apart from my brother everybody was there** außer meinem Bruder waren alle da

**apologize** VERB sich entschuldigen; **he apologized for his mistake** er enschuldigte sich für seinen Fehler, **he apologized to Sam** er hat sich bei Sam entschuldigt

**apology** NOUN Entschuldigung die *(PLURAL die Entschuldigungen)*

**apostrophe** NOUN Apostroph der *(PLURAL die Apostrophe)*

**apparent** ADJECTIVE offensichtlich

**apparently** ADVERB offensichtlich

**appeal** NOUN Appell der *(PLURAL die Appelle)*

**appeal** VERB ❶ to appeal for something um etwas (DAT) bitten◇ ❷ to appeal to somebody sich an jemanden wenden◇, horror films don't appeal to me Horrorfilme sind nicht mein Geschmack

**appear** VERB ❶ erscheinen◇ (PERF sein); Mick appeared at breakfast Mick erschien zum Frühstück ❷ to appear on television im Fernsehen auftreten◇ (SEP) (PERF sein) ❸ (seem) scheinen◇; it appears that somebody has stolen the key es scheint, dass jemand den Schlüssel gestohlen hat

**appendicitis** NOUN Blinddarmentzündung die

**appetite** NOUN Appetit der; it'll spoil your appetite das verdirbt dir den Appetit

**applaud** VERB Beifall klatschen

**applause** NOUN Beifall der

**apple** NOUN Apfel der (PLURAL die Äpfel)

**apple tree** NOUN Apfelbaum der (PLURAL die Apfelbäume)

**applicant** NOUN Bewerber der (PLURAL die Bewerber) Bewerberin die (PLURAL die Bewerberinnen)

**application** NOUN Bewerbung die (PLURAL die Bewerbungen)

**application form** NOUN (for a job) Bewerbungsformular das (PLURAL die Bewerbungsformulare)

**apply** VERB ❶ to apply for a job sich um eine Stelle bewerben◇ ❷ to apply for university sich um einen Studienplatz bewerben◇ ❸ to apply for a passport einen Pass beantragen ❹ to apply to zutreffen◇ (SEP) auf (+ACC), that doesn't apply to students das trifft nicht auf Studenten zu

**appointment** NOUN Termin der (PLURAL die Termine); to make a dental appointment einen Zahnarzttermin vereinbaren, I've got a hair appointment at four ich habe um vier einen Friseurtermin

**appreciate** VERB I appreciate your advice ich bin dir für deinen Rat dankbar, I'd appreciate it if you could tidy up afterwards es wäre nett von dir, wenn du danach aufräumen würdest

**apprentice** NOUN Lehrling der (PLURAL die Lehrlinge)

**apprenticeship** NOUN Lehre die (PLURAL die Lehren)

**approach** VERB sich nähern (+DAT) (PERF sein); we were approaching the village wir näherten uns dem Dorf

**approve** VERB to approve of something mit etwas (DAT) einverstanden sein, they don't approve of her friends sie lehnen ihre Freunde ab

**approximate** ADJECTIVE ungefähr

**approximately** ADVERB ungefähr; approximately fifty people ungefähr fünfzig Personen

**apricot** NOUN Aprikose die (PLURAL die Aprikosen)

**April** NOUN April der; in April im April

**April Fool** NOUN (trick) Aprilscherz der (PLURAL die Aprilscherze); April fool! April, April!

**April Fool's Day** NOUN der erste April

a
b
c
d
e
f
g
h
i
j
k
l
m
n
o
p
q
r
s
t
u
v
w
x
y
z

**apron** NOUN Schürze die (PLURAL die Schürzen)

**aquarium** NOUN Aquarium das (PLURAL die Aquarien)

**Aquarius** NOUN Wassermann der; **Sharon's Aquarius** Sharon ist Wassermann

**Arab** NOUN Araber der (PLURAL die Araber) Araberin die (PLURAL die Araberinnen)

**Arab** ADJECTIVE arabisch; **the Arab countries** die arabischen Länder

**arch** NOUN Bogen der (PLURAL die Bogen)

**archaeologist** NOUN Archäologe der (PLURAL die Archäologen) Archäologin die (PLURAL die Archäologinnen); **she's an archaeologist** sie ist Archäologin

**archaeology** NOUN Archäologie die

**architect** NOUN Architekt der (PLURAL die Architekten) Architektin die (PLURAL die Architektinnen); **he's an architect** er ist Architekt

**architecture** NOUN Architektur die

**are** VERB ▶ SEE **be**

**area** NOUN ❶ (part of a town, a region) Gegend die (PLURAL die Gegenden); **a nice area** eine nette Gegend, **in the Leeds area** in der Gegend von Leeds ❷ **picnic area** der Picknickplatz

**argue** VERB sich streiten◇; **to argue about something** sich über etwas (ACC) streiten, **they're arguing about the result** sie streiten sich über das Ergebnis

**argument** NOUN Streit der (PLURAL die Streite); **to get into an argument with somebody** mit jemandem in Streit geraten◇, **to have an argument** sich streiten◇

**Aries** NOUN Widder der; **Pauline's Aries** Pauline ist Widder

**arm** NOUN Arm der (PLURAL die Arme); **arm in arm** Arm in Arm, **to break your arm** sich (DAT) den Arm brechen

**armchair** NOUN Sessel der (PLURAL die Sessel)

**armed** ADJECTIVE bewaffnet

**army** NOUN ❶ Heer das (PLURAL die Heere) ❷ (profession) Militär das; **to join the army** zum Militär gehen

**around** PREPOSITION, ADVERB ❶ (with time of day) gegen (+ACC); **we'll be there around ten** wir werden gegen zehn da sein ❷ (with ages or amounts) etwa; **she's around fifteen** sie ist etwa fünfzehn, **we need around six kilos** wir brauchen etwa sechs Kilo ❸ (with dates) um (+ACC herum); **around 10 August** um den 10. August herum ❹ (surrounding) um ... herum; **the countryside around Edinburgh** die Landschaft um Edinburgh herum ❺ (near) **is there a post office around here?** gibt es hier in der Gegend eine Post?, **is Phil around?** ist Phil da?

**arrange** VERB **to arrange something** etwas vereinbaren, **we've arranged to go to the cinema on Saturday** wir haben vereinbart, am Samstag ins Kino zu gehen

**arrest** NOUN **to be under arrest** verhaftet sein

**arrest** VERB verhaften

**arrival** NOUN Ankunft die (PLURAL die Ankünfte)

**arrive** VERB ankommen◇ (SEP) (PERF sein); **they arrived at 3 p.m.** sie kamen um fünfzehn Uhr an

**arrow** NOUN Pfeil der (PLURAL die Pfeile)

**art** NOUN ❶ Kunst die (PLURAL die Künste); **modern art** moderne Kunst ❷ (school subject) Kunsterziehung die

**artery** NOUN Arterie die (PLURAL die Arterien)

**art gallery** NOUN Kunstgalerie die (PLURAL die Kunstgalerien)

**article** NOUN ❶ (in a newspaper or magazine) Artikel der (PLURAL die Artikel) ❷ (object) Stück das (PLURAL die Stücke)

**artificial** ADJECTIVE künstlich

**artist** NOUN Künstler der (PLURAL die Künstler) Künstlerin die (PLURAL die Künstlerinnen); **he's an artist** er ist Künstler

**artistic** ADJECTIVE künstlerisch

**art school** NOUN Kunsthochschule die (PLURAL die Kunsthochschulen)

**as** CONJUNCTION, ADVERB ❶ wie; **as you know** wie du weißt, **as usual** wie üblich, **as I told you** wie ich dir gesagt habe ❷ (because) da; **as there was no bus, we took a taxi** da es keinen Bus gab, nahmen wir ein Taxi ❸ **as ... as ...** so ... wie, **he's as tall as his brother** er ist so groß wie sein Bruder, **come as quickly as possible** komm so schnell wie möglich ❹ **as much ... as** so viel ... wie, **you have**

**as much time as I do** du hast so viel Zeit wie ich ❺ **as many ... as** so viele ... wie
**we have as many problems as he does** wir haben genauso viele Probleme wie er ❻ **as long as** vorausgesetzt, **we'll go tomorrow, as long as it's a nice day** wir gehen morgen, vorausgesetzt es ist schönes Wetter ❼ **for as long as** solange, **you can stay for as long as you like** du kannst bleiben, solange du willst ❽ **as soon as possible** so bald wie möglich ❾ **to work as** arbeiten als, **he works as a waiter in the evenings** abends arbeitet er als Kellner, **as well** auch

**ash** NOUN ❶ Asche die (PLURAL die Aschen) ❷ (tree) Esche die (PLURAL die Eschen)

**ashamed** ADJECTIVE **to be ashamed of something** sich wegen etwas (DAT) schämen, **you should be ashamed of yourself!** du solltest dich schämen!

**ashtray** NOUN Aschenbecher der (PLURAL die Aschenbecher)

**Asia** NOUN Asien das; **in Asia** in Asien

**Asian** NOUN Asiate der (PLURAL die Asiaten) Asiatin die (PLURAL die Asiatinnen)

**Asian** ADJECTIVE asiatisch

**ask** VERB ❶ fragen; **to ask somebody something** jemanden nach etwas (DAT) fragen, **I asked him the way** ich fragte ihn nach dem Weg ❷ **to ask something** um etwas (ACC) bitten, **to ask somebody a favour** jemanden um einen Gefallen bitten, **to ask somebody to do something** jemanden bitten, etwas zu tun, **ask Danny to give you a hand**

**asleep**                             **Atlantic**

bitte Danny, dir zu helfen ❸ **to ask somebody a question** jemandem eine Frage stellen, **I asked him a few questions** ich habe ihm ein paar Fragen gestellt ❹ einladen◇ *(SEP)*; **they've asked us to a party** sie haben uns auf eine Party eingeladen, **Paul's asked Janie out on Friday** Paul hat Janie Freitag eingeladen ❺ **to ask for** verlangen **how much are they asking for the car?** wieviel verlangen sie für das Auto?

**asleep** *ADJECTIVE* **to be asleep** schlafen◇, **the baby's asleep** das Baby schläft, **to fall asleep** einschlafen◇ *(SEP)* *(PERF* sein)

**asparagus** *NOUN* Spargel der *(PLURAL* die Spargel)

**aspirin** *NOUN* Aspirin das

**assembly** *NOUN* *(at school)* Morgenandacht die *(PLURAL* die Morgenandachten)

**assess** *VERB* beurteilen

**assignment** *NOUN* *(at school)* Aufgabe die *(PLURAL* die Aufgaben)

**assist** *VERB* helfen *(+DAT)*

**assistance** *NOUN* Hilfe die

**assistant** *NOUN* ❶ Helfer der *(PLURAL* die Helfer) Helferin die *(PLURAL* die Helferinnen) ❷ *(in school)* Assistent der *(PLURAL* die Assistenten), Assistentin die *(PLURAL* die Assistentinnen) ❸ **shop assistant** der Verkäufer, die Verkäuferin

**association** *NOUN* Verband der *(PLURAL* die Verbände)

**assorted** *ADJECTIVE* gemischt

**assortment** *NOUN* Auswahl die

**assume** *VERB* annehmen◇ *(SEP)*; **I assume** ich nehme an

**asthma** *NOUN* Asthma das

**astrology** *NOUN* Astrologie die

**astronaut** *NOUN* Astronaut der *(PLURAL* die Astronauten) Astronautin die *(PLURAL* die Astronautinnen)

**astronomy** *NOUN* Astronomie die

**at** *PREPOSITION* ❶ in *(+DAT)*; **at school** in der Schule, **at my office** in meinem Büro, **at the supermarket** im Supermarket ❷ an *(+DAT)*; **at the station** am Bahnhof, **at the bus stop** an der Bushaltestelle ❸ bei *(+DAT)*; **at the dentist** beim Zahnarzt, **at Emma's** bei Emma, **she's at her brother's this evening** sie ist heute Abend bei ihrem Bruder, **at the hairdresser's** beim Friseur ❹ **at a party** auf einer Party ❺ **at home** zu Hause ❻ *(talking about the time)* um; **at eight o'clock** um acht Uhr ❼ **at night** nachts, **at Christmas** zu Weihnachten, **at the weekend** am Wochenende ❽ *(@ in e-mail addresses)* Klammeraffe der; **john-dot-smith@easycom-dot-com** john-punkt-smith-Klammeraffe-easycom-punkt-com ❾ **at last** endlich, **she's found a job at last** sie hat endlich einen Job gefunden

**athlete** *NOUN* Athlet der *(PLURAL* die Athleten) Athletin die *(PLURAL* die Athletinnen)

**athletic** *ADJECTIVE* sportlich

**athletics** *NOUN* Leichtathletik die

**Atlantic** *NOUN* **the Atlantic (Ocean)** der Atlantik

**atlas** NOUN Atlas der (PLURAL die Atlanten)

**atmosphere** NOUN Atmosphäre die (PLURAL die Atmosphären)

**atom** NOUN Atom das (PLURAL die Atome)

**atomic** ADJECTIVE Atom-; an atomic bomb eine Atombombe

**attach** VERB befestigen

**attached** ADJECTIVE (emotionally) to be attached to somebody/something an jemandem/etwas (DAT) hängen◇

**attachment** NOUN ❶ (in a letter) Anlage die (PLURAL die Anlagen) ❷ (in an email) Attachment das (PLURAL die Attachments)

**attack** NOUN Angriff der (PLURAL die Angriffe)

**attack** VERB ❶ angreifen◇ (SEP) ❷ (mug or raid) überfallen◇

**attempt** NOUN Versuch der (PLURAL die Versuche); at the first attempt beim ersten Versuch

**attempt** VERB to attempt to do something versuchen, etwas zu tun

**attend** VERB teilnehmen◇ (SEP) an (+DAT); to attend a meeting an einer Besprechung teilnehmen, to attend an evening class einen Abendkurs besuchen

**attention** NOUN ❶ Aufmerksamkeit die; to pay attention aufpassen (SEP), I wasn't paying attention ich habe nicht aufgepasst ❷ he wasn't paying attention to the teacher er hörte dem Lehrer nicht zu

**attic** NOUN Dachboden der (PLURAL die Dachböden); in the attic auf dem Dachboden

**attitude** NOUN ❶ (way of thinking) Einstellung die ❷ (way of acting) Haltung die

**attract** VERB anziehen◇ (SEP)

**attraction** NOUN ❶ Anziehung die ❷ (a thing that attracts) Attraktion die (PLURAL die Attraktionen); the whale was a big attraction der Wal war eine große Attraktion

**attractive** ADJECTIVE attraktiv

**aubergine** NOUN Aubergine die (PLURAL die Auberginen)

**audience** NOUN Publikum das; the television audience die Fernsehzuschauer (plural)

**August** NOUN August der; in August im August

**aunt**, **auntie** NOUN Tante die (PLURAL die Tanten)

**au pair** NOUN Aupairmädchen das (PLURAL die Aupairmädchen); I'm looking for a job as an au pair ich suche eine Aupair-Stelle

**Australia** NOUN Australien das; to Australia nach Australien

**Australian** NOUN Australier der (PLURAL die Australier) Australierin die (PLURAL die Australierinnen)

**Australian** ADJECTIVE australisch; she's Australian sie ist Australierin

**Austria** NOUN Österreich das; in Austria in Österreich

**Austrian** NOUN Österreicher der (PLURAL die Österreicher) Österreicherin die (PLURAL die Österreicherinnen)

**Austrian** ADJECTIVE österreichisch; he's Austrian er ist Österreicher

a
b
c
d
e
f
g
h
i
j
k
l
m
n
o
p
q
r
s
t
u
v
w
x
y
z

**author** NOUN Autor der (PLURAL die Autoren) Autorin die (PLURAL die Autorinnen)

**autograph** NOUN Autogramm das (PLURAL die Autogramme)

**automatic** ADJECTIVE automatisch

**automatically** ADVERB automatisch

**autumn** NOUN Herbst der (PLURAL die Herbste); **in autumn** im Herbst

**available** ADJECTIVE (on sale) erhältlich

**average** NOUN Durchschnitt der (PLURAL die Durchschnitte); **on average** im Durchschnitt, **above average** über dem Durchschnitt

**average** ADJECTIVE durchschnittlich; **the average height** die durchschnittliche Größe

**avocado** NOUN Avocado die (PLURAL die Avocados)

**avoid** VERB ❶ vermeiden◇; **to avoid doing something** es vermeiden, etwas zu tun, **I avoid speaking to him** ich vermeide es, mit ihm zu reden ❷ (keep away from somebody or a place) meiden◇; **she avoids me** sie meidet mich

**awake** ADJECTIVE **to be awake** wach sein, **are you still awake?** bist du noch wach?

**award** NOUN Preis der (PLURAL die Preise); **to win an award** einen Preis gewinnen

**aware** ADJECTIVE **to be aware of a problem** sich (DAT) eines Problems bewusst sein, **I'm aware of the danger** ich bin mir der Gefahr bewusst, **as far as I'm aware** soweit ich weiß

**away** ADVERB ❶ **to be away** nicht da sein, **I'll be away next week** ich bin nächste Woche nicht da ❷ **to go away** verreisen (PERF sein), **Laura's gone away for a week** Laura ist auf eine Woche verreist, **go away!** geh weg! ❸ **to run away** weglaufen◇ (SEP) (PERF sein), **the thieves ran away** die Diebe liefen weg ❹ **the school is two kilometres away** die Schule ist zwei Kilometer entfernt, **how far away is it?** wie weit entfernt ist es?, **not far away** nicht weit entfernt ❺ **to put something away** etwas wegräumen (SEP), **I'm just putting my books away** ich räume gerade meine Bücher weg ❻ **to give something away** etwas weggeben◇ (SEP), (as a present) etwas verschenken, **she's given away all her cassettes** sie hat alle ihre Kassetten verschenkt

**away match** NOUN Auswärtsspiel das (PLURAL die Auswärtsspiele)

**awful** ADJECTIVE furchtbar; **the film was awful** der Film war furchtbar, **I feel awful** (ill) ich fühle mich furchtbar, **I feel awful about it** es ist mir furchtbar unangenehm, **an awful lot of mistakes** furchtbar viele Fehler

**awkward** ADJECTIVE ❶ schwierig; **it's an awkward situation** das ist eine schwierige Situation, **it's a bit awkward** das ist ein bisschen schwierig, **an awkward child** ein schwieriges Kind ❷ **an awkward question** eine peinliche Frage

**axe** NOUN Axt die (PLURAL die Äxte)

# Bb

**baby** NOUN **Baby** das (PLURAL die **Babys**)

**babysit** VERB **babysitten**

**babysitter** NOUN **Babysitter** der (PLURAL die **Babysitter**) **Babysitterin** die (PLURAL die **Babysitterinnen**)

**babysitting** NOUN **Babysitten** das

**back** NOUN ❶ (of a person or animal) **Rücken** der (PLURAL die **Rücken**); **he did it behind my back** er hat es hinter meinem Rücken getan ❷ (of a piece of paper, or building) **Rückseite** die (PLURAL die **Rückseiten**); **on the back** auf der Rückseite ❸ **the back of your hand** der **Handrücken** ❹ **at the back** hinten, **at the back of the room** hinten im Zimmer, **we sat at the back** wir saßen hinten, **a garden at the back of the house** ein Garten hinter dem Haus ❺ (of a chair or sofa) **Rückenlehne** die (PLURAL die **Rückenlehnen**) ❻ (in football or hockey) **Verteidiger** der (PLURAL die **Verteidiger**), **Verteidigerin** die (PLURAL die **Verteidigerinnen**); **left back** der Linksverteidiger

**back** ADJECTIVE ❶ **the back seat** (of a car) der **Rücksitz** ❷ **the back door** die Hintertür, **the back garden** der Garten hinter dem Haus

**back** ADVERB ❶ **zurück**; **there and back** hin und zurück, **to go back** (on foot) zurückgehen◇ (SEP) (PERF sein), (in a vehicle) zurückfahren◇ (SEP) (PERF sein) ❷ **to come back** zurückkommen◇ (SEP) (PERF sein), **they've come back from Italy** sie sind aus Italien zurückgekommen, **I'll be back at 8 o'clock** ich bin um acht Uhr zurück, **Sue's not back yet** Sue ist noch nicht zurück ❸ **to phone back** zurückrufen◇ (SEP), **I'll ring back later** ich rufe dich später zurück ❹ **to give something back to somebody** jemandem etwas zurückgeben◇ (SEP), **give it back!** gib es zurück!

**back** VERB (bet on) **setzen auf** (+ACC)
- **to back up** (computing) **sichern**, **to back up a file** eine Sicherungskopie machen
- **to back somebody up** jemanden unterstützen

**backache** NOUN **Rückenschmerzen** (plural)

**background** NOUN ❶ (of a person) **Verhältnisse** (plural); **she comes from a poor background** sie kommt aus ärmlichen Verhältnissen ❷ (in a picture, view, or situation) **Hintergrund** der (PLURAL die **Hintergründe**); **background noise** Hintergrundgeräusche (plural) ❸ (to events or problems) **Hintergründe** (plural)

**backhand** NOUN **Rückhand** die

**backing** NOUN ❶ (on sticky-back plastic, for example) **Verstärkung** die (PLURAL die **Verstärkungen**) ❷ (moral support) **Unterstützung** die ❸ (in music) **Begleitung** die; **a backing group** eine Begleitband

**backpack** NOUN **Rucksack** der (PLURAL die **Rucksäcke**)

**backpack** VERB to go backpacking trampen (PERF sein)

**back seat** NOUN Rücksitz der (PLURAL die Rücksitze)

**backstroke** NOUN Rückenschwimmen das

**back to front** ADVERB verkehrt herum; your jumper's back to front du hast deinen Pullover verkehrt herum an

**backup** NOUN ❶ (support) Unterstützung die ❷ (in computing) Sicherungskopie die (PLURAL die Sicherungskopien); a backup disk eine Sicherungsdiskette

**backwards** ADVERB ❶ rückwärts ❷ to lean backwards sich nach hinten lehnen, to fall backwards nach hinten fallen

**bacon** NOUN Speck der; bacon and eggs Eier mit Speck

**bad** ADJECTIVE ❶ (not good) schlecht; a bad idea eine schlechte Idee, a bad meal ein schlechtes Essen, his new film's not bad sein neuer Film ist nicht schlecht, it's bad for your health das ist ungesund, I'm bad at physics ich bin schlecht in Physik ❷ (serious) schlimm; a bad mistake ein schlimmer Fehler, a bad cold eine schlimme Erkältung ❸ a bad accident ein schwerer Unfall ❹ (rotten) schlecht; to go bad schlecht werden ❺ a bad apple ein fauler Apfel ❻ bad language Kraftausdrücke (plural)
• too bad! schade!, so ein Pech!

**badge** NOUN Abzeichen das (PLURAL die Abzeichen)

**badly** ADVERB ❶ (poorly) schlecht; he writes badly er schreibt schlecht, I slept badly ich habe schlecht geschlafen ❷ (seriously) schwer; they were badly injured sie waren schwer verletzt ❸ (very much) dringend; to need something badly etwas dringend brauchen

**bad-mannered** ADJECTIVE to be bad-mannered schlechte Manieren haben

**badminton** NOUN Badminton das

**bad-tempered** ADJECTIVE schlecht gelaunt; a bad-tempered old man ein schlecht gelaunter alter Mann

**bag** NOUN ❶ Tasche die (PLURAL die Taschen) ❷ (made of paper or plastic) Tüte die (PLURAL die Tüten)

**baggage** NOUN Gepäck das

**bagpipes** PLURAL NOUN Dudelsack der (PLURAL die Dudelsäke)

**bags** PLURAL NOUN Gepäck das; to pack your bags (sein Gepäck) packen
• to have bags under your eyes Ringe unter den Augen haben (informal)

**bake** VERB ❶ backen; to bake a cake einen Kuchen backen ❷ I'm baking mir ist furchtbar heiß

**baked** ADJECTIVE ❶ (fish or fruit) überbacken; baked apples Bratäpfel ❷ baked potatoes die Ofenkartoffeln

**baked beans** PLURAL NOUN Bohnen in Tomatensoße

**baker** NOUN Bäcker der (PLURAL die Bäcker); to go to the baker's zum Bäcker gehen

**bakery** NOUN Bäckerei die (PLURAL die Bäckereien)

**balance** NOUN ❶ **Gleichgewicht** das; to lose your balance das Gleichgewicht verlieren ❷ (in a bank account) **Kontostand** der

**balanced** ADJECTIVE **ausgeglichen**

**balcony** NOUN **Balkon** der (PLURAL die **Balkons**)

**bald** ADJECTIVE ❶ **kahl** ❷ (of a person) **kahlköpfig**; to go bald eine Glatze bekommen

**ball** NOUN ❶ (for tennis, football, or golf) **Ball** der (PLURAL die **Bälle**) ❷ (for billiards, croquet) **Kugel** die (PLURAL die **Kugeln**) ❸ (of string or wool) **Knäuel** das (PLURAL die **Knäuel**)

**ballet** NOUN **Ballett** das (PLURAL die **Ballette**)

**ballet dancer** NOUN **Balletttänzer** der (PLURAL die **Balletttänzer**) **Balletttänzerin** die (PLURAL die **Balletttänzerinnen**)

**balloon** NOUN ❶ **Luftballon** der (PLURAL die **Luftballons**) ❷ (hot-air) **Ballon** der (PLURAL die **Ballons**)

**ballpoint (pen)** NOUN **Kugelschreiber** der (PLURAL die **Kugelschreiber**)

**ban** NOUN **Verbot** das (PLURAL die **Verbote**); a ban on smoking ein Rauchverbot

**ban** VERB **verbieten**◇; to ban someone from smoking jemandem verbieten zu rauchen

**banana** NOUN ❶ **Banane** die (PLURAL die **Bananen**) ❷ a banana yoghurt ein Bananenjoghurt

**band** NOUN ❶ (playing music) **Band** die (PLURAL die **Bands**); rock band die Rockband, brass band die

Blaskapelle ❷ rubber band das Gummiband

**bandage** NOUN **Verband** der (PLURAL die **Verbände**)

**bandage** VERB **verbinden**◇

**bang** NOUN (noise) **Knall** der (PLURAL die **Knalle**)

**bang** VERB ❶ (hit, knock) **schlagen**◇; he banged his fist on the table er schlug mit der Faust auf den Tisch, to bang on the door gegen die Tür schlagen ❷ I banged my head on the door ich habe mir den Kopf an der Tür gestoßen ❸ to bang into something gegen etwas (ACC) knallen ❹ (shut loudly) **zuknallen** (SEP); he banged the door er knallte die Tür zu

**bang** EXCLAMATION **peng!**

**bank** NOUN ❶ (for money) **Bank** die (PLURAL die **Banken**); I'm going to the bank ich gehe auf die Bank ❷ (of a river or lake) **Ufer** das (PLURAL die **Ufer**)

**bank account** NOUN **Bankkonto** das (PLURAL die **Bankkonten**)

**bank balance** NOUN **Kontostand** der (PLURAL die **Kontostände**)

**bank card** NOUN **Scheckkarte** die (PLURAL die **Scheckkarten**)

**bank holiday** NOUN **gesetzliche Feiertag** der (PLURAL die **gesetzlichen Feiertage**)

**banknote** NOUN **Geldschein** der (PLURAL die **Geldscheine**)

**bank statement** NOUN **Kontoauszug** der (PLURAL die **Kontoauszüge**)

**bar** NOUN ❶ (selling drinks) Bar die (PLURAL die Bars); **Janet works in a bar** Janet arbeitet in einer Bar ❷ (counter) Theke die (PLURAL die Theken); **on the bar** auf der Theke ❸ **a bar of chocolate** eine Tafel Schokolade ❹ **a bar of soap** ein Stück Seife ❺ (made of wood or metal) Stange die (PLURAL die Stangen); **an iron bar** eine Eisenstange ❻ (in music) Takt der (PLURAL die Takte)

**barbecue** NOUN ❶ (apparatus) Grill der (PLURAL die Grills) ❷ (party) Grillfest das (PLURAL die Grillfeste)

**barbecue** VERB **to barbecue a chicken** ein Hühnchen grillen, **barbecued chicken** gegrilltes Hühnchen

**bare** ADJECTIVE nackt

**barefoot** ADJECTIVE **to be barefoot** barfuß sein, **to walk barefoot** barfuß gehen

**bargain** NOUN (a good buy) gute Kauf der (PLURAL die guten Käufe); **I got a bargain** ich habe einen guten Kauf gemacht, **it's a bargain!** das ist ein Schnäppchen!

**barge** NOUN Kahn der (PLURAL die Kähne)

**bark** NOUN ❶ (of a tree) Rinde die (PLURAL die Rinden) ❷ (of a dog) Bellen das

**bark** VERB bellen

**barmaid** NOUN Bardame die (PLURAL die Bardamen)

**barman** NOUN Barkeeper der (PLURAL die Barkeeper)

**barn** NOUN Scheune die (PLURAL die Scheunen)

**barrel** NOUN Fass das (PLURAL die Fässer)

**barrier** NOUN Absperrung die (PLURAL die Absperrungen)

**base** NOUN (bottom part) Fuß der (PLURAL die Füße)

**baseball** NOUN Baseball der

**based** ADJECTIVE ❶ **to be based on** basieren auf (+DAT), **the film is based on a true story** der Film basiert auf einer wahren Geschichte ❷ **to be based in** wohnen in (+DAT), **he's based in Bristol** er wohnt in Bristol

**basement** NOUN Kellergeschoss das (PLURAL die Kellergeschosse)

**bash** NOUN ❶ Schlag der (PLURAL die Schläge) ❷ **I'll have a bash** ich probier's mal

**bash** VERB **I bashed my head** ich habe mir den Kopf angestoßen

**basic** ADJECTIVE ❶ grundlegend, Grund-; **basic knowledge** Grundkenntnisse (plural), **her basic salary** ihr Grundgehalt ❷ **the basic problem** das Hauptproblem ❸ (not luxurious) einfach

**basically** ADVERB ❶ grundsätzlich; **it's basically all right** grundsätzlich ist es okay ❷ **basically, I don't want to come** eigentlich will ich nicht kommen

**basics** PLURAL NOUN **the basics** das Wesentliche

**basin** NOUN Becken das (PLURAL die Becken)

**basis** NOUN ❶ Basis die ❷ **on a regular basis** regelmäßig

**basket** NOUN Korb der (PLURAL die Körbe); **a basket of apples** ein Korb Äpfel, **waste-paper basket** der Papierkorb

**basketball** NOUN Basketball der

**bass** NOUN ❶ Bass der (PLURAL die Bässe) ❷ **double bass** der Kontrabass

**bass guitar** NOUN Bassgitarre die (PLURAL die Bassgitarren)

**bassoon** NOUN Fagott das (PLURAL die Fagotte)

**bat** NOUN ❶ (for games) Schläger der (PLURAL die Schläger) ❷ (animal) Fledermaus die (PLURAL die Fledermäuse)

**bath** NOUN ❶ Bad das (PLURAL die Bäder); **to have a bath** baden ❷ (tub) Badewanne die (PLURAL die Badewannen)

**bathroom** NOUN Badezimmer das (PLURAL die Badezimmer)

**baths** PLURAL NOUN Badeanstalt die (PLURAL die Badeanstalten)

**bath towel** NOUN Badetuch das (PLURAL die Badetücher)

**batter** NOUN Teig der (PLURAL die Teige); **fish in batter** ausgebackener Fisch

**battery** NOUN Batterie die (PLURAL die Batterien)

**battle** NOUN ❶ (in war) Schlacht die (PLURAL die Schlachten) ❷ (contest) Kampf der (PLURAL die Kämpfe)

**Bavaria** NOUN Bayern das

**bay** NOUN ❶ (on coast) Bucht die (PLURAL die Buchten) ❷ (in bus station) Haltebucht die (PLURAL die Haltebuchten)

**BC** ABBREVIATION (short for **before Christ**) v.Chr. (short for vor Christus)

**be** VERB ❶ sein◇ (PERF sein); **Melanie is in the kitchen** Melanie ist in der Küche, **where is the butter?** wo ist die Butter?, **I'm tired** ich bin müde, **when we were in Germany** als wir in Deutschland waren ❷ (with jobs and professions) sein◇ (PERF sein); **she's a teacher** sie ist Lehrerin, **he's a taxi driver** er ist Taxifahrer ❸ (in clock times, days of the week, dates, and age) sein◇ (PERF sein); **it's three o'clock** es ist drei Uhr, **it's half past five** es ist halb sechs, **what day is it today?** welcher Tag ist heute?, **it's Tuesday today** heute ist Dienstag, **it's the twentieth of May** heute ist der zwanzigste Mai, **what's the date today?** der Wievielte ist heute?, **how old are you?** wie alt bist du?, **I'm fifteen** ich bin fünfzehn ❹ (cold, hot, ill) sein◇ (PERF sein); **I'm hot** mir ist heiß, **I'm cold** mir ist kalt, **to be ill** krank sein ❺ (weather) sein◇ (PERF sein); **it's cold today** heute ist es kalt, **it's a nice day** es ist schönes Wetter, **it's raining** es regnet ❻ **I'm hungry** ich habe Hunger, **she's thirsty** sie hat Durst ❼ (saying how much something costs) kosten; **how much are the bananas?** wie viel kosten die Bananen? ❽ (go, come, or visit) sein◇ (PERF sein); **I've never been to Berlin** ich war noch nie in Berlin gewesen, **have you been to England before?** warst du schon einmal in England? **has the postman been?** war der Briefträger schon da? ❾ (forming the passive) werden◇ (PERF sein); **to be loved** geliebt werden, **he has been promoted** er ist befördert worden ❿ **there is/are** es gibt, **is there a bank near here?** gibt es hier in der Nähe eine Bank?

a
b
c
d
e
f
g
h
i
j
k
l
m
n
o
p
q
r
s
t
u
v
w
x
y
z

**beach** NOUN Strand der (PLURAL die Strände); to go to the beach zum Strand gehen, on the beach am Strand

**bead** NOUN Perle die (PLURAL die Perlen)

**beak** NOUN Schnabel der (PLURAL die Schnäbel)

**beam** NOUN ❶ (of light) Strahl der (PLURAL die Strahlen) ❷ (for a roof) Balken der (PLURAL die Balken)

**bean** NOUN Bohne die (PLURAL die Bohnen); green beans grüne Bohnen

**bear** NOUN Bär der (PLURAL die Bären)

**bear** VERB ❶ ertragen◇; I can't bear the idea ich kann den Gedanken nicht ertragen ❷ to bear something in mind an etwas (ACC) denken, I'll bear it in mind ich denke daran

**beard** NOUN Bart der (PLURAL die Bärte)

**bearded** ADJECTIVE bärtig

**bearings** PLURAL NOUN to get one's bearings sich orientieren

**beast** NOUN ❶ (animal) Tier das (PLURAL die Tiere) ❷ you beast! du Biest!

**beat** NOUN (in music) Takt der

**beat** VERB ❶ (defeat) schlagen◇; we beat them! wir haben sie geschlagen ❷ you can't beat a good meal es geht doch nichts über ein gutes Essen
• to beat somebody up jemanden verprügeln

**beautiful** ADJECTIVE schön

**beauty** NOUN ❶ Schönheit die (PLURAL die Schönheiten) ❷ the beauty of

it is that ... das Schöne daran ist, dass ...

**because** CONJUNCTION ❶ weil; because it's cold weil es kalt ist ❷ because of wegen (+GEN), because of the accident wegen des Unfalls, because of you deinetwegen

**become** VERB werden◇ (PERF sein); she's become a painter sie ist Malerin geworden

**bed** NOUN ❶ Bett das (PLURAL die Betten); double bed das Doppelbett, in bed im Bett, to go to bed ins Bett gehen ❷ (flower bed) Beet das (PLURAL die Beete)

**bedclothes** PLURAL NOUN Bettwäsche die

**bedding** NOUN Bettzeug das

**bedroom** NOUN Schlafzimmer das (PLURAL die Schlafzimmer); bedroom furniture Schlafzimmermöbel (plural), my bedroom window mein Schlafzimmerfenster

**bedside table** NOUN Nachttisch der (PLURAL die Nachttische)

**bedsit, bedsitter** NOUN möblierte Zimmer das (PLURAL die möblierten Zimmer)

**bedspread** NOUN Tagesdecke die (PLURAL die Tagesdecken)

**bedtime** NOUN Schlafenszeit die; at bedtime vor dem Schlafengehen

**bee** NOUN Biene die (PLURAL die Bienen)

**beech** NOUN Buche die (PLURAL die Buchen)

**beef** NOUN Rindfleisch das; we had roast beef wir haben Rinderbraten gegessen

**beefburger** NOUN Hamburger der (PLURAL die **Hamburger**)

**beer** NOUN Bier das (PLURAL die **Biere**); **two beers please** zwei Bier bitte, **beer can** die Bierdose

**beetle** NOUN Käfer der (PLURAL die **Käfer**)

**beetroot** NOUN Rote Bete die

**before** PREPOSITION ❶ vor (+DAT); **before Monday** vor Montag, **he left before me** er ist vor mir gegangen, **the day before the wedding** am Tag vor der Hochzeit ❷ **the day before** am Tag zuvor, **the day before yesterday** vorgestern, **the week before** in der Woche zuvor ❸ (already) schon einmal; **I've seen him before somewhere** ich habe ihn schon einmal irgendwo gesehen, **I had seen the film before** ich hatte den Film schon einmal gesehen

**before** CONJUNCTION bevor; **I closed the windows before leaving** (or **before I left**) ich habe die Fenster zugemacht, bevor ich wegging, **before the train leaves** bevor der Zug abfährt, **oh, before I forget ...** oh, bevor ich es vergesse ...

**beforehand** ADVERB (ahead of time) vorher; **phone beforehand** rufe vorher an

**beg** VERB ❶ betteln; **to beg for money** um Geld betteln ❷ (ask) bitten◇; **he begged her not to say anything** er bat sie, nichts zu sagen ❸ **I beg your pardon** entschuldigen Sie bitte

**begin** VERB anfangen◇ (SEP), beginnen◇; **the meeting begins at ten** die Besprechung fängt um zehn an, **the words beginning with P** die Wörter, die mit P anfangen, **to begin to do something** anfangen, etwas zu tun, beginnen, etwas zu tun, **I'm beginning to understand why ...** ich beginne zu verstehen, warum ...

**beginner** NOUN Anfänger der (PLURAL die **Anfänger**) Anfängerin die (PLURAL die **Anfängerinnen**)

**beginning** NOUN Anfang der (PLURAL die **Anfänge**); **at the beginning** am Anfang, **at the beginning of the holidays** am Anfang der Ferien

**behalf** NOUN **on behalf of** im Namen von (+DAT), **on behalf of Mr and Mrs Smith** im Namen von Herrn und Frau Smith

**behave** VERB ❶ sich benehmen◇; **he behaved badly** er hat sich schlecht benommen ❷ **to behave oneself** sich benehmen◇, **behave yourself!** benimm dich!

**behaviour** NOUN Benehmen das

**behind** NOUN Hintern der (informal) (PLURAL die **Hintern**)

**behind** PREPOSITION, ADVERB ❶ hinter (+DAT or, with movement towards a place, +ACC); **behind the sofa** hinter dem Sofa, **behind them** hinter ihnen, **the car behind** das Auto hinter ihnen/uns ❷ **to leave something behind** (belongings) etwas vergessen

**beige** ADJECTIVE beige

**Belgian** NOUN Belgier der (PLURAL die **Belgier**) Belgierin die (PLURAL die **Belgierinnen**)

**Belgian** ADJECTIVE belgisch; **he's Belgian** er ist Belgier

**Belgium** NOUN Belgien das; **to Belgium** nach Belgien

**belief** NOUN Glaube der (PLURAL die Glauben); **his political beliefs** seine politische Überzeugung

**believe** VERB ❶ glauben; **I believe so** ich glaube schon, **they believed what I said** sie glaubten, was ich sagte, **I don't believe you** das glaube ich dir nicht ❷ **to believe in something** an etwas (ACC) glauben, **to believe in God** an Gott glauben

**bell** NOUN ❶ (in a church) Glocke die (PLURAL die Glocken) ❷ (on a door) Klingel die (PLURAL die Klingeln); **to ring the bell** klingeln ❸ (for a cat or toy) Glöckchen das (PLURAL die Glöckchen)
• **that name rings a bell** der Name sagt mir etwas (literally: says something to me)

**belong** VERB ❶ **to belong to** gehören (+DAT), **that belongs to my mother** das gehört meiner Mutter ❷ **to belong to a club** einem Klub angehören ❸ (go) gehören; **where does this vase belong?** wo gehört diese Vase hin?

**belongings** PLURAL NOUN Sachen (plural); **all my belongings** alle meine Sachen

**below** PREPOSITION unter (+DAT or, with movement towards a place, +ACC); **below the window** unter dem Fenster, **the flat below yours** die Wohnung unter dir

**below** ADVERB ❶ (further down) unten; **he called from below** er rief von unten herauf ❷ **the flat below** die Wohnung darunter

**belt** NOUN Gürtel der (PLURAL die Gürtel)

**bench** NOUN Bank die (PLURAL die Bänke)

**bend** NOUN ❶ (in a road) Kurve die (PLURAL die Kurven) ❷ (in a river) Biegung die (PLURAL die Biegungen)

**bend** VERB ❶ (make a bend in) biegen◇ (a pipe or wire), beugen (your knee, arm, or head) ❷ (curve) eine Biegung machen ❸ **to bend down** sich bücken

**beneath** PREPOSITION unter (+DAT)

**benefit** NOUN ❶ Vorteil der (PLURAL die Vorteile) ❷ **unemployment benefit** die Arbeitslosenunterstützung

**bent** ADJECTIVE verbogen

**beret** NOUN Baskenmütze die (PLURAL die Baskenmützen)

**beside** PREPOSITION (next to) neben (+DAT or, with movement towards a place, +ACC); **she was sitting beside me** sie saß neben mir **she sat down beside me** sie hat sich neben mich gesetzt
• **that's beside the point** das hat nichts damit zu tun

**besides** ADVERB (anyway) außerdem; **besides, it's too late** außerdem ist es zu spät, (as well) **four dogs, and six cats besides** vier Hunde und außerdem sechs Katzen

**best** ADJECTIVE ❶ bester/beste/ bestes; **she's my best friend** sie ist meine beste Freundin ❷ **she's the best at tennis** im Tennis ist sie die Beste, **it's best to wait** das Beste ist zu warten

**best** ADVERB am besten; **he plays best**

er spielt am besten, **I like Munich best** München gefällt mir am besten, **best of all** am allerbesten **I like grapes best** ich mag Weintrauben am liebsten
• **all the best!** alles Gute!
• **to make the best of it** das Beste daraus machen
• **to do your best** sein Bestes tun; **I did my best to help her** ich habe mein Bestes getan, um ihr zu helfen

**best man** NOUN Trauzeuge der (PLURAL die Trauzeugen)

**bet** NOUN Wette die (PLURAL die Wetten)

**bet** VERB wetten; **to bet on a horse** auf ein Pferd wetten, **I bet you he'll forget it** ich wette mit dir, dass er es vergisst

**better** ADJECTIVE, ADVERB ❶ besser; **she's found a better flat** sie hat eine bessere Wohnung gefunden ❷ **it works better than the other one** dieser geht besser als der andere, **even better** noch besser, **it's even better than before** das ist noch besser als vorher ❸ (less ill) **I'm better** es geht mir besser, **he's a bit better today** es geht ihm heute ein bisschen besser, **I feel better** ich fühle mich besser ❹ **to get better** besser werden, **my German is getting better** mein Deutsch wird besser ❺ **so much the better** umso besser, **the sooner the better** je eher, desto besser

**better** ADVERB **it's better to phone at once** es wäre besser, sofort anzurufen, **he'd better not go** er sollte besser nicht gehen, **I'd better go now** ich gehe jetzt besser

**better off** ADJECTIVE ❶ (richer) besser gestellt; **they're better off than us** sie sind besser gestellt als wir

❷ (more comfortable) **to be better off** besser dran sein, **you'd be better off in bed** im Bett wärst du besser aufgehoben

**between** PREPOSITION ❶ zwischen (+DAT or, with movement towards a place, +ACC); **between London and Dover** zwischen London und Dover, **between Monday and Friday** zwischen Montag und Freitag ❷ (sharing) unter (+DAT); **between ourselves** unter uns, **between the two of them** unter sich

**beyond** PREPOSITION ❶ (in space) jenseits (+GEN); **beyond the border** jenseits der Grenze ❷ (in time) nach (+DAT); **beyond midnight** nach Mitternacht ❸ **it's beyond me!** das ist mir unverständlich

**Bible** NOUN **the Bible** die Bibel

**bicycle** NOUN Fahrrad das (PLURAL die Fahrräder); **she rides a bicycle** sie fährt Rad

**bicycle lane** NOUN Fahrradweg der (PLURAL die Fahrradwege)

**big** ADJECTIVE groß; **a big house** ein großes Haus, **my big sister** meine große Schwester, **a big mistake** ein großer Fehler, **it's too big for me** das ist mir zu groß

**big toe** NOUN große Zehe die (PLURAL die großen Zehen)

**bike** NOUN ❶ (with pedals) Rad das (PLURAL die Räder); **by bike** mit dem Rad ❷ (with motor) Motorrad das (PLURAL die Motorräder)

**bikini** NOUN Bikini der (PLURAL die Bikinis)

**bilingual** ADJECTIVE zweisprachig

**bill** NOUN Rechnung die (PLURAL die

a b c d e f g h i j k l m n o p q r s t u v w x y z

Rechnungen); **can we have the bill, please?** die Rechnung bitte

**billiards** NOUN Billard das; **to play billiards** Billard spielen

**billion** NOUN Milliarde die (PLURAL die Milliarden) Billion die (PLURAL die Billionen); **two billion euros** zwei Milliarden Euro

**bin** NOUN Mülleimer der (PLURAL die Mülleimer)

**binoculars** PLURAL NOUN Fernglas das (PLURAL die Ferngläser)

**biochemistry** NOUN Biochemie die

**biology** NOUN Biologie die

**bird** NOUN Vogel der (PLURAL die Vögel)

**bird sanctuary** NOUN Vogelschutzgebiet das (PLURAL die Vogelschutzgebiete)

**birdwatching** NOUN das Beobachten von Vögeln; **to go birdwatching** Vögel beobachten

**Biro** NOUN Kugelschreiber der (PLURAL die Kugelschreiber)

**birth** NOUN Geburt die (PLURAL die Geburten)

**birth certificate** NOUN Geburtsurkunde die (PLURAL die Geburtsurkunden)

**birthday** NOUN Geburtstag der (PLURAL die Geburtstage); **happy birthday!** herzlichen Glückwunsch zum Geburtstag!

**birthday party** NOUN Geburtstagsfeier die (PLURAL die Geburtstagsfeiern)

**biscuit** NOUN Keks der (PLURAL die Kekse)

**bishop** NOUN ❶ (churchman) Bischof der (PLURAL die Bischöfe) ❷ (in chess) Läufer der (PLURAL die Läufer)

**bit** NOUN ❶ (piece) Stückchen das (PLURAL die Stückchen); **a bit of chocolate** ein Stückchen Schokolade ❷ (a small amount) **a bit of** ein bisschen, **a bit of sugar** ein bisschen Zucker ❸ (in a book, film, etc.) Teil der (PLURAL die Teile); **this bit is brilliant** dieser Teil ist hervorragend ❹ **a bit** ein bisschen, **a bit too early** ein bisschen zu früh, **wait a bit!** warte ein bisschen! ❺ **he's a bit of a show-off** er ist ein ziemlicher Angeber ❻ **bit by bit** nach und nach

**bite** NOUN ❶ (snack) Happen der (PLURAL die Happen); **we'll just have a bite before we go** wir essen noch einen kleinen Happen, bevor wir gehen ❷ (from an insect) Stich der (PLURAL die Stiche); **mosquito bite** der Mückenstich ❸ (from a dog) Biss der (PLURAL die Bisse)

**bite** VERB ❶ (person or dog) beißen◇ ❷ (insect) stechen◇

**bitter** ADJECTIVE (taste) bitter

**black** ADJECTIVE ❶ schwarz; **my black jacket** meine schwarze Jacke ❷ **a black man** ein Schwarzer, **a black woman** eine Schwarze

**blackberry** NOUN Brombeere die (PLURAL die Brombeeren)

**blackbird** NOUN Amsel die (PLURAL die Amseln)

**blackboard** NOUN Tafel die (PLURAL die Tafeln)

**blackcurrant** NOUN Schwarze Johannisbeere die (PLURAL die Schwarzen Johannisbeeren)

A B C D E F G H I J K L M N O P Q R S T U V W X Y Z

**black pudding** NOUN Blutwurst die (PLURAL die Blutwürste)

**blade** NOUN Klinge die (PLURAL die Klingen)

**blame** NOUN Schuld die; **to take the blame for something** die Schuld für etwas (ACC) auf sich (ACC) nehmen, **to put the blame on somebody** die Schuld auf jemanden schieben

**blame** VERB **to blame somebody for something** jemandem die Schuld an etwas (DAT) geben, **they blamed him for the accident** sie haben ihm die Schuld an dem Unfall gegeben, **she is to blame for it** sie ist daran schuld, **I blame the parents** ich gebe den Eltern Schuld, **I don't blame you** ich kann es dir nicht verdenken

**blank** NOUN Lücke die (PLURAL die Lücken)

**blank** ADJECTIVE ❶ (page) leer (tape or disk) unbespielt ❷ **blank cheque** der Blankoscheck

**blanket** NOUN Decke die (PLURAL die Decken)

**blaze** NOUN Feuer das (PLURAL die Feuer)

**blaze** VERB brennen◇

**bleach** NOUN Bleichmittel das (PLURAL die Bleichmittel)

**bleed** VERB bluten; **my nose is bleeding** meine Nase blutet

**blend** VERB mischen

**blender** NOUN Mixer der (PLURAL die Mixer)

**bless** VERB segnen; **bless you!** (after a sneeze) Gesundheit!

**blind** NOUN (in a window) Rollo das (PLURAL die Rollos)

**blind** ADJECTIVE blind

**blink** VERB (mit den Augen) blinzeln

**blister** NOUN Blase die (PLURAL die Blasen)

**blizzard** NOUN Schneesturm der (PLURAL die Schneestürme)

**block** NOUN (a building or buildings) Block der (PLURAL die Blocks); **block of flats** der Wohnblock, **office block** das Bürohaus, **to drive round the block** um den Block fahren

**block** VERB ❶ sperren (an exit or a road) ❷ **the sink's blocked** das Spülbecken ist verstopft

**blonde** ADJECTIVE blond

**blood** NOUN Blut das

**blood test** NOUN Blutprobe die (PLURAL die Blutproben)

**blouse** NOUN Bluse die (PLURAL die Blusen)

**blow** NOUN Schlag der (PLURAL die Schläge)

**blow** VERB ❶ (a person) blasen◇ ❷ (the wind) wehen ❸ **the bomb blew the bridge to pieces** die Bombe hat die Brücke in die Luft gesprengt ❹ **to blow your nose** sich (DAT) die Nase putzen
- **to blow something out** etwas ausblasen◇ (SEP)
- **to blow up** (explode) explodieren (PERF sein)
- **to blow something up** (a tyre or balloon) etwas aufblasen◇ (SEP), (with explosives) etwas sprengen

**blow-dry** NOUN Föhnen das; **a cut and blow-dry** Schneiden und Föhnen

**blue** | **bomb**

**blue** ADJECTIVE **blau**; **blue eyes** blaue Augen

**blunder** NOUN **Fehler** der (PLURAL die **Fehler**)

**blunt** ADJECTIVE ❶ (a knife, pencil, or scissors) **stumpf** ❷ (a person or question) **direkt**

**blurred** ADJECTIVE ❶ (not distinct) **verschwommen** ❷ (photo) **unscharf**

**blush** VERB **erröten** (PERF **sein**)

**board** NOUN ❶ (plank, notice board, game) **Brett** das (PLURAL die **Bretter**); **chess board** das Schachbrett ❷ (blackboard) **Tafel** die (PLURAL die **Tafeln**) ❸ (accommodation in a hotel) **full board** die Vollpension, **half board** die Halbpension, **board and lodging** Unterkunft und Verpflegung

**boarder** NOUN (in a school) **Internatsschüler** der (PLURAL die **Internatsschüler**), **Internatsschülerin** die (PLURAL die **Internatsschülerinnen**)

**board game** NOUN **Brettspiel** das (PLURAL die **Brettspiele**)

**boarding** NOUN (on a plane, train) **Einsteigen** das

**boarding card** NOUN **Bordkarte** die (PLURAL die **Bordkarten**)

**boarding school** NOUN **Internat** das (PLURAL die **Internate**)

**boast** VERB **prahlen**; **he was boasting about his new bike** er prahlte mit seinem neuen Rad

**boat** NOUN ❶ **Boot** das (PLURAL die **Boote**); **rowing boat** das Ruderboot ❷ (larger boat) **Schiff** das (PLURAL die **Schiffe**); **to go by boat** mit dem Schiff fahren

**body** NOUN ❶ **Körper** der (PLURAL die **Körper**) ❷ (corpse) **Leiche** die (PLURAL die **Leichen**)

**bodybuilding** NOUN **Bodybuilding** das

**bodyguard** NOUN **Leibwächter** der (PLURAL die **Leibwächter**)

**body odour** NOUN **Körpergeruch** der

**boil** NOUN ❶ **to bring the water to the boil** das Wasser zum Kochen bringen ❷ (swelling) **Furunkel** der (PLURAL die **Furunkel**)

**boil** VERB ❶ **kochen**; **the water's boiling** das Wasser kocht, **to boil vegetables** Gemüse kochen ❷ (put the kettle on) **to boil some water** Wasser aufsetzen (SEP)
• **to boil over** überkochen (SEP) (PERF sein)

**boiled egg** NOUN **gekochte Ei** das (PLURAL die **gekochten Eier**)

**boiled potato** NOUN **Salzkartoffel** die (PLURAL die **Salzkartoffeln**)

**boiler** NOUN (for central heating) **Heizkessel** der (PLURAL die **Heizkessel**)

**boiling** ADJECTIVE ❶ (water) **kochend** ❷ **it's boiling hot today** heute ist es wahnsinnig heiß

**bolt** NOUN (on a door) **Riegel** der (PLURAL die **Riegel**)

**bolt** VERB ❶ (lock) **verriegeln** ❷ (gobble down) **runterschlingen**◇ (SEP) (informal)

**bomb** NOUN **Bombe** die (PLURAL die **Bomben**)

**bomb** VERB **bombardieren**

**bombing** NOUN ❶ (in war) Bombardierung die (PLURAL die Bombardierungen) ❷ (a terrorist attack) Bombenattentat das (PLURAL die Bombenattentate)

**bone** NOUN ❶ Knochen der (PLURAL die Knochen) ❷ (of a fish) Gräte die (PLURAL die Gräten)

**bonfire** NOUN Feuer das (PLURAL die Feuer)

**bonnet** NOUN ❶ (of a car) Kühlerhaube die (PLURAL die Kühlerhauben) ❷ (clothing) Haube die (PLURAL die Hauben)

**boo** VERB ausbuhen (SEP); the crowd booed the referee die Menge buhte den Schiedsrichter aus

**book** NOUN ❶ Buch das (PLURAL die Bücher); a book about dinosaurs ein Buch über Dinosaurier, my biology book mein Biologiebuch ❷ (of stamps, tickets) Heft das (PLURAL die Hefte) ❸ exercise book das Heft, cheque book das Scheckbuch

**book** VERB ❶ buchen (holiday, flight) ❷ bestellen (a table, theatre, or cinema tickets); I booked a table for 8 p.m. ich habe einen Tisch für zwanzig Uhr bestellt

**bookcase** NOUN Bücherregal das (PLURAL die Bücherregale)

**booking** NOUN (for a flight or a holiday, for example) Buchung die (PLURAL die Buchungen)

**booking office** NOUN ❶ (at a train station) Fahrkartenschalter der (PLURAL die Fahrkartenschalter) ❷ (in a theatre or cinema) Kasse die (PLURAL die Kassen)

**booklet** NOUN Broschüre die (PLURAL die Broschüren)

**bookshelf** NOUN Bücherregal das (PLURAL die Bücherregale)

**bookshop** NOUN Buchhandlung die (PLURAL die Buchhandlungen)

**boot** NOUN ❶ Stiefel der (PLURAL die Stiefel) ❷ (for football, walking, climbing, or skiing) Schuh der (PLURAL die Schuhe); football boots Fußballschuhe ❸ (of a car) Kofferraum der (PLURAL die Kofferräume)

**border** NOUN (between countries) Grenze die (PLURAL die Grenzen); at the border an der Grenze

**bore** NOUN ❶ (a boring person) langweilige Mensch der (PLURAL die langweiligen Menschen) ❷ (a nuisance) what a bore! wie ärgerlich!

**bored** ADJECTIVE to be bored sich langweilen, I'm bored ich langweile mich

**boring** ADJECTIVE langweilig

**born** ADJECTIVE geboren; to be born geboren werden, she was born in Germany sie ist in Deutschland geboren

**borrow** VERB sich (DAT) borgen; can I borrow your bike? kann ich mir dein Rad borgen?, to borrow something from somebody sich etwas von jemandem borgen, I borrowed some money from Dad ich habe mir Geld von Vati geborgt

a
**b**
c
d
e
f
g
h
i
j
k
l
m
n
o
p
q
r
s
t
u
v
w
x
y
z

**boss** NOUN Chef der (PLURAL die Chefs) Chefin die (PLURAL die Chefinnen)

**bossy** ADJECTIVE herrisch

**both** PRONOUN beide; **they both came** sie kamen beide, **both my sisters were there** meine beiden Schwestern waren da, **both of us** wir beide, **they are both sold** beide sind verkauft

**both** ADVERB **both at home and at school** sowohl zu Hause als auch in der Schule, **both in summer and in winter** sowohl im Sommer als auch im Winter

**bother** NOUN ❶ (minor trouble) Ärger der; **I've had a lot of bother with the car** ich hatte viel Ärger mit dem Auto ❷ **if it isn't too much bother** wenn es nicht zu viel Mühe macht, **it's no bother** das ist kein Problem, **the children were no bother** die Kinder waren kein Problem, **without any bother** ohne irgendwelche Schwierigkeiten

**bother** VERB ❶ (disturb) stören; **I'm sorry to bother you** es tut mir Leid, dich zu stören ❷ (worry) stören; **what's bothering you?** was stört dich?, **it doesn't bother me at all** das stört mich überhaupt nicht ❸ (take trouble) **don't bother to write** du brauchst nicht zu schreiben, **she didn't even bother to wait** sie hat nicht einmal gewartet, **don't bother!** lass es! (informal), **I can't be bothered** ich habe keine Lust

**bottle** NOUN Flasche die (PLURAL die Flaschen)

**bottle bank** NOUN Altglascontainer der (PLURAL die Altglascontainer)

**bottle opener** NOUN Flaschenöffner der (PLURAL die Flaschenöffner)

**bottom** NOUN ❶ (of a bag, bottle, hole, or stretch of water) Boden der (PLURAL die Böden); **at the bottom of the lake** am Boden des Sees, **at the bottom of the well** auf dem Grund des Brunnens ❷ (of a hill or building) Fuß der (PLURAL die Füße); **at the bottom of the tower** am Fuß des Turms ❸ (of a garden, street, list) Ende das (PLURAL die Enden); **at the bottom of the street** am Ende der Straße ❹ **at the bottom of the page** unten auf der Seite ❺ (buttocks) Hintern der (informal) (PLURAL die Hintern)

**bottom** ADJECTIVE ❶ unterster/ unterste/unterstes; **the bottom shelf** das unterste Regalbrett ❷ **the bottom flat** die Wohnung im Erdgeschoss

**bounce** VERB (jump) springen◇ (PERF sein)

**bouncer** NOUN Rausschmeißer der (PLURAL die Rausschmeißer)

**bound** ADJECTIVE (certain) **he's bound to be late** er kommt ganz bestimmt zu spät, **that was bound to happen** das musste ja kommen

**boundary** NOUN Grenze die (PLURAL die Grenzen)

**bow** NOUN ❶ (in a shoelace or ribbon) Schleife die (PLURAL die Schleifen) ❷ (for a violin or with arrows) Bogen der (PLURAL die Bogen); **with bow and arrow** mit Pfeil und Bogen

**bowl** NOUN ❶ (large, for salad, mixing, or washing up) Schüssel die (PLURAL die Schüsseln) ❷ (smaller) Schale die (PLURAL die Schalen)

**bowler** NOUN *(in cricket)* **Werfer** der *(PLURAL* die **Werfer)**, **Werferin** die *(PLURAL* die **Werferinnen)**

**bowling** NOUN *(tenpin)* **Bowling** das; **to go bowling** kegeln gehen

**bow tie** NOUN **Fliege** die *(PLURAL* die **Fliegen)**

**box** NOUN ❶ **Schachtel** die *(PLURAL* die **Schachteln)**; **a box of chocolates** eine Schachtel Pralinen ❷ **cardboard box** der **Karton** ❸ *(on a form)* **Kästchen** das *(PLURAL* die **Kästchen)**

**boxer** NOUN **Boxer** der *(PLURAL* die **Boxer)**

**boxing** NOUN ❶ **Boxen** das ❷ **boxing match** der **Boxkampf**

**Boxing Day** NOUN **zweite Weihnachtsfeiertag** der

**box office** NOUN **Kasse** die *(PLURAL* die **Kassen)**

**boy** NOUN **Junge** der *(PLURAL* die **Jungen)**; **a little boy** ein kleiner Junge

**boyfriend** NOUN **Freund** der *(PLURAL* die **Freunde)**

**bra** NOUN **BH** der *(PLURAL* die **BHs)**

**brace** NOUN *(for teeth)* **Spange** die *(PLURAL* die **Spangen)**

**bracelet** NOUN **Armband** das *(PLURAL* die **Armbänder)**

**bracket** NOUN **Klammer** die *(PLURAL* die **Klammern)**; **in brackets** in Klammern

**brain** NOUN **Gehirn** das *(PLURAL* die **Gehirne)**

**brainwave** NOUN **Geistesblitz** der *(PLURAL* die **Geistesblitze)**

**brake** NOUN **Bremse** die *(PLURAL* die **Bremsen)**

**brake** VERB **bremsen**

**branch** NOUN ❶ *(of a tree)* **Ast** der *(PLURAL* die **Äste)** ❷ *(of a shop)* **Filiale** die *(PLURAL* die **Filialen)** ❸ *(of a bank)* **Zweigstelle** die *(PLURAL* die **Zweigstellen)**

**brand** NOUN **Marke** die *(PLURAL* die **Marken)**

**brand new** ADJECTIVE **nagelneu**

**brandy** NOUN **Weinbrand** der *(PLURAL* die **Weinbrände)**

**brass** NOUN ❶ *(metal)* **Messing** das ❷ *(in an orchestra)* **the brass** die **Blechbläser**

**brass band** NOUN **Blaskapelle** die *(PLURAL* die **Blaskapellen)**

**brave** ADJECTIVE **tapfer**

**bravery** NOUN **Tapferkeit** die

**Brazilian** ADJECTIVE **brasilianisch**

**Brazilian** NOUN **Brasilianer** der *(PLURAL* die **Brasilianer)** **Brasilianerin** die *(PLURAL* die **Brasilianerinnen)**

**bread** NOUN **Brot** das *(PLURAL* die **Brote)**; **a slice of bread** eine Scheibe Brot, **a piece of bread and butter** ein Butterbrot

**break** NOUN ❶ *(a short rest or at school)* **Pause** die *(PLURAL* die **Pausen)**; **ten minutes' break** eine Pause von zehn Minuten, **to take a break** Pause machen, **at break** in der Pause ❷ **the Christmas break** die Weihnachtsferien *(plural)*

a b c d e f g h i j k l m n o p q r s t u v w x y z

**break** VERB ❶ zerbrechen◇, kaputtmachen (SEP) (informal); **he broke a glass** er hat ein Glas zerbrochen, **don't break the doll** mach die Puppe nicht kaputt ❷ (get damaged) zerbrechen◇ (PERF sein), kaputtgehen◇ (SEP) (informal) (PERF sein); **the glass broke** das Glas zerbrach, **the eggs broke** die Eier sind kaputtgegangen ❸ **to break your arm** sich (DAT) den Arm brechen ❹ brechen◇ (rules, promise); **to break one's promise** sein Versprechen brechen ❺ **to break the record** den Rekord brechen◇ ❻ **to break the news that ...** melden, dass ...

• **to break down** ❶ (car) eine Panne haben; **the car broke down** das Auto hatte eine Panne ❷ (talks, negotiations) scheitern (PERF sein)

• **to break in** einbrechen◇ (SEP) (PERF sein)

• **to break up** ❶ (couple) sich trennen ❷ (crowd) sich auflösen (SEP) ❸ **we break up on Thursday** die Ferien fangen Donnerstag an

**breakdown** NOUN ❶ (of a vehicle) Panne die (PLURAL die Pannen); **we had a breakdown on the motorway** wir hatten eine Panne auf der Autobahn ❷ (in talks or negotiations) Scheitern das ❸ (a nervous collapse) Zusammenbruch der (PLURAL die Zusammenbrüche); **to have a nervous breakdown** einen Nervenzusammenbruch haben

**breakdown truck** NOUN Abschleppwagen der (PLURAL die Abschleppwagen)

**breakfast** NOUN Frühstück das (PLURAL die Frühstücke); **we have breakfast at eight** wir frühstücken um acht Uhr

**break-in** NOUN Einbruch der (PLURAL die Einbrüche)

**breast** NOUN Brust die (PLURAL die Brüste)

**breaststroke** NOUN Brustschwimmen das

**breath** NOUN Atem der; **out of breath** außer Atem, **to hold your breath** den Atem anhalten, **to get your breath back** wieder zu Atem kommen, **to take a deep breath** tief einatmen

**breathe** VERB atmen

**breathing** NOUN Atmen das

**breed** NOUN (of animal) Rasse die (PLURAL die Rassen)

**breeze** NOUN Brise die (PLURAL die Brisen)

**brew** VERB ❶ brauen (beer) ❷ aufbrühen (SEP) (tea); **the tea's brewing** der Tee zieht noch

**brewery** NOUN Brauerei die (PLURAL die Brauereien)

**brick** NOUN Ziegel der (PLURAL die Ziegel); **a brick wall** eine Ziegelmauer

**bride** NOUN Braut die (PLURAL die Bräute); **the bride and groom** das Brautpaar

**bridegroom** NOUN Bräutigam der (PLURAL die Bräutigame)

**bridesmaid** NOUN Brautjungfer die (PLURAL die Brautjungfern)

**bridge** NOUN ❶ (over a river) Brücke die (PLURAL die Brücken) ❷ (card game) Bridge das

**bridle** NOUN Zaumzeug das (PLURAL die Zaumzeuge)

**brief** ADJECTIVE kurz

**briefcase** NOUN Aktentasche die (PLURAL die Aktentaschen)

**briefly** ADVERB kurz

**briefs** PLURAL NOUN Slip der (PLURAL die Slips)

**bright** ADJECTIVE ❶ (colour) leuchtend; **bright green socks** leuchtend grüne Socken ❷ (eyes, sunshine) strahlend ❸ (light) hell ❹ (clever) intelligent; **she's not very bright** sie ist nicht sehr intelligent
• **to look on the bright side** die Sache positiv sehen (literally: to see things positively)

**brilliant** ADJECTIVE ❶ (very clever) glänzend; **he's a brilliant surgeon** er ist ein glänzender Chirurg ❷ (wonderful) toll; **the party was brilliant!** die Party war toll!

**bring** VERB ❶ mitbringen◇ (SEP); **he brought a present** er brachte ein Geschenk mit, **bring your camera** bring deinen Fotoapparat mit ❷ (to a place) bringen◇; **she's bringing the children home** sie bringt die Kinder nach Hause
• **to bring somebody up** jemanden großziehen◇ (SEP); **he was brought up by his aunt** er wurde von seiner Tante großgezogen

**Britain** NOUN Großbritannien das; **to Britain** nach Großbritannien

**British** PLURAL NOUN **the British** die Briten

**British** ADJECTIVE ❶ britisch; **the British Isles** die Britischen Inseln ❷ **he's British** er ist Brite, **she's British** sie ist Britin

**broad** ADJECTIVE ❶ (wide) breit ❷ (extensive) weit

**broad bean** NOUN dicke Bohne die (PLURAL die dicken Bohnen)

**broadcast** NOUN Sendung die (PLURAL die Sendungen)

**broadcast** VERB senden

**broccoli** NOUN Brokkoli der (PLURAL die Brokkolis)

**brochure** NOUN Broschüre die (PLURAL die Broschüren)

**broke** ADJECTIVE **to be broke** pleite sein (informal)

**broken** ADJECTIVE zerbrochen, kaputt (informal); **the window's broken** das Fenster ist kaputt, **to have a broken leg** ein gebrochenes Bein haben

**bronchitis** NOUN Bronchitis die

**brooch** NOUN Brosche die (PLURAL die Broschen)

**broom** NOUN Besen der (PLURAL die Besen)

**brother** NOUN Bruder der (PLURAL die Brüder); **my mother's brother** der Bruder meiner Mutter

**brother-in-law** NOUN Schwager der (PLURAL die Schwäger)

**brown** ADJECTIVE braun; **my brown shoes** meine braunen Schuhe, **light brown** hellbraun, **dark brown** dunkelbraun, **to go brown** (suntanned) braun werden

**brown bread** NOUN Mischbrot das (PLURAL die Mischbrote)

**bruise** NOUN ❶ (on a person) blaue Fleck der (PLURAL die blauen

a
b
c
d
e
f
g
h
i
j
k
l
m
n
o
p
q
r
s
t
u
v
w
x
y
z

Flecken) ❷ (on fruit) Druckstelle die (PLURAL die Druckstellen)

**brush** NOUN ❶ (for your hair, clothes, nails, or shoes) Bürste die (PLURAL die Bürsten); my hair brush meine Haarbürste ❷ (for sweeping) Besen der (PLURAL die Besen) ❸ (for paint) Pinsel der (PLURAL die Pinsel)

**brush** VERB ❶ bürsten; to brush your hair sich (DAT) die Haare bürsten, I brushed my hair ich habe mir die Haare gebürstet ❷ to brush your teeth sich (DAT) die Zähne putzen

**Brussels** NOUN Brüssel das

**Brussels sprout** NOUN Rosenkohl der; he likes Brussels sprouts er mag Rosenkohl

**bubble** NOUN Blase die (PLURAL die Blasen)

**bubble bath** NOUN Badeschaum der

**bucket** NOUN Eimer der (PLURAL die Eimer)

**buckle** NOUN Schnalle die (PLURAL die Schnallen)

**Buddhism** NOUN Buddhismus der

**Buddhist** NOUN Buddhist der (PLURAL die Buddhisten) Buddhistin die (PLURAL die Buddhistinnen)

**budget** NOUN Budget das (PLURAL die Budgets)

**budgie** NOUN Wellensittich der (PLURAL die Wellensittiche)

**buffet** NOUN Büffet das (PLURAL die Büffets)

**buffet car** NOUN Speisewagen der (PLURAL die Speisewagen)

**bug** NOUN ❶ (insect) Wanze die (PLURAL die Wanzen) ❷ (germ) Bazillus der (PLURAL die Bazillen); a stomach bug eine Magengrippe ❸ a computer bug ein Programmierfehler

**build** VERB bauen

**builder** NOUN Bauarbeiter der (PLURAL die Bauarbeiter)

**building** NOUN Gebäude das (PLURAL die Gebäude)

**building site** NOUN Baustelle die (PLURAL die Baustellen)

**building society** NOUN Bausparkasse die (PLURAL die Bausparkassen)

**built-up** ADJECTIVE ❶ bebaut ❷ built-up area das Wohngebiet

**bulb** NOUN ❶ (lightbulb) Glühbirne die (PLURAL die Glühbirnen) ❷ (flower bulb) Blumenzwiebel die (PLURAL die Zwiebeln)

**bull** NOUN Bulle der (PLURAL die Bullen)

**bulldozer** NOUN Planierraupe die (PLURAL die Planierraupen)

**bullet** NOUN Kugel die (PLURAL die Kugeln)

**bulletin** NOUN ❶ (written) Bulletin das (PLURAL die Bulletins) ❷ (on TV, radio) news bulletin die Kurzmeldung

**bully** NOUN ❶ (in school) Rabauke der (PLURAL die Rabauken) ❷ (adult) Tyrann der (PLURAL die Tyrannen)

**bully** VERB schikanieren

**bum** NOUN Hintern der (informal) (PLURAL die Hintern)

**bump** NOUN ❶ (on a surface) Unebenheit die (PLURAL die Unebenheiten); there are lots of bumps in the road die Straße ist sehr uneben ❷ (swelling) Beule die (PLURAL die Beulen); a bump on the head eine Beule am Kopf ❸ (jolt) Stoß der (PLURAL die Stöße) ❹ (noise) Bums der (PLURAL die Bumse)

**bump** VERB ❶ (bang) stoßen◊; I bumped my head ich habe mir den Kopf gestoßen, to bump into something gegen etwas (ACC) stoßen ❷ to bump into somebody (meet by chance) jemanden zufällig treffen

**bumper** NOUN Stoßstange die (PLURAL die Stoßstangen)

**bumpy** ADJECTIVE holperig

**bun** NOUN ❶ (for a burger) Brötchen das (PLURAL die Brötchen), Semmel die (PLURAL die Semmeln) ❷ (sweet) süße Brötchen das (PLURAL die süßen Brötchen)

**bunch** NOUN ❶ (of flowers) Strauß der (PLURAL die Sträuße) ❷ (of carrots, radishes) Bund das (PLURAL die Bunde); a bunch of keys ein Schlüsselbund ❸ a bunch of grapes eine ganze Weintraube

**bundle** NOUN Bündel das (PLURAL die Bündel)

**bungalow** NOUN Bungalow der (PLURAL die Bungalows)

**bunk** NOUN ❶ (on a boat) Koje die (PLURAL die Kojen) ❷ (on a train) Bett das (PLURAL die Betten)

**bunk bed** NOUN Etagenbett das (PLURAL die Etagenbetten)

**burger** NOUN Hamburger der (PLURAL die Hamburger)

**burglar** NOUN Einbrecher der (PLURAL die Einbrecher) Einbrecherin die (PLURAL die Einbrecherinnen)

**burglar alarm** NOUN Alarmanlage die (PLURAL die Alarmanlagen)

**burglary** NOUN Einbruch der (PLURAL die Einbrüche)

**burn** NOUN ❶ (on the skin) Verbrennung die (PLURAL die Verbrennungen) ❷ (on fabric, object) Brandstelle die (PLURAL die Brandstellen)

**burn** VERB ❶ verbrennen◊; she burnt his letters sie hat seine Briefe verbrannt ❷ (fire, candle) brennen◊ ❸ (injure) verbrennen◊; to burn yourself sich verbrennen, you'll burn your fingers! du verbrennst dir die Finger! ❹ (cake, meat, etc.) anbrennen◊ (SEP); Mum's burnt the cake Mutti hat den Kuchen anbrennen lassen

**burnt** ADJECTIVE ❶ (papers, rubbish) verbrannt ❷ (cake, meat, etc.) angebrannt

**burst** VERB ❶ platzen lassen (a balloon); the tyre has burst der Reifen ist geplatzt ❷ to burst out laughing in Lachen ausbrechen◊ (SEP) (PERF sein), to burst into tears in Tränen ausbrechen◊ (SEP) (PERF sein) ❸ to burst into flames in Flammen aufgehen◊ (SEP) (PERF sein)

**bury** VERB ❶ begraben◊ (a dead person) ❷ vergraben◊ (treasure or a bone)

**bus** NOUN Bus der (PLURAL die Busse); on the bus im Bus, by bus mit dem Bus

**bus driver** NOUN Busfahrer der (PLURAL die Busfahrer) Busfahrerin die (PLURAL die Busfahrerinnen)

**bush** NOUN Busch der (PLURAL die Büsche)

**business** NOUN ❶ (commercial dealings) Geschäfte (plural); business is bad die Geschäfte gehen schlecht, he's in Leeds on business er ist geschäftlich in Leeds ❷ (a line of business or profession) Branche die (PLURAL die Branchen); he's in the insurance business er ist in der Versicherungsbranche ❸ (firm or company) Betrieb der (PLURAL die Betriebe); small businesses kleine Betriebe ❹ (personal concern) Angelegenheit die (PLURAL die Angelegenheiten); mind your own business! kümmere dich um deine eigenen Angelegenheiten!

**businessman** NOUN Geschäftsmann der (PLURAL die Geschäftsleute)

**business trip** NOUN Geschäftsreise die (PLURAL die Geschäftsreisen)

**businesswoman** NOUN Geschäftsfrau die (PLURAL die Geschäftsfrauen)

**bus pass** NOUN Zeitkarte die (PLURAL die Zeitkarten)

**bus route** NOUN Buslinie die (PLURAL die Buslinien)

**bus shelter** NOUN Wartehäuschen das (PLURAL die Wartehäuschen)

**bus station** NOUN Busbahnhof der (PLURAL die Busbahnhöfe)

**bus stop** NOUN Bushaltestelle die (PLURAL die Bushaltestellen)

**bus ticket** NOUN Busfahrkarte die (PLURAL die Busfahrkarten)

**busy** ADJECTIVE ❶ beschäftigt; he's busy er ist beschäftigt, she was busy packing sie war mit Packen beschäftigt ❷ to have a busy day viel zu tun haben ❸ the shops were busy in den Läden war sehr viel los ❹ (phone) besetzt

**but** CONJUNCTION ❶ aber; small but strong klein aber stark ❷ (after a negative statement) sondern; not Thursday but Friday nicht Donnerstag, sondern Freitag, not only ... but also nicht nur ... sondern auch

**but** PREPOSITION ❶ außer (+DAT); everyone but Winston alle außer Winston, anything but that! nur das nicht! ❷ the last but one der/die/ das Vorletzte

**butcher** NOUN ❶ Fleischer der (PLURAL die Fleischer) Fleischerin die (PLURAL die Fleischerinnen) Metzger der (PLURAL die Metzger) Metzgerin die (PLURAL die Metzgerinnen); he's a butcher er ist Fleischer, er ist Metzger ❷ the butcher's die Fleischerei, die Metzgerei

**butter** NOUN Butter die

**butter** VERB buttern

**butterfly** NOUN Schmetterling der (PLURAL die Schmetterlinge)

**button** NOUN Knopf der (PLURAL die Knöpfe); the record button die Aufnahmetaste

**buttonhole** NOUN Knopfloch das (PLURAL die Knopflöcher)

**buy** NOUN **Kauf** der *(PLURAL* die **Käufe)**; a bad buy ein schlechter Kauf

**buy** VERB **kaufen**; I bought the tickets ich habe die Karten gekauft, **to buy something for somebody** jemandem etwas kaufen, **Sarah bought him a sweater** Sarah hat ihm einen Pullover gekauft

**buzz** VERB *(a fly or bee)* **summen**

**buzzer** NOUN **Summer** der *(PLURAL* die **Summer)**

**by** PREPOSITION **❶ von** *(+DAT)*; **I was bitten by a dog** ich bin von einem Hund gebissen worden, **by Mozart** von Mozart **❷ by mistake** versehentlich **❸** *(travel)* **mit** *(+DAT)*; **to come by bus** mit dem Bus kommen, **to go by train** mit dem Zug fahren, **by bike** mit dem Rad **❹** *(near)* **an** *(+DAT)*; **by the sea** am Meer, **the stop by the school** die Haltestelle an der Schule **❺** *(before)* **bis**; **it'll be ready by Monday** es wird bis Montag fertig sein, **I'll be back by four** ich bin bis vier Uhr zurück **❻ by now** inzwischen **❼ by yourself** ganz allein, **I was by myself in the house** ich war ganz allein im Haus, **she did it by herself** sie hat es ganz allein gemacht **❽ by the way** übrigens **❾ to go by** vorbeigehen◇ *(SEP)* *(PERF* **sein)**

**bye** EXCLAMATION **tschüs!** *(informal)*

**bypass** NOUN **Umgehungsstraße** die *(PLURAL* die **Umgehungsstraßen)**

# Cc

**cab** NOUN **❶ Taxi** das *(PLURAL* die **Taxis)**; **to call a cab** ein Taxi rufen **❷** *(on a lorry)* **Führerhaus** das *(PLURAL* die **Führerhäuser)**

**cabbage** NOUN **Kohl** der

**cable** NOUN **Kabel** das *(PLURAL* die **Kabel)**

**café** NOUN **Café** das *(PLURAL* die **Cafés)**

**cage** NOUN **Käfig** der *(PLURAL* die **Käfige)**

**cagoule** NOUN **Anorak** der *(PLURAL* die **Anoraks)**

**cake** NOUN **Kuchen** der *(PLURAL* die **Kuchen)**; **would you like a piece of cake?** möchtest du ein Stück Kuchen?

**calculate** VERB **berechnen**

**calculation** NOUN **Rechnung** die *(PLURAL* die **Rechnungen)**

**calculator** NOUN **Taschenrechner** der *(PLURAL* die **Taschenrechner)**

**calendar** NOUN **Kalender** der *(PLURAL* die **Kalender)**

**calf** NOUN **❶** *(animal)* **Kalb** das *(PLURAL* die **Kälber)** **❷** *(of your leg)* **Wade** die *(PLURAL* die **Waden)**

**call** NOUN *(telephone)* **Anruf** der *(PLURAL* die **Anrufe)**; **I had several calls this morning** ich erhielt heute Morgen mehrere Anrufe, **thank you for your**

**call** danke für deinen Anruf, **a phone call** ein Telefonanruf

**call** VERB ❶ rufen◇; **to call a taxi** ein Taxi rufen, **to call the doctor** einen Arzt rufen, **they called the police** sie riefen die Polizei ❷ *(phone)* anrufen◇ *(SEP)*; **call me later** ruf mich später an, **thank you for calling** danke für deinen Anruf, **I'll call you back later** ich rufe dich später zurück ❸ nennen◇; **they've called the baby Julie** sie haben das Baby Julie genannt ❹ **to be called** heißen◇, **her brother is called Dan** ihr Bruder heißt Dan, **what's he called?** wie heißt er?

**call box** NOUN Telefonzelle die *(PLURAL die Telefonzellen)*

**calm** ADJECTIVE ruhig

**calm** VERB beruhigen
• **to calm down** sich beruhigen; **he's calmed down a bit** er hat sich etwas beruhigt
• **to calm somebody down** jemanden beruhigen; **I tried to calm her down** ich habe versucht, sie zu beruhigen

**calmly** ADVERB ruhig

**calorie** NOUN Kalorie die *(PLURAL die Kalorien)*

**camcorder** NOUN Camcorder der *(PLURAL die Camcorder)*

**camel** NOUN Kamel das *(PLURAL die Kamele)*

**camera** NOUN ❶ Fotoapparat der *(PLURAL die Fotoapparate)* ❷ *(film or video camera)* Kamera die *(PLURAL die Kameras)*

**camp** NOUN Lager das *(PLURAL die Lager)*

**camp** VERB campen, zelten

**campaign** NOUN Kampagne die *(PLURAL die Kampagnen)*

**camper** NOUN ❶ *(person)* Camper der *(PLURAL die Camper)*, Camperin die *(PLURAL die Camperinnen)* ❷ *(vehicle)* Campingbus der *(PLURAL die Campingbusse)*

**camper van** NOUN Wohnmobil das *(PLURAL die Wohnmobile)*

**camping** NOUN Camping das; **to go camping** zelten, **we're going camping in Bavaria this summer** diesen Sommer zelten wir in Bayern

**campsite** NOUN Campingplatz der *(PLURAL die Campingplätze)*

**can¹** NOUN ❶ Dose die *(PLURAL die Dosen)*; **a can of tomatoes** eine Dose Tomaten ❷ *(for petrol or oil)* Kanister der *(PLURAL die Kanister)*

**can²** VERB ❶ können◇; **I can't be there before ten** ich kann vor zehn Uhr nicht da sein, **can you open the door, please?** kannst du die Tür bitte aufmachen?, **can I help you?** kann ich Ihnen helfen?, **they couldn't come** sie konnten nicht kommen, **you could have told me** das hättest du mir wirklich sagen können, **I can't see him** ich kann ihn nicht sehen, **I can't remember it** ich kann mich nicht daran erinnern, **she can't drive** sich kann nicht Auto fahren ❷ *(be allowed)* dürfen◇; **you can't smoke here** Sie dürfen hier nicht rauchen

**Canada** NOUN Kanada das; **to Canada** nach Kanada

**Canadian** NOUN Kanadier der *(PLURAL die Kanadier)* Kanadierin die *(PLURAL die Kanadierinnen)*

**Canadian** *ADJECTIVE* **kanadisch**; **he is Canadian** er ist Kanadier

**canal** *NOUN* **Kanal** der *(PLURAL die Kanäle)*

**cancel** *VERB* **absagen** *(SEP)*; **the concert's been cancelled** das Konzert ist abgesagt worden

**cancer** *NOUN* **Krebs** der; **to have lung cancer** Lungenkrebs haben

**Cancer** *NOUN* **Krebs** der *(PLURAL die Krebse)*; **I'm Cancer** ich bin Krebs

**candidate** *NOUN* **Kandidat** der *(PLURAL die Kandidaten)* **Kandidatin** die *(PLURAL die Kandidatinnen)*

**candle** *NOUN* **Kerze** die *(PLURAL die Kerzen)*

**candlestick** *NOUN* **Kerzenständer** der *(PLURAL die Kerzenständer)*

**canned** *ADJECTIVE* **in Dosen**; **canned tomatoes** Tomaten in Dosen

**canoe** *NOUN* **Kanu** das *(PLURAL die Kanus)*

**canoeing** *NOUN* **to go canoeing** Kanu fahren◇ *(PERF sein)*, **I like canoeing** ich fahre gerne Kanu

**can-opener** *NOUN* **Dosenöffner** der *(PLURAL die Dosenöffner)*

**canteen** *NOUN* **Kantine** die *(PLURAL die Kantinen)*

**canvas** *NOUN* **❶** *(of a tent or bag)* **Segeltuch** das **❷** *(for painting on)* **Leinwand** die

**cap** *NOUN* **❶** *(hat)* **Kappe** die *(PLURAL die Kappen)*; **baseball cap** Baseballkappe **❷** *(on a bottle or tube)* **Verschluss** der *(PLURAL die Verschlüsse)*

**capable** *ADJECTIVE* **fähig**

**capital** *NOUN* **❶** *(city)* **Hauptstadt** die *(PLURAL die Hauptstädte)*; **Berlin is the capital of Germany** Berlin ist die Hauptstadt von Deutschland **❷** *(letter)* **Großbuchstabe** der *(PLURAL die Großbuchstaben)*; **in capitals** mit Großbuchstaben

**capitalism** *NOUN* **Kapitalismus** der

**Capricorn** *NOUN* **Steinbock** der *(PLURAL die Steinböcke)*; **Linda's Capricorn** Linda ist Steinbock

**captain** *NOUN* **Kapitän** der *(PLURAL die Kapitäne)*

**capture** *VERB* **festnehmen**◇ *(SEP)*

**car** *NOUN* **Auto** das *(PLURAL die Autos)*; **to park the car** das Auto einparken, **we're going by car** wir fahren mit dem Auto, **car crash** der Autounfall

**caramel** *NOUN* **Karamell** der *(PLURAL die Karamells)*

**caravan** *NOUN* **Wohnwagen** der *(PLURAL die Wohnwagen)*

**card** *NOUN* **Karte** die *(PLURAL die Karten)*; **card game** das Kartenspiel, **to have a game of cards** Karten spielen

**cardboard** *NOUN* **Pappe** die

**cardigan** *NOUN* **Strickjacke** die *(PLURAL die Strickjacken)*

**cardphone** *NOUN* **Kartentelefon** das *(PLURAL die Kartentelefone)*

**care** *NOUN* **❶** **Vorsicht** die; **to take care crossing the road** beim Überqueren der Straße vorsichtig sein, **take care!** *(be careful)* sei vorsichtig!, *(when saying goodbye)* mach's gut! **❷** **to take care to do**

a
b
c
d
e
f
g
h
i
j
k
l
m
n
o
p
q
r
s
t
u
v
w
x
y
z

**something** darauf achten, dass man etwas tut, **to take care of somebody** auf jemanden aufpassen

**care** VERB ❶ **to care about something** sich für etwas (ACC) interessieren, **she cares about the environment** die Umwelt liegt ihr am Herzen ❷ **she doesn't care** es ist ihr egal, **I couldn't care less!** das ist mir völlig egal!

**career** NOUN Karriere die (PLURAL die Karrieren)

**careful** ADJECTIVE vorsichtig; **a careful driver** ein vorsichtiger Fahrer, eine vorsichtige Fahrerin, **be careful!** sei vorsichtig!

**carefully** ADVERB ❶ sorgfältig; **to read the instructions carefully** die Anweisungen sorgfältig lesen ❷ vorsichtig; **she put the vase down carefully** sie stellte die Vase vorsichtig hin, **drive carefully!** fahr vorsichtig! ❸ **listen carefully!** hören Sie gut zu!

**careless** ADJECTIVE ❶ **he's very careless** er ist sehr nachlässig, **this is careless work** das ist eine schlampige Arbeit ❷ **a careless mistake** ein Flüchtigkeitsfehler ❸ **a careless driver** ein leichtsinniger Fahrer

**car ferry** NOUN Autofähre die (PLURAL die Autofähren)

**car hire** NOUN Autovermietung die

**Caribbean** NOUN **the Caribbean (islands)** die Karibik (SINGULAR)

**carnation** NOUN Nelke die (PLURAL die Nelken)

**carnival** NOUN Karneval der (PLURAL die Karnevale)

**car park** NOUN Parkplatz der (PLURAL die Parkplätze), (multistorey) Parkhaus das (PLURAL die Parkhäuser)

**carpenter** NOUN Tischler der (PLURAL die Tischler) Tischlerin die (PLURAL die Tischlerinnen)

**carpentry** NOUN Tischlerhandwerk das

**carpet** NOUN Teppich der (PLURAL die Teppiche)

**car phone** NOUN Autotelefon das (PLURAL die Autotelefone)

**car radio** NOUN Autoradio das (PLURAL die Autoradios)

**carriage** NOUN (of a train) Abteil das (PLURAL die Abteile)

**carrier bag** NOUN Tragetasche die (PLURAL die Tragetaschen)

**carrot** NOUN Karotte die (PLURAL die Karotten) Möhre die (PLURAL die Möhren)

**carry** VERB tragen; **she was carrying a case** sie trug einen Koffer
• **to carry on** weitermachen (SEP); **they carried on working** sie arbeiteten weiter

**carrycot** NOUN Babytragetasche die (PLURAL die Babytragetaschen)

**carsick** ADJECTIVE **he gets carsick** ihm wird beim Autofahren schlecht

**carton** NOUN ❶ (of cream or yoghurt) Becher der (PLURAL die Becher) ❷ (of milk or orange) Tüte die (PLURAL die Tüten)

**cartoon** NOUN ❶ (a film) Zeichentrickfilm der (PLURAL die Zeichentrickfilme) ❷ (a comic strip) **Cartoon** der *(PLURAL die* **Cartoons)** ❸ *(a drawing)* **Karikatur** die *(PLURAL die* **Karikaturen)**

**cartridge** NOUN *(for a pen)* **Patrone** die *(PLURAL die* **Patronen)**

**case¹** NOUN ❶ *(suitcase)* **Koffer** der *(PLURAL die* **Koffer)**; **to pack a case** einen Koffer packen ❷ *(a large wooden box)* **Kiste** die *(PLURAL die* **Kisten)** ❸ *(for spectacles or small things)* **Etui** das *(PLURAL die* **Etuis)**

**case²** NOUN ❶ **Fall** der *(PLURAL die* **Fälle)**; **in that case** in dem Fall, **that's not the case** das ist nicht der Fall, **in case of fire** bei Feuer ❷ **in case** falls, **in case he comes** falls er kommt ❸ **just in case** für alle Fälle ❹ **in any case** sowieso, **in any case, it's too late** es ist sowieso zu spät

**cash** NOUN ❶ *(money in general)* **Geld** das; **I haven't any cash on me** ich habe kein Geld dabei ❷ *(money rather than a cheque)* **Bargeld** das; **to pay in cash** bar zahlen, **£50 in cash** fünfzig Pfund in bar

**cash card** NOUN **Bankkarte** die *(PLURAL die* **Bankkarten)**

**cash desk** NOUN **Kasse** die *(PLURAL die* **Kassen)**; **to pay at the cash desk** an der Kasse zahlen

**cash dispenser** NOUN **Geldautomat** der *(PLURAL die* **Geldautomaten)**

**cashier** NOUN **Kassierer** der *(PLURAL die* **Kassierer)** **Kassiererin** die *(PLURAL die* **Kassiererinnen)**

**cash point** NOUN **Geldautomat** der *(PLURAL die* **Geldautomaten)**

**cassette** NOUN **Kassette** die *(PLURAL die* **Kassetten)**

**cassette recorder** NOUN **Kassettenrekorder** der *(PLURAL die* **Kassettenrekorder)**

**cast** NOUN *(of a play)* **Besetzung** die

**castle** NOUN ❶ **Burg** die *(PLURAL die* **Burgen)** ❷ *(in chess)* **Turm** der *(PLURAL die* **Türme)**

**casual** ADJECTIVE **zwanglos**

**casualty** NOUN ❶ *(in an accident)* **Verletzte** der/die *(PLURAL die* **Verletzten)** ❷ *(hospital department)* **Unfallstation** die *(PLURAL die* **Unfallstationen)**; **he's in casualty** er ist auf der Unfallstation

**cat** NOUN **Katze** die *(PLURAL die* **Katzen)**, *(tomcat)* **Kater** der *(PLURAL die* **Kater)**
• **it's raining cats and dogs** es regnet in Strömen *(literally: it's raining in streams)*

**catalogue** NOUN **Katalog** der *(PLURAL die* **Kataloge)**

**catastrophe** NOUN **Katastrophe** die *(PLURAL die* **Katastrophen)**

**catch** NOUN ❶ *(on a door)* **Schnappriegel** der *(PLURAL die* **Schnappriegel)** ❷ *(a drawback)* **Haken** der *(PLURAL die* **Haken)**; **where's the catch?** wo ist der Haken?

**catch** VERB ❶ **fangen**◇; **Tom caught the ball** Tom hat den Ball gefangen, **she caught a fish** sie hat einen Fisch gefangen, **catch me!** fang mich! ❷ **to catch somebody doing something** jemanden bei etwas *(DAT)* **erwischen**, **he was caught stealing money** er wurde beim Geldstehlen erwischt ❸ *(be in time for)* **noch erreichen**; **did Tim catch his plane?** hat Tim sein Flugzeug noch erreicht? **❹** *(become ill with)* **bekommen**◇; **she's caught chickenpox** sie hat die Windpocken bekommen **❺** **verstehen**◇ *(what somebody says)*; **I didn't catch your name** ich habe Ihren Namen nicht verstanden

• **to catch up with somebody** jemanden einholen *(SEP)*

**category** *NOUN* Kategorie die *(PLURAL* die **Kategorien***)*

**catering** *NOUN* **❶** *(trade)* Gastronomie die **❷** **who's doing the catering?** wer liefert das Essen und die Getränke?

**caterpillar** *NOUN* Raupe die *(PLURAL* die **Raupen***)*

**cathedral** *NOUN* Kathedrale die *(PLURAL* die **Kathedralen***)*; **Cologne cathedral** der Kölner Dom

**Catholic** *NOUN* Katholik der *(PLURAL* die **Katholiken***)* Katholikin die *(PLURAL* die **Katholikinnen***)*

**Catholic** *ADJECTIVE* katholisch

**cattle** *PLURAL NOUN* Vieh das

**cauliflower** *NOUN* Blumenkohl der; **cauliflower cheese** mit Käse überbackener Blumenkohl

**cause** *NOUN* **❶** Ursache die *(PLURAL* die **Ursachen***)*; **the cause of the accident** die Unfallursache **❷** **for a good cause** für eine gute Sache

**cause** *VERB* verursachen; **to cause difficulties** Schwierigkeiten verursachen

**cave** *NOUN* Höhle die *(PLURAL* die **Höhlen***)*

**caving** *NOUN* Höhlenforschung die; **to go caving** auf Höhlenforschung gehen

**CD** *NOUN* CD die *(PLURAL* die **CDs***)*

**CD player** *NOUN* CD-Player der *(PLURAL* die **CD-Player***)*

**CD-ROM** *NOUN* CD-ROM die *(PLURAL* die **CD-ROMs***)*

**ceiling** *NOUN* Decke die *(PLURAL* die **Decken***)*; **on the ceiling** an der Decke

**celebrate** *VERB* feiern; **he's celebrating his birthday** er feiert seinen Geburtstag

**celebrity** *NOUN* Berühmtheit die *(PLURAL* die **Berühmtheiten***)*

**celery** *NOUN* Sellerie der *(PLURAL* die Sellerie*)*

**cell** *NOUN* Zelle die *(PLURAL* die **Zellen***)*

**cellar** *NOUN* Keller der *(PLURAL* die Keller*)*

**cello** *NOUN* Cello das *(PLURAL* die **Cellos***)*; **to play the cello** Cello spielen

**cement** *NOUN* Zement der

**cemetery** *NOUN* Friedhof der *(PLURAL* die **Friedhöfe***)*

**cent** *NOUN* **❶** *(in euro system)* Eurocent der *(PLURAL* die **Eurocents***)*, Cent der *(PLURAL* die **Cents***)*; **50 cents** 50 (Euro)cent **❷** *(in dollar system)* Cent der *(PLURAL* die **Cents***)*; **25 cents** 25 Cent

**centigrade** *ADJECTIVE* Celsius; **ten degrees centigrade** zehn Grad Celsius

**centimetre** *NOUN* Zentimeter der *(PLURAL* die **Zentimeter***)*

**central** ADJECTIVE ❶ zentral; **the office is very central** das Büro ist sehr zentral gelegen ❷ **in central London** im Zentrum von London

**Central Europe** NOUN Mitteleuropa das

**central heating** NOUN Zentralheizung die

**centre** NOUN Zentrum das (PLURAL die Zentren); **in the centre of** im Zentrum von (+DAT), **in the town centre** im Stadtzentrum, **a shopping centre** ein Einkaufszentrum

**century** NOUN Jahrhundert das (PLURAL die Jahrhunderte); **in the twentieth century** im zwanzigsten Jahrhundert

**cereal** NOUN **breakfast cereal** Frühstücksflocken (plural)

**ceremony** NOUN Zeremonie die (PLURAL die Zeremonien)

**certain** ADJECTIVE ❶ (definite) bestimmt; **a certain number of** eine bestimmte Zahl von (+DAT) ❷ (confident) sicher; **to be certain** sich (DAT) sicher sein; **are you certain of the address?** bist du sicher, dass das die richtige Adresse ist?, **I'm absolutely certain** ich bin mir ganz sicher, **to be certain that ...** sicher sein, dass ... ❸ **nobody knows for certain** niemand weiß es genau

**certainly** ADVERB bestimmt; **certainly not** bestimmt nicht

**certificate** NOUN ❶ Bescheinigung die (PLURAL die Bescheinigungen) ❷ **birth certificate** die Geburtsurkunde ❸ (at school) Zeugnis das (PLURAL die Zeugnisse)

**chain** NOUN Kette die (PLURAL die Ketten)

**chair** NOUN ❶ (upright) Stuhl der (PLURAL die Stühle); **a kitchen chair** ein Küchenstuhl ❷ (with arms) Sessel der (PLURAL die Sessel)

**chair lift** NOUN Sessellift der (PLURAL die Sessellifte)

**chalet** NOUN ❶ (in the mountains) Chalet das (PLURAL die Chalets) ❷ (in a holiday camp) Ferienhaus das (PLURAL die Ferienhäuser)

**challenge** NOUN Herausforderung die (PLURAL die Herausforderungen)

**champion** NOUN Meister der (PLURAL die Meister) Meisterin die (PLURAL die Meisterinnen); **the world slalom champion** der Weltmeister im Slalom, die Weltmeisterin im Slalom

**chance** NOUN ❶ (opportunity) Gelegenheit die (PLURAL die Gelegenheiten); **to have the chance to do something** die Gelegenheit haben, etwas zu tun, **if you have the chance to go to New York** wenn du die Gelegenheit hast, nach New York zu fahren, **I had no chance to speak to him** ich hatte keine Gelegenheit, mit ihm zu reden ❷ (likelihood) Aussicht die (PLURAL die Aussichten); **he's got no chance of winning** er hat keine Aussicht zu gewinnen ❸ (luck) Zufall der; **by chance** zufällig, **do you have her address, by any chance?** hast du zufällig ihre Adresse?

**change** NOUN ❶ (from one thing to another) Änderung die (PLURAL die Änderungen); **a change of address** eine Adressänderung, **there's been a change of plan**

a b c d e f g h i j k l m n o p q r s t u v w x y z

der Plan ist geändert worden
❷ *(alteration)* Veränderung die
*(PLURAL die* Veränderungen*)*;
**they've made some changes to the
house** sie haben im Haus ein paar
Veränderungen vorgenommen,
**a change in the weather** eine
Wetterumschwung ❸ *(for the sake
of variety)* **for a change, we could
go to a restaurant** zur Abwechslung
könnten wir in ein Restaurant
gehen, **it makes a change from
hamburgers** das ist mal etwas
anderes als Hamburger, **a change
of clothes** etwas anderes zum
Anziehen ❹ *(cash)* Wechselgeld
das; **I haven't any change** ich habe
kein Wechselgeld

**change** VERB ❶ *(make different)*
ändern; **you can't change her**
du kannst sie nicht ändern,
**to change your address** seine
Adresse ändern ❷ *(become
different)* sich verändern; **Liz has
changed a lot** Liz hat sich sehr
verändert ❸ *(transform completely)*
verwandeln; **the prince changed
into a frog** der Prinz verwandelte
sich in einen Frosch ❹ *(exchange
in a shop)* umtauschen *(SEP)*; **just
change it for a larger size** tauschen
Sie es einfach gegen eine Nummer
größer um ❺ *(change clothes)*
sich umziehen◇ *(SEP)*; **Mike's just
changing** Mike zieht sich gerade
um ❻ *(switch from one train or bus
to another)* umsteigen◇ *(SEP) (PERF
sein)*; **we changed trains at Crewe**
wir stiegen in Crewe um ❼ *(switch
one thing for another)* wechseln; **I
want to change my job** ich möchte
meinen Arbeitsplatz wechseln, **they
changed places** sie haben die Plätze
gewechselt ❽ **to change your mind**
sich anders entschließen◇

**changing room** NOUN *(for sport or
swimming)* Umkleideraum der
*(PLURAL die* Umkleideräume*)*

**channel** NOUN ❶ *(on TV)* Kanal der
*(PLURAL die* Kanäle*)*; **to change
channels** auf einen anderen Kanal
umschalten ❷ **the Channel** der
Ärmelkanal

**Channel Tunnel** NOUN Eurotunnel
der

**chaos** NOUN Chaos das; **it was chaos!**
das war ein Chaos!

**chapel** NOUN Kapelle die *(PLURAL die
Kapellen)*

**chapter** NOUN Kapitel das *(PLURAL die
Kapitel)*; **in chapter two** im zweiten
Kapitel

**character** NOUN ❶ *(personality)*
Charakter der ❷ *(somebody in a
book)* Charakter der *(PLURAL die
Charaktere)* ❸ *(part in a play or
film)* Rolle die *(PLURAL die* Rollen*)*;
**the main character** die Hauptrolle

**charcoal** NOUN ❶ *(for burning)*
Holzkohle die ❷ *(for drawing)*
Kohle die

**charge** NOUN ❶ *(what you
pay)* Gebühr die *(PLURAL die
Gebühren)*; **a booking charge**
eine Buchungsgebühr, **an extra or
additional charge** eine zusätzliche
Gebühr, **there's no charge** das
ist kostenlos ❷ **to be in charge**
für etwas *(ACC)* verantwortlich
sein, **who's in charge of the
children?** wer ist für die Kinder
verantwortlich? ❸ **to be on a
charge of theft** wegen Diebstahls
angeklagt sein

**charge** VERB ❶ *(ask to pay)*
berechnen; **they charge us fifteen**

**pounds an hour** sie berechnen uns fünfzehn Pfund pro Stunde, **they didn't charge for delivery** sie haben die Lieferung nicht berechnet, **we won't charge you for it** wir berechnen Ihnen nichts dafür ❷ **to charge somebody with something** jemanden wegen etwas (+GEN) anklagen (SEP)

**charity** NOUN Wohltätigkeitsverein der (PLURAL die Wohltätigkeitsvereine)

**charming** ADJECTIVE reizend

**chart** NOUN ❶ (table) Tabelle die (PLURAL die Tabellen) ❷ **the weather chart** die Wetterkarte ❸ **the charts** die Hitparade

**charter flight** NOUN Charterflug der (PLURAL die Charterflüge)

**chase** NOUN Verfolgungsjagd die (PLURAL die Verfolgungsjagden); **a car chase** eine Verfolgungsjagd mit dem Auto

**chase** VERB jagen

**chat** NOUN Plauderei die (PLURAL die Plaudereien); **to have a chat with somebody** mit jemandem plaudern

**chatroom** NOUN Chatroom der (PLURAL die Chatrooms)

**chat show** NOUN Talkshow die (PLURAL die Talkshows)

**chatter** VERB ❶ (talk) schwatzen ❷ **my teeth were chattering** ich klapperte mit den Zähnen

**cheap** ADJECTIVE billig; **cheap shoes** billige Schuhe, **that's very cheap** das ist sehr billig

**cheaply** ADVERB billig; **to eat cheaply** billig essen

**cheap-rate** ADJECTIVE verbilligt; **a cheap-rate phone call** ein Gespräch zum Billigtarif

**cheat** NOUN ❶ Betrüger der (PLURAL die Betrüger) Betrügerin die (PLURAL die Betrügerinnen) ❷ (in games) Mogler der (PLURAL die Mogler), Moglerin die (PLURAL die Moglerinnen)

**cheat** VERB ❶ betrügen◇ ❷ (in games) mogeln

**check** NOUN ❶ (in a factory or at a border control) Kontrolle die (PLURAL die Kontrollen); **passport check** die Passkontrolle ❷ (in chess) **check!** Schach!

**check** VERB ❶ (make sure) prüfen; **he checked their statements** er prüfte ihre Aussagen ❷ (make sure by looking) nachsehen◇ (SEP); **to check the time** auf die Uhr sehen, **check they're all back** sieh nach, ob alle wieder da sind ❸ (inspect) kontrollieren; **to check the tickets** die Fahrkarten kontrollieren

• **to check in** sich anmelden (SEP); **to check in at the airport** am Flughafen einchecken

• **to check out** abreisen◇ (SEP) (PERF sein); **to check out of the hotel** das Hotel verlassen

**check-in** NOUN Abfertigungsschalter der (PLURAL die Abfertigungsschalter)

**checkout** NOUN Kasse die (PLURAL die Kassen); **at the checkout** an der Kasse

**check-up** NOUN Untersuchung die (PLURAL die Untersuchungen)

**cheek** NOUN ❶ (part of face) Backe die (PLURAL die Backen) ❷ (nerve)

Frechheit die; **what a cheek!** so eine Frechheit!

**cheeky** ADJECTIVE frech

**cheer** NOUN ❶ **three cheers for Tom!** ein dreifaches Hoch auf Tom! ❷ (when drinking) **cheers!** prost!

**cheer** VERB (shout hurray) Hurra schreien◇
- **to cheer somebody up** jemanden aufmuntern (SEP); **your visits always cheer me up** deine Besuche muntern mich immer auf, **cheer up!** Kopf hoch!

**cheerful** ADJECTIVE fröhlich

**cheese** NOUN Käse der; **a cheese sandwich** ein Käsebrot

**chef** NOUN Koch der (PLURAL die Köche) Köchin die (PLURAL die Köchinnen)

**chemical** NOUN Chemikalie die (PLURAL die Chemikalien)

**chemist** NOUN ❶ (in a pharmacy) Apotheker der (PLURAL die Apotheker), Apothekerin die (PLURAL die Apothekerinnen) ❷ **chemist's** (dispensing) Apotheke die (PLURAL die Apotheken), **at the chemist's** in der Apotheke ❸ (scientist) Chemiker der (PLURAL die Chemiker), Chemikerin die (PLURAL die Chemikerinnen)

**chemistry** NOUN Chemie die

**cheque** NOUN Scheck der (PLURAL die Schecks); **to pay by cheque** mit Scheck bezahlen, **to write a cheque** einen Scheck ausstellen

**cheque book** NOUN Scheckbuch das (PLURAL die Scheckbücher)

**cherry** NOUN Kirsche die (PLURAL die Kirschen)

**chess** NOUN Schach das; **to play chess** Schach spielen

**chessboard** NOUN Schachbrett das (PLURAL die Schachbretter)

**chest** NOUN ❶ (part of the body) Brust die (PLURAL die Brüste) ❷ (box) Truhe die (PLURAL die Truhen) ❸ **a chest of drawers** eine Kommode

**chestnut** NOUN Esskastanie die (PLURAL die Esskastanien)

**chestnut tree** NOUN ❶ (horse-chestnut) Rosskastanie die (PLURAL die Rosskastanien) ❷ (sweet chestnut) Edelkastanie die (PLURAL die Edelkastanien)

**chew** VERB kauen

**chewing gum** NOUN Kaugummi der (PLURAL die Kaugummis)

**chicken** NOUN Huhn das (PLURAL die Hühner); **roast chicken** das Brathähnchen, **chicken breast** die Hühnerbrust

**chickenpox** NOUN Windpocken (plural)

**child** NOUN Kind das (PLURAL die Kinder); **when I was a child ...** als Kind ...

**childish** ADJECTIVE kindisch

**childminder** NOUN Tagesmutter die (PLURAL die Tagesmütter)

**chill** NOUN ❶ Kälte die ❷ **to have a chill** eine Erkältung haben

**chilled** ADJECTIVE gekühlt

**chilli** NOUN Chili der

**chimney** NOUN Schornstein der (PLURAL die Schornsteine)

**chimpanzee** NOUN Schimpanse der (PLURAL die Schimpansen)

**chin** NOUN Kinn das (PLURAL die Kinne)

**china** NOUN Porzellan das; the china bowl die Porzellanschüssel

**China** NOUN China das

**Chinese** NOUN ❶ the Chinese (people) die Chinesen ❷ (language) Chinesisch das

**Chinese** ADJECTIVE ❶ chinesisch; a Chinese man ein Chinese, a Chinese woman eine Chinesin ❷ to have a Chinese meal chinesisch essen

**chip** NOUN ❶ (fried potato) chips Pommes frites (plural), fish and chips ausgebackener Fisch mit Pommes frites ❷ (microchip) Chip der (PLURAL die Chips) ❸ (in glass or china) angeschlagene Stelle die (PLURAL die angeschlagenen Stellen)

**chipped** ADJECTIVE angeschlagen

**chocolate** NOUN ❶ Schokolade die; a box of chocolates eine Schachtel Pralinen ❷ chocolate ice cream das Schokoladeneis ❸ a cup of hot chocolate eine Tasse Kakao

**choice** NOUN ❶ Wahl die (PLURAL die Wahlen); to make a good choice eine gute Wahl treffen ❷ (variety) Auswahl die; you have a choice of two flights du hast zwei Flüge zur Auswahl

**choir** NOUN Chor der (PLURAL die Chöre)

**choke** NOUN (on a car) Choke der (PLURAL die Chokes)

**choke** VERB (by yourself) sich verschlucken; she choked on a bone sie hat sich an einer Gräte verschluckt

**choose** VERB ❶ wählen; you chose well du hast gut gewählt, it's hard to choose from all these colours es ist schwer, unter allen diesen Farben zu wählen ❷ (select from a group of things) sich (DAT) aussuchen (SEP); Cathy chose the red skirt Cathy suchte sich den roten Rock aus

**chop** NOUN Kotelett das (PLURAL die Koteletts); a pork chop ein Schweinekotelett

**chop** VERB hacken

**chord** NOUN Akkord der (PLURAL die Akkorde)

**chorus** NOUN ❶ (when you all join in the song) Refrain der (PLURAL die Refrains) ❷ (a group of singers) Chor der (PLURAL die Chöre)

**Christ** NOUN Christus der

**christening** NOUN Taufe die (PLURAL die Taufen)

**Christian** NOUN Christ der (PLURAL die Christen) Christin die (PLURAL die Christinnen)

**Christian** ADJECTIVE christlich

**Christianity** NOUN Christentum das

**Christian name** NOUN Vorname der (PLURAL die Vornamen)

**Christmas** NOUN Weihnachten das (PLURAL die Weihnachten); at Christmas zu Weihnachten, what did you get for Christmas? was hast du zu Weihnachten bekommen?, Happy Christmas! Frohe Weihnachten!

**Christmas card** NOUN
Weihnachtskarte die (PLURAL die
Weihnachtskarten)

**Christmas carol** NOUN
Weihnachtslied das (PLURAL die
Weihnachtslieder)

**Christmas cracker** NOUN
Knallbonbon der (PLURAL die
Knallbonbons)

**Christmas Day** NOUN erste
Weihnachtstag der

**Christmas Eve** NOUN Heiligabend
der; on Christmas Eve Heiligabend

**Christmas present** NOUN
Weihnachtsgeschenk das (PLURAL
die Weihnachtsgeschenke)

**Christmas tree** NOUN
Weihnachtsbaum der (PLURAL die
Weihnachtsbäume)

**church** NOUN Kirche die (PLURAL die
Kirchen); to go to church in die
Kirche gehen

**chute** NOUN (in a swimming pool or
playground) Rutsche die (PLURAL die
Rutschen)

**cider** NOUN Apfelwein der (PLURAL die
Apfelweine)

**cigar** NOUN Zigarre die (PLURAL die
Zigarren)

**cigarette** NOUN Zigarette die (PLURAL
die Zigaretten)

**cinema** NOUN Kino das (PLURAL die
Kinos); to go to the cinema ins Kino
gehen

**circle** NOUN Kreis der (PLURAL die
Kreise); to sit in a circle im Kreis
sitzen, to go round in circles sich im
Kreis drehen

**circuit** NOUN ❶ (for athletes) Bahn
die (PLURAL die Bahnen) ❷ (for
cars) Rennbahn die (PLURAL die
Rennbahnen)

**circumstance** NOUN Umstand
der (PLURAL die Umstände); under
these circumstances unter diesen
Umständen

**circus** NOUN Zirkus der (PLURAL die
Zirkusse)

**citizen** NOUN Bürger der (PLURAL die
Bürger) Bürgerin die (PLURAL die
Bürgerinnen)

**city** NOUN Stadt die (PLURAL die
Städte); the city of Berlin die Stadt
Berlin

**city centre** NOUN Stadtzentrum das
(PLURAL die Stadtzentren); in the
city centre im Stadtzentrum, in der
Innenstadt

**civilization** NOUN Zivilisation die
(PLURAL die Zivilisationen)

**civil servant** NOUN Beamte der
(PLURAL die Beamten) Beamtin
die (PLURAL die Beamtinnen); she's a
civil servant sie ist Beamtin

**claim** VERB behaupten; he claims
to know who ... er behauptet zu
wissen, wer ...

**claim** NOUN ❶ (statement)
Behauptung die (PLURAL
die Behauptungen) ❷ (for
compensation) Anspruch der
(PLURAL die Ansprüche); to make
a claim on insurance seine
Versicherungsansprüche geltend
machen

**clap** VERB ❶ klatschen; everyone
clapped alle klatschten ❷ to clap
your hands in die Hände klatschen

**clarinet** NOUN Klarinette die (PLURAL die Klarinetten); **to play the clarinet** Klarinette spielen

**clash** NOUN (between two groups) Zusammenstoß der (PLURAL die Zusammenstöße)

**clash** VERB ❶ (rival groups) zusammenstoßen◇ (SEP) ❷ (colours) sich beißen◇; **the curtains clash with the wallpaper** die Vorhänge passen farblich nicht zur Tapete

**class** NOUN ❶ (a group of students or pupils) Klasse die (PLURAL die Klassen); **she's in my class** sie geht in meine Klasse ❷ (a lesson) Stunde die (PLURAL die Stunden); **history class** die Geschichtsstunde, **in class** im Unterricht ❸ (category) Klasse die (PLURAL die Klassen); **social class** die Gesellschaftsschicht

**classic** ADJECTIVE klassisch

**classical** ADJECTIVE klassisch; **classical music** die klassische Musik

**classroom** NOUN Klassenzimmer das (PLURAL die Klassenzimmer)

**clay** NOUN Ton der

**clean** ADJECTIVE sauber; **a clean shirt** ein sauberes Hemd, **my hands are clean** ich habe saubere Hände

**clean** VERB ❶ putzen; **I cleaned the windows** ich habe die Fenster geputzt ❷ **to clean your teeth** sich (DAT) die Zähne putzen, **I'm going to clean my teeth** ich putze mir jetzt die Zähne

**cleaner** NOUN ❶ (cleaning lady) Putzfrau die (PLURAL die Putzfrauen) ❷ (in a public place) Reinigungskraft die (PLURAL die Reinigungskräfte) ❸ **dry cleaner's** die (chemische) Reinigung

**cleaning** NOUN **to do the cleaning** putzen

**cleanser** NOUN ❶ (for the house) Reinigungsmittel das (PLURAL die Reinigungsmittel) ❷ (for your face) Reinigungsmilch die

**clear** ADJECTIVE ❶ (that you can see through) klar; **clear water** klares Wasser ❷ (cloudless) klar ❸ (easy to understand) klar; **clear instructions** klare Anweisungen, **is that clear?** ist das klar? (informal), **to make something clear** etwas klar machen

**clear** VERB ❶ räumen; **have you cleared your stuff out of your room?** hast du deine Sachen aus deinem Zimmer geräumt? ❷ **can I clear the table?** kann ich den Tisch abräumen (SEP) ? ❸ **to clear your throat** sich räuspern

• **to clear up** ❶ (tidy up) aufräumen (SEP) ❷ (the weather) sich aufklären (SEP); **the weather's clearing up a bit** das Wetter klärt sich ein bisschen auf

**clearly** ADVERB ❶ (to think, speak, or hear) deutlich ❷ (obviously) eindeutig; **she was clearly better** sie war eindeutig besser

**clementine** NOUN Klementine die (PLURAL die Klementinen)

**clever** ADJECTIVE klug; **their children are all very clever** ihre Kinder sind alle sehr klug ❷ (ingenious) clever; **a clever idea** eine clevere Idee

**click** NOUN ❶ (noise) Klicken das ❷ (with mouse) Klick der (PLURAL die Klicks); **a double click** ein Doppelklick

**click** *VERB* **to click on something** etwas anklicken *(SEP)*, **click on the icon twice** doppelklicken Sie das Icon!

**client** *NOUN* **Klient** der *(PLURAL die Klienten)* **Klientin** die *(PLURAL die Klientinnen)*

**cliff** *NOUN* **Klippe** die *(PLURAL die Klippen)*

**climate** *NOUN* **Klima** das *(PLURAL die Klimata)*

**climate change** *NOUN* **Klimawandel** der

**climb** *VERB* ❶ *(the stairs, a hill)* **hinaufgehen⬦** *(SEP) (PERF sein)*; **to climb a mountain** einen Berg besteigen⬦ *(PERF sein)* ❷ *(a wall, tree, or rock)* **klettern** *(PERF sein)*, **auf** *(+ACC)*; **to climb a tree** auf einen Baum klettern

**climber** *NOUN* **Bergsteiger** der *(PLURAL die Bergsteiger)* **Bergsteigerin** die *(PLURAL die Bergsteigerinnen)*

**climbing** *NOUN* **Bergsteigen** das; **they go climbing in Italy** sie gehen in Italien bergsteigen

**clinic** *NOUN* **Klinik** die *(PLURAL die Kliniken)*

**clip** *NOUN* ❶ *(from a film)* **Ausschnitt** der *(PLURAL die Ausschnitte)* ❷ *(for your hair)* **Klammer** die *(PLURAL die Klammern)*

**cloakroom** *NOUN* *(for coats)* **Garderobe** die *(PLURAL die Garderoben)*

**clock** *NOUN* ❶ **Uhr** die *(PLURAL die Uhren)*; **to put the clocks forward an hour** die Uhr eine Stunde vorstellen, **to put the clocks back**

die Uhr zurückstellen ❷ **an alarm clock** ein Wecker

**close¹** *ADJECTIVE, ADVERB* ❶ *(result)* **knapp** ❷ *(friend, connection)* **eng** ❸ *(relation or acquaintance)* **nahe** ❹ *(near)* **in der Nähe; the station's very close** der Bahnhof ist ganz in der Nähe, **she lives close by** sie wohnt in der Nähe ❺ **close to** nahe, nah *(informal)* *(+DAT)*, **close to the cinema** nahe am Kino, **not very close** nicht sehr nah

**close²** *NOUN* **Ende** das; **at the close** am Ende

**close** *VERB* **zumachen** *(SEP)*, **schließen⬦**; **close your eyes!** mach die Augen zu!, **she closed the door** sie machte die Tür zu, **the post office closes at six** die Post macht um sechs zu, die Post schließt um sechs

**closed** *ADJECTIVE* **geschlossen; 'closed on Mondays'** 'Montags geschlossen'

**closely** *ADVERB* ❶ *(in distance)* **eng** ❷ *(carefully)* **genau; to look at something closely** sich etwas genau ansehen

**closing date** *NOUN* **the closing date for entries** *(for a competition)* der Einsendeschluss, *(for a sporting event)* der Meldeschluss

**closing time** *NOUN* ❶ **Ladenschluss** der ❷ *(of a pub)* **Polizeistunde** die

**cloth** *NOUN* ❶ *(for drying up and polishing)* **Tuch** das *(PLURAL die Tücher)* ❷ *(for the floor)* **Lappen** der *(PLURAL die Lappen)* ❸ *(fabric)* **Stoff** der *(PLURAL die Stoffe)*

**clothes** *PLURAL NOUN* ❶ **Kleider** *(plural)* ❷ **to put your clothes on** sich anziehen⬦ *(SEP)*, **to take**

**your clothes off** sich ausziehen◇ (SEP), **to change your clothes** sich umziehen◇ (SEP)

**clothes peg** NOUN Wäscheklammer die (PLURAL die Wäscheklammern)

**clothing** NOUN Kleidung die

**cloud** NOUN Wolke die (PLURAL die Wolken)

**cloudy** ADJECTIVE bewölkt

**clown** NOUN Clown der (PLURAL die Clowns)

**club** NOUN ❶ (association, for tennis-players, golfers) Klub der (PLURAL die Klubs), (for footballers) Verein der (PLURAL die Vereine); **a football club** ein Fußballverein ❷ (in cards) Kreuz das (PLURAL die Kreuze); **the four of clubs** die Kreuz-Vier ❸ (golfing iron) Schläger der (PLURAL die Schläger)

**clue** NOUN ❶ Anhaltspunkt der (PLURAL die Anhaltspunkte); **they have a few clues** sie haben ein paar Anhaltspunkte ❷ (in a crossword) Frage die (PLURAL die Fragen)
• **I haven't a clue** ich habe keine Ahnung

**clumsy** ADJECTIVE ungeschickt

**clutch** NOUN (in a car) Kupplung die (PLURAL die Kupplungen)

**clutch** VERB **to clutch something** etwas festhalten◇ (SEP)

**coach** NOUN ❶ (bus) Bus der (PLURAL die Busse); **on the coach** im Bus, **to travel by coach** mit dem Bus fahren ❷ (sports trainer) Trainer der (PLURAL die Trainer), Trainerin die (PLURAL die Trainerinnen) ❸ (railway carriage) Wagen der (PLURAL die Wagen)

**coach station** NOUN Busbahnhof der (PLURAL die Busbahnhöfe)

**coach trip** NOUN Busausflug der (PLURAL die Busausflüge); **to go on a coach trip** einen Busausflug machen

**coal** NOUN Kohle die (PLURAL die Kohlen)

**coarse** ADJECTIVE grob

**coast** NOUN Küste die (PLURAL die Küsten); **on the east coast** an der Ostküste

**coat** NOUN ❶ Mantel der (PLURAL die Mäntel) ❷ **coat of paint** der Anstrich

**coat hanger** NOUN Kleiderbügel der (PLURAL die Kleiderbügel)

**cobweb** NOUN Spinnennetz das (PLURAL die Spinnennetze)

**cocaine** NOUN Kokain das

**cock** NOUN Hahn der (PLURAL die Hähne)

**cocoa** NOUN Kakao der

**coconut** NOUN Kokosnuss die (PLURAL die Kokosnüsse)

**cod** NOUN Kabeljau der (PLURAL die Kabeljaue)

**code** NOUN ❶ (in law) Gesetzbuch das; **the highway code** die Straßenverkehrsordnung ❷ **the dialling code for Hull** die Vorwahl für Hull

**coffee** NOUN Kaffee der (PLURAL die Kaffees); **a cup of coffee** eine Tasse Kaffee, **a black coffee, please** einen Kaffee ohne Milch bitte, **a white coffee, please** einen Kaffee mit Milch bitte

**English—German**

**coffee break** NOUN Kaffeepause die (PLURAL die Kaffeepausen)

**coffee cup** NOUN Kaffeetasse die (PLURAL die Kaffeetassen)

**coffee machine** NOUN Kaffeemaschine die (PLURAL die Kaffeemaschinen)

**coffin** NOUN Sarg der (PLURAL die Särge)

**coin** NOUN ❶ Münze die (PLURAL die Münzen); **she collects old coins** sie sammelt alte Münzen ❷ **a pound coin** ein Einpfundstück

**coincidence** NOUN Zufall der (PLURAL die Zufälle)

**Coke** NOUN Cola die; **two Cokes please** zwei Cola bitte

**cold** NOUN ❶ (cold weather) Kälte die; **to be out in the cold** draußen in der Kälte sein ❷ (illness) Schnupfen der (PLURAL die Schnupfen), Erkältung die (PLURAL die Erkältungen); **to have a cold** Schnupfen haben, **Carol's got a cold** Carol hat Schnupfen, **a bad cold** eine schlimme Erkältung

**cold** ADJECTIVE ❶ kalt; **your hands are cold** du hast kalte Hände, **cold milk** kalte Milch ❷ (weather, temperature) **it's cold today** heute ist es kalt ❸ (feeling) **I'm cold** mir ist kalt

**collapse** VERB ❶ (a roof or wall) einstürzen (SEP) (PERF sein) ❷ (a person) zusammenbrechen◇ (SEP) (PERF sein); **he collapsed in his office** er brach in seinem Büro zusammen

**collar** NOUN ❶ (on a garment) Kragen der (PLURAL die Kragen) ❷ (for an animal) Halsband das (PLURAL die Halsbänder)

**colleague** NOUN Kollege der (PLURAL die Kollegen) Kollegin die (PLURAL die Kolleginnen)

**collect** VERB ❶ (as a hobby) sammeln; **do you collect stamps?** sammelst du Briefmarken? ❷ (fetch) abholen (SEP); **she collects the children from school** sie holt die Kinder von der Schule ab ❸ **to collect up the exercise books** die Hefte einsammeln (SEP)

**collection** NOUN (of stamps, money, etc.) Sammlung die (PLURAL die Sammlungen)

**collector** NOUN Sammler der (PLURAL die Sammler) Sammlerin die (PLURAL die Sammlerinnen)

**college** NOUN ❶ (for higher education) Hochschule die (PLURAL die Hochschulen); **to go to college** studieren ❷ (a school) College das (PLURAL die Colleges)

**Cologne** NOUN Köln das

**colour** NOUN Farbe die (PLURAL die Farben); **what colour is it?** welche Farbe hat es?, **do you have it in a different colour?** haben Sie es in einer anderen Farbe?

**colour** VERB ❶ (with paints or crayons) anmalen (SEP); **to colour something red** etwas rot anmalen ❷ (with dye) färben

**colour blind** ADJECTIVE farbenblind

**colour film** NOUN Farbfilm der (PLURAL die Farbfilme)

**colourful** ADJECTIVE bunt

**column** NOUN ❶ (of a building) Säule die (PLURAL die Säulen) ❷ (on a page) Spalte die (PLURAL die Spalten)

**comb** NOUN **Kamm** der (PLURAL die **Kämme**)

**comb** VERB **kämmen**; to comb your hair sich (DAT) die Haare kämmen, I'll just comb my hair ich kämme mir nur die Haare

**come** VERB ❶ **kommen**◇ (PERF **sein**); come quick! komm schnell!, come here! komm mal her!, Nick came by car Nick kam mit dem Auto, can you come over for a coffee? kannst du auf eine Tasse Kaffe kommen?, did Jess come to school yesterday? war Jess gestern in der Schule? ❷ (arrive) coming! ich komme schon!, the bus is coming der Bus kommt gerade, come along! komm schon!
- to come back **zurückkommen**◇ (SEP) (PERF **sein**); he's coming back to collect us er kommt zurück, um uns abzuholen
- to come down **herunterkommen**◇ (SEP) (PERF **sein**)
- to come for (collect) **abholen** (SEP); my father's coming for me mein Vater holt mich ab
- to come in **hereinkommen**◇ (SEP) (PERF **sein**); come in! herein!, she came into the kitchen sie kam in die Küche
- to come off (a button) **abgehen**◇ (SEP) (PERF **sein**)
- to come out **herauskommen**◇ (SEP) (PERF **sein**); they came out when I called als ich rief, kamen sie heraus, the new CD's coming out soon die neue CD kommt bald heraus
- to come up **heraufkommen**◇ (SEP) (PERF **sein**); can you come up a moment? kannst du eine Sekunde heraufkommen?
- to come up to somebody auf jemanden **zukommen**◇ (SEP) (PERF **sein**)

**comedian** NOUN **Komiker** der (PLURAL die **Komiker**) **Komikerin** die (PLURAL die **Komikerinnen**)

**comedy** NOUN **Komödie** die

**comfortable** ADJECTIVE ❶ **bequem**; this chair's really comfortable dieser Sessel ist wirklich bequem ❷ to feel comfortable (a person) sich wohl fühlen

**comfortably** ADVERB **bequem**

**comic** NOUN (magazine) **Comicheft** das (PLURAL die **Comichefte**)

**comic strip** NOUN **Comic** der (PLURAL die **Comics**)

**comma** NOUN **Komma** das (PLURAL die **Kommas**)

**command** NOUN **Befehl** der (PLURAL die **Befehle**)

**comment** NOUN (remark) **Bemerkung** die (PLURAL die **Bemerkungen**); he made some rude comments about my friends er hat ein paar unhöfliche Bemerkungen über meine Freunde gemacht

**commentary** NOUN **Reportage** die (PLURAL die **Reportagen**); the commentary on the soccer match die Reportage über das Fußballspiel

**commentator** NOUN **Reporter** der (PLURAL die **Reporter**) **Reporterin** die (PLURAL die **Reporterinnen**); sports commentator der Sportreporter

**commercial** NOUN **Werbespot** der (PLURAL die **Werbespots**)

**commercial** ADJECTIVE **kommerziell**

**commit** VERB ❶ **begehen**◇ (a crime)
❷ **to commit yourself to** sich
festlegen (SEP) : auf (+ACC)

**committee** NOUN **Ausschuss** der
(PLURAL die **Ausschüsse**)

**common** ADJECTIVE ❶ **häufig; it's a
common problem** das Problem
kommt häufig vor ❷ **in common**
gemeinsam, **they have nothing
in common** sie haben nichts
gemeinsam

**common sense** NOUN **gesunde
Menschenverstand** der

**communicate** VERB
**kommunizieren**

**communication** NOUN
**Verständigung** die

**communion** NOUN (in a Catholic
church) **Kommunion** die, (in a
Protestant church) **Abendmahl** das

**communism** NOUN **Kommunismus**
der

**community** NOUN **Gemeinschaft**
die (PLURAL die **Gemeinschaften**);
**the European Community** die
Europäische Gemeinschaft

**commute** VERB **to commute
between Oxford and London**
zwischen Oxford und London
pendeln (PERF **sein**)

**commuter** NOUN **Pendler** der (PLURAL
die **Pendler**) **Pendlerin** die (PLURAL
die **Pendlerinnen**)

**compact disc** NOUN **Compactdisc**
die (PLURAL die **Compactdiscs**)

**compact disc player** NOUN
**Compactdisc-Player** der (PLURAL die
**Compactdisc-Player**)

**company** NOUN ❶ (business)
**Gesellschaft** die (PLURAL die
**Gesellschaften**); **an airline
company** eine Fluggesellschaft,
**she's set up a company** sie hat eine
Firma gegründet ❷ (group) **Truppe**
die (PLURAL die **Truppen**); **a theatre
company** eine Theatertruppe
❸ **to keep somebody company**
jemandem Gesellschaft leisten, **the
dog keeps me company** der Hund
leistet mir Gesellschaft

**compare** VERB **vergleichen**◇; **if
you compare the German phrase
with the English** wenn man den
deutschen mit dem englischen
Ausdruck vergleicht, **our house
is small compared with yours**
verglichen mit eurem ist unser Haus
klein

**compartment** NOUN **Abteil** das
(PLURAL die **Abteile**)

**compass** NOUN **Kompass** der (PLURAL
die **Kompasse**)

**compatible** ADJECTIVE ❶ **zueinander
passend** ❷ (in computing)
**kompatibel**

**compete** VERB ❶ **to compete
in something** (race, event) an
etwas (DAT) teilnehmen◇ (SEP)
❷ **to compete with each other**
miteinander konkurrieren ❸ **to
compete for something** um etwas
(ACC) kämpfen, **thirty people are
competing for one job** dreißig
Leute kämpfen um eine Stelle

**competent** ADJECTIVE **fähig**

**competition** NOUN ❶ (a contest) Wettbewerb der (PLURAL die Wettbewerbe) ❷ (in a magazine) Preisausschreiben das (PLURAL die Preisausschreiben)

**competitor** NOUN Konkurrent der (PLURAL die Konkurrenten) Konkurrentin die (PLURAL die Konkurrentinnen)

**complain** VERB sich beschweren; we complained about the meals wir haben uns über das Essen beschwert

**complaint** NOUN Beschwerde die (PLURAL die Beschwerden); to make a complaint sich beschweren, she made a complaint to the manager about the poor service sie beschwerte sich bei dem Geschäftsführer über den schlechten Service

**complete** ADJECTIVE ❶ (whole) vollständig; the complete collection die vollständige Sammlung ❷ (absolute) völlig; a complete idiot ein völliger Idiot (informal)

**complete** VERB (to finish) beenden

**completely** ADVERB völlig

**complexion** NOUN Teint der (PLURAL die Teints)

**complicated** ADJECTIVE kompliziert

**compliment** NOUN Kompliment das (PLURAL die Komplimente); to pay somebody a compliment jemandem ein Kompliment machen

**composer** NOUN Komponist der (PLURAL die Komponisten) Komponistin die (PLURAL die Komponistinnen)

**comprehension** NOUN Verständnis das; a comprehension test ein Test zum Textverständnis

**comprehensive school** NOUN Gesamtschule die (PLURAL die Gesamtschulen)

**compulsory** ADJECTIVE ❶ obligatorisch ❷ (at school) compulsory subject das Pflichtfach

**computer** NOUN Computer der (PLURAL die Computer); to work on a computer am Computer arbeiten, to have something on computer etwas im Computer gespeichert haben

**computer engineer** NOUN Computertechniker der (PLURAL die Computertechniker) Computertechnikerin die (PLURAL die Computertechnikerinnen)

**computer game** NOUN Computerspiel das (PLURAL die Computerspiele)

**computer program** NOUN Computerprogramm das (PLURAL die Computerprogramme)

**computer programmer** NOUN Programmierer der (PLURAL die Programmierer) Programmiererin die (PLURAL die Programmiererinnen)

**computer science** NOUN Informatik die

**computing** NOUN Informatik die

**concentrate** VERB sich konzentrieren; I can't concentrate ich kann mich nicht konzentrieren, I was concentrating on the film ich konzentrierte mich auf den Film

a
b
c
d
e
f
g
h
i
j
k
l
m
n
o
p
q
r
s
t
u
v
w
x
y
z

**concentration** NOUN
Konzentration die

**concern** VERB (to affect) betreffen◇;
this doesn't concern you das
betrifft Sie nicht, as far as I'm
concerned was mich betrifft

**concert** NOUN ❶ Konzert das (PLURAL
die Konzerte); to go to a concert
ins Konzert gehen ❷ concert ticket
die Konzertkarte

**conclusion** NOUN Schluss der (PLURAL
die Schlüsse)

**concrete** NOUN Beton der; the
concrete floor der Betonboden

**condemn** VERB verurteilen; to
condemn somebody to death
jemanden zum Tode verurteilen

**condition** NOUN ❶ Zustand
der (PLURAL die Zustände);
in good condition in gutem
Zustand, weather conditions
die Wetterlage ❷ (something you
insist on) Bedingung die (PLURAL die
Bedingungen); on condition that
you let me pay unter der Bedingung,
dass du mich zahlen lässt

**conditional** NOUN Konditional das

**conditioner** NOUN (for your hair)
Spülung die (PLURAL die Spülungen)

**condom** NOUN Kondom das (PLURAL
die Kondome)

**conduct** NOUN Benehmen das

**conduct** VERB dirigieren (an
orchestra or a piece of music)

**conductor** NOUN (of an orchestra)
Dirigent der (PLURAL die
Dirigenten), Dirigentin die (PLURAL
die Dirigentinnen)

**cone** NOUN ❶ (for ice cream) Eistüte
die (PLURAL die Eistüten) ❷ (for
traffic) Verkehrshütchen das
(PLURAL die Verkehrshütchen)

**conference** NOUN Konferenz die
(PLURAL die Konferenzen)

**confess** VERB gestehen◇

**confession** NOUN Geständnis das
(PLURAL die Geständnisse)

**confidence** NOUN ❶ (self-confidence)
Selbstvertrauen das; to be lacking
in confidence kein Selbstvertrauen
haben ❷ (faith in somebody else)
Vertrauen das; to have confidence
in somebody jemandem vertrauen

**confident** ADJECTIVE ❶ (sure of
yourself) selbstbewusst ❷ (sure
that something will happen)
zuversichtlich

**confirm** VERB bestätigen; he
confirmed the date er bestätigte das
Datum

**confuse** VERB ❶ verwirren (a
person) ❷ to confuse someone
with somebody else jemanden (mit
jemandem anderem) verwechseln,
I confuse him with his brother ich
verwechsle ihn immer mit seinem
Bruder

**confused** ADJECTIVE ❶ wirr;
a confused story eine wirre
Geschichte ❷ durcheinander;
I'm confused about the holiday
plans ich bin mit den Ferienplänen
durcheinander, now I'm completely
confused jetzt bin ich völlig
durcheinander

**confusing** ADJECTIVE verwirrend;
the instructions are confusing die
Anweisungen sind verwirrend

**confusion** NOUN Verwirrung die

**congratulate** VERB gratulieren; **I congratulated Tim on passing his exam** ich gratulierte Tim zur bestandenen Prüfung

**congratulations** PLURAL NOUN Glückwünsche (plural); **congratulations on the baby!** herzlichen Glückwunsch zum Baby!

**connect** VERB (to plug in to the mains) anschließen◇ (SEP) (a dishwasher or TV, for example)

**connection** NOUN ❶ (between two ideas or events) Zusammenhang der (PLURAL die Zusammenhänge); **there's no connection between his letter and my decision** es besteht kein Zusammenhang zwischen seinem Brief und meiner Entscheidung ❷ (between trains, planes, on phone, and electrical) Anschluss der (PLURAL die Anschlüsse); **Sally missed her connection** Sally hat ihren Anschluss verpasst

**conscience** NOUN Gewissen das; **to have a guilty conscience** ein schlechtes Gewissen haben

**conscious** ADJECTIVE bei Bewusstsein sein◇; **she is not fully conscious yet** sie ist noch nicht wieder bei vollem Bewusstsein, **I was conscious that he was a policeman** es war mir bewusst, dass er Polizist war

**conservation** NOUN (of nature) Schutz der; **environmental conservation** der Umweltschutz

**conservative** NOUN Konservative der/die (PLURAL die Konservativen)

**conservative** ADJECTIVE konservativ

**conservatory** NOUN Wintergarten der (PLURAL die Wintergärten)

**consider** VERB ❶ sich (DAT) überlegen (a suggestion or idea); **all things considered** alles in allem ❷ (think about (doing)) erwägen◇; **we are considering buying a flat** wir erwägen, eine Wohnung zu kaufen

**considerate** ADJECTIVE rücksichtsvoll

**considering** PREPOSITION wenn man bedenkt; **considering her age** wenn man ihr Alter bedenkt, **considering he did it all himself** wenn man bedenkt, dass er es ganz allein gemacht hat

**consist** VERB to consist of bestehen◇ aus (+DAT)

**consonant** NOUN Konsonant der (PLURAL die Konsonanten)

**constant** ADJECTIVE ständig

**constipated** ADJECTIVE verstopft

**construct** VERB bauen

**construction** NOUN ❶ (building) Gebäude das (PLURAL die Gebäude); **a construction site** eine Baustelle ❷ (in grammar) Konstruktion die (PLURAL die Konstruktionen)

**consul** NOUN Konsul der (PLURAL die Konsuln)

**consulate** NOUN Konsulat das (PLURAL die Konsulate)

**consult** VERB konsultieren

**consumer** NOUN Verbraucher der (PLURAL die Verbraucher) Verbraucherin die (PLURAL die Verbraucherinnen)

a
b
c
d
e
f
g
h
i
j
k
l
m
n
o
p
q
r
s
t
u
v
w
x
y
z

**contact** NOUN Kontakt der (PLURAL die Kontakte); **to be in contact with somebody** mit jemandem in Kontakt sein, **we've lost contact** wir haben den Kontakt verloren, **Rob has contacts in the music business** Rob hat Kontakte zur Musikindustrie

**contact** VERB sich in Verbindung setzen mit (+DAT); **I'll contact you tomorrow** ich setze mich morgen mit dir in Verbindung

**contact lens** NOUN Kontaktlinse die (PLURAL die Kontaktlinsen)

**contain** VERB enthalten◇

**container** NOUN Behälter der (PLURAL die Behälter)

**contaminate** VERB verseuchen

**contemporary** ADJECTIVE ❶ (around today) zeitgenössisch ❷ (modern) modern

**contents** PLURAL NOUN Inhalt der; **the contents of my suitcase** der Inhalt meines Koffers

**contest** NOUN Wettbewerb der (PLURAL die Wettbewerbe)

**contestant** NOUN Teilnehmer der (PLURAL die Teilnehmer) Teilnehmerin die (PLURAL die Teilnehmerinnen)

**continent** NOUN Kontinent der (PLURAL die Kontinente)

**continue** VERB ❶ fortsetzen (SEP); **we continued (with) our journey** wir setzten unsere Reise fort ❷ **to continue to do something** etwas weiter tun, **Jill continued talking** Jill redete weiter ❸ 'to be continued' 'Fortsetzung folgt'

**continuous** ADJECTIVE ununterbrochen

**contraception** NOUN Verhütung die

**contraceptive** NOUN Verhütungsmittel das (PLURAL die Verhütungsmittel)

**contract** NOUN Vertrag der (PLURAL die Verträge)

**contradict** VERB widersprechen◇ (+DAT)

**contradiction** NOUN Widerspruch der (PLURAL die Widersprüche)

**contrary** NOUN Gegenteil das; **on the contrary** im Gegenteil

**contrast** NOUN Kontrast der (PLURAL die Kontraste)

**contribute** VERB beisteuern (SEP) (money)

**contribution** NOUN (to charity or an appeal) Spende die (PLURAL die Spenden)

**control** NOUN (of a crowd or animals) Kontrolle die; **the police are in control of the situation** die Polizei hat die Situation unter Kontrolle, **keep your dogs under control** halten Sie Ihre Hunde unter Kontrolle, **everything's under control** alles ist unter Kontrolle, **to get out of control** außer Kontrolle geraten

**control** VERB **to control yourself** sich beherrschen

**convenient** ADJECTIVE ❶ praktisch; **frozen food is very convenient** Tiefkühlkost ist sehr praktisch ❷ **to be convenient for somebody** jemandem passen, **whenever's convenient for you** wann immer es dir passt

**conventional** ADJECTIVE
konventionell

**conversation** NOUN Gespräch das
(PLURAL die Gespräche)

**convert** VERB ❶ umwandeln (SEP)
❷ (adapt a building) umbauen
(SEP); **we're going to convert the
garage into a workshop** wir wollen
die Garage zu einer Werkstatt
umbauen

**convince** VERB überzeugen; **I'm
convinced he's wrong** ich bin davon
überzeugt, dass er sich irrt

**convincing** ADJECTIVE überzeugend

**cook** NOUN Koch der (PLURAL die
Köche) Köchin die (PLURAL die
Köchinnen)

**cook** VERB ❶ kochen; **who's cooking
tonight?** wer kocht heute Abend?,
**I like cooking** ich koche gern,
**to cook vegetables and pasta**
Gemüse und Nudeln kochen, **cook
the cabbage for five minutes** lass
den Kohl fünf Minuten kochen ❷ (prepare food or a meal) **machen**;
**Fran's busy cooking supper** Fran
macht gerade Abendessen, **how
do you cook duck?** wie macht man
Ente? ❸ (boil) **kochen**, (fry or roast)
**braten**◇; **the potatoes are cooking**
die Kartoffeln kochen, **the sausages
are cooking** die Würstchen braten

**cooker** NOUN Herd der (PLURAL
die Herde); **electric cooker** der
Elektroherd, **gas cooker** der
Gasherd

**cookery** NOUN Kochen das

**cookery book** NOUN Kochbuch das
(PLURAL die Kochbücher)

**cooking** NOUN ❶ (preparing food)
Kochen das; **cooking is fun**
Kochen macht Spaß, **who's doing
the cooking?** wer kocht? ❷ (food)
Küche die; **Italian cooking** die
italienische Küche

**cool** NOUN ❶ (coldness) Kühle
die ❷ (calm) **to lose one's cool**
durchdrehen (SEP) (PERF sein)
(informal), **don't lose your cool!**
dreh nicht durch!, **he kept his cool**
er blieb gelassen

**cool** ADJECTIVE ❶ (cold) kühl; **it's cool
inside** drinnen ist es kühl ❷ (laid
back) gelassen; **to stay cool**
gelassen bleiben (PERF sein)

**cool** VERB abkühlen (SEP) (PERF sein)

**cop** NOUN Polizist der (PLURAL die
Polizisten)

**cope** VERB zurechtkommen◇ (SEP)
(PERF sein); **she copes well** sie
kommt gut zurecht, **to cope with
the children** mit den Kindern
zurechtkommen, **she's had a lot to
cope with** sie musste mit viel fertig
werden

**copy** NOUN ❶ (photocopy) Kopie
die (PLURAL die Kopien) ❷ (of a
book) Exemplar das (PLURAL die
Exemplare)

**copy** VERB ❶ (imitate) kopieren
❷ (make a copy of) abschreiben◇
(SEP); **I copied (down) the address** ich
habe die Adresse abgeschrieben, (in
an exam) **to copy from somebody** bei
jemandem abschreiben

**cord** NOUN (for a blind, for example)
Schnur die (PLURAL die Schnüre)

**cordless telephone** NOUN
schnurlose Telefon das (PLURAL die
schnurlosen Telefone)

a
b
c
d
e
f
g
h
i
j
k
l
m
n
o
p
q
r
s
t
u
v
w
x
y
z

**core** NOUN (of an apple or a pear) Kerngehäuse das (PLURAL die Kerngehäuse)

**cork** NOUN ❶ (in a bottle) Korken der (PLURAL die Korken) ❷ (material) Kork der

**corkscrew** NOUN Korkenzieher der (PLURAL die Korkenzieher)

**corn** NOUN ❶ (wheat) Korn das ❷ (sweetcorn) Mais der

**corner** NOUN ❶ Ecke die (PLURAL die Ecken); at the corner of the street an der Straßenecke, it's just round the corner es ist gleich um die Ecke ❷ (of mouth) Mundwinkel ❸ (of eye) Augenwinkel der (PLURAL die Augenwinkel); out of the corner of your eye aus den Augenwinkeln heraus ❹ (bend in the road) Kurve die (PLURAL die Kurven) ❺ (in football) Eckball der (PLURAL die Eckbälle)

**cornflakes** PLURAL NOUN die Cornflakes (plural)

**corpse** NOUN Leiche die (PLURAL die Leichen)

**correct** ADJECTIVE ❶ richtig; the correct answer die richtige Antwort ❷ yes, that's correct ja, das stimmt

**correct** VERB ❶ verbessern ❷ (teacher) korrigieren; the teacher has already corrected our homework der Lehrer hat unsere Hausaufgaben schon korrigiert

**correction** NOUN Verbesserung die (PLURAL die Verbesserungen)

**correctly** ADVERB richtig; have you filled in the form correctly? hast du das Formular richtig ausgefüllt?

**corridor** NOUN Korridor der (PLURAL die Korridore)

**cosmetics** PLURAL NOUN Kosmetik die

**cost** NOUN ❶ Kosten (plural); the cost of living die Lebenshaltungskosten (plural) ❷ the cost of a new computer der Preis für einen neuen Computer

**cost** VERB kosten; how much does it cost? was kostet es?, the tickets cost £10 die Karten kosten zehn Pfund, it costs too much das ist zu teuer

**costume** NOUN Kostüm das (PLURAL die Kostüme)

**cosy** ADJECTIVE (a room) gemütlich

**cot** NOUN Kinderbett das (PLURAL die Kinderbetten)

**cottage** NOUN Häuschen das (PLURAL die Häuschen)

**cotton** NOUN ❶ (fabric) Baumwolle die; cotton shirt das Baumwollhemd ❷ (thread) Nähgarn das (PLURAL die Nähgarne)

**cotton wool** NOUN Watte die

**couch** NOUN Couch die (PLURAL die Couchs)

**cough** NOUN Husten der; a nasty cough ein schlimmer Husten, to have a cough Husten haben

**cough** VERB husten

**could** VERB ❶ (the past tense of können is used to translate 'was able to') I couldn't open it ich konnte es nicht aufmachen, they couldn't come sie konnten nicht kommen, she did all she could sie hat getan, was sie konnte, he couldn't drive er konnte nicht Auto fahren, **she couldn't see anything** sie konnte überhaupt nichts sehen ❷ *(the past tense of dürfen is used to translate 'was allowed to')* **they couldn't smoke there** sie durften dort nicht rauchen ❸ *(might) (the subjunctive of können is used to translate a wish or suggestion)* **could I speak to David?** könnte ich mit David sprechen?, **you could try phoning** du könntest versuchen anzurufen, **if he could pay** wenn er zahlen könnte, **he could be right** er könnte recht haben

**council** NOUN Stadtrat der *(PLURAL die Stadträte)*

**count** VERB ❶ *(reckon up)* zählen; **I counted my money** ich habe mein Geld gezählt ❷ *(include)* mitzählen *(SEP)*; **thirty-five not counting the children** fünfunddreißig, die Kinder nicht mitgezählt

**counter** NOUN ❶ *(in a shop)* Ladentisch der *(PLURAL die Ladentische)* ❷ *(in a post office or bank)* Schalter der *(PLURAL die Schalter)* ❸ *(in a bar or café)* Theke die *(PLURAL die Theken)* ❹ *(for board games)* Spielmarke die *(PLURAL die Spielmarken)*

**country** NOUN ❶ *(Germany, etc.)* Land das *(PLURAL die Länder)* ❷ *(in a post office a foreign country* ein fremdes Land, **from another country** aus einem anderen Land ❷ *(not town)* Land das; **in the country** auf dem Land, **country road** die Landstraße

**country dancing** NOUN Volkstanz der

**countryside** NOUN ❶ *(not town)* Land das ❷ *(scenery)* Landschaft die

**county** NOUN Grafschaft die *(PLURAL die Grafschaften)*

**couple** NOUN ❶ *(a pair)* Paar das *(PLURAL die Paare)* ❷ **a couple of** ein paar **a couple of times** ein paar Mal, **I've got a couple of things to do** ich habe ein paar Sachen zu tun

**courage** NOUN Mut der

**courgette** NOUN Zucchini die *(PLURAL die Zucchini)*

**courier** NOUN ❶ *(for tourist group)* Reiseleiter der *(PLURAL die Reiseleiter)*, Reiseleiterin die *(PLURAL die Reiseleiterinnen)* ❷ *(delivery person)* Kurier der *(PLURAL die Kuriere)*; **it will be delivered by courier** es wird mit Kurierdienst gebracht

**course** NOUN ❶ *(lessons)* Kurs der *(PLURAL die Kurse)*; **computer course** der Computerkurs, **to go on a course** einen Kurs machen ❷ *(part of a meal)* Gang der *(PLURAL die Gänge)*; **the main course** der Hauptgang ❸ **golf course** der Golfplatz ❹ **of course** natürlich, **yes, of course!** ja, natürlich!, **he's forgotten, of course** er hat es natürlich vergessen

**court** NOUN ❶ *(for playing sports)* Platz der *(PLURAL die Plätze)* ❷ *(lawcourt)* Gericht das; **to go to court** vor Gericht gehen

**cousin** NOUN Cousin der *(PLURAL die Cousins)* Kusine die *(PLURAL die Kusinen)*; **my cousin Sonia** meine Kusine Sonia

**cover** NOUN ❶ *(of a book)* Einband der *(PLURAL die Einbände)* ❷ *(for a duvet or cushion)* Bezug der *(PLURAL die Bezüge)*

**cover** VERB ❶ (to cover up) **zudecken** (SEP); **he covered her with a blanket** er hat sie mit einer Decke zugedeckt ❷ **he was covered in spots** er war mit Pickeln übersät, **the room was covered in dust** das Zimmer war völlig verstaubt ❸ (with leaves, snow, or for protection) **bedecken**; **the ground was covered with snow** der Boden war mit Schnee bedeckt ❹ (with fabric) **beziehen**◇

**cow** NOUN **Kuh** die (PLURAL die **Kühe**); **mad cow disease** der **Rinderwahn**

**coward** NOUN **Feigling** der (PLURAL die **Feiglinge**)

**cowboy** NOUN **Cowboy** der (PLURAL die **Cowboys**)

**crab** NOUN **Krabbe** die (PLURAL die **Krabben**)

**crack** NOUN ❶ (in a glass or cup) **Sprung** der (PLURAL die **Sprünge**) ❷ (in wood or a wall) **Riss** der (PLURAL die **Risse**) ❸ (a cracking noise) **Knacks** der (PLURAL die **Knackse**)

**crack** VERB ❶ (to make a crack in) **anschlagen**◇ (SEP) ❷ (to break) **zerbrechen**◇ ❸ (to make a noise) (a twig) **knacken**

**cracker** NOUN ❶ (biscuit) **Cracker** der (PLURAL die **Cracker**) ❷ (Christmas cracker) **Knallbonbon** der (PLURAL die **Knallbonbons**)

**craft** NOUN (at school) **Werken** das

**cramp** NOUN **Krampf** der (PLURAL die **Krämpfe**); **to have cramp in your leg** einen Krampf im Bein haben

**crane** NOUN **Kran** der (PLURAL die **Kräne**)

**crash** NOUN ❶ (an accident) **Unfall** der (PLURAL die **Unfälle**); **car crash** der **Autounfall** ❷ (a noise) **Krachen** das

**crash** VERB ❶ (a plane) **abstürzen** (SEP) (PERF **sein**); **the plane crashed** das Flugzeug ist abgestürzt ❷ (have a collision in a car) **einen Unfall haben** ❸ **to crash into something** gegen etwas (ACC) **krachen** (PERF **sein**); **the car crashed into a tree** das Auto krachte gegen einen Baum

**crash course** NOUN **Schnellkurs** der (PLURAL die **Schnellkurse**)

**crash helmet** NOUN **Sturzhelm** der (PLURAL die **Sturzhelme**)

**crate** NOUN **Kiste** die (PLURAL die **Kisten**)

**crawl** NOUN (in swimming) **Kraulen** das

**crawl** VERB ❶ (a person) **kriechen**◇ (PERF **sein**), (a baby) **krabbeln** (PERF **sein**) ❷ (cars in a jam) **im Schneckentempo fahren**◇ (PERF **sein**); **we were crawling along** wir fuhren im Schneckentempo

**crayon** NOUN ❶ (wax) **Wachsmalstift** der (PLURAL die **Wachsmalstifte**) ❷ (coloured pencil) **Buntstift** der (PLURAL die **Buntstifte**)

**craze** NOUN **Mode** die; **the craze for rollerblades** die **Inlinerwelle**

**crazy** ADJECTIVE **verrückt**; **to be crazy for something** verrückt auf etwas (ACC) **sein**

**cream** NOUN **Sahne** die; **strawberries and cream** Erdbeeren mit Sahne

**cream cheese** NOUN **Frischkäse** der

**creased** ADJECTIVE **zerknittert**

**create** VERB **(er)schaffen**◇

**creative** ADJECTIVE **kreativ**

**creature** NOUN **Geschöpf** das (PLURAL die **Geschöpfe**)

**crèche** NOUN Kinderkrippe die
(PLURAL die **Kinderkrippen**)

**credit** NOUN Kredit der; **to buy
something on credit** etwas auf
Kredit kaufen

**credit card** NOUN Kreditkarte die
(PLURAL die **Kreditkarten**)

**cress** NOUN Kresse die

**crew** NOUN ❶ (on a ship or plane)
Besatzung die ❷ camera crew
das Kamerateam ❸ (in water
sports) Mannschaft die (PLURAL die
Mannschaften)

**crew cut** NOUN Bürstenschnitt der
(PLURAL die **Bürstenschnitte**)

**cricket** NOUN ❶ (game) Kricket das; **to
play cricket** Kricket spielen ❷ (insect)
Grille die (PLURAL die **Grillen**)

**cricket bat** NOUN Kricketschläger
der (PLURAL die **Kricketschläger**)

**crime** NOUN ❶ Verbrechen das
(PLURAL die **Verbrechen**); **theft is a
crime** Diebstahl ist ein Verbrechen
❷ (criminality) Kriminalität die;
**to fight crime** die Kriminalität
bekämpfen

**criminal** NOUN Kriminelle der/die
(PLURAL die **Kriminellen**)

**criminal** ADJECTIVE kriminell

**crisis** NOUN Krise die (PLURAL die **Krisen**)

**crisp** NOUN Chip der (PLURAL die
Chips); **a packet of potato crisps**
eine Tüte Kartoffelchips

**crisp** ADJECTIVE ❶ (biscuit) knusprig
❷ (apple) knackig

**critical** ADJECTIVE ❶ kritisch (remark,
medical condition) ❷ entscheidend
(moment)

**criticism** NOUN Kritik die

**criticize** VERB kritisieren

**crocodile** NOUN Krokodil das (PLURAL
die **Krokodile**)

**crook** NOUN (criminal) Gauner der
(PLURAL die **Gauner**), Gaunerin die
(PLURAL die **Gaunerinnen**)

**crop** NOUN Ernte die

**cross** NOUN Kreuz das (PLURAL die
Kreuze)

**cross** ADJECTIVE ärgerlich; **she was
very cross** sie war sehr ärgerlich,
**I'm cross with you** ich bin sehr
ärgerlich auf dich

**cross** VERB ❶ (to cross over)
überqueren; **to cross the road**
die Straße überqueren ❷ **to cross
your legs** die Beine übereinander
schlagen◇ ❸ (to cross each other)
sich kreuzen; **the two roads cross
here** die beiden Straßen kreuzen
sich hier
• **to cross out** durchstreichen◇ (SEP)

**cross-Channel** ADJECTIVE **a cross-
Channel ferry** eine Fähre über den
Ärmelkanal

**cross-country** NOUN ❶ Crosslauf
der ❷ **cross-country skiing** der
Langlauf

**crossing** NOUN ❶ (from one place to
another) Überquerung die (PLURAL
die **Überquerungen**) ❷ (a sea
journey) Überfahrt die (PLURAL die
**Überfahrten**); **Channel crossing**
die Überfahrt über den Ärmelkanal
❸ **pedestrian crossing** der
Fußgängerübergang, **level crossing**
der Bahnübergang

a
b
c
d
e
f
g
h
i
j
k
l
m
n
o
p
q
r
s
t
u
v
w
x
y
z

**crossroads** NOUN Kreuzung die (PLURAL die **Kreuzungen**); **at the crossroads** an der Kreuzung

**crossword** NOUN Kreuzworträtsel das (PLURAL die **Kreuzworträtsel**); **to do the crossword** ein Kreuzworträtsel machen

**crow** NOUN Krähe die (PLURAL die **Krähen**)

**crow** VERB (a cock) krähen

**crowd** NOUN ❶ Menschenmenge die (PLURAL die **Menschenmengen**); **in the crowd** in der Menschenmenge ❷ (spectators) **a crowd of five thousand** fünftausend Zuschauer (plural)

**crowd** VERB **to crowd into** or **onto something** sich in etwas (ACC) drängen, **we all crowded into the train** wir drängten uns alle in den Zug

**crowded** ADJECTIVE überfüllt

**crown** NOUN Krone die (PLURAL die **Kronen**)

**crude** ADJECTIVE ❶ (rough and ready) primitiv ❷ (vulgar) ordinär

**cruel** ADJECTIVE grausam

**cruise** NOUN Kreuzfahrt die (PLURAL die **Kreuzfahrten**); **to go on a cruise** eine Kreuzfahrt machen

**crumb** NOUN Krümel der (PLURAL die **Krümel**)

**crumpled** ADJECTIVE zerknittert

**crunchy** ADJECTIVE knusprig

**crush** VERB zerquetschen

**crust** NOUN Kruste die (PLURAL die **Krusten**)

**crusty** ADJECTIVE knusprig

**crutch** NOUN Krücke die (PLURAL die **Krücken**); **to be on crutches** an Krücken gehen

**cry** NOUN Schrei der (PLURAL die **Schreie**)

**cry** VERB ❶ (weep) weinen ❷ (call out) schreien◇

**cub** NOUN ❶ (animal) Junge das (PLURAL die **Jungen**) ❷ (boy scout) Wölfling der (PLURAL die **Wölflinge**)

**cube** NOUN Würfel der (PLURAL die **Würfel**); **ice cube** der Eiswürfel

**cubic** ADJECTIVE (in measurements) Kubik-; **three cubic metres** drei Kubikmeter

**cubicle** NOUN ❶ (in a changing room) Kabine die ❷ (in a public lavatory) Toilette die (PLURAL die **Toiletten**)

**cuckoo** NOUN Kuckuck der (PLURAL die **Kuckucke**)

**cucumber** NOUN Gurke die (PLURAL die **Gurken**)

**cuddle** NOUN **to give somebody a cuddle** jemanden in den Arm nehmen

**cuddle** VERB schmusen

**cue** NOUN (billiards, pool, snooker) Queue das (PLURAL die **Queues**)

**cuff** NOUN (on a shirt) Manschette die (PLURAL die **Manschetten**)

**cul-de-sac** NOUN Sackgasse die (PLURAL die **Sackgassen**)

**culture** NOUN Kultur die (PLURAL die **Kulturen**)

**cunning** ADJECTIVE listig

**cup** NOUN ❶ (for drinking) Tasse die (PLURAL die Tassen); **a cup of tea** eine Tasse Tee ❷ (a trophy) Pokal der (PLURAL die Pokale)

**cupboard** NOUN Schrank der (PLURAL die Schränke); **in the kitchen cupboard** im Küchenschrank

**cup tie** NOUN Pokalspiel das (PLURAL die Pokalspiele)

**cure** NOUN Heilmittel das (PLURAL die Heilmittel)

**cure** VERB heilen

**curiosity** NOUN Neugier die

**curious** ADJECTIVE neugierig

**curl** NOUN Locke die (PLURAL die Locken)

**curl** VERB ❶ locken (hair) ❷ (of hair) sich locken

**currant** NOUN Korinthe die (PLURAL die Korinthen)

**currency** NOUN Währung die (PLURAL die Währungen); **the Japanese currency** die japanische Währung, **foreign currencies** Devisen (plural)

**current** NOUN ❶ (electricity) Strom der ❷ (in water or air) Strömung die (PLURAL die Strömungen)

**current** ADJECTIVE aktuell

**current affairs** NOUN Tagespolitik die

**curriculum** NOUN Lehrplan der (PLURAL die Lehrpläne)

**curry** NOUN Curry das; **vegetable curry** das Gemüse in Currysoße

**cursor** NOUN Cursor der (PLURAL die Cursors)

**curtain** NOUN Vorhang der (PLURAL die Vorhänge)

**cushion** NOUN Kissen das (PLURAL die Kissen)

**custard** NOUN Vanillesoße die (PLURAL die Vanillesoßen)

**custom** NOUN Brauch der (PLURAL die Bräuche)

**customer** NOUN Kunde der (PLURAL die Kunden) Kundin die (PLURAL die Kundinnen); **customer services** Kundendienst der

**customs** PLURAL NOUN Zoll der; **to go through customs** durch den Zoll gehen

**customs hall** NOUN Zollabfertigung die

**customs officer** NOUN Zollbeamte der (PLURAL die Zollbeamten) Zollbeamtin die (PLURAL die Zollbeamtinnen)

**cut** NOUN ❶ (injury) Schnittwunde die (PLURAL die Schnittwunden) ❷ (haircut) Schnitt der (PLURAL die Schnitte)

**cut** VERB ❶ schneiden◇; **can you cut the bread please?** kannst du bitte das Brot schneiden?, **you'll cut yourself!** du schneidest dich!, **Kevin's cut his finger** Kevin hat sich in den Finger geschnitten ❷ **to cut the grass** den Rasen mähen ❸ **to get your hair cut** sich (DAT) die Haare schneiden lassen, **I had my hair cut** ich habe mir die Haare schneiden lassen ❹ **to cut prices** die Preise senken
• **to cut down** ❶ fällen (a tree) ❷ **to cut down on cigarettes** seinen Zigarettenkonsum einschränken (SEP)

- **to cut out something ❶** etwas ausschneiden◇ *(SEP) (a shape, a newspaper article)* **❷** etwas streichen◇ *(sugar, fatty food, holidays, for example)*
- **to cut something up** etwas klein schneiden◇ *(food)*

**cutlery** *NOUN* Besteck das *(PLURAL die Bestecke)*

**CV** *NOUN* Lebenslauf der *(PLURAL die Lebensläufe)*

**cyberbullying** *NOUN* Cybermobbing das

**cycle** *NOUN (bike)* Rad das *(PLURAL die Räder)*

**cycle** *VERB* Rad fahren◇ *(PERF sein)*; **do you like cycling?** fährst du gerne Rad?, **we cycle to school** wir fahren mit dem Rad zur Schule

**cycle lane** *NOUN* Fahrradweg die *(PLURAL die Fahrradwege)*

**cycle race** *NOUN* Radrennen das *(PLURAL die Radrennen)*

**cycling** *NOUN* Radfahren das

**cycling shorts** *NOUN* Radlerhose die *(PLURAL die Radlerhosen)*

**cyclist** *NOUN* Radfahrer der *(PLURAL die Radfahrer)* Radfahrerin die *(PLURAL die Radfahrerinnen)*

# Dd

**dad** *NOUN* Vati der *(PLURAL die Vatis)*

**daffodil** *NOUN* Osterglocke die *(PLURAL die Osterglocken)*

**daily** *ADJECTIVE* täglich; **his daily visit** sein täglicher Besuch

**daily** *ADVERB* täglich; **she visits him daily** sie besucht ihn täglich

**dairy products** *PLURAL NOUN* Milchprodukte *(plural)*

**daisy** *NOUN* Gänseblümchen das *(PLURAL die Gänseblümchen)*

**dam** *NOUN* Damm der *(PLURAL die Dämme)*

**damage** *NOUN* Schaden der *(PLURAL die Schäden)*; **to do a lot of damage** großen Schaden anrichten

**damage** *VERB* beschädigen

**damn** *NOUN* **I don't give a damn** das ist mir piepegal *(informal)*

**damn** *EXCLAMATION* **damn!** verdammt!

**damp** *ADJECTIVE* feucht

**damp** *NOUN* Feuchtigkeit die

**dance** *NOUN* Tanz der *(PLURAL die Tänze)*; **a folk dance** ein Volkstanz

**dance** *VERB* tanzen; **I like dancing** ich tanze gerne

**dancer** *NOUN* Tänzer der *(PLURAL die Tänzer)* Tänzerin die *(PLURAL die Tänzerinnen)*

**dancing** NOUN Tanzen das

**dancing class** NOUN Tanzstunde die (PLURAL die **Tanzstunden**); **to go to dancing classes** in die Tanzstunde gehen

**dandruff** NOUN Schuppen (plural)

**danger** NOUN Gefahr die (PLURAL die **Gefahren**); **to be in danger** in Gefahr sein

**dangerous** ADJECTIVE gefährlich; **it's dangerous to drive too fast** es ist gefährlich, zu schnell zu fahren

**Danish** NOUN Dänisch das

**Danish** ADJECTIVE dänisch; **he's Danish** er ist Däne, **she's Danish** sie ist Dänin

**dare** VERB ❶ wagen; **to dare to do something** es wagen, etwas zu tun, **I didn't dare suggest it** ich habe es nicht gewagt, das vorzuschlagen ❷ **don't you dare tell her I'm here!** untersteh dich, ihr zu sagen, dass ich hier bin! ❸ **I dare you!** du traust dich doch nicht!, **I dare you to tell him!** sag's ihm doch wenn du dich traust!

**daring** ADJECTIVE gewagt; **that was a bit daring** das war etwas gewagt

**dark** NOUN **in the dark** im Dunkeln, **after dark** nach Einbruch der Dunkelheit, **to be afraid of the dark** Angst im Dunkeln haben

**dark** ADJECTIVE ❶ (colour) dunkel (adjectives ending in -el drop the e when followed by a vowel, which means that dunkel becomes dunkler/ dunkle/dunkles); **a dark colour** eine dunkle Farbe, **it gets dark around five** es wird gegen fünf dunkel ❷ **a dark blue skirt** ein dunkelblauer

Rock, **she has dark brown hair** sie hat dunkelbraune Haare

**darkness** NOUN Dunkelheit die; **in darkness** in der Dunkelheit

**darling** NOUN Liebling der (PLURAL die **Lieblinge**); **see you later, darling!** bis später, Liebling!

**dart** NOUN ❶ Wurfpfeil der (PLURAL die **Wurfpfeile**) ❷ (game) **darts** Darts das, **to play darts** Darts spielen

**data** PLURAL NOUN Daten (plural)

**database** NOUN Datenbank die (PLURAL die **Datenbanken**)

**date** NOUN ❶ Datum das (PLURAL die **Daten**); **what's the date today?** welches Datum haben wir heute?, **the date of the meeting** das Datum für das Treffen, **what date is he coming?** wann kommt er? ❷ Termin der (PLURAL die **Termine**); **the last date for payment** der letzte Zahlungstermin ❸ **out of date** ungültig, **my passport's out of date** mein Pass ist ungültig ❹ (appointment) Verabredung die (PLURAL die **Verabredungen**); **Laura's got a date with Frank** Laura ist mit Frank verabredet ❺ (fruit) Dattel die (PLURAL die **Datteln**)

**date of birth** NOUN Geburtsdatum das (PLURAL die **Geburtsdaten**)

**daughter** NOUN Tochter die (PLURAL die **Töchter**); **Tina's daughter** Tinas Tochter

**daughter-in-law** NOUN Schwiegertochter die (PLURAL die **Schwiegertöchter**)

**dawn** NOUN Morgendämmerung die (PLURAL die **Morgendämmerungen**)

**day** NOUN ❶ Tag der *(PLURAL* die **Tage)**; **three days later** drei Tage später, **a few days ago** vor ein paar Tagen, **the day I went to London** an dem Tag, an dem ich nach London gefahren bin, **we spent the day in London** wir haben den Tag in London verbracht, **it rained all day** es hat den ganzen Tag geregnet, **the day after** am Tag danach, **the day after the wedding** am Tag nach der Hochzeit, **the day before** am Tag davor, **the day before the wedding** am Tag vor der Hochzeit ❷ **the day after tomorrow** übermorgen, **my sister's arriving the day after tomorrow** meine Schwester kommt übermorgen an ❸ **the day before yesterday** vorgestern, **my brother arrived the day before yesterday** mein Bruder kam vorgestern an ❹ **during the day** tagsüber

**dead** ADJECTIVE tot; **her father's dead** ihr Vater ist tot

**dead** ADVERB *(really)* **irre** *(informal)*; **he's dead nice** er ist irre nett, **it was dead good** es war irre gut, **it was dead easy** es war kinderleicht, **you're dead right** du hast völlig Recht, **she arrived dead on time** sie kam auf die Minute pünktlich an

**dead end** NOUN Sackgasse die *(PLURAL* die **Sackgassen)**

**deadline** NOUN letzte Termin der *(PLURAL* die **letzten Termine)**

**deaf** ADJECTIVE taub

**deafening** ADJECTIVE ohrenbetäubend

**deal** NOUN ❶ *(involving money)* Geschäft das *(PLURAL* die **Geschäfte)**; **it's a good deal** das ist ein gutes Geschäft ❷ *(agreement)* Vereinbarung die *(PLURAL* die **Vereinbarungen)**; **to make a deal with somebody** mit jemandem eine Vereinbarung treffen, **it's a deal!** abgemacht! ❸ **a great deal of** viel, **I don't have a great deal of time** ich habe nicht viel Zeit

**deal** VERB *(in cards)* geben; **it's you to deal** du gibst
• **to deal with something** sich um etwas *(ACC)* kümmern; **Linda deals with the accounts** Linda kümmert sich um die Buchführung, **I'll deal with it as soon as possible** ich kümmere mich so schnell wie möglich darum

**dear** ADJECTIVE ❶ lieb; **Dear Franz** Lieber Franz, **Dear Mr Smith** Sehr geehrter Herr Smith ❷ *(expensive)* teuer

**death** NOUN Tod der; **after his father's death** nach dem Tod seines Vaters **three deaths** drei Todesfälle
• **I was bored to death** ich habe mich zu Tode gelangweilt
• **I'm sick to death of it** ich habe es gründlich satt

**death penalty** NOUN Todesstrafe die

**debate** NOUN Debatte die *(PLURAL* die **Debatten)**

**debate** VERB debattieren

**debt** NOUN *(money owed)* Schulden *(plural)*; **to get into debt** in Schulden geraten

**decade** NOUN Jahrzehnt das *(PLURAL* die **Jahrzehnte)**

**decaffeinated** ADJECTIVE koffeinfrei

**deceive** VERB betrügen◇

**December** NOUN Dezember der *(PLURAL* die **Dezember)**; **in December** im Dezember

**decent** *ADJECTIVE* anständig; **a decent salary** ein anständiges Gehalt, **a decent meal** ein anständiges Essen

**decide** *VERB* ❶ entscheiden◇; **to decide on something** sich für etwas (*ACC*) entscheiden, **he's decided against buying a new car** er hat sich entschieden, kein neues Auto zu kaufen ❷ **to decide to do something** sich entschließen◇, etwas zu tun

**they've decided to buy a house** sie haben sich entschlossen, ein Haus zu kaufen

**decimal** *ADJECTIVE* Dezimal-; **decimal number** die Dezimalzahl

**decimal point** *NOUN* Komma das (*PLURAL* die Kommas)

**decision** *NOUN* Entscheidung die (*PLURAL* die Entscheidungen); **to make a decision** eine Entscheidung treffen

**deckchair** *NOUN* Liegestuhl der (*PLURAL* die Liegestühle)

**declare** *VERB* ❶ erklären ❷ *(at customs)* **nothing to declare** nichts zu verzollen

**decorate** *VERB* ❶ schmücken; **to decorate the Christmas tree** den Weihnachtsbaum schmücken ❷ *(with paint)* streichen◇, *(with wallpaper)* tapezieren; **we're decorating the kitchen this weekend** wir streichen dieses Wochenende die Küche

**decoration** *NOUN* Verzierung die (*PLURAL* die Verzierungen); **Christmas decorations** der Weihnachtsschmuck

**decrease** *NOUN* Rückgang der (*PLURAL* die Rückgänge); **a decrease in the**

**number of accidents** ein Rückgang in der Anzahl der Unfälle

**decrease** *VERB* zurückgehen◇ *(SEP)* *(PERF* sein), abnehmen◇ *(SEP)*

**deep** *ADJECTIVE* tief; **a deep feeling of gratitude** ein tiefes Dankbarkeitsgefühl, **how deep is the swimming pool?** wie tief ist das Schwimmbecken?, **a hole two metres deep** ein zwei Meter tiefes Loch

**deep end** *NOUN* Schwimmerbecken das (*PLURAL* die Schwimmerbecken); **deep end: 2 metres** Wassertiefe: 2 Meter

**deep freeze** *NOUN* Tiefkühltruhe die (*PLURAL* die Tiefkühltruhen), *(upright)* Tiefkühlschrank der (*PLURAL* die Tiefkühlschränke)

**deeply** *ADVERB* tief

**deer** *NOUN* ❶ Hirsch der (*PLURAL* die Hirsche) ❷ *(roe deer)* Reh das (*PLURAL* die Rehe)

**defeat** *NOUN* Niederlage die (*PLURAL* die Niederlagen)

**defeat** *VERB* schlagen◇

**defence** *NOUN* Verteidigung die

**defend** *VERB* verteidigen

**defender** *NOUN* Verteidiger der (*PLURAL* die Verteidiger) Verteidigerin die (*PLURAL* die Verteidigerinnen)

**definite** *ADJECTIVE* ❶ eindeutig; **a definite improvement** eine eindeutige Besserung ❷ *(certain)* sicher; **it's not definite yet** es ist noch nicht sicher ❸ *(exact)* klar; **a definite answer** eine klare Antwort

**definite article** *NOUN* bestimmter Artikel der (*PLURAL* die bestimmten Artikel)

a
b
c
d
e
f
g
h
i
j
k
l
m
n
o
p
q
r
s
t
u
v
w
x
y
z

**definitely** ADVERB ❶ *(when giving your opinion about something)* **eindeutig**; **your German is definitely better than mine** dein Deutsch ist eindeutig besser als meins ❷ *(without doubt)* **bestimmt**; **she's definitely going to be there** sie wird bestimmt dort sein, **I'm definitely not coming** ich komme ganz bestimmt nicht ❸ 'are you sure you like this one better?' – 'definitely!' 'gefällt dir diese wirklich besser?' – 'auf jeden Fall!'

**definition** NOUN **Definition** die *(PLURAL* die *Definitionen)*

**degree** NOUN ❶ **Grad** der *(PLURAL* die *Grade)*; **thirty degrees** dreißig Grad ❷ **a university degree** ein akademischer Grad

**delay** NOUN **Verspätung** die *(PLURAL* die *Verspätungen)*; **a two-hour delay** eine zweistündige Verspätung

**delay** VERB ❶ *(hold up)* **aufhalten**◇ *(SEP)*; **she was delayed in the office** sie ist im Büro aufgehalten worden ❷ *train, plane* **to be delayed** Verspätung haben, **the flight was delayed by bad weather** der Flug hatte wegen des schlechten Wetters Verspätung ❸ *(postpone)* **aufschieben**◇ *(SEP)*; **the decision has been delayed until Thursday** die Entscheidung wurde bis Donnerstag aufgeschoben

**delete** VERB ❶ **streichen**◇ ❷ *(in computing)* **löschen**

**deliberate** ADJECTIVE **absichtlich**

**deliberately** ADVERB **absichtlich**; **she did it deliberately** sie hat das absichtlich getan

**delicate** ADJECTIVE ❶ *(fabric, health)* **zart** ❷ *(situation, question)* **heikel** ❸ *(taste, smell)* **fein**

**delicatessen** NOUN **Feinkostgeschäft** das *(PLURAL* die *Feinkostgeschäfte)*

**delicious** ADJECTIVE **köstlich**

**delighted** ADJECTIVE **hocherfreut**; **to be delighted** begeistert sein, **they're delighted with their new flat** sie sind von ihrer neuen Wohnung begeistert, **I'm delighted that you can come** ich freue mich sehr, dass ihr kommen könnt

**deliver** VERB ❶ **liefern**; **they're delivering the washing machine tomorrow** die Waschmaschine wird morgen geliefert ❷ *(mail, newspapers)* **zustellen** *(SEP)*

**delivery** NOUN ❶ **Lieferung** die *(PLURAL* die *Lieferungen)* ❷ *(of mail, newspapers)* **Zustellung** die *(PLURAL* die *Zustellungen)*

**demand** NOUN **Nachfrage** die *(PLURAL* die *Nachfragen)*; **much in demand** sehr gefragt

**demand** VERB **verlangen**

**demo** NOUN *(protest)* **Demo** die *(informal) (PLURAL* die *Demos)*

**democracy** NOUN **Demokratie** die *(PLURAL* die *Demokratien)*

**democratic** ADJECTIVE **demokratisch**

**demolish** VERB **abreißen**◇ *(SEP)*

**demonstrate** VERB ❶ *(a machine, product, or technique)* **vorführen** *(SEP)* ❷ *(protest)* **demonstrieren**; **to demonstrate against something** gegen etwas *(ACC)* demonstrieren

**demonstration** NOUN ❶ (of a machine, product, or technique) Vorführung die (PLURAL die Vorführungen) ❷ (protest) Demonstration die (PLURAL die Demonstrationen)

**demonstrator** NOUN Demonstrant der (PLURAL die Demonstranten) Demonstrantin die (PLURAL die Demonstrantinnen)

**denim** NOUN Jeansstoff der (PLURAL die Jeansstoffe); a denim jacket eine Jeansjacke

**Denmark** NOUN Dänemark das

**dental** ADJECTIVE ❶ Zahn-; dental floss die Zahnseide, dental hygiene die Zahnpflege ❷ to have a dental appointment einen Zahnarzt Termin haben

**dental surgeon** NOUN Zahnarzt der (PLURAL die Zahnärzte) Zahnäztin die (PLURAL die Zahnärztinnen)

**dentist** NOUN Zahnarzt der (PLURAL die Zahnärzte) Zahnärztin die (PLURAL die Zahnärztinnen); my mum's a dentist meine Mutter ist Zahnärztin

**deny** VERB bestreiten◇

**deodorant** NOUN Deodorant das (PLURAL die Deodorants)

**depart** VERB ❶ (set out on a journey) abreisen (SEP) (PERF sein) ❷ (train, coach) abfahren◇ (SEP) (PERF sein) ❸ (plane) abfliegen◇ (SEP) (PERF sein)

**department** NOUN ❶ (in a shop, firm, or hospital) Abteilung die (PLURAL die Abteilungen); the men's department die Herrenabteilung ❷ (of a university) Seminar das (PLURAL die Seminare); the history department das Seminar für Geschichte ❸ (in school) Fachbereich der (PLURAL die Fachbereiche)

**department store** NOUN Kaufhaus das (PLURAL die Kaufhäuser)

**departure** NOUN ❶ (of a person) Abreise die ❷ (of a car, train) Abfahrt die ❸ (of a plane) Abflug der

**departure lounge** NOUN Abflughalle die (PLURAL die Abflughallen)

**depend** VERB ❶ to depend on abhängen◇ (SEP) von (+DAT), it depends on the price das hängt vom Preis ab, it depends on what you want das hängt davon ab, was du willst ❷ it depends es kommt darauf an

**deposit** NOUN ❶ (when renting or hiring) Kaution die (PLURAL die Kautionen) ❷ (when booking a holiday or hotel room) Anzahlung die (PLURAL die Anzahlungen); to pay a deposit eine Anzahlung leisten ❸ (on a bottle) Pfand das

**depressed** ADJECTIVE deprimiert

**depressing** ADJECTIVE deprimierend

**depth** NOUN Tiefe die

**deputy** NOUN Stellvertreter der (PLURAL die Stellvertreter), Stellvertreterin die (PLURAL die Stellvertreterinnen); the deputy headteacher Konrektor der (PLURAL die Konrektoren), Konrektorin die (PLURAL die Konrektorinnen)

**describe** VERB beschreiben◇

**description** NOUN Beschreibung die (PLURAL die Beschreibungen)

**desert** NOUN Wüste die (PLURAL die Wüsten)

**desert island** NOUN verlassene Insel die (PLURAL die verlassenen Inseln)

**deserve** VERB verdienen

**design** NOUN ❶ Konstruktion die (PLURAL die Konstruktionen); **the design of the plane** die Flugzeugkonstruktion ❷ (artistic design) Design das (PLURAL die Designs); **modern design** modernes Design ❸ (pattern) Muster das (PLURAL die Muster); **a floral design** ein Blumenmuster ❹ (sketch) Entwurf der (PLURAL die Entwürfe)

**design** VERB ❶ konstruieren (a machine, plane, system) ❷ entwerfen◇ (costumes, fabric, scenery)

**designer** NOUN Designer der (PLURAL die Designer), Designerin die (PLURAL die Designerinnen)

**desk** NOUN ❶ (in an office or at home) Schreibtisch der (PLURAL die Schreibtische) ❷ (pupil's) Pult das (PLURAL die Pulte) ❸ **the reception desk** die Rezeption, **the information desk** die Auskunft

**despair** NOUN Verzweiflung die

**despair** VERB **to despair of doing something** alle Hoffnung aufgeben◇ (SEP), etwas zu tun

**desperate** ADJECTIVE ❶ verzweifelt; **a desperate attempt** ein verzweifelter Versuch ❷ **to be desperate to do something** etwas dringend tun müssen, **I'm desperate to speak to you** ich muss dich dringend sprechen, **to**

**be desperate for something** etwas dringend brauchen

**dessert** NOUN Nachtisch der (PLURAL die Nachtische); **what's for dessert?** was gibts zum Nachtisch?

**destination** NOUN Ziel das (PLURAL die Ziele)

**destroy** VERB zerstören

**destruction** NOUN Zerstörung die

**detached house** NOUN Einfamilienhaus das (PLURAL die Einfamilienhäuser)

**detail** NOUN Einzelheit die (PLURAL die Einzelheiten)

**detailed** ADJECTIVE ausführlich

**detective** NOUN ❶ (in the police) Kriminalbeamte der (PLURAL die Kriminalbeamten), Kriminalbeamtin die (PLURAL die Kriminalbeamtinnen) ❷ **private detective** der Detektiv, die Detektivin

**detective story** NOUN Detektivgeschichte die (PLURAL die Detektivgeschichten)

**detention** NOUN ❶ (at school) Nachsitzen das ❷ (in prison) Haft die

**detergent** NOUN Waschmittel das (PLURAL die Waschmittel)

**determined** ADJECTIVE entschlossen; **he's determined to leave** er ist fest entschlossen zu gehen

**detour** NOUN Umweg der (PLURAL die Umwege)

**develop** VERB ❶ entwickeln; **to get a film developed** einen Film entwickeln lassen ❷ sich entwickeln; **how children develop** wie Kinder sich entwickeln

**developing country** NOUN Entwicklungsland das (PLURAL die Entwicklungsländer)

**development** NOUN Entwicklung die (PLURAL die Entwicklungen)

**devil** NOUN Teufel der (PLURAL die Teufel)

**devoted** ADJECTIVE treu

**diabetes** NOUN Zuckerkrankheit die

**diabetic** NOUN Diabetiker der (PLURAL die Diabetiker), Diabetikerin die (PLURAL die Diabetikerinnen)

**diabetic** ADJECTIVE zuckerkrank; **to be diabetic** zuckerkrank sein

**diagnosis** NOUN Diagnose die (PLURAL die Diagnosen)

**diagonal** ADJECTIVE diagonal

**diagram** NOUN Diagramm das (PLURAL die Diagramme)

**dial** VERB wählen; **I dialled the wrong number** ich habe die falsche Nummer gewählt, **dial 00 49 for Germany** wählen Sie die Vorwahl 00 49 für Deutschland

**dialling tone** NOUN Freizeichen das

**dialogue** NOUN Dialog der (PLURAL die Dialoge)

**diamond** NOUN ❶ Diamant der (PLURAL die Diamanten), (gemstone) Brillant der (PLURAL die Brillanten) ❷ (in cards) Karo das; **the jack of diamonds** der Karobube ❸ (shape) Raute die (PLURAL die Rauten)

**diarrhoea** NOUN Durchfall der

**diary** NOUN ❶ (for appointments) Terminkalender der (PLURAL die Terminkalender) ❷ Tagebuch das (PLURAL die Tagebücher); **to keep a diary** ein Tagebuch führen

**dice** NOUN Würfel der (PLURAL die Würfel); **to throw the dice** würfeln

**dictation** NOUN Diktat das (PLURAL die Diktate)

**dictionary** NOUN Wörterbuch das (PLURAL die Wörterbücher)

**did** VERB ▸ SEE **do**

**die** VERB ❶ sterben✧ (PERF sein); **my grannie died in January** meine Oma starb im Januar ❷ **to be dying to do something** darauf brennen, etwas zu tun, **I'm dying to meet her** ich brenne darauf, sie kennen zu lernen

**diesel** NOUN ❶ Dieselöl das ❷ **diesel engine** der Dieselmotor, **diesel car** der Diesel

**diet** NOUN ❶ Ernährung die; **a healthy diet** eine gesunde Ernährung ❷ (slimming or special) Diät die (PLURAL die Diäten); **to be on a diet** Diät machen

**difference** NOUN ❶ Unterschied der (PLURAL die Unterschiede); **I can't see any difference between the two** ich erkenne keinen Unterschied zwischen den beiden, **what's the difference between ...?** was ist der Unterschied zwischen ...? ❷ **it makes a difference** es ist ein Unterschied, **it makes no difference** es ist egal, **it makes no difference what I say** es ist egal, was ich sage

**different** ADJECTIVE ❶ verschieden; **the two sisters are very different** die beiden Schwestern sind sehr verschieden ❷ **to be different from**

anders sein als, **she's very different from her sister** sie ist ganz anders als ihre Schwester ❸ *(separate)* anderer/andere/anderes; **she reads a different book every day** sie liest jeden Tag ein anderes Buch

**difficult** ADJECTIVE schwer; **it's really difficult** es ist sehr schwer, **he finds it difficult** es fällt ihm schwer

**difficulty** NOUN Schwierigkeit die *(PLURAL* die Schwierigkeiten*)*; **to have difficulty doing something** Schwierigkeiten haben, etwas zu tun, **I had difficulty finding your house** ich hatte Schwierigkeiten, dein Haus zu finden

**dig** VERB graben✧; **to dig a hole** ein Loch graben

**digestion** NOUN Verdauung die

**digital** ADJECTIVE digital; **digital watch** die Digitaluhr, **digital recording** die Digitalaufnahme

**dim** ADJECTIVE ❶ schwach; **a dim light** ein schwaches Licht ❷ beschränkt; **she's a bit dim** sie ist ein bisschen beschränkt

**din** NOUN Lärm der; **stop making such a din!** hör auf, so einen Lärm zu machen!

**dinghy** NOUN ❶ **sailing dinghy** das Dingi ❷ **rubber dinghy** das Schlauchboot

**dining room** NOUN Esszimmer das *(PLURAL* die Esszimmer*)*; **in the dining room** im Esszimmer

**dinner** NOUN ❶ *(evening)* Abendessen das *(PLURAL* die Abendessen*)*; **to invite somebody to dinner** jemanden zum Abendessen einladen ❷ *(midday)* Mittagessen das *(PLURAL* die Mittagessen*)*; **to have school dinner** in der Schulkantine zu Mittag essen

**dinner party** NOUN Abendessen das *(PLURAL* die Abendessen*)*

**dinner time** NOUN Essenszeit die

**dinosaur** NOUN Dinosaurier der *(PLURAL* die Dinosaurier*)*

**diploma** NOUN Diplom das *(PLURAL* die Diplome*)*

**direct** ADJECTIVE direkt; **a direct flight** ein Direktflug

**direct** ADVERB direkt; **the bus goes direct to the airport** der Bus fährt direkt zum Flughafen

**direct** VERB ❶ **to direct a film or a play** bei einem Film oder einem Theaterstück Regie führen ❷ regeln *(traffic)*

**direction** NOUN ❶ Richtung die *(PLURAL* die Richtungen*)*; **to go in the other direction** in die andere Richtung gehen ❷ **to ask somebody for directions** jemanden nach dem Weg fragen ❸ **directions for use** die Gebrauchsanweisung *(SINGULAR)*

**directly** ADVERB direkt; **directly afterwards** gleich danach

**director** NOUN ❶ *(of a company)* Direktor der *(PLURAL* die Direktoren*)*, Direktorin die *(PLURAL* die Direktorinnen*)* ❷ *(of a play, film)* Regisseur der *(PLURAL* die Regisseure*)*, Regisseurin die *(PLURAL* die Regisseurinnen*)* ❸ *(of a programme)* Leiter der *(PLURAL* die Leiter*)*, Leiterin die *(PLURAL* die Leiterinnen*)*

**directory** NOUN Telefonbuch das (PLURAL die Telefonbücher); **he's ex-directory** seine Nummer steht nicht im Telefonbuch

**dirt** NOUN Schmutz der

**dirty** ADJECTIVE schmutzig; **my hands are dirty** ich habe schmutzige Hände, **to get something dirty** etwas schmutzig machen, **you'll get your dress dirty** du machst dir das Kleid schmutzig, **to get dirty** schmutzig werden, **the curtains get dirty quickly** die Vorhänge werden sehr schnell schmutzig

**disability** NOUN Behinderung die (PLURAL die Behinderungen); **does he have a disability?** ist er behindert?

**disabled** ADJECTIVE behindert; **disabled people** Behinderte (plural)

**disadvantage** NOUN ❶ Nachteil der (PLURAL die Nachteile) ❷ **to be at a disadvantage** im Nachteil sein

**disagree** VERB ❶ **I disagree** ich bin anderer Meinung ❷ **to disagree with somebody** mit jemandem nicht übereinstimmen (SEP), **I disagree with James** ich stimme mit James nicht überein

**disappear** VERB verschwinden◇ (PERF sein)

**disappearance** NOUN Verschwinden das

**disappointed** ADJECTIVE enttäuscht; **I'm disappointed with my marks** ich bin über meine Noten enttäuscht

**disappointment** NOUN Enttäuschung die (PLURAL die Enttäuschungen)

**disaster** NOUN Katastrophe die (PLURAL die Katastrophen); **it was a complete disaster** es war eine komplette Katastrophe

**disastrous** ADJECTIVE katastrophal

**disc** NOUN ❶ compact disc die Compactdisc ❷ tax disc (for a vehicle) die Steuerplakette ❸ slipped disc der Bandscheibenvorfall

**discipline** NOUN Disziplin die

**disc-jockey** NOUN Diskjockey der (PLURAL die Diskjockeys)

**disco** NOUN ❶ Disko die (PLURAL die Diskos); **they're having a disco** sie veranstalten eine Disko ❷ (club) Disko die (PLURAL die Diskos); **to go to a disco** in eine Disko gehen

**discount** NOUN Rabatt der (PLURAL die Rabatte)

**discover** VERB entdecken

**discovery** NOUN Entdeckung die (PLURAL die Entdeckungen)

**discreet** ADJECTIVE diskret

**discrimination** NOUN Diskriminierung die; **discrimination against women** die Diskriminierung von Frauen, **racial discrimination** die Rassendiskriminierung

**discuss** VERB **to discuss something** etwas besprechen◇, **we'll discuss the problem tomorrow** wir besprechen das Problem morgen, **I'm going to discuss it with Phil** ich werde es mit Phil besprechen

**discussion** NOUN Gespräch das (PLURAL die Gespräche)

**disease** NOUN Krankheit die (PLURAL die Krankheiten)

a
b
c

e
f
g
h
i
j
k
l
m
n
o
p
q
r
s
t
u
v
w
x
y
z

**disguise** NOUN Verkleidung die (PLURAL die **Verkleidungen**); **to be in disguise** verkleidet sein

**disguise** VERB verkleiden; **disguised as a woman** als Frau verkleidet

**disgust** NOUN Ekel der

**disgusted** ADJECTIVE ❶ (filled with indignation) empört ❷ (nauseated) angeekelt

**disgusting** ADJECTIVE eklig

**dish** NOUN ❶ Schüssel die (PLURAL die **Schüsseln**); **a large white dish** eine große weiße Schüssel, **satellite dish** die Satellitenschüssel ❷ (type of food) Gericht das (PLURAL die **Gerichte**); **risotto is my favourite dish** Risotto ist mein Lieblingsgericht ❸ (crockery) **the dishes** das Geschirr, **to do the dishes** Geschirr spülen

**dishcloth** NOUN Spültuch das (PLURAL die **Spültücher**)

**dishonest** ADJECTIVE unehrlich

**dishonesty** NOUN Unehrlichkeit die

**dishwasher** NOUN Geschirrspülmaschine die (PLURAL die **Geschirrspülmaschinen**)

**disinfect** VERB desinfizieren

**disinfectant** NOUN Desinfektionsmittel das

**disk** NOUN Diskette die (PLURAL die **Disketten**); **hard disk** die Festplatte

**disk drive** NOUN Diskettenlaufwerk das (PLURAL die **Diskettenlaufwerke**)

**dismiss** VERB entlassen◇ (an employee)

**disobedient** ADJECTIVE ungehorsam

**display** NOUN ❶ Ausstellung die (PLURAL die **Ausstellungen**); **handicrafts display** die Handarbeitsausstellung, **to be on display** ausgestellt sein ❷ **window display** die Auslage ❸ **firework display** das Feuerwerk

**display** VERB ausstellen (SEP)

**disposable** ADJECTIVE Wegwerf-; **disposable towel** das Wegwerfhandtuch

**disqualify** VERB disqualifizieren

**disrupt** VERB stören

**dissolve** VERB auflösen (SEP)

**distance** NOUN Entfernung die (PLURAL die **Entfernungen**); **from this distance** aus dieser Entfernung, **from a distance** von weitem, **in the distance** in der Ferne, **it's within walking distance** es ist zu Fuß erreichbar

**distant** ADJECTIVE fern

**distinct** ADJECTIVE deutlich

**distinctly** ADVERB ❶ deutlich ❷ **it's distinctly odd** es ist äußerst komisch

**distract** VERB ablenken (SEP)

**distribute** VERB verteilen

**district** NOUN ❶ (of a town) Stadtteil der (PLURAL die **Stadtteile**); **a poor district of Berlin** ein ärmlicher Stadtteil von Berlin ❷ (in the country) Gebiet das (PLURAL die **Gebiete**)

**disturb** VERB stören; **sorry to disturb you** Entschuldigung, dass ich störe

**dive** NOUN **Kopfsprung** der (PLURAL die **Kopfsprünge**)

**dive** VERB ❶ **einen Kopfsprung machen** ❷ (swim underwater) **tauchen** (PERF sein)

**diver** NOUN ❶ (underwater) **Taucher** der (PLURAL die **Taucher**), **Taucherin** die (PLURAL die **Taucherinnen**) ❷ (from a diving board) **Kunstspringer** der (PLURAL die **Kunstspringer**), **Kunstspringerin** die (PLURAL die **Kunstspringerinnen**)

**diversion** NOUN (of traffic) **Umleitung** die (PLURAL die **Umleitungen**)

**divide** VERB **teilen**

**diving** NOUN ❶ (underwater) **Tauchen** das ❷ (from a diving board) **Kunstspringen** das

**diving board** NOUN **Sprungbrett** das (PLURAL die **Sprungbretter**)

**division** NOUN ❶ **Teilung** die (PLURAL die **Teilungen**) ❷ (in maths) **Division** die (PLURAL die **Divisionen**) ❸ (sports league) **Liga** die (PLURAL die **Ligen**)

**divorce** NOUN **Scheidung** die (PLURAL die **Scheidungen**)

**divorce** VERB **sich scheiden lassen**◇; **they divorced in May** sie haben sich im Mai scheiden lassen

**divorced** ADJECTIVE **geschieden**

**DIY** NOUN ❶ **Heimwerken** das ❷ **to do DIY** heimwerken ❸ **DIY shop** der **Baumarkt** (PLURAL die **Baumärkte**)

**dizzy** ADJECTIVE **I feel dizzy** mir ist schwindlig

**DJ** NOUN **DJ** der (PLURAL die **DJs**)

**do** VERB ❶ **tun**◇, **machen**; **what are you doing?** was machst du?, **I'm doing my homework** ich mache meine Hausaufgaben, **what have you done with the hammer?** was hast du mit dem Hammer gemacht?, **can you do me a favour?** kannst du mir einen Gefallen tun?, **do as I say** tu was ich sage ❷ **she's doing the cleaning** sie putzt, **I'll do the washing up** ich wasche ab, **I must do the shopping** ich muss einkaufen gehen ❸ (in questions) **do you like it?** gefällt es dir?, **when does the film start?** wann fängt der Film an?, **how do you open the door?** wie macht man die Tür auf?, **do you know him?** kennst du ihn? ❹ (in negative sentences) **I don't like mushrooms** ich mag keine Pilze, **Rosie doesn't like spinach** Rosie mag keinen Spinat, **you didn't shut the door** du hast die Tür nicht zugemacht, **it doesn't matter** das macht nichts ❺ (when it refers back to another verb, 'do' is not translated) **'do you live here?' – 'yes, I do'** 'wohnst du hier?' – 'ja', **she has more money than I do** sie hat mehr Geld als ich, **'I live in Oxford' – 'so do I'** 'ich wohne in Oxford' – 'ich auch', **'I didn't phone Gemma' – 'neither did I'** 'ich habe Gemma nicht angerufen' – 'ich auch nicht' ❻ **don't you?, doesn't he?** nicht wahr?, **you know Helen, don't you?** du kennst Helen, nicht wahr?, **she left on Thursday, didn't she?** sie ist Donnerstag abgefahren, nicht wahr? ❼ **that'll do** das reicht, **it'll do like that** das geht so
• **to do something up** ❶ **etwas zubinden**◇ (SEP) (shoes) ❷ **etwas zumachen** (SEP) (a cardigan, jacket) ❸ **etwas renovieren** (a house)

- **to do without something** ohne etwas *(ACC)* auskommen◇ *(SEP) (PERF sein)*; **we can do without knives** wir können ohne Messer auskommen

**doctor** *NOUN* Arzt der *(PLURAL die Ärzte)*, Ärztin die *(PLURAL die Ärztinnen)*; **her mother's a doctor** ihre Mutter ist Ärztin

**document** *NOUN* Dokument das *(PLURAL die Dokumente)*

**documentary** *NOUN* Dokumentarfilm der *(PLURAL die Dokumentarfilme)*

**dodgems** *PLURAL NOUN* **the dodgems** Autoskooter der *(PLURAL die Autoskooter)*

**dog** *NOUN* Hund der *(PLURAL die Hunde)*

**do-it-yourself** *NOUN* Heimwerken das

**dole** *NOUN* Arbeitslosgeld das; **to be on the dole** arbeitslos sein

**doll** *NOUN* Puppe die *(PLURAL die Puppen)*

**dollar** *NOUN* Dollar der *(PLURAL die Dollars)*

**dolphin** *NOUN* Delfin der *(PLURAL die Delfine)*

**domino** *NOUN* **❶** Dominostein der *(PLURAL die Dominosteine)* **❷** *(game)* **dominoes** Domino das, **to play dominoes** Domino spielen

**donkey** *NOUN* Esel der *(PLURAL die Esel)*

**don't** ▸ SEE do

**door** *NOUN* Tür die *(PLURAL die Türen)*; **to open the door** die Tür aufmachen, **to shut the door** die Tür zumachen

**doorbell** *NOUN* Türklingel die *(PLURAL die Türklingeln)*; **to ring the doorbell** klingeln

**dot** *NOUN* **❶** Punkt der *(PLURAL die Punkte)*; **at ten on the dot** Punkt zehn Uhr **❷** *(small dot on fabric)* Pünktchen das *(PLURAL die Pünktchen)*

**double** *ADJECTIVE, ADVERB* **❶** doppelt; **a double helping** eine doppelte Portion, **double the size** doppelt so groß, **double the time** doppelt so viel Zeit, **at double the price** zum doppelten Preis **❷** **double room** das Doppelzimmer **❸** **double bed** das Doppelbett

**double bass** *NOUN* Kontrabass der *(PLURAL die Kontrabässe)*

**double-decker bus** *NOUN* Doppeldeckerbus der *(PLURAL die Doppeldeckerbusse)*

**doubles** *NOUN* *(in tennis)* Doppel das *(PLURAL die Doppel)*

**doubt** *NOUN* Zweifel der *(PLURAL die Zweifel)*; **there's no doubt about it** es besteht kein Zweifel daran, **I have my doubts** ich habe gewisse Zweifel

**doubt** *VERB* **to doubt something** etwas bezweifeln, **I doubt it** das bezweifle ich, **I doubt that ...** ich bezweifle, dass ..., **I doubt they'll buy it** ich bezweifle, dass sie es kaufen

**doubtful** *ADJECTIVE* **❶** fraglich; **it's doubtful** es ist fraglich **❷** **to be doubtful about doing something** Bedenken haben, ob man etwas tun soll, **I'm doubtful about inviting them together** ich habe Bedenken, ob ich sie zusammen einladen soll

**dough** *NOUN* Teig der

**doughnut** NOUN Krapfen der (PLURAL die **Krapfen**)

**down** ADVERB, PREPOSITION ❶ unten; he's down in the cellar er ist unten im Keller, it's down there es ist da unten ❷ down the road (nearby) in der Nähe, there's a chemist's just down the road da ist eine Apotheke ganz in der Nähe ❸ to go down nach unten gehen, I went down to open the door ich ging nach unten, um die Tür aufzumachen, to walk down the street die Straße entlanggehen◇ (SEP) (PERF sein), to run down the stairs die Treppe runterrennen (SEP) (PERF sein) (informal) ❹ to come down herunterkommen◇ (SEP) (PERF sein), she came down into the kitchen sie kam in die Küche herunter ❺ to sit down sich setzen, she sat down on the chair sie setzte sich auf den Stuhl ❻ to write something down etwas aufschreiben◇ (SEP)

**download** VERB herunterladen, downloaden

**downstairs** ADVERB ❶ unten; she's downstairs sie ist unten ❷ (with movement) nach unten; to go downstairs nach unten gehen ❸ im Erdgeschoss; the flat downstairs die Wohnung im Erdgeschoss

**doze** VERB dösen

**dozen** NOUN Dutzend das (PLURAL die **Dutzende**)

**drag** NOUN ❶ what a drag! so'n Mist! (informal) ❷ what a drag she is! Mann, ist die langweilig! (informal)

**drag** VERB schleppen

**dragon** NOUN Drache der (PLURAL die **Drachen**)

**drain** NOUN ❶ (outlet pipe) Abflussrohr das (PLURAL die **Abflussrohre**) ❷ the drains Kanalisation die (PLURAL die **Kanalisationen**)

**drain** VERB abgießen◇ (SEP) (vegetables), trockenlegen (SEP) (fields, land)

**drama** NOUN ❶ (play) Drama das (PLURAL die **Dramen**); he made a big drama out of it er hat ein großes Drama daraus gemacht (informal) ❷ (dramatic nature) Dramatik die

**dramatic** ADJECTIVE dramatisch

**draught** NOUN Luftzug der; there's a draught in here hier zieht es

**draughts** NOUN Damespiel das; to play draughts Dame spielen

**draw** NOUN ❶ (in a match) Unentschieden das; to end in a draw mit einem Unentschieden enden ❷ (lottery) Ziehung die (PLURAL die **Ziehungen**)

**draw** VERB ❶ zeichnen; she can draw really well sie kann wirklich sehr gut zeichnen ❷ to draw the curtains (open) die Vorhänge aufziehen◇ (SEP), (close) die Vorhänge zuziehen◇ (SEP) ❸ (in a match) unentschieden spielen; we drew three all wir haben drei zu drei unentschieden gespielt

**drawer** NOUN Schublade die (PLURAL die **Schubladen**)

**drawing** NOUN Zeichnung die (PLURAL die **Zeichnungen**)

**drawing pin** NOUN Reißzwecke die (PLURAL die **Reißzwecken**)

**dreadful** ADJECTIVE furchtbar

**dreadfully** *ADVERB* furchtbar; **I'm dreadfully late** ich habe mich furchtbar verspätet, **I'm dreadfully sorry** es tut mir furchtbar Leid

**dream** *NOUN* Traum der *(PLURAL* die Träume); **to have a dream** einen Traum haben

**dream** *VERB* träumen; **to dream about something** von etwas *(DAT)* träumen

**dress** *NOUN* Kleid das *(PLURAL* die Kleider)

**dress** *VERB* **to dress a child** ein Kind anziehen◇ *(SEP)*
• **to dress up** sich verkleiden; **to dress up as a vampire** sich als Vampir verkleiden

**dressed** *ADJECTIVE* ❶ angezogen; **is Tom dressed yet?** ist Tom schon angezogen? ❷ **she was dressed in black trousers and a yellow shirt** sie trug eine schwarze Hose und ein gelbes Hemd ❸ **to get dressed** sich anziehen◇ *(SEP)*, **I got dressed quickly** ich zog mich schnell an

**dressing gown** *NOUN* Morgenrock der *(PLURAL* die Morgenröcke)

**dressing table** *NOUN* Frisierkommode die *(PLURAL* die Frisierkommoden)

**drier** *NOUN* **hair drier** der Föhn, **tumble drier** der Wäschetrockner

**drill** *NOUN* Bohrer der *(PLURAL* die Bohrer)

**drink** *NOUN* ❶ Getränk das *(PLURAL* die Getränke); **to have a drink** etwas trinken; **would you like a drink of water?** möchtest du etwas Wasser trinken? ❷ *(an alcoholic drink)* Drink der *(PLURAL* die Drinks);

they've invited us round for drinks sie haben uns auf einen Drink eingeladen, **let's have a drink!** trinken wir einen! *(informal)*

**drink** *VERB* trinken◇; **he drank a glass of water** er trank ein Glas Wasser

**drive** *NOUN* ❶ **to go for a drive** eine Autofahrt machen ❷ *(in front of a house)* Einfahrt die *(PLURAL* die Einfahrten)

**drive** *VERB* ❶ fahren◇ *(PERF* sein); **she drives very fast** sie fährt sehr schnell, **to drive a car** Auto fahren, **I'd like to learn to drive** ich möchte Autofahren lernen, **can you drive?** kannst du Auto fahren? ❷ **we drove to Berlin** wir sind mit dem Auto nach Berlin gefahren ❸ **to drive somebody (to a place)** jemanden (irgendwohin) fahren *(PERF* haben), **Mum drove me to the station** Mutti hat mich zum Bahnhof gefahren, **to drive somebody home** jemanden nach Hause fahren
• **she drives me mad!** sie macht mich verrückt!

**driver** *NOUN* ❶ Fahrer der *(PLURAL* die Fahrer), Fahrerin die *(PLURAL* die Fahrerinnen) ❷ *(of a locomotive)* Lokomotivführer der *(PLURAL* die Lokomotivführer), Lokomotivführerin die *(PLURAL* die Lokomotivführerinnen)

**driving instructor** *NOUN* Fahrlehrer der *(PLURAL* die Fahrlehrer), Fahrlehrerin die *(PLURAL* die Fahrlehrerinnen)

**driving lesson** *NOUN* Fahrstunde die *(PLURAL* die Fahrstunden)

**driving licence** *NOUN* Führerschein der *(PLURAL* die Führerscheine)

A B C D E F G H I J K L M N O P Q R S T U V W X Y Z

**driving test** NOUN Fahrprüfung die; **to take your driving test** die Fahrprüfung machen, **Jenny's passed her driving test** Jenny hat die Fahrprüfung bestanden

**drop** NOUN Tropfen der (PLURAL die Tropfen)

**drop** VERB ❶ **to drop something** etwas fallen lassen, **I dropped my glasses** ich habe meine Brille fallen lassen ❷ **drop it!** lass das! ❸ **I'm going to drop history next year** nächstes Jahr lege ich Geschichte ab ❹ absetzen (SEP) (a person); **could you drop me at the station?** könntest du mich am Bahnhof absetzen?

**drought** NOUN Dürre die (PLURAL die Dürren)

**drown** VERB ertrinken◇ (PERF sein); **she drowned in the lake** sie ertrank im See

**drug** NOUN (medicine) Medikament das (PLURAL die Medikamente) ❷ (illegal) **drugs** Drogen (plural)

**drug abuse** NOUN Drogenmissbrauch der

**drug addict** NOUN Drogenabhängige der/die (PLURAL die Drogenabhängigen)

**drug addiction** NOUN Drogenabhängigkeit die

**drum** NOUN ❶ Trommel die (PLURAL die Trommeln) ❷ **drums** das Schlagzeug, **to play drums** Schlagzeug spielen

**drummer** NOUN Schlagzeuger der (PLURAL die Schlagzeuger) Schlagerzeugerin die (PLURAL die Schlagzeugerinnen)

**drunk** NOUN Betrunkene der/die (PLURAL die Betrunkenen)

**drunk** ADJECTIVE betrunken; **to get drunk** sich betrinken◇

**dry** ADJECTIVE trocken

**dry** VERB ❶ trocknen; **to let something dry** etwas trocknen lassen, **to dry your hair** sich (DAT) die Haare trocknen, **to dry the washing** die Wäsche trocknen ❷ **to dry your hands** sich (DAT) die Hände abtrocknen (SEP), **I dried my feet** ich trocknete mir die Füße ab, **to dry the dishes** das Geschirr abtrocknen

**dry cleaner's** NOUN chemische Reinigung die

**dryer** NOUN ▶ SEE drier

**dual carriageway** NOUN zweispurige Straße die (PLURAL die zweispurigen Straßen)

**dubbed** ADJECTIVE **a dubbed film** ein synchronisierter Film

**duck** NOUN Ente die (PLURAL die Enten)

**due** ADJECTIVE, ADVERB ❶ **to be due to do something** etwas tun müssen, **Paul's due back soon** Paul muss bald zurück sein, **we're due to leave on Thursday** wir müssen Donnerstag abfahren ❷ **due to** wegen (+GEN), **due to bad weather** wegen schlechten Wetters

**dull** ADJECTIVE ❶ **dull weather** trübes Wetter, **it's a dull day today** heute ist ein trüber Tag ❷ (boring) langweilig

**dumb** ADJECTIVE ❶ stumm ❷ (stupid) dumm; **he asked some dumb questions** er hat ein paar dumme Fragen gestellt

# dump

**dump** VERB ❶ abladen◇ (SEP) (rubbish) ❷ (put down) hinwerfen◇ (SEP); **he dumped it in the rubbish** er hat es in den Müll geworfen ❸ abschieben◇ (SEP) (a person) (informal); **she's dumped her boyfriend** sie hat ihren Freund abgeschoben

**dungarees** PLURAL NOUN Latzhose die (PLURAL die Latzhosen)

**during** PREPOSITION während (+GEN); **during the night** während der Nacht, **I saw her during the holidays** ich habe sie während der Ferien gesehen

**dusk** NOUN Dämmerung die (PLURAL die Dämmerungen); **at dusk** bei Einbruch der Dunkelheit

**dust** NOUN Staub der

**dust** VERB ❶ abstauben (SEP) (furniture, objects) ❷ (in a room) Staub wischen; **she's dusting** sie wischt Staub

**dustbin** NOUN Mülltonne die (PLURAL die Mülltonnen)

**dustman** NOUN Müllmann der (PLURAL die Müllmänner)

**dusty** ADJECTIVE staubig

**Dutch** NOUN ❶ (language) Holländisch das ❷ the Dutch (people) die Holländer

**Dutch** ADJECTIVE holländisch; **he's Dutch** er ist Holländer, **she's Dutch** sie ist Holländerin

**duty** NOUN ❶ Pflicht die (PLURAL die Pflichten); **to have a duty to do something** die Pflicht haben, etwas zu tun, **you have a duty to inform us** du hast die Pflicht, uns zu benachrichtigen ❷ **to be on**

# dyslexic

**duty** Dienst haben, **to be on night duty** Nachtdienst haben, **I'm off duty tonight** ich habe heute Abend keinen Dienst

**duty-free** ADJECTIVE zollfrei; **duty-free shop** der Dutyfreeshop, **duty-free goods** zollfreie Waren (plural)

**duvet** NOUN Bettdecke die (PLURAL die Bettedecken)

**duvet cover** NOUN Bettbezug der (PLURAL die Bettbezüge)

**dye** NOUN Färbemittel das (PLURAL die Färbemittel)

**dye** VERB färben; **to dye your hair** sich die Haare färben, **I'm going to dye my hair black** ich werde mir die Haare schwarz färben, **I'm going to have my hair dyed pink** ich lasse mir die Haare rosa färben

**dynamic** ADJECTIVE dynamisch

**dyslexia** NOUN Legasthenie die

**dyslexic** ADJECTIVE legasthenisch; **to be dyslexic** Legastheniker sein, Legasthenikerin sein

# Ee

**each** ADJECTIVE, PRONOUN ❶ jeder/
jede/jedes; **each Sunday** jeden
Sonntag, **each time** jedes Mal, **at
the beginning of each year** am
Anfang jedes Jahres, **we each have
an invitation** jeder von uns hat eine
Einladung, **my sisters each have a
computer** jede meiner Schwestern
hat einen Computer, **she gave us an
apple each** sie hat jedem von uns
einen Apfel gegeben, **each of you**
jeder von euch/jede von euch, **we
each got a present** jeder Einzelne
hat ein Geschenk bekommen ❷ **the
tickets cost ten pounds each** die
Karten kosten je zehn Pfund, £5 each
*(per person)* fünf Pfund pro Person,
*(per item)* fünf Pfund pro Stück

**each other** PRONOUN *('each other' is
usually translated using a reflexive
pronoun)* **they love each other** sie
lieben sich, **we know each other** wir
kennen uns, **do you see each other
often?** seht ihr euch oft?

**eagle** NOUN **Adler** der *(PLURAL* die **Adler)**

**ear** NOUN **Ohr** das *(PLURAL* die **Ohren)**

**earache** NOUN **to have earache**
Ohrenschmerzen haben

**earlier** ADVERB ❶ *(a while ago)* **vor
kurzem**; **your brother phoned
earlier** dein Bruder hat vor kurzem
angerufen ❷ *(not as late)* **früher**;
**we should have started earlier** wir
hätten früher anfangen sollen

**early** ADVERB ❶ *(in the morning)* **früh**;
**to get up early** früh aufstehen, **it's
too early** es ist zu früh ❷ *(for an
appointment)* **to be early** (zu) früh
dran sein, **we're early, the train
doesn't leave until ten** wir sind früh
dran, der Zug fährt erst um zehn
Uhr ab

**early** ADJECTIVE ❶ *(one of the first)*
**in the early months** während der
ersten Monate, **I'm getting the
early train** ich nehme den früheren
Zug ❷ **to have an early lunch** früh
zu Mittag essen, **Jan's having an
early night** Jan geht früh zu Bett
❸ **in the early afternoon** am frühen
Nachmittag, **in the early hours** in
den frühen Morgenstunden

**earn** VERB **verdienen**; **Richard earns
five pounds an hour** Richard
verdient fünf Pfund die Stunde

**earphone** NOUN **Ohrhörer** der
*(PLURAL* die **Ohrhörer)**

**earring** NOUN **Ohrring** der *(PLURAL* die
**Ohrringe)**

**earth** NOUN **Erde** die; **life on earth** das
Leben auf der Erde
• **what on earth are you doing?** was
in aller Welt machst du da?

**earthquake** NOUN **Erdbeben** das
*(PLURAL* die **Erdbeben)**

**easily** ADVERB **leicht**; **he's easily the
best** er ist mit Abstand der Beste

**east** NOUN **Osten** der; **in the east** im
Osten

**east** ADJECTIVE, ADVERB **östlich, Ost-**; **the
east side** die Ostseite, **an east wind**
ein Ostwind, **east of Munich** östlich
von München

**Easter** NOUN Ostern das (PLURAL die Ostern); **they're coming at Easter** sie kommen zu Ostern, **Happy Easter** Frohe Ostern

**Easter bunny** NOUN Osterhase die

**Easter Day** NOUN Ostersonntag der (PLURAL die Ostersonntage)

**Easter egg** NOUN Osterei das (PLURAL die Ostereier)

**Eastern Europe** NOUN Osteuropa das

**easy** ADJECTIVE leicht; **it's easy!** das ist leicht!, **it was easy to decide** die Entscheidung fiel uns leicht

**eat** VERB ❶ essen◇; **he was eating a banana** er aß eine Banane, **we're going to have something to eat** wir essen jetzt etwas ❷ **to eat your breakfast** frühstücken

**EC** NOUN EG die (Europäische Gemeinschaft)

**echo** NOUN Echo das (PLURAL die Echos)

**echo** VERB wiederholen

**ecological** ADJECTIVE ökologisch

**ecology** NOUN Ökologie die

**economical** ADJECTIVE sparsam

**economics** NOUN Wirtschaftswissenschaften (plural)

**economy** NOUN Wirtschaft die

**edge** NOUN ❶ Kante die (PLURAL die Kanten); **the edge of the table** die Tischkante ❷ (of a road, sheet of paper, or cliff) Rand der (PLURAL die Ränder); **at the edge of the forest** am Waldrand

**edible** ADJECTIVE essbar

**edit** VERB redigieren

**editor** NOUN ❶ (of a newspaper or magazine) Chefredakteur der (PLURAL die Chefredakteure), Chefredakteurin die (PLURAL die Chefredakteurinnen) ❷ (of a book) Redakteur der (PLURAL die Redakteure), Redakteurin die (PLURAL die Redakteurinnen)

**educate** VERB erziehen◇

**education** NOUN Ausbildung die

**effect** NOUN ❶ Wirkung die (PLURAL die Wirkungen); **the effect of the explosion was horrific** die Wirkung der Explosion war entsetzlich ❷ **to have an effect on something** eine Auswirkung auf etwas (ACC) haben, **it had a good effect on the whole family** es hatte eine gute Auswirkung auf die ganze Familie ❸ (in a film) Effekt der (PLURAL die Effekte); **special effects** die Specialeffekte

**effective** ADJECTIVE effektiv

**efficient** ADJECTIVE ❶ (person) tüchtig ❷ (machine or organization) leistungsfähig

**effort** NOUN ❶ Mühe die (PLURAL die Mühen) ❷ **to make an effort** sich bemühen, **Toya made an effort to help us** Toya hat sich bemüht, uns zu helfen, **he didn't even make the effort to apologize** er hat sich nicht einmal die Mühe gemacht, sich zu entschuldigen

**e.g.** ABBREVIATION z.B. (short for zum Beispiel)

**egg** NOUN Ei das (PLURAL die Eier); **a fried egg** ein Spiegelei, **a hard-boiled egg** ein hart gekochtes Ei

**egg-cup** NOUN **Eierbecher** der (PLURAL die **Eierbecher**)

**eggshell** NOUN **Eierschale** die (PLURAL die **Eierschalen**)

**egg-white** NOUN **Eiweiß** das (PLURAL die **Eiweiße**)

**egg-yolk** NOUN **Eigelb** das (PLURAL die **Eigelbe**)

**eight** NUMBER **acht**; **Maya's eight** Maya ist acht, **at eight o'clock** um acht Uhr

**eighteen** NUMBER **achtzehn**; **Jason's eighteen** Jason ist achtzehn

**eighth** NUMBER **achter/achte/achtes**; **on the eighth of July** am achten Juli

**eighty** NUMBER **achtzig**; **eighty-five** fünfundachtzig

**either** PRONOUN ❶ (one or the other) **einer von beiden/eine von beiden/eins von beiden**; **take either (of them)** nimm einen von beiden/eine von beiden/eins von beiden, **I don't like either (of them)** ich mag keinen von beiden/keine von beiden/keins von beiden ❷ (both) **beide** (plural); **either is possible** beide sind möglich, **on either side** auf beiden Seiten

**either** CONJUNCTION ❶ **either ... or** entweder ... oder, **either Susie or Judy** entweder Susie oder Judy ❷ (with a negative) **either ... or** weder ... noch, **he didn't ring either Sam or Emma** er hat weder Sam noch Emma angerufen ❸ **I don't know them either** ich kenne sie auch nicht

**elastic** NOUN **Gummiband** das (PLURAL die **Gummibänder**)

**elastic band** NOUN **Gummiband** das (PLURAL die **Gummibänder**)

**elbow** NOUN **Ellbogen** der (PLURAL die **Ellbogen**)

**elder** ADJECTIVE **älterer/ältere/älteres**; **her elder brother** ihr älterer Bruder

**elderly** ADJECTIVE **alt**; **the elderly** ältere Menschen (plural)

**eldest** ADJECTIVE **ältester/älteste/ältestes**; **her eldest brother** ihr ältester Bruder

**elect** VERB **wählen**; **she has been elected** sie ist gewählt worden

**election** NOUN **Wahl** die (PLURAL die **Wahlen**); **in the election** bei den Wahlen, **to call an election** allgemeine Wahlen ausrufen (SEP)

**electric** ADJECTIVE **elektrisch**

**electrical** ADJECTIVE **elektrisch**, **Elektro-**; **electrical equipment** Elektrogeräte (plural)

**electrician** NOUN **Elektriker** der (PLURAL die **Elektriker**), **Elektrikerin** die (PLURAL die **Elektrikerinnen**)

**electricity** NOUN **Strom** der

**electronic** ADJECTIVE **elektronisch**

**electronics** NOUN **Elektronik** die

**elegant** ADJECTIVE **elegant**

**elephant** NOUN **Elefant** der (PLURAL die **Elefanten**)

**eleven** NUMBER **elf**; **Josh is eleven** Josh ist elf, **at eleven o'clock** um elf Uhr, **a football eleven** eine Fußballelf

**eleventh** NUMBER **elfter/elfte/elftes**; **the eleventh of September** der elfte September, **on the eleventh floor** im elften Stock

a
b
c
d
e
f
g
h
i
j
k
l
m
n
o
p
q
r
s
t
u
v
w
x
y
z

**else** ADVERB ❶ (in addition) sonst; **who else?** wer sonst?, **did you see anyone else?** hast du sonst noch jemanden gesehen?, **nothing else** sonst nichts, **I don't want anything else** ich will sonst nichts ❷ **would you like something else?** möchten Sie sonst noch etwas? ❸ (instead or different) anderer/ andere/anderes; **somewhere else** irgendwo anders, **everyone else** alle anderen, **somebody else** jemand anders, **something else** etwas anderes ❹ **or else** sonst, **hurry up, or else we'll be late** beeil dich, sonst kommen wir zu spät

**email** NOUN E-Mail die (PLURAL die E-Mails)

**email** VERB mailen

**embarrassed** ADJECTIVE verlegen; **he was very embarrassed** er war ganz verlegen

**embarrassing** ADJECTIVE peinlich

**embassy** NOUN Botschaft die (PLURAL die Botschaften); **the German Embassy** die Deutsche Botschaft

**emergency** NOUN Notfall der (PLURAL die Notfälle)

**emergency exit** NOUN Notausgang der (PLURAL die Notausgänge)

**emotion** NOUN Gefühl das (PLURAL die Gefühle)

**emotional** ADJECTIVE ❶ (person) emotional ❷ (speech or occasion) emotionsgeladen

**emperor** NOUN Kaiser der (PLURAL die Kaiser)

**emphasize** VERB betonen; **he emphasized that it was voluntary** er betonte, dass es freiwillig war

**empire** NOUN Reich das (PLURAL die Reiche); **the Roman Empire** das Römische Reich

**employ** VERB ❶ (have working for you) beschäftigen ❷ (take on a worker) einstellen (SEP)

**employee** NOUN Angestellte der/die (PLURAL die Angestellten)

**employer** NOUN Arbeitgeber der (PLURAL die Arbeitgeber), Arbeitgeberin die (PLURAL die Arbeitgeberinnen)

**employment** NOUN Arbeit die

**empty** ADJECTIVE leer; **an empty bottle** eine leere Flasche

**empty** VERB ❶ (empty out) ausleeren (SEP) ❷ (pour) schütten

**enclose** VERB (in a letter) beilegen (SEP); **please find enclosed a cheque** ein Scheck liegt bei

**encourage** VERB ermutigen; **to encourage somebody to do something** jemanden (dazu) ermutigen, etwas zu tun, **Mum encouraged me to try again** Mutti hat mich dazu ermutigt, es noch einmal zu versuchen

**encouragement** NOUN Ermutigung die (PLURAL die Ermutigungen)

**encouraging** ADJECTIVE ermutigend

**encyclopedia** NOUN Lexikon das (PLURAL die Lexika)

**end** NOUN ❶ Ende das (PLURAL die Enden); **'The End'** 'Ende', **at the end of the film** am Ende des Films, **by the end of the lesson** als die Stunde zu Ende war, **in the end I went home** schließlich bin ich nach Hause gegangen, **Sally's coming at**

**the end of June** Sally kommt Ende Juni, **I read to the end of the page** ich habe die Seite zu Ende gelesen, **hold the other end** halte das andere Ende fest, **at the end of the street** am Ende der Straße ❷ *(in sports)* Spielfeldhälfte die *(PLURAL die Spielfeldhälften)*; **to change ends** die Seiten wechseln

**end** VERB ❶ *(to put an end to)* beenden; **they've ended the strike** sie haben den Streik beendet ❷ *(to come to an end)* enden; **the day ended with a meal** der Tag endete mit einem Essen

• **to end up** ❶ **to end up doing something** am Ende etwas tun, **we ended up taking a taxi** am Ende haben wir ein Taxi genommen ❷ **to end up somewhere** irgendwo landen *(PERF sein) (informal)*, **Rob ended up in Berlin** Rob landete schließlich in Berlin

**endangered** ADJECTIVE gefährdet; **an endangered species** eine von Aussterben bedrohte Art

**ending** NOUN ❶ Ende das *(PLURAL die Enden)* ❷ *(in grammar)* Endung die *(PLURAL die Endungen)*

**endless** ADJECTIVE endlos *(day or journey, for example)*

**enemy** NOUN Feind der *(PLURAL die Feinde)*; **to make enemies** sich *(DAT)* Feinde machen

**energetic** ADJECTIVE energiegeladen

**energy** NOUN Energie die

**engaged** ADJECTIVE ❶ *(to be married)* verlobt; **they're engaged** sie sind verlobt, **to get engaged** sich verloben ❷ *(a phone or toilet)* besetzt; **it's engaged, I'll ring later** es ist besetzt, ich rufe später an

**engagement** NOUN *(to marry)* Verlobung die *(PLURAL die Verlobungen)*

**engagement ring** NOUN Verlobungsring der *(PLURAL die Verlobungsringe)*

**engine** NOUN ❶ *(in a car)* Motor der *(PLURAL die Motoren)* ❷ *(pulling a train)* Lokomotive die *(PLURAL die Lokomotiven)*

**engineer** NOUN ❶ *(who comes for repairs)* Techniker der *(PLURAL die Techniker)*, Technikerin die *(PLURAL die Technikerinnen)* ❷ *(who builds roads and bridges)* Ingenieur der *(PLURAL die Ingenieure)*, Ingenieurin die *(PLURAL die Ingenieurinnen)*

**England** NOUN England das; **I'm from England** ich bin Engländer, ich bin Engländerin

**English** NOUN ❶ *(the language)* Englisch das; **do you speak English?** sprechen Sie Englisch?, **he answered in English** er hat auf Englisch geantwortet ❷ *(the people)* the English die Engländer

**English** ADJECTIVE ❶ *(of or from England)* englisch; **the English team** die englische Mannschaft, **he's English** er ist Engländer, **she's English** sie ist Engländerin ❷ **an English lesson** eine Englischstunde, **our English teacher** unser Englischlehrer, unsere Englischlehrerin

**English Channel** NOUN the English Channel der Ärmelkanal

**Englishman** NOUN Engländer der *(PLURAL die Engländer)*

**Englishwoman** NOUN Engländerin die *(PLURAL die Engländerinnen)*

**enjoy** ... **environment-friendly**

**enjoy** VERB ❶ did you enjoy the party? hat dir die Party gefallen?, we really enjoyed the concert das Konzert hat uns wirklich gut gefallen ❷ to enjoy doing something etwas gerne tun◇, I enjoy reading ich lese gerne, do you enjoy living in York? wohnst du gerne in York? ❸ to enjoy oneself sich gut amüsieren, we really enjoyed ourselves wir haben uns richtig gut amüsiert, enjoy yourselves! viel Vergnügen!, did you enjoy yourself? hast du dich gut amüsiert?

**enjoyable** ADJECTIVE nett

**enormous** ADJECTIVE riesig

**enough** ADVERB, ADJECTIVE, PRONOUN ❶ genug; there's enough for everyone es gibt genug für alle, big enough groß genug, have we got enough bread? haben wir genug Brot? ❷ that's enough das reicht

**enquire** VERB to enquire about sich erkundigen nach (+DAT); I'm going to enquire about the trains ich werde mich nach den Zügen erkundigen

**enrol** VERB sich anmelden (SEP); I want to enrol on the course ich möchte mich zu dem Kurs anmelden

**enter** VERB ❶ (to go inside) gehen◇ (PERF sein) in (+ACC), (a room or a building); we all entered the church wir gingen alle in die Kirche hinein ❷ (in computing) eingeben◇ (SEP) ❸ to enter for sich anmelden zu (+DAT), (an exam or a race), to enter for a competition an einem Preisausschreiben teilnehmen◇ (SEP)

**entertain** VERB ❶ (to keep amused) unterhalten◇ ❷ (to have people round) Gäste haben◇; they don't entertain much sie haben selten Gäste

**entertainment** NOUN (fun) Unterhaltung die; there wasn't much entertainment in the evenings abends war wenig Unterhaltung geboten

**enthusiasm** NOUN Begeisterung die

**enthusiast** NOUN ❶ Enthusiast der (PLURAL die Enthusiasten), Enthusiastin die (PLURAL die Enthusiastinnen) ❷ (for sports) Fan der (PLURAL die Fans); he's a rugby enthusiast er ist ein Rugbyfan

**enthusiastic** ADJECTIVE begeistert

**entire** ADJECTIVE ganz; the entire class die ganze Klasse

**entirely** ADVERB ganz

**entrance** NOUN ❶ (fee) Eintritt der ❷ (way in) Eingang der (PLURAL die Eingänge)

**entry** NOUN ❶ (way in) Eingang der (PLURAL die Eingänge), (for cars) Einfahrt die (PLURAL die Einfahrten) ❷ 'no entry' 'Zutritt verboten', (to cars) 'Einfahrt verboten'

**entry phone** NOUN Sprechanlage die (PLURAL die Sprechanlagen)

**envelope** NOUN Briefumschlag der (PLURAL die Briefumschläge)

**environment** NOUN Umwelt die

**environmental** ADJECTIVE Umwelt-; environmental pollution die Umweltverschmutzung

**environment-friendly** ADJECTIVE umweltfreundlich

**epidemic** NOUN Epidemie die (PLURAL die **Epidemien**)

**epileptic** ADJECTIVE epileptisch

**episode** NOUN ❶ (an event) Episode die (PLURAL die **Episoden**) ❷ (on TV or radio) Folge die (PLURAL die **Folgen**)

**equal** ADJECTIVE gleich; **milk and water in equal quantities** gleich viel Milch und Wasser

**equal** VERB gleichen◇ (+DAT)

**equality** NOUN Gleichberechtigung die

**equalize** VERB ausgleichen◇ (SEP); **they equalized in the last minute** sie haben in der letzten Minute ausgeglichen

**equally** ADVERB (to share) gleichmäßig; **we divided it equally** wir haben es gleichmäßig verteilt

**equator** NOUN Äquator der

**equip** VERB ausrüsten (SEP); **well equipped for the hike** für die Wanderung gut ausgerüstet, **equipped with rucksacks** mit Rucksäcken ausgerüstet

**equipment** NOUN ❶ (for sport) Ausrüstung die (PLURAL die **Ausrüstungen**) ❷ Ausstattung die (PLURAL die **Ausstattungen**); **laboratory equipment** die Laborausstattung ❸ (something needed for an activity) Geräte (plural); **recording equipment** Aufnahmegeräte

**equivalent** ADJECTIVE gleichwertig; **to be equivalent to** etwas (DAT) entsprechen, **1 litre is equivalent to about 1.75 pints** ein Liter entspricht ungefähr 1,75 Pints

**error** NOUN ❶ (in spelling, typing, on a computer, or in maths) Fehler der (PLURAL die **Fehler**); **spelling error** der Rechtschreibfehler ❷ (wrong opinion) Irrtum der (PLURAL die **Irrtümer**)

**error message** NOUN Fehlermeldung die (PLURAL die **Fehlermeldungen**)

**escalator** NOUN Rolltreppe die (PLURAL die **Rolltreppen**)

**escape** NOUN (from prison) Ausbruch der (PLURAL die **Ausbrüche**)

**escape** VERB ❶ (from prison) ausbrechen◇ (SEP) (PERF sein) ❷ entkommen◇ (PERF sein); **to escape from somebody** jemandem entkommen

**especially** ADVERB besonders

**essay** NOUN Aufsatz der (PLURAL die **Aufsätze**); **an essay on German reunification** ein Aufsatz über die deutsche Wiedervereinigung

**essential** ADJECTIVE unbedingt erforderlich; **it's essential to reply quickly** es ist unbedingt erforderlich, sofort zu antworten

**estate** NOUN ❶ (a housing estate) Wohnsiedlung die (PLURAL die **Wohnsiedlungen**) ❷ (a big house and grounds) Landsitz der (PLURAL die **Landsitze**)

**estate agent** NOUN Immobilienmakler der (PLURAL die **Immobilienmakler**), Immobilienmaklerin die (PLURAL die **Immobilienmaklerinnen**)

**estate car** NOUN Kombiwagen der (PLURAL die **Kombiwagen**)

413

**estimate** NOUN ❶ (a quote for work) Kostenvoranschlag der (PLURAL die Kostenvoranschläge) ❷ (a rough guess) Schätzung die (PLURAL die Schätzungen)

**estimate** VERB schätzen

**etc.** ABBREVIATION usw. (short for und so weiter)

**ethnic** ADJECTIVE ethnisch; **an ethnic minority** eine ethnische Minderheit

**EU** NOUN EU die (Europäische Union)

**euro** NOUN Euro der (PLURAL die Euros); **the euro is divided into 100 cents** ein Euro hat 100 Cent

**Europe** NOUN Europa das

**European** NOUN Europäer der (PLURAL die Europäer), Europäerin die (PLURAL die Europäerinnen)

**European** ADJECTIVE europäisch

**European Union** NOUN Europäische Union die

**eurozone** NOUN Euroland das

**even¹** ADVERB ❶ sogar; **even Lisa is coming** sogar Lisa kommt ❷ **not even** nicht einmal, **I don't like animals, not even dogs** ich mag keine Tiere, nicht einmal Hunde ❸ **without even asking** ohne wenigstens zu fragen ❹ **even if** selbst wenn, **even if they arrive late** selbst wenn sie spät ankommen ❺ (with a comparison) (sogar) noch; **even bigger** sogar noch größer, **even faster** noch schneller, **even better than** sogar noch besser als, **the song is even better than their last one** das Lied ist sogar noch besser als ihr letztes ❻ **even so** trotzdem, **even so, we had a good time** trotzdem haben wir uns gut amüsiert

**even²** ADJECTIVE ❶ (surface or layer) eben ❷ (number) gerade; **six is an even number** sechs ist eine gerade Zahl ❸ (equal) gleich (distance, value); **the score is even** die Punktzahl ist gleich ❹ **to get even with somebody** es jemandem heimzahlen

**evening** NOUN ❶ Abend der (PLURAL die Abende); **in the evening** am Abend, **this evening** heute Abend, **tomorrow evening** morgen Abend, **on Monday evening** am Montagabend, **every Thursday evening** jeden Donnerstagabend, **the evening before** am Abend zuvor, **the evening meal** das Abendessen ❷ **at six o'clock in the evening** um sechs Uhr abends, **the other evening** neulich abends, **I work in the evening(s)** ich arbeite abends

**evening class** NOUN Abendkurs der (PLURAL die Abendkurse)

**event** NOUN ❶ (a happening) Ereignis das (PLURAL die Ereignisse) ❷ (in athletics) Disziplin die (PLURAL die Disziplinen)

**eventually** ADVERB schließlich

**ever** ADVERB ❶ (at any time) je; **have you ever noticed that?** hast du das je bemerkt?, **more than ever** mehr denn je, **colder than ever** kälter denn je, **he drove more slowly than ever** er fuhr langsamer als je zuvor ❷ **not ever** nie, **nobody ever came** es kam nie jemand, **hardly ever** fast nie ❸ (always) immer; **as cheerful as ever** so vergnügt wie immer, **the same as ever** so wie immer ❹ **ever since** seitdem, **and it's been raining ever since** und seitdem regnet es

**every** *ADJECTIVE* ❶ jeder/jede/jedes; **every house has a garden** jedes Haus hat einen Garten, **every day** jeden Tag, **every Monday** jeden Montag, **every time** jedes Mal ❷ **every few days** alle paar Tage, **every ten kilometres** alle zehn Kilometer ❸ **every one** jeder Einzelne/jede Einzelne/jedes Einzelne, **I've seen every one of his films** ich habe jeden Einzelnen seiner Filme gesehen ❹ **every now and then** ab und zu

**everybody**, **everyone** *PRONOUN* ❶ alle *(plural)*; **everybody knows that ...** alle wissen, dass ..., **everyone else** alle anderen ❷ *(each one)* jeder; **not everybody can afford it** das kann sich nicht jeder leisten

**everything** *PRONOUN* alles; **everything is ready** es ist alles fertig, **everything's fine** es ist alles okay *(informal)*, **everything else** alles andere, **he gets everything he wants** er bekommt alles, was er will

**everywhere** *ADVERB* ❶ überall; **there was dirt everywhere** überall war Dreck, **she went everywhere** sie ist überall hingegangen, **everywhere else** sonst überall ❷ **everywhere she went** wohin sie auch ging

**evidently** *ADVERB* offensichtlich

**evil** *NOUN* Böse das

**evil** *ADJECTIVE* böse

**exact** *ADJECTIVE* genau; **the exact fare** das genaue Fahrgeld, **it's the exact opposite** das ist das genaue Gegenteil

**exactly** *ADVERB* genau; **they're exactly the right age** sie sind genau im richtigen Alter, **yes, exactly!** ja, genau!

**exaggerate** *VERB* übertreiben◇

**exaggeration** *NOUN* Übertreibung die *(PLURAL* die **Übertreibungen)**

**exam** *NOUN* Prüfung die *(PLURAL* die **Prüfungen)**; **history exam** die Geschichtsprüfung, **to sit an exam** eine Prüfung machen, **to pass an exam** eine Prüfung bestehen, **to fail an exam** durch eine Prüfung fallen

**examination** *NOUN* Prüfung die *(PLURAL* die **Prüfungen)**

**examine** *VERB* ❶ *(at school or university)* prüfen ❷ *(at the doctor's)* untersuchen

**examiner** *NOUN* Prüfer der *(PLURAL* die **Prüfer)**, Prüferin die *(PLURAL* die **Prüferinnen)**

**example** *NOUN* Beispiel das *(PLURAL* die **Beispiele)**; **for example** zum Beispiel, **to set a good example** ein gutes Beispiel geben

**excellent** *ADJECTIVE* ausgezeichnet

**except** *PREPOSITION* ❶ außer *(+DAT)*; **every day except Tuesday** täglich außer Dienstag, **we play except when it rains** wir spielen, außer wenn es regnet, **except in March** außer März ❷ **except for** außer *(+DAT)*, **except for the children** außer den Kindern

**exception** *NOUN* Ausnahme die *(PLURAL* die **Ausnahmen)**; **without exception** ohne Ausnahme, **with the exception of** mit Ausnahme von *(+DAT)*

**exchange** NOUN ❶ Austausch der; **the students are coming to London on an exchange** die Schüler kommen auf einen Schüleraustausch nach London, **exchange student** der Austauschstudent, die Austauschstudentin, **an exchange of pupils** ein Schüleraustausch ❷ **in exchange for his help** für seine Hilfe

**exchange** VERB umtauschen (SEP); **can I exchange this shirt for a smaller one?** kann ich dieses Hemd gegen ein kleineres umtauschen?

**exchange rate** NOUN Wechselkurs der (PLURAL die Wechselkurse)

**excite** VERB ❶ (thrill) begeistern ❷ (agitate) aufregen (SEP)

**excited** ADJECTIVE ❶ aufgeregt; **the children are excited** die Kinder sind aufgeregt, **the dogs get excited when they hear the car** die Hunde geraten in Aufregung, wenn sie das Auto hören ❷ (annoyed or angry) **to get excited** sich aufregen (SEP)

**exciting** ADJECTIVE aufregend; **a very exciting film** ein sehr aufregender Film

**exclamation mark** NOUN Ausrufezeichen das (PLURAL die Ausrufezeichen)

**excursion** NOUN Ausflug der (PLURAL die Ausflüge)

**excuse** NOUN Entschuldigung die (PLURAL die Entschuldigungen)

**excuse** VERB (apologizing) **excuse me!** Entschuldigung!

**exercise** NOUN ❶ Übung die (PLURAL die Übungen); **a maths exercise** eine Matheübung ❷ physical

exercise körperliche Bewegung, **to get exercise** sich Bewegung verschaffen

**exercise bike** NOUN Heimtrainer der (PLURAL die Heimtrainer)

**exercise book** NOUN Heft das (PLURAL die Hefte); **my German exercise book** mein Deutschheft

**exhaust (pipe)** NOUN Auspuff der (PLURAL die Auspuffe)

**exhausted** ADJECTIVE erschöpft

**exhaust fumes** NOUN Abgase die (plural)

**exhibition** NOUN Ausstellung die (PLURAL die Ausstellungen); **the Dürer exhibition** die Dürer-Ausstellung

**exist** VERB existieren

**exit** NOUN ❶ Ausgang der (PLURAL die Ausgänge) ❷ (from a motorway) Ausfahrt die (PLURAL die Ausfahrten)

**expect** VERB ❶ erwarten (guests or a baby); **we're expecting thirty visitors** wir erwarten dreißig Besucher ❷ (require something) **to expect somebody to do something** von jemandem erwarten, dass er etwas tut ❸ rechnen mit (+DAT), (something to happen); **I didn't expect that** damit habe ich nicht gerechnet, **I didn't expect it at all** damit habe ich überhaupt nicht gerechnet ❹ (suppose) glauben; **I expect she'll bring her boyfriend** ich glaube, sie bringt ihren Freund mit, **yes, I expect so** ich glaube ja

**expedition** NOUN Expedition die (PLURAL die Expeditionen)

**expel** VERB **to be expelled** (from school) von der Schule verwiesen werden

**expensive** ADJECTIVE **teuer**; **those shoes are too expensive for me** diese Schuhe sind mir zu teuer, **the most expensive CDs** die teuersten CDs

**experience** NOUN ❶ **Erfahrung** die (PLURAL die **Erfahrungen**) ❷ (an event) **Erlebnis** das (PLURAL die **Erlebnisse**)

**experienced** ADJECTIVE **erfahren**

**experiment** NOUN **Experiment** das (PLURAL die **Experimente**); **to do an experiment** ein Experiment machen

**expert** NOUN **Experte** der (PLURAL die **Experten**), **Expertin** die (PLURAL die **Expertinnen**); **he's a computer expert** er ist ein Computerexperte

**expire** VERB **ablaufen**◇ (SEP) (PERF **sein**)

**expiry date** NOUN **Verfallsdatum** das (PLURAL die **Verfallsdaten**)

**explain** VERB **erklären**

**explanation** NOUN **Erklärung** die (PLURAL die **Erklärungen**)

**explode** VERB **explodieren** (PERF **sein**)

**explore** VERB **erforschen**

**explosion** NOUN **Explosion** die (PLURAL die **Explosionen**)

**export** NOUN **Export** der (PLURAL die **Exporte**); **the chief export is wool** das wichtigste Exportgut ist Wolle

**export** VERB **exportieren**; **Russia exports a lot of oil and timber** Russland exportiert viel Öl und Holz

**exposure** NOUN (of a film) **Belichtung** die; **a 24-exposure film** ein Film mit 24 Aufnahmen

**express** NOUN (train) **Schnellzug** der (PLURAL die **Schnellzüge**)

**express** VERB ❶ **ausdrücken** (SEP) ❷ **to express yourself** sich ausdrücken

**expression** NOUN **Ausdruck** der (PLURAL die **Ausdrücke**)

**extend** VERB ❶ **verlängern** ❷ **ausbauen** (SEP) (a house)

**extension** NOUN ❶ (to a house) **Anbau** der (PLURAL die **Anbauten**) ❷ (telephone) **Apparat** der (PLURAL die **Apparate**); **can I have extension 2347 please?** bitte verbinden Sie mich mit Apparat 2347 (note that in spoken German telephone numbers are usually broken down into groups of two figures) ❸ (electrical) **Verlängerung** die (PLURAL die **Verlängerungen**)

**extension number** NOUN **Apparatnummer** die (PLURAL die **Apparatnummern**)

**exterior** ADJECTIVE **äußerer/äußere/äußeres**

**extinct** ADJECTIVE ❶ (animal) **ausgestorben** ❷ (volcano) **erloschen**

**extinguish** VERB ❶ **löschen** (a fire) ❷ **to extinguish a cigarette** eine Zigarette ausmachen (SEP)

**extinguisher** NOUN **Feuerlöscher** der (PLURAL die **Feuerlöscher**)

**extra** ADJECTIVE ❶ **zusätzlich**, **extra** (informal) (extra never has an ending); **extra homework** zusätzliche Hausaufgaben, **wine is extra** Wein kostet extra, **you have to pay extra** das wird extra berechnet ❷ **at no extra charge** ohne Aufschlag

A B C D E F G H I J K L M N O P Q R S T U V W X Y Z

**extra** *ADVERB* ❶ besonders; he was extra careful er war besonders vorsichtig ❷ extra large extragroß

**extraordinary** *ADJECTIVE* außerordentlich

**extra time** *NOUN* (in football) Verlängerung die (PLURAL die Verlängerungen); to go into extra time in die Verlängerung gehen

**extravagant** *ADJECTIVE* verschwenderisch (person)

**extreme** *NOUN* Extrem das (PLURAL die Extreme); to go from one extreme to another von einem Extrem ins andere fallen

**extreme** *ADJECTIVE* extrem

**extremely** *ADVERB* äußerst; extremely fast äußerst schnell

**eye** *NOUN* Auge das (PLURAL die Augen); a girl with blue eyes ein Mädchen mit blauen Augen, shut your eyes! mach die Augen zu!
• to keep an eye on something auf etwas (ACC) aufpassen (SEP)

**eyebrow** *NOUN* Augenbraue die (PLURAL die Augenbrauen)

**eyelash** *NOUN* Augenwimper die (PLURAL die Augenwimpern)

**eyelid** *NOUN* Augenlid das (PLURAL die Augenlider)

**eyeliner** *NOUN* Eyeliner der (PLURAL die Eyeliner)

**eye shadow** *NOUN* Lidschatten der (PLURAL die Lidschatten)

**eyesight** *NOUN* to have good eyesight gute Augen haben, to have bad eyesight schlechte Augen haben

**fabric** *NOUN* (cloth) Stoff der (PLURAL die Stoffe)

**fabulous** *ADJECTIVE* phantastisch

**face** *NOUN* ❶ (of a person) Gesicht das (PLURAL die Gesichter); to pull a face eine Grimasse schneiden ❷ (of a clock or watch) Zifferblatt das (PLURAL die Zifferblätter)

**face** *VERB* ❶ gegenüberstehen◇ (SEP) (PERF sein) (+DAT); she was facing him sie stand ihm gegenüber ❷ the house faces the park das Haus befindet sich gegenüber dem Park ❸ (to stand the idea of) verkraften; I can't face going back ich bringe es nicht über mich zurückzugehen ❹ to face up to something sich etwas (DAT) stellen

**facilities** *PLURAL NOUN* ❶ the school has good sports facilities die Schule hat gute Sportanlagen ❷ the flat has no cooking facilities die Wohnung hat keine Kochgelegenheit

**fact** *NOUN* Tatsache die (PLURAL die Tatsachen); the fact is that ... Tatsache ist, dass ..., in fact tatsächlich, is that a fact? Tatsache?

**factory** *NOUN* Fabrik die (PLURAL die Fabriken)

**fade** *VERB* ❶ (fabric) ausbleichen◇ (SEP) (PERF sein); faded jeans ausgeblichene Jeans ❷ (a colour or

418

memory) verblassen *(PERF* sein); **the colours have faded** die Farben sind verblasst

**fail** *VERB* ❶ nicht bestehen◇ *(a test or an exam)*; **I failed my driving test** ich habe meine Fahrprüfung nicht bestanden ❷ *(in a test or an exam)* **durchfallen◇** *(SEP) (PERF* sein); **three students failed** drei Studenten sind durchgefallen ❸ **to fail to do something** etwas nicht tun, **he failed to inform us** er hat uns nicht benachrichtigt
• **without fail** auf jeden Fall; **ring me without fail** ruf mich auf jeden Fall an

**failure** *NOUN* ❶ Misserfolg der *(PLURAL* die Misserfolge); **it was a terrible failure** es war ein schrecklicher Misserfolg ❷ *(of equipment)* Ausfall der *(PLURAL* die Ausfälle); **a power failure** ein Stromausfall

**faint** *ADJECTIVE* ❶ *(slight)* leicht; **a faint smell of gas** ein leichter Gasgeruch, **I haven't the faintest idea** ich habe nicht die blasseste Ahnung *(informal)* ❷ *(voice or sound)* leise

**faint** *VERB* ohnmächtig werden; **Lisa fainted** Lisa wurde ohnmächtig

**fair** *NOUN* Jahrmarkt der *(PLURAL* die Jahrmärkte)

**fair** *ADJECTIVE* ❶ *(not unfair)* gerecht ❷ *(hair)* blond; **he's fair-haired** er ist blond ❸ *(skin)* hell; **fair-skinned** hellhäutig ❹ *(fairly good)* ganz gut *(chance, condition, or performance)* ❺ *(weather)* schön; **if it's fair tomorrow** wenn es morgen schön ist

**fairground** *NOUN* Jahrmarkt der *(PLURAL* die Jahrmärkte)

**fairly** *ADVERB* *(quite)* ziemlich

**fairy** *NOUN* Fee die *(PLURAL* die Feen)

**fairy tale** *NOUN* Märchen das *(PLURAL* die Märchen)

**faith** *NOUN* ❶ *(trust)* Vertrauen das; **to have faith in somebody** Vertrauen zu jemandem haben ❷ *(religious belief)* Glaube der *(PLURAL* die Glauben)

**faithful** *ADJECTIVE* treu; **to be faithful to somebody** jemandem treu sein

**faithfully** *ADVERB* **Yours faithfully** Hochachtungsvoll

**fake** *NOUN* ❶ Imitation die *(PLURAL* die Imitationen); **the diamonds were fakes** die Brillanten waren eine Imitation ❷ *(a painting or money)* Fälschung die *(PLURAL* die Fälschungen)

**fake** *ADJECTIVE* gefälscht; **a fake passport** ein gefälschter Pass

**fall** *NOUN* Fall der *(PLURAL* die Fälle); **to have a fall** stürzen *(PERF* sein)

**fall** *VERB* ❶ fallen◇ *(PERF* sein); **mind, you'll fall** pass auf, dass du nicht hinfällst, **Tony fell off his bike** Tony ist vom Rad gefallen, **she fell down the stairs** sie ist die Treppe hinuntergefallen ❷ *(of temperature, prices)* sinken◇ *(PERF* sein)

**false** *ADJECTIVE* falsch; **a false alarm** ein falscher Alarm

**fame** *NOUN* Ruhm der

**familiar** *ADJECTIVE* bekannt; **his face is familiar** sein Gesicht kommt mir bekannt vor

**family** *NOUN* Familie die *(PLURAL* die Familien); **a family of six** eine sechsköpfige Familie, **Ben's one of the family** Ben gehört zur Familie, **the Morris family** Familie Morris

**famous** ADJECTIVE **berühmt**

**fan** NOUN ❶ (a supporter) **Fan** der (PLURAL die **Fans**); **Will's a Chelsea fan** Will ist ein Fan von Chelsea ❷ (electric, for cooling) **Ventilator** der (PLURAL die **Ventilatoren**) ❸ (hand-held) **Fächer** der (PLURAL die **Fächer**)

**fanatic** NOUN **Fanatiker** der (PLURAL die **Fanatiker**) **Fanatikerin** die (PLURAL die **Fanatikerinnen**)

**fancy** NOUN **to take somebody's fancy** jemandem gefallen⬦, **the picture took his fancy** das Bild hat es ihm angetan

**fancy** ADJECTIVE (equipment) **ausgefallen**

**fancy** VERB ❶ (to want) **(do you) fancy a coffee?** hast du Lust auf einen Kaffee?, **do you fancy going to the cinema?** hast du Lust, ins Kino zu gehen? ❷ **I really fancy him** ich stehe total auf ihn ❸ (just) **fancy that!** stell dir vor!, **fancy you being here!** na so was, dich hier zu treffen!

**fancy dress** NOUN **in fancy dress** verkleidet, **fancy-dress party** das Kostümfest

**fantastic** ADJECTIVE **fantastisch**; **really? that's fantastic!** wirklich? das ist ja fantastisch!, **a fantastic holiday** fantastische Ferien

**far** ADVERB, ADJECTIVE ❶ **weit**; **it's not far** es ist nicht weit, **is it far to Carlisle?** ist es weit nach Carlisle?, **how far is it to Bristol?** wie weit ist es bis nach Bristol? ❷ **he took us as far as Newport** er hat uns bis Newport

mitgenommen ❸ **by far** bei weitem, **the prettiest by far** bei weitem das hübscheste ❹ (much) **viel**; **far better** viel besser, **far faster** viel schneller, **far too many people** viel zu viele Leute ❺ **so far** bis jetzt, **so far everything's going well** bis jetzt läuft alles gut ❻ **as far as I know** soweit ich weiß

**fare** NOUN ❶ (on a bus, train, or the underground) **Fahrpreis** der (PLURAL die **Fahrpreise**) ❷ (on a plane) **Flugpreis** der (PLURAL die **Flugpreise**); **half fare** der halbe Fahrpreis, **full fare** der volle Fahrpreis

**Far East** NOUN **der Ferne Osten**, **Fernost** das

**farm** NOUN **Bauernhof** der (PLURAL die **Bauernhöfe**)

**farmer** NOUN **Bauer** der (PLURAL die **Bauern**) **Bäuerin** die (PLURAL die **Bäuerinnen**)

**farming** NOUN **Landwirtschaft** die

**fascinating** ADJECTIVE **faszinierend**

**fashion** NOUN **Mode** die (PLURAL die **Moden**); **in fashion** in Mode, **to go out of fashion** aus der Mode kommen

**fashionable** ADJECTIVE **modisch**

**fashion model** NOUN **Mannequin** das (PLURAL die **Mannequins**)

**fashion show** NOUN **Modenschau** die (PLURAL die **Modenschauen**)

**fast** ADJECTIVE ❶ **schnell**; **a fast car** ein schnelles Auto ❷ (of a clock or watch) **to be fast** vorgehen⬦ (SEP) (PERF **sein**), **my watch is fast** meine Uhr geht vor, **you're ten minutes fast** deine Uhr geht zehn Minuten vor

**fast** ADVERB ❶ schnell; he swims fast er schwimmt schnell ❷ to be fast asleep fest schlafen

**fast food** NOUN Fastfood das

**fast forward** NOUN Vorlauf der

**fat** NOUN Fett das (PLURAL die Fette)

**fat** ADJECTIVE ❶ (meat) fett ❷ (person) dick, fett (informal); a fat man ein dicker Mann, to get fat fett werden (informal)

**fatal** ADJECTIVE tödlich

**father** NOUN Vater der (PLURAL die Väter); my father's office das Büro von meinem Vater

**Father Christmas** NOUN der Weihnachtsmann

**father-in-law** NOUN Schwiegervater der (PLURAL die Schwiegerväter)

**fault** NOUN ❶ (when you are responsible) Schuld die; it's Stephen's fault Stephen ist schuld, it's not my fault es ist nicht meine Schuld ❷ (in tennis) double fault der Doppelfehler

**favour** NOUN ❶ (a kindness) Gefallen der (PLURAL die Gefallen); to do somebody a favour jemandem einen Gefallen tun, can you do me a favour? kannst du mir einen Gefallen tun?, to ask a favour of somebody jemanden um einen Gefallen bitten ❷ to be in favour of something für etwas (ACC) sein

**favourite** ADJECTIVE Lieblings-; my favourite band meine Lieblingsband

**fear** NOUN Angst die (PLURAL die Ängste)

**fear** VERB fürchten

**feather** NOUN Feder die (PLURAL die Federn)

**feature** NOUN ❶ (of your face) Gesichtszug der (PLURAL die Gesichtszüge); to have delicate features feine Gesichtszüge haben ❷ (of a car or a machine) Merkmal das (PLURAL die Merkmale)

**February** NOUN Februar der; in February im Februar

**fed up** ADJECTIVE ❶ I'm fed up ich habe die Nase voll (informal), he's fed up with her er hat die Nase voll von ihr ❷ to be fed up with something etwas (ACC) satt haben (informal), I'm fed up with working every day ich habe es satt, jeden Tag zu arbeiten

**feed** VERB füttern; have you fed the dog? hast du den Hund gefüttert?

**feel** VERB ❶ sich fühlen; I don't feel well ich fühle mich nicht gut ❷ spüren; I didn't feel a thing ich habe nichts gespürt ❸ I feel tired ich bin müde, I feel cold mir ist kalt ❹ to feel afraid Angst haben, to feel thirsty Durst haben ❺ to feel like doing something Lust haben, etwas zu tun, I feel like going to the cinema ich habe Lust, ins Kino zu gehen ❻ (touch) fühlen ❼ (to the touch) sich anfühlen (SEP); to feel soft sich weich anfühlen

**feeling** NOUN ❶ Gefühl das (PLURAL die Gefühle); to show your feelings seine Gefühle zeigen, a dizzy feeling ein Schwindelgefühl, I have the feeling James doesn't like me ich habe das Gefühl, dass James mich nicht mag ❷ to hurt somebody's feelings jemanden verletzen

a b c d e f g h i j k l m n o p q r s t u v w x y z

**felt-tip (pen)** NOUN Filzstift der
(PLURAL die Filzstifte)

**female** NOUN (animal) Weibchen das
(PLURAL die Weibchen)

**female** ADJECTIVE weiblich

**feminine** ADJECTIVE weiblich

**feminist** NOUN Feministin die (PLURAL
die Feministinnen), Feminist der
(PLURAL die Feministen)

**feminist** ADJECTIVE feministisch

**fence** NOUN Zaun der (PLURAL die Zäune)

**ferry** NOUN Fähre die (PLURAL die
Fähren)

**fertilizer** NOUN Dünger der

**festival** NOUN (of films, art, or music)
Festspiele (plural)

**fetch** VERB ❶ (collect) abholen (SEP);
Tom's fetching the children Tom
holt die Kinder ab ❷ holen; fetch
me the other knife hol mir das
andere Messer

**fever** NOUN Fieber das

**few** ADJECTIVE, PRONOUN ❶ wenige; few
people know that ... wenige Leute
wissen, dass ... ❷ a few (several)
ein paar (ein paar never changes); a
few weeks ein paar Wochen, in a
few minutes in ein paar Minuten,
have you got any tomatoes? we
want a few for the salad haben Sie
Tomaten? wir brauchen ein paar für
den Salat ❸ quite a few eine ganze
Menge, there were quite a few
questions es gab eine ganze Menge
Fragen

**fewer** ADJECTIVE weniger; there are
fewer mosquitoes this year dieses
Jahr gibt es weniger Mücken

**fiancé** NOUN Verlobte der (PLURAL die
Verlobten)

**fiancée** NOUN Verlobte die (PLURAL die
Verlobten)

**field** NOUN ❶ (with grass or crops)
Feld das (PLURAL die Felder); a
field of wheat ein Kornfeld ❷ (for
sport) Spielfeld das (PLURAL die
Spielfelder)

**fierce** ADJECTIVE ❶ wild (animal or
person) ❷ heftig (storm or battle)

**fifteen** NUMBER fünfzehn

**fifth** NUMBER fünfter/fünfte/fünftes;
the fifth of January der fünfte
Januar, on the fifth floor im fünften
Stock

**fifty** NUMBER fünfzig

**fig** NOUN Feige die (PLURAL die Feigen)

**fight** NOUN ❶ (a scuffle) Schlägerei
die (PLURAL die Schlägereien) ❷ (in
boxing or against illness) Kampf der
(PLURAL die Kämpfe)

**fight** VERB ❶ (to have a fight) sich
prügeln; they were fighting sie
haben sich geprügelt ❷ (to quarrel)
sich streiten◇; they're always
fighting sie streiten sich immer
❸ (struggle against) kämpfen
gegen (+ACC), (poverty or a disease)

**figure** NOUN ❶ (number) Zahl die
(PLURAL die Zahlen); a four-figure
number eine vierstellige Zahl
❷ (body shape) Figur die; good
for your figure gut für die Figur
❸ (a person) Gestalt die (PLURAL die
Gestalten)

**figure** VERB to figure something
out etwas herausfinden◇ (SEP) (the
answer or reason)

**file** NOUN ❶ *(for records of a person or case)* **Akte** die *(PLURAL* die **Akten)** ❷ *(ring binder or folder)* **Ordner** der *(PLURAL* die **Ordner)** ❸ *(on a computer)* **Datei** die *(PLURAL* die **Dateien)** ❹ **a nail file** eine **Nagelfeile**

**file** VERB ❶ **ablegen** *(SEP) (documents)* ❷ **to file your nails** sich *(DAT)* die **Nägel feilen**

**fill** VERB ❶ **füllen** *(a container)*; **she filled my glass** sie füllte mein Glas ❷ **to be filled with people** voller Menschen sein, **filled with smoke** voller Rauch
• **to fill in** **ausfüllen** *(SEP) (a form)*

**filling** NOUN ❶ *(of a pie)* **Füllung** die *(PLURAL* die **Füllungen)** ❷ *(in a tooth)* **Füllung** die *(PLURAL* die **Füllungen)**

**film** NOUN *(in a cinema and for a camera)* **Film** der *(PLURAL* die **Filme)**; **shall we go and see the new film about Freud?** wollen wir uns den neuen Film über Freud ansehen?, **to make a film** einen Film drehen, **a 24-exposure colour film** ein Farbfilm mit 24 Aufnahmen

**film star** NOUN **Filmstar** der *(PLURAL* die **Filmstars)**

**filter** NOUN **Filter** der *(PLURAL* die **Filter)**

**filthy** ADJECTIVE **dreckig**

**final** NOUN *(in sport)* **Endspiel** das *(PLURAL* die **Endspiele)**

**final** ADJECTIVE **letzter/letzte/ letztes**; **the final instalment** die letzte Folge, **the final result** das **Endergebnis**

**finally** ADVERB **schließlich**

**find** VERB **finden**◇; **did you find your passport?** hast du deinen Pass gefunden?, **I can't find my keys** ich kann meine Schlüssel nicht finden
• **to find out** ❶ *(to enquire)* sich **informieren**; **I don't know, I'll find out** das weiß ich nicht, ich werde mich informieren ❷ **to find something out** etwas *(ACC)* **herausfinden**◇ *(SEP) (the facts or an answer)*, **when she found out the truth** als sie die Wahrheit herausfand

**fine** NOUN **Bußgeld** das *(PLURAL* die **Bußgelder)** *(for parking or speeding)*

**fine** ADJECTIVE ❶ *(in good health)* **gut**; **'how are you?' – 'fine, thanks'** 'wie gehts?' – 'danke, gut', **I'm fine** mir geht es gut ❷ *(convenient)* in **Ordnung**; **ten o'clock? yes, that's fine** zehn Uhr? ja, in Ordnung!, **Friday will be fine** Freitag geht in Ordnung ❸ *(sunny)* **schön**; *(weather or day)* if it's fine wenn es schön ist, **in fine weather** bei schönem Wetter ❹ *(not coarse or thick)* **fein**

**finely** ADVERB **fein** *(chopped or grated)*

**finger** NOUN **Finger** der *(PLURAL* die **Finger)**
• **I'll keep my fingers crossed for you** ich drücke dir den Daumen

**fingernail** NOUN **Fingernagel** der *(PLURAL* die **Fingernägel)**

**finish** NOUN ❶ *(end)* **Schluss** der *(PLURAL* die **Schlüsse)** ❷ *(in a race)* **Ziel** das *(PLURAL* die **Ziele)**

**finish** VERB ❶ **beenden** *(a conversation or quarrel)*; **to finish a discussion** ein Gespräch beenden, **to be finished with something** mit etwas *(DAT)* fertig sein *(work or a project)*, **have**

a
b
c
d
e
f
g
h
i
j
k
l
m
n
o
p
q
r
s
t
u
v
w
x
y
z

you finished your homework? bist du mit den Hausaufgaben fertig?, **wait, I haven't finished!** warte, ich bin noch nicht fertig! ❷ *(to finish off)* **to finish doing something** etwas zu beenden, **have you finished (reading) the letter?** hast du den Brief zu Ende gelesen?, **he hasn't yet finished (writing) the report** er hat den Bericht noch nicht zu Ende geschrieben ❸ *(come to an end)* **zu Ende sein, aus sein** *(informal) (a meeting or performance)*; **the film finishes at ten o'clock** der Film ist um zehn Uhr zu Ende, **when does school finish?** wann ist die Schule aus?

• **to finish with** *(complete your use of)* nicht mehr brauchen; **when you've finished with these clothes, give them back to me** wenn du die Sachen nicht mehr brauchst, gib sie mir zurück, **have you finished with the computer?** brauchen Sie den Computer noch?

**Finland** NOUN Finnland das

**Finnish** NOUN *(the language)* Finnisch das

**Finnish** ADJECTIVE finnisch; **he's Finnish** er ist Finne, **she's Finnish** sie ist Finnin

**fire** NOUN ❶ *(in a grate)* Kaminfeuer das *(PLURAL die Kaminfeuer)*; **to light the fire** das Feuer im Kamin anmachen ❷ *(accidental)* Feuer das *(PLURAL die Feuer)*; **to catch fire** *(fabric, furnishings)* Feuer fangen ❸ *(in a building or forest)* Brand der *(PLURAL die Brände)*; **to set fire to a factory** eine Fabrik in Brand stecken ❹ **to be on fire** brennen◇

**fire** VERB ❶ *(with a gun)* schießen◇; **to fire at somebody** auf jemanden schießen ❷ abfeuern *(SEP) (a gun)*

**fire alarm** NOUN Feuermelder der *(PLURAL die Feuermelder)*

**fire brigade** NOUN Feuerwehr die

**fire engine** NOUN Feuerwehrauto das *(PLURAL die Feuerwehrautos)*

**fire escape** NOUN Feuertreppe die *(PLURAL die Feuertreppen)*

**fire extinguisher** NOUN Feuerlöscher der *(PLURAL die Feuerlöscher)*

**firefighter** NOUN Feuerwehrmann der *(PLURAL die Feuerwehrleute)*

**fireplace** NOUN Kamin der *(PLURAL die Kamine)*

**fire station** NOUN Feuerwache die *(PLURAL die Feuerwachen)*

**firework** NOUN Feuerwerkskörper der *(PLURAL die Feuerwerkskörper)*; **firework display** das Feuerwerk

**firm** NOUN *(business)* Firma die *(PLURAL die Firmen)*

**firm** ADJECTIVE ❶ fest ❷ *(strict)* streng

**first** ADJECTIVE erster/erste/erstes; **the first of May** der erste Mai, **for the first time** zum ersten Mal, **I was the first to arrive** ich kam als Erster/Erste an, **Susan was first** Susan war die Erste, **to come first in the 100 metres** beim Hundertmeterlauf Erster/Erste werden

**first** ADVERB ❶ *(to begin with)* zuerst; **first, I'm going to make some tea** zuerst mache ich Tee ❷ **at first** zuerst, **at first he was shy** er war zuerst schüchtern

**first aid** NOUN erste Hilfe die

**first class** ADJECTIVE *(ticket, carriage, or hotel)* **erster Klasse** *(goes* *after the noun)*; **a first-class hotel** ein Hotel erster Klasse, **he always travels first class** er reist immer erster Klasse, **a first-class compartment** ein Erste-Klasse-Abteil

**first floor** NOUN **erste Stock** der; **on the first floor** im ersten Stock

**firstly** ADVERB **zunächst**

**first name** NOUN **Vorname** der *(PLURAL die* **Vornamen***)*

**fir tree** NOUN **Tanne** die *(PLURAL die* **Tannen***)*

**fish** NOUN **Fisch** der *(PLURAL die* **Fische***)*

**fish** VERB **fischen**, *(with a rod)* **angeln**

**fish and chips** NOUN **ausgebackener Fisch mit Pommes frites**

**fisherman** NOUN **Fischer** der *(PLURAL die* **Fischer***)*

**fishing** NOUN **Fischen** das, *(with a rod)* **Angeln** das; **to go fishing** fischen/angeln gehen

**fishing rod** NOUN **Angel** die *(PLURAL die* **Angeln***)*

**fishing tackle** NOUN **Angelausrüstung** die

**fist** NOUN **Faust** die *(PLURAL die* **Fäuste***)*

**fit** NOUN **❶** *(of rage)* **Anfall** der *(PLURAL die* **Anfälle***)*; **your dad'll have a fit when he sees your hair** dein Vater kriegt bestimmt einen Anfall, wenn er deine Haare sieht **❷ an epileptic fit** ein epileptischer Anfall

**fit** ADJECTIVE *(healthy)* **fit**; **I feel really fit** ich fühle mich richtig fit, **to keep fit** fit bleiben

**fit** VERB **❶** *(be the right size for) (of shoes or a garment)* **passen** *(+DAT)*; **this skirt doesn't fit me** der Rock passt mir nicht **❷** *(be able to be put into)* **passen in** *(+ACC)*; **will my cases all fit in the car?** passen meine Koffer alle in das Auto?, **the key doesn't fit in the lock** der Schlüssel passt nicht ins Schloss **❸** *(install)* **einbauen** *(SEP)*

**fitted carpet** NOUN **Teppichboden** der *(PLURAL die* **Teppichböden***)*

**fitted kitchen** NOUN **Einbauküche** die *(PLURAL die* **Einbauküchen***)*

**fitting room** NOUN **Umkleidekabine** die *(PLURAL die* **Umkleidekabinen***)*

**five** NUMBER **fünf**; **it's five o'clock** es ist fünf Uhr

**fix** VERB **❶** *(repair)* **reparieren**; **Mum's fixed the computer** Mutti hat den Computer repariert **❷** *(decide on)* **festlegen**◇ *(SEP)*; **to fix a date** einen Termin festlegen **❸ machen** *(a meal)*; **I'll fix supper** ich mache Abendessen

**fizzy** ADJECTIVE **sprudelnd**; **fizzy water** das Sprudelwasser

**flag** NOUN **Fahne** die *(PLURAL die* **Fahnen***)*

**flame** NOUN **Flamme** die *(PLURAL die* **Flammen***)*

**flan** NOUN **Torte** die *(PLURAL die* **Torten***)*; **fruit flan** die Obsttorte

**flap** VERB *(of a bird)* **to flap its wings** mit den Flügeln schlagen◇

**flash** NOUN *(on a camera)* **Blitz** der *(PLURAL die* **Blitze***)*; **flash of lightning** der Blitz

**flash** VERB ❶ (a light) aufleuchten (SEP), (repeatedly) blinken ❷ to flash by or past vorbeiflitzen (SEP) (informal)

**flashback** NOUN Rückblende die (PLURAL die Rückblenden)

**flat** NOUN Wohnung die (PLURAL die Wohnungen); a third-floor flat eine Wohnung im dritten Stock

**flat** ADJECTIVE ❶ flach; flat shoes flache Schuhe, a flat landscape eine flache Landschaft ❷ a flat tyre ein platter Reifen

**flatmate** NOUN Mitbewohner der (PLURAL die Mitbewohner), Mitbewohnerin die (PLURAL die Mitbewohnerinnen)

**flatter** NOUN schmeicheln (+DAT)

**flavour** NOUN ❶ Geschmack der (PLURAL die Geschmäcke); the sauce has a bitter flavour die Soße hat einen bitteren Geschmack, strawberry flavour Erdbeergeschmack ❷ (of drinks, coffee, or tea) Aroma das (PLURAL die Aromen)

**flavour** VERB würzen; vanilla-flavoured mit Vanillegeschmack

**flea** NOUN Floh der (PLURAL die Flöhe)

**flesh** NOUN Fleisch das

**flex** NOUN Kabel das (PLURAL die Kabel)

**flight** NOUN ❶ Flug der (PLURAL die Flüge); the flight was delayed der Flug hatte Verspätung, charter flight der Charterflug, the flight from Munich to London takes an hour and a half die Flugzeit von München nach London beträgt eineinhalb Stunden ❷ flight of stairs die Treppe

**flight attendant** NOUN Flugbegleiter der (PLURAL die Flugbegleiter), Flugbegleiterin die (PLURAL die Flugbegleiterinnen)

**flipper** NOUN Flosse die (PLURAL die Flossen)

**flirt** VERB flirten

**float** VERB ❶ (on water) treiben◇ ❷ (in the air) schweben

**flood** NOUN ❶ (of water) Überschwemmung die (PLURAL die Überschwemmungen) ❷ to be in floods of tears in Tränen aufgelöst sein ❸ (of letters or complaints) Flut die

**flood** VERB überschwemmen

**floodlight** NOUN Flutlicht das

**floor** NOUN ❶ Boden der (PLURAL die Böden); your glasses are on the floor deine Brille liegt auf dem Boden ❷ to sweep the floor fegen, to sweep the kitchen floor die Küche fegen ❸ (a storey) Stock der (PLURAL die Stock); on the second floor im zweiten Stock

**florist** NOUN Blumenhändler der (PLURAL die Blumenhändler), Blumenhändlerin die (PLURAL die Blumenhändlerinnen)

**flour** NOUN Mehl das

**flow** VERB fließen◇ (PERF sein)

**flower** NOUN Blume die (PLURAL die Blumen); bunch of flowers der Blumenstrauß

**flower** VERB blühen

**flu** NOUN Grippe die (PLURAL die Grippen); to have flu die Grippe haben

**fluent** ADJECTIVE **she speaks fluent Italian** sie spricht fließend Italienisch

**fluently** ADVERB fließend

**flute** NOUN Flöte die (PLURAL die Flöten); **to play the flute** Flöte spielen

**fly** NOUN Fliege die (PLURAL die Fliegen)

**fly** VERB ❶ fliegen◇ (PERF sein); **we flew to Berlin** wir sind nach Berlin geflogen ❷ **steigen lassen** (a kite) ❸ fliegen◇ (PERF haben) (a plane or helicopter) ❹ (to pass quickly) schnell vergehen◇ (PERF sein)

**foam** NOUN ❶ (foam rubber) Schaumgummi der; **foam mattress** die Schaumgummimatratze ❷ (on a drink) Schaum der

**focus** NOUN Brennpunkt der (PLURAL die Brennpunkte) **to be in focus** scharf sein, **to be out of focus** unscharf sein

**focus** VERB scharf stellen (a camera)

**fog** NOUN Nebel der

**foggy** ADJECTIVE neblig

**foil** NOUN (kitchen foil) Alufolie die

**fold** NOUN ❶ (in fabric or skin) Falte die (PLURAL die Falten) ❷ (in paper) Falz der (PLURAL die Falze)

**fold** VERB falten; **to fold something up** etwas zusammenfalten (SEP)

**folder** NOUN Mappe die (PLURAL die Mappen)

**follow** VERB ❶ folgen (PERF sein) (+DAT); **follow me!** folgen Sie mir! ❷ **do you follow me?** verstehst du, was ich meine?

**following** ADJECTIVE folgend; **the following evening** am folgenden Abend

**fond** ADJECTIVE **to be fond of somebody** jemanden gern haben, **I'm very fond of him** ich habe ihn sehr gern

**food** NOUN ❶ Essen das; **I have to buy some food** ich muss noch etwas zu essen einkaufen ❷ **I like German food** ich mag die deutsche Küche ❸ (stocks) Lebensmittel (plural); **we bought food for the holiday** wir haben Lebensmittel für die Ferien eingekauft

**food poisoning** NOUN Lebensmittelvergiftung

**fool** NOUN Dummkopf der (PLURAL die Dummköpfe)

**foot** NOUN Fuß der (PLURAL die Füße); **Lucy came on foot** Lucy ist zu Fuß gekommen

**football** NOUN Fußball der (PLURAL die Fußbälle); **to play football** Fußball spielen

**footballer** NOUN Fußballspieler der (PLURAL die Fußballspieler), Fußballspielerin die (PLURAL die Fußballspielerinnen)

**footpath** NOUN Fußweg der (PLURAL die Fußwege)

**footprint** NOUN Fußabdruck der (PLURAL die Fußabdrücke)

**footstep** NOUN Schritt der (PLURAL die Schritte)

**for** PREPOSITION ❶ für (+ACC); **a present for my mother** ein Geschenk für meine Mutter, **what's it for?** wofür ist das? ❷ (for a particular occasion or event) zu (+DAT); **sausages for**

**lunch** Würstchen zum Mittagessen, **Sam got a bike for Christmas** Sam hat zu Weihnachten ein Rad bekommen, **what for?** wozu? ❸ *(time expressions in the past but continuing in the present)* **seit** *(+DAT)*; **I've been waiting here for an hour** *(and I'm still waiting)* ich warte hier seit einer Stunde, **my brother's been living in Berlin for three years** *(and he still lives there)* mein Bruder wohnt seit drei Jahren in Berlin ❹ *(time expressions in the past or the future)* **I studied French for six years** *(but I no longer do)* ich habe sechs Jahre lang Französisch gelernt, **I'll be away for four days** ich werde vier Tage nicht da sein ❺ *(with a price)* **für** *(+ACC)*; **I sold my bike for fifty pounds** ich habe mein Rad für fünfzig Pfund verkauft ❻ **what's the German for 'bee'?** wie heißt 'bee' auf Deutsch?

**forbid** *VERB* verbieten◊; **to forbid somebody to do something** jemandem verbieten, etwas zu tun

**forbidden** *ADJECTIVE* verboten

**force** *NOUN* Kraft die *(PLURAL die Kräfte)*

**force** *VERB* zwingen◊; **to force somebody to do something** jemanden zwingen, etwas zu tun

**forecast** *NOUN* Vorhersage die *(PLURAL die Vorhersagen)*

**foreground** *NOUN* Vordergrund der; **in the foreground** im Vordergrund

**forehead** *NOUN* Stirn die *(PLURAL die Stirnen)*

**foreign** *ADJECTIVE* ❶ ausländisch; **in a foreign country** im Ausland, **from a foreign country** aus dem Ausland ❷ **foreign language** die Fremdsprache

**foreigner** *NOUN* Ausländer der *(PLURAL die Ausländer)*, Ausländerin die *(PLURAL die Ausländerinnen)*

**forest** *NOUN* Wald der *(PLURAL die Wälder)*

**forever** *ADVERB* ❶ immer; **I'd like to stay here forever** ich möchte für immer hier bleiben ❷ *(non-stop)* ständig; **he's forever asking questions** er fragt ständig

**forget** *VERB* vergessen◊; **to forget about something** etwas vergessen, **we've forgotten the bread** wir haben das Brot vergessen, **to forget to do something** vergessen, etwas zu tun, **I forgot to phone** ich habe vergessen anzurufen

**forgive** *VERB* verzeihen◊ *(+DAT)*; **to forgive somebody** jemandem verzeihen, **I forgave him** ich habe ihm verziehen, **to forgive somebody for doing something** jemandem verzeihen, dass er/sie etwas getan hat, **I forgave her for losing my ring** ich habe ihr verziehen, dass sie meinen Ring verloren hat

**fork** *NOUN* Gabel die *(PLURAL die Gabeln)*

**form** *NOUN* ❶ Formular das *(PLURAL die Formulare)*; **to fill in a form** ein Formular ausfüllen ❷ *(shape or kind)* Form die *(PLURAL die Formen)*; **in the form of** in Form von, **to be on form** gut in Form sein ❸ *(in school)* Klasse die *(PLURAL die Klassen)*

**form** *VERB* bilden

**formal** *ADJECTIVE* formell *(invitation, event)*

**format** *NOUN* Format das *(PLURAL die Formate)*

**former** *ADJECTIVE* ehemalig; a former pupil ein ehemaliger Schüler, eine ehemalige Schülerin

**fortnight** *NOUN* vierzehn Tage *(plural)*; we're going to Spain for a fortnight wir fahren vierzehn Tage nach Spanien

**fortunately** *ADVERB* glücklicherweise

**fortune** *NOUN* Vermögen das *(PLURAL* die Vermögen)*; to make a fortune ein Vermögen machen

**forty** *NUMBER* vierzig

**forward** *NOUN (in sport)* Stürmer der *(PLURAL* die Stürmer)*

**forward** *ADVERB (to the front)* nach vorn; to move forward vorrücken *(SEP) (PERF* sein)*, a seat further forward ein Platz weiter vorn

**forward slash** *NOUN* Schrägstrich der *(PLURAL* die dieSchrägstriche)*

**foster child** *NOUN* Pflegekind das *(PLURAL* die Pflegekinder)*

**foul** *NOUN (in sport)* Foul das *(PLURAL* die Fouls)*

**foul** *ADJECTIVE* scheußlich; the weather's foul das Wetter ist scheußlich

**fountain** *NOUN* Brunnen der *(PLURAL* die Brunnen)*

**fountain pen** *NOUN* Füllfederhalter der *(PLURAL* die Füllfederhalter)*

**four** *NUMBER* vier; it's four o'clock es ist vier Uhr
• on all fours auf allen vieren

**fourteen** *NUMBER* vierzehn

**fourth** *NUMBER* vierter/vierte/ viertes; the fourth of July der vierte Juli, on the fourth floor im vierten Stock

**fox** *NOUN* Fuchs der *(PLURAL* die Füchse)*

**fragile** *ADJECTIVE* zerbrechlich

**frame** *NOUN* ❶ Rahmen der *(PLURAL* die Rahmen)* ❷ *(of spectacles)* Gestell das *(PLURAL* die Gestelle)*

**franc** *NOUN* ❶ *(Swiss)* Franken der *(PLURAL* die Franken)*; a fifty-franc note ein Fünfzig-Franken-Schein ❷ *(former French and Belgian currencies)* Franc der *(PLURAL* die Francs)*

**France** *NOUN* Frankreich das; to France nach Frankreich

**frantic** *ADJECTIVE* ❶ *(very upset)* to be frantic außer sich *(DAT)* sein, I was frantic with worry ich war außer mir vor Sorge ❷ *(desperate)* fieberhaft *(effort or search)*

**freckle** *NOUN* Sommersprosse die *(PLURAL* die Sommersprossen)*

**free** *ADJECTIVE* ❶ *(when you don't pay)* kostenlos; a free ride eine kostenlose Fahrt, a free ticket eine Freikarte ❷ *(without charge)* umsonst; to do something for free etwas umsonst machen ❸ *(not occupied)* frei; are you free on Thursday? haben Sie am Donnerstag Zeit? ❹ sugar-free ohne Zucker, lead-free bleifrei

**free** *VERB* befreien

**freedom** *NOUN* Freiheit die

**free gift** *NOUN* Werbegeschenk das *(PLURAL* die Werbegeschenke)*

**English—German** (side tab)

A B C D E F G H I J K L M N O P Q R S T U V W X Y Z (side tab)

**free kick** NOUN Freistoß der (PLURAL die Freistöße)

**freeze** VERB ❶ (in a freezer) einfrieren◇ (SEP); to freeze raspberries Himbeeren einfrieren ❷ (in cold weather) frieren◇; it's freezing es friert ❸ (become covered with ice) zufrieren◇ (SEP) (PERF sein); the pond is frozen der Teich ist zugefroren

**freezer** NOUN Gefrierschrank der (PLURAL die Gefrierschränke)

**freezing** NOUN below freezing unter Null, three degrees above freezing drei Grad über Null

**freezing** ADJECTIVE ❶ I'm freezing ich friere sehr ❷ it's freezing outside es ist eiskalt draußen

**French** NOUN ❶ (the language) Französisch das ❷ (the people) the French die Franzosen

**French** ADJECTIVE ❶ französisch; Jean-Marc is French Jean-Marc ist Franzose ❷ (teacher or lesson) Französisch-; the French class der Französischunterricht

**French bean** NOUN grüne Bohne die (PLURAL die grünen Bohnen)

**French dressing** NOUN Vinaigrette die

**French fries** PLURAL NOUN Pommes frites (plural)

**Frenchman** NOUN Franzose der (PLURAL die Franzosen)

**French window** NOUN Terrassentür die (PLURAL die Terrassentüren)

**Frenchwoman** NOUN Französin die (PLURAL die Französinnen)

**frequent** ADJECTIVE häufig

**fresh** ADJECTIVE frisch; fresh eggs frische Eier, I'm going out for some fresh air ich gehe ein bisschen frische Luft schnappen

**Friday** NOUN ❶ Freitag der (PLURAL die Freitage); next Friday nächsten Freitag, last Friday letzten Freitag, on Friday (am) Freitag, I'll phone you on Friday evening ich rufe dich Freitagabend an, every Friday jeden Freitag, Good Friday Karfreitag ❷ on Fridays freitags, closed on Fridays freitags geschlossen

**fridge** NOUN Kühlschrank der (PLURAL die Kühlschränke); put it in the fridge stell es in den Kühlschrank

**friend** NOUN ❶ Freund der (PLURAL die Freunde), Freundin die (PLURAL die Freundinnen); a friend of mine ein Freund von mir ❷ to make friends sich anfreunden, he made friends with Danny er hat sich mit Danny angefreundet, he is friends with Danny er ist mit Danny befreundet

**friendly** ADJECTIVE freundlich

**friendship** NOUN Freundschaft die (PLURAL die Freundschaften)

**fries** PLURAL NOUN Pommes frites (plural)

**fright** NOUN ❶ Schreck der (PLURAL die Schrecke); to have or get a fright einen Schreck bekommen ❷ you gave me a fright! du hast mich erschreckt!

**frighten** VERB ❶ (of an explosion or shot) erschrecken ❷ (scare or threaten) to frighten somebody jemandem Angst machen

**frightened** ADJECTIVE **to be frightened** Angst haben, **Martin's frightened of snakes** Martin hat Angst vor Schlangen

**frightening** ADJECTIVE beängstigend

**fringe** NOUN ❶ *(hairstyle)* Pony der *(PLURAL* die **Ponys)* ❷ *(on clothes or a curtain)* Fransen *(plural)*

**frog** NOUN Frosch der *(PLURAL* die **Frösche)*

**from** PREPOSITION ❶ von *(+DAT)*; **ten metres from the cinema** zehn Meter vom Kino, **a letter from Tom** ein Brief von Tom, **from Monday to Friday** von Montag bis Freitag, **from now on** von jetzt an ❷ aus *(+DAT)*; **he comes from Dublin** er kommt aus Dublin, **the train from London** der Zug aus London ❸ **from seven o'clock onwards** ab sieben Uhr, **from then on** von da ab

**front** NOUN ❶ *(of a cupboard, card, or envelope)* Vorderseite die *(PLURAL* die **Vorderseiten)**, *(of a building)* Vorderfront die *(PLURAL* die **Vorderfronten)* ❷ *(of a garment or in an interior)* Vorderteil das *(PLURAL* die **Vorderteile)* ❸ *(at the seaside)* Strandpromenade die *(PLURAL* die **Strandpromenaden)* ❹ *(of a car)* **to sit in (the) front** vorne sitzen ❺ *(of a train or queue)* **vordere Ende** das *(PLURAL* die **vordere Ende)* ❻ *(of a procession or in a race)* Spitze die ❼ **in/at the front** vorne **in/at the front of** vorne in *(+DAT or, with movement towards a place, +ACC)*, **there are still seats at the front of the train** es gibt noch Plätze vorne im Zug, **we got on at the front of the train** wir sind vorne in den Zug eingestiegen ❽ **in front of** vor *(+DAT or, with movement towards a place, +ACC)*, **in front of the TV** vor dem Fernseher, **in front of me** vor mir

**front** ADJECTIVE ❶ vorderer/vordere/ vorderes; **in the front rows** in den vorderen Reihen ❷ **Vorder-**; **front seat** *(of a car)* der Vordersitz, **front wheel** das Vorderrad

**front door** NOUN Haustür die *(PLURAL* die **Haustüren)*

**frontier** NOUN Grenze die *(PLURAL* die **Grenzen)*

**frost** NOUN Frost der

**frosty** ADJECTIVE frostig

**frown** VERB die Stirn runzeln; **he frowned at us** er blickte uns mit gerunzelter Stirn an

**frozen** ADJECTIVE *(in a freezer)* tiefgekühlt; **a frozen pizza** eine Tiefkühlpizza

**fruit** NOUN ❶ *(a single fruit or type of fruit)* Frucht die *(PLURAL* die **Früchte)* ❷ *(various fruits)* Obst das; **we bought cheese and fruit** wir haben Käse und Obst gekauft

**fruit juice** NOUN Fruchtsaft der *(PLURAL* die **Fruchtsäfte)*

**fruit machine** NOUN Spielautomat der *(PLURAL* die **Spielautomaten)*

**fruit salad** NOUN Obstsalat der *(PLURAL* die **Obstsalate)*

**frustrated** ADJECTIVE frustriert

**fry** VERB braten◇; **we fried fish** wir haben Fisch gebraten, **fried potatoes** Bratkartoffeln, **fried egg** das Spiegelei

**frying pan** NOUN Bratpfanne die *(PLURAL* die **Bratpfannen)*

a b c d e f g h i j k l m n o p q r s t u v w x y z

**fuel** *NOUN (for a car)* **Kraftstoff** der

**full** *ADJECTIVE* ❶ **voll**; **the glass is full** das Glas ist voll, **I'm full** ich bin voll *(informal)* ❷ **full of voller** *(+GEN)*, **the train was full of tourists** der Zug war voller Touristen ❸ **at full speed** in voller Fahrt ❹ **to write something out in full** etwas voll ausschreiben

**full stop** *NOUN* **Punkt** der *(PLURAL die Punkte)*

**full-time** *ADJECTIVE* **a full-time job** eine Ganztagsstelle

**fully** *ADVERB* **voll**

**fun** *NOUN* ❶ **Spaß** der; **have fun!** viel Spaß!, **we had fun catching the ponies** die Ponys einzufangen machte uns Spaß, **skiing is fun** Skifahren macht Spaß, **I do it for fun** ich mache es aus Spaß ❷ **to have fun** sich amüsieren
• **to make fun of somebody** sich über jemanden lustig machen

**funds** *PLURAL NOUN* **Geldmittel** *(plural)*

**funeral** *NOUN* **Beerdigung** die *(PLURAL die Beerdigungen)*

**funfair** *NOUN* **Jahrmarkt** der *(PLURAL die Jahrmärkte)*

**funny** *ADJECTIVE* ❶ *(amusing)* **lustig**; **a funny story** eine lustige Geschichte, **he's so funny** er ist so witzig ❷ *(strange)* **komisch**; **a funny noise** ein komisches Geräusch, **that's funny, I'm sure I paid** das ist komisch, ich bin mir sicher, dass ich gezahlt habe

**fur** *NOUN* ❶ *(on an animal)* **Fell** das *(PLURAL die Felle)* ❷ *(for a coat)* **Pelz** der *(PLURAL die Pelze)*; **fur coat** der Pelzmantel

**furious** *ADJECTIVE* **wütend**; **she was furious with Steve** sie war wütend auf Steve

**furniture** *NOUN* **Möbel** *(plural)*; **to buy some furniture** Möbel kaufen, **piece of furniture** das Möbelstück

**further** *ADVERB* **weiter**; **further than the station** weiter als der Bahnhof, **ten kilometres further on** zehn Kilometer weiter, **further off** weiter entfernt, **further forward** weiter vorn, **further back** weiter hinten

**fuse** *NOUN* **Sicherung** die *(PLURAL die Sicherungen)*

**fuss** *NOUN* **Theater** das; **to make a fuss** ein Theater machen, **to make a big fuss about the bill** ein großes Theater um die Rechnung machen

**fussy** *ADJECTIVE* **to be fussy about something** wählerisch in etwas *(DAT)* sein *(food, for example)*

**future** *NOUN* **Zukunft** die; **in future** in Zukunft

**gadget** NOUN Gerät das (PLURAL die Geräte)

**gain** VERB ❶ gewinnen◇; **in order to gain time** um Zeit zu gewinnen ❷ profitieren; **to gain by something** von etwas profitieren

**gale** NOUN Sturm der (PLURAL die Stürme)

**gallery** NOUN Galerie die (PLURAL die Galerien)

**gamble** VERB spielen (for money)

**game** NOUN ❶ Spiel das (PLURAL die Spiele); **game of chance** das Glücksspiel, **board game** das Brettspiel ❷ **to have a game of cards** eine Partie Karten spielen ❸ **to have a game of football** Fußball spielen ❹ **games** (at school) Sport der

**games console** NOUN Spielkonsole die (PLURAL die Spielkonsolen)

**gang** NOUN Bande die (PLURAL die Banden); **all the gang were there** die ganze Bande war da

**gap** NOUN ❶ (hole) Lücke die (PLURAL die Lücken) ❷ (in time) Pause die (PLURAL die Pausen); **a two-hour gap** eine zweistündige Pause ❸ **age gap** der Altersunterschied

**gap year** NOUN Orientierungsjahr das (PLURAL die Orientierungsjahre)

**garage** NOUN ❶ (for keeping your car) Garage die (PLURAL die Garagen) ❷ (for repairing cars) Autowerkstatt die (PLURAL die Autowerkstätten) ❸ (for petrol) Tankstelle die (PLURAL die Tankstellen)

**garden** NOUN Garten der (PLURAL die Gärten)

**gardener** NOUN Gärtner der (PLURAL die Gärtner), Gärtnerin die (PLURAL die Gärtnerinnen)

**gardening** NOUN Gartenarbeit die

**garlic** NOUN Knoblauch der

**garment** NOUN Kleidungsstück das (PLURAL die Kleidungsstücke)

**gas** NOUN Gas das

**gas cooker** NOUN Gasherd der (PLURAL die Gasherde)

**gas fire** NOUN Gasofen der (PLURAL die Gasöfen)

**gas meter** NOUN Gaszähler der (PLURAL die Gaszähler)

**gate** NOUN ❶ (in garden) Pforte die (PLURAL die Pforten) ❷ (in field) Gatter das (PLURAL die Gatter) ❸ (at an airport) Flugsteig der (PLURAL die Flugsteige)

**gather** VERB ❶ (of people) sich versammeln ❷ sammeln (fruit, vegetables, flowers) ❸ **as far as I can gather** soweit ich weiß

**gay** ADJECTIVE (homosexual) schwul (informal)

**gaze** VERB **to gaze at something** etwas anstarren (SEP)

**GCSEs** NOUN PLURAL
*(You can explain GCSEs briefly as follows: Dies sind Prüfungen, die im Alter von ca 16 Jahren in bis zu 12 Fächern abgelegt werden. Sie werden von A\* (beste Note) bis N (nicht bestanden) benotet. Viele Schüler und Schülerinnen machen nach den GCSEs weiter und legen die A-level Prüfungen ab)* ▸ SEE **A levels**

**gear** NOUN ❶ *(in a car)* Gang der *(PLURAL die Gänge)*; **to change gear** schalten ❷ *(equipment)* Ausrüstung die; **camping gear** die Campingausrüstung ❸ *(things)* Sachen *(plural)*; **I've left all my gear at Gary's** ich habe alle meine Sachen bei Gary gelassen

**gear lever** NOUN Schalthebel der *(PLURAL die Schalthebel)*

**gel** NOUN Gel das *(PLURAL die Gele)*

**Gemini** NOUN Zwillinge *(plural)*; **Steph's Gemini** Steph ist Zwilling

**gender** NOUN *(of a word)* Geschlecht das *(PLURAL die Geschlechter)*; **what is the gender of 'Haus'?** welches Geschlecht hat 'Haus'?

**general** NOUN General der *(PLURAL die Generäle)*

**general** ADJECTIVE allgemein; **in general** im Allgemeinen, **the general election** die allgemeinen Wahlen

**general knowledge** NOUN Allgemeinwissen das

**generally** ADVERB im Allgemeinen

**generation** NOUN Generation die *(PLURAL die Generationen)*

**generator** NOUN Generator der *(PLURAL die Generatoren)*

**generous** ADJECTIVE großzügig

**genetics** NOUN Genetik die

**Geneva** NOUN Genf das; **Lake Geneva** der Genfer See

**genius** NOUN Genie das *(PLURAL die Genies)*; **Lisa, you're a genius!** Lisa, du bis ein Genie!

**gentle** ADJECTIVE sanft

**gentleman** NOUN Herr der *(PLURAL die Herren)*; **ladies and gentlemen!** meine Damen und Herren!

**gently** ADVERB sanft

**gents** NOUN *(lavatory)* Herrentoilette die *(PLURAL die Herrentoiletten)*; *(on a sign)* **'Gents'** 'Herren', **where's the gents?** wo ist die Herrentoilette?

**genuine** ADJECTIVE ❶ *(real, authentic)* echt; **a genuine diamond** ein echter Brillant ❷ aufrichtig *(person)*; **she's very genuine** sie ist sehr aufrichtig

**geography** NOUN Geographie die, *(at school)* Erdkunde die

**germ** NOUN ❶ Keim der *(PLURAL die Keime)* ❷ *(causing a cold)* **germs** Bazillen *(plural)*

**German** NOUN ❶ *(person)* Deutsche der/die *(PLURAL die Deutschen)* ❷ *(language)* Deutsch das; **in German** auf Deutsch

**German** ADJECTIVE deutsch; **he is German** er ist Deutscher **she is German** sie ist Deutsche, **our German teacher** unser Deutschlehrer, unsere Deutschlehrerin

**Germany** NOUN Deutschland das; **to Germany** nach Deutschland, **from Germany** aus Deutschland

**get** VERB ❶ (obtain, receive) bekommen◇, kriegen (informal); **I got a bike for my birthday** ich habe ein Rad zum Geburtstag bekommen, **Fred got the job** Fred hat die Stelle bekommen, **she got a shock** sie hat einen Schreck gekriegt, **I got a good mark for my German homework** ich habe auf meine Deutschhausaufgaben eine gute Note bekommen ❷ **he's got lots of money** er hat viel Geld, **she's got long hair** sie hat lange Haare, **I've got a headache** ich habe Kopfschmerzen ❸ (fetch) holen; **I'll get some bread** ich hole Brot, **I'll get your bag for you** ich hole dir deine Tasche ❹ **to have got to do something** etwas tun müssen◇, **I've got to phone before midday** ich muss vor Mittag anrufen ❺ **to get (to) somewhere** irgendwo ankommen◇ (SEP) (PERF sein), **when I got to London** als ich in London ankam, **we got here this morning** wir sind heute Morgen angekommen, **what time did they get there?** wann sind sie angekommen? ❻ (become) werden◇ (PERF sein); **it's getting late** es wird spät, **it's getting dark** es wird dunkel ❼ **to get something done** etwas machen lassen◇, **I'm getting my hair cut today** ich lasse mir heute die Haare schneiden

- **to get back** zurückkommen◇ (SEP) (PERF sein); **Mum gets back at six** Mutti kommt um sechs zurück
- **to get something back** etwas zurückbekommen◇ (SEP), etwas zurückkriegen (SEP) (informal); **did you get your books back?** hast du deine Bücher zurückbekommen?
- **to get into something** (a vehicle) in etwas (ACC) einsteigen◇ (SEP) (PERF sein); **he got into the car** er ist ins Auto eingestiegen

- **to get off something** (a vehicle) aus etwas (DAT) aussteigen◇ (SEP) (PERF sein); **I got off the train at Banbury** ich bin in Banbury aus dem Zug ausgestiegen
- **to get on how's Amanda getting on?** wie gehts Amanda?
- **to get on something** (a vehicle) in etwas (ACC) einsteigen◇ (SEP) (PERF sein); **she got on the train at Reading** sie ist in Reading in den Zug eingestiegen
- **to get on with somebody** sich mit jemandem verstehen◇; **she doesn't get on with her brother** sie versteht sich nicht mit ihrem Bruder
- **to get out of something** (a vehicle) aus etwas (DAT) austeigen◇ (SEP) (PERF sein); **Laura got out of the car** Laura ist aus dem Auto ausgestiegen
- **to get together** sich wieder sehen◇ (SEP); **we must get together soon** wir müssen uns bald mal wieder sehen
- **to get up** aufstehen◇ (SEP) (PERF sein); **I get up at seven** ich stehe um sieben auf

**ghost** NOUN **Geist** der (PLURAL die Geister)

**giant** NOUN **Riese** der (PLURAL die Riesen)

**giant** ADJECTIVE **riesig**; **a giant lorry** ein riesiger Lastwagen

**gift** NOUN ❶ **Geschenk** das (PLURAL die Geschenke); **a Christmas gift** ein Weihnachtsgeschenk ❷ **Begabung** die; **to have a gift for something** für etwas (ACC) begabt sein, **Jo has a real gift for languages** Jo ist wirklich sprachbegabt

a b c d e f  h i j k l m n o p q r s t u v w x y z

**gigabyte** NOUN Gigabyte das (PLURAL die Gigabytes); **a fifty gigabyte hard disk** eine Festplatte mit fünfzig Gigabyte Speicherkapazität

**gigantic** ADJECTIVE riesig

**gin** NOUN Gin der (PLURAL die Gins)

**ginger** NOUN Ingwer der (PLURAL die Ingwer)

**gipsy** NOUN Zigeuner der (PLURAL die Zigeuner), Zigeunerin die (PLURAL die Zigeunerinnen)

**giraffe** NOUN Giraffe die (PLURAL die Giraffen)

**girl** NOUN Mädchen das (PLURAL die Mädchen); **three boys and four girls** drei Jungen und vier Mädchen, **when I was a little girl I had …** als kleines Mädchen hatte ich …

**girlfriend** NOUN Freundin die (PLURAL die Freundinnen)

**give** VERB ❶ geben◇; **to give something to somebody** jemandem etwas geben, **I'll give you my address** ich gebe dir meine Adresse, **give me the key** gib mir den Schlüssel, **Yasmin's dad gave her the money** Yasmins Vater hat ihr das Geld gegeben ❷ (give as a gift) schenken; **to give somebody a present** jemandem etwas schenken
• **to give something away** etwas weggeben◇ (SEP); **she's given away all her books** sie hat alle ihre Bücher weggegeben
• **to give something back to somebody** jemandem etwas zurückgeben◇ (SEP); **I gave her back the keys** ich habe ihr die Schlüssel zurückgegeben
• **to give in** nachgeben◇ (SEP); **my mum said no but she gave in in the end** meine Mutti hat nein gesagt, aber schließlich hat sie nachgegeben
• **to give up** aufgeben◇ (SEP); **I give up!** ich gebe auf!
• **to give up doing something** etwas aufgeben◇ (SEP); **she's given up smoking** sie hat das Rauchen aufgegeben

**glad** ADJECTIVE froh; **I'm glad to hear he's better** ich bin froh, dass es ihm besser geht, **I'm glad to be back** ich bin froh, dass ich wieder zurück bin

**glass** NOUN Glas das (PLURAL die Gläser); **a glass of water** ein Glas Wasser, **a glass table** ein Glastisch

**glasses** PLURAL NOUN Brille die (PLURAL die Brillen); **to wear glasses** eine Brille tragen

**glider** NOUN Segelflugzeug das (PLURAL die Segelflugzeuge)

**global warming** NOUN globale Temperaturanstieg der

**glove** NOUN Handschuh der (PLURAL die Handschuhe); **a pair of gloves** ein Paar Handschuhe

**glove compartment** NOUN Handschuhfach das (PLURAL die Handschuhfächer)

**glue** NOUN Klebstoff der (PLURAL die Klebstoffe)

**go** NOUN ❶ (in a game) whose go is it? wer ist dran?, **it's my go** ich bin dran ❷ **to have a go at doing something** versuchen, etwas zu tun, **I'll have a go at mending it** ich versuche, es zu reparieren

**go** VERB ❶ (on foot) gehen◇ (PERF sein); **to go to school** in die Schule gehen, **Mark's gone to the dentist's** Mark ist zum Zahnarzt gegangen, **to go shopping** einkaufen gehen ❷ *(in a vehicle)* **fahren**◇ *(PERF* **sein)**; **we're going to London** wir fahren nach London, **we're planning to go early** wir wollen früh losfahren, **to go on holiday** in die Ferien fahren ❸ *(by plane)* **fliegen**◇ *(PERF* **sein)** ❹ **to go for a walk** spazieren gehen◇ *(SEP)* *(PERF* **sein)** ❺ *(with another verb)* **I'm going to do it** ich werde es tun, **I'm going to make some tea** ich mache Tee, **he was going to phone you** er wollte dich anrufen ❻ *(leave)* **gehen**◇ *(PERF* **sein)**; **Pauline's already gone** Pauline ist schon gegangen ❼ *(on a journey)* **abfahren**◇ *(SEP)* *(PERF* **sein)**; **when does the train go?** wann fährt der Zug ab? ❽ *(turn out)* **verlaufen**◇ *(PERF* **sein)** *(event)*; **how did your evening go?** wie ist dein Abend verlaufen?, **the party went well** die Party war gut

- **to go away** ❶ **weggehen**◇ *(SEP)* *(PERF* **sein)**; **go away!** geh weg! ❷ *(on holiday)* **verreisen** *(PERF* **sein)**
- **to go back** ❶ **zurückgehen**◇ *(SEP)* *(PERF* **sein)**; **I'm going back to Germany in March** ich werde im März nach Deutschland zurückkehren, **I'm not going back there again!** ich gehe da nicht wieder zurück! ❷ **I went back home** ich bin nach Hause gegangen
- **to go down** ❶ **hinuntergehen**◇ *(SEP)* *(PERF* **sein)**; **she's gone down to the kitchen** sie ist in die Küche hinuntergegangen, **to go down the stairs** die Treppe hinuntergehen ❷ *(price, temperature)* **fallen**◇ *(PERF* **sein)** ❸ *(tyre, balloon, airbed)* Luft verlieren◇
- **to go in** hineingehen◇ *(SEP)* *(PERF* **sein)**; **he went in and shut the door** er ist hineingegangen und hat die

Tür zugemacht
- **to go into** ❶ *(person)* gehen in *(+ACC)* *(PERF* **sein)**; **Fran went into the kitchen** Fran ging in die Küche ❷ *(object)* passen in *(+ACC)*; **this book won't go into my bag** dieses Buch passt nicht in meine Tasche
- **to go off** ❶ *(bomb)* explodieren *(PERF* **sein)** ❷ *(alarm clock)* klingeln; **my alarm clock went off at six** mein Wecker hat um sechs geklingelt ❸ *(fire or burglar alarm)* losgehen◇ *(SEP)* *(PERF* **sein)**; **the fire alarm went off** der Feuermelder ging los
- **to go on** ❶ **what's going on?** was ist los? ❷ **to go on doing something** weiter etwas tun, **she went on talking** sie hat weitergeredet ❸ **to go on about something** stundenlang von etwas *(DAT)* reden, **he's always going on about his dog** er redet stundenlang von seinem Hund
- **to go out** ❶ *(for an evening)* ausgehen◇ *(SEP)*, weggehen◇ *(SEP)* *(PERF* **sein)** *(informal)*; **we're going out tonight** wir gehen heute Abend aus ❷ *(leave)* **she went out of the kitchen** sie ist aus der Küche gegangen ❸ **to be going out with somebody** mit jemandem gehen◇ *(PERF* **sein)** *(informal)*, **she's going out with my brother** sie geht mit meinem Bruder ❹ *(light, fire)* ausgehen◇ *(SEP)* *(PERF* **sein)**; **the light went out** das Licht ist ausgegangen
- **to go past something** an etwas *(DAT)* vorbeigehen◇ *(SEP)*; **we went past your house** wir sind an eurem Haus vorbeigegangen
- **to go round to somebody's house** jemanden besuchen, **we went round to Fred's last night** wir haben gestern Abend Fred besucht
- **to go round something** ❶ um

**A B C D E F G H I J K L M N O P Q R S T U V W X Y Z**

etwas *(AC)* herumgehen◇ *(SEP)* *(PERF* sein*)* *(building, park, garden)* ❷ besichtigen *(museum, monument)*
• to go through ❶ the train goes through Cologne der Zug fährt durch Köln ❷ to go through a room durch ein Zimmer gehen ❸ *(search)* durchsuchen
• to go up ❶ *(person)* hinaufgehen◇ *(SEP)* *(PERF* sein*)*; she's gone up to her room sie ist in ihr Zimmer hinaufgegangen, to go up the stairs die Treppe hinaufgehen ❷ *(prices)* steigen◇ *(PERF* sein*)*; the price of petrol has gone up die Benzinpreise sind gestiegen

**goal** NOUN Tor das *(PLURAL* die Tore*)*; to score a goal ein Tor schießen, to win by 3 goals to 2 mit 3 zu 2 Toren gewinnen

**goalkeeper** NOUN Torwart der *(PLURAL* die Torwarte*)*, Torfrau die *(PLURAL* die Torfrauen*)*

**goat** NOUN Ziege die *(PLURAL* die Ziegen*)*

**god** NOUN Gott der *(PLURAL* die Götter*)*

**God** NOUN Gott der; to believe in God an Gott glauben

**godchild** NOUN Patenkind das *(PLURAL* die Patenkinder*)*

**goddaughter** NOUN Patentochter die *(PLURAL* die Patentöchter*)*

**goddess** NOUN Göttin die *(PLURAL* die Göttinnen*)*

**godfather** NOUN Pate der *(PLURAL* die Paten*)*

**godmother** NOUN Patin die *(PLURAL* die Patinnen*)*

**godson** NOUN Patensohn der *(PLURAL* die Patensöhne*)*

**goggles** PLURAL NOUN Schutzbrille die *(PLURAL* die Schutzbrillen*)*; swimming goggles Schwimmbrille die *(PLURAL* die Schwimmbrillen*)*, skiing goggles Skibrille die *(PLURAL* die Skibrillen*)*

**gold** NOUN Gold das; a gold bracelet ein Goldarmband

**goldfish** NOUN Goldfisch der *(PLURAL* die Goldfische*)*

**golf** NOUN Golf das; to play golf Golf spielen

**golf club** NOUN ❶ *(place)* Golfklub der *(PLURAL* die Golfklubs*)* ❷ *(iron)* Golfschläger der *(PLURAL* die Golfschläger*)*

**golf course** NOUN Golfplatz der *(PLURAL* die Golfplätze*)*

**golfer** NOUN Golfspieler der *(PLURAL* die Golfspieler*)*, Golfspielerin die *(PLURAL* die Golfspielerinnen*)*

**good** ADJECTIVE ❶ gut; she's a good teacher sie ist eine gute Lehrerin, the cherries are very good die Kirschen sind sehr gut ❷ to be good for you gesund sein, tomatoes are good for you Tomaten sind gesund ❸ good at gut in *(+DAT)*, she's good at maths sie ist gut in Mathe, he's good at drawing er kann gut zeichnen ❹ *(well-behaved)* brav; be good! sei brav! ❺ *(kind)* nett; she's been very good to me sie ist sehr nett zu mir gewesen ❻ for good endgültig, I've stopped smoking for good ich habe das Rauchen endgültig aufgegeben

**good afternoon** EXCLAMATION guten Tag!

**goodbye** EXCLAMATION auf Wiedersehen!

**good evening** *EXCLAMATION* **guten Abend!**

**Good Friday** *NOUN* **Karfreitag** der *(PLURAL* die **Karfreitage)**

**good-looking** *ADJECTIVE* **gut aussehend**

**good morning** *EXCLAMATION* **guten Morgen!**

**goodness** *EXCLAMATION* **meine Güte!; for goodness sake!** um Himmels willen!

**good night** *EXCLAMATION* **gute Nacht!**

**goods** *PLURAL NOUN* **Waren** *(plural)*

**goods train** *NOUN* **Güterzug** der *(PLURAL* die **Güterzüge)**

**goose** *NOUN* **Gans** die *(PLURAL* die **Gänse)**

**gorgeous** *ADJECTIVE* **herrlich; it's a gorgeous day** es ist ein herrlicher Tag

**gorilla** *NOUN* **Gorilla** der *(PLURAL* die **Gorillas)**

**gosh** *EXCLAMATION* **Mensch!**

**gossip** *NOUN* ❶ *(person)* **Klatschbase** die *(PLURAL* die **Klatschbasen)** ❷ *(scandal)* **Klatsch** der

**gossip** *VERB* **klatschen**

**government** *NOUN* **Regierung** die *(PLURAL* die **Regierungen)**

**grab** *VERB* ❶ **packen; she grabbed my arm** sie packte mich am Arm ❷ **to grab something from somebody** jemandem etwas *(ACC)* entreißen◇, **he grabbed the book from me** er hat mir das Buch entrissen

**grade** *NOUN (mark)* **Note** die *(PLURAL* die **Noten); to get good grades** gute Noten bekommen

**gradual** *ADJECTIVE* **allmählich**

**gradually** *ADVERB* **allmählich; the weather got gradually better** das Wetter wurde allmählich besser

**graffiti** *PLURAL NOUN* **Graffiti** *(plural)*

**grain** *NOUN* **Korn** das *(PLURAL* die **Körner)**

**gram** *NOUN* **Gramm** das; **100 grams of salami** hundert Gramm Salami

**grammar** *NOUN* **Grammatik** die

**grammar school** *NOUN* **Gymnasium** das *(PLURAL* die **Gymnasien)**

**grammatical** *ADJECTIVE* **grammatikalisch; a grammatical error** eine Grammatikfehler

**gran** *NOUN* **Oma** die *(PLURAL* die **Omas)**

**grandchildren** *PLURAL NOUN* **Enkelkinder** *(plural)*

**granddad** *NOUN* **Opa** der *(PLURAL* die **Opas)**

**granddaughter** *NOUN* **Enkelin** die *(PLURAL* die **Enkelinnen)**

**grandfather** *NOUN* **Großvater** der *(PLURAL* die **Großväter)**

**grandma** *NOUN* **Oma** die *(PLURAL* die **Omas)**

**grandmother** *NOUN* **Großmutter** die *(PLURAL* die **Großmütter)**

**grandpa** *NOUN* **Opa** der *(PLURAL* die **Opas)**

**grandparents** *PLURAL NOUN* **Großeltern** *(plural)*

A
B
C
D
E
F
G
H
I
J
K
L
M
N
O
P
Q
R
S
T
U
V
W
X
Y
Z

**grandson** NOUN Enkel der (PLURAL die Enkel)

**granny** NOUN Omi die (PLURAL die Omis)

**grape** NOUN Weintraube die (PLURAL die Weintrauben); **a grape** eine Weintraube, **to buy some grapes** Weintrauben kaufen, **do you like grapes?** magst du Weintrauben?, **a bunch of grapes** eine ganze Weintraube

**grapefruit** NOUN Grapefruit die (PLURAL die Grapefruits)

**graph** NOUN Grafik die (PLURAL die Grafiken)

**grasp** VERB festhalten◇ (SEP)

**grass** NOUN ❶ Gras das; **to lie on the grass** im Gras liegen ❷ (lawn) Rasen der (PLURAL die Rasen); **to cut the grass** den Rasen mähen

**grasshopper** NOUN Heuschrecke die (PLURAL die Heuschrecken)

**grate** VERB reiben◇; **grated cheese** geriebener Käse

**grateful** ADJECTIVE dankbar; **to be grateful to somebody** jemandem dankbar sein

**grater** NOUN Reibe die (PLURAL die Reiben)

**grave** NOUN Grab das (PLURAL die Gräber)

**graveyard** NOUN Friedhof der (PLURAL die Friedhöfe)

**gravy** NOUN Soße die (PLURAL die Soßen)

**grease** NOUN Fett das

**greasy** ADJECTIVE ❶ fettig; **to have greasy skin** fettige Haut haben ❷ (food) fett

**great** ADJECTIVE ❶ groß; **a great poet** ein großer Dichter ❷ (terrific) großartig; **it was a great party** das war eine großartige Party, **great!** großartig!, prima! (informal) ❸ **a great deal of** sehr viel, **a great many** sehr viele

**Great Britain** NOUN Großbritannien das

**Greece** NOUN Griechenland das

**greedy** ADJECTIVE gierig, (with food) gefräßig

**Greek** NOUN ❶ (person) Grieche der (PLURAL die Griechen), Griechin die (PLURAL die Griechinnen) ❷ (language) Griechisch das

**Greek** ADJECTIVE griechisch; **she's Greek** sie ist Griechin

**green** NOUN ❶ (colour) Grün das; **a pale green** ein Hellgrün ❷ **the Greens** (ecologists) die Grünen

**green** ADJECTIVE ❶ grün; **a green door** eine grüne Tür ❷ **the Green Party** die Grünen (plural)

**greengrocer** NOUN Obst- und Gemüsehändler der (PLURAL die Obst- und Gemüsehändler)

**greenhouse** NOUN Gewächshaus das (PLURAL die Gewächshäuser)

**greenhouse effect** NOUN Treibhauseffekt der

**greetings** PLURAL NOUN Grüße (plural); **Season's Greetings** fröhliche Weihnachten und ein glückliches neues Jahr

**greetings card** NOUN
Glückwunschkarte die (PLURAL die
Glückwunschkarten)

**grey** ADJECTIVE grau

**greyhound** NOUN Windhund der
(PLURAL die Windhunde)

**grid** NOUN ❶ (grating) Gitter das
(PLURAL die Gitter) ❷ (network) Netz
das (PLURAL die Netze)

**grief** NOUN Trauer die

**grill** NOUN Grill der (PLURAL die Grills)

**grill** VERB grillen; I'm going to
grill the sausages ich grille die
Würstchen

**grim** ADJECTIVE grauenvoll

**grin** VERB grinsen

**grind** VERB mahlen

**grip** VERB (hold on to) festhalten◇
(SEP)

**groan** NOUN Stöhnen das

**groan** VERB stöhnen

**grocer** NOUN Lebensmittelhändler
der (PLURAL die
Lebensmittelhändler)

**groceries** PLURAL NOUN Lebensmittel
(plural)

**grocer's** NOUN
Lebensmittelgeschäft das (PLURAL
die Lebensmittelgeschäfte)

**groom** NOUN Bräutigam der (PLURAL
die Bräutigame); the bride and
groom das Brautpaar

**gross** ADJECTIVE ❶ a gross injustice
eine schreiende Ungerechtigkeit
❷ grob; a gross error ein grober
Fehler ❸ (disgusting) ekelhaft; the

food was gross! das Essen war
ekelhaft!

**ground** NOUN ❶ Boden der; to sit on
the ground auf dem Boden sitzen
❷ (for sport) Sportplatz der (PLURAL
die Sportplätze); football ground
der Fußballplatz

**ground** ADJECTIVE gemahlen; ground
coffee gemahlener Kaffee

**ground floor** NOUN Erdgeschoss
das; they live on the ground floor
sie wohnen im Erdgeschoss

**group** NOUN Gruppe die (PLURAL die
Gruppen)

**grow** VERB (get bigger) ❶ wachsen◇
(PERF sein); your hair grows very
quickly deine Haare wachsen sehr
schnell, my little sister's grown
quite a bit this year meine kleine
Schwester ist dieses Jahr ein ganzes
Stück gewachsen, the number
of students is still growing die
Zahl der Studenten wächst noch
❷ anbauen (SEP) (fruit, vegetables)
❸ to grow a beard sich (DAT) einen
Bart wachsen lassen ❹ (become)
werden◇ (PERF sein); to grow old
alt werden
• to grow up ❶ erwachsen werden;
the children are growing up
die Kinder werden erwachsen
❷ aufwachsen◇ (SEP) (PERF sein);
she grew up in Scotland sie ist in
Schottland aufgewachsen

**growl** VERB knurren

**grown-up** NOUN Erwachsene der/
die (PLURAL die Erwachsenen)

**growth** NOUN Wachstum das

**grudge** NOUN to bear a grudge against somebody etwas gegen jemanden haben, **she bears me a grudge** sie hat etwas gegen mich

**grumble** VERB ❶ murren; he's always grumbling er murrt immer ❷ to grumble about something sich über etwas (ACC) beklagen, **what's she grumbling about?** worüber beklagt sie sich?

**guarantee** NOUN Garantie die (PLURAL die Garantien); a year's guarantee ein Jahr Garantie

**guarantee** VERB garantieren

**guard** NOUN ❶ prison guard der Gefängniswärter, die Gefängniswärterin ❷ (on a train) Zugführer der (PLURAL die Zugführer), Zugführerin die (PLURAL die Zugführerinnen) ❸ security guard der Wächter, die Wächterin

**guard** VERB bewachen

**guard dog** NOUN Wachhund der (PLURAL die Wachhunde)

**guess** NOUN have a guess! rate mal!, it's a good guess gut geraten

**guess** VERB ❶ raten◊; guess who I saw last night rate mal, wen ich gestern Abend gesehen habe ❷ (guess something correctly) es erraten◊; you'll never guess! du errätst es nie!

**guest** NOUN Gast der (PLURAL die Gäste); we've got guests coming tonight wir haben heute Abend Gäste, a paying guest ein zahlender Gast

**guide** NOUN ❶ (person) Führer der (PLURAL die Führer), Führerin die (PLURAL die Führerinnen) ❷ (book) Reiseführer der (PLURAL die Reiseführer) ❸ (girl guide) Pfadfinderin die (PLURAL die Pfadfinderinnen)

**guidebook** NOUN ❶ Reiseführer der (PLURAL die Reiseführer) ❷ (to a museum or monument) Handbuch das (PLURAL die Handbücher)

**guide dog** NOUN Blindenhund der (PLURAL die Blindenhunde)

**guideline** NOUN Richtlinie die (PLURAL die Richtlinien)

**guilty** ADJECTIVE ❶ schuldig ❷ to feel guilty ein schlechtes Gewissen haben, I felt guilty about the noise ich hatte ein schlechtes Gewissen wegen des Lärms

**guinea pig** NOUN ❶ (pet) Meerschweinchen das (PLURAL die Meerschweinchen) ❷ (in an experiment) Versuchskaninchen das (PLURAL die Versuchskaninchen)

**guitar** NOUN Gitarre die (PLURAL die Gitarren); to play the guitar Gitarre spielen

**gum** NOUN ❶ (in your mouth) Zahnfleisch das ❷ (chewing gum) Kaugummi der (PLURAL die Kaugummis)

**gun** NOUN ❶ Pistole die (PLURAL die Pistolen) ❷ (rifle) Gewehr das (PLURAL die Gewehre)

**gutter** NOUN ❶ (in the street) Rinnstein der (PLURAL die Rinnsteine) ❷ (on roof edge) Dachrinne die (PLURAL die Dachrinnen)

**guy** NOUN Typ der (PLURAL die Typen)
(informal); **he's a nice guy** er ist
ein netter Typ, **that guy from
Newcastle** der Typ aus Newcastle

**gym** NOUN ❶ (school lesson) Turnen
das ❷ (building) Turnhalle die
(PLURAL die Turnhallen) ❸ (health
club) Fitnesscenter das (PLURAL die
Fitnesscenter); **to go to the gym**
ins Fitnesscenter gehen

**gymnasium** NOUN Turnhalle die
(PLURAL die Turnhallen)

**gymnast** NOUN Turner der (PLURAL
die Turner), Turnerin die (PLURAL die
Turnerinnen)

**gymnastics** NOUN Turnen das

**gym shoe** NOUN Turnschuh der
(PLURAL die Turnschuhe)

# Hh

**habit** NOUN Gewohnheit die
(PLURAL die Gewohnheiten); **it's
a bad habit** es ist eine schlechte
Gewohnheit

**haddock** NOUN Schellfisch der;
**smoked haddock** geräucherter
Schellfisch

**hail** NOUN Hagel der

**hailstone** NOUN Hagelkorn das
(PLURAL die Hagelkörner)

**hailstorm** NOUN Hagelschauer der
(PLURAL die Hagelschauer)

**hair** NOUN ❶ Haare (plural); **to comb
your hair** sich (DAT) die Haare
kämmen, **to wash your hair** sich
(DAT) die Haare waschen, **to have
your hair cut** sich (DAT) die Haare
schneiden lassen, **she's had her hair
cut** sie hat sich die Haare schneiden
lassen ❷ **a hair** ein Haar

**hairbrush** NOUN Haarbürste die
(PLURAL die Haarbürsten)

**haircut** NOUN ❶ Haarschnitt der
(PLURAL die Haarschnitte) ❷ **to
have a haircut** sich (DAT) die Haare
schneiden lassen

**hairdresser** NOUN Friseur der
(PLURAL die Friseure), Friseurin die
(PLURAL die Friseurinnen); **at the
hairdresser's** beim Friseur

**hair drier** NOUN Föhn der (PLURAL die
Föhne)

a
b
c
d
e
f
g
h
i
j
k
l
m
n
o
p
q
r
s
t
u
v
w
x
y
z

**hair gel** NOUN Haargel das (PLURAL die Haargele)

**hairgrip** NOUN Haarklemme die (PLURAL die Haarklemmen)

**hairslide** NOUN Haarspange die (PLURAL die Haarspangen)

**hairspray** NOUN Haarspray das (PLURAL die Haarsprays)

**hairstyle** NOUN Frisur die (PLURAL die Frisuren)

**hairy** ADJECTIVE behaart

**half** NOUN ❶ Hälfte die (PLURAL die Hälften); half of die Hälfte von (+DAT), I gave him half of the money ich habe ihm die Hälfte von dem Geld gegeben, half of it die Hälfte davon ❷ half an apple ein halber Apfel ❸ to cut something in half etwas halbieren ❹ (as a fraction) halb; three and a half dreieinhalb ❺ (in time) halb; half an hour eine halbe Stunde, an hour and a half anderthalb Stunden, it's half past three es ist halb vier (literally: half on the way to four) ❻ (in weights and measures) halb; half a litre ein halber Liter

**half hour** NOUN halbe Stunde die; every half hour jede halbe Stunde

**half price** ADJECTIVE, ADVERB zum halben Preis; half-price CDs CDs zum halben Preis

**half-time** NOUN Halbzeit die; at half-time the score is 0-0 zur Halbzeit steht es null zu null

**halfway** ADVERB ❶ auf halbem Weg; halfway to Frankfurt auf halbem Weg nach Frankfurt ❷ to be halfway through doing something mit etwas halb fertig sein, I'm halfway through my homework ich bin mit meinen Hausaufgaben halb fertig

**hall** NOUN ❶ (in a house) Diele die (PLURAL die Dielen) ❷ (public) Saal der (PLURAL die Säle); village hall der Gemeindesaal, concert hall der Konzertsaal

**Hallowe'en** NOUN der Tag vor Allerheiligen (in Germany there are no particular customs for this date)

**ham** NOUN Schinken der; a ham sandwich ein Schinkenbrot

**hamburger** NOUN Hamburger der (PLURAL die Hamburger)

**hammer** NOUN Hammer der (PLURAL die Hammer)

**hamster** NOUN Hamster der (PLURAL die Hamster)

**hand** NOUN ❶ Hand die (PLURAL die Hände); to have something in your hand etwas in der Hand haben, to hold somebody's hand jemandes Hand halten ❷ to give somebody a hand jemandem helfen◇, can you give me a hand to move the table into the corner? kannst du mir helfen, den Tisch in die Ecke zu rücken?, do you need a hand? kann ich dir helfen? ❸ on the other hand ... andererseits ... ❹ (of a watch or clock) Zeiger der (PLURAL die Zeiger); the hour hand der Stundenzeiger

**hand** VERB to hand something to somebody jemandem etwas geben◇, I handed him the keys ich gab ihm die Schlüssel

• to hand something in etwas abgeben◇ (SEP); hand in your homework gebt eure Hausaufgaben ab

- **to hand something out** etwas austeilen *(SEP)*

**handbag** *NOUN* Handtasche die *(PLURAL die Handtaschen)*

**handcuffs** *PLURAL NOUN* Handschellen *(plural)*

**handful** *NOUN* **a handful of** eine Hand voll

**handkerchief** *NOUN* Taschentuch das *(PLURAL die Taschentücher)*

**handle** *NOUN* **①** *(of a door, drawer, bag, or knife)* Griff der *(PLURAL die Griffe)* **②** *(on a cup, jug, or basket)* Henkel der *(PLURAL die Henkel)* **③** *(of a frying pan or broom)* Stiel der *(PLURAL die Stiele)*

**handle** *VERB* **①** erledigen; **Gina handles the correspondence** Gina erledigt die Korrespondenz **②** umgehen◇ *(SEP)* *(PERF* sein*)* mit; **she's good at handling people** sie kann gut mit Menschen umgehen **③** fertig werden◇ *(PERF* sein*)* mit; **he can't handle problems** er kann mit Problemen nicht fertig werden

**handlebars** *PLURAL NOUN* Lenkstange die *(PLURAL die Lenkstangen)*

**hand luggage** *NOUN* Handgepäck das

**handmade** *ADJECTIVE* handgemacht

**handsome** *ADJECTIVE* gut aussehend; **he's a handsome guy** er ist ein gut aussehender Typ

**handwriting** *NOUN* Handschrift die *(PLURAL die Handschriften)*

**handy** *ADJECTIVE* **①** praktisch; **this little knife's very handy** dieses kleine Messer ist sehr praktisch **②** griffbereit; **I always keep a notebook handy** ich habe immer ein kleines Notizbuch griffbereit

**hang** *VERB* **①** hängen◇; **there was a mirror hanging on the wall** an der Wand hing ein Spiegel **②** aufhängen *(SEP)*; **to hang a mirror on the wall** einen Spiegel an der Wand aufhängen
- **to hang around** rumhängen◇ *(SEP)* *(PERF* sein*)* *(informal)*; **we were hanging around outside the cinema** wir haben vor dem Kino rumgehangen
- **to hang on** warten; **hang on a second!** warten Sie einen Moment!
- **to hang up** *(on the phone)* auflegen *(SEP)*; **she hung up on me** sie hat einfach aufgelegt
- **to hang something up** etwas aufhängen *(SEP)*

**hang-gliding** *NOUN* Drachenfliegen das; **to go hang-gliding** Drachenfliegen gehen

**hangover** *NOUN* Kater der *(PLURAL die Kater)*

**happen** *VERB* **①** passieren *(PERF* sein*)*; **what happened?** was ist passiert?, **it happened in June** es ist im Juni passiert **②** **what's happening?** was ist los?, **what's happened to Jill?** was ist mit Jill los? **③** **what's happened to the can-opener?** wo ist der Dosenöffner? **④** **if you happen to see him** wenn du ihn zufällig triffst, **Leila happened to be there** Leila war zufällig da

**happily** *ADVERB* **①** glücklich **②** *(willingly)* gerne; **I'll happily do it for you** ich tu es gerne für dich

**happiness** NOUN Glück das

**happy** ADJECTIVE glücklich; a happy child ein glückliches Kind, Happy Birthday herzlichen Glückwunsch zum Geburtstag

**harbour** NOUN Hafen der (PLURAL die Häfen)

**hard** ADJECTIVE ❶ hart ❷ (difficult) schwer; a hard question eine schwere Frage, it's hard to say es ist schwer zu sagen

**hard** ADVERB ❶ to work hard hart arbeiten ❷ to try hard sich sehr bemühen

**hard disk** NOUN Festplatte die (PLURAL die Festplatten)

**hardly** ADVERB ❶ kaum; I can hardly hear him ich kann ihn kaum hören, there was hardly anybody there es war kaum jemand da, we've got hardly any milk wir haben kaum Milch, hardly anything kaum etwas, he ate hardly anything er hat kaum etwas gegessen ❷ hardly ever fast nie, I hardly ever see him ich sehe ihn fast nie

**hard up** ADJECTIVE to be hard up knapp bei Kasse sein

**hare** NOUN Hase der (PLURAL die Hasen)

**harm** NOUN it won't do any harm es kann nichts schaden

**harm** VERB ❶ to harm somebody jemandem etwas tun, they didn't harm him sie haben ihm nichts getan ❷ schaden (+DAT), (health, environment, reputation); a cup of coffee won't harm you eine Tasse Kaffee schadet nicht

**harmful** ADJECTIVE schädlich

**harmless** ADJECTIVE unschädlich

**harvest** NOUN Ernte die (PLURAL die Ernten); to get the harvest in die Ernte einbringen

**hat** NOUN Hut der (PLURAL die Hüte)

**hate** VERB hassen; I hate geography ich hasse Erdkunde

**hatred** NOUN Hass der

**have** VERB ❶ haben◇; Anna has three brothers Anna hat drei Brüder, how many sisters do you have? wie viele Schwestern hast du? ❷ what have you got in your hand? was hast du in der Hand?, he has (got) flu er hat die Grippe ❸ (to form past tenses, some verbs in German take 'haben' and others 'sein') I've finished ich bin fertig, have you seen the film? hast du den Film gesehen?, Rosie hasn't arrived yet Rosie ist noch nicht angekommen ❹ to have to do something etwas tun müssen◇, I have to phone my mum ich muss meine Mutter anrufen ❺ ('have' is often translated by a more specific German verb) we had a coffee wir haben einen Kaffee getrunken, what will you have? was nehmen Sie?, I'll have an omelette ich nehme ein Omelett, I'm going to have a shower ich dusche jetzt, to have lunch zu Mittag essen, to have dinner (in the evening) zu Abend essen ❻ (get) bekommen◇; Emma had a letter from Sam yesterday gestern bekam Emma einen Brief von Sam, she had a baby sie hat ein Baby bekommen ❼ to have something done etwas machen lassen◇, I'm going to have my hair cut ich lasse mir die Haare schneiden ❽ to have on (be *wearing)* anhaben◊ *(SEP)*, **to have nothing on** nichts anhaben

**hawk** *NOUN* Habicht der *(PLURAL* die Habichte)

**hay** *NOUN* Heu das

**hay fever** *NOUN* Heuschnupfen der

**hazelnut** *NOUN* Haselnuss die *(PLURAL* die Haselnüsse)

**he** *PRONOUN* er; **he lives in Manchester** er wohnt in Manchester

**head** *NOUN* ❶ Kopf der *(PLURAL* die Köpfe); **he shook his head** er schüttelte den Kopf ❷ *(of a school)* Direktor der *(PLURAL* die Direktoren)*, Direktorin die *(PLURAL* die Direktorinnen)* ❸ *(of a firm)* Chef der *(PLURAL* die Chefs), Chefin die *(PLURAL* die Chefinnen)* ❹ *(when tossing a coin)* **'heads or tails?'** 'Kopf oder Zahl?'
• **to head for something** auf etwas *(ACC)* zusteuern *(SEP)* *(PERF* sein); **Liz headed for the door** Liz steuerte auf die Tür zu

**headache** *NOUN* Kopfschmerzen *(plural)*; **I've got a headache** ich habe Kopfschmerzen

**headlight** *NOUN* Scheinwerfer der *(PLURAL* die Scheinwerfer)

**headline** *NOUN* Schlagzeile die *(PLURAL* die Schlagzeilen)

**headmaster** *NOUN* Direktor der *(PLURAL* die Direktoren)

**headmistress** *NOUN* Direktorin die *(PLURAL* die Direktorinnen)

**headphones** *NOUN* Kopfhörer der *(PLURAL* die Kopfhörer)

**headteacher** *NOUN* Direktor der *(PLURAL* die Direktoren), Direktorin die *(PLURAL* die Direktorinnen)

**health** *NOUN* Gesundheit die

**health centre** *NOUN* Ärztezentrum das *(PLURAL* die Ärztezentren)

**healthy** *ADJECTIVE* gesund

**heap** *NOUN* Haufen der *(PLURAL* die Haufen)*; **I've got heaps of work** ich habe einen Haufen Arbeit *(informal)*

**hear** *VERB* hören; **I can't hear anything** ich kann überhaupt nichts hören, **I hear you've bought a dog** ich habe gehört, dass ihr einen Hund gekauft habt
• **to hear about something** von etwas *(DAT)* hören; **have you heard about the concert?** hast du von dem Konzert gehört?
• **to hear from somebody** von jemandem hören

**hearing aid** *NOUN* Hörgerät das *(PLURAL* die Hörgeräte)

**heart** *NOUN* ❶ Herz das *(PLURAL* die Herzen) ❷ **to learn something by heart** etwas auswendig lernen ❸ *(in cards)* Herz das; **the jack of hearts** der Herzbube

**heart attack** *NOUN* Herzinfarkt der *(PLURAL* die Herzinfarkte)

**heat** *NOUN* Hitze die

**heat** *VERB* ❶ **to heat something** etwas heiß machen, **I'll go and heat the soup** ich mache die Suppe heiß ❷ **the soup's heating** die Suppe wird warm ❸ **heizen** *(a room)*
• **to heat something up** etwas aufwärmen *(SEP)*; **I'm heating the sauce up** ich wärme die Soße auf

a b c d e f g h i j k l m n o p q r s t u v w x y z

**heater** NOUN Heizgerät das (PLURAL die Heizgeräte)

**heather** NOUN Heidekraut das

**heating** NOUN Heizung die

**heatwave** NOUN Hitzewelle die (PLURAL die Hitzewellen)

**heaven** NOUN Himmel der

**heavy** ADJECTIVE ❶ schwer; my rucksack's really heavy mein Rucksack ist sehr schwer ❷ (busy) I've got a heavy day tomorrow ich habe morgen viel zu tun ❸ (in quantity) stark; heavy rain starker Regen

**hectic** ADJECTIVE hektisch; a hectic day ein hektischer Tag

**hedge** NOUN Hecke die (PLURAL die Hecken)

**hedgehog** NOUN Igel der (PLURAL die Igel)

**heel** NOUN ❶ (of foot or sock) Ferse die (PLURAL die Fersen) ❷ (of a shoe) Absatz der (PLURAL die Absätze)

**height** NOUN ❶ (of a person) Größe die; what height are you? wie groß bist du? ❷ (of a building, mountain) Höhe die; what height is it? wie hoch ist es?

**helicopter** NOUN Hubschrauber der (PLURAL die Hubschrauber)

**hell** NOUN Hölle die; hell! verdammt! (informal)

**hello** EXCLAMATION ❶ (polite) guten Tag! ❷ (informal, and on the phone) hallo!

**helmet** NOUN Helm der (PLURAL die Helme)

**help** NOUN Hilfe die; do you need any help? kann ich dir helfen?, (in a shop) kann ich Ihnen behilflich sein?

**help** VERB ❶ helfen◇ (+DAT); to help somebody (to) do something jemandem helfen, etwas zu tun, can you help me lay the table? kannst du mir helfen, den Tisch zu decken? ❷ to help yourself to something sich (DAT) etwas nehmen◇, help yourself to vegetables nimm dir Gemüse, help yourself! greif zu! ❸ help! Hilfe! ❹ he can't help it er kann nichts dafür

**helper** NOUN Helfer der (PLURAL die Helfer), Helferin die (PLURAL die Helferinnen)

**helpful** ADJECTIVE (person) hilfsbereit

**helping** NOUN Portion die (PLURAL die Portionen); would you like a second helping? möchtest du eine zweite Portion?

**hem** NOUN Saum der (PLURAL die Säume)

**hen** NOUN Henne die (PLURAL die Hennen)

**her** PRONOUN (in German this pronoun changes according to the function it has in the sentence or the preposition it follows) ❶ (as a direct object in the accusative) sie; I know her ich kenne sie, I saw her last week ich habe sie letzte Woche gesehen ❷ (after prepositions +ACC) sie; without her ohne sie, we've heard a lot about her wir haben viel über sie gehört ❸ (as an indirect object or after verbs that take the dative) ihr; I gave her

**my address** ich habe ihr meine Adresse gegeben, **we helped her** wir haben ihr geholfen ❹ *(after prepositions +DAT)* **ihr; with her** mit ihr ❺ *(in comparisons)* **sie; he's older than her** er ist älter als sie ❻ *(in the nominative)* **sie; it was her** sie war es

**her** *DETERMINER* ❶ *(before a masculine noun)* **ihr; her brother** ihr Bruder ❷ *(before a feminine noun)* **ihre; her sister** ihre Schwester ❸ *(before a neuter noun)* **ihr; her house** ihr Haus ❹ *(before a plural noun)* **ihre; her children** ihre Kinder ❺ *(with parts of the body)* **der/die/das** *(PLURAL die)*; **she had a glass in her hand** sie hatte ein Glas in der Hand, **she's washing her hands** sie wäscht sich die Hände

**herb** *NOUN* Kraut das *(PLURAL die Kräuter)*

**herd** *NOUN (of cattle, goats)* Herde die *(PLURAL die Herden)*

**here** *ADVERB* ❶ *(in or at this place)* **hier; not far from here** nicht weit von hier, **here's my address** hier ist meine Adresse, **I want to stay here** ich möchte hier bleiben ❷ *(to this place)* **hierher; when Peter came here** als Peter hierher kam ❸ **here they are!** da sind sie!, **Tom isn't here at the moment** Tom ist im Moment nicht da

**hero** *NOUN* Held der *(PLURAL die Helden)*

**heroin** *NOUN* Heroin das

**heroine** *NOUN* Heldin die *(PLURAL die Heldinnen)*

**herring** *NOUN* Hering der *(PLURAL die Heringe)*

**hers** *PRONOUN* ❶ *(for a masculine noun)* **ihrer; my coat is blue and hers is red** mein Mantel ist blau und ihrer ist rot, **I took my hat and she took hers** ich nahm meinen Hut und sie nahm ihren ❷ *(for a feminine noun)* **ihre; I gave Ann my address and she gave me hers** ich habe Ann meine Adresse gegeben und sie hat mir ihre gegeben ❸ *(for a neuter noun)* **ihr(e)s; my bike is new but hers is old** mein Rad ist neu, aber ihrs ist alt ❹ *(for masculine/feminine/neuter plural nouns)* **ihre; I showed Emma my photos and she showed me hers** ich habe Emma meine Fotos gezeigt und sie hat mir ihre gezeigt ❺ **the CDs are hers** die CDs gehören ihr, **it's hers** das gehört ihr

**herself** *PRONOUN* ❶ *(reflexive)* **sich; she's hurt herself** sie hat sich wehgetan ❷ *(stressing something)* **selbst; she said it herself** sie hat es selbst gesagt ❸ **she did it by herself** sie hat es ganz allein gemacht

**hesitate** *VERB* zögern

**heterosexual** *ADJECTIVE* heterosexuell

**heterosexual** *NOUN* Heterosexuelle der/die *(PLURAL die Heterosexuellen)*

**hi** *EXCLAMATION* hallo!

**hiccups** *PLURAL NOUN* **to have the hiccups** einen Schluckauf haben

**hidden** *ADJECTIVE* verborgen

**hide** *VERB* ❶ sich verstecken; **she hid behind the door** sie hat sich hinter der Tür versteckt ❷ **to hide something** etwas verstecken

**hi-fi** NOUN **Hi-Fi-Anlage** die (PLURAL die Hi-Fi-Anlagen)

**high** ADJECTIVE ❶ **hoch; how high is the wall?** wie hoch ist die Mauer?, **the wall is two metres high** die Mauer ist zwei Meter hoch, **the shelf is too high** das Regal ist zu hoch, (the adjective 'hoch' loses its c when it has an ending, becoming hoher/hohe/hohes) **a high tower** ein hoher Turm, **a high wall** eine hohe Mauer, **at high speed** mit hoher Geschwindigkeit, **a high voice** eine hohe Stimme ❷ **high winds** starker Wind

**high** ADVERB **hoch**

**Highers, Advanced Highers** NOUN PLURAL **Abitur** das (Students take 'Abitur' at about 19 years of age. You can explain Highers briefly as follows: Highers werden im vorletzten Jahr der Sekundarstufe in bis zu fünf Fächern abgelegt. Manche Schüler legen zusätzlich Advanced Highers in ihrem letzten Schuljahr ab. Advanced Highers werden in bis zu drei Fächern, die bereits für Highers belegt wurden, abgelegt. Beide Qualifikationen werden von A bis C benotet und sind Hochschulzugangsberechtigungen)
▸ SEE **Abitur**

**high-heeled** ADJECTIVE **hochhackig**

**high jump** NOUN **Hochsprung** der

**hijack** VERB **to hijack a plane** ein Flugzeug entführen

**hijacker** NOUN **Entführer** der (PLURAL die Entführer)

**hijacking** NOUN **Entführung** die (PLURAL die Entführungen)

**hike** NOUN **Wanderung** die (PLURAL die Wanderungen)

**hiker** NOUN **Wanderer** der (PLURAL die Wanderer), **Wanderin** die (PLURAL die Wanderinnen)

**hiking** NOUN **Wandern** das

**hilarious** ADJECTIVE **lustig**

**hill** NOUN ❶ (large hill) **Berg** der (PLURAL die Berge); **you can see the hills** man kann die Berge sehen ❷ (smaller) **Hügel** der (PLURAL die Hügel); **to walk up the hill** den Hügel hinaufgehen ❸ (hillside) **Hang** der (PLURAL die Hänge); **the house on the hill** das Haus am Hang

**him** PRONOUN
(in German this pronoun changes according to the function it has in the sentence or the preposition it follows) ❶ (as a direct object in the accusative) **ihn; I know him** ich kenne ihn, **I saw him last week** ich habe ihn letzte Woche gesehen ❷ (after prepositions +ACC) **ihn; he fought against him** er hat gegen ihn gekämpft, **without him** ohne ihn ❸ (as an indirect object or after verbs that take the dative) **ihm; I gave him my address** ich habe ihm meine Adresse gegeben, **you must help him** du musst ihm helfen ❹ (after prepositions +DAT) **ihm; with him** mit ihm ❺ (in comparisons) **er; she's older than him** sie ist älter als er ❻ (in the nominative) **er; it was him** er war es

**himself** PRONOUN ❶ (reflexive) **sich; he's hurt himself** er hat sich wehgetan ❷ (stressing something) **selbst; he said it himself** er hat es selbst gesagt ❸ **he did it by himself** er hat es ganz allein gemacht

**Hindu** *ADJECTIVE* hinduistisch

**hip** *NOUN* Hüfte die (*PLURAL* die **Hüften**)

**hippie** *NOUN* Hippie der (*PLURAL* die **Hippies**)

**hippopotamus** *NOUN* Nilpferd das (*PLURAL* die **Nilpferde**)

**hire** *NOUN* ❶ Vermietung die; **car hire** die Autovermietung ❷ **for hire** zu vermieten

**hire** *VERB* mieten

**his** *DETERMINER* ❶ (before a masculine noun) sein; **his brother** sein Bruder ❷ (before a feminine noun) seine; **his sister** seine Schwester ❸ (before a neuter noun) sein; **his house** sein Haus ❹ (before a plural noun) seine; **his children** seine Kinder ❺ (with parts of the body) der/die/das (*PLURAL* die); **he had a glass in his hand** er hatte ein Glas in der Hand, **he's washing his hands** er wäscht sich (*DAT*) die Hände

**his** *PRONOUN* ❶ (for a masculine noun) seiner; **my hat is red and his is blue** mein Hut ist rot und seiner ist blau ❷ (for a feminine noun) seine; **I gave him my address and he gave me his** ich habe ihm meine Adresse gegeben und er hat mir seine gegeben ❸ (for a neuter noun) sein(e)s; **my book is new but his is old** mein Buch ist neu, aber seins ist alt ❹ (for masculine/feminine/neuter plural nouns) seine; **I've invited my parents and Steve's invited his** ich habe meine Eltern eingeladen und Steve hat seine eingeladen ❺ **the green car's his** das grüne Auto gehört ihm, **it's his** das gehört ihm

**historic** *ADJECTIVE* historisch

**history** *NOUN* Geschichte die

**hit** *NOUN* ❶ (song) Hit der (*PLURAL* die **Hits**); **their latest hit** ihr neuester Hit ❷ (success) Erfolg der (*PLURAL* die **Erfolge**); **the film is a huge hit** der Film ist ein großer Erfolg

**hit** *VERB* ❶ treffen⋄; **to hit the ball** den Ball treffen ❷ **to hit your head on something** sich (*DAT*) den Kopf an etwas (*DAT*) stoßen, **I hit my head on the door** ich habe mir den Kopf an der Tür gestoßen ❸ prallen gegen (+*ACC*) (*PERF* sein); **the car hit a wall** das Auto ist gegen eine Wand geprallt ❹ **to be hit by a car** von einem Auto angefahren werden

**hitch** *NOUN* Problem das (*PLURAL* die **Probleme**); **there's been a slight hitch** ein kleines Problem ist aufgetaucht

**hitch** *VERB* **to hitch a lift** per Anhalter fahren⋄ (*PERF* sein)

**hitchhike** *VERB* per Anhalter fahren⋄ (*PERF* sein); **we hitchhiked to Heidelberg** wir sind per Anhalter nach Heidelberg gefahren

**hitchhiker** *NOUN* Anhalter der (*PLURAL* die **Anhalter**), Anhalterin die (*PLURAL* die **Anhalterinnen**)

**hitchhiking** *NOUN* Trampen das

**HIV-negative** *ADJECTIVE* HIV-negativ

**HIV-positive** *ADJECTIVE* HIV-positiv

**hobby** *NOUN* Hobby das (*PLURAL* die **Hobbys**)

**hockey** *NOUN* Hockey das

**hockey stick** *NOUN* Hockeyschläger der (*PLURAL* die **Hockeyschläger**)

a
b
c
d
e
f
g
h
i
j
k
l
m
n
o
p
q
r
s
t
u
v
w
x
y
z

**hold** VERB ❶ halten◇; **to hold something in your hand** etwas in der Hand halten, **can you hold the torch?** kannst du die Taschenlampe halten? ❷ (be able to contain) fassen; **the jug holds a litre** der Krug fasst einen Liter ❸ **to hold a meeting** eine Versammlung abhalten◇ (SEP) ❹ **can you hold the line, please?** bleiben Sie bitte am Apparat ❺ **hold on!** (wait) warten Sie! (on the phone) bleiben Sie am Apparat

- **to hold on to something** (to stop yourself from falling) sich an etwas (DAT) festhalten◇ (SEP)
- **to hold somebody up** (delay) jemanden aufhalten◇ (SEP); **I was held up at the dentist's** ich bin beim Zahnarzt aufgehalten worden
- **to hold something up** (raise) etwas hochhalten◇ (SEP)

**hold-up** NOUN ❶ Verzögerung die (PLURAL die Verzögerungen) ❷ (traffic jam) Stau der (PLURAL die Staus) ❸ (robbery) Überfall der (PLURAL die Überfälle)

**hole** NOUN Loch das (PLURAL die Löcher)

**holiday** NOUN ❶ Ferien (plural), Urlaub der (PLURAL die Urlaube) (students, schoolchildren, and families usually have 'Ferien'; people in paid employment usually have 'Urlaub'); **where are you going for your holiday?** wo fahrt ihr in den Ferien hin?, **have a good holiday!** schöne Ferien!, schönen Urlaub!, **to be away on holiday** auf Urlaub sein, in den Ferien sein, **to go on holiday** in Urlaub fahren, in die Ferien fahren, **the school holidays** die Schulferien ❷ (day off work) freie Tag der (PLURAL die freien Tage);

**I'm taking two days' holiday next week** ich nehme mir nächste Woche zwei Tage frei ❸ **public holiday** der Feiertag, **Monday's a holiday** Montag ist ein Feiertag

**holiday home** NOUN Ferienhaus das (PLURAL die Ferienhäuser)

**Holland** NOUN Holland das

**hollow** ADJECTIVE hohl

**holy** ADJECTIVE heilig

**home** NOUN ❶ **I was at home** ich war zu Hause, **to stay at home** zu Hause bleiben ❷ **make yourself at home** mach es dir bequem

**home** ADVERB ❶ (to home) nach Hause; **Susie's gone home** Susie ist nach Hause gegangen, **on my way home** auf dem Weg nach Hause, **to get home** nach Hause kommen, **we got home at midnight** wir sind um Mitternacht nach Hause gekommen ❷ (at home) zu Hause; **I'll be home in the afternoon** ich bin am Nachmittag zu Hause

**homeless** ADJECTIVE obdachlos; **the homeless** die Obdachlosen

**homemade** ADJECTIVE selbst gemacht; **homemade biscuits** selbst gebackene Kekse

**homeopathic** ADJECTIVE homöopathisch

**homesick** ADJECTIVE **to be homesick** Heimweh haben

**homework** NOUN Hausaufgaben (plural); **I did my homework** ich habe meine Hausaufgaben gemacht, **my German homework** meine Deutschhausaufgaben

**homosexual** ADJECTIVE homosexuell

**homosexual** NOUN Homosexuelle der/die (PLURAL die Homosexuellen)

**honest** ADJECTIVE ehrlich

**honestly** ADVERB ehrlich

**honesty** NOUN Ehrlichkeit die

**honey** NOUN Honig der (PLURAL die Honige)

**honeymoon** NOUN Flitterwochen die, (plural); they're going to Italy on their honeymoon sie fahren nach Italien in die Flitterwochen

**honour** NOUN Ehre die

**hood** NOUN ❶ Kapuze die (PLURAL die Kapuzen) ❷ (on a car) Verdeck das (PLURAL die Verdecke)

**hook** NOUN ❶ Haken der (PLURAL die Haken) ❷ to take the phone off the hook das Telefon aushängen (SEP)

**hooligan** NOUN Hooligan der (PLURAL die Hooligans)

**hooray** EXCLAMATION hurra!

**hoover** VERB saugen; I hoovered my bedroom ich habe mein Schlafzimmer gesaugt

**Hoover** NOUN Staubsauger der (PLURAL die Staubsauger)

**hope** NOUN Hoffnung die (PLURAL die Hoffnungen); to give up hope die Hoffnung aufgeben

**hope** VERB ❶ hoffen; we hope you'll be able to come wir hoffen, ihr könnt kommen, I'm hoping to see you on Friday ich hoffe, dich am Freitag zu sehen ❷ I hope so hoffentlich, I hope not hoffentlich nicht

**hopefully** ADVERB hoffentlich; hopefully, the film won't have started hoffentlich hat der Film noch nicht angefangen

**hopeless** ADJECTIVE miserabel (informal); I'm hopeless at geography ich bin miserabel in Erdkunde

**horizontal** ADJECTIVE horizontal, waagrecht; the flag has three horizontal bars die Flagge hat drei waagrechte Streifen

**horn** NOUN ❶ (of an animal, instrument) Horn das (PLURAL die Hörner) ❷ (of a car) Hupe die (PLURAL die Hupen)

**horoscope** NOUN Horoskop das (PLURAL die Horoskope)

**horrible** ADJECTIVE ❶ furchtbar; the weather was horrible das Wetter war furchtbar ❷ (person) gemein; she's really horrible sie ist richtig gemein, he was really horrible to me er war richtig gemein zu mir

**horror** NOUN Entsetzen das

**horror film** NOUN Horrorfilm der (PLURAL die Horrorfilme)

**horse** NOUN Pferd das (PLURAL die Pferde)

**horse chestnut** NOUN (tree and nut) Rosskastanie die (PLURAL die Rosskastanien)

**horseshoe** NOUN Hufeisen das (PLURAL die Hufeisen)

**hose** NOUN Schlauch der (PLURAL die Schläuche)

**hosepipe** NOUN Schlauch der (PLURAL die Schläuche)

A
B
C
D
E
F
G
**H**
I
J
K
L
M
N
O
P
Q
R
S
T
U
V
W
X
Y
Z

**hospital** NOUN **Krankenhaus** das
(PLURAL die **Krankenhäuser**); **in
hospital** im Krankenhaus, **to be
taken into hospital** ins Krankenhaus
kommen

**hospitality** NOUN **Gastfreundschaft**
die

**host** NOUN ❶ **Gastgeber** der
(PLURAL die **Gastgeber**) ❷ (on a TV
programme) **Moderator** der (PLURAL
die **Moderatoren**)

**hostage** NOUN **Geisel** die (PLURAL die
**Geiseln**)

**hostel** NOUN **youth hostel** die
Jugendherberge

**hostess** NOUN ❶ **Gastgeberin** die
(PLURAL die **Gastgeberinnen**) ❷ (on
a TV programme) **Moderatorin** die
(PLURAL die **Moderatorinnen**) ❸ **air
hostess** die Stewardess

**host family** NOUN **Gastfamilie** die
Gastfamilien

**hot** ADJECTIVE ❶ **heiß**; **be careful, the
plates are hot** sei vorsichtig, die
Teller sind heiß, **it's hot today** heute
ist es heiß ❷ person **I'm very hot** mir
ist sehr heiß ❸ (spicy) **scharf**; **the
curry's too hot for me** das Curry
ist mir zu scharf ❹ **a hot meal** ein
warmes Essen

**hot dog** NOUN **Hotdog** das or der
(PLURAL die **Hotdogs**)

**hotel** NOUN **Hotel** das (PLURAL die
**Hotels**)

**hour** NOUN **Stunde** die (PLURAL die
**Stunden**); **two hours later** zwei
Stunden später, **we waited for two
hours** wir haben zwei Stunden lang
gewartet, **I've been waiting for
hours** ich warte schon seit Stunden,

**two hours ago** vor zwei Stunden,
**to be paid by the hour** pro Stunde
bezahlt werden, **every hour** jede
Stunde, **half an hour** eine halbe
Stunde, **a quarter of an hour** eine
Viertelstunde, **an hour and a half**
anderthalb Stunden

**house** NOUN ❶ **Haus** das (PLURAL
die **Häuser**) ❷ **at somebody's
house** bei jemandem, **I'm at Judy's
house** ich bin bei Judy, **I'm going
to Sid's house tonight** ich gehe
heute Abend zu Sid, **I phoned from
Jill's house** ich habe von Jill aus
angerufen

**housewife** NOUN **Hausfrau** die
(PLURAL die **Hausfrauen**)

**housework** NOUN **Hausarbeit** die;
**he does the housework** er macht
den Haushalt (informal)

**hovercraft** NOUN
**Luftkissenfahrzeug** das (PLURAL die
**Luftkissenfahrzeuge**)

**how** ADVERB ❶ **wie**; **how did you
do it?** wie hast du das gemacht?,
**how are you?** wie geht es dir?,
**how many?** wie viele?, **how many
brothers do you have?** wie viele
Brüder hast du?, **how old are you?**
wie alt bist du?, **how far is it?** wie
weit ist es?, **how far is it to York?**
wie weit ist es bis York?, **how long
will it take?** wie lange dauert es?,
**how long have you known her?** wie
lange kennst du sie? ❷ **how much?**
wie viel?, **how much money do you
have?** wie viel Geld hast du?, **how
much is it?** wie viel kostet das?

**however** ADVERB ❶ **jedoch** ❷ (in
questions) **however did she do
it?** wie hat sie das nur gemacht?
❸ **however famous he is** wie
berühmt er auch sein mag

**hug** NOUN to give somebody a hug jemanden umarmen, **she gave me a hug** sie hat mich umarmt

**huge** ADJECTIVE **riesig**

**hum** VERB **summen**

**human** ADJECTIVE **menschlich**

**human being** NOUN **Mensch** der (PLURAL die **Menschen**)

**humour** NOUN **Humor** der; to have a sense of humour Humor haben

**hundred** NUMBER **hundert**; two hundred zweihundert, **two hundred and ten** zweihundertzehn, **a hundred people** hundert Menschen, **about a hundred** um die hundert, **hundreds of people** hunderte von Menschen

**Hungary** NOUN **Ungarn** das

**hunger** NOUN **Hunger** der

**hungry** ADJECTIVE to be hungry Hunger haben, **I'm hungry** ich habe Hunger

**hunt** VERB ❶ **jagen** (an animal) ❷ **suchen** (a person)

**hunting** NOUN **Jagd** die; fox-hunting die Fuchsjagd

**hurry** NOUN to be in a hurry es eilig haben, **I'm in a hurry** ich habe es eilig, **there's no hurry** es eilt nicht

**hurry** VERB ❶ **sich beeilen**; I must hurry ich muss mich beeilen, **hurry up!** beeil dich! ❷ **he hurried home** er ging schnell nach Hause

**hurt** VERB ❶ to hurt somebody jemandem wehtun◇ (SEP), **you're hurting me!** du tust mir weh!, **that hurts!** das tut weh! ❷ **my arm hurts** der Arm tut mir weh ❸ to hurt yourself sich (DAT) wehtun◇ (SEP), **did you hurt yourself?** hast du dir wehgetan?

**hurt** ADJECTIVE ❶ (in an accident) **verletzt**; three people were hurt drei Menschen wurden verletzt ❷ (in feelings) **gekränkt**; she felt hurt sie fühlte sich gekränkt

**husband** NOUN **Ehemann** der (PLURAL die **Ehemänner**)

**hygienic** ADJECTIVE **hygienisch**

**hymn** NOUN **Kirchenlied** das (PLURAL die **Kirchenlieder**)

**hypermarket** NOUN **Großmarkt** der (PLURAL die **Großmärkte**)

**hyphen** NOUN **Bindestrich** der (PLURAL die **Bindestriche**)

a
b
c
d
e
f
g
h
i
j
k
l
m
n
o
p
q
r
s
t
u
v
w
x
y
z

**I** PRONOUN ich; **I have two sisters** ich habe zwei Schwestern

**ice** NOUN Eis das

**ice cream** NOUN Eis das; **two chocolate ice creams** zwei Schokoladeneis

**ice hockey** NOUN Eishockey das

**ice rink** NOUN Eisbahn die (PLURAL die Eisbahnen)

**ice-skating** NOUN **to go ice-skating** Schlittschuh laufen◇ (PERF sein)

**icy** ADJECTIVE ❶ vereist (road) ❷ (very cold) eiskalt

**idea** NOUN ❶ Idee die (PLURAL die Ideen); **what a good idea!** was für eine gute Idee! ❷ **I've no idea** ich habe keine Ahnung

**ideal** ADJECTIVE ideal

**identical** ADJECTIVE identisch

**identification** NOUN ❶ Identifizierung die ❷ (proof of identity) Ausweispapiere (plural)

**identity card** NOUN Personalausweis der (PLURAL die Personalausweise)

**idiot** NOUN Idiot der (PLURAL die Idioten)

**idiotic** ADJECTIVE idiotisch

**i.e.** ABBREVIATION d. h. (short for das heißt)

**if** CONJUNCTION ❶ wenn; **if it rains** wenn es regnet, **if I won the lottery** wenn ich in der Lotterie gewinnen sollte, **if not** wenn nicht, **if only** wenn nur, **if only you'd told me** wenn du mir das nur gesagt hättest ❷ **even if** selbst wenn, **even if it snows** selbst wenn es schneit ❸ **if I were you** an deiner Stelle ❹ (whether) ob; **I wonder if he'll come** ich bin gespannt, ob er kommt, **as if** als ob

**ignore** VERB ❶ ignorieren ❷ überhören (what somebody says)

**ill** ADJECTIVE krank; **to fall ill, to be taken ill** krank werden, **I feel ill** ich fühle mich krank

**illegal** ADJECTIVE illegal

**illness** NOUN Krankheit die (PLURAL die Krankheiten)

**illusion** NOUN Illusion die (PLURAL die Illusionen)

**illustration** NOUN Illustration die (PLURAL die Illustrationen)

**image** NOUN Bild das (PLURAL die Bilder)
• **he's the spitting image of his father** er ist das Ebenbild seines Vaters

**imagination** NOUN Phantasie die

**imaginative** ADJECTIVE phantasievoll

**imagine** VERB sich (DAT) vorstellen; **imagine that you're very rich** stell dir vor, du bist sehr reich, **you can't imagine how hard it was** du kannst dir nicht vorstellen, wie schwer es war

**imitate** VERB nachahmen (SEP)

**immediate** ADJECTIVE ❶ (without delay) unmittelbar ❷ the

A
B
C
D
E
F
G
H
I
J
K
L
M
N
O
P
Q
R
S
T
U
V
W
X
Y
Z

**immediate family** die engste Familie

**immediately** ADVERB ❶ sofort; **I rang them immediately** ich habe sie sofort angerufen ❷ **immediately before** unmittelbar davor, **immediately after** unmittelbar danach

**immigrant** NOUN Einwanderer der (PLURAL die Einwanderer) Einwanderin die (PLURAL die Einwanderinnen)

**immigration** NOUN Einwanderung die

**impatience** NOUN Ungeduld die

**impatient** ADJECTIVE ❶ ungeduldig ❷ **to be impatient with somebody** ungeduldig mit jemandem sein

**impatiently** ADVERB ungeduldig

**imperfect** NOUN (verb tense) Imperfekt das; "ich schlug" **is in the imperfect** "ich schlug" steht im Imperfekt

**import** NOUN Import der (PLURAL die Importe)

**import** VERB importieren

**importance** NOUN Wichtigkeit die

**important** ADJECTIVE wichtig

**impossible** ADJECTIVE unmöglich; **it's impossible to find a telephone** es ist unmöglich, ein Telefon zu finden

**impressed** ADJECTIVE beeindruckt; **to be impressed by something** von etwas (DAT) beeindruckt sein

**impression** NOUN Eindruck der (PLURAL die Eindrücke); **to make a good impression on somebody** einen guten Eindruck auf jemanden

machen, **I got the impression he was hiding something** ich hatte den Eindruck, dass er etwas verheimlichte

**impressive** ADJECTIVE eindrucksvoll

**improve** VERB ❶ **to improve something** etwas verbessern ❷ (get better) besser werden; **the weather is improving** das Wetter wird besser

**improvement** NOUN Verbesserung die (PLURAL die Verbesserungen)

**in** PREPOSITION ❶ in (+DAT or, with movement into, +ACC); **it is in my pocket** es ist in meiner Tasche, (with movement) **he put it in his pocket** er hat es in die Tasche gesteckt, **she sat in the sun** sie saß in der Sonne, **I read it in the newspaper** ich habe es in der Zeitung gelesen, **in Oxford** in Oxford, **in Germany** in Deutschland ❷ **the biggest city in the world** die größte Stadt der Welt, **a house in the country** ein Haus auf dem Land, **in the street** auf der Straße ❸ (wearing and with colours) **in** (+DAT); **the girl in the pink shirt** das Mädchen im rosa Hemd ❹ **in German** auf Deutsch ❺ (time expressions) **in** (+DAT); **in May** im Mai, **in 1994** (im Jahre) 1994, **in winter** im Winter, **in summer** im Sommer, **in the night** in der Nacht, **I'll phone you in ten minutes** ich rufe dich in zehn Minuten an, **she was ready in five minutes** sie war in fünf Minuten fertig ❻ **in the morning** am Morgen, **at eight in the morning** um acht Uhr morgens ❼ (among people or in literature) **bei** (+DAT); **it's rare in children** das ist selten bei Kindern, **in Shakespeare** bei Shakespeare, **in the army** beim Militär ❽ **in time** rechtzeitig

**in** ADVERB ❶ (inside) **hinein-, herein-, rein-** (informal) (Herein-, hinein-, and rein- form prefixes to separable verbs. 'Herein-' is used with verbs like kommen, which have the sense of moving towards the speaker. 'Hinein-' is used with verbs like gehen, which have the sense of going away from the speaker. The informal 'rein-' can be used with either movement); **to come in hereinkommen◇** (SEP) (PERF **sein), to go in hineingehen◇** (SEP) (PERF **sein), he was not allowed to go into the room** er durfte nicht ins Zimmer reingehen, **to run in reinlaufen◇** (SEP) (PERF **sein**) (informal) ❷ **to be in** da sein, **Mick's not in at the moment** Mick ist im Moment nicht da ❸ (at home) **zu Hause** ❹ (indoors) **drinnen; in here** hier drinnen, **in there** da drinnen

**include** VERB **einschließen◇** (SEP); **service is included in the price** die Bedienung ist im Preis inbegriffen

**including** PREPOSITION ❶ **einschließlich** (+GEN); **everyone, including the children** alle, einschließlich der Kinder, **£50 including postage** fünfzig Pfund einschließlich Porto, **including Sundays** einschließlich sonntags ❷ **not including Sundays** außer sonntags

**income** NOUN **Einkommen** das (PLURAL die **Einkommen**)

**income tax** NOUN **Einkommenssteuer** die (PLURAL die **Einkommenssteuern**)

**increase** NOUN **Erhöhung** die (PLURAL die **Erhöhungen**) (in price, for example)

**increase** VERB ❶ **steigen◇** (PERF **sein**); **the price has increased by £10** der Preis ist um zehn Pfund gestiegen ❷ **erhöhen** (salary)

**incredible** ADJECTIVE **unglaublich**

**incredibly** ADVERB (very) **unglaublich; the film's incredibly boring** der Film ist unglaublich langweilig

**indeed** ADVERB ❶ (to emphasize) **wirklich; she's very pleased indeed** sie hat sich wirklich sehr gefreut ❷ (certainly) **natürlich; 'can you hear the radio?' – 'indeed I can!'** 'kannst du das Radio hören?' – 'ja, natürlich!' ❸ **thank you very much indeed** vielen herzlichen Dank

**indefinite article** NOUN **unbestimmte Artikel** der (PLURAL die **umbestimmten Artikel**)

**independence** NOUN **Unabhängigkeit** die

**independent** ADJECTIVE **unabhängig; independent school** die **Privatschule**

**index** NOUN **Register** das (PLURAL die **Register**)

**India** NOUN **Indien** das

**Indian** NOUN ❶ **Inder** der (PLURAL die **Inder**), **Inderin** die (PLURAL die **Inderinnen**) ❷ (a Native American) **Indianer** der (PLURAL die **Indianer**), **Indianerin** die (PLURAL die **Indianerinnen**)

**Indian** ADJECTIVE ❶ **indisch; he's Indian** er ist Inder ❷ (Native American) **indianisch; she's Indian** sie ist Indianerin

**indicate** VERB ❶ zeigen auf (+ACC), (a person or a thing) ❷ (of a car or driver) blinken

**indigestion** NOUN Magenverstimmung die (PLURAL die Magenverstimmungen)

**individual** NOUN Einzelne der/die (PLURAL die Einzelnen)

**individual** ADJECTIVE ❶ einzeln (serving, contribution) ❷ individual tuition der Einzelunterricht

**indoor** ADJECTIVE an indoor swimming pool ein Hallenbad, indoor games Spiele im Haus, (in sports) Hallenspiele

**indoors** ADVERB drinnen; it's cooler indoors drinnen ist es kühler, to go indoors ins Haus gehen

**industrial** ADJECTIVE industriell

**industrial estate** NOUN Industriegebiet das (PLURAL die Industriegebiete)

**industry** NOUN Industrie die (PLURAL die Industrien); the car industry die Autoindustrie

**inefficient** ADJECTIVE uneffektiv

**inevitable** ADJECTIVE unvermeidlich

**inevitably** ADVERB zwangsläufig

**inexperienced** ADJECTIVE unerfahren

**infant school** NOUN Vorschule die (PLURAL die Vorschulen)

**infection** NOUN Infektion die (PLURAL die Infektionen); eye infection die Augeninfektion, throat infection die Halsentzündung

**infectious** ADJECTIVE ansteckend

**infinitive** NOUN Infinitiv der (PLURAL die Infinitive)

**inflammable** ADJECTIVE leicht entflammbar

**inflatable** ADJECTIVE inflatable mattress die Luftmatratze, inflatable boat das Schlauchboot

**inflate** VERB aufblasen◇ (SEP) (a mattress or boat)

**inflation** NOUN Inflation die (PLURAL die Inflationen)

**influence** NOUN Einfluss der (PLURAL die Einflüsse); to be a good influence on somebody einen guten Einfluss auf jemanden haben

**influence** VERB beeinflussen

**inform** VERB informieren; to inform somebody of something jemanden über etwas (ACC) informieren

**informal** ADJECTIVE ❶ zwanglos (meal or event) ❷ ungezwungen (language, tone)

**information** NOUN Auskunft die; where can I get information about flights to Berlin? wo kann ich Auskunft über Flüge nach Berlin bekommen?

**information desk**, **information office** NOUN Auskunftsbüro das (PLURAL die Auskunftsbüros)

**information technology** NOUN Informatik die

**ingredient** NOUN Zutat die (PLURAL die Zutaten)

a
b
c
d
e
f
g
h
i
j
k
l
m
n
o
p
q
r
s
t
u
v
w
x
y
z

**inhabitant** NOUN Einwohner der (PLURAL die Einwohner), Einwohnerin die (PLURAL die Einwohnerinnen)

**initials** PLURAL NOUN Initialen (plural)

**initiative** NOUN Initiative die (PLURAL die Initiativen); **you must use your initiative** du musst die Initiative ergreifen

**injection** NOUN Spritze die (PLURAL die Spritzen)

**injure** VERB verletzen

**injury** NOUN Verletzung die (PLURAL die Verletzungen)

**ink** NOUN Tinte die (PLURAL die Tinten)

**in-laws** NOUN Schwiegereltern (plural)

**inner** ADJECTIVE inner

**innocent** ADJECTIVE unschuldig

**insane** ADJECTIVE ❶ geisteskrank ❷ (foolish) wahnsinnig

**insect** NOUN Insekt das (PLURAL die Insekten); **insect bite** der Insektenstich

**insect repellent** NOUN Insektenvertilgungsmittel das

**inside** NOUN on the inside innen, **the inside of the oven is black** innen ist der Herd schwarz

**inside** PREPOSITION in (+DAT or, with movement towards a place, +ACC); **inside the cinema** im Kino, **to go inside (the house)** ins Haus gehen

**inside** ADVERB drinnen; **she's inside, I think** ich glaube, sie ist drinnen

**inside out** ADJECTIVE, ADVERB (clothing) links

**insist** VERB darauf bestehen◇; **if you insist** wenn du darauf bestehst, **to insist on doing something** darauf bestehen, etwas zu tun, **he insists on paying** er besteht darauf zu zahlen, **to insist that ...** darauf bestehen, dass ..., **Ruth insisted I was wrong** Ruth hat darauf bestanden, dass ich Unrecht hatte

**inspector** NOUN ❶ (on a bus or train) Kontrolleur der (PLURAL die Kontrolleure), Kontrolleurin die (PLURAL die Kontrolleurinnen) ❷ (in the police) Kommissar der (PLURAL die Kommissare), Kommissarin die (PLURAL die Kommissarinnen)

**install** VERB installieren

**instalment** NOUN (of a story or serial) Folge die (PLURAL die Folgen)

**instance** NOUN for instance zum Beispiel

**instant** NOUN Augenblick der (PLURAL die Augenblicke); **come here this instant!** komm sofort her!

**instant** ADJECTIVE ❶ Instant- (coffee, tea) ❷ (immediate) sofortig

**instantly** ADVERB sofort

**instead** ADVERB ❶ Ted couldn't come, so I came instead (of him) Ted konnte nicht kommen, also bin ich an seiner Stelle gekommen ❷ instead of statt (+GEN) or (+DAT) **he bought a bike instead of a car** statt eines Autos hat er ein Fahrrad gekauft, **instead of cake I had cheese** statt Kuchen habe ich Käse genommen, **instead of playing tennis we went swimming** statt Tennis zu spielen, sind wir schwimmen gegangen

**instinct** NOUN Instinkt der (PLURAL die Instinkte)

**institute** NOUN Institut das (PLURAL die Institute)

**instructions** PLURAL NOUN Anweisung die (PLURAL die Anweisungen); **follow the instructions on the packet** befolgen Sie die Anweisung auf der Packung, **'instructions for use'** 'Gebrauchsanweisung'

**instructor** NOUN Lehrer der (PLURAL die Lehrer), Lehrerin die (PLURAL die Lehrerinnen); **my skiing instructor** mein Skilehrer

**instrument** NOUN Instrument das (PLURAL die Instrumente); **to play an instrument** ein Instrument spielen

**insulin** NOUN Insulin das

**insult** NOUN Beleidigung die (PLURAL die Beleidigungen)

**insult** VERB beleidigen

**insurance** NOUN Versicherung die (PLURAL die Versicherungen); **travel insurance** die Reiseversicherung, **do you have holiday medical insurance?** bist du urlaubskrankenversichert?

**intelligence** NOUN Intelligenz die

**intelligent** ADJECTIVE intelligent

**intend** VERB beabsichtigen; **as I intended** wie beabsichtigt, **to intend to do something** beabsichtigen, etwas zu tun, **we intend to spend the night in Rome** wir beabsichtigen, in Rom zu übernachten

**intensive care** NOUN Intensivpflege die; **he's now in intensive care** er ist jetzt auf der Intensivstation

**intention** NOUN Absicht die (PLURAL die Absichten); **I have no intention of paying** ich habe nicht die Absicht zu zahlen

**interest** NOUN ❶ Interesse das (PLURAL die Interessen); **to have lots of interests** viele Interessen haben, **he has an interest in jazz** er hat Interesse an Jazz ❷ (financial) Zinsen (plural)

**interest** VERB interessieren; **that doesn't interest me** das interessiert mich nicht

**interested** ADJECTIVE **to be interested in something** sich für etwas (ACC) interessieren, **Sean's interested in cooking** Sean interessiert sich für Kochen

**interesting** ADJECTIVE interessant

**interfere** VERB ❶ **to interfere with something** (to fiddle with it) sich (DAT) an etwas (DAT) zu schaffen machen, **don't interfere with my computer!** mach dir nicht an meinem Computer zu schaffen! ❷ **to interfere in something** sich in etwas (ACC) einmischen (SEP) (somebody else's affairs)

**interior designer** NOUN Innenarchitekt der (PLURAL die Innenarchitekten), Innenarchitektin die (PLURAL die Innenarchitektinnen)

**international** ADJECTIVE international

**Internet** NOUN Internet das; **on the Internet** im Internet

A
B
C
D
E
F
G
H
I
J
K
L
M
N
O
P
Q
R
S
T
U
V
W
X
Y
Z

**interpret** VERB *(act as an interpreter)* dolmetschen

**interpreter** NOUN Dometscher der *(PLURAL die Dolmetscher)* Dolmetscherin die *(PLURAL die Dometscherinnen)*

**interrupt** VERB unterbrechen◇

**interruption** NOUN Unterbrechung die *(PLURAL die Unterbrechungen)*

**interval** NOUN *(in a play or concert)* Pause die *(PLURAL die Pausen)*

**interview** NOUN ❶ *(for a job)* Vorstellungsgespräch das *(PLURAL die Vorstellungsgespräche)*; **to go for an interview** sich vorstellen *(SEP)* ❷ *(in a newspaper, on TV, or radio)* Interview das *(PLURAL die Interviews)*

**interview** VERB interviewen *(on TV, radio)*

**interviewer** NOUN Interviewer der *(PLURAL die Interviewer)*, Interviewerin die *(PLURAL die Interviewerinnen)*

**into** PREPOSITION ❶ in *(+ACC)*; **he's gone into the garden** er ist in den Garten gegangen, **I put the ball into the bag** ich habe den Ball in die Tasche getan, **we all got into the car** wir sind alle ins Auto gestiegen, **to go into town** in die Stadt gehen, **to get into bed** ins Bett gehen, **to translate into German** ins Deutsche übersetzen, **to change pounds into euros** Pfund in Euro wechseln ❷ *(against)* gegen *(+ACC)*; **he drove into the wall** er ist gegen die Wand gefahren ❸ **to be into jazz** auf Jazz abfahren◇ *(SEP) (PERF sein) (informal)*

**introduce** VERB vorstellen *(SEP)*; **she introduced me to her brother** sie hat mich ihrem Bruder vorgestellt, **she introduced her brother to me** sie hat mir ihren Bruder vorgestellt, **can I introduce you to my mother?** darf ich Sie meiner Mutter vorstellen?

**introduction** NOUN *(in a book)* Einleitung die *(PLURAL die Einleitungen)*

**invade** VERB einfallen◇ *(SEP)* in *(PERF sein) (+ACC)*

**invalid** NOUN Kranke der/die *(PLURAL die Kranken)*

**invent** VERB erfinden◇

**invention** NOUN Erfindung die *(PLURAL die Erfindungen)*

**inverted commas** PLURAL NOUN Anführungszeichen *(plural)*; **in inverted commas** in Anführungszeichen

**investigation** NOUN Untersuchung die *(PLURAL die Untersuchungen)*; **an investigation into the incident** eine Untersuchung des Vorfalls

**invisible** ADJECTIVE unsichtbar

**invitation** NOUN Einladung die *(PLURAL die Einladungen)*; **an invitation to dinner** eine Einladung zum Abendessen

**invite** VERB einladen◇ *(SEP)*; **Kirsty invited me to lunch** Kirsty hat mich zum Mittagessen eingeladen, **he's invited me out on Tuesday** er hat mich eingeladen, Dienstag mit ihm auszugehen, **they invited us round** sie haben uns zu sich eingeladen

**inviting** *ADJECTIVE* verlockend

**involve** *VERB* ❶ erfordern; **it involves a lot of time** es erfordert viel Zeit ❷ *(include)* beteiligen; **the game will involve everybody** alle können sich an dem Spiel beteiligen, **to be involved in something** an etwas *(DAT)* beteiligt sein, **I am involved in the new project** ich bin an dem neuen Projekt beteiligt ❸ *(implicate)* verwickeln; **to get involved in something** in etwas *(ACC)* verwickelt werden, **two cars were involved in the accident** zwei Autos waren in den Unfall verwickelt ❹ **to get involved with somebody** sich mit jemandem einlassen◇ *(SEP)*

**Iran** *NOUN* Iran der

**Iraq** *NOUN* Irak der

**Ireland** *NOUN* Irland das; **the Republic of Ireland** die Republik Irland

**Irish** *NOUN* ❶ *(the language)* Irisch das ❷ *(the people)* **the Irish** die Iren

**Irish** *ADJECTIVE* irisch; **he's Irish** er ist Ire, **she's Irish** sie ist Irin

**Irishman** *NOUN* Ire der *(PLURAL die Iren)*

**Irish Sea** *NOUN* Irische See die

**Irishwoman** *NOUN* Irin die *(PLURAL die Irinnen)*

**iron** *NOUN* ❶ *(for clothes)* Bügeleisen das *(PLURAL die Bügeleisen)* ❷ *(the metal)* Eisen das

**iron** *VERB* bügeln

**ironing** *NOUN* Bügeln das; **to do the ironing** bügeln

**ironing board** *NOUN* Bügelbrett das *(PLURAL die Bügelbretter)*

**ironmonger's** *NOUN* Haushaltswarengeschäft das *(PLURAL die Haushaltswarengeschäfte)*

**irregular** *ADJECTIVE* unregelmäßig

**irritable** *ADJECTIVE* reizbar

**irritate** *VERB* ärgern

**irritating** *ADJECTIVE* ärgerlich

**Islam** *NOUN* Islam der

**Islamic** *ADJECTIVE* islamisch

**island** *NOUN* Insel die *(PLURAL die Inseln)*

**isolated** *ADJECTIVE* ❶ *(remote)* abgelegen ❷ *(single)* einzeln; **isolated cases** Einzelfälle

**Israel** *NOUN* Israel das

**Israeli** *NOUN* Israeli der/die *(PLURAL die Iraelis)*

**Israeli** *ADJECTIVE* israelisch

**issue** *NOUN* ❶ *(something you discuss)* Frage die *(PLURAL die Fragen)*; **a political issue** eine politische Frage ❷ *(of a magazine)* Ausgabe die *(PLURAL die Ausgaben)*

**issue** *VERB* *(hand out)* ausgeben◇ *(SEP)*

**it** *PRONOUN* ❶ *(as the subject)* er *(standing for a masculine noun)*, sie *(standing for a feminine noun)*, es *(standing for a neuter noun)*; **'where's my key?' – 'it's in the kitchen'** 'wo ist mein Schlüssel?' – 'er ist in der Küche', **'where's my bag?' – 'it's in the living-room'** 'wo ist meine Tasche?' – 'sie ist im Wohnzimmer' **'how old is your**

car?' – 'it's five years old' 'wie alt ist dein Auto?' – 'es ist fünf Jahre alt' ❷ *(as the direct object, in the accusative)* **ihn** *(standing for a masculine noun)*, **sie** *(standing for a feminine noun)*, **es** *(standing for a neuter noun)*; **'where's your umbrella?' – 'I've lost it'** 'wo ist dein Regenschirm?' – 'ich habe ihn verloren', **'have you seen my bag?' –'I saw it in the kitchen'** 'hast du meine Tasche gesehen?' – 'ich habe sie in der Küche gesehen', **'have you read his new book?' – 'I've just bought it'** 'hast du sein neues Buch gelesen?' – 'ich habe es gerade gekauft' ❸ **to it** ihm *(masculine)*, ihr *(feminine)*, ihm *(neuter)* ❹ **yes, it's true** ja, das stimmt, **it doesn't matter** das macht nichts ❺ **who is it?** wer ist da?, **it's me** ich bins, **what is it?** was ist los? ❻ **it's raining** es regnet, **it's Monday** es ist Montag, **it's two o'clock** es ist zwei Uhr ❼ **of it** davon ❽ **out of it** daraus

**Italian** NOUN ❶ *(the language)* **Italienisch** das ❷ *(person)* **Italiener** der *(PLURAL die* **Italiener***)*, **Italienerin** die *(PLURAL die* **Italienerinnen***)*

**Italian** ADJECTIVE ❶ **italienisch**; **Italian food** die italienische Küche ❷ **my Italian class** mein Italienischunterricht

**italics** NOUN **Kursivschrift** die; **in italics** kursiv

**Italy** NOUN **Italien** das

**itch** VERB ❶ **my back's itching** mein Rücken juckt ❷ **this jumper itches** dieser Pullover kratzt

**item** NOUN ❶ **Gegenstand** der *(PLURAL die* **Gegenstände***)* ❷ *(for sale in a shop)* **Artikel** der *(PLURAL die* **Artikel***)*

**its** ADJECTIVE ❶ **sein** *(for a masculine noun)*, **ihr** *(for a feminine noun)*, **sein** *(for a neuter noun)*; **the dog has lost its collar** der Hund hat sein Halsband verloren, **the cat's in its basket** die Katze ist in ihrem Korb, **the horse is brown and its mane is black** das Pferd ist braun und seine Mähne ist schwarz ❷ *(for a plural noun)* **seine** *(standing for a feminine noun)*, *(standing for a masculine noun)* **ihre, seine** *(standing for a neuter noun)*; **its toys** seine Spielsachen, ihre Spielsachen

**itself** PRONOUN ❶ *(reflexive)* **sich**; **the cat's washing itself** die Katze putzt sich ❷ **he left the dog by itself** er hat den Hund allein gelassen

**ivy** NOUN **Efeu** der

**jack** NOUN ❶ *(in cards)* Bube der *(PLURAL* die Buben)*; **the jack of clubs** der Kreuzbube ❷ *(for a car)* Wagenheber der *(PLURAL* die Wagenheber)*

**jacket** NOUN Jacke die *(PLURAL* die Jacken)*

**jacket potatoes** NOUN in der Schale gebackenen Kartoffeln

**jackpot** NOUN Jackpot der *(PLURAL* die Jackpots)*; **to win the jackpot** den Hauptgewinn bekommen, **to hit the jackpot** das große Los ziehen

**jam** NOUN ❶ Marmelade die *(PLURAL* die Marmeladen)*; **raspberry jam** die Himbeermarmelade ❷ **traffic jam** der Stau

**January** NOUN Januar der; **in January** im Januar

**Japan** NOUN Japan das

**Japanese** NOUN ❶ *(the language)* Japanisch das ❷ *(person)* Japaner der *(PLURAL* die Japaner)*, Japanerin die *(PLURAL* die Japanerinnen)*; **the Japanese** die Japaner

**Japanese** ADJECTIVE japanisch

**jar** NOUN ❶ *(small)* Glas das *(PLURAL* die Gläser)*; **a jar of jam** ein Glas Marmelade ❷ *(large)* Topf der *(PLURAL* die Töpfe)*

**javelin** NOUN Speer der *(PLURAL* die Speere)*

**jaw** NOUN Kiefer der *(PLURAL* die Kiefer)*

**jazz** NOUN Jazz der

**jealous** ADJECTIVE eifersüchtig; **to be jealous of somebody** eifersüchtig auf jemanden sein

**jeans** PLURAL NOUN Jeans *(plural)*; **my jeans** meine Jeans, **a pair of jeans** ein Paar Jeans

**jelly** NOUN ❶ Gelee das *(PLURAL* die Gelees)* ❷ *(dessert)* Götterspeise die *(PLURAL* die Götterspeisen)*

**jellyfish** NOUN Qualle die *(PLURAL* die Quallen)*

**jersey** NOUN ❶ *(jumper)* Pullover der *(PLURAL* die Pullover)* ❷ *(for football)* Trikot das *(PLURAL* die Trikots)*

**Jesus** NOUN Jesus der; **Jesus Christ** Jesus Christus

**jet** NOUN *(a plane)* Jet der *(PLURAL* die Jets)*

**jet lag** NOUN Jetlag der

**Jew** NOUN Jude der *(PLURAL* die Juden)*, Jüdin die *(PLURAL* die Jüdinnen)*

**jewel** NOUN Edelstein der *(PLURAL* die Edelsteine)*

**jeweller** NOUN Juwelier der *(PLURAL* die Juweliere)*

**jeweller's** NOUN Juweliergeschäft das

**jewellery** NOUN Schmuck der

**Jewish** ADJECTIVE jüdisch

**jigsaw** NOUN Puzzlespiel das *(PLURAL* die Puzzlespiele)*

**job** | **jumper**

**job** NOUN ❶ (paid work) Stelle die (PLURAL die Stellen), Job der (PLURAL die Jobs) (informal); **a job as a secretary** eine Stelle als Sekretärin ❷ (a task) Arbeit die (PLURAL die Arbeiten); **it's not an easy job** das ist keine leichte Arbeit ❸ **she made a good job of it** sie hat es gut gemacht

**jobless** ADJECTIVE arbeitslos

**jog** VERB joggen◇ (PERF sein)

**join** VERB ❶ (become a member of) beitreten◇ (SEP) (+DAT) (PERF sein); **I've joined the tennis club** ich bin dem Tennisklub beigetreten ❷ (to meet up with) treffen◇; **I'll join you later** ich treffe euch später
• **to join in** ❶ mitmachen (SEP); **Kylie never joins in** Kylie macht nie mit ❷ **to join in something** bei etwas (DAT) mitmachen (SEP), **won't you join in the game?** willst du bei dem Spiel nicht mitmachen?

**joint** NOUN ❶ (of meat) Braten der (PLURAL die Braten); **a joint of beef** ein Rinderbraten ❷ (in your body) Gelenk das (PLURAL die Gelenke)

**joke** NOUN Witz der (PLURAL die Witze); **to tell a joke** einen Witz erzählen

**joke** VERB Witze machen; **you must be joking!** du machst wohl Witze!

**joker** NOUN (in cards) Joker der (PLURAL die Joker)

**journalism** NOUN Journalismus der

**journalist** NOUN Journalist der (PLURAL die Journalisten), Journalistin die (PLURAL die Journalistinnen); **Sean's a journalist** Sean ist Journalist

**journey** NOUN ❶ (a long one) Reise die (PLURAL die Reisen); **on our journey to Italy** auf unserer Reise nach Italien ❷ (shorter; to work or school) Fahrt die (PLURAL die Fahrten); **bus journey** die Busfahrt

**joy** NOUN Freude die (PLURAL die Freuden)

**joystick** NOUN (for computer games) Joystick der (PLURAL die Joysticks)

**Judaism** NOUN Judentum das

**judge** NOUN ❶ (in court) Richter der (PLURAL die Richter) ❷ (in sporting events) Schiedsrichter der (PLURAL die Schiedsrichter) ❸ (in a competition) Preisrichter der (PLURAL die Preisrichter)

**judge** VERB schätzen (time or distance)

**judo** NOUN Judo das; **he does judo** er macht Judo

**jug** NOUN Krug der (PLURAL die Krüge)

**juice** NOUN Saft der; **two orange juices please** zwei Orangensaft bitte

**juicy** ADJECTIVE saftig

**jukebox** NOUN Jukebox die (PLURAL die Jukeboxes)

**July** NOUN Juli der; **in July** im Juli

**jumble sale** NOUN Basar der (PLURAL die Basare)

**jump** NOUN Sprung der (PLURAL die Sprünge); **parachute jump** der Fallschirmsprung

**jump** VERB springen◇ (PERF sein)

**jumper** NOUN Pullover der (PLURAL die Pullover)

## junction

**junction** NOUN ❶ (of roads) **Kreuzung** die (PLURAL die **Kreuzungen**) ❷ (on railway) **Gleisanschluss** der (PLURAL die **Gleisanschlüsse**)

**June** NOUN **Juni** der; **in June** im Juni

**jungle** NOUN **Dschungel** der

**junior** ADJECTIVE **jünger**; **junior school** die **Grundschule**, **the juniors** (at primary school) die **Grundschüler**, die **Grundschülerinnen**

**junk** NOUN **Trödel** der

**junk food** NOUN **ungesunde Essen** das

**just** ADVERB ❶ (very recently) **gerade**; **to have just done something** gerade etwas getan haben, **Tom has just arrived** Tom ist gerade angekommen ❷ **to be just doing something** gerade dabei sein, etwas zu tun, **I'm just doing the food** ich bin gerade dabei, Essen zu machen ❸ **just before midday** kurz vor Mittag, **just after 4 o'clock** kurz nach vier Uhr ❹ (only) **nur**; **just for fun** nur zum Vergnügen, **he's just a child** er ist doch nur ein Kind, **just me and Justine are coming** nur ich und Justine kommen ❺ **just a minute!** einen Moment! ❻ **just coming!** ich komme schon! ❼ (exactly) **just as** genauso wie, **he's got just as many friends** er hat genauso viele Freunde

**justice** NOUN **Gerechtigkeit** die

## keep

**kangaroo** NOUN **Känguru** das (PLURAL die **Kängurus**)

**karate** NOUN **Karate** das

**karting** NOUN **Gokarten** das; **to go go-karting** Gokarten gehen

**kebab** NOUN **Kebab** der (PLURAL die **Kebabs**)

**keen** ADJECTIVE ❶ (enthusiastic or committed) **begeistert**; **he's a keen photographer** er ist ein begeisterter Fotograf, **you don't seem too keen** du scheinst nicht gerade begeistert zu sein ❷ **to be keen on mögen**◇, **I'm not keen on fish** ich mag Fisch nicht ❸ **to be keen on doing** (or **to do**) **something** etwas gerne tun

**keep** VERB ❶ **behalten**◇; **you can keep the book** du kannst das Buch behalten, **to keep a secret** ein Geheimnis für sich behalten ❷ **will you keep my seat?** können Sie meinen Platz freihalten? ❸ **to keep somebody waiting** jemanden warten lassen ❹ (store) **aufbewahren** (SEP); **can I keep my watch in your desk?** kann ich meine Uhr in deinem Schreibtisch aufbewahren?, **where do you keep saucepans?** wo sind die Töpfe? ❺ (not throw away) **aufheben**◇ (SEP); **I kept all his letters** ich habe alle seine Briefe aufgehoben ❻ **to keep on doing something** etwas weiter tun, **she kept on talking** sie

467

hat weitergeredet, **keep straight on** weiter geradeaus gehen ❼ **to keep on doing something** *(time after time)* dauernd etwas tun

he keeps on ringing me up er ruft mich dauernd an ❽ *(maintain)* halten◇; **to keep the food warm** das Essen warm halten, **to keep a promise** ein Versprechen halten ❾ *(stay)* bleiben◇ *(PERF sein)*; **to keep calm** ruhig bleiben, **to keep out of the sun** im Schatten bleiben

**kennel** NOUN ❶ *(for one dog)* Hundehütte die *(PLURAL die Hundehütten)* ❷ *(for boarding)* **kennels** Hundepension die *(PLURAL die Hundepensionen)*

**kerb** NOUN Randstein der

**kettle** NOUN Kessel der *(PLURAL die Kessel)*; **to put the kettle on** Wasser aufsetzen

**key** NOUN ❶ *(for a lock)* Schlüssel der *(PLURAL die Schlüssel)*; **bunch of keys** der Schlüsselbund ❷ *(on a piano or keyboard)* Taste die

**keyboard** NOUN *(for a computer)* Tastatur die *(PLURAL die Tastaturen)*

**keyring** NOUN Schlüsselring der *(PLURAL die Schlüsselringe)*

**keyword** NOUN Schlüsselwort das *(PLURAL die Speicherkarten)*

**kick** NOUN ❶ *(from a person or a horse)* Tritt der *(PLURAL die Tritte)*; **to give somebody a kick** jemandem einen Tritt geben ❷ *(in football)* Schuss der *(PLURAL die Schüsse)*

• **to get a kick out of doing something** etwas leidenschaftlich gerne tun

**kick** VERB ❶ **to kick somebody** jemandem einen Tritt geben ❷ **to**

**kick the ball** den Ball schießen

• **to kick off** anstoßen◇ *(SEP)*

**kick-off** NOUN Anstoß der

**kid** NOUN *(child)* Kind das *(PLURAL die Kinder)*; **Dad's looking after the kids** Vati passt auf die Kinder auf

**kidnap** VERB entführen

**kidnapper** NOUN Entführer der *(PLURAL die Entführer)*, Entführerin die *(PLURAL die Entführerinnen)*

**kidney** NOUN Niere die *(PLURAL die Nieren)*

**kill** VERB ❶ töten *(an animal)* ❷ *(murder)* umbringen◇ *(SEP)*; **he killed the girl** er brachte das Mädchen um ❸ **she was killed in a car accident** sie kam bei einem Autounfall ums Leben

**killer** NOUN Mörder der *(PLURAL die Mörder)*, Mörderin die *(PLURAL die Mörderinnen)*

**kilo** NOUN Kilo das *(PLURAL die Kilo)*; **a kilo of sugar** ein Kilo Zucker, **two euros a kilo** zwei Euro das Kilo

**kilogram** NOUN Kilogramm das *(PLURAL die Kilogramm)*

**kilometre** NOUN Kilometer der *(PLURAL die Kilometer)*

**kilt** NOUN Kilt der *(PLURAL die Kilts)*

**kind** NOUN ❶ Art die *(PLURAL die Arten)*; **this kind of book** diese Art Buch, **all kinds of people** alle möglichen Leute ❷ *(brand)* Sorte die *(PLURAL die Sorten)*

**kind** ADJECTIVE nett; **she was very kind to me** sie war sehr nett zu mir

**kindness** NOUN Freundlichkeit die

**king** NOUN König der *(PLURAL die Könige)*; **the king of hearts** der Herzkönig

**kingdom** NOUN Königreich das *(PLURAL die Königreiche)*; **the United Kingdom** das Vereinigte Königreich

**kiosk** NOUN **❶** *(for newspapers or snacks)* Kiosk das *(PLURAL die Kioske)* **❷** *(for a phone)* Telefonzelle die *(PLURAL die Telefonzellen)*

**kipper** NOUN Räucherhering der *(PLURAL die Räucherheringe)*

**kiss** NOUN Kuss der *(PLURAL die Küsse)*; **to give somebody a kiss** jemandem einen Kuss geben

**kiss** VERB küssen; **kiss me!** küss mich!, **we kissed each other** wir haben uns geküsst

**kit** NOUN **❶** *(of tools)* Werkzeug das **❷** *(in a box)* **a tool kit** ein Werkzeugkasten **❸** *(clothes)* Sachen *(plural)*; **where's my football kit?** wo sind meine Fußballsachen? **❹** *(for making a model, a piece of furniture, etc.)* Bausatz der *(PLURAL die Bausätze)*

**kitchen** NOUN Küche die *(PLURAL die Küchen)*; **the kitchen table** der Küchentisch

**kitchen foil** NOUN Alufolie die

**kitchen roll** NOUN Küchenrolle die *(PLURAL die Küchenrollen)*

**kite** NOUN Drachen der; **to fly a kite** einen Drachen steigen lassen

**kitten** NOUN Kätzchen das *(PLURAL die Kätzchen)*

**kiwi fruit** NOUN Kiwi die *(PLURAL die Kiwis)*

**knee** NOUN Knie das *(PLURAL die Knie)*; **on (your) hands and knees** auf allen vieren

**kneel** VERB knien◇; **to kneel (down)** sich hinknien *(SEP)*

**knickers** PLURAL NOUN Schlüpfer der *(PLURAL die Schlüpfer)*; **two pairs of knickers** zwei Schlüpfer

**knife** NOUN Messer das *(PLURAL die Messer)*

**knife** VERB einstechen◇ *(SEP)* auf *(+ACC)*, *(kill)* erstechen◇

**knight** NOUN *(in chess)* Springer der *(PLURAL die Springer)*

**knit** VERB stricken

**knitting** NOUN Strickerei die

**knob** NOUN **❶** *(on a door or walking stick)* Knauf der *(PLURAL die Knäufe)* **❷** *(control on a radio or machine)* Knopf der *(PLURAL die Knöpfe)* **❸** **knob of butter** das kleine Stückchen Butter

**knock** NOUN Schlag der *(PLURAL die Schläge)*; **a knock on the head** ein Schlag auf den Kopf, **a knock at the door** ein Klopfen an der Tür

**knock** VERB **❶** *(to bang)* stoßen◇; **I knocked my arm on the table** ich habe mir den Arm am Tisch gestoßen **❷** **to knock on something** an etwas *(ACC)* klopfen
- **to knock down ❶** *(in a traffic accident)* anfahren◇ *(SEP)* *(a person)* **❷** *(to demolish)* abreißen◇ *(SEP)* *(an old building)*
- **to knock out ❶** *(to make unconscious)* bewusstlos schlagen◇ **❷** *(in sport, to eliminate)* k.o. schlagen◇

**knot** NOUN **Knoten** der *(PLURAL* die **Knoten)**; **to tie a knot** einen Knoten machen

**know** VERB ❶ *(know a fact)* **wissen**◇; **do you know where Tim is?** weißt du, wo Tim ist?, **I know they've moved house** ich weiß, dass sie umgezogen sind, **yes, I know** ja, weiß ich, **you never know!** man kann nie wissen!, **I know how to get to town** ich weiß, wie man in die Stadt kommt ❷ *(be personally acquainted with)* **kennen**◇; **do you know the Jacksons?** kennst du die Jacksons?, **all the people I know** alle Leute, die ich kenne, **I don't know his mother** ich kenne seine Mutter nicht ❸ **to know how to do something** wissen, wie man etwas macht, **Steve knows how to make potato salad** Steve kann Kartoffelsalat machen, **Liz knows how to mend it** Liz kann es reparieren ❹ **to know about** Bescheid wissen über *(+ACC)*, *(items in the news)* ❺ **to know about** sich auskennen◇ *(SEP)* mit *(machines, cars, etc.)*, **Lindy knows about computers** Lindy kennt sich mit Computern aus ❻ **to get to know somebody** jemanden kennen lernen

**knowledge** NOUN **Wissen** das

**Koran** NOUN **Koran** der

**kosher** ADJECTIVE **koscher**

**LI**

**lab** NOUN **Labor** das *(PLURAL* die **Labors)**

**label** NOUN **Etikett** das *(PLURAL* die **Etikette)**

**laboratory** NOUN **Labor** das *(PLURAL* die **Labors)**

**lace** NOUN ❶ *(for a shoe)* **Schnürsenkel** der *(PLURAL* die **Schnürsenkel)**; **to tie your laces** sich *(DAT)* die Schnürsenkel binden ❷ *(fabric or trimming)* **Spitze** die

**ladder** NOUN ❶ *(for climbing)* **Leiter** die *(PLURAL* die **Leitern)** ❷ *(in your tights)* **Laufmasche** die *(PLURAL* die **Laufmaschen)**

**ladies** NOUN *(lavatory)* **Damentoilette** die *(PLURAL* die **Damentoiletten)**; *(on a sign)* 'Ladies' 'Damen'

**lady** NOUN **Dame** die *(PLURAL* die **Damen)**; **ladies and gentlemen** meine Damen und Herren

**ladybird** NOUN **Marienkäfer** der *(PLURAL* die **Marienkäfer)**

**lager** NOUN **helle Bier** das *(PLURAL* die **hellen Biere)**, **Helle** das *(PLURAL* die **Hellen)** *(informal)*; **a lager, please** ein Helles bitte

**laid-back** ADJECTIVE **gelassen**

**lake** NOUN **See** der *(PLURAL* die **Seen)**; **Lake Geneva** der Genfer See

**landlady** NOUN ❶ *(of a house or room)* **Vermieterin** die *(PLURAL die* **Vermieterinnen**) ❷ *(of a pub)* **Gastwirtin** die *(PLURAL die* **Gastwirtinnen**)

**landlord** NOUN ❶ *(of a house or room)* **Vermieter** der *(PLURAL die* **Vermieter**) ❷ *(of a pub)* **Gastwirt** der *(PLURAL die* **Gastwirte**)

**lane** NOUN ❶ *(small road)* **Weg** der *(PLURAL die* **Wege**) ❷ *(of a motorway)* **Spur** die *(PLURAL die* **Spuren**)

**language** NOUN ❶ *(German, Italian, etc.)* **Sprache** die *(PLURAL die* **Sprachen**); **foreign language** **Fremdsprache** die ❷ *(way of speaking)* **Ausdrucksweise** die; **bad language** **Kraftausdrücke** *(plural)*

**lap** NOUN ❶ **Schoß** der *(PLURAL die* **Schöße**) ❷ *(in races)* **Runde** die *(PLURAL die* **Runden**)

**laptop** NOUN **Laptop** der *(PLURAL die* **Laptops**)

**larder** NOUN **Speisekammer** die *(PLURAL die* **Speisekammern**)

**large** ADJECTIVE **groß**

**laser** NOUN **Laser** der *(PLURAL die* **Laser**)

**laser beam** NOUN **Laserstrahl** der *(PLURAL die* **Laserstrahlen**)

**laser printer** NOUN **Laserdrucker** der *(PLURAL die* **Laserdrucker**)

**laser surgery** NOUN **Laseroperation** die *(PLURAL die* **Laseroperationen**)

**last** ADJECTIVE **letzter/letzte/letztes**; **last week** letzte Woche, **for the last time** zum letzten Mal, **last night** gestern Nacht

**last** ADVERB ❶ *(in final position)* **als Letzter/als Letzte/als Letztes**; **Rob arrived last** Rob kam als Letzter an ❷ *(at last!)* endlich! ❸ *(most recently)* **zuletzt**; **I last saw him in May** ich habe ihn zuletzt im Mai gesehen

**last** VERB **dauern**; **the film lasted two hours** der Film dauerte zwei Stunden

**late** ADJECTIVE, ADVERB ❶ **spät**; **I'm late** ich bin spät dran, **we were five minutes late** wir haben uns fünf Minuten verspätet, **they arrived late** sie sind zu spät angekommen, **to be late for something** zu spät zu etwas *(DAT)* kommen, **we were late for the party** wir kamen zu spät zur Party ❷ **to be late** *(of a bus or train)* **Verspätung haben**, **the train was an hour late** der Zug hatte eine Stunde Verspätung ❸ *(late in the day)* **spät**; **we got up late** wir sind spät aufgestanden, **the chemist is open late** die Apotheke hat bis spät auf, **late last night** gestern spät in der Nacht, **too late!** zu spät!

**lately** ADVERB **in letzter Zeit**

**later** ADVERB **später**; **I'll explain later** ich erkläre es später, **see you later!** bis später!

**latest** ADJECTIVE ❶ **neuester/neueste/neuestes**; **the latest news** die neuesten Nachrichten, **the latest in audio equipment** das Neueste an Audioausrüstung ❷ **at the latest** **spätestens**

**Latin** NOUN **Latein** das

**laugh** NOUN **Lachen** das; **to do something for a laugh** etwas aus Spaß machen

**laugh** VERB ❶ lachen; **everybody laughed** alle haben gelacht, **to laugh about something** über etwas (ACC) lachen ❷ **to laugh at somebody** jemanden auslachen (SEP), **they'll only laugh at me** sie lachen mich bestimmt aus

**launch** NOUN ❶ (of a ship) Stapellauf der ❷ (of a product) Einführung die ❸ (of a spacecraft) Abschuss der

**launch** VERB ❶ auf den Markt bringen◇ (a product) ❷ ins All schiessen◇ (a spacecraft) ❸ zu Wasser lassen◇ (a ship)

**launderette** NOUN Waschsalon der (PLURAL die Waschsalons)

**lavatory** NOUN Toilette die (PLURAL die Toiletten); **to go to the lavatory** auf die Toilette gehen

**lavender** NOUN Lavendel der

**law** NOUN ❶ Gesetz das (PLURAL die Gesetze); **to break the law** gegen das Gesetz verstoßen ❷ **it's against the law** das ist verboten ❸ (subject of study) Jura die (NO PLURAL)

**lawn** NOUN Rasen der (PLURAL die Rasen)

**lawnmower** NOUN Rasenmäher der (PLURAL die Rasenmäher)

**lawyer** NOUN Rechtsanwalt der (PLURAL die Rechtsanwälte), Rechtsanwältin die (PLURAL die Rechtsanwältinnen)

**lay** VERB ❶ (put) legen; **she laid the cards on the table** sie legte die Karten auf den Tisch ❷ **to lay the table** den Tisch decken

**lay-by** NOUN Parkplatz der (PLURAL die Parkplätze)

**layer** NOUN Schicht die (PLURAL die Schichten)

**lazy** ADJECTIVE faul

**lead**[1] NOUN ❶ (when you are ahead) Führung die; **to be in the lead** in Führung liegen, **Baxter's in the lead** Baxter liegt in Führung, **to take the lead** in Führung gehen ❷ (electric) Kabel das (PLURAL die Kabel) ❸ (for a dog) Leine die (PLURAL die Leinen); **on a lead** an der Leine ❹ (role) Hauptrolle die (PLURAL die Hauptrollen) ❺ (an actor) Hauptdarsteller der (PLURAL die Hauptdarsteller), Hauptdarstellerin die (PLURAL die Hauptdarstellerinnen)

**lead** VERB ❶ führen; **the path leads to the sea** der Weg führt zum Meer, **to lead by three points** mit drei Punkten führen ❷ **to lead the way** vorangehen◇ (SEP) (PERF sein) ❸ **to lead to something** zu etwas (DAT) führen (an accident or problems, for example)

**lead**[2] NOUN (metal) Blei das

**leader** NOUN ❶ (of a political party) Vorsitzende der/die (PLURAL die Vorsitzenden) ❷ (of an expedition or group) Leiter der (PLURAL die Leiter), Leiterin die (PLURAL die Leiterinnen) ❸ (in a competition) Erste der/die (PLURAL die Ersten) ❹ (of a gang) Anführer der (PLURAL die Anführer), Anführerin die (PLURAL die Anführerinnen)

**lead singer** NOUN Leadsänger der (PLURAL die Leadsänger), Leadsängerin die (PLURAL die Leadsängerinnen)

**leaf** NOUN Blatt das (PLURAL die Blätter)

**leaflet** NOUN ❶ (with instructions) Merkblatt das (PLURAL die Merkblätter) ❷ (for advertising) Reklameblatt das (PLURAL die Reklameblätter)

**leak** NOUN ❶ (in a roof, tent) undichte Stelle die (PLURAL die undichten Stellen) ❷ gas leak die undichte Gasleitung ❸ (in a boat) Leck das (PLURAL die Lecks)

**leak** VERB (bottle or roof) undicht sein

**lean** ADJECTIVE (meat) mager

**lean** VERB ❶ to lean on something sich an etwas (ACC) lehnen, he leaned against the door er hat sich gegen die Tür gelehnt ❷ sich lehnen; she was leaning out of the window sie lehnte sich aus dem Fenster ❸ to lean forward sich vorbeugen (SEP)

**leap year** NOUN Schaltjahr das (PLURAL die Schaltjahre)

**learn** VERB lernen; to learn German Deutsch lernen, to learn (how to) drive Autofahren lernen

**learner** NOUN ❶ Lerner der (PLURAL die Lerner); to be a fast learner schnell lernen ❷ (beginner) Anfänger der (PLURAL die Anfänger), Anfängerin die (PLURAL die Anfängerinnen)

**least** ADJECTIVE, PRONOUN ❶ wenigster/wenigste/wenigstes; to have least time am wenigsten Zeit haben, Tony has the least money Tony hat das wenigste Geld ❷ (the slightest) geringster/geringste/geringstes; I haven't the least idea ich habe nicht die geringste Ahnung

**least** ADVERB ❶ am wenigsten; I like the blue shirt least ich mag das blaue Hemd am wenigsten ❷ the

least expensive hotel das billigste Hotel ❸ at least (at a minimum) mindestens, at least twenty people mindestens zwanzig Leute ❹ at least (at any rate) wenigstens, she's a teacher, at least I think she is sie ist Lehrerin, glaube ich wenigstens

**leather** NOUN Leder das; leather jacket die Lederjacke

**leave** NOUN Urlaub der; three days' leave drei Tage Urlaub

**leave** VERB ❶ (go away) gehen◇ (PERF sein), (by car) fahren◇ (SEP) (PERF sein), (a train or bus) abfahren◇ (SEP) (PERF sein); they're leaving tomorrow evening sie fahren morgen Abend, we left at six wir sind um sechs Uhr gegangen, the train leaves Munich at ten der Zug fährt um zehn Uhr von München ab ❷ (go away from or go out of) verlassen◇; I left the office at five ich habe das Büro um fünf verlassen, he left his wife er hat seine Frau verlassen ❸ (deposit or allow to remain in the same state) lassen◇; you can leave your coats in the hall Sie können Ihre Mäntel in der Diele lassen, to leave the door open die Tür offen lassen, leave it until tomorrow lass es bis morgen ❹ to leave somebody something jemandem etwas hinterlassen◇ (a message or money) he didn't leave a message er hat keine Nachricht hinterlassen ❺ (not do) stehen lassen◇; leave the washing up lass den Abwasch stehen ❻ (forget) vergessen◇; he left his umbrella on the train er hat seinen Regenschirm im Zug vergessen ❼ be left übrig sein (PERF sein), there are two pancakes left zwei Pfannkuchen sind noch übrig, I don't have any money left ich habe kein Geld mehr übrig, **we have ten minutes left** wir haben noch zehn Minuten Zeit

**lecture** NOUN ❶ *(at university)* **Vorlesung** die *(PLURAL die* **Vorlesungen)** ❷ *(public)* **Vortrag** der *(PLURAL die* **Vorträge)**

**leek** NOUN **Lauch** der

**left** NOUN **on the left** links, **to drive on the left** links fahren, **on my left** links von mir

**left** ADVERB **links; turn left at the church** an der Kirche links abbiegen

**left** ADJECTIVE **linker/linke/linkes; his left foot** sein linker Fuß

**left-click** NOUN **Klick** der, **(mit der linken Maustaste)**

**left-click** VERB **left-click the icon** das Icon mit der linken Maustaste anklicken

**left-hand** ADJECTIVE **the left-hand side** die linke Seite

**left-handed** ADJECTIVE **linkshändig**

**left-luggage office** NOUN **Gepäckaufbewahrung** die *(PLURAL die* **Gepäckaufbewahrungen)**

**leg** NOUN ❶ **Bein** das *(PLURAL die* **Beine)**; **my left leg** mein linkes Bein, **to break your leg** sich *(DAT)* das Bein brechen ❷ *(in cooking)* **Keule** die *(PLURAL die* **Keulen)**; **leg of lamb** die Lammkeule
- **to pull somebody's leg** jemanden auf den Arm nehmen

**legal** ADJECTIVE **gesetzlich**

**leggings** PLURAL NOUN **Leggings** *(plural)*

**leisure** NOUN **Freizeit** die; **in my leisure time** in meiner Freizeit

**lemon** NOUN **Zitrone** die *(PLURAL die* **Zitronen)**

**lemonade** NOUN **Limonade** die *(PLURAL die* **Limonaden)**

**lemon juice** NOUN **Zitronensaft** der

**lend** VERB **leihen**✧; **to lend something to somebody** jemandem etwas leihen, **I lent Judy my bike** ich habe Judy mein Rad geliehen, **will you lend it to me?** kannst du es mir leihen?

**length** NOUN **Länge** die *(PLURAL die* **Längen)**

**lens** NOUN ❶ *(in a camera)* **Objektiv** das *(PLURAL die* **Objektive)** ❷ *(in spectacles)* **Brillenglas** das *(PLURAL die* **Brillengläser)** ❸ **contact lenses** Kontaktlinsen *(plural)*

**Lent** NOUN **Fastenzeit** die

**lentil** NOUN **Linse** die *(PLURAL die* **Linsen)**

**Leo** NOUN **Löwe** der *(PLURAL die* **Löwen)** **I'm a Leo** ich bin Löwe

**leotard** NOUN **Turnanzug** der *(PLURAL die* **Turnanzüge)**

**lesbian** ADJECTIVE **lesbisch**

**less** PRONOUN, DETERMINER, ADVERB **weniger** *('weniger' never changes)*; **Ben eats less** Ben isst weniger, **less time** weniger Zeit, **less than** weniger als, **less than three hours** weniger als drei Stunden, **you spent less than me** du hast weniger als ich ausgegeben, **less and less** immer weniger

**lesson** NOUN (class) Stunde die (PLURAL die Stunden); German lesson die Deutschstunde, driving lesson die Fahrstunde

**let¹** VERB ❶ (allow) lassen◇; to let somebody do something jemanden etwas tun lassen, she lets me drive her car sie lässt mich mit ihrem Auto fahren, the police let us through die Polizei hat uns durchgelassen, let me in lass mich hinein ❷ (as a suggestion or a command) let's go! gehen wir!, let's not talk about it reden wir nicht mehr darüber, let's eat out essen wir im Restaurant
• to let off ❶ abfeuern◇ (fireworks) ❷ (to excuse from) befreien von (+DAT), (homework)

**let²** VERB (to rent out) vermieten; 'flat to let' 'Wohnung zu vermieten'

**letter** NOUN ❶ Brief der (PLURAL die Briefe); a letter for you from Delia ein Brief für dich von Delia ❷ (of the alphabet) Buchstabe der (PLURAL die Buchstaben)

**letter box** NOUN Briefkasten der (PLURAL die Briefkästen)

**lettuce** NOUN Salat der; two lettuces zwei Salatköpfe

**leukaemia** NOUN Leukämie die

**level** NOUN Höhe die; at eye level in Augenhöhe

**level** ADJECTIVE ❶ eben (ground or floor) ❷ (horizontal) waagerecht (shelf) ❸ (at the same height) auf gleicher Höhe; to be level with the ground auf gleicher Höhe mit dem Boden sein

**level crossing** NOUN Bahnübergang der (PLURAL die Bahnübergänge)

**lever** NOUN Hebel der (PLURAL die Hebel)

**liar** NOUN Lügner der (PLURAL die Lügner), Lügnerin die (PLURAL die Lügnerinnen)

**liberal** ADJECTIVE ❶ tolerant ❷ (in politics) liberal; the Liberal Democrats die Liberaldemokraten

**Libra** NOUN Waage die; Sean's Libra Sean ist Waage

**librarian** NOUN Bibliothekar der (PLURAL die Bibliothekare), Bibliothekarin die (PLURAL die Bibliothekarinnen)

**library** NOUN Bibliothek die (PLURAL die Bibliotheken); public library die öffentliche Bücherei

**licence** NOUN ❶ (for a TV) Genehmigung die (PLURAL die Genehmigungen) ❷ (driving licence) Führerschein der (PLURAL die Führerscheine)

**lick** VERB lecken

**lid** NOUN Deckel der (PLURAL die Deckel)

**lie** NOUN Lüge die (PLURAL die Lügen); to tell a lie (or lies) lügen◇

**lie** VERB ❶ (to be stretched out) liegen◇; he's lying on the sofa er liegt auf dem Sofa, my coat lay on the bed mein Mantel lag auf dem Bett ❷ to lie down (for a rest) sich hinlegen (SEP), I'm going to lie down for a little ich lege mich ein bisschen hin ❸ (tell lies) lügen◇

**lie-in** NOUN **to have a lie-in** ausschlafen✧ (SEP)

**life** NOUN **Leben** das (PLURAL die Leben); **all her life** ihr ganzes Leben lang, **full of life** voller Leben, **that's life!** so ist das Leben!

**lifeboat** NOUN **Rettungsboot** das (PLURAL die **Rettungsboote**)

**lifeguard** NOUN **Rettungsschwimmer** der (PLURAL die **Rettungsschwimmer**), **Rettungsschwimmerin** die (PLURAL die **Rettungsschwimmerinnen**); **is there a lifeguard at the pool?** gibt es einen Bademeister im Schwimmbad?

**life jacket** NOUN **Schwimmweste** die (PLURAL die **Schwimmwesten**)

**life-style** NOUN **Lebensstil** der (PLURAL die **Lebensstile**)

**lift** NOUN ❶ **Aufzug** der (PLURAL die **Aufzüge**); **let's take the lift** fahren wir mit dem Aufzug ❷ (a ride) **to give somebody a lift to the station** jemanden zum Bahnhof mitnehmen✧ (SEP), **Khaled's giving me a lift** Khaled nimmt mich mit, **would you like a lift?** möchtest du mitfahren?

**lift** VERB **hochheben**✧ (SEP); **he lifted the box** er hob die Kiste hoch

**light** NOUN ❶ **Licht** das; **will you turn the light on?** kannst du das Licht anmachen?, **to turn off the light** das Licht ausmachen, **are your lights on?** hast du das Licht an? ❷ (in the street) **Straßenlampe** die (PLURAL die **Straßenlampen**) ❸ (a lamp) **Lampe** die (PLURAL die **Lampen**) ❹ **traffic lights** die Ampel (SINGULAR), **the lights are green** die Ampel ist

grün ❺ (for a cigarette) **have you got a light?** hast du Feuer?

**light** ADJECTIVE ❶ (not dark) **hell**; **a light blue dress** ein hellblaues Kleid, **it gets light at six** es wird um sechs hell ❷ (not heavy) **leicht**; **a light coat** ein leichter Mantel, **a light breeze** eine leichte Brise

**light** VERB ❶ **anzünden** (SEP) (the fire, a match, the gas); **we lit a fire** wir zündeten ein Feuer an ❷ **to light a cigarette** sich (DAT) eine Zigarette anzünden

**light bulb** NOUN **Glühbirne** die (PLURAL die **Glühbirnen**)

**lighter** NOUN **Feuerzeug** das (PLURAL die **Feuerzeuge**)

**lighthouse** NOUN **Leuchtturm** der (PLURAL die **Leuchttürme**)

**lightning** NOUN **Blitz** der; **flash of lightning** der Blitz, **to be struck by lightning** vom Blitz getroffen werden

**like¹** PREPOSITION, CONJUNCTION ❶ **wie**; **like me** wie ich, **like a duck** wie eine Ente, **like I said** wie gesagt, **what's it like?** wie ist es?, **what was the weather like?** wie war das Wetter? ❷ **like this/that** so ❸ **ähnlich** (+DAT); **to look like somebody** jemandem ähnlich sehen, **Cindy looks like her father** Cindy sieht ihrem Vater ähnlich

**like²** VERB ❶ **mögen**✧; **I like vegetables** ich mag Gemüse, **I don't like meat** ich mag kein Fleisch, **I like Dürer best** ich mag Dürer am liebsten ❷ **to like doing something** etwas gerne tun, **Mum likes reading** Mutti liest gerne ❸ **I would like ...** ich möchte gerne ..., **would you like a coffee?** möchten Sie einen Kaffee?,

what would you like to eat? was
möchten Sie essen?, **yes, if you like**
ja, wenn du willst ❹ **I like the dress**
das Kleid gefällt mir, **how do you
like it?** wie gefällt es dir?

**likely** ADJECTIVE **wahrscheinlich; she's
likely to phone** wahrscheinlich ruft
sie an

**lime** NOUN **Kalk** der

**limit** NOUN **Grenze** die (PLURAL
die **Grenzen**); **speed limit** die
Geschwindigkeitsbeschränkung

**limp** NOUN **to have a limp** hinken

**line** NOUN ❶ **Linie** die (PLURAL die
**Linien**); **a straight line** eine
gerade Linie, **to draw a line**
eine Linie ziehen ❷ (in writing)
**Zeile** die (PLURAL die **Zeilen**); **six
lines of text** sechs Zeilen Text
❸ (railway) **Bahnlinie** die (PLURAL
die **Bahnlinien**) (from one place
to another); **on the line** (the track)
auf der Strecke ❹ (a queue of
people or cars) **Schlange** die (PLURAL
die **Schlangen**); **to stand in line**
Schlange stehen ❺ (telephone)
**Leitung** die (PLURAL die **Leitungen**);
**the line's bad** die Verbindung ist
schlecht, **hold the line, please** bitte
bleiben Sie am Apparat

**line** VERB **füttern** (a coat)

**linen** NOUN **Leinen** das; **a linen jacket**
eine Leinenjacke

**lining** NOUN **Futter** das (PLURAL die
**Futter**)

**link** NOUN **Verbindung** die (PLURAL die
**Verbindungen**); **what's the link
between the two?** was für eine
Verbindung besteht zwischen den
beiden?

**link** VERB **verbinden**◇ (two places);
**the two towns are linked by a
railway line** die beiden Städte sind
durch eine Bahnlinie miteinander
verbunden

**lion** NOUN **Löwe** der (PLURAL die
**Löwen**)

**lip** NOUN **Lippe** die (PLURAL die **Lippen**)

**lip-read** VERB **von den Lippen
lesen**◇

**lipstick** NOUN **Lippenstift** der (PLURAL
die **Lippenstifte**)

**liquid** NOUN **Flüssigkeit** die (PLURAL
die **Flüssigkeiten**)

**liquid** ADJECTIVE **flüssig**

**liquidizer** NOUN **Mixer** der (PLURAL
die **Mixer**)

**list** NOUN **Liste** die (PLURAL die **Listen**)

**listen** VERB ❶ **zuhören** (SEP); **I wasn't
listening** ich habe nicht zugehört,
**to listen to somebody** jemandem
zuhören, **you're not listening to me**
du hörst mir nicht zu ❷ **to listen to
something** etwas (ACC) hören, **to
listen to the radio** Radio hören

**listener** NOUN (to the radio) **Hörer**
der (PLURAL die **Hörer**), **Hörerin** die
(PLURAL die **Hörerinnen**)

**literature** NOUN **Literatur** die (PLURAL
die **Literaturen**)

**litre** NOUN **Liter** der (PLURAL die **Liter**);
**a litre of milk** ein Liter Milch

**litter** NOUN (rubbish) **Abfall** der

**litter bin** NOUN **Abfalleimer** der
(PLURAL die **Abfalleimer**)

**little** ADJECTIVE, PRONOUN ❶ (small)
**klein; a little boy** ein kleiner Junge,

**a little break** eine kleine Pause **②** *(not much)* wenig; **we have very little time** wir haben sehr wenig Zeit **③ a little** ein wenig, **we have a little left** wir haben ein wenig übrig **④ just a little, please** nur ein bisschen, bitte, **it's a little late** es ist ein bisschen spät, **a little more** ein bisschen mehr, **a little less** ein bisschen weniger

• **little by little** nach und nach

**little finger** NOUN kleine Finger der *(PLURAL* die **kleinen Finger)**

**live¹** VERB **①** *(in a house or town)* wohnen; **she lives in York** sie wohnt in York, **we live in a flat** wir wohnen in einer Wohnung **②** *(be or stay alive, spend one's life)* leben; **we're living in the country now** wir leben jetzt auf dem Land, **they live on fruit** sie leben von Obst, **they live apart** sie leben getrennt

**live²** ADJECTIVE, ADVERB **①** live *(broadcast)*; **a live programme** eine Livesendung, **live music** die Livemusik, **a broadcast live from Wembley** eine Liveübertragung aus Wembley, **to broadcast a concert live** ein Konzert live senden **②** *(alive)* lebend

**lively** ADJECTIVE lebhaft

**liver** NOUN Leber die *(PLURAL* die **Lebern)**

**living** NOUN Lebensunterhalt der; **to earn a living** sich *(DAT)* seinen Lebensunterhalt verdienen

**living room** NOUN Wohnzimmer das *(PLURAL* die **Wohnzimmer)**

**lizard** NOUN Eidechse die *(PLURAL* die **Eidechsen)**

**load** NOUN **①** *(on a lorry)* Ladung die *(PLURAL* die **Ladungen)**; **a (lorry-)load of bricks** eine Ladung Ziegelsteine **②** **a bus-load of tourists** ein Bus voll Touristen **③** **loads of** massenhaft *(informal)*, **loads of tourists** massenhaft Touristen, **they've got loads of money** sie haben einen Haufen Geld *(informal)*

**load** VERB **①** beladen◇ *(a vehicle)* **②** **to load a camera** einen Film einlegen *(SEP)*

**loaf** NOUN Brot das *(PLURAL* die **Brote)**; **a loaf of white bread** ein Weißbrot

**loan** NOUN **①** *(from a person)* Leihgabe die *(PLURAL* die **Leihgaben)** **②** *(by a bank)* Kredit der *(PLURAL* die **Kredite)**

**loan** VERB leihen◇

**loathe** VERB hassen; **I loathe getting up early** ich hasse es, früh aufzustehen

**local** NOUN **①** *(a pub)* Stammkneipe die *(PLURAL* die **Stammkneipen)** **②** **the locals** *(people)* die Einheimischen

**local** ADJECTIVE **①** hiesig; **the local library** die hiesige Bücherei **②** **local newspaper** die Lokalzeitung

**lock** NOUN Schloss das *(PLURAL* die **Schlösser)**

**lock** VERB abschließen◇ *(SEP) (a door, room, or bicycle)*; **have you locked the door?** hast du abgeschlossen?

**lodger** NOUN Untermieter der *(PLURAL* die **Untermieter)**, Untermieterin die *(PLURAL* die **Untermieterinnen)**

**loft** NOUN Dachboden der *(PLURAL* die **Dachböden)**

**log** NOUN ❶ **Baumstamm** der
(PLURAL die **Baumstämme**) ❷ (as
firewood) **Holzscheit** das (PLURAL die
**Holzscheite**); **a log fire** ein offenes
Feuer

**lollipop** NOUN **Lutscher** der (PLURAL
die **Lutscher**)

**London** NOUN **London** das

**Londoner** NOUN **Londoner** der
(PLURAL die **Londoner**), **Londonerin**
die (PLURAL die **Londonerinnen**)

**lonely** ADJECTIVE **einsam**; **to feel
lonely** sich einsam fühlen

**long** ADJECTIVE, ADVERB ❶ **lang**; **a long
film** ein langer Film, **a long day** ein
langer Tag, **it's five metres long**
es ist fünf Meter lang, **the film is
an hour long** der Film dauert eine
Stunde ❷ **a long time** lange, **he
stayed for a long time** er ist lange
geblieben, **I've been here for a long
time** ich bin schon lange hier, **a long
time ago** vor langer Zeit, **this won't
take long** das dauert nicht lange
❸ **how long?** wie lange?, **how long
have you been here?** wie lange sind
Sie schon hier?, **long ago** vor langer
Zeit ❹ **a long way** weit, **it's a long
way to the cinema** bis zum Kino ist
es weit ❺ **all night long** die ganze
Nacht ❻ **no longer** nicht mehr, **he
doesn't work here any longer** er
arbeitet nicht mehr hier

**long** VERB **to long to do something**
sich danach sehnen, etwas zu tun,
**I'm longing to see you** ich sehne
mich danach, dich zu sehen

**long-distance call** NOUN (within the
country) **Ferngespräch** das (PLURAL
die **Ferngespräche**)

**long jump** NOUN **Weitsprung** der

**longlife milk** NOUN **H-Milch** die

**loo** NOUN **Klo** das (PLURAL die **Klos**)
(informal)

**look** NOUN ❶ (a glance) **Blick** der
(PLURAL die **Blicke**); **to take a look at
somebody** einen Blick auf jemanden
werfen ❷ (a tour) **to have a look
at the school** sich (DAT) die Schule
ansehen, **to have a look round the
town** sich (DAT) die Stadt ansehen
❸ **to have a look for** suchen

**look** VERB ❶ **sehen**◇; **to look out
of the window** aus dem Fenster
sehen, **I wasn't looking** ich habe
nicht hingesehen ❷ **to look at**
ansehen◇ (SEP), **he looked at the
girl** er hat das Mädchen angesehen,
**to look at something** sich (DAT)
etwas ansehen, **I'm looking at the
photos** ich sehe mir die Fotos an
❸ (to seem) **aussehen**◇ (SEP); **she
looks sad** sie sieht traurig aus, **the
salad looks delicious** der Salat sieht
köstlich aus, **to look like** aussehen
wie, **what does the house look like?**
wie sieht das Haus aus? ❹ (resemble)
**to look like somebody** jemandem
ähnlich sehen, **she looks like her
aunt** sie sieht ihrer Tante ähnlich,
**they look like each other** sie sehen
sich ähnlich

• **to look after** ❶ sich kümmern
um (+ACC); **Dad's looking after the
children** Vati kümmert sich um die
Kinder ❷ **aufpassen** (SEP) auf (+ACC),
(luggage)

• **to look for** suchen; **I'm looking for
my keys** ich suche meine Schlüssel

• **to look forward to** sich freuen auf
(+ACC), (a party or a trip, for example)

• **to look out** (to be careful) **aufpassen**
(SEP); **look out, it's hot!** pass auf, das
ist heiß!

• **to look up** nachschlagen◇ (SEP) (in a

*dictionary or directory)*; **he's looking it up in the dictionary** er schlägt es im Wörterbuch nach

**loose** *ADJECTIVE* ❶ *(screw or knot)* locker ❷ *(garment)* weit ❸ **loose change** das Kleingeld
• **I'm at a loose end** ich habe nichts zu tun

**lorry** *NOUN* Lastwagen der *(PLURAL die Lastwagen)*

**lorry driver** *NOUN* Lastwagenfahrer der *(PLURAL die Lastwagenfahrer)*, Lastwagenfahrerin die *(PLURAL die Lastwagenfahrerinnen)*

**lose** *VERB* ❶ verlieren◇; **we lost** wir haben verloren, **we lost the match** wir haben das Spiel verloren, **Sam's lost his watch** Sam hat seine Uhr verloren ❷ **to get lost** sich verlaufen◇, **we got lost in the woods** wir haben uns im Wald verlaufen ❸ **to lose weight** abnehmen◇ *(SEP)*

**loss** *NOUN* Verlust der *(PLURAL die Verluste)*

**lost property** *NOUN* Fundsachen *(plural)*

**lot** *NOUN* ❶ **a lot** viel, **Wilbur eats a lot** Wilbur isst viel, **I spent a lot** ich habe viel ausgegeben, **he's a lot better** es geht ihm viel besser, **a lot of** viel, **a lot of coffee** viel Kaffee ❷ *(many)* **a lot of** viele, **a lot of books** viele Bücher ❸ **lots of** eine Menge *(informal)*, **lots of people** eine Menge Leute

**lottery** *NOUN* Lotterie die *(PLURAL die Lotterien)*; **to win the lottery** in der Lotterie gewinnen

**loud** *ADJECTIVE* ❶ laut; **in a loud voice** mit lauter Stimme ❷ **to say something out loud** etwas laut sagen

**loudly** *ADVERB* laut

**loudspeaker** *NOUN* Lautsprecher der *(PLURAL die Lautsprecher)*

**lounge** *NOUN* ❶ *(in a house)* Wohnzimmer das *(PLURAL die Wohnzimmer)* ❷ *(in a hotel or an airport)* Halle die *(PLURAL die Hallen)*; **departure lounge** die Abflughalle

**love** *NOUN* ❶ Liebe die; **for love** aus Liebe ❷ **to be in love with somebody** in jemanden verliebt sein, **she's in love with Jake** sie ist in Jake verliebt ❸ **Gina sends her love** Gina lässt grüßen, **with love from Charlie** herzliche Grüße von Charlie ❹ *(in tennis)* null

**love** *VERB* ❶ lieben *(a person)*; **I love you** ich liebe dich ❷ sehr gerne mögen◇ *(a place or food)*; **she loves London** sie mag London sehr gerne, **Wayne loves chocolate** Wayne mag Schokolade sehr gerne ❸ **to love doing something** etwas sehr gerne tun, **I love dancing** ich tanze sehr gerne ❹ **I'd love to come** ich würde sehr gerne kommen

**lovely** *ADJECTIVE* schön; **a lovely dress** ein schönes Kleid, **we had lovely weather** wir hatten schönes Wetter, **we had a lovely day** der Tag war sehr schön

**low** *ADJECTIVE* ❶ niedrig; **a low table** ein niedriger Tisch, **at a low price** zu einem niedrigen Preis ❷ *(not loud)* leise; **in a low voice** mit leiser Stimme

**lower** *ADJECTIVE (not as high)* **tiefer**

**lower** *VERB* **senken**

**loyalty** *NOUN* **Loyalität die** *(PLURAL die Loyalitäten)*

**loyalty card** *NOUN* **Treuekarte die** *(PLURAL die Treuekarten)*

**luck** *NOUN* ❶ **Glück das; good luck!** viel Glück!, **with a bit of luck** wenn wir Glück haben ❷ **bad luck!** so ein Pech!

**luckily** *ADVERB* **zum Glück; luckily for them** zu ihrem Glück

**lucky** *ADJECTIVE* ❶ **to be lucky** Glück haben, **we were lucky** wir haben Glück gehabt ❷ **to be lucky** *(bringing luck)* Glück bringen, **it's supposed to be lucky** es soll Glück bringen, **my lucky number** meine Glückszahl

**luggage** *NOUN* **Gepäck das; my luggage is in the boot** mein Gepäck ist im Kofferraum

**lump** *NOUN* ❶ **Klumpen der** *(PLURAL die Klumpen)* ❷ *(of sugar or butter)* **Stück das** *(PLURAL die Stücke)*

**lunch** *NOUN* **Mittagessen das** *(PLURAL die Mittagessen)*; **to have lunch** zu Mittag essen, **we had lunch in Oxford** wir haben in Oxford zu Mittag gegessen

**lunch break** *NOUN* **Mittagspause die** *(PLURAL die Mittagspausen)*

**lunch hour**, **lunch time** *NOUN* **Mittagszeit die**

**lung** *NOUN* **Lungenflügel der; lungs** die Lunge *(SINGULAR)*

**luxurious** *ADJECTIVE* **luxuriös**

**lyrics** *PLURAL NOUN* **Text der**

**Mm**

**mac** *NOUN* **Regenmantel der** *(PLURAL die Regenmäntel)*

**macaroni** *NOUN* **Makkaroni** *(plural)*

**machine** *NOUN* ❶ **Maschine die** *(PLURAL die Maschinen)* ❷ *(a slot machine)* **Automat der** *(PLURAL die Automaten)*

**machinery** *NOUN* **die Maschinen** *(plural)*

**mackerel** *NOUN* **Makrele die** *(PLURAL die Makrelen)*

**mad** *ADJECTIVE* ❶ **verrückt; she's completely mad!** sie ist total verrückt! ❷ *(angry)* **wütend; to be mad at somebody** wütend auf jemanden sein ❸ **to be mad about something** ganz verrückt auf etwas *(ACC)* sein, **she's mad about horses** sie ist ganz verrückt auf Pferde

**madman** *NOUN* **Verrückte der** *(PLURAL die Verrückten)*

**madness** *NOUN* **Wahnsinn der**

**magazine** *NOUN* **Zeitschrift die** *(PLURAL die Zeitschriften)*, *(with mostly photos)* **Magazin das** *(PLURAL die Magazine)*

**magic** *NOUN* **Zauber der**, *(conjuring tricks)* **Zauberei die**

**magic** _ADJECTIVE_ **❶** Zauber-; **magic wand** der Zauberstab **❷** (great) super (informal)

**magician** _NOUN_ **❶** (wizard) Zauberer der (PLURAL die Zauberer) **❷** (conjurer) Zauberkünstler der (PLURAL die Zauberkünstler)

**magnificent** _ADJECTIVE_ wundervoll

**magnifying glass** _NOUN_ Lupe die (PLURAL die Lupen)

**maiden name** _NOUN_ Mädchenname der (PLURAL die Mädchennamen)

**mail** _NOUN_ Post die

**mail order** _NOUN_ Bestellung per Post die; **to buy something by mail order** etwas bei einem Versandhaus bestellen, **mail order catalogue** der Versandhauskatalog

**main** _ADJECTIVE_ Haupt-; **main entrance** der Haupteingang

**main course** _NOUN_ Hauptgericht das (PLURAL die Hauptgerichte)

**mainly** _ADVERB_ hauptsächlich

**main road** _NOUN_ Hauptstraße die (PLURAL die Hauptstraßen)

**maize** _NOUN_ Mais der

**major** _ADJECTIVE_ **❶** (important) groß **❷** (serious) schwer; **a major accident** ein schwerer Unfall

**Majorca** _NOUN_ Mallorca das

**majority** _NOUN_ Mehrheit die

**make** _NOUN_ Marke die (PLURAL die Marken); **the make of a car** die Automarke

**make** _VERB_ **❶** machen; **to make a meal** Essen machen, **I made breakfast** ich habe Frühstück gemacht, **she made her bed** sie hat ihr Bett gemacht, **to make somebody happy** jemanden glücklich machen, **it makes you tired** das macht einen müde **❷** herstellen (SEP); **they make computers** sie stellen Computer her, **'made in Germany'** 'in Deutschland hergestellt' **❸** **he made me wait** er ließ mich warten, **she makes me laugh** sie bringt mich zum Lachen **❹** verdienen; **he makes forty pounds a day** er verdient vierzig Pfund pro Tag, **to make a living** seinen Lebensunterhalt verdienen **❺** (force) zwingen◇; **to make somebody do something** jemanden zwingen, etwas zu tun, **she made him give the money back** sie hat ihn gezwungen, das Geld zurückzugeben **❻** (the verb 'make' is often translated by a more specific verb) **to make a cake** einen Kuchen backen, **to make a phone call** telefonieren, **to make a dress** ein Kleid nähen **❼** **to make friends with somebody** sich mit jemandem anfreunden (SEP) **❽** **I can't make it tonight** ich kann heute Abend nicht kommen **❾** **two and three make five** zwei und drei ist fünf

- **to make something up ❶** etwas erfinden◇; **she made up an excuse** sie hat eine Ausrede erfunden **❷** **to make it up** (after a quarrel) sich versöhnen, **they've made it up again** sie haben sich wieder versöhnt

**make-up** _NOUN_ **❶** Make-up das; **I don't wear make-up** ich trage kein Make-up **❷** **to put on your make-up** sich schminken, **Jo's putting on her make-up** Jo schminkt sich

**male** *ADJECTIVE* ❶ männlich; **male voice** die Männerstimme ❷ **male animal** das Männchen, **male rat** das Rattenmännchen ❸ **male student** der Student

**male chauvinist** *NOUN* Chauvinist der *(PLURAL* die **Chauvinisten)**

**man** *NOUN* ❶ Mann der *(PLURAL* die **Männer)**; **an old man** ein alter Mann ❷ *(the human race)* der Mensch

**manage** *VERB* ❶ leiten *(a business, team)*; **she manages a travel agency** sie leitet ein Reisebüro ❷ *(cope)* zurechtkommen◇ *(SEP)* *(PERF sein)*; **I can manage** ich komme schon zurecht ❸ **to manage to do something** es schaffen, etwas zu tun, **he managed to push the door open** er hat es geschafft, die Tür aufzustoßen, **I didn't manage to get in touch with her** ich habe es nicht geschafft, sie zu erreichen

**management** *NOUN* ❶ Management das *(PLURAL* die **Managements)**; **management course** der Managementkurs ❷ Leitung die

**manager** *NOUN* ❶ *(of a company or bank)* Direktor der *(PLURAL* die **Direktoren)**, Direktorin die *(PLURAL* die **Direktorinnen)** ❷ *(of a shop or restaurant)* Geschäftsführer der *(PLURAL* die **Geschäftsführer)**, Geschäftsfürerin die *(PLURAL* die **Geschäftsführerinnen)** ❸ *(in football)* Trainer der *(PLURAL* die **Trainer)**, Manegerin die *(PLURAL* die **Managerinnen)**, Trainerin die *(PLURAL* die **Trainerinnen)** ❹ *(in entertainment)* Manager der *(PLURAL* die **Manager)**, Manegerin die *(PLURAL* die **Managerinnen)**

**manageress** *NOUN* *(of a shop or restaurant)* Geschäftsführerin die *(PLURAL* die **Geschäftsführerinnen)**

**mania** *NOUN* Manie die *(PLURAL* die **Manien)**

**maniac** *NOUN* Wahnsinnige der/ die *(PLURAL* die **Wahnsinnigen)**; **she drives like a maniac** sie fährt wie eine Wahnsinnige

**man-made** *ADJECTIVE* **man-made fibre** die Kunstfaser

**manner** *NOUN* ❶ **in a manner of speaking** mehr oder weniger ❷ **manners** Manieren *(plural)*, **to have good manners** gute Manieren haben, **it's bad manners to talk like that** es gehört sich nicht, so zu reden

**mantelpiece** *NOUN* Kaminsims der *(PLURAL* die **Kaminsimse)**

**manual** *NOUN* Handbuch das *(PLURAL* die **Handbücher)**

**manufacture** *VERB* herstellen *(SEP)*

**manufacturer** *NOUN* Hersteller der *(PLURAL* die **Hersteller)**

**many** *DETERMINER, PRONOUN* ❶ viele; **does she have many friends?** hat sie viele Freunde?, **we didn't see many people** wir haben nicht viele Leute gesehen, **not many** nicht viele, **many of them forgot** viele haben es vergessen, **there were too many people** es waren zu viele (Leute) da, **how many?** wie viele?, **how many were there?** wie viele waren da?, **how many sisters have you got?** wie viele Schwestern hast du?, **how many are there left?** wie viele sind übrig geblieben?, **I've never had so many presents** ich habe noch nie so viele Geschenke bekommen

a b c d e f g h i j k l m n o p q r s t u v w x y z

❷ *(a lot)* **so many** so viel, **I have so many things to do** ich habe so viel zu tun ❸ *(as much as)* **as many as** so viel wie, **take as many as you like** nimm so viel wie du willst ❹ *(too much)* **that's far too many** das ist viel zu viel

**map** NOUN ❶ **Karte** die *(PLURAL die Karten)* ❷ *(of a town)* **Stadtplan** *(PLURAL die Stadtpläne)*

**marathon** NOUN **Marathonlauf** der *(PLURAL die Marathonläufe)*

**marble** NOUN ❶ **Marmor** der ❷ *(for playing)* **Murmel** die *(PLURAL die Murmeln)*; **to play marbles** Murmeln spielen

**march** NOUN **Marsch** der *(PLURAL die Märsche)*

**march** VERB **marschieren** *(PERF sein)*

**March** NOUN **März** der; **in March** im März

**mare** NOUN **Stute** die *(PLURAL die Stuten)*

**margarine** NOUN **Margarine** die

**margin** NOUN **Rand** der *(PLURAL die Ränder)*

**marijuana** NOUN **Marihuana** das

**mark** NOUN ❶ *(at school)* **Note** die *(PLURAL die Noten)*; **I got a good mark in German** ich habe eine gute Note in Deutsch bekommen ❷ *(stain)* **Fleck** der *(PLURAL die Flecke)* ❸ *(German currency until replaced by the euro; one hundred marks = 51.13 euros)* **Mark** die *(PLURAL die Mark)*

**mark** VERB ❶ **korrigieren**; **the teacher marks our homework** die Lehrerin korrigiert unsere Hausaufgaben ❷ *(in sports)* **decken**

**market** NOUN **Markt** der *(PLURAL die Märkte)*

**marketing** NOUN **Marketing** das

**marmalade** NOUN **Orangenmarmelade** die

**maroon** ADJECTIVE **kastanienbraun**

**marriage** NOUN ❶ **Ehe** die ❷ *(wedding)* **Hochzeit** die *(PLURAL die Hochzeiten)*

**married** ADJECTIVE ❶ **verheiratet**; **they've been married for twenty years** sie sind seit zwanzig Jahren verheiratet ❷ **married couple** das **Ehepaar**

**marry** VERB ❶ **to marry somebody** jemanden heiraten, **she married a Frenchman** sie hat einen Franzosen geheiratet ❷ **to get married** heiraten, **they got married in July** sie haben im Juli geheiratet

**marvellous** ADJECTIVE **wunderbar**

**marzipan** NOUN **Marzipan** das

**mascara** NOUN **Wimperntusche** die

**masculine** NOUN *(in German and other grammars)* **männlich**

**mash** VERB **stampfen**

**mashed potatoes** PLURAL NOUN **Kartoffelbrei** der *(SINGULAR)*

**mask** NOUN **Maske** die *(PLURAL die Masken)*

**mass** NOUN ❶ **a mass of** eine **Menge** ❷ **masses of** massenhaft *(informal)*, **they've got masses of money** sie haben massenhaft Geld, **there's masses left over** es ist massenhaft übrig geblieben ❸ *(religious)* Messe die *(PLURAL die* Messen); **to go to mass** zur Messe gehen

**massage** *NOUN* Massage die *(PLURAL die* Massagen)

**massive** *ADJECTIVE* riesig

**master** *VERB* ❶ meistern ❷ to **master a language** eine Sprache beherrschen

**masterpiece** *NOUN* Meisterwerk das *(PLURAL die* Meisterwerke)

**mat** *NOUN* ❶ *(doormat)* Matte die *(PLURAL die* Matten) ❷ *(to put under a hot dish)* Untersetzer der *(PLURAL die* Untersetzer) ❸ **table mat** das Platzdeckchen

**match** *NOUN* ❶ *(for lighting)* Streichholz das *(PLURAL die* Streichhölzer); **box of matches** die Streichholzschachtel ❷ *(in sports)* Spiel das *(PLURAL die* Spiele); **football match** das Fußballspiel, **to watch the match** das Spiel sehen, **to win the match** das Spiel gewinnen, **to lose the match** das Spiel verlieren

**match** *VERB* passen zu *(+DAT)*; **the jacket matches the skirt** die Jacke passt zu dem Rock

**mate** *NOUN* Freund der *(PLURAL die* Freunde); **I'm going to the pub with my mates** ich gehe mit meinen Freunden in die Kneipe

**material** *NOUN* ❶ *(fabric, also information)* Stoff der *(PLURAL die* Stoffe) ❷ *(substance)* Material das *(PLURAL die* Materialien)

**mathematics** *NOUN* Mathematik die

**maths** *NOUN* Mathe die *(informal)*; **I like maths** ich mag Mathe gerne, **Anna's good at maths** Anna ist gut in Mathe

**matter** *NOUN* **what's the matter?** was ist los?

**matter** *VERB* ❶ **that's what matters most** das ist am wichtigsten, **it matters a lot to me** es ist mir sehr wichtig, **does it really matter?** ist das wirklich so wichtig? ❷ **it doesn't matter** es macht nichts, **it doesn't matter if it rains** es macht nichts, wenn es regnet ❸ **you can write it in German or English, it doesn't matter** du kannst es auf Deutsch oder Englisch schreiben, das ist egal ❹ **to matter to somebody** jemandem etwas ausmachen *(SEP)*; **does it matter to you if I leave earlier?** macht es dir etwas aus, wenn ich früher gehe?

**mattress** *NOUN* Matratze die *(PLURAL die* Matratzen)

**maximum** *NOUN* Maximum das *(PLURAL die* Maxima); **the maximum number/speed possible is 200** die Höchstzahl/Höchstgeschwindigkeit ist 200

**maximum** *ADJECTIVE* maximal; **the maximum temperature** die Höchsttemperatur, **she got the maximum points** sie erreichte die Höchstpunktzahl

**may** *VERB* ❶ **she may be ill** vielleicht ist sie krank, **we may go to Spain** wir fahren vielleicht nach Spanien ❷ *(expressing permission)* dürfen◇; **may I close the door?** darf ich die Tür zumachen?

**May** NOUN **Mai** der; **in May** im Mai

**maybe** ADVERB **vielleicht**; **maybe they've got lost** vielleicht haben sie sich verlaufen

**May Day** NOUN **der Erste Mai**

**mayonnaise** NOUN **Majonäse** die

**mayor** NOUN **Bürgermeister** der (PLURAL die **Bürgermeister**), **Bürgermeisterin** die (PLURAL die **Bürgermeisterinnen**)

**me** PRONOUN
*(in German this pronoun changes according to the function it has in the sentence or the preposition it follows)* ❶ *(as a direct object in the accusative)* **mich**; **she knows me** sie kennt mich ❷ *(after a preposition that takes the accusative)* **mich**; **they left without me** sie sind ohne mich losgefahren, **wait for me!** warte auf mich! ❸ *(as an indirect object or following a verb that takes the dative)* **mir**; **can you give me your address?** kannst du mir deine Adresse geben?, **he helped me** er hat mir geholfen ❹ *(after a preposition that takes the dative)* **mir**; **she never talks to me** sie redet nie mit mir ❺ *(in comparisons)* **than me** als ich, **she's older than me** sie ist älter als ich ❻ *(in the nominative)* **ich**; **it's me** ich bin's, **not me** ich nicht

**meadow** NOUN **Wiese** die (PLURAL die **Wiesen**)

**meal** NOUN ❶ **Essen** das (PLURAL die **Essen**); **to cook a meal** Essen kochen ❷ **to go for a meal** essen gehen

**mean** VERB ❶ *(signify)* **bedeuten**; **what does that mean?** was bedeutet das? ❷ *(intend to say)*

**meinen** ❸ **what do you mean?** was meinst du?, **that's not what I meant** das habe ich nicht gemeint ❹ **to mean to do something** etwas tun wollen, **I meant to phone my mother** ich wollte meine Mutter anrufen ❺ **to be meant to do something** etwas tun sollen, **she was meant to be here at six** sie sollte um sechs hier sein

**mean** ADJECTIVE ❶ *(with money)* **geizig** ❷ *(unkind)* **gemein**; **she's really mean to her brother** sie ist richtig gemein zu ihrem Bruder, **what a mean thing to do!** das ist gemein!

**meaning** NOUN **Bedeutung** die (PLURAL die **Bedeutungen**)

**means** NOUN ❶ **Mittel** das (PLURAL die **Mittel**); **means of transport** das Verkehrsmittel ❷ **a means of** eine Möglichkeit, **a means of earning money** eine Möglichkeit, Geld zu verdienen ❸ **by means of** mit Hilfe (+GEN) ❹ **by all means!** selbstverständlich!

**meantime** ADVERB **for the meantime** einstweilen, **in the meantime** in der Zwischenzeit

**meanwhile** ADVERB **in der Zwischenzeit**; **meanwhile she was waiting at the station** in der Zwischenzeit wartete sie am Bahnhof

**measles** NOUN **Masern** (plural)

**measure** VERB **messen**◇

**measurements** PLURAL NOUN **Maße** (plural); **the measurements of the room** die Maße des Zimmers, **my measurements** meine Maße

**meat** NOUN **Fleisch** das; **I don't like meat** ich mag kein Fleisch

**mechanic** NOUN **Mechaniker** der (PLURAL die **Mechaniker**), **Mechanikerin** die (PLURAL die **Mechanikerinnen**)

**mechanical** ADJECTIVE **mechanisch**

**medal** NOUN **Medaille** die (PLURAL die **Medaillen**); the gold medal die **Goldmedaille**

**media** NOUN the media die **Medien** (plural)

**medical** NOUN ❶ **ärztliche Untersuchung** die (PLURAL die **ärztlichen Untersuchungen**) ❷ to have a medical sich untersuchen lassen

**medical** ADJECTIVE ❶ **medizinisch** ❷ **ärztlich** (examination, treatment)

**medicine** NOUN ❶ (drug) **Medikament** das (PLURAL die **Medikamente**) ❷ (subject of study) **Medizin** die; she's studying medicine sie studiert Medizin ❸ alternative medicine die **Alternativmedizin**

**Mediterranean** NOUN the Mediterranean (Sea) das **Mittelmeer**

**medium** ADJECTIVE **mittlerer/ mittlere/mittleres**

**medium-sized** ADJECTIVE **mittelgroß**

**meet** VERB ❶ (by chance) **treffen**◇; I met Rosie at the baker's ich habe Rosie beim Bäcker getroffen ❷ (by appointment) **sich treffen mit** (+DAT); I'll meet you outside the cinema ich treffe mich mit dir vor dem Kino ❸ **sich treffen**; we're meeting at six wir treffen uns um sechs ❹ (get to know) **kennen lernen**; I met a German girl last week ich habe letzte Woche eine Deutsche kennen gelernt ❺ I've never met Oskar ich kenne Oskar nicht ❻ (off a train or bus, for example) **abholen** (SEP); my dad's meeting me at the station mein Vater holt mich vom Bahnhof ab

**meeting** NOUN ❶ (by arrangement) **Treffen** das (PLURAL die **Treffen**) ❷ (in business) **Besprechung** die (PLURAL die **Besprechungen**); she's in a meeting sie ist in einer Besprechung ❸ (by chance, in sports) **Begegnung** die (PLURAL die **Begegnungen**)

**megabyte** NOUN **Megabyte** das (PLURAL die **Megabytes**)

**melon** NOUN **Melone** die (PLURAL die **Melonen**)

**melt** VERB ❶ **schmelzen**◇ (PERF **sein**); the snow has melted der Schnee ist geschmolzen ❷ (in cookery) **zerlassen**◇ (butter, fat); melt the butter in a saucepan Butter im Topf zerlassen

**member** NOUN **Mitglied** das (PLURAL die **Mitglieder**)

**Member of Parliament** NOUN **Abgeordnete** der/die (PLURAL die **Abgeordneten**)

**membership** NOUN **Mitgliedschaft** die

**membership card** NOUN **Mitgliedskarte** die (PLURAL die **Mitgliedskarten**)

**membership fee** NOUN **Mitgliedsbeitrag** der (PLURAL die **Mitgliedsbeiträge**)

**memorial** NOUN Denkmal das (PLURAL die **Denkmäler**); **a war memorial** ein Kriegsdenkmal

**memorize** VERB to memorize something etwas auswendig lernen

**memory** NOUN ❶ (of a person) Gedächtnis das; **you have a good memory** du hast ein gutes Gedächtnis ❷ (of the past) Erinnerung die (PLURAL die **Erinnerungen**); **I have good memories of our stay in Italy** ich habe schöne Erinnerungen an unseren Urlaub in Italien ❸ (of a computer) Speicher der

**memory card** NOUN Speicherkart die **Speicherkarten**

**mend** VERB ❶ reparieren ❷ (by sewing) ausbessern (SEP)

**meningitis** NOUN Hirnhautentzündung die

**mental** ADJECTIVE ❶ geistig ❷ mental illness die Geisteskrankheit, **mental hospital** die psychiatrische Klinik

**mention** VERB erwähnen

**menu** NOUN ❶ (in a restaurant) Speisekarte die (PLURAL die **Speisekarten**); **is there a set menu?** gibt es ein Menü? ❷ (in computing) Menü das (PLURAL die **Menüs**)

**meringue** NOUN Baiser das (PLURAL die **Baisers**)

**merit** NOUN ❶ Verdienst das (PLURAL die **Verdienste**) ❷ (good feature or advantage) Vorzug der (PLURAL die **Vorzüge**)

**merry** ADJECTIVE ❶ fröhlich; Merry Christmas fröhliche Weihnachten ❷ (from drinking) angeheitert

**merry-go-round** NOUN Karussell das (PLURAL die **Karussells**)

**mess** NOUN ❶ Durcheinander das; **my papers are in a complete mess** meine Unterlagen sind ein einziges Durcheinander, **what a mess!** was für ein Durcheinander! ❷ **to make a mess** Unordnung machen ❸ **to clear up the mess** aufräumen (SEP)
• **to mess about** herumalbern (SEP); **stop messing about!** hör auf herumzualbern!
• **to mess about with something** mit etwas (DAT) herumspielen (SEP); **it's dangerous to mess about with matches** es ist gefährlich, mit Streichhölzern herumzuspielen
• **to mess something up** ❶ etwas durcheinander bringen◇; **you've messed up all my papers** Sie haben meine Unterlagen völlig durcheinander gebracht ❷ (make dirty) etwas schmutzig machen ❸ (botch) etwas verpfuschen

**message** NOUN ❶ Nachricht die (PLURAL die **Nachrichten**); **a telephone message** eine telefonische Nachricht ❷ **to give somebody a message** jemandem etwas ausrichten (SEP)

**messy** ADJECTIVE ❶ (dirty) **it's a messy job** das ist eine schmutzige Arbeit ❷ **he's a messy eater** er bekleckert sich beim Essen ❸ **her writing's really messy** sie hat eine furchtbare Schrift ❹ (untidy) **she's very messy** sie ist sehr unordentlich

**metal** NOUN Metall das (PLURAL die **Metalle**)

**meter** NOUN ❶ (electricity, gas, taxi) Zähler der (PLURAL die **Zähler**); **to read the meter** den Zähler ablesen◇ (SEP) ❷ **parking meter** die Parkuhr

**method** *NOUN* Methode die *(PLURAL die* Methoden*)*

**Methodist** *NOUN* Methodist der *(PLURAL die* Methodisten*)*, Methodistin die *(PLURAL die* Methodistinnen*)*

**metre** *NOUN* Meter der *(PLURAL die* Meter*)*

**metric** *ADJECTIVE* metrisch

**microchip** *NOUN* Mikrochip der *(PLURAL die* Mikrochips*)*

**microphone** *NOUN* Mikrofon das *(PLURAL die* Mikrofone*)*

**microscope** *NOUN* Mikroskop das *(PLURAL die* Mikroskope*)*

**microwave (oven)** *NOUN* Mikrowellenherd der *(PLURAL die* Mikrowellenherde*)*

**midday** *NOUN* Mittag der; **at midday** mittags

**middle** *NOUN* ❶ Mitte die; **in the middle of the room** in der Mitte des Zimmers, **in the middle of June** Mitte Juni, **in the middle of the night** mitten in der Nacht ❷ **to be in the middle of doing something** gerade dabei sein, etwas zu tun, **when she phoned I was in the middle of washing my hair** als sie anrief, war ich gerade dabei, mir die Haare zu waschen

**middle-aged** *ADJECTIVE* mittleren Alters; **a middle-aged lady** eine Dame mittleren Alters

**middle-class** *ADJECTIVE* der Mittelschicht; **a middle-class family** eine Familie der Mittelschicht

**Middle-East** *NOUN* **the Middle East** der Nahe Osten

**midge** *NOUN* Mücke die *(PLURAL die* Mücken*)*

**midnight** *NOUN* Mitternacht die; **at midnight** um Mitternacht

**Midsummer's Day** *NOUN* Sommersonnenwende die

**might** *VERB* ❶ 'are you going to phone him?' – 'I might' 'rufst du ihn an?' – 'vielleicht', **I might invite Jo** vielleicht lade ich Jo ein, **he might have forgotten** vielleicht hat er es vergessen ❷ **she might be right** sie könnte Recht haben

**migraine** *NOUN* Migräne die

**mike** *NOUN* (microphone) Mikro das *(PLURAL die* Mikros*)* (informal)

**mild** *ADJECTIVE* mild

**mile** *NOUN* ❶ Meile die *(PLURAL die* Meilen*)* (Germans use kilometres for distances; to convert miles to kilometres, multiply by 8 and divide by 5); **it's ten miles to Oxford** es sind sechzehn Kilometer bis Oxford ❷ **it's miles better** das ist viel besser

**military** *ADJECTIVE* militärisch

**milk** *NOUN* Milch die; **full-cream milk** die Vollmilch, **skimmed milk** die Magermilch, **semi-skimmed milk** die fettarme Milch

**milk** *VERB* melken

**milk chocolate** *NOUN* Milchschokolade die

**milkman** *NOUN* Milchmann der *(PLURAL die* Milchmänner*)*

**milk shake** *NOUN* Milchshake der *(PLURAL die* Milchshakes*)*

**millennium** NOUN **Jahrtausend** das (PLURAL die **Jahrtausende**)

**millimetre** NOUN **Millimeter** der (PLURAL die **Millimeter**)

**million** NOUN **Million** die (PLURAL die **Millionen**); **a million people** eine Million Menschen, **two million people** zwei Millionen Menschen

**millionaire** NOUN **Millionär** der (PLURAL die **Millionäre**), **Millionärin** die (PLURAL die **Millionärinnen**)

**mimic** VERB **nachmachen** (SEP)

**mince** NOUN **Hackfleisch** das

**mind** NOUN ❶ **Sinn** der; **it never crossed my mind to ask them for help** es kam mir überhaupt nicht in den Sinn, sie um Hilfe zu bitten ❷ **Meinung** die; **to change your mind** seine Meinung ändern, **I've changed my mind** ich habe meine Meinung geändert ❸ **to make up your mind to do something** sich entschließen◊, etwas zu tun, **I can't make up my mind which dress to wear** ich kann mich nicht entschließen, welches Kleid ich anziehe ❹ **I've made up my mind** ich habe mich entschieden

**mind** VERB ❶ **aufpassen** (SEP) auf (+ACC); **can you mind my bag for me?** können Sie auf meine Handtasche aufpassen?, **could you mind the baby for ten minutes?** könntest du zehn Minuten auf das Baby aufpassen? ❷ **do you mind closing the door?** würden Sie bitte die Tür zumachen? ❸ **do you mind if ...?** würde es Ihnen etwas ausmachen (SEP), wenn ...?, **do you mind if I open the window?** würde es Ihnen etwas ausmachen, wenn ich das Fenster aufmache?,

**I don't mind** es macht mir nichts aus, **I don't mind the heat** die Hitze macht mir nichts aus ❹ **never mind** macht nichts

**mine**[1] NOUN **Bergwerk** das (PLURAL die **Bergwerke**); **coal mine** das Kohlenbergwerk

**mine**[2] PRONOUN ❶ (for a masculine noun) **mein**; **she took her coat and I took mine** sie hat ihren Mantel genommen und ich habe meinen genommen ❷ (for a feminine noun) **meine**; **she gave me her address and I gave her mine** sie hat mir ihre Adresse gegeben und ich habe ihr meine gegeben ❸ (for a neuter noun) **meins**; **her dress is red and mine is blue** ihr Kleid ist rot und meins ist blau ❹ (for masculine/feminine/neuter plural nouns) **meine**; **she showed me her photos and I showed her mine** sie hat mir ihre Fotos gezeigt und ich habe ihr meine gezeigt ❺ **a friend of mine** ein Freund von mir, **it's mine** das gehört mir

**miner** NOUN **Bergarbeiter** der (PLURAL die **Bergarbeiter**)

**mineral water** NOUN **Mineralwasser** das

**miniature** NOUN **Miniatur** die (PLURAL die **Miniaturen**)

**miniature** ADJECTIVE **Miniatur-**; **miniature model** Miniaturmodell das

**minibus** NOUN **Kleinbus** der (PLURAL die **Kleinbusse**)

**minimum** NOUN **Minimum** das (PLURAL die **Minima**); **a minimum of** ein Minimum von

**minimum** *ADJECTIVE* Mindest-; **the minimum age** das Mindestalter, **minimum wage** der Mindestlohn

**miniskirt** *NOUN* Minirock der *(PLURAL* die Miniröcke)

**minister** *NOUN* ❶ *(in government)* Minister der *(PLURAL* die Minister), Ministerin die *(PLURAL* die Ministerinnen) ❷ *(of a church)* Geistliche der/die *(PLURAL* die Geistlichen)

**ministry** *NOUN* Ministerium das *(PLURAL* die Ministerien)

**minor** *ADJECTIVE* kleiner

**minority** *NOUN* Minderheit die *(PLURAL* die Minderheiten)

**mint** *NOUN* ❶ *(herb)* Minze die *(PLURAL* die Minzen) ❷ *(sweet)* Pfefferminzbonbon der *(PLURAL* die Pfefferminzbonbons)

**minus** *PREPOSITION* minus *(+GEN)*; **seven minus three is four** sieben minus drei ist vier, **it was minus ten this morning** es war minus zehn heute Morgen

**minute¹** *NOUN* ❶ Minute die *(PLURAL* die Minuten)*; **I'll be ready in two minutes** ich bin in zwei Minuten fertig, **it's five minutes' walk from here** es ist fünf Minuten zu Fuß von hier ❷ Moment der; **just a minute!** einen Moment bitte! ❸ **in a minute** gleich

**minute²** *ADJECTIVE* winzig; **the bedrooms are minute** die Schlafzimmer sind winzig

**miracle** *NOUN* Wunder das *(PLURAL* die Wunder)*

**mirror** *NOUN* Spiegel der *(PLURAL* die Spiegel)*; **he looked at himself in the mirror** er hat sich im Spiegel betrachtet

**misbehave** *VERB* sich schlecht benehmen◊

**miserable** *ADJECTIVE* ❶ elend; **he was miserable without her** ohne sie fühlte er sich elend ❷ **I feel really miserable today** ich fühle mich heute richtig elend ❸ mies; **it's miserable weather** das Wetter ist mies, **she gets paid a miserable salary** sie bekommt ein mieses Gehalt

**miss** *VERB* ❶ verpassen; **she missed her train** sie hat ihren Zug verpasst, **I missed the film** ich habe den Film verpasst, **to miss an opportunity** eine Gelegenheit verpassen ❷ nicht treffen◊; **the stone missed me** der Stein hat mich nicht getroffen, **the ball missed the goal** der Schuss ging am Tor vorbei, **missed!** nicht getroffen! ❸ versäumen; **he's missed his classes** er hat den Unterricht versäumt ❹ vermissen *(a person or thing)*; **I miss you** ich vermisse dich, **she's missing her sister** sie vermisst ihre Schwester, **I miss England** ich vermisse England

**Miss** *NOUN* Fräulein das; **Miss Jones** Fräulein Jones, Frau Jones *(adult women are usually addressed as 'Frau', whether or not they are married)*

**missing** *ADJECTIVE* ❶ fehlend; **she's found the missing pieces** sie hat die fehlenden Teile gefunden, **the missing link** das fehlende Glied ❷ **to be missing** fehlen, **there's a plate missing** ein Teller fehlt, **there are three forks missing** drei

**missionary**                                   **mock**

Gabeln fehlen ❸ **to go missing** verschwinden◇ *(PERF* **sein)**, **several things have gone missing lately** mehrere Sachen sind kürzlich verschwunden ❹ **three children are missing** drei Kinder werden vermisst

**missionary** *NOUN* **Missionar** der *(PLURAL* die **Missionare)**, **Missionarin** die *(PLURAL* die **Missionarinnen)**

**mist** *NOUN* **Nebel** der

**mistake** *NOUN* ❶ **Fehler** der *(PLURAL* die **Fehler)**; **spelling mistake** der **Rechtschreibfehler**, **you've made lots of mistakes** du hast viele Fehler gemacht ❷ **to make a mistake** *(be mistaken)* sich irren, **sorry, I made a mistake** Entschuldigung, ich habe mich geirrt ❸ **by mistake** aus Versehen

**mistake** *VERB* **I mistook you for your brother** ich habe dich mit deinem Bruder verwechselt

**mistaken** *ADJECTIVE* **to be mistaken** sich täuschen, **you're mistaken** du täuschst dich

**mistletoe** *NOUN* **Mistel** die *(PLURAL* die **Misteln)**

**misty** *ADJECTIVE* **dunstig**; **a misty morning** ein dunstiger Morgen

**misunderstand** *VERB* **missverstehen◇**; **I misunderstood** ich habe es missverstanden

**misunderstanding** *NOUN* **Missverständnis** das *(PLURAL* die **Missverständnisse)**; **there's been a misunderstanding** da liegt ein Missverständnis vor

**mix** *NOUN* **Mischung** die *(PLURAL* die **Mischungen)**; **a good mix** eine gute Mischung, **cake mix** die **Backmischung**

**mix** *VERB* ❶ **vermischen**; **mix the ingredients together** die Zutaten vermischen, **mix the cream into the sauce** die Sahne in die Soße rühren ❷ **to mix with** verkehren mit *(+DAT)*, **she mixes with lots of interesting people** sie verkehrt mit vielen interessanten Leuten

• **to mix up** ❶ **durcheinander bringen◇**; **you've mixed up all the papers** du hast alle Unterlagen durcheinander gebracht, **you've got it all mixed up** du hast alles durcheinander gebracht ❷ *(confuse)* **verwechseln**; **I get him mixed up with his brother** ich verwechsele ihn mit seinem Bruder

**mixed** *ADJECTIVE* ❶ **bunt**; **a mixed programme** ein buntes Programm ❷ **gemischt**; **a mixed salad** ein gemischter Salat

**mixture** *NOUN* **Mischung** die *(PLURAL* die **Mischungen)**; **it's a mixture of jazz and rock** es ist eine Mischung aus Jazz und Rock

**moan** *VERB* *(complain)* **jammern**; **stop moaning!** hör auf zu jammern!

**mobile home** *NOUN* **Wohnwagen** der *(PLURAL* die **Wohnwagen)**

**mobile phone** *NOUN* **Handy** das *(PLURAL* die **Handys)**

**mock** *NOUN* *(mock exam)* **Übungsprüfung** die *(PLURAL* die **Übungsprüfungen)**

**mock** *VERB* **sich lustig machen über** *(+ACC)*; **stop mocking me** hör auf, dich über mich lustig zu machen

**model** NOUN **①** Modell das (PLURAL die Modelle); **his car is the latest model** sein Auto ist das neueste Modell, **a model of Westminster Abbey** ein Modell von der Westminsterabtei **②** (fashion model) Mannequin das (PLURAL die Mannequins); **she's a model** sie ist Fotomodell

**model aeroplane** NOUN Modellflugzeug das (PLURAL die Modellflugzeuge)

**model railway** NOUN Modelleisenbahn die (PLURAL die Modelleisenbahnen)

**modem** NOUN Modem der (PLURAL die Modems)

**modern** ADJECTIVE modern

**modernize** VERB modernisieren

**modern languages** NOUN neuere Sprachen (plural)

**modest** ADJECTIVE bescheiden

**modify** VERB abändern (SEP)

**moisture** NOUN Feuchtigkeit die

**moisturizer** NOUN Feuchtigkeitscreme die

**mole** NOUN **①** (animal) Maulwurf der (PLURAL die Maulwürfe) **②** (on the skin) Leberfleck der (PLURAL die Leberflecke)

**molecule** NOUN Molekül das (PLURAL die Moleküle)

**molehill** NOUN Maulwurfshügel der (PLURAL die Maulwurfshügel)

**moment** NOUN **①** Moment der (PLURAL die Momente); **at any moment** jeden Moment, **at the moment** im Moment, im Augenblick, **at the right moment** im richtigen Moment **②** Augenblick der (PLURAL die Augenblicke); **wait a moment!** einen Augenblick! **③** **he'll be ready in a moment** er ist gleich fertig

**monarchy** NOUN Monarchie die

**monastery** NOUN Kloster das (PLURAL die Klöster)

**Monday** NOUN **①** Montag der; **on Monday** am Montag, **I'm going to see him on Monday** ich sehe ihn am Montag, **see you on Monday!** bis Montag!, **every Monday** jeden Montag, **last Monday** letzten Montag, **next Monday** nächsten Montag **②** **on Mondays** montags, **the museum is closed on Mondays** das Museum ist montags geschlossen

**money** NOUN Geld das; **I don't have enough money** ich habe nicht genug Geld, **to make money** Geld verdienen

**money box** NOUN Sparbüchse die (PLURAL die Sparbüchsen)

**monitor** NOUN (of a computer) Monitor der (PLURAL die Monitoren)

**monk** NOUN Mönch der (PLURAL die Mönche)

**monkey** NOUN Affe der (PLURAL die Affen)

**monotonous** ADJECTIVE eintönig

**monster** NOUN Ungeheuer das (PLURAL die Ungeheuer)

**month** NOUN Monat der; **in the month of May** im Mai, **this month** diesen Monat, **next month** nächsten Monat, **last month** letzten Monat, **for three months** drei Monate lang,

**every month** jeden Monat, **every three months** alle drei Monate, **in two months' time** in zwei Monaten, **at the end of the month** am Monatsende

**monthly** ADJECTIVE monatlich; **monthly payment** die monatliche Zahlung, **monthly ticket** die Monatskarte

**monument** NOUN Denkmal das (PLURAL die **Denkmäler**)

**mood** NOUN ❶ Laune die (PLURAL die **Launen**); **to be in a good mood** gute Laune haben, **to be in a bad mood** schlechte Laune haben ❷ **I'm not in the mood** ich habe keine Lust dazu, **I'm not in the mood for working** ich habe keine Lust zum Arbeiten

**moon** NOUN Mond der (PLURAL die **Monde**); **by the light of the moon** im Mondschein
• **to be over the moon** im siebten Himmel sein (literally: to be in seventh heaven)

**moonlight** NOUN Mondschein der; **by moonlight** im Mondschein

**moped** NOUN Moped das (PLURAL die **Mopeds**)

**moral** NOUN Moral die; **the moral of the story** die Moral der Geschichte

**moral** ADJECTIVE moralisch

**morals** NOUN Moral die

**more** ADVERB ❶ (followed by an adjective) (in German the ending '-er' is added to the adjective to show the comparative) **more interesting** interessanter, **the book's more interesting than the film** das Buch ist interessanter als der Film, **more**

**difficult** schwieriger, **more slowly** langsamer, **more easily** einfacher, **books are getting more and more expensive** Bücher werden immer teurer ❷ not any more (no longer) nicht mehr, **she doesn't live here any more** sie wohnt nicht mehr hier

**more** DETERMINER ❶ mehr ('mehr' never changes); **more friends** mehr Freunde, **more ... than** mehr ... als, **they have more money than we do** sie haben mehr Geld als wir ❷ **no more** kein, **there's no more milk** es ist keine Milch mehr da ❸ (of something you have already) noch; **would you like some more cake?** möchtest du noch etwas Kuchen?, **a few more glasses** noch ein paar Gläser

**more** PRONOUN ❶ mehr; **he eats more than me** er isst mehr als ich, **no more, thank you** nichts mehr, danke ❷ (of something you have already) noch; **we need three more** wir brauchen noch drei, **any more?** noch etwas? ❸ **more and more** immer mehr, **it takes more and more time** es beansprucht immer mehr Zeit ❹ **more or less** mehr oder weniger, **it's more or less finished** es ist mehr oder weniger fertig

**morning** NOUN ❶ Morgen der (PLURAL die **Morgen**); **in the morning** am Morgen, **this morning** heute Morgen, **tomorrow morning** morgen früh, **yesterday morning** gestern Morgen, **on Friday morning** am Freitagmorgen ❷ **in the morning** (regularly) morgens, **she doesn't work in the morning** sie arbeitet morgens nicht, **on Friday mornings** freitagmorgens, **at six o'clock in the morning** um sechs Uhr morgens ❸ (as opposed to afternoon) Vormittag der (PLURAL die **Vormittage**); **I spent the whole morning waiting for him** ich habe den ganzen Vormittag auf ihn gewartet

**Moscow** NOUN Moskau das

**Moslem** NOUN Moslem der (PLURAL die **Moslems**), Moslemin die (PLURAL die **Mosleminnen**)

**mosque** NOUN Moschee die (PLURAL die **Moscheen**)

**mosquito** NOUN Mücke die (PLURAL die **Mücken**); **mosquito bite** der Mückenstich

**most** DETERMINER, PRONOUN ❶ (followed by a plural noun) die meisten; **most children like chocolate** die meister Kinder mögen Schokolade, **most of my friends** die meisten meinen Freunden ❷ (followed by a singular noun) der meiste/die meiste/das meiste; **they've eaten most of the ice-cream** sie haben das meiste Eis gegessen ❸ **the most** (followed by a noun or a verb) am meisten, **I've got the most time** ich habe am meisten Zeit ❹ **most of the time** die meiste Zeit, **most of them** die meisten

**most** ADVERB ❶ (followed by an adjective in German the ending '-(e)st' is added to the adjective to show the superlative) **the most interesting film** der interessanteste Film, **the most exciting story** die spannendste Geschichte, **the most boring book** das langweiligste Buch ❷ **am meisten**; **the noise bothers me most** der Lärm stört mich am meisten ❸ (very) höchst; **it's most unlikely** es ist höchst unwahrscheinlich

**moth** NOUN ❶ Nachtfalter der (PLURAL die **Nachtfalter**) ❷ (clothes moth) Motte die (PLURAL die **Motten**)

**mother** NOUN Mutter die (PLURAL die **Mütter**); **Kate's mother** Kates Mutter

**mother-in-law** NOUN Schwiegermutter die (PLURAL die **Schwiegermütter**)

**Mother's Day** NOUN Muttertag der (PLURAL die **Muttertage**)

**motivation** NOUN Motivation die

**motor** NOUN Motor der (PLURAL die **Motoren**)

**motorbike** NOUN Motorrad das (PLURAL die **Motorräder**)

**motorcyclist** NOUN Motorradfahrer der (PLURAL die **Motorradfahrer**), Motorradfahrerin die (PLURAL die **Motorradfahrerinnen**)

**motorist** NOUN Autofahrer der (PLURAL die **Autofahrer**), Autofahrerin die (PLURAL die **Autofahrerinnen**)

**motor racing** NOUN Autorennsport der

**motorway** NOUN Autobahn die (PLURAL die **Autobahnen**)

**mouldy** ADJECTIVE schimmelig

**mountain** NOUN Berg der (PLURAL die **Berge**); **in the mountains** in den Bergen

**mountain bike** NOUN Mountainbike das (PLURAL die **Mountainbikes**)

a
b
c
d
e
f
g
h
i
j
k
l
m
n
o
p
q
r
s
t
u
v
w
x
y
z

**mountaineer** NOUN Bergsteiger der (PLURAL die Bergsteiger), Bergsteigerin die (PLURAL die Bergsteigerinnen)

**mountaineering** NOUN Bergsteigen das; to go mountaineering Bergsteigen gehen

**mountainous** ADJECTIVE gebirgig

**mouse** NOUN Maus die (PLURAL die Mäuse) (also for a computer)

**mousse** NOUN Mousse die (PLURAL die Mousses)

**moustache** NOUN Schnurrbart der (PLURAL die Schnurrbärte)

**mouth** NOUN ❶ (of a person) Mund der (PLURAL die Münder) ❷ (of an animal) Maul das (PLURAL die Mäuler) ❸ (of a river) Mündung die (PLURAL die Mündungen)

**mouthful** NOUN (food) Bissen der (PLURAL die Bissen) (informal)

**mouth organ** NOUN Mundharmonika die (PLURAL die Mundharmonikas); to play the mouth organ Mundharmonika spielen

**move** NOUN ❶ (to a different house) Umzug der (PLURAL die Umzüge) ❷ (in a game) Zug der (PLURAL die Züge); your move! du bist am Zug!

**move** VERB ❶ sich bewegen; she didn't move sie hat sich nicht bewegt ❷ to move up vorrücken (SEP) (PERF sein), move up a bit rücken Sie etwas vor ❸ wegnehmen◇ (SEP); can you move your bag, please? können Sie Ihre Handtasche bitte wegnehmen? ❹ to move something somewhere else etwas woandershin stellen,

I've moved the chest into the cellar ich habe die Truhe in den Keller gestellt ❺ (car) fahren◇ (PERF sein) ❻ (traffic) vorwärtskommen◇ (SEP) (PERF sein) ❼ (driver) wegfahren◇ (SEP); could you move your car, please? würden Sie bitte Ihr Auto wegfahren? ❽ to move forward (person) vorrücken (SEP) (PERF sein) (vehicle) vorwärts fahren◇ (PERF sein) ❾ (move house) umziehen◇ (SEP) (PERF sein); we're moving on Tuesday wir ziehen am Dienstag um, they've moved to London sie sind nach London umgezogen

• to move away wegziehen (SEP) (PERF sein)

• to move in einziehen (SEP) (PERF sein); she's moving in with friends sie zieht bei Freunden ein

• to move out ausziehen (SEP) (PERF sein); we're moving out next week wir ziehen nächste Woche aus

**movement** NOUN Bewegung die (PLURAL die Bewegungen)

**movie** NOUN Film der (PLURAL die Filme); to go to the movies ins Kino gehen

**moving** ADJECTIVE ❶ fahrend; a moving car ein fahrendes Auto ❷ (emotionally) ergreifend

**mow** VERB mähen

**mower** NOUN Rasenmäher der (PLURAL die Rasenmäher)

**MP** NOUN Abgeordnete der/die (PLURAL die Abgeordneten)

**Mr** NOUN Herr der; (in an address) Mr Angus Brown Herrn Angus Brown, (in a letter) Dear Mr Brown Sehr geehrter Herr Brown

**Mrs** NOUN **Frau** die; **Mrs Mary Hendry** Frau Mary Hendry, *(in a letter)* **Dear Mrs Hendry** Sehr geehrte Frau Hendry

**Ms** NOUN **Frau** die *(there is no direct equivalent to 'Ms' in German, but 'Frau' may be used whether the woman is married or not)*

**much** DETERIMINER, ADVERB, PRONOUN **❶ viel**; **she doesn't eat much for breakfast** sie isst nicht viel zum Frühstück, **much more** viel mehr, **much quicker** viel schneller, **we don't have much time** wir haben nicht viel Zeit **❷ not much** nicht viel, **'do you have a lot of work?' – 'no, not much'** 'hast du viel Arbeit?' – ' nein, nicht viel' **❸ so much** so viel, **I have so much to do** ich habe so viel zu tun, **you shouldn't have given me so much** du hättest mir nicht so viel geben sollen **❹ as much as** so viel, **take as much as you like** nimm so viel du willst **❺ too much** zu viel, **she gets too much money from her parents** sie bekommt zu viel Geld von ihren Eltern, **that's far too much** das ist viel zu viel **❻ how much?** wie viel?, **how much is it?** wie viel kostet es?, **how much do you want?** wie viel möchten Sie?, **how much money do you need?** wie viel Geld brauchst du? **❼** *(greatly)* **sehr**; **he loved her very much** er hat sie sehr geliebt, **too much** zu sehr, **so much** (so) sehr, **we liked it so much** es hat uns sehr gefallen **❽** *(often)* **oft**; **I don't watch television much** ich sehe nicht oft fern, **we don't go out much** wir gehen nicht oft aus **❾ thank you very much** vielen Dank

**mud** NOUN **Schlamm** der

**muddle** NOUN **❶ Durcheinander** das **❷ to be in a muddle** durcheinander sein

**mug** NOUN **Becher** der *(PLURAL* die Becher)*; **a mug of milk** ein Becher Milch

**mug** VERB **to mug somebody** jemanden überfallen◇, **to be mugged** überfallen werden

**mugging** NOUN **Straßenraub** der

**multiplication** NOUN **Multiplikation** die

**multiply** VERB **multiplizieren**; **six multiplied by four** sechs multipliziert mit vier

**mum, mummy** NOUN **Mutti** die *(PLURAL* die Muttis)*; **Tom's mum** Toms Mutti, **I'll ask my mum** ich frage Mutti

**mumps** NOUN **Mumps** der

**Munich** NOUN **München** das

**murder** NOUN **Mord** der *(PLURAL* die Morde)*

**murder** VERB **ermorden**

**murderer** NOUN **Mörder** der *(PLURAL* die Mörder)*, **Mörderin** die *(PLURAL* die Mörderinnen)*

**muscle** NOUN **Muskel** der *(PLURAL* die Muskeln)*

**muscular** ADJECTIVE **muskulös**

**museum** NOUN **Museum** das *(PLURAL* die Museen)*; **to go to the museum** ins Museum gehen

**mushroom** NOUN **Pilz** der *(PLURAL* die Pilze)*, **Champignon** der *(PLURAL* die Champignons)*; **mushroom salad** der Champignonsalat

**music** NOUN Musik die; **pop music** die Popmusik, **classical music** die klassische Musik

**musical** NOUN Musical das (PLURAL die Musicals)

**musical** ADJECTIVE ❶ **musical instrument** das Musikinstrument ❷ **they're a very musical family** sie sind eine sehr musikalische Familie

**musician** NOUN Musiker der (PLURAL die Musiker), Musikerin die (PLURAL die Musikerinnen)

**Muslim** NOUN Muslem der (PLURAL die Muslim), Muslimin die (PLURAL die Musliminnen)

**mussel** NOUN Muschel die (PLURAL die Muscheln)

**must** VERB ❶ müssen◇; **we must leave now** wir müssen jetzt gehen, **you must learn the vocabulary** du musst die Vokabeln lernen ❷ (with a negative) dürfen◇; **you mustn't do that** das darfst du nicht tun ❸ (expressing probability) müssen◇; **you must be tired** ihr müsst müde sein, **it must be five o'clock** es muss fünf Uhr sein, **he must have forgotten** er muss es vergessen haben

**mustard** NOUN Senf der (PLURAL die Senfe)

**mutter** VERB murmeln

**my** DETERMINER ❶ (before a masculine noun) mein; **my brother** mein Bruder, **they don't like my dog** sie mögen meinen Hund nicht ❷ (before a feminine noun) meine; **my sister** meine Schwester ❸ (before a neuter noun) mein; **that's my new car** das ist mein neues Auto, **we can go in my car** wir

können mit meinem Auto fahren ❹ (before masculine/feminine/neuter plural nouns) meine; **my children** meine Kinder ❺ (with parts of the body) der/die/das; **I had a glass in my hand** ich hatte ein Glas in der Hand, **I'm washing my hands** ich wasche mir die Hände

**myself** PRONOUN ❶ (reflexive and after a preposition taking the accusative) mich; **I've cut myself** ich habe mich geschnitten, **I've addressed the letter to myself** ich habe den Brief an mich adressiert ❷ (reflexive and after a preposition taking the dative) mir; **I've hurt myself** ich habe mir wehgetan, **I said to myself** ich habe mir gesagt ❸ (stressing something) selbst; **I said it myself** ich habe es selbst gesagt ❹ **by myself** allein

**mysterious** ADJECTIVE rätselhaft

**mystery** NOUN ❶ Rätsel das (PLURAL die Rätsel) ❷ (book) Krimi der (PLURAL die Krimis) (informal)

**myth** NOUN Mythos der (PLURAL die Mythen)

**mythology** NOUN Mythologie die (PLURAL die Mythologien)

**nail** NOUN (on your finger or toe, also metal) Nagel der (PLURAL die Nägel)

**nail** VERB nageln

**nailbrush** NOUN Nagelbürste die (PLURAL die Nagelbürsten)

**nailfile** NOUN Nagelfeile die (PLURAL die Nagelfeilen)

**nail polish** NOUN Nagellack der

**nail polish remover** NOUN Nagellackentferner der

**naked** ADJECTIVE nackt

**name** NOUN ❶ Name der (PLURAL die Namen); I've forgotten her name ich habe ihren Namen vergessen, what's your name? wie heißt du?, my name's Joy ich heiße Joy ❷ (of a book or film) Titel der (PLURAL die Titel)

**napkin** NOUN Serviette die (PLURAL die Servietten)

**nappy** NOUN Windel die (PLURAL die Windeln)

**narrow** ADJECTIVE schmal; a narrow street eine schmale Straße

**nasty** ADJECTIVE ❶ (mean) gemein; that was a nasty thing to do das war gemein ❷ (unpleasant, bad) scheußlich; that's a nasty job das ist eine scheußliche Arbeit, a nasty smell ein scheußlicher Geruch

**nation** NOUN Nation die (PLURAL die Nationen)

**national** ADJECTIVE national

**national anthem** NOUN Nationalhymne die (PLURAL die Nationalhymnen)

**nationality** NOUN Nationalität die (PLURAL die Nationalitäten)

**national park** NOUN Nationalpark der (PLURAL die Nationalparks)

**natural** ADJECTIVE natürlich

**naturally** ADVERB natürlich

**nature** NOUN Natur die

**nature reserve** NOUN Naturschutzgebiet das (PLURAL die Naturschutzgebiete)

**naughty** ADJECTIVE unartig

**navy** NOUN Marine die; my uncle's in the navy mein Onkel ist bei der Marine

**navy-blue** ADJECTIVE marineblau

**near** ADJECTIVE ❶ nah(e) ❷ (the superlative of nah(e) is der/die/das nächste) the nearest park der nächste Park, the nearest bank die nächste Bank, the nearest shop das nächste Geschäft

**near** PREPOSITION nahe an (+DAT); near (to) the station nahe am Bahnhof

**near** ADVERB ❶ nah(e) (in spoken German 'nah' is more common); they live quite near sie wohnen ganz nah ❷ to come nearer näher kommen

**nearby** ADVERB nahe gelegen; there's a park nearby hier in der Nähe ist ein Park

a
b
c
d
e
f
g
h
i
j
k
l
m
n
o
p
q
r
s
t
u
v
w
x
y
z

**nearly** ADVERB fast; **nearly empty** fast leer

**neat** ADJECTIVE ❶ (well organized, tidy) ordentlich; **a neat room** ein ordentliches Zimmer ❷ adrett (clothes or the way you look)

**necessarily** ADVERB **not necessarily** nicht unbedingt

**necessary** ADJECTIVE nötig; **if necessary** falls nötig

**neck** NOUN ❶ (of a person) Hals der (PLURAL die Hälse) ❷ (of a garment) Kragen der (PLURAL die Kragen)

**necklace** NOUN Halskette die (PLURAL die Halsketten)

**need** NOUN **there's no need, I've already done it** das ist nicht nötig, ich habe es schon gemacht, **there's no need to wait** du brauchst nicht zu warten

**need** VERB ❶ brauchen; **we need bread** wir brauchen Brot, **everything you need** alles, was man braucht ❷ (to have to) müssen◊; **I need to go to the bank** ich muss zur Bank gehen ❸ (with a negative) **you needn't wait** du brauchst nicht zu warten

**needle** NOUN Nadel die (PLURAL die Nadeln)

**negative** NOUN (of a photo) Negativ das (PLURAL die Negative)

**neglected** ADJECTIVE vernachlässigt

**neighbour** NOUN Nachbar der (PLURAL die Nachbarn), Nachbarin die (PLURAL die Nachbarinnen); **we're going round to the neighbours'** wir besuchen die Nachbarn

**neighbourhood** NOUN Nachbarschaft die; **in our neighbourhood** in unserer Nachbarschaft

**neither** CONJUNCTION ❶ **neither … nor** weder … noch, **I have neither the time nor the money** ich habe weder die Zeit noch das Geld ❷ **neither do I** ich auch nicht, **'I don't like fish' – 'neither do I'** 'ich mag keinen Fisch' – 'ich auch nicht', **'I didn't like the film' – 'neither did Kirsty'** 'mir hat der Film nicht gefallen' – 'Kirsty hat er auch nicht gefallen'

**neither** PRONOUN keiner von beiden/keine von beiden/keins von beiden; **'which do you like?' – 'neither'** 'welches gefällt dir?' – 'keins von beiden'

**nephew** NOUN Neffe der (PLURAL die Neffen)

**nerve** NOUN ❶ Nerv der (PLURAL die Nerven) ❷ **to lose your nerve** die Nerven verlieren, **you've got a nerve!** du hast Nerven! (informal) ❸ **what a nerve!** so eine Frechheit!
• **he gets on my nerves** er geht mir auf die Nerven (informal)

**nervous** ADJECTIVE ❶ (afraid) ängstlich; **to feel nervous about something** Angst vor etwas (DAT) haben ❷ (highly strung) nervös (person)

**nest** NOUN Nest das (PLURAL die Nester)

**net** NOUN Netz das (PLURAL die Netze)

**Netherlands** NOUN Niederlande (plural); **in the Netherlands** in den Niederlanden

**nettle** NOUN Nessel die (PLURAL die Nesseln)

**network** NOUN Netzwerk das (PLURAL die Netzwerke)

**neutral** NOUN (neutral gear) Leerlauf der; **to be in neutral** im Leerlauf sein

**neutral** ADJECTIVE neutral

**never** ADVERB ❶ nie; **Ben never smokes** Ben raucht nie, **I've never told him** ich habe es ihm nie gesagt, **never again** nie wieder ❷ noch nie; **'have you ever been to Spain?' – 'no, never'** 'warst du schon mal in Spanien?' – 'nein, noch nie' ❸ **never mind** macht nichts

**new** ADJECTIVE neu; **have you seen their new house?** hast du ihr neues Haus gesehen?

**news** NOUN ❶ (new information) Nachricht die (PLURAL die Nachrichten); **I've got good news** ich habe gute Nachrichten ❷ **a piece of news** eine Neuigkeit, **any news?** was gibt es Neues? ❸ (on TV or the radio) Nachrichten (plural); **we saw it on the news** wir haben es in den Nachrichten gesehen

**newsagent** NOUN Zeitungshändler der (PLURAL die Zeitungshändler)

**newspaper** NOUN Zeitung die (PLURAL die Zeitungen)

**newsreader** NOUN Nachrichtensprecher der (PLURAL die Nachrichtensprecher), Nachrichtensprecherin die (PLURAL die Nachrichtensprecherinnen)

**New Year** NOUN Neujahr das; **Happy New Year!** ein gutes neues Jahr!

**New Year's Day** NOUN Neujahr das

**New Year's Eve** NOUN Silvester der

**New Zealand** NOUN Neuseeland das

**next** ADJECTIVE ❶ nächster/nächste/ nächstes; **the next train leaves at ten** der nächste Zug fährt um zehn ab, **next week** nächste Woche, **next Thursday** nächsten Donnerstag, **next year** nächstes Jahr, **next time I see you** nächstes Mal, wenn ich dich sehe ❷ (following) der Nächste bitte/die Nächste bitte, **the next thing** das Nächste, **the next day** am nächsten Tag, **the letter arrived the next day** der Brief kam am nächsten Tag ❸ **the week after next** übernächste Woche ❹ (next-door) nebenan; **I'm in the next room** ich bin nebenan

**next** ADVERB ❶ (afterwards) danach; **what did he say next?** was hat er danach gesagt? ❷ (now) als Nächstes; **what shall we do next?** was machen wir als Nächstes? ❸ **next to** neben (+DAT or, with movement towards a place, +ACC), **the house next to the baker's** das Haus neben dem Bäcker, **I sat down next to her** ich habe mich neben sie gesetzt

**next door** ADVERB nebenan; **they live next door** sie wohnen nebenan, **the girl next door** das Mädchen von nebenan

**nice** ADJECTIVE ❶ (pleasant) schön; **we had a nice evening** wir haben einen schönen Abend verbracht, **Brighton's a nice town** Brighton ist eine schöne Stadt, **we had nice weather** wir hatten schönes Wetter ❷ **to have a nice time** sich amüsieren, **have a nice day!** viel Spaß! ❸ (attractive to look at) hübsch; **that's a nice dress** das ist ein hübsches Kleid ❹ (kind, friendly) nett (person); **she's really nice** sie ist wirklich nett ❺ **to be nice to**

a
b
c
d
e
f
g
h
i
j
k
l
m
**n**
o
p
q
r
s
t
u
v
w
x
y
z

somebody nett zu jemandem sein,
she's been very nice to me sie war
sehr nett zu mir ❻ *(tasting good)*
gut; it tastes nice es schmeckt gut

**nickname** NOUN Spitzname der
*(PLURAL die Spitznamen)*

**niece** NOUN Nichte die *(PLURAL die
Nichten)*

**night** NOUN ❶ *(after bedtime)* Nacht
die *(PLURAL die Nächte)*; during the
night während der Nacht, Sunday
night Sonntag Nacht, it's cold at
night nachts ist es kalt, to stay the
night über Nacht bleiben, I stayed
the night at Emma's ich habe bei
Emma übernachtet ❷ *(before you
go to bed)* Abend der *(PLURAL die
Abende)*; what are you doing
tonight? was macht ihr heute
Abend?, one night eines Abends,
tomorrow night morgen Abend,
I met Greg last night ich habe Greg
gestern Abend getroffen, on Friday
night am Freitagabend, see you
tonight! bis heute Abend!

**night club** NOUN Nachtklub der
*(PLURAL die Nachtklubs)*

**nightie** NOUN Nachthemd das *(PLURAL
die Nachthemden)*

**nightmare** NOUN Albtraum der
*(PLURAL die Albträume)*

**nil** NOUN *(in sport)* null; they won four-
nil sie haben vier zu null gewonnen

**nine** NUMBER neun

**nineteen** NUMBER neunzehn

**ninety** NUMBER neunzig

**ninth** NUMBER neunter/neunte/
neuntes; on the ninth floor im
neunten Stock, on the ninth of June
am neunten Juni

**no** ADVERB nein; I said no ich habe nein
gesagt, no thank you nein danke

**no** ADJECTIVE ❶ kein; we've got no
bread wir haben kein Brot, no
problem! kein Problem! ❷ *(on a
notice)* 'no smoking' 'Rauchen
verboten', 'no parking' 'Parken
verboten'

**nobody** PRONOUN niemand; 'who's
there?' – 'nobody' 'wer ist da?'
– 'niemand', there's nobody in the
kitchen es ist niemand in der Küche,
nobody was at home niemand war
zu Hause

**nod** VERB nicken; he nodded in
agreement er hat zustimmend
genickt

**noise** NOUN Lärm der; to make a
noise Lärm machen

**noise pollution** NOUN
Lärmbelästigung die

**noisy** ADJECTIVE laut

**none** PRONOUN ❶ *(not one)* keiner/
keine/keins; none of us keiner
von uns/keine von uns, 'how many
students failed the exam?' – 'none'
'wie viele Schüler sind durch die
Prüfung gefallen?' – 'keine', none
of the boys knows him keiner der
Jungen kennt ihn ❷ there's none
left es ist nichts mehr übrig

**nonsense** NOUN Unsinn der; to talk
nonsense Unsinn reden, nonsense!
Unsinn!

**non-smoker** NOUN Nichtraucher
der *(PLURAL die Nichtraucher)*,
Nichtraucherin die *(PLURAL die
Nichtraucherinnen)*

**non-stop** ADJECTIVE **durchgehend** *(train)*, **Nonstop-** *(flight)*

**non-stop** ADVERB **ununterbrochen**; **she talks non-stop** sie redet ununterbrochen

**noodles** PLURAL NOUN **Nudeln** die *(plural)*

**noon** NOUN **Mittag** der; **at (twelve) noon** um zwölf (Uhr mittags)

**no-one** PRONOUN **niemand**; **'who's there?' – 'no-one'** 'wer ist da?' – 'niemand', **there's no-one in the kitchen** es ist niemand in der Küche, **no-one was at home** niemand war zu Hause

**nor** CONJUNCTION ❶ **neither ... nor** weder ... noch, **I have neither the time nor the money** ich habe weder die Zeit noch das Geld ❷ **nor do I** ich auch nicht, **'I don't like fish' – 'nor do I'** 'ich mag keinen Fisch' – 'ich auch nicht', **nor do we** wir auch nicht

**normal** ADJECTIVE **normal**

**normally** ADVERB ❶ *(usually)* **normalerweise** ❷ *(in a normal way)* **normal**

**north** NOUN **Norden** der; **in the north** im Norden

**north** ADJECTIVE **nördlich**, **Nord-**; **the north side** die Nordseite, **north wind** der Nordwind

**north** ADVERB ❶ *(towards the north)* **nach Norden**; **to travel north** nach Norden fahren ❷ **north of London** nördlich von London

**North America** NOUN **Nordamerika** das

**North American** NOUN **Nordamerikaner** der *(PLURAL die **Nordamerikaner**)*, **Nordamerikanerin** die *(PLURAL die **Nordamerikanerinnen**)*

**North American** ADJECTIVE **nordamerikanisch**

**northeast** NOUN **Nordosten** der

**northeast** ADJECTIVE **in northeast England** in Nordostengland

**Northern Ireland** NOUN **Nordirland** das

**North Pole** NOUN **Nordpol** der

**North Sea** NOUN **the North Sea** die **Nordsee**

**northwest** NOUN **Nordwesten** der

**northwest** ADJECTIVE **in northwest England** in Nordwestengland

**Norway** NOUN **Norwegen** das

**Norwegian** NOUN ❶ *(person)* **Norweger** der *(PLURAL die **Norweger**)*, **Norwegerin** die *(PLURAL die **Norwegerinnen**)* ❷ *(language)* **Norwegisch** das

**Norwegian** ADJECTIVE **norwegisch**

**nose** NOUN **Nase** die *(PLURAL die **Nasen**)*; **to blow your nose** sich *(DAT)* die Nase putzen

**not** ADVERB ❶ **nicht**; **not on Sundays** sonntags nicht, **not all alone!** nicht ganz allein!, **not bad** nicht schlecht, **not at all** überhaupt nicht, **not yet** noch nicht, **Sam didn't phone** Sam hat nicht angerufen, **I hope not** hoffentlich nicht ❷ **not a** kein/keine, **he's not a specialist** er ist kein Fachmann, **not a bit** kein bisschen

**note** NOUN ❶ *(a short letter)* Zettel der *(PLURAL* die **Zettel)**, *(informal)* Brief der *(PLURAL* die **Briefe)** ❷ *(in a class)* Notiz die *(PLURAL* die **Notizen)**; **to take notes** sich *(DAT)* Notizen machen ❸ *(a banknote)* Schein der *(PLURAL* die **Scheine)**; **a ten-pound note** ein Zehnpfundschein ❹ *(in music)* Note die *(PLURAL* die **Noten)**

**notebook** NOUN Notizbuch das *(PLURAL* die **Notizbücher)**

**notepad** NOUN Notizblock der *(PLURAL* die **Notizblöcke)**

**nothing** PRONOUN nichts; 'what did you say?' – 'nothing' 'was hast du gesagt?' – 'nichts', **nothing special** nichts Besonderes, **nothing new** nichts Neues, **I saw nothing** ich habe nichts gesehen, **there's nothing left** es ist nichts mehr übrig

**notice** NOUN ❶ *(a sign)* Schild das *(PLURAL* die **Schilder)** ❷ *(an advertisement)* Anzeige die *(PLURAL* die **Anzeigen)** ❸ *(advance warning)* Ankündigung die ❹ **don't take any notice of her** nimm keine Notiz von ihr ❺ **at short notice** kurzfristig

**notice** VERB bemerken; **I didn't notice anything** ich habe nichts bemerkt

**notice board** NOUN Anschlagbrett das *(PLURAL* die **Anschlagbretter)**

**nought** NOUN Null die *(PLURAL* die **Nullen)**

**noun** NOUN Substantiv das *(PLURAL* die **Substantive)**

**novel** NOUN Roman der *(PLURAL* die **Romane)**

**novelist** NOUN Romanautor der *(PLURAL* die **Romanautoren)**,

Romanautorin die *(PLURAL* die **Romanautorinnen)**

**November** NOUN November der; **in November** im November

**now** ADVERB ❶ jetzt; **where is he now?** wo ist er jetzt?, **from now on** von jetzt an ❷ **he left just now** er ist gerade eben gegangen, **I saw her just now in the corridor** ich habe sie gerade eben im Gang gesehen ❸ **do it right now!** mach es sofort! ❹ **now and then** hin und wieder

**nowadays** ADVERB heutzutage; **nowadays they are quite common** heutzutage sind sie ziemlich häufig

**nowhere** ADJECTIVE nirgends; **there's nowhere to park** man kann nirgends parken

**nuclear** ADJECTIVE Kern-; **nuclear power** die Kernenergie, **nuclear power station** das Kernkraftwerk

**nude** NOUN **in the nude** nackt

**nude** ADJECTIVE nackt

**nuisance** NOUN **it's a nuisance** das ist ärgerlich, **what a nuisance!** wie ärgerlich!

**numb** ADJECTIVE ❶ *(with cold)* gefühllos ❷ *(emotionally)* benommen

**number** NOUN ❶ *(of a house, telephone, or account)* Nummer die *(PLURAL* die **Nummern)**; **I live at number five** ich wohne in der Nummer fünf, **my new phone number** meine neue Telefonnummer ❷ *(a written figure)* Zahl die *(PLURAL* die **Zahlen)** ❸ *(amount)* Anzahl die; **the number of visitors** die Anzahl der Besucher

**number plate** NOUN
Nummernschild das (PLURAL die
Nummernschilder)

**nun** NOUN Nonne die (PLURAL die
Nonnen)

**nurse** NOUN ❶ (female)
Krankenschwester die (PLURAL die
Krankenschwestern); Janet's a
nurse Janet ist Krankenschwester
❷ (male) Krankenpfleger der
(PLURAL die Krankenpfleger)

**nursery** NOUN ❶ (for children)
Kindertagesstätte die (PLURAL
die Kindertagesstätten) ❷ (for
plants) Gärtnerei die (PLURAL die
Gärtnereien)

**nursery school** NOUN
Kindergarten der (PLURAL die
Kindergärten)

**nut** NOUN ❶ Nuss die (PLURAL die
Nüsse) ❷ (for a bolt) Mutter die
(PLURAL die Muttern)

**nylon** NOUN Nylon das

## Oo

**oak** NOUN Eiche die (PLURAL die Eichen)

**oar** NOUN Ruder das (PLURAL die Ruder)

**oats** NOUN Hafer der; porridge oats
Haferflocken (plural)

**obedient** ADJECTIVE gehorsam

**obey** VERB ❶ gehorchen (+DAT);
to obey somebody jemandem
gehorchen ❷ to obey the rules sich
an die Vorschriften halten◇

**object** NOUN ❶ (thing) Gegenstand
der (PLURAL die Gegenstände)
❷ (aim) Zweck der ❸ (in grammar)
Objekt das (PLURAL die Objekte)

**object** VERB etwas dagegen
haben◇; if you don't object wenn
Sie nichts dagegen haben

**objection** NOUN Einwand der (PLURAL
die Einwände)

**oboe** NOUN Oboe die (PLURAL die
Oboen); to play the oboe Oboe
spielen

**obscene** ADJECTIVE obszön

**observe** VERB beobachten

**obsessed** ADJECTIVE besessen; she's
really obsessed with her diet sie
ist von ihrer Schlankheitskur ganz
besessen

**obstacle** NOUN Hindernis das (PLURAL
die Hindernisse)

A
B
C
D
E
F
G
H
I
J
K
L
M
N
O
P
Q
R
S
T
U
V
W
X
Y
Z

**obstinate** ADJECTIVE **starrsinnig**

**obtain** VERB **erhalten**◇

**obvious** ADJECTIVE **eindeutig**

**obviously** ADVERB ❶ (of course)
**natürlich** ❷ (looking at something)
**offensichtlich; the house is
obviously empty** das Haus steht
offensichtlich leer

**occasion** NOUN **Gelegenheit** die
(PLURAL die **Gelegenheiten**); on
**special occasions** zu besonderen
Gelegenheiten

**occasionally** ADVERB **gelegentlich**

**occupation** NOUN **Beruf** der (PLURAL
die **Berufe**)

**occupied** ADJECTIVE ❶ (taken) **besetzt;
the seat is occupied** der Platz ist
besetzt ❷ (lived in) **bewohnt**

**occur** VERB ❶ **to occur to somebody**
jemandem einfallen◇ (SEP) (PERF
sein), **it occurs to me that ...**
mir fällt ein, dass ... ❷ **it never
occurred to me** darauf wäre ich
nie gekommen ❸ (happen) **sich
ereignen**

**ocean** NOUN **Ozean** der (PLURAL die
**Ozeane**)

**o'clock** ADVERB **at ten o'clock** um zehn
Uhr, **it's three o'clock** es ist drei Uhr

**October** NOUN **Oktober** der; **in
October** im Oktober

**octopus** NOUN **Tintenfisch** der
(PLURAL die **Tintenfische**)

**odd** ADJECTIVE ❶ (strange) **komisch;
that's odd, I'm sure I heard the
bell** das ist komisch, ich habe
es bestimmt klingeln gehört
❷ (number) **ungerade; three is an**

**odd number** drei ist eine ungerade
Zahl ❸ **the odd one out** die
Ausnahme

**odds and ends** PLURAL NOUN
**Kleinkram** der

**of** PREPOSITION ❶ **von** (+DAT); (instead
of translating 'of' with 'von', the
genitive case can be used) **the
parents of the children** die Eltern
von den Kindern, die Eltern der
Kinder, **the name of the flower**
der Name der Blume, **it's very
kind of you** das ist sehr nett von
Ihnen ❷ (with quantities 'of' is not
translated) **a kilo of tomatoes** ein
Kilo Tomaten, **a bottle of milk** eine
Flasche Milch, **the three of us** wir
drei ❸ **of it/them** davon (things)
**of them** von ihnen (people), **how
many of them didn't pay?** wie viele
von ihnen haben nicht gezahlt?,
**Ray has four cars but he's selling
three of them** Ray hat vier Autos,
aber er verkauft drei davon, **half of
it** die Hälfte davon, **we ate a lot of
it** wir haben viel davon gegessen
❹ **the sixth of June** der sechste Juni
❺ **made of** aus, **a bracelet made of
silver** ein Armband aus Silber

**off** ADVERB, ADJECTIVE, PREPOSITION
❶ (switched off) **aus; is the telly off?**
ist der Fernseher aus?, **to turn off
the lights** das Licht ausmachen (SEP)
❷ (electricity, water, gas) **abgestellt;
the gas and electricity were off**
Gas und Strom waren abgestellt, **to
turn off the tap** den Wasserhahn
zudrehen (SEP) ❸ **to be off** (to leave)
**gehen**◇ (PERF sein), (in a vehicle)
**fahren**◇ (PERF sein), **I must be off**
ich muss gehen ❹ **on my day off** an
meinem freien Tag, **to take three
days off work** sich (DAT) drei Tage
frei nehmen, **we were given two
days off school** wir hatten zwei

Tage schulfrei, **to be off sick** wegen Krankheit fehlen, **Maya's off school today** Maya fehlt heute in der Schule ❺ *(cancelled)* **abgesagt**; **the match is off** das Spiel ist abgesagt worden ❻ **'20% off shoes'** 'Schuhe 20% reduziert'

**offence** *NOUN* ❶ *(crime)* **Straftat** die *(PLURAL* die **Straftaten)* ❷ **to take offence** beleidigt sein, **he takes offence easily** er ist schnell beleidigt

**offer** *NOUN* ❶ **Angebot** das *(PLURAL* die **Angebote)**; **job offer** das Stellenangebot ❷ **on special offer** im Sonderangebot

**offer** *VERB* **anbieten**◇ *(SEP) (a present, a reward, or a job)*; **he offered her a chair** er bot ihr einen Stuhl an, **to offer to do something** anbieten, etwas zu tun, **he offered to drive me to the station** er hat angeboten, mich zum Bahnhof zu fahren

**office** *NOUN* **Büro** das *(PLURAL* die **Büros)**; **he's still at the office** er ist noch im Büro

**office block** *NOUN* **Bürohaus** das *(PLURAL* die **Bürohäuser)**

**officer** *NOUN* **Offizier** der *(PLURAL* die **Offiziere)**

**official** *ADJECTIVE* **offiziell**

**off-licence** *NOUN* **Wein- und Spirituosenhandlung** die *(PLURAL* die **Wein- und Spirituosenhandlungen)**

**often** *ADVERB* ❶ **oft**; **he's often late** er kommt oft zu spät, **how often?** wie oft? ❷ **more often** öfter, **couldn't you come more often?** könntest du nicht öfter kommen?

**oil** *NOUN* ❶ *(crude oil)* **Öl** das ❷ **olive oil** das Olivenöl, **suntan oil** das Sonnenöl

**oil slick** *NOUN* **Ölteppich** der *(PLURAL* die **Ölteppiche)**

**ointment** *NOUN* **Salbe** die *(PLURAL* die **Salben)**

**okay** *ADJECTIVE* ❶ **okay** *(informal)*; **tomorrow at ten, okay?** morgen um zehn, okay?, **is it okay if I don't come till Friday?** ist es okay, wenn ich erst Freitag komme? ❷ *(person)* **in Ordnung**; **Daisy's okay** Daisy ist in Ordnung ❸ *(nothing special, not ill)* **ganz gut**; **the film was okay** der Film war ganz gut, **I've been ill but I'm okay now** ich war krank, aber jetzt geht es mir ganz gut, **'how are you?' – 'okay'** 'wie geht's?' – 'ganz gut' ❹ **it's okay by me** mir ist es recht

**old** *ADJECTIVE* ❶ *(not young, not new, previous)* **alt**; **an old man** ein alter Mann, **an old lady** eine alte Dame, **an old tree** ein alter Baum, **old people** alte Leute, **bring some old clothes** bring ein paar alte Sachen mit, **I've only got their old address** ich habe nur ihre alte Adresse ❷ *(talking about age)* **how old are you?** wie alt bist du?, **James is ten years old** James ist zehn Jahre alt ❸ **a two-year-old child** ein zweijähriges Kind ❹ **my older sister** meine ältere Schwester, **she's older than me** sie ist älter als ich, **he's a year older than me** er ist ein Jahr älter als ich

**old age** *NOUN* **Alter** das

**old age pensioner** *NOUN* **Rentner** der *(PLURAL* die **Rentner)**, **Rentnerin** die *(PLURAL* die **Rentnerinnen)**

**old-fashioned** NOUN altmodisch

**old people's home** NOUN Altenheim das (PLURAL die Altenheime)

**olive** NOUN Olive die (PLURAL die Oliven)

**olive oil** NOUN Olivenöl das (PLURAL die Olivenöle)

**Olympic Games, Olympics** PLURAL NOUN Olympische Spiele (plural)

**omelette** NOUN Omelett das (PLURAL die Omelette); a cheese omelette ein Käseomelett

**on** PREPOSITION **❶** auf (+DAT or, with movement towards a place, +ACC); it's on the desk es ist auf dem Schreibtisch **❷** (attached to) an (+DAT or, with movement towards a place, +ACC); on the wall an der Wand **❸** on the beach am Strand, on the right/left rechts/links **❹** (in expressions of time) on March 21st am 21. März, he's arriving on Tuesday er kommt am Dienstag an, it's shut on Sundays es ist sonntags geschlossen, on rainy days an Regentagen **❺** (for buses, trains, etc.) to go on the bus mit dem Bus fahren, I met Jackie on the train ich habe Jackie im Zug getroffen, let's go on our bikes fahren wir mit dem Rad **❻** on TV im Fernsehen, on the radio im Radio, on video auf Video **❼** on holiday in den Ferien

**on** ADJECTIVE **❶** (switched on) to be on an sein, the lights are on das Licht ist an, is the radio on? ist das Radio an? **❷** (happening) what's on TV? was gibts im Fernsehen?, what's on this week at the cinema? was läuft diese Woche im Kino?

**once** ADVERB **❶** einmal; I've tried once already ich habe es schon einmal versucht, try once more versuch es noch einmal, once a day einmal täglich, once upon a time ... es war einmal ... **❷** more than once mehrmals **❸** at once (immediately) sofort, the doctor came at once der Arzt kam sofort **❹** at once (at the same time) gleichzeitig, I can't do two things at once ich kann nicht zwei Sachen gleichzeitig machen

**one** NUMBER (when counting) eins, (with a noun) ein; one son ein Sohn, one apple ein Apfel, if you want a biro I've got one falls du einen Kugelschreiber brauchst, habe ich einen, at one o'clock um ein Uhr

**one** PRONOUN **❶** einer/eine/eines; I saw the photos, can I have one of them? ich habe die Fotos gesehen, kann ich eins davon haben? **❷** this one dieser/diese/dieses, I'd prefer that bike, but this one's cheaper ich würde lieber das Rad haben, aber dieses ist billiger **❸** that one der da/die da/das da, 'which video?' – 'that one' 'welches Video?' – 'das da' **❹** which one? welcher/welche/welches?, 'my foot's hurting' – 'which one?' 'mir tut der Fuß weh' – 'welcher?', 'she borrowed a skirt from me' – 'which one?' 'sie hat sich einen Rock von mir geliehen' – 'welchen?' **❺** (you) man; one never knows man kann nie wissen

**one's** ADJECTIVE sein/seine/sein; one pays for one's car man zahlt für sein Auto

**oneself** PRONOUN **❶** (reflexive) sich; to wash oneself sich waschen **❷** (stressing something) selbst; one has to do everything oneself man muss alles selbst machen

**one-way street** NOUN Einbahnstraße die (PLURAL die Einbahnstraßen)

**onion** NOUN Zwiebel die (PLURAL die Zwiebeln)

**online** ADVERB online

**only** ADJECTIVE ❶ einziger/einzige/einziges; the only free seat der einzige freie Platz, the only thing you could do das Einzige, was du machen könntest ❷ an only child ein Einzelkind

**only** ADVERB, CONJUNCTION ❶ nur; they've only got two bedrooms sie haben nur zwei Schlafzimmer, Anne's only free on Fridays Anne hat nur freitags Zeit, there are only three left es sind nur noch drei übrig, I'd walk, only it's raining ich würde zu Fuß gehen, nur regnet es ❷ (very recently) gerade erst; he's only just got the message er hat die Nachricht gerade erst bekommen ❸ (barely) gerade noch; we've only just made it on time wir sind gerade noch rechtzeitig angekommen

**onto** PREPOSITION auf (+ACC)

**open** NOUN in the open im Freien

**open** ADJECTIVE ❶ offen; the door's open die Tür ist offen, the baker's is not open die Bäckerei ist nicht geöffnet ❷ in the open air im Freien

**open** VERB ❶ aufmachen (SEP); can you open the door for me? kannst du mir die Tür aufmachen?, the bank opens at nine die Bank macht um neun auf ❷ (open up) sich öffnen; the door opened slowly die Tür öffnete sich langsam

**opera** NOUN Oper die (PLURAL die Opern)

**operate** VERB ❶ (medically) operieren; will they have to operate (on him/her)? werden sie ihn/sie operieren müssen? ❷ bedienen (a machine)

**operation** NOUN ❶ Operation die (PLURAL die Operationen) ❷ to have an operation operiert werden

**opinion** NOUN Meinung die (PLURAL die Meinungen); in my opinion meiner Meinung nach

**opinion poll** NOUN Meinungsumfrage die (PLURAL die Meinungsumfragen)

**opponent** NOUN Gegner der (PLURAL die Gegner), Gegnerin die (PLURAL die Gegnerinnen)

**opportunity** NOUN Gelegenheit die (PLURAL die Gelegenheiten); to have the opportunity of doing something die Gelegenheit haben, etwas zu tun

**opposite** NOUN Gegenteil das (PLURAL die Gegenteile); no, quite the opposite nein, ganz im Gegenteil

**opposite** ADJECTIVE ❶ entgegengesetzt (direction); she went off in the opposite direction sie ging in die entgegengesetzte Richtung ❷ (facing) gegenüberliegend; in the house opposite im gegenüberliegenden Haus

**opposite** ADVERB gegenüber; they live opposite sie wohnen gegenüber

a
b
c
d
e
f
g
h
i
j
k
l
m
n
o
p
q
r
s
t
u
v
w
x
y
z

**opposite** PREPOSITION **gegenüber** (+DAT); **opposite the station** gegenüber dem Bahnhof

**optician** NOUN Optiker der (PLURAL die Optiker), Optikerin die (PLURAL die Optikerinnen)

**optimistic** ADJECTIVE **zuversichtlich, optimistisch**

**option** NOUN Wahl die; **we have no option** wir haben keine andere Wahl

**optional** ADJECTIVE **auf Wunsch erhältlich**; **optional subject** das Wahlfach

**or** CONJUNCTION ❶ **oder**; **English or German?** Englisch oder Deutsch?, **today or Tuesday?** heute oder Dienstag? ❷ (in negatives) **noch**; **I don't have a cat or a dog** ich habe weder eine Katze noch einen Hund, **not in June or July** weder im Juni noch im Juli ❸ (or else) **sonst**; **phone Mum, or she'll worry** ruf Mutti an, sonst macht sie sich Sorgen

**oral** NOUN (an exam) **Mündliche** das (informal); **my German oral** meine mündliche Deutschprüfung

**orange** NOUN (the fruit) **Orange** die (PLURAL die Orangen); **orange juice** der Orangensaft

**orange** ADJECTIVE **orange** ('orange' never changes); **my orange socks** meine orange Socken

**orchestra** NOUN Orchester das (PLURAL die Orchester)

**order** NOUN ❶ (sequence) **Reihenfolge** die (PLURAL die Reihenfolgen); **in the right order** in der richtigen Reihenfolge, **in the wrong order** in der falschen

Reihenfolge, **in alphabetical order** in alphabetischer Reihenfolge ❷ (in a restaurant, cafe, or shop) **Bestellung** die (PLURAL die Bestellungen) ❸ 'out of order' 'außer Betrieb' ❹ **in order to do something** um etwas zu tun

**order** VERB ❶ (in a restaurant or a shop) **bestellen**; **we ordered soup** wir haben Suppe bestellt, **have you ordered?** haben Sie schon bestellt? ❷ **bestellen** (a taxi)

**ordinary** ADJECTIVE **normal**

**organ** NOUN ❶ (the instrument) **Orgel** die (PLURAL die Orgeln) ❷ (of the body) **Organ** das (PLURAL die Organe)

**organic** ADJECTIVE **Bio-** (food); **organic food** die Biokost

**organization** NOUN Organisation die (PLURAL die Organisationen)

**organize** VERB ❶ **organisieren** ❷ **veranstalten** (a conference or festival)

**orienteering** NOUN Orientierungslauf der

**original** ADJECTIVE ❶ **ursprünglich**; **the original plan was better** der ursprüngliche Plan war besser ❷ **originell**; **it's a really original novel** das ist ein wirklich origineller Roman

**originally** ADVERB **ursprünglich**; **originally we wanted to go by car** ursprünglich wollten wir mit dem Auto fahren

**orphan** NOUN Waise die (PLURAL die Waisen); **he is an orphan** er ist Waise

**ostrich** NOUN **Strauß** der (PLURAL die Sträuße)

**other** ADJECTIVE ❶ **anderer/andere/ anderes**; **we took the other road** wir haben die andere Straße genommen, **where are the others?** wo sind die anderen?, **the other two cars** die anderen beiden Autos ❷ **give me the other one** gib mir den anderen/die andere/das andere (the translation of 'the other one' depends on the gender of the noun it refers to) ❸ **the other day** neulich ❹ **every other week** jede zweite Woche ❺ **somebody or other** irgendjemand, **something or other** irgendetwas, **somewhere or other** irgendwo ❻ **any other questions?** sonst noch Fragen?

**otherwise** ADVERB, CONJUNCTION **sonst**

**ought** VERB ('ought' is usually translated by the subjunctive of 'sollen') **I ought to go** ich sollte eigentlich gehen, **they ought to have known the address** sie hätten die Adresse kennen sollen, **you oughtn't to have any problems** du solltest keine Probleme haben

**our** ADJECTIVE ❶ (before a masculine noun) **unser**; **our father** unser Vater ❷ (before a feminine noun) **unsere**; **our mother** unsere Mutter ❸ (before a neuter noun) **our house** unser Haus ❹ (before masculine/feminine/neuter plural nouns) **unsere**; **our parents** unsere Eltern ❺ (with parts of the body) **der/die/das** (plural die); **we'll go and wash our hands** wir waschen uns die Hände

**ours** PRONOUN ❶ (for a masculine noun) **unserer**; **their garden's bigger than ours** ihr Garten ist größer als unserer ❷ (for a feminine noun) **unsere**; **their kitchen is smaller than ours** ihre Küche ist kleiner als unsere ❸ (for a neuter noun) **unseres**; **their child is younger than ours** ihr Kind ist jünger als unseres ❹ (for plural nouns) **unsere**; **they've invited their friends and we've invited ours** sie haben ihre Freunde eingeladen und wir haben unsere eingeladen ❺ **the green car is ours** das grüne Auto gehört uns, **it's ours** es gehört uns, **a friend of ours** ein Freund von uns

**ourselves** PRONOUN ❶ (reflexive) **uns**; **we introduced ourselves** wir haben uns vorgestellt ❷ (for emphasis) **selbst**; **in the end we did it ourselves** schließlich haben wir es selbst gemacht

**out** ADVERB ❶ (outside) **draußen**; **it's cold out there** es ist kalt da draußen, **they're out in the garden** sie sind draußen im Garten ❷ **to go out** hinausgehen◇ (SEP) (PERF **sein**) rausgehen◇ (SEP) (PERF **sein**) (informal), **to go out shopping** einkaufen gehen ❸ **get out!** raus! (informal) ❹ **the ball is out** der Ball ist aus ❺ (absent) **to be out** nicht da sein, **Mr Barnes is out** Herr Barnes ist nicht da ❻ **to go out** (for an evening or to the theatre or cinema) **ausgehen**◇ (SEP) (PERF **sein**), **weggehen**◇ (SEP) (PERF **sein**) (informal), **are you going out this evening?** gehst du heute Abend weg?, **to be going out with somebody** mit jemandem gehen, **Alison's going out with Danny now** Alison geht jetzt mit Danny ❼ **to ask somebody out** jemanden einladen◇ *(SEP)*, **he's asked me out** er hat mich eingeladen ❽ **(light, fire) aus**; **are all the lights out?** ist das Licht aus?

**out** *PREPOSITION* **out of aus** *(+DAT)*, **to go out of the room** aus dem Zimmer gehen, **he threw it out of the window** er hat es aus dem Fenster geworfen, **to drink out of a glass** aus einem Glas trinken, **she took the photo out of her bag** sie hat das Foto aus der Tasche genommen

**outdoor** *ADJECTIVE (activity or sport)* **im Freien**; **outdoor games** Spiele im Freien

**outdoors** *ADVERB* **draußen**; **to go outdoors** nach draußen gehen

**outing** *NOUN* **Ausflug** der *(PLURAL* die **Ausflüge)**; **to go on an outing** einen Ausflug machen

**outline** *NOUN (of an object)* **Umriss** der *(PLURAL* die **Umrisse)**

**out-of-date** *ADJECTIVE* ❶ *(no longer valid)* **ungültig**; **my passport's out of date** mein Pass ist ungültig ❷ *(old-fashioned)* **altmodisch** *(clothes, music)*

**outside** *NOUN* **Außenseite** die; **it's blue on the outside** außen ist es blau

**outside** *ADJECTIVE* **Außen-**

**outside** *ADVERB* **draußen**; **it's cold outside** es ist kalt draußen

**outside** *PREPOSITION* **vor** *(+DAT)*; **I'll meet you outside the cinema** ich treffe mich vor dem Kino mit dir

**outskirts** *PLURAL NOUN* **Stadtrand** der; **on the outskirts of Lübeck** am Stadtrand von Lübeck

**oven** *NOUN* **Ofen** der *(PLURAL* die **Öfen)**; **to put something in the oven** etwas in den Ofen tun

**over** *PREPOSITION* ❶ *(above)* **über** *(+DAT)*; **there's a mirror over the sink** über dem Waschbecken hängt ein Spiegel ❷ *(involving movement)* **über** *(+ACC)*; **he threw the ball over the wall** er hat den Ball über die Mauer geworfen ❸ **over here** hier drüben, **the food is over here** das Essen ist hier drüben ❹ **over there** da drüben, **she's over there** sie ist da drüben ❺ *(more than)* **über**; **it will cost over a hundred pounds** es wird über hundert Pfund kosten, **he's over sixty** er ist über sechzig ❻ *(during)* **über** *(+ACC)*; **over Christmas** über Weihnachten, **over the weekend** übers Wochenende ❼ *(finished)* **zu Ende**; **when the meeting's over** wenn die Besprechung zu Ende ist, **it's all over** es ist vorbei ❽ **over the phone** am Telefon, **to ask someone over** jemanden einladen◇ *(SEP)*, **to come over** herüberkommen◇ *(SEP)*, **come over on Saturday** komm am Samstag zu uns herüber ❾ **all over the place** überall, **I've been looking for it all over** ich habe überall danach gesucht

**overdose** *NOUN* **Überdosis** die *(PLURAL* die **Überdosen)**

**overtake** *VERB* **überholen**

**overtime** *NOUN* **to work overtime** Überstunden machen

**overweight** *ADJECTIVE* **to be overweight** Übergewicht haben

**owe** *VERB* **schulden**; **I owe him ten pounds** ich schulde ihm zehn Pfund

**owing** ADJECTIVE ❶ (outstanding) ausstehend; **there's five pounds owing** fünf Pfund stehen aus ❷ **owing to** wegen (+GEN), **owing to the snow** wegen des Schnees

**owl** NOUN Eule die (PLURAL die Eulen)

**own** ADJECTIVE ❶ eigen; **my own computer** mein eigener Computer, **I've got my own room** ich habe mein eigenes Zimmer ❷ **on your own** allein, **Annie did it on her own** Annie hat es allein gemacht

**own** VERB besitzen◇

**owner** NOUN Besitzer der (PLURAL die Besitzer), Besitzerin die (PLURAL die Besitzerinnen)

**oxygen** NOUN Sauerstoff der

**oyster** NOUN Auster die (PLURAL die Austern)

**ozone layer** NOUN Ozonschicht die

**pace** NOUN ❶ (a step) Schritt der (PLURAL die Schritte) ❷ (the speed you walk at) Tempo das (PLURAL die Tempos)

**Pacific** NOUN **the Pacific (Ocean)** der Pazifik

**pack** NOUN ❶ Packung die (PLURAL die Packungen) ❷ **pack of cards** das Kartenspiel

**pack** VERB ❶ packen (your case); **I haven't packed yet** ich habe noch nicht gepackt, **I'll pack my case tonight** ich packe meinen Koffer heute Abend ❷ einpacken (SEP) (clothes, shoes, etc.); **have you packed my red shirt?** hast du mein rotes Hemd eingepackt?

**package** NOUN Paket das (PLURAL die Pakete)

**package holiday** NOUN Pauschalurlaub der (PLURAL die Pauschalurlaube)

**packed lunch** NOUN Lunchpaket das (PLURAL die Lunchpakete)

**packet** NOUN ❶ Päckchen das (PLURAL die Päckchen); **a packet of tea** ein Päckchen Tee ❷ (box) Schachtel die (PLURAL die Schachteln) ❸ (bag) Tüte die (PLURAL die Tüten); **a packet of crisps** eine Tüte Chips

**pad** NOUN (of paper) **Block** der (PLURAL die **Blöcke**)

**paddle** NOUN (for a canoe) **Paddel** das (PLURAL die **Paddel**)

**paddle** VERB ❶ (at the seaside) **plauschen** (PERF **sein**); **to go paddling** plauschen gehen ❷ (a canoe) **paddeln**

**padlock** NOUN **Vorhängeschloss** das (PLURAL die **Vorhängeschlösser**)

**page** NOUN **Seite** die (PLURAL die **Seiten**); **on page seven** auf Seite sieben

**pain** NOUN **Schmerz** der (PLURAL die **Schmerzen**); **to be in pain** Schmerzen haben, **I've got a pain in my leg** ich habe Schmerzen im Bein
- **Eric's a real pain (in the neck)** Eric geht einem richtig auf den Wecker (informal)

**painful** ADJECTIVE **schmerzhaft**

**painkiller** NOUN **Schmerzmittel** das (PLURAL die **Schmerzmittel**)

**paint** NOUN **Farbe** die (PLURAL die **Farben**); **'wet paint'** 'frisch gestrichen'

**paint** VERB **malen** (a picture), **streichen**◇ (a room); **to paint a room pink** ein Zimmer rosa streichen

**paintbrush** NOUN **Pinsel** der (PLURAL die **Pinsel**)

**painter** NOUN **Maler** der (PLURAL die **Maler**), **Malerin** die (PLURAL die **Malerinnen**)

**painting** NOUN (picture) **Gemälde** das (PLURAL die **Gemälde**); **a painting by Picasso** ein Gemälde von Picasso

**pair** NOUN ❶ **Paar** das (PLURAL die **Paare**); **a pair of socks** ein Paar Socken ❷ **a pair of scissors** eine Schere ❸ **a pair of trousers** eine Hose, **a pair of knickers** eine Unterhose ❹ **to work in pairs** paarweise arbeiten

**Pakistan** NOUN **Pakistan** das

**palace** NOUN **Palast** der (PLURAL die **Paläste**)

**pale** ADJECTIVE **blass**; **to turn pale** blass werden, **pale green** zartgrün

**palm** NOUN ❶ (of your hand) **Handfläche** die (PLURAL die **Handflächen**) ❷ (a palm tree) **Palme** die (PLURAL die **Palmen**)

**pan** NOUN ❶ (saucepan) **Topf** der (PLURAL die **Töpfe**); **a pan of water** ein Topf Wasser ❷ (frying-pan) **Pfanne** die (PLURAL die **Pfannen**)

**pancake** NOUN **Pfannkuchen** der (PLURAL die **Pfannkuchen**)

**panel** NOUN ❶ (for a discussion) **Diskussionsrunde** die, (for a quiz) **Rateteam** das ❷ (a piece of wood) **Tafel** die (PLURAL die **Tafeln**)

**panic** NOUN **Panik** die

**panic** VERB **in Panik geraten**◇; **don't panic!** keine Panik!

**pantomime** NOUN **Märchenvorstellung** die (PLURAL die **Märchenvorstellungen**)

**pants** PLURAL NOUN **Unterhose** die (PLURAL die **Unterhosen**)

**paper** NOUN ❶ **Papier** das; **a sheet of paper** ein Blatt Papier ❷ **paper hanky** das Papiertaschentuch ❸ **paper cup** der Pappbecher ❹ (newspaper) **Zeitung** die (PLURAL die **Zeitungen**); it was in the paper es stand in der Zeitung ❺ **papers** (*documents*) Unterlagen (*plural*)

**paperback** *NOUN* Taschenbuch das (*PLURAL* die **Taschenbücher**)

**paperclip** *NOUN* Büroklammer die (*PLURAL* die **Büroklammern**)

**paper towel** *NOUN* Papierhandtuch das (*PLURAL* die **Papierhandtücher**)

**parachute** *NOUN* Fallschirm der (*PLURAL* die **Fallschirme**)

**parade** *NOUN* Umzug der (*PLURAL* die **Umzüge**)

**paraffin** *NOUN* Petroleum das

**paragraph** *NOUN* Absatz der (*PLURAL* die **Absätze**); 'new paragraph' 'Absatz'

**parallel** *ADJECTIVE* parallel

**paralysed** *ADJECTIVE* gelähmt

**parcel** *NOUN* Paket das (*PLURAL* die **Pakete**)

**pardon** *NOUN* I beg your pardon (*as an apology*) Entschuldigung!, **pardon?** wie bitte?

**parent** *NOUN* Elternteil der; **parents** Eltern (*plural*), **my parents live in Germany** meine Eltern wohnen in Deutschland, **parents' evening** der Elternabend

**park** *NOUN* ❶ Park der (*PLURAL* die **Parks**); **theme park** der (thematische) Freizeitpark ❷ **car park** der Parkplatz

**park** *VERB* ❶ parken; **you can park outside the house** du kannst vor dem Haus parken ❷ **to find somewhere to park** einen Parkplatz finden

**parking** *NOUN* Parken das; 'no parking' 'Parken verboten'

**parking meter** *NOUN* Parkuhr die (*PLURAL* die **Parkuhren**)

**parking space** *NOUN* Parklücke die (*PLURAL* die **Parklücken**)

**parking ticket** *NOUN* Strafzettel der (*PLURAL* die **Strafzettel**)

**parliament** *NOUN* Parlament das (*PLURAL* die **Parlamente**)

**parrot** *NOUN* Papagei der (*PLURAL* die **Papageien**)

**parsley** *NOUN* Petersilie die

**part** *NOUN* ❶ Teil der (*PLURAL* die **Teile**); **part of the garden** Teil des Gartens, **the last part of the book** der letzte Teil des Buches ❷ **that's part of your job** das gehört dazu ❸ **to take part in something** an etwas (*DAT*) teilnehmen◇ (*SEP*) ❹ (*spare part*) Teil das (*PLURAL* die **Teile**) (*for a machine or an engine*) ❺ (*a role in a play*) Rolle die (*PLURAL* die **Rollen**)

**particular** *ADJECTIVE* besonderer/besondere/besonderes; **nothing in particular** nichts Besonderes

**particularly** *ADVERB* besonders; **not particularly interesting** nicht besonders interessant

**parting** *NOUN* ❶ (*in your hair*) Scheitel der (*PLURAL* die **Scheitel**) ❷ (*departure*) Abschied der (*PLURAL* die **Abschiede**)

**partly** *ADVERB* teilweise

**partner** *NOUN* Partner der (*PLURAL* die **Partner**), Partnerin die (*PLURAL* die **Partnerinnen**)

**part-time** *ADJECTIVE* Teilzeit-; part-time work die Teilzeitarbeit

**part-time** *ADVERB* to work part-time Teilzeit arbeiten

**party** *NOUN* ❶ *(small, private)* Party die *(PLURAL* die **Partys**), Feier die *(PLURAL* die **Feiern**); a Christmas party eine Weihnachtsfeier, to have a birthday party eine Geburtstagsparty machen ❷ *(more formal, in the evening)* Gesellschaft die *(PLURAL* die **Gesellschaften**); we've been invited to a party at the Smiths' house wir sind zu einer Gesellschaft bei Smiths eingeladen worden ❸ *(group)* Gruppe die *(PLURAL* die **Gruppen**); a party of schoolchildren eine Gruppe Schulkinder ❹ *(in politics)* Partei die *(PLURAL* die **Parteien**)

**party game** *NOUN* Gesellschaftsspiel das *(PLURAL* die **Gesellschaftsspiele**)

**pass** *NOUN* ❶ *(to let you in)* Ausweis der *(PLURAL* die **Ausweise**) ❷ bus pass die Buskarte ❸ *(over the mountains)* Pass der *(PLURAL* die **Pässe**) ❹ *(in an exam)* to get a pass in maths die Mathematikprüfung bestehen

**pass** *VERB* ❶ *(walk past)* vorbeigehen◇ *(SEP)* *(PERF* sein) an *(+DAT)*, *(a place or building)*; we passed your house wir sind an deinem Haus vorbeigegangen ❷ *(drive past)* vorbeifahren◇ *(SEP)* *(PERF* sein) an *(+DAT)*, *(a place or building)* ❸ *(overtake)* überholen *(a car)* ❹ *(give)* reichen; could you pass me the sugar please? könnten Sie mir bitte den Zucker reichen? ❺ *(time)* vergehen◇ *(PERF* sein); the time passed slowly die Zeit verging

langsam ❻ bestehen◇ *(an exam)*; to pass an exam eine Prüfung bestehen, did you pass in German? hast du die Deutschprüfung bestanden?

**passage** *NOUN* ❶ *(corridor)* Gang der *(PLURAL* die **Gänge**) ❷ *(a piece of text)* Passage die *(PLURAL* die **Passagen**)

**passenger** *NOUN* ❶ *(in a plane or ship)* Passagier der *(PLURAL* die **Passagiere**) ❷ *(in a train or bus)* Fahrgast der *(PLURAL* die **Fahrgäste**) ❸ *(in a car)* Mitfahrer der *(PLURAL* die **Mitfahrer**)

**passive** *NOUN* Passiv das

**passive** *ADJECTIVE* passiv

**Passover** *NOUN* Passah das

**passport** *NOUN* Reisepass der *(PLURAL* die **Reisepässe**) Pass der *(PLURAL* die **Pässe**)

**password** *NOUN* ❶ *(to gain entry)* Kennwort das *(PLURAL* die **Kennwörter**) ❷ *(for access to data)* Passwort das *(PLURAL* die **Passwörter**); to give the password das Passwort eingeben

**past** *NOUN* Vergangenheit die; in the past in der Vergangenheit

**past** *ADJECTIVE* ❶ *(recent)* letzter/ letzte/letztes; in the past few weeks in den letzten paar Wochen ❷ *(over)* vorbei; winter is past der Winter ist vorbei

**past** *PREPOSITION, ADVERB* ❶ to walk past something an etwas *(DAT)* vorbeigehen◇ *(SEP)* *(PERF* sein), we went past the school wir sind an der Schule vorbeigegangen, to go past vorbeifahren◇ *(PERF* sein) ❷ *(after)* nach *(+DAT)*; it's just past

**the post office** es ist kurz nach der Post ❸ *(talking about time)* **ten past six** zehn nach sechs, **half past four** halb fünf, **a quarter past two** Viertel nach zwei

**pasta** NOUN **Nudeln** *(plural)*; **I don't like pasta** ich mag keine Nudeln

**pastry** NOUN ❶ *(for baking)* **Teig** der ❷ *(cake)* **Gebäck** das

**patch** NOUN ❶ *(for mending)* **Flicken** der *(PLURAL die* **Flicken***)* ❷ *(of snow or ice)* **Stelle** die *(PLURAL die* **Stellen***)* ❸ *(of blue sky)* **Stückchen** das *(PLURAL die* **Stückchen***)*

**path** NOUN **Weg** der *(PLURAL die* **Wege***)*, *(very narrow)* **Pfad** der *(PLURAL die* **Pfade***)*

**pathetic** ADJECTIVE *(useless, hopeless)* **jämmerlich**

**patience** NOUN ❶ **Geduld** die ❷ *(card game)* **Patience** die

**patient** NOUN **Patient** der *(PLURAL die* **Patienten***)*, **Patientin** die *(PLURAL die* **Patientinnen***)*

**patient** ADJECTIVE **geduldig**

**patiently** ADVERB **geduldig**

**patio** NOUN **Terrasse** die *(PLURAL die* **Terrassen***)*

**pattern** NOUN ❶ *(on wallpaper or fabric)* **Muster** das *(PLURAL die* **Muster***)* ❷ *(dressmaking, knitting)* **Schnitt** der *(PLURAL die* **Schnitte***)*

**pause** NOUN **Pause** die *(PLURAL die* **Pausen***)*

**pavement** NOUN **Bürgersteig** der *(PLURAL die* **Bürgersteige***)*; **on the pavement** auf dem Bürgersteig

**paw** NOUN **Pfote** die *(PLURAL die* **Pfoten***)*

**pawn** NOUN *(in chess)* **Bauer** der *(PLURAL die* **Bauern***)*

**pay** NOUN *(wage)* **Lohn** der *(PLURAL die* **Löhne***)*, *(salary)* **Gehalt** das *(PLURAL die* **Gehälter***)*

**pay** VERB ❶ **zahlen**; **I'm paying** ich zahle, **to pay cash** bar zahlen, **to pay by credit card** mit Kreditkarte zahlen, **they pay £8 an hour** sie zahlen acht Pfund die Stunde, **to pay by cheque** mit Scheck zahlen ❷ **bezahlen** *('bezahlen' is used when you pay a person, a bill or for something)*; **to pay for something** etwas bezahlen, **Tony paid for the drinks** Tony hat die Getränke bezahlt, **it's all paid for** es ist alles bezahlt ❸ **to pay somebody back** *(money)* jemandem Geld zurückzahlen *(SEP)* ❹ **to pay attention** aufpassen *(SEP)* ❺ **to pay a visit to somebody** jemanden besuchen

**payment** NOUN ❶ **Bezahlung** die *(of sum, bill, debt, or fine)* ❷ **Zahlung** die *(PLURAL die* **Zahlungen***)* *(of interest, tax, or fee)*

**pay phone** NOUN **Münzfernsprecher** der *(PLURAL die* **Münzfernsprecher***)*

**PC** NOUN *(computer)* **PC** der *(PLURAL die* **PC***)*

**pea** NOUN **Erbse** die *(PLURAL die* **Erbsen***)*

**peace** NOUN **Frieden** der

**peaceful** ADJECTIVE **friedlich**

**peach** NOUN **Pfirsich** der *(PLURAL die* **Pfirsiche***)*

a
b
c
d
e
f
g
h
i
j
k
l
m
n
o
p
q
r
s
t
u
v
w
x
y
z

**peacock** NOUN Pfau der (PLURAL die Pfauen)

**peak period** (for holidays) Hauptferienzeit die (PLURAL die Hauptferienzeiten)

**peak rate** NOUN (for phoning) Höchsttarif der (PLURAL die Höchsttarife)

**peak time** NOUN (for traffic) Stoßzeit die (PLURAL die Stoßzeiten)

**peanut** NOUN Erdnuss die (PLURAL die Erdnüsse)

**peanut butter** NOUN Erdnussbutter die

**pear** NOUN Birne die (PLURAL die Birnen)

**pearl** NOUN Perle die (PLURAL die Perlen)

**pebble** NOUN Kieselstein der (PLURAL die Kieselsteine)

**peculiar** ADJECTIVE komisch

**pedal** NOUN Pedal das (PLURAL die Pedale)

**pedal** VERB (on a bike) to pedal off (mit dem Rad) wegfahren◇ (PERF sein)

**pedestrian** NOUN Fußgänger der (PLURAL die Fußgänger), Fußgängerin die (PLURAL die Fußgängerinnen)

**pedestrian crossing** NOUN Fußgängerüberweg der (PLURAL die Fußgängerüberwege)

**pedestrian precinct** NOUN Fußgängerzone die (PLURAL die Fußgängerzonen)

**pee** NOUN to have a pee pinkeln (informal)

**peel** NOUN Schale die (PLURAL die Schalen)

**peel** VERB schälen (fruit, vegetables)

**peg** NOUN ❶ (hook) Haken der (PLURAL die Haken) ❷ clothes peg die Wäscheklammer (PLURAL die Wäscheklammern) ❸ (for a tent) Hering der (PLURAL die Heringe)

**pen** NOUN (ball-point) Kugelschreiber der (PLURAL die Kugelschreiber); felt pen der Filzstift

**penalty** NOUN ❶ (a fine) Geldstrafe die (PLURAL die Geldstrafen) ❷ (in football) Elfmeter der (PLURAL die Elfmeter)

**pence** PLURAL NOUN Pence (plural)

**pencil** NOUN Bleistift der (PLURAL die Bleistifte); to write in pencil mit Bleistift schreiben

**pencil case** NOUN Federmäppchen das (PLURAL die Federmäppchen)

**pencil sharpener** NOUN Bleistiftanspitzer der (PLURAL die Bleistiftanspitzer)

**penfriend** NOUN Brieffreund der (PLURAL die Brieffreunde), Brieffreundin die (PLURAL die Brieffreundinnen); my German pen-friend is called Heidi meine deutsche Brieffreundin heißt Heidi

**penguin** NOUN Pinguin der (PLURAL die Pinguine)

**penis** NOUN Penis der (PLURAL die Penisse)

**penknife** NOUN Taschenmesser das (PLURAL die Taschenmesser)

**penny** NOUN Penny der (PLURAL die Pence)

**pension** NOUN Rente die (PLURAL die Renten)

**pensioner** NOUN Rentner der (PLURAL die Rentner) Rentnerin die (PLURAL die Rentnerinnen)

**people** PLURAL NOUN ❶ Leute (plural), Menschen (plural), ('Menschen' is used in a more formal context); **most people round here** die meisten Leute hier, **several people** verschiedene Leute, **nice people** nette Leute, **all the people in the world** alle Menschen auf der Welt, **a crowd of people** eine Menschenmenge ❷ (when you're counting them) Personen (plural); **for ten people** für zehn Personen, **how many people have you invited?** wie viele Personen hast du eingeladen? ❸ **people say that ...** man sagt, dass ...

**pepper** NOUN ❶ (spice) Pfeffer der ❷ (vegetable) Paprikaschote die (PLURAL die Paprikaschoten)

**peppermill** NOUN Pfeffermühle die (PLURAL die Pfeffermühlen)

**peppermint** NOUN (plant) Pfefferminze die; **peppermint tea** der Pfefferminztee

**per** PREPOSITION pro (+ACC); **ten pounds per person** zehn Pfund pro Person

**per cent** ADVERB Prozent das; **sixty per cent of students** sechzig Prozent der Studenten

**percentage** NOUN Prozentsatz der (PLURAL die Prozentsätze)

**percussion** NOUN Schlagzeug das; **to play percussion** Schlagzeug spielen

**perfect** ADJECTIVE ❶ perfekt; **she speaks perfect English** sie spricht perfekt Englisch ❷ (ideal) herrlich (day or weather)

**perfectly** ADVERB ❶ (absolutely) vollkommen ❷ (faultlessly) perfekt

**perform** VERB ❶ spielen (a piece of music or a part) ❷ singen◇ (a song) ❸ **to perform a play** ein Theaterstück aufführen (SEP)

**performance** NOUN ❶ (playing or acting) Darstellung die (PLURAL die Darstellungen); **his performance as Hamlet** seine Darstellung des Hamlet ❷ (show or film) Vorstellung die (PLURAL die Vorstellungen); **the performance starts at eight** die Vorstellung fängt um acht Uhr an ❸ (of a play or opera) Aufführung die (PLURAL die Aufführungen)

**performer** NOUN Künstler der (PLURAL die Künstler), Künstlerin die (PLURAL die Künstlerinnen)

**perfume** NOUN Parfüm das (PLURAL die Parfüme)

**perhaps** ADVERB vielleicht; **perhaps he's missed the train** vielleicht hat er den Zug verpasst

**period** NOUN ❶ (length of time) Zeit die (PLURAL die Zeiten); **trial period** die Probezeit ❷ (a portion of time) Zeitraum der; **a two-year period** ein Zeitraum von zwei Jahren ❸ (in school) Stunde die (PLURAL die Stunden) ❹ (menstruation) Periode die (PLURAL die Perioden)

**perm** NOUN Dauerwelle die (PLURAL die Dauerwellen)

**permanent** *ADJECTIVE* ❶ ständig ❷ fest *(job or address, for example)*

**permanently** *ADVERB* ❶ dauernd ❷ to be permanently employed fest angestellt sein

**permission** *NOUN* Erlaubnis die; to get permission to do something Erlaubnis zu etwas *(DAT)* erhalten

**permit** *NOUN* Genehmigung die *(PLURAL die Genehmigungen)*

**permit** *VERB* ❶ erlauben; to permit somebody to do something jemandem erlauben, etwas zu tun, smoking is not permitted Rauchen ist nicht gestattet ❷ weather permitting bei entsprechendem Wetter

**person** *NOUN* ❶ Person die *(PLURAL die Personen)*; there's still room for one more person wir haben noch Platz für eine Person ❷ in person persönlich

**personal** *ADJECTIVE* persönlich

**personality** *NOUN* Persönlichkeit die *(PLURAL die Persönlichkeiten)*

**personally** *ADVERB* persönlich; personally, I'm against it ich persönlich bin dagegen

**perspiration** *NOUN* Schweiß der

**persuade** *VERB* überreden; to persuade somebody to come jemanden überreden zu kommen

**pessimistic** *ADJECTIVE* pessimistisch

**pest** *NOUN* ❶ *(greenfly, for example)* Schädling der *(PLURAL die Schädlinge)* ❷ *(annoying person)* Nervensäge die *(PLURAL die Nervensägen) (informal)*

**pet** *NOUN* ❶ Haustier das *(PLURAL die Haustiere)*; do you have a pet? habt ihr Haustiere?, a pet dog ein Hund ❷ Julie is teacher's pet Julie ist der Liebling des Lehrers

**petrol** *NOUN* Benzin das *(PLURAL die Benzine)*; to fill up with petrol tanken, to run out of petrol kein Benzin mehr haben

**petrol station** *NOUN* Tankstelle die *(PLURAL die Tankstellen)*

**pharmacy** *NOUN* Apotheke die *(PLURAL die Apotheken)*

**pheasant** *NOUN* Fasan der *(PLURAL die Fasane)*

**philosophy** *NOUN* Philosophie die *(PLURAL die Philosophien)*

**phone** *NOUN* Telefon das *(PLURAL die Telefone)*; she's on the phone sie telefoniert, I was on the phone to Sophie ich habe mit Sophie telefoniert, you can book by phone du kannst telefonisch buchen

**phone** *VERB* ❶ telefonieren; while I was phoning während ich telefonierte ❷ to phone somebody jemanden anrufen◇ *(SEP)*, I'll phone you tonight ich rufe dich heute Abend an

**phone book** *NOUN* Telefonbuch das *(PLURAL die Telefonbücher)*

**phone box** *NOUN* Telefonzelle die *(PLURAL die Telefonzellen)*

**phone call** *NOUN* ❶ Anruf der *(PLURAL die Anrufe)*; to get a phone call einen Anruf erhalten ❷ to make a phone call ein Telefongespräch führen, phone calls are free Telefongespräche sind gebührenfrei

**phone card** NOUN Telefonkarte die (PLURAL die **Telefonkarten**)

**phone number** NOUN Telefonnummer die (PLURAL die **Telefonnummern**)

**photo** NOUN Foto das (PLURAL die **Fotos**); to take a photo ein Foto machen, to take a photo of somebody ein Foto von jemandem machen

**photocopier** NOUN Fotokopiergerät das (PLURAL die **Fotokopiergeräte**)

**photocopy** NOUN Fotokopie die (PLURAL die **Fotokopien**)

**photocopy** VERB fotokopieren

**photograph** NOUN Fotografie die (PLURAL die **Fotografien**); to take a photograph ein Foto machen

**photograph** VERB fotografieren

**photographer** NOUN Fotograf der (PLURAL die **Fotografen**), Fotografin die (PLURAL die **Fotografinnen**)

**photography** NOUN Fotografie die

**phrase** NOUN Phrase die (PLURAL die **Phrasen**); an idiomatic phrase eine Redewendung

**phrase-book** NOUN Sprachführer der (PLURAL die **Sprachführer**)

**physical** ADJECTIVE körperlich

**physics** NOUN Physik die

**physiotherapist** NOUN Physiotherapeut der (PLURAL die **Physiotherapeuten**), Physiotherapeutin die (PLURAL die **Physiotherapeutinnen**)

**physiotherapy** NOUN Physiotherapie die

**piano** NOUN Klavier das (PLURAL die **Klaviere**); to play the piano Klavier spielen, piano lesson die Klavierstunde

**pick** NOUN to take your pick sich (DAT) etwas aussuchen (SEP)

**pick** VERB ❶ (to select) wählen; he picked his words carefully er wählte seine Worte mit Bedacht ❷ (choose for oneself) sich (DAT) aussuchen (SEP); pick any book such dir irgendein Buch aus ❸ to pick a team eine Mannschaft aufstellen ❹ pflücken (fruit); to pick strawberries Erdbeeren pflücken
• to pick up ❶ (lift) (in die Hand) nehmen◇; he picked up the papers er nahm die Unterlagen ❷ (collect) abholen (SEP); I'll pick you up at six ich hole dich um sechs Uhr ab, I'll pick up the keys tomorrow ich hole die Schlüssel morgen ab

**pickpocket** NOUN Taschendieb der (PLURAL die **Taschendiebe**)

**picnic** NOUN Picknick das (PLURAL die **Picknicke**); to have a picnic ein Picknick machen

**picture** NOUN ❶ Bild das (PLURAL die **Bilder**) ❷ to go to the pictures (the cinema) ins Kino gehen

**pie** NOUN ❶ (sweet) Kuchen der (PLURAL die **Kuchen**); apple pie der Apfelkuchen ❷ (savoury) Pastete die (PLURAL die **Pasteten**)

**piece** NOUN ❶ (a bit) Stück das (PLURAL die **Stücke**); a big piece of cheese ein großes Stück Käse ❷ (that you fit together) Teil das (PLURAL die **Teile**); the pieces of a jigsaw die Teile von einem Puzzle, to take something

**to pieces** etwas in Einzelteile zerlegen ❸ **piece of furniture** das Möbelstück, **a piece of information** eine Information, **a piece of luck** ein Glücksfall ❹ *(coin)* Stück das *(PLURAL die Stücke)*; **a five-pence piece** ein Fünf-Pence-Stück

**pierce** VERB ❶ durchstechen◇ *(SEP)* ❷ **to have pierced ears** Löcher in den Ohrläppchen haben

**pig** NOUN Schwein das *(PLURAL die Schweine)*

**pigeon** NOUN Taube die *(PLURAL die Tauben)*

**piggy bank** NOUN Sparschwein das *(PLURAL die Sparschweine)*

**pigtail** NOUN Zopf der *(PLURAL die Zöpfe)*

**pile** NOUN ❶ *(a neat stack)* Stapel der *(PLURAL die Stapel)*; **a pile of plates** ein Stapel Teller ❷ *(a heap)* Haufen der *(PLURAL die Haufen)*
• **to pile something up** *(neatly)* etwas aufstapeln *(SEP)*, *(in a heap)* etwas auftürmen *(SEP)*

**pill** NOUN Pille die *(PLURAL die Pillen)*

**pillar** NOUN Säule die *(PLURAL die Säulen)*

**pillow** NOUN Kopfkissen das *(PLURAL die Kopfkissen)*

**pilot** NOUN Pilot der *(PLURAL die Piloten)*, Pilotin die *(PLURAL die Pilotinnen)*

**pimple** NOUN Pickel der *(PLURAL die Pickel)*

**pin** NOUN ❶ *(for sewing)* Stecknadel die *(PLURAL die Stecknadeln)* ❷ **a three-pin plug** ein dreipoliger Stecker

• **to pin up** ❶ hochstecken *(SEP)* *(a hem)* ❷ anschlagen◇ *(SEP)* *(a notice)*

**PIN** NOUN *(short for **personal identification number**)* Geheimnummer die

**pinball** NOUN Flippern das; **to play pinball** flippern, **pinball machine** der Flipper

**pinch** NOUN *(of salt, for example)* Prise die *(PLURAL die Prisen)*

**pinch** VERB ❶ kneifen◇; **she pinched my arm** sie hat mich in den Arm gekniffen ❷ *(to steal)* klauen; **somebody's pinched my bike** jemand hat mein Rad geklaut

**pine** NOUN Kiefer die *(PLURAL die Kiefern)*; **pine furniture** Kiefernmöbel *(plural)*

**pineapple** NOUN Ananas die *(PLURAL die Ananas)*

**pine cone** NOUN Kiefernzapfen der *(PLURAL die Kiefernzapfen)*

**ping-pong** NOUN Tischtennis das; **to play ping-pong** Tischtennis spielen

**pink** ADJECTIVE rosa *('rosa' never changes)*; **pink hats** rosa Hüte

**pip** NOUN *(in a fruit)* Kern der *(PLURAL die Kerne)*

**pipe** NOUN ❶ *(for gas or water)* Rohr das *(PLURAL die Rohre)* ❷ *(for smoking)* Pfeife die *(PLURAL die Pfeifen)*; **he smokes a pipe** er raucht Pfeife

**pirate** NOUN Pirat der *(PLURAL die Piraten)*

**Pisces** NOUN Fische *(plural)*; **Amanda is Pisces** Amanda ist Fisch

**pitch** NOUN Platz der (PLURAL die Plätze); football pitch der Fußballplatz

**pitch** VERB to pitch a tent ein Zelt aufstellen (SEP)

**pity** NOUN ❶ (feeling sorry for somebody) Mitleid das ❷ what a pity! wie schade!, it would be a pity to miss the beginning es wäre schade, den Anfang zu verpassen

**pity** VERB to pity somebody jemanden bemitleiden

**pizza** NOUN Pizza die (PLURAL die Pizzas)

**place** NOUN ❶ Ort der (PLURAL die Orte); Salzburg is a wonderful place Salzburg ist ein sehr schöner Ort, in place an Ort und Stelle ❷ all over the place überall ❸ (a space) Platz der (PLURAL die Plätze); a place for the car ein Platz für das Auto, is there a place for me? ist Platz für mich?, will you keep my place? kannst du mir den Platz freihalten?, to change places die Plätze tauschen ❹ (spot) Stelle die (PLURAL die Stellen); this is a good place to stop das ist eine gute Stelle zum Halten ❺ (in a race) Platz der (PLURAL die Plätze); to gain first place den ersten Platz belegen ❻ at your place bei dir, we'll go round to Zafir's place wir gehen zu Zafir ❼ to take place stattfinden◇ (SEP), the competition will take place at four der Wettbewerb findet um vier Uhr statt

**place** VERB (upright) stellen, (lying flat) legen

**plain** NOUN Ebene die (PLURAL die Ebenen)

**plain** ADJECTIVE ❶ einfach; plain food einfaches Essen ❷ (unflavoured) Natur-; plain yoghurt der Naturjoghurt ❸ (not patterned) einfarbig; plain curtains einfarbige Vorhänge

**plait** NOUN Zopf der (PLURAL die Zöpfe)

**plan** NOUN Plan der (PLURAL die Pläne); we've made plans for the summer wir haben Pläne für den Sommer gemacht, to go according to plan nach Plan gehen, everything went according to plan alles ging nach Plan

**plan** VERB ❶ to plan to do something etwas vorhaben◇ (SEP), we're planning to leave at eight wir haben vor, um acht abzufahren ❷ (make plans for, organize, design) planen; she's planning a trip to Italy sie plant eine Reise nach Italien

**plane** NOUN Flugzeug das (PLURAL die Flugzeuge); we went by plane wir sind geflogen

**planet** NOUN Planet der (PLURAL die Planeten)

**plant** NOUN Pflanze die (PLURAL die Pflanzen); a house plant eine Topfpflanze

**plant** VERB pflanzen

**plaster** NOUN ❶ (sticking plaster) Pflaster das (PLURAL die Pflaster) ❷ (for walls) Verputz der ❸ Gips der; to have your leg in plaster das Bein in Gips haben

**plastic** NOUN Plastik das; plastic bag die Plastiktüte

**plate** NOUN Teller der (PLURAL die Teller)

**platform** NOUN ❶ (in a station) Bahnsteig der (PLURAL die Bahnsteige) ❷ the train is arriving at platform six der Zug fährt auf Gleis sechs ein ❸ (for lecturing or performing) Podium das (PLURAL die Podien)

**play** NOUN (in the theatre) Stück das (PLURAL die Stücke); television play das Fernsehspiel, we are putting on a play by Brecht at school wir führen ein Stück von Brecht in der Schule auf

**play** VERB ❶ spielen; the children are playing with a ball die Kinder spielen Ball, they play the piano and the guitar sie spielen Klavier und Gitarre, who's playing Hamlet? wer spielt Hamlet?, to play tennis Tennis spielen, they were playing cards sie haben Karten gespielt ❷ (in sport) to play somebody gegen jemanden spielen, Italy are playing Germany Italien spielt gegen Deutschland ❸ spielen (a record); play your new song spiel mal deine neue Lied

**player** NOUN ❶ Spieler der (PLURAL die Spieler), Spielerin die (PLURAL die Spielerinnen); football player der Fußballspieler ❷ (in the theatre) Schauspieler der (PLURAL die Schauspieler), Schauspielerin die (PLURAL die Schauspielerinnen)

**playground** NOUN Spielplatz der (PLURAL die Spielplätze); school playground der Schulhof

**playgroup** NOUN Spielgruppe die (PLURAL die Spielgruppen)

**playing field** NOUN Sportplatz der (PLURAL die Sportplätze)

**pleasant** ADJECTIVE angenehm

**please** ADVERB bitte; two coffees, please zwei Kaffee bitte, could you turn the TV off, please? könntest du bitte den Fernseher ausmachen?

**pleased** ADJECTIVE ❶ erfreut; I'm really pleased! das freut mich wirklich! ❷ she was pleased with her present sie hat sich über ihr Geschenk gefreut ❸ pleased to meet you! freut mich!

**pleasure** NOUN ❶ (amusement) Vergnügen das ❷ (joy) Freude die; to get a lot of pleasure out of something viel Freude an etwas (DAT) haben

**plenty** PRONOUN ❶ (lots) viel; he's got plenty of money er hat viel Geld ❷ (enough) genug; that's plenty! das ist genug!, we've got plenty of time left wir haben noch genug Zeit

**plot** NOUN (of a film or novel) Handlung die

**plough** NOUN Pflug der (PLURAL die Pflüge)

**plough** VERB pflügen

**plug** NOUN ❶ (electrical) Stecker der (PLURAL die Stecker) ❷ (in a bath or sink) Stöpsel der (PLURAL die Stöpsel); to pull out the plug den Stöpsel herausziehen

**plum** NOUN Pflaume die (PLURAL die Pflaumen); plum tart der Pflaumenkuchen

**plumber** NOUN Installateur der (PLURAL die Installateure)

**plural** NOUN Mehrzahl die, Plural der; in the plural in der Mehrzahl, im Plural

**plus** *PREPOSITION* **plus** *(+DAT)*; **three children plus a baby** drei Kinder und ein Baby

**p.m.** *ABBREVIATION* **nachmittags** *(for times up to 6 p.m.)*, **abends** *(for times after 6 p.m.)*; **at two p.m.** um zwei Uhr nachmittags, um vierzehn Uhr, **at nine p.m.** um neun Uhr abends, um einundzwanzig Uhr *(in German you usually express times after midday in terms of the 24-hour clock)*

**pocket** *NOUN* **Tasche** die *(PLURAL die Taschen)*

**pocket money** *NOUN* **Taschengeld** das

**poem** *NOUN* **Gedicht** das *(PLURAL die Gedichte)*

**poet** *NOUN* **Dichter** der *(PLURAL die Dichter)*, **Dichterin** die *(PLURAL die Dichterinnen)*

**poetry** *NOUN* **Dichtung** die

**point** *NOUN* ❶ *(tip)* **Spitze** die *(PLURAL die Spitzen)*; **the point of a nail** die Spitze eines Nagels ❷ *(a tiny mark or dot)* **Punkt** der *(PLURAL die Punkte)* ❸ *(in time)* **Zeitpunkt** der *(PLURAL die Zeitpunkte)*; **at that point** zu diesem Zeitpunkt, **to be on the point of doing something** gerade etwas tun wollen ❹ **that's not the point** darum geht es nicht, **there's no point phoning, he's out** es hat keinen Sinn anzurufen, er ist nicht da, **what's the point?** wozu? ❺ **that's a good point!** das stimmt!, **the point is ...** es geht darum ... ❻ **point of view** der Standpunkt, **from my point of view** von meinem Standpunkt aus ❼ **her strong point** ihre Stärke ❽ *(in scoring)* **Punkt** der *(PLURAL die Punkte)*; **to win by**

**fifteen points** mit fünfzehn Punkten Vorsprung gewinnen ❾ *(in decimals)* **6 point 4** sechs Komma vier *(in German, a comma is used for the decimal point)*

**point** *VERB* ❶ **hinweisen**◇ *(SEP)* **auf** *(+ACC)*; **a notice pointing to the station** ein Schild, das in Richtung Bahnhof zeigt ❷ *(with your finger)* **zeigen auf** *(+ACC)*; **he pointed at Tom** er zeigte auf Tom

**pointless** *ADJECTIVE* **sinnlos**; **it's pointless to keep on ringing** es ist sinnlos, dauernd zu klingeln

**poison** *NOUN* **Gift** das *(PLURAL die Gifte)*

**poison** *VERB* **vergiften**

**poisonous** *ADJECTIVE* **giftig**

**Poland** *NOUN* **Polen** das

**polar bear** *NOUN* **Eisbär** der *(PLURAL die Eisbären)*

**pole** *NOUN* ❶ *(for a tent)* **Stange** die *(PLURAL die Stangen)* ❷ *(for skiing)* **Stock** der *(PLURAL die Stöcke)* ❸ **the North Pole** der Nordpol

**Pole** *NOUN* *(a Polish person)* **Pole** der *(PLURAL die Polen)*, **Polin** die *(PLURAL die Polinnen)*

**police** *NOUN* **the police** die Polizei, **the police are coming** die Polizei kommt

**police car** *NOUN* **Streifenwagen** der *(PLURAL die Streifenwagen)*

**policeman** *NOUN* **Polizist** der *(PLURAL die Polizisten)*

**police station** *NOUN* **Polizeiwache** die *(PLURAL die Polizeiwachen)*

## policewoman                                pork

**policewoman** NOUN Polizistin die
(PLURAL die Polizistinnen)

**policy** NOUN ❶ (plan of action)
Vorgehensweise die (PLURAL
die Vorgehensweisen); the
policy on immigration die
Einwanderungspolitik ❷ (document)
Versicherungsschein der (PLURAL
die Versicherungsscheine)

**polish** NOUN ❶ (for furniture) Politur
die ❷ (for shoes) Schuhcreme die
❸ (for the floor) Bohnerwachs das

**polish** VERB ❶ polieren (furniture,
silver) ❷ to polish your shoes seine
Schuhe putzen

**Polish** NOUN (language) Polnisch das

**Polish** ADJECTIVE polnisch

**polite** ADJECTIVE höflich; to be polite
to somebody höflich zu jemandem
sein

**political** ADJECTIVE politisch

**politician** NOUN Politiker der (PLURAL
die Politiker), Politikerin die
(PLURAL die Politikerinnen)

**politics** NOUN Politik die

**pollen** NOUN Pollen der; the pollen
count for today is ... die Pollenzahl
heute ist ...

**polluted** ADJECTIVE verschmutzt

**pollution** NOUN
Umweltverschmutzung die

**polo-necked** ADJECTIVE Rollkragen-;
a polo-necked jumper ein
Rollkragenpullover

**pond** NOUN Teich der (PLURAL die
Teiche)

**pony** NOUN Pony das (PLURAL die
Ponys)

**ponytail** NOUN Pferdeschwanz der
(PLURAL die Pferdeschwänze)

**poodle** NOUN Pudel der (PLURAL die
Pudel)

**pool** NOUN ❶ (swimming pool)
Schwimmbecken das (PLURAL
die Schwimmbecken) ❷ (pond)
Tümpel der (PLURAL die Tümpel)
❸ (puddle) Lache die (PLURAL die
Lachen) ❹ (game) Poolbillard das
❺ the football pools das Toto, to do
the pools Toto spielen

**poor** ADJECTIVE ❶ arm; a poor country
ein armes Land, a poor family
eine arme Familie ❷ poor Tanya's
failed her exam die arme Tanya ist
durch die Prüfung gefallen ❸ (bad)
schlecht; that's a poor result
das ist ein schlechtes Ergebnis,
the weather was pretty poor das
Wetter war ziemlich schlecht

**pop** NOUN Popmusik die; pop concert
das Popkonzert, pop star der
Popstar, pop song der Popsong
• to pop into I'll just pop into the
bank ich gehe kurz auf die Bank

**popcorn** NOUN Popcorn das

**pope** NOUN Papst der (PLURAL die
Päpste)

**poppy** NOUN Mohn der

**popular** ADJECTIVE beliebt

**population** NOUN Bevölkerung die

**porch** NOUN Vorbau der (PLURAL die
Vorbauten)

**pork** NOUN Schweinefleisch das;
pork chop das Schweinekotelett

**porridge** NOUN Haferbrei der

**port** NOUN ❶ Hafen der (PLURAL die Häfen) ❷ (wine) Portwein der (PLURAL die Portweine)

**porter** NOUN ❶ (at a station or an airport) Gepäckträger der (PLURAL die Gepäckträger) ❷ (in a hotel) Portier der (PLURAL die Portiers)

**portion** NOUN (of food) Portion die (PLURAL die Portionen)

**portrait** NOUN Porträt das (PLURAL die Porträts)

**Portugal** NOUN Portugal das

**Portuguese** NOUN ❶ (language) Portugiesisch das ❷ (a person) Portugiese der (PLURAL die Portugiesen), Portugiesin die (PLURAL die Portugiesinnen)

**Portuguese** ADJECTIVE portugiesisch

**posh** ADJECTIVE vornehm; a posh area eine vornehme Gegend

**position** NOUN ❶ Platz der (PLURAL die Plätze) ❷ (situation) Lage die (PLURAL die Lagen) ❸ (status, job) Stellung die (PLURAL die Stellungen)

**positive** ADJECTIVE ❶ (sure) sicher; I'm positive he's left ich bin mir sicher, dass er gegangen ist ❷ (enthusiastic) positiv; her reaction was very positive ihre Reaktion war sehr positiv

**possess** VERB besitzen◇

**possessions** PLURAL NOUN Sachen (plural); all my possessions are in the flat alle meine Sachen sind in der Wohnung

**possibility** NOUN Möglichkeit die (PLURAL die Möglichkeiten)

**possible** ADJECTIVE möglich; it's possible es ist gut möglich, if possible wenn möglich, as quickly as possible so schnell wie möglich

**possibly** ADVERB ❶ (maybe) möglicherweise; 'will you be at home at midday?' – 'possibly' 'bist du mittags zu Hause?' – 'möglicherweise' ❷ how can you possibly believe that? wie kannst du das nur glauben?, I can't possibly arrive before Thursday ich kann unmöglich vor Donnerstag ankommen

**post** NOUN ❶ Post die; to send something by post etwas per Post schicken, (letters) is there any post for me? ist Post für mich gekommen? ❷ (a pole) Pfosten der (PLURAL die Pfosten) ❸ (a job) Stelle die (PLURAL die Stellen)

**post** VERB to post a letter einen Brief abschicken (SEP)

**postbox** NOUN Briefkasten der (PLURAL die Briefkästen)

**postcard** NOUN Postkarte die (PLURAL die Postkarten)

**postcode** NOUN Postleitzahl die (PLURAL die Postleitzahlen)

**poster** NOUN ❶ (for decoration) Poster das (PLURAL die Poster); I've bought an Oasis poster ich habe ein Poster von Oasis gekauft ❷ (advertising) Plakat das (PLURAL die Plakate); I saw a poster for the concert ich habe ein Plakat für das Konzert gesehen

**postman** NOUN Briefträger der (PLURAL die Briefträger)

**post office** | **prawn**

**post office** NOUN Post die; **the post office is on the right** die Post ist auf der rechten Seite

**postpone** VERB verschieben◇; **we've postponed the meeting until next week** wir haben die Besprechung auf nächste Woche verschoben

**postwoman** NOUN Briefträgerin die (PLURAL die Briefträgerinnen)

**pot** NOUN ❶ (jar) Topf der (PLURAL die Töpfe); **a pot of honey** ein Topf Honig ❷ (teapot) Kanne die (PLURAL die Kannen) ❸ **the pots and pans** die Töpfe und Pfannen

**potato** NOUN Kartoffel die (PLURAL die Kartoffeln); **fried potatoes** Bratkartoffeln (plural), **mashed potatoes** der Kartoffelbrei

**potato crisps** PLURAL NOUN Kartoffelchips (plural)

**pottery** NOUN ❶ (craft) Töpferei die ❷ (objects) Töpferwaren (plural)

**pound** NOUN ❶ (money) Pfund das (PLURAL die Pfunde); **fourteen pounds** vierzehn Pfund, **1.6 euros to the pound** 1,6 Euro für ein Pfund, **a five pound note** ein Fünfpfundschein ❷ (in weight) Pfund das; **two pounds of apples** zwei Pfund Äpfel

**pour** VERB ❶ gießen◇ (liquid); **he poured milk into the pan** er hat Milch in den Topf gegossen ❷ eingießen◇ (SEP) (a drink); **to pour the tea** den Tee eingießen, **I poured him a drink** ich habe ihm etwas zu trinken eingeschenkt ❸ (with rain) **it's pouring** es gießt

**poverty** NOUN Armut die

**powder** NOUN ❶ Pulver das (PLURAL die Pulver) ❷ (for face or body) Puder der (PLURAL die Puder)

**power** NOUN ❶ (electricity) Strom der; **a power cut** eine Stromsperre ❷ (energy) Energie die; **nuclear power** die Kernenergie ❸ (strength) Kraft die ❹ (over other people) Macht die; **to be in power** an der Macht sein

**powerful** ADJECTIVE (strong) stark, (influential) mächtig

**power point** NOUN Steckdose die (PLURAL die Steckdosen)

**power station** NOUN Kraftwerk das (PLURAL die Kraftwerke)

**practical** ADJECTIVE praktisch

**practically** ADVERB fast

**practice** NOUN ❶ (for sport) Training das; **hockey practice** das Hockeytraining ❷ Übung die; **to do your piano practice** Klavier üben, **to be out of practice** aus der Übung sein

**practise** VERB ❶ üben (an instrument, exercise, or skill); **to practise the piano** Klavier üben ❷ anwenden (SEP) (a language); **a week in Berlin to practise my German** eine Woche in Berlin, um mein Deutsch anzuwenden ❸ (in sport) trainieren; **the team practises on Wednesday** die Mannschaft trainiert mittwochs

**praise** VERB loben; **to praise somebody for something** jemanden für etwas (ACC) loben

**pram** NOUN Kinderwagen der (PLURAL die Kinderwagen)

**prawn** NOUN Garnele die (PLURAL die Garnelen)

**pray** *VERB* **beten**

**prayer** *NOUN* **Gebet** das *(PLURAL* die **Gebete)**

**precaution** *NOUN*
**Vorsichtsmaßnahme** die *(PLURAL* die **Vorsichtsmaßnahmen)**;
**to take precautions against something** Vorsichtsmaßnahmen gegen *(+ACC)* etwas ergreifen

**precinct** *NOUN* **shopping precinct** das Einkaufszentrum, **pedestrian precinct** die Fußgängerzone

**precisely** *ADVERB* **genau**; **at eleven o'clock precisely** um genau elf Uhr

**prefer** *VERB* ❶ **vorziehen**◇ *(SEP)*;
**I prefer Anna to her sister** ich mag Anna lieber als ihre Schwester ❷ **to prefer to do something** etwas lieber tun, **I prefer to stay at home** ich bleibe lieber zu Hause

**pregnant** *ADJECTIVE* **schwanger**

**prejudice** *NOUN* **Vorurteil** das *(PLURAL* die **Vorurteile)**; **to fight against racial prejudice** gegen Rassenvorurteile ankämpfen

**prejudiced** *ADJECTIVE* **to be prejudiced** voreingenommen sein

**prep** *NOUN* **Hausaufgaben** *(plural)*; **my English prep** meine Englischhausaufgaben

**preparation** *NOUN* **Vorbereitung** die *(PLURAL* die **Vorbereitungen)**;
**in preparation for something** in Vorbereitung auf etwas *(ACC)*, **our preparations for Christmas** unsere Weihnachtsvorbereitungen

**prepare** *VERB* ❶ **vorbereiten** *(SEP)*; **to prepare somebody for something** jemanden auf etwas *(ACC)* vorbereiten ❷ **to be prepared for**

**the worst** sich auf das Schlimmste gefasst machen

**prepared** *ADJECTIVE* **bereit**; **I'm prepared to pay half** ich bin bereit, die Hälfte zu zahlen

**preposition** *NOUN* **Präposition** die *(PLURAL* die **Präpositionen)**

**prep school** *NOUN* **private Grundschule** die

**prescription** *NOUN* **Rezept** das *(PLURAL* die **Rezepte)**; **on prescription** auf Rezept

**presence** *NOUN* **Anwesenheit** die; **he admitted it in my presence** er gab es in meiner Anwesenheit zu

**present** *NOUN* ❶ *(a gift)* **Geschenk** das *(PLURAL* die **Geschenke)**; **to give somebody a present** jemandem ein Geschenk machen ❷ *(the time now)* **Gegenwart** die; **in the present (tense)** im Präsens ❸ **that's all for the present** das ist vorläufig alles

**present** *ADJECTIVE* ❶ *(attending)* **anwesend**; **Mr Blair is not present** Herr Blair ist nicht anwesend, **to be present at something** bei etwas *(DAT)* anwesend sein, **fifty people were present at the funeral** fünfzig Personen waren bei der Beerdigung anwesend ❷ *(existing now)* **gegenwärtig**; **the present situation** die gegenwärtige Lage ❸ **at the present time** zur Zeit

**present** *VERB* ❶ **überreichen** *(a prize)* ❷ *(introduce)* **vorstellen** *(SEP)* ❸ *(on TV, radio)* **moderieren** *(a programme)*

**presenter** *NOUN* *(on TV)* **Moderator** der *(PLURAL* die **Moderatoren)**, **Moderatorin** die *(PLURAL* die **Moderatorinnen)**

**presently** ADVERB ❶ (now) momentan ❷ (soon) bald

**president** NOUN Präsident der (PLURAL die Präsidenten), Präsidentin die (PLURAL die Präsidentinnen)

**press** NOUN the press die Presse

**press** VERB ❶ (to push) drücken; press here! hier drücken! ❷ drücken auf (+ACC), (a button or switch); she pressed the button sie hat auf den Knopf gedrückt

**press conference** NOUN Pressekonferenz die (PLURAL die Pressekonferenzen)

**pressure** NOUN Druck der; to put pressure on somebody jemanden unter Druck setzen

**pressure gauge** NOUN Druckluftmesser der (PLURAL die Druckluftmesser)

**pressure group** NOUN Interessengruppe die (PLURAL die Interessengruppen)

**pretend** VERB to pretend that ... so tun, als ob ..., he's pretending not to hear er tut so, als ob er nicht hört

**pretty** ADJECTIVE hübsch; a pretty dress ein hübsches Kleid

**pretty** ADVERB ziemlich; it was pretty silly das war ziemlich blöd

**prevent** VERB to prevent somebody from doing something jemanden daran hindern, etwas zu tun, there's nothing to prevent you from leaving niemand kann dich daran hindern zu gehen

**previous** ADJECTIVE ❶ (earlier) früher (years, opportunity, or job)

❷ (immediately preceding) vorig; on the previous Tuesday am vorigen Dienstag

**price** NOUN Preis der (PLURAL die Preise); the price per kilo der Preis pro Kilo, what is the price of this? was kostet das?

**price list** NOUN Preisliste die (PLURAL die Preislisten)

**price ticket** NOUN Preisschild das (PLURAL die Preisschilder)

**prick** VERB stechen◇; to prick your finger sich in den Finger stechen

**pride** NOUN Stolz der

**priest** NOUN Priester der (PLURAL die Priester)

**primary (school) teacher** NOUN Grundschullehrer der (PLURAL die Grundschullehrer), Grundschullehrerin die (PLURAL die Grundschullehrerinnen)

**primary school** NOUN Grundschule die (PLURAL die Grundschulen)

**prime minister** NOUN Premierminister der (PLURAL die Premierminister), Premierministerin die (PLURAL die Premierministerinnen)

**prince** NOUN Prinz der (PLURAL die Prinzen)

**princess** NOUN Prinzessin die (PLURAL die Prinzessinnen)

**principal** NOUN (of a college) Direktor der (PLURAL die Direktoren), Direktorin die (PLURAL die Direktorinnen)

**principal** ADJECTIVE (main) Haupt-

**principle** NOUN Prinzip das (PLURAL die Prinzipien); **on principle** im Prinzip, **that's true in principle** im Prinzip stimmt das

**print** NOUN ❶ (letters) Druck der; **in small print** klein gedruckt ❷ (a photo) Abzug der (PLURAL die Abzüge); **colour print** der Farbabzug

**printer** NOUN (for a computer) Drucker der (PLURAL die Drucker)

**print-out** NOUN Ausdruck der (PLURAL die Ausdrucke)

**prison** NOUN Gefängnis das (PLURAL die Gefängnisse); **in prison** im Gefängnis

**prisoner** NOUN Gefangene der/die (PLURAL die Gefangenen)

**private** ADJECTIVE ❶ Privat-, privat; **private school** die Privatschule, **private property** das Privateigentum, **to have private lessons** Privatstunden nehmen ❷ **in private** privat

**prize** NOUN Preis der (PLURAL die Preise); **to win a prize** einen Preis gewinnen

**prize-giving** NOUN Preisverleihung die (PLURAL die Preisverleihungen)

**prizewinner** NOUN Gewinner der (PLURAL die Gewinner), Gewinnerin die (PLURAL die Gewinnerinnen)

**probable** ADJECTIVE wahrscheinlich

**probably** ADVERB wahrscheinlich

**problem** NOUN Problem das (PLURAL die Probleme); **it's a serious problem** das ist ein ernstes Problem, **no problem!** kein Problem!

**process** NOUN ❶ Prozess der (PLURAL die Prozesse) ❷ **to be in the process of doing something** dabei sein, etwas zu tun

**procession** NOUN ❶ (in parade) Umzug der (PLURAL die Umzüge) ❷ (at religious festival) Prozession die (PLURAL die Prozessionen)

**produce** NOUN (food) Erzeugnisse (plural)

**produce** VERB ❶ herstellen (SEP) (goods, food) ❷ vorzeigen (SEP) (a ticket, document); **I produced my passport** ich habe meinen Pass vorgezeigt ❸ erzeugen (interest, tension); **it produces heat** es erzeugt Wärme ❹ **to produce a film** einen Film produzieren ❺ **to produce a play** ein Theaterstück inszenieren

**producer** NOUN (of a film or programme) Produzent der (PLURAL die Produzenten)

**product** NOUN Produkt das (PLURAL die Produkte)

**production** NOUN ❶ (of a film or an opera) Produktion die (PLURAL die Produktionen) ❷ (of a play) Inszenierung die (PLURAL die Inszenierungen); **a new production of Hamlet** eine neue Inszenierung von Hamlet ❸ (by a factory) Produktion die

**profession** NOUN Beruf der (PLURAL die Berufe)

**professional** NOUN ❶ (a trained person) Fachmann der (PLURAL die Fachleute) ❷ (in sport) Profi der (PLURAL die Profis)

**professional** ADJECTIVE ❶ professionell (work, sportsman); **a professional footballer**

a
b
c
d
e
f
g
h
i
j
k
l
m
n
o
p
q
r
s
t
u
v
w
x
y
z

ein professioneller Fußballer
**❷ beruflich** *(career, success)*; **she's a professional singer** sie ist Sängerin von Beruf

**professor** NOUN **Professor** der *(PLURAL* die **Professoren)*, **Professorin** die *(PLURAL* die **Professorinnen)*

**profile** NOUN **Profil** das *(PLURAL* die **Profile)*

**profit** NOUN **Gewinn** der *(PLURAL* die **Gewinne)*

**profitable** ADJECTIVE **rentabel**

**program** NOUN **computer program** das **Programm**

**programme** NOUN **❶** *(for a play or an event)* **Programm** das *(PLURAL* die **Programme)* **❷** *(on TV or radio)* **Sendung** die *(PLURAL* die **Sendungen)*

**programmer** NOUN **Programmierer** der *(PLURAL* die **Programmierer)*, **Programmiererin** die *(PLURAL* die **Programmiererinnen)*

**progress** NOUN **❶ Fortschritt** der *(PLURAL* die **Fortschritte)*; **to make progress** Fortschritte machen **❷ to be in progress** im Gange sein

**project** NOUN **❶** *(at school)* **Arbeit** die *(PLURAL* die **Arbeiten)* **❷** *(a plan)* **Projekt** das *(PLURAL* die **Projekte)*; **a project to build a bridge** ein Brückenbauprojekt

**promise** NOUN **Versprechen** das *(PLURAL* die **Versprechen)*; **to make somebody a promise** jemandem ein Versprechen geben, **to keep a promise** ein Versprechen halten, **it's a promise!** versprochen!

**promise** VERB **to promise something** etwas versprechen◊, **I've promised to ring my mother** ich habe versprochen, meine Mutter anzurufen

**promote** VERB **to be promoted** *(in football)* aufsteigen◊ *(SEP)* *(PERF* **sein)*, *(at work)* befördert werden

**promotion** NOUN **❶ Beförderung** die **❷** *(in football)* **Aufstieg** der **❸** *(in advertising)* **Werbung** die

**promptly** ADVERB **❶** *(at once)* **sofort**; **he promptly fell off again** er fiel sofort wieder herunter **❷** *(quickly)* **schnell**; **please reply promptly** bitte antworten Sie unverzüglich **❸** *(puntually)* **pünktlich**; **they left promptly at five o'clock** sie fuhren pünktlich um 5 Uhr ab

**pronoun** NOUN **Pronomen** das *(PLURAL* die **Pronomen)*

**pronounce** VERB **aussprechen◊** *(SEP)*; **you don't pronounce the 'c'** das 'c' spricht man nicht aus

**pronunciation** NOUN **Aussprache** die

**proof** NOUN **Beweis** der *(PLURAL* die **Beweise)*; **there's no proof that ...** es gibt keine Beweise dafür, dass ...

**propaganda** NOUN **Propaganda** die

**propeller** NOUN **Propeller** der *(PLURAL* die **Propeller)*

**proper** ADJECTIVE **❶** *(correct, real, genuine)* **richtig**; **the proper answer** die richtige Antwort, **he's not a proper doctor** er ist kein richtiger Arzt **❷** *(decent)* **anständig**; **I need a proper meal** ich brauche ein anständiges Essen **❸ in its proper place** an den richtigen Ort

**properly** ADVERB ❶ richtig ❷ (decent) anständig

**property** NOUN ❶ (your belongings) Eigentum das ❷ (land, premises) Besitz der; 'private property' 'Privatbesitz' ❸ (house) Haus das (PLURAL die Häuser)

**propose** VERB ❶ (suggest) vorschlagen◇ (SEP) ❷ (marriage) he proposed to her er hat ihr einen Heiratsantrag gemacht

**protect** VERB schützen; to protect somebody from something jemanden vor etwas (DAT) schützen

**protection** NOUN Schutz der

**protein** NOUN Protein das (PLURAL die Proteine)

**protest** NOUN ❶ Beschwerde die (PLURAL die Beschwerden); to make a protest eine Beschwerde einlegen (SEP) ❷ (disapproval) Protest der (PLURAL die Proteste); in protest against something aus Protest gegen etwas (ACC)

**protest** VERB protestieren; to protest about something gegen etwas (ACC) protestieren

**Protestant** NOUN Protestant der (PLURAL die Protestanten), Protestantin die (PLURAL die Protestantinnen)

**Protestant** ADJECTIVE protestantisch

**protest march** NOUN Protestmarsch der (PLURAL die Protestmärsche)

**proud** ADJECTIVE stolz; to be proud about something stolz auf etwas (ACC) sein

**prove** VERB beweisen◇

**proverb** NOUN Sprichwort das (PLURAL die Sprichwörter)

**provide** VERB zur Verfügung stellen

**provided, providing** CONJUNCTION vorausgesetzt; provided it doesn't rain vorausgesetzt, es regnet nicht

**prune** NOUN Backpflaume die (PLURAL die Backpflaumen)

**psychiatrist** NOUN Psychiater der (PLURAL die Psychiater), Psychiaterin die (PLURAL die Psychiaterinnen)

**psychological** ADJECTIVE psychologisch

**psychologist** NOUN Psychologe der (PLURAL die Psychologen) Psychologin die (PLURAL die Psychologinnen)

**psychology** NOUN Psychologie die

**PTO** ABBREVIATION b.w. (short for bitte wenden)

**pub** NOUN Kneipe die (PLURAL die Kneipen) (informal)

**public** NOUN the public die Öffentlichkeit, in public in aller Öffentlichkeit

**public** ADJECTIVE öffentlich

**public holiday** NOUN gesetzliche Feiertag der (PLURAL die gesetzlichen Feiertage); January 1st is a public holiday der erste Januar ist ein gesetzlicher Feiertag

**publicity** NOUN ❶ Publicity die ❷ (advertising) Werbung die

**public school** NOUN Privatschule die (PLURAL die Privatschulen)

**public transport** NOUN öffentliche Verkehrsmittel (plural)

**publish** VERB veröffentlichen

**publisher** NOUN ❶ Verleger der (PLURAL die Verleger), Verlegerin die (PLURAL die Verlegerinnen) ❷ (company) Verlag der (PLURAL die Verlage)

**pudding** NOUN (dessert) Nachtisch der (PLURAL die Nachtische); for pudding we've got strawberries zum Nachtisch gibt es Erdbeeren

**puddle** NOUN Pfütze die (PLURAL die Pfützen)

**puff** NOUN (of smoke) Wölkchen das (PLURAL die Wölkchen)

**puff pastry** NOUN Blätterteig der

**pull** VERB ❶ ziehen◇; to pull a cart einen Wagen ziehen ❷ ziehen◇ (+DAT); to pull a rope an einem Seil ziehen, he pulled a letter out of his pocket er hat einen Brief aus der Tasche gezogen
- he's pulling your leg! er nimmt dich auf den Arm (literally: he's picking you up in his arms)
- to pull down ❶ herunterziehen◇ (SEP) ❷ (demolish) abreißen◇ (SEP) (a building)
- to pull in (at the roadside) an den Straßenrand fahren◇ (PERF sein)

**pullover** NOUN Pullover der (PLURAL die Pullover)

**pulse** NOUN Puls der; the doctor took my pulse der Arzt maß meinen Puls

**pump** NOUN Pumpe die (PLURAL die Pumpen); bicycle pump die Fahrradpumpe

**pump** VERB pumpen
- to pump up aufpumpen (SEP)

**pumpkin** NOUN Kürbis der (PLURAL die Kürbisse)

**punch** NOUN ❶ (in boxing) Faustschlag der (PLURAL die Faustschläge) ❷ (drink) Bowle die (PLURAL die Bowlen)

**punch** VERB ❶ he punched me in the stomach er hat mich in den Magen geboxt ❷ lochen (a ticket)

**punctual** ADJECTIVE pünktlich

**punctuation** NOUN Zeichensetzung die

**punctuation mark** NOUN Satzzeichen das (PLURAL die Satzzeichen)

**puncture** NOUN (flat tyre) Reifenpanne die (PLURAL die Reifenpannen)

**punish** VERB bestrafen

**punishment** NOUN Strafe die (PLURAL die Strafen)

**pupil** NOUN Schüler der (PLURAL die Schüler), Schülerin die (PLURAL die Schülerinnen)

**puppet** NOUN Puppe die (PLURAL die Puppen)

**puppy** NOUN junge Hund der (PLURAL die jungen Hunde); a boxer puppy ein junger Boxer

**pure** ADJECTIVE rein

**purple** ADJECTIVE lila ('lila' never changes)

**purpose** NOUN ❶ Zweck der (PLURAL die Zwecke); what's the purpose of it? was hat das für einen Zweck? ❷ on purpose absichtlich, she did it on purpose das hat sie absichtlich getan, he closed the door on

**purpose** er hat die Tür absichtlich zugemacht

**purr** VERB **schnurren**

**purse** NOUN **Portemonee** das (PLURAL die **Portemonees**)

**push** NOUN **to give something a push** etwas schieben◇

**push** VERB ❶ **schubsen**; he pushed me er hat mich geschubst ❷ (to press) **drücken auf** (+ACC), (a bell or button) ❸ **to push somebody to do something** jemanden zu etwas drängen, his teacher is pushing him to sit the exam sein Lehrer drängt ihn, die Prüfung zu machen ❹ **to push your way through the crowd** sich durch die Menge drängeln
• **to push something away** etwas wegschieben◇ (SEP); she pushed her plate away sie schob ihren Teller weg

**pushchair** NOUN **Sportwagen** der (PLURAL die **Sportwagen**)

**put** VERB ❶ (place generally) **tun**◇; put some milk in your tea tu etwas Milch in den Tee, you can put the butter in the fridge du kannst die Butter in den Kühlschrank tun ❷ (lay flat) **legen**; she put the pencil on the desk sie hat den Bleistift auf den Schreibtisch gelegt ❸ (place upright) **stellen**; where did you put my bag? wo hast du meine Handtasche hingestellt? ❹ (write) **schreiben**◇; put your address here schreiben Sie Ihre Adresse hierhin
• **to put away** wegräumen (SEP); put away your things räume deine Sachen weg
• **to put back** ❶ zurücktun (SEP), zurücklegen (SEP), zurückstellen (SEP) (the translation of 'put back' depends on the way it is done: if it's

placed lying down, use 'zurücklegen', if placed upright use 'zurückstellen' and if it could be either, use 'zurücktun'); I put it back in the drawer ich habe es in die Schublade zurückgetan ❷ (postpone) **verschieben**◇; the meeting has been put back until Thursday die Besprechung ist auf Donnerstag verschoben worden
• **to put down** (lying down) hinlegen (SEP), (upright) hinstellen (SEP); where can I put the vase down? wo soll ich die Vase hinstellen?
• **to put off** ❶ (postpone) verschieben◇; he's put off my lesson till Thursday er hat meine Stunde auf Donnerstag verschoben ❷ (turn off) ausmachen (SEP); don't forget to put off the lights vergiss nicht, das Licht auszumachen ❸ **to put somebody off something** jemandem die Lust an etwas (DAT) verderben◇, it really put me off my food das hat mir wirklich den Apettit verdorben ❹ **to put somebody off doing something** jemanden davon abbringen◇ (SEP), etwas zu tun, don't be put off lass dich nicht davon abbringen
• **to put on** ❶ anziehen◇ (SEP) (clothes); I'll just put my shoes on ich ziehe nur schnell meine Schuhe an ❷ auflegen (SEP) (a record); I'm putting on Oasis ich lege Oasis auf ❸ (switch on) anmachen (SEP) (a light or the heating); could you put the lamp on? kannst du die Lampe anmachen?
• **to put out** ❶ (put outside) nach draußen tun◇, raustun◇ (SEP) (informal); have you put the rubbish out? hast du den Müll rausgebracht? ❷ ausmachen (SEP) (a light or cigarette); I've put the lights out ich habe das Licht ausgemacht

❸ **to put out your hand** die Hand
ausstrecken *(SEP)*
- **to put up** ❶ heben◇ *(your hand)*
❷ aufhängen *(SEP) (a picture or
poster)*; **I've put up some posters in
my room** ich habe ein paar Poster
in meinem Zimmer aufgehängt
❸ anschlagen◇ *(SEP) (a notice)*
❹ erhöhen *(the price)*; **they've put
up the fare** sie haben den Fahrpreis
erhöht ❺ *(for the night)* **friends
put me up** ich habe bei Freunden
übernachtet, **can you put me up on
Friday?** kann ich Freitag bei euch
übernachten?
- **to put up with something** etwas
aushalten◇ *(SEP)*; **I don't know how
she puts up with it** ich weiß nicht,
wie sie das aushält

**puzzle** *NOUN (jigsaw)* **Puzzle** das
*(PLURAL* die **Puzzles)**

**puzzled** *ADJECTIVE* **verdutzt**

**pyjamas** *PLURAL NOUN* **Schlafanzug**
der *(PLURAL* die **Schlafanzüge)**; **a
pair of pyjamas** ein Schlafanzug,
**where are my pyjamas?** wo ist mein
Schlafanzug?

# Qq

**qualification** *NOUN* ❶ *(ability,
experience)* **Qualifikation** die
*(PLURAL* die **Qualifikationen)** ❷ *(on
paper)* **Zeugnis** das *(PLURAL* die
**Zeugnisse)**

**qualified** *ADJECTIVE* ❶ **ausgebildet;
she's a qualified ski instructor** sie
ist eine ausgebildete Skilehrerin
❷ *(having a degree or a diploma)*
**Diplom-; a qualified engineer** ein
Diplomingenieur

**qualify** *VERB* ❶ *(to be eligible)*
**berechtigt sein; we don't qualify
for a reduction** wir bekommen
keine Ermäßigung ❷ *(in sport)* **sich
qualifizieren; they qualified for
the third round** sie haben sich für
die dritte Runde qualifiziert

**quality** *NOUN* **Qualität** die; **good
quality products** Waren von guter
Qualität

**quantity** *NOUN* **Menge** die *(PLURAL* die
**Mengen)**

**quarrel** *NOUN* **Streit** der *(PLURAL* die
**Streite)**; **to have a quarrel** Streit
haben

**quarrel** *VERB* **sich streiten◇; they're
always quarrelling** sie streiten sich
dauernd

**quarry** NOUN **Steinbruch** der (PLURAL die **Steinbrüche**)

**quarter** NOUN ❶ **Viertel** das (PLURAL die **Viertel**); **a quarter of the price** ein Viertel des Preises, **three quarters of the class** drei Viertel der Klasse, **it's a quarter past ten** es ist Viertel nach zehn, **it's a quarter to ten** es ist Viertel vor zehn ❷ **we meet at quarter to eight** wir treffen uns um Viertel vor acht ❸ **a quarter of an hour** eine Viertelstunde ❹ **three quarters of an hour** eine Dreiviertelstunde ❺ **an hour and a quarter** eineinviertel Stunden

**quarter finals** NOUN **Viertelfinale** das (PLURAL die **Viertelfinale**)

**queen** NOUN ❶ **Königin** die (PLURAL die **Königinnen**) ❷ (in chess, cards) **Dame** die (PLURAL die **Damen**)

**query** NOUN **Frage** die (PLURAL die **Fragen**); **are there any queries?** gibt es irgendwelche Fragen?

**question** NOUN **Frage** die (PLURAL die **Fragen**); **to ask somebody a question** jemandem eine Frage stellen, **I asked her a question** ich habe ihr eine Frage gestellt, **it's out of the question** das kommt nicht in Frage

**question** VERB **befragen** (a person)

**question mark** NOUN **Fragezeichen** das (PLURAL die **Fragezeichen**)

**questionnaire** NOUN **Fragebogen** der (PLURAL die **Fragebögen**)

**queue** NOUN (of people, cars) **Schlange** die (PLURAL die **Schlangen**); **to stand in a queue** Schlange stehen, **a queue of cars** eine Autoschlange

**quick** ADJECTIVE **schnell**; **to have a quick lunch** schnell etwas zu Mittag essen, **it's quicker on the motorway** auf der Autobahn geht es schneller, **to have a quick look at something** sich (DAT) etwas schnell ansehen, **be quick!** mach schnell!

**quickly** ADVERB **schnell**; **I'll just quickly phone my mother** ich rufe nur schnell meine Mutter an

**quiet** ADJECTIVE ❶ (silent) **still**; **to keep quiet** still sein, **please keep quiet** sei bitte still ❷ (not loud) **leise**; **the children are very quiet** die Kinder sind ganz leise, **in a quiet voice** mit leiser Stimme ❸ (peaceful) **ruhig**; **a quiet street** eine ruhige Straße

**quietly** ADVERB ❶ (speak, move) **leise**; **he got up quietly** er ist leise aufgestanden ❷ (read or play) **ruhig**; **to sit quietly** ruhig sitzen

**quilt** NOUN **Steppdecke** die (PLURAL die **Steppdecken**)

**quite** ADVERB ❶ (fairly) **ziemlich**; **it's quite cold outside** es ist ziemlich kalt draußen, **quite often** ziemlich oft, **quite a few** ziemlich viele, **quite a few of our friends came** ziemlich viele unserer Freunde sind gekommen, **quite a few people** ziemlich viele Leute, **that's quite a good idea** das ist eine ganz gute Idee ❷ (completely) **völlig**; **it was quite amazing** es war einfach fantastisch, **not quite** nicht ganz, **she's not quite ready** sie ist noch nicht ganz fertig ❸ **genau**; **I don't quite know what he wants** ich weiß nicht genau, was er will, **quite!** genau!

**quiz** NOUN **Quiz** das (PLURAL die **Quiz**)

**quotation** NOUN (from a book) **Zitat** das (PLURAL die **Zitate**)

**quotation marks** PLURAL NOUN **Anführungszeichen** (plural); **in quotation marks** in Anführungszeichen

**quote** NOUN ❶ (from a book) **Zitat** das (PLURAL die **Zitate**) ❷ (estimate) **Kostenvoranschlag** der (PLURAL die **Kostenvoranschläge**)

**quote** VERB **zitieren**

**rabbi** NOUN **Rabbi** der (PLURAL die **Rabbis**)

**rabbit** NOUN **Kaninchen** das (PLURAL die **Kaninchen**)

**rabies** NOUN **Tollwut** die

**race** NOUN ❶ (a sports event) **Rennen** das (PLURAL die **Rennen**); **cycle race** das Radrennen ❷ **to have a race** (running) um die Wette laufen◇ (PERF **sein**), (swimming) um die Wette schwimmen◇ (PERF **sein**) ❸ (an ethnic group) **Rasse** die (PLURAL die **Rassen**)

**racetrack** NOUN **Rennbahn** die (PLURAL die **Rennbahnen**)

**racial** ADJECTIVE **rassisch, Rassen-**; **racial discrimination** die Rassendiskriminierung

**racing car** NOUN **Rennwagen** der (PLURAL die **Rennwagen**), **Rennfahrerin** die (PLURAL die **Rennfahrerinnen**)

**racing driver** NOUN **Rennfahrer** der (PLURAL die **Rennfahrer**)

**racism** NOUN **Rassismus** der

**racist** NOUN **Rassist** der (PLURAL die **Rassisten**), **Rassistin** die (PLURAL die **Rassistinnen**)

**racist** ADJECTIVE **rassistisch**

**racket** NOUN ❶ (for tennis) Schläger der (PLURAL die Schläger); my tennis racket mein Tennisschläger ❷ (noise) Krach der

**radiation** NOUN Strahlung die (PLURAL die Strahlungen)

**radiator** NOUN Heizkörper der (PLURAL die Heizkörper)

**radio** NOUN Radio das (PLURAL die Radios); to listen to the radio Radio hören, to hear something on the radio etwas im Radio hören

**radioactive** ADJECTIVE radioaktiv

**radio-controlled** ADJECTIVE ferngesteuert

**radio station** NOUN Rundfunkstation die (PLURAL die Rundfunkstationen)

**radish** NOUN Radieschen das (PLURAL die Radieschen)

**rag** NOUN Lumpen der (PLURAL die Lumpen)

**rage** NOUN Wut die; to fly into a rage in Wut geraten◇ (PERF sein), she's in a rage sie ist wütend
• it's all the rage das ist der letzte Schrei (literally: it's the last scream)

**rail** NOUN ❶ (for a train) Schiene die (PLURAL die Schienen) ❷ (the railway) to go by rail mit der Bahn fahren ❸ (on a balcony, bridge, or stairs) Geländer das (PLURAL die Geländer)

**rail card** NOUN Bahnpass der (PLURAL die Bahnpässe)

**railing(s)** NOUN Geländer das (PLURAL die Geländer)

**railway** NOUN ❶ (the system) Bahn die; the railways die Bahn ❷ railway line (from one place to another) die Bahnstrecke ❸ on the railway line (the track) auf dem Gleis

**railway carriage** NOUN Eisenbahnwagen der (PLURAL die Eisenbahnwagen)

**railway station** NOUN Bahnhof der (PLURAL die Bahnhöfe)

**rain** NOUN Regen der; in the rain im Regen

**rain** VERB regnen; it's raining es regnet, it's going to rain es wird regnen

**rainbow** NOUN Regenbogen der (PLURAL die Regenbogen)

**raincoat** NOUN Regenmantel der (PLURAL die Regenmäntel)

**rainy** ADJECTIVE regnerisch

**raise** VERB ❶ (lift up) hochheben◇ (SEP) ❷ (increase) erhöhen (prices) ❸ to raise money for something Geld für etwas aufbringen◇ (SEP)

**raisin** NOUN Rosine die (PLURAL die Rosinen)

**rake** NOUN Rechen der (PLURAL die Rechen)

**rally** NOUN ❶ (a meeting) Versammlung die (PLURAL die Versammlungen) ❷ (for cars) Rallye die (PLURAL die Rallyes) ❸ (in tennis) Ballwechsel der (PLURAL die Ballwechsel)

**rambler** NOUN Wanderer der (PLURAL die Wanderer), Wanderin die (PLURAL die Wanderinnen)

**rambling** NOUN Wandern das

A
B
C
D
E
F
G
H
I
J
K
L
M
N
O
P
Q
R
S
T
U
V
W
X
Y
Z

**range** NOUN ❶ (a choice) **Auswahl**
die; **a wide range of travel
brochures** eine große Auswahl
an Reiseprospekten ❷ **a range of
subjects** verschiedene Fächer, **in a
range of colours** in verschiedenen
Farben ❸ **a computer in this price
range** ein Computer in dieser
Preislage, **that's out of my price
range** das kann ich mir nicht leisten

**rap** NOUN **Rap** der (music)

**rape** NOUN **Vergewaltigung** die
(PLURAL die **Vergewaltigungen**)

**rape** VERB **vergewaltigen**

**rare** ADJECTIVE ❶ **selten**; **a rare bird**
ein seltener Vogel ❷ **englisch
gebraten** (steak)

**rarely** ADVERB **selten**

**rash** NOUN **Ausschlag** der (PLURAL die
**Ausschläge**)

**rash** ADJECTIVE **voreilig**

**raspberry** NOUN **Himbeere** die
(PLURAL die **Himbeeren**); **raspberry
jam** die Himbeermarmelade

**rat** NOUN **Ratte** die (PLURAL die **Ratten**)

**rate** NOUN ❶ (a charge) **Gebühren**
(plural); **postage rates**
Postgebühren ❷ **are there
special rates for children?** gibt
es Sonderpreise für Kinder?, **at
reduced rates** zu ermäßigten
Preisen ❸ **rate of exchange** der
Wechselkurs ❹ **rate of pay** der
Lohnsatz ❺ (a level) **Rate** die (PLURAL
die **Raten**); **a high cancellation rate**
eine hohe Absagerate ❻ **at any rate**
auf jeden Fall

**rather** ADVERB ❶ **lieber**; **I'd rather
wait** ich warte lieber, **I'd rather
you didn't go** es wäre mir lieber,

wenn du nicht gingest ❷ **ziemlich**;
**I'm rather busy** ich habe ziemlich
viel zu tun, **I've got rather a lot
of shopping to do** ich muss noch
ziemlich viel einkaufen ❸ **rather
than** eher als, **in summer rather
than winter** eher im Sommer als
im Winter

**rave** NOUN (party) **Fete** die (PLURAL die
**Feten**) (informal)

**raw** ADJECTIVE **roh**

**razor** NOUN **Rasierapparat** der (PLURAL
die **Rasierapparate**)

**razor blade** NOUN **Rasierklinge** die
(PLURAL die **Rasierklingen**)

**RE** NOUN **Religionsunterricht** der

**reach** NOUN **Reichweite** die; **out of
reach** außer Reichweite, **within
reach** leicht ereichbar, **to be within
easy reach of Munich** von München
aus leicht erreichbar sein

**reach** VERB ❶ **ankommen**◇ (SEP)
(PERF **sein**) **an** (+DAT) (a place or point),
**ankommen**◇ (SEP) (PERF **sein**) **in**
(+DAT) (a town or country); **when
you reach the station** wenn du am
Bahnhof ankommst ❷ **kommen**◇
(PERF **sein**) **zu** (+DAT) (an agreement,
a conclusion); **to reach a decision** zu
einer Entscheidung kommen ❸ **to
reach for something** nach etwas
(DAT) **greifen**◇

**react** VERB **reagieren**

**reaction** NOUN **Reaktion** die (PLURAL
die **Reaktionen**)

**read** VERB ❶ **lesen**◇; **what are you
reading at the moment?** was liest
du zur Zeit?, **I'm reading a detective
novel** ich lese einen Krimi ❷ **to read
out** vorlesen◇ (SEP), **he read out the**

list to the students er hat die Liste den Studenten vorgelesen

**reading** NOUN ❶ (action) **Lesen** das ❷ (reading matter) **Lektüre** die; some easy reading for the holidays eine leichte Lektüre für die Ferien

**ready** ADJECTIVE ❶ **fertig**; supper's not ready yet das Essen ist noch nicht fertig, we are not quite ready wir sind noch nicht ganz fertig, are you ready to leave? seid ihr fertig?, (on a journey) seid ihr reisefertig?, to get ready sich fertig machen, I'm getting ready to play tennis ich mache mich zum Tennisspielen fertig, I was getting ready for bed ich war gerade dabei, ins Bett zu gehen ❷ to get something ready (complete) etwas fertig machen, etwas vorbereiten (SEP) (a room or food), I'll get your room ready ich bereite dein Zimmer vor

**real** ADJECTIVE ❶ (genuine) **echt**; it's a real diamond das ist ein echter Brillant, he's a real coward er ist ein echter Feigling ❷ (true) **richtig**; is that her real name? ist das ihr richtiger Name? ❸ (not imagined) **wirklich**; it's a real pity you can't come es ist wirklich schade, dass du nicht kommen kannst

**realistic** ADJECTIVE **realistisch**

**reality** NOUN **Wirklichkeit** die; a reality show eine Reality-Show

**realize** VERB **wissen**◇; I hadn't realized das wusste ich nicht, I didn't realize he was French ich wusste nicht, dass er Franzose ist, do you realize what time it is? weißt du, wie viel Uhr es ist?

**really** ADVERB ❶ **wirklich**; the film was really good der Film war wirklich gut, really? wirklich? ❷ not really eigentlich nicht

**reason** NOUN **Grund** der (PLURAL die **Gründe**); for that reason aus diesem Grund, the reason why I phoned der Grund meines Anrufs

**reasonable** ADJECTIVE **vernünftig**

**receipt** NOUN **Quittung** die (PLURAL die **Quittungen**)

**receive** VERB **erhalten**◇

**receiver** NOUN **Hörer** der (PLURAL die **Hörer**); to pick up the receiver den Hörer abnehmen◇ (SEP)

**recent** ADJECTIVE ❶ **kürzlich erfolgter/kürzlich erfolgte/ kürzlich erfolgtes**; the recent closure die kürzlich erfolgte Schließung ❷ in recent years in den letzten Jahren

**recently** ADVERB ❶ (at a time not long ago) **kürzlich** ❷ (over the recent period) **in letzter Zeit**

**reception** NOUN ❶ **Rezeption** die (PLURAL die **Rezeptionen**); he's waiting at reception er wartet an der Rezeption ❷ **Empfang** der (PLURAL die **Empfänge**); a big wedding reception ein großer Hochzeitsempfang ❸ to get a good reception gut aufgenommen werden

**receptionist** NOUN ❶ **Empfangsdame** die (PLURAL die **Empfangsdamen**) ❷ (in a doctor's surgery) **Sprechstundenhilfe** die (PLURAL die **Sprechstundenhilfen**)

**recipe** NOUN **Rezept** das (PLURAL die **Rezepte**)

**reckon** *VERB* glauben; **I reckon it's a good idea** ich glaube, das ist eine gute Idee

**recognize** *VERB* erkennen◇

**recommend** *VERB* empfehlen◇; **can you recommend a dentist?** kannst du mir einen Zahnarzt empfehlen?, **I recommend the fish soup** ich empfehle die Fischsuppe

**record** *NOUN* ❶ Rekord der (*PLURAL* die Rekorde); **it's a world record** das ist ein Weltrekord, **record sales** Verkaufsrekorde ❷ *(of events)* Aufzeichnung die (*PLURAL* die Aufzeichnungen); **on record** aufgezeichnet, **to keep a record of something** über etwas Buch führen ❸ *(music)* Platte die (*PLURAL* die Platten); **a Miles Davis record** eine Platte von Miles Davis ❹ **records** *(office files)* Unterlagen *(plural)*, **I'll just check your records** ich prüfe nur Ihre Unterlagen

**record** *VERB (on tape)* aufnehmen◇ *(SEP)*

**recorder** *NOUN* Blockflöte die (*PLURAL* die Blockflöten); **to play the recorder** Blockflöte spielen

**recording** *NOUN (on tape)* Aufnahme die (*PLURAL* die Aufnahmen), *(on video)* Aufzeichnung die (*PLURAL* die Aufzeichnungen)

**record player** *NOUN* Plattenspieler der (*PLURAL* die Plattenspieler)

**recover** *VERB* sich erholen; **she's recovered now** sie hat sich wieder erholt

**recovery** *NOUN (from an illness)* Erholung die; **to make a good recovery** sich gut erholen

**rectangle** *NOUN* Rechteck das (*PLURAL* die Rechtecke)

**rectangular** *ADJECTIVE* rechteckig

**recycle** *VERB* recyceln

**red** *ADJECTIVE* rot; **a red car** ein rotes Auto, **to go red** rot werden, **to have red hair** rote Haare haben

**Red Cross** *NOUN* **the Red Cross** das Rote Kreuz

**redcurrant** *NOUN* Johannisbeere die (*PLURAL* die Johannisbeeren); **redcurrant jelly** das Johannisbeergelee

**redecorate** *VERB (with paint)* neu streichen◇, *(with wallpaper)* neu tapezieren; **they've redecorated the kitchen** sie haben die Küche neu gestrichen

**redo** *VERB* noch einmal machen

**reduce** *VERB* ❶ **to reduce prices** die Preise herabsetzen *(SEP)* ❷ **to reduce speed** die Geschwindigkeit verringern

**reduction** *NOUN* ❶ *(in price)* Ermäßigung die (*PLURAL* die Ermäßigungen) ❷ *(in speed or number)* Reduzierung die

**redundant** *ADJECTIVE* **to be made redundant** entlassen werden

**referee** *NOUN (in sport)* Schiedsrichter der (*PLURAL* die Schiedsrichter), Schiedsrichterin die (*PLURAL* die Schiedsrichterinnen)

**reference** *NOUN* Referenz die (*PLURAL* die Referenzen); *(for a job)* **she gave me a good reference** sie hat mir eine gute Referenz gegeben

**reference book** *NOUN*
Nachschlagewerk das *(PLURAL die Nachschlagewerke)*

**refill** *VERB* nachfüllen *(SEP)*

**reflect** *VERB* spiegeln; to be reflected sich spiegeln

**reflection** *NOUN* ❶ *(in a mirror or on water)* Spiegelung die *(PLURAL die Spiegelungen)*; to see your reflection in the mirror sich im Spiegel sehen ❷ *(thought)* Überlegung die; on reflection nach nochmaliger Überlegung

**reflexive** *ADJECTIVE* a reflexive verb ein reflexives Verb

**refreshing** *ADJECTIVE* erfrischend

**refreshment** *NOUN* Erfrischung die *(PLURAL die Erfrischungen)*

**refrigerator** *NOUN* Kühlschrank der *(PLURAL die Kühlschränke)*

**refuge** *NOUN* Zuflucht die; a mountain refuge eine Schutzhütte, to take refuge in sich flüchten in *(+DAT)*

**refugee** *NOUN* Flüchtling der *(PLURAL die Flüchtlinge)*

**refund** *NOUN* Rückzahlung die *(PLURAL die Rückzahlungen)*

**refund** *VERB* zurückerstatten *(SEP)*

**refusal** *NOUN* ❶ Weigerung die *(PLURAL die Weigerungen)* ❷ *(for a job)* Absage die *(PLURAL die Absagen)* to get a refusal eine Absage bekommen

**refuse** *NOUN* *(rubbish)* Abfall der

**refuse** *VERB* sich weigern; I refused ich habe mich geweigert, he refuses to help er weigert sich zu helfen

**regards** *PLURAL NOUN* Grüße *(plural)*; regards to your parents viele Grüße an deine Eltern, **Nat sends his regards** Nat lässt grüßen

**reggae** *NOUN* Reggae der

**region** *NOUN* Gebiet das *(PLURAL die Gebiete)*

**regional** *ADJECTIVE* regional

**register** *NOUN* *(in school)* Anwesenheitsliste die *(PLURAL die Anwesenheitslisten)*

**register** *VERB* ❶ eintragen✧ *(SEP) (a name)* ❷ *(report)* anmelden *(SEP)*

**registered letter** *NOUN* Einschreiben das *(PLURAL die Einschreiben)*

**registration number** *NOUN* Autonummer die *(PLURAL die Autonummern)*

**regret** *VERB* bedauern

**regular** *ADJECTIVE* regelmäßig; regular visits regelmäßige Besuche

**regularly** *ADVERB* regelmäßig

**regulation** *NOUN* Vorschrift die *(PLURAL die Vorschriften)*

**rehearsal** *NOUN* Probe die *(PLURAL die Proben)*

**rehearse** *VERB* proben

**reheat** *VERB* aufwärmen *(SEP)*

**reject** *VERB* ablehnen *(SEP)*

**related** *ADJECTIVE* verwandt; we're not related wir sind nicht verwandt

**relation** *NOUN* Verwandte der/die *(PLURAL die Verwandten)*

**relationship** NOUN Beziehung die
(PLURAL die Beziehungen); I have a
good relationship with my parents
ich habe eine gute Beziehung zu
meinen Eltern

**relative** NOUN Verwandte der/die
(PLURAL die Verwandten)

**relatively** ADVERB relativ

**relax** VERB entspannen; I'm going to
relax and watch telly tonight heute
Abend entspanne ich und sehe fern

**relaxed** ADJECTIVE entspannt

**relaxing** ADJECTIVE entspannend

**relay race** NOUN Staffel die (PLURAL
die Staffeln)

**release** NOUN (a film or book)
❶ Neuerscheinung die (PLURAL
die Neuerscheinungen); this
week's new releases die neuen
Filme der Woche ❷ (of a prisoner or
hostage) Freilassung die (PLURAL die
Freilassungen)

**release** VERB ❶ herausbringen◇
(SEP) (a record, film, or video)
❷ freilassen◇ (SEP) (a person)

**reliable** ADJECTIVE zuverlässig

**relief** NOUN Erleichterung die; what
a relief! da bin ich aber erleichtert!

**relieve** VERB stillen (pain)

**relieved** ADJECTIVE erleichtert; I was
relieved to hear you'd arrived ich
war erleichtert zu hören, dass du
angekommen bist

**religion** NOUN Religion die (PLURAL die
Religionen)

**religious** ADJECTIVE religiös

**rely** VERB ❶ (trust) to rely on
somebody sich auf jemanden
verlassen◇, I'm relying on your
help for Saturday ich verlasse mich
darauf, dass du mir am Samstag
hilfst ❷ (be dependent on) to rely on
angewiesen sein auf (+ACC)

**remain** VERB (be left over) übrig
bleiben◇ (PERF sein), (stay)
bleiben◇ (PERF sein)

**remark** NOUN Bemerkung die
(PLURAL die Bemerkungen); to
make remarks about something
Bemerkungen über etwas (ACC)
machen

**remarkable** ADJECTIVE
bemerkenswert

**remarkably** ADVERB
bemerkenswert

**remember** VERB ❶ sich erinnern
an (+ACC), (a person or an occasion);
I don't remember daran kann
ich mich nicht erinnern, do you
remember the holiday in Italy?
erinnerst du dich noch an die Ferien
in Italien? ❷ I can't remember his
number seine Nummer fällt mir
nicht ein ❸ to remember to do
something daran denken◇, etwas
zu tun, remember to lock the
door denk daran abzuschließen,
I remembered to bring the CDs
ich habe daran gedacht, die CDs
mitzubringen

**remind** VERB ❶ erinnern; to remind
somebody to do something
jemanden daran erinnern, etwas zu
tun, remind your mother to pick
me up erinnere deine Mutter daran,
mich abzuholen, he reminds me
of my brother er erinnert mich an
meinen Bruder ❷ oh, that reminds
me … dabei fällt mir ein …

**remote** *ADJECTIVE* abgelegen

**remote control** *NOUN* ❶ *(for a car or plane)* Fernsteuerung die *(PLURAL die Fernsteuerungen)* ❷ *(for TV or video)* Fernbedienung die *(PLURAL die Fernbedienungen)*

**remove** *VERB* ❶ entfernen *(a stain, mark, or obstacle)* ❷ ausziehen◇ *(SEP)* *(clothes)*

**renew** *VERB* verlängern *(a passport or licence)*

**rent** *NOUN* Miete die *(PLURAL die Mieten)*

**rent** *VERB* mieten; Simon's rented a flat Simon hat eine Wohnung gemietet

**reorganize** *VERB* umorganisieren

**repair** *NOUN* Reparatur die *(PLURAL die Reparaturen)*

**repair** *VERB* reparieren; to get something repaired etwas reparieren lassen, we've had the television repaired wir haben unseren Fernseher reparieren lassen

**repay** *VERB* zurückzahlen *(SEP)*

**repeat** *NOUN* Wiederholung die *(PLURAL die Wiederholungen)*

**repeat** *VERB* wiederholen

**repeatedly** *ADVERB* wiederholt

**repetitive** *ADJECTIVE* eintönig

**replace** *VERB* ersetzen

**reply** *NOUN* Antwort die *(PLURAL die Antworten)*; I didn't get a reply to my letter ich habe keine Antwort auf meinen Brief bekommen, there's no reply niemand antwortet

**reply** *VERB* antworten; I still haven't replied to the letter ich habe immer noch nicht auf den Brief geantwortet

**report** *NOUN* ❶ *(of an event)* Bericht der *(PLURAL die Berichte)* ❷ *(school report)* Zeugnis das *(PLURAL die Zeugnisse)*

**report** *VERB* ❶ melden *(a problem or an accident)*; we've reported the theft wir haben den Diebstahl gemeldet ❷ sich melden; I had to report to reception ich musste mich an der Rezeption melden ❸ *(in the news)* berichten; to report on the strike über den Streik berichten

**reporter** *NOUN* Reporter der *(PLURAL die Reporter)*, Reporterin die *(PLURAL die Reporterinnen)*

**represent** *VERB* ❶ darstellen *(SEP)* *(a word, a thing, an idea)* ❷ vertreten◇ *(a group or company)*

**representative** *NOUN* Vertreter der *(PLURAL die Vertreter)*, Vertreterin die *(PLURAL die Vertreterinnen)*

**reproduction** *NOUN* ❶ *(process)* Fortpflanzung die *(PLURAL die Fortpflanzungen)* ❷ *(of sound etc)* Wiedergabe die ❸ *(copy)* Reproduktion die *(PLURAL die Reproduktionen)*

**republic** *NOUN* Republik die *(PLURAL die Republiken)*

**reputation** *NOUN* ❶ Ruf der; to have a good reputation einen guten Ruf haben ❷ she has a reputation for honesty sie gilt als ehrlich

**request** *NOUN* Bitte die *(PLURAL die Bitten)*; at my mother's request auf Bitte meiner Mutter

**request** _VERB_ bitten◊; to request something um etwas (_ACC_) bitten

**rescue** _NOUN_ Rettung die; rescue operation die Rettungsaktion, to come to somebody's rescue jemandem zu Hilfe kommen

**rescue** _VERB_ retten; they rescued the dog sie haben den Hund gerettet

**rescue party** _NOUN_ Rettungsmannschaft die (_PLURAL_ die Rettungsmannschaften)

**research** _NOUN_ ❶ Forschung die; for research into Aids für die Aidsforschung ❷ to do research forschen

**research** _VERB_ to research into something etwas erforschen

**resemblance** _NOUN_ Ähnlichkeit die (_PLURAL_ die Ähnlichkeiten)

**reservation** _NOUN_ (a booking) Reservierung die (_PLURAL_ die Reservierungen); to make a reservation (for a room) (ein Zimmer) reservieren lassen

**reserve** _NOUN_ ❶ Reserve die (_PLURAL_ die Reserven); we have a few in reserve wir haben ein paar in Reserve ❷ nature reserve das Naturschutzgebiet ❸ (for a match) Reservespieler der (_PLURAL_ die Reservespieler), Reservespielerin die (_PLURAL_ die Reservespielerinnen)

**reserve** _VERB_ reservieren; this table is reserved dieser Tisch ist reserviert

**reservoir** _NOUN_ Reservoir das (_PLURAL_ die Reservoirs)

**resident** _NOUN_ Bewohner der (_PLURAL_ die Bewohner), Bewohnerin die (_PLURAL_ die Bewohnerinnen)

**residential** _ADJECTIVE_ Wohn-; a residential area eine Wohngegend

**resign** _VERB_ ❶ (from your job) kündigen ❷ (from an official post) zurücktreten◊ (_SEP_)

**resignation** _NOUN_ ❶ Kündigung die (_PLURAL_ die Kündigungen) ❷ (from an official post) Rücktritt der

**resist** _VERB_ widerstehen◊ (+_DAT_), (an offer or temptation)

**resit** _VERB_ wiederholen (an exam)

**resort** _NOUN_ ❶ (for holidays) holiday resort der Urlaubsort, ski resort der Wintersportsort, seaside resort das Seebad ❷ as a last resort als letzter Ausweg

**respect** _NOUN_ Respekt der

**respect** _VERB_ respektieren

**respectable** _ADJECTIVE_ anständig

**responsibility** _NOUN_ Verantwortung die (_PLURAL_ die Verantwortungen)

**responsible** _ADJECTIVE_ ❶ verantwortlich; he was responsible for the accident er war für den Unfall verantwortlich, I'm responsible for booking the rooms ich bin für die Zimmerreservierung verantwortlich ❷ (reliable) verantwortungsbewusst; he's not very responsible er ist nicht sehr verantwortungsbewusst

**rest** _NOUN_ ❶ the rest der Rest, the rest of the day der Rest des Tages, the rest of the bread der Brotrest, der Rest von dem Brot ❷ (the others) the rest die Übrigen, **the rest have gone home** die Übrigen sind nach Hause gegangen ❸ **Erholung** die; **he's going to the mountains for a rest** er fährt zur Erholung ins Gebirge, **ten days' rest** zehn Tage Erholung, **to have a rest** sich ausruhen *(SEP)* ❹ *(a short break)* **Pause** die *(PLURAL* die **Pausen)**; **to stop for a rest** eine Pause machen

**rest** VERB *(have a rest)* **sich ausruhen** *(SEP)*

**restaurant** NOUN **Restaurant** das *(PLURAL die **Restaurants)***

**restful** ADJECTIVE **erholsam**

**restless** ADJECTIVE **unruhig**

**restrain** VERB **zurückhalten**◇ *(SEP)*

**result** NOUN ❶ **Ergebnis** das *(PLURAL die **Ergebnisse)**; **the exam results** die Prüfungsergebnisse ❷ **as a result** infolgedessen, **as a result we missed the train** infolgedessen haben wir den Zug verpasst

**retire** VERB ❶ *(from work)* **in den Ruhestand gehen**◇, *(civil servant, teacher, soldier)* **in Pension gehen**◇; **she retires in June** sie geht im Juni in Pension ❷ **to be retired** im Ruhestand sein◇

**retirement** NOUN **Ruhestand** der; **since his retirement** seitdem er in den Ruhestand gegangen ist

**return** NOUN ❶ *(coming back)* **Rückkehr** die; **the return journey** die Rückreise ❷ **by return of post** postwendend ❸ **in return for** für, **in return for his help** für seine Hilfe ❹ **in return** dafür
• **many happy returns!** herzlichen Glückwunsch zum Geburtstag

**return** VERB ❶ *(come back)* **zurückkommen**◇ *(SEP)* *(PERF* **sein)**; **he returned ten minutes later** er kam zehn Minuten später zurück, **to return from holiday** aus den Ferien zurückkommen ❷ *(go back)* **zurückgehen**◇ *(SEP)* *(PERF* **sein)**, *(drive)* **zurückfahren**◇ *(SEP)* *(PERF* **sein)**; **we are planning to return in the evening** wir wollen am Abend zurückfahren ❸ *(to give back)* **zurückgeben**◇ *(SEP)*; **Gemma's never returned the video** Gemma hat das Video nie zurückgegeben

**return fare** NOUN **Preis für eine Rückfahrkarte** der, *(for a flight)* **Preis für einen Rückflugschein** der

**return ticket** NOUN **Rückfahrkarte** die *(PLURAL die **Rückfahrkarten)**, *(for a flight)* **Rückflugticket** das *(PLURAL die **Rückflugtickets)***

**reveal** VERB **enthüllen**

**reverse** VERB ❶ *(in a car)* **rückwärts fahren**◇ *(PERF* **sein)** ❷ **to reverse the charges** ein R-Gespräch führen

**review** NOUN *(of a book, play, or film)* **Kritik** die *(PLURAL die **Kritiken)***

**review** VERB **rezensieren** *(a book, play, or film)*

**revise** VERB ❶ **lernen** *(for an exam)*; **Tessa's busy revising for her exams** Tessa lernt jetzt für ihre Prüfung ❷ **wiederholen**; **to revise maths** Mathe wiederholen

**revision** NOUN **Wiederholung** die

**revive** VERB ❶ *(a person)* **wiederbeleben** *(SEP)* ❷ *(to recover)* **sich erholen**

**revolting** ADJECTIVE **eklig**

a
b
c
d
e
f
g
h
i
j
k
l
m
n
o
p
q
r
s
t
u
v
w
x
y
z

**revolution** NOUN Revolution die (PLURAL die **Revolutionen**)

**reward** NOUN Belohnung die (PLURAL die **Belohnungen**)

**reward** VERB belohnen

**rewind** VERB zurückspulen (SEP) (a video)

**rhinoceros** NOUN Nashorn das (PLURAL die **Nashörner**)

**rhubarb** NOUN Rhabarber der

**rhyme** NOUN Reim der (PLURAL die **Reime**)

**rhythm** NOUN Rhythmus der (PLURAL die **Rhythmen**)

**rib** NOUN Rippe die (PLURAL die **Rippen**)

**ribbon** NOUN Band das (PLURAL die **Bänder**)

**rice** NOUN Reis der; **rice pudding** der Milchreis

**rich** ADJECTIVE ❶ reich; **they are very rich** sie sind sehr reich ❷ **the rich** die Reichen

**rid** ADJECTIVE **to get rid of something** etwas loswerden◇ (SEP) (PERF sein) (informal), **we got rid of the car** wir sind das Auto losgeworden

**riddle** NOUN Rätsel das (PLURAL die **Rätsel**)

**ride** NOUN Fahrt die (PLURAL die **Fahrten**); **to go for a ride (on a bike)** eine Fahrt machen, **to go for a ride (on a horse)** reiten gehen◇ (PERF sein)

**ride** VERB ❶ **to ride a bike** Rad fahren◇ (PERF sein), **can you ride a bike?** kannst du Rad fahren?, **I've never ridden a bike** ich bin noch nie Rad

gefahren ❷ **to ride (a horse)** reiten◇ (PERF sein), **I've never ridden a horse** ich bin noch nie auf einem Pferd geritten

**rider** NOUN ❶ (on a horse) Reiter der (PLURAL die **Reiter**), Reiterin die (PLURAL die **Reiterinnen**) ❷ (on a bike) Radler der (PLURAL die **Radler**), Radlerin die (PLURAL die **Radlerinnen**) ❸ (on a motorbike) Fahrer der (PLURAL die **Fahrer**), Fahrerin die (PLURAL die **Fahrerinnen**)

**ridiculous** ADJECTIVE lächerlich

**riding** NOUN Reiten das; **to go riding** reiten gehen◇

**riding school** NOUN Reitschule die (PLURAL die **Reitschulen**)

**rifle** NOUN Gewehr das (PLURAL die **Gewehre**)

**right** NOUN ❶ (not left) rechte Seite die; **on the right** auf der rechten Seite, **on my right** rechts von mir ❷ (to do something) Recht das (PLURAL die **Rechte**); **to have the right to something** ein Recht auf etwas (ACC) haben, **the right to work** das Recht auf Arbeit, **you have no right to say that** du hast kein Recht, das zu sagen

**right** ADJECTIVE ❶ (not left) rechter/ rechte/rechtes; **my right hand** meine rechte Hand ❷ (correct) richtig; **the right answer** die richtige Antwort, **is this the right address?** ist das die richtige Adresse? ❸ **to be right** (of a person) Recht haben, **you see, I was right** siehst du, ich hatte Recht ❹ **you were right not to say anything** du hattest Recht, nichts zu sagen ❺ **the clock is right** die Uhr geht richtig

**❻** yes, that's right ja, das stimmt, is that right? stimmt das?

**right** ADVERB **❶** (direction) rechts; turn right at the lights biege an der Ampel rechts ab **❷** (correctly) richtig; you're not doing it right du machst das nicht richtig **❸** (completely) ganz; right at the bottom ganz unten, right at the beginning ganz am Anfang **❹** (exactly) genau; right in the middle genau in der Mitte **❺** right now sofort **❻** (okay) gut; right, let's go gut, gehen wir

**right-click** NOUN Klick der, mit der rechten Maustaste (PLURAL die Klicks mit der rechten Maustaste)

**right-hand** ADJECTIVE on the right-hand side rechts

**right-handed** ADJECTIVE rechtshändig

**ring** NOUN **❶** (on the phone) to give somebody a ring jemanden anrufen◇ (SEP) **❷** (for your finger) Ring der (PLURAL die Ringe) **❸** (circle) Kreis der (PLURAL die Kreise) **❹** there was a ring at the door es hat geklingelt

**ring** VERB **❶** (a bell or phone) klingeln; the phone rang das Telefon klingelte **❷** (phone) anrufen◇ (SEP); I'll ring you tomorrow ich rufe dich morgen an **❸** to ring for a taxi ein Taxi rufen
• to ring back zurückrufen◇ (SEP); I'll ring you back later ich rufe dich später zurück
• to ring off auflegen (SEP)

**ring road** NOUN Ringstraße die (PLURAL die Ringstraßen)

**ringtone** NOUN Klingelton der (PLURAL die Klingeltöne)

**rinse** VERB spülen

**riot** NOUN Aufstand der (PLURAL die Aufstände)

**rioting** NOUN Unruhen (plural)

**rip** VERB zerreißen◇

**ripe** ADJECTIVE reif; are the tomatoes ripe? sind die Tomaten reif?

**rip-off** NOUN it's a rip-off das ist Nepp (informal)

**rise** NOUN **❶** Anstieg der; a rise in temperature ein Temperaturanstieg **❷** pay rise die Gehaltserhöhung

**rise** VERB **❶** (the sun) aufgehen◇ (SEP) (PERF sein) **❷** (prices) steigen◇ (PERF sein)

**risk** NOUN Risiko das (PLURAL die Risiken); to take a risk ein Risiko eingehen

**risk** VERB riskieren; he risks losing his job er riskiert es, seine Stelle zu verlieren

**river** NOUN Fluss der (PLURAL die Flüsse)

**road** NOUN **❶** Straße die (PLURAL die Straßen); the road to London die Straße nach London **❷** the baker's is on the other side of the road die Bäckerei ist auf der anderen Straßenseite **❸** across the road gegenüber, they live across the road from us sie wohnen bei uns gegenüber

**road accident** NOUN Verkehrsunfall der (PLURAL die Verkehrsunfälle)

A
B
C
D
E
F
G
H
I
J
K
L
M
N
O
P
Q
R
S
T
U
V
W
X
Y
Z

**road map** NOUN Straßenkarte die (PLURAL die **Straßenkarten**)

**roadside** NOUN by the roadside am Straßenrand

**road sign** NOUN Straßenschild das (PLURAL die **Straßenschilder**)

**roadworks** PLURAL NOUN Straßenarbeiten (plural)

**roast** NOUN Braten der (PLURAL die **Braten**)

**roast** ADJECTIVE gebraten; roast potatoes Bratkartoffeln, roast beef der Rinderbraten

**rob** VERB ❶ berauben (a person) ❷ ausrauben (SEP) (a bank)

**robber** NOUN Räuber der (PLURAL die **Räuber**)

**robbery** NOUN Raub der (PLURAL die **Raube**); bank robbery der Bankraub

**robot** NOUN Roboter der (PLURAL die **Roboter**)

**rock** NOUN ❶ (a big stone) Felsen der (PLURAL die **Felsen**) ❷ (the material) Fels der ❸ (music) Rock der; rock band die Rockband, to dance rock and roll Rock 'n' Roll tanzen

**rock climbing** NOUN Klettern das; to go rock climbing (zum) Klettern gehen

**rocket** NOUN Rakete die (PLURAL die **Raketen**)

**rock music** NOUN Rockmusik die

**rock star** NOUN Rockstar der (PLURAL die **Rockstars**)

**rocky** ADJECTIVE felsig

**rod** NOUN a fishing rod eine Angel

**role** NOUN Rolle die (PLURAL die **Rollen**); to play the role of Hamlet die Rolle des Hamlet spielen

**roll** NOUN ❶ Rolle die (PLURAL die **Rollen**); a roll of film eine Rolle Film, a toilet roll eine Rolle Toilettenpapier ❷ bread roll das Brötchen, die Semmel (South German)

**roll** VERB rollen (PERF sein)

**roller** NOUN ❶ (for hair) Lockenwickler der (PLURAL die **Lockenwickler**) ❷ (for paint) Rolle die (PLURAL die **Rollen**)

**rollerblades** PLURAL NOUN Inlineskates (plural), Inliners (plural)

**rollercoaster** NOUN Achterbahn die (PLURAL die **Achterbahnen**)

**roller skates** PLURAL NOUN Rollschuhe (plural)

**Roman Catholic** ADJECTIVE römisch-katholisch

**romantic** ADJECTIVE romantisch

**roof** NOUN Dach das (PLURAL die **Dächer**)

**roof rack** NOUN Gepäckträger der (PLURAL die **Gepäckträger**)

**rook** NOUN ❶ (in chess) Turm der (PLURAL die **Türme**) ❷ (bird) Saatkrähe die (PLURAL die **Saatkrähen**)

**room** NOUN ❶ Zimmer das (PLURAL die **Zimmer**); she's in the other room sie ist im anderen Zimmer, a three-room flat eine Dreizimmerwohnung ❷ (space) Platz der; enough room for two genug Platz für zwei, very little room wenig Platz, to make room Platz machen

**root** NOUN **Wurzel** die (PLURAL die **Wurzeln**)

**rope** NOUN **Seil** das (PLURAL die **Seile**)

**rose** NOUN **Rose** die (PLURAL die **Rosen**)

**rot** VERB **verfaulen** (PERF **sein**)

**rotten** ADJECTIVE **verfault**

**rough** ADJECTIVE ❶ (scratchy) **rau** ❷ (vague) **grob** (plan or estimate) ❸ a rough idea eine vage Vorstellung ❹ (stormy) **stürmisch**; a rough sea eine stürmische See ❺ (difficult) to have a rough time es schwer haben ❻ to sleep rough im Freien schlafen

**roughly** ADVERB (approximately) **ungefähr**; roughly ten per cent ungefähr zehn Prozent, it takes roughly three hours es dauert ungefähr drei Stunden

**round** NOUN **Runde** die (PLURAL die **Runden**); a round of talks eine Gesprächsrunde, a round of drinks eine Runde

**round** ADJECTIVE **rund**; a round table ein runder Tisch

**round** PREPOSITION ❶ **um** (+ACC); round the city um die Stadt, round my arm um meinen Arm, they were sitting round the table sie haben um den Tisch gesessen, it's just round the corner es ist gleich um die Ecke ❷ to go round a museum ein Museum besuchen

**round** ADVERB ❶ to go round to somebody's house jemanden besuchen (+DAT) ❷ to invite somebody round jemanden zu sich (DAT) einladen◇ (SEP), we invited Sally round for lunch wir haben Sally zum Mittagessen eingeladen

❸ to look round the shops sich in den Geschäften umsehen◇ (SEP) ❹ all the year round das ganze Jahr hindurch

**roundabout** NOUN ❶ (for traffic) **Kreisverkehr** der ❷ (in a fairground) **Karussell** das (PLURAL die **Karussells**)

**route** NOUN ❶ (that you plan) **Route** die (PLURAL die **Routen**); the best route is via Calais die beste Route führt über Calais ❷ bus route die Buslinie

**routine** NOUN **Routine** die (PLURAL die **Routinen**)

**row**¹ NOUN ❶ **Reihe** die (PLURAL die **Reihen**); in the front row in der ersten Reihe, in the back row in der letzten Reihe ❷ in a row hintereinander, four times in a row viermal hintereinander

**row** VERB (in a boat) **rudern** (PERF **sein**), (a boat, a person) **rudern** (PERF **haben**); we rowed across the lake wir sind über den See gerudert, he rowed us across the lake er hat uns über den See gerudert

**row**² NOUN ❶ (a quarrel) **Krach** der (informal) (PLURAL die **Kräche**); to have a row Krach haben, they've had a row sie haben Krach gehabt, I had a row with my parents ich habe Krach mit meinen Eltern gehabt ❷ (noise) **Krach** der; they were making a terrible row sie haben einen furchtbaren Krach gemacht

**rowing** NOUN **Rudern** das; to go rowing rudern gehen

**rowing boat** NOUN **Ruderboot** das (PLURAL die **Ruderboote**)

**royal** *ADJECTIVE* **königlich; the royal family** die königliche Familie

**rub** *VERB* **reiben**◇; **to rub your eyes** sich *(DAT)* die Augen reiben
- **to rub something out** etwas ausradieren *(SEP)*

**rubber** *NOUN* ❶ *(an eraser)* **Radiergummi** der *(PLURAL die Radiergummis)* ❷ *(material)* **Gummi** der; **rubber soles** Gummisohlen

**rubbish** *NOUN* ❶ *(for the bin)* **Müll** der ❷ *(nonsense)* **Quatsch** der *(informal)*; **you're talking rubbish!** du redest Quatsch

**rubbish** *ADJECTIVE* **schlecht; the film was rubbish** der Film war schlecht, **they're a rubbish band** sie sind eine lausige Band

**rubbish bin** *NOUN* **Mülleimer** der *(PLURAL die Mülleimer)*

**rucksack** *NOUN* **Rucksack** der *(PLURAL die Rucksäcke)*

**rude** *ADJECTIVE* ❶ **unhöflich; that's rude** das ist unhöflich ❷ **unanständig; a rude joke** ein unanständiger Witz

**rug** *NOUN* ❶ **Teppich** der *(PLURAL die Teppiche)* ❷ *(a blanket)* **Decke** die *(PLURAL die Decken)*

**rugby** *NOUN* **Rugby** das

**ruin** *NOUN* *(remains)* **Ruine** die *(PLURAL die Ruinen)*; **in ruins** in Trümmern

**ruin** *VERB* ❶ **ruinieren; you'll ruin your jacket** du ruinierst dir die Jacke ❷ **verderben**◇ *(day, holiday)*; **it ruined my evening** das hat mir den Abend verdorben

**rule** *NOUN* ❶ **Regel** die *(PLURAL die Regeln)*; **the rules of the game** die Spielregeln, **as a rule** in der Regel ❷ *(administrative)* **Vorschrift** die *(PLURAL die Vorschriften)*; **according to the school rules** nach den Schulvorschriften

**ruler** *NOUN* **Lineal** das *(PLURAL die Lineale)*; **I've lost my ruler** ich habe mein Lineal verloren

**rum** *NOUN* **Rum** der

**rumour** *NOUN* **Gerücht** das *(PLURAL die Gerüchte)*

**run** *NOUN* ❶ *(in games, sport, and for fitness)* **Lauf** der *(PLURAL die Läufe)*; **to go for a run** laufen gehen *(PERF sein)*, joggen gehen *(PERF sein)* ❷ *(of a play)* **Laufzeit** die ❸ *(in skiing)* **Abfahrt** die *(PLURAL die Abfahrten)* ❹ **in the long run** auf lange Sicht

**run** *VERB* ❶ **laufen**◇ *(PERF sein)*; **I ran ten kilometres** ich bin zehn Kilometer gelaufen, **he ran across the pitch** er ist über das Spielfeld gelaufen ❷ *(run fast)* **rennen**◇ *(PERF sein)*; **Kitty ran for the bus** Kitty rannte, um den Bus zu kriegen ❸ *(drive)* **fahren**◇; **I'll run you home later** ich fahre dich später nach Hause ❹ *(organize)* **veranstalten** *(a course or competition)*; **who's running this competition?** wer veranstaltet diesen Wettbewerb? ❺ *(manage)* **leiten** *(a business)*; **she's been running the firm for years** sie leitet die Firma schon seit Jahren, **to run a shop** ein Geschäft leiten ❻ *(a train or a bus)* **fahren**◇ *(PERF sein)*; **the buses don't run on Sundays** sonntags fahren keine Busse ❼ **to run a bath** ein Bad einlaufen lassen
- **to run away** weglaufen◇ *(SEP)* *(PERF sein)*

- **to run into something** gegen etwas (ACC) fahren◇ (PERF **sein**); **the car ran into a tree** das Auto ist gegen einen Baum gefahren
- **to run out of something we've run out of bread** wir haben kein Brot mehr, **I'm running out of money** ich habe kaum noch Geld
- **to run somebody over** jemanden überfahren◇; **he nearly got run over** er ist beinahe überfahren worden

**runner** NOUN **Läufer** der (PLURAL die **Läufer**), **Läuferin** die (PLURAL die **Läuferinnen**)

**runner-up** NOUN **Zweite** der/die (PLURAL die **Zweiten**)

**running** NOUN (for exercise) **Laufen** das, **Jogging** das

**running** ADJECTIVE ❶ **running water** fließendes Wasser ❷ **three days running** drei Tage hintereinander, **to win three times running** dreimal hintereinander gewinnen

**runway** NOUN ❶ (for take-off) **Startbahn** die (PLURAL die **Startbahnen**) ❷ (for landing) **Landebahn** die (PLURAL die **Landebahnen**)

**rush** NOUN (a hurry) **to be in a rush** in Eile sein, **sorry, I'm in a rush** Entschuldigung, ich bin in Eile

**rush** VERB ❶ (hurry) **sich beeilen**; **I must rush!** ich muss mich beeilen ❷ (run) **hetzen** (PERF **sein**); **she rushed out** sie stürmte raus (informal) ❸ **Louise was rushed to hospital** Louise ist schnellstens ins Krankenhaus gebracht worden

**rush hour** NOUN **Stoßzeit** die (PLURAL die **Stoßzeiten**); **in the rush hour** während der Stoßzeit

**Russia** NOUN **Russland** das

**Russian** NOUN ❶ (a person) **Russe** der (PLURAL die **Russen**), **Russin** die (PLURAL die **Russinnen**) ❷ (the language) **Russisch** das

**Russian** ADJECTIVE **russisch**; **he's Russian** er ist Russe

**rust** NOUN **Rost** der

**rusty** ADJECTIVE **rostig**

**rye** NOUN **Roggen** der

# Ss

**Sabbath** NOUN ❶ (Jewish) Sabbat der (PLURAL die Sabbate) ❷ (Christian) Sonntag der (PLURAL die Sonntage)

**sack** NOUN ❶ Sack der (PLURAL die Säcke) ❷ to get the sack rausgeschmissen werden (informal)

**sack** VERB to sack somebody jemanden rausschmeißen◇ (SEP) (informal)

**sad** ADJECTIVE traurig

**saddle** NOUN Sattel der (PLURAL die Sättel)

**saddlebag** NOUN Satteltasche die (PLURAL die Satteltaschen)

**sadly** ADVERB ❶ traurig; she looked at me sadly sie hat mich traurig angesehen ❷ (unfortunately) leider

**safe** ADJECTIVE ❶ (out of danger) sicher; to feel safe from something sich vor etwas (DAT) sicher fühlen ❷ she's safe sie ist in Sicherheit ❸ (not dangerous) ungefährlich; the path is safe der Weg ist ungefährlich, it's not safe das ist gefährlich

**safety** NOUN Sicherheit die

**safety belt** NOUN Sicherheitsgurt der (PLURAL die Sicherheitsgurte)

**safety pin** NOUN Sicherheitsnadel die (PLURAL die Sicherheitsnadeln)

**Sagittarius** NOUN Schütze der; Kylie's Sagittarius Kylie ist Schütze

**sail** NOUN Segel das (PLURAL die Segel)

**sailing** NOUN Segeln das; to go sailing segeln

**sailing boat** NOUN Segelboot das (PLURAL die Segelboote)

**sailor** NOUN Seemann der (PLURAL die Seeleute)

**saint** NOUN Heilige der/die (PLURAL die Heiligen)

**sake** NOUN ❶ for your mother's sake deiner Mutter zuliebe ❷ for heaven's sake um Gottes willen

**salad** NOUN Salat der (PLURAL die Salate); tomato salad der Tomatensalat

**salad dressing** NOUN Salatsoße die (PLURAL die Salatsoßen)

**salami** NOUN Salami die (PLURAL die Salamis)

**salary** NOUN Gehalt das (PLURAL die Gehälter)

**sale** NOUN ❶ (selling) Verkauf der (PLURAL die Verkäufe); the sale of the house der Verkauf des Hauses, 'for sale' 'zu verkaufen' ❷ the sales der Ausverkauf, I bought it in the sales ich habe es im Ausverkauf gekauft

**sales assistant** NOUN Verkäufer der (PLURAL die Verkäufer) Verkäuferin die (PLURAL die Verkäuferinnen)

**salesman** NOUN Verkäufer der (PLURAL die Verkäufer)

**saleswoman** NOUN Verkäuferin die (PLURAL die Verkäuferinnen)

**salmon** NOUN Lachs der (PLURAL die Lachse)

A B C D E F G H I J K L M N O P Q R S T U V W X Y Z

**salt** NOUN **Salz** das

**salty** ADJECTIVE **salzig**

**same** ADJECTIVE **the same** der gleiche/
die gleiche/das gleiche, **she said
the same thing** sie hat das gleiche
gesagt, **her birthday's the same
day as mine** sie hat am gleichen Tag
Geburtstag wie ich, **at the same
time** zur gleichen Zeit, **their car's
the same as ours** sie haben das
gleiche Auto wie wir

**same** ADVERB ❶ **the same** gleich, **the
two bikes look the same** die beiden
Fahrräder sehen gleich aus ❷ **all the
same** trotzdem

**sample** NOUN **Muster** das (PLURAL
die **Muster**); **a free sample** ein
unverkäufliches Muster, eine
Warenprobe

**sand** NOUN **Sand** der

**sandal** NOUN **Sandale** die (PLURAL die
**Sandalen**); **a pair of sandals** ein
Paar Sandalen

**sandpaper** NOUN **Sandpapier** das
(PLURAL die **Sandpapiere**)

**sandwich** NOUN **Sandwich** das
(PLURAL die **Sandwichs**), **belegte
Brot** das (PLURAL die **belegten
Brote**); **ham sandwich** das
Schinkenbrot

**sanitary towel** NOUN **Damenbinde**
die (PLURAL die **Damenbinden**)

**Santa Claus** NOUN der
**Weihnachtsmann**

**sarcastic** ADJECTIVE **sarkastisch**

**sardine** NOUN **Sardine** die (PLURAL die
**Sardinen**)

**SARS** NOUN **SARS** das

**satchel** NOUN **Ranzen** der (PLURAL die
**Ranzen**)

**satellite** NOUN **Satellit** der (PLURAL die
**Satelliten**)

**satellite dish** NOUN
**Satellitenschüssel** die (PLURAL die
**Satellitenschüsseln**)

**satellite television** NOUN
**Satellitenfernsehen** das

**satisfactory** ADJECTIVE **befriedigend**

**satisfied** ADJECTIVE **zufrieden**

**satisfy** VERB **befriedigen**

**satisfying** ADJECTIVE ❶ **befriedigend**
❷ **a satisfying meal** ein sättigendes
Essen

**Saturday** NOUN ❶ **Samstag** der
(PLURAL die **Samstage**) **Sonnabend**
der (North German), (PLURAL die
**Sonnabende**); **on Saturday**
am Sonnabend/am Samstag,
**I'm going out on Saturday** ich
gehe Sonnabend aus, **see you on
Saturday!** bis Samstag!, **every
Saturday** jeden Samstag, **last
Saturday** vorigen Sonnabend, **next
Saturday** nächsten Sonnabend
❷ **on Saturdays** samstags,
sonnabends (North German), **the
museum is closed on Saturdays** das
Museum ist sonnabends/samstags
geschlossen, **to have a Saturday job**
sonnabends/samstags arbeiten

**sauce** NOUN **Soße** die (PLURAL die
**Soßen**)

**saucepan** NOUN **Kochtopf** der (PLURAL
die **Kochtöpfe**)

**saucer** NOUN **Untertasse** die (PLURAL
die **Untertassen**)

**sausage** NOUN **Wurst** die (PLURAL die **Würste**)

**save** VERB ❶ **retten** (life); to save somebody's life jemandem das Leben retten, the doctors saved his life die Ärzte haben ihm das Leben gerettet ❷ **sparen** (money); I've saved £60 ich habe sechzig Pfund gespart, I cycle to school to save money ich fahre mit dem Rad zur Schule, um Geld zu sparen, we'll take a taxi to save time um Zeit zu sparen, nehmen wir ein Taxi ❸ (on a computer) **speichern** ❹ (stop) **abwehren** (SEP) (a shot); to save a penalty einen Elfmeter abwehren
• to save up sparen; I'm saving up for a car ich spare auf ein Auto

**savings** PLURAL NOUN **Ersparnisse** (plural)

**savoury** ADJECTIVE (not sweet) **pikant**

**saw** NOUN **Säge** die (PLURAL die **Sägen**)

**sax** NOUN **Saxophon** das (PLURAL die **Saxophone**)

**saxophone** NOUN **Saxophon** das (PLURAL die **Saxophone**); to play the saxophone Saxophon spielen

**say** VERB ❶ **sagen**; what did you say? was hast du gesagt?, she says she's tired sie sagt, dass sie müde ist, he said to wait here er hat gesagt, wir sollen hier warten, they say man sagt ❷ to say something again etwas wiederholen ❸ that's to say das heißt

**saying** NOUN **Redensart** die (PLURAL die **Redensarten**); it's just a saying das ist so eine Redensart, as the saying goes wie man so sagt

**scab** NOUN **Wundschorf** der (PLURAL die **Wundschorfe**)

**scale** NOUN ❶ (of a map or model) **Maßstab** der (PLURAL die **Maßstäbe**) ❷ (extent) **Ausmaß** das (PLURAL die **Ausmaße**); the scale of the disaster das Ausmaß der Katastrophe ❸ (in music) **Tonleiter** die (PLURAL die **Tonleitern**)

**scales** NOUN **Waage** die (PLURAL die **Waagen**); bathroom scales die Personenwaage

**scandal** NOUN ❶ **Skandal** der (PLURAL die **Skandale**) ❷ (gossip) **Klatsch** der (informal)

**Scandinavia** NOUN **Skandinavien** das

**Scandinavian** ADJECTIVE **skandinavisch**

**scanner** NOUN **Scanner** der (PLURAL die **Scanner**)

**scar** NOUN **Narbe** die (PLURAL die **Narben**)

**scarce** ADJECTIVE **knapp**

**scare** NOUN ❶ **Schrecken** der (PLURAL die **Schrecken**); to give somebody a scare jemandem einen Schrecken einjagen (SEP) ❷ (general alarm) **Panik** die (PLURAL die **Paniken**); to cause a scare eine Panik auslösen ❸ bomb scare die Bombendrohung

**scare** VERB to scare somebody jemanden erschrecken, you scared me! du hast mich erschreckt!

**scarecrow** NOUN **Vogelscheuche** die (PLURAL die **Vogelscheuchen**)

**scared** ADJECTIVE ❶ to be scared Angst haben, I'm scared ich habe Angst, to be scared of something vor etwas (DAT) Angst haben, he's scared of dogs er hat vor Hunden Angst ❷ to be scared of doing something sich nicht trauen, etwas zu tun, **I'm scared of telling him the truth** ich traue mich nicht, ihm die Wahrheit zu sagen

**scarf** NOUN ❶ (silky) **Tuch** das (PLURAL die **Tücher**) ❷ (long, warm) **Schal** der (PLURAL die **Schals**)

**scary** ADJECTIVE **unheimlich**

**scene** NOUN ❶ (of an incident or event) **Schauplatz** der (PLURAL die **Schauplätze**); **to be on the scene** am Schauplatz sein, **the scene of the crime** der Tatort ❷ (world) the music scene die Musikszene, **on the fashion scene** in der Modewelt ❸ (argument) **Szene** die (PLURAL die **Szenen**); **to make a scene** eine Szene machen

**scenery** NOUN ❶ (landscape) **Landschaft** die ❷ (in the theatre) **Bühnenbild** das

**schedule** NOUN **Programm** das (PLURAL die **Programme**)

**scheduled flight** NOUN **Linienflug** der (PLURAL die **Linienflüge**)

**scheme** NOUN **Projekt** das (PLURAL die **Projekte**)

**scholarship** NOUN **Stipendium** das (PLURAL die **Stipendien**)

**school** NOUN **Schule** die (PLURAL die **Schulen**); **at school** in der Schule, **to go to school** zur Schule gehen

**schoolbook** NOUN **Schulbuch** das (PLURAL die **Schulbücher**)

**schoolboy** NOUN **Schüler** der (PLURAL die **Schüler**)

**schoolchildren** PLURAL NOUN **Schulkinder** (plural)

**schoolfriend** NOUN **Schulfreund** der (PLURAL die **Schulfreunde**), **Schulfreundin** die (PLURAL die **Schulfreundinnen**)

**schoolgirl** NOUN **Schülerin** die (PLURAL die **Schülerinnen**)

**science** NOUN **Wissenschaft** die (PLURAL die **Wissenschaften**)

**science fiction** NOUN **Sciencefiction** die

**scientific** ADJECTIVE **wissenschaftlich**

**scientist** NOUN **Wissenschaftler** der (PLURAL die **Wissenschaftler**), **Wissenschaftlerin** die (PLURAL die **Wissenschaftlerinnen**)

**scissors** PLURAL NOUN **Schere** die (PLURAL die **Scheren**); **a pair of scissors** eine Schere

**scoop** NOUN ❶ (implement) **Eisportionierer** der (PLURAL die **Eisportionierer**) ❷ (quantity) **Eiskugel** die (PLURAL die **Eiskugeln**); **how many scoops would you like?** wieviele Kugeln Eis möchtest du? ❸ (in journalism) **Knüller** der (PLURAL die **Knüller**)

**scooter** NOUN ❶ (motor scooter) **Motorroller** der (PLURAL die **Motorroller**) ❷ (for a child) **Roller** der (PLURAL die **Roller**)

**score** NOUN **Spielstand** der (PLURAL die **Spielstände**); **the score was three two** es stand drei zu zwei

**score** VERB ❶ **to score a goal** ein Tor schießen◇ ❷ **to score three points** drei Punkte erzielen ❸ (keep score) **zählen**

**Scorpio** NOUN **Skorpion** der; **Neil is Scorpio** Neil ist Skorpion

**Scot** NOUN **Schotte** der (PLURAL die **Schotten**), **Schottin** die (PLURAL die **Schottinnen**); **the Scots** die **Schotten**

**Scotland** NOUN **Schottland** das; **from Scotland** aus Schottland, **Pauline's from Scotland** Pauline kommt aus Schottland, **to Scotland** nach Schottland

**Scots** ADJECTIVE **schottisch**

**Scotsman** NOUN **Schotte** der (PLURAL die **Schotten**)

**Scotswoman** NOUN **Schottin** die (PLURAL die **Schottinnen**)

**Scottish** ADJECTIVE **schottisch**; **he's Scottish** er ist Schotte

**scout** NOUN **Pfadfinder** der (PLURAL die **Pfadfinder**)

**scrambled eggs** NOUN **Rührei** das

**scrap** NOUN **Stück** das (PLURAL die **Stücke**); **a scrap of paper** ein Stück Papier

**scrapbook** NOUN **Sammelalbum** das (PLURAL die **Sammelalben**)

**scrape** VERB ❶ **schaben** (potatoes or carrots) ❷ (remove dirt or paint) **abkratzen** (SEP) ❸ (damage) **schrammen**

**scratch** NOUN (on your skin or a surface) **Kratzer** der (PLURAL die **Kratzer**)
- **to start from scratch** von vorn anfangen◇ (SEP)

**scratch** VERB (scratch yourself) **sich kratzen**; **to scratch your head** sich am Kopf kratzen

**scream** NOUN **Schrei** der (PLURAL die **Schreie**)

**scream** VERB **schreien**◇

**screen** NOUN ❶ **Bildschirm** der (PLURAL die **Bildschirme**) (of a TV or computer); **on the screen** auf dem Bildschirm ❷ (in the cinema) **Leinwand** die (PLURAL die **Leinwände**)

**screw** NOUN **Schraube** die (PLURAL die **Schrauben**)

**screw** VERB **schrauben**

**screwdriver** NOUN **Schraubenzieher** der (PLURAL die **Schraubenzieher**)

**scribble** VERB **kritzeln**

**scrub** VERB **scheuern** (a saucepan or the floor); **to scrub your nails** sich (DAT) die Nägel bürsten

**scuba diving** NOUN **Gerätetauchen** das

**sculptor** NOUN **Bildhauer** der (PLURAL die **Bildhauer**), **Bildhauerin** die (PLURAL die **Bildhauerinnen**); **Rebecca's a sculptor** Rebecca ist Bildhauerin

**sculpture** NOUN **Skulptur** die (PLURAL die **Skulpturen**)

**sea** NOUN **Meer** das (PLURAL die **Meere**), **See** die; **by the sea** am Meer, an der See

**seafood** NOUN **Meeresfrüchte** (plural); **I love seafood** ich esse Meeresfrüchte sehr gern

**seagull** NOUN **Möwe** die (PLURAL die **Möwen**)

**seal** NOUN (animal) **Robbe** die (PLURAL die **Robben**), **Seehund** der (PLURAL die **Seehunde**)

**seal** VERB **zukleben** (SEP) (an envelope)

**search** VERB ❶ absuchen (SEP); **I've searched my desk but I can't find the letter** ich habe meinen Schreibtisch abgesucht, aber ich kann den Brief nicht finden ❷ durchsuchen; **they searched the building for him** sie haben das Gebäude nach ihm durchsucht ❸ suchen; **to search for something** nach etwas (DAT) suchen, **I've been searching everywhere for my scissors** ich habe überall nach meiner Schere gesucht

**seashell** NOUN Muschel die (PLURAL die Muscheln)

**seasick** ADJECTIVE **to be seasick** seekrank sein

**seaside** NOUN **at the seaside** am Meer

**season** NOUN ❶ Jahreszeit die (PLURAL die Jahreszeiten); **the four seasons** die vier Jahreszeiten ❷ (period of social or sporting activity) Saison die (PLURAL die Saisons); **the tennis season** die Tennissaison, **off-season prices** Preise außerhalb der Saison ❸ **strawberries are not in season at the moment** jetzt ist nicht die richtige Zeit für Erdbeeren

**season ticket** NOUN Dauerkarte die (PLURAL die Dauerkarten)

**seat** NOUN ❶ Sitz der (PLURAL die Sitze); **the front seat** (in a car) der Vordersitz, **the back seat** der Rücksitz, **take a seat** nehmen Sie Platz (formal), setz dich (informal) ❷ (on a bus, in the theatre, etc.) Platz der (PLURAL die Plätze); **to book a seat** einen Platz reservieren, **can you keep my seat?** kannst du mir meinen Platz freihalten?

**seatbelt** NOUN Sicherheitsgurt der (PLURAL die Sicherheitsgurte)

**seaweed** NOUN Tang der

**second** NOUN Sekunde die (PLURAL die Sekunden); **can you wait a second?** kannst du eine Sekunde warten?

**second** ADJECTIVE ❶ zweiter/zweite/zweites; **for the second time** zum zweiten Mal ❷ **the second of July** der zweite Juli

**secondary school** NOUN ❶ weiterführende Schule die (PLURAL die weiterführenden Schulen) (Germans define the type of secondary school) ❷ Gymnasium das (PLURAL die Gymnasien) (grammar school, from age 10 to 19 when Abitur is taken) ❸ Realschule die (PLURAL die Realschulen) (from age 10 to 16, less academic than a Gymnasium)

**secondhand** ADJECTIVE, ADVERB gebraucht; **a secondhand bike** ein gebrauchtes Fahrrad, **secondhand car** der Gebrauchtwagen, **I bought it secondhand** ich habe es gebraucht gekauft

**secondly** ADVERB zweitens

**secret** NOUN Geheimnis das (PLURAL die Geheimnisse); **to tell somebody a secret** jemandem ein Geheimnis verraten, **in secret** heimlich

**secret** ADJECTIVE geheim; **a secret plan** ein geheimer Plan, **to keep something secret** etwas geheim halten

**secretary** NOUN Sekretär der (PLURAL die Sekretäre), Sekretärin die (PLURAL die Sekretärinnen); **the secretary's office** das Sekretariat

**secretly** ADVERB heimlich

**sect** *NOUN* Sekte die *(PLURAL die Sekten)*

**section** *NOUN* Teil der *(PLURAL die Teile)*

**security** *NOUN* Sicherheit die

**security guard** *NOUN* Wächter der *(PLURAL die Wächter)*, Wächterin die *(PLURAL die Wächterinnen)*

**see** *VERB* ❶ sehen◇; I saw Lindy yesterday ich habe Lindy gestern gesehen, have you seen the film? hast du den Film gesehen?, I can't see anything ich kann überhaupt nichts sehen ❷ to go and see nachsehen◇ *(SEP)*, I'll go and see ich sehe nach ❸ *(visit)* besuchen; why don't you come and see us in the summer? warum besucht ihr uns nicht im Sommer? ❹ to see somebody home jemanden nach Hause begleiten ❺ see you! tschüs! *(informal)*, see you on Saturday! bis Samstag!, see you soon! bis bald!
- to see to something sich um etwas *(ACC)* kümmern; Jo's seeing to the drinks Jo kümmert sich um die Getränke

**seed** *NOUN* Samen der *(PLURAL die Samen)*

**seem** *VERB* ❶ scheinen◇; his story seems odd to me seine Geschichte kommt mir komisch vor, he seems shy er scheint schüchtern zu sein, the museum seems to be closed das Museum scheint geschlossen zu sein ❷ it seems (that) ... anscheinend ..., it seems he's left anscheinend ist er weggegangen, it seems that there are problems anscheinend gibt es Probleme

**seesaw** *NOUN* Wippe die *(PLURAL die Wippen)*

**select** *VERB* auswählen *(SEP)*

**self-confidence** *NOUN* Selbstbewusstsein das; she doesn't have much self-confidence sie hat sehr wenig Selbstbewusstsein

**self-employed** *ADJECTIVE* to be self-employed selbstständig sein, my parents are self-employed meine Eltern sind selbstständig

**selfish** *ADJECTIVE* egoistisch

**self-service** *ADJECTIVE* a self-service restaurant ein Selbstbedienungsrestaurant

**sell** *VERB* ❶ verkaufen; to sell something to somebody jemandem etwas verkaufen, I sold him my bike ich habe ihm mein Rad verkauft, the house sold for a million das Haus wurde für eine Million verkauft ❷ the concert's sold out das Konzert ist ausverkauft, the tickets sold out very quickly die Karten waren schnell ausverkauft

**sell-by date** *NOUN* Verfallsdatum das *(PLURAL die Verfallsdaten)*

**Sellotape** *NOUN* Tesafilm der

**sellotape** *VERB* to sellotape something etwas mit Tesafilm kleben

**semi** *NOUN* Doppelhaushälfte die *(PLURAL die Doppelhaushälften)*

**semicircle** *NOUN* Halbkreis der *(PLURAL die Halbkreise)*

**semicolon** *NOUN* Strichpunkt der *(PLURAL die Strichpunkte)*

**semi-detached house** *NOUN* Doppelhaushälfte die *(PLURAL die Doppelhaushälften)*

**semi-final** *NOUN* Halbfinale das (*PLURAL* die **Halbfinale**)

**send** *VERB* schicken; to send something to somebody jemandem etwas schicken, I sent her a present for her birthday ich habe ihr zum Geburtstag ein Geschenk geschickt
- to send somebody back jemanden zurückschicken (*SEP*)
- to send something back etwas zurückschicken (*SEP*)

**sender** *NOUN* Absender der (*PLURAL* die **Absender**)

**senior citizen** *NOUN* Senior der (*PLURAL* die **Senioren**), Seniorin die (*PLURAL* die **Seniorinnen**)

**sensation** *NOUN* ❶ (*feeling*) Gefühl das ❷ (*impact*) Sensation die (*PLURAL* die **Sensationen**); she caused a sensation sie erregte viel Aufsehen

**sensational** *ADJECTIVE* sensationell

**sense** *NOUN* ❶ (*common sense*) Verstand der ❷ (*faculty*) Sinn der (*PLURAL* die **Sinne**); sense of smell der Geruchssinn, sense of touch der Tastsinn, to have a sense of humour Humor haben, she has no sense of humour sie hat keinen Sinn für Humor ❸ (*meaning*) Sinn der; this sentence makes no sense dieser Satz ergibt keinen Sinn, it doesn't make sense to do that es ist Unsinn, das zu machen, it makes sense to collect her first es ist sinnvoll, sie erst abzuholen

**sensible** *ADJECTIVE* vernünftig; be sensible sei vernünftig, that's a sensible suggestion das ist ein vernünftiger Vorschlag

**sensitive** *ADJECTIVE* empfindlich; for sensitive skin für empfindliche Haut

**sentence** *NOUN* ❶ (*words*) Satz der (*PLURAL* die **Sätze**) ❷ (*prison*) Strafe die (*PLURAL* die **Strafen**); the death sentence die Todesstrafe

**sentence** *VERB* verurteilen; to be sentenced to death zum Tode verurteilt werden, to sentence somebody to a year in prison jemanden zu einem Jahr Gefängnis verurteilen

**sentimental** *ADJECTIVE* sentimental

**separate** *ADJECTIVE* ❶ extra (*'extra' never has an ending*); a separate pile ein extra Stapel, she wrote it on a separate sheet of paper sie hat es auf ein anderes Blatt Papier geschrieben, the drinks are separate die Getränke gehen extra ❷ (*different*) verschieden; two separate problems zwei verschiedene Probleme ❸ they have separate rooms sie haben getrennte Zimmer

**separate** *VERB* ❶ trennen ❷ (*a couple*) sich trennen

**separately** *ADVERB* ❶ extra ❷ getrennt; they live separately sie leben getrennt

**separation** *NOUN* Trennung die (*PLURAL* die **Trennungen**)

**September** *NOUN* September der; in September im September

**sequel** *NOUN* Folge die (*PLURAL* die **Folgen**)

**sequence** *NOUN* ❶ (*series*) Reihe die (*PLURAL* die **Reihen**); a sequence of events eine Reihe von Ereignissen, in sequence in der richtigen Reihenfolge ❷ (*in a film*) Sequenz die (*PLURAL* die **Sequenzen**)

A
B
C
D
E
F
G
H
I
J
K
L
M
N
O
P
Q
R
S
T
U
V
W
X
Y
Z

**sergeant** NOUN ❶ (in the police) **Polizeimeister** der (PLURAL die **Polizeimeister**), **Polizeimeisterin** die (PLURAL die **Polizeimeisterinnen**) ❷ (in the army) **Feldwebel** der (PLURAL die **Feldwebel**)

**serial** NOUN
❶ **Fortsetzungsgeschichte** die (PLURAL die **Fortsetzungsgeschichten**) ❷ (on TV or radio) **Serie** die (PLURAL die **Serien**)

**series** NOUN **Serie** die (PLURAL die **Serien**); **television series** die **Fernsehserie**

**serious** ADJECTIVE ❶ **ernst**; a **serious discussion** eine ernste Unterhaltung, **to be serious about something** etwas ernst nehmen, **are you serious?** ist das dein Ernst? ❷ **schwer** (accident or mistake)

**seriously** ADVERB ❶ **im Ernst**; **seriously, I have to go now** im Ernst, ich muss jetzt gehen, **seriously?** im Ernst? ❷ **to take somebody seriously** jemanden ernst nehmen ❸ (gravely) **schwer**; **she is seriously ill** sie ist schwer krank

**servant** NOUN **Bedienstete** der/die (PLURAL die **Bediensteten**)

**serve** NOUN (in tennis) **Aufschlag** der (PLURAL die **Aufschläge**); **it's my serve** ich habe Aufschlag

**serve** VERB ❶ (in tennis) **aufschlagen**◇ (SEP); **Becker is serving** Becker schlägt auf ❷ **servieren**; **can you serve the vegetables, please?** können Sie bitte das Gemüse servieren?
• **it serves him right** das geschieht ihm recht

**service** NOUN ❶ (in a restaurant, shop, etc.) **Bedienung** die; **service is included** inklusive Bedienung ❷ (from a company or firm to a customer) **Service** der ❸ **the emergency services** der Notdienst ❹ (church service) **Gottesdienst** der (PLURAL die **Gottesdienste**) ❺ (of a car or machine) **Wartung** die (PLURAL die **Wartungen**)

**service area** NOUN **Raststätte** die (PLURAL die **Raststätten**)

**service charge** NOUN **Bedienung** die; **there is no service charge** die Bedienung wird nicht extra berechnet

**service station** NOUN **Tankstelle** die (PLURAL die **Tankstellen**)

**serviette** NOUN **Serviette** die (PLURAL die **Servietten**)

**session** NOUN **Sitzung** die (PLURAL die **Sitzungen**)

**set** NOUN ❶ (for playing a game) **Spiel** das (PLURAL die **Spiele**); **chess set** das Schachspiel ❷ **train set** die Spielzeugeisenbahn ❸ (in tennis) **Satz** der (PLURAL die **Sätze**)

**set** ADJECTIVE ❶ **fest** (hours, habits); a **set date** ein festes Datum, **at a set time** zu einer festgesetzten Zeit ❷ **set menu** das Menü

**set** VERB ❶ **festlegen** (SEP) (a date, time) ❷ **aufstellen** (SEP) (a record) ❸ **to set the table** den Tisch decken, **to set an alarm clock** einen Wecker stellen, **I've set my alarm for seven** ich habe meinen Wecker auf sieben gestellt ❹ **to set your watch** seine Uhr richtig stellen ❺ (sun) **untergehen**◇ (SEP)
• **to set off** aufbrechen◇ (SEP) (PERF

sein); we're setting off at ten wir brechen um zehn auf, they set off for Vienna yesterday sie sind gestern nach Wien aufgebrochen
- to set off something ❶ etwas auslösen *(SEP) (an alarm, reaction)* ❷ etwas abbrennen◇ *(SEP) (a firework)* ❸ etwas explodieren lassen *(a bomb)*
- to set out aufbrechen◇ *(SEP) (PERF sein)*; they set out for Hamburg at ten sie sind um zehn nach Hamburg aufgebrochen

**settee** *NOUN* Sofa das *(PLURAL die Sofas)*

**settle** *VERB* ❶ bezahlen *(a bill)* ❷ lösen *(a problem)* ❸ beilegen *(SEP) (an argument)*

**seven** *NUMBER* sieben; Rosie's seven Rosie ist sieben

**seventeen** *NUMBER* siebzehn; I'm seventeen ich bin siebzehn

**seventh** *ADJECTIVE* siebter/siebte/siebtes; on the seventh floor im siebten Stock, the seventh of July der siebte Juli

**seventies** *PLURAL NOUN* the seventies die Siebzigerjahre, in the seventies in den Siebzigerjahren

**seventieth** *ADJECTIVE* siebzigster/siebzigste/siebzigstes; it's her seventieth birthday es ist ihr siebzigster Geburtstag

**seventy** *NUMBER* siebzig; my granny's seventy meine Oma ist siebzig

**several** *ADJECTIVE, PRONOUN* ❶ mehrere; I've read several of her novels ich habe mehrere ihrer Romane gelesen ❷ I've seen her several times ich habe sie mehrmals gesehen

**sew** *VERB* nähen

**sewing** *NOUN* Nähen das; I like sewing ich nähe gern

**sewing machine** *NOUN* Nähmaschine die *(PLURAL die Nähmaschinen)*

**sex** *NOUN* ❶ *(gender)* Geschlecht das *(PLURAL die Geschlechter)* ❷ *(intercourse)* Sex der; to have sex with someone mit jemandem Sex haben

**sex education** *NOUN* Aufklärungsunterricht der

**sexism** *NOUN* Sexismus der

**sexist** *ADJECTIVE* sexistisch; sexist remarks sexistische Bemerkungen

**sexual** *ADJECTIVE* sexuell

**sexual harassment** *NOUN* sexuelle Belästigung die

**sexuality** *NOUN* Sexualität die

**sexy** *ADJECTIVE* sexy

**shabby** *ADJECTIVE* schäbig

**shade** *NOUN* ❶ Ton der *(PLURAL die Töne)*; a shade of green ein Grünton ❷ Schatten der; in the shade im Schatten

**shadow** *NOUN* Schatten der *(PLURAL die Schatten)*

**shake** *VERB* ❶ *(tremble)* zittern; I was shaking with fear ich zitterte vor Angst ❷ to shake something etwas schütteln, to shake your head *(meaning no)* den Kopf schütteln ❸ to shake hands with somebody jemandem die Hand geben◇, she shook hands with me sie hat mir die Hand gegeben, we shook hands wir gaben uns die Hand

A B C D E F G H I J K L M N O P Q R S T U V W X Y Z

**shaken** ADJECTIVE erschüttert; **I was shaken by the news** die Nachricht hat mich erschüttert

**shall** VERB **shall I come with you?** soll ich mitkommen?, **shall we stop now?** sollen wir jetzt aufhören?

**shallow** ADJECTIVE flach; **stay in the shallow end of the pool** bleib am flachen Ende des Beckens

**shambles** NOUN Chaos das; **it was a total shambles!** es war ein völliges Chaos!

**shame** NOUN ❶ Schande die; **the shame of it!** was für eine Schande! ❷ **what a shame!** wie schade!, **it's a shame she can't come** schade, dass sie nicht kommen kann

**shampoo** NOUN Shampoo das (PLURAL die Shampoos); **I bought some shampoo** ich habe Shampoo gekauft

**shamrock** NOUN Klee der

**shandy** NOUN Radler der (PLURAL die Radler) (South German), Alsterwasser das (PLURAL die Alsterwasser) (North German)

**shape** NOUN Form die (PLURAL die Formen)

**share** NOUN ❶ Anteil der (PLURAL die Anteile); **your share of the money** dein Anteil am Geld, **he paid his share** er hat seinen Anteil gezahlt ❷ (in a company) Aktie die (PLURAL die Aktien)

**share** VERB teilen; **I'm sharing a room with Lucy** ich teile ein Zimmer mit Lucy

**shark** NOUN Hai der (PLURAL die Haie), Haifisch der (PLURAL die Haifische)

**sharp** ADJECTIVE ❶ (knife) scharf; **this knife isn't very sharp** dieses Messer ist nicht sehr scharf ❷ (pointed) spitz; **a sharp pencil** ein spitzer Bleistift ❸ **a sharp bend** eine scharfe Kurve ❹ (clever) clever

**shave** VERB ❶ (have a shave) sich rasieren ❷ **to shave your legs** sich (DAT) die Beine rasieren ❸ **to shave off your beard** den Bart abrasieren (SEP)

**shaver** NOUN Rasierapparat der (PLURAL die Rasierapparate); **electric shaver** der Elektrorasierer

**shaving cream** NOUN Rasiercreme die (PLURAL die Rasiercremes)

**shaving foam** NOUN Rasierschaum der

**she** PRONOUN sie; **she's a student** sie ist Studentin, **she's a very good teacher** sie ist eine sehr gute Lehrerin

**shed** NOUN Schuppen der (PLURAL die Schuppen)

**sheep** NOUN Schaf das (PLURAL die Schafe)

**sheepdog** NOUN Schäferhund der (PLURAL die Schäferhunde)

**sheer** ADJECTIVE rein; **it's sheer stupidity** das ist reine Dummheit

**sheet** NOUN ❶ (for a bed) Laken das (PLURAL die Laken) ❷ **a sheet of paper** ein Blatt Papier, **a blank sheet** ein leeres Blatt ❸ (of glass or metal) Platte die (PLURAL die Platten)
• **to be as white as a sheet** leichenblass sein

**shelf** NOUN ❶ (in the home or a shop) Regal das (PLURAL die Regale); **a set of shelves** ein Regal ❷ (in an oven) Schiene die (PLURAL die Schienen)

**shell** NOUN ❶ (of an egg or a nut) **Schale** die (PLURAL die **Schalen**) ❷ (seashell) **Muschel** die (PLURAL die **Muscheln**)

**shellfish** NOUN ❶ **Schalentier** das (PLURAL die **Schalentiere**) ❷ (in cookery) **Meeresfrüchte** (plural)

**shelter** NOUN **Schutz** der; **in the shelter of** im Schutz (+GEN), **to take shelter from the rain** sich unterstellen (SEP)

**shepherd** NOUN **Schäfer** der (PLURAL die **Schäfer**)

**sherry** NOUN **Sherry** der (PLURAL die **Sherrys**)

**Shetland Islands** NOUN **Shetlandinseln** (plural)

**shield** NOUN **Schild** der (PLURAL die **Schilde**)

**shift** NOUN **Schicht** die (PLURAL die **Schichten**); **the night shift** die Nachtschicht, **to be on night shift** Nachtschicht haben

**shift** VERB **to shift something** etwas verrücken

**shifty** ADJECTIVE **verschlagen**; **he looks shifty** er sieht verschlagen aus, **a shifty-looking guy** ein verschlagener Typ

**shin** NOUN **Schienbein** das (PLURAL die **Schienbeine**)

**shine** VERB **scheinen**◇; **the sun is shining** die Sonne scheint

**shiny** ADJECTIVE **glänzend**

**ship** NOUN **Schiff** das (PLURAL die **Schiffe**)

**shipyard** NOUN **Werft** die (PLURAL die **Werften**)

**shirt** NOUN ❶ (man's) **Hemd** das (PLURAL die **Hemden**) ❷ (woman's) **Bluse** die (PLURAL die **Blusen**)

**shiver** VERB **zittern**

**shock** NOUN ❶ **Schock** der (PLURAL die **Schocks**); **to get a shock** einen Schock bekommen, **it gave me a shock** das hat mir einen Schock versetzt ❷ **electric shock** der elektrische Schlag

**shock** VERB (upset) **erschüttern** (cause scandal) **schockieren**

**shocked** ADJECTIVE **schockiert**

**shocking** ADJECTIVE **schockierend**

**shoe** NOUN **Schuh** der (PLURAL die **Schuhe**); **a pair of shoes** ein Paar Schuhe

**shoelace** NOUN **Schnürsenkel** der (PLURAL die **Schnürsenkel**)

**shoe polish** NOUN **Schuhcreme** die (PLURAL die **Schuhcremes**)

**shoe shop** NOUN **Schuhgeschäft** das (PLURAL die **Schuhgeschäfte**)

**shoot** VERB ❶ (fire) **schießen**◇; **to shoot at somebody** auf jemanden schießen, **she shot him in the leg** sie hat ihm ins Bein geschossen, **he was shot in the arm** er wurde am Arm getroffen ❷ (kill, execute) **erschießen**◇; **he was shot by terrorists** er wurde von Terroristen erschossen ❸ (in football, hockey) **schießen**◇ ❹ **to shoot a film** einen Film drehen

**shop** NOUN **Geschäft** das (PLURAL die **Geschäfte**) **Laden** der (PLURAL die **Läden**); **shoe shop** das Schuhgeschäft, **to go round the shops** einen Einkaufsbummel machen

**shop assistant** *NOUN* Verkäufer der
*(PLURAL* die **Verkäufer)**, Verkäuferin
die *(PLURAL* die **Verkäuferinnen)**

**shopkeeper** *NOUN* Ladenbesitzer
der *(PLURAL* die **Ladenbesitzer)**,
**Ladenbesitzerin** die *(PLURAL* die
**Ladenbesitzerinnen)**

**shoplifter** *NOUN* Ladendieb
der *(PLURAL* die **Ladendiebe)**,
**Ladendiebin** die *(PLURAL* die
**Ladendiebinnen)**

**shoplifting** *NOUN* Ladendiebstahl der

**shopping** *NOUN* ❶ Einkäufe *(plural)*;
**can you put the shopping away?**
kannst du die Einkäufe wegräumen?
❷ *(activity)* Einkaufen das;
**shopping is fun** Einkaufen macht
Spaß, **to go shopping** einkaufen
gehen◇

**shopping trolley** *NOUN*
Einkaufswagen der *(PLURAL* die
**Einkaufswagen)**

**shop window** *NOUN* Schaufenster
das *(PLURAL* die **Schaufenster)**

**short** *ADJECTIVE* ❶ kurz; **a short dress**
ein kurzes Kleid, **she has short hair**
sie hat kurze Haare ❷ **a short break**
eine kurze Pause, **to go for a short
walk** einen kurzen Spaziergang
machen, **it's a short walk from the
bus stop** es ist nicht weit zu Fuß von
der Bushaltestelle ❸ **to be short of
something** knapp mit etwas *(DAT)*
sein, **we're a bit short of money at
the moment** wir sind im Moment
etwas knapp bei Kasse, **we're
getting short of time** die Zeit wird
uns knapp

**shortage** *NOUN* Mangel der

**shortbread** *NOUN* Buttergebäck
das

**shortcrust pastry** *NOUN*
Mürbeteig der

**short cut** *NOUN* Abkürzung die
*(PLURAL* die **Abkürzungen)**

**shortly** *ADVERB* gleich; **shortly before
I left** kurz bevor ich ging, **shortly
after** kurz danach

**shorts** *PLURAL NOUN* Shorts *(plural)*; **a
pair of shorts** ein Paar Shorts, **my
red shorts** meine roten Shorts

**short-sighted** *ADJECTIVE* kurzsichtig;
**I'm short-sighted** ich bin kurzsichtig

**shot** *NOUN* ❶ *(from a gun)* Schuss
der *(PLURAL* die **Schüsse)** ❷ *(a
photo)* Aufnahme die *(PLURAL* die
**Aufnahmen)**

**should** *VERB* ❶ sollen◇ *('should' is
usually translated by the imperfect
subjunctive of 'sollen')*; **you should
ask Simon** du solltest Simon fragen,
**the potatoes should be ready now**
die Kartoffeln sollten jetzt fertig
sein ❷ *('should have' is translated by
'hätte sollen')* **you should have told
me** du hättest es mir sagen sollen,
**I shouldn't have stayed** ich hätte
nicht bleiben sollen, **you shouldn't
have said that** das hättest du nicht
sagen sollen ❸ *('should' meaning
'would' is translated by 'würde')* **I
should forget it if I were you** an
deiner Stelle würde ich es vergessen
❹ **I should think** ich würde sagen,
**I should think he's forgotten** ich
würde sagen, er hat's vergessen
❺ **this should be enough** das
müsste eigentlich reichen

**shoulder** *NOUN* Schulter die *(PLURAL*
die **Schultern)**

**shoulder bag** NOUN Umhängetasche die (PLURAL die Umhängetaschen)

**shout** NOUN Schrei der (PLURAL die Schreie)

**shout** VERB ❶ schreien◇; stop shouting! hör auf zu schreien! ❷ (call) rufen◇; he shouted at us to come back er rief uns zu, wir sollten zurückkommen

**shovel** NOUN Schaufel die (PLURAL die Schaufeln)

**show** NOUN ❶ (on stage) Show die (PLURAL die Shows); we went to see a show wir haben eine Show gesehen ❷ (on TV, radio) Sendung die (PLURAL die Sendungen) ❸ (exhibition) Ausstellung die (PLURAL die Ausstellungen); fashion show die Modenschau

**show** VERB ❶ zeigen; to show something to somebody jemandem etwas zeigen, I'll show you my photos ich zeige dir meine Fotos, to show somebody how something works jemandem zeigen, wie etwas funktioniert, he showed me how to make pancakes er hat mir gezeigt, wie man Pfannkuchen macht ❷ it shows! das sieht man!
• to show off angeben◇ (SEP)

**shower** NOUN ❶ (in a bathroom) Dusche die (PLURAL die Duschen); to have a shower duschen ❷ (of rain) Schauer der (PLURAL die Schauer)

**show-jumping** NOUN Springreiten das

**show-off** NOUN Angeber der (PLURAL die Angeber), Angeberin die (PLURAL die Angeberinnen)

**shriek** VERB kreischen

**shrimp** NOUN Krabbe die (PLURAL die Krabben)

**shrink** VERB ❶ schrumpfen (PERF sein) ❷ (clothes) einlaufen◇ (SEP) (PERF sein); my sweater has shrunk mein Pullover ist eingelaufen

**Shrove Tuesday** NOUN Fastnachtsdienstag der

**shrug** VERB to shrug your shoulders mit den Achseln zucken

**shuffle** VERB to shuffle the cards die Karten mischen

**shut** ADJECTIVE zu; the shops are shut die Geschäfte haben zu

**shut** VERB zumachen (SEP); can you shut the door please? kannst du die Tür bitte zumachen?, the shops shut at six die Geschäfte machen um sechs zu
• to shut up den Mund halten◇ (informal); shut up! halt den Mund!

**shuttlecock** NOUN Federball der (PLURAL die Federbälle)

**shuttle service** NOUN Pendelverkehr der; there's a shuttle service from the airport es gibt einen Shuttledienst vom Flughafen

**shy** ADJECTIVE schüchtern

**shyness** NOUN Schüchternheit die

**Sicily** NOUN Sizilien das

**sick** ADJECTIVE ❶ (ill) krank ❷ to be sick (vomit) sich übergeben◇, I was sick several times ich habe mich mehrmals übergeben ❸ I feel sick mir ist schlecht ❹ übel; a sick joke ein übler Witz ❺ to be sick of something etwas satt haben, I'm sick of staying at home every day ich habe es satt, jeden Tag zu Hause zu sitzen

**sickness** NOUN Krankheit die (PLURAL die Krankheiten)

**side** NOUN ❶ Seite die (PLURAL die Seiten); **on the other side of the street** auf der anderen Straßenseite, **on the wrong side** auf der falschen Seite, **I'm on your side** (I agree with you) ich bin auf deiner Seite ❷ (edge) Rand der (PLURAL die Ränder) (of a pool, river); **at the side of the road** am Straßenrand ❸ (team) Mannschaft die (PLURAL die Mannschaften); **the winning side** die siegreiche Mannschaft, **she plays on our side** sie spielt bei uns mit ❹ **to take sides** Partei ergreifen◇, **he always takes sides against her** er ergreift immer gegen sie Partei ❺ **side by side** nebeneinander

**sideboard** NOUN Anrichte die (PLURAL die Anrichten)

**sideburns** NOUN Koteletten (plural)

**side-effect** NOUN Nebenwirkung die (PLURAL die Nebenwirkungen)

**side street** NOUN Seitenstraße die (PLURAL die Seitenstraßen)

**sieve** NOUN Sieb das (PLURAL die Siebe)

**sigh** NOUN Seufzer der (PLURAL die Seufzer)

**sigh** VERB seufzen

**sight** NOUN ❶ Anblick der; **it was a marvellous sight** es war ein herrlicher Anblick ❷ **at first sight** auf den ersten Blick ❸ (eyesight) **to have poor sight** schlechte Augen haben, **to know somebody by sight** jemanden vom Sehen kennen, **out of sight** außer Sicht

**to lose sight of somebody** jemanden aus den Augen verlieren ❹ **the sights** die Sehenswürdigkeiten, **to see the sights** die Sehenswürdigkeiten besichtigen

**sightseeing** NOUN Sightseeing das; **to do some sightseeing** einige Sehenswürdigkeiten besichtigen

**sign** NOUN ❶ (notice) Schild das (PLURAL die Schilder); **there's a sign on the door** da ist ein Schild an der Tür ❷ (trace, indication) Zeichen das (PLURAL die Zeichen) ❸ (of the zodiac) Sternzeichen das (PLURAL die Sternzeichen); **what sign are you?** was für ein Sternzeichen bist du?

**sign** VERB ❶ unterschreiben◇; **to sign a cheque** einen Scheck unterschreiben ❷ (using sign language) sich durch Zeichensprache verständigen
• **to sign on** sich arbeitslos melden

**signal** NOUN Signal das (PLURAL die Signale)

**signature** NOUN Unterschrift die (PLURAL die Unterschriften)

**significant** ADJECTIVE bedeutend

**sign language** NOUN Zeichensprache die (PLURAL die Zeichensprachen)

**signpost** NOUN Wegweiser der (PLURAL die Wegweiser)

**silence** NOUN Stille die

**silent** ADJECTIVE still

**silk** NOUN Seide die

**silk** ADJECTIVE Seiden-; **a silk blouse** eine Seidenbluse

**silky** ADJECTIVE seidig

**silly** ADJECTIVE **dumm**; **it was a really silly thing to do** das war wirklich dumm

**silver** NOUN **Silber** das

**silver** ADJECTIVE **Silber-**; **a silver medal** eine Silbermedaille

**similar** ADJECTIVE **ähnlich**; **it looks similar to my old bike** es sieht so ähnlich wie mein altes Rad aus

**similarity** NOUN **Ähnlichkeit** die (PLURAL die **Ähnlichkeiten**)

**simple** ADJECTIVE **einfach**

**simply** ADVERB **einfach**

**sin** NOUN **Sünde** die (PLURAL die **Sünden**)

**since** PREPOSITION **❶ seit** (+DAT), (notice that German uses the present tense for an action starting in the past and still going on in the present); **I have been in Berlin since Saturday** ich bin seit Samstag in Berlin, **since when?** seit wann? **❷** (with a negative the perfect tense is used) **I haven't seen her since Monday** ich habe sie seit Montag nicht gesehen

**since** CONJUNCTION **❶ seit**; **since I have known him** seit ich ihn kenne, **since I've been learning German** seitdem ich Deutsch lerne **❷** (because) **da**; **since it was raining, the match was cancelled** da es regnete, wurde das Spiel abgesagt

**since** ADVERB **seitdem**; **I haven't seen him since** ich habe ihn seitdem nicht mehr gesehen

**sincere** ADJECTIVE **aufrichtig**

**sincerely** ADVERB **Yours sincerely** Mit freundlichen Grüßen

**sing** VERB **singen**◊

**singer** NOUN **Sänger** der (PLURAL die **Sänger**) **Sängerin** die (PLURAL die **Sängerinnen**)

**singing** NOUN **❶ Singen** das; **a singing lesson** eine Singstunde **❷ I like singing** ich singe gern

**single** NOUN **❶** (ticket) **einfache Fahrkarte** die (PLURAL die **einfachen Fahrkarten**); **a single to Munich, please** eine einfache Fahrkarte nach München bitte **❷** (record) **Single** die (PLURAL die **Singles**)

**single** ADJECTIVE **❶** (not married) **allein stehend**; **a single woman** eine allein stehende Frau, (on forms) **ledig ❷** (just one) **einzig**; **I haven't had a single reply** ich habe keine einzige Antwort bekommen **❸ not a single one** kein Einziger/keine Einzige/kein Einziges **❹ single room** das Einzelzimmer, **single bed** das Einzelbett

**single parent** NOUN **allein Erziehende** der/die (PLURAL die **allein Erziehenden**); **she's a single parent** sie ist allein erziehende Mutter, **a single-parent family** eine Einelternfamilie

**singles** PLURAL NOUN (in tennis) **Einzel** das (PLURAL die **Einzel**); **the women's singles** das Dameneinzel, **the men's singles** das Herreneinzel

**singular** NOUN **Einzahl** die; **in the singular** in der Einzahl

**sink** NOUN **Spülbecken** das (PLURAL die **Spülbecken**)

**sink** VERB **sinken**◊ (PERF **sein**)

**sir** NOUN **Herr** der (PLURAL die **Herren**); (in German,' Sir' is usually not

A
B
C
D
E
F
G
H
I
J
K
L
M
N
O
P
Q
R
S
T
U
V
W
X
Y
Z

*translated)* **would you like another one, sir?** möchten Sie noch eins?, **yes, sir** ja, mein Herr

**sister** NOUN **Schwester** die *(PLURAL* die **Schwestern)**; **my sister's ten** meine Schwester ist zehn

**sister-in-law** NOUN **Schwägerin** die *(PLURAL* die **Schwägerinnen)**

**sit** VERB ❶ *(to sit down)* **sich setzen**; **you can sit on the sofa** ihr könnt euch aufs Sofa setzen, **sit on the floor** setz dich auf den Boden ❷ *(to be sitting)* **sitzen**◇; **Leila was sitting on the sofa** Leila saß auf dem Sofa, **to sit on the floor** auf dem Boden sitzen ❸ **to sit an exam** eine Prüfung machen
• **to sit down** sich setzen; **he sat down on the chair** er setzte sich auf den Stuhl, **do sit down** setzen Sie sich

**sitcom** NOUN **Situationskomödie** die *(PLURAL* die **Situationskomödien)**

**site** NOUN ❶ **building site** die Baustelle ❷ **camping site** der Campingplatz ❸ **archaeological site** die archäologische Stätte

**sitting room** NOUN **Wohnzimmer** das *(PLURAL* die **Wohnzimmer)**

**situated** ADJECTIVE **to be situated** sich befinden◇, **the house is situated in a small village** das Haus befindet sich in einem kleinen Dorf

**situation** NOUN ❶ *(location)* **Lage** die *(PLURAL* die **Lagen)** ❷ *(circumstances)* **Situation** die *(PLURAL* die **Situationen)**

**six** NUMBER **sechs**; **Harry's six** Harry ist sechs

**sixteen** NUMBER **sechzehn**; **Alice is sixteen** Alice ist sechzehn

**sixth** ADJECTIVE **sechster/sechste/ sechstes**; **on the sixth floor** im sechsten Stock, **on the sixth of July** am sechsten Juli

**sixty** NUMBER **sechzig**; **she's sixty** sie ist sechzig

**size** NOUN ❶ **Größe** die *(PLURAL* die **Größen)**; **it depends on the size of the house** es kommt auf die Größe des Hauses an ❷ **what size is the window?** wie groß ist das Fenster? ❸ *(in clothes)* **Größe** die *(PLURAL* die **Größen)**; **what size do you take?** welche Größe haben Sie? ❹ *(of shoes)* **Schuhgröße** die *(PLURAL* die **Schuhgrößen)**; **I take a size thirty-eight** ich habe Schuhgröße achtunddreißig

**skate** NOUN ❶ *(an ice skate)* **Schlittschuh** der *(PLURAL* die **Schlittschuhe)** ❷ *(a roller skate)* **Rollschuh** der *(PLURAL* die **Rollschuhe)**

**skate** VERB ❶ *(ice-skate)* **Schlittschuh laufen**◇ *(PERF* **sein)** ❷ *(roller-skate)* **Rollschuh laufen**◇ *(PERF* **sein)**

**skateboard** NOUN **Skateboard** das *(PLURAL* die **Skateboards)**

**skateboarding** NOUN **Skateboardfahren** das; **to go skateboarding** Skateboard fahren◇ *(PERF* **sein)**

**skater** NOUN ❶ *(on rollerskates)* **Rollschuhfahrer** der *(PLURAL* die **Rollschuhfahrer)**, **Rollschuhfahrerin** die *(PLURAL* die **Rollschuhfahrerinnen)** ❷ *(on ice)* **Eisläufer** der *(PLURAL* die **Eisläufer)**, **Eisläuferin** die *(PLURAL* die **Eisläuferinnen)** ❸ *(on a skateboard)* **Skater** der *(PLURAL* die **Skater)**

**skating** NOUN ❶ (on ice) Schlittschuhlaufen das; to go skating Schlittschuh laufen◇ (PERF sein) ❷ (roller-skating) Rollschuhlaufen das; to go roller-skating Rollschuh laufen◇ (PERF sein)

**skating rink** NOUN ❶ (ice rink) Eisbahn die (PLURAL die Eisbahnen) ❷ (for roller-skating) Rollschuhbahn die (PLURAL die Rollschuhbahnen)

**skeleton** NOUN Skelett das (PLURAL die Skelette)

**sketch** NOUN ❶ Skizze die (PLURAL die Skizzen) ❷ (comedy routine) Sketch der (PLURAL die Sketche)

**ski** NOUN Ski der (PLURAL die Skier)

**ski** VERB Ski fahren◇ (PERF sein); he can ski er kann Ski fahren

**ski boot** NOUN Skistiefel der (PLURAL die Skistiefel)

**skid** VERB schleudern (PERF sein); the car skidded das Auto kam ins Schleudern

**skier** NOUN Skifahrer der (PLURAL die Skifahrer), Skifahrerin die (PLURAL die Skifahrerinnen)

**skiing** NOUN Skifahren das; to go skiing Ski fahren◇ (PERF sein)

**ski lift** NOUN Skilift der (PLURAL die Skilifte)

**skimmed milk** NOUN fettarme Milch die

**skin** NOUN Haut die (PLURAL die Häute)

**skinhead** NOUN Skinhead der (PLURAL die Skinheads)

**skinny** ADJECTIVE dünn

**skip** NOUN (for rubbish) Container der (PLURAL die Container)

**skip** VERB ❶ auslassen◇ (SEP) (a meal, part of a book); I skipped a few chapters ich ließ ein paar Kapitel aus ❷ to skip a lesson eine Stunde schwänzen (informal)

**skirt** NOUN Rock der (PLURAL die Röcke); a long skirt ein langer Rock, a tight skirt ein enger Rock, a miniskirt ein Minirock

**ski suit** NOUN Skianzug der (PLURAL die Skianzüge)

**skittles** PLURAL NOUN Kegeln das

**skull** NOUN Schädel der (PLURAL die Schädel)

**sky** NOUN Himmel der (PLURAL die Himmel)

**skyscraper** NOUN Wolkenkratzer der (PLURAL die Wolkenkratzer)

**slam** VERB zuknallen (SEP); she slammed the door sie hat die Tür zugeknallt, the door slammed die Tür ist zugeknallt

**slang** NOUN Slang der (PLURAL die Slangs)

**slap** NOUN Klaps der (PLURAL die Klapse), (in the face) Ohrfeige die (PLURAL die Ohrfeigen)

**slap** VERB to slap somebody (across the face) jemanden ohrfeigen, (on the bottom) jemandem einen Klaps geben

**sledge** NOUN Schlitten der (PLURAL die Schlitten)

**sledging** NOUN to go sledging Schlitten fahren◇ (PERF sein)

**sleep** NOUN Schlaf der; **you need more sleep** du brauchst mehr Schlaf, **I had a good sleep** ich habe gut geschlafen, **to go to sleep** einschlafen◇ (SEP) (PERF sein), **he's gone back to sleep** er ist wieder eingeschlafen

**sleep** VERB schlafen◇; **she's sleeping** sie schläft

**sleeping bag** NOUN Schlafsack der (PLURAL die Schlafsäcke)

**sleeping pill** NOUN Schlaftablette die (PLURAL die Schlaftabletten)

**sleepy** ADJECTIVE **to be sleepy** schläfrig sein, **he was getting sleepy** er wurde schläfrig

**sleet** NOUN Schneeregen der

**sleeve** NOUN Ärmel der (PLURAL die Ärmel); **a long-sleeved jumper** ein Pullover mit langen Ärmeln, **a short-sleeved shirt** ein Hemd mit kurzen Ärmeln, **to roll up your sleeves** die Ärmel hochkrempeln

**slice** NOUN Scheibe die (PLURAL die Scheiben); **a slice of bread** eine Scheibe Brot

**slice** VERB **to slice something** etwas in Scheiben schneiden◇

**slide** NOUN ❶ (photo) Dia das (PLURAL die Dias) ❷ (hairslide) Haarspange die (PLURAL die Haarspangen) ❸ (for sliding down) Rutschbahn die (PLURAL die Rutschbahnen)

**slight** ADJECTIVE klein; **there is a slight problem** es gibt ein kleines Problem

**slightly** ADVERB etwas

**slim** ADJECTIVE schlank

**slim** VERB abnehmen◇ (SEP); **I'm slimming** ich mache eine Schlankheitskur

**sling** NOUN Schlinge die (PLURAL die Schlingen); **to have your arm in a sling** den Arm in der Schlinge haben

**slip** NOUN ❶ (mistake) Fehler der (PLURAL die Fehler) ❷ (petticoat) Unterrock der (PLURAL die Unterröcke)

**slip** VERB ❶ (slide) ausrutschen (SEP) (PERF sein) ❷ **it slipped my mind** es ist mir entfallen
• **to slip up** einen Fehler machen

**slipper** NOUN Hausschuh der (PLURAL die Hausschuhe)

**slippery** ADJECTIVE glatt

**slope** NOUN Hang der (PLURAL die Hänge)

**slot** NOUN Schlitz der (PLURAL die Schlitze)

**slot machine** NOUN ❶ (vending machine) Automat der (PLURAL die Automaten) ❷ (games machine) Spielautomat der (PLURAL die Spielautomaten)

**slow** ADJECTIVE ❶ langsam; **the service is a bit slow** die Bedienung ist etwas langsam ❷ (of a clock or watch) **to be slow** nachgehen◇ (SEP) (PERF sein), **my watch is slow** meine Uhr geht nach
• **to slow down** langsamer werden

**slowly** ADVERB langsam; **he got up slowly** er ist langsam aufgestanden, **can you speak more slowly, please?** können Sie bitte etwas langsamer sprechen?

**slug** NOUN Nacktschnecke die (PLURAL die Nacktschnecken)

**sly** ADJECTIVE **gerissen** (a person)
• **on the sly** heimlich

**smack** NOUN **Klaps** der (PLURAL die **Klapse**)

**smack** VERB **to smack somebody** jemandem einen Klaps geben◇

**small** ADJECTIVE **klein**; **a small dog** ein kleiner Hund

**smart** ADJECTIVE ❶ (well-dressed, posh) **elegant**; **a smart restaurant** ein elegantes Restaurant ❷ (clever) **clever**

**smash** NOUN (collision) **Zusammenstoß** der (PLURAL die **Zusammenstöße**)

**smash** VERB ❶ (break) **zerschlagen**◇; **they smashed a window pane** sie haben eine Fensterscheibe zerschlagen ❷ (get broken) **zerbrechen**◇ (PERF **sein**); **the plate smashed** der Teller ist zerbrochen

**smashing** ADJECTIVE **klasse** (informal)

**smell** NOUN **Geruch** der (PLURAL die **Gerüche**); **a nasty smell** ein scheußlicher Geruch, **a smell of gas** ein Gasgeruch

**smell** VERB ❶ **riechen**◇; **I can't smell anything** ich kann nichts riechen, **to smell of perfume** nach Parfüm riechen ❷ (smell bad) **stinken**◇; **the drains smell** der Abfluss stinkt

**smelly** ADJECTIVE ❶ **stinkend**; **her smelly dog** ihr stinkender Hund ❷ **to be smelly** stinken◇

**smile** NOUN **Lächeln** das

**smile** VERB **lächeln**; **to smile at somebody** jemanden anlächeln (SEP)

**smoke** NOUN **Rauch** der

**smoke** VERB **rauchen**; **she doesn't smoke** sie raucht nicht

**smoked** ADJECTIVE **geräuchert**; **smoked salmon** Räucherlachs der

**smoker** NOUN **Raucher** der (PLURAL die **Raucher**), **Raucherin** die (PLURAL die **Raucherinnen**)

**smoking** NOUN **'no smoking'** 'Rauchen verboten', **to give up smoking** mit dem Rauchen aufhören

**smooth** ADJECTIVE ❶ **glatt**; **a smooth surface** eine glatte Oberfläche ❷ (person) **aalglatt**

**smug** ADJECTIVE **selbstgefällig**

**smuggle** VERB **to smuggle something** etwas schmuggeln

**smuggler** NOUN ❶ **Schmuggler** der (PLURAL die **Schmuggler**), **Schmugglerin** die (PLURAL die **Schmugglerinnen**) ❷ **drugs smuggler** der Drogenschmuggler

**snack** NOUN **Snack** der (PLURAL die **Snacks**)

**snail** NOUN **Schnecke** die (PLURAL die **Schnecken**)

**snake** NOUN **Schlange** die (PLURAL die **Schlangen**)

**snap** NOUN (card game) **Schnippschnapp** das (PLURAL die **Schnippschnapp**)

**snap** VERB ❶ (break) **brechen**◇ (PERF **sein**) ❷ **to snap something** etwas zerbrechen◇ ❸ **to snap your fingers** mit den Fingern schnalzen

**snapshot** NOUN **Schnappschuss** der (PLURAL die **Schnappschüsse**)

**snarl** VERB **knurren**

**snatch** VERB ❶ entreißen◇; to snatch something from somebody jemandem etwas entreißen, she had her bag snatched man hat ihr die Handtasche entrissen ❷ he snatched it out of my hand er hat es mir aus der Hand gerissen

**sneak** VERB ❶ to sneak in sich hineinschleichen◇ (SEP), to sneak out sich hinausschleichen◇ (SEP) ❷ to sneak on somebody jemanden verpetzen (informal)

**sneeze** VERB niesen

**sniff** VERB schnüffeln

**snob** NOUN Snob der (PLURAL die Snobs)

**snobbery** NOUN Snobismus der

**snooker** NOUN Snooker das

**snooze** VERB Nickerchen das (PLURAL die Nickerchen); to have a snooze ein Nickerchen machen

**snore** VERB schnarchen

**snow** NOUN Schnee der

**snow** VERB schneien; it's snowing es schneit

**snowball** NOUN Schneeball der (PLURAL die Schneebälle)

**snow drift** NOUN Schneewehe die (PLURAL die Schneewehen)

**snowman** NOUN Schneemann der (PLURAL die Schneemänner)

**so** CONJUNCTION, ADVERB ❶ so; he's so lazy er ist so faul, not so nicht so, our house is a bit like yours, but not so big unser Haus ist so ähnlich wie eures, aber nicht so groß ❷ so much so sehr, I hate it so much ich hasse es so sehr ❸ so much so viel, I

have so much work ich habe so viel Arbeit ❹ so many so viele, we've got so many problems wir haben so viele Probleme ❺ (therefore) also; he got up late, so he missed his train er ist zu spät aufgestanden und hat deshalb den Zug verpasst, so what shall we do? also, was machen wir? ❻ so what? na und? ❼ (also) so do I, so did I ich auch, 'I live in Leeds' – 'so do I' 'ich wohne in Leeds' – 'ich auch', I liked the film and so did he ich fand den Film gut und er auch, so am I ich auch, so do we wir auch ❽ I think so ich glaube schon ❾ I hope so hoffentlich

**soak** VERB einweichen (SEP)

**soaked** ADJECTIVE patschnass
• to be soaked to the skin patschnass sein

**soap** NOUN ❶ Seife, die (PLURAL die Seifen) ❷ (soap opera) Seifenoper die (PLURAL die Seifenopern)

**soap powder** NOUN Seifenpulver das

**sober** ADJECTIVE nüchtern
• to sober up nüchtern werden◇ (PERF sein)

**soccer** NOUN Fußball der

**social** ADJECTIVE ❶ sozial; social problems soziale Probleme ❷ gesellschaftlich (engagement, ambition); social engagements gesellschaftliche Verpflichtungen, social class die gesellschaftliche Schicht ❸ (sociable) gesellig (evening, person)

**socialism** NOUN Sozialismus der

**socialist** NOUN Sozialist der (PLURAL die Sozialisten), Sozialistin die (PLURAL die Sozialistinnen)

**social security** NOUN ❶ Sozialhilfe die; to be on social security Sozialhilfe bekommen ❷ *(the system)* Sozialversicherung die

**social worker** NOUN Sozialarbeiter der *(PLURAL die Sozialarbeiter)*, Sozialarbeiterin die *(PLURAL die Sozialarbeiterinnen)*

**society** NOUN Gesellschaft die *(PLURAL die Gesellschaften)*

**sociology** NOUN Soziologie die

**sock** NOUN Socke die *(PLURAL die Socken)*; a pair of socks ein Paar Socken

**socket** NOUN *(power point)* Steckdose die *(PLURAL die Steckdosen)*

**sofa** NOUN Sofa das *(PLURAL die Sofas)*

**sofa bed** NOUN Schlafcouch die *(PLURAL die Schlafcouchs)*

**soft** ADJECTIVE ❶ weich ❷ a soft option eine bequeme Lösung
• to have a soft spot for somebody eine Schwäche für jemanden haben

**soft drink** NOUN alkoholfreie Getränk das *(PLURAL die alkoholfreien Getränke)*

**soft toy** NOUN Stofftier das *(PLURAL die Stofftiere)*

**software** NOUN Software die

**soil** NOUN Erde die

**solar energy** NOUN Sonnenenergie die

**soldier** NOUN Soldat der *(PLURAL die Soldaten)*

**solicitor** NOUN ❶ *(dealing with lawsuits)* Rechtsanwalt der *(PLURAL die Rechtsanwälte)*,

Rechtsanwältin die *(PLURAL die Rechtsanwältinnen)* ❷ *(dealing with property or documents)* Notar der *(PLURAL die Notare)*, Notarin die *(PLURAL die Notarinnen)*

**solid** ADJECTIVE ❶ *(not flimsy)* stabil; a solid structure ein stabiler Bau ❷ massiv; a table made of solid oak ein Tisch aus massiver Eiche, solid silver massives Silber

**solo** NOUN Solo das *(PLURAL die Solos)*; guitar solo das Gitarrensolo

**solo** ADJECTIVE Solo-; a solo act eine Solonummer

**solo** ADVERB solo

**soloist** NOUN Solist der *(PLURAL die Solisten)*, Solistin die *(PLURAL die Solistinnen)*

**solution** NOUN Lösung die *(PLURAL die Lösungen)*

**solve** VERB lösen

**some** ADJECTIVE, ADVERB ❶ *(followed by a singular noun)* etwas; would you like some salad? möchtest du etwas Salat?, can you lend me some money? kannst du mir etwas Geld leihen?, have you got some bread? *(some is often not translated)* hast du Brot? ❷ *(followed by a plural noun) (a few)* ein paar; I've bought some apples ich habe ein paar Äpfel gekauft ❸ *(followed by a plural noun) (a certain number but not all)* einige; some of his films are too violent einige von seinen Filmen sind zu brutal ❹ *(referring to something that has been mentioned)* 'would you like tea?' – 'thanks, I've got some' 'möchten Sie Tee?' – 'nein danke, ich habe schon welchen', he's eaten some of it er hat etwas davon gegessen, I'd like some ich

**somebody** | **sort**

möchte etwas, *(with a plural noun)* ich möchte welche **⑤** *(certain people or things)* **manche**; **some people think he's right** manche Leute glauben, dass er Recht hat **⑥ some day** eines Tages

**somebody, someone** PRONOUN jemand; **there's somebody in the garden** da ist jemand im Garten

**somehow** ADVERB irgendwie; **I've got to finish this essay somehow** ich muss diesen Aufsatz irgendwie fertig schreiben

**something** PRONOUN **❶ etwas**; **there's something I've got to tell you** ich muss dir etwas erzählen, **something new** etwas Neues, **something interesting** etwas Interessantes, **there's something wrong** irgendetwas stimmt nicht **❷ their house is really something!** ihr Haus ist einfach Klasse!

**sometime** ADVERB irgendwann; **give me a ring sometime next week** ruf mich irgendwann nächste Woche an

**sometimes** ADVERB manchmal; **I sometimes take the train** manchmal fahre ich mit der Bahn

**somewhere** ADVERB **❶** *(in a place)* irgendwo; **I've left my bag somewhere here** ich habe meine Handtasche hier irgendwo liegen lassen **❷** *(to a place)* irgendwohin; **I'd like to go somewhere warm** ich möchte irgendwohin fahren, wo es warm ist

**son** NOUN Sohn der *(PLURAL die Söhne)*

**song** NOUN Lied das *(PLURAL die Lieder)*

**son-in-law** NOUN Schwiegersohn der *(PLURAL die Schwiegersöhne)*

**soon** ADVERB **❶ bald**; **we'll soon be on holiday** wir haben bald Ferien, **see you soon!** bis bald! **❷ as soon as she arrives** sobald sie ankommt, **as soon as possible** so bald wie möglich **❸ it's too soon** es ist zu früh

**sooner** ADVERB **❶ früher**; **we should have started sooner** wir hätten früher anfangen sollen, **sooner or later** früher oder später **❷ I'd sooner wait** ich würde lieber warten

**soprano** NOUN Sopran der *(PLURAL die Soprane)*

**sore** NOUN wunde Stelle die *(PLURAL die wunden Stellen)*

**sore** ADJECTIVE **❶** *(inflamed)* wund; **to have a sore throat** Halsschmerzen haben **❷ he has a sore leg** ihm tut das Bein weh, **my arm's sore** mir tut der Arm weh
• **it's a sore point** das ist ein wunder Punkt

**sorry** ADJECTIVE **❶ I'm really sorry** es tut mir wirklich Leid, **sorry to disturb you** es tut mir Leid, dass ich dich störe, **I'm sorry I forgot your birthday** es tut mir Leid, dass ich deinen Geburtstag vergessen habe, **I'm sorry, were closing** es tut mir Leid, aber wir machen jetzt zu **❷ sorry!** Entschuldigung! **❸ sorry?** wie bitte? **❹ I feel sorry for him** er tut mir Leid

**sort** NOUN Art die *(PLURAL die Arten)*; **a sort of dance music** eine Art Tanzmusik, **what sort of car have you got?** was für ein Auto hast du?, **all sorts of people** alle möglichen Leute, **for all sorts of reasons** aus allen möglichen Gründen
• **to sort something out ❶** Ordnung schaffen◇ in *(+DAT)*, *(papers, desk,*

*room, possessions);* **I must sort out my room tonight** ich muss heute Abend in meinem Zimmer Ordnung schaffen ❷ klären *(a problem, arrangement);* **Liz is sorting it out** Liz klärt es

**so-so** ADJECTIVE so lala *(informal);* **'how was the film?' – 'so-so'** 'wie war der Film?' – 'mittelmäßig'

**soul** NOUN ❶ Seele die *(PLURAL die Seelen)* ❷ *(music)* Soul der

**sound** NOUN ❶ *(noise)* Geräusch das *(PLURAL die Geräusche)* ❷ *(of voices, laughter, bell)* Klang der; **the sound of her voice** der Klang ihrer Stimme, **I can hear the sound of voices** ich kann Stimmen hören ❸ **without a sound** lautlos ❹ *(volume)* Lautstärke die; **to turn the sound down** leiser stellen

**sound** VERB ❶ **it sounds easy** es hört sich einfach an ❷ **it sounds as if she's happy** sie scheint glücklich zu sein

**sound asleep** ADVERB **to be sound asleep** fest schlafen⬦

**sound effect** NOUN Geräuscheffekt der *(PLURAL die Geräuscheffekte)*

**soundtrack** NOUN Soundtrack der *(PLURAL die Soundtracks)*

**soup** NOUN Suppe die *(PLURAL die Suppen);* **mushroom soup** die Pilzsuppe

**soup plate** NOUN Suppenteller der *(PLURAL die Suppenteller)*

**soup spoon** NOUN Suppenlöffel der *(PLURAL die Suppenlöffel)*

**sour** ADJECTIVE sauer

**south** NOUN Süden der; **in the south** im Süden

**south** ADJECTIVE Süd-, südlich; **the south side** die Südseite, **south wind** der Südwind

**south** ADVERB **south of Berlin** südlich von Berlin, **they went south** sie sind nach Süden gefahren

**South Africa** NOUN Südafrika das

**South America** NOUN Südamerika das

**southeast** NOUN Südosten der

**southeast** ADJECTIVE **in southeast England** in Südostengland

**South Pole** NOUN Südpol der

**southwest** NOUN Südwesten der

**southwest** ADJECTIVE **in southwest England** in Südwestengland

**souvenir** NOUN Souvenir das *(PLURAL die Souvenirs)*

**soya** NOUN Soja die

**space** NOUN ❶ *(room)* Platz der; **there's enough space** es ist genug Platz, **we've got enough space for two** wir haben genug Platz für zwei ❷ *(gap)* Zwischenraum der *(PLURAL die Zwischenräume);* **to leave a large space between lines** viel Platz zwischen den Zeilen lassen ❸ **(parking) space** die Parklücke ❹ *(outer space)* Weltraum der; **in space** im Weltraum

**spacecraft** NOUN Raumschiff das *(PLURAL die Raumschiffe)*

**spade** NOUN ❶ Spaten der *(PLURAL die Spaten)* ❷ *(in cards)* Pik das; **the queen of spades** die Pikdame

**Spain** *NOUN* Spanien das; from Spain aus Spanien, to Spain nach Spanien

**Spaniard** *NOUN* Spanier der *(PLURAL die Spanier)*, Spanierin die *(PLURAL die Spanierinnen)*

**spaniel** *NOUN* Spaniel der *(PLURAL die Spaniels)*

**Spanish** *NOUN* ❶ *(language)* Spanisch das; I'm learning Spanish ich lerne Spanisch ❷ the Spanish *(people)* die Spanier

**Spanish** *ADJECTIVE* spanisch; Pedro is Spanish Pedro ist Spanier

**spanner** *NOUN* Schraubenschlüssel der *(PLURAL die Schraubenschlüssel)*

**spare** *ADJECTIVE* Extra-; we have a spare ticket wir haben eine Karte übrig

**spare** *VERB* to have time to spare Zeit haben, can you spare a moment? hast du einen Moment Zeit?

**spare part** *NOUN* Ersatzteil das *(PLURAL die Ersatzteile)*

**spare room** *NOUN* Gästezimmer das *(PLURAL die Gästezimmer)*

**spare time** *NOUN* Freizeit die; in my spare time in meiner Freizeit

**spare wheel** *NOUN* Reserverad das *(PLURAL die Reserveräder)*

**sparkling** *ADJECTIVE* sparkling mineral water Mineralwasser mit Kohlensäure, sparkling wine der Schaumwein

**sparrow** *NOUN* Spatz der *(PLURAL die Spatzen)*

**speak** *VERB* ❶ sprechen◇; do you speak German? sprechen Sie Deutsch?, spoken German gesprochenes Deutsch, to speak to somebody about something mit jemandem über etwas *(ACC)* sprechen, she's speaking to Mike about it sie spricht mit Mike darüber ❷ who's speaking? *(on the phone)* wer ist am Apparat?

**speaker** *NOUN* ❶ *(on a music system)* Lautsprecher der *(PLURAL die Lautsprecher)* ❷ *(at a public lecture)* Redner der *(PLURAL die Redner)*, Rednerin die *(PLURAL die Rednerinnen)*

**special** *ADJECTIVE* ❶ besonderer/besondere/besonderes; on special occasions bei besonderen Anlässen ❷ special offer das Sonderangebot

**specialist** *NOUN* Fachmann der *(PLURAL die Fachleute)* Fachfrau die *(PLURAL die Fachfrauen)*

**specialize** *VERB* sich spezialisieren auf *(+ACC)*; to specialize in I'm specializing in business studies ich spezialisiere mich auf Wirtschaftswissenschaften

**specially** *ADVERB* ❶ besonders; not specially nicht besonders, it's specially good for babies es ist besonders gut für Babys ❷ *(specifically)* speziell; I made this cake specially for you ich habe diesen Kuchen speziell für dich gebacken

**species** *NOUN* Art die *(PLURAL die Arten)*

**spectacles** *NOUN* Brille die *(PLURAL die Brillen)*

**spectacular** *ADJECTIVE* spektakulär

**spectator** *NOUN* Zuschauer der *(PLURAL die Zuschauer)*, Zuschauerin die *(PLURAL die Zuschauerinnen)*

**speech** NOUN **Rede** die (PLURAL die **Reden**); to make a speech eine Rede halten

**speechless** ADJECTIVE **sprachlos**; to be speechless: she was speechless with rage sie war sprachlos vor Wut

**speed** NOUN ❶ **Geschwindigkeit** die (PLURAL die **Geschwindigkeiten**); at top speed mit Höchstgeschwindigkeit, what speed was he doing? wie schnell ist er gefahren? ❷ (gear) **Gang** der (PLURAL die **Gänge**); a twelve-speed bike ein Rad mit zwölf Gängen
• to speed up ❶ beschleunigen (a car) ❷ (of a person, car) schneller werden

**speeding** NOUN **zu schnelle Fahren** das; he was fined for speeding er hat wegen zu schnellen Fahrens ein Bußgeld bekommen

**speed limit** NOUN **Geschwindigkeitsbeschränkung** die

**spell** NOUN ❶ (of time) **Weile** die; for a spell eine Weile ❷ cold spell die Kälteperiode, sunny spells sonnige Abschnitte

**spell** VERB ❶ (in writing) **schreiben**◇; how do you spell it? wie schreibt man das?, how do you spell your surname? wie schreibt man Ihren Nachnamen? ❷ (out loud) **buchstabieren**

**spell checker** NOUN **Rechtschreibprogramm** das (PLURAL die **Rechtschreibprogramme**)

**spelling** NOUN **Rechtschreibung** die; spelling mistake der Rechtschreibfehler

**spend** VERB ❶ **ausgeben**◇ (SEP) (money); I've spent all my money ich habe mein ganzes Geld ausgegeben ❷ **verbringen**◇ (time); we spent three days in Munich wir haben drei Tage in München verbracht, she spends her time reading sie verbringt ihre Zeit mit Lesen

**spice** NOUN **Gewürz** das (PLURAL die **Gewürze**)

**spicy** ADJECTIVE **scharf**; he doesn't like spicy food er mag kein scharfes Essen

**spider** NOUN **Spinne** die (PLURAL die **Spinnen**)

**spill** VERB **verschütten**; I've spilled my wine on the carpet ich habe meinen Wein auf dem Teppich verschüttet

**spinach** NOUN **Spinat** der

**spine** NOUN **Wirbelsäule** die (PLURAL die **Wirbelsäulen**)

**spire** NOUN **Kirchturm** der (PLURAL die **Kirchtürme**)

**spirit** NOUN ❶ (energy) **Energie** die ❷ in the right spirit mit der richtigen Einstellung

**spirits** NOUN ❶ (alcohol) **Spirituosen** (plural) ❷ to be in good spirits guter Laune sein

**spit** VERB ❶ **spucken** ❷ to spit something out etwas ausspucken (SEP), spit it out! spuck es aus!

**spite** NOUN ❶ in spite of trotz (+GEN), we decided to go in spite of the rain wir beschlossen trotz des Regens zu gehen ❷ (nastiness) **Boshaftigkeit** die; to do something out of spite etwas aus Boshaftigkeit tun

**spiteful** ADJECTIVE gehässig

**splash** NOUN ❶ *(noise)* Platsch der ❷ **splash of colour** der Farbfleck

**splash** VERB bespritzen

**splendid** ADJECTIVE herrlich

**splinter** NOUN Splitter der *(PLURAL die Splitter)*

**split** VERB ❶ *(with an axe or a knife)* spalten; **to split wood** Holz spalten ❷ *(come apart)* zerreißen◇ *(PERF sein)*; **the lining has split** das Futter ist zerrissen ❸ *(divide up)* teilen; **they split the money between them** sie haben das Geld untereinander geteilt
• **to split up** ❶ *(a group or crowd)* sich auflösen *(SEP)* ❷ *(a couple)* sich trennen; **she's split up with her husband** sie hat sich von ihrem Mann getrennt, **she's split up with Sam** sie hat mit Sam Schluss gemacht *(informal)*

**spoil** VERB verderben◇; **it completely spoiled our evening** das hat uns den Abend völlig verdorben, **to spoil somebody's fun** jemandem den Spaß verderben

**spoiled** ADJECTIVE verwöhnt; **a spoiled child** ein verwöhntes Kind

**spoilsport** NOUN Spielverderber der *(PLURAL die Spielverderber)*, Spielverderberin die *(PLURAL die Spielverderberinnen)*

**spoke** NOUN *(of a wheel)* Speiche die *(PLURAL die Speichen)*

**spokesman** NOUN Sprecher der *(PLURAL die Sprecher)*

**spokeswoman** NOUN Sprecherin die *(PLURAL die Sprecherinnen)*

**sponge** NOUN Schwamm der *(PLURAL die Schwämme)*

**sponge cake** NOUN Rührkuchen der *(PLURAL die Rührkuchen)*

**sponsor** NOUN Sponsor der *(PLURAL die Sponsoren)*

**sponsor** VERB sponsern

**spooky** ADJECTIVE gruselig; **a spooky story** eine gruselige Geschichte

**spoon** NOUN Löffel der *(PLURAL die Löffel)*; **a spoon of sugar** ein Löffel Zucker, **soup spoon** der Suppenlöffel, **teaspoon** der Teelöffel

**spoonful** NOUN Löffel der *(PLURAL die Löffel)*

**sport** NOUN ❶ Sport der; **to be good at sport** gut im Sport sein, **my favourite sport** mein Lieblingssport ❷ *(in games)* **to be a good sport** ein guter Verlierer sein

**sports bag** NOUN Sporttasche die *(PLURAL die Sporttaschen)*

**sports car** NOUN Sportwagen der *(PLURAL die Sportwagen)*

**sports centre** NOUN Sportzentrum das *(PLURAL die Sportzentren)*

**sports club** NOUN Sportverein der *(PLURAL die Sportvereine)*

**sportsman** NOUN Sportler der *(PLURAL die Sportler)*

**sportswear** NOUN Sportbekleidung die

**sportswoman** NOUN Sportlerin die *(PLURAL die Sportlerinnen)*

**sporty** ADJECTIVE sportlich; **she's very sporty** sie ist sehr sportlich

**spot** NOUN ❶ (pattern in fabric) **Punkt** der (PLURAL die **Punkte**); **a red shirt with black spots** ein rotes Hemd mit schwarzen Punkten ❷ (on your skin) **Pickel** der (PLURAL die **Pickel**); **I've got spots** ich habe Pickel, **to be covered in spots** völlig verpickelt sein ❸ (stain) **Fleck** der (PLURAL die **Flecke**); **you've got a spot on your shirt** du hast einen Fleck auf dem Hemd ❹ (spotlight) **Scheinwerfer** der (PLURAL die **Scheinwerfer**), (in the home) **Spot** der (PLURAL die **Spots**) ❺ **on the spot** (immediately) auf der Stelle, **we'll do it for you on the spot** wir machen es Ihnen auf der Stelle ❻ (at hand) **on the spot** zur Stelle ❼ (at the same place) **on the spot** an Ort und Stelle

**spot** VERB **entdecken**; **he spotted his friend in the crowd** er entdeckte seinen Freund in der Menge

**spotlight** NOUN ❶ **Scheinwerfer** der (PLURAL die **Scheinwerfer**) ❷ (in the home) **Spot** der (PLURAL die **Spots**)

**spotty** ADJECTIVE (pimply) **pickelig**

**spouse** NOUN ❶ (male) **Ehemann** der (PLURAL die **Ehemänner**) ❷ (female) **Ehefrau** die (PLURAL die **Ehefrauen**)

**sprain** NOUN **Verstauchung** die (PLURAL die **Verstauchungen**)

**sprain** VERB **to sprain your ankle** sich (DAT) den Fuß verstauchen

**spray** NOUN (spray can) **Spray** das (PLURAL die **Sprays**)

**spray** VERB **sprühen**

**spread** NOUN **Brotaufstrich** der; **cheese spread** der Streichkäse

**spread** VERB ❶ (of news or a disease) **sich verbreiten** ❷ **streichen**◇ (butter, jam, glue)

**spreadsheet** NOUN (on a computer) **Tabellenkalkulation** die

**spring** NOUN ❶ (the season) **Frühling** der (PLURAL die **Frühlinge**); **in the spring** im Frühling, **spring flowers** Frühlingsblumen ❷ (made of metal) **Feder** die (PLURAL die **Federn**) ❸ (providing water) **Quelle** die (PLURAL die **Quellen**)

**springtime** NOUN **Frühjahr** das; **in springtime** im Frühjahr

**spring water** NOUN **Quellwasser** das

**sprint** NOUN **Sprint** der (PLURAL die **Sprints**)

**sprint** VERB **rennen**◇ (PERF **sein**)

**sprinter** NOUN **Sprinter** der (PLURAL die **Sprinter**), **Sprinterin** die (PLURAL die **Sprinterinnen**)

**sprout** NOUN (Brussels sprout) **Rosenkohl** der; **he likes sprouts** er mag Rosenkohl

**spy** NOUN **Spion** der (PLURAL die **Spione**), **Spionin** die (PLURAL die **Spioninnen**)

**spy** VERB **to spy on somebody** jemandem nachspionieren (SEP), **he's spying on me** er spioniert mir nach

**squabble** VERB **sich zanken**

**square** NOUN ❶ (shape) **Quadrat** das (PLURAL die **Quadrate**) ❷ (in a town or village) **Platz** der (PLURAL die **Plätze**); **the village square** der Dorfplatz

A
B
C
D
E
F
G
H
I
J
K
L
M
N
O
P
Q
R
**S**
T
U
V
W
X
Y
Z

**square** *ADJECTIVE* **quadratisch**; a square box **eine viereckige Schachtel**, three square metres **drei Quadratmeter**, the room is four metres square **das Zimmer ist vier mal vier Meter**
• to go back to square one **noch einmal von vorn anfangen**

**squash** *NOUN* ❶ *(drink)* **Saft** der; orange squash **der Orangensaft** ❷ *(sport)* **Squash** das

**squash** *VERB* **zerquetschen**

**squeak** *VERB* ❶ *(door, hinge)* **quietschen** ❷ *(person, animal)* **quieken**

**squeeze** *VERB* ❶ **drücken**; to squeeze somebody's hand **jemandem die Hand drücken** ❷ **drücken** *(toothpaste)*

**squirrel** *NOUN* **Eichhörnchen** das *(PLURAL* die **Eichhörnchen)*

**stab** *VERB* **stechen**◇; to stab somebody *(kill)* **jemanden erstechen**◇

**stable** *NOUN* **Stall** der *(PLURAL* die **Ställe)*

**stable** *ADJECTIVE* **stabil**

**stack** *NOUN* ❶ **Stapel** der *(PLURAL* die **Stapel)* ❷ stacks of **ein Haufen**, she's got stacks of CDs **sie hat einen Haufen CDs**

**stadium** *NOUN* **Stadion** das *(PLURAL* die **Stadien)*

**staff** *NOUN* ❶ *(of a company)* **Personal** das ❷ *(in a school)* **Lehrkräfte** *(plural)*

**stage** *NOUN* ❶ *(for a performance)* **Bühne** die *(PLURAL* die **Bühnen)*; on stage **auf der Bühne** ❷ *(phase)*

**Phase** die *(PLURAL* die **Phasen)*; at this stage of the project **in dieser Phase des Projekts**, at this stage it's hard to say **im Augenblick ist es schwer zu sagen**

**staggered** *ADJECTIVE* *(amazed)* **verblüfft**

**stain** *NOUN* **Fleck** der *(PLURAL* die **Flecke)*

**stain** *VERB* **beflecken**

**stainless steel** *NOUN* **Edelstahl** der; a stainless steel sink **ein Spülbecken aus Edelstahl**

**stair** *NOUN* ❶ *(step)* **Stufe** die *(PLURAL* die **Stufen)* ❷ the stairs **die Treppe** *(singular)*, I met her on the stairs **ich habe sie auf der Treppe getroffen**

**staircase** *NOUN* **Treppe** die *(PLURAL* die **Treppen)*

**stale** *ADJECTIVE* **alt**

**stalemate** *NOUN* *(in chess)* **Patt** das *(PLURAL* die **Patts)*

**stall** *NOUN* ❶ *(at a market or fair)* **Stand** der *(PLURAL* die **Stände)* ❷ *(in a theatre)* the stalls **das Parkett**

**stammer** *NOUN* to have a stammer **stottern**

**stamp** *NOUN* **Briefmarke** die *(PLURAL* die **Briefmarken)*

**stamp** *VERB* ❶ **frankieren** *(a letter)* ❷ to stamp your foot **mit dem Fuß aufstampfen**

**stamp album** *NOUN* **Briefmarkenalbum** das *(PLURAL* die **Briefmarkenalben)*

**stamp collection** *NOUN* **Briefmarkensammlung** die *(PLURAL* die **Briefmarkensammlungen)*

**stand¹** VERB ❶ **stehen**◇; several
people were standing viele Leute
standen, we stood outside the
cinema wir haben vor dem Kino
gestanden ❷ (bear) **ausstehen**◇
(SEP); I can't stand her ich kann
sie nicht ausstehen, I can't stand
waiting ich kann es nicht ausstehen,
wenn man warten muss ❸ (keep
going) **aushalten**◇ (SEP); I can't
stand it any longer ich halte es
nicht mehr aus

**stand** NOUN (in a stadium) **Tribüne**
die (PLURAL die **Tribünen**)
- to stand for something (be short
for) **bedeuten**; UN stands for
United Nations UN bedeutet United
Nations
- stand up **aufstehen**◇ (SEP) (PERF
sein); everybody stood up alle
standen auf

**stand²** NOUN ❶ (in a stadium) **Tribüne**
die (PLURAL die **Tribünen**) ❷ (in fair)
**Stand** der (PLURAL die **Stände**)

**standard** NOUN ❶ (level) **Niveau**
das; of high standard von hohem
Niveau ❷ standard of living der
Lebensstandard ❸ she sets herself
high standards sie stellt hohe
Ansprüche an sich selbst

**standard** ADJECTIVE **normal**; the
standard size die Normalgröße

**Standard grades** NOUN PLURAL
(You can explain Standard grades
as follows: Diese Prüfungen werden
im Alter von ca 16 Jahren in sechs
oder sieben Fächern abgelegt. Sie
werden von 1 (beste Note) bis 7
(Kurs abgeschlossen) benotet. Viele
Schüler machen nach Standard
Grades weiter, und legen Highers
und Advanced Highers ab)
▸ SEE **Highers**

**staple** NOUN **Heftklammer** die (PLURAL
die **Heftklammern**)

**staple** VERB **heften**; to staple
the pages together die Seiten
zusammenheften

**stapler** NOUN **Hefter** der (PLURAL die
**Hefter**)

**star** NOUN ❶ (in the sky) **Stern** der
(PLURAL die **Sterne**) ❷ (person) **Star**
der (PLURAL die **Stars**); he's a film star
er ist ein Filmstar

**star** VERB to star in a film in einem
Film die Hauptrolle spielen,
starring ... in der Hauptrolle ...

**stare** VERB ❶ **starren**; what are you
staring at? was starrst du so? ❷ to
stare at somebody jemanden
anstarren (SEP); he's staring at the
wall er starrt die Wand an

**start** NOUN ❶ **Anfang** der; at the
start am Anfang, at the start of the
film am Anfang des Films, from the
start von Anfang an, we knew from
the start that it was dangerous
wir wussten von Anfang an, dass
es gefährlich war ❷ to make a
start on something mit etwas (DAT)
anfangen◇ (SEP), I've made a start
on my homework ich habe mit
meinen Hausaufgaben angefangen
❸ (of a race) **Start** der (PLURAL die
**Starts**)

**start** VERB ❶ **anfangen**◇ (SEP); the
film starts at eight der Film fängt
um acht an, I've started the book
ich habe das Buch angefangen, to
start doing something anfangen,
etwas zu tun, I've started learning
Spanish ich habe angefangen,
Spanisch zu lernen, to start crying
anfangen zu weinen ❷ to start
a business ein Geschäft gründen

❸ **to start a car** ein Auto starten, **she started the car** sie hat das Auto gestartet ❹ **the car won't start** das Auto springt nicht an

**starter** *NOUN (first course)* Vorspeise die *(PLURAL* die **Vorspeisen)**

**starve** *VERB* verhungern; **I'm starving!** ich bin schon am Verhungern!

**state** *NOUN* ❶ Zustand der *(PLURAL* die Zustände); **the house is in a very bad state** das Haus ist in einem sehr schlechten Zustand ❷ *(country)* Staat der *(PLURAL* die **Staaten)**; **the state** der Staat ❸ **the States** *(USA)* die Staaten, **they live in the States** sie leben in den Staaten

**state** *VERB* ❶ erklären *(intention, reason)* ❷ angeben◇ *(SEP) (an address, income, a reason)*

**stately home** *NOUN* herrschaftliche Anwesen das *(PLURAL* die herrschaftlichen Anwesen)

**statement** *NOUN* Erklärung die *(PLURAL* die **Erklärungen)**

**station** *NOUN* ❶ Bahnhof der *(PLURAL* die Bahnhöfe); **at the railway station** am Bahnhof, **bus station** der Busbahnhof ❷ **police station** die Polizeiwache ❸ **radio station** der Rundfunksender

**stationer's** *NOUN* Schreibwarengeschäft das *(PLURAL* die Schreibwarengeschäfte)

**statistics** *NOUN (subject)* Statistik die; **the statistics** *(figures)* die Statistik

**statue** *NOUN* Statue die *(PLURAL* die Statuen)

**stay** *NOUN* Aufenthalt der *(PLURAL* die Aufenthalte); **our stay in Cologne** unser Aufenthalt in Köln, **enjoy your stay!** einen schönen Aufenthalt!

**stay** *VERB* ❶ bleiben◇ *(PERF* sein); **I'll stay here** ich bleibe hier, **how long are you staying?** wie lange bleibst du? ❷ *(spend the night)* **you can stay with us** du kannst bei uns übernachten, **to stay the night with friends** bei Freunden übernachten ❸ *(be temporarily lodged)* wohnen; **where are you staying?** wo wohnst du?, **I'm staying in a hotel** ich wohne im Hotel ❹ *(be on a visit)* sein◇ *(PERF* sein), **I'm going to stay with my sister this weekend** ich bin am Wochenende bei meiner Schwester, **I stayed in Munich for a couple of days** ich war ein paar Tage in München
- **to stay in** zu Hause bleiben◇ *(PERF* sein); **I'm staying in tonight** heute Abend bleibe ich zu Hause

**steady** *ADJECTIVE* ❶ fest; **a steady job** eine feste Stelle ❷ gleichmäßig; **at a steady pace** mit gleichmäßiger Geschwindigkeit ❸ *(hand, voice)* ruhig; **to hold something steady** etwas ruhig halten ❹ *(dependable)* zuverlässig

**steak** *NOUN* Steak das *(PLURAL* die Steaks); **steak and chips** Steak mit Pommes frites

**steal** *VERB* stehlen◇

**steam** *NOUN* Dampf der

**steel** *NOUN* Stahl der

**steep** *ADJECTIVE* steil; **a steep slope** ein steiler Hang

**steeple** *NOUN (spire)* Kirchturm der *(PLURAL* die Kirchtürme)

**steering wheel** *NOUN* Lenkrad das *(PLURAL* die **Lenkräder)**

**step** *NOUN* ❶ Schritt der *(PLURAL* die **Schritte)**; to take a step forwards einen Schritt nach vorn machen, to take a step backwards einen Schritt zurück machen ❷ *(stair)* Stufe die *(PLURAL* die **Stufen)**

• to step back zurücktreten◇ *(SEP)* *(PERF* **sein)**

• to step forward vortreten◇ *(SEP)* *(PERF* **sein)**

**stepbrother** *NOUN* Stiefbruder der *(PLURAL* die **Stiefbrüder)**

**stepdaughter** *NOUN* Stieftochter die *(PLURAL* die **Stieftöchter)**

**stepfather** *NOUN* Stiefvater der *(PLURAL* die **Stiefväter)**

**stepladder** *NOUN* Trittleiter die *(PLURAL* die **Trittleitern)**

**stepmother** *NOUN* Stiefmutter die *(PLURAL* die **Stiefmütter)**

**stepsister** *NOUN* Stiefschwester die *(PLURAL* die **Stiefschwestern)**

**stepson** *NOUN* Stiefsohn der *(PLURAL* die **Stiefsöhne)**

**stereo** *NOUN* Stereoanlage die *(PLURAL* die **Stereoanlagen)**

**sterling** *NOUN* Sterling der; in sterling in Pfund (Sterling)

**stew** *NOUN* Eintopf der *(PLURAL* die **Eintöpfe)**

**steward** *NOUN* Steward der *(PLURAL* die **Stewards)**

**stewardess** *NOUN* Stewardess die *(PLURAL* die **Stewardessen)**

**stick** *NOUN* ❶ Stock der *(PLURAL* die **Stöcke)** ❷ hockey stick der Hockeyschläger

**stick** *VERB* ❶ *(with glue)* kleben ❷ *(put)* tun◇; stick them on my desk tu sie auf meinen Schreibtisch

**sticker** *NOUN* Aufkleber der *(PLURAL* die **Aufkleber)**

**sticky** *ADJECTIVE* ❶ klebrig; I've got sticky hands ich habe klebrige Hände ❷ a sticky label ein Aufkleber

**sticky tape** *NOUN* Klebestreifen der

**stiff** *ADJECTIVE* ❶ steif; to feel stiff steif sein, *(after exercise)* Muskelkater haben, to have a stiff neck einen steifen Hals haben ❷ to be bored stiff sich zu Tode langweilen ❸ to be scared stiff furchtbare Angst haben

**still** *ADJECTIVE* ❶ sit still! sitz still!, keep still! halt still! ❷ still mineral water Mineralwasser ohne Kohlensäure

**still** *ADVERB* ❶ noch; do you still live in London? wohnst du noch in London?, I've still not finished ich bin immer noch nicht fertig, he's still working er arbeitet noch ❷ *(nevertheless)* trotzdem; I told her not to, but she still did it ich habe es ihr verboten, aber sie hat es trotzdem gemacht ❸ better still noch besser

**sting** *NOUN* Stich der *(PLURAL* die **Stiche)**

**sting** *VERB* stechen◇

**stink** *NOUN* Gestank der

**stink** *VERB* stinken◇; it stinks of fish in here es stinkt hier nach Fisch

**stir** *VERB* rühren

**stitch** NOUN ❶ (in sewing, surgical) **Stich** der (PLURAL die **Stiche**) ❷ (in knitting) **Masche** die (PLURAL die **Maschen**) ❸ (pain) **Seitenstechen** das

**stock** NOUN ❶ (in a shop) **Warenbestand** der; to have something in stock etwas auf Lager haben, to be out of stock ausverkauft sein ❷ (supply) **Vorrat** der (PLURAL die **Vorräte**); I always have a stock of pencils ich habe immer einen Bleistiftvorrat ❸ (for cooking) **Brühe** die; chicken stock die Hühnerbrühe

**stock** VERB (in a shop) **führen**; they don't stock books sie führen keine Bücher

**stock cube** NOUN **Brühwürfel** der (PLURAL die **Brühwürfel**)

**stock exchange** NOUN **Börse** die (PLURAL die **Börsen**)

**stocking** NOUN **Strumpf** der (PLURAL die **Strümpfe**)

**stomach** NOUN **Magen** der (PLURAL die **Mägen**)

**stomach-ache** NOUN **Magenschmerzen** (plural); to have stomach-ache Magenschmerzen haben

**stone** NOUN **Stein** der (PLURAL die **Steine**); stone wall die Steinmauer

**stool** NOUN **Hocker** der (PLURAL die **Hocker**)

**stop** NOUN **Haltestelle** die (PLURAL die **Haltestellen**); bus stop die Bushaltestelle

**stop** VERB ❶ **halten**◇; does the train stop in Stuttgart? hält der Zug in Stuttgart? ❷ to stop somebody/

something jemanden/etwas anhalten◇ (SEP), the police stopped the car die Polizei hielt den Wagen an ❸ (cease) **aufhören** (SEP); the noise has stopped der Lärm hat aufgehört, to stop doing something aufhören, etwas zu tun, he's stopped smoking er hat aufgehört zu rauchen, she never stops asking questions sie hört nie auf, Fragen zu stellen, stop it! hör auf! ❹ to stop somebody doing something jemanden daran hindern, etwas zu tun, I can't stop her ringing him ich kann sie nicht daran hindern, ihn anzurufen ❺ (prevent) **verhindern** (an accident, a crime)

**stopwatch** NOUN **Stoppuhr** die (PLURAL die **Stoppuhren**)

**store** NOUN (shop) **Geschäft** das (PLURAL die **Geschäfte**); department store das Kaufhaus

**store** VERB ❶ **aufbewahren** (SEP), (in a warehouse) **lagern** ❷ (on a computer) **speichern**

**storey** NOUN **Stockwerk** das (PLURAL die **Stockwerke**); a four-storey house ein vierstöckiges Haus

**storm** NOUN ❶ **Sturm** der (PLURAL die **Stürme**) ❷ (thunderstorm) **Gewitter** das (PLURAL die **Gewitter**)

**stormy** ADJECTIVE **stürmisch**

**story** NOUN **Geschichte** die (PLURAL die **Geschichten**); to tell a story eine Geschichte erzählen

**stove** NOUN (cooker) **Herd** der (PLURAL die **Herde**)

**straight** ADJECTIVE ❶ **gerade**; a straight line eine gerade Linie ❷ to have straight hair glatte Haare haben

**straight** ADVERB ❶ (in direction) straight ahead geradeaus, to go straight ahead geradeaus gehen ❷ (immediately, directly) sofort; straight away sofort, he went straight to the doctor's er ging sofort zum Arzt

**straightforward** ADJECTIVE einfach

**strain** NOUN Stress der; the strain of the last few weeks der Stress in den letzten Wochen, to be a strain anstrengend sein

**strain** VERB ❶ zerren (a muscle) ❷ verrenken (your arm, back); he's strained his back er hat sich (DAT) den Rücken verrenkt

**strange** ADJECTIVE seltsam; his strange behaviour sein seltsames Verhalten

**stranger** NOUN Fremde der/die (PLURAL die Fremden)

**strangle** VERB erwürgen

**strap** NOUN ❶ (on a case, bag, camera) Riemen der (PLURAL die Riemen) ❷ (on a garment) Träger der (PLURAL die Träger) ❸ (of a watch) Armband das (PLURAL die Armbänder)

**strapless** ADJECTIVE trägerlos

**straw** NOUN ❶ (for drinking) Strohhalm der (PLURAL die Strohhalme) ❷ (the material) Stroh das; straw hat der Strohhut

**strawberry** NOUN Erdbeere die (PLURAL die Erdbeeren); strawberry jam die Erdbeermarmelade

**stray** ADJECTIVE a stray dog ein streunender Hund

**stream** NOUN Bach der (PLURAL die Bäche)

**street** NOUN Straße die (PLURAL die Straßen); I met Simon in the street ich habe Simon auf der Straße getroffen

**streetlamp** NOUN Straßenlaterne die (PLURAL die Straßenlaternen)

**street map** NOUN Stadtplan der (PLURAL die Stadtpläne)

**streetwise** ADJECTIVE gewieft

**strength** NOUN Kraft die (PLURAL die Kräfte)

**stress** NOUN Stress der

**stress** VERB betonen; to stress the importance of something die Wichtigkeit von etwas betonen

**stretch** VERB ❶ (garment, shoes) sich dehnen; this jumper has stretched der Pullover hat sich gedehnt ❷ to stretch your legs sich (DAT) die Beine vertreten◇

**stretcher** NOUN Trage die (PLURAL die Tragen)

**stretchy** ADJECTIVE elastisch

**strict** ADJECTIVE streng

**strike** NOUN Streik der (PLURAL die Streiks); to go on strike in den Streik treten◇ (PERF sein), to be/go on strike streiken

**strike** VERB ❶ (hit) schlagen◇; the clock struck six die Uhr schlug sechs ❷ (be/go on strike) streiken

**striker** NOUN ❶ (in football) Stürmer der (PLURAL die Stürmer), Stürmerin die (PLURAL die Stürmerinnen) ❷ (person on strike) Streikende der/die (PLURAL die Streikenden)

a
b
c
d
e
f
g
h
i
j
k
l
m
n
o
p
q
r
s
t
u
v
w
x
y
z

**string** NOUN ❶ (for tying) **Schnur** die (PLURAL die **Schnüre**) ❷ (on a musical instrument) **Saite** die (PLURAL die **Saiten**)

**strip** NOUN **Streifen** der (PLURAL die **Streifen**)

**strip** VERB ❶ (undress) **sich ausziehen**◇ (SEP) ❷ (remove paint from) **abbeizen** (SEP)

**strip cartoon** NOUN **Comicstrip** der (PLURAL die **Comicstrips**)

**stripe** NOUN **Streifen** der (PLURAL die **Streifen**)

**striped** ADJECTIVE **gestreift**

**stroke** NOUN ❶ (style of swimming) **Stil** der (PLURAL die **Stile**) ❷ (medical) **Schlaganfall** der (PLURAL die **Schlaganfälle**); **to have a stroke** einen Schlaganfall bekommen
• **a stroke of luck** ein Glücksfall; **to have a stroke of luck** Glück haben

**stroke** VERB **streicheln**

**strong** ADJECTIVE ❶ (person, drink, feeling) **stark** ❷ (sturdy) **stabil** (furniture); **strong shoes** feste Schuhe

**strongly** ADVERB ❶ (believe, oppose) **fest** ❷ (support) **nachdrücklich** ❸ (advise, recommend) **dringend** ❹ **she smelt strongly of garlic** sie hat stark nach Knoblauch gerochen

**struggle** NOUN **Kampf** der (PLURAL die **Kämpfe**); **the struggle for freedom** der Kampf für die Freiheit, **it's been a struggle** es war ein Kampf

**struggle** VERB ❶ (to obtain something) **kämpfen**; **to struggle to do something** kämpfen, um etwas zu tun, **she struggled for a place** sie kämpfte um einen

Platz ❷ (physically, in order to escape or reach something) **sich wehren** ❸ (have difficulty in doing something) **sich abmühen** (SEP); **they are struggling to pay the rent** sie mühen sich ab, ihre Miete zu zahlen, **he's struggling with his homework** er müht sich mit seinen Hausaufgaben ab

**stub** NOUN **cigarette stub** die Kippe
• **to stub out** ausdrücken (SEP)

**stubborn** ADJECTIVE **stur**

**stuck** ADJECTIVE ❶ (jammed) **it's stuck** es klemmt, **the drawer's stuck** die Schublade klemmt ❷ **to get stuck** (person) **stecken bleiben**◇ (in a lift, traffic jam, or place)

**stud** NOUN ❶ (on clothes) **Niete** die (PLURAL die **Nieten**) ❷ (on a boot) **Stollen** der (PLURAL die **Stollen**) ❸ (earring) **Ohrstecker** der (PLURAL die **Ohrstecker**)

**student** NOUN ❶ (at college or university) **Student** der (PLURAL die **Studenten**), **Studentin** die (PLURAL die **Studentinnen**) ❷ (at school) **Schüler** der (PLURAL die **Schüler**), **Schülerin** die (PLURAL die **Schülerinnen**)

**studio** NOUN ❶ (film, TV) **Studio** das (PLURAL die **Studios**) ❷ (artist's) **Atelier** das (PLURAL die **Ateliers**)

**study** VERB ❶ **lernen**; **he's busy studying for his exams** er lernt fleißig für seine Prüfung ❷ **studieren**; **she's studying medicine** sie studiert Medizin

**stuff** NOUN (things, personal belongings) **Zeug** das (informal); **we can put all that stuff in the attic** wir können das ganze Zeug auf den Dachboden bringen, **you can leave**

your stuff at my house du kannst dein Zeug bei mir lassen

**stuff** *VERB* ❶ *(shove)* stopfen; she stuffed some things into a suitcase sie hat ein paar Sachen in einen Koffer gestopft ❷ füllen *(vegetables, turkey)*; stuffed peppers gefüllte Paprikaschoten

**stuffing** *NOUN* *(in cooking)* Füllung die *(PLURAL* die Füllungen)

**stuffy** *ADJECTIVE* *(airless)* stickig

**stumble** *VERB* stolpern *(PERF* sein)

**stunned** *ADJECTIVE* sprachlos

**stunning** *ADJECTIVE* toll *(informal)*

**stunt** *NOUN* *(in a film)* Stunt der *(PLURAL* die Stunts)

**stuntman** *NOUN* Stuntman der *(PLURAL* die Stuntmen)

**stupid** *ADJECTIVE* dumm; that was really stupid das war wirklich dumm, I did something stupid ich habe etwas Blödes gemacht

**stutter** *NOUN* to have a stutter stottern

**stutter** *VERB* stottern

**style** *NOUN* ❶ Stil der *(PLURAL* die Stile); style of living der Lebensstil, he has his own style er hat seinen eigenen Stil ❷ *(fashion)* Mode die; it's the latest style das ist die neueste Mode

**subject** *NOUN* ❶ Thema das *(PLURAL* die Themen); the subject of my talk das Thema meiner Rede ❷ *(at school)* Fach das *(PLURAL* die Fächer); my favourite subject is biology mein Lieblingsfach ist Biologie

**submarine** *NOUN* Unterseeboot das *(PLURAL* die Unterseeboote), U-Boot das *(PLURAL* die U-Boote)

**subscription** *NOUN* Abonnement das *(PLURAL* die Abonnements); to take out a subscription to a magazine eine Zeitschrift abonnieren

**subsidize** *VERB* subventionieren

**subsidy** *NOUN* Subvention die *(PLURAL* die Subventionen)

**substance** *NOUN* Substanz die *(PLURAL* die Substanzen)

**substitute** *NOUN* *(in sport)* Ersatzspieler der *(PLURAL* die Ersatzspieler), Ersatzspielerin die *(PLURAL* die Ersatzspielerinnen)

**substitute** *VERB* ersetzen

**subtitled** *ADJECTIVE* mit Untertiteln

**subtitles** *PLURAL NOUN* Untertitel *(plural)*

**subtle** *ADJECTIVE* subtil

**subtract** *VERB* abziehen◇ *(SEP)*

**suburb** *NOUN* Vorort der *(PLURAL* die Vororte); a suburb of Edinburgh ein Vorort von Edinburgh, in the suburbs of London in den Londoner Vororten

**suburban** *ADJECTIVE* Vorort-; a suburban train ein Vorortzug

**subway** *NOUN* *(underpass)* Unterführung die *(PLURAL* die Unterführungen)

**succeed** *VERB* gelingen◇ *(PERF* sein); we've succeeded in contacting her es ist uns gelungen, sie zu erreichen

a b c d e f g h i j k l m n o p q r s t u v w x y z

**success** NOUN **Erfolg** der (PLURAL die **Erfolge**); a great success ein großer Erfolg

**successful** ADJECTIVE ❶ **erfolgreich**; he's a successful writer er ist ein erfolgreicher Schriftsteller ❷ to be successful in doing something etwas mit Erfolg tun

**successfully** ADVERB **mit Erfolg**

**such** ADJECTIVE, ADVERB ❶ **so**; they're such nice people das sind so nette Leute, I've had such a busy day ich habe so einen hektischen Tag gehabt, it's such a long way es ist so weit, it's such a pity es ist so schade ❷ such a lot of (followed by a singular noun) so viel they've got such a lot of money sie haben so viel Geld ❸ such a lot of (followed by a plural noun) so viele, she's got such a lot of problems sie hat so viele Probleme ❹ such as wie, in big cities such as Glasgow in großen Städten wie Glasgow ❺ there's no such thing so etwas gibt es nicht

**suck** VERB **lutschen**; to suck your thumb am Daumen lutschen

**sudden** ADJECTIVE **plötzlich**
• all of a sudden plötzlich

**suddenly** ADVERB **plötzlich**; he suddenly started to laugh plötzlich hat er angefangen zu lachen, suddenly the light went out plötzlich ging das Licht aus

**suede** NOUN **Wildleder** das; suede jacket die Wildlederjacke

**suffer** VERB **leiden**◇; to suffer from asthma an Asthma leiden

**sufficiently** ADVERB **genug**

**sugar** NOUN **Zucker** der; do you take sugar? nimmst du Zucker?

**suggest** VERB **vorschlagen**◇ (SEP); he suggested I should speak to you about it er hat vorgeschlagen, dass ich mit dir darüber sprechen soll

**suggestion** NOUN **Vorschlag** der (PLURAL die **Vorschläge**); to make a suggestion einen Vorschlag machen

**suicide** NOUN **Selbstmord** der (PLURAL die **Selbstmorde**); to commit suicide Selbstmord begehen

**suit** NOUN ❶ (man's) **Anzug** der (PLURAL die **Anzüge**) ❷ (woman's) **Kostüm** das (PLURAL die **Kostüme**)

**suit** VERB ❶ (be convenient) **passen** (+DAT); does Monday suit you? passt Ihnen Montag? ❷ (look good on) **stehen**◇ (+DAT); hats suit her ihr stehen Hüte

**suitable** ADJECTIVE ❶ **geeignet**; to be suitable for something für etwas geeignet sein, it's suitable for children es ist für Kinder geeignet ❷ (convenient) **passend**; at a suitable time zur passenden Zeit, Saturday is the most suitable day for me Samstag passt mir am besten ❸ (for a social occasion) **angemessen** (clothes)

**suitcase** NOUN **Koffer** der (PLURAL die **Koffer**)

**sulk** VERB **schmollen**

**sum** NOUN ❶ **Summe** die (PLURAL die **Summen**); a sum of money eine Geldsumme ❷ (calculation) **Rechenaufgabe** die (PLURAL die **Rechenaufgaben**)
• to sum up zusammenfassen (SEP)

**summarize** *VERB* zusammenfassen (*SEP*)

**summary** *NOUN*
Zusammenfassung die (*PLURAL* die Zusammenfassungen)

**summer** *NOUN* Sommer der (*PLURAL* die Sommer); in summer im Sommer, summer clothes die Sommerkleidung, the summer holidays die Sommerferien

**summertime** *NOUN* Sommer der; in summertime im Sommer

**summit** *NOUN* Gipfel der (*PLURAL* die Gipfel)

**sun** *NOUN* Sonne die (*PLURAL* die Sonnen); in the sun in der Sonne

**sunbathe** *VERB* sich sonnen

**sunblock** *NOUN* Sunblocker der (*PLURAL* die Sunblocker)

**sunburn** *NOUN* Sonnenbrand der (*PLURAL* die Sonnenbrände)

**sunburned** *ADJECTIVE* to get sunburned einen Sonnenbrand bekommen

**Sunday** *NOUN* ❶ Sonntag der (*PLURAL* die Sonntage); on Sunday am Sonntag, I'm going to the cinema on Sunday ich gehe (am) Sonntag ins Kino, see you on Sunday! bis Sonntag!, every Sunday jeden Sonntag, last Sunday vorigen Sonntag, next Sunday nächsten Sonntag ❷ on Sundays sonntags, the museum is closed on Sundays das Museum ist sonntags geschlossen

**sunflower** *NOUN* Sonnenblume die (*PLURAL* die Sonnenblumen); sunflower oil das Sonnenblumenöl

**sunglasses** *PLURAL NOUN*
Sonnenbrille die (*PLURAL* die Sonnenbrillen)

**sunlight** *NOUN* Sonnenlicht das

**sunny** *ADJECTIVE* sonnig; a sunny day ein sonniger Tag, sunny intervals sonnige Abschitte

**sunrise** *NOUN* Sonnenaufgang der (*PLURAL* die Sonnenaufgänge)

**sunroof** *NOUN* Schiebedach das (*PLURAL* die Schiebedächer)

**sunscreen** *NOUN*
Sonnenschutzcreme die (*PLURAL* die Sonnenschutzcremes)

**sunset** *NOUN* Sonnenuntergang der (*PLURAL* die Sonnenuntergänge)

**sunshine** *NOUN* Sonnenschein der

**sunstroke** *NOUN* Sonnenstich der (*PLURAL* die Sonnenstiche); to get sunstroke einen Sonnenstich bekommen

**suntan** *NOUN* Bräune die; to have a suntan braun sein, to get a suntan braun werden

**suntan lotion** *NOUN* Sonnenmilch die

**suntan oil** *NOUN* Sonnenöl das

**super** *ADJECTIVE* klasse (informal) ('klasse' never changes); we had a super time es war wirklich klasse

**supermarket** *NOUN* Supermarkt der (*PLURAL* die Supermärkte)

**supernatural** *ADJECTIVE*
übernatürlich

**superstitious** *ADJECTIVE*
abergläubisch

**supervise** *VERB* beaufsichtigen

**supervisor** | **surgery**

**supervisor** NOUN Aufseher der (PLURAL die Aufseher), Aufseherin die (PLURAL die Aufseherinnen)

**supper** NOUN Abendessen das (PLURAL die Abendessen); **I had supper at Sandy's** ich war bei Sandy zum Abendessen

**supplement** NOUN ❶ (to newspaper) Beilage die (PLURAL die Beilagen) ❷ (to fare) Zuschlag der (PLURAL die Zuschläge)

**supplies** PLURAL NOUN Vorrat der (PLURAL die Vorräte)

**supply** NOUN ❶ (stock) Vorrat der (PLURAL die Vorräte) ❷ **to be in short supply** knapp sein

**supply** VERB ❶ stellen; **the school supplies the books** die Schule stellt die Bücher ❷ (deliver) liefern; **to supply somebody with something** jemandem etwas liefern

**supply teacher** NOUN Aushilfslehrer der (PLURAL die Aushilfslehrer), Aushilfslehrerin die (PLURAL die Aushilfslehrerinnen)

**support** NOUN Unterstützung die; **in support** zur Unterstützung

**support** VERB ❶ (back up) unterstützen; **her teachers have really supported her** die Lehrer haben sie sehr unterstützt, **to support somebody financially** jemanden finanziell unterstützen ❷ **Will supports Chelsea** Will ist ein Chelsea-Fan, **what team do you support?** für welche Mannschaft bist du? ❸ (keep, provide for) ernähren; **to support a family** eine Familie ernähren

**supporter** NOUN ❶ Fan der (PLURAL die Fans); **she's a Manchester United supporter** sie ist ein Manchester-United-Fan ❷ (of a party or cause) Anhänger der (PLURAL die Anhänger), Anhängerin die (PLURAL die Anhängerinnen)

**suppose** VERB annehmen◇ (SEP); **I suppose she's forgotten** ich nehme an, sie hat es vergessen

**supposed** ADJECTIVE **to be supposed to do something** etwas tun sollen, **you were supposed to be here at six** du solltest um sechs hier sein

**sure** ADJECTIVE ❶ sicher; **are you sure?** bist du sicher?, **are you sure you saw her?** bis du sicher, dass du sie gesehen hast? ❷ **sure!** klar!

**surely** ADVERB doch sicherlich; **surely she hasn't forgotten** sie hat es doch sicherlich nicht vergessen

**surf** NOUN Surfen das

**surf** VERB **to surf the Net/Web** im Internet surfen

**surface** NOUN Oberfläche die (PLURAL die Oberflächen)

**surfboard** NOUN Surfbrett das (PLURAL die Surfbretter)

**surfer** NOUN (on the sea and Internet) Surfer der (PLURAL die Surfer), Surferin die (PLURAL die Surferinnen)

**surfing** NOUN Surfen das

**surgeon** NOUN Chirurg der (PLURAL die Chirurgen), Chirurgin die (PLURAL die Chirurginnen)

**surgery** NOUN ❶ **to have surgery** operiert werden ❷ (doctor's) Praxis die (PLURAL die Praxen); **the dentist's surgery** die Zahnarztpraxis ❸ (surgery hours) Sprechstunde die

**surname** NOUN Nachname der (PLURAL die Nachnamen)

**surprise** NOUN Überraschung die (PLURAL die Überraschungen); **what a surprise!** was für eine Überraschung!

**surprised** ADJECTIVE überrascht; **I was surprised to see her** ich war überrascht, sie zu sehen

**surprising** ADJECTIVE überraschend

**surround** VERB umgeben; **surrounded by** umgeben von (+DAT), **she was surrounded by friends** sie war von Freunden umgeben

**survey** NOUN Umfrage die (PLURAL die Umfragen)

**survive** VERB überleben

**survivor** NOUN Überlebende der/die (PLURAL die Überlebenden)

**suspect** NOUN Verdächtige der/die (PLURAL die Verdächtigen)

**suspect** ADJECTIVE verdächtig

**suspect** VERB verdächtigen

**suspend** VERB ❶ **to be suspended** (from school) vom Unterricht ausgeschlossen werden ❷ (from a team) sperren; **to suspend a player for four weeks** einen Spieler für vier Wochen sperren

**suspense** NOUN Spannung die

**suspicious** ADJECTIVE ❶ misstrauisch; **to be suspicious of somebody** jemandem misstrauen ❷ (suspicious looking) verdächtig

**swallow** NOUN (bird) Schwalbe die (PLURAL die Schwalben)

**swallow** VERB schlucken

**swan** NOUN Schwan der (PLURAL die Schwäne)

**swap** VERB tauschen; **do you want to swap?** willst du tauschen?, **he swapped his bike for a computer** er hat sein Rad gegen einen Computer getauscht, **we swapped seats** wir tauschten die Plätze

**swear** VERB (use bad language) fluchen

**swearword** NOUN Kraftausdruck der (PLURAL die Kraftausdrücke)

**sweat** NOUN Schweiß der

**sweat** VERB schwitzen

**sweater** NOUN Pullover der (PLURAL die Pullover)

**swede** NOUN Kohlrübe die (PLURAL die Kohlrüben)

**Swede** NOUN Schwede der (PLURAL die Schweden), Schwedin die (PLURAL die Schwedinnen)

**Sweden** NOUN Schweden das; **from Sweden** aus Schweden, **to Sweden** nach Schweden

**Swedish** NOUN (the language) Schwedisch das

**Swedish** ADJECTIVE schwedisch; **he's Swedish** er ist Schwede, **she's Swedish** sie ist Schwedin

**sweep** VERB fegen

**sweet** NOUN ❶ Bonbon der (PLURAL die Bonbons) ❷ (dessert) Nachtisch der (PLURAL die Nachtische)

**sweet** ADJECTIVE ❶ süß; **I try not to eat sweet things** ich versuche nichts Süßes zu essen, **she looks really sweet in that hat** mit dem Hut sieht sie richtig süß aus ❷ (kind) lieb; **she's a really sweet person** sie ist wirklich ein sehr lieber Mensch, **how sweet of him** wie lieb von ihm

**sweetcorn** NOUN **Mais** der

**swell** VERB *(part of the body)* **anschwellen**◇ *(SEP)* *(PERF* **sein***)*

**swelling** NOUN **Schwellung** die *(PLURAL* die **Schwellungen***)*

**swim** NOUN **to go for a swim** schwimmen gehen◇ *(PERF* **sein***)*

**swim** VERB **schwimmen**◇ *(PERF* **sein***)*; **can he swim?** kann er schwimmen?, **to swim across a lake** an die gegenüberliegende Seite des Sees schwimmen

**swimmer** NOUN **Schwimmer** der *(PLURAL* die **Schwimmer***)*, **Schwimmerin** die *(PLURAL* die **Schwimmerinnen***)*; **she's a strong swimmer** sie ist eine gute Schwimmerin

**swimming** NOUN **Schwimmen** das; **to go swimming** schwimmen gehen◇

**swimming cap** NOUN **Badekappe** die *(PLURAL* die **Badekappen***)*

**swimming costume** NOUN **Badeanzug** der *(PLURAL* die **Badeanzüge***)*

**swimming pool** NOUN **Schwimmbecken** das *(PLURAL* die **Schwimmbecken***)*

**swimming trunks** NOUN **Badehose** die *(PLURAL* die **Badehosen***)*

**swimsuit** NOUN **Badeanzug** der *(PLURAL* die **Badeanzüge***)*

**swindle** NOUN **Betrug** der *(PLURAL* die **Betrüge***)*; **what a swindle!** was für ein Betrug!

**swindle** VERB **betrügen**

**swing** NOUN **Schaukel** die *(PLURAL* die **Schaukeln***)*

**Swiss** NOUN *(person)* **Schweizer** der *(PLURAL* die **Schweizer***)*, **Schweizerin** die *(PLURAL* die **Schweizerinnen***)*; **the Swiss** die Schweizer

**Swiss** ADJECTIVE **schweizerisch**; **she is Swiss** sie ist Schweizerin

**switch** NOUN *(for a light, radio, etc.)* **Schalter** der *(PLURAL* die **Schalter***)*

**switch** VERB *(change)* **wechseln**; **to switch places** die Plätze wechseln
- **to switch something off** etwas ausschalten *(SEP)*
- **to switch something on** etwas anschalten *(SEP)*

**Switzerland** NOUN **die Schweiz**; **from Switzerland** aus der Schweiz, **in Switzerland** in der Schweiz, **to Switzerland** in die Schweiz

**swollen** ADJECTIVE **geschwollen**

**swop** VERB ▸ SEE **swap**

**sword** NOUN **Schwert** das *(PLURAL* die **Schwerter***)*

**syllabus** NOUN **Lehrplan** der *(PLURAL* die **Lehrpläne***)*; **to be on the syllabus** auf dem Lehrplan stehen

**symbol** NOUN **Symbol** das *(PLURAL* die **Symbole***)*

**symbolic** ADJECTIVE **symbolisch**

**sympathetic** ADJECTIVE **verständnisvoll**

**sympathize** *VERB* to sympathize with somebody mit jemandem mitfühlen *(SEP)*, I sympathize with you ich kann mit Ihnen mitfühlen

**sympathy** *NOUN* Mitleid das

**symphony** *NOUN* Sinfonie die *(PLURAL* die **Sinfonien***)*

**symptom** *NOUN* Symptom das *(PLURAL* die **Symptome***)*

**synagogue** *NOUN* Synagoge die *(PLURAL* die **Synagogen***)*

**synthesizer** *NOUN* Synthesizer der *(PLURAL* die **Synthesizer***)*

**synthetic** *ADJECTIVE* synthetisch

**syringe** *NOUN* Spritze die *(PLURAL* die **Spritzen***)*

**system** *NOUN* System das *(PLURAL* die **Systeme***)*

**table** *NOUN* Tisch der *(PLURAL* die **Tische***)*; to lay the table den Tisch decken, to clear the table den Tisch abräumen *(SEP)*

**tablecloth** *NOUN* Tischdecke die *(PLURAL* die **Tischdecken***)*

**tablespoon** *NOUN* Esslöffel der *(PLURAL* die **Esslöffel***)*; a tablespoon of flour ein Esslöffel Mehl

**tablet** *NOUN* Tablette die *(PLURAL* die **Tabletten***)*

**table tennis** *NOUN* Tischtennis das

**tackle** *VERB* ❶ *(in football or hockey)* angreifen◇ *(SEP)* ❷ angehen◇ *(SEP)* *(PERF* **sein***)* *(a job or a problem)*

**tact** *NOUN* Takt der

**tactful** *ADJECTIVE* taktvoll; that wasn't very tactful das war nicht sehr taktvoll

**tadpole** *NOUN* Kaulquappe die *(PLURAL* die **Kaulquappen***)*

**tail** *NOUN* ❶ Schwanz der *(PLURAL* die **Schwänze***)* ❷ 'heads or tails?' – 'tails' 'Kopf oder Zahl?' – 'Zahl'

**take** *VERB* ❶ nehmen◇; he took a sweet er nahm einen Bonbon, take my hand nimm meine Hand, I took the bus ich habe den Bus genommen, do you take sugar? nimmst du Zucker? ❷ *(with time)* dauern; it takes two hours es dauert zwei Stunden ❸ *(react to)* **aufnehmen**◇ *(SEP)*; **he took the news calmly** er hat die Nachricht gelassen aufgenommen ❹ *(take to a place)* **bringen**◇; **I'm taking Jake to my parents** ich bringe Jake zu meinen Eltern, **I must take the car to the garage** ich muss das Auto in die Werkstatt bringen, **to take somebody home** jemanden nach Hause bringen ❺ **to take something up(stairs)** etwas hinaufbringen◇ *(SEP)*, **could you take the towels up?** könntest du die Handtücher heraufbringen? ❻ **to take something down(stairs)** etwas hinunterbringen◇ *(SEP)*, **Cheryl's taken the cups down** Cheryl hat die Tassen heruntergebracht ❼ *(carry with you)* **mitnehmen**◇ *(SEP)*; **she's taken some of the files home** sie hat einige der Akten mit nach Hause genommen, **I'm taking my Walkman** ich nehme meinen Walkman mit, **I'll take him next time** nächstes Mal nehme ich ihn mit ❽ **nehmen**◇ *(SEP)* *(a credit card or a cheque)*; **do you take cheques?** nehmen Sie Schecks? ❾ **machen** *(an exam, a holiday, or a photo)*; **she's taking her driving test tomorrow** sie macht morgen ihre Fahrprüfung, **to take a holiday** Ferien machen ❿ *(need)* **brauchen**; **it takes a lot of courage** dazu braucht man viel Mut, **it takes me at least two hours to read it** ich brauche mindestens zwei Stunden, um es zu lesen ⓫ **haben**◇ *(clothes size)*; **what size do you take?** welche Größe haben Sie?

• **to take something apart** etwas auseinander nehmen◇

• **to take something back** etwas zurückbringen◇ *(SEP)*

• **to take off** ❶ *(plane)* **abfliegen**◇

*(SEP)* *(PERF* **sein***)* ❷ **ausziehen**◇ *(SEP)* *(clothes, shoes)*; **take your jacket off** zieh die Jacke aus, **to take your clothes off** sich ausziehen ❸ **abziehen**◇ *(SEP)* *(money)*; **he took five pounds off the price** er hat fünf Pfund vom Preis abgezogen

• **to take out something** *(from a bag or pocket)* **herausnehmen**◇ *(SEP)*; **Eric took out his wallet** Eric nahm seine Brieftasche heraus

• **to take somebody out** jemanden ausführen *(SEP)*; **to take somebody out for a meal** jemanden zum Essen in ein Restaurant einladen◇ *(SEP)*

**takeaway** NOUN ❶ *(meal)* **Essen zum Mitnehmen** das *(PLURAL die Essen zum Mitnehmen)*; **an Indian takeaway** ein indisches Essen zum Mitnehmen ❷ *(where you buy it)* **Restaurant mit Straßenverkauf** das *(PLURAL die Restaurants mit Straßenverkauf)*

**take-off** NOUN *(of a plane)* **Abflug** der *(PLURAL die Abflüge)*

**talent** NOUN **Talent** das *(PLURAL die Talente)*; **to have a talent for painting** ein Talent zum Malen haben

**talented** ADJECTIVE **talentiert**; **he's really talented** er ist wirklich talentiert

**talk** NOUN ❶ *(a chat)* **Gespräch** das *(PLURAL die Gespräche)*; **we had a serious talk about it** wir hatten ein ernstes Gespräch darüber ❷ **Vortrag** der *(PLURAL die Vorträge)*; **she's giving a talk on Hungary** sie hält einen Vortrag über Ungarn

**talk** VERB ❶ **reden**; **to talk to somebody** mit jemandem reden, **we talked about football** wir haben über Fußball geredet, **what's he talking about?** wovon redet er?, **we'll talk about it later** darüber reden wir später, **they're always talking** sie reden immer ❷ **to talk to somebody on the phone** mit jemandem telefonieren

**tall** ADJECTIVE ❶ groß; **she's very tall** sie ist sehr groß, **I'm 1.7 metres tall** ich bin ein Meter siebzig groß ❷ hoch (building or tree)

**tame** ADJECTIVE zahm

**tampon** NOUN Tampon der (PLURAL die Tampons)

**tan** NOUN Bräune die; **to have a tan** braun sein, **to get a tan** braun werden

**tank** NOUN ❶ (for petrol or water) Tank der (PLURAL die Tanks) ❷ (for fish) Aquarium das (PLURAL die Aquarien) ❸ (military) Panzer der (PLURAL die Panzer)

**tanker** NOUN ❶ (on sea) Tanker der (PLURAL die Tanker) ❷ (on the road) Tankwagen der (PLURAL die Tankwagen)

**tanned** ADJECTIVE braun

**tap** NOUN Wasserhahn der (PLURAL die Wasserhähne); **to turn on the tap** den Wasserhahn aufdrehen (SEP), **to turn off the tap** den Wasserhahn zudrehen (SEP), **the hot tap** der Warmwasserhahn

**tap** VERB klopfen; **to tap on the door** an die Tür klopfen

**tap-dancing** NOUN Stepptanzen das

**tape** NOUN ❶ Kassette die (PLURAL die Kassetten); **my tape of the Stones** meine Kassette von den Stones, **I've got it on tape** ich habe

es auf Kassette ❷ **sticky tape** der Klebestreifen

**tape** VERB aufnehmen◇ (SEP); **I want to tape the film** ich will den Film aufnehmen

**tape measure** NOUN Metermaß das (PLURAL die Metermaße)

**tape recorder** NOUN Tonbandgerät das (PLURAL die Tonbandgeräte)

**tapestry** NOUN Wandteppich der (PLURAL die Wandteppiche)

**target** NOUN Ziel das (PLURAL die Ziele)

**tart** NOUN Kuchen der (PLURAL die Kuchen); **apple tart** der Apfelkuchen

**tartan** ADJECTIVE Schotten-; **a tartan skirt** ein Schottenrock

**task** NOUN Aufgabe die (PLURAL die Aufgaben)

**taste** NOUN ❶ Geschmack der (PLURAL die Geschmäcke); **a taste of onions** ein Zwiebelgeschmack, **she's got no taste** sie hat keinen Geschmack ❷ **in bad taste** geschmacklos

**taste** VERB ❶ schmecken; **the soup tastes horrible** die Suppe schmeckt furchtbar ❷ **to taste of something** nach etwas (DAT) schmecken, **it tastes of garlic** es schmeckt nach Knoblauch ❸ (try a little) probieren; **do you want to taste?** möchtest du mal probieren?

**tasty** ADJECTIVE schmackhaft

**tattoo** NOUN Tätowierung die (PLURAL die Tätowierungen); **he's got a tattoo on his arm** er hat eine Tätowierung am Arm

**Taurus** NOUN Stier der; **Josephine's Taurus** Josephine ist (ein) Stier

a b c d e f g h i j k l m n o p q r s **t** u v w x y z

597

**tax** NOUN **Steuer** die (PLURAL die **Steuern**) (on goods, income)

**taxi** NOUN **Taxi** das (PLURAL die **Taxis**); to go by taxi mit dem **Taxi** fahren, to take a taxi ein **Taxi** nehmen

**taxi driver** NOUN **Taxifahrer** der (PLURAL die **Taxifahrer**) **Taxifahrerin** die (PLURAL die **Taxifahrerinnen**)

**taxi rank** NOUN **Taxistand** der (PLURAL die **Taxistände**)

**tea** NOUN ❶ **Tee** der (PLURAL die **Tees**); a cup of tea eine **Tasse Tee**, to have tea **Tee** trinken ❷ (evening meal) **Abendessen** das (PLURAL die **Abendessen**)

**teabag** NOUN **Teebeutel** der (PLURAL die **Teebeutel**)

**teach** VERB ❶ **beibringen**◇ (SEP); she's teaching me to drive sie bringt mir das **Autofahren** bei ❷ to teach yourself something sich (DAT) etwas **beibringen**◇ (SEP), I taught myself Italian ich habe mir **Italienisch** beigebracht ❸ that'll teach you! das wird dir eine **Lehre** sein! ❹ **unterrichten**; her mum teaches maths ihre Mutter unterrichtet **Mathematik**

**teacher** NOUN **Lehrer** der (PLURAL die **Lehrer**), **Lehrerin** die (PLURAL die **Lehrerinnen**)

**teaching** NOUN **Unterrichten** das

**team** NOUN **Mannschaft** die (PLURAL die **Mannschaften**); football team die **Fußballmannschaft**

**teapot** NOUN **Teekanne** die (PLURAL die **Teekannen**)

**tear**[1] NOUN (a rip) **Riss** der (PLURAL die **Risse**)

**tear** VERB ❶ **zerreißen**◇; she tore up my letter sie hat meinen Brief zerrissen ❷ **reißen**◇ (PERF **sein**); the net has torn das **Netz** ist gerissen, be careful, it tears easily sei vorsichtig, es reißt leicht

**tear**[2] NOUN (when you cry) **Träne** die (PLURAL die **Tränen**); to be in tears in **Tränen aufgelöst** sein, to burst into tears in **Tränen ausbrechen**

**tease** VERB ❶ **necken** (a person) ❷ **quälen** (an animal)

**teaspoon** NOUN **Teelöffel** der (PLURAL die **Teelöffel**); a teaspoon of vinegar ein **Teelöffel Essig**

**teatime** NOUN (evening meal) **Abendessenszeit** die; it's teatime! es gibt **Abendessen**!

**tea towel** NOUN **Geschirrtuch** das (PLURAL die **Geschirrtücher**)

**technical** ADJECTIVE **technisch**

**technical college** NOUN **Fachhochschule** die (PLURAL die **Fachhochschulen**)

**technician** NOUN **Techniker** der (PLURAL die **Techniker**), **Technikerin** die (PLURAL die **Technikerinnen**)

**technique** NOUN **Technik** die (PLURAL die **Techniken**)

**techno** NOUN (music) **Techno** der

**technological** ADJECTIVE **technologisch**

**technology** NOUN ❶ **Technologie** die ❷ information technology die **Informatik**

**teddy bear** NOUN **Teddybär** der (PLURAL die **Teddybären**)

**teenage** *ADJECTIVE* **❶ Teenage-
❷** they have a teenage son sie
haben einen Sohn im Teenageralter
**❸** *(films, magazines, etc.)* **für
Teenager**; a teenage magazine
eine Jugendzeitschrift

**teenager** *NOUN* **Teenager** der
*(PLURAL* die **Teenager***)*; a group
of teenagers eine Gruppe von
Teenagern

**teens** *PLURAL NOUN* the teens die
Teenagerjahre, he's in his teens er
ist ein Teenager

**tee-shirt** *NOUN* **T-Shirt** das *(PLURAL* die
**T-Shirts***)*

**telephone** *NOUN* **Telefon** das *(PLURAL*
die **Telefone***)*; on the telephone am
Telefon

**telephone** *VERB* **anrufen**◇ *(SEP)*; I'll
telephone the bank ich rufe die
Bank an

**telephone box** *NOUN* **Telefonzelle**
die *(PLURAL* die **Telefonzellen***)*

**telephone call** *NOUN*
**Telefongespräch** das *(PLURAL* die
**Telefongespräche***)*

**telephone directory** *NOUN*
**Telefonbuch** das *(PLURAL* die
**Telefonbücher***)*

**telephone number** *NOUN*
**Telefonnummer** die *(PLURAL* die
**Telefonnummern***)*

**telescope** *NOUN* **Fernrohr** das *(PLURAL*
die **Fernrohre***)*, **Teleskop** das
*(PLURAL* die **Teleskope***)*

**televise** *VERB* **im Fernsehen
übertragen**◇; they're televising
the match sie übertragen das Spiel
im Fernsehen

**television** *NOUN* **❶ Fernsehen** das;
I saw it on television ich habe es
im Fernsehen gesehen **❷** to watch
television fernsehen◇ *(SEP)*, I'm
watching television ich sehe fern

**television programme** *NOUN*
**Fernsehsendung** die *(PLURAL* die
**Fernsehsendungen***)*

**tell** *VERB* **❶ sagen**; to tell somebody
something jemandem etwas sagen,
if she asks, tell her sag's ihr, wenn
sie fragt **❷** to tell somebody to do
something jemandem sagen, er/sie
soll etwas tun, he told me to do it
myself er hat mir gesagt, ich soll
es selbst machen, she told me not
to wait sie sagte ich solle nicht
warten **❸** *(explain)* can you tell me
how to do it? kannst du mir sagen,
wie man das macht? **❹ erzählen** *(a
story)*; tell me about your holiday
erzähl mir von deinen Ferien **❺** *(to
see)* **sehen**◇; you can tell it's old
man sieht, dass es alt ist, I can't
tell them apart ich kann sie nicht
unterscheiden

**telly** *NOUN* **❶** *(set)* **Fernseher** der
*(PLURAL* die **Fernseher***)* **❷** to watch
telly fernsehen◇ *(SEP)*, I saw her
on telly ich habe sie im Fernsehen
gesehen

**temp** *NOUN* **Aushilfskraft** die *(PLURAL*
die **Aushilfskräfte***)*

**temper** *NOUN* to lose your temper
wütend werden

**temperature** *NOUN* **❶ Temperatur**
die *(PLURAL* die **Temperaturen***)*;
what is the temperature? wie
viel Grad sind es? **❷** to have a
temperature Fieber haben

**temporary** *ADJECTIVE*
**vorübergehend**

a
b
c
d
e
f
g
h
i
j
k
l
m
n
o
p
q
r
s
t
u
v
w
x
y
z

**temptation** NOUN Versuchung die
(PLURAL die **Versuchungen**)

**tempted** ADJECTIVE versucht; **I'm
really tempted to come** ich würde
am liebsten kommen

**tempting** ADJECTIVE verlockend

**ten** NUMBER zehn; **Harry's ten** Harry
ist zehn

**tend** VERB **to tend to do something**
dazu neigen, etwas zu tun

**tender** ADJECTIVE ❶ (loving) zärtlich
❷ (painful) empfindlich

**tennis** NOUN Tennis das; **to play
tennis** Tennis spielen

**tennis ball** NOUN Tennisball der
(PLURAL die **Tennisbälle**)

**tennis court** NOUN Tennisplatz der
(PLURAL die **Tennisplätze**)

**tennis player** NOUN Tennisspieler
der (PLURAL die **Tennisspieler**),
Tennisspielerin die (PLURAL die
**Tennisspielerinnen**)

**tennis racket** NOUN Tennisschläger
der (PLURAL die **Tennisschläger**)

**tenor** NOUN Tenor der (PLURAL die
**Tenöre**)

**tenpin bowling** NOUN Bowling das

**tense** NOUN Zeit die; **the present
tense** das Präsens, **in the future
tense** im Futur

**tense** ADJECTIVE gespannt

**tent** NOUN Zelt das (PLURAL die **Zelte**)

**tenth** NUMBER zehnter/zehnte/
zehntes; **on the tenth floor** im
zehnten Stock, **the tenth of April**
der zehnte April

**term** NOUN (in school) Halbjahr das
(PLURAL die **Halbjahre**), (at university)
Semester das (PLURAL die **Semester**)

**terminal** NOUN ❶ (at an airport)
Terminal der (PLURAL die **Terminals**)
❷ bus terminal die Endstation
❸ (computer terminal) Terminal das
(PLURAL die **Terminals**)

**terrace** NOUN ❶ (outside a house)
Terrasse die (PLURAL die **Terrassen**)
❷ (row of houses) Häuserreihe die
(PLURAL die **Häuserreihen**) ❸ **the
terraces** (at a stadium) die Ränge
(plural)

**terrible** ADJECTIVE furchtbar

**terribly** ADVERB ❶ (very) sehr; **not
terribly clean** nicht sehr sauber
❷ (badly) furchtbar; **I played
terribly** ich habe furchtbar gespielt

**terrific** ADJECTIVE ❶ irre (informal);
**a terrific amount** eine irre Menge
❷ **terrific!** super! (informal)

**terrified** ADJECTIVE verängstigt; **to be
terrified** furchtbare Angst haben

**terrorism** NOUN Terrorismus der

**terrorist** NOUN Terrorist der (PLURAL
die **Terroristen**) Terroristin die
(PLURAL die **Terroristinnen**)

**test** NOUN ❶ (in school) Klassenarbeit
die (PLURAL die **Klassenarbeiten**);
**we've got a maths test tomorrow**
wir schreiben morgen eine
Mathearbeit ❷ (medical check,
trial) Test der (PLURAL die **Tests**);
**eye test** der Sehtest, **blood test**
die Blutprobe ❸ **driving test** die
Fahrprüfung, **she's taking her
driving test on Friday** sie macht
am Freitag ihre Fahrprüfung, **he
passed his driving test** er hat seine
Fahrprüfung bestanden

**test** *VERB (in school)* prüfen; **can you test me?** kannst du mich abfragen?

**test tube** *NOUN* Reagenzglas das *(PLURAL die Reagenzgläser)*

**text** *VERB* simsen

**text** *NOUN* **❶** Text die *(PLURAL die Texte)* **❷** SMSD die *(PLURAL die SMS)*

**textbook** *NOUN* Lehrbuch das *(PLURAL die Lehrbücher)*

**text message** *NOUN* SMS die *(PLURAL die SMS)*

**Thames** *NOUN* **the Thames** die Themse

**than** *CONJUNCTION* als; **they have more money than we do** sie haben mehr Geld als wir, **more than forty** mehr als vierzig, **more than thirty years** mehr als dreißig Jahre

**thank** *VERB* **❶** **to thank somebody for something** sich bei jemandem für etwas *(ACC)* bedanken **❷** **thank you** danke, **thank you for looking after the children** danke, dass du auf die Kinder aufgepasst hast

**thanks** *PLURAL NOUN* **❶** Dank der; **thanks a lot!** vielen Dank!, **many thanks** vielen Dank **❷** **no thanks** nein danke, **thanks for your letter** danke für deinen Brief **❸** **thanks to** dank *(+DAT)*, **it was thanks to him that we made it** dank ihm haben wir es geschafft

**thank you** *ADVERB* danke; **thank you very much for the cheque** herzlichen Dank für den Scheck, **no thank you** nein danke, **a thank-you letter** ein Dankbrief

**that** *DETERMINER* **❶** dieser/diese/dieses; **that boy** dieser Junge, **that woman** diese Frau, **that house**

dieses Haus **❷** **that one** der da/die da/das da, **'which cake would you like?' – 'that one, please'** 'welchen Kuchen möchten Sie?' – 'den da, bitte', **I like all the dresses but I'm going to buy that one** mir gefallen alle Kleider, aber ich kaufe das da

**that** *ADVERB* so; **it's not that easy** es ist nicht so einfach

**that** *PRONOUN* **❶** das; **what's that?** was ist das?, **who's that?** wer ist das?, **where's that?** wo ist das?, **is that Mandy?** ist das Mandy? **❷** das; **did you see that?** hast du das gesehen?, **that's my bedroom** das ist mein Schlafzimmer **❸** *(in relative clauses)* der/die/das *(depending on the gender of the noun 'that' refers to)*; **the train that's leaving now** der Zug, der jetzt abfährt, **the flower that I picked** die Blume, die ich gepflückt habe, **the car that's red** das Auto, das rot ist

**that** *CONJUNCTION* dass; **I knew that he was lying** ich wußte, dass er log

**the** *DETERMINER* **❶** der/die/das *(the determiner changes according to the gender of the noun)*; *(before a masculine noun)* **the dog** der Hund, *(before a feminine noun)* **the cat** die Katze, *(before a neuter noun)* **the car** das Auto **❷** *(before all plural nouns)* die; **the windows** die Fenster

**theatre** *NOUN* Theater das *(PLURAL die Theater)*; **to go to the theatre** ins Theater gehen

**theft** *NOUN* Diebstahl der *(PLURAL die Diebstähle)*

**their** *DETERMINER* ihr *(PLURAL ihre)*; **their son** ihr Sohn, **their daughter** ihre Tochter, **their car** ihr Auto, **their presents** ihre Geschenke

**theirs** PRONOUN ❶ **ihrer** *(when standing for a masculine noun)*; **our garden's smaller than theirs** unser Garten ist kleiner als ihrer ❷ **ihre** *(when standing for a feminine noun)*; **your flat is bigger than theirs** deine Wohnung ist größer als ihre ❸ **ihrs** *(when standing for a neuter noun)*; **our car was cheaper than theirs** unser Auto war billiger als ihrs ❹ **ihre** *(when standing for a plural noun)*; **our children are older than theirs** unsere Kinder sind älter als ihre ❺ **the yellow car's theirs** das gelbe Auto gehört ihnen, **it's theirs** das gehört ihnen

**them** PRONOUN ❶ *(as a direct object in the accusative)* **sie**; **I know them** ich kenne sie, **I don't know them** ich kenne sie nicht ❷ *(after prepositions +ACC)* **sie**; **it's for them** das ist für sie ❸ *(as an indirect object or following a verb that takes the dative)* **ihnen**; **I told them a story** ich habe ihnen eine Geschichte erzählt ❹ *(to them)* **ihnen**; **I gave them my address** ich habe ihnen meine Adresse gegeben ❺ *(after prepositions +DAT)* **ihnen**; **I'll go with them** ich gehe mit ihnen mit ❻ *(in comparisons)* **he's older than them** er ist älter als sie

**theme** NOUN **Thema** das *(PLURAL die Themen)*

**theme park** NOUN **Themenpark** der *(PLURAL die Themenparks)*

**themselves** PRONOUN ❶ **sich**; **they enjoyed themselves** sie haben sich amüsiert ❷ *(for emphasis)* **selbst**; **the boys can do it themselves** die Jungen können es selbst machen

**then** ADVERB ❶ *(next)* **dann**; **I get up and then I make the bed** ich stehe auf und dann mache ich das Bett,

**I went to the post office and then the bank** ich bin zur Post und dann auf die Bank gegangen ❷ *(at that time)* **damals**; **we were living in York then** wir haben damals in York gewohnt ❸ *(in that case)* **dann**; **then why worry?** warum machst du dir dann Sorgen? ❹ *(since then)* **seitdem** ❺ *(from then on)* **von da an**

**theory** NOUN ❶ **Theorie** die *(PLURAL die Theorien)* ❷ **in theory** theoretisch

**there** ADVERB ❶ *(in a fixed location)* **da**; **up there** da oben, **down there** da unten, **in there** da drin, **stay there** bleib da ❷ **over there** da drüben, **she's over there with Mark** sie ist da drüben mit Mark ❸ *(with movement to a place)* **dahin**; **put it there** leg es dahin, **we're going there on Tuesday** wir fahren am Dienstag dahin ❹ *(further away)* **dort**; **I've seen photos of Oxford but I've never been there** ich habe Fotos von Oxford gesehen, aber ich war noch nie dort ❺ **there is** *(there exists)* **da ist, es ist**, **there's a cat in the garden** da ist eine Katze im Garten, **there's enough bread** es ist genug Brot da, **no, there's not enough** nein, es ist nicht genug da ❻ **there is** es **es gibt**, **there's only one hospital in this town** in dieser Stadt gibt es nur ein Krankenhaus ❼ **there are** **da sind, es sind**, **there were lots of people in town** es waren viele Leute in der Stadt ❽ **there are** *(there exist)* **es gibt**, **there are lots of museums here** es gibt hier viele Museen ❾ *(when drawing attention)* **da**; **there they are!** da sind sie!, **there's the bus coming!** da kommt der Bus!

**therefore** ADVERB **deshalb**

**thermometer** NOUN **Thermometer** das (PLURAL die **Thermometer**)

**these** DETERMINER **diese**; these glasses diese Gläser

**these** PRONOUN **die**; these are cheaper die sind billiger

**they** PRONOUN ❶ **sie**; 'where are the knives?' – 'they're in the drawer' 'wo sind die Messer?' – 'sie sind in der Schublade' ❷ **man**; they say man sagt

**thick** ADJECTIVE **dick**; a thick layer of butter eine dicke Schicht Butter

**thief** NOUN **Dieb** der (PLURAL die **Diebe**) **Diebin** die (PLURAL die **Diebinnen**)

**thigh** NOUN **Oberschenkel** der (PLURAL die **Oberschenkel**)

**thin** ADJECTIVE **dünn**

**thing** NOUN ❶ (an object) **Ding** das (PLURAL die **Dinge**); they have lots of nice things sie haben viele schöne Dinge, she told me some strange things sie hat mir ein paar seltsame Dinge erzählt, that thing next to the hammer das Ding da neben dem Hammer ❷ things (belongings) **Sachen** (plural), you can leave your things in my room du kannst deine Sachen in meinem Zimmer lassen ❸ the best thing to do is ... am besten wäre es ... ❹ (subject, affair) **Sache** die (PLURAL die **Sachen**); the thing is, I've lost her address die Sache ist die, ich habe ihre Adresse verloren ❺ how are things? wie geht's?

**think** VERB ❶ (believe) **glauben**; do you think they'll come? glaubst du, sie kommen? no, I don't think so nein, ich glaube nicht, I think so ich glaube schon, I think he's already paid ich glaube, er hat schon gezahlt ❷ **denken**◇; I'm thinking about you ich denke an dich, what are you thinking about? woran denkst du? ❸ what do you think of that? was halten Sie davon?, I don't think much of her proposal ich halte nicht viel von ihrem Vorschlag ❹ what do you think of my new jacket? wie findest du meine neue Jacke? ❺ (remember) to think to do something daran denken, etwas zu tun, he didn't think of locking the door er hat nicht daran gedacht, die Tür abzuschließen ❻ (to think carefully) **nachdenken**◇ (SEP); he thought for a moment er hat einen Moment lang nachgedacht, think about it! denk darüber nach! ❼ I've thought it over carefully ich habe es mir genau überlegt ❽ (imagine) **sich** (DAT) **vorstellen** (SEP); just think, we'll soon be in Spain! stell dir nur vor, bald sind wir in Spanien!, I never thought it would be like this so habe ich es nie vorgestellt, dass es so sein würde

**third** NOUN **Drittel** das (PLURAL die **Drittel**); a third of the population ein Drittel der Bevölkerung

**third** ADJECTIVE **dritter/dritte/drittes**; on the third floor im dritten Stock, on the third of March am dritten März

**thirdly** ADVERB **drittens**

**Third World** NOUN **Dritte Welt** die

**thirst** NOUN **Durst** der

**thirsty** ADJECTIVE **durstig**; to be thirsty Durst haben, I'm thirsty ich habe Durst, we were all thirsty wir hatten alle Durst

**thirteen** NUMBER **dreizehn; Ahmed's thirteen** Ahmed ist dreizehn

**thirty** NUMBER **dreißig**

**this** DETERMINER ❶ **dieser/diese/ dieses; this boy** dieser Junge, **this flower** diese Blume, **this car** dieses Auto, **at the end of this week** Ende dieser Woche ❷ **this morning** heute Morgen, **this evening** heute Abend, **this afternoon** heute Nachmittag ❸ **this one** der/die/das, *(with more emphasis)* dieser/diese/dieses, **if you need a pen you can have this one** wenn du einen Kugelschreiber brauchst, kannst du das haben, **I'll take this one** ich nehme diesen

**this** PRONOUN ❶ **das; can you hold this?** kannst du das festhalten?, **what's this?** was ist das? ❷ **this is my sister Carla** *(in introductions)* das ist meine Schwester Carla ❸ **this is Tracy speaking** *(on the phone)* hier spricht Tracy

**thistle** NOUN **Distel** die *(PLURAL die Disteln)*

**thorn** NOUN **Dorn** der *(PLURAL die Dornen)*

**those** ADJECTIVE **diese; those books** diese Bücher

**those** PRONOUN **die da; if you need more knives you can take those** wenn du mehr Messer brauchst, kannst du die da nehmen

**though** CONJUNCTION **obwohl; though it's cold** obwohl es kalt ist

**though** ADVERB **dennoch; it was a good idea, though** es war dennoch eine gute Idee

**thought** NOUN **Gedanke** der *(PLURAL die Gedanken)*

**thousand** NUMBER ❶ **tausend; a thousand** eintausend, **three thousand** dreitausend ❷ **thousands of** Tausende von, **there were thousands of tourists in Venice** Tausende von Touristen waren in Venedig

**thread** NOUN **Faden** der *(PLURAL die Fäden)*

**thread** VERB **einfädeln** *(a needle)*

**threat** NOUN **Drohung** die *(PLURAL die Drohungen)*; **is that a threat?** soll das eine Drohung sein?

**threaten** VERB **drohen** *(+DAT)*; **he threatened her** er hat ihr gedroht, **to threaten to do something** damit drohen, etwas zu tun

**three** NUMBER **drei; Oskar's three** Oskar ist drei

**three-quarters** NOUN **drei Viertel** die

**three-quarters** ADVERB **three-quarters full** drei viertel voll

**thrilled** ADJECTIVE **to be thrilled** sich wahnsinnig freuen

**thriller** NOUN **Thriller** der *(PLURAL die Thriller)*

**thrilling** ADJECTIVE **spannend**

**throat** NOUN **Hals** der *(PLURAL die Hälse)*; **to have a sore throat** Halsschmerzen haben

**through** PREPOSITION ❶ *(across, via)* **durch** *(+ACC)*; **through the forest** durch den Wald, **the train goes through Leeds** der Zug fährt durch Leeds, **through the window** durch das Fenster ❷ **to let somebody through** jemanden durchlassen◇ *(SEP)*, **the police let us through** die

Polizei ließ uns durch **❸ I know them through my cousin** ich kenne sie über meinen Vetter

**throw** VERB **❶** werfen◇; **I threw the letter in the bin** ich habe den Brief in den Mülleimer geworfen **❷ to throw something to somebody** jemandem etwas zuwerfen◇ (SEP), **throw me the ball** wirf mir den Ball zu, **to throw something at somebody** etwas nach jemandem werfen

- **to throw something away** etwas wegwerfen◇ (SEP); **I'm throwing away the old newspapers** ich werfe die alten Zeitungen weg
- **to throw somebody out** jemanden rauswerfen◇ (SEP)
- **to throw something out** etwas wegwerfen◇ (SEP) (rubbish)

**thumb** NOUN **Daumen** der (PLURAL die **Daumen**)

**thump** VERB schlagen◇, auf (+ACC); **he thumped the radio to see if it would work** er schlug auf das Radio, um zu sehen ob es dann funktionierte

**thunder** NOUN **Donner** der; **peal of thunder** der Donnerschlag

**thunderstorm** NOUN **Gewitter** das (PLURAL die **Gewitter**)

**thundery** ADJECTIVE gewittrig

**Thursday** NOUN **❶ Donnerstag** der (PLURAL die **Donnerstage**); **on Thursday** (am) Donnerstag, **I'm leaving on Thursday** ich fahre am Donnerstag ab, **see you on Thursday** bis Donnerstag, **every Thursday** jeden Donnerstag, **last Thursday** vorigen Donnerstag, **next Thursday** nächsten Donnerstag **❷ on Thursdays** donnerstags, **the**

**museum is closed on Thursdays** das Museum ist donnerstags geschlossen

**thyme** NOUN **Thymian** der

**tick** VERB **❶** (clock, watch) **ticken ❷** (on paper) **abhaken** (SEP)

**ticket** NOUN **❶** (for an exhibition, theatre, or cinema) **Karte** die (PLURAL die **Karten**); **two tickets for the concert** zwei Karten für das Konzert **❷** (for the underground, a bus, or a train) **Fahrkarte** die (PLURAL die **Fahrkarten**); **a plane ticket** ein Flugschein, ein Ticket **❸** (for left luggage, parking) **Zettel** der (PLURAL die **Zettel**) **❹** (for a lottery or raffle) **Los** das (PLURAL die **Lose**) **❺** parking ticket der Strafzettel

**ticket inspector** NOUN **Schaffner** der (PLURAL die **Schaffner**), **Schaffnerin** die (PLURAL die **Schaffnerinnen**)

**ticket office** NOUN (at a station) **Fahrkartenschalter** der (PLURAL die **Fahrkartenschalter**)

**tickle** VERB kitzeln

**tide** NOUN **❶** (high) **Flut** die (PLURAL die **Fluten**); **at high tide** bei Flut **❷** (low) **Ebbe** die (PLURAL die **Ebben**); **the tide is out** es ist Ebbe

**tidy** ADJECTIVE ordentlich

**tidy** VERB aufräumen (SEP); **I'll tidy (up) the kitchen** ich räume die Küche auf

**tie** NOUN **❶** (necktie) **Krawatte** die (PLURAL die **Krawatten**) **❷** (in a match) **Unentschieden** das

**tie** VERB **❶** binden◇; **to tie your shoelaces** sich (DAT) die Schnürsenkel binden **❷ to tie a**

A
B
C
D
E
F
G
H
I
J
K
L
M
N
O
P
Q
R
S
**T**
U
V
W
X
Y
Z

knot in something einen Knoten in etwas (ACC) machen ❸ (in a match) we tied two all wir haben zwei zu zwei gespielt

**tiger** NOUN **Tiger** der (PLURAL die **Tiger**)

**tight** ADJECTIVE (close-fitting) **eng**; the skirt's a bit tight der Rock ist etwas eng, these shoes are too tight diese Schuhe sind zu eng, she was wearing tight jeans sie hatte enge Jeans an

**tighten** VERB **anziehen**◇ (SEP) (a screw, knot); he tightened his belt er schnallte seinen Gürtel enger, he tightened his grip er griff fester zu

**tightly** ADVERB **fest**

**tights** PLURAL NOUN **Strumpfhose** die (PLURAL die **Strumpfhosen**); a pair of purple tights eine lila Strumpfhose

**tile** NOUN ❶ (on a floor) **Fliese** die (PLURAL die **Fliesen**) ❷ (on a wall) **Kachel** die (PLURAL die **Kacheln**) ❸ (on a roof) **Ziegel** der (PLURAL die **Ziegel**)

**till**¹ PREPOSITION, CONJUNCTION ❶ **bis**; they're staying till Sunday sie bleiben bis Sonntag, till then bis dann, till now bis jetzt ❷ (when 'till' is followed by a noun it is usually translated as 'bis zu' +DAT) till the evening bis zum Abend ❸ not till erst, she won't be back till ten sie kommt erst um zehn zurück, we won't know till Monday wir werden erst am Montag Bescheid wissen

**till**² NOUN **Kasse** die (PLURAL die **Kassen**); please pay at the till bitte zahlen Sie an der Kasse

**time** NOUN ❶ (on the clock) **Zeit** die; it's time for breakfast es ist Zeit

zum Frühstücken ❷ what time is it? wie viel Uhr ist es?, at what time does it start? um wie viel Uhr fängt es an?, ten o'clock German time zehn Uhr, deutsche Zeit ❸ on time pünktlich ❹ (an amount of time) **Zeit** die; we've got lots of time wir haben viel Zeit, I haven't got time now ich habe jetzt keine Zeit, there's no time left to do it dafür bleibt keine Zeit mehr, from time to time von Zeit zu Zeit, for a long time lange ❺ (moment) **Moment** der (PLURAL die **Momente**); this isn't a good time to discuss it das ist kein guter Moment, um darüber zu sprechen, at the right time im richtigen Moment, for the time being im Moment, any time now jeden Moment ❻ at times manchmal ❼ (in a series) **Mal** das (PLURAL die **Male**); eight times achtmal, for the first time zum ersten Mal, the first time I saw you das erste Mal, als ich dich sah, three times a year dreimal jährlich ❽ three times two is six drei mal zwei ist sechs ❾ to have a good time sich amüsieren, we had a really good time wir haben uns richtig gut amüsiert, have a good time! viel Vergnügen!

**timetable** NOUN ❶ (in school) **Stundenplan** der (PLURAL die **Stundenpläne**) ❷ (for trains or buses) **Fahrplan** der (PLURAL die **Fahrpläne**); bus timetable der Busfahrplan

**tin** NOUN **Dose** die (PLURAL die **Dosen**); a tin of tomatoes eine Dose Tomaten

**tinned** ADJECTIVE **in Dosen**; tinned peas Erbsen in Dosen

**tin opener** NOUN **Dosenöffner** der *(PLURAL die* **Dosenöffner***)*

**tiny** ADJECTIVE **winzig**

**tip** NOUN ❶ *(end)* **Spitze** die *(PLURAL die* **Spitzen***)* ❷ *(money)* **Trinkgeld** das ❸ *(useful hint)* **Tipp** der *(PLURAL die* **Tipps***) (informal)*

**tip** VERB *(give money)* **ein Trinkgeld geben**✧ *(+DAT)*; **we tipped the waiter** wir haben dem Kellner ein Trinkgeld gegeben

**tiptoe** NOUN **on tiptoe** auf Zehenspitzen

**tired** ADJECTIVE ❶ **müde**; **I'm tired** ich bin müde, **you look tired** du siehst müde aus ❷ **to be tired of something** etwas satt haben, **I'm tired of London** ich habe London satt, **I'm tired of watching TV every evening** ich habe es satt, jeden Abend fernzusehen

**tiring** ADJECTIVE **ermüdend**

**tissue** NOUN *(a paper hanky)* **Papiertaschentuch** das *(PLURAL die* **Papiertaschentücher***)*

**tissue paper** NOUN **Seidenpapier** das

**title** NOUN **Titel** der *(PLURAL die* **Titel***)*

**to** PREPOSITION ❶ *(to a country or town)* **nach**; **to go to London** nach London fahren, **the motorway to Italy** die Autobahn nach Italien, **they're going to Switzerland** sie fahren in die Schweiz ❷ *(to the cinema, theatre, school, office)* **in** *(+ACC)*; **I'm going to school** ich gehe in die Schule, **she's gone to the office** sie ist ins Büro gegangen, **we want to go to town** wir wollen in die Stadt gehen ❸ *(to a wedding, party, university, the toilet)* **auf** *(+ACC)*; **she's**
gone to the toilet sie ist auf die Toilette gegangen ❹ *(addressed or attached to)* **an** *(+ACC)*; **a letter to my parents** ein Brief an meine Eltern ❺ **give the book to her** gib ihr das Buch, **he said to me that ...** er hat mir gesagt, dass ... ❻ *(to somebody's house, a particular place, or person)* **zu** *(+DAT)*; **I went round to Paul's house** ich bin zu Paul nach Hause gegangen, **we're going to the Browns' for supper** wir gehen zu Browns zum Abendessen, **I'm going to the dentist tomorrow** morgen gehe ich zum Zahnarzt ❼ *(talking about the time)* **it's ten to nine** es ist zehn vor neun, **from eight to ten** von acht bis zehn, **from Monday to Friday** von Montag bis Freitag ❽ *(in order to)* **um ... zu** *(+ INFINITIVE)*; **he gave me some money to buy a sandwich** er hat mir Geld gegeben, um ein Sandwich zu kaufen ❾ *(in verbal phrases with the infinitive)* **zu**; **I have nothing to do** ich habe nichts zu tun, **have you got something to eat?** hast du etwas zu essen?

**toast** NOUN ❶ **Toast** der *(PLURAL die* **Toasts***)*; **two slices of toast** zwei Scheiben Toast ❷ *(to your health)* **Toast** der *(PLURAL die* **Toasts***)*; **to drink a toast to somebody** auf jemanden trinken

**toaster** NOUN **Toaster** der *(PLURAL die* **Toaster***)*

**tobacco** NOUN **Tabak** der

**tobacconist's** NOUN **Tabakladen** der *(PLURAL die* **Tabakläden***)*

**today** ADVERB **heute**; **today's her birthday** sie hat heute Geburtstag

**toe** NOUN **Zeh** der *(PLURAL die* **Zehen***)*

**toffee** NOUN **Karamell** der

a b c d e f g h i j k l m n o p q r s t u v w x y z

**together** ADVERB ❶ zusammen; **we did it together** wir haben es zusammen gemacht ❷ *(at the same time)* gleichzeitig; **they all left together** sie sind alle gleichzeitig weggegangen

**toilet** NOUN Toilette die *(PLURAL die Toiletten)*; **she's gone to the toilet** sie ist auf die Toilette gegangen

**toilet paper** NOUN Toilettenpapier das

**toilet roll** NOUN Rolle Toilettenpapier die *(PLURAL die Rollen Toilettenpapier)*

**token** NOUN ❶ *(for a machine or game)* Marke die *(PLURAL die Marken)* ❷ *(voucher)* Gutschein der *(PLURAL die Gutscheine)*; **gift token** der Geschenkgutschein

**tolerant** ADJECTIVE tolerant

**toll** NOUN ❶ *(payment)* Gebühr die *(PLURAL die Gebühren)* ❷ *(number)* Zahl die; **the death toll has risen to 25** die Zahl der Todesopfer ist jetzt bei 25

**tomato** NOUN Tomate die *(PLURAL die Tomaten)*; **tomato salad** der Tomatensalat, **tomato sauce** die Tomatensoße

**tomorrow** ADVERB ❶ morgen; **I'll do it tomorrow** ich mache es morgen, **tomorrow afternoon** morgen Nachmittag, **tomorrow morning** morgen früh, **tomorrow night** morgen Abend ❷ **the day after tomorrow** übermorgen

**tone** NOUN *(on an answerphone, of a voice, or letter)* Ton der *(PLURAL die Töne)*

**tongue** NOUN Zunge die *(PLURAL die Zungen)*; **to stick your tongue out at somebody** jemandem die Zunge herausstrecken
• **it's on the tip of my tongue** es liegt mir auf der Zunge

**tonic** NOUN Tonic das *(PLURAL die Tonics)*; **a gin and tonic** ein Gin Tonic

**tonight** ADVERB ❶ *(this evening)* heute Abend; **I'm going out with my friends tonight** ich gehe heute Abend mit meinen Freunden weg ❷ *(after bedtime)* heute Nacht

**tonsillitis** NOUN Mandelentzündung die; **Ahlem's got tonsillitis** Ahlem hat eine Mandelentzündung

**too** ADVERB ❶ zu; **it's too expensive** es ist zu teuer, **too often** zu oft ❷ **too much** zu viel, **I've spent too much** ich habe zu viel ausgegeben, **too many** zu viele ❸ *(as well)* auch; **Karen's coming too** Karen kommt auch, **me too!** ich auch!

**tool** NOUN Werkzeug das *(PLURAL die Werkzeuge)*

**tool box** NOUN Werkzeugkasten der *(PLURAL die Werkzeugkästen)*

**tool kit** NOUN Werkzeug das

**tooth** NOUN Zahn der *(PLURAL die Zähne)*; **to brush your teeth** sich *(DAT)* die Zähne putzen

**toothache** NOUN Zahnschmerzen *(plural)*

**toothbrush** NOUN Zahnbürste die *(PLURAL die Zahnbürsten)*

**toothpaste** NOUN Zahnpasta die *(PLURAL die Zahnpasten)*

**top** NOUN ❶ *(highest part)* Spitze die *(PLURAL die* Spitzen) *(of a tree)* ❷ at the top of oben auf *(+DAT)*, at the top of the ladder oben auf der Leiter, it's on top of the chest of drawers es liegt oben auf der Kommode ❸ at the top oben, there are four rooms at the top oben sind vier Zimmer, from top to bottom von oben bis unten ❹ *(of a container, jar, or box)* Deckel der *(PLURAL die* Deckel) ❺ *(of a mountain)* Gipfel der *(PLURAL die* Gipfel) ❻ *(a lid)* Kappe die *(PLURAL die* Kappen) *(of a pen)*, Verschluss der *(PLURAL die* Verschlüsse) *(of a bottle)* ❼ *(of a garment)* Oberteil das *(PLURAL die* Oberteile) ❽ *(in sport)* the top of the table die Tabellenspitze
- and on top of all that obendrein
- it was a bit over the top es war leicht übertrieben

**top** ADJECTIVE oberster/oberste/ oberstes *(step or floor)*; on the top floor im obersten Stockwerk

**topic** NOUN Thema das *(PLURAL die* Themen)

**topping** NOUN Belag der *(PLURAL die* Beläge)*; which topping would you like? welchen Belag hättest du gerne?

**torch** NOUN Taschenlampe die *(PLURAL die* Taschenlampen)

**torn** ADJECTIVE zerrissen

**tortoise** NOUN Schildkröte die *(PLURAL die* Schildkröten)

**torture** NOUN ❶ Folter die *(PLURAL die* Foltern) ❷ the exam was torture die Prüfung war die Hölle *(informal)*

**torture** VERB quälen

**Tory** NOUN Konservative der/die *(PLURAL die* Konservativen)

**total** NOUN ❶ *(number)* Gesamtzahl die *(PLURAL die* Gesamtzahlen) ❷ *(result of addition)* Summe die *(PLURAL die* Summen)

**total** ADJECTIVE gesamt

**totally** ADVERB völlig

**touch** NOUN ❶ *(contact)* to get in touch with somebody sich mit jemandem in Verbindung setzen, to stay in touch with somebody mit jemandem Kontakt halten ❷ we've lost touch wir haben keinen Kontakt mehr, I've lost touch with Peter ich habe keinen Kontakt mehr zu Peter ❸ *(a little bit)* a touch of salt eine Spur Salz, it was a touch embarrassing es war ein bisschen peinlich

**touch** VERB ❶ berühren ❷ *(get hold of)* anfassen *(SEP)*; don't touch that fass das nicht an

**touched** ADJECTIVE gerührt

**touching** ADJECTIVE rührend

**touchscreen** NOUN Touchscreen der *(PLURAL die* Touchscreens)

**tough** ADJECTIVE ❶ hart; she's had a tough time sie hat eine harte Zeit hinter sich, a tough guy ein harter Kerl ❷ zäh; the meat's tough das Fleisch ist zäh ❸ fest *(material, shoes, etc.)* ❹ tough luck! Pech!, tough, you're too late so'n Pech, du bist zu spät dran

**tour** NOUN ❶ Besichtigung die *(PLURAL die* Besichtigungen); a tour of the city eine Stadtbesichtigung, we did a tour of the castle wir haben das Schloss besichtigt ❷ guided

a
b
c
d
e
f
g
h
i
j
k
l
m
n
o
p
q
r
s
t
u
v
w
x
y
z

**tour** die Führung ❸ package tour
die Pauschalreise ❹ (by a band or
theatre group) Tournee die (PLURAL
die Tournees); to go on tour auf
Tournee gehen

**tour** VERB (performer) auf Tournee
sein◇ (PERF sein); they're touring
America sie sind auf Tournee in
Amerika

**tour guide** NOUN Reiseleiter
der (PLURAL die Reiseleiter),
Reiseleiterin die (PLURAL die
Reiseleiterinnen)

**tourism** NOUN Tourismus der

**tourist** NOUN Tourist der (PLURAL die
Touristen), Touristin die (PLURAL die
Touristinnen)

**tourist information office** NOUN
Fremdenverkehrsbüro das (PLURAL
die Fremdenverkehrsbüros)

**tournament** NOUN Turnier das
(PLURAL die Turniere); tennis
tournament das Tennisturnier

**tow** VERB to be towed away
abgeschlept werden◇ (PERF sein)

**towards** PREPOSITION zu (+DAT); she
went off towards the lake sie
ist zum See gegangen; to come
towards somebody auf jemanden
zukommen◇ (SEP) (PERF sein)

**towel** NOUN Handtuch das (PLURAL die
Handtücher)

**tower** NOUN Turm der (PLURAL die
Türme)

**tower block** NOUN Hochhaus das
(PLURAL die Hochhäuser)

**town** NOUN Stadt die (PLURAL die
Städte); to go into town in die
Stadt gehen

**town centre** NOUN Stadtmitte die
(PLURAL die Stadtmitten)

**town hall** NOUN Rathaus das (PLURAL
die Rathäuser)

**toy** NOUN Spielzeug das

**toyshop** NOUN Spielzeuggeschäft
das (PLURAL die Spielzeuggeschäfte)

**trace** NOUN Spur die (PLURAL die
Spuren); there was no trace of the
thieves es fehlte jede Spur von den
Dieben

**trace** VERB ❶ (find) finden◇ ❷ (follow)
verfolgen ❸ (copy) durchpausen
(SEP)

**tracing paper** NOUN Pauspapier
das

**track** NOUN ❶ (for sport) Bahn die
(PLURAL die Bahnen); cycling track
die Radrennbahn, racing track (for
cars) die Rennstrecke ❷ (a path)
Weg der (PLURAL die Wege) ❸ (song)
Stück das (PLURAL die Stücke); this
is my favourite track das ist mein
Lieblingsstück

**track suit** NOUN Trainingsanzug der
(PLURAL die Trainingsanzüge)

**tractor** NOUN Traktor der (PLURAL die
Traktoren)

**trade** NOUN ❶ (a profession) Gewerbe
das ❷ (skill, craft) Handwerk das;
to learn a trade ein Handwerk
erlernen

**trade union** NOUN Gewerkschaft
die (PLURAL die Gewerkschaften)

**tradition** NOUN Tradition die (PLURAL
die Traditionen)

**traditional** ADJECTIVE traditionell

**traffic** NOUN Verkehr der

**traffic island** NOUN **Verkehrsinsel** die *(PLURAL* die **Verkehrsinseln***)*

**traffic jam** NOUN **Stau** der *(PLURAL* die **Staus***)*

**traffic lights** PLURAL NOUN **Ampel** die *(PLURAL* die **Ampeln***)*

**traffic warden** NOUN **Verkehrsüberwacher** der *(PLURAL* die **Verkehrsüberwacher***)*, **Politesse** die *(PLURAL* die **Politessen***)*

**tragedy** NOUN **Tragödie** die *(PLURAL* die **Tragödien***)*

**tragic** ADJECTIVE **tragisch**

**trail** NOUN *(a path)* **Pfad** der *(PLURAL* die **Pfade***)*; a nature trail ein Naturlehrpfad

**trailer** NOUN **Anhänger** der *(PLURAL* die **Anhänger***)*

**train** NOUN **Zug** der *(PLURAL* die **Züge***)*; he's coming by train er kommt mit dem Zug, I met her on the train ich habe sie im Zug getroffen, the train for York der Zug nach York

**train** VERB ❶ *(for a career)* **ausbilden** *(SEP)* ❷ she's training to be a nurse sie macht eine Ausbidung zur Krankenschwester ❸ *(in sport)* **trainieren**; the team trains on Wednesdays die Mannschaft trainiert mittwochs

**trainee** NOUN **Auszubildende** der/die *(PLURAL* die **Auszubildenden***)*

**trainer** NOUN ❶ *(of an athlete or horse)* **Trainer** der *(PLURAL* die **Trainer***)*, **Trainerin** die *(PLURAL* die **Trainerinnen***)* ❷ trainers **Turnschuhe** *(plural)*

**training** NOUN ❶ *(for a career)* **Ausbildung** die ❷ *(for sport)* **Training** das

**train ticket** NOUN **Zugfahrkarte** die *(PLURAL* die **Zugfahrkarten***)*

**train timetable** NOUN **Bahnfahrplan** der *(PLURAL* die **Bahnfahrpläne***)*

**tram** NOUN **Straßenbahn** die *(PLURAL* die **Straßenbahnen***)*

**tramp** NOUN **Landstreicher** der *(PLURAL* die **Landstreicher***)*, **Landstreicherin** die *(PLURAL* die **Landstreicherinnen***)*

**transfer** NOUN **Abziehbild** das *(PLURAL* die **Abziehbilder***)*

**transform** VERB **verwandeln**

**transistor** NOUN **Transistor** der *(PLURAL* die **Transistoren***)*

**translate** VERB **übersetzen**; to translate something into German etwas ins Deutsche übersetzen

**translation** NOUN **Übersetzung** die *(PLURAL* die **Übersetzungen***)*

**translator** NOUN **Übersetzer** der *(PLURAL* die **Übersetzer***)*, **Übersetzerin** die *(PLURAL* die **Übersetzerinnen***)*

**transparent** ADJECTIVE **durchsichtig**

**transplant** NOUN **Transplantation** die *(PLURAL* die **Transplantationen***)*

**transport** NOUN **Transport** der *(PLURAL* die **Transporte***)*, the transport of goods der Warentransport, public transport öffentliche Verkehrsmittel *(plural)*

**trap** NOUN **Falle** die *(PLURAL* die **Fallen***)*

**travel** NOUN Reisen das; **foreign travel** Auslandsreisen (plural)

**travel** VERB reisen (PERF sein)

**travel agency** NOUN Reisebüro das (PLURAL die **Reisebüros**)

**travel agent's** NOUN Reisebüro das (PLURAL die **Reisebüros**)

**traveller** NOUN ❶ Reisende der/die (PLURAL die **Reisenden**) ❷ (gypsy) Zigeuner der (PLURAL die **Zigeuner**), Zigeunerin die (PLURAL die **Zigeunerinnen**)

**traveller's cheque** NOUN Reisescheck der (PLURAL die **Reiseschecks**)

**travel-sick** ADJECTIVE reisekrank; **I get travel-sick** ich werde reisekrank

**tray** NOUN Tablett das (PLURAL die **Tabletts**)

**tread** VERB **to tread on something** auf etwas (ACC) treten◇ (PERF sein), **she trod on my foot** sie ist mir auf den Fuß getreten

**treasure** NOUN Schatz der (PLURAL die **Schätze**)

**treat** NOUN ❶ **I took them to the circus as a treat** ich habe ihnen eine besondere Freude gemacht und sie in den Zirkus eingeladen ❷ (food) Leckerbissen der (PLURAL die **Leckerbissen**)

**treat** VERB ❶ behandeln; **he treats his dog well** er behandelt seinen Hund gut, **the doctor who treated you** der Arzt, der dich behandelt hat ❷ **to treat somebody to something** jemandem etwas spendieren, **I'll treat you to an ice cream** ich spendiere euch ein Eis

**treatment** NOUN Behandlung die (PLURAL die **Behandlungen**)

**tree** NOUN Baum der (PLURAL die **Bäume**)

**tremble** VERB zittern

**trend** NOUN ❶ (a fashion) Trend der (PLURAL die **Trends**) ❷ (a tendency) Tendenz die (PLURAL die **Tendenzen**)

**trendy** ADJECTIVE modern

**trial** NOUN (in court) Prozess der (PLURAL die **Prozesse**)

**triangle** NOUN Dreieck das (PLURAL die **Dreiecke**)

**trick** NOUN ❶ (a joke) Streich der (PLURAL die **Streiche**); **to play a trick on somebody** jemandem einen Streich spielen ❷ (a knack or by a conjuror) Trick der (PLURAL die **Tricks**); **there must be a trick to it** da muss ein Trick dabei sein

**trick** VERB hereinlegen (SEP); **he tricked me!** er hat mich hereingelegt!

**tricky** ADJECTIVE verzwickt; **it's a tricky situation** das ist eine verzwickte Situation

**tricycle** NOUN Dreirad das (PLURAL die **Dreiräder**)

**trim** VERB schneiden◇ (hair)

**trip** NOUN ❶ Reise die (PLURAL die **Reisen**); **a trip to Florida** eine Reise nach Florida, **he's going on a business trip** er macht eine Geschäftsreise ❷ (a day out) Ausflug der (PLURAL die **Ausflüge**); **a day trip to France** ein Tagesausflug nach Frankreich

**trip** VERB (to stumble) **stolpern** (PERF **sein**); **Nicky tripped over a stone** Nicky ist über einen Stein gestolpert

**triumph** NOUN **Triumph** der (PLURAL die **Triumphe**)

**trolley** NOUN ❶ (for shopping) **Einkaufswagen** der (PLURAL die **Einkaufswagen**) ❷ (for luggage) **Kofferkuli** der (PLURAL die **Kofferkulis**)

**trombone** NOUN **Posaune** die (PLURAL die **Posaunen**)

**troops** PLURAL NOUN **Truppen** (plural)

**trophy** NOUN **Trophäe** die (PLURAL die **Trophäen**), (in competitions) **Pokal** der (PLURAL die **Pokale**)

**trot** VERB **traben** (PERF **sein**)

**trouble** NOUN ❶ (general difficulties) **Ärger** der; **to make trouble** Ärger machen; **to get into trouble** Ärger bekommen; **we had trouble with the travel agency** wir hatten Ärger mit dem Reisebüro ❷ (problem) **Problem** das (PLURAL die **Probleme**); **the trouble is, I've lost his phone number** das Problem ist, dass ich seine Telefonnummer verloren habe, **Steph's in trouble** Steph hat Probleme, **what's the trouble?** was ist los?, **it's no trouble!** das ist kein Problem ❸ (difficulty, effort) **Mühe** die; **to have trouble doing something** Mühe haben, etwas zu tun, **I had trouble finding a seat** ich hatte Mühe, einen Platz zu finden, **it's not worth the trouble** das ist nicht der Mühe wert

**trousers** PLURAL NOUN **Hose** die (PLURAL die **Hosen**); **my old trousers** meine alte Hose, **a new pair of trousers** eine neue Hose

**trout** NOUN **Forelle** die (PLURAL die **Forellen**)

**truant** NOUN **Schulschwänzer** der (PLURAL die **Schulschwänzer**), **Schulschwänzerin** die (PLURAL die **Schulschwänzerinnen**); **she's playing truant** sie schwänzt die Schule

**truck** NOUN **Lastwagen** der (PLURAL die **Lastwagen**)

**true** ADJECTIVE ❶ **wahr**; **a true story** eine wahre Geschichte ❷ **is that true?** stimmt das?, **it's true she's absent-minded** das stimmt, sie ist sehr vergesslich

**trump** NOUN **Trumpf** der (PLURAL die **Trümpfe**); **hearts are trumps** Herz ist Trumpf

**trumpet** NOUN **Trompete** die (PLURAL die **Trompeten**)

**trunk** NOUN ❶ (of a tree) **Stamm** der (PLURAL die **Stämme**) ❷ (of an elephant) **Rüssel** der (PLURAL die **Rüssel**)

**trunks** PLURAL NOUN **swimming trunks Badehose** die (PLURAL die **Badehosen**)

**trust** NOUN **Vertrauen** das

**trust** VERB ❶ (believe) **to trust somebody** jemandem vertrauen ❷ (rely on) **you can trust him** man kann sich auf ihn verlassen

**truth** NOUN **Wahrheit** die

**try** NOUN **Versuch** der (PLURAL die **Versuche**); **it's my first try** es ist mein erster Versuch, **to have a try** es versuchen, **give it a try!** versuch's doch mal!

**try** VERB ❶ **versuchen**; to try to do something **versuchen**, etwas zu tun, I'm trying to open the door ich versuche, die Tür aufzumachen ❷ *(taste)* **probieren**
• to try something on etwas **anprobieren** *(SEP)* *(a garment)*

**T-shirt** NOUN **T-Shirt** das *(PLURAL die T-Shirts)*

**tube** NOUN ❶ **Tube** die *(PLURAL die Tuben)* ❷ *(the Underground)* the Tube die **U-Bahn**

**tuberculosis** NOUN **Tuberkulose** die

**Tuesday** NOUN ❶ **Dienstag** der *(PLURAL die Dienstage)*; on Tuesday (am) Dienstag, I'm going to the cinema on Tuesday ich gehe Dienstag ins Kino, see you on Tuesday! bis Dienstag!, every Tuesday jeden Dienstag, last Tuesday vorigen Dienstag, next Tuesday nächsten Dienstag ❷ on Tuesdays dienstags, the museum is closed on Tuesdays das Museum ist dienstags geschlossen

**tuition** NOUN ❶ **Unterricht** der; piano tuition der Klavierunterricht ❷ extra tuition **Nachhilfestunden** *(plural)*

**tulip** NOUN **Tulpe** die *(PLURAL die Tulpen)*

**tumble-drier** NOUN **Wäschetrockner** der *(PLURAL die Wäschetrockner)*

**tumbler** NOUN **Becherglas** das *(PLURAL die Bechergläser)*

**tuna** NOUN **Thunfisch** der

**tune** NOUN **Melodie** die *(PLURAL die Melodien)*

**tunnel** NOUN **Tunnel** der *(PLURAL die Tunnel)*; the Channel Tunnel der Eurotunnel

**turkey** NOUN **Pute** die *(PLURAL die Puten)*

**Turkey** NOUN **die Türkei**; from Turkey aus der Türkei, in Turkey in der Türkei, to Turkey in die Türkei

**Turkish** NOUN *(language)* **Türkisch** das

**Turkish** ADJECTIVE **türkisch**; he is Turkish er ist Türke, she is Turkish sie ist Türkin

**turn** NOUN ❶ *(in a game)* it's your turn du bist an der Reihe, whose turn is it? wer ist an der Reihe?, it's Jane's turn Jane ist an der Reihe ❷ to take turns sich abwechseln, to take it in turns to do something abwechselnd etwas tun ❸ *(in a road)* **Kurve** die *(PLURAL die Kurven)*; to take a right/left turn nach rechts/links abbiegen

**turn** VERB ❶ **drehen**; turn the key to the right dreh den Schlüssel nach rechts, turn your chair round dreh deinen Stuhl herum ❷ *(person, car)* **abbiegen**◇ *(SEP)* *(PERF sein)*; turn left at the next set of lights biegen Sie an der nächsten Ampel links ab ❸ *(become)* **werden**◇ *(PERF sein)*; she turned red sie wurde rot
• to turn back **umkehren** *(SEP)* *(PERF sein)*
• to turn off ❶ *(from a road)* **abbiegen**◇ *(SEP)* *(PERF sein)* ❷ *(switch off)* **ausmachen** *(SEP)* *(a light, an oven, a TV, or radio)*, **zudrehen** *(SEP)* *(a tap)*, **abstellen** *(SEP)* *(gas, electricity, or water)*, **ausschalten** *(SEP)* *(an engine)*
• to turn on **anmachen** *(SEP)* *(a TV, radio, or light)*, **aufdrehen** *(SEP)* *(a tap)*, **anschalten** *(SEP)* *(an oven)*,

anlassen◇ *(SEP) (an engine)*

- to turn out ❶ to turn out well gut ausgehen◇ *(SEP) (PERF* **sein***)*, the discussions turned out badly die Gespräche sind schlecht ausgegangen, it all turned out all right in the end am Ende ging alles gut aus ❷ it turned out that I was right es stellte sich heraus, dass ich Recht hatte
- to turn up ❶ *(to arrive)* aufkreuzen *(SEP) (PERF* **sein***)*; they turned up an hour later sie sind eine Stunde später aufgekreuzt ❷ *(to make louder)* lauter machen

**turning** *NOUN* **Abzweigung** die *(PLURAL* die **Abzweigungen***)*; take the third turning on the right nimm die dritte Abzweigung rechts

**turnip** *NOUN* **Steckrübe** die *(PLURAL* die **Steckrüben***)*

**turquoise** *ADJECTIVE* **türkis**

**turtle** *NOUN* **Schildkröte** die *(PLURAL* die **Schildkröten***)*

**TV** *NOUN* **Fernsehen** das; I saw her on TV ich habe sie im Fernsehen gesehen

**tweezers** *NOUN* **Pinzette** die *(PLURAL* die **Pinzetten***)*

**twelfth** *NUMBER* **zwölfter/zwölfte/ zwölftes**; on the twelfth floor im zwölften Stock, the twelfth of May der zwölfte Mai

**twelve** *NUMBER* ❶ **zwölf**; Tara's twelve Tara ist zwölf ❷ at twelve o'clock um zwölf Uhr

**twenty** *NUMBER* **zwanzig**; Marie's twenty Marie ist zwanzig, twenty-one einundzwanzig

**twice** *ADVERB* ❶ **zweimal**; I've asked him twice ich habe ihn zweimal gefragt, twice a day zweimal täglich ❷ twice as much doppelt so viel

**twig** *NOUN* **Zweig** der *(PLURAL* die **Zweige***)*

**twin** *NOUN* **Zwilling** der *(PLURAL* die **Zwillinge***)*; Helen and Tim are twins Helen und Tim sind Zwillinge, her twin sister ihre Zwillingsschwester

**twin** *VERB* Richmond is twinned with Konstanz Richmond und Konstanz sind Partnerstädte

**twist** *VERB* ❶ *(bend out of shape)* **verbiegen◇** ❷ **verdrehen** *(words, meaning)* ❸ to twist your ankle sich den Knöchel verrenken

**two** *NUMBER* **zwei**; Ben's two Ben ist zwei, two by two zu zweit

**type** *NOUN* **Art** die; what type of computer is it? welche Art Computer ist es?

**type** *VERB (on a typewriter)* **Schreibmaschine schreiben◇**, **tippen** *(informal)*; I'm learning to type ich lerne Schreibmaschine schreiben, I'm just typing some letters ich tippe gerade ein paar Briefe

**typewriter** *NOUN* **Schreibmaschine** die *(PLURAL* die **Schreibmaschinen***)*

**typical** *ADJECTIVE* **typisch**

**tyre** *NOUN* **Reifen** der *(PLURAL* die **Reifen***)*

a
b
c
d
e
f
g
h
i
j
k
l
m
n
o
p
q
r
s
t
u
v
w
x
y
z

# Uu

**ugly** ADJECTIVE **hässlich**

**UK** NOUN (United Kingdom) **Vereinigte Königreich das**

**ulcer** NOUN **Geschwür das** (PLURAL die **Geschwüre**)

**Ulster** NOUN **Ulster**; **from Ulster aus Ulster, aus Nordirland**

**umbrella** NOUN **Regenschirm der** (PLURAL die **Regenschirme**)

**umpire** NOUN **Schiedsrichter der** (PLURAL die **Schiedsrichter**), **Schiedsrichterin die** (PLURAL die **Schiedsrichterinnen**)

**UN** ABBREVIATION (short for **United Nations**) **UN** (plural)

**unable** ADJECTIVE **to be unable to do something etwas nicht tun können, he's unable to come er kann nicht kommen**

**unavoidable** ADJECTIVE **unvermeidlich**

**unbearable** ADJECTIVE **unerträglich**

**unbelievable** ADJECTIVE **unglaublich**

**uncertain** ADJECTIVE ❶ (not sure) **to be uncertain whether ... sich** (DAT) **nicht sicher sein, ob ...** ❷ (unpredictable) **ungewiss** (future or result)

**uncle** NOUN **Onkel der** (PLURAL die **Onkel**)

**uncomfortable** ADJECTIVE ❶ **unbequem** (shoes, chair, or journey) ❷ **unangenehm** (situation, heat)

**unconscious** ADJECTIVE (out cold) **bewusstlos**

**under** PREPOSITION ❶ (underneath) **unter** (+DAT, or +ACC when there is movement towards a place); **the dog's under the bed der Hund ist unter dem Bett, the ball rolled under the bed der Ball ist unter das Bett gerollt** ❷ **under there da drunter, perhaps it's under there vielleicht ist es da drunter** ❸ (less than) **unter** (+DAT); **under £20 unter zwanzig Pfund, children under five Kinder unter fünf**

**under-age** ADJECTIVE **to be under-age minderjährig sein**

**underclothes** PLURAL NOUN **Unterwäsche die**

**undercooked** ADJECTIVE **nicht gar**

**underestimate** VERB **unterschätzen**

**underground** NOUN (railway) **U-Bahn die** (PLURAL die **U-Bahnen**); **I saw her on the underground ich habe sie in der U-Bahn gesehen, shall we go by underground? fahren wir mit der U-Bahn?**

**underground** ADJECTIVE **unterirdisch** (cave); **underground car park die Tiefgarage**

**underline** VERB **unterstreichen**◊

**underneath** PREPOSITION **unter** (+DAT or, with movement towards a place, +ACC); **it's underneath the newspaper es ist unter der Zeitung, I put it underneath the newspaper ich habe es unter die Zeitung gelegt**

**underneath** ADVERB darunter; **check underneath** sieh darunter nach

**underpants** PLURAL NOUN Unterhose die (PLURAL die **Unterhosen**); **my underpants** meine Unterhose

**underpass** NOUN Unterführung die (PLURAL die **Unterführungen**)

**understand** VERB verstehen◇; **do you understand?** verstehst du?, **I couldn't understand what he was saying** ich konnte ihn nicht verstehen, **I can't understand why she doesn't want to see him** ich kann nicht verstehen, warum sie ihn nicht sehen will

**understandable** ADJECTIVE **that's understandable** das ist verständlich

**understanding** NOUN Verständnis das

**understanding** ADJECTIVE verständnisvoll

**underwear** NOUN Unterwäsche die

**undo** VERB aufmachen (SEP)

**undone** ADJECTIVE **to come undone** aufgehen◇ (SEP) (PERF **sein**)

**undress** VERB **to get undressed** sich ausziehen◇ (SEP)

**unemployed** NOUN **the unemployed** die Arbeitslosen (plural)

**unemployed** ADJECTIVE arbeitslos

**unemployment** NOUN Arbeitslosigkeit die

**uneven** ADJECTIVE uneben (surface); **her pulse is uneven** ihr Puls ist unregelmäßig, **your writing is very uneven** deine Schrift ist sehr ungleichmäßig, **the icing is uneven** diese Kuchenglasur ist nicht glatt

**unexpected** ADJECTIVE unerwartet

**unexpectedly** ADVERB (to happen, arrive) überraschend

**unfair** ADJECTIVE unfair; **it's unfair on young people** es ist jungen Leuten gegenüber unfair

**unfashionable** ADJECTIVE unmodern

**unfasten** VERB aufmachen (SEP)

**unfit** ADJECTIVE nicht fit; **I'm terribly unfit** ich bin nicht sehr fit

**unfold** VERB ❶ (a map) ausbreiten (SEP) ❷ (to develop) spielen, **the story unfolds in Africa** die Geschichte spielt in Afrika

**unfortunate** ADJECTIVE unglücklich

**unfortunately** ADVERB leider

**unfriendly** ADJECTIVE unfreundlich

**ungrateful** ADJECTIVE undankbar

**unhappy** ADJECTIVE ❶ unglücklich ❷ (not satisfied) unzufrieden; **to be unhappy about something** mit etwas unzufrieden sein

**unhealthy** ADJECTIVE ungesund

**uniform** NOUN Uniform die (PLURAL die **Uniformen**)

**union** NOUN (trade union) Gewerkschaft die (PLURAL die **Gewerkschaften**)

**Union Jack** NOUN **the Union Jack** die britische Nationalflagge

**unique** ADJECTIVE einzigartig

**unit** NOUN ❶ (for measuring, for example) Einheit die (PLURAL die **Einheiten**) ❷ (in a kitchen) Einbauschrank der (PLURAL die **Einbauschränke**) ❸ (a department)

**Abteilung** die *(PLURAL* die **Abteilungen)**; the research unit die Forschungsabteilung

**United Kingdom** *NOUN* **Vereinigte Königreich** das

**United Nations** *NOUN* **Vereinte Nationen** *(plural)*

**United States (of America)** *PLURAL NOUN* **Vereinigte Staaten (von Amerika)** *(plural)*

**universe** *NOUN* **Universum** das, **Weltall** das

**university** *NOUN* **Universität** die *(PLURAL* die **Universitäten)**; to go to university auf die Universität gehen

**unkind** *ADJECTIVE* **unfreundlich**

**unknown** *ADJECTIVE* **unbekannt**

**unleaded petrol** *NOUN* **bleifreie Benzin** das

**unless** *CONJUNCTION* **es sei denn**; unless he does it es sei denn, er macht es, unless you write es sei denn, du schreibst

**unlike** *ADJECTIVE* ❶ im Gegensatz zu *(+DAT)*; unlike me, she hates dogs im Gegensatz zu mir hasst sie Hunde ❷ it's unlike her to be late es sieht ihr gar nicht ähnlich, zu spät zu kommen

**unlikely** *ADJECTIVE* **unwahrscheinlich**

**unlimited** *ADJECTIVE* **unbegrenzt**

**unload** *VERB* ❶ **ausladen**◇ *(SEP)* *(luggage, car)* ❷ **entladen**◇ *(lorry)*

**unlock** *VERB* **aufschließen**◇ *(SEP)*

**unlucky** *ADJECTIVE* ❶ to be unlucky *(person)* Pech haben, I was unlucky, the shop was shut ich hatte Pech,

das Geschäft war zu ❷ *(bringing bad luck)* **Unglücks-**; thirteen is an unlucky number dreizehn ist eine Unglückszahl, it's unlucky es bringt Unglück

**unmarried** *ADJECTIVE* **ledig**

**unnecessary** *ADJECTIVE* **unnötig**

**unpack** *VERB* **auspacken** *(SEP)*; I'm just unpacking my rucksack ich packe gerade meinen Rucksack aus, I'll just unpack and then come down ich packe nur noch aus und dann komme ich runter

**unpaid** *ADJECTIVE* **unbezahlt**

**unpleasant** *ADJECTIVE* **unangenehm**

**unplug** *VERB* to unplug the lamp den Stecker der Lampe herausziehen◇ *(SEP)*

**unpopular** *ADJECTIVE* **unbeliebt**

**unreasonable** *ADJECTIVE* **uneinsichtig**; he's being really unreasonable er ist so uneinsichtig

**unrecognizable** *ADJECTIVE* **nicht wieder zu erkennen**

**unreliable** *ADJECTIVE* **unzuverlässig**; he's unreliable er ist unzuverlässig

**unsafe** *ADJECTIVE* **gefährlich** *(wiring, for example)*

**unsatisfactory** *ADJECTIVE* **unbefriedigend**

**unscrew** *VERB* **aufschrauben** *(SEP)*

**unshaven** *ADJECTIVE* **unrasiert**

**unsuccessful** *ADJECTIVE* ❶ **erfolglos**; an unsuccessful attempt ein erfolgloser Versuch ❷ to be unsuccessful keinen Erfolg haben, I tried, but I was unsuccessful ich habe es versucht, aber ich hatte keinen Erfolg

**unsuitable** ADJECTIVE **unpassend**

**untidy** ADJECTIVE **unordentlich**; the house is always untidy das Haus ist immer unordentlich

**until** PREPOSITION, CONJUNCTION ❶ **bis**; until Monday bis Montag, until now bis jetzt, until then bis dahin ❷ (when 'until' is followed by a noun it is usually translated as 'bis zu' +DAT) until the tenth bis zum Zehnten, until the morning bis zum Morgen ❸ not until **erst**, not until September erst im September, it won't be finished until Friday es wird erst Freitag fertig sein

**unusual** ADJECTIVE **ungewöhnlich**; an unusual face ein ungewöhnliches Gesicht

**unwilling** ADJECTIVE to be unwilling to do something etwas nicht tun wollen

**unwrap** VERB **auspacken** (SEP)

**up** PREPOSITION, ADVERB ❶ (out of bed) to be up auf sein◇ (PERF **sein**), Liz isn't up yet Liz ist noch nicht auf, I was up late last night ich war gestern bis spät auf ❷ to get up **aufstehen**◇ (SEP) (PERF **sein**), we got up at six wir sind um sechs aufgestanden ❸ (higher up) **auf** (+DAT or, with movement towards a place, +ACC); up on the roof auf dem Dach ◆ up here hier oben, up there da oben, to go up (upstairs) nach oben gehen, I went up ich bin nach oben gegangen ❺ to go up the road die Straße entlanggehen◇ (SEP) (PERF **sein**), it's further up the road es ist weiter die Straße entlang ❻ to go up the hill (on

foot) **hinaufgehen**◇ (SEP) (PERF **sein**), (in a vehicle) **hinauffahren**◇ (SEP) (PERF **sein**), (in spoken German the prefix 'rauf-' is most common) does the bus go up the hill? fährt der Bus den Berg rauf? ❼ to come up **heraufkommen**◇ (SEP) (PERF **sein**) **raufkommen**◇ (SEP) (PERF **sein**) (informal) ❽ (wrong) what's up? was ist los? (informal), what's up with him? was ist mit ihm los? ❾ up to **bis**, up to here bis hier, up to last week bis zur letzten Woche ❿ she came up to me sie kam auf mich zu ⓫ what's she up to? was hat sie vor? ⓬ it's up to you (it's for you to decide) das hängt von dir ab, (it concerns only you) das ist deine Sache
• time's up! die Zeit ist um

**up-date** NOUN **Aktualisierung** die (PLURAL die **Aktualisierungen**); here's an up-date on our plans dies ist der neueste Stand unserer Pläne

**up-date** VERB ❶ (to revise) **überarbeiten** (timetables, information) ❷ (to modernize) **auf den neuesten Stand bringen**◇ (styles, furnishings)

**upheaval** NOUN **Unruhe** die (PLURAL die **Unruhen**)

**upload** VERB **hochladen**, **uploaden**

**upper-class** ADJECTIVE **der Oberschicht**; an upper-class family eine Familie der Oberschicht

**upright** ADJECTIVE **aufrecht**; put it upright stell es aufrecht, to stand upright aufrecht stehen

**upset** NOUN stomach upset die **Magenverstimmung**

**upset** | **usually**

**upset** ADJECTIVE ❶ (annoyed) ärgerlich; **he's upset** er ist ärgerlich ❷ (distressed) bestürzt, (sad) betrübt

**upset** VERB **to upset somebody** (hurt) jemanden kränken, (annoy) jemanden ärgern

**upside down** ADJECTIVE verkehrt herum

**upstairs** ADVERB ❶ oben; **Mum's upstairs** Mutti ist oben ❷ (with movement) nach oben; **to go upstairs** nach oben gehen

**up-to-date** ADJECTIVE ❶ (in fashion) modern ❷ (information) aktuell

**upwards** ADJECTIVE nach oben

**urgent** ADJECTIVE dringend

**us** PRONOUN uns; **she knows us** sie kennt uns, **they saw us** sie haben uns gesehen, **with us** mit uns

**US** NOUN USA (plural)

**USA** NOUN USA (plural)

**use** NOUN ❶ Gebrauch der; **instructions for use** die Gebrauchsanweisung (SINGULAR) ❷ **it's no use** es hat keinen Zweck, **it's no use phoning** es hat keinen Zweck anzurufen

**use** VERB benutzen; **we used the dictionary** wir haben das Wörterbuch benutzt, **to use something to do something** etwas zu etwas (DAT) benutzen, **I used a towel to dry myself** ich habe ein Handtuch zum Abtrocknen benutzt
• **to use up** ❶ aufbrauchen (SEP) (food) ❷ verbrauchen (money)

**used** ADJECTIVE ❶ **to be used to something** an etwas (ACC) gewöhnt sein, **I'm used to cats** ich bin an Katzen gewöhnt, **I'm not used to it!** das bin ich nicht gewohnt!, **I'm not used to eating in restaurants** ich bin nicht daran gewöhnt, in Restaurants zu essen ❷ **to get used to something** sich an etwas (ACC) gewöhnen, **you'll soon get used to the new car** du wirst dich schnell an das neue Auto gewöhnen, **I've got used to living here** ich habe mich daran gewöhnt, hier zu wohnen, **you'll get used to it** du wirst dich schon daran gewöhnen

**used** VERB **they used to live in the country** sie haben früher auf dem Land gewohnt, **she used to smoke** sie hat früher geraucht

**useful** ADJECTIVE nützlich

**useless** ADJECTIVE ❶ unbrauchbar; **this knife's useless** dieses Messer ist unbrauchbar, **you're completely useless!** du bist wirklich zu nichts zu gebrauchen! ❷ nutzlos (advice, information, or facts, for example); **useless knowledge** nutzloses Wissen ❸ (pointless) zwecklos

**user** NOUN Benutzer der (PLURAL die Benutzer), Benutzerin die (PLURAL die Benutzerinnen)

**user-friendly** ADJECTIVE benutzerfreundlich

**usual** ADJECTIVE ❶ üblich; **it's the usual problem** es ist das übliche Problem, **as usual** wie üblich ❷ **it's colder than usual** es ist kälter als gewöhnlich

**usually** ADJECTIVE normalerweise; **I usually leave at eight** normalerweise gehe ich um acht weg

**vacancy** NOUN ❶ (in a hotel) **'vacancies'** 'Zimmer frei', **'no vacancies'** 'belegt' ❷ **job vacancy** die freie Stelle

**vacant** ADJECTIVE **frei**

**vaccinate** NOUN **impfen**

**vaccination** NOUN **Impfung** die (PLURAL die **Impfungen**)

**vacuum** VERB **saugen**; **I'm going to vacuum my room** ich sauge mein Zimmer

**vacuum cleaner** NOUN **Staubsauger** der (PLURAL die **Staubsauger**)

**vagina** NOUN **Vagina** die (PLURAL die **Vaginen**)

**vague** ADJECTIVE **vage**

**vain** ADJECTIVE **eitel**; **in vain** vergeblich

**valentine card** NOUN **Valentinskarte** die (PLURAL die **Valentinskarten**)

**Valentine's Day** NOUN **Valentinstag** der (PLURAL die **Valentinstage**)

**valid** ADJECTIVE **gültig**

**valley** NOUN **Tal** das (PLURAL die **Täler**)

**valuable** ADJECTIVE **wertvoll**

**value** NOUN **Wert** der (PLURAL die **Werte**)

**value** VERB **schätzen**

**van** NOUN **Lieferwagen** der (PLURAL die **Lieferwagen**)

**vandal** NOUN **Rowdy** der (PLURAL die **Rowdys**)

**vandalism** NOUN **Vandalismus** der

**vandalize** VERB **mutwillig zerstören**

**vanilla** NOUN **Vanille** die; **vanilla ice cream** das Vanilleeis

**vanish** VERB **verschwinden**◇ (PERF **sein**)

**variety** NOUN ❶ **Abwechslung** die (in a routine, diet, or style); **for the sake of variety** zur Abwechslung ❷ (kind) **Sorte** die (PLURAL die **Sorten**); **a new variety of apple** eine neue Apfelsorte ❸ (assortment) **Auswahl** die

**various** ADJECTIVE **verschieden**; **there are various ways of doing it** man kann es auf verschiedene Art und Weise machen

**vary** VERB ❶ (become different) **sich ändern** ❷ **it varies a lot** es ist sehr unterschiedlich ❸ (make different) **ändern** (a programme or method)

**vase** NOUN **Vase** die (PLURAL die **Vasen**)

**VAT** NOUN **Mehrwertsteuer** die

**VCR** NOUN **Videorekorder** der (PLURAL die **Videorekorder**)

**VDU** NOUN **Bildschirm** der (PLURAL die **Bildschirme**)

**veal** NOUN **Kalbfleisch** das

**vegan** NOUN **Veganer** der (PLURAL die **Veganer**), **Veganerin** die (PLURAL die **Veganerinnen**)

**vegetable** NOUN **Gemüse** das; fresh vegetables frisches Gemüse

**vegetarian** NOUN **Vegetarier** der (PLURAL die **Vegetarier**), **Vegetarierin** die (PLURAL die **Vegetarierinnen**)

**vegetarian** ADJECTIVE **vegetarisch**

**vehicle** NOUN **Fahrzeug** das (PLURAL die **Fahrzeuge**)

**vein** NOUN **Vene** die (PLURAL die **Venen**)

**velvet** NOUN **Samt** der

**vending machine** NOUN **Automat** der (PLURAL die **Automaten**)

**verb** NOUN **Verb** das (PLURAL die **Verben**)

**verdict** NOUN **Urteil** das (PLURAL die **Urteile**)

**verge** NOUN ❶ (roadside) **Bankett** das (PLURAL die **Banketten**) ❷ to be on the verge of doing something im Begriff sein, etwas zu tun, I was on the verge of leaving ich war im Begriff zu gehen

**version** NOUN **Version** die (PLURAL die **Versionen**)

**versus** PREPOSITION **gegen** (+ACC); Arsenal versus Chelsea Arsenal gegen Chelsea

**vertical** ADJECTIVE **senkrecht**

**very** ADVERB **sehr**; it's very difficult es ist sehr schwer, very much sehr viel, very little sehr wenig

**very** ADJECTIVE ❶ the very person I need! genau der Mann, den ich brauche, genau die Frau, die ich brauche, the very thing he's looking for genau das, was er sucht, in the very middle genau in der Mitte ❷ at the very end ganz am Ende, at the very front ganz vorne

**vest** NOUN **Unterhemd** das (PLURAL die **Unterhemden**)

**vet** NOUN **Tierarzt** der (PLURAL die **Tierärzte**), **Tierärztin** die (PLURAL die **Tierärztinnen**); she's a vet sie ist Tierärztin

**via** PREPOSITION **über** (+ACC); we're going to Frankfurt via Brussels wir fahren über Brüssel nach Frankfurt

**vicar** NOUN **Pfarrer** der (PLURAL die **Pfarrer**)

**vicious** ADJECTIVE ❶ **bösartig** (dog) ❷ **brutal** (attack)

**victim** NOUN **Opfer** das (PLURAL die **Opfer**)

**victory** NOUN **Sieg** der (PLURAL die **Siege**)

**video** NOUN ❶ (film, cassette) **Video** das (PLURAL die **Videos**); to watch a video ein Video ansehen, I've got it on video ich habe es auf Video ❷ (video recorder) **Videorekorder** der (PLURAL die **Videorekorder**)

**video** VERB **aufzeichnen** (SEP); I'll video it for you ich zeichne es für dich auf

**video camera** NOUN **Videokamera** die (PLURAL die **Videokameras**)

**video game** NOUN **Videospiel** das (PLURAL die **Videospiele**)

**video recorder** NOUN **Videorekorder** der (PLURAL die **Videorekorder**)

**Vienna** NOUN **Wien** das; to Vienna nach Wien

**view** *NOUN* ❶ **Aussicht** die; a room with a view of the lake ein Zimmer mit Aussicht auf den See ❷ *(opinion)* **Meinung** die *(PLURAL die* **Meinungen***)*; in my view meiner Meinung nach, point of view der Standpunkt

**viewer** *NOUN* **Zuschauer** der *(PLURAL die* **Zuschauer***)*, **Zuschauerin** die *(PLURAL die* **Zuschauerinnen***)*

**vile** *ADJECTIVE* **ekelhaft**

**villa** *NOUN* **Villa** die *(PLURAL die* **Villen***)*

**village** *NOUN* **Dorf** das *(PLURAL die* **Dörfer***)*

**vine** *NOUN* **Weinrebe** die *(PLURAL die* **Weinreben***)*

**vinegar** *NOUN* **Essig** der

**vineyard** *NOUN* **Weinberg** der *(PLURAL die* **Weinberge***)*

**violence** *NOUN* **Gewalt** die

**violent** *ADJECTIVE* ❶ **gewalttätig** *(person, film, behaviour)* ❷ **heftig** *(jolt, punch)*

**violin** *NOUN* **Geige** die *(PLURAL die* **Geigen***)*; to play the violin Geige spielen

**violinist** *NOUN* **Geiger** der *(PLURAL die* **Geiger***)*, **Geigerin** die *(PLURAL die* **Geigerinnen***)*

**virgin** *NOUN* **Jungfrau** die *(PLURAL die* **Jungfrauen***)*

**Virgo** *NOUN* **Jungfrau** die; Robert's Virgo Robert ist Jungfrau

**virtual reality** *NOUN* **virtuelle Realität** die

**virus** *NOUN (in medicine and IT)* **Virus** der *(PLURAL die* **Viren***)*; anti-virus software Antivirenprogramm das *(PLURAL die* **Antivirenprogramme***)*

**visa** *NOUN* **Visum** das *(PLURAL die* **Visa***)*

**visible** *ADJECTIVE* **sichtbar**

**visit** *NOUN* **Besuch** der *(PLURAL die* **Besuche***)*; I was in Berlin on a visit to friends ich war in Berlin bei Freunden zu Besuch, my last visit to Germany mein letzter Deutschlandbesuch

**visit** *VERB* ❶ **besuchen** *(a person)* ❷ **besichtigen** *(a building, town)*

**visitor** *NOUN* ❶ **Besucher** der *(PLURAL die* **Besucher***)*, **Besucherin** die *(PLURAL die* **Besucherinnen***)* ❷ we've got visitors tonight wir haben heute Abend Besuch ❸ *(in a hotel)* **Gast** der *(PLURAL die* **Gäste***)*

**visual** *ADJECTIVE* **visuell**

**vital** *ADJECTIVE* **unbedingt erforderlich**; it's vital to book man muss unbedingt buchen

**vitamin** *NOUN* **Vitamin** das *(PLURAL die* **Vitamine***)*

**vivid** *ADJECTIVE* **lebhaft** *(colours, memory)*; to have a vivid imagination eine lebhafte Phantasie haben

**vocabulary** *NOUN* **Wortschatz** der

**vocational** *ADJECTIVE* **beruflich**

**vodka** *NOUN* **Wodka** der *(PLURAL die* **Wodkas***)*

**voice** *NOUN* **Stimme** die *(PLURAL die* **Stimmen***)*

**volcano** *NOUN* **Vulkan** der *(PLURAL die* **Vulkane***)*

a
b
c
d
e
f
g
h
i
j
k
l
m
n
o
p
q
r
s
t
u
v
w
x
y
z

**volleyball** NOUN Volleyball der; **to play volleyball** Volleyball spielen

**volume** NOUN ❶ Lautstärke die; **could you turn down the volume?** könntest du etwas leiser stellen? ❷ (book) Band der (PLURAL die Bände)

**voluntary** ADJECTIVE ❶ freiwillig; **a voluntary worker** ein freiwilliger Helfer, eine freiwillige Helferin ❷ **to do voluntary work** für einen wohltätigen Zweck arbeiten

**volunteer** NOUN Freiwillige der/die (PLURAL die Freiwilligen)

**volunteer** VERB **to volunteer to do something** sich bereit erklären, etwas zu tun

**vomit** VERB sich übergeben◇

**vote** VERB wählen; **to vote for somebody** jemanden wählen, **she always votes Green** sie wählt immer die Grünen

**voucher** NOUN Gutschein der (PLURAL die Gutscheine)

**vowel** NOUN Vokal der (PLURAL die Vokale)

**vulgar** ADJECTIVE vulgär

# Ww

**waffle** NOUN Waffel die (PLURAL die Waffeln)

**wage(s)** NOUN Lohn der (PLURAL die Löhne)

**waist** NOUN Taille die (PLURAL die Taillen)

**waistcoat** NOUN Weste die (PLURAL die Westen)

**waist measurement** NOUN Taillenweite die

**wait** NOUN Wartezeit die; **an hour's wait** eine Stunde Wartezeit

**wait** VERB ❶ warten; **they're waiting in the car** sie warten im Auto, **she kept me waiting** sie hat mich warten lassen ❷ **to wait for somebody** auf jemanden warten, **wait for me** warte auf mich, **to wait for something** auf etwas (ACC) warten, **we waited for a taxi** wir haben auf ein Taxi gewartet ❸ **to wait for somebody to do something** darauf warten, dass jemand etwas tut
**I'm waiting for him to ring** ich warte darauf, dass er anruft ❹ **I can't wait to open it** ich kann's kaum erwarten, es aufzumachen

**waiter** NOUN Kellner der (PLURAL die Kellner); **waiter!** Herr Ober!

**waiting list** NOUN Warteliste die (PLURAL die Wartelisten)

**waiting room** NOUN Wartezimmer das (PLURAL die **Wartezimmer**), (at a station) Warteraum der (PLURAL die Warteräume)

**waitress** NOUN Kellnerin die (PLURAL die **Kellnerinnen**); **waitress!** Fräulein!

**wake** VERB ❶ wecken (somebody); **Jess woke me at six** Jess hat mich um sechs geweckt ❷ aufwachen (SEP) (PERF sein); **I woke (up) at six** ich bin um sechs aufgewacht, **wake up!** wach auf!

**Wales** NOUN Wales das; **from Wales** aus Wales, **to Wales** nach Wales

**walk** NOUN ❶ Spaziergang der (PLURAL die **Spaziergänge**); **to go for a walk** einen Spaziergang machen, **we'll go for a little walk round the village** wir machen einen kleinen Spaziergang durchs Dorf ❷ **to take the dog for a walk** mit dem Hund spazieren gehen◇ (PERF sein) ❸ **it's about five minutes' walk from here** es ist ungefähr fünf Minuten zu Fuß von hier

**walk** VERB ❶ (go, not run) gehen◇ (PERF sein); **he walks very slowly** er geht sehr langsam, **I'll walk to the bus stop with you** ich gehe mit dir zur Bushaltestelle ❷ (on foot rather than by car or bus) zu Fuß gehen◇ (PERF sein); **it's not far, we can walk** es ist nicht weit, wir können zu Fuß gehen ❸ (walk around) spazieren gehen◇ (PERF sein); **we walked around the old town** wir sind in der Altstadt spazieren gegangen ❹ (move on foot) laufen◇ (PERF sein); **to learn to walk** laufen lernen, **the child can't walk yet** das Kind kann noch nicht laufen

**walking** NOUN (hiking) Wandern das; **to go walking** wandern (PERF sein)

**walking distance** NOUN **to be within walking distance** zu Fuß zu erreichen sein, **it's within walking distance of the sea** man kann das Meer zu Fuß erreichen

**wall** NOUN ❶ (inside a building) Wand die (PLURAL die **Wände**); **there's a picture on every wall** an jeder Wand hängt ein Bild ❷ (outside) Mauer die (PLURAL die **Mauern**)

**wallet** NOUN Brieftasche die (PLURAL die **Brieftaschen**)

**wallpaper** NOUN Tapete die (PLURAL die **Tapeten**)

**walnut** NOUN Walnuss die (PLURAL die **Walnüsse**)

**wander** VERB **to wander around town** durch die Stadt bummeln (PERF sein), **to wander off** weggehen◇ (SEP) (PERF sein)

**want** VERB ❶ wollen◇; **do you want to come?** willst du mitkommen?, **what do you want to do?** was willst du machen?, **I don't want to bother him** ich will ihn nicht stören ❷ (more polite) mögen◇ ('ich möchte' is much politer than 'ich will'); **do you want some more coffee?** möchtest du noch Kaffee?, **I want two pounds of apples please** ich möchte gern zwei Pfund Äpfel ('möchte gern' is particularly used when shopping)

**war** NOUN Krieg der (PLURAL die Kriege)

**ward** NOUN Station die (PLURAL die Stationen)

**wardrobe** NOUN **Kleiderschrank** der (PLURAL die **Kleiderschränke**)

**warm** ADJECTIVE ❶ **warm**; a warm coat ein warmer Mantel, it's warm today heute ist es warm, I'll keep your dinner warm ich halte dir das Essen warm, it's warm inside drinnen ist es warm, I am warm mir ist warm ❷ (friendly) **herzlich**; a warm welcome ein herzlicher Empfang

**warm** VERB **wärmen**; to warm the plates die Teller wärmen
• to warm up ❶ (weather) warm werden ❷ (an athlete) sich aufwärmen (SEP) ❸ (to heat up) aufwärmen (SEP); I'll warm the soup up for you ich wärme dir die Suppe auf

**warmth** NOUN **Wärme** die

**warn** VERB ❶ **warnen**; I warn you, it's expensive ich warne dich, es ist teuer, to warn somebody not to do something jemanden davor warnen, etwas zu tun, she warned me not to let him drive sie hat mich davor gewarnt, ihn fahren zu lassen ❷ he warned me to lock the car er hat mich ermahnt, das Auto abzuschließen

**warning** NOUN **Warnung** die (PLURAL die **Warnungen**)

**wart** NOUN **Warze** die (PLURAL die **Warzen**)

**wash** NOUN to give something a wash etwas waschen◇, to have a wash sich waschen

**wash** VERB ❶ **waschen**◇; I've washed your jeans ich habe deine Jeans gewaschen ❷ (have a wash) **sich waschen**◇; to get washed sich

waschen ❸ to wash your hands sich (DAT) die Hände waschen, I washed my hands ich habe mir die Hände gewaschen, to wash your hair sich (DAT) die Haare waschen ❹ to wash the dishes abwaschen◇ (SEP)
• to wash up abwaschen◇ (SEP)

**washbasin** NOUN **Waschbecken** das (PLURAL die **Waschbecken**)

**washing** NOUN **Wäsche** die; to do the washing Wäsche waschen

**washing machine** NOUN **Waschmaschine** die (PLURAL die **Waschmaschinen**)

**washing powder** NOUN **Waschpulver** das

**washing-up** NOUN **Abwasch** der; to do the washing-up den Abwasch machen

**washing-up liquid** NOUN **Spülmittel** das (PLURAL die **Spülmittel**)

**wasp** NOUN **Wespe** die (PLURAL die **Wespen**)

**waste** NOUN **Verschwendung** die; it's a waste of time das ist eine Zeitverschwendung

**waste** VERB **verschwenden**

**waste-bin** NOUN **Mülltonne** die (PLURAL die **Mülltonnen**)

**waste-paper basket** NOUN **Papierkorb** der (PLURAL die **Papierkörbe**)

**watch** NOUN **Uhr** die (PLURAL die **Uhren**); my watch is fast meine Uhr geht vor, my watch is slow meine Uhr geht nach

**watch** VERB ❶ (to look at) **sich** (DAT) **ansehen**◇ (SEP); I was watching a film ich habe mir einen Film angesehen ❷ to watch TV fernsehen◇ *(SEP)* ❸ *(keep a check on, look after)* **achten auf** *(+ACC)*; watch the children achte auf die Kinder ❹ *(to be careful)* **aufpassen** *(SEP)*; watch you don't spill it pass auf, dass du es nicht verschüttest, watch out! pass auf! ❺ *(observe)* **beobachten**; they were being watched sie wurden beobachtet

**water** *NOUN* **Wasser** das

**water** *VERB* **gießen◇** *(plants)*

**waterfall** *NOUN* **Wasserfall** der *(PLURAL* die **Wasserfälle)**

**watering can** *NOUN* **Gießkanne** die *(PLURAL* die **Gießkannen)**

**water melon** *NOUN* **Wassermelone** die *(PLURAL* die **Wassermelonen)**

**waterproof** *ADJECTIVE* **wasserdicht**

**water-skiing** *NOUN* **Wasserskifahren** das; to go water-skiing **Wasserski fahren◇**

**water sports** *PLURAL NOUN* **Wassersport** der

**wave** *NOUN* ❶ *(in the sea)* **Welle** die *(PLURAL* die **Wellen)** ❷ *(with your hand)* to give somebody a wave jemandem zuwinken *(SEP)*, she gave him a wave from the bus sie winkte ihm vom Bus zu

**wave** *VERB* ❶ *(with your hand)* **winken** ❷ *(flap)* **schwenken** *(a flag, for example)*

**wax** *NOUN* **Wachs** das

**way** *NOUN* ❶ *(a route or road)* **Weg** der *(PLURAL* die **Wege)**; the way to town der Weg in die Stadt, we asked the way to the station

wir haben gefragt, wie man zum Bahnhof kommt, on the way back auf dem Rückweg, on the way unterwegs, to be in the way im Weg sein, to be in somebody's way jemandem im Weg sein, to get out of the way aus dem Weg gehen ❷ to lose your way sich verlaufen◇, *(in a car)* sich verfahren◇ ❸ 'way in' 'Eingang', 'way out' 'Ausgang' ❹ *(direction)* **Richtung** die *(PLURAL* die **Richtungen)**; which way did he go? in welche Richtung ist er gegangen?, this way in diese Richtung ❺ *(side)* the right way up richtig herum, the wrong way round falsch herum, the other way round andersherum ❻ *(distance)* it's a long way es ist weit weg, we still had a little way to go wir mussten noch ein kleines Stück gehen ❼ *(manner)* **Art und Weise** die; my way of learning German meine Art und Weise, Deutsch zu lernen, he does it his way er macht es auf seine Art und Weise, I've done it the wrong way ich habe es falsch gemacht, in a way in gewisser Weise ❽ no way! auf keinen Fall! ❾ by the way übrigens

**we** *PRONOUN* **wir**; we're going to the cinema tonight wir gehen heute Abend ins Kino

**weak** *ADJECTIVE* ❶ *(feeble)* **schwach**; in a weak voice mit schwacher Stimme ❷ **dünn** *(coffee or tea)*

**wealthy** *ADJECTIVE* **reich**

**weapon** *NOUN* **Waffe** die *(PLURAL* die **Waffen)**; weapons of mass destruction Massenvernichtungswaffen die *(plural)*

**wear** ‖ **welcome**

**wear** NOUN **children's wear** die Kinderkleidung, **sports wear** die Sportkleidung

**wear** VERB tragen◇, anhaben◇ (SEP) (informal); **she often wears red** sie trägt oft Rot, **Tamsin's wearing her jeans** Tamsin hat ihre Jeans an

**weather** NOUN ❶ Wetter das; **what's the weather like?** wie ist das Wetter?, **in fine weather** bei schönem Wetter, **the weather is terrible** das Wetter ist furchtbar ❷ **in wet weather** wenn es regnet, **the weather was cold** es war kalt

**weather forecast** NOUN Wettervorhersage die; **the weather forecast says it will rain** der Wettervorhersage zufolge soll es regnen

**web** NOUN ❶ (spider's) Spinnennetz das (PLURAL die Spinnennetze) ❷ **the Web** Netz das

**webcam** NOUN Webcam die (PLURAL die Webcams)

**web page** NOUN Webseite die (PLURAL die Webseiten)

**web site** NOUN Website die (PLURAL die Websites)

**wedding** NOUN Hochzeit die (PLURAL die Hochzeiten)

**Wednesday** NOUN ❶ Mittwoch der (PLURAL die Mittwoche); **on Wednesday** (am) Mittwoch, **I'm going to the cinema on Wednesday** ich gehe Mittwoch ins Kino, **see you on Wednesday!** bis Mittwoch!, **every Wednesday** jeden Mittwoch, **last Wednesday** vorigen Mittwoch, **next Wednesday** nächsten Mittwoch ❷ **on Wednesdays** mittwochs, **the museum is closed**

**on Wednesdays** das Museum ist mittwochs geschlossen

**weed** NOUN Unkraut das

**week** NOUN Woche die (PLURAL die Wochen); **last week** vorige Woche, **next week** nächste Woche, **this week** diese Woche, **for weeks** wochenlang, **a week today** heute in einer Woche, **in three weeks' time** in drei Wochen

**weekday** NOUN **on weekdays** wochentags

**weekend** NOUN Wochenende das (PLURAL die Wochenenden); **last weekend** voriges Wochenende, **next weekend** nächstes Wochenende, **they're coming for the weekend** sie kommen übers Wochenende, **I'll do it at the weekend** ich mache es am Wochenende, **have a nice weekend!** (ein) schönes Wochenende!

**weigh** VERB ❶ wiegen◇; **to weigh something** etwas wiegen, **to weigh yourself** sich wiegen ❷ **how much do you weigh?** wie viel wiegst du?, **I weigh 50 kilos** ich wiege fünfzig Kilo

**weight** NOUN ❶ Gewicht das (PLURAL die Gewichte) ❷ **to put on weight** zunehmen◇ (SEP) ❸ **to lose weight** abnehmen◇ (SEP)

**weird** ADJECTIVE seltsam

**welcome** NOUN ❶ **they gave us a warm welcome** sie haben uns herzlich empfangen ❷ **welcome to Oxford!** herzlich willkommen in Oxford!

**welcome** ADJECTIVE willkommen; **you're welcome any time** du bist immer willkommen, **'thank you!' – 'you're welcome!'** 'danke!' – 'bitte!'

**welcome** VERB begrüßen; **to welcome somebody** jemanden begrüßen

**well**[1] ADVERB ❶ to be well gesund sein, **I'm very well, thank you** danke, es geht mir gut, **get well soon!** gute Besserung! ❷ gut; **Terry played well** Terry hat gut gespielt, **it's well paid** es wird gut bezahlt, **well done!** gut gemacht! ❸ as well auch, **Kevin's coming as well** Kevin kommt auch ❹ na ja; **well, never mind** na ja, macht nichts ❺ gut; **it may well be that ...** es ist gut möglich, dass ..., **very well then, you can go** also gut, du kannst gehen

**well**[2] NOUN Brunnen der (PLURAL die Brunnen)

**well-behaved** ADJECTIVE artig

**well-done** ADJECTIVE durchgebraten (steak)

**wellington (boot)** NOUN Gummistiefel der (PLURAL die Gummistiefel)

**well-known** ADJECTIVE bekannt

**well-off** ADJECTIVE wohlhabend

**Welsh** NOUN ❶ the Welsh (people) die Waliser (plural) ❷ (language) Walisisch das

**Welsh** ADJECTIVE walisisch; he's Welsh er ist Waliser, **she's Welsh** sie ist Waliserin

**Welshman** NOUN Waliser der (PLURAL die Waliser)

**Welshwoman** NOUN Waliserin die (PLURAL die Waliserinnen)

**west** NOUN Westen der; in the west im Westen

**west** ADJECTIVE West-; the west side die Westseite, **west wind** der Westwind, **west of** westlich von, **it's west of Munich** es liegt westlich von München

**west** ADVERB nach Westen

**western** NOUN (film) Western der (PLURAL die Western)

**West Indian** NOUN Westinder der (PLURAL die Westinder), Westinderin die (PLURAL die Westinderinnen)

**West Indian** ADJECTIVE westindisch

**West Indies** PLURAL NOUN die Westindischen Inseln (plural); **in the West Indies** auf den Westindischen Inseln

**wet** ADJECTIVE ❶ nass; we got wet wir sind nass geworden ❷ a wet day ein regnerischer Tag

**whale** NOUN Wal der (PLURAL die Wale)

**what** PRONOUN, ADJECTIVE ❶ (in questions) was; **what did you say?** was hast du gesagt?, **what's she doing?** was macht sie?, **what did you buy?** was hast du gekauft?, **what is it?** was ist das?, **what's the matter?** was ist los?, **what's happened?** was ist passiert?, **what?** was? ❷ what's your address? wie ist Ihre Adresse?, **what's her name?** wie heißt sie?, **what was it like?** wie war's? ❸ (asking for an amount) wie viel; **at what time?** um wie viel Uhr? ❹ (that which) was (relative pronoun); **she told me what had happened** sie hat mir gesagt, was passiert ist, **do what I tell you** tu, was ich dir sage ❺ (which) welcher/welche/welches; **what country is**

it in? in welchem Land ist es?, what colour is it? welche Farbe hat es?, what make is it? welche Marke ist es? ❻ what for? wozu?

**wheat** NOUN **Weizen** der

**wheel** NOUN **Rad** das (PLURAL die **Räder**); the spare wheel das Reserverad, the steering wheel das Lenkrad

**wheelbarrow** NOUN **Schubkarre** die (PLURAL die **Schubkarren**)

**wheelchair** NOUN **Rollstuhl** der (PLURAL die **Rollstühle**)

**when** ADVERB **wann**; when is she arriving? wann kommt sie an?, when's your birthday? wann hast du Geburtstag?

**when** CONJUNCTION ❶ (with the past) **als**; I was out shopping when you rang ich war beim Einkaufen, als du anriefst ❷ (with the present or future) **wenn**; when she comes I'll ring wenn sie kommt, rufe ich an

**where** ADVERB, CONJUNCTION **wo**; where do you live? wo wohnst du?, where are you going? wo gehst du hin?, I don't know where they live ich weiß nicht, wo sie wohnen

**whether** CONJUNCTION **ob**; I don't know whether he's back ich weiß nicht, ob er schon zurück ist

**which** ADJECTIVE, PRONOUN ❶ **welcher/ welche/welches**; which song did you buy? welche Lied hast du gekauft? ❷ which (one) **welcher/ welche/welches** (depending on the gender of the noun the question refers back to), 'I met your brother' - 'which one?' 'ich habe deinen Bruder getroffen' - 'welchen?', 'I met your sister' - 'which one?'

'ich habe deine Schwester getroffen' - 'welche?', 'have you seen my book?' - 'which one?' 'hast du mein Buch gesehen?' - 'welches?' ❸ (relative pronoun) **der/ die/das** (PLURAL **die**); (depending on the gender of the noun 'which' refers to) the film which is showing now der Film, der gerade läuft, the lamp which is on the table die Lampe, die auf dem Tisch steht, the book which I lent you das Buch, das ich dir geliehen habe, the books which I've read die Bücher, die ich gelesen habe

**while** NOUN for a while eine Weile, she worked here for a while sie hat eine Weile hier gearbeitet, after a while nach einer Weile

**while** CONJUNCTION **während**; you can make some coffee while I'm finishing my homework du kannst Kaffee kochen, während ich meine Hausaufgaben fertig mache

**whip** NOUN **Peitsche** die (PLURAL die **Peitschen**)

**whip** VERB **schlagen**◇ (cream); whipped cream die Schlagsahne

**whisker** NOUN **Schnurrhaar** das (PLURAL die **Schnurrhaare**)

**whisky** NOUN **Whisky** der (PLURAL die **Whiskys**)

**whisper** NOUN **Flüstern** das; in a whisper im Flüsterton

**whisper** VERB **flüstern**

**whistle** NOUN **Pfeife** die (PLURAL die **Pfeifen**)

**whistle** VERB **pfeifen**◇

**white** NOUN **Weiß** das; egg white das Eiweiß

**white** ADJECTIVE weiß; **a white shirt** ein weißes Hemd

**white coffee** NOUN Kaffee mit Milch der (PLURAL die **Kaffees mit Milch**)

**Whitsun** NOUN Pfingsten das (PLURAL die **Pfingsten**)

**who** PRONOUN ❶ (in questions) wer; **who wants some chocolate?** wer möchte Schokolade? ❷ (in the accusative) wen; **who did you ring?** wen hast du angerufen? ❸ (in the dative) wem; **who did you give it to?** wem hast du es gegeben? ❹ (relative pronoun) der/die/das (PLURAL die); (depending on the gender of the noun 'who' refers to) **my boy friend who lives in Liverpool** mein Freund, der in Liverpool wohnt, **my girl friend who lives in Berlin** meine Freundin, die in Berlin wohnt, **the child who's staying with us** das Kind, das bei uns wohnt, **the friends who are coming to see us tonight** die Freunde, die heute Abend zu Besuch kommen

**whole** NOUN **the whole of the class** die ganze Klasse, **the whole of Germany** ganz Deutschland, **on the whole** im Großen und Ganzen

**whole** ADJECTIVE ganz; **the whole family** die ganze Familie, **the whole morning** den ganzen Morgen, **the whole time** die ganze Zeit, **the whole world** die ganze Welt

**wholemeal** ADJECTIVE Vollkorn-; **wholemeal bread** das Vollkornbrot

**whom** PRONOUN ❶ den/die/das, (PLURAL die); **the man whom I saw** der Mann, den ich sah, **the woman whom I saw** die Frau, die ich sah, **the child whom I saw** das Kind, das ich sah ❷ (in the dative) dem/ der/dem (PLURAL denen); **the girl to whom I wrote** das Mädchen, dem ich geschrieben habe ❸ (in questions) wen; **whom did you see?** wen haben Sie gesehen? ❹ **to whom did you give it?** wem haben Sie es gegeben?

**whose** PRONOUN, ADJECTIVE ❶ (in questions) wessen; **whose is this jacket?** wessen Jacke ist das?, **whose shoes are these?** wessen Schuhe sind das? ❷ **whose is it?** wem gehört das?, **I know whose it is** ich weiß, wem es gehört ❸ (as a relative pronoun) dessen/deren/dessen (PLURAL deren); (depending on the gender of the noun 'whose' refers to) **the man whose car I'm buying** der Mann, dessen Auto ich kaufe, **the woman whose bag I found** die Frau, deren Tasche ich gefunden habe, **the girl whose sister I know** das Mädchen, dessen Schwester ich kenne, **the people whose children he teaches** die Leute, deren Kinder er unterrichtet

**why** ADVERB ❶ warum; **why did she phone?** warum hat sie angerufen?, **why not?** warum nicht? ❷ **that's why I don't want to come** deswegen will ich nicht kommen

**wicked** ADJECTIVE ❶ (bad) böse ❷ (brilliant) geil (informal)

**wide** ADJECTIVE ❶ breit; **it's a very wide road** es ist eine sehr breite Straße, **the shelf is 30 cm wide** das Regal ist dreißig Zentimeter breit, **wide screen** das Breitbild ❷ groß; **a wide range** eine große Auswahl

**wide** ADVERB **the door was wide open** die Tür stand weit offen

**wide awake** ADJECTIVE hellwach

a
b
c
d
e
f
g
h
i
j
k
l
m
n
o
p
q
r
s
t
u
v
w
x
y
z

**widow** NOUN Witwe die (PLURAL die Witwen)

**widower** NOUN Witwer der (PLURAL die Witwer)

**width** NOUN Breite die

**wife** NOUN Ehefrau die (PLURAL die Ehefrauen)

**wi-fi** NOUN WLAN das

**wig** NOUN Perücke die (PLURAL die Perücken)

**wild** ADJECTIVE ❶ wild; wild animals wilde Tiere ❷ (crazy) verrückt (idea, party, person) ❸ to be wild about something scharf auf etwas (ACC) sein

**wildlife** NOUN Tierwelt die; a programme on wildlife in Africa eine Sendung über die afrikanische Tierwelt

**wildlife park** NOUN Wildpark der (PLURAL die Wildparks)

**will** VERB ❶ (in German the present tense is often used to express future actions and intentions) I'll wait for you at the bus stop ich warte an der Bushaltestelle auf dich, he'll be pleased to help you er hilft dir gern, that won't be a problem das ist kein Problem, I'll phone them at once ich rufe sie sofort an ❷ (the German future tense is used when firm intention is stressed, when referring to the more distant future and when some doubt about the future is expressed) werden◇; he will definitely come er wird ganz bestimmt kommen, she'll probably ring before leaving sie wird wahrscheinlich anrufen, bevor sie geht ❸ (in questions and requests) will you have some more tea?

möchten Sie noch Tee?, will you help me? hilfst du mir?, 'will you write to me?' - 'of course I will!' 'schreibst du mir?' - 'ja, natürlich', 'he won't like it' - 'yes he will' 'es wird ihm nicht gefallen' - 'doch' ❹ wollen◇; he won't help us er will uns nicht helfen, the car won't start das Auto will nicht anspringen

**willing** ADJECTIVE to be willing to do something bereit sein, etwas zu tun, I'm willing to pay half ich bin bereit, die Hälfte zu zahlen

**willingly** ADVERB gern

**willow** NOUN Weide die (PLURAL die Weiden)

**win** NOUN Sieg der (PLURAL die Siege); our win over Everton unser Sieg über Everton

**win** VERB ❶ gewinnen◇; we won! wir haben gewonnen! ❷ to win a prize einen Preis bekommen

**wind**[1] NOUN Wind der (PLURAL die Winde)

**wind**[2] VERB ❶ wickeln (a wire or rope, for example) ❷ aufziehen◇ (SEP) (a clock)

**wind farm** NOUN Windpark der (PLURAL die Windparks)

**wind instrument** NOUN Blasinstrument das (PLURAL die Blasinstrumente)

**window** NOUN ❶ Fenster das (PLURAL die Fenster); to look out of the window aus dem Fenster sehen ❷ (in a shop) Schaufenster das (PLURAL die Schaufenster)

**windscreen** NOUN Windschutzscheibe die (PLURAL die Windschutzscheiben)

**windscreen wiper** *NOUN* Scheibenwischer der *(PLURAL* die Scheibenwischer)

**windsurfing** *NOUN* Windsurfen das; **to go windsurfing** windsurfen gehen

**windy** *ADJECTIVE* windig; **it's windy today** heute ist es windig

**wine** *NOUN* Wein der *(PLURAL* die Weine); **a glass of white wine** ein Glas Weißwein

**wing** *NOUN* Flügel der *(PLURAL* die Flügel)

**wink** *VERB* **to wink at somebody** jemandem zuzwinkern *(SEP)*

**winner** *NOUN* Sieger der *(PLURAL* die Sieger) Siegerin die *(PLURAL* die Siegerinnen)*

**winning** *ADJECTIVE* siegreich

**winnings** *PLURAL NOUN* Gewinn der

**winter** *NOUN* Winter der *(PLURAL* die Winter); **in winter** im Winter

**wipe** *VERB* ❶ abwischen *(SEP)*; **I'll just wipe the table** ich wische schnell den Tisch ab, **to wipe your nose** sich *(DAT)* die Nase abwischen ❷ **to wipe the floor** den Boden wischen ❸ **to wipe your feet** sich *(DAT)* die Schuhe abtreten *(SEP)*

• **to wipe up** abtrocknen *(SEP)* (dishes)

**wire** *NOUN* Draht der *(PLURAL* die Drähte); **electric wire** die Leitung

**wise** *ADJECTIVE* weise

**wish** *NOUN* ❶ Wunsch der *(PLURAL* die Wünsche); **to make a wish** sich *(DAT)* etwas wünschen, **make a wish!** wünsch dir was! ❷ **best wishes on your birthday** alles Gute zum Geburtstag ❸ *(in a letter)* **with best wishes** mit freundlichen Grüßen

**wish** *VERB* ❶ **I wish she were here** ich wünschte, sie wäre hier ❷ **to wish for something** sich *(DAT)* etwas wünschen ❸ **to wish somebody a happy Christmas** jemandem frohe Weihnachten wünschen, **I wished him happy birthday** ich habe ihm alles Gute zum Geburtstag gewünscht

**wit** *NOUN* Geist der

**with** *PREPOSITION* ❶ mit *(+DAT)*; **with me** mit mir, **with pleasure** mit Vergnügen, **he went on holiday with his friends** er ist mit seinen Freunden in die Ferien gefahren, **a girl with red hair** ein Mädchen mit roten Haaren ❷ *(at the house of)* bei *(+ACC)*; **we're staying the night with friends** wir übernachten bei Freunden ❸ vor *(+DAT)*; **to shiver with cold** vor Kälte zittern, **to tremble with fear** vor Angst zittern ❹ **I haven't got any money with me** ich habe kein Geld dabei

**without** *PREPOSITION* ohne *(+ACC)*; **without you** ohne dich, **without a sweater** ohne einen Pullover, **without knowing** ohne zu wissen

**witness** *NOUN* Zeuge der *(PLURAL* die Zeugen) Zeugin die *(PLURAL* die Zeuginnen)*

**witty** *ADJECTIVE* geistreich

**wolf** *NOUN* Wolf der *(PLURAL* die Wölfe)

**woman** *NOUN* Frau die *(PLURAL* die Frauen); **a woman friend** eine Freundin, **a woman doctor** eine Ärztin

**wonder** *NOUN* Wunder das *(PLURAL* die Wunder); **it's no wonder you're tired** es ist kein Wunder, dass du müde bist

**wonder** VERB ❶ sich fragen; **I wonder why she did that** ich frage mich, warum sie das getan hat ❷ **I wonder who?** wer wohl?, **I wonder where Jake is** wo Jake wohl ist? ❸ (in polite requests) **I wonder if you could tell me ...?** könnten Sie mir vielleicht sagen ...?

**wonderful** ADJECTIVE wunderbar

**wood** NOUN Holz das; **the lamp is made of wood** die Lampe ist aus Holz

**wooden** ADJECTIVE Holz-, hölzern; **wooden toys** das Holzspielzeug

**woodwork** NOUN (craft) Tischlerei die

**wool** NOUN Wolle die

**word** NOUN ❶ Wort das (PLURAL die Wörter) (the plural 'Wörter' is used when the words are unrelated); **a long word** ein langes Wort, **what's the German word for 'window'?** wie heißt 'window' auf Deutsch?, **I've learned ten German words today** ich habe heute zehn deutsche Wörter gelernt, **words in the dictionary** Wörter im Wörterbuch ❷ Wort das (PLURAL die Worte) (the plural 'Worte' is used when the words are connected in a text or conversation); **he wanted to say a few words** er wollte ein paar Worte sagen, **in other words** mit anderen Worten, **to have a word with somebody** mit jemandem sprechen ❸ (promise) Wort das; **to keep your word** sein Wort halten, **he broke his word** er hat sein Wort gebrochen ❹ **the words of a song** der Text von einem Lied

**word processing** NOUN Textverarbeitung die

**word processor** NOUN Textverarbeitungssystem das (PLURAL die Textverbeitungssysteme)

**work** NOUN Arbeit die; **I enjoy my work** meine Arbeit macht mir Spaß, **she's looking for work** sie sucht Arbeit, **I've got some work to do** ich habe noch etwas Arbeit, **he's out of work** er hat keine Arbeit, **to be off work** nicht arbeiten, **Ben's off work** (sick) Ben ist krank, **to go to work on the tube** mit der U-Bahn zur Arbeit fahren

**work** VERB ❶ arbeiten; **she works in an office** sie arbeitet in einem Büro, **Mum works as a dentist** Mutti ist Zahnärztin, **he works part-time** er arbeitet halbtags ❷ (to operate) sich auskennen⋄ (SEP) mit; **can you work the video?** kennst du dich mit dem Videorekorder aus? ❸ (function) funktionieren; **the washing machine's not working** die Waschmaschine funktioniert nicht ❹ (a plan or idea) klappen; **that worked really well** das hat prima geklappt

• **to work out** ❶ (understand) verstehen⋄; **I can't work out why** ich kann nicht verstehen, warum ❷ (exercise) trainieren ❸ (to go well) klappen ❹ (calculate) ausrechnen (SEP) (a sum); **I'll work out how much it would cost** ich rechne aus, wie viel es kosten würde ❺ (solve) lösen (a problem)

**worker** NOUN Arbeiter der (PLURAL die Arbeiter), Arbeiterin die (PLURAL die Arbeiterinnen)

**work experience** NOUN Praktikum das (PLURAL die Praktika); **to do work experience** ein Praktikum machen

**working-class** *ADJECTIVE* **der Arbeiterschicht**; **a working-class family** eine Familie der Arbeiterschicht

**work of art** *NOUN* **Kunstwerk** das *(PLURAL* die **Kunstwerke)**

**workshop** *NOUN* **Werkstatt** die *(PLURAL* die **Werkstätten)**

**world** *NOUN* **Welt** die; **the biggest tree in the world** der größte Baum der Welt, **all over the world** auf der ganzen Welt, **the Western world** die westliche Welt

**World Cup** *NOUN* **the World Cup** die Weltmeisterschaft

**world war** *NOUN* **Weltkrieg** der *(PLURAL* die **Weltkriege)**; **the Second World War** der Zweite Weltkrieg

**worm** *NOUN* **Wurm** der *(PLURAL* die **Würmer)**

**worn out** *ADJECTIVE* **❶** *(person)* **erschöpft ❷** *(clothes or shoes)* **abgetragen**

**worried** *ADJECTIVE* **❶ besorgt**; **his worried parents** seine besorgten Eltern, **❷ to be worried about somebody** sich *(DAT)* um jemanden Sorgen machen, **we're worried about Susan** wir machen uns um Susan Sorgen

**worry** *NOUN* **Sorge** die *(PLURAL* die **Sorgen)**

**worry** *VERB* **sich** *(DAT)* **Sorgen machen**; **don't worry!** keine Sorge!, **don't worry about it** mach dir darum keine Sorgen

**worrying** *ADJECTIVE* **beunruhigend**

**worse** *ADJECTIVE* **❶** *(more unpleasant)* **schlimmer** *(problem, pain, illness),*

**things couldn't be worse** es kann nicht schlimmer kommen **❷** *(less good)* **schlechter**; **it was even worse than the last time** es war noch schlechter als letztes Mal, **to get worse** schlechter werden, **the weather's getting worse** das Wetter wird schlechter, **she's getting worse** *(in health)* es geht ihr schlechter

**worst** *ADJECTIVE* **❶** *(most unpleasant)* **schlimmster/schlimmste/ schlimmstes**; **the worst** der/ die/das schlimmste, **it was the worst day of my life** es war der schlimmste Tag meines Lebens, **if the worst comes to the worst** wenn es zum Schlimmsten kommt **❷** *(least good)* **schlechtester/ schlechteste/schlechtestes**; **it's his worst film** das ist sein schlechtester Film, **French is my worst subject** in Französisch bin ich am schlechtesten

**worth** *ADJECTIVE* **to be worth** wert sein, **how much is it worth?** wie viel ist es wert?, **it's worth buying** das lohnt sich zu kaufen, **it's worth it** das lohnt sich, **it's not worth it** es lohnt sich nicht

**would** *VERB* **❶ would you like something to eat?** möchtest du etwas essen?, **what would you like?** was möchten Sie? **❷ I wouldn't do it** ich würde das nicht machen, **I would buy it, but I haven't got any money at the moment** ich würde es kaufen, aber ich habe zur Zeit kein Geld, **I'd like to go to the cinema** ich würde gern ins Kino gehen, **she said she'd help us** sie hat gesagt, sie würde uns helfen **❸ that would be a good idea** das wäre eine gute Idee, **if we had asked her she would have helped us** wenn wir sie gefragt

## wound          wrong

hätten, hätte sie uns geholfen ❹ **he wouldn't answer** er wollte nicht antworten, **the car wouldn't start** das Auto wollte nicht anspringen

**wound** NOUN Wunde die (PLURAL die Wunden)

**wound** VERB verwunden

**wrap** VERB einwickeln (SEP); **I'm going to wrap (up) my presents** ich wickele meine Geschenke ein, **could you wrap it for me please?** können Sie es bitte in Geschenkpapier einwickeln?

**wrapping paper** NOUN Geschenkpapier das

**wreck** NOUN ❶ Wrack das (PLURAL die Wracks) ❷ **I feel a wreck** ich bin völlig kaputt

**wreck** VERB ❶ zerstören (a building or machinery) ❷ kaputtfahren◇ (SEP) (a car) ❸ verderben◇ (a party, holidays); **it completely wrecked my evening** das hat mir den Abend völlig verdorben ❹ zunichte machen (plans)

**wrestler** NOUN Ringer der (PLURAL die Ringer), Ringerin die (PLURAL die Ringerinnen)

**wrestling** NOUN Ringen das

**wrist** NOUN Handgelenk das (PLURAL die Handgelenke)

**write** VERB schreiben◇; **to write to somebody** jemandem schreiben, **I'll write her a letter** ich schreibe ihr einen Brief, **to write to a firm** an eine Firma schreiben

• **to write down** aufschreiben◇ (SEP); **I wrote down her name** ich schrieb ihren Namen auf, **she wrote it down for me** sie hat es mir aufgeschrieben

**writer** NOUN Schriftsteller der (PLURAL die Schriftsteller), Schriftstellerin die (PLURAL die Schriftstellerinnen)

**writing** NOUN Schrift die

**wrong** ADJECTIVE ❶ (not correct) falsch; **the wrong answer** die falsche Antwort, **it's the wrong address** das ist die falsche Adresse ❷ **you've got the wrong number** Sie haben sich verwählt ❸ **to be wrong** (be mistaken) sich irren, **I must have been wrong** ich muss mich geirrt haben ❹ (out of order) **to be wrong** nicht stimmen, **there's something wrong** etwas stimmt nicht ❺ (dishonest) **nicht richtig**; **it's wrong to make him pay for it** es ist nicht richtig, dass er dafür zahlen muss, **he's wrong** er hat Unrecht, **you're quite wrong there, cars pollute the environment** da haben Sie aber Unrecht, Autos verschmutzen die Umwelt ❻ **what's wrong?** was ist los?

**wrong** ADVERB ❶ (false) falsch; **he's got it wrong** er hat es falsch gemacht ❷ **to go wrong** (break) kaputtgehen◇ (SEP) (PERF sein) (informal) ❸ **to go wrong** schief gehen◇ (plan)

**xerox** NOUN **Fotokopie** die *(PLURAL* die **Fotokopien)**

**xerox** VERB **fotokopieren**

**X-ray** NOUN **Röntgenaufnahme** die *(PLURAL* die **Röntgenaufnahmen)**; **to have an X-ray** geröntgt werden◇ *(PERF* **sein)**

**X-ray** VERB **röntgen**; **they X-rayed her ankle** sie haben ihren Knöchel geröntgt

**yacht** NOUN ❶ *(sailing boat)* **Segelboot** das *(PLURAL* die **Segelboote)** ❷ *(large luxury boat)* **Jacht** die *(PLURAL* die **Jachten)**

**yawn** VERB **gähnen**

**year** NOUN ❶ **Jahr** das *(PLURAL* die **Jahre)**; **six years ago** vor sechs Jahren, **the whole year** das ganze Jahr ❷ **they lived in Moscow for years** sie haben jahrelang in Moskau gewohnt ❸ **to be seventeen years old** siebzehn Jahre alt sein, **a two-year-old child** ein zweijähriges Kind ❹ *(in school)* **Klasse** die *(PLURAL* die **Klassen)** *(in German secondary schools the years go from the 'fünfte Klasse' to the 'dreizehnte Klasse')*; **I'm in Year 10** *(in Britain)* ich gehe in die zehnte Klasse, **he'll be in Year 11** *(in Britain)* er kommt in die elfte Klasse

**yell** VERB **schreien**◇

**yellow** ADJECTIVE **gelb**

**yes** ADVERB ❶ **ja**; **yes please** ja bitte, **'is Tom in his room?' – 'yes, he is'** 'ist Tom im Zimmer?' – 'ja' ❷ *(answering a negative)* **doch**; **'you don't want to come with us, do you?' – ' yes, I do!'** 'du willst nicht mitkommen?' – 'doch!', **'you haven't finished, have you?' – 'yes, I have'** 'Sie sind noch nicht fertig, oder?' – 'doch!'

**yesterday** *ADVERB* **❶** gestern; **I saw her yesterday** ich habe sie gestern gesehen, **yesterday afternoon** gestern Nachmittag, **yesterday morning** gestern früh **❷ the day before yesterday** vorgestern

**yet** *ADVERB* **❶ not yet** noch nicht, **it's not ready yet** es ist noch nicht fertig **❷** *(in questions)* **schon**; **has she mentioned it yet?** hat sie es schon erwähnt?

**yoghurt** *NOUN* Joghurt der *(PLURAL* die Joghurt)

**yolk** *NOUN* Eigelb das *(PLURAL* die Eigelbe)

**you** *PRONOUN* **❶** *(as the subject of the sentence and in comparisons)* **du** *(familiar form, singular)*, **Sie** *(polite form, singular and plural)*; *('du' is the familiar way of talking to family members, close friends, and people of your own age; 'Sie' is more polite)* **do you want to go to the cinema tonight?** möchtest du heute Abend ins Kino gehen?, **can you tell me where the station is, please?** können Sie mir bitte sagen, wo der Bahnhof ist?, **he's older than you** er ist älter als du, er ist älter als Sie **❷** *(the object form of 'du' and 'Sie', in the dative)* **dir** *(familiar form, singular)*, **Ihnen** *(polite form, singular and plural)*; **I'll lend you my bike** ich leihe dir mein Rad, **I'll write to you** ich schreibe Ihnen, **I'll come with you** ich komme mit Ihnen mit **❸** *(the object form of 'du' and 'Sie', in the accusative)* **dich** *(familiar form, singular)*, **Sie** *(polite form, singular and plural)*; **I saw you** ich habe dich gesehen, ich habe Sie gesehen **❹** *(as the subject of the sentence)* **ihr**, *(familiar form, plural)*; **do you all want to come?** wollt ihr alle kommen? **❺** *(the object form, in

the accusative and the dative)* **euch**; **I'll invite you all!** ich lade euch alle ein!, **I'll give it to you later** ich gebe es euch später

**young** *ADJECTIVE* jung; **young people** junge Leute, **he's younger than me** er ist jünger als ich, **Tessa's two years younger than me** Tessa ist zwei Jahre jünger als ich

**your** *DETERMINER* **❶** *(familiar form, singular)* **dein** *(this is the familiar way of talking to family members, close friends, and people of your own age; 'Ihr' is more polite)*; **I met your brother** ich habe deinen Bruder getroffen, **I met your sister** ich habe deine Schwester getroffen, **I drove your car** ich bin mit deinem Auto gefahren, **I know your brothers** ich kenne deine Brüder **❷** *(familiar form, plural)* **euer**; **your brother** euer Bruder, **your sister** eure Schwester, **your car** euer Auto, **your friends are waiting downstairs** eure Freunde warten unten **❸** *(polite form, singular and plural)* **Ihr**; **your brother** Ihr Bruder, **your sister** Ihre Schwester, **your car is in the garage** Ihr Auto ist in der Garage, **you can all bring your friends** Sie können alle Ihre Freunde mitbringen

**yours** *PRONOUN* **❶** *(familiar form, singular)* **deiner/deine/deins** *(this is the familiar way of talking to family members, close friends, and people of your own age, 'Ihrer/Ihre/Ihrs' is more polite)*; **my brother's younger than yours** mein Bruder ist jünger als deiner, **my sister is older than yours** meine Schwester ist älter als deine, **I enjoyed that book – is it yours?** das Buch hat mir gefallen – ist es deins?, **my shoes are more expensive than yours** meine Schuhe sind teureried als deine **❷** *(familiar form, plural)* **euer/eure/eures**; **my children are younger than yours** meine Kinder sind jünger als yours **❸** *(polite form, singular and plural)* **Ihrer/Ihre/Ihrs**; **his father must be older than yours** sein Vater muss älter als Ihrer sein **❹ she's a friend of yours** sie ist eine Freundin von Ihnen, **these books are yours** diese Bücher gehören Ihnen **❺** *(in letters)* **Yours sincerely** Mit freundlichen Grüßen

**yourself** *PRONOUN* **❶** *(when translated by a reflexive verb in German)* **dich**, *(formal)* **sich**; **ask yourself** frage dich, fragen Sie sich **❷** *(as a reflexive dative pronoun)* **dir**, *(formal)* **sich**; **did you hurt yourself?** hast du dir wehgetan?, haben Sie sich wehgetan? **❸** *(for emphasis)* **selbst**; **did you do it yourself?** hast du es selbst gemacht? **❹ all by yourself** ganz allein

**yourselves** *PRONOUN* **❶ euch**, *(formal)* **sich**; **make yourselves comfortable** macht es euch gemütlich, machen Sie es sich gemütlich **❷** *(for emphasis)* **selbst**; **did you do it yourselves?** habt ihr es selbst gemacht? **❸ by yourselves** allein

**youth** *NOUN* **❶** *(stage in life)* **Jugend** die **❷** *(young people)* **die Jugendlichen**; **today's youth** die Jugend von heute **❸** *(young male)* **Jugendliche** der *(PLURAL die Jugendlichen)*

**youth hostel** *NOUN* **Jugendherberge** die *(PLURAL die Jugendherbergen)*

**Yugoslavia** *NOUN* **Jugoslawien** das; **in the former Yugoslavia** im ehemaligen Jugoslawien

# Zz

**zany** *ADJECTIVE* **verrückt**

**zebra** *NOUN* **Zebra** das *(PLURAL die Zebras)*

**zebra crossing** *NOUN* **Zebrastreifen** der *(PLURAL die Zebrastreifen)*

**zero** *NOUN* **Null** die *(PLURAL die Nullen)*

**zigzag** *VERB* **❶ im Zickzack laufen**✧ *(PERF* **sein)** **❷** *(in a car)* **im Zickzack fahren**✧ *(PERF* **sein)**

**zip** *NOUN* **Reißverschluss** der *(PLURAL die Reißverschlüsse)*

**zodiac** *NOUN* **Tierkreis** der; **the signs of the zodiac** die Sternzeichen *(plural)*

**zone** *NOUN* **Zone** die *(PLURAL die Zonen)*

**zoo** *NOUN* **Zoo** der *(PLURAL die Zoos)*

**zoom lens** *NOUN* **Zoomobjektiv** das *(PLURAL die Zoomobjektive)*

# LIFE AND CULTURE

# At school

| | |
|---|---|
| das Abitur | This is the exam taken by students who have stayed at school to the age of 18 or 19. The equivalent exam in Austria and Switzerland is called die Matura. |
| hitzefrei | This means literally 'heat free'. In many schools, students are sent home early if the thermometer reaches 27° C. |
| die Klassen | As most German students begin school when they are six, they are usually in Klasse 6 at the age of 11: |

6. Klasse = Year 7
7. Klasse = Year 8
8. Klasse = Year 9
9. Klasse = Year 10

| | |
|---|---|
| die Noten | These are school marks. In Germany, Note 1 is the best. In Austria, Note 1 is the best and Note 5 is the worst. In Switzerland, Note 1 is the worst and Note 6 is the best. |
| die Schule | At the age of 10, students in Germany move from primary school (Grundschule) to one of three types of secondary school: Gymnasium (the most academic), Hauptschule (the most vocational), or Realschule (between the other two). In some areas, there are comprehensive schools (Gesamtschulen). In Switzerland, some cantons have only one type of secondary school, whilst other cantons have three types. In Austria, students move to a Hauptschule, a Gymnasium, or a neue Mittelschule. |
| die Schulferien | These are the school holidays. Different parts of Germany have their summer holidays at different times. There may be: |

- one or two weeks in October / November
- two weeks at Christmas
- one or two weeks in February
- two weeks at Easter
- a week at Whitsun
- six or seven weeks in summer

| | |
|---|---|
| der Schultag | This is the school day. The German school day is usually from 8.00 a.m. to 1 p.m. for younger students, with older students often having afternoon classes on one or more afternoons a week. |

**Did you know ...**
- that students do not wear uniforms?
- that students who fail in too many subjects have to repeat the year (sitzen bleiben or, formally, Nichtversetzung) instead of going on to a higher class?

| | |
|---|---|
| Ich gehe zu Fuß zur Schule. | I walk to school. |
| Ich bin in der sechsten (6.) Klasse. | I'm in Year 7. |
| In meiner Klasse sind 25 Schüler. | There are 25 students in my class. |
| Der Unterricht beginnt um neun Uhr. | Lessons start at 9 o'clock. |
| Mittags esse ich in der Schulkantine. | At lunchtime, I have lunch in the canteen. |
| | |
| Ich bin in ... gut. | I'm good at ... |
| Ich bin in ... nicht sehr gut. | I'm not very good at ... |
| Ich lerne für eine Prüfung, die ... genannt wird. | I'm working towards an exam called ... |
| Wir haben viele Hausaufgaben. | We have a lot of homework. |
| Herein! | Come in! |
| Packt eure Hefte aus. | Take out your exercise books. |
| Schlagt eure Bücher auf Seite 23 auf. | Open your books at page 23. |
| Arbeitet mit einem Partner. | Work in pairs. |
| Hört zu und wiederholt. | Listen and repeat. |

**Ich brauche ...**
**I need ...**

| | | | |
|---|---|---|---|
| mein Schulbuch. | my textbook. | meinen Bleistiftspitzer. | my pencil sharpener. |
| meinen Bleistift. | my pencil. | meine Schere. | my scissors. |
| meinen Kuli. | my Biro®. | meinen Taschenrechner. | my calculator. |
| meine Filzstifte. | my felt-tips. | | |
| mein Lineal. | my ruler. | mein Federmäppchen. | my pencil case. |
| mein Radiergummi. | my rubber. | mein Heft. | my exercise book. |

**Mein Lieblingsfach ist ...**
**My favourite subject is ...**

| | | | |
|---|---|---|---|
| Biologie. | Biology. | Kunst. | Art. |
| Chemie. | Chemistry. | Mathe. | Maths. |
| Deutsch. | German. | Musik. | Music. |
| Englisch. | English. | Naturwissenschaften. | Science. |
| Französisch. | French. | Physik. | Physics. |
| Geschichte. | History. | Religion. | RE. |
| Erdkunde | Geography. | Spanisch. | Spanish. |
| Informatik. | IT. | Sport. | PE. |

**Später möchte ich ...**
**Later, I want to ...**

| | | | |
|---|---|---|---|
| auf die Universität gehen. | go to university. | Arzt / Ärztin werden ... | become a doctor ... |
| ... studieren. | study ... | ... denn ... | ... because ... |
| ins Ausland gehen ... | go abroad ... | es ist interessant. | it's interesting. |
| | | es ist gut bezahlt. | it's well paid. |

## At home

| | |
|---|---|
| Wir sind zu fünft in unserer Familie. | There are five of us in our family. |

**Ich habe ...**
**I've got ...**

| | |
|---|---|
| einen Bruder / eine Schwester. | a brother / a sister. |
| einen Halbbruder / eine Halbschwester. | a half-brother / a half-sister. |
| einen Zwillingsbruder / eine Zwillingsschwester. | a twin brother / a twin sister. |
| Ich bin (ein) Einzelkind. | I'm an only child. |

**Ich wohne ...**
**I live ...**

| | | | |
|---|---|---|---|
| in einem Haus. | in a house. | in einer Wohnung. | in a flat. |

## Es gibt ...
## There is ...

| | | | |
|---|---|---|---|
| eine Küche. | a kitchen. | ein Bad / | |
| ein Wohnzimmer. | a living room. | Badezimmer. | a bathroom. |
| eine Toilette. | a toilet. | einen Garten. | a garden. |
| drei Schlafzimmer. | three bedrooms. | | |

## Meine Lieblingsbeschäftigung ist ...
## My favourite pastime is ...

| | | | |
|---|---|---|---|
| mit Freunden ausgehen. | going out with friends. | Rad fahren. | going cycling. |
| lesen. | reading. | mountainbiken. | mountain biking. |
| Musik hören. | listening to music. | Fußball / Volleyball spielen. | playing football / volleyball. |
| fernsehen. | watching TV. | | |
| an einer Spielkonsole spielen. | playing on a games console. | skaten / skateboarden. | skateboarding. |
| | | inlineskaten. | roller-blading. |

## Ich werde mir ... ansehen.
## I'm going to watch ...

| | | | |
|---|---|---|---|
| einen Film | a film. | eine Spielshow | a game show. |
| eine Sportsendung | a sports programme. | meine Lieblingsserie | my favourite series. |

## Ich habe ...
## I've got ...

| | | | |
|---|---|---|---|
| eine Spielkonsole. | a games console. | ein iPad®. | an iPad®. |
| ein Handy. | a (mobile) phone. | eine Satellitenschüssel. | a satellite dish. |
| einen Laptop. | a laptop. | eine Webcam. | a webcam. |
| eine Digitalkamera. | a digital camera. | einen Computer. | a computer. |

## On the computer

| | |
|---|---|
| Mit meinem Computer ... | On my computer ... |
| mache ich Hausaufgaben. | I do my homework. |
| lade ich Musik herunter. | I download music. |
| schaue ich etwas im Internet nach. | I look something up on the Internet. |
| chatte ich mit meinen Freunden. | I chat with my friends. |
| besuche ich Chatrooms. | I visit chatrooms. |
| gehe ich auf soziale Netzwerk-Sites. | I go on social networking sites. |
| twittere ich. | I tweet. |

## Email

| | |
|---|---|
| eine E-Mail | an email |
| eine E-Mail-Adresse | an email address |
| eine E-Mail schicken | to send an email |
| eine E-Mail bekommen | to get an email |

## On the phone

| | |
|---|---|
| Hallo! | Hello! |
| Kann ich ... sprechen? | Can I speak to ...? |
| Wer ist am Apparat? | Who's calling? |
| Einen Moment, bitte. | Hold on, please. |
| Kann ich eine Nachricht hinterlassen? | Can I leave a message? |
| Ich rufe später zurück. | I'll call back later. |
| eine SMS | a text |
| eine SMS schicken / simsen | to send a text |

---

**Did you know ...**

- that in an email address, @ is called ein At-Zeichen (or just 'at'), or ein Klammeraffe, and dot is called Punkt?
- that many German Internet sites end with .de; many Austrian sites end with .at; many Swiss sites end with .ch?

# Shopping

**Ich gehe ... einkaufen.**
**I go shopping (for food) ...**

| | |
|---|---|
| in der Konditorei | at the cake shop. |
| beim Lebensmittelhändler | at the grocer's. |
| beim Bäcker | at the baker's. |
| beim Metzger *(southern Germany)* | |
| \| Schlachter *(northern Germany)* | at the butcher's. |
| im Feinkostgeschäft | at the delicatessen. |
| auf dem Markt | at the market. |
| im Supermarkt | at the supermarket. |
| im Internet | on the Internet. |

**Ich möchte ...**
**I'd like ...**

| | | | |
|---|---|---|---|
| ein Brot. | a loaf of bread. | Was kostet es? | How much is it? |
| vier Brötchen. | four rolls. | ein Kilo Zucker. | a kilo of sugar. |

eine Bäckerei    This is a baker's shop which usually sells cakes, pastries and many types of bread some with whole cereal seeds. They also sell rolls, called Brötchen in the north of Germany, and Semmeln in the south.

eine Konditorei    This is a cake shop which will sells a wide range of cakes (Kuchen) and gateaux (Torten).

# Food and eating out

**Was darf es sein?**
What would you like?

**Als Vorspeise nehme ich ...**
For a starter I'll have ...

| Zwiebelsuppe. | onion soup. | Tomatensalat. | tomato salad. |

**Als Hauptgericht möchte ich ...**
For my main course I'll have ...

| Hähnchen in Sahnesoße. | chicken in cream sauce | einen Hamburger. | a burger. |
| **mit ...** with ... | Pommes. chips. | | Salat. salad. |

**Als Nachtisch möchte ich ...**
For dessert I'd like ...

| Apfelstrudel. | apple strudel. | Milchreis. | rice pudding. |

**Zu trinken nehme ich ...**
To drink I'll have ...

| Mineralwasser. | mineral water. | eine Tasse Tee. | a cup of tea. |
| eine Cola. | a Coke®. | | |
| einen Orangensaft | an orange juice. | einen Kaffee. | a coffee. |

| Ich habe Hunger. | I'm hungry. | Ich habe eine Allergie. | I have an allergy. |
| Ich habe Durst. | I'm thirsty. | | |
| Das ist lecker! | It's delicious! | Zahlen, bitte. | The bill, please. |

## Meals

| Frühstück | breakfast | Kaffee und Kuchen | coffee and cakes |
| Mittagessen | lunch | | or afternoon tea |
| Abendessen / Abendbrot | dinner | | |

## Food

| | |
|---|---|
| Apfelschorle | This is a drink consisting of apple juice and fizzy mineral water. In Austria it is known as Apfelsaft gespritzt. |
| Apfelstrudel | This is a traditional Austrian dessert made of thin pastry rolled around a filling of apples and raisins. It is often served warm with whipped cream or thin vanilla custard. |
| Brötchen | These are bread rolls. They are also called Semmeln, especially in southern Germany and Austria. People often go out early to buy them for breakfast. |
| Brezeln | This is twisted pieces of firm, salted bread. |
| Chips | These are crisps. Chips are called Pommes frites, or just Pommes. |
| Eis | ice cream |
| Emmentaler | a Swiss cheese with a strong flavour and holes |
| Käsefondue | This is a cheese fondue. It is made from cheese melted in white wine, and is eaten by dipping bits of bread into a communal pot. The south does it with sausages, in the north you get it with boiled ham too. |
| Lebkuchen | This is soft gingerbread and it is traditionally made at Christmas, and may be covered with icing or chocolate. |
| Sauerkraut | This is boiled pickled white cabbage. It has a strong, vinegary flavour and is usually eaten with sausages. Many people consider it to be Germany's most typical dish. |
| Sachertorte | rich chocolate cake, originally from Vienna |
| Schlagsahne | This is whipped cream. In Austria it is also called Schlagobers or Schlag. |
| Schnitzel | a slice of pork, fried in breadcrumbs |
| Stollen | A rich bread-like cake, containing dried fruit and often marzipan. It is traditionally eaten at Christmas. |
| Wurst | Germany has a huge range of Wurst or sausages, which can be boiled (Bockwurst), fried or grilled (Bratwurst), or served cold like salami. |

**Did you know ...?**
- that a Berliner is a jam doughnut, a Wiener a sausage, and a Hamburger, of course, a hamburger?
- that, in Austria, potatoes are often called Erdäpfel (apples of the earth) and tomatoes Paradeiser (fruits of paradise)?
- that chocolates are Pralinen, and chocolate is Schokolade?

## On holiday

| | |
|---|---|
| Letzten Sommer bin ich nach Deutschland gefahren. | Last summer, I went to Germany. |
| Nächsten Sommer werde ich nach Berlin fahren. | Next summer, I'll be going to Berlin. |

**Ich war ...**
**I stayed ...**

| | |
|---|---|
| in einem Hotel. | in a hotel. |
| in einem Ferienhaus auf dem Land. | in a holiday home in the country. |
| auf einem Campingplatz. | on a campsite. |

**Wir sind mit ... gefahren.**
**We travelled by ...**

| | | | |
|---|---|---|---|
| dem Schiff | ship. | dem (Reise)bus | coach. |
| dem Zug | train. | dem Fahrrad | bike. |
| dem Auto | car. | Wir sind geflogen. | We flew. |

| | |
|---|---|
| Biergärten | These are beer gardens. In a Biergarten coffee, cake, soft drinks, and small meals can be ordered, as well as beer. |
| der Föhn | This is a wind which brings warm air from the Mediterranean to Austria, southern Germany, and parts of Switzerland. Some people believe that it causes headaches and other health problems. |
| ins Freibad gehen | This means going to an outdoor swimming pool. Freibäder are very popular because the weather gets very hot in summer. |
| Hochdeutsch | This means High German (standard German). Each area of Germany, Austria, and German-speaking Switzerland has its own dialect. |
| Kaffee und Kuchen | This means coffee and cake. Germany, Switzerland, and Austria are all famous for their mouth-watering cakes. |
| Kantone | Each of the 26 individual states in Switzerland is called a Kanton (canton). |
| Länder | Each of the individual states in Germany and Austria is called a Land. Germany has 16 Länder; Austria has nine. |
| der Marktplatz | This is the market square. |

| Personalausweise | These are identity cards. German, Austrian, and Swiss citizens can use their Personalausweis instead of a passport for some travel. |
| das Rathaus | This is the town hall. It is often a grand building in the main square. |

**Did you know ...**

- that you can be fined if you cross the road when the traffic light (Ampel) is red for pedestrians?
- that German post boxes (Briefkästen) are yellow?
- that the usual way of greeting people is:
  - Guten Tag in northern Germany,
  - Grüß Gott in southern Germany,
  - Grüezi in Switzerland,
  - Servus in Austria,

  but that you can also say Hallo everywhere?
- that a minority of Swiss people speak Romantsch, a language derived from Latin?
- that, in towns which have several railway stations, the main railway station is usually called the Hauptbahnhof?
- that Germany's fastest trains are called InterCity Express? You pay a supplement to travel in them, and have to book a seat.
- that many towns have a tram system (Straßenbahn)?
- that underground trains are called the U-Bahn?
- that services on the motorway (Autobahn) are called Raststätte or Autohof?
- that to travel on Swiss or Austrian motorways, you have to buy a sticker called a Vignette, and display the sticker on the car windscreen?
- that the biggest city in Switzerland is Zürich, but the capital city (Hauptstadt) is Bern?
- that the capital of Austria is Vienna?
- that West and East Germany were reunified in 1990, having been divided into two states after World War II?
- that before reunification, the West German government had its seat in Bonn, and that after reunification Berlin was re-established as the capital?

# Places of interest

| | |
|---|---|
| die Alpen | **The Alps** cover much of Austria and Switzerland, and stretch along the southern border of Germany.<br>They are a popular holiday area in both summer and winter. The highest points in the three countries are:<br><br>Germany: **Zugspitze** 2962m<br>Austria: **Großglockner** 3798m<br>Switzerland: **Monte Rosa** 4634m |
| Bayern | **Bavaria,** Germany's biggest Land, is in the south, with the Alps along its southern border. Its capital is Munich. Bavaria is famous for its big wooden farmhouses and its many local beers. |
| Brandenburger Tor | This gateway, built in 1791, is Berlin's most famous landmark. |
| Berliner Mauer | **The Berlin Wall.** East Germany was separated from West Germany, and governed by a Communist government, from 1948 to 1990. In Berlin, the Communists built a wall around West Berlin, to prevent people from East Germany fleeing to the West. The wall was taken down in 1989; some parts of it remain, as a reminder of the past. |
| Liechtenstein | A tiny country of 160 km$^2$ bordering Switzerland and Austria. It has its own government and issues its own stamps, but uses Swiss francs. |
| Neuschwanstein | A fairy-tale castle in the Bavarian Alps. Many people in Britain recognize Neuschwanstein as the castle from the film 'Chitty Chitty Bang Bang' and the inspiration for the castle in Disney's 'Cinderella'. |
| Ostsee | **The Baltic Sea.** With large sandy beaches, this is a popular holiday area, especially as parts of it are within easy reach of Berlin. |
| Reichstag | Built in 1894, the Reichstag was the seat of the German parliament. Destroyed by fire in 1933, it was rebuilt following the reunification of Germany, and the German parliament now sits there again. |
| Rhein | **The River Rhine.** It cuts through the hills in a deep valley, with vines on the hillsides and castles on the tops. Barges carry goods along the Rhine. |
| Südtirol | **South Tyrol:** part of Italy, in the Alps, where people speak both German and Italian. |

| | |
|---|---|
| Wien | **Vienna,** the capital of Austria. It is known for its music, its museums and cafes, the white horses in the Spanish Riding School and the Riesenrad, an enormous Ferris wheel built in 1897. |

## Festivals and celebrations

| | |
|---|---|
| Neujahr | **New Year's Day** |
| Heilige Drei Könige | **Epiphany, or Twelfth Night, 6th January.** In Austria and parts of Germany, people dress up as kings and collect money to help children in developing countries. |
| Valentinstag | **St Valentine's Day** |
| Fasching / Fastnacht / Karneval | This is the celebration before Lent, with some people having fancy dress parties and processions. Shrove Tuesday is known as **Fastnachtsdienstag** or **Faschingsdienstag,** and the Monday before as **Rosenmontag.** |
| Ostern | **Easter.** Children hunt for chocolate eggs brought by the Osterhase (the Easter Hare), and many families decorate branches in a vase and hang them with decorated eggs. Germans also boil eggs in special food colours for Easter Sunday breakfast. Good Friday is known as **Karfreitag** and Easter Monday as **Ostermontag.** |
| der 1. Mai/ Tag der Arbeit Maifeiertag | **May Day.** The public holiday is always on 1st May, whereas in Britain it is on the first Monday in May. |
| Christi Himmelfahrt | **Ascension Day.** This is a public holiday on the Thursday that is forty days after Easter. |
| Pfingsten | **Whitsun (Pentecost).** This is fifty days after Easter. Pfingstmontag (Whit Monday) is a public holiday. |
| Schweizer Nationalfeiertag | **Swiss National Day.** This is always on 1st August. |
| Oktoberfest | This is a famous festival in Munich, with funfairs and beer tents. It actually begins in late September. |
| Tag der Deutschen Einheit | **Day of German Unity.** The public holiday on 3rd October commemorates the reunification of East and West Germany in 1989. |
| Österreichischer Nationalfeiertag | **Austrian National Day. T**his is always on 26th October. |

| | |
|---|---|
| Reformationstag | **Reformation Day.** This is always on 1st October. This is a public holiday in 5 of the 16 federal states of Germany. |
| Allerheiligen | **1st November.** All Saints' Day. On this day many people put flowers on the graves of loved ones. It is a public holiday in most Roman Catholic parts of Germany and Switzerland, and in Austria. |
| Nikolaus | **6th December.** The Feast of Saint Nicholas. On the evening before, children put a shoe outside their door. In the morning, they find that der Nikolaus (Saint Nicholas) has filled the shoe with chocolates, nuts, and other goodies. (Traditionally, this happens only if they have been good.) |
| der Heiligabend / der Heilige Abend | **24th December, Christmas Eve.** Most families have a real Christmas tree. The main celebration is the in the evening when people open their present after decorating the Christmas tree. Many people go to midnight mass. |
| Weihnachtsmärkte | **Christmas markets.** These are stalls decorated with greenery and smelling of mulled wine and roast almonds. A Weihnachtsmarkt is a beautiful setting for buying Christmas gifts. |
| Weihnachten | **25th December, Christmas.** Der erste Weihnachtstag (Christmas Day) often begins with a lie-in after the celebrations of the night before. There is a big midday meal. Christmas Day is Christtag in Austria and Weihnachtstag in Switzerland. (Boxing Day) is also a public holiday. Boxing Day is Stefanitag in Austria and Stephanstag in Switzerland. |
| Silvester | **31st December, New Year's Eve** |

**Did you know ...**
- that some other religious festivals are celebrated, mainly in Roman Catholic regions?
- that people who live in southern Germany get more public holidays (Feiertage) than those who live in the north?
- that Germany has more public holidays (Feiertage) than most countries in Europe, but if a public holiday falls on a Saturday or Sunday, it is lost (verloren) and the following Monday is a working day as usual?

## Dates

| | | | |
|---|---|---|---|
| am ersten Januar | on the 1st January | zwölfte | 12th |
| der erste Januar | the 1st of January | dreizehnte | 13th |
| zweite (2.) | 2nd | vierzehnte | 14th |
| dritte (3.) | 3rd | fünfzehnte | 15th |
| vierte (4.) | 4th | sechzehnte | 16th |
| fünfte | 5th | siebzehnte | 17th |
| sechste | 6th | achtzehnte | 18th |
| siebte | 7th | neunzehnte | 19th |
| achte | 8th | zwanzigste | 20th |
| neunte | 9th | einundzwanzigste | 21st |
| zehnte | 10th | dreißigste | 30th |
| elfte | 11th | | |

## Days

| | | | |
|---|---|---|---|
| Montag | Monday | Freitag | Friday |
| Dienstag | Tuesday | Samstag / Sonnabend *(northern Germany)* | Saturday |
| Mittwoch | Wednesday | | |
| Donnerstag | Thursday | Sonntag | Sunday |

## Months

| | | | |
|---|---|---|---|
| Januar | January | Juli | July |
| Februar | February | August | August |
| März | March | September | September |
| April | April | Oktober | October |
| Mai | May | November | November |
| Juni | June | Dezember | December |

## Seasons

| | | | |
|---|---|---|---|
| der Winter | winter | der Sommer | summer |
| der Frühling | spring | der Herbst | autumn |

# Time

Wie spät ist es?
What time is it?

| | |
|---|---|
| Es ist ein Uhr. | It's one o'clock. |
| Es ist halb fünf. | It's half past four. |
| Es ist Viertel nach sechs. | It's quarter past six. |
| Es ist Viertel vor sechs. | It's quarter to six. |
| Es ist zehn nach neun. | It's ten past nine. |
| Es ist zehn vor neun. | It's ten to nine. |
| Es ist Mittag. | It's midday. |
| Es ist Mitternacht. | It's midnight. |
| Es ist 7 Uhr abends (19 Uhr). | It's 7 p.m. (19.00). |
| Es ist dreizehn Uhr fünfzehn. | It's 1.15 p.m. |

| | |
|---|---|
| jeden Tag | every day |
| einmal die Woche | once a week |
| gelegentlich | from time to time |
| nie | never |
| immer | always |

# Numbers

| | |
|---|---|
| null | 0 |
| eins | 1 |
| zwei | 2 |
| drei | 3 |
| vier | 4 |
| fünf | 5 |
| sechs | 6 |
| sieben | 7 |
| acht | 8 |
| neun | 9 |
| zehn | 10 |
| elf | 11 |
| zwölf | 12 |
| dreizehn | 13 |
| vierzehn | 14 |
| fünfzehn | 15 |
| sechzehn | 16 |
| siebzehn | 17 |
| achtzehn | 18 |
| neunzehn | 19 |
| zwanzig | 20 |
| einundzwanzig | 21 |
| zweiundzwanzig | 22 |
| dreiundzwanzig | 23 |
| vierundzwanzig | 24 |
| fünfundzwanzig | 25 |
| sechsundzwanzig | 26 |
| siebenundzwanzig | 27 |
| achtundzwanzig | 28 |
| neunundzwanzig | 29 |
| dreißig | 30 |

| | |
|---|---|
| vierzig | 40 |
| fünfzig | 50 |
| sechzig | 60 |
| siebzig | 70 |
| einundsiebzig | 71 |
| achtzig | 80 |
| einundachtzig | 81 |
| zweiundachtzig | 82 |
| neunzig | 90 |
| einundneunzig | 91 |
| zweiundneunzig | 92 |
| neunundneunzig | 99 |
| hundert | 100 |
| hunderteins | 101 |
| hundertzwei | 102 |
| zweihundert | 200 |
| zweihunderteins | 201 |
| zweihundertzwei | 202 |

| | |
|---|---|
| tausend | 1000 |
| tausendeins | 1001 |
| tausendzwei | 1002 |
| zweitausend | 2000 |
| eine Million | 1 000 000 |
| eine Milliarde | 1 000 000 000 |
| eine Billion | 1 000 000 000 000 |

# States and cantons

Germany and Austria are divided into Bundesländer (states).
Germany has sixteen Bundesländer, and Austria has nine.
Switzerland is divided into 26 Kantone (cantons).

| Bundesland | German Federal State |
| --- | --- |
| Baden-Württemberg | Baden-Württemberg |
| Bayern | Bavaria |
| Berlin | Berlin |
| Brandenburg | Brandenburg |
| Bremen | Bremen |
| Hamburg | Hamburg |
| Hessen | Hesse |
| Mecklenburg-Vorpommern | Mecklenburg-Western Pomerania |
| Niedersachsen | Lower Saxony |
| Nordrhein-Westfalen | North-Rhine Westphalia |
| Rheinland-Pfalz | Rhineland-Palatinate |
| Saarland | Saarland |
| Sachsen | Saxony |
| Sachsen-Anhalt | Saxony-Anhalt |
| Schleswig-Holstein | Schleswig-Holstein |
| Thüringen | Thuringia |

| Bundesland | Austrian State |
| --- | --- |
| Burgenland | Burgenland |
| Kärnten | Carinthia |
| Niederösterreich | Lower Austria |
| Oberösterreich | Upper Austria |
| Salzburg | Salzburg |
| Steiermark | Styria |
| Tirol | Tyrol |
| Vorarlberg | Vorarlberg |
| Wien | Vienna |

| Kanton | Main language spoken | Canton *(common English name)* |
|---|---|---|
| Aargau | German | Aargau |
| Appenzell Ausserrhoden Ausserrhoden | German | Appenzell |
| Appenzell Innerrhoden | German | Appenzell Innerrhoden |
| Basel-Stadt | German | Basel-Stadt |
| Basel-Landschaft | German | Basel-Landschaft |
| Bern | German | Bern |
| Freiburg | French | Fribourg |
| Genf | French | Geneva |
| Glarus | German | Glarus |
| Graubünden | German | Graubünden |
| Jura | French | Jura |
| Luzern | German | Lucerne |
| Neuenburg | French | Neuchâtel |
| Nidwalden | German | Nidwalden |
| Obwalden | German | Obwalden |
| St. Gallen | German | St Gallen |
| Schaffhausen | German | Schaffhausen |
| Schwyz | German | Schwyz |
| Solothurn | German | Solothurn |
| Tessin | Italian | Ticino |
| Thurgau | German | Thurgau |
| Uri | German | Uri |
| Waadt | French | Vaud |
| Wallis | French | Valais |
| Zug | German | Zug |
| Zürich | German | Zürich |

## NOTES

# NOTES